SELECTING A DESCRIPTIVE STATISTICAL PROCEDURE

Type of data	*Individual scores*	*Central tendency*	*Variability*	*Correlation coefficient*
Nominal	frequency, rel. frequency, or percent	Mode	Range	ϕ
Ordinal	frequency, rel. frequency, or percent	Median	Range	Spearman r_s
Interval or ratio (skewed distribution)	frequency, rel. frequency, or percent	Median	Range or semi-interquartile range	none
Interval or ratio (normally distributed)	frequency, rel. frequency, percent, or *z*-score	Mean	Standard deviation or variance	Pearson r and regression

The point-biserial r_{pb} is used with one interval or ratio variable and one dichotomous variable.

PARAMETRIC PROCEDURES AND THEIR NONPARAMETRIC COUNTERPARTS

Type of design	*Parametric test*	*Nonparametric test*
Two independent samples	Independent-samples *t*-test	Mann-Whitney *U* or Rank Sums test
Two dependent samples	Dependent-samples *t*-test	Wilcoxon *T*-test
Three or more independent samples	Between-subjects ANOVA (Post hoc test: protected *t*-test)	Kruskal-Wallis *H* test (Post hoc test: Rank Sums test)
Three or more dependent samples	Within-subjects ANOVA (Post hoc test: Tukey's *HSD*)	Friedman χ^2 test (Post hoc test: Nemenyi's procedure)

UNDERSTANDING RESEARCH METHODS AND STATISTICS

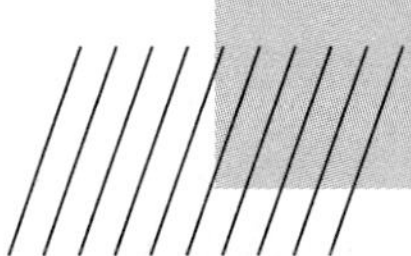

Brief Contents

Preface xix

Part 1

Introduction to Psychological Research

1 Introduction to the Scientific Method 2
2 The Logic of Designing and Interpreting Research 28
3 Understanding Reliability and Validity 54
4 Design Issues and Ethical Concerns in Experiments 79
5 Design Issues and Ethical Concerns in Descriptive Research 108

Part 2

Descriptive Statistics

6 Summarizing Research Using Frequency Distributions and Percentiles 134
7 Summarizing Research Using Measures of Central Tendency 163
8 Summarizing Research Using Measures of Variability 191
9 Summarizing Research Using *z*-Scores 218

Part 3

Correlational Research and Correlational Statistics

10 Correlational Research and the Correlation Coefficient 248
11 Using Linear Regression to Predict Scores 282

Part 4

Introduction to Inferential Statistics

12 Probability and Making Decisions About Chance Events 312
13 Overview of Statistical Hypothesis Testing: The *z*-Test 336
14 The Single-Sample Study: Testing a Sample Mean or Correlation Coefficient 368

Part 5

Designing and Analyzing Two-Sample Experiments

15 The Two-Sample Between-Subjects Experiment and the Independent-Samples *t*-Test 400
16 The Two-Sample Within-Subjects Experiment and the Dependent-Samples *t*-Test 429

Part 6

Designing and Analyzing Complex Experiments

17 The One-Way Between-Subjects Experiment and the One-Way Analysis of Variance 456
18 The Two-Way Between-Subjects Experiment and the Two-Way Analysis of Variance 488
19 Within-Subjects Experiments and Other Multifactor Designs 528

Part 7

Alternative Approaches to Design and Analysis

20 Quasi-Experiments and Single-Subject Designs 558
21 Chi Square and Other Nonparametric Statistical Procedures 587

Appendices

A Organizing and Communicating Research Using APA Format 615
B Additional Statistical Formulas 659
C Statistical Tables 703
D Answers to Odd-Numbered Review Questions and Practice Problems 725

Glossary 751
References 765
Index 769

Key Terms 105
Review Questions 106
Practice Problems 106

5

Design Issues and Ethical Concerns in Descriptive Research 108

The Uses of Descriptive Research 109
Observational Studies 109
Field Surveys 113
Types of Sampling Techniques 114
Designing Interviews and Questionnaires 117
Ethical Issues in Descriptive Research 126
Putting It All Together 127
Chapter Summary 127
Key Terms 129
Review Questions 129
Practice Problems 130

Part 2

Descriptive Statistics

6

Summarizing Research Using Frequency Distributions and Percentiles 134

More Statistical Notation 135
Types of Measurement Scales 136
Creating Simple Frequency Distributions 139
Types of Simple Frequency Distributions 143
Creating Relative Frequency Distributions 148
Creating Cumulative Frequency Distributions 153
Computing Percentile 155
A Word About Grouped Frequency Distributions 156
Putting It All Together 157
Chapter Summary 157
Key Terms 159

Review Questions 159
Practice Problems 160
Summary of Formulas 162

7

Summarizing Research Using Measures of Central Tendency 163

More Statistical Notation 164
Understanding Central Tendency 164
The Mode 166
The Median 168
The Mean 170
Using the Mean in Research 175
Summarizing Research Using Central Tendency 178
Designing a Powerful Experiment 184
APA Format for Statistical Notation 185
Putting It All Together 186
Chapter Summary 186
Key Terms 187
Review Questions 187
Practice Problems 188
Summary of Formulas 190

8

Summarizing Research Using Measures of Variability 191

More Statistical Notation 192
Understanding Variability 193
Describing the Sample Variance 197
Describing the Sample Standard Deviation 200
The Population Standard Deviation and the Population Variance 204
Variance as the Error in Predictions 209
Summarizing Research Using the Mean and Standard Deviation 210
APA Format for Statistical Notation 213
Putting It All Together 213
Chapter Summary 213
Key Terms 214
Review Questions 215

To Karen, my wife and best friend

Senior Sponsoring Editor: Kerry Baruth
Development Editor: Marianne Stepanian
Senior Project Editor: Kathryn Dinovo
Senior Manufacturing Coordinator: Marie Barnes
Marketing Associate: Carolyn Guy

Cover design: Diana Coe/ko Design Studio
Cover image: © Minoru Toi/Photonica. © Hiroshi Sakuramoto/Photonica

Printed in the U.S.A.

Library of Congress Catalog Card Number: 00-133834

ISBN: 0-618-04304-7

3456789-VH-04 03 02 01

UNDERSTANDING RESEARCH METHODS AND STATISTICS

AN INTEGRATED INTRODUCTION FOR PSYCHOLOGY

Second Edition

Gary W. Heiman

Buffalo State College

HOUGHTON MIFFLIN COMPANY Boston New York

Practice Problems 333
Summary of Formulas 335

13

Overview of Statistical Hypothesis Testing: The *z*-Test 336

More Statistical Notation 337
The Role of Inferential Statistics in Research 337
Setting Up Inferential Procedures 339
Testing a Mean When σ_X Is Known: The *z*-Test 345
Interpreting z_{obt} 347
Summary of Statistical Hypothesis Testing 352
The One-Tailed Test 353
Errors in Statistical Decision Making 355
APA Format for Statistical Notation 362
Putting It All Together 362
Chapter Summary 363
Key Terms 364
Review Questions 364
Practice Problems 365
Summary of Formulas 366

14

The Single-Sample Study: Testing a Sample Mean or Correlation Coefficient 368

More Statistical Notation 369
Understanding the *t*-Test for a Single-Sample Mean 369
Calculating the Single-Sample *t*-Test 371
Estimating the Population μ by Computing a Confidence Interval 379
Summary of the *t*-Test 382
Significance Tests for Correlation Coefficients 382
Summary of Testing a Correlation Coefficient 391
Maximizing the Power of the *t*-Test and Correlation Coefficient 391
APA Format for Statistical Notation 393
Putting It All Together 393
Chapter Summary 393
Key Terms 394
Review Questions 394

Practice Problems 395
Summary of Formulas 397

Part 5

Designing and Analyzing Two-Sample Experiments

15

The Two-Sample Between-Subjects Experiment and the Independent-Samples *t*-Test 400

More Statistical Notation 401
Designing the Two-Sample Experiment 401
Controlling Participant Variables in a Between-Subjects Design 403
The Independent-Samples *t*-Test 409
Describing the Relationship in a Two-Sample Experiment 418
Power and the Independent-Samples *t*-Test 422
Eliminating Participants from the Data 423
APA Format for Statistical Notation 423
Putting It All Together 423
Chapter Summary 424
Key Terms 425
Review Questions 425
Practice Problems 426
Summary of Formulas 428

16

The Two-Sample Within-Subjects Experiment and the Dependent-Samples *t*-Test 429

More Statistical Notation 430
Designs That Directly Control Participant Variables 430
Choosing a Design 436
The Dependent-Samples *t*-Test 438
Power and the Dependent-Samples *t*-Test 447
APA Format for Statistical Notation 448
Putting It All Together 448
Chapter Summary 449

Key Terms 450
Review Questions 450
Practice Problems 451
Summary of Formulas 453

Part 6

Designing and Analyzing Complex Experiments

17

The One-Way Between-Subjects Experiment and the One-Way Analysis of Variance 456

More Statistical Notation 457
Designing Multilevel Experiments 457
Overview of ANOVA 459
Components of the *F*-Statistic 462
Computing the *F*-Ratio 468
Performing Post Hoc Comparisons 474
Summary of the Steps in Performing a One-Way ANOVA 477
Describing the Relationship in a One-Way ANOVA 478
Power and the ANOVA 480
APA Format for Statistical Notation 480
Putting It All Together 481
Chapter Summary 481
Key Terms 482
Review Questions 483
Practice Problems 483
Summary of Formulas 486

18

The Two-Way Between-Subjects Experiment and the Two-Way Analysis of Variance 488

More Statistical Notation 489
The Reason for Multifactor Studies 491
Overview of the Two-Way ANOVA 491
Computing the Two-Way ANOVA 499
Interpreting the Two-Way Experiment 507

Summary of the Steps in Performing a Two-Way ANOVA 517
APA Format for Statistical Notation 518
Putting It All Together 518
Chapter Summary 518
Key Terms 519
Review Questions 519
Practice Problems 520
Summary of Formulas 524

19

Within-Subjects Experiments and Other Multifactor Designs 528

Controlling Participant Variables in Complex Designs 529
The One-Way Within-Subjects Analysis of Variance 533
The Two-Way Within-Subjects Design 537
The Two-Way Mixed Design 538
The Three-Way Design 541
The Test for Homogeneity of Variance: The F_{max} Test 545
Other Ways to Compare the Means in a Factorial Design 546
Going Beyond the Analysis of Variance 547
APA Format for Statistical Notation 548
Putting It All Together 548
Chapter Summary 549
Key Terms 550
Review Questions 550
Practice Problems 551
Summary of Formulas 555

Part 7

Alternative Approaches to Design and Analysis

20

Quasi-Experiments and Single-Subject Designs 558

Understanding Quasi-Experiments 558
Quasi-Independent Variables Involving Participant Variables 560

Contents

Preface xix

Part 1

Introduction to Psychological Research

1

Introduction to the Scientific Method 2

Introduction (Or Why Am I Here?) 2
The Scientific Method 5
The Goals of Psychological Research 11
Scientific Hypotheses 14
The Flaws in Scientific Research 19
Putting It All Together 23
Chapter Summary 24
Key Terms 25
Review Questions 25
Practice Problems 26

2

The Logic of Designing and Interpreting Research 28

Beginning the Design: Asking the Question 29

Testing a Hypothesis by Discovering a Relationship 33
The Role of Statistical Procedures 38
Summary of the Flow of a Study 40
Experimental Research Methods 42
Descriptive Research Methods 47
Putting It All Together 48
Chapter Summary 48
Key Terms 50
Review Questions 50
Practice Problems 51

3

Understanding Reliability and Validity 54

Designing an Example Study 55
Critically Evaluating the Study 57
Understanding Reliability 61
Understanding Validity 62
Minimizing Threats to Validity and Reliability 66
Issues of Validity and Reliability in Descriptive Studies 68
Issues of Validity and Reliability in Experiments 70
Putting It All Together 74
Chapter Summary 75
Key Terms 76
Review Questions 76
Practice Problems 77

4

Design Issues and Ethical Concerns in Experiments 79

Two Example Studies 80
Designing the Independent Variable 80
Designing the Dependent Variable 82
Controlling Extraneous Variables 88
Demand Characteristics 90
Research Involving Animals 95
Research Ethics 96
Putting It All Together 103
Chapter Summary 104

Key Terms 276
Review Questions 276
Practice Problems 277
Summary of Formulas 280

11

Using Linear Regression to Predict Scores 282

More Statistical Notation 283
Understanding Linear Regression 283
The Linear Regression Equation 285
Describing Errors in Prediction When Using the Linear Regression Equation 291
Predicting Variability: The Proportion of Variance Accounted For 298
A Word About Multiple Correlation and Regression 303
APA Format for Statistical Notation 304
Putting It All Together 304
Chapter Summary 304
Key Terms 305
Review Questions 306
Practice Problems 306
Summary of Formulas 308

Part 4

Introduction to Inferential Statistics

12

Probability and Making Decisions About Chance Events 312

More Statistical Notation 313
The Logic of Probability 313
Computing Probability 315
Obtaining Probability From the Standard Normal Curve 317
Making Decisions Based on Probability 321
Making Decisions About a Sample Mean 323
Putting It All Together 330
Chapter Summary 331
Key Terms 332
Review Questions 332

Practice Problems 215
Summary of Formulas 217

9

Summarizing Research Using *z*-Scores 218

More Statistical Notation 219
Understanding *z*-Scores 219
Interpreting *z*-Scores: The *z*-Distribution 224
Using the *z*-Distribution to Compare Different Distributions 225
Using the *z*-Distribution to Describe Individual Scores 227
Using *z*-Scores to Describe Sample Means 236
APA Format for Statistical Notation 242
Putting It All Together 242
Chapter Summary 242
Key Terms 243
Review Questions 244
Practice Problems 244
Summary of Formulas 246

Part 3

Correlational Research and Correlational Statistics

10

Correlational Research and the Correlation Coefficient 248

More Statistical Notation 249
Understanding Correlational Research 249
Distinguishing Characteristics of Correlational Analysis 252
Types of Relationships 254
Strength of the Relationship 257
Using the Correlation Coefficient in Research 261
Computing the Correlation Coefficient 264
Creating a Powerful Correlational Design 272
Correlations in the Population 274
APA Format for Statistical Notation 274
Putting It All Together 274
Chapter Summary 275

Quasi-Independent Variables Involving Environmental Events: The Time-Series Design 563
The Quasi-Independent Variable of the Passage of Time 570
Understanding Small *N* Research and the Single-Subject Design 573
A Word About Program Evaluation 581
Putting It All Together 582
Chapter Summary 582
Key Terms 584
Review Questions 584
Practice Problems 585

21

Chi Square and Other Nonparametric Statistical Procedures 587

The Reasons for Using Nonparametric Procedures 588
Chi Square Procedures 589
The One-Way Chi Square: The Goodness of Fit Test 589
The Two-Way Chi Square: The Test of Independence 596
Nonparametric Procedures for Ranked Data 602
APA Format for Statistical Notation 609
Putting It All Together 609
Chapter Summary 609
Key Terms 610
Review Questions 610
Practice Problems 611
Summary of Formulas 613

Appendices

A

Organizing and Communicating Research Using APA Format 615

An Example Study 616
The Research Literature 617
Organization of a Research Article 622
The Components of an APA-Style Research Article 626

Putting It All Together 641
Chapter Summary 642
Key Terms 643
Review Questions 643
Practice Problems 644
Sample APA-Style Research Report 646

B

Additional Statistical Formulas 659

B.1. Computing Percentiles 660
B.2. Computing the Semi-Interquartile Range 667
B.3. Performing Linear Interpolation 667
B.4. Additional Formulas for Computing Probability 670
B.5. The One-Way Within-Subjects Analysis of Variance 674
B.6. The Two-Way Within-Subjects Analysis of Variance 679
B.7. The Two-Way Mixed-Design Analysis of Variance 687
B.8. Nonparametric Procedures for Ranked Data 693

C

Statistical Tables 703

D

Answers to Odd-Numbered Review Questions and Practice Problems 725

Glossary 751

References 765

Index 769

Preface

This text actively teaches research design and statistical procedures in an integrated fashion. It is intended primarily for an introductory two-semester psychology course that covers the material usually found in separate, one-semester courses in statistics and methods. Therefore, I have included the complete set of descriptive and experimental research methods, as well as all common primary and secondary statistical procedures. (The text can also be used in a one-semester course by assigning only some chapters.) Using one integrated text eliminates the confusion that results when separate statistics and methods texts differ in perspective, sequence, terminology, and symbols. Further, because I have previously written both a statistics textbook and a research methods textbook for use in separate courses, I am especially sensitive to the need to introduce design issues when teaching statistics, and to include statistical procedures in any discussion of research design. I am also sensitive to the times when, for clarity, it is necessary simply to teach a design principle that applies regardless of the statistics being employed, or to teach a statistical formula, without raising design concerns that only confuse the issue.

Approach

This text's approach places students in the role of researchers, focusing on the actual decisions and conclusions they make. I believe this is the way for students to develop the critical thinking skills necessary to understand and design research. At the same time, I've attempted to explain each concept clearly using a writing style that anticipates students' questions and provides many examples. In particular, statistical formulas and calculations are presented in a way that responds to students' math anxiety without pandering to them. The result is that students successfully learn complex design issues and statistical analyses, so that they are well-prepared for advanced undergraduate courses — including independent research projects — as well as for reading the professional literature.

The central idea in this text is that the question a researcher asks leads to a particular research method, and this in turn leads to a specific statistical procedure, which is a tool the researcher uses. The researcher then considers the strengths and weaknesses of the design, and these in turn determine the interpretation of the results. The text stresses the interrelatedness of topics and continually reviews previous material while building on it. Throughout, intuitive explanations and easily grasped examples accompany more formal explanations, and all material is presented in a logical, step-by-step fashion. Overall, the approach recognizes the initial limitations of students, yet brings them up to the sophisticated level needed to understand the methods and statistics used in modern psychological research.

For the topics in methods, my goal was that students (1) understand the terminology, logic, and procedures used in research; (2) integrate statistical procedures with research methods; (3) develop critical thinking skills regarding research; and (4) learn how to design and conduct research and write APA-style reports. My goal was not to train graduate-level researchers nor to treat methods as an abstract academic discipline. Rather, I sought a middle ground of giving students a solid understanding of the basic designs and statistics found in psychological research so that students can apply them to their research activities.

For the topics in statistics, I assumed that students have a weak background in mathematics and some degree of "math phobia." My goal was that, by the end of the course, these students should understand and perform the descriptive and inferential statistical procedures commonly used in psychological research. Therefore, I have included the calculations for *t*-tests, for linear correlation and regression, and for between-subjects, within-subjects, and mixed two-way factorial designs. I also discuss the logic and interpretation of three-way designs and advanced correlational techniques. In addition, the formulas for nonparametric procedures are complete, so that the text serves as a reference source for such procedures. The importance of computing measures of effect size for each type of design is also stressed. Throughout, however, the perspective is that of a psychologist, not a statistician, so I avoid dwelling on the remarkable things statisticians can do with statistics and instead discuss the things researchers commonly do to make sense out of data. Each procedure is therefore introduced in a research example, focusing on the examination of relationships between variables. Then, specific procedures for describing or inferring such relationships are introduced, finally returning to the conceptual purpose and behavioral interpretation of the study.

Organization

The text employs a "top-down" approach that stresses context and the interrelatedness of topics. Initial chapters give students a background in thinking scientifically and understanding research. These chapters discuss the general design and statistical issues involved in the research process. I envision that students can begin conducting their own laboratory exercises as early as Chapters 4 or 5. Later chapters then describe specific statistical procedures and fill in additional design details along with more complex designs. Appendix A, dealing with reading and writing APA-style research papers, can be assigned at any time.

Chapter 1 shows students what we mean by "critical thinking" and how to apply the logic of the scientific method. Chapter 2 then gives an overview of how hypotheses are developed and tested, based on demonstrating a relationship between variables. Chapter 3 explains the issues of reliability and validity so that students understand how to critique and evaluate research. Chapter 4 discusses the details of conducting experiments and the ethical issues that arise. Chapter 5 presents descriptive designs—including questionnaire development—and the corresponding ethical issues.

With this background, basic descriptive statistics are presented, including how they are used to interpret research. Chapters 6 through 8 present graphs and distributions, measures of central tendency, and measures of variability, and introduce the issues in creating powerful designs. (Procedures for computing percentiles using class intervals are presented in Appendix B.) Chapter 9 discusses *z*-scores, including sampling distributions and computing a *z*-score for a sample mean, to prepare students for understanding inferential statistics as essentially computing *z*-scores.

Chapter 10 presents several correlation coefficients, and Chapter 11 covers linear regression and the proportion of variance accounted for. These procedures are introduced as descriptive statistics rather than later as inferential procedures, because breaking up the discussion of hypothesis testing to introduce the concept of correlation is confusing. The importance of significance testing, however, is emphasized when correlation is introduced.

The presentation of inferential statistics begins with Chapter 12, introducing probability and a preview of hypothesis testing, focusing on using the normal curve to compute probability. (Advanced probability formulas are provided in Appendix B.) Chapter 13 formalizes hypothesis testing using the *z*-test. Chapter 14 presents the single-sample *t*-test and significance testing of correlation coefficients, and begins discussing the relationship between powerful designs and statistical power. Chapter 15 covers the design and analysis of two-sample between-subject designs, and introduces measures of effect size. Chapter 16 covers the issues of controlling participant variables and the design and analysis of two-sample within-subject designs.

Chapter 17 introduces the logic of multilevel designs, and presents the one-way between-subjects ANOVA, including post hoc tests for equal and unequal *n*s and a measure of effect size. Chapter 18 discusses the logic and design of factorial experiments, and presents the two-way between-subjects ANOVA, including post hoc tests for main effects and interactions. Chapter 19 discusses the logic of the one-way and two-way within-subjects ANOVA, mixed-design ANOVAs, and three-way factorial designs and ANOVAs. (The computational procedures for these one- and two-way designs are demonstrated in Appendix B.)

Chapter 20 discusses the design and analysis of various quasi-experimental designs, as well as the reasons for, and types of, single-subject designs. Chapter 21 presents the one-way and two-way chi square, as well as identifying the nonparametric versions of all previous parametric tests, with appropriate post hoc tests and measures of effect size. (The computational steps for these procedures are shown in Appendix B.)

Appendix A provides a comprehensive look at how to search the literature and how to read and write a research report in APA format. A complete example manuscript describes a simple yet engaging two-sample experiment.

Pedagogical Features

The text is designed to be an effective learning tool during the course, and a useful reference source after the course:

- Each chapter begins with a "GETTING STARTED" section that identifies relevant concepts from previous chapters for students to review, and then lists the learning objectives for the chapter.

- In chapters that primarily describe statistics, a "MORE STATISTICAL NOTATION" section at the beginning of the chapter introduces new statistical notation, separate from the conceptual issues that the chapter then presents.
- Important points are emphasized by "REMEMBER" statements, which are summary reminders set off from the text.
- Key terms are highlighted in **bold** type, reviewed in the chapter summary, and listed in a new "KEY TERMS" section at the end of the chapter. (There is also a complete end-of-text glossary.) Formal definitions are accompanied by numerous mnemonics and analogies to promote retention and understanding.
- All concepts, formulas, and statistical statements are presented with complete explanations. Both definitional and computational formulas are introduced in terms of what they accomplish, and computational examples for each statistic are completely worked out, including for those in the appendices.
- All graphs and diagrams are thoroughly explained in captions and fully integrated into the discussion.
- The "PUTTING IT ALL TOGETHER" section at the end of each chapter provides advice, cautions, and ways to integrate material from different chapters.
- Each "CHAPTER SUMMARY" provides a substantive review of the material, not merely a list of the topics covered.
- A minimum of 25 challenging end-of-chapter questions accompany each chapter. Often containing multiple parts, roughly half of the questions per chapter are "REVIEW QUESTIONS" that test definitions and procedural knowledge, while the remaining "PRACTICE PROBLEMS" test applications to real-world data and research situations. Answers to odd-numbered items (with final and intermediate answers) are found in Appendix D. Even-numbered items (with answers in the Instructor's Manual) can be used as assigned homework.
- A "SUMMARY OF FORMULAS" appears at the end of appropriate chapters.
- Appendix B provides computational formulas for computing percentiles using class intervals, linear interpolation, advanced probability, the one-way and two-way within-subjects ANOVA, the two-way mixed-design ANOVA, and nonparametric procedures for ranked data. Practice problems are also included with these sections.
- Reference tables for selecting among designs and statistical procedures are presented on the inside front cover, and a glossary of symbols appears on the inside back cover.
- A unique "capstone" chapter of review information created by me is available on the Houghton Mifflin Website. This presents a series of research topics in which students are led through the development, design, analysis, and interpretation of each study in a guided, stepwise fashion, to provide them experience in applying the principles they have learned. (See "Supplements" below.)

General Changes to the Second Edition

For this edition, the entire text was extensively revised and edited to streamline the narrative, without removing content or losing understandability. I also tightened the conceptual presentations and incorporated a number of new explanatory techniques.

- In appropriate chapters, a new "APA FORMAT FOR STATISTICAL NOTATION" section was added that shows students the symbols and techniques used to present results in published reports.
- A number of new summary and integrative review tables were added to help students organize the material when complex topics are discussed.
- Given the prevalence of computerized statistical programs, the presentation of statistical procedures now de-emphasizes computational issues.
- The introduction of statistical notation now emphasizes the importance of uppercase or lowercase in the symbols.
- The headings and instructions for the statistical tables were improved.
- A list of "KEY TERMS" was added to the end of each chapter.
- Existing end-of-chapter questions were revised, and new questions were added, to give a minimum of 25 "REVIEW QUESTIONS" and "PRACTICE PROBLEMS" per chapter. More questions that deal with graphing, interpreting statistical results, and interpreting statements similar to those encountered in published research were added.

Specific Chapter Changes

Chapter 1 Was revised and organized to better integrate the components of the scientific method.

Chapter 2 Now more clearly shows how descriptive and experimental research demonstrate relationships, and the role that descriptive and inferential statistics play.

Chapter 3 Was drastically revised to show students how to identify and deal with potential flaws in research and how to label them as involving reliability or validity.

Chapter 4 Now essentially completely prepares students to conduct an experiment, and shows how ethical issues arise and how to deal with them.

Chapter 5 Presents a clearer discussion of the issues involved in creating questionnaires and the ethical issues in observational research.

Chapter 6 Includes new and better examples of and instructions for creating frequency distributions.

Chapter 7 Includes a new section describing why central tendency is important and a major revision of how to use central tendency to summarize an experiment. This is the first chapter in which the "APA FORMAT FOR STATISTICAL NOTATION" section appears.

Chapter 8 Contains expanded discussions of how variability relates to the normal curve and of the differences and similarities between the sample, population, and estimated versions of the standard deviation and variance.

Chapter 9 Presents a revised in-depth discussion of z-scores and the z-distribution and how they are used, a new summary of the steps involved when using the z-tables, and a clearer explanation of the central limit theorem and the sampling distribution of means.

Chapter 10 Now better relates individual differences to the size of a correlation coefficient.

Chapter 11 Revisions include a major change in how the proportion of variance accounted for is explained.

Chapter 12 Presents a shortened discussion of computing probability in the abstract, an expanded discussion of using z-scores to compute probability, and a major revision of how statistics use probability to determine the representativeness of a sample.

Chapter 13 Provides an expanded discussion of sampling error, a revised presentation of the z-test, and a very different, more easily understood discussion of Type I and Type II errors.

Chapter 14 Presents a more streamlined discussion of t-tests and confidence intervals, with a reduced emphasis on one-tailed tests.

Chapter 15 Now better integrates the control of participant variables and related design issues with the two-sample experiment, along with revised discussions of interpreting the experiment and computing effect size.

Chapter 16 Now presents counterbalancing of conditions only as it applies to a two-sample experiment, with complex counterbalancing moved to Chapter 19.

Chapter 17 Presents a completely revised and simplified explanation of what the components of the F-ratio estimate in the population and de-emphasizes the mathematical steps in calculating F.

Chapter 18 Presents an expanded discussion of understanding interaction effects and generally interpreting a two-way ANOVA, with de-emphasis on its calculations.

Chapter 19 Now contains a full discussion of complete and partial counterbalancing and randomization of the order of conditions to fit with the discussion of a multilevel, repeated-measures design. Also, now describes the logic of the one-way within-subjects ANOVA, but with the calculations moved to Appendix B, to better fit the chapter's conceptual discussions of two-way and three-way designs.

Chapter 20 Presents a revised, clearer description of quasi-experiments, and a shorter introduction to single-subject designs.

Chapter 21 Although the computations of chi square procedures remain, only the uses and logic of the Mann-Whitney, ranked sums, Wilcoxon, Kruskal-Wallis, and Friedman tests are now discussed, with their computations moved to Appendix B.

Appendix A Revisions more clearly present the techniques for searching the literature and the steps taken when creating an APA-style report.

Appendix B Now contains the formulas—with a completed example and practice problems—for the one-way within-subjects ANOVA and the nonparametric procedures for ranked data, as well as for the two-way within-subjects and mixed-design ANOVAs.

Supplements

Several additional resources support the instructional and learning processes.

- *Instructor's Manual and Test Bank* provides multiple-choice, short-answer, and discussion questions. The test questions are also available on disk in a program that allows instructors to edit items, add their own items, and generate exams.
- The student *Study Guide* provides guided review, additional practice problems, and example test questions for each chapter of the text. Answers are included for the student.
- *SPSS for Windows*, by Charles Stangor, with several accompanying data sets can be shrinkwrapped with my text for students learning to use that software.
- The capstone chapter for this book on Houghton Mifflin's Psychology Website can be reached at the Houghton Mifflin home page at http://www.hmco.com by going to the College Division Psychology page. This chapter provides an integrative review of the entire course by describing a number of published research studies, with prompts that guide students through the researchers' decision-making and interpretive processes.

Acknowledgments

Many people contributed to the production of this text. At Houghton Mifflin Company, I want to thank Kerry Baruth, Senior Sponsoring Editor for Psychology, for his support, and Marianne Stepanian, Development Editor, for her patience and hard work. Thanks too to all those who saw the project through to completion, including Kathryn Dinovo, Charline Lake, and Merrill Peterson.

Finally, I am grateful to the following reviewers who provided valuable feedback:

David Anderson, Allegheny College

Cole Barton, Davidson College

Chrismarie Baxter, Frostburg State College

Russell Bennett, Bemidji State University

Alberto dos Santos, Southern Adventist University

Deborah Foss, Massachusetts College of Liberal Arts

Gary Gillund, The College of Wooster

Christopher M. Hakala, Lycoming College

Daniel Mayes, University of Central Florida

Monicarol Nickelson, Wichita State University

P. Michael Politano, The Citadel
Kavintha Srinivas, Boston College
M. Stewart, Willamette University
Zoe Warwick, University of Maryland, Baltimore

Gary W. Heiman

UNDERSTANDING RESEARCH METHODS AND STATISTICS

PART 1

INTRODUCTION TO PSYCHOLOGICAL RESEARCH

Okay, so you're taking a course in research methods and statistics. You probably wonder what that means. Well, essentially, you're going to learn the basics of conducting scientific psychological research: you'll learn when and how to use the methods that researchers use to conduct a study, as well as when and how to perform the different statistical procedures they use to analyze their results. To begin this journey, the following five chapters provide an overview of psychological research. The first chapter explains why students in psychology learn the scientific method and what it is. The second chapter shows you the steps involved in a psychological study. Chapter 3 describes the major pitfalls researchers face when interpreting research. Chapters 4 and 5 show the details of how psychological research is conducted.

If you're a little nervous about studying statistics, you'll be happy to see that there isn't much about statistics in these chapters. To understand how psychologists use statistics, you must first understand why and how they conduct research. As you begin to understand behavioral research, you'll see how statistics fit in, and they'll become much less threatening. (Honest!)

1

Introduction to the Scientific Method

GETTING STARTED

As you read this chapter, your goals are to learn:

- How to approach statistics and research methods.
- The assumptions and attitudes of scientists, and the goals of science.
- The difference between basic and applied research.
- The criteria for scientific hypotheses and for acceptable evidence for testing them.
- Why literal and conceptual replication are necessary.

This chapter first discusses the purpose and goals of studying research and statistics. Then it examines the scientific method and the process that leads to psychological knowledge. The discussion is rather general, without many details. The purpose here is to show you the broad perspective that researchers take toward conducting research. Once you've adopted this perspective, the rules, procedures, and details in later chapters make much more sense.

INTRODUCTION (OR WHY AM I HERE?)

The following sections address some of the questions students commonly ask about statistics and research methods. The answers to these questions will teach you something about psychological research (and possibly alleviate any anxiety you have.)

Why Do I Need to Learn about Research Methods and Statistics?

Psychology is the science of human and nonhuman behavior. Because you are a student of psychology, you are training to be a scientist so that you can study part of "nature," just as biologists, physicists, and other scientists do. And, as in all other sciences, there is only one acceptable source for your "facts": everything that psychologists think they know in the science of psychology is obtained through research. Therefore, understanding research is an essential part of being a psychologist.

But I'm Not Interested in Research, I Just Want to Help People!

Even if you're not interested in being a researcher yourself, you must understand psychological research so that you can comprehend other people's research. Let's say that you become a therapist and you don't consider yourself a "scientist." You hear of a new therapy that says the way to cure people of some psychological problem is to scare the living daylights out of them. This sounds crazy, but what is important is the quality of the research that does or does not support the therapy. As a responsible professional, you would evaluate the research supporting this therapy before you would use it. You could not do so without understanding research methods and statistics.

So What Am I Learning?

Research methods and statistics are the most enjoyable—and the easiest to learn—when you are actively involved, so this book's approach is to place you in the role of a researcher who wants to answer questions scientifically. Then, you'll learn how to phrase questions scientifically, how to design and conduct scientific research, and how to analyze, interpret, and communicate your results. Along the way, you'll also learn how scientists operate. This involves a combination of thinking logically, being creative, and, more than anything else, applying a critical eye to all phases of a study so that you recognize its imperfections and limitations. Ultimately, you'll not only understand the research of others, but you'll be able to conduct and interpret your own research.

Where Do Statistics Fit In?

Scientists conduct research because they have a question in mind, and statistics help to answer the question. Psychological research measures the behaviors of organisms, resulting in numbers or scores. For example, to study intelligence, researchers measure the IQ scores of different individuals; to study how rats learn a maze, researchers measure the time it takes each rat to escape the maze. Such scores are **data**. (The word *data*, by the way, is plural, so say "the data *are* . . . .") In virtually any study, the researcher ends up with a large batch of data, which must be made manageable and meaningful. Statistical procedures are used to *organize*, *summarize*, and *communicate* data and then to *conclude* what the data indicate. In essence, statistics help a researcher to make sense out of data.

What If I'm Not Very Good at Statistics?

In the grand scheme of things, performing statistics is one small, although extremely important, step in the research process. But, there are not a great number of different statistical procedures for you to learn, and these fancy "procedures" include such mundane things as computing an average or identifying the highest and lowest scores in the data. Also, statisticians have already developed the procedures you'll encounter, so you won't be solving strange formulas, performing proofs, or doing other mystery math. Instead, your job is to learn how to *apply* statistics correctly. Understand that statistics are simply a tool used in the behavioral sciences, just like a wrench is a tool used in the repair of automobile engines. A mechanic need not be an expert "wrencher," and a psychologist need not be an expert "statistician." Rather, in the same way that a mechanic must understand the correct use of wrenches in order to fix an engine, you must understand the correct use of statistics: to identify which research situation calls for which statistics and to understand what a statistical result indicates about a study.

But Statistics Aren't Even Written in English!

There's no denying that statistics involve many strange symbols and unfamiliar terms. But the symbols and terms are simply the shorthand "code" for communicating statistical results and for simplifying statistical formulas. This code even has a name: It's called **statistical notation**. A major part of learning statistics is merely learning the code. Once you speak this language, much of the mystery surrounding statistics evaporates.

What If I'm Not Good at Math?

Although statistics do involve math, it's simple math. You need to know only how to add, subtract, multiply, divide, square, find square roots, and draw simple graphs. What makes statistical procedures *appear* difficult is that they involve a sequence of operations (first you square the numbers, then you add them together, then you subtract some other number, and so on). Working through the formulas is not difficult, but because they're in code, it takes a little practice. So, keep an open mind, be prepared to do some work, and you'll be amazed by what happens. Although statistics are a little unusual, they are not incomprehensible and they do not require you to be a math wizard.

So All I Have to Do Is Learn to Compute Statistical Answers?

No! Don't get so carried away with formulas and calculations that you lose sight of the big picture. In the big picture, a statistical answer tells you something about data and therefore something about your research. Ultimately, you want to make sense of data, and to do that you must compute the appropriate statistic and correctly interpret it. You need to concentrate on learning *when* and *why* to use each procedure and *how to interpret* its answer. Be sure to put as much effort into this as you do into learning how to perform the calculations.

All Right, So How Do I Learn Methods and Statistics?

Study. Think. Practice. Think. Practice some more. Psychological research has its own language involving very specific terms—with very specific meanings—that you must learn. The way to learn a foreign language is to speak it every day, so practice the vocabulary of research every day. Likewise, although knowing the rules of science is important, you must practice generalizing the rules to the different types of research you'll encounter later when on your own.

Recognize that because you do not yet speak the language, you won't learn anything by simply skimming a chapter. You must learn to translate the terminology and symbols into words that you understand and this takes time and effort. Also, you cannot "cram" this material. If you try, you won't learn much (and your brain will melt). Instead, work on the material a little bit every day. Then you'll be able to digest the material in bite-sized pieces. This is the most effective—and least painful—way to learn research methods and statistics.

What's with This Book?

There are several ways this book helps you master the material. At the beginning of each chapter is a list of the important concepts to review before beginning, followed by a list of the major points you should learn from the chapter. After you finish the chapter, check that you understand everything in the list. Also, throughout each chapter, you'll see statements labeled "**REMEMBER**." These describe concepts and principles that are especially important. You'll also encounter a number of tables that help you to integrate different concepts, or that organize the steps to follow when performing exercises or conducting your own research. At the end of each chapter is a list of summary statements: Be sure you understand each one. Then there are review questions and practice problems that will help you identify weak spots in your knowledge (use these as a self-test to prepare for the real test). Answers to odd-numbered questions and problems are provided in Appendix D.

Each chapter that focuses on statistics will open with a section titled "More Statistical Notation." Here you can become familiar with new symbols used in the chapter before being immersed in the concepts of the chapter. Then every new formula will be presented with some example data so that you can see how to use the formula. Master the formulas and codes at each step, because they often reappear later as part of more complicated formulas. (The examples are unrealistically simple, containing only a few scores. But, if you understand a procedure using simple numbers, you'll be able to perform it with more complex data.) For quick reference, a list of the formulas discussed in a chapter is provided at the end of the chapter.

Okay! Now that you have some idea of what this course involves, let's look at the basics of scientific research.

THE SCIENTIFIC METHOD

If you are at all curious about behavior, you're already on your way toward becoming a researcher. All sciences are based on curiosity about nature, and psychology is based on curiosity about behavior. Your curiosity is important because it is the basis for deciding what you want to learn about a behavior and how to go about learning it.

But being curious is not enough. Creating, conducting, and interpreting research requires mental effort because nature is very secretive and not easily understood. On the one hand, psychological research is fun because of the challenge in devising ways to unlock the mysteries of behavior. But, on the other hand, caution is needed at every step because it is easy to draw *incorrect* conclusions about a behavior. This is a critical problem because psychology is used by society in ways that have a serious impact on the lives and well-being of others. For example, at one time, people with a criminal history were thought to have "defective" personalities, which were "remedied" by the removal of portions of their brains! Unfortunately for those undergoing the surgery, this approach was just plain wrong! Thus, because the knowledge produced by research can drastically influence the lives of others, psychology's goal is to be perfectly accurate.

To try to meet this goal, psychology uses the "scientific method." This is a rather broad term, but essentially, the **scientific method** is a set of rules consisting of certain assumptions, attitudes, goals, and procedures for creating and answering questions about nature.

Why should psychologists—including yourself—use the scientific method? We could use our intuitions and personal experiences, or logical deductions and common sense, or we could defer to the pronouncements of authority figures. But! We don't trust intuitions or personal experience because everyone has different feelings about, and experiences of, the world. (Whose should we believe?) Likewise, we do not trust logic because nature does not always conform to our logic. Also, we cannot rely on common sense because it is often contradictory. (Which is true: "Absence makes the heart grow fonder" or "Out of sight, out of mind"?) And, we cannot rely on what the "experts" say because there's no reason to believe that they correctly understand how nature works either. The problem with all of these sources of knowledge is that they ultimately rely on opinions or beliefs that may be created by someone who is biased or wrong or downright crazy! After all, merely because someone says something is true does not make it true.

Psychology relies on the scientific method because it is the best approach for eliminating bias and opinion, for reaching a consensus about how a behavior truly operates, and for correcting errors. It does this by requiring that, whenever someone makes a statement about behavior, we ask "How do you know that?" We don't mean "believe," "feel," or "think"—we mean *know*! In science—just as in a court of law—it is the *evidence* supporting a statement that is most important. The scientific method provides the most convincing evidence about nature because, instead of reflecting our own biases or intuitions, scientific evidence is based on the events that occur in nature.

The remainder of this chapter examines the scientific approach to studying behavior. To start with, the following sections look at how scientists approach the task of science.

The Assumptions of Science

What first distinguishes scientists from nonscientists is the philosophy about nature that scientists adopt. At first glance, any aspect of nature, especially human behavior, seems overwhelmingly complex, verging on the chaotic. Scientists have the audacity to try to understand such a complicated topic because they do not consider nature to be chaotic. Instead, scientists make certain assumptions about nature that allow them to approach it as a regulated and consistent system. These assumptions are that nature is lawful, deterministic, and understandable.

By saying that nature is **lawful**, we mean that every event can be understood as a predictable sequence of natural causes and effects. We assume that behavior is lawful, because if it isn't (and instead is random), then we could never understand it. Thus, in the same way that the "law of gravity" governs the behavior of planets or the "laws of aerodynamics" govern the behavior of airplanes, psychologists assume there are laws of nature that govern the behavior of living organisms. Although some laws do not apply to all species (for example, laws dealing with nest building among birds do not apply to humans), a specific law does apply to all members of a group. Thus, when psychologists study the mating behavior of penguins, or the development of language in people, they are studying laws of nature.

Viewing behavior as lawful leads to a second, related assumption: We assume that behavior is "determined." **Determinism** means that behavior is solely influenced by natural causes and does not depend on an individual's choice or "free will." If, instead, we assumed that organisms freely decide their behavior, then behavior truly would be chaotic, because the only explanation for every behavior would be "because he or she wanted to." Therefore, we reject the idea that free will plays a role. After all, you cannot walk off a cliff and "will" yourself not to fall, because the law of gravity forces you to fall. Anyone else in the same situation will also fall because that is how gravity operates. Likewise, we assume that you cannot freely choose to exhibit a particular personality or respond in a particular way in a given situation. The laws of behavior force you to have certain attributes and to behave in a certain way in a given situation. Anyone else in that situation will be similarly influenced, because that is how the laws of behavior operate. (Note that "determinism" is different from "predestination." *Predestination* suggests that our actions follow some grand plan that is already laid out for us. *Determinism* means that, while there is no overall plan, there are natural causes for every behavior.)

The third assumption of science is that the laws of nature are *understandable*. Regardless of how complicated nature may appear or how confused we currently are about it, we assume that we will eventually understand it (or there is no point in studying it). Thus, any scientific statement must logically and rationally fit with the known facts so that it can be understood. Part of an explanation can never be that we must accept an unexplainable mystery or an unresolvable contradiction. If two statements contradict each other at present, it must be logically possible to resolve the debate eventually so that only one statement applies.

> ***REMEMBER*** To be studied scientifically, any behavior must be assumed to be lawful, determined, and understandable.

Notice that the above assumptions exclude certain topics from being studied scientifically. For example, miracles cannot be studied scientifically because, by definition, miracles do not obey the laws of nature. Likewise, because of determinism we cannot study free will. (We can, however, study people's *perceptions* of miracles or free will, because their perceptions are behaviors that fit the above assumptions.) Further, because nature is assumed to be understandable, any topic that requires faith cannot be studied scientifically. Faith is the acceptance of the truth of a statement without questions or needing proof. But in science it is *always* appropriate to question and to ask for proof. Thus, although scientists are entitled to the same religions and beliefs as anyone else, they cannot allow these beliefs to play a part when producing and evaluating scientific evidence. After all, if science did allow statements of faith, whose faith would we use . . . yours or mine?

The Attitudes of Scientists

To help prevent their own biases and beliefs from creeping into their conclusions, scientists explicitly adopt specific attitudes toward the process of learning about nature. As a scientist, you should be uncertain, open-minded, skeptical, cautious, and ethical.

The starting point is to recognize that the purpose of science is to learn about nature, admitting that no one already knows everything about how nature operates. There is always some degree of *uncertainty*. For psychologists, this means that no one knows precisely what a particular behavior entails, what the factors are that influence it, or what the one correct way to study it is. All other steps in scientific research stem from this simple admission.

If no one knows for certain how nature operates, then any explanation or description of it may be just as appropriate as any other. Therefore, as a scientist you should be **open-minded**, leaving your biases and preconceptions behind. An explanation may offend your sensibilities or contradict your beliefs, but that is no reason to dismiss it. You must look in all directions, at all possible explanations, when trying to understand a behavior.

At the same time, you should be very *skeptical*: Never automatically accept the truth of a scientific statement. Because no one already knows how nature works, any description of a behavior or interpretation of a study may be incorrect. After all, the history of science is littered with descriptions that at first appeared accurate but later turned out to misrepresent nature. (The earth is not flat!) Therefore, you must skeptically and critically evaluate the evidence produced by any study: Using logic and your knowledge of psychology, always question whether the factors proposed as important might actually be irrelevant (or at least not the whole story) and whether the factors proposed as irrelevant might actually be important. To aid in this process, researchers share their research findings through professional publications, meetings, and so on. Then, eventually, psychology will identify and rectify any mistakes, to arrive at the best, most accurate information.

If we assume that critical analysis will eventually produce an error-free understanding of nature, then we must also recognize that we are currently in the process of discovering which parts of our information are incorrect. Therefore, be **cautious** when dealing with scientific findings. Any scientific conclusion implicitly contains the qualifying statement "given our present knowledge and abilities." Never treat the results of any single study as a "fact" in the usual sense. Instead, always remember that a research finding is a piece of evidence that provides some degree of confidence in a description of nature, but that at the same time may actually misrepresent nature.

Finally, there is one other attitude that scientists adopt: Scientists must behave *ethically* when conducting research. Later chapters examine the specific guidelines for **research ethics**, but the basic principle is that neither researchers nor their research should cause harm to others.

Table 1.1 will help you to remember these attitudes by relating each one to the approach that scientists take. Whenever you conduct research or encounter that of others, be sure that these attitudes are present.

TABLE 1.1 How the Attitudes of Researchers Influence Their Approach to Psychological Findings

Attitude	*Approach*
Uncertain	No one already knows how a behavior operates.
Open-minded	Any approach or statement may be correct.
Skeptical	Any approach or statement may contain error.
Cautious	Any conclusion is not a "fact."
Ethical	Research should not harm others.

REMEMBER Scientists are uncertain, open-minded, skeptical, and cautious. They are also ethical.

As scientists, psychologists are led by their attitudes to continually evaluate their research and the research of others. Evaluating a study means evaluating the evidence the study provides. As with the rules of evidence in a court of law, science has rules governing what evidence is admissible and how it must be gathered.

The Criteria for Scientific Evidence

When people think of scientific research, they usually think of "experiments." Although psychologists perform experiments, they also conduct other types of research. In fact, there is an infinite number of different ways to "design" a study. The **design** of a study is the specific manner in which the study is set up and conducted. First, the design must identify the specific people or animals to study. (Note that historically, published psychological research has referred to these individuals as **subjects**. However, in publications after 1994 the preference is to refer to them as **participants**.) In addition, a design includes the specific situation or sequence of situations under which participants are studied, the way their behavior is examined, and the components of the situation and behavior that are considered.

As an example of a behavior we might design a study for, let's discuss one simple, familiar behavior: the irritating tendency of people to "channel surf"—to grab the television remote control and change the channel whenever a commercial appears. (If this seems too mundane a behavior to be "psychological," stay tuned . . . .) To study this behavior, remember that we seek the most convincing evidence for answering the question "How do you know that?" In science, convincing evidence is empirical, objective, systematic, and controlled.

First, scientific evidence must be **empirical**—meaning learned by *observation*. Psychologists study everything that an individual does, feels, thinks, wants, or remembers, from the microlevel of neurological functioning to the macrolevel of complex, lifelong behaviors. Yet ultimately, all evidence is collected and all debates are resolved by attending to observable, public behaviors. Thus, to understand channel changing, we should *observe* channel changing. Because anyone else can potentially observe this behavior in the same way, everyone shares the same basis for determining how it operates.

Second, several people can observe the same event and still have different personal impressions of it. Therefore, science requires **objectivity**. This means that, ideally, a researcher's personal biases, attitudes, or subjective impressions do not influence the observations or conclusions. Scientists strive for this by obtaining *measurements* that are as empirical, objective, and precise as possible. It is through objective measurement of behavior that a researcher obtains the data in a study. For example, counting the number of times someone changes channels during a specified period results in objective, precise data. Or, in other studies, we may use equipment that times participants' responses or measures their physiological reactions, we may interview participants or have them perform mental or physical tests, we may observe subjects surreptitiously, and so on. In any of these approaches, we try to be as objective as possible, so that the data reflect what participants actually do in a given situation and not our personal interpretations of what they do.

Third, nature is very complex. Consequently, the research situation must be simplified so that we are not confused by all that is going on. Therefore, evidence is gathered systematically. Being **systematic** means that observations are obtained in a methodical, step-by-step fashion. For example, say we think that boring commercials cause channel changing. After we've objectively measured "boring," we would then measure the channel changing that occurs with very boring commercials, with less boring commercials, and again with interesting commercials. If we also think that the number of people in the room influences channel changing, we would observe participants' responses to the above commercials first when alone, then when another person is present, then when two other people are present, and so on. By being systematic, we determine the role of each factor and combination of factors as they apply to a behavior.

Finally, evidence must be obtained under controlled conditions. **Control** is another way to simplify the situation by eliminating factors that might influence the behavior being observed and thus create confusion. For example, while observing whether more boring commercials produce more channel changing, we would try to control how boring the television program is, so that this factor could not influence channel changing. Likewise, we'd control the situation by having participants only watch television so that other distractions won't influence their channel changing. In short, with control, researchers attempt to create a clearly defined situation in which they observe only the specific behavior and the relevant factors that interest them.

Table 1.2 will help you remember the above criteria by relating them to the rules for designing research. The more that a study deviates from these rules, the more that its results are likely to misrepresent nature, and so the less confidence we have in its conclusions.

TABLE 1.2 How the Criteria for Scientific Research Translate into the Rules for Designing Research

Criteria	*Rule*
Empirical	Information is based on observation.
Objective	Observations are free from bias.
Systematic	Observations are made in a step-by-step fashion.
Controlled	Potentially confusing factors are eliminated.

REMEMBER Acceptable scientific evidence is obtained through empirical, objective, systematic, and controlled research.

As you will see, many different research designs are possible that meet the above criteria. Which design you should use depends first upon the type of question being asked—the specific goal of the study.

THE GOALS OF PSYCHOLOGICAL RESEARCH

Overall, the goal of psychology is to understand behavior. But what does "understand" mean? Science has come to define understanding an event in terms of the four simultaneous and equally important goals of being able to describe, explain, predict, and control the event.

Obviously, psychologists want to know what behavior does and does not occur in nature, so the first goal is to *describe* each behavior and the conditions under which it occurs. To describe channel changing, we would specify how frequently channels are changed, whether they are changed during all commercials, at all times of the day, and so on. We could also describe channel changing from various perspectives, in terms of the hand movements necessary to operate the remote control, or the cognitive decision making involved, or the neurological activity occurring in the brain.

Mere description of a behavior, however, is not enough to understand it; we also need to know *why* the behavior occurs. Therefore, another goal is to *explain* behaviors in terms of their specific causes. Thus, we want to explain what aspect of a commercial, either present or absent, causes channel changing, and why. We also want to explain the factors—the channel changer's personality, the type of program, the presence of other people in the room—that cause more or less channel changing, and why. And again, there are various perspectives we can take, such as neurological, cognitive, motivational, or environmental causes.

Note that in explaining a behavior, it is important to avoid pseudo-explanations. A **pseudo-explanation** is circular, giving as the reason for an event another name for that event. For example, a pseudo-explanation of channel changing is that it is caused by the motivation to see what is on other channels—really just another way of saying that people change channels because they want to change channels. The key to avoiding a pseudo-explanation is to provide an *independent* verification of the supposed cause. If, for example, we could discover a gene that motivates people to change channels, then we would be confident that we were talking about two different things—a cause (the gene) and an effect (changing channels)—and not merely renaming one thing.

Another aspect of understanding a behavior is to know when it will occur or what will bring it about, so an additional goal of psychology is to *predict* behaviors. Thus, we want to be able to accurately predict when channel changing will and will not occur, the amount or degree of the behavior to expect from a particular person, or when and how the behavior will change as a person's physiological, cognitive, social, or environmental conditions change. In addition, notice that the accuracy with which a behavior can be predicted is an indication of how well we have explained it. If we say that a behavior has a particular cause, but the presence of the cause does not allow us to accurately predict the behavior, then the explanation is wrong, or at least incomplete.

TABLE 1.3 How the Goals of Science Translate into the Activities of Psychologists

Goal	*Activity*
Describe	Learn what a behavior entails and the situations in which it occurs.
Explain	Learn the causes that determine when and why a behavior occurs.
Predict	Learn to identify the factors needed to predict when a behavior will occur.
Control	Learn to manipulate the factors needed to produce or eliminate a behavior.

Finally, if we truly understand a behavior, we should be able to create the situation in which it occurs. Therefore, the fourth goal is to *control* behavior. Thus, in studying channel changing, we want to know how to alter the situation to produce, increase, decrease, or eliminate the behavior. And note that being able to control events is another important test of an explanation. If a cause of a behavior is identified, then *manipulating* that cause—turning it on and off or providing more or less of it—should produce changes in the behavior. If it does not, the explanation is again either wrong or incomplete.

Table 1.3 will help you to remember these goals by relating them to the types of activities psychologists pursue when conducting research. Any psychological study will entail one or more of these activities.

REMEMBER To completely understand a behavior, researchers strive to describe it, explain its causes, and predict and control its occurrence.

Meeting the Goals of Science

Now you can see how the science of psychology proceeds: As shown in Figure 1.1, it is through the combination of the required attitudes plus the requirements of research that we expect to understand behavior. That is, researchers attempt to learn about a behavior by obtaining empirical, objective, systematic, and controlled observations that allow them to describe, explain, predict, and control the behavior. Each finding is rigorously evaluated in a skeptical yet open-minded manner, so that an accurate understanding of the laws of behavior can be developed.

FIGURE 1.1 How a Scientist's Attitudes Plus the Criteria for Acceptable Evidence Lead to Meeting the Goals of Science

Attitudes of Scientists		*Criteria for Research*		*Accurate Understanding*
Uncertain Open-minded Skeptical Cautious Ethical	+	Empirical Objective Systematic Controlled	=	Describe Explain Predict Control

You may think that this approach is massive overkill when studying a behavior as mundane as channel changing. Is it really necessary to be that fussy? Well, yes, if we want to *fully* understand the behavior. Granted, it's easier to see why we should be so fussy if, for example, we were studying something like airplane pilots who turn off their planes' engines in midflight. There is an urgency to this behavior so that understanding it in such great detail would not be overkill (pardon the pun). But recognize that channel changing is not so mundane. This behavior involves major psychological processes, such as decision making, information processing, communication, neural-pathways control, motivation, and social processes. Thus, an in-depth study of channel changing is worthwhile because, for example, by studying the decision making involved in channel changing, we can learn about decision-making processes in general. Further, another reason for a detailed study of channel changing is that research often leads to *serendipitous* findings: In the process of studying one aspect of nature, researchers may accidentally discover another aspect, unrelated to the original topic. (In studying channel changing, we may stumble onto a cure for boredom.) Thus, because we never know where an investigation will lead, we take the study of every behavior very seriously and do the best, most complete job we can.

Applied and Basic Research

There is a greater urgency for studying something like the errors an airplane pilot makes, because this behavior represents a real-life problem. Such research is called applied research. **Applied research** is conducted for the purpose of solving an existing, real-life problem. For example, the companies that pay for television commercials might conduct applied research into channel changing during their commercials so that they can eliminate the resulting problem of wasted advertising money.

On the other hand, **basic research** is conducted simply for the knowledge it produces. Thus, we might study channel changing simply because it adds to our understanding of behavior in general. Although people often have a hard time understanding why it's important to conduct basic research, such activity is justified first and foremost because science seeks to understand *all* aspects of nature. Also, basic and applied research often overlap. For example, basic research into channel changing might provide information that advertising companies can apply to solve their problem (and applied research designed to eliminate channel changing will add to our basic understanding of the behavior). A third justification of basic research is that past basic research may someday be valuable in a future applied setting. Say that we learn that channel changing and turning off airplane engines in midflight share a common factor (perhaps both are caused by boredom). At that point, our basic research into channel changing would be very useful for the applied problem of preventing airplane crashes. And, finally, a justification for basic research is that it often results in serendipitous applied findings. For example, some of the most common medicinal drugs have been discovered totally by accident during the course of basic research.

In sum, the terms *basic* and *applied* are general, describing a study in terms of its obvious, stated purposes. In reality, we never know the ultimate purpose that research will serve (which is another reason for employing very rigorous methods).

REMEMBER The primary purpose of basic research is to obtain knowledge; the primary purpose of applied research is to solve an existing problem.

The Role of a Single Study

Regardless of whether we conduct applied or basic research, *completely* describing, explaining, predicting, and controlling a behavior are the *ultimate* goals of research. But, because of the extreme complexity of behaviors, no single study can fully meet this goal. Instead, a systematic and controlled study simplifies nature by examining one factor and taking one perspective at a time. Thus, one study will describe certain aspects of a behavior, another will examine an explanation, other studies will investigate ways to predict the behavior, and still others will focus on controlling it. Any specific study is therefore a momentary "snapshot" of one small portion of a behavior. (In fact, because any study has such an extremely narrow focus, most psychologists would think it too grandiose to claim that their study directly examines a law of nature.) As a result of this piecemeal approach, the discipline of psychology—and publications describing it—may appear to be disjointed and unfocused, going off in many directions at once. Yet, we assume that eventually all of these individual pieces of information will be integrated so that we can truly understand the laws of nature.

> *REMEMBER* Any study represents a very limited and simplified view of the complexity found in nature and contributes minutely to the goals of describing, explaining, predicting, and controlling a behavior.

Every decision researchers make depends first and foremost on whether their primary goal is to describe, explain, predict, or control a behavior. Therefore, the first step in any study is to formulate the specific question you wish to answer. That question is called a hypothesis.

SCIENTIFIC HYPOTHESES

To begin our study, we might ask the question, "What causes channel changing?" However, this is actually a very ambiguous question, with no hint as to the type of "snapshot" needed to answer it. Do we mean "what" in terms of the cognitive, the physiological, or the environmental causes? And which aspect of the cognitive, physiological, or environmental causes are we talking about? Such an ambiguous question cannot be directly answered by a study. After all, at some point we must go out and actually collect some data, so sooner or later we need to know precisely which behavior to examine and how to examine it. Therefore, we must translate any general question into a specific hypothesis that directs the research.

Creating Scientific Hypotheses

A **hypothesis** is a formally stated expectation about how a behavior operates. It is, in essence, a tentative guess about a behavior that usually relates a behavior to some other behavior or influence. Rather than asking a question beginning with "Why" or "What," a hypothesis is phrased as a declarative statement or description. Then we test the hypothesis: We conduct an empirical, controlled, systematic study that provides data that help us determine if the statement is correct or not.

There are two general types of hypotheses. In keeping with the goal of explaining and controlling the causes of behavior, one type is a **causal hypothesis**: This tentatively identifies a particular cause for, or influence on, a behavior. For example, we might hypothesize that "channel changing is caused by the boring content of commercials." (Implicitly, we recognize there may be many other influences on channel changing, but for now, this is the one we'd study.)

On the other hand, in keeping with the goal of describing and predicting behavior, the other type is a **descriptive hypothesis**: This tentatively describes a behavior in terms of its characteristics or the situation in which it occurs, and allows us to predict when it occurs. For example, we might hypothesize that "channel changing occurs more frequently when someone is watching television alone than when other people are present." Notice that even though the number of people present might partially cause channel changing, we have not stated this. A descriptive hypothesis does *not* attempt to identify the causes of a behavior. In fact, sometimes it states simply that certain behaviors occur and can be observed and measured, giving a general goal and direction to a study. For example, we might hypothesize that "channel changers have certain personality characteristics" and then set out to describe them.

> *REMEMBER* A causal hypothesis postulates a causal influence on a behavior, and a descriptive hypothesis postulates characteristics of the behavior or provides a goal for observations.

It is very important to state explicitly whether a study examines the causes of a behavior, because, as you'll see, this is a critical factor in determining the design of the study. Before designing the study, however, you must be sure the hypothesis reflects our assumptions about the lawfulness and understandability of nature. If it does not, then the hypothesis is not scientific, and the evidence that supports it is not scientifically admissible. Therefore, there are specific rules for creating scientific hypotheses.

The Criteria for Scientific Hypotheses

Regardless of whether it's a causal or descriptive hypothesis, there are five attributes that a scientific hypothesis should have: it should be testable, falsifiable, precise, rational, and parsimonious.

A hypothesis must first be testable and falsifiable. **Testable** means that it is possible to devise a test of a hypothesis. **Falsifiable** means that the test can potentially show that the hypothesis is incorrect. Our previous channel-changing hypotheses are testable and falsifiable because we can devise a study to test them, and we might find evidence indicating they are incorrect. It is possible, however, to create hypotheses that are not testable or falsifiable. Consider the hypothesis "When people die, they see a bright light." This is not a testable hypothesis because it's not possible to study people's experience after death—they're dead! Because it's not testable, the hypothesis is also not falsifiable. Or, consider Sigmund Freud's hypothesis that the "id" leads people to express aggression directly as well as indirectly through superficially nonaggressive behaviors. We can determine whether aggression occurs, but regardless of what is observed, it isn't possible to show that the hypothesis is false: If we observe aggression, it's because of the id. If we don't observe aggression, it's still because of the id, expressing its aggression through nonaggressive behavior. Given the circular logic here, this hypothesis cannot tell us anything about the id. If a hypothesis is not testable or falsifiable, it is impossible to determine its accuracy. Instead, we must accept the hypothesis on faith, a nonscientific approach.

A hypothesis must also add to knowledge about the laws of nature in a meaningful and understandable way, so a hypothesis must be precise and rational. A **precise** hypothesis contains terms that are clearly defined. The use of ambiguous terms opens the hypothesis to interpretation and opinion, making it less clearly testable and falsifiable. A **rational** hypothesis logically fits what is already known about the laws of behavior. For example, our hypothesis about boring commercials causing channel changing will, if correct, mesh easily with existing knowledge. In contrast, consider the claim that some people exhibit "ESP," the ability to send and receive mental messages. A hypothesis about this supposed ability is not rational, because it contradicts existing knowledge about the brain and physical energy already developed in psychology, biology, and physics.

Finally, a hypothesis must be parsimonious. A **parsimonious** hypothesis is one that is as simple as possible. The assumption that nature is lawful implies that many diverse events can be accounted for by an economical combination of relatively few laws. If we propose new laws or mechanisms for every situation, we are merely renaming nature without explaining it. Therefore, the rule of parsimony says that we begin with relatively simple hypotheses that apply to broad categories of behaviors. Then, only if the simple explanations fail to account for a behavior are we justified in proposing new, more complex ones. Thus, any hypothesis about ESP would not be parsimonious, because it would require proposing all sorts of new brain components and new energy waves, just to make it a viable hypothesis. To be parsimonious, however, there would first need to be scientific evidence for ESP that could not be explained using brain mechanisms and energy forms that are already established by previous research. Only then would it be acceptable to propose the existence of new brain components and new energy waves.

Table 1.4 will help you remember the criteria for an acceptable hypothesis by relating each of them to a question you should ask about the hypothesis. The more that a hypothesis deviates from these criteria, the less confidence we have in any conclusions about it.

> ***REMEMBER*** Scientific hypotheses must be falsifiable, testable, precise, rational, and parsimonious.

Sources of Hypotheses

How do you come up with a hypothesis? One obvious source is a researcher's own opinions, observations, or experiences. It is perfectly acceptable to base a hypothesis on

TABLE 1.4 Questions to Consider When Determining Whether a Hypothesis Meets the Five Criteria for Scientific Acceptability

Criteria	*Questions about the hypothesis*
Testable	Can a test be designed for it?
Falsifiable	Can it be possibly proved false?
Precise	Are its terms clearly defined?
Rational	Does it fit with the known information?
Parsimonious	Does it involve the simplest possible approach?

such sources, as long as you then conduct an empirical, objective study to provide evidence for the hypothesis. A second source is existing research: When reading the results of a study that tested one hypothesis, you'll usually see the basis for several additional hypotheses. For example, if we find that channel changing increases when someone is alone, we would then want to determine why, identify the factors that modify this influence, and so on. A third source of a hypothesis, as we'll see, is the retesting of a hypothesis previously tested by another researcher.

Theories are another source of hypotheses. A **theory** is an integrated set of proposals that defines, explains, organizcs, and interrelates knowledge about many behaviors. Theoreticians may develop a theory beginning with proposals and concepts for which there is little scientific evidence. Or, they may develop a theory after substantial evidence has been collected, in order to tie together many diverse findings. Either way, a theory is a framework of abstract concepts that helps to explain and describe a broad range of behaviors in a parsimonious way. For example, "Freudian theory" attempted to explain a vast array of normal and abnormal behaviors using the theoretical concepts of id, ego, and superego.

Theories serve two major functions. First, they help to *organize* empirical findings. Additional research can then be tied to the theory, providing a framework for developing the "big picture" regarding a behavior. At the same time, theories serve to *guide* research. To test or add to a theory, researchers derive a specific hypothesis, test it in a study, and then use the study's outcome to either add to or correct the theory. Then, from the modified theory, researchers develop additional hypotheses, which, after testing, are used to further modify the theory. (*Note*: A study cannot test a theory; it can test a hypothesis derived from a theory. Be careful when using the word *theory*.)

> ***REMEMBER*** A theory is an organized body of research that describes and explains a wide range of behaviors.

A final, related source of hypotheses is a model. A **model** is a description that, by analogy, explains the process underlying particular behaviors. Whereas a theory tends to be very broad in scope, a model tends to be more specific and concrete. Consider a model airplane: It provides a solid way to discuss and understand how the components of an actual airplane operate. Contrast this with the theory of aerodynamics that explains the general principles of flight. Likewise, in psychology, a theory describes broad, abstract components of a behavior, while a model provides a more specific analogy for discussing and understanding the components of the behavior. A psychological model usually involves a flow chart or diagram. For example, Figure 1.2 shows the typical Information-Processing Model of human memory.

FIGURE 1.2 The Information-Processing Model of Memory

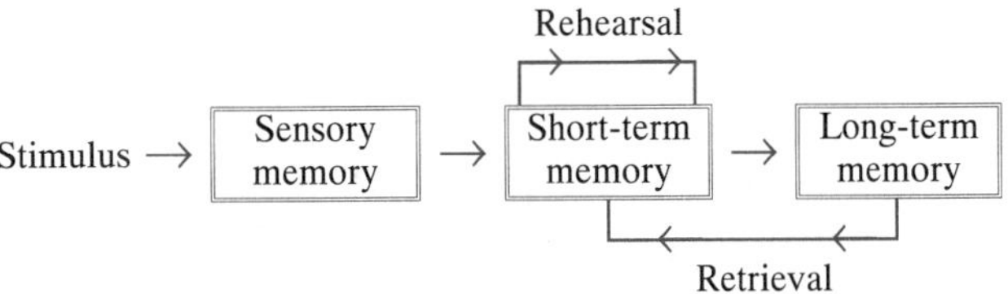

Each box in the figure represents the flow of information through different types of memories. Although no one believes that your brain actually contains little boxes labeled short-term and long-term memory, this is a useful analogy for deriving specific hypotheses about how and when information remains in temporary or in more permanent memory. Researchers then test these hypotheses and use the results to modify the model, in the same way that theories are modified.

Testing Hypotheses Through Research

The "model" in Figure 1.3 summarizes how hypotheses are tested and how the results are incorporated into scientific knowledge. The first step is to create an acceptable hypothesis—using theoretical concepts, models, or our observations about behavior—so that we can better describe, explain, predict, and control a behavior.

Next, we design a study to test the hypothesis. Just how you do that is the topic of this book. Suffice it to say that there are many designs to choose from, depending on whether the goal of the study is to describe, explain, predict, or control the behavior. Regardless of the design, we attempt to obtain objective, systematic, and controlled measurements of the intended behavior, so that we clearly and confidently test the hypothesis.

As part of the design, researchers distinguish between a hypothesis and a prediction. Whereas a hypothesis is a general statement about how a behavior operates, a **prediction** is a specific statement about how we will see the behavior manifested in the research situation, describing the specific results that we expect in a study. We test the

FIGURE 1.3 The Flow of Scientific Research

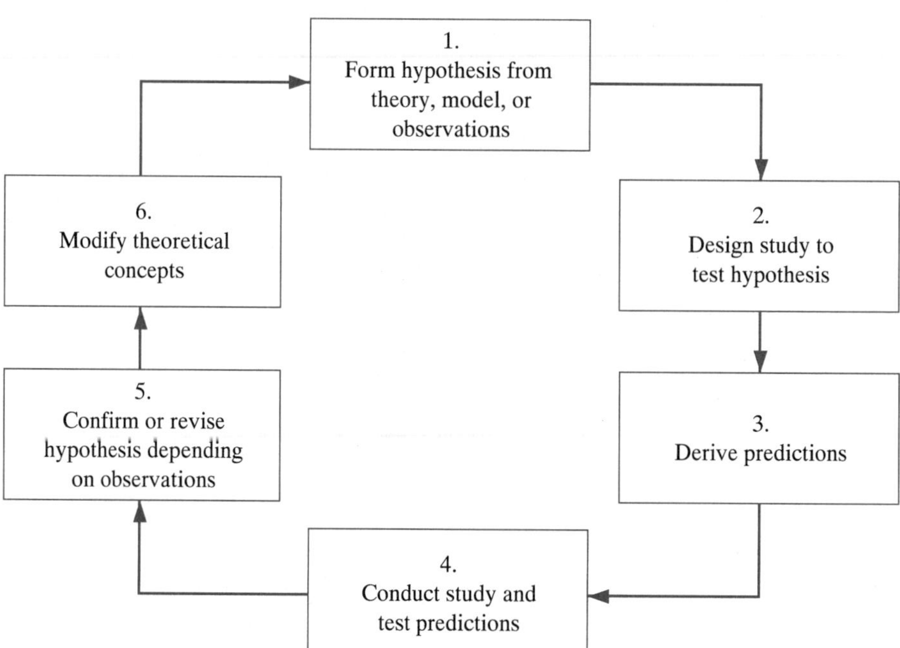

accuracy of a hypothesis using the logic that, if the hypothesis is correct, then participants should behave in a certain way, resulting in certain data: The behavior should occur in such a way that the corresponding scores will be high or low, or will change in a predictable manner. For example, if we hypothesized that boring commercials cause channel changing, we'd predict that as more boring commercials occur, participants' scores will reflect more frequent, more rapid, or more motivated channel changing.

With a prediction in hand, researchers conduct the study and collect the data. Then statistical procedures come into play. There are various types of statistics to use, depending on the specific design of a study. All statistics, however, essentially make sense out of data so that it is possible to see if the scores form the predicted pattern. Thus, if we are testing whether more frequent channel changing occurs with more boring commercials, we'll use statistical procedures to determine if this pattern occurs in the data.

If the data fit the prediction, there is evidence to support the original hypothesis. If they do not, there is not support for the hypothesis. Then, from the conclusions about the hypothesis, we work back to the theoretical concepts, model, or proposals we started with in step 1, either adding to or correcting them. Future research then uses this modified description, testing additional hypotheses that will further modify the description, and the cycle begins again. It is through this continual cycle that the science of psychology collates, organizes, and resolves the diverse "snapshots" of behaviors that individual studies provide, so that we can eventually understand the broader laws of nature.

THE FLAWS IN SCIENTIFIC RESEARCH

Recall that it's easy to make mistakes when learning about nature because nature is complex and mysterious, and it's not already clear to us how it works. Although the rules we've examined may seem sufficient to eliminate error, they do not guarantee this. There will always be many opportunities for researchers to make errors. Therefore, you must be skeptical, remembering that what we know—or think we know—depends on (1) the evidence presented and (2) how it is interpreted.

First, let's consider the evidence.

The Flaws in the Evidence

An ideal study would produce perfectly accurate measurements of the exact behavior we seek to describe, with only the relevant factors coming into play. However, no study is ideal. Rather, there are four general aspects of any study that can weaken our confidence in its data and conclusions.

First, some behaviors cannot be studied in a completely empirical, objective, systematic, and controlled manner. For example, it is impossible to directly observe "thinking." Instead, we must observe some other behavior—such as the errors in logic that people make—from which to draw inferences about thinking. However, the greater the inferential leap from the observed to the unseen behavior, the less confidence we have in our conclusions. Also, there is no "yardstick" for objectively measuring some behaviors, such as aggressiveness or love. Instead, we must employ more subjective measurement procedures that may include bias and error. Finally, researchers cannot always observe a behavior in a systematic and controlled fashion. For example, in studying the attitudes of women toward childbearing, we cannot separate the fact that participants have female personalities from the fact that they have female genes. Therefore, it is impossible to be sure whether a woman's personality or her physiology (or both) influences her attitudes. Because similar limitations are found in every study, we never have complete confidence that we *know* what the measurements reflect about the behavior, or which factors were truly operating.

Second, the decisions made when designing a study may also reduce confidence in the findings. For example, if we study channel changing as it occurs in someone's living room, we cannot control such distractions as whether the phone rings in the middle of a commercial and thus prevents channel changing. But, if we study channel changing in a controlled "laboratory" setting, we create an artificial and thus biased picture of the behavior: People do not normally watch television in a laboratory! Likewise, the particular participants in a study, the way a behavior is measured, and the way factors are controlled may all bias the results.

Third, often there are technical limitations that produce misleading information. For example, in the late 1800s, psychologists studied "phrenology," the idea that various personality traits are reflected by the size of bumps on the skull. Considering current techniques for studying personality and brain physiology, however, phrenology now seems silly. Always consider the inherent limitations arising from current technical abilities.

And, finally, the results of one study can never tell the whole story. Because a single study is a "snapshot," it necessarily provides a biased perspective, considering certain factors and ignoring others (some of which we don't even know about). Depending on what is ignored, a study may seriously misrepresent nature. This is illustrated by an old fable about several blind men trying to describe an elephant. One, touching the animal's trunk, describes the elephant as like a snake. Another, touching the ear, says the elephant is like a fan. Another, touching the leg, describes the elephant as resembling a tree. And so on. In studying a behavior, researchers are like the blind men, trying to describe the entire elephant from one limited perspective. For example, say that our study suggests that channel changing is caused by boring commercials. If we do not consider the television program during which the commercials appear, however, then a different study may indicate that channel changing is caused by boring programs. The problem is that either study alone does not give the complete picture if channel changing is actually caused by a combination of boring commercials and a boring program. Remember, being skeptical means not falling for the obvious explanation provided. Always consider whether your attention has been misdirected by the limited perspective of a study.

Thus, individual studies can vary greatly in the extent to which they provide "good" data that accurately reflect the behavior and situation as they occur in nature. The bottom line here is that not all research is created equal! Therefore, you must critically evaluate any study to determine the extent that it might possibly misrepresent nature. The most important factor to consider is the design of the study. As you will see again and again, the design and interpretation of a study are completely interrelated: Whether the design is flawed determines whether the data is flawed, which determines whether the conclusions of the study are flawed. So, whether you're evaluating a study performed by you or by someone else, always consider whether there are flaws in the design that suggest reasons for doubting the study's conclusions.

REMEMBER A study's design determines the "snapshot" of a behavior it produces and thus, ultimately, the evidence for a particular hypothesis.

Even when a study contains a minimum of flaws, you still cannot have as much confidence in the conclusions as you might think. This is because of the intrinsic difficulty in "proving" that a hypothesis is true.

The Flaws in Testing Hypotheses

When our data do not fit our hypothesis, the conclusion is rather straightforward. Say that we test the hypothesis that people change channels more frequently with more boring commercials. But we find that people change channels about the same amount regardless of how boring the commercial is. Here we have evidence that the hypothesis is false, providing **disconfirmation**. However, although we have disconfirmed the hypothesis as stated, it may contain some element of truth. Maybe more boring commercials *do* produce more channel changing, but only when a boring program is also present.

On the other hand, say that participants *do* change channels more frequently with more boring commercials. Here our finding is consistent with the hypothesis, providing **confirmation**. But is confirmation the same as proving that the hypothesis is true? Absolutely not! It looks like we've "proven" the hypothesis to be true, because you're thinking only in terms of this one hypothesis, so it becomes a yes/no situation: "Yes, the data fit the hypothesis, so it must be true." You can see the error here by considering that another, different explanation is always possible for any situation, and that *this rival hypothesis might coincidentally produce exactly the same outcome that you've observed*.

For example, it might be that, unknown to us, our more boring commercials coincidentally contain less visual stimulation. The correct hypothesis might be that participants change channels to obtain more visual stimulation, and would do so *regardless* of how boring the commercial is. The hypothesis about boredom could be totally wrong, but we've simply observed results that *coincidentally* support it because of the nature of the true explanation. Given this possibility, we cannot be sure whether the amount of boredom or the amount of visual stimulation in a commercial actually causes channel changing. And, because our observations fit and confirm two, very different hypotheses, we certainly have not "proven" our original hypothesis.

Researchers use two tactics to minimize this problem. First, they try to anticipate and eliminate potential rival hypotheses when designing the study: If we produce boring and nonboring commercials having the same degree of visual stimulation then this issue is moot. Second, researchers perform experiments in which they attempt to simultaneously confirm their hypothesis while disconfirming any rival hypotheses: We'd devise a study to confirm our original boredom hypothesis while disconfirming the visual stimulation hypothesis. The more rival hypotheses that we disconfirm while confirming our hypothesis, the more confident we can be that it really is boring commercials that cause channel changing. Thus, when designing a study, you must fight the urge to seek only confirming evidence. The best evidence comes from disconfirming competing hypotheses while simultaneously confirming your hypothesis.

Even then, however, *confirming a hypothesis is never the same as proving it.* Confirming a hypothesis is actually a failure to "disprove" it. We may fail for one of two reasons: (1) The hypothesis is correct, or (2) The hypothesis is incorrect, but coincidentally the observations fit it and thus did not disprove it. We can never "prove" that our original hypothesis is correct, because no matter how many studies we conduct, someone can always suggest a rival hypothesis that would produce the same results, and so one more study might be the one to disconfirm our original hypothesis. For this reason, *never* use the terms "proof" or "proved."

Although the above is a serious objection after conducting only one or a few studies, it becomes less convincing as we complete more research. After enough tries, we can argue that if a disproving instance were out there, we would have found it. If we continually fail to disconfirm a hypothesis, we come to believe that the hypothesis is not disprovable—that it is correct. Thus, the goal is to repeatedly confirm a hypothesis while disconfirming competing hypotheses. Eventually, with enough data, we will become confident in the truth of the hypothesis, even though, technically, we never "prove" it.

REMEMBER If we confirm a hypothesis, we are merely more confident that it is true than we were before we tested it.

Testing hypotheses in real research is especially difficult, because some data may confirm a hypothesis, while other data may disconfirm it. Therefore, it is essential to critically evaluate the various lines of evidence. For example, do you accept the hypothesis that dreams predict the future? If you do, it's probably because you've occasionally dreamt of events that later occurred. But consider the quality and quantity of this evidence. First, such a hypothesis is suspect because it is neither rational nor parsimonious. Second, your feelings that you accurately recall a dream and that it matches real events lack objectivity and thus are also suspect. Third, your conclusion is based only on confirmation: Your observation is consistent with the hypothesis that dreams predict the future. But weigh this weak evidence against the amount of disconfirmation that is available. How many times have your dreams *failed* to come true? On balance, the preponderance of evidence heavily disconfirms the hypothesis that dreams predict the future. It makes much more sense to say that those few confirming instances are nothing more than mere coincidence: Some event occurred after you had coincidentally dreamt about it.

REMEMBER Our confidence in any scientific hypothesis is based on the quantity and quality of evidence that confirms and disconfirms it.

At the same time, a conclusion must accurately reflect *all* of the available evidence. For example, most scientists are not convinced that UFOs exist, because there has not been enough confirming, scientifically acceptable evidence. As in all scientific debates, additional evidence must be gathered so that, eventually, we will all be convinced one way or the other. However, notice that, in the meantime, I said that we are not convinced that UFOs exist—I did not say that UFOs don't exist. You must be open-minded and cautious, so when one hypothesis has not been confirmed sufficiently to accept with confidence, the conclusion is that the jury is still out, not that the opposite of the hypothesis is true.

Using Replication to Build Confidence in Psychological Findings

As you've seen, researchers ultimately develop confidence in a hypothesis by repeatedly confirming the hypothesis while disconfirming rival, competing hypotheses. This final component of the scientific method is called replication. *Replication* is the process of repeatedly conducting studies that test and confirm a hypothesis so that we develop confidence in its truth. The logic behind replication is that because nature is lawful, it is also consistent. Over many studies, therefore, the correct hypotheses will be consistently supported, while the erroneous, coincidental ones will not.

Researchers perform two types of replication. In **literal replication**, the researcher tries to duplicate precisely the specific design and results of a previous study. This approach, also called *direct* or *exact* replication, is used because there are always chance factors at work—the particular individuals studied, the unique environment of the study, and so on—that may mislead us. But chance factors that appear in one study are unlikely to appear consistently in others. Therefore, literal replication demonstrates that the original results are not likely to be due to chance factors. If different researchers can repeatedly obtain the same evidence in the same situation, we are more confident that the hypothesis is correct.

On the other hand, in **conceptual replication**, the researcher provides additional confirmation of a hypothesis, but does so while measuring the behavior in a different way, examining different types of participants, or using a different design. Conceptual or *indirect* replication provides for greater confidence in the general applicability of the hypothesis while testing and disconfirming competing hypotheses. Thus, for example, conceptual replications of our channel-changing study might involve observing children watching Saturday-morning cartoons and adults watching late-night shows, or include various commercials for toys, automobiles, and so on. Then, by combining the findings from these different studies, researchers can determine how the behavior generally operates and which factors influence it.

Thus, scientists use replication to build confidence in their "facts" in the same way that lawyers build a legal case. Literal replication is analogous to repeatedly questioning the same witnesses to make sure they keep their stories straight. Conceptual replication is akin to finding a number of witnesses who, from different vantage points, all report the same event. With enough consistent evidence from both sources, we eventually come to believe that we have discovered a law of nature.

The need for replication is often frustrating because society thinks science should quickly provide a solution to every problem. For example, a newspaper story may report the discovery of a new drug for treating cancer, but sadly, the researcher notes that it could be many years before the drug is available to the public. This reflects the recognition that consistent, convincing evidence of the effectiveness of the drug can be obtained only through time-consuming replication. After all, we accept the "law" of gravity because it always works, in every situation, from every perspective. The same logic must be used when making any other scientific claim as well.

PUTTING IT ALL TOGETHER

As should be painfully obvious by now, a study never provides unquestionable "proof." First, we can never be completely confident that the data reflect the precise behavior we wish to measure, in the precise situation we wish to observe. Further, even with good, convincing data that confirm a hypothesis, the hypothesis may still be incorrect. For that matter, even when a hypothesis is disconfirmed, it may still contain some elements of truth.

Given these problems, you may wonder why we even bother to conduct research. Well, the issues we've discussed are reasons for being skeptical about any single research finding, not for being negative about the research process. Instead of being paralyzed by such limitations, we view dealing with them as a challenge. Simply recognize that testing a hypothesis involves translating a general statement about a behavior into a concrete measurable situation, and then translating the measurements back into conclusions about the general behavior. There is always room for error in the translation.

Therefore, do not automatically accept or dismiss any single study. On the one hand, researchers try to design the best study they can, providing the clearest evidence for answering the question at hand. Thus, even with flaws, a study usually tells us something about a behavior. On the other hand, what seems to describe a behavior correctly from one perspective may be incorrect when viewed from a different perspective. Look for that different perspective. And always keep in mind that a single study will not tell us everything about a behavior. A complete understanding can be gained only by replication, as we repeatedly obtain numerous and varied "snapshots" of the behavior.

CHAPTER SUMMARY

1. The *scientific method* includes certain assumptions, attitudes, goals, and procedures for creating and answering questions about nature.
2. The assumptions of psychology are that behaviors are *lawful*, *determined*, and *understandable*.
3. Scientists are *uncertain*, *open-minded*, *skeptical*, *cautious*, and *ethical*.
4. The *design* of a study is the specific manner in which the study is conducted. It should provide for *empirical*, *objective*, *systematic*, and *controlled* observations of a behavior.
5. Statistical procedures are used to *organize*, *summarize*, and *communicate* data and to *draw conclusions* about what the data indicate.
6. The goals of psychological research are to *describe*, *explain*, *predict*, and *control* behavior.
7. A *pseudo-explanation* is circular, explaining the causes of an event by renaming the event. To avoid pseudo-explanations, scientists obtain independent verification of a supposed cause.
8. The primary purpose of *basic research* is to obtain knowledge. The primary purpose of *applied research* is to solve an existing problem.
9. A *hypothesis* is a formally stated expectation about how a behavior operates. A *causal hypothesis* postulates a causal influence on a behavior. A *descriptive hypothesis* postulates characteristics or aspects of the behavior.

10. Scientific hypotheses must be *testable*, *falsifiable*, *precise*, *rational*, and *parsimonious*.

11. A *theory* is an organized set of proposals that defines, explains, organizes, and interrelates knowledge about many behaviors.

12. A *model* is a description that, by analogy, explains the process underlying a set of common behaviors.

13. A *prediction* is a statement about the data that are expected in a specific study if the hypothesis is correct.

14. The more a study deviates from the ideal criteria, the more likely it is to misrepresent nature, and the less *confidence* we have in its findings.

15. The fact that the results of a study *confirm* a hypothesis does not prove that the hypothesis is true, because the results may coincidentally fit it. *Disconfirming* a hypothesis provides the greatest confidence in a conclusion about the hypothesis.

16. *Replication* is the process of repeatedly conducting studies to build confidence in a hypothesis. *Literal replication* precisely duplicates a previous study. *Conceptual replication* repeats the test of a hypothesis, but uses a different design.

KEY TERMS (with page references)

applied research (13)
basic research (13)
causal hypothesis (14)
conceptual replication (23)
confirmation (21)
control (10)
data (3)
descriptive hypothesis (15)
design (9)
determinism (7)
disconfirmation (21)
empirical (9)
falsifiable (15)
hypothesis (14)
lawful (7)
literal replication (23)
model (17)
objectivity (10)
open-minded (8)
parsimonious (16)
participants (9)
precise (16)
prediction (18)
pseudo-explanation (11)
rational (16)
research ethics (8)
scientific method (6)
statistical notation (4)
subjects (9)
systematic (10)
testable (15)
theory (17)

REVIEW QUESTIONS

(Answers for odd-numbered questions and problems are provided in Appendix D.)

1. Why do researchers need to learn about research and statistics?
2. As a student learning statistics, what are your goals?

3. A researcher measures the IQ scores of a group of college students. What four things will the researcher use statistics for?
4. What three assumptions do scientists make about nature?
5. (a) What are the five attitudes that characterize scientists? (b) Why are they necessary?
6. What are the four criteria for scientific evidence, and what does each term mean?
7. What are the four goals of research?
8. (a) What is the difference between a theory and a model? (b) What two general functions do theories serve?
9. What are the five criteria for a scientific hypothesis, and what does each term mean?
10. What is the scientific method?
11. What is the difference between a causal hypothesis and a descriptive hypothesis?
12. What is the difference between a hypothesis and a prediction?
13. Why must you critically evaluate the design of any study?
14. Why does disconfirmation provide greater confidence than confirmation?
15. What is replication, and why does science rely on it?
16. What is the difference between literal replication and conceptual replication?

PRACTICE PROBLEMS

17. On a television talk show, a panelist says that listening to rock and roll music causes the listener to become a devil worshiper, a homicidal maniac, or a suicide victim. What questions would you ask this panelist before voting to ban rock and roll?
18. A theorist claims that men become homosexual when, as they are growing up, their mother either (a) tried to control them or (b) did not try to control them. Scientifically speaking, what is wrong with this hypothesis?
19. You've read some research in a developmental psychology text that contradicts what you've observed about your younger brother. Whose claim should you believe, your own or the researcher's? Why?
20. The government has announced a very large monetary grant awarded to a scientist to study the sex life of a nearly extinct butterfly. A commentator claims that this research is a waste of money. Why do you agree or disagree?
21. Researchers who accept the existence of extrasensory perception (ESP) argue that the reason others have not found convincing evidence for it is that they do not believe such mental powers exist. What rule of science is violated by this argument?
22. A researcher explains that the reason people can remember smells is because they have a memory for smells. What is wrong with this explanation?
23. There's a rumor that if you dream you're falling off a cliff and you don't wake up before you hit the ground, you will actually die. (a) What is wrong with trying to confirm this hypothesis? (b) What is the way to test this hypothesis? (c) Even if you collect the appropriate dream information, what problems remain?
24. When people debate the idea of evolution, one common argument is that it's only a "theory" and therefore has no basis in fact. What error is in this statement?
25. Some people argue that, along with the theory of evolution, high-school students should also be taught the "science of creationism"—the Christian-Judeo belief

that God originally created the humans and animals we see today. Why is calling creationism a science a contradiction in terms?

26. I find that people change channels less when there are more people with them than when they're alone. I claim this proves the hypothesis that boredom causes channel changing, because with more people present, a person is less bored and so changes channels less. (a) Why isn't this proof? (b) What rival hypothesis do you see?

27. I conduct an experiment "to test the theory that adequate amounts of sleep are necessary for emotional balance." What errors are in this statement?

28. (a) Select a behavior and create both a descriptive hypothesis and a causal hypothesis about it. (b) In general terms, how would you go about testing each hypothesis?

2

The Logic of Designing and Interpreting Research

Getting Started

To understand this chapter, recall the following:

- We create either a descriptive or a causal hypothesis about a behavior.
- Then we conduct a study that measures the behavior of participants.
- Depending on whether the data support our predictions, we have evidence that either confirms or disconfirms the hypothesis.

Your goals in this chapter are to learn:

- How to translate a hypothetical construct into a variable and then an operational definition.
- What a relationship is and what is meant by the "strength" of a relationship.
- How a relationship in a sample of scores is used to draw inferences about the behavior of a population.
- When and why descriptive and inferential statistical procedures are used.
- What the difference between experimental and descriptive research is, and what true experiments, quasi-experiments, and correlational designs are.
- What the independent variable, conditions, and dependent variable are in an experiment.

You already know that in research, we translate a general, abstract hypothesis about a behavior into objective measurements and then translate the measurements back into conclusions about the behavior. In this chapter, we'll expand on this translation process, covering three major topics: first, we'll discuss in depth how to derive a testable, empirical hypothesis; then, we'll discuss how data are generally interpreted and the major uses of statistical analysis; and, finally, we'll introduce the two major types of research designs.

BEGINNING THE DESIGN: ASKING THE QUESTION

It's pointless to design a study by simply grabbing some behavior out of the blue to examine; you'll end up with an answer in search of a question. Research proceeds well only if you first determine the question you want to answer and then design a study to answer it. For example, we've all heard the rumor that "the more you study, the more you learn." Let's say we set out to examine this proposal.

The key to developing a hypothesis lies in fitting it into previous research and theory in a rational and parsimonious manner. Therefore, an important first step in any study is to examine the psychological research literature. The term "research literature" refers to published reports of research found in professional-level books and journals. This is where you will find numerous ideas for interesting studies, established procedures that you can employ, and theories, models, and previous research that ensure that your hypothesis fits with known psychological processes. (A discussion of how to "search" the literature is presented in Appendix A.)

As you read the literature, the design of the study will emerge. As you'll see, all design decisions are ultimately made simultaneously, because any one decision has an impact on all other decisions. However, a useful starting point is to identify the relevant population and sample.

Identifying the Population and Sample

By saying that studying improves learning, we have essentially hypothesized a component of a law of nature. Any law of nature applies to a specific group of individuals (all mammals, all humans, all male white rats, whatever). The entire group to which the law applies is called the **population**. Part of designing a study is to specifically define the target population. Are we talking about young children, college students, senior citizens, or all of the above? Does the hypothesis apply to all cultures, socioeconomic classes, intelligence levels, and personality types? Say we define the population for our study as college-aged men and women who are psychology majors. Notice that now we also know the specific participants we will observe (and we are most concerned with reading the literature dealing with such individuals).

A population is usually considered to be infinitely large (but it need not be). To examine the behaviors of an infinitely large population would take forever, so instead, we usually study a sample. A **sample** is a subset of a population that is intended to represent, or stand in for, the population. It is the sample or samples of participants that are measured in a study, and the scores from the sample(s) constitute the data.

Although psychologists ultimately discuss the population of *individuals*, in statistics we will talk of the population of *scores*, as if we had already measured the behavior of everyone in the population in a particular situation. Thus, you can think of a population as the group of all possible scores we would obtain if we could measure the behavior of everyone of interest in a particular situation. Likewise, we discuss a sample of scores as if we had already measured the participants in a particular situation.

The definitions of a sample and a population depend on your perspective. Say that we measure the students in your class. If these are the only individuals we're interested in, then we've measured the population. But, if we're interested in the population of all college students taking this course, then we have a sample of scores that represents this population. Or, if we are interested in both the population of males and the population of females taking this course, then the males in the class are one sample, the females are another sample, and each sample represents its respective population. And finally, scores from *one* student can be a sample representing the population of all scores that the student might produce. Thus, a population is any complete group of scores found in a particular situation, and a sample is a subset of those scores that we actually measure in that situation.

The logic behind samples and populations is this: We assume that the participants (or scores) in a sample are basically interchangeable with any other participants (or scores) we might obtain from the population. Therefore, any sample should produce scores similar to those of any and all others in the population. In other words, we assume the sample will be representative of the population. In a **representative sample**, the characteristics of the participants—and thus their behaviors—accurately reflect the characteristics and behaviors of individuals in the population. Thus, a representative sample of college students will contain the same proportion of good and poor, motivated and unmotivated, and male and female students as in the population. Then, the sample's scores will be a good example of the scores we would find in the population. Therefore, in research, we measure a sample and use the scores to estimate or *infer* the scores we would find if we could measure the entire population.

And, remember: Scores reflect behavior. By translating the scores in a sample back into the behaviors they reflect, we can infer the behavior of everyone in the population. Everyone in the population is everyone that a law of nature applies to; so, at this point, we *are* describing how nature operates. Thus, when the nightly news predicts who will win the presidential election based on the results of a survey, researchers are using the scores from a sample (usually containing about 1200 voters) to infer the voting *behavior* of over 80 million voters in the population.

The basis for creating a representative sample is random sampling. **Random sampling** is a method of selecting a sample in which (1) all members of the population have the same chance of being selected for a sample and (2) all possible samples have the same chance of being selected. Although we'll discuss the details later, random sampling basically relies on the luck of the draw so that participants are chosen in an unbiased and unselective manner. Thus, think of random sampling as if the names of everyone in the population have been placed in a large hat and then, with our eyes closed, we draw participants for the sample. Because we are unbiased in our selections, we should select from all segments of the population so that the sample *should be* a good example of the population. (But as you'll see, it may not be!)

Once you have identified the population to be studied, completing the design involves deciding exactly what behavior to observe and how to measure it.

Identifying the Hypothetical Constructs

To investigate how studying and learning operate in nature, we must first decide what we mean by these terms. Like most concepts in psychology—memory, thinking, motivation, personality, or intelligence—the terms *studying* and *learning* are general terms that refer to a wide variety of behaviors. Such terms have an important name. They represent general ideas that researchers "construct" from many observations, so they are called hypothetical constructs. A **hypothetical construct** is an abstract concept used in a particular theoretical manner to relate different behaviors according to their underlying features or causes. It is used to describe, organize, summarize, and communicate our interpretations of behaviors. Thus, we describe the differences in people's mental capabilities using the construct of "intelligence." Or, we summarize an individual's traits and characteristics as his or her "personality." And, in our study, "learning" describes a person's mental integration of new information, and "studying" refers to the activities involved when acquiring such information.

> ***REMEMBER*** A hypothetical construct is an abstract term used to summarize and describe behaviors that share certain attributes.

It is important that you recognize the hypothetical constructs involved in your study, because the way to ensure that a hypothesis is rational and parsimonious is to incorporate accepted hypothetical concepts. That's because when we talk about understanding a behavior, we are really talking about understanding the constructs that describe and govern the behavior.

We *study* constructs, however, by observing components of the physical world that we think reflect them. But because constructs are intentionally general, they may be examined from many perspectives (think of all the ways one can study and learn.) Therefore, in designing a study, you must define each hypothetical construct in terms of a specific measurable event that reflects the construct. You accomplish this using variables.

Identifying the Component Variables of a Construct

The way we learn about a hypothetical construct is by measuring a variable that reflects the construct. In psychological research, a **variable** is any measurable aspect of a behavior or influence on a behavior that may change. A measurable aspect of a behavior may be a physical action, a mental reaction, or a physiological response. A measurable influence on behavior may be a characteristic of the participants, of the situation, or of a stimulus to which subjects respond. A few of the variables found in psychological research include your age, gender, and personality type; how anxious, angry, or aggressive you are; and how hard you will work at a task or how accurately you recall a situation.

When selecting the variables for a study, first, consider the many variables that may reflect a construct. Then, select the specific variables that you'll examine. However, not all variables are created equal, and which you should use in a specific study depends on a number of important considerations (discussed in later chapters.) Essentially, though, a variable should be a good example of the hypothetical construct as psychologists conceptualize it, it should allow for objective and precise measurement as much as possible, and it must be compatible with other aspects of the study's design.

REMEMBER We examine an aspect of a hypothetical construct by selecting a specific variable that we will measure.

Variables fall into one of two general categories. If a score indicates the amount of a variable that is present, it is a **quantitative** variable. A person's height, for example, is a quantitative variable because a score indicates the quantity of height that is present. Some variables, however, cannot be measured in amounts. Instead, a score classifies an individual on the basis of some characteristic. Such variables are called **qualitative** variables. A person's gender, for example, is a qualitative variable, because the "score" of male or female indicates a quality, or category.

Thus, we could measure "studying" using such variables as the effort put into studying or the number of times a chapter is read, but say we select the variable of the number of hours spent studying for a college exam. We could measure "learning" by measuring how well new concepts can be explained or how quickly information can be recalled. But say we select the variable of performance on the exam.

Notice we have now translated the general hypothesis that studying leads to learning into the more specific hypothesis that the number of hours spent studying for a test is related to performance on the test. However, this is still too general.

Creating Operational Definitions

Even after selecting a variable, there are still a variety of ways to measure it. Ultimately, you must specifically define each variable, and the way to do that is through an operational definition. An **operational definition** defines a variable by the specific operations used to measure it. Operational definitions are very important because they eliminate ambiguity. For example, although you and I may disagree about exactly what the construct of intelligence means, in a study I might operationally define it as a score on the XYZ intelligence test. Now, at least, there is no debate about what I had my participants do, how I've measured their intelligence, and what you'd need to do to replicate my study. This is far clearer than simply stating, "I determined each person's intelligence."

Thus, you must devise an operational definition of each variable in a study, and you should give considerable thought to each. Operational definitions are a major source of potential flaws in a study and can produce all kinds of controversy among researchers. (When studying intelligence, for example, I would be in big trouble if most researchers did not accept that the XYZ test measures intelligence.) Therefore, first generate a list of potential approaches, and then select the best one. As with all phases of a design, consult the research literature for definitions that have been used successfully in previous research.

In the example, we might define "hours of study" as the number of hours that students report they studied for a statistics test from Chapter 6 of this book the evening before the test. Or we might define it as the length of time we observe them studying during the afternoon before the test. Likewise, we might define "performance on a test" as the number of multiple-choice questions answered correctly on the Chapter 6 test, or the number of errors made when calculating statistical answers on the test.

Thus, we translate a hypothetical construct into a variable and translate the variable into the specific operations used to measure it. Then, measuring the variable produces the data of the study. It is through this process that researchers whittle away at the com-

TABLE 2.1 The Steps in Defining a Research Concept

Step	*Definition*
1. Hypothetical construct	General theoretical term that summarizes common behaviors or processes.
2. Variable	Measurable component of a construct.
3. Operational definition	Definition of variable in terms of the method used to measure it.

plexity of a behavior to produce a "snapshot" of it that meets the scientific goals of obtaining empirical, objective, systematic, and controlled observations. Likewise, designing the remainder of a study essentially involves operationally defining all other variables that characterize the situation in which we examine the behavior. Thus, we must define what we mean by "studying" (is it reading the textbook, highlighting it, or outlining it?); where the studying will take place (the dorm, the library, or our laboratory); what "performance on the test" is (is it number correct or number of errors?); and so on, for every aspect of the behavior, participants, and situation that we will examine.

> ***REMEMBER*** Each variable in a study must be operationally defined in terms of the procedure that is used to measure it.

So that you remember the preceding terminology, Table 2.1 summarizes the steps in defining a concept in psychological research.

By operationally defining the variables, we translate our original, general hypothesis into a specific *prediction* about the scores that will be observed: Above, if our hypothesis is correct, then the longer that students study for the statistics test, the better their performance on the test will be. To test this prediction, we would simply need to measure some students and *see* if different amounts of learning do occur with different amounts of studying.

TESTING A HYPOTHESIS BY DISCOVERING A RELATIONSHIP

The most basic assumption in scientific research is this: If Y is influenced by or otherwise tied to X by a law of nature, then *different* amounts or categories of Y will occur when *different* amounts or categories of X occur. Thus, if nature ties those mental activities we call studying to those mental activities we call learning, then different amounts of our learning variable should occur with different amounts of our studying variable. In other words, the test of a prediction is to look for a *relationship* in the data. A **relationship** occurs when a change in one variable is accompanied by a consistent change in another variable. Because we measure scores, a mathematical relationship is a *pattern* in which specific scores on one variable are paired with certain scores on another variable, so that as scores on one variable change (increase or decrease), scores on the other variable change in a consistent manner.

TABLE 2.2 Scores Showing a Relationship Between the Variables of Study Time and Test Grades

Student	*Study time in hours*	*Test grades*
Jane	1	F
Bob	1	F
Sue	2	D
Tony	3	C
Sidney	3	C
Ann	4	B
Rose	4	B
Lou	5	A

What might our relationship look like? Say that we asked some students how long they studied for the test and their subsequent grades on the test. We might obtain the scores shown in Table 2.2.[1] These variables form a relationship, because as the study time scores change (increase), the test grades also change in a consistent fashion (also increase). Further, when study time scores do *not* change (for example, Jane and Bob both studied for 1 hour), scores on the grade variable do not change either (they both received Fs). In research, we often use the term *association* when talking about relationships: Here, low study times are associated with low test grades, and high study times are associated with high test grades.

> ***REMEMBER*** In a relationship, specific scores on one variable are associated with certain scores on the other variable, so that as scores on one variable change, scores on the other variable change in a consistent fashion.

The simplest relationships fit either the pattern "the more you *X*, the *more* you *Y*," or the pattern "the more you *X*, the *less* you *Y*." Thus, "the bigger they are, the harder they fall" describes a relationship, as does that old saying "the more you practice statistics, the less difficult they are." Relationships may also form more complicated patterns where, for example, more *X* at first leads to more *Y*, but beyond a certain point, even more *X* leads to *less Y*. For example, at first, the more you exercise, the better you feel. Beyond a certain point, however, more exercise leads to feeling less well, as pain and exhaustion set in.

Although the above examples involve quantitative variables, relationships may also involve qualitative variables. For example, typically men are taller than women. If you think of male and female as "scores" on the qualitative variable of gender, then this is a relationship: As gender scores change (going from male to female), height scores change in a consistent fashion (decrease).

[1] The data presented in this book are a work of fiction. Any resemblance to real data is purely a coincidence.

Strength of a Relationship

Table 2.2 showed perfectly consistent association, because all those who studied the same amount received the same grade. In the real world, however, not all people who study the same amount will receive the same grade. (Life is not fair.) A relationship can be present, however, even if the association between scores is not perfectly consistent. There can be some *degree* of consistency so that as the scores on one variable change, the scores on the other variable *tend* to change in a consistent fashion. For example, Table 2.3 shows a relationship between the number of hours spent studying and number of errors made on a test. Higher scores on the study time variable *tend* to be associated with lower scores on the error variable, but not every increase in study time is matched perfectly with a decrease in errors, and sometimes the same studying score produces different error scores.

In research, the consistency found in a particular relationship is called its strength: The **strength of a relationship** is the extent to which one value of Y is consistently associated with one and only one value of X. It is the *degree of association* between the variables.

There are two reasons that relationships are not perfectly consistent. First, there may be external influences operating on the participants. For example, among those students who studied for two hours, perhaps for some their dorm was particularly noisy, so their studying was less effective. Because of this, different test scores occur among these students, even though they all studied the same amount. (A major purpose of studying research methods is for you to learn how to eliminate—*control*—such external influences.)

The other reason for weaker relationships is individual differences. The term **individual differences** refers to the fact that no two individuals are identical and that differences in genetic make-up, experience, intelligence, personality, and many other variables all influence behavior in a given situation. Because of individual differences, a particular law of nature operates in *more or less* the same way for all members of a population. Thus, our participants will exhibit individual differences in terms of their intelligence, aptitude, and motivation, so they will score differently on the test,

TABLE 2.3 Scores Showing a Relationship Between Study Time and Number of Errors on Test

Student	*Study time in hours*	*Number of errors on test*
Amy	1	12
Karen	1	13
Joe	1	11
Cleo	2	11
Jack	2	10
Maria	2	9
Terry	3	9
Manny	3	10
Chris	4	9
Sam	4	8
Gary	5	7

even when they study the same amount. Because individual differences produce differences in test scores for a particular study time, scores will be only somewhat consistently associated with study times. (Later, you'll also learn ways of controlling individual differences.)

Mathematically, the scores from two variables can form a relationship of any strength, from perfectly consistent to no association, in which case there is no relationship. For example, there is (I think) no relationship between the number of chocolate bars people consume each day and the number of times they blink each minute. Measuring individuals on these two variables might produce the data shown in Table 2.4. Here there is no consistent change in the scores on one variable as the scores on the other variable change. Instead, the same blinking scores tend to show up for each chocolate bar score.

Real research never produces a perfectly consistent relationship; we can never perfectly control external influences and individual differences. Instead, most research produces relationships that are consistent only to some degree. Therefore, it is never enough merely to say that you have observed a relationship—you must also describe the strength of the relationship. As you'll see, knowing the strength of a relationship is extremely important for ultimately interpreting how nature operates in a particular situation.

> ***REMEMBER*** In research, we are concerned not only with the existence of a relationship but also with its strength.

Graphing Relationships

Researchers often use graphs to show a relationship, so it's important that you recognize a relationship and its strength when looking at a graph. Recall that the horizontal line across the bottom of a graph is called the *X* axis, and the vertical line at the left-hand side is called the *Y* axis. How do we decide which variable to call *X* or *Y*? Any study implicitly asks this question: For a *given* score on one variable, what scores occur on the other variable? The "given" variable is called the *X* variable (plotted on the *X* axis), and the other variable is the *Y* variable (plotted on the *Y* axis). Thus, we asked, "For a given amount of study time, what test grade occurs?", so study time is the *X* variable and test grade is the *Y* variable.

TABLE 2.4 Scores Showing No Relationship Between Number of Chocolate Bars Consumed per Day and Number of Eye Blinks per Minute

Student	*Number of chocolate bars consumed per day*	*Number of eye blinks per minute*
Mark	1	20
Ted	1	22
Ray	2	20
Denise	2	23
Maria	3	23
Irene	3	20

Once you have identified the X and Y variables, there is a special way of communicating the relationship between them. The general format is this: "Scores on the Y variable change **as a function of** changes in the X variable." Thus, we have discussed relationships involving "test grades as a function of study time" and "number of eye blinks as a function of amount of chocolate consumed." Likewise, if you hear of a study titled "Differences in Career Choices as a Function of Personality Type," you know that the researcher looked at how Y scores that measure career choices changed as X scores that measure personality types changed.

> ***REMEMBER*** The "given" variable in a study is designated the X variable, and we describe a relationship as "changes in Y as a function of changes in X."

Figure 2.1 shows the graphs from four sets of data. Graph A plots the original test-grade and study-time data from Table 2.2. To fill in the graph, we plot a dot to represent each pair of X and Y scores. Each dot is called a **data point**. For example, for a person who studied 1 hour, by traveling vertically from 1 to the data point and then horizontally back to the Y axis, we see the corresponding test grade was F. (Notice that two

FIGURE 2.1 Plots of Data Points from Four Sets of Data

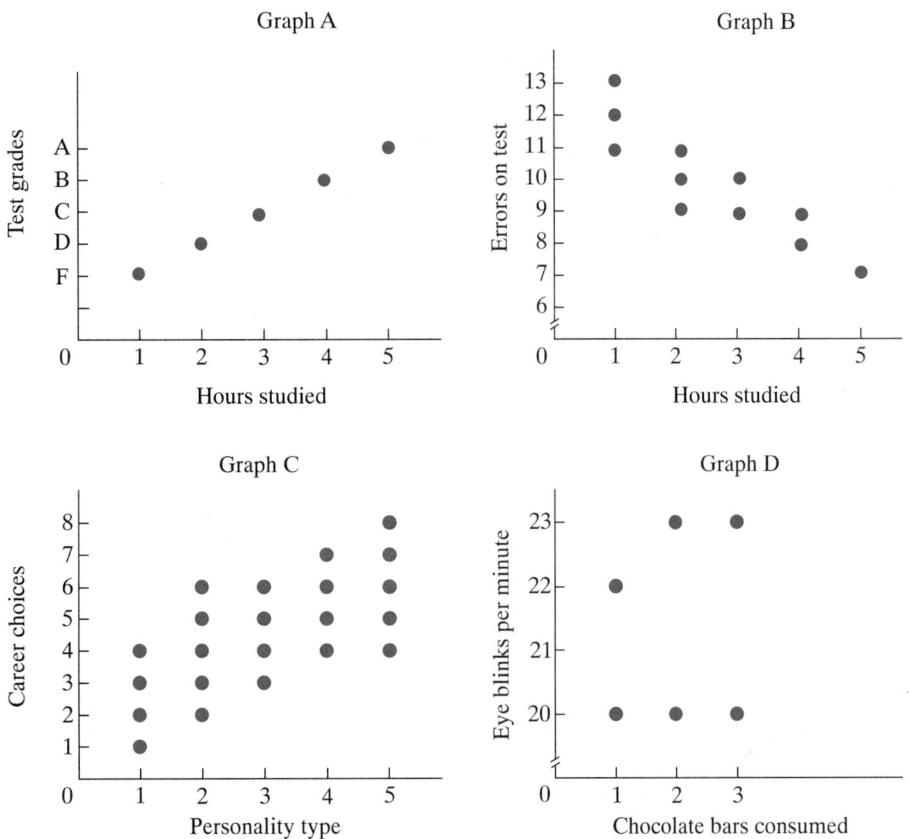

people originally studied for 1 hour and received an F, so their data points are on top of one another.)

To see the overall relationship, read the graph from left to right along the *X* axis, simultaneously observing the pattern of change in the *Y* scores. In essence, you should ask, "As the scores on the *X* axis increase, what happens to the scores on the *Y* axis?" In Graph A, as the *X* scores increase, the *Y* scores also increase. Further, there is perfectly consistent association here because everyone with a particular *X* score obtained the same *Y* score.

Graph B shows test errors as a function of number of hours studied, from Table 2.3. Here, increasing *X* scores are associated with decreasing values of *Y*. But, because there are different values of *Y* at an *X* score, this relationship is weaker than in Graph A and is not perfectly consistent. (Notice the two diagonal lines (//) on the *Y* axis: Whenever there is a gap between 0 and the lowest score being plotted, the axis is compressed using this symbol. Here we "cut out" the *Y* axis between 0 and 6 and slid the remaining *Y* values closer to 0.)

Say that Graph C shows the relationship between *Y* scores reflecting different career choices and *X* scores reflecting different personality types. Again, there is a relationship here, but a relatively wide range of different career-choice scores are paired with each personality-type score. Therefore, this is an even weaker, less-consistent relationship than in Graph B.

Graph D shows the eye-blink and chocolate-bar data from Table 2.4. There is no consistent pattern of change in *Y* scores, with more or less the same values of *Y* occurring with each value of *X*. As here, whenever a graph shows an essentially flat pattern—so that *Y* scores tend to neither increase nor decrease as *X* scores increase—the graph reflects zero association and no relationship.

Later, you'll learn when to create other types of graphs. Regardless of the final form, always label the *X* and *Y* axes to indicate what the scores measure (not just *X* and *Y*), and create the graph in a way that honestly presents the data, without exaggerating or minimizing the pattern formed by the data.

THE ROLE OF STATISTICAL PROCEDURES

As you've seen, the key to research is this: If the data show the relationship we've predicted, then we have confirming evidence that supports our original hypothesis. We originally hypothesized that studying is linked to learning, and the relationship between our variables that we observed supports this hypothesis. However, the data from real research seldom produce as clear a picture as in this example. Instead, researchers are usually confronted with a mind-boggling array of different numbers that may have a relationship hidden in it. Therefore, we employ statistical procedures to help bring order to this chaos. There are two general types of procedures—descriptive and inferential statistics.

Descriptive Statistics

To understand the sample data and the relationship they form, we employ descriptive statistics. **Descriptive statistics** are procedures for organizing and summarizing scores so that we can describe and communicate the important characteristics of the sample data. (When you see *descriptive*, think *describe*.) Descriptive statistics have three general purposes.

First, they tell us whether a relationship is present. For example, if we are studying test errors as a function of hours studied, then we first want to determine whether there is a relationship between error scores and amount of time studied.

Second, descriptive statistics summarize the scores and describe the particular relationship we've found. Thus, we want to know how many errors are associated with a particular amount of study time, how much errors decrease with increased study time, how consistently errors decrease, and so on.

Third, descriptive statistics help us to meet the scientific goal of predicting behavior because we can use a participant's score on one variable to predict his or her score on the other variable. Thus, once we establish the relationship in our study, we will know the typical score that a student obtains for a given amount of study. Using this relationship, we can then predict the scores of any other students, if we know how long they studied.

> ***REMEMBER*** Descriptive statistics are used to determine whether a relationship is present, to describe the relationship and the scores in it, and to predict the scores on one variable using the scores on another variable.

Inferential Statistics

After we describe and understand the relationship in the sample, we want to do the same thing for the population represented by the sample because then we are describing how the variables and underlying behaviors relate for *everyone* in nature. Usually, however, we must *infer* the description of the population, based on the sample data. Thus, in our study-time research, if the sample who studied 1 hour made between 11 and 15 errors on the test, we'd expect that if *all* students studied for 1 hour, they would produce a population consisting of error scores generally between 11 and 15. However, if participants who studied for 2 hours produced between 7 and 10 errors, we'd expect that if we had all students study for 2 hours, they would produce a different population consisting of scores between 7 and 10 errors. And so on.

At least we *hope* it works that way! But this all assumes that the sample is representative of the population. What if the sample is *unrepresentative*, so that the characteristics of the sample *do not* match those in the population? The trouble is that whether a sample is representative is determined by which participants we select, and that is determined by random chance. Therefore, we can, just by the luck of the draw, obtain a very unusual sample whose characteristics do not match those of the population. Then, we will misinterpret how nature works. For example, we might unknowingly select a group of very poor students to study for 1 hour, so their test grades will not reflect those of all students who have studied for 1 hour. Or, by luck, we might select only exceptionally good students to study for 2 hours, so their scores will not represent the typical student either. And so on. If the samples are unrepresentative of the population, then the *relationship* in the sample data does not accurately represent the relationship we'd find in the population. Then, if we could study the population of all students, we might find a relationship very different from this one, or we might find *no* relationship!

REMEMBER Never automatically assume that a sample accurately represents the population.

Thus, random sampling is a double-edged sword. Usually, it works pretty well in producing a representative sample. But it can backfire, producing a very unrepresentative sample. For help in this dilemma, we apply inferential statistics. **Inferential statistics** are procedures for deciding whether the sample data represent a particular relationship in the population. As the name implies, inferential procedures are for making *inferences* about the population represented by a sample.

For now, think of inferential statistics as tools for deciding whether sample data are "believable": Should we believe that we would find similar data, forming a similar relationship, in the population? If the answer is yes, we then ask the same things about the population we asked about the sample: What are the characteristics of the scores and of the relationship that would be found in the population, and can we use the scores in the population on one variable to predict the scores on the other variable?

REMEMBER Inferential statistics help us to draw inferences about the population.

SUMMARY OF THE FLOW OF A STUDY

Now you can see how it all comes together. A typical research study involves translating from the general to the specific and then back to the general again, as illustrated by the double funnels in Figure 2.2.

Begin with broad hypothetical constructs regarding a behavior. We originally hypothesized that, in nature, studying is related to learning. Then, narrow the scope by identifying the applicable population and specify the hypothesis as a relationship between variables. Whittle down the situation to a very specific one by creating operational definitions of the variables, and then predict the relationship between the scores that you seek. We predicted a relationship where, as scores reflecting more study time occur, scores reflecting higher test performance also tend to occur.

Next, select a random sample from the population, and employ the materials and method for measuring participants. After obtaining the scores, use descriptive statistical procedures to identify and examine the relationship between the scores in the sample.

If you find the relationship between the scores in the sample, begin widening the scope by using inferential statistics to decide whether the relationship is likely to be found in the population. Then you can infer that the variables are related in this way for everyone in the population. Then, interpret this relationship, describing how the scores are related and what the consistency of the relationship indicates about nature in general.

By claiming that our specific observations provide evidence for the general case, we are generalizing. To **generalize** means to apply conclusions to other individuals or situations. When interpreting research, we generalize in two ways. First, as above, we generalize the relationship between the variables in the sample to a relationship between the variables in the population. Second, we then generalize the relationship between the

FIGURE 2.2 The Steps in a Typical Research Study

The flow of a study is from a general hypothesis to the specifics of the study, and then back to the general hypothesis.

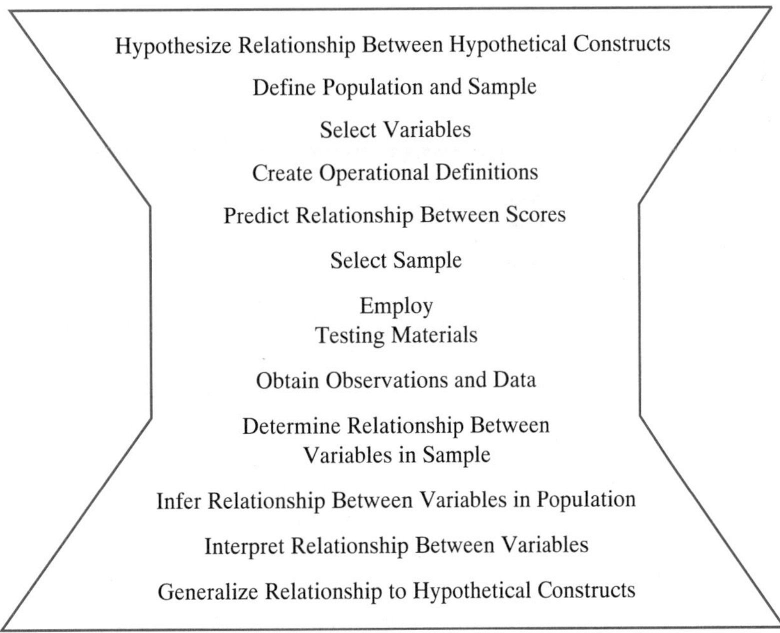

variables in the population to the relationship between the broader hypothetical constructs that we originally set out to study. That is, we translate the scores back into the general behaviors and events they reflect, and then argue that a similar relationship would be found with other variables and operational definitions. Thus, ultimately, we want to say that as scores on *any* variable reflecting amount of studying increase, scores on *any* variable reflecting amount learned will also increase. Then we have come full circle, confirming the original hypothesis that nature lawfully operates in such a way that when more of the process we call studying occurs, more of the behavior we call learning also occurs.

> ***REMEMBER*** The focus of research is to generalize a sample relationship to the relationship between hypothetical constructs.

The above flow from the general to the specific and back to the general is mirrored in the organization that psychologists use when publishing reports of research in the psychological literature. This organization was created by the American Psychological Association or "APA," the national association of psychologists in the United States, and is known as "APA style" or "APA format." (This format is presented in Appendix A in detail.) A published report will basically follow the above discussion, although the sequence may not be so obvious. The trick to reading the literature is to look for what the author is saying about each step.

When reading the literature, you will come across a variety of research designs, because there are many ways to go about demonstrating a relationship. However, research can be broken into two major types: experiments and descriptive studies.

EXPERIMENTAL RESEARCH METHODS

Recall that a causal hypothesis proposes the causes of a behavior. To test such a hypothesis, we usually employ *experimental methods*. The logic of an experiment is this: If my hypothesis is correct, then if I *do* this or that to participants, I should see an influence or change in their behaviors. Therefore, in an **experiment**, the researcher actively changes or *manipulates* one variable and measures the participant's resulting behavior by measuring another variable. Then we look to see if the manipulation changed the behavior so that the predicted relationship is produced.

Usually an experiment implies a laboratory setting, but this need not be the case. Thus, if we originally hypothesized that more studying *causes* fewer test errors, we would systematically manipulate amount of study time and then measure the number of resulting test errors. For example, to compare 1, 2, 3, and 4 hours of study time, we could randomly select four samples of students. Then, we'd give one sample 1 hour of study time, administer the test, and then count the number of errors each participant makes. We could give another sample 2 hours of study time, administer the test, and then count the errors, and so on. If we understand the laws of nature governing learning and test taking, then as the length of time that students study increases, the number of errors they make should decrease.

There are names for the components of any experiment, and you will use them daily.

The Independent Variable

An **independent variable** is a variable that is directly changed or manipulated by the experimenter. Implicitly, it is the variable that we think causes a change in behavior. Above, we manipulate study time because we think it influences test errors, so amount of study time is the independent variable. Or, in an experiment to determine whether eating more chocolate causes people to blink more, amount of chocolate consumed would be the independent variable. You can remember the independent variable as the variable that the experimenter manipulates *independent* of what the participant wishes: Some students will study for 4 hours whether they want to or not. (An independent variable is also called a **factor**.)

We select an independent variable because it is relevant to our hypothetical construct. Then we create an operational definition of the variable, stating how we will measure and manipulate it. An independent variable may be quantitative (manipulating the amount of a variable that is present), or an independent variable may be qualitative (manipulating a quality or attribute of the situation). For example, if in a different study, we compare the test performance of students who study in either their dorm room or a library room, we are manipulating a quality of the room.

Although there is an unlimited variety of independent variables, common approaches to manipulating them include changing a physical aspect of stimuli (e.g., changing the color or brightness of geometric shapes or the loudness or pitch of tones that people must recognize) or changing the meaning of stimuli (e.g., manipulating whether words to be remembered have similar meanings or have a positive or negative emotional connotation). Sometimes researchers manipulate the environment (e.g., changing the color of the walls in a room where participants study, altering the furniture arrangement in an office, or varying the number of people present when someone gives a speech). Or, we change the attributes of the stimuli or task (e.g., providing different instructions or varying the rewards or punishments given); or, we alter the social setting in which participants are placed.

Note that one way researchers manipulate a social setting is through confederates. **Confederates** are people enlisted by a researcher to act as other participants or "accidental" passers-by, thus creating a particular social situation in which the "real" participants are observed.

> ***REMEMBER*** A researcher changes the independent variable to produce a corresponding change in participants' behavior and thus demonstrate a relationship.

Conditions of the Independent Variable

An independent variable is the *overall* variable a researcher examines that may have many different amounts or categories we could examine. A **condition** is a specific amount or category of the independent variable that the researcher selects to create the situation under which the participants are observed. Thus, although our independent variable of amount of study time could be any amount, our conditions were 1, 2, 3, or 4 hours of study. Likewise, if we compare studying in a dorm room to studying in a library room, the independent variable is type of room, and the conditions are "dorm" and "library." (A condition is also known as a **level** or a **treatment**.)

> ***REMEMBER*** The independent variable is the entire causal variable of interest. Conditions are the specific amounts or categories of the variable under which participants are tested.

We have a special name for the condition in which we present zero amount of the independent variable. A **control group** is a group of participants that is measured on the dependent variable but receives zero amount of the independent variable, or otherwise does not receive any treatment. A control group shows how participants behave without the treatment, providing a "baseline" or starting point for evaluating the influence of the variable when it is present. On the other hand groups that receive a nonzero amount of the independent variable or otherwise do experience the treatment are called **experimental groups**. Thus, in our study-time experiment, a control group would be students who spend zero time studying for the exam. Their test scores then provide a starting point for determining, literally, whether the other amounts of study time are better than nothing.

Sometimes it is not possible to administer zero amount of the independent variable, and then the control group is tested under a "normal" or "neutral" condition. For example, if the independent variable is temperature, there must be some temperature present, so the control condition might be normal room temperature. Or, if we are presenting cheerful or sad statements to alter participants' moods, the control condition might involve emotionally neutral statements. And sometimes a control condition involves comparing participants' performance to the result we would expect if they were guessing. For example, to study "psychic abilities," researchers "send" participants a telepathic message about a card drawn from a deck of playing cards. The number of cards correctly selected is then compared to the number we'd expect if a person were merely guessing. ("Psychics" do not perform above a chance level; Hanssel, 1980.)

True versus Quasi-Experiments

Not all experiments are true experiments involving true independent variables. In a **true experiment** the independent variable is controlled *by the researcher* so that a **true independent variable** is something that the experimenter does *to* participants. You can recognize a true independent variable because participants can be randomly assigned to any condition. **Random assignment** means that the condition of the independent variable a participant experiences is determined by random chance. Random assignment is a second step that occurs after we use random sampling to select the individuals for a study. For example, we might write the names of the study-time conditions (1, 2, 3, or 4) on slips of paper and, when a participant we've randomly selected arrives for the study, we would select a slip to randomly assign him or her to one of the conditions.

> ***REMEMBER*** A true experiment, with a true independent variable, allows random assignment of participants to any condition.

Although a true independent variable is something that a researcher exposes participants to, there are many behavior-influencing variables that we cannot manipulate in this way, such as age, race, background, or personality. Such variables are called **quasi-independent variables**, and studies that employ them are called **quasi-experiments**. A quasi-independent variable is *not* something that the experimenter does *to* participants, and so they cannot be randomly assigned to conditions. Instead, participants are assigned to a particular condition because they already qualify for that condition based upon some inherent characteristic. For example, say in a different study we hypothesize that growing older causes higher test scores. We can't randomly select participants and *make* some of them 20 years old and others 40 years old. Instead, we would randomly select one sample of 20-year-olds and one sample of 40-year-olds. Similarly, if we wanted to examine whether a qualitative variable such as gender was related to test scores, we would select a sample of females and a sample of males.

> ***REMEMBER*** A quasi-experiment does not involve random assignment of participants to conditions.

Note that with a true or quasi-independent variable, the experimenter always determines a participant's "score" on the independent variable. Thus, students who studied 1 hour have a score of 1 on our study-time variable, or people in the 20-year-olds sample have a score of 20 on our age variable. Thus, both a true and a quasi-experiment have the same purpose: to demonstrate a relationship in which as the conditions of the independent variable change, participants' scores on the other variable change. This other variable is called the dependent variable.

The Dependent Variable

The **dependent variable** reflects some aspect of participants or their behavior. You can identify the dependent variable as the one in which scores are presumably caused or influenced by the independent variable, so scores on the dependent variable *depend* on the conditions of the independent variable. In our studying experiment, the number of errors on the test is the dependent variable, because we believe that errors depend on how long students study. Or, if we manipulate the amount of chocolate people consume and then measure their eye blinking, eye blinking is the dependent variable. (The dependent variable is also called the **dependent measure**.)

As with everything else, you must also operationally define a dependent variable. Most of the time, the dependent variable *quantifies* a behavior: It measures the amount or degree of a behavior—how strongly it is exhibited, or its frequency of occurrence. At other times, the variable *qualifies* the behavior, distinguishing one behavior from another in terms of a quality or characteristic. For example, if we look at the causes of different personalities, personality type is the dependent variable, even though instead of measuring more or less personality, we would just identify different ones.

Essentially, the dependent variable measures participants' responses. Some of the dependent variables you'll find in the literature include those that measure physical actions, such as coordination or ability, perceptual and sensory responses, or internal physiological reactions. They may also measure how well or how often a behavior is performed to reflect the unseen behavior of the participant's degree of learning, memory, or motivation. Also, **reaction time**, which is the amount of time a participant takes to respond to a stimulus, is used to infer aspects of an underlying mental process.

Researchers also examine participants' judgments about events or other people. Such judgments may involve a **forced-choice procedure**, in which participants select from a limited set of choices (e.g., a multiple-choice test), or participants may perform a **sorting task**, in which they indicate similarities or differences by sorting stimuli into different groups. Other dependent measures include asking participants to describe their feelings, beliefs, or attitudes that a situation elicits, in which case they are providing **self-reports**. Often, self-reports involve completing **Likert-type questions**. Here, participants rate a series of statements, typically using a scale of 1 to 5, where 1 indicates "strongly agree" and 5 indicates "strongly disagree." In other forms of self-reports, subjects provide a running commentary of their mental activities or keep a diary.

Also, note that researchers may not directly influence the dependent variable. Instead, they manipulate a variable because they believe it changes an internal psychological state, which then influences the behavior. This internal state is called an intervening variable. An **intervening variable** is influenced by the independent variable, which in turn influences the dependent variable. It "intervenes" or comes between the independent and dependent variables. Thus, say we propose that frustration results in anger and that greater anger then leads to greater amounts of aggressive behavior. We would manipulate the independent variable of how frustrated participants are so that we change the intervening variable of their anger, which should then influence the dependent variable of their aggressiveness.

> ***REMEMBER*** Changing the independent variable presumably causes participants' behavior to change, and the dependent variable measures that behavior.

TABLE 2.5 Summary of Terminology Used in Experiments

Term	*Definition*
Independent variable	The variable manipulated to cause a change in a behavior
Condition	A specific amount or category of the independent variable that participants experience
Dependent variable	The variable measuring the behavior being changed
True independent variable	Produces conditions to which participants can be randomly assigned
Quasi-independent variable	Produces conditions to which participants cannot be randomly assigned
Random assignment	Using random chance to determine which condition a participant will experience

Table 2.5 will help you remember the previous terminology used to describe the components of an experiment.

After conducting the study-time experiment, we need to examine the results. Table 2.6 shows a useful way to diagram the design of an experiment, label the components, and organize the data. Each column is a condition of the independent variable—study time—under which three participants were tested. Each number in a column is a student's score on the dependent variable of number of test errors. Is there a relationship here? Yes. Why? Because as scores on the variable of amount of study time change (increase), scores on the variable of number of test errors also tend to change (decrease).

Notice that in an experiment, we ask, "What scores occur on the dependent variable for a *given* amount of the independent variable?" In other words, we always ask, "Are there consistent changes in the dependent variable *as a function of* changes in the independent variable?" Above, we are asking, "For a given study time, what error scores occur" or "Do error scores decrease as a function of increasing study time?"

As you'll see, there are special descriptive statistics for summarizing the relationship found in an experiment, and there are special inferential statistics for deciding whether the sample data are likely to represent the relationship that would be found if we tested

TABLE 2.6 Diagram of an Experiment Involving the Independent Variable of Number of Hours Spent Studying and the Dependent Variable of Number of Errors Made on a Statistics Test

Each column contains participants' scores measured under one condition of the independent variable.

	Independent variable: number of hours spent studying			
	Condition 1: 1 hour	*Condition 2: 2 hours*	*Condition 3: 3 hours*	*Condition 4: 4 hours*
Dependent variable: number of errors made on a statistics test	13 12 11	9 8 7	7 6 5	5 3 2

everyone from the population in the experiment. If so, we then proceed to generalize the results to the original hypothetical constructs as we discussed earlier.

> ***REMEMBER*** In experiments, we look for a relationship where, as the conditions of the independent variable change, scores on the dependent variable tend to change in a consistent fashion.

DESCRIPTIVE RESEARCH METHODS

In addition to testing causal hypotheses, recall that we may also create a descriptive hypothesis that describes a behavior without identifying its causes. Researchers test such hypotheses using *descriptive* or *nonexperimental methods*. In a **descriptive design**, we simply observe behaviors or relationships so that we may describe them, without manipulating the variables of interest. The logic behind descriptive methods is this: If my hypothesis is correct, then I should observe the predicted characteristics of the behavior, participants, or situation. To test such hypotheses, we may interview participants, directly measure their behavior, or examine their history. We may study only one subject or conduct a survey of many people. Or we may surreptitiously watch people or animals in their natural habitat.

Don't confuse descriptive *hypotheses* and descriptive *research* with descriptive *statistics*. Descriptive statistics are used to describe *data* from any type of design, whether it be experimental or descriptive. Descriptive hypotheses and descriptive research pertain to a research approach where we seek to describe *behaviors*.

The most common descriptive method is a correlational design. In a **correlational design**, we measure participants' scores on at least two variables (which, as usual, we operationally define) and then determine whether the scores form the predicted relationship. Originally, for example, we used a correlational design to study the relationship between amount of study time and test grades: We *asked* a random sample of students how long they studied for a test and what their grade was, and then we looked for a relationship. (This is different from the above experiment where we *made* students study for a particular amount of time.) Or, in a different study, we would have a correlational design if we measured participants' career choices and their personality type, asking, "Is career choice related to personality type?" Notice, here we have no independent or dependent variable, and we simply look to see if Y scores consistently change *as a function of* changes in a "given" X variable.

> ***REMEMBER*** In a correlational design, the researcher passively measures both variables, asking whether a relationship can be *found*. But in an experiment, the researcher actively changes one variable and measures the other, asking whether a relationship can be *produced*.

A correlational design may test a hypothesis that specific variables are related, or we may set out to discover which variables are related. In doing so, researchers often look for a relationship between scores on two tests or questionnaires (e.g., determining whether higher IQ scores occur with higher creativity test scores). We can also "correlate" test scores with some measure of physical or mental performance (e.g., relating personality type to problem-solving ability). Or we might relate a participant's record to his or her performance (e.g., relating school-attendance records to measures of subsequent job success).

Correlational procedures are especially useful in predicting behaviors. Researchers often conduct such studies in natural "field" settings, where a wide range of natural behaviors is likely. This makes the data useful for predicting future, natural behaviors. Thus, we may test the hypothesis that scores on a certain variable can be used to accurately predict a behavior, or we may set out to discover variables that are useful for making predictions.

Not all descriptive designs are correlational designs. Sometimes the hypothesis is simply that certain behaviors or situations operate in a certain way, and we merely observe participants on one or more variables, without predicting that they form a relationship. Thus, we might surreptitiously observe people while they study, simply to describe this behavior. Or we might distribute a survey regarding various variables that we think constitute studying, so we can describe what studying is, develop theoretical constructs, or derive additional hypotheses for later study.

REMEMBER Descriptive designs are used to demonstrate a relationship, predict behaviors, and describe a behavior or participant.

In later chapters, you'll see specific descriptive statistics for summarizing the data from descriptive studies, especially when they are correlational designs. There are also special inferential procedures for deciding whether similar results are likely to be found in the population. If so, then as usual, we generalize from the specific variables we have observed to a more general description in terms of the corresponding hypothetical constructs.

PUTTING IT ALL TOGETHER

The terms and logic introduced in this chapter are used throughout the scientific world. Psychologists thoroughly understand such terms as relationship, independent and dependent variable, condition, and descriptive statistics. These terms are part of their everyday vocabulary, and they think in these terms. For you to understand research and apply statistical procedures (let alone understand this book), you too must learn to think in these terms. The first step is to always try to use the appropriate terminology.

But don't let the terminology obscure your ultimate purpose. Always remember the overall logic of research, which can be summarized as follows: Based on a hypothesized law of nature, design either an experiment or a descriptive study to observe a relationship in the sample's scores. Then, use descriptive statistics to understand the relationship in the sample, and use inferential procedures to decide if a similar relationship would be found if you could study everyone in the population. Because scores reflect behaviors and events, by describing the scores that would be found in the population, you are actually describing the behavior of everyone of interest in a particular situation. Describing the behavior of everyone in a particular situation *is* describing how a law of nature operates.

CHAPTER SUMMARY

1. A *sample* is a subset of a *population*, which consists of all the members of a specific group. In statistics, the population is the entire group of scores being described, and a sample is a subset of those scores.

2. A *hypothetical construct* is an abstract concept used in a particular theoretical manner to relate different behaviors according to their underlying features or causes.
3. A hypothetical construct is studied by measuring a *variable*, which is any measurable aspect of a behavior or influence on behavior that may change. Variables may be *quantitative*, measuring a quantity or amount, or *qualitative*, measuring a quality or category.
4. An *operational definition* defines a construct or variable in terms of the operations used to measure it.
5. Most studies focus on demonstrating a *relationship*, a pattern in which, as the scores on one variable change, scores on another variable also change in a consistent fashion. On a graph, the pattern is formed by the *data points*.
6. The *strength* of a relationship is the degree of consistent association between the scores on the two variables.
7. The term *individual differences* refers to the fact that no two individuals are identical.
8. The "given" variable in any study is always designated the X variable, and a relationship is described in terms of "changes in Y *as a function of* changes in X." Experiments investigate changes in the *dependent variable* as a function of changes in the *independent variable.*
9. *Random sampling* is the method for selecting a sample so that all individuals in the population have the same chance of being selected and all possible samples have the same chance of being selected.
10. Random sampling should produce *representative samples*, in which the characteristics of the sample match the characteristics of the population. By chance, however, a sample may be unrepresentative.
11. *Descriptive statistics* are used to organize, summarize, and describe sample data. *Inferential statistics* are for deciding whether sample data represent a particular relationship in the population.
12. Causal hypotheses are tested using *experiments*, in which the researcher demonstrates a relationship by manipulating the *independent variable* and then measuring participants' scores on the *dependent variable.*
13. Each specific amount or category of the independent variable is a *condition.* A *control group* receives zero amount of the independent variable, as opposed to an *experimental group*, which does receive the treatment.
14. In a *true experiment*, with a *true independent variable*, participants can be randomly assigned to any condition. *Random assignment* means that the condition a participant experiences is determined in a random manner.
15. In a *quasi-experiment*, with a *quasi-independent variable*, participants cannot be randomly assigned to any condition because they already belong to a particular condition based upon some inherent characteristic.
16. *Confederates* are people enlisted by a researcher to create a particular social situation for participants.

17. An *intervening variable* is an internal characteristic that is influenced by the independent variable, which in turn influences the dependent variable.

18. Dependent measures may include *forced-choice procedures* (including *sorting tasks*) and *self-reports* (including *Likert-type questions*).

19. Descriptive hypotheses are tested using *descriptive designs*, in which no variables are manipulated. Instead, variables are simply measured as they occur. In a *correlational study*, two or more variables are measured to determine whether the predicted relationship occurs.

KEY TERMS (with page references)

as a function of (37)
condition (43)
confederates (43)
control group (43)
correlational design (47)
data point (37)
dependent measure (45)
dependent variable (45)
descriptive design (46)
descriptive statistics (38)
experiment (42)
experimental group (43)
factor (42)
forced-choice procedure (45)
generalize (40)
hypothetical construct (31)
independent variable (42)
individual differences (35)
inferential statistics (40)
intervening variable (45)
level (43)
Likert-type question (45)
operational definition (32)
population (29)
qualitative (32)
quantitative (32)
quasi-experiment (44)
quasi-independent variable (44)
random assignment (44)
random sampling (30)
reaction time (45)
relationship (33)
representative sample (30)
sample (29)
self-reports (45)
sorting task (45)
strength of a relationship (35)
treatment (43)
true experiment (44)
true independent variable (44)
variable (31)

REVIEW QUESTIONS

(Answers for odd-numbered questions and problems are provided in Appendix D.)

1. (a) How can you recognize when a relationship exists between two variables? (b) Why do researchers look for relationships between variables?

2. (a) What does the term *hypothetical construct* mean? (b) How do hypothetical constructs simplify nature? (c) Why does incorporating hypothetical constructs help you create scientifically acceptable hypotheses?

3. (a) What's the difference between a sample and a population? (b) How are samples used in research?

4. Why can't you expect to observe a perfectly consistent relationship between variables?
5. What is a data point?
6. What is random sampling?
7. (a) Why do random samples occur that are representative of the population? (b) Why do unrepresentative samples occur?
8. What are descriptive statistics used for?
9. What are inferential statistics used for?
10. (a) What is the difference between descriptive and experimental research methods? (b) What is the primary consideration for selecting one approach over the other?
11. (a) What is the difference between the independent variable and the conditions of the independent variable? (b) What is the dependent variable?
12. (a) What is a control group? (b) What is an experimental group? (c) Why do we employ control groups?
13. What is the difference between a true independent variable and a quasi-independent variable?
14. What does it mean to use (a) a "forced-choice procedure"? (b) "Likert-type" questions? (c) a "sorting task"? (d) "self-reports"?
15. What is the difference between an experiment and a descriptive design?
16. (a) What is the difference between a correlational study and other descriptive research methods? (b) What is the difference between an experiment and a correlational study?

PRACTICE PROBLEMS

17. In study A, a researcher gives groups of participants various amounts of alcohol and then observes any decrease in their ability to walk. In study B, a researcher notes the various amounts of alcohol that people drink at a party, and then observes any decrease in their ability to walk. What is the name for each type of design? Why?
18. In each of the following, identify the independent variable, the conditions, and the dependent variable: (a) Studying whether scores on a final exam are influenced by whether background music is played softly, is played loudly, or is absent. (b) Comparing freshmen, sophomores, juniors, and seniors with respect to how much fun they have while attending college. (c) Comparing whether being first-born, second-born, or third-born is related to intelligence. (d) Studying whether length of daily exposure to a sun lamp (15 minutes versus 60 minutes) accounts for differences in self-reported depression. (e) Investigating whether being in a room with blue walls, green walls, red walls, or beige walls influences aggressive behavior in a group of adolescents.
19. In problem 18, which are true experiments and which are quasi-experiments?
20. A student, Foofy, conducts a survey of the beverage preferences of college students on a random sample of students. Based on her findings, she concludes that most college students prefer sauerkraut juice to other beverages. What statistical argument can you give for not accepting her conclusions?
21. For the following data sets, which sample or samples have a relationship present?

Sample A		*Sample B*		*Sample C*		*Sample D*	
X	*Y*	*X*	*Y*	*X*	*Y*	*X*	*Y*
1	1	20	40	13	20	92	71
1	1	20	42	13	19	93	77
1	1	22	40	13	18	93	77
2	2	22	41	13	17	95	79
2	2	23	40	13	15	96	74
3	3	24	40	13	14	97	71
3	3	24	42	13	13	98	69

22. In which sample in problem 21 is there the strongest relationship? How do you know?

23. Below are graphs of data from three studies. Which depict a relationship? How do you know?

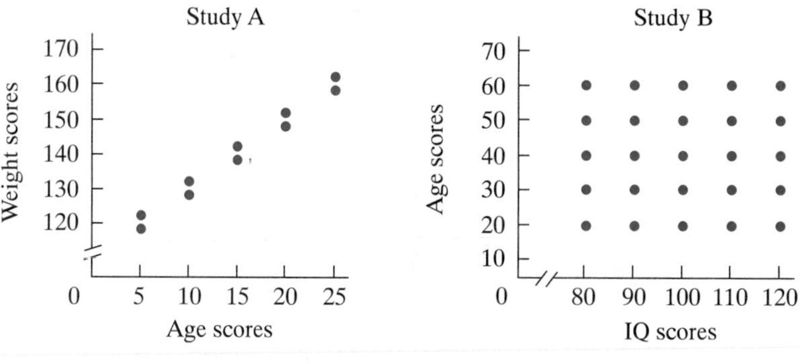

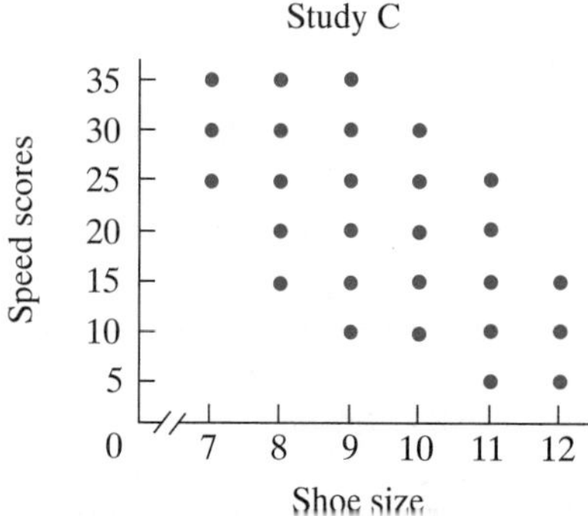

24. Which study in problem 23 demonstrates the strongest relationship between the variables? How do you know?

25. In problem 23, why does each relationship suggest that a law of nature is at work?

26. (a) Another student, Poindexter, says that Study A in problem 23 examines age scores as a function of weight scores. Is he correct? (b) Poindexter also claims that in Study C, the researcher is asking, "For a given shoe size, what speed scores occur?" Is he correct? (c) Let's say the studies in problem 23 were experiments. In each, which variable is the independent (or quasi-independent) variable, and which is the dependent variable?

27. A researcher proposes that happier students perform better on a test. To alter their mood when taking a test, students are tested in a room with either red, blue, or green walls. (a) What do we call the variable of wall color in this study? (b) What do we call the variable of test grades in this study? (c) What do we call the variable of mood in this study?

28. A nurse claims that when she wore one of those silly-looking hats, patients followed instructions better than they do now that she no longer wears it. What hypothetical constructs might this situation reflect?

3

Understanding Reliability and Validity

Getting Started

To understand this chapter, recall the following:

- From Chapter 1, recall how flaws in the evidence and the difficulty of proving a hypothesis can weaken a conclusion.
- From Chapter 2, understand the flow of a study, what a relationship is, and how experimental and descriptive designs differ.

Your goals in this chapter are to learn:

- The strategy for critically evaluating a study.
- What is meant by reliability and validity.
- What the various types of validity are.
- How participant, environmental, researcher, and measurement variables threaten reliability and validity.
- What a confounding is.
- How to control threats to reliability and validity.
- How experimental and descriptive designs differ in terms of reliability and validity.

In Chapter 2, you saw what is *apparently* a pretty straightforward process: We predict and then examine a relationship between variables and then use the relationship to draw conclusions about a hypothesis. You may be wondering why then, in Chapter 1, I made such a big deal of the potential flaws in research and the need for skeptical and critical evaluation of every research finding. Well, although *overall* a study is straightforward, it is in the specifics of a study that all sorts of errors can creep in. This is because nature is very complex, and so any research situation is loaded with all sorts of unwanted variables. Any of these variables may be a design flaw that ultimately misleads us about a behavior. Therefore, *the* issue when designing research is to identify and deal with these variables.

There are three major aspects to this chapter: We'll discuss how to critically identify the flaws in a study, then you'll see the names for the common flaws, and then you'll see how they influence the interpretation of descriptive and experimental designs. First, though, let's design an example study in which such flaws might occur.

DESIGNING AN EXAMPLE STUDY

Say that while in the student lounge, you observe that your friends are more successful at meeting members of the opposite sex than you are (aren't they always?). You believe this is because they are better-looking than you (aren't they always!). You decide to investigate this topic. Your observation is related to the broad hypothetical constructs of "first impressions" and "physical attractiveness," and in the research literature, you find many social psychology studies that show that first impressions are influenced by physical attractiveness (e.g., Eagly, Ashmore, MaKijani & Longo, 1991). Although this finding holds for *both* genders, you'll examine the descriptive hypothesis that females form more positive first impressions of males who are more physically attractive. (If this hypothesis offends you because it suggests people are shallow and insensitive, remember that scientists must be open-minded and accept nature as it is, warts and all.)

Your first step in testing this hypothesis should be to take a moment and think about the behavior.

Considering the Context of the Behavior

When designing any study, first consider the overall context or situation in which the behavior occurs. Using your knowledge of psychology and some common sense, try to identify all of the factors that may influence the behavior and your study of it. This will not only provide numerous ideas for the specific study, but it will also allow you to foresee potential problems. So, what's involved when a woman forms a first impression and judges a man as attractive?

First, what might a female consider when determining a male's attractiveness? She probably considers his facial attractiveness, the color and style of his hair, his height and weight, his posture, his body's shape, his style of dress, his cleanliness, and so on. She might also consider his behavior when they meet: Whether he is silent or talkative, what he says and how he says it, whether he is friendly or condescending. Does he exhibit nervous tics or irritating mannerisms? Does he make eye contact? Does he smile? Does he make physical contact, and how? (Is his handshake firm or mushy?)

The personal characteristics of the woman can also influence her perceptions. Her height and weight determine whether she judges a male as tall or short, heavy or thin. Also, is she different from him in age, style of dress, educational level, culture, or language? Is she actively seeking to meet men, or is she happily married and thus disinterested? Further, how does she form a first impression? It may involve whether she judges him to be intelligent, creative, sexy, likable, interesting, decisive, or some combination of these qualities. How long after she meets him is she beyond first impressions and getting to know him?

We should also consider the environment for the meeting. Is she interviewing him for a job, or is the meeting social? Is the meeting in a crowded room or an empty one? Does it occur at a shopping mall, a party, or a funeral? Is the environment noisy or quiet, dark or well-lit? Remember, too, that we must somehow observe her behavior. Doing so may make her nervous and interfere with her "normal" reactions. Does the gender of the researcher make her more or less self-conscious? How will we measure her impressions? Will she answer questions honestly?

The above provides only a partial list of the many questions to consider when studying how a female forms a first impression and judges a male's attractiveness. Notice, however, that these questions center around four general components found in any study. The *researcher* observes the *participants* in a specific *environment* and applies a *measurement procedure*. When designing a study, you must consider variables related to each component.

1. **Participant variables:** The personal characteristics and experiences of participants that may influence their responses.
2. **Researcher variables:** The behaviors and characteristics of the researcher that may influence the reactions of participants.
3. **Environmental variables:** The aspects of the environment that can influence scores.
4. **Measurement variables:** The aspects of the stimuli presented or the measurement procedure employed that may influence scores.

It is by dealing with these variables that you reduce a complex situation into a controlled and understandable one. Therefore, much of designing a study involves deciding how you'll deal with these variables.

Refining the Design

Let's first identify the population (and the sample). Physical appearance is probably irrelevant to blind people when forming first impressions, so we limit the population to adult, sighted females who are citizens of this country. We must locate a random sample of such women, and given your initial observations at the lounge, we'll sample from among the women attending your college. In fact, we'll go to the most common source for participants—the current introductory psychology course.

From reading the literature, it appears that a good way to determine a male's physical attractiveness is to measure the variable of his "facial attractiveness." Of the many ways we might operationally define facial attractiveness (e.g., rating it ourselves or having a panel of judges rate it), we will directly ask female participants how attractive a man is. We also decide that an important component of a first impression is how much he is initially "liked" by the woman. Although we might measure the variable of "likability" by determining whether a female agrees that he meets some definition of likability, or by recording the number of times she uses "like" when describing him, we decide to simply ask her how much she likes him. To quantify a woman's judgment of a man's likability and attractiveness, we'll use a 6-point rating scale (a "Likert scale") and have participants answer these two questions:

How much do you like this person?
1 2 3 4 5 6
DISLIKE LIKE

How attractive is this person's face?
1 2 3 4 5 6
UNATTRACTIVE ATTRACTIVE

You can now see the prediction: At an initial meeting between a male and our participants, women who produce higher attractiveness ratings for a man should also produce higher likability scores for him. Completing the design involves defining the individual components of "an initial meeting between a male and our participants." Say we define "participants" as 12 females from an introductory psychology class. We define the "meeting" as a social, one-on-one introduction, and "initial" as lasting about 2 minutes. And we define "meeting males" as bringing each woman to a student lounge and introducing her to each of 10 of our male friends—we'll call each man a *model*. After each meeting, a participant will rate the model's likability and attractiveness, answering our questions using pencil and paper.

You may think that the design is finished. However, it's not a good design, because we have not completely thought it through.

CRITICALLY EVALUATING THE STUDY

Say that we conducted the likability study and obtained the data in Table 3.1. For simplicity, the likability scores are separated into two groups based on whether a model was less attractive (rated a 3 or below) or more attractive (rated a 4 or above). Sure enough, higher likability scores were given to the more attractive models. It looks like a woman's first impression of a man is related to his physical attractiveness.

But, recall that the goal is to *know* how a behavior operates. However, in any study, the only thing we "know" is that each participant obtained a particular score—a number—at a particular time. We *don't* know what these numbers actually mean: We don't know that participants are really—and only—reacting to the variables we want them to,

TABLE 3.1 Summary of Data from the Likability Study

	Less Attractive Models	***More Attractive Models***
Likability scores →	2	5
	1	6
	2	6
	1	5
	3	4
	3	6
	3	5

so we don't know what a score really measures, and so we don't know what the relationship really reflects. That's why you must always critically evaluate a study. Critically evaluating a study means answering the question, "How confident are you that the scores actually reflect the hypothetical constructs, variables, and behaviors you think they reflect, and that the observed relationship actually reflects the relationship you think it reflects?"

Because, there are many aspects of the likability study that we took for granted, there are many potential flaws that reduce our confidence that the scores indicate what we think they indicate, and that the relationship reflects what we think it reflects. These flaws can also be grouped in terms of those four types of variables—participant, researcher, measurement, and environment—that define a study. Here are just some of the things that could go wrong:

Participant variables

- Some females barely speak English. Their answers to the questions are partially a test of their English.
- Some participants are extremely nearsighted (but don't wear glasses). They can barely see the model and, instead, guess at his attractiveness.
- Some participants already know the models. Our measurements do not reflect an *initial* anything.

Environmental variables

- The lounge is usually lit by sunlight, but when clouds pass by, some participants meet the models in a darkened room. Everyone looks more attractive in the dark.
- Sometimes the lounge is hot, sometimes it's noisy, and sometimes other people are wandering through it. Therefore, some participants don't pay much attention to the model.

Researcher variables

- The researcher is a female who introduces the more attractive models in a more positive manner. Or, the researcher is a male who's jealous of the attractive males and gives negative introductions for them. Either way, likability scores reflect the tone of the introduction.
- An introduction of a model sometimes lasts only 30 seconds and sometimes lasts over 2 minutes, so we don't always measure the same kind of first impression.

Measurement variables

- The truth is that "facial attractiveness" and "likability" cannot be accurately measured by this procedure.
- Some females cannot decide between a "4" and a "5" on the rating scales, and mentally flip a coin when responding.
- Some models wear a more pleasant aftershave, have more muscular bodies, and dress better than others, and some talk warmly to the females while others talk only of car engines and beer blasts. Some models will be rated as more attractive, but *not* because of their faces.
- Two females are inadvertently given a pencil with a broken point and think that their reaction to this is what is actually being studied. They focus not on attractiveness or likability but on where the hidden camera might be.

Although such problems may strike you as unlikely, they can and do occur. For example, May and Hamilton (1980) found that something as mundane as the type of background music being played influenced how females rated a male's attractiveness. Therefore, because you are skeptical and open-minded, always consider whether such things might be occurring in a study so that the scores do not really reflect what we think they do.

> ***REMEMBER*** Critically evaluating a study means questioning whether the scores and relationship actually reflect what we think they do.

When evaluating a study, you should follow two general strategies. First, always consider the operational definitions being used. A particular definition may provide a perspective that is misleading or incorrect. For example, maybe when answering the likability question about a model, a female in no way taps into her "first impression" of him, so that measuring the variable in this way is just plain wrong. Rely on the research literature for accepted definitions that produce the most precise and accurate data possible.

Second, look for fluctuations in extraneous variables. An **extraneous variable** is a variable that can influence the results, but is not a variable we wish to study. Such variables come from those four components of a study—the researcher, participants, environment, and measurement task. Evaluating a study boils down to looking for fluctuating extraneous variables from each component that may inadvertently alter the results. For example, the extraneous variables of a researcher's rudeness and the environment's temperature may flaw the attractiveness scores, and participants' nearsightedness and their difficulty with English may flaw likability scores. The more that such variables are operating, the more that the scores and the relationship do not reflect what we think they do.

Ideally, of course, you want to identify and eliminate important extraneous variables when *designing* a study so that they cannot influence the results. Therefore, look for extraneous variables when initially considering the context of the behavior. When we originally considered the context of first impressions and attractiveness, we were actually identifying potential extraneous variables. And, as above, also look for anything that can go wrong that might produce unexpected variables. Always remember that if you miss an important extraneous variable, it then comes back to haunt you, causing problems when interpreting the study.

Look for extraneous variables that fluctuate in either of two ways. Sometimes a variable changes **unsystematically**, changing with no consistent pattern. If, for example, the lounge is sometimes dark and sometimes light in a random pattern, then lounge lighting changes unsystematically. On the other hand, an extraneous variable may also change **systematically**, either increasing or decreasing in a way that forms a consistent pattern. For example, if the researcher is more polite when introducing later models, then politeness systematically changed.

> ***REMEMBER*** The flaws that decrease confidence in a study come from inappropriate operational definitions and from systematic and unsystematic extraneous variables.

Understand that systematic and unsystematic extraneous variables influence a study in two ways. First, as above, they lead to errors when interpreting and generalizing the study, because the variables that we think are operating are not those that are really operating. Above, we think we are seeing the relationship between attractiveness and likability, but really it may involve the influence of lounge lighting and how polite an introduction was.

Second, before you even get to the interpretation, extraneous variables can influence the scores and thus the mathematical relationship produced. Recall that our first concern is producing a consistent relationship in the sample data. But extraneous variables may increase or decrease scores, and thus alter the *strength* of the relationship. For example, on the left side of Table 3.2 are data when few extraneous variables are operating. Then a fairly consistent pattern occurs, showing that more attractive models do tend to receive higher likability ratings. On the right side of the table, however, say that unsystematic extraneous variables are operating: Maybe lighting in the lounge fluctuates so that likability ratings are now sometimes higher and sometimes lower than if the lighting were constant. The result is that scores *within* each attractiveness group now span the full range between low and high, producing a weaker, *less consistent relationship*. In fact, the scores might be so inconsistent that there is no relationship, so that we think our variables are not related (when in nature they may be.)

Likewise, a systematic extraneous variable might raise or lower scores in a consistent way so that the sample relationship is different than it would be if the variable were not operating. For example, the researcher might—out of pity—give especially nice introductions for the less attractive models, and more abrupt introductions for the attractive models. This could raise all scores for the less attractive group while lowering scores for the attractive group. Then the data will show that as attractiveness goes up, likability goes *down*, even though normally in nature the reverse may be true.

> ***REMEMBER*** Extraneous variables can produce misleading scores and a misleading relationship, as well as a misleading interpretation of how nature operates.

So, as we've seen, the process of interpreting a relationship and testing a hypothesis is *not* so straightforward after all. The ultimate question is always whether the data actually reflect what we think they do. Because of the complexity of this question,

TABLE 3.2 Examples of Likability Scores Without and With the Influence of Extraneous Variables.

Without extraneous variables		*With extraneous variables*	
Less attractive models	***More attractive models***	***Less attractive models***	***More attractive models***
2	5	1	6
1	6	4	4
1	4	3	2
2	3	5	6
3	6	2	1
3	6	1	2

however, researchers have special terminology for communicating different aspects of it. These aspects fall under two general concerns, called reliability and validity.

UNDERSTANDING RELIABILITY

One component of asking whether the data actually reflect what we think they do is asking whether the data are reliable. **Reliability** is the degree to which the same event or behavior produces the same score each time it is measured. With reliability we ask, "Regardless of what the scores actually measure, do they at least measure it consistently, without introducing random error?" In other words, a reliable measurement is repeatable and stable over time. Reliability is necessary because a law of nature is consistent and stable over time, so a measurement reflecting the law should also be consistent and stable. For example, we assume a female's liking of a particular male will not change rapidly. If she likes him now, she should like him to the same degree five minutes from now. If her two ratings for him differ, however, then we have some measurement error: Either the first, the second, or both scores contain error in measuring her behavior.

The problem with *unreliable* scores is that different scores each time we measure the behavior will lead to different conclusions each time, so then we don't know which conclusion is correct. Thus, unreliable data are "untrustworthy" in the sense that they reflect error and lead to inconsistent conclusions. Therefore, how reliable the data are influences our confidence in a study.

To obtain reliable data, the goal is to design a study in which the research situation is as consistent as possible. Anything that adds sloppiness or random errors when measuring a variable—whether an independent, a dependent, or other variable—threatens reliability. Often reliability is reduced by unsystematic extraneous variables, so again you should consider those four components of a study, and ask, "Might a particular score be different if we measured it again in the same situation?" Thus, we have an unreliable measurement of the duration of a meeting if our stopwatch is inaccurate. Or, we have unreliable attractiveness ratings if, because of their eyesight, females guess when responding.

> ***REMEMBER*** Reliability is the degree to which measurements are consistent and do not contain error.

Although previously, we used the term *consistency* when referring to the strength of a relationship, a reliable relationship is *not* the same as a consistent relationship. A reliable relationship is one that—whether strong or weak—is found repeatedly every time a particular situation is examined. On the other hand, reliability when measuring any *single* variable does influence the strength of the relationship. For example, as we saw with extraneous variables back in Table 3.2, if the measurement procedure produces larger differences in likability scores within an attractiveness group, then we will have a less consistent relationship than would otherwise be observed. And if enough inconsistency is present, we may be misled into thinking no relationship exists. Thus, unreliability in measuring a variable can lead to an inconsistent relationship and/or a faulty interpretation of it.

UNDERSTANDING VALIDITY

Our other concern when asking what the data actually reflect is in terms of whether the data accurately reflect the constructs, variables, and relationships we think they do. Any time researchers question whether they are drawing the correct inferences from results, they are concerned with validity. **Validity** is the extent to which a procedure measures what it is intended to measure. When a procedure lacks validity, it is "untrustworthy" because it reflects the "wrong" aspects of a situation to some degree, so we cannot trust our inferences about the situation.

As you'll see below, researchers break the issue of validity into several subparts, depending on the particular inference being drawn.

Drawing Valid Inferences about Measurements

First, we are concerned with whether a score actually reflects what we think it does, in terms of the variable and in terms of the hypothetical construct we wish to measure. For each type of inference, we have a corresponding type of validity.

Content validity is the degree to which measurements actually reflect the *variable* of interest. Here, we question whether a procedure actually and only measures all dimensions of the behavior we seek (are we tapping the appropriate "contents" of the target behavior?). Thus, when females are supposedly rating attractiveness, we ask, "Are their scores actually and only measuring the attractiveness of the model?"

A procedure lacks content validity, first, if it lacks reliability. For example, if participants are guessing somewhat when rating a model's attractiveness, then a score partly reflects his attractiveness and partly reflects guessing. Second, content validity is decreased if any systematic or unsystematic extraneous variable is also measured by a score. Thus, we lose content validity in measuring attractiveness when participants barely speak English, because their scores partially reflect their language ability. Likewise, content validity is decreased if a woman's rating partially reflects her response to a model's behavior or style of dress. By reflecting these other variables, such scores can mislead us about the variable of facial attractiveness. In essence, we don't know what we're talking about when it comes to facial attractiveness, because we have not measured facial attractiveness alone.

On the other hand, **construct validity** is the extent to which a measurement reflects the *hypothetical construct* of interest. Here, we question whether the variable we are measuring actually reflects the construct as it is conceptualized from a particular theoretical viewpoint. If a procedure lacks construct validity, then any inferences drawn about the broad underlying psychological processes will be in error.

A classic question of construct validity occurs with intelligence tests, which measure people on such variables as vocabulary or problem-solving ability. While content validity is the question of whether we really measure these variables, construct validity is the question of whether these variables really measure "intelligence." Perhaps some other variables more accurately reflect this construct. Likewise, some females might argue that they are not so shallow as to judge a man's attractiveness based on his facial appearance. They are essentially theorizing about what should constitute the construct of attractiveness and its relationship to first impressions. For them, our study lacks construct validity because it examines the "wrong" variable—facial attractiveness—and thus will lead to an incorrect interpretation of behavior.

> ***REMEMBER*** Content validity refers to whether we actually and only measure an intended variable. Construct validity refers to whether a variable actually and only reflects the intended hypothetical construct.

In addition to considering the content and construct validity of any *single* variable, as above, we are also concerned with the validity of our inferences about the relationship *between* the variables. Because we may consider the relationship either in terms of the sample data or when generalizing, we have two types of validity here—internal and external.

Drawing Internally Valid Inferences about the Relationship

Internal validity is the degree to which the mathematical relationship we observe between the *scores* actually and only reflects the relationship between the *variables* of interest. Thus, we have internal validity if the X and Y scores reflect only the relationship between the intended X and Y variables, so that we draw the correct inferences about what was going on *in* ("internal" to) the study. Internal validity is reduced, however, if other variables are also being measured, so that the *apparent* relationship between the X and Y scores actually reflects another relationship involving *other* variables. This is important because if we do not know what the sample's relationship reflects, we cannot draw correct inferences about the relationship in nature.

Don't confuse internal validity with content or construct validity. If, for example, our questions do accurately measure a model's likability and attractiveness, then we have content and construct validity. But, say that also the researcher inadvertently gave some models a more positive introduction, simultaneously making them both more attractive and more likable. Then internal validity is reduced, because the "real" relationship we've observed also involves the changing variable of how positive the introduction is. Thus, internal validity is threatened whenever changes in our X variable do not relate directly and only to changes in the Y variable.

> ***REMEMBER*** Internal validity is the degree to which the relationship between the scores reflects only the relationship between the intended variables.

The primary threat to internal validity is from confounding variables.

Confounding Variables

A **confounding** variable is an extraneous variable that systematically changes along with a variable of interest. Then, we cannot tell which variable is actually operating in the study (we are confused or "confounded.") For example, say that coincidentally our more attractive models were also better dressed, while less attractive models were poorly dressed. Then, we would say that "style of dress is a confounding variable" or that "attractiveness and manner of dress are confounded." This confounding is illustrated in Table 3.3

TABLE 3.3 Diagram of a Confounded Relationship

Intended variable →	*Less attractive models*	*More attractive models*
Confounding variable →	*Poorly dressed*	*Well dressed*
Likability scores →	2	5
	1	6
	2	6
	1	5
	3	4
	3	6

Again the likability scores in the table have been separated into two groups, labeled as either less attractive or more attractive. However, because of the confounding, the less attractive models can also be labeled as poorly dressed, while the more attractive models can be described as well-dressed. The problem is that then we don't know which is the correct label for the groups. Maybe facial attractiveness was irrelevant in this situation. Maybe we should be calling the groups "poorly dressed" and "well-dressed" because this was the variable that is actually related to likability.

> ***REMEMBER*** If an extraneous variable changes simultaneously with a variable of interest, then the variables are confounded.

Identifying a confounding after the study is conducted makes interpreting it impossible: Above, we don't know whether females were reacting to a male's attractiveness or to his manner of dress. Therefore, the goal is to identify and eliminate *potential* confounding variables when designing the study. Confounding variables arise from any source. There's a confounding if a male researcher introduces the unattractive models and a female researcher introduces the attractive ones. Also, confoundings occur if, with more attractive models, there are systematic changes in the temperature or noise level of the lounge, or in how interested participants are in meeting men. Or, say that in a different study we examine the influence of background music on the models' likability, comparing a song that has lyrics with another that does not. Confoundings are present if one song is louder than the other, or if one is more familiar than the other. In every case, we will not be able to determine which variable is the one that produced differences in likability scores.

> ***REMEMBER*** Always consider the internal validity of a study by looking for confounding variables.

Drawing Externally Valid Inferences about the Relationship

After we conclude what was going on *in* a study, we then *generalize* the conclusions beyond the study to everyone in the population. But, are we correct in this conclusion? **External validity** is the degree to which the results accurately generalize to other individuals and other situations. Thus, external validity is the question of whether the study provides a good example of the relationship that occurs in situations "external" to our study.

External validity is threatened by any extraneous variable that makes observations unique and atypical, so that they are unrepresentative of the relationship generally found in nature. For example, our female participants are all from the same college, so the sample represents the type of women who attend that college. And by testing only college women, we have less confidence that the relationship generalizes to the population of all women, including those who don't go to college. Likewise, the way we operationally defined the variables and the specifics of the procedure may result in scores or a relationship that would not be found in other settings. If a similar relationship cannot be found with other participants in other settings, then we have a biased and misleading perspective: We will incorrectly describe the relationship between likability and facial attractiveness—as well as incorrectly describing the relationship between the constructs of first impressions and physical attractiveness.

> ***REMEMBER*** External validity is the degree to which we can draw the correct inferences when generalizing beyond a study.

Several subparts to external validity arise, depending on the researcher's perspective when generalizing. One important subpart is ecological validity.

Ecological validity **Ecological validity** is the extent to which research can be generalized to common behaviors and natural situations. If a design does not have ecological validity, we end up focusing on what participants *can* do in a study instead of what they *usually* do in everyday life. This issue is most important in highly controlled laboratory experiments. For example, for years researchers studied "paired-associate learning," in which participants learned pairs of nonsense syllables (e.g., learning that BIM goes with YOB). But learning nonsense syllables is not an everyday, real-life behavior, and so such research lacks ecological validity: We cannot be confident that it accurately describes, natural learning processes.

Researchers often lose ecological validity in their quest for internal validity, developing a rather unusual measurement task in order to control and simplify the behavior. (Paired-associate learning allows for much more controlled observations than, say, classroom learning.) However, where possible, a balance between internal and ecological validity is best. The challenge is to maintain control while having participants perform tasks that bear some resemblance to those found in the real world.

TABLE 3.4 A Researcher's Terminology for Questioning the Different Aspects of a Study

Question	*Research term*
Do the scores reflect error?	Reliability
Do the scores reflect the variable?	Content validity
Do the scores reflect the hypothetical construct?	Construct validity
Does the relationship reflect the variables in the study?	Internal validity
Does the relationship generalize beyond the study?	External validity
Do the results generalize to natural behaviors and situations?	Ecological validity

REMEMBER Ecological validity is the extent to which the situation and behaviors in a study are found in the natural environment.

The preceding issues of reliability and validity are *the* issues in designing research, so they are summarized for you in Table 3.4. (You need to know these terms.)

MINIMIZING THREATS TO VALIDITY AND RELIABILITY

All research suffers to some extent from problems of reliability and validity. The best you can do is minimize the *major* threats to reliability and validity, so that you are as confident in a conclusion as possible. The problem with the likability study was that we did not take the necessary steps to minimize these threats. After a study is completed, however, there is no way to solve such problems. The design and interpretation of a study are completely interwoven, so the appropriate time to worry about the interpretation is when you are designing the study.

Notice that although we focus on identifying threats to reliability and validity, such issues are ultimately empirical questions. That is, we rely on replication to determine whether we've made a mistake when interpreting a study. In particular, literal or direct replications—studies that duplicate a previous study—increase our confidence that a particular approach is reliable and internally valid. Conceptual replications—studies that employ somewhat different procedures—increase our confidence that the overall approach is externally valid.

Consequently, researchers rely first on the psychological literature to find operational definitions of constructs and variables that are reliable and have the various types of validity. Instead, you can devise your own procedures, but you run the risk that they will have weak validity and reliability. Therefore, you must demonstrate that a procedure is reliable and valid. (Some techniques for demonstrating this are discussed in Chapter 10.) Whenever possible, however, it is best to adopt procedures that are commonly accepted in the literature.

In addition, you'll make decisions about how to test a hypothesis so that in some ways your study is unique, with its own threats to validity and reliability. The first step in dealing with such threats is to identify potentially important extraneous variables. Use your knowledge of research and psychology to examine the general context of the behavior, as we did in our likability study. Throughout, look for variables that reduce your confidence that the scores and relationship actually reflect what you think they reflect.

Once you identify serious threats, you need to control them.

Controlling Extraneous Variables

It is by controlling extraneous variables that we meet the scientific goal of obtaining controlled observations. To do so, the basic approach is to employ a more precise operational definition of each component. More precise definitions automatically limit extraneous variables.

Typically, researchers control extraneous variables in one of three ways—by eliminating them, keeping them constant, or balancing them.

Many problems can be eliminated by *eliminating extraneous variables*. For example, in the likability study, we could improve reliability and content validity by eliminating distracting noises by moving to a lounge where they do not occur. We could refuse to admit intruders who might distract participants. We could ensure the models are all unknown to participants by obtaining them from a different school, and we could avoid the use of broken pencils.

If we cannot eliminate an extraneous variable, we may keep it *constant* for all participants. For example, to improve reliability, and eliminate potential confoundings, we should keep the temperature and illumination in the lounge at constant, normal levels, and we should keep the researcher's behavior constant, precisely defining how all participants are treated. Also, we could redefine our participants, selecting females who all speak English well and have corrected vision. Likewise, we could select models with the same body type and manner of dress, and provide them with a "script" of what to say and how to behave.

Sometimes an extraneous variable cannot be eliminated (for example, we cannot eliminate the variable of a researcher's gender). Likewise, keeping the variable constant may not be feasible, because if it is present in one particular way, it may create a rather unique situation, reducing external validity for generalizing our findings (employing only a male researcher or only a female researcher might influence participants in a particular way, and this would reduce generalizability). In such cases, we may intentionally change the variable to *balance* its biasing influence. For example, we could balance the researcher's gender as shown in Table 3.5. We would have a male researcher introduce half of the less attractive and half of the more attractive models, while a female researcher would introduce the remaining models. In one sense, this design is consistent, because across all participants and all models, the potential positive or negative influence of the male researcher should balance out any potential effects of the female researcher. Then we show a more general relationship between attractiveness and likability that occurs despite the sex of the researcher.

Likewise, if we thought the time of day participants were tested might have an influence, we'd balance those tested early in the day with those tested later. Or, if we thought a particular lounge could influence first impressions, we'd balance testing

TABLE 3.5 Diagram of Likability Study Where Researcher's Gender Is Balanced

	Less attractive models	*More attractive models*
Likability scores with male experimenter	2 2 3 1	5 5 6 6
Likability scores with female experimenter	2 1 1 3	4 6 5 4

some participants in each of several different lounges. (We'll see more about balancing variables in the next chapter.)

> ***REMEMBER*** To control extraneous variables, we eliminate them, keep them constant, or balance their influence.

Deciding on the Controls to Employ

Ideally, of course, you want the best possible study from all perspectives, so always correct any flaws that you can. It is a fact of life, however, that the things that influence reliability and validity are interrelated. There are always trade-offs, so that improving one aspect of a study may negatively impact another aspect (e.g., the most reliable procedure may not be construct valid). In particular, as you'll see repeatedly, those procedures that increase internal validity often decrease external validity, and vice versa.

Therefore, there is no set of rules to follow when deciding whether to control an extraneous variable. How to deal with any issue of reliability and validity depends on your particular research hypothesis and how you examine the behavior. You may simply accept a threat to reliability or to a certain type of validity because the threat is not all that important to your study. In doing so, however, recognize the limitations produced by the threat and refrain from drawing inferences that are invalid because of them.

> ***REMEMBER*** Whether you should deal with a threat to reliability or validity depends on whether it seriously threatens the purpose of your study.

How to deal with threats to reliability and validity is determined primarily by the type of hypothesis you are testing and thus by whether you conduct a descriptive study or an experiment.

ISSUES OF VALIDITY AND RELIABILITY IN DESCRIPTIVE STUDIES

Recall that in descriptive designs, the researcher does not manipulate the variables of interest. The original likability study in the lounge was a descriptive, correlational design because we simply measured the reactions of females when first meeting a model.

Descriptive studies are usually conducted outside of the laboratory in natural "field" settings where few variables are controlled and so a wide range of natural behaviors are likely. Therefore, descriptive studies tend to produce high external validity: They tend to be repeatable with other participants and settings. For example, even with the controls we've discussed, the likability study has much in common with the way people meet in the real world. Therefore, our results should generalize to other such meetings in the real world.

It is because of their high external validity that descriptive methods are best for testing descriptive hypotheses. Here, the goal is to describe behaviors as they normally occur and to predict their occurrence in natural settings. Therefore, we use the methods that produce observations and relationships that are typical of such behaviors in the real world.

Different designs result in trade-offs, however: The cost of high external validity in a descriptive study is reduced control. Uncontrolled fluctuating variables in the student lounge, for example, reduce the reliability, content validity, and construct validity of the measurements. And most important:

> **Descriptive research tends to have weak internal validity because of likely confoundings.**

Internal validity in descriptive/correlational research is the extent that changes in the *X* variable relate directly and only to changes in the *Y* variable. But, recall that our models rated as more attractive might also coincidentally be better dressed or be given a better introduction. Likewise numerous other extraneous variables might also be operating because we have males and females who can behave in all sorts of ways, and who are interacting in an uncontrolled environment. Because such confounding variables are so likely, we have little confidence that the relationship between scores that we observe *actually and only* reflects the relationship between attractiveness and likability.

> ***REMEMBER*** Descriptive approaches tend to have greater external validity but less internal validity than experiments.

It is because of their weak internal validity that descriptive approaches cannot be used to make valid inferences about the causes of a behavior.

Problems in Inferring the Causes of a Behavior

Recall that experimental methods are used to test causal hypotheses. It's not that we can't test causal hypotheses using descriptive procedures, it's just that they provide minimal confidence in our conclusions. This is because merely showing a relationship between *X* and *Y* does not automatically mean that changes in *X cause* changes in *Y*. One variable can be related to another variable without causing it to change: A person's weight is related to his or her height, but greater weight does not cause greater height. The key to inferring a causal relationship lies in the *manner* in which the relationship is demonstrated. Two components are needed.

First, it is necessary to produce the correct temporal sequence: To say that *X* causes *Y*, we must show that *X* occurs *before Y*. Descriptive studies do not establish positively which variable occurs first. In the likability study, we cannot say that greater attractiveness causes greater likability, because we are unsure of the order in which these reactions occur. Perhaps, females first perceived a model as more attractive and this then caused greater likability. Or, perhaps, females first decided they liked the model, and his greater likability then caused him to be rated as more attractive.

The second requirement for demonstrating a behavior's cause is to be sure that no extraneous variable could actually be the cause—in other words, that there are no confoundings. We have the least confidence about causality in descriptive studies because they are so likely to contain confoundings. Thus, although the original likability study in the lounge might *appear* to show that greater attractiveness causes greater likability, with so many other causes possibly present, we have virtually no internal validity for making this claim.

Thus, with descriptive designs, we only *describe* the relationship between the variables, without inferring that one causes the other. Changes in *X* might cause changes in *Y*, but it's also possible that (1) Changes in *Y* cause changes in *X*, or (2) Some other, third variable causes both *X* and *Y* to change. (This latter idea is often called "the third variable problem.") Therefore, all we can say with confidence is that there is a relationship, or association, between the scores on the two variables.

> ***REMEMBER*** In descriptive designs, we are unsure that changes in *X* cause changes in *Y*, because we cannot be sure that *X* changes first or that it is the only variable that could cause *Y* to change.

The way to demonstrate a relationship so that we have greater confidence about the causes of a behavior is to conduct an experiment.

ISSUES OF VALIDITY AND RELIABILITY IN EXPERIMENTS

The way to increase internal validity is through greater control. If we could control all extraneous variables so that the only variable that systematically distinguished the models was their facial attractiveness, then we could confidently claim that attractiveness causes likability. To provide this type of control, we conduct an experiment. Laboratory experiments typically yield the greatest control, because we solicit participants to come to our controlled environment and be tested under situations we determine.

For example, here are some controls we could employ in a likability experiment. We might have a panel of judges rate different models' facial attractiveness prior to the study, and then create conditions of the independent variable of attractiveness by, for example, selecting one model consistently rated as low to create a "low attractiveness" condition, one rated as medium to create a "medium attractiveness" condition, and so on. We could control extraneous participant variables by selecting English-speaking females with corrected eyesight. To eliminate extraneous variables stemming from a model's behavior, dress, or body type, we could show participants a photograph of each model's face (as in May & Hamilton, 1980). To give all models the same personality characteristics, all participants would read the same paragraph describing the model. Finally, we could conduct the study in a controlled laboratory, keeping the environment constant, keeping the researcher's behavior constant, and balancing the researcher's gender in each condition. As the conditions change so that the model's attractiveness increases, his likability score should also increase. Now, however, by controlling these extraneous variables, we have a much clearer idea of what the scores and the relationship reflect.

In particular, the above controls eliminate potential confoundings, improving internal validity. Internal validity in experiments is our confidence that changing the independent variable *alone* caused the dependent variable to change. Thus, we have greater confidence that our relationship involves only facial attractiveness and likability: Because participants don't experience a model's behavior or dress, it makes no sense to argue that differences in likability were caused by these variables. Because the environment and the researcher are more consistent, it's unlikely that these variables influenced the ratings. And so on.

However, recall there is a trade-off between internal and external validity. More controls produce a more atypical and unnatural situation. For example, above we've created a rather strange situation, because females do not normally form first impressions from meetings with a photograph! Such an unusual situation reduces external validity: These results probably generalize poorly to other individuals and settings. Thus, with experimental methods, we have greater internal validity for understanding a particular relationship, but at the cost of getting results that may be atypical of, and thus less generalizable to, other settings.

REMEMBER Experiments tend to have greater internal validity but less external validity than descriptive methods.

Not all experiments, however, are equally strong in internal validity or equally weak in external validity. Two aspects of an experiment that influence its validity are whether we have a quasi-independent variable, and whether the study is a field experiment.

Internal Validity in True versus Quasi-Experiments

Recall that with a true independent variable participants can be randomly assigned to any condition, but with a quasi-independent variable this is not the case. Random assignment is very important because it is a way of "balancing" and thus controlling extraneous participant variables. Quasi-experiments, by not allowing for random assignment, are likely to be confounded by participant variables.

For example, say we conduct a quasi-experiment to determine whether a model's likability changes as a function of a female's age, comparing the conditions of 18- or 22-year-olds. We cannot randomly assign females to be a particular age, so we must select participants for each condition who are already that age. In the process, however, we may end up with two groups who also differ in terms of all sorts of other participant variables. For example, older women have probably had a greater amount of dating experience. Thus, we might have the study shown in Table 3.6, in which the quasi-

TABLE 3.6 Diagram of Quasi-Experiment Showing a Confounding of the Independent Variable of Age with Amount of Dating Experience

	Condition 1	*Condition 2*
Independent variable	*18-year-olds*	*22-year-olds*
Confounding variable	*Little dating experience*	*Much dating experience*
Likability scores →	*X* *X* *X* *X* *X*	*X* *X* *X* *X* *X*

independent variable of age is confounded by the extraneous variable of dating experience. Further, the women in these groups may also differ in terms of their year in college, their maturity, their preferences in men, and so on. Differences in any of these variables might actually be causing the differences in likability scores. Therefore, we cannot confidently claim that age is actually the causal variable. In other words, the absence of random assignment severely reduces internal validity.

Note that the lack of random assignment also limits the internal validity of descriptive designs. Here, we simply measure participants on the variables, so we cannot prevent extraneous participant variables from producing a confounding. For example, when we measured likability and attractiveness in the lounge, those women who found certain models less attractive might coincidentally have been younger, shorter, or less experienced. These variables might have then determined likability.

On the other hand, the likability experiment in the laboratory that we proposed is, coincidentally, an example of a true independent variable: Here, we can randomly assign each participant to see the photo in either the low, medium, or high attractiveness condition. Then we would be confident that the above confoundings do not occur, because by luck, we should obtain various types of females in each condition, so that differences in participant variables should balance out. That is, we'd expect each condition to contain some women who are experienced daters and some not, some older and some younger, some taller and some shorter, some freshmen and some seniors, and so on. Overall, each condition should contain a balanced mix of the same types of subjects as the other conditions. Therefore, we have greater confidence that the independent variable is not confounded by extraneous participant variables.

> ***REMEMBER*** Random assignment to conditions balances participant variables, so true independent variables provide greater internal validity than quasi-independent variables.

Thus, on the one hand, a well-designed true experiment provides the most confidence that we have demonstrated a causal relationship. First, by presenting the conditions of the independent variable and *then* measuring the dependent variable, we're confident of the temporal sequence between the supposed cause and its effect. Second, random assignment balances extraneous participant variables, reducing their potential as confoundings. And third, by adding controls that eliminate other extraneous variables, *hopefully* the only variable that systematically changes will be the independent variable, so that it must be causing the dependent scores to change.

On the other hand, you can never be *totally* confident in a conclusion. I said "hopefully" above because there is no guarantee that we have, in fact, identified the variable that is actually causing the behavior. Instead, being skeptical, we recognize that we've eliminated only *some* of the many extraneous variables that are possible, and so we may have missed an important one. (Also, the measurements are probably not otherwise perfectly valid and reliable.)

Thus, although a well-controlled, true experiment provides substantial confidence that we have demonstrated a causal relationship, it is not "proof." Recall from Chapter 1 that the difficulty in "proving" a hypothesis was the possibility of there always being a rival hypothesis that would explain our results. Essentially, the possibility of a hidden confounding variable is what provides a potential rival hypothesis. Thus, even with our controls, an unknown, confounding variable may still be operating, so that the rival hypothesis that this variable is the causal variable may actually be true. A quasi-experiment has the added problem of lacking random assignment, so we have even less confidence in conclusions about causality with these designs.

Therefore, the results of any single experiment allow us to *argue* to some degree that we have identified a causal relationship. However, only as researchers conduct replication studies that control different extraneous variables do we become truly confident of the cause of a behavior.

We also influence internal and external validity by creating either a laboratory or field experiment.

Issues of Validity in Laboratory versus Field Experiments

Laboratory experiments have reduced external validity because a laboratory setting is not a slice of real life. The situation is artificial, participants know they are being tested, and a researcher is present who is "studying" them. Also, participants may be unrepresentative because we can study only individuals who will come to our laboratory. Therefore, the results may generalize poorly to other individuals and settings.

Sometimes this is an acceptable state of affairs. Typically, for basic research that seeks the underlying causes of behavior or tests hypotheses derived from theories, we are usually concerned with internal validity and thus lean toward highly controlled laboratory experiments. Such research adds to our understanding of basic processes, even though it may create a unique or artificial situation that is less externally valid. (For example, laboratory studies involving reaction time do not generalize well to everyday behaviors, but they do tell us how basic cognitive processes operate.) Likewise, a vast amount of research has studied participants drawn from college Introductory Psychology courses. Such subjects may decrease external validity, because they primarily represent the population of Introductory Psychology students. Usually, however, this is acceptable because the primary emphasis of the study is not external validity.

When we seek greater external validity, however, we may leave the laboratory and conduct **field research**. When studying a causal relationship, we perform a field experiment. A **field experiment** is a true or quasi-experiment conducted in a natural setting. Field experiments are common in applied research, to observe complex behaviors in a natural setting, or to determine whether theoretical explanations are supported in the real world. The setting may be a factory, a school, a shopping mall, a street corner, or any place the behavior occurs. Yet a field experiment is still an experiment, so we try to randomly assign participants to conditions, systematically manipulate the independent variable, control extraneous variables, and measure the dependent variable in a reliable manner. Then, because we conduct an experiment, we have internal validity for arguing that changing the independent variable caused the dependent scores to change. And, because the experiment is in the field, we also have external validity when generalizing the results.

> ***REMEMBER*** Field experiments are conducted to increase external validity while studying a causal relationship.

One common approach to field experiments is to disguise the fact that an experiment is being conducted while observing the general public. Often, the researcher manipulates an environmental condition. For example, Barefoot, Hoople, and McClay (1972) investigated violations of "personal space" by observing whether people used a public drinking fountain if someone else was sitting close by. Or, Ellsworth, Carlsmith, and Henson (1972) stared at drivers who were stopped at an intersection, to determine if staring prompted them to take flight and depart more rapidly (it did). Researchers also use confederates to create a particular social situation. For example, Shaffer, Rogel, and Hendrick (1975) had a confederate leave his belongings with a subject in the college library, and then another confederate searched the belongings and stole a wallet. The dependent variable was whether the subject tried to stop the thief. Or Crusco and Wetzel (1984) examined whether restaurant patrons left a larger tip depending on whether they had been touched by their (confederate) waitress.

The other common approach to field experiments is studying an existing group, because a behavior occurs only in certain situations or with certain individuals. For example, Neri, Shappell, and DeJohn (1992) studied the errors made by airplane pilots on flight simulators as a function of different conditions of fatigue. Likewise, we may study police officers or nurses on the job, because they exhibit specific types of behavior, operate in a role of authority, normally wear uniforms, and so on.

In any of the above, the more natural setting should produce more generalizable results. However, field experiments are far from perfect. They may lose ecological validity because the situation is somewhat contrived: Would a real thief steal a wallet when another person is sitting at the same table watching? Even external validity is still limited to situations and participants similar to the ones we study: Helping was studied when a nonviolent theft occurred, and participants were the type who sit alone in the library. Most important, however, because of lessened control of extraneous variables, there is the usual trade-off where we lose internal validity. For example, the size of a tip people leave may be confounded by how much money they have, or by the perceived quality of the waitress's service. Also, confederates' behaviors may be inconsistent, because they must react to a participant's uncontrolled behavior. And we have less control over environmental variables, such as wind and temperature conditions, or traffic noises and other distractions. Thus, the lessened control of field experiments means we study a more natural situation that generalizes better, but we have less confidence about what specifically influenced the behavior.

> ***REMEMBER*** Field experiments tend to have greater external validity but weakened internal validity. Laboratory experiments tend to have greater internal validity but weakened external validity.

PUTTING IT ALL TOGETHER

Although validity and reliability are always important concerns, recognize that some behaviors simply cannot be studied using certain methods, and that your options may be limited because you must always be ethical and not harm participants. Therefore, any design is always guided by the questions "What is it you wish to study?" and then "What potential flaws must you deal with?" Select a procedure for its strengths while trying to minimize its weaknesses.

The key to minimizing a study's weaknesses is to anticipate potential threats and build in controls that eliminate them. Therefore, keep these points in mind. (1) State the hypothesis clearly, asking one question about one specific behavior. (2) Be a psychologist, using your knowledge of behavior to identify potential flaws in the design. (3) Rely on the research literature, employing solutions that others have already developed. And (4) Assume that "Murphy's Law" always applies: Anything that can go wrong will go wrong. Design the study accordingly.

At the same time, recognize that you cannot control every aspect of a situation. Therefore, deal with the *serious* threats to validity and reliability. You can never create the perfect study, so every decision must necessarily involve "the lesser of two evils." Any study ultimately involves two major concerns: First, try to eliminate the flaws that can be dealt with practically. Second, consider any remaining flaws when interpreting the results. Leave everything else for the next study.

CHAPTER SUMMARY

1. *Extraneous variables* are variables that can influence the results, but are not variables we intend to study. They may be *participant*, *environmental*, *measurement*, or *researcher variables*, and they may be *systematic* or *unsystematic*. Extraneous variables are a problem because they (1) can influence scores and alter the sample relationship, and (2) lead to errors when interpreting the study, because they are operating in addition to the variables we think are operating.
2. *Reliability* is the degree to which the same event or behavior produces the same score each time it is measured, so that a measurement is consistent and repeatable.
3. *Content validity* is the degree to which a measurement reflects the variable of interest.
4. *Construct validity* is the degree to which a measurement reflects the hypothetical construct of interest.
5. *Internal validity* is the degree to which the relationship found in a study reflects only the relationship between the variables of interest.
6. When an extraneous variable changes systematically with a variable of interest, then the extraneous variable is a *confounding* variable.
7. *External validity* is the degree to which the relationship found in a study generalizes to other individuals and situations.
8. *Ecological validity* is the extent to which a study's results generalize to natural settings and natural behaviors.
9. Extraneous variables are controlled by *eliminating them*, *keeping them constant*, or *balancing their influence*.
10. To demonstrate that changes in variable *X cause* changes in variable *Y*, a study must show that *X* occurs first and is the only variable that could be causing the change.
11. *Descriptive methods* are best for testing a descriptive hypothesis because they tend to have greater external validity. However, they also have less internal validity.

12. *Experimental methods* are best for testing a causal hypothesis because they tend to have greater internal validity. However, they also have less external validity.

13. In a *true experiment*, with a true independent variable, participants are randomly assigned to a particular condition. This helps to balance out participant variables between the conditions and thus prevent confounding.

14. In a *quasi-experiment*, with a quasi-independent variable, participants cannot be randomly assigned to conditions, and thus participant variables may confound the independent variable.

15. A *field experiment* is an experiment conducted in a natural setting. Field research tends to have greater external validity, but reduced internal validity.

KEY TERMS (with page references)

confounding (63)
construct validity (62)
content validity (62)
ecological validity (65)
environmental variables (56)
external validity (64)
extraneous variable (59)
field experiment (73)
field research (73)
internal validity (63)
measurement variables (56)
participant variables (56)
reliability (61)
researcher variables (56)
systematic (59)
unsystematic (59)
validity (62)

REVIEW QUESTIONS

(Answers for odd-numbered questions and problems are provided in Appendix D.)

1. What is the general question to ask about the data when evaluating any study?
2. What are the two strategies to follow when critically evaluating a study?
3. (a) What is an extraneous variable? (b) What is the difference between a systematic and unsystematic extraneous variable? (c) How do extraneous variables influence the sample relationship? (d) How do they influence our interpretation of nature?
4. (a) In general, what does the term *validity* mean? (b) Why must scientists be concerned about drawing valid inferences?
5. Define the following: (a) content validity, (b) construct validity, (c) internal validity, (d) external validity.
6. (a) What does reliability mean? (b) Why is reliability a necessary part of science? (c) How does unreliability influence the relationship in the sample data?
7. How do you control an extraneous variable by (a) eliminating it? (b) keeping it constant? (c) balancing it?
8. What do we mean by the term *confounding variable*?
9. What question about a study is raised by the term *ecological validity*?

10. How does randomly assigning participants to conditions prevent confounding from participant variables?

11. (a) Why does increasing internal validity tend to decrease external validity? (b) Why does increasing external validity tend to decrease internal validity?

12. (a) What are the advantages and disadvantages of descriptive research methods? (b) How do they influence a researcher's conclusions?

13. (a) What are the advantages and disadvantages of experimental methods? (b) How do they influence a researcher's conclusions?

14. (a) What are field experiments? (b) What is their major advantage? (c) What is their major potential weakness?

15. (a) What is the difference between a true independent variable and a quasi-independent variable? (b) What is the problem with using the latter to draw causal inferences?

PRACTICE PROBLEMS

16. After taking a test, you hear the following complaints. Each is actually about whether the test is reliable or valid. Identify the specific issue raised by each. (a) "The test is unfair because it does not reflect my knowledge of the material." (b) "The questions were 'tricky' and required that I be good at solving riddles." (c) "My essay makes the same points as my friend's, but I obtained a lower grade." (d) "Based on my grade and how I studied in this course, I believe I know how well I'll do in other courses." (e) "I doubt that what caused students to perform poorly or well on the test was how much they studied."

17. While testing the less attractive models in the likability study, you are in a nasty mood. Coincidentally, while testing the more attractive models, you are in a good mood. (a) What do we call the variable of your mood? (b) What two techniques could you use to deal with this variable?

18. You study participants' memory for a story, comparing the recall of those who read it silently to that of others who read it out loud. (a) Will you have greater external validity if you test only males or only females, or if you test both genders? (b) Draw a diagram to show how you would balance participants' gender.

19. To test the hypothesis that drinking red wine daily prevents heart disease, we select elderly people who have consumed either zero, one, or two glasses of red wine daily during their lives and determine the health of their hearts. (a) What type of design is this? (b) What term do we use to refer to the amount of wine a person drinks? (c) What do we call the amounts we examine? (d) What do we call the healthiness of participants' hearts? (e) How confident can we be when concluding that drinking more wine reduces heart disease? Why?

20. How would you conduct the above study using a correlational design?

21. Red wine contains an acid that causes headaches, so people who drink more red wine probably take more aspirin. Taking aspirin may prevent heart disease. (a) In question 19, what term do we use to refer to the amount of aspirin that people take? (b) What problem of validity pertains to this situation, and how does it affect our conclusions?

22. In question 19, describe how you would control the variable of aspirin by (a) eliminating it, (b) keeping it constant, and (c) balancing it.

23. We hypothesize that the greater a person's fear of sexually transmitted diseases, the fewer sexual partners the person has had. (a) How should we study this relationship? (b) What inherent flaw must we accept?
24. Poindexter conducted a survey. In his sample, 83% of females employed outside the home would rather be in the home raising children. After performing all the necessary statistical analysis, he concluded that "the statistical analyses prove that most working women would rather be at home." What is the problem with this conclusion?
25. A researcher reads numerous traffic accident reports and finds that red-colored automobiles are involved in the most traffic accidents. He concludes that certain colors cause more accidents. (a) What type of research method was used? (b) Are the researcher's inferences correct? Why? (c) What specific confounding variables might be operating? (*Hint:* Think participant variables.) (d) What design is needed to bolster his inference? Describe this study.
26. You test the effectiveness of motivational training by providing it to half of your college's football team. The remaining members form the control group, and the dependent variable is the coach's evaluation of each player. (a) What type of design is this? (b) What is the advantage to testing the football team, instead of testing introductory psychology students? (c) What specific flaws occur as a result of your design?

4

Design Issues and Ethical Concerns in Experiments

GETTING STARTED

To understand this chapter, recall the following:

- From Chapter 2, recall the components of an experiment.
- From Chapter 3, understand what extraneous variables are, how they produce confoundings, and how they threaten reliability and validity.

Your goals in this chapter are to learn:

- How to design reliable and valid independent and dependent variables and the basic mechanisms for maintaining consistency.
- What order effects are and how to deal with them.
- What demand characteristics are and how to deal with them.
- What research ethics are and how to conduct an ethical study.
- What animal research involves and the ethical issues in animal research.

You are now ready to begin designing reliable and valid research. This chapter discusses *true* experiments, but similar techniques are used in quasi-experiments and descriptive research. The chapter presents two major topics. First, you'll learn how to design a well-controlled experiment. Then, we'll discuss the ethical issues that arise with human and animal participants, and how to handle them. (*Note*: The concepts here are not difficult, but be prepared for some new vocabulary.)

To begin, let's propose two studies.

TWO EXAMPLE STUDIES

In this chapter we will refer to two rather "classic" experiments. The first investigated the hypothesis that the facial muscles used for smiling provide feedback that improves mood. (In other words, not only does being happy make you smile, but smiling makes you happy.) To test this hypothesis, Strack, Martin, and Stepper (1988) measured the dependent variable of mood after college students experienced a condition of the independent variable of either holding a pen in their mouths using their teeth (which mimics smiling) or holding the pen using their puckered lips (which does not mimic smiling). The second study tested whether people become more aggressive as room temperature increases. Bell (1980) placed students in a laboratory under different conditions of the independent variable of room temperature and then provoked them by being rude. Participants later evaluated the experimenter, and the dependent variable for measuring aggressiveness was how negative the evaluation was.

As above, we begin a design by creating an acceptable scientific hypothesis, identifying the relevant population, and selecting the variables. Now the task is to fill in all of the details to produce reliable and valid data. There are essentially three simultaneous steps to completing the design: completing the operational definition of the independent variable, defining the dependent variable, and designing the testing situation. We'll begin with the independent variable.

DESIGNING THE INDEPENDENT VARIABLE

As with any variable, an independent variable should reflect the hypothetical construct of interest (have construct validity) and should generalize well (have external validity). Also, our measurements of it should reflect that variable (have content validity), and it should involve real-life events (have ecological validity). Then, the next step is to select the specific conditions of the independent variable to present to participants. This entails choosing the number of conditions and the amount in each condition.

Choosing the Number of Conditions

You can examine virtually any number of conditions in an experiment. The number selected depends first on how many conditions are needed to adequately test a hypothesis. The smile study is an adequate test with only two conditions—the presence or absence of smiling. The temperature study could involve only two conditions (hot versus not-so-hot), or we could include several temperatures to investigate the relationship more fully. (This also relates to some statistical issues you'll see later.)

Choosing the Amount of the Variable for Each Condition

The specific amount or category of the variable to be present in each condition also depends primarily on the hypothesis. The temperature study, for example, investigates the influence of hot temperatures, so we don't want conditions where it's very cold. So, we might compare the conditions of 70 versus 90 degrees Fahrenheit.

Recall that sometimes a *control group* is also included: A condition containing zero or a "normal" amount of the independent variable is presented, providing a comparison for other conditions. Thus, we might include a normal, cooler temperature condition to compare to when hot temperatures occur.

An important part of selecting the conditions is to be sure they will have a visible impact on the behavior being studied. After all, if the independent variable does influence the behavior in nature, we want to see this in the data. This translates into creating conditions that are likely to produce large differences in dependent scores. Thus, to be convinced that higher temperature produces more aggression, we would like to see rather low aggression scores with low temperature, and very different, high aggression scores with higher temperature. Therefore, we want to manipulate temperature in ways that are likely to produce such differences. This is called creating a strong manipulation. A **strong manipulation** is likely to produce large changes in behavior and, thus, large differences in dependent scores between the conditions. Conversely, a weak manipulation involves conditions that produce little or no change in scores, so that even if the independent variable would otherwise work as predicted, we will see a weak or no relationship. Then we may miss the relationship that actually exists in nature.

Create strong manipulations using two approaches. First, select amounts or categories of the independent variable that are substantially different from one another. Using 70- and 90-degree temperature conditions is a reasonably strong manipulation, because if temperature does influence aggression, increasing it by 20 degrees should produce visible and convincing differences in aggression scores. Or, in a different study, say we are presenting happy or sad words to influence participants' mood. For a strong manipulation, the happy words should be *very* happy and the sad ones should be *very* sad.

The second aspect of a strong manipulation is to have participants experience a condition sufficiently for it to influence their behavior. For example, a strong manipulation will expose participants to each temperature long enough to substantially influence their aggression. Or, participants should hold the pen in their mouths sufficiently to alter their mood. Or, with happy and sad words, there should be a sufficient number of each, and participants should deal with them for enough time to be substantially influenced.

> ***REMEMBER*** A strong manipulation produces conditions so that, if the hypothesis is correct, we are likely to see large differences in scores between the conditions.

Controlling Threats to the Reliability and Validity of a Treatment

Once the conditions have been selected, you must precisely define how to create and present them, while eliminating the influence of extraneous variables. Once again, consider those four components of a study: the participants, the researcher, the measurement procedure, and the environment. For each, try to anticipate and eliminate anything that might threaten reliability and validity.

Recall that a key element in experiments is maintaining *internal validity* by eliminating any *confoundings*. This means that there should be no systematic differences between the conditions other than the independent variable. This is why participants in the smile study hold the pen in either their lips or their teeth, because then the "only" difference between conditions is whether the smile muscles are engaged. If, instead, they either held a pen between their teeth (smile) or held nothing, the conditions would differ in whether participants held *something* in their mouths or not, as well as in whether they employed their smile muscles or not.

Remember also to be concerned with reliability. A reliable independent variable is measured and manipulated consistently and without error, so that all participants in a condition receive the same amount of the variable, and when we change to another condition, all subjects there receive the same, new amount. Thus, in the temperature study, the room should be precisely 70 degrees for everyone in one condition and precisely 90 degrees for everyone in the other condition.

Inconsistency in a manipulation presents two problems we've seen previously. The first is with the interpretation: if we are not always presenting precisely the condition we think we are, then our conclusions and generalizations about the behavior will be based on the wrong amounts of the variable. The second problem is with the scores and sample relationship: Inconsistent conditions will produce inconsistency among the scores. If, for example, temperature does influence aggression, but the temperature fluctuates between participants *within* a condition, then aggression scores will fluctuate within a condition. With fluctuating scores in each condition, there will be a less consistent—weaker—relationship, or perhaps no relationship at all.

Manipulation Checks

So far, we've been *planning* conditions that *should* influence participants in the predicted way. But, you can also "check" that a manipulation actually did work as intended. A **manipulation check** is a measurement, in addition to the dependent variable, that determines whether each condition of the independent variable had its intended effect. Usually, this check is made after measuring participants on the dependent variable. Then they may answer questions about their experience in a condition, or perform a task that reflects its influence. So, if the goal was to test people in a hot room, we can check that they thought it really was hot. Or, if the intent was to make participants happy, we will check that they really were happy. Such checks increase our confidence that the independent variable worked as intended, which then increases internal validity for explaining why dependent scores changed as they did.

Manipulation checks are especially important for checking an *intervening variable.* Thus, if we thought that higher room temperature produced greater aggressiveness by way of intervening anger, we could also directly measure participants' anger.

> ***REMEMBER*** Designing the independent variable involves selecting the number of conditions and their amounts, minimizing confoundings, employing a strong manipulation, and performing a manipulation check.

DESIGNING THE DEPENDENT VARIABLE

The dependent variable should also have construct validity, external validity, content validity, and ecological validity. Then, the next step is to decide how you will apply it. For this you need scoring criteria.

Creating the Scoring Criteria

Scoring criteria define the system for assigning scores to different responses. These criteria determine whether a response is correct or not, what constitutes the beginning and end of a response, how to distinguish one response from another, and all of the other decisions necessary for consistently assigning a particular score to a particular response. Then, we'll "know" what participants did or did not do to receive a certain score, and that anyone else who received that score did the same things.

You need scoring criteria even for straightforward variables. For example, say we test participants' memory by presenting a list of words, and then counting the number of words they recall. Is it a correct response if someone writes "bare" but the list contained "bear"? What if for "mother" they recall "mom"? What if participants recall the correct words but in a different order than in the list?

Scoring criteria will be even more elaborate when a behavior is more difficult to quantify, as when measuring aggressiveness, sexism, or motivation, because here you must evaluate a participant's behavior subjectively. For example, in the temperature study, we might define an aggression score as the number of aggressive acts exhibited toward the researcher. But what do we mean by an aggressive act? The strategy is always to minimize inconsistency and bias by minimizing the interpretation you must give to a behavior. Instead, look for observable, concrete behaviors that have a distinct beginning and end. Thus, we could define aggressive acts in terms of such observable behaviors as yelling, hitting, slamming things on the desk, and so on.

You must also define how to assign scores when such behaviors occur. Does each word a participant yells count as one aggressive act, or is each uninterrupted string of yelling one aggressive act? Does a nasty look receive the same score as a punch? And so on. Or, if you are observing whether someone smiles in response to a stimulus, how soon after the stimulus must a smile occur in order to be considered a response to that stimulus? How long must a smile last for it to be counted?

Recognize that participants *never* behave in an ideal way. You must try to anticipate every possible variation on the expected response, so if it happens, you know how to score it. For help, refer to the literature to find acceptable scoring criteria. Beyond this, your decisions are usually arbitrary: Simply define one way to score each behavior so that you eliminate inconsistency, sloppiness, and error.

> ***REMEMBER*** Precise scoring criteria that focus on observable behaviors are necessary for measuring a behavior reliably.

One important goal for your scoring criteria is that they result in a sensitive measure.

Creating a Sensitive Dependent Measure

Recall that the goal is to observe different behaviors as the conditions change. Therefore, the measurement procedure must *discriminate* or distinguish between behaviors, giving a different score each time a behavior is even slightly different. Only when two individuals exhibit the identical behavior should they receive the same score. Therefore, we seek a sensitive dependent measure. A **sensitive measure** produces different scores for small differences in behavior. This lets us detect even a small influence on responses that a manipulation may produce.

Sensitivity is increased through observing responses that can differ subtly, and by precisely measuring those differences. For example, if we're judging a person's aggressiveness, a five-point rating scale is more sensitive than a simple yes-no judgment. This is because if someone is either somewhat aggressive or very aggressive, we could still answer only "yes." Then, we could not distinguish differences in aggression, instead lumping participants together as if they're the same. The result would be that, even though the temperature conditions produce differences in aggressive behavior, we might not see these differences in the scores (and the experiment will be a failure). Using a rating scale, however, we could assign a "3" to somewhat aggressive people and a "5" to very aggressive people, and now we'll see these differences in the data. Using a physiological or physical measurement would be even more sensitive. Thus, always try to measure a *quantitative* variable that measures the amount or degree of a behavior precisely. Try to avoid measuring a *qualitative* variable that merely categorizes behaviors (like yes-no or pass-fail.)

Another part of creating a sensitive measure is to avoid restricting the range.

Avoiding a Restricted Range of Scores

So that we can distinguish subtle differences in participants' behavior, it should be possible for them to obtain any of a wide range of scores. If the design artificially limits participants to only a few possible scores, then we have a restricted range. **Restriction of range** occurs when the range of possible scores on a variable is limited. For example, people can exhibit great differences in aggressiveness, so the procedure should allow scores that also reflect these differences. If we restrict the range, however, everyone scores close to, or at, the same score, *regardless* of the independent variable. Therefore, we are less likely to see different scores as the conditions of the independent variable change.

To avoid a restricted range, first consider the scores you will assign. If, in the temperature study, participants can obtain a score of only 1, 2, or 3, the range is restricted. But, if they can score anywhere between 0 and 100, the range is not restricted. Second, look for aspects of the testing situation that, *practically speaking*, limit the behaviors or scores that may occur.

One such aspect is when the task is too easy or otherwise biased so that all scores are likely to be near the highest possible score. In that case, the data will show **ceiling effects**: The lowest potential scores—from the worst-scoring participants—are very high, so scores cannot differ much because would-be higher-scoring individuals cannot get much higher (everyone's scores are "hitting the ceiling"). For example, if we accept almost any action as being aggressive, then not-so-aggressive people will have a high score. Then the range is restricted, because those who get seriously aggressive cannot score higher, and we will fail to discriminate between differences in aggressive behavior.

The range is also restricted if the task is too hard or otherwise biased toward producing low scores. Here, the data will show **floor effects**: The highest potential scores—from the best-scoring participants—are very low, so scores cannot differ much because would-be lower-scoring participants cannot get much lower (everyone's scores are "hitting the floor"). For example, most laboratory subjects will not physically assault a researcher, so it's unreasonable to make a high aggressiveness score depend on such actions: Realistically, no one will obtain such scores and everyone will have low scores. Then, truly nonaggressive participants cannot score lower than more aggressive ones, and, again, we will fail to discriminate between behaviors.

Thus, a sensitive procedure is, in part, one that avoids ceiling and floor effects. To achieve this, the typical participant should start off with scores in the middle between very low scores and very high scores. But, it should also be realistically possible to obtain higher or lower scores as the independent variable changes.

> ***REMEMBER*** Strive for a sensitive procedure that will reflect slight differences in behavior and that will produce an unrestricted range of scores.

Observing Reliable Behaviors

So far we've discussed reliability in terms of inconsistency on the experimenter's part when measuring a variable that reflects a behavior. However, unreliability can also come from the *behavior*. If a participant's behavior is an atypical, unrepresentative response to a condition, then it and the resulting score will be misleading. Instead, we want participants' scores in a condition to reflect their typical, representative behavior in this situation.

There are two strategies for increasing the reliability of the behaviors we observe: Practice trials and multiple trials.

Practice trials A participant's behavior—and score—may be unrepresentative because he or she has not "warmed up" on the measurement task. When this is a possibility, we provide **practice trials**: We test participants as in the real study, but then ignore the scores from these trials when analyzing the results. (A "trial" is one complete measurement or observation.) Practice trials are especially useful when studying physical reactions, as in a reaction-time task. Also, if the task is complicated or involves elaborate equipment, practice trials ensure that participants understand the task. And, practice trials allow participants to become accustomed to being observed, so they behave more naturally when providing the real data.

Multiple trials A major component of reliability is the number of real trials a participant performs in a condition. A score that is based on only one trial may reflect all sorts of extraneous factors: A participant may be momentarily distracted or may guess well; the trial may be especially easy or difficult; or some other aspect of the situation may make the trial peculiar. In such cases, the response and score are not representative of the participant's typical response and score.

To avoid the bias from one unique trial, we observe each participant several times in a condition, observing **multiple trials**. Again, this involves the strategy of balancing out extraneous variables. We assume that differences in a participant's motivation or attention on different trials balance out, that easy trials balance with hard ones, and so on. We then compute each participant's total score or average score for all trials. When interpreting these summary scores, we are more confident that they reliably reflect the typical response, because we have balanced out the random fluctuations found in individual trials.

There is no magic number of trials to observe per condition. Depending on the study, there may be as few as 1 or 2 trials or as many as several hundred. To prevent confounding, all conditions should involve the same number of trials. Observe more trials when each trial is easily influenced by extraneous variables and is thus likely to be unreliable.

REMEMBER Provide practice trials and test multiple trials to increase the reliability of the data.

Although multiple trials add reliability, they also create the problem of order effects.

The Problem of Order Effects

Multiple trials introduce a new extraneous variable called order effects. **Order effects** are the influence on a particular trial that arises from its position in the sequence of trials. Order effects have two sub-components.

Practice effects are the influence on performance that arises from practicing a task. Even after practice trials, participants may perform initial trials poorly because they are still not warmed up. After more trials, performance may improve because participants become quicker or more accurate. With even more trials, however, performance may decrease again because participants become fatigued or bored.

The other component is **carryover effects**, the influence that a particular trial has on performance of subsequent trials. Carryover effects may arise first from simply experiencing a trial. For example, if one trial happens to be very frustrating, this feeling may "carry over," lowering performance on subsequent trials. Trials might also be especially boring, easy, or anxiety-provoking, all of which may influence responses to later trials.

A special type of carryover effect is a **response set**. This is a bias toward responding in a particular way because of previous responses made. Essentially, responding becomes more of a habit than a natural reaction to a stimulus. Thus, you have a response set when completing a multiple-choice exam if, after the first few questions, you superstitiously believe the correct answer is always choice 4. You might also develop response sets from strategies that have proven successful. For example, unscramble each of the words below:

ookb reet oatc oabt

You can solve the first three words quickly because of the response set that says to always place the final letter first. If you stumble on the fourth word, however, it's because this strategy no longer works.

The problem with practice and carryover effects is that a response is somewhat unique because of where in the sequence it occurs. (Above, your solution of each word is faster or slower than it would be if the word was in a different location in the sequence.) Therefore, participants' overall performance is tied to the unique order used, and so the summary score is an unreliable indication of the typical response, especially when compared to other orders.

Counterbalancing Order Effects

To solve the problem of order effects, we again use the strategy of balancing. Here we balance the effect of any single order by including several different orders. Balancing order effects is called counterbalancing. **Counterbalancing** is systematically changing the order of trials for different participants in a *balanced* way to *counter* the biasing influence of any one order. For example, say that in the temperature study, we measure how aggressive participants feel toward the experimenter by having them answer 10

TABLE 4.1 Diagram of Temperature Experiment with the Order of Trials Within Each Condition Counterbalanced

Each X Represents a Participant's Summary Score from 10 Questions.

	Independent variable of temperature	
	70 degrees	***90 degrees***
Participant's scores obtained with order 1–10	*X* *X* *X* *X*	*X* *X* *X* *X*
Participant's scores obtained with order 10–1	*X* *X* *X* *X*	*X* *X* *X* *X*

different questions. If we number the questions 1 through 10, a simple counterbalancing scheme is to present the questions to half of the participants in each condition in the order 1 through 10, and to present the questions to the remaining subjects in the order 10 through 1. This design is shown in Table 4.1. Each *X* represents a participant's summary score for the 10 questions. We then ignore the order in which participants completed the questions and look at all aggression scores found in each condition (each column). Higher scores in the 90-degree condition will support the hypothesis that increasing temperature increases aggressiveness. Further, we are confident that the results are not biased by the order in which questions were answered, because in each condition there is not one particular order present. To be even more confident that the order of trials was not biasing the results, we could test additional people using other orders. (Several variations of this technique are discussed in Chapter 19.)

> ***REMEMBER*** When you measure multiple trials, counterbalance the order of trials.

Some researchers use the term *counterbalancing* when balancing any extraneous variable, in addition to the variable of order. Thus, if a male experimenter tests half the participants in each condition and a female tests the remainder, we have counterbalanced for experimenter gender. If half the participants in each condition are male and half are female, we have counterbalanced for participant gender.

> ***REMEMBER*** To create a valid and reliable dependent variable, establish scoring criteria, create a sensitive procedure that avoids a restricted range (and floor/ceiling effects), include practice trials, observe multiple trials, and counterbalance the order of trials or other extraneous variables.

After designing the independent and dependent variables, the next step is to control any remaining extraneous variables.

CONTROLLING EXTRANEOUS VARIABLES

The final step in designing an experiment is to control extraneous variables. The goal is to prevent them from fluctuating *within a condition* (so that all participants experience the condition in the same way) and *between the conditions* (so that, except for the independent variable, everything is the same in the different conditions). You can view all fluctuating extraneous variables as essentially resulting in inconsistency either within or between conditions. Therefore, the basic strategy is to build in consistency. Thus, everyone in the smile study should hold the same type of pen in their mouths, for the same period of time, all the while maintaining the same posture and performing the same tasks. In the temperature study, all participants should be dressed the same way, seated the same distance from the heater, acclimated to the temperature to the same extent, and so on.

Consistency is important for two reasons. First, recall that we cannot support a hypothesis unless we find a consistent relationship in the data. Inconsistent extraneous variables will cause participants' scores to fluctuate inconsistently, producing a weak, inconsistent relationship. Second, if everything *is* the same for all participants except for the conditions of the independent variable, then we have greater confidence that we "know" what the scores and relationship reflect.

> ***REMEMBER*** The key to designing a convincing experiment is to build in consistency within and between conditions.

Although every study will necessitate its own controls, there are several general techniques for creating consistency.

Instructions to Participants

Always provide instructions to participants that clearly explain what the task is and how they should approach it: Describe the sequence of events, identify the stimuli they should attend to, and explain how to respond. The goal is to have all participants perform the same intended task, without introducing extraneous stimuli or behaviors that make the task different for different participants.

Creating effective yet consistent instructions requires considerable effort. They should be clear for the least sophisticated subjects, avoiding psychological jargon and unfamiliar words. They should anticipate participants' questions. (Should people guess when responding? Should they hurry?) Instructions should also prohibit unwanted behaviors. (Participants should not look around, fidget, or talk, so they don't miss crucial aspects of the task.) And, the same instructions should be presented to everyone. (When manipulating a variable through instructions, change only the necessary parts and avoid a confounding by keeping constant all other aspects.) Never "ad lib" instructions, because you can't reproduce them reliably. Instead, read from a prepared script, using an easily reproduced, neutral voice, or, better yet, play a tape recording of them.

Using Automation

The way we present stimuli, obtain responses, and assign and record scores while measuring participants can be additional sources of inconsistency. The way to control extraneous variables here is through **automation**: using electronic or mechanical devices to present stimuli and to measure and record responses. Electronic timers, slide projectors, video and audio tape recorders, and computers ensure controlled and reliable stimulus presentations. Automating the data-collection process ensures that the scoring system is consistently and accurately applied, and provides for more reliable and sensitive measures. Automation also eliminates experimenter errors and inconsistency that may result because (1) the experimenter is so busy directing the study that parts of a behavior are missed, and (2) the experimenter has expectations about how the study should turn out and thus inadvertently influences participants or records scores accordingly.

With automation, however, you must guard against instrumentation effects. **Instrumentation effects** are changes in the measurement materials that occur because of use, making the measurements less reliable. This occurs when, over the course of a study, slides, films, and videotapes become scratched and blurred, paper materials get mutilated, or equipment becomes worn and timers become inaccurate. Part of the "instrumentation" is also the experimenter, who may become more experienced, more bored, or more crazed as time passes, and who may inadvertently change the procedure. Because of changes in the material or procedure, the measurements obtained late in a study can be different from those obtained early on, making the experiment unreliable overall.

To minimize instrumentation effects, always keep equipment in order and make copies of materials so that all participants can be presented with pristine stimuli. Also, keep the experimenter's behavior constant. Finally, test some participants from each condition during the early, middle, and late stages of the study, so that potential instrumentation effects are balanced in all conditions and thus cannot confound the study.

Testing Participants in Groups

When building in consistency, an important issue is whether to test participants individually or in groups. Group testing is most common when the task requires written responses, such as on a questionnaire. The advantages of group testing are (1) data collection is more efficient, and (2) if you can test everyone in a condition at once, all participants will experience the same consistent condition. The disadvantage is that participants may make noise, block one another's view, or otherwise distract each other so that extraneous variables are introduced. Therefore, you need to control participants carefully when testing groups. Usually, we can do this through particularly explicit instructions. But, how successful you'll be—and the wisdom of group testing in general—depends on the particular experiment and how susceptible participants will be to the presence of others.

Pilot Studies

To be sure that they have developed a reliable and valid procedure, researchers often conduct a pilot study. A **pilot study** is a miniature version of a study that tests the procedure prior to the actual study. (*Note*: A pilot study is different from a manipulation check; pilot studies occur *before* a study, manipulation checks *during* the study.) Using participants similar to those in the actual study, a pilot study determines such matters as whether the instructions are clear; whether the task can be performed given time constraints or other demands; and whether you have developed a workable, sensitive, and reliable scoring procedure. It also allows the experimenter to work out any bugs in the equipment or procedure so that the study runs smoothly and consistently.

Pilot studies are also used to create and validate stimuli. For example, say that an independent variable involves showing participants films that contain different amounts of violence. Our personal judgment is of little help in determining the amount of violence in a film, because we might be particularly sensitive or insensitive to violence. Therefore, we would show the films to pilot subjects and have them rate the amount of violence each contains.

For any problems identified, we alter the stimuli, task, or instructions and conduct more pilot studies until we have the desired situation in each condition.

> ***REMEMBER*** To maintain consistency, create clear instructions, employ automation but limit instrumentation effects, consider group testing, and conduct pilot studies.

There is one more major threat to reliability and validity. In any study, we must deal with demand characteristics.

DEMAND CHARACTERISTICS

Imagine you are a subject in an "experiment" taking place in a "laboratory." A "psychologist" with lab coat and clipboard puts a plate of cookies in front of you and says, "Normal people crave cookies at this time of day, so eat if you want." I bet you'll eat one. On the other hand, imagine the psychologist says, "Only people who have no self-control eat at this time, but eat if you want." I'll bet you don't. In any situation, the social and physical surroundings provide cues that essentially "demand" that we behave in a certain way. In research, these cues are called demand characteristics. A **demand characteristic** is an extraneous cue that guides or biases a participant's behavior. Participants rely on demand characteristics to answer such questions as "What's really going on here?" "What am I supposed to do?" and "How will my response be interpreted?" Demand characteristics arise despite the instructions we provide, and participants don't necessarily respond to them intentionally, or even consciously.

To identify potential demand characteristics, again consider those four components of a study. Some are so common that we have names for them.

First, participants bring with them certain attitudes that influence their behavior. Research procedures are mysterious, and rumor has it that psychologists do strange things to people and study only intelligence, sexual deviance, and crazy people. Therefore, participants tend to be on guard: They are sensitive to being "studied" and may alter their behavior accordingly. This is the demand characteristic called reactivity. **Reactivity** is the bias in responses that occurs because participants are aware that they are being observed. Participants know they're under the gun, and they "react" to the mere presence of the experimenter who is observing their behavior. Therefore, they may respond in very different ways than if they weren't being observed.

A similar demand characteristic is the **Hawthorne effect**, which refers to the influence on participants' performance—usually an improvement—that occurs due to the novelty of being in a study. This effect was named for a study of worker productivity conducted at the Western Electric Company's Hawthorne factory. The researchers manipulated numerous variables that should have decreased productivity, but the participants instead continuously increased their productivity. They later indicated that, because the researchers had given them special attention, they felt compelled to increase productivity (Roethlisberger & Dickson, 1939). (There is, however, some controversy over this account; see Bramel & Friend, 1981.)

The Hawthorne effect is different from reactivity. If participants are unnaturally motivated to perform a boring task because of their enthusiasm for the study, we have the Hawthorne effect. If their performance is then unnatural due to nervousness about being videotaped, we have reactivity.

Participants also respond to another demand characteristic called **social desirability**. This occurs when people provide what they consider to be the socially acceptable response. Essentially, participants "edit" their responses so that they aren't embarrassed or so they won't appear weird or abnormal. Thus, in the smile study, some participants might act happy, not so much because they are happy, but because they think it's expected. Others may want to act happy, but inhibit this because they're afraid it's inappropriate.

The environment and measurement task also produce demand characteristics. The surroundings may cause participants to react to extraneous factors. This is especially true in fancy laboratories with one-way mirrors and complex equipment that can play upon a person's fears. (Once, when using a bank of electronic timers, I had to convince subjects they would not be electrocuted by having them look under their chair to see that there were no wires!) Likewise, participants react to the measurement procedure. For example, participants may interpret our 10 questions for measuring aggressiveness as really being a personality test. Then, instead of honestly answering the questions, they may respond in ways they think will project the ideal personality.

Finally, the experimenter is an important source of demand characteristics. Researchers usually dress and behave rather formally to inspire cooperation from participants. But, this formality may inhibit participants. On the other hand, if we act and dress too informally, we may encourage inattentiveness and sloppiness. Further, people are very sensitive to **experimenter expectancies**, which are cues the experimenter provides about the responses that participants should give in a particular condition. These cues occur because the researcher knows the predictions of the study and may inadvertently communicate them to participants. Then, the ultimate self-fulfilling prophecy is produced. In the smile study, for example, we expect people to be happier when mimicking a smile. Subtle actions on our part can register on participants and, sure enough, they'll respond with the predicted mood.

As these examples illustrate, demand characteristics cause people to play a role, being good (or not so good) participants who perform on cue. The problem is that they are responding to these cues, instead of to our variables. Then, we may observe a restricted range and reduced sensitivity: When we measure aggressiveness, for example, participants might stifle their aggression so they don't look bad. This will produce low scores for all conditions, producing floor effects. If we measured "niceness," however, we might see ceiling effects. We also lose internal validity because it is the cues that cause a particular response, instead of the independent variable. (If people act happy when smiling because they think it's expected, then we'll conclude that the manipulation works when it really does not.) We lose reliability, because not all participants react to the same cues in the same way, so scores will be inconsistent. And, we lose external validity because the results will not generalize to other situations where such demand characteristics are not present.

> ***REMEMBER*** Demand characteristics are cues that bias participants, resulting in responses that are not valid, reliable reactions to our variables.

There are several techniques, however, for controlling demand characteristics.

General Controls for Demand Characteristics

Our first line of defense against demand characteristics is to provide participants with as few cues as possible. If they have no cues, their only recourse is to act naturally. Thus, instructions should not divulge the specific purpose, manipulation, or predictions of a study. (*Note*: anytime we keep participants in the dark regarding the specifics about a condition they receive, we are using a **single-blind procedure**.) In addition, instructions should not include extraneous, distracting information (such as placing an unnecessary time limit on a task). Also, hide threatening equipment, and avoid threatening actions by the experimenter.

In addition, limit the cues from the experimenter. A prime reason for using automation is that equipment will not communicate experimenter expectations. When a potentially biasing experimenter must be present, however, employ a double blind. In a **double-blind procedure**, both the participants and the researcher who interacts with them are unaware of the specific condition being presented. The original researcher trains others to conduct the study, but they do not know the conditions or predictions—they are "blind" to them. Such procedures are especially common when testing the effect of a drug or other medical treatment. If the researcher knows when a particular drug is being administered, his or her expectations about its effects may be communicated to patients. These expectations *alone* can produce the expected physical reaction. If the experimenter is blind to such information, however, no expectations can be communicated.

Our second defense against demand characteristics is to make those cues that must be present as neutral as possible. Thus, the researcher tries to be rather bland, being neither overly friendly nor unfriendly. In the instructions, we try to neutralize participants' fears and suspicions by presenting the task without implying that it is difficult or easy and without indicating what the "normal" or expected response is. Also, we try to provide a response format that participants are comfortable with: We have children act out responses using toys, or we give college students a paper-and-pencil test. And we try to select a researcher with whom participants will be comfortable too (in terms of gender, age, etc.). We also make participants comfortable by allowing them to "habituate" to the procedure. With **habituation**, we familiarize participants with a procedure before beginning actual data collection. For example, practice trials allow participants to habituate to the researcher and task. Or, when testing children, we may first play with them until our presence is no longer disruptive. If we are videotaping responses, we allow participants to become comfortable with being recorded before the study begins.

Our final defense is to have participants ignore demand characteristics by creating experimental realism. **Experimental realism** is the extent to which the measurement task engages participants. The goal is to create a task that people find so engrossing that they "forget" about demand characteristics. Thus, in the smile study, if participants are so engrossed that they forget about the pen in their mouths, the results will be less influenced by demand characteristics. Experimental realism does not mean, however, that the task is like real life, so experimental realism is different from ecological validity. With experimental realism, the task may be very strange and unreal, but participants' responses are actual, honest responses to it.

> ***REMEMBER*** Single- and double-blind procedures, habituation, and experimental realism help to reduce demand characteristics.

The above approaches are used in all types of designs. Sometimes, however, such strong demand characteristics are likely that two additional techniques are used: You may employ unobtrusive measures and deception, or try to conceal the entire experiment.

Using Unobtrusive Measures and Deception

When the procedure for measuring the dependent variable will strongly encourage reactivity and social desirability, unobtrusive measures may be needed. With an **unobtrusive measure**, we measure participants' behavior without their being aware of the measurement. Thus, an unobtrusive measure of aggressiveness would be observing participants through a one-way mirror. Other unobtrusive measures include the use of hidden cameras and recorders. Or we may observe telltale evidence left by participants (for example, to measure how far people sit from each other, we could measure the distance separating their chairs after they've left the room). In each case, participants cannot be overly influenced by demand characteristics if they are unaware of the measurement being made.

Sometimes an unobtrusive measure is used in conjunction with deception. **Deception** involves the creation of an artificial situation or "cover story" that disguises a study. Participants are then unaware of the manipulation or the behavior being studied, so they do not feel pressured to respond in a certain way. For example, in the smile study, imagine what you would do if a researcher simply said, "Here, hold this pen in your lips." You'd probably feel very self-conscious and behave unnaturally. The original researchers eliminated such problems by telling participants that the study investigated how physically impaired people use their mouths to do tasks that others do by hand. Then, while holding the pen in either their lips or teeth, participants used the pen for various tasks, including marking various stimuli. Among the stimuli were several cartoons, and participants' rating of how humorous they found the cartoons to be was the dependent variable for measuring their mood. Thus, what might have been a bizarre task was transformed into a rational, engaging task in which participants were less self-conscious and responded in a more natural way.

A special type of deception is often used in conjunction with a control condition. Because only the experimental group receives the treatment, only it experiences the associated demand characteristics. Therefore, we have a confounding: The experimental group behaves differently from the control group either because of the treatment or because of the accompanying demand characteristics. For example, let's say we give an experimental group a drink of alcohol while a control group receives nothing. Any impairment the experimental group exhibits may be due to the alcohol, or it may arise because giving people alcohol implies that we expect them to act drunkenly, so they do.

To keep such demand characteristics constant, control groups are given a placebo. A **placebo** provides the demand characteristics of a treatment. Thus, we would give the above control group something that smells and tastes like alcohol, but that is not alcohol. Then we communicate to both groups the same demand characteristics for acting drunkenly, so any differences in their behavior are due to the real alcohol given to the experimental group. Similarly, in studies that require the experimental group to perform an involved task prior to making a response, we have the control group perform a similar, placebo task to eliminate differences between the groups in terms of motivation or fatigue.

> ***REMEMBER*** Deception—including placebos—is a way to control demand characteristics.

Deception is not always necessary or wise (as with everything in research, you must balance the pros and cons). Research has shown, for example, that we should not try to hide that we are manipulating room temperature. If we offhandedly remark that the room's thermostat is broken, participants often guess that the study deals with temperature anyway (Bell & Baron, 1976). Catching the researcher in a lie worsens demand characteristics, because now participants *know* they should be on guard.

Concealing the Experiment

When researchers are especially concerned about reactivity and social desirability, the final approach is to conceal the entire experiment. Many studies, for example, have been performed while participants sit in a waiting room, supposedly waiting to be taken into the experiment. Mathews and Cannon (1975) studied how the noise level in a room influenced a person's willingness to help a confederate who dropped some books. Doing this in a formal laboratory with the experimenter watching might communicate that helping behavior was being studied and that the expected behavior was to help. Instead, a confederate dropped the books while walking past the participant in the "waiting room," and the person's response was unobtrusively observed.

The most extreme way to conceal an experiment is to move out of the laboratory and conduct a *field experiment* with the general public. Recall that here we unobtrusively conduct the experiment by observing people in shopping malls, student unions, and so on. One reason that field experiments have greater external validity is that with them we can disguise the fact that an experiment is being conducted. For example, Isen and Levin (1972) discreetly manipulated participants' mood by allowing some people the pleasant experience of "finding" money in the change return of a pay phone. Then, a passing confederate dropped a manila folder, and the dependent variable was whether participants helped the confederate. Such field studies overcome the reactivity or social desirability that occurs with laboratory experiments, because reactivity, experimenter cues, and so on are minimized, and the situation tends to have high experimental realism.

> ***REMEMBER*** Reduce demand characteristics through minimizing cues, habituation, experimental realism, unobtrusive measures, deception, and field experiments.

Believe it or not, with the information you've learned from this chapter, you are ready to begin designing experiments. (There are a few more issues to consider, but they're best left until you've gotten some statistics under your belt.) To summarize the discussions so far, Table 4.2 presents a list of the major issues for you to consider when designing an experiment.

Similar techniques are used when conducting research involving animals.

RESEARCH INVOLVING ANIMALS

Psychological research is not limited to the study of humans. Psychologists study other animals, in part, simply because they demonstrate interesting behaviors. Researchers also study animals to test models of behavior that then generalize to all species, including humans. For example, much of what we know about basic brain functioning is based on models that originated from animal research. A common design is to surgically alter an area of the brain and then determine how a behavior is different relative to the behavior in unaltered animals. For example, researchers have learned a great deal about the role that the hypothalamus plays in eating behavior by surgically damaging different parts of the hypothalamus in rats. Researchers also test animal models without using surgical techniques. For example, much of what we know about genetics comes from the breeding of rats and mice. Similarly, animal research has been the basis for many developments in learning and conditioning: Ivan Pavlov's principles of classical conditioning were based on the behavior of dogs, and B. F. Skinner's work on operant conditioning was based on the behavior of rats and pigeons.

TABLE 4.2 Issues to Consider When Designing an Experiment

Create valid and reliable independent variable
- Minimize confounding
- Specify type and number of conditions
- Create a strong manipulation
- Include manipulation check

Create valid and reliable dependent variable
- Establish scoring criteria
- Create a sensitive procedure
- Avoid restricted range and floor/ceiling effects
- Include practice trials
- Observe multiple trials
- Counterbalance order of trials

Maintain consistency of testing procedure
- Create clear instructions
- Employ automation but limit instrumentation effects
- Consider group testing
- Conduct a pilot study

Control demand characteristics
- Minimize reactivity, social desirability, experimenter expectancies
- Consider Hawthorne effect
- Include habituation, double-blind, and experimental realism
- Consider deception and unobtrusive techniques
- Consider field experiment

Though some people are incensed by the comparisons, animal research often has substantial external validity, generalizing well to many aspects of human behavior, such as education, clinical therapy, and the workplace. Humans are animals too, and some laws of nature apply to all animals in the same ways. For example, a hypothalamus is a hypothalamus, and the model of how a rat's hypothalamus influences eating behavior has generalized well to humans. Likewise, animal research is often the first step in the development of a new drug or physical treatment. When the treatment works with animals, it often works with humans.

Controls Used with Animal Research

Many animal studies are true experiments conducted in a laboratory: We obtain a random sample of animals (sometimes trapped in the wild but usually purchased from commercial suppliers), randomly assign them to conditions, and apply all of the previous controls for reliably and validly manipulating the independent variable. For internal validity, we keep constant extraneous variables that might produce a confounding, so we maintain the environment consistently for all participants, test them in the same manner, and so on. Also, for a valid and reliable dependent variable, we define scoring criteria, provide practice trials, observe multiple trials and counterbalance order effects.

Believe it or not, experimenter expectancies and demand characteristics are a problem even in animal studies. A researcher can inadvertently make errors in measuring or recording scores that are biased toward confirming the research hypothesis. And a researcher's expectations can produce subtle differences in the way that animals are handled and tested, biasing their behavior so that they confirm the hypothesis. Researchers minimize such biases by handling all animals in the same way, automating data collection, and employing double-blinds.

Further, control groups are often used to identify the influences of merely handling and testing the animals. For example, when testing a drug or surgical procedure, control animals are injected with a placebo or undergo the anesthesia and surgery without receiving the actual treatment. As a result, they experience the same trauma that experimental animals experience.

> ***REMEMBER*** Control extraneous variables in animal research in the same ways as in research involving humans.

Regardless of whether we test animal or human participants, as you'll see in the final sections in this chapter, we must conduct an experiment in an ethical manner.

RESEARCH ETHICS

As a researcher in psychology, you face a dilemma: On the one hand, you need a well-controlled, informative study, even if this means being deceptive, eliciting responses that participants want to keep private, or doing things that cause them discomfort. We justify these actions on the grounds that sound scientific knowledge is needed to benefit humanity. On the other hand, you should treat participants properly because they have basic rights to privacy, to respect, and to safety. Therefore, the issue of **research ethics** can be summed up as a concern for balancing a researcher's right to study a behavior with the right of participants to be protected from abuse.

The Cooperativeness of Participants

Why do people allow themselves to be mistreated by a researcher? First, researchers are often viewed as authority figures and, as with all authority figures, people tend to think that they are benevolent and honest. Second, people assume that research is valuable for society, so they believe their participation is important. The result is that participants respect the goals of research and trust the researcher, so they are open to abuse.

An example of how motivated participants are was demonstrated by Orne (1962), who tried to give participants a task they would refuse. He gave each person 2,000 sheets of paper, each of which contained 224 addition problems. No justification for the task was given, and participants were merely told that the researcher would return "sometime." Five and one-half hours later, the participants were still working, but the experimenter gave up! In the next attempt, participants were told that, after completing each sheet, they should tear it up into a minimum of 32 pieces and then continue with the next sheet. Participants performed this task for *several hours* until, again, the experimenter gave up. Subjects later reported that they viewed this task as an important psychological endurance test.

As the above illustrates, an overriding demand characteristic in any study is for participants to be cooperative. In fact, people cooperate even to their own detriment. The classic example of this is Milgram (1963), who convinced participants that they were assisting him to train a "learner" confederate to learn verbal stimuli. Each time the learner made an error, the participants pressed a switch that he or she believed administered an increasingly larger electrical shock to the learner. Despite protests from the learner (who could be heard but not seen, and who eventually emitted deathly silence), and despite the fact that the electrical switches were labeled "DANGER: SEVERE SHOCK," a *majority* of participants delivered what they believed was as much as 450 volts of electricity! (This is much more voltage than is in the electrical outlets in your home!)

Milgram applied no coercion other than to tell participants to continue, using only the authority that they had implicitly given him. Yet they complied, even though they believed they were harming another person, and in many cases became *very* emotionally and physically distressed themselves. Further, these were not young, impressionable freshman college students, but adults of various ages and backgrounds.

Milgram was soundly criticized for his tactics, but there are many studies suggesting that a researcher can probably get participants to do almost anything: They are willing to suffer great mental or physical discomfort, and they are reluctant to protest or to protect themselves. However, merely because people volunteer for a study does not mean that we have the right to take advantage of them. In essence, there is an implicit contract between participants and researchers. Their side of the contract is to help in the study and to trust us. Our side of the contract is to not abuse their trust. Being ethical means living up to our part of the contract.

REMEMBER Conducting ethical research means protecting participants from abuse.

The APA Principles of Ethical Conduct

To assist researchers when dealing with ethical issues, the American Psychological Association adopted the Ethical Principles of Psychologists and Code of Conduct (1992). These principles govern the full range of a psychologist's activities. In particular, they deal with the care of human and nonhuman research participants, and apply to any type of study (not just experiments). Essentially, there are five general components to the APA principles.

1. **Identify potential risks** First, identify potential *physical* risks: Is there anything in the study that could physically endanger participants? Are you manipulating a potentially dangerous independent variable or could measuring the dependent variable be harmful? Is all equipment working properly and safely, and will presenting stimuli cause pain or physical damage? Are you adhering to all accepted procedures when injecting drugs, drawing blood, and the like?

Second, identify potential *psychological* risks: Will participants experience undue anxiety, depression, or other unpleasant feelings because you are invading their privacy, producing negative emotions, or lowering their self-esteem? Distress can occur directly as the result of a manipulation, as when we intentionally cause people to become sad or depressed. Distress may also result indirectly. For example, you might think Milgram's study was not so bad because no one actually got hurt. But if Milgram had not disconnected the electrical wires, the participants would have killed—murdered—the learner! Think about how they felt when *that* dawned on them.

When identifying potential risks, consider not only the procedure, but also the participants. Having healthy teenagers perform strenuous exercise may not be risky, but it is risky for the elderly and for people with heart conditions. Likewise, films containing sex, violence, and mayhem are standard fare for some adult moviegoers, but they may be upsetting for others, or for children.

Dealing with deception is a particularly difficult issue. On the one hand, Christensen (1988) found that among people who had participated in deceptive and nondeceptive experiments, those in the deceptive studies enjoyed the experience more, became better educated about psychological research, and did not mind being deceived. On the other hand, this does not mean we can freely deceive participants on a whim. Deception may be harmful because, when participants learn of it, they may feel foolish, depressed, or angry. Therefore, the APA guidelines explicitly require that deception be used *only* when it is necessary!

Thus, in evaluating the ethics of deception, first consider whether it is necessary for producing the desired study. (It is doubtful, for example, that Milgram could have elicited such extreme obedience without employing deception.) Second, consider the amount of deception involved. The greater the deception—the bigger the lie—the more objectionable it is. Finally, and most important, consider how severe the psychological impact of the deception will be. The extreme emotional reactions resulting from Milgram's deception are a serious ethical concern, while the more minor reactions arising from the deception in our smile study are much less objectionable.

2. **Protect participants from physical and psychological harm** Once the potential risks have been identified, try to eliminate or at least minimize them. If participants will be stressed or embarrassed, can you alter the design to eliminate these feelings and still get at the intended behaviors? In particular, recall that we seek a strong manipulation by giving participants a substantial exposure to the independent variable. Balance this, however, with minimizing the negative impact of a treatment: Can you "tone down" the manipulation so that it affects participants but still is not too extreme? Thus, if we want to make one group more depressed than another, we don't need to make the first group suicidal! In fact, consider whether the study will work if, instead, we make one group happier than another. We can also minimize risks by screening out high-risk individuals. If the study involves exercise, for example, screen out people having a heart condition. If manipulating depression, screen out people who are already clinically depressed.

One important rule is to minimize participants' anxiety by keeping all information about them confidential. They are never identified in publications or discussed in casual conversations. (Often we assign participants a number instead of recording their names so they remain anonymous.)

3. **Justify remaining risks** For any risks to participants that remain, fairly and honestly decide whether they are justified by the study's scientific worth. The knowledge to be gained from a study must clearly and convincingly justify the risk to participants. Thus, ask whether the study will demonstrate something *new* and *important* about a behavior. Is exposing participants to a risky independent variable really necessary? Will a risky dependent variable tell you that much more than a safe one? Throughout, recognize that as the potential for physical or psychological risk increases, there must be a corresponding increase in the scientific worth of the study. If not, don't conduct the study.

> ***REMEMBER*** The primary ethical concern in any study is to minimize potential physical or psychological harm to participants and to ensure that any remaining risk is justified.

Ethical issues are not always clear-cut, so seek the advice of others. In fact, the APA's Ethical Principles (as well as federal and state regulations) require that colleges and research institutions maintain a **Human Subjects Review Committee** (also called an Institutional Review Board, or IRB). This committee consists of individuals from various disciplines so a broad perspective is represented. The committee's job is to review a study's procedures to ensure the ethical treatment of participants. All researchers must obtain approval from their IRB *before* conducting any type of study. And yes, *student* research projects must also be approved.

One thing a review committee always looks at is how you'll deal with the issue of informed consent.

4. **Obtain informed consent** Out of respect for the participants' right to control what happens to them, you must inform them about the study *prior* to their participation, and then let them decide whether they wish to participate. That is, obtain **informed consent**. The APA's Ethical Principles state that informed consent is required unless there is minimal risk, such as when merely observing anonymous people in a field setting. But always obtain informed consent when conducting laboratory experiments. The usual procedure is to provide participants with a written description that contains four components.

First, describe the purpose and procedures of the study. Sometimes you must withhold specific details because of demand characteristics, but usually you can provide general information without biasing participants. Tell them as much as you can.

Second, explicitly warn participants of any physical or psychological risks associated with the procedure, describing any details that could reasonably be expected to influence a person's decision to participate in the study. Even if you cannot divulge all aspects of a procedure, you must warn participants of any negative consequences of it. (For example, Milgram should have at least warned his subjects that they might learn some unpleasant things about themselves.)

Third, inform participants that they are free to discontinue their participation at any time during the study, *without penalty*. Volunteering for a study produces such strong demand characteristics to be cooperative that this option *does not occur* to people. Be sure that withdrawing is a realistic option, without any hidden coercion because participants are enrolled in a class or have a job where the study is being conducted.

Finally, obtain participants' signatures as their explicit consent to participate. In the case of minors and others who are not capable of making this decision, obtain consent from their parents or guardians.

5. **Take care of participants after the study** Finally, after the study, remove any negative consequences of the procedure so that participants feel as good about themselves as when they entered the study. First, alleviate any concerns they have by providing a **debriefing**. Here, we fully inform participants about all aspects of the study, including about the manipulation and any deception used and why. Second, remove any adverse physical or emotional reactions in participants that may have been created. Thus, if we tested the effects of alcohol, we care for subjects until they are sober. If we created anxiety or depression, we try to reverse these feelings, explaining why we think they are normal reactions to our manipulation. If follow-up counseling or check-ups may be needed, we provide qualified, professional help. Finally, give participants a means of contacting you later in case unforeseen problems arise.

REMEMBER Always obtain informed consent, debrief participants, and care for them after the study.

Regardless of the specific design of a study, approach the ethical issues in the same manner. Table 4.3 will help you remember them all.

The Ethics of Unobtrusive Measures and Field Experiments

Ethical issues get particularly complicated with unobtrusive and deceptive procedures, especially in terms of the issue of informed consent. In a laboratory setting, participants are aware that they will be observed even if they cannot see the observer, so using one-way mirrors and such is usually acceptable. Likewise, in a waiting-room situation, participants have given their tacit agreement to be observed by showing up for the study. However, if an unobtrusive procedure might embarrass, victimize, or otherwise harm a person, then explicit prior informed consent is needed.

TABLE 4.3 Checklist of Ethical Issues to Consider When Designing an Experiment

- Identify physical risks to participants
- Identify psychological risks to participants
- Eliminate or minimize risks
- Justify risks in terms of scientific value of results
- Submit planned procedure to IRB for review
- Obtain informed consent
- Provide debriefing and care for participants after the study

When people know they are participating in a field experiment, we deal with informed consent and debriefing as described above. However, the most difficult ethical situation arises with unobtrusive or hidden field experiments. After all, they involve the ultimate deception, because participants are not even aware a study is being conducted! Therefore, they have not formally volunteered, nor have they been given a chance to provide informed consent. As usual, the first step is to minimize the risks and then be sure the remaining risks are scientifically justified.

Risk is especially important in field experiments, because they allow us to manipulate all sorts of real-life situations. However, we are *not* free to abuse the unsuspecting public in the name of "science." (You don't have the right to yell "fire" in a crowded theater just to see what happens!) In a laboratory setting, informed consent and a lack of experimental realism are protection for participants: Because they have volunteered to experience our artificial situation, it has less of a real impact on them. In field experiments, however, this is not the case. Our deceptions and pranks can cause people to become really frightened, really angry, or really dangerous! Therefore, researchers have an even greater responsibility to respect and protect participants. In short, there are limits to our right to conduct field studies that impose on others. And, as usual, after resolving the ethical issues for ourselves, we obtain approval from our Human Subjects Review Committee.

Role Playing and Simulations

One possible solution when a laboratory or field procedure is just too risky is to have people simulate being in the experiment through **role playing**: Participants pretend they are in a particular situation and we either observe their behavior or have them describe how they would behave. Because the situation is not real, physical or psychological harm is unlikely. However, caution must still be exercised. For example, Haney, Banks, and Zimbardo (1973) created a notorious prison simulation that unexpectedly turned sinister: College men pretending to be guards or prisoners exhibited the worst, most dangerous behaviors associated with a real prison.

In practice, role playing is used infrequently because it has very limited validity and reliability. First, demand characteristics can run rampant: Participants may alter their reactions or descriptions to conform to perceived expectations or to keep their real behaviors private. (Would people simulating the Milgram electric-shock study actually admit that they'd electrocute someone?) Second, people often cannot accurately predict how they would respond. For example, in studies of personal space, participants have given verbal descriptions, manipulated dolls, or drawn lines on paper to indicate how far they would stand from someone else. Yet, such predictions seldom match the person's actual behavior when observed under real conditions (Hayduk, 1983).

Ethics and Animal Research

Scientists and the general public continue to debate the ethics of conducting laboratory experiments with animals. It is true that such research often exposes animals to unpleasant and harmful manipulations, such as surgical procedures, electric shock, or food or water deprivation. Further, the way to conduct a manipulation check of a surgical procedure is to perform an autopsy. And, even with nonsurgical procedures, animals may be physically or psychologically altered by the treatments, so they usually cannot be studied again and are destroyed.

On the one hand, some animal rights advocates say that animal experiments are unethical because they violate the rights of animals to live free and unharmed. They argue that even though humans have the *ability* to exploit other animals, they do not have the *right* to do so. Some even make the more radical argument that laboratory studies of animals do not even provide useful information, so there is no justification for what is seen as animal abuse. From these perspectives, the only ethical way to study animals is through descriptive studies conducted in natural settings.

On the other hand, animal researchers argue that such experiments are justified by the knowledge they produce: The previous criticism is wrong in that animal research has definitely added substantially to the well-being of humans (and other animals). Animal research has been the basis for virtually all modern drugs and surgical techniques, for the identification of numerous toxins and carcinogens, and for many psychological principles. From this perspective, it would be *un*ethical if researchers did *not* conduct animal research to benefit society. Thus, they argue that researchers have the right—and the responsibility—to pursue any useful scientific information.

This issue boils down to whether you think the goal of benefitting humans takes precedence over the rights of other animals. If you think it does, then animal research is justified, because there is no other way to obtain the data. It would be more unethical to perform experimental surgical or medical procedures on humans: We cannot undo surgical alterations, and, when first testing a drug, we often have no idea of the harmful side effects that can occur. Likewise, we cannot control the breeding practices of humans in order to study genetics, nor can we administer to humans the aversive conditions that have led to important discoveries with animals.

In addition, there are scientific and practical reasons for conducting animal laboratory studies. Field research limits the variables and controls we can employ, so this approach is an inadequate substitute. Also, laboratory research with animals can be conducted quickly and efficiently: Animals are easily obtained and housed, their environment can be controlled and manipulated easily, and, for genetic studies, they have a short gestation period.

Regardless of where your personal feelings fall in this debate, it is wrong to think of animal research as involving the mindless torture of abused animals. As with all people, some researchers are less than ethical and may mistreat their animals. However, for the vast majority of researchers, laboratory animals are valued subjects in whom much time, energy, and expense have been invested. It is in the researchers' interest to treat them well, because animals who are abused make poor subjects for a reliable and valid study. Furthermore, the APA's Ethical Principles (1992) provide guidelines for the treatment of research animals, and there are federal, state, and local regulations for the housing and care of animals as well. Because of such rules, animals are well cared for, undergo surgery in sterile settings with anesthesia, and are disposed of in a humane manner.

Finally, APA's ethical guidelines require that we evaluate animal research in the same way we do human research. First, the harm caused to an animal must be minimized. Thus, we prefer designs that provide positive events as opposed to aversive ones, we prefer mildly aversive events to drastic ones, and we prefer temporary physical alterations to permanent surgical ones. Second, we are not frivolous in the treatment of animals, so every aspect of a procedure must be necessary. As usual, the key issue is whether the procedure is justified by the scientific importance of the information that may be learned. Finally, every research institution must have an institutional review board that ensures the ethical treatment of animals.

> ***REMEMBER*** Acceptable animal research minimizes the harm done to subjects and must be justified as scientifically important.

Scientific Fraud

There is one more aspect of ethics to consider. Unfortunately, one reason that scientists must always be skeptical about research findings is that other scientists are sometimes guilty of fraud. They may report data from a study inaccurately, or they may publish data when no research was conducted. Often, their motivation is to provide further support for their previous conclusions: They needed a replication that failed to materialize, so they "faked" the data. At other times, they are responding to professional pressures to be productive researchers.

Science tries to prevent fraud in two ways. First, most published research reports have undergone *peer review*: Prior to publication, a report's manuscript is sent to several psychologists who are knowledgeable about the research topic. They check that conclusions make sense, appropriate procedures are followed, ideas are not plagiarized, and so on, so that sound and convincing evidence and not fraudulent research gets into the research literature. Second, science prevents fraud through replication: Fraudulent conclusions that do make it into the literature will not be replicated. Then, even though not identified as fraudulent, these conclusions are dropped from the accepted literature.

Regardless, it is unethical to commit scientific fraud. This includes falsifying results, as well as keeping secret a result that contradicts one's views. (This also includes plagiarism: When writing a research report, always reference the source for any idea that you got from reading other research.)

Fraud not only violates every rule of science, but causes enormous harm: Given the extent to which researchers share and integrate research findings, a fraudulent report can undermine many areas of psychological knowledge. There is no justification for research fraud.

PUTTING IT ALL TOGETHER

With this chapter, you're a little more familiar with the issues in designing a good study (actually, you're a lot more familiar). However, don't develop a false sense of security about the "proof" that a controlled experiment provides. We are still only collecting evidence. The techniques we've discussed are necessary for producing "good" convincing evidence.

For the best evidence, remember to keep everything as consistent as possible, both *within* and *between* each condition. Also, don't underestimate the influence that demand characteristics can have—especially reactivity and social desirability. Therefore, play psychologist: Use what you know about human nature, defense mechanisms, anxiety, and the like to anticipate demand characteristics. Imagine how people like you, and people very different from you, will feel. If it is rather uncomfortable, then alter the situation.

And finally, remember that research ethics are not some stuffy topic to merely give lip service to. There usually is no convincing scientific justification for a very risky procedure, and practically speaking, you'll never get it past an Institutional Review Board. As we've seen, one study never definitively "proves" a hypothesis anyway, so conducting an unethical or dangerous study is just not worth it.

CHAPTER SUMMARY

1. A *strong manipulation* involves conditions that are likely to produce large changes in behavior and thus large differences in dependent scores between the conditions.
2. A *manipulation check* is used to check that participants were influenced as intended.
3. *Scoring criteria* define the system for assigning a score to a response. They should produce a *sensitive measure*, producing different scores for small differences in behavior.
4. *Restriction of range* occurs when the range of possible scores on a variable is limited. With *ceiling effects*, all scores tend to be high, so scores cannot get much higher. With *floor effects*, all scores tend to be low, so scores cannot get much lower.
5. Reliability is improved with *practice trials* and by observing participants on *multiple trials* within each condition.
6. *Order effects* are the influence on a particular trial due to its position in a sequence of trials. *Practice effects* are the influence due to practicing a task, and *carryover effects* are the influence that a trial has on performance of subsequent trials. A *response set* is a bias in responding because of previous responses made.
7. *Counterbalancing* controls for order effects by presenting different orders of trials within each condition.
8. The key to designing a convincing experiment is to build in *consistency*, both *within* and *between* conditions. Consider *automation*, *instrumentation effects* (changes in equipment and materials that occur through use), *instructions*, *group testing*, and *pilot studies*.
9. *Demand characteristics* are extraneous cues that guide or bias a participant's behavior.

10. *Reactivity* is the demand characteristic occurring because participants are aware that they are being observed.
11. The *Hawthorne effect* is the influence due to the novelty of being in a study.
12. *Social desirability* is the demand characteristic occurring because participants want to behave in a socially acceptable manner.
13. *Experimenter expectancies* is the demand characteristic from cues the researcher provides about the responses participants should give.
14. Demand characteristics are reduced through *habituation*, *unobtrusive measures*, *deception*, and *unobtrusive field experiments*.
15. With *experimental realism*, participants are engaged by the task and thus are less concerned with demand characteristics.
16. A *placebo* provides the demand characteristics of a treatment.
17. In a *single-blind* procedure, participants are unaware of the nature of the treatment. In a *double-blind* procedure, both the researcher who tests participants and the participants themselves are unaware of the nature of the treatment.
18. *Research ethics* deal with balancing the right of a researcher to study a behavior with the right of participants to be protected from abuse.
19. The *APA's Ethical Principles of Psychologists and Code of Conduct* require that animal and human participants be protected from physical or psychological harm and that potential harm is scientifically justified.
20. All research is reviewed by the appropriate institutional review committee.
21. Researchers should obtain *informed consent*, should *debrief* participants, and should take care of them after the study.
22. In *role playing*, participants pretend they are in a particular situation.

KEY TERMS (with page references)

automation (89)
carryover effects (86)
ceiling effects (84)
counterbalancing (86)
debriefing (100)
deception (93)
demand characteristic (90)
double-blind procedure (92)
experimental realism (92)
experimenter expectancies (91)
floor effects (84)
habituation (92)
Hawthorne effect (90)
Human Subjects Review Committee (99)
informed consent (99)
instrumentation effects (89)
manipulation check (82)
multiple trials (85)
order effects (86)
pilot study (89)
placebo (94)
practice effects (86)
practice trials (85)
reactivity (90)
research ethics (96)

response set (86)
restriction of range (84)
role playing (101)
scoring criteria (83)
sensitive measure (83)
single-blind procedure (92)
social desirability (91)
strong manipulation (81)
unobtrusive measure (93)

REVIEW QUESTIONS

(Answers for odd-numbered questions and problems are provided in Appendix D.)

1. (a) What is a strong manipulation? (b) Why should you seek one? (c) What are the two approaches to creating one?
2. (a) What does it mean to manipulate the independent variable reliably? (b) What effect does an unreliable manipulation have?
3. (a) What is a manipulation check? (b) What is the difference between a pilot study and a manipulation check?
4. (a) Why do we include practice trials? (b) Why are multiple trials generally better than a single observation? (c) What problem arises with multiple trials?
5. (a) What are practice effects? (b) What are carryover effects? (c) What is a response set?
6. What is counterbalancing?
7. What is a sensitive measurement procedure?
8. What are the pros and cons of testing participants in groups?
9. (a) What do we mean by automation? (b) Why can automation be good for a study? (c) Why can automation be bad for a study?
10. (a) What do we mean by demand characteristics? (b) In terms of reliability, internal validity, and external validity, how do demand characteristics harm a study?
11. (a) What is experimental realism and why do we seek it? (b) How is experimental realism different from ecological validity?
12. (a) What are unobtrusive measures? (b) Why do researchers employ unobtrusive measures and/or deception?
13. What is meant by research ethics?
14. What are the three major issues about risks you must resolve to *design* an ethical study?
15. What are the two major steps you must include to *conduct* an ethical study?
16. (a) Why is informed consent needed? (b) What four things must you include when obtaining informed consent?
17. (a) What is role playing? (b) What is the advantage of this approach? (c) What is the disadvantage of this approach?

PRACTICE PROBLEMS

18. In the smile study discussed in this chapter, should participants be tested individually or in groups? Why?
19. In a study of memory, you read out loud one list of either similar or dissimilar words and then measure participants' memory for the list. (a) What problems

with reliability may occur because you read the lists? (b) In terms of demand characteristics, what is the problem with reading the lists? (c) How can you eliminate the problems in (a) and (b) above? (d) What problem may then arise over the course of testing many people?

20. In question 19, you ask participants to write down the list of words. (a) To score recall reliably, what decisions should you make? (b) How could you ensure that the person scoring the responses was unbiased?

21. In question 19, (a) What would constitute a strong manipulation? (b) What preliminary task can you add to increase reliability of the dependent scores? (c) How can you expand your observations of each participant to improve reliability? (d) What problem have you created? (e) Precisely describe how you would deal with the problem.

22. You wish to test the proposal that women become more sexually aroused by erotic films as a function of whether the plot has a weak or strong theme of love and romance. After showing participants one type of film, you measure the dependent variable using a questionnaire about their arousal. (a) What demand characteristics are a major problem? (b) How would you reduce these demand characteristics? (c) What ethical problems might arise with this study?

23. (a) In problem 22, why should you test each participant in a condition with more than one film? (b) What possible bias must you then eliminate? (c) Describe how you would accomplish this.

24. (a) What are two major criticisms of laboratory animal research? (b) How would you answer these criticisms?

25. When conducting a study, a researcher wears a white lab coat and carries a clipboard and stopwatch. How might these details influence the internal and external validity of the study?

26. Consider the hypothesis that greater exposure to violence on television results in more aggressive behavior. (a) For ethical reasons, what may be the best design for determining whether this relationship exists? (b) What is the trade-off involved in being ethical?

27. You deliver different speeches to make participants more or less sexist. Then you examine how sexism influences whether they help a confederate of the opposite sex. (a) Why could your manipulation appear to work even though it does not really alter participants' views? (b) Why could your manipulation appear not to have worked although it really did alter participants' views? (c) What can you do to check that your speech altered their sexism?

28. In the previous chapter, we discussed having students study for different amounts of time before taking a statistics exam. Ethically speaking, what's wrong with this design?

5

Design Issues and Ethical Concerns in Descriptive Research

GETTING STARTED

To understand this chapter, recall the following:

- From Chapter 2, understand what a representative sample is.
- From Chapter 3, understand the terms *true experiment*, *quasi-experiment*, and *descriptive research*.
- From Chapter 4, understand how to design a study, especially the counterbalancing of order effects.

Your goals in this chapter are to learn:

- The different approaches to observational research.
- How field surveys are conducted.
- The different sampling procedures researchers use.
- How to design questionnaires and interviews.
- The ethical issues in descriptive research.

This chapter addresses the basics of descriptive research. In it, we discuss procedures for observing participants and for asking them questions through questionnaires and interviews, as well as different sampling techniques and, as usual, ethical concerns. Although the focus here is description, recognize that many of these procedures also can be used in experiments.

THE USES OF DESCRIPTIVE RESEARCH

Descriptive research involves the observation and description of a behavior, the situation it occurs in, or the individuals exhibiting it. You've seen that a common descriptive procedure is a correlational design—a descriptive study that examines the relationship between two or more variables. Other types of descriptive studies may *not* look for a specific relationship. Instead, they may measure only one variable or involve only one participant, with the goal here of simply describing a certain behavior or type of individual. Regardless of the specific design, however, the purpose is to describe natural behaviors, so descriptive research is usually conducted as field research in order to minimize demand characteristics and increase external validity.

On the one hand, the disadvantage of such descriptions is that we examine a behavior without much control, so there is great potential for confoundings, and we may miss hidden influences or misinterpret what we see. Therefore, with descriptive research we can only speculate on the causes of a behavior. On the other hand, there are three advantages to descriptive research:

1. Descriptions are informative. For example, we might describe the mating rituals of frogs in the wild or the actions of drivers in a large city, because these are interesting behaviors. For applied research, we may describe consumer attitudes or the behaviors of drug addicts.

2. Descriptions are the starting point for identifying variables and building hypothetical constructs that can be tested later using other methods. For example, much research in clinical psychology developed from the constructs of Sigmund Freud, even though he only observed and described behaviors. Likewise, descriptions can provide an indirect test of a theory or model. (A researcher might ask, for example, "Are the predictions from a Freudian model confirmed by a description of a schizophrenic?")

3. Description is sometimes the only way to study a behavior or situation, because it is either practically or ethically impossible to produce it in an experiment. For example, the only way to learn about the migratory behaviors of whales or the childhood experiences of a serial killer is by observing and describing them.

Thus, descriptive research is a legitimate approach, even though we cannot use it with confidence to infer the causes of behavior. In addition to correlational designs, descriptive research falls into the following two general categories: Observational studies and field surveys.

OBSERVATIONAL STUDIES

In **observational research**, we do not directly ask participants to respond. Rather, we observe them in an unobtrusive manner. There are three general observational methods.

In **naturalistic observation**, the researcher observes a wide variety of behaviors in an unobtrusive manner. Naturalistic observation usually implies a rather unstructured and unsystematic approach in which we have not identified a limited behavior or situation to study. To be unobtrusive, we may use hidden cameras, observe from camouflaged hiding places, or simply blend in with the crowd in a public place. If unobtrusive techniques are not possible, then at a minimum we *habituate* participants to our presence before beginning the study. For example, the famous studies performed by Jane Goodall (1986, 1990) involved naturalistic observation of chimpanzees in which she observed their general lifestyles in the wild.

More commonly, researchers perform **systematic naturalistic observation**. We are again unobtrusive, but here we identify a particular behavior to observe, and are more systematic in our observations. For example, Heslin and Boss (1980) observed people being met at an airport, categorizing their various nonverbal actions. This approach is also common when studying animal behavior, such as when Boesch-Acherman and Boesch (1993) observed the use of natural tools by wild chimpanzees.

Sometimes the behavior of interest involves private interactions between members of a group that cannot be observed from afar. Then, we engage in **participant observation**. Here, the researcher is a "participating" member of the group being observed. Usually, the researcher's activities are "disguised" or hidden from subjects. In a classic example, Rosenhan (1973) arranged for "normal" people to be admitted to a psychiatric hospital to observe how patients were treated. Less frequently, the participant observer is "undisguised."

> *REMEMBER* The basic approaches to observational research are naturalistic observation, systematic naturalistic observation, and participant observation.

The Pros and Cons of Observational Designs

The overriding advantage of observational designs is that, through unobtrusive observation, we are describing behaviors in a natural setting that are not influenced by reactivity or other demand characteristics. There are, however, several disadvantages:

1. Descriptions are highly susceptible to experimenter expectations, so that we may see only what we expect to see. This is especially a problem with participant observation because the researcher may inadvertently cause participants to behave in the expected way.
2. We may be very limited in the individuals that we can find to observe, and so we may have an unrepresentative sample.
3. We often have only our verbal descriptions of a behavior. Such *qualitative* data may lack precision and accuracy, and they are not very sensitive for identifying subtle differences in behavior.
4. We do not obtain informed consent.
5. Because we do not control any variables, there is little internal validity for identifying even the variables involved in a relationship, let alone identifying a causal relationship.

To minimize the above problems, we can try to build in more control. For example, we may develop specific quantitative scoring criteria, looking for certain movements, speech patterns, facial expressions, and so on. Then, we may count the frequency of each behavior, measure its duration, or determine whether it occurs during a given time period. To facilitate accurate data recording and to minimize the time spent not observing, we may produce structured scoring sheets so that we can simply check off categories of behavior, or we may automate by tape-recording participants for later scoring.

An especially important control is to eliminate experimenter biases through the use of multiple raters.

The Problem of Multiple Raters and Inter-rater Reliability

Special reliability concerns occur when, in either descriptive or experimental designs, a score is based on a researcher's subjective *judgment* about a participant's behavior. Because of experimenter expectancies, a researcher may not produce objective, valid, and reliable judgments. Therefore, we enlist the aid of others, called *raters*, who are usually "blind" to the hypothesis and are trained (often in a pilot study) to use our scoring criteria. For example, in research into whether chimpanzees learn American Sign Language, the researcher might inadvertently cue the chimp as to the correct sign or erroneously give the chimp credit for a sign because it's "close enough" to the desired sign. To eliminate these biases, one researcher shows the object, and another "rater," who cannot see the object, observes and records the chimp's sign. Raters are also common in studies that involve scoring such behaviors as creativity or aggressiveness.

Of course, a rater might not reliably score a behavior. At times the rater might miss or forget part of a participant's actions, or, over the course of a study, become more attuned and sensitive, or become fatigued and less motivated. And, finally, one rater might judge a behavior differently from another. (What you call a neutral facial expression, I might call an aggressive glare.) Any rater can introduce such errors, and we usually cannot eliminate them.

As you know, when we cannot eliminate an extraneous influence, we try to balance it. The approach with raters is to employ **multiple raters**, having more than one rater judge each participant's behavior. Then, we combine the ratings from different judges, usually computing the average rating given to each participant. This average should balance out the biases of individual raters, giving us a more reliable measure of each subject's behavior. Further, multiple raters form a sample of observers from which we can infer that any observer would judge the behavior in roughly the same way, so we can generalize the results with greater confidence.

To be convinced that raters are consistent, we determine their inter-rater reliability. **Inter-rater reliability** is the extent to which raters agree on the scores they assign to a participant's behavior. To determine inter-rater reliability, we may first conduct a pilot study where we examine the ratings and train the raters so that, hopefully, they will be reliable. Then, to be sure they *were* reliable, the inter-rater reliability in the actual completed study is determined. One way to do so is to compute the percentage of agreements between raters—for example, the percentage of times that two raters agreed on the sign a chimp produced. Usually, better than 90% agreement is needed to be considered reliable. Or, as discussed in Chapter 10, we may "correlate" the scores from two raters, and a high correlation indicates high inter-rater reliability.

> ***REMEMBER*** Using multiple raters who have high inter-rater reliability is a major concern in *any* design where data are obtained by subjectively evaluating participants.

Additional Sources of Data in Descriptive Approaches

The term *observational research* usually implies that a researcher was physically present to observe participants. The research literature, however, contains three common terms that indicate that other procedures were employed: Archival research, ex post facto research, and case studies.

Archival research In **archival research**, the source of the data is written records. Typically, the records come from schools, hospitals, government agencies, or police. For example, Faustman and White (1989) examined medical and psychiatric records to describe stress disorders found in some war veterans. Archival research is also used to describe social trends and events, as in Connors and Alpher's (1989) analysis of alcohol-related themes in country-western music. (They concluded that in such songs alcohol is usually used for drowning one's sorrows.) As above, usually archival research involves a descriptive, correlational design, but we may also assign participants to different groups to then compare, creating a quasi-experiment.

The advantage of archival research is that it allows access to behaviors that would otherwise be unobservable. It also allows us to verify participants' self-reports (e.g., we can compare actual college-grade records to participants' reported grades). However, archival research also presents three disadvantages. First, obtaining access to records may be very difficult. Second, usually, the records are not made with a researcher's question in mind, so they may not address our variables, and they may contain verbose, indirect descriptions, requiring much subjective interpretation on our part. And, third, there are often few controls in place to prevent the inclusion of the record-keeper's personal biases or errors. Thus, we often have considerably less confidence in archival data than in data derived from our own direct observations.

Ex post facto research In **ex post facto research**, a descriptive or experimental study is conducted after the events of interest have occurred (*ex post facto* means "after the fact"). Usually, this approach involves examining archival records. For example, in an ex post facto (correlational) study, Anderson and Anderson (1984) examined police records and meteorological records to determine whether the number of criminal assaults increased with increased daily temperature. Less commonly, ex post facto research may involve having participants report a past event, such as completing a questionnaire regarding their stress levels before and after an earthquake.

The problem with ex post facto designs is again that we obtain potentially unreliable data. Often, we cannot precisely quantify the variables and events that occurred, nor ensure that they reliably occurred for all participants. Likewise, written records are only as accurate as the people keeping them, and participants' self-reports may be biased and erroneous.

Case studies A **case study** is an in-depth study of one situation or "case." Usually, the case is a person, and such studies are frequently found in clinical research, providing an in-depth description of a particular patient's clinical symptoms and reactions to therapy (e.g., Martorano, 1991; Stagray & Truitt, 1992). However, a case may also involve a specific event or organization, as in Anderson's (1983) study of the government's decision-making procedures during the "case" of the Cuban missile crisis.

The advantage of case studies is that they provide an in-depth description of an individual or event. Their disadvantage is that they may yield data with poor reliability and validity. Further, their generalizability may be poor because our one case probably does not typify other cases.

> ***REMEMBER*** Archival research, ex post facto research, and case studies are common forms of descriptive research.

FIELD SURVEYS

Another common approach in descriptive research is the field survey. In a **field survey**, people complete a questionnaire or interview in a natural setting so that we can infer the responses we would see if we could poll the population. Field surveys may apply to a narrow population, as when, for example, surveying nurses treating AIDS patients to gauge their burn-out rates (George, Reed, Ballard, Colin, & Fielding, 1993). They are also used to describe the attitudes of the general population, as when, for example, describing consumer attitudes (Fornell, 1992). Field surveys may also describe less common experiences: The Roper Organization (1992) asked Americans if they ever experienced ghosts or UFOs (more than 30% reported they had!).

When developing a survey, developing reliable and valid questions is of paramount importance, and, as you'll see later in this chapter, requires considerable work. In addition to asking good questions, however, the key to field surveys is to reach the target sample and population. Therefore, we typically survey a large sample involving hundreds of participants. This may occur at a shopping mall or other public place, because members of the target population frequent that location. Or, if we are unable to obtain a representative sample at any one place, we try to reach a broader segment of the population either by mailing the survey or by conducting it over the telephone.

Mailed versus Telephone Surveys

A mailed survey is most useful when a large sample is needed and/or a lengthy questionnaire is being used—and when the researcher is not in a hurry to get the data. A telephone survey is typically shorter and can be completed quickly. For example, telephone surveys are conducted overnight during election campaigns to get the momentary "pulse" of the voters. The major difficulty with mailed or telephone surveys is in getting people to participate. Many will not bother mailing a survey back (even though we always should provide a stamped, addressed return envelope), so the "return rate" may be only 10% or 20%. People may also refuse to participate in a telephone survey, especially because "psychological surveys" have frequently been used as a cover for obscene phone calls or telemarketing scams.

There are many techniques for improving the return rates of mailed surveys (see Kanuk & Berenson, 1975), and for enlisting participants in a telephone survey (see Lavrakas, 1993). Essentially, the approach is to introduce the survey as an above-board, scientifically important, and professional project. Participants are informed about the purpose of the research, who the researchers are, and how they can be contacted. Then, brief questions are asked that can be accurately and rapidly completed. Throughout, the

TABLE 5.1 Summary of Terminology Used in Descriptive Research

Observational research:	Observation of participants
Naturalistic observation:	Unobtrusive, rather unstructured observation
Systematic observation:	Unobtrusive but rather structured observations
Participant observation:	Unobtrusive, systematic observations, with researcher a member of group being observed
Archival research:	Any type of design in which data are collected from formal records
Ex post facto research:	Any type of design in which data are collected after events have occurred
Case study:	In-depth description of one individual, group, or event
Field survey:	Polling people in the field

goal is to convince participants of the legitimacy of the research and to elicit their interest and cooperation.

The Flaws in Field Surveys

Recognize first that field surveys reflect how people feel at the time of the survey: They probably do *not* describe how people will feel later. Also, a survey can be biased if there are hidden criteria that eliminate certain types of participants. For example, surveys distributed at a shopping mall in the evening will reach only certain types of people, and thus produce a biased sample.

Another problem is that surveys are especially prone to the volunteer bias. The **volunteer bias** is the bias that arises from the particular people who participate in a study. This is a problem in both descriptive and experimental studies, because there are considerable differences between people who volunteer for a study and those who do not (Rosenthal & Rosnow, 1975). Among other things, volunteers tend to have a higher social status and intelligence, and to exhibit a greater need for social approval. An especially important factor is how strongly people feel about the issues being raised in a survey. For example, a mailed survey about abortion in the United States is most likely to be completed by those who very strongly favor abortion or very strongly oppose it. This is the danger with radio and television call-in surveys: The callers are probably a biased sample, consisting of those people who are especially motivated to make the call. In field surveys, always consider whether the "silent majority" has been missed.

> ***REMEMBER*** Field surveys can be influenced by low return rates, biased sampling, and the volunteer bias.

So that you can remember the previous terms used in different descriptive research, a summary is presented in Table 5.1.

TYPES OF SAMPLING TECHNIQUES

Recall that an aspect of external validity is how well our conclusions generalize to the broader population, so we are always concerned with obtaining a representative sample. Although external validity is an issue in experiments, we are especially concerned about it in descriptive field research. Therefore, by taking the study to the participants, we can be more selective in defining the target population and in the techniques used to select participants.

Researchers often identify potential participants from governmental or commercial mailing lists, or from membership lists of social or civic groups. On the one hand, such lists should not include people from outside the target population. A survey of voter attitudes, for example, should include only people who vote, so we may use a list of people who voted in the last election (although this does not mean they will vote the next time). On the other hand, we should not exclude any important segments of the population—a list of voters from the last election does not include people who are voting for the first time. Likewise, a survey about gun control should not include only registered gun owners, but it should not totally exclude them either. Thus, to obtain a representative sample, the goal is to include all of the important subgroups in the target population.

How we go about obtaining a sample is referred to as our "sampling technique." There are two general types of sampling techniques: probability sampling and nonprobability sampling.

Probability Sampling Techniques

Probability sampling relies on random sampling to select participants. The most common type of probability sampling is simple random sampling. With **simple random sampling** we select participants so that all members of the population have an equal chance of being selected and all samples have an equal chance of being selected. Ideally, by giving everyone an equal chance, the type of individuals found in the population should occur with the same frequency in the sample. One way to randomly sample is to use books containing tables of random numbers: Close your eyes and point to a number in the table, and then select the individual having the same identification number. You may also program a computer to select participants in this way.

Another probability technique is **systematic random sampling**, in which every *n*th person is selected from a list of the population. For example, after randomly selecting a starting point in the list, we might then select every third, or every tenth, name in the list. A variation of this approach used in field research is to survey, for example, every tenth person entering a shopping mall. Be careful, however, that there is no hidden bias here: If, for example, people are listed by age, then you may fill the sample with young people before getting to older ones further down the line.

Both simple and systematic random sampling rely on chance, so we may miss some types of individuals found in the population. To avoid this, we may instead employ stratified sampling. In **stratified random sampling**, we randomly select from the important subgroups so that their representation in the sample is proportional to their representation in the population. For example, if government records reveal that 60% of the target population is male, then 60% of a sample should be male. If the sample will contain 100 people, then, from the pool of identified men, we randomly select 60. If someone declines to participate, we select another male to replace him. We may also combine selection criteria: For example, if 5% of the population are females who own guns, we randomly select 5 participants from the pool of female gun owners. Other "strata" that are typically included in field research are socio-economic level, race, and geographic location.

Sometimes it is too expensive or too difficult to contact the individuals in a population. In such cases, we might use an alternative technique called cluster sampling. In **cluster sampling**, certain groups or "clusters" are randomly selected, and then all members of each group are observed. To study homeless people, for example, we might randomly select a few areas in a city where homeless people are found and then study all subjects in each area. Similarly, to study workers at a large factory, we might randomly select a few departments and study the workers in each. Because the clusters are randomly selected, there should be no bias in selecting participants, so the sample should be representative.

Nonprobability Sampling Techniques

Nonprobability sampling does not rely on random sampling. Therefore, not every member of the population has an equal opportunity to be selected, and so we are likely to miss certain types of individuals and obtain a less representative sample.

A common form of this approach is **convenience sampling**, in which we study participants who are conveniently available. Testing the students sitting in the student union or the people riding on a bus involves convenience samples. These are not random samples, because only those people who are present at the one place and time of the study have any chance of being selected, and the reason they are present is usually not a random event. Therefore, a convenience sample is representative of a very limited population.

Recognize that, to at least some extent, most "random" samples are also convenience samples: Given a researcher's limitations in terms of travel, time, and cost, there will always be some members of the population who have no chance of being selected. In reality, then, a truly random sample is an ideal that is seldom attained. In particular, the vast majority of psychological research—both descriptive and experimental—is based on convenience sampling of college-level, introductory psychology students. Therefore, participants are technically representative only of the population of introductory psychology students.

Another type of nonprobability sampling that may produce a more representative sample is **quota sampling**. As in stratified sampling, we ensure that the sample has the same percentage—the same "quota"—of each subgroup as in the population. Unlike stratified sampling, however, we do not randomly sample from each subgroup. Instead, convenience samples are used to fill each quota. For example, say that we want 20 six-year-olds and 20 seven-year-olds in a sample. If we obtain these participants from a convenient class of first-graders and a convenient class of second-graders, we are using quota sampling.

Finally, sometimes we seek to study a "hidden" population, as when studying drug addicts or prostitutes. Then we may use **snowball sampling**. Here, we identify one participant, and from him or her we identify other potential participants, and from them we identify others, so that the sample tends to build or "snowball." Note that such a sample is probably not very representative, because only those people within our network of acquaintances have any chance of being selected, and they may be different from others in the population.

For a summary of the above sampling techniques, consult Table 5.2.

TABLE 5.2 Summary of Sampling Techniques

Probability sampling	
Simple	Randomly select participants from the population.
Systematic	Select every *n*th individual from the population.
Stratified	Randomly select from subgroups, proportionate to each group's representation in the population.
Cluster	Randomly select clusters and test all members per cluster.
Nonprobability sampling	
Convenience	Select subjects who are conveniently available.
Quota	Obtain convenience samples to represent subgroups, proportionate to each group's representation in the population.
Snowball	Locate participants through other participants.

DESIGNING INTERVIEWS AND QUESTIONNAIRES

A common method of gathering data in descriptive research is to ask people questions using interviews and questionnaires. However, such self-reports are often used in experiments to measure the dependent variable and as a manipulation check.

When developing an interview or questionnaire, your first step should be to search the psychological literature for existing questionnaires and tests. The advantage of using existing procedures is that their reliability and validity have already been established. Detailed descriptions of various psychological tests can be found in research reports, as well as in specific reference books (e.g., Robinson, Shaver & Wrightsman, 1991).

On the other hand, creating your own questions involves a lot of work, and then *you* must demonstrate their reliability and validity. As you'll see below, when developing your own questions, you first have a number of decisions to make. As an example, say that from industrial-organizational psychology you learn about the construct of "job satisfaction," the degree to which workers find working a satisfying experience. How would you go about measuring job satisfaction?

The first step is to consider the type of questions to ask.

Using Closed-Ended versus Open-Ended Questions

In a **closed-ended question**, the researcher provides the alternatives from which the participant selects. Multiple-choice, true-false, yes-no, and rating-scale questions are all closed-ended questions. Some closed-ended questions that might reflect job satisfaction are:

(a) At work, my favorite activity is
1. Working with my hands.
2. Solving mental problems.
3. Supervising others.
4. Completing paperwork.

(b) At work, I become angry
1. Never.
2. Once in a while.
3. Frequently.
4. Most of the time.

(c) Mark all the words that describe your co-workers:
— Stimulating
— Stupid
— Helpful
— Boring

(d) On most days, do you look forward to going to work?
1. Yes
2. No

Closed-ended questions are also called "objective" questions, and that is their overwhelming strength: A response can be assigned a score objectively and reliably, with a minimum of subjective interpretation or error on the researcher's part. For example, in question (a) above, when participants select choice 1, we can assign them a score of 1 on that question, reliably assigning the same score to all people who gave the same response.

The disadvantage of closed-ended questions is that they yield limited information. First, they measure only the variable(s) we've selected. In question (b) above, we ask about anger at work, but participants may feel that happiness is the more relevant emotion. Second, participants can select only from the choices provided, even if they would like to give a different response. In question (c) above, perhaps a worker considers co-workers to be "intelligent," a response that is not available. For these reasons, closed-ended questions are used when reliability is a major concern but we are not interested in discovering new variables that may be relevant.

Conversely, in an **open-ended question**, the participant determines both the alternatives to choose from and the response. Any question equivalent to an essay question, whether written or oral, is open-ended. Thus, we might ask the open-ended questions "Describe your favorite activities at work" and "How often do you become angry at work?" The advantages of open-ended questions are the opposite of those of closed-ended questions. Open-ended questions allow for a wide range of responses, so researchers may discover new relevant variables. Further, participants can respond in their own words, so they are not limited to just the one perspective or phrasing that is present in a closed-ended question. On the other hand, the disadvantage of open-ended questions is that scoring each response requires subjective interpretation by the researcher, so scores may not be reliable. Two people who should be given the same score because their behaviors are the same may obtain different scores because of differences in the wording of their responses. (How would you score the responses "The paperwork is easy" versus "The paperwork is very easy"?) Further, the scoring of open-ended questions is highly susceptible to experimenter biases and expectations.

As usual, we counteract problems of subjective scoring by using double-blinds and multiple scorers who demonstrate high inter-rater reliability. The crucial component, however, is the scoring criteria. One technique for scoring open-ended questions is called content analysis. In **content analysis**, we score a participant's written or spoken answer by counting specified types of responses. We can assign a score based on the number of times a certain word, a certain feeling, or a particular perspective occurs. For example, a worker's score might simply reflect the number of positive references made to paperwork, regardless of whether the word "very" occurs.

Content analysis is also applied in other contexts, such as when scoring physical actions in observational research, or when scoring subjects' diaries or conversations. (See Krippendorf, 1980, for further information on content analysis.)

Even with strict scoring criteria, open-ended questions tend to provide less reliable and objective data, so they are used when reliability is not a major concern. In particular, open-ended questions are used when we are beginning to study a previously unexplored behavior so that we can identify potentially relevant variables, or we use this technique when each participant's response is likely to be unique.

Of course, you can employ both open-ended and closed-ended questions in the same questionnaire. This mix has the advantage of providing both reliable questions that are narrow in scope and less reliable but wider-ranging questions.

Using Interviews versus Questionnaires

You must also decide whether to use an interviewer to ask the questions or to provide participants with a questionnaire to complete. The advantage of interviewers is that they ensure that participants complete the questions as instructed. In addition, an interviewer can react to the information provided by a participant, either requesting clarifying information or exploring new topics that arise. The drawback to interviewers, however, is that they may inadvertently heighten the demand characteristics of reactivity and social desirability, or they may communicate expectancies about the desired response.

Just the opposite is true of questionnaires: The interaction between the researcher and participant is minimal, so there is less risk of transmitting experimenter expectations. Reactivity and social desirability also may be reduced, because completing a questionnaire anonymously can be much less threatening than talking to another person. Questionnaires also provide more efficient data collection, because many people can be tested at one time. The disadvantages of questionnaires, however, are that participants may not complete them as instructed, and the information obtained is limited to the inflexible questions presented.

The role of an interviewer is not all-or-nothing. At one extreme is the structured interview. In a **structured interview**, participants are asked specific, predetermined questions in a controlled manner. The most structured interview is when the interviewer simply reads closed-ended questions to participants and records their responses. Questions are read in a neutral manner with no additional comments or hints, and the response to a participant's comments is to merely repeat the question. (This approach is common in telephone surveys or when testing young children.) A less structured interview may involve asking open-ended questions, but the interviewer follows a script to ensure that all participants are treated in a consistent fashion. (This approach is commonly used in intelligence tests.)

At the opposite extreme is an unstructured interview. In an **unstructured interview**, the researcher has a general idea of the open-ended questions that will be asked, but there is freedom of discussion and interaction between participant and interviewer. Such interviews are commonly used when a researcher begins studying a behavior or is developing a complete description of an individual, such as during a clinical diagnosis. The lack of structure allows us to explore a wide range of issues, but the trade-off is reduced reliability, and the interviewer may lead participants into saying things they do not mean.

REMEMBER Interviews are preferred when the researcher must react to participant responses, but questionnaires are more reliable and less susceptible to demand characteristics.

Constructing Questions

The principles for creating questions for interviews or for questionnaires are largely the same. Think of any question as a *trial*, where what we ask is a stimulus and a participant's answer is his or her response. Exercise the same concerns when designing a question that we did when presenting an independent variable and measuring a dependent variable.

First, recognize that participants must interpret the meaning of a question and that you must interpret the meaning of their response. For valid inferences, minimize the extent to which participants must decide what it is you are asking. For example, the question "Do you experience job satisfaction with your job?" is a problem because most workers will not know what we mean by job satisfaction. Instead, we should ask participants to report specific behaviors. If, for example, job satisfaction is related to being paid enough, we should ask workers whether they are paid enough. Then *we* translate their responses back into our variables and constructs. Therefore, the elements of a question should have construct validity (reflecting the hypothetical construct as it's defined), as well as content validity, so that the question and the response actually and only reflect the variable or behavior you seek to measure.

Second, design questions that are sensitive to the subtle differences that exist between people. A question should *discriminate* or differentiate between participants on the variable being measured. After all, we assume that there are differences between people on the variable because, otherwise, why bother to measure it? Therefore, design sensitive and precise questions that participants will answer differently, to reflect such differences. Also, design questions that avoid ceiling effects, floor effects, or any other restriction of range in participants' scores. This includes avoiding questions that bias participants toward selecting a particular response.

Finally, recall that a score should reflect a participant's "typical" behavior. However, a response to a particular question might be atypical because of the question's unique wording or perspective, or because the participant experiences a momentary distraction or misinterprets the question. As usual, we counter such problems by increasing reliability through multiple trials: We create a number of different questions designed to measure the same variable or behavior. By varying the wording and perspective across different questions, we should balance out the unique aspects of any one question. Then, we compute a summary score for each participant, such as a total score or average score. This should provide a more reliable estimate of a person's typical response to such items.

REMEMBER The goal of question construction is to reliably and validly discriminate between participants on the variable being studied.

When generating questions, try to create many examples that reflect a variable. Then select those questions that are best suited to your purposes. Select questions using the following criteria.

Wording the questions Phrase questions so that you are confident you know what participants are communicating by their response and so that you can discriminate between different people. To meet these goals, avoid the following types of questions.

First, avoid **double-barreled questions**. These are questions that have more than one component. Consider the question "Should you be given more flexibility and less supervision on your job?" What if a person agrees to one part but not the other? The meaning of any response here will be unclear, so instead, ask two separate questions. Always phrase a question so that it states just one idea.

Second, avoid **leading questions**. These are questions that communicate social desirability or experimenter expectancies so that there is only one obvious response. Consider the question "Should very bad workers who are always late receive low pay?" This question won't discriminate between participants, because everyone knows what the correct answer "should be." Always phrase questions in a neutral manner, avoiding biased or inflammatory statements.

Third, avoid **Barnum statements**. These are questions that are so global and vague that everyone would agree with them or select the same response for them. (They are named after P. T. Barnum, who was famous for such statements.) For example, asking "Do you sometimes worry?" or "Have you had difficulty in some college courses?" will elicit the same answer from virtually everyone. This is the problem with horoscopes and palm readings: They are so general that people can always think of personal experiences that seem to fit. Always phrase a question so that it targets a specific behavior.

Finally, avoid questions that contain **undefined terms**. For example, asking "Should workers who are always late receive low pay?" will leave you wondering how participants interpret "always" and "low." Instead, either define such terms in the question, or have participants provide the definition in their response. Thus, you might ask "What pay should a worker receive who is late for work an average of twice a week?" In this version, you define "always late" and you allow participants to define "low pay" in their response.

> *REMEMBER* A question should be a clear, precise, and unbiased statement of a single idea, to which different participants are likely to respond differently.

Creating the Responses for Closed-Ended Questions The above guidelines also apply to the wording of the responses in closed-ended questions. Each alternative should be constructed to maximize your confidence that you know what participants wish to communicate when they select it. Therefore, the choices should be worded in a precise and unbiased manner, should convey one idea each, and should be mutually exclusive.

You must also determine the **response scale**, which is the number and type of choices to provide for each question. Be sure to provide enough choices. For example, we might ask yes-no (or true-false) questions, such as "Do you deserve a raise in pay?" Then we could assign a score of 1 for "yes" and a 2 for "no" (or any other two numbers). With only two scores, however, we have a *restricted range*, so that we cannot finely discriminate between participants: we'll gloss over differences between those who firmly believe a statement is true and those who think it is only sometimes true. Also, if we are scoring a test in terms of right or wrong answers, someone's *apparent* correct response might actually be a lucky guess. To alleviate problems of restricted range, sensitivity, and guessing, increase the number of response choices.

Multiple-choice questions are most appropriate for measuring factual information or discrete responses. For example, we might ask

Do you deserve a raise in pay?

1. No
2. Yes, a $1 raise
3. Yes, a $2 raise
4. Yes, more than a $2 raise

Four choices allow for more precise discrimination. However, the fourth choice does not distinguish between those who seek a $3 raise and those who seek a $4 or $5 raise. To obtain finer discriminations, we'd provide additional choices.

Likert-type questions are appropriate when measuring responses that fall along a continuum. Each consists of a declarative statement accompanied by a rating scale. Most often, the scale is "anchored" at each end by the words *agree* and *disagree*. Thus, we might ask

My hourly salary is sufficient for me.

1 2 3 4 5

STRONGLY AGREE   STRONGLY DISAGREE

You can also change the wording of the question to measure other experiences and attitudes, using such anchors as *seldom/frequently* or *like/dislike*.

Notice that creating a Likert-type question involves three decisions. First, consider the wording of the anchors. For example, including the word "strongly" implies extreme feelings. Because of social desirability, participants may be less likely to select the extreme positions of 1 or 5. Labeling the anchors with only *agree/disagree* would imply less extreme feelings, and thus would be more likely to get a wider range of responses. However, we'd also have a less clear definition of what participants were communicating. The way to resolve this issue depends on how threatening a particular question is. Usually, we define the anchors clearly and then attempt to minimize demand characteristics by our wording of the statement being rated.

Second, you must select the number of response alternatives. A five-point rating scale discriminates among only five levels of agreement. When greater sensitivity is needed, include more alternatives. (Do not allow participants to place responses between the points on the scale, because such responses cannot be scored reliably.) How large a scale you should select depends on participants' ability to differentiate their feelings. On a scale of 1 to 20, for instance, people probably cannot distinguish between a 16 and a 17. Instead, they are likely to guess between the two, and then your interpretation of what a 16 or 17 indicates is in error. Resolving this issue depends on the particular question, but we usually use scales with between 5 and 7 choices.

Finally, note that with five, seven, or any odd number of choices, there is one neutral, "middle of the road" choice. The more threatening an issue, the more likely it is that people will play it safe and choose the midpoint. This defeats our primary purpose of discriminating among participants. The solution is to use an even number of choices. With six options, for example, there is no middle ground, so participants must commit one way or the other. In general, use an odd-numbered scale when you assume that people can be legitimately neutral on an issue, and use an even-numbered scale to force participants to take a stand.

Completing the Questions Once you have created the basic questions to ask, you can often generate additional, comparable questions to create multiple trials for reliability merely by changing the wording and perspective. For example, to measure how interesting workers find their job, we can ask them to answer these two questions:

My job is interesting.					My job is boring.				
1	2	3	4	5	1	2	3	4	5
STRONGLY AGREE				STRONGLY DISAGREE	STRONGLY AGREE				STRONGLY DISAGREE

Then we "code" similar responses across related questions so that a particular score always means the same thing. That is, strongly agreeing with "My job is interesting" is equivalent to strongly disagreeing with "My job is boring." Therefore, we can record a response of 5 on the "boring" question as a score of 1, a 4 as a 2, and so on. Then, for both questions, the lower the score, the more interesting the job. Likewise, with multiple-choice questions, we score the choices so that each score reflects the same response (e.g., a 1 is assigned to any choice implying minimum job satisfaction).

Note that pilot studies are extremely valuable when developing questionnaires and interviews because you can ask participants questions about your questions. Thus, you can check that the questions have the intended meaning, that the rating scale is appropriate for differentiating their feelings, that the response scale fits the question, or that minimal demand characteristics are present. Alter problem questions and conduct additional pilot studies until you have created the desired questions.

Dealing with Order Effects

By presenting participants with a series of questions to answer, we once again create the problem of order effects. Practice effects, for example, occur if participants first find the questions to be novel or they feel great reactivity, but with more questions, they become comfortable, or later, they become fatigued or bored. Likewise, carry-over effects occur if participants respond in a biased fashion to later questions because of earlier questions. (Have you ever found that the way one question on an exam is worded provides the answer to a later question?) Participants may also develop response sets, especially over repeated closed-ended questions. If, for example, initial multiple-choice questions consistently call for choice 1, participants may superstitiously select choice 1 for subsequent questions. Or, if people select the strongly agree option on initial Likert-type questions, they may continue to make this response automatically.

There are several techniques for dealing with order effects:

1. **Provide practice questions** By providing practice questions prior to presenting the questions of interest, we allow participants to warm up to the questions and to habituate to their content, without contaminating the data.

2. **Counterbalance order effects** Balance out the effects of one particular order by creating different orders of questions for different participants so that questions that appear early in some questionnaires appear later in others, and vice versa. Across all participants completing the different versions, the total sample will not be biased by one unique order of questions.

3. **Prevent response sets** To prevent rote responding, vary the question format to try to force participants to read and think about each question. Thus, in multiple-choice questions, randomly vary which choice is correct. In Likert-type questions, present both positive and negative statements to be rated, and vary the scale by mixing agree/disagree with frequently/infrequently, and so on. You may also intermix multiple-choice with Likert-type questions, but do not change the format from question to question. This will confuse participants and lead to increased errors. Rather, present a block of one type of question containing, say, 10 questions before changing to a different format for the next block.
4. **Use alternate forms** **Alternate forms** are different versions of the same questionnaire. Here we change the order, wording, and perspective of questions so that the questionnaires appear to be different, yet still measure the same variables. Alternate forms are especially necessary when we must measure the same participants repeatedly. For example, say we wanted to measure workers' job satisfaction immediately before and after giving them a raise. If we used the identical questionnaire both times, people might duplicate their previous responses on the second testing in order to appear consistent, or they might intentionally change their responses because they think we expect them to. Ideally, the alternate forms will hide the similarity of participants' past and present responses so that they answer the second version honestly. (Alternate forms involve different questionnaires, so you must ensure that they are comparable in terms of validity and reliability.)

Creating Catch Trials

Sometimes participants do not follow instructions when completing questionnaires and interviews. Some people may give no thought to the questions, selecting answers randomly, just so they can be finished. Others may be untruthful, responding solely to demand characteristics. And still others may make errors when responding. Researchers incorporate special questions to "catch" such participants.

To identify people who may be answering questions randomly, we include a specific question several times throughout the questionnaire, but reorder the choices. Consider these examples:

When working, I prefer to be
1. Left alone.
2. Supervised occasionally.
3. Supervised frequently.

When working, I prefer to be
1. Supervised occasionally.
2. Supervised frequently.
3. Left alone.

A person's preference should be the same on both questions. Anyone who fails to be consistent is either responding randomly or recording responses erroneously.

To identify participants who are responding to demand characteristics, we create questions for which we know the truthful response. For example, say that when questioning teenagers about their experience with recreational drugs, we are concerned that peer pressure may cause some participants to overstate their drug use. To identify these people, we might ask the following:

I have taken the pill known as a "watermelon"

1. Never.
2. Between 1 and 5 times.
3. Between 5 and 10 times.
4. More than 10 times.

There is no pill known as a watermelon. All participants should select response 1, unless they are untruthful or made an error when responding.

With such questions, we can estimate the frequency with which participants were untruthful or made errors when responding to all other questions. Also, we may use such questions to prevent untrustworthy participants from being included in the data.

Administering the Questionnaire or Interview

Administering a questionnaire or interview requires the same controls that are found in experiments. Thus, control the environment so that there are no extraneous distractions, provide unbiased instructions for completing the questions (even if they seem self-explanatory), and keep the behaviors of the researcher neutral and consistent.

To minimize demand characteristics, be careful when creating a title for a questionnaire. Is a title necessary? Does it bias participants? (e.g., How you would respond to a questionnaire titled "Survey of Deviant Sexual Fantasies." What if it were titled "Survey of Common Sexual Fantasies"?) Second, consider whether deception is needed in the form of "filler" or "distracter" questions. These are not included in the data, but they alter the overall appearance of the questionnaire and disguise its actual purpose. (e.g., You might include filler questions about nonsexual fantasies to reduce reactivity to sexually oriented questions, and title the questionnaire "Survey of Common Fantasies.")

Last, but certainly not least, you are usually obligated to use the statistical techniques discussed in Chapter 10 to demonstrate that the questions have a minimum level of reliability and validity. After all, without this, you are not measuring what you seek to measure, so you're just wasting time.

To help you remember the various issues when constructing questions, Table 5.3 summarizes the previous sections.

TABLE 5.3 Issues to Consider in Question Construction

Use closed- or open-ended questions?
- Is reliability or breadth of information most needed?

Use interview or questionnaire format?
- How strong are demand characteristics?
- Must responding be structured for participants?
- What breadth of information is needed?

Are questions worded correctly?
- Avoid double-barreled questions.
- Avoid leading questions.
- Avoid Barnum statements.
- Avoid undefined terms.

What is response scale?
- Are measurements sensitive to subtle differences?
- Use multiple-choice or Likert scale?
- What description should anchor Likert scales?
- How many choices in each scale?
- Is odd or even number of points needed?

How to administer questioning?
- Avoid order effects, especially response sets.
- Are alternate forms needed?
- Are catch trials needed?
- Include clear instructions.
- Is pilot study needed?

ETHICAL ISSUES IN DESCRIPTIVE RESEARCH

The ethical issues in descriptive research are the same as in experiments: to minimize the potential risks to participants, and to have any remaining risks justified by the knowledge to be gained. The "risks" we're talking about here occur because being observed by a researcher or completing a survey may be embarrassing, stressful, or unpleasant for participants. As with all research, your procedure should first be approved by your institution's Human Subjects Review Committee.

If the participants are aware a study is being conducted, follow the usual rules: All responses are kept confidential, and alleviate participants' fears about what the data will divulge about them or what it will be used for. As always, obtain explicit informed consent. The fact that participants complete a questionnaire or interview is *not* informed consent, because they may feel coerced to do so. Upon completion of testing, provide a debriefing.

The principal ethical dilemma arises with unobtrusive research. From one perspective, observational techniques are another name for spying on people. With participant observation, we are present under false pretenses, and we violate a person's expectation of privacy. With archival studies, we examine private records without obtaining informed consent. In fact, in any form of unobtrusive field research, participants are not even aware that a study is being conducted, we do not obtain their informed consent, and so we may be violating their rights.

A classic example of this dilemma is a study by Middlemist, Knowles, and Matter (1976). They were studying the "personal space" that people use to separate themselves from others, and they wanted to eliminate demand characteristics while measuring whether an invasion of one's personal space created physical tension. Their solution was to observe males as they visited the urinal in a public restroom! They invaded personal space by having a confederate use the adjacent urinal, and the measure of a participant's resulting tension was the amount of time he took to urinate. To be unobtrusive, a researcher occupied one of the stalls and used a periscope to observe each participant, timing the interval between unzipping and rezipping.

Although technically this was a field experiment, the ethical problem is with the secret observation of participants. We might justify this study by claiming that it is "scientific research" for the "good of humanity." But, some would argue, this is no different from when a government agency or the police spy on citizens, claiming that it helps catch criminals. After all, spying is spying, and it is wrong to invade people's privacy and violate their rights, regardless of whether it is for scientific advancement and the good of humanity, or for national security and rooting out evil.

Others would argue that a public behavior is just that—public—and so it's open to anyone's observation. Thus, a male who uses a public restroom has tacitly agreed to be observed by other males. If a male wishes to keep his urinal behavior private, he should not use a public restroom. From this perspective, some researchers claim that it is unethical for scientists *not* to conduct unobtrusive field research, because then they would miss potentially valuable information.

There is no easy resolution to this debate. You might suggest that we obtain informed consent after the study, but by then the person's rights are already violated (and telling participants afterwards would likely be more upsetting than not informing them at all). Instead, as usual, it is the researcher's responsibility to weigh the violation of participants' rights against the potential scientific information to be gained. Therefore, first decide just how "public" participants consider a behavior to be. Are you invading their expected privacy? How strenuously would they object if you asked their permission? How upset would they be if they found out about your spying after the fact? (If you are unsure of the answers, conduct a pilot study in which you ask people these questions.)

Then, weigh the invasion of privacy against the potential scientific benefits. For example, Koocher (1977) argued that the above urinal study needlessly invaded participants' privacy, because it replicated findings already demonstrated by other, less questionable techniques. (But see the reply of Middlemist et al., 1977.) Also, consider whether the procedure really needs to be conducted as an unobtrusive study. Remember that the APA's Ethical Principles (1992) state that deception must be necessary and that informed consent is needed unless the risk to participants is minimal. Therefore, the more the behavior being studied is an innocuous, mundane public behavior, and the greater the necessity for an unobtrusive field study, the more the study can be justified ethically.

REMEMBER Be particularly sensitive to the ethics of unobtrusive field research.

PUTTING IT ALL TOGETHER

Because we always want valid and reliable data, there are actually few differences in the mechanics of how to conduct descriptive or experimental research. The issues are largely the same, so any of the procedures you learned in the previous chapter apply to the descriptive research discussed in this chapter, and vice versa. Thus, for example, in any research, you should create clear instructions or consider automating. Also, always consider multiple raters and inter-rater reliability, the volunteer bias, and using the appropriate sampling technique to obtain the most representative sample. Essentially, from these chapters, you've been developing a collection of techniques that, depending upon the specific hypothesis, you may mix and match as needed.

CHAPTER SUMMARY

1. In *descriptive research*, the goal is to describe a behavior, the situation it occurs in, or the individuals exhibiting it. The three major types of descriptive designs are *correlational studies*, *observational studies*, and *field surveys*.
2. In *naturalistic observation*, the researcher observes participants' behaviors in an unsystematic manner. In *systematic naturalistic observation*, the researcher observes a behavior systematically. In *participant observation*, the researcher is a member of the group being observed.
3. *Ex post facto* research is conducted after a phenomenon has occurred. *Archival research* is conducted using participants' records. A *case study* is an in-depth description of one individual, organization, or event.

4. When a score involves subjectively evaluating a participant, we use *multiple raters*. They should have high *inter-rater reliability*, which is the extent to which raters agree in the scores they assign a particular behavior.
5. In a *field survey*, participants complete a questionnaire or interview, either in person, by mail, or over the telephone.
6. The *volunteer bias* is the bias that arises because people who will participate in a study are different from those who will not.
7. In *probability sampling techniques*, every member of the population has an equal likelihood of being selected. In *simple random sampling*, participants are selected in a random fashion. In *systematic random sampling*, every *n*th individual is selected from a list of the population. With *stratified random sampling*, participants are randomly selected proportionately from subgroups in the population. With *cluster sampling*, some groups are randomly selected and all members of each group are observed.
8. In *nonprobability sampling*, not every member of the population has an equal likelihood of being selected. In *convenience sampling*, participants are those who are available. In *quota sampling*, the population is proportionately sampled using convenience samples to fill each quota. With *snowball sampling*, potential participants are identified by other participants.
9. The goal of question construction is to reliably and validly discriminate among participants on the variable of interest. With *closed-ended questions*, participants select from alternatives provided by the researcher. With *open-ended questions*, participants determine the alternatives to choose from.
10. *Content analysis* is the procedure for scoring open-ended questions by looking for specific words, themes, or actions.
11. In a *structured interview*, participants are asked predetermined questions. In an *unstructured interview*, the questions are less rigidly predetermined.
12. Researchers should avoid (a) *double-barreled questions*, which have more than one component; (b) *leading questions*, which are biased so that there is only one obvious response; (c) *Barnum statements*, which are global truisms to which everyone responds in the same way; and (d) questions that contain *undefined terms*.
13. The *response scale* is the number and type of choices provided for each question. When using Likert-type questions, the scale should (a) have anchors that are not overly biasing, (b) contain choices that participants can discriminate among, and (c) force participants to indicate a preference.
14. Order effects in questionnaires can be controlled by (a) including practice questions, (b) counterbalancing different orders so the influence of any one order is balanced out, (c) alternating between different question formats, and (d) using *alternate forms* of a questionnaire that contain questions that are worded differently but measure the same behaviors.
15. The central ethical issue in unobtrusive field research is that by not obtaining *informed consent*, the researcher may violate participants' rights.

KEY TERMS (with page references)

alternate forms (124)
archival research (112)
Barnum statements (121)
case study (112)
closed-ended question (117)
cluster sampling (116)
content analysis (118)
convenience sampling (116)
descriptive research (109)
double-barreled questions (121)
ex post facto research (112)
field survey (113)
inter-rater reliability (111)
leading questions (121)
multiple raters (111)
naturalistic observation (109)
nonprobability sampling (116)
observational research (109)
open-ended question (118)
participant observation (110)
probability sampling (115)
quota sampling (116)
response scale (121)
simple random sampling (115)
snowball sampling (116)
stratified random sampling (115)
structured interview (119)
systematic naturalistic observation (110)
systematic random sampling (115)
undefined terms (121)
unstructured interview (119)
volunteer bias (114)

REVIEW QUESTIONS

(Answers for odd-numbered questions and problems are provided in Appendix D.)

1. What does the term *descriptive research* convey?
2. What are the differences among naturalistic observation, systematic observation, and participant observation?
3. (a) What are the strengths of observational designs? (b) What are their weaknesses?
4. (a) What is archival research? (b) What is ex post facto research? (c) What are the major weaknesses of these designs? (d) Why do researchers employ them?
5. (a) What is a case study? (b) What is the strength of this approach? (c) What is its weakness?
6. (a) What important ethical issue pertains to unobtrusive observational research? (b) According to the APA's Ethical Principles, when may we not obtain informed consent with these approaches?
7. (a) What is the difference between simple and systematic random sampling? (b) What is stratified random sampling? (c) What is cluster sampling?
8. (a) What is the difference between probability and nonprobability sampling techniques? (b) Why are probability techniques more likely to produce a representative sample? (c) Which probability technique should produce the most representative sample?
9. (a) What is quota sampling? (b) What is snowball sampling?
10. (a) What is convenience sampling? (b) Why are all samples somewhat convenience samples? (c) How do such samples influence external validity?

11. (a) When do researchers mail surveys? (b) When do they employ telephone surveys? (c) Why is it important to ensure high subject-participation rates in both types of surveys?

12. (a) What is the difference between open-ended and closed-ended questions? (b) What are the advantages and disadvantages of each?

13. How do you create scoring criteria for an observational study?

14. (a) What is the volunteer bias? (b) How does it adversely affect the results of a survey or experiment?

15. (a) What are alternate forms? (b) With what type of procedure are they especially necessary?

PRACTICE PROBLEMS

16. What is the difference between a structured and an unstructured interview in terms of (a) the actions of the researcher? (b) the reliability of the data? (c) the information obtained?

17. You wish to examine how well people do on a test of problem-solving ability as a function of how anxious they are. (a) Why and how would you conduct this as an experiment? (b) Why and how would you conduct this as a descriptive design?

18. For each of the following, indicate whether you should use a written questionnaire, a structured interview, or an unstructured interview: (a) When measuring the attitudes of first-graders; (b) When measuring the contents of people's daydreams; (c) When measuring people's attitudes toward researchers.

19. Here are two questions developed for a survey about college. What three problems in each need to be corrected?

a. I enjoy living in the dorm with my roommate.

VERY STRONGLY AGREE		VERY STRONGLY DISAGREE
1	2	3

b. People who don't study much will do poorly.

FREQUENTLY				SELDOM
1	2	3	4	5

20. I ask students in my class to rate their agreement with the following statements. Give the term that identifies what is wrong with the wording of each statement. (a) The material in this textbook is sometimes difficult. (b) Students like reading this book, but dislike the statistics. (c) A good student will like my book. (d) With this book students can get an acceptable grade.

21. On a personality test, the question "Do you prefer raw or cooked carrots?" occurs several times. Why?

22. (a) In what types of situations are multiple raters used? (b) What must you always examine regarding their ratings? (c) When in a study do you examine it? (d) What flaws occur in a study if there is a problem with the ratings?

23. In the "urinal study" discussed in this chapter, what changes can you propose to lessen the objections to this procedure?

24. A student complains that a college exam was unfair because it contained some questions that very few students could answer correctly. How would a researcher justify the inclusion of such questions?

25. A researcher wants to observe children unobtrusively at a day-care center, judging how aggressively they behave after watching an adult behave aggressively. (a) What problem arises with this scoring technique? (b) In terms of the scoring criteria, how would you ensure reliability? (c) In terms of the scorer, how would you ensure reliability? (d) What must you then do to show you have reliability?

26. In problem 25, what are the major ethical issues in this design, and how should you handle them?

PART 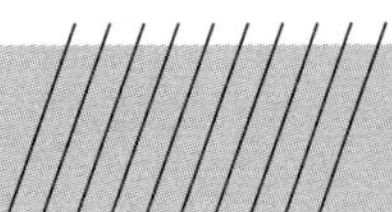

DESCRIPTIVE STATISTICS

Now that you understand the basics of descriptive and experimental research, it's time to see how statistical procedures fit in. Our starting point is descriptive statistics that summarize the important characteristics of data. What do we mean by important characteristics? Essentially, they involve answering the following five questions about the data:

1. *Which scores occurred?* We answer this question by presenting the scores in tables and graphs.
2. *Are the scores generally high scores or generally low scores?* We can describe the scores with one number that represents the "typical" score.
3. *Are the scores very different from each other, or are they close together?* There are mathematical ways to describe "close."
4. *How does any one particular score compare to all other scores?* We have a system for evaluating any score relative to the other scores.
5. *What is the nature of the relationship we have found?* We can summarize a relationship and then use it to predict scores on one variable if we know a score on another variable.

The following four chapters show how to answer the first four questions. In Part 3, we answer the final question.

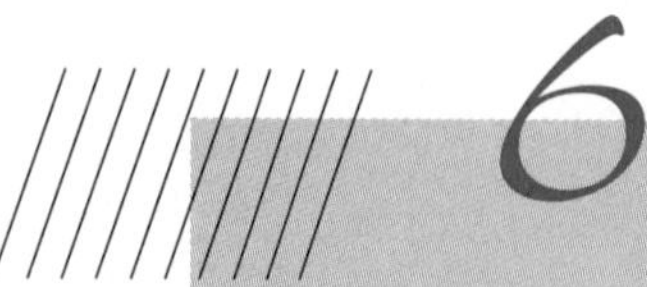

Summarizing Research Using Frequency Distributions and Percentiles

GETTING STARTED

To understand this chapter, recall the following:

- From Chapter 2, recall the difference between a sample and population of scores, how a sample is used to draw inferences about a population, what a data point is, and what the phrase "as a function of" means.

Your goals in this chapter are to learn:

- The scales of measurement that researchers use.
- How simple frequency, relative frequency, cumulative frequency, and percentile are computed, and what each tells you.
- How the different types of frequency tables, bar graphs, histograms, and polygons are created.
- What normal, skewed, bimodal, and rectangular distributions are.
- How the proportion of the total area under the normal curve corresponds to the relative frequency of scores.

Recall that statistics are for making sense out of data. This chapter shows how to do that by displaying data in graphs and tables. Always create a table or graph. As the saying goes, "A picture is worth a thousand words," and nowhere is this more appropriate than when trying to make sense out of data. Also, part of science is to communicate our results to others, and a table or graph is often the best way to do this. Finally, a table or graph makes it easier to see the relationship hidden in data.

Before we examine the relationship between the scores of two variables, however, we first summarize the scores on each individual variable, asking "Which scores occurred?" In fact, buried in any batch of scores are two important questions: Which scores occurred, and how often did each score occur? We answer both questions simultaneously with certain types of tables and graphs. But first, let's look at some basic statistical rules and notation.

MORE STATISTICAL NOTATION

The scores we measure in a study are the *raw scores*: They are "raw" and not yet "digestible." Descriptive statistics help us cook down the raw scores into an interpretable form. One way to do this is to create a **distribution**, which is the general name for any organized set of data. Then, we can see the pattern the scores form, or in statistical language, see how the scores are *distributed.*

Another way to make raw scores interpretable is through transformations. A **transformation** is a mathematical procedure for converting a set of scores into a different set of scores. One reason for transformations is to make different kinds of scores comparable. For example, it's difficult to compare an 8 out of 10 on a math quiz to a 75 out of 100 on an English quiz. However, by transforming each score to, for example, a percent of the total, we are no longer comparing apples to oranges. Second, transformations make scores easier to work with. For example, if the scores contain one decimal place, multiplying every score by 10 eliminates the decimals.

Speaking of decimals, "close" counts in statistics, so carry out calculations to the appropriate number of decimal places before you "round off" an answer. The convention is that the *final* answer after rounding should have two more decimal places than the original scores. For example, if you have whole-number raw scores, the final answer should contain two decimal places. However, do not round off at each intermediate step in the calculations: *Round off only at the end!* So, if the final answer will contain two decimals, carry out the intermediate calculations to at least three decimals, and then round off the final answer. Use the following rules when rounding:

- If the number in the next decimal place is 5 or greater than 5, round up. For example, if rounding to two decimal places, 2.366 is rounded to 2.370, which becomes 2.37.
- If the number in the next decimal place is less than 5, round down: 3.524 is rounded to 3.520, which becomes 3.52.

Recognize that we add zeroes to the right of the decimal point to indicate our level of precision. Rounding 4.996 to two decimal places produces 5, but to show the precision of two decimal places, we report it as 5.00.

Finally, we often count how *many* scores we have. The symbol N stands for the total number of scores in a set of data. (Notice that this is a *capitalized* N, and so, when you see N, think *Number*.) An N of 10 means that we have 10 scores, or $N = 43$ means there are 43 scores. In statistical terminology, N is the *sample size*, indicating how big a sample is. When we have one score for each participant, N also corresponds to the number of individuals in the sample. So, N is the *total number* of scores, *not* the number of different scores. For example, if the 43 scores in a sample are all the same score, N still equals 43. Get in the habit of treating N as a quantity itself so that you understand such statements as "increasing N" or "this sample's N is larger than that sample's N."

We also count how *often* each score occurs. How often a score occurs is the score's **frequency**, symbolized by f. Notice that this is the *lowercase* f. (Always pay attention to whether a symbol involves an upper- or lowercase letter.) Also, learn to treat f as a quantity: One score's f may be larger than another score's f, we can add the fs of different scores, and so on. As you'll see, there are several ways to describe a score's frequency, so we often combine the term frequency (and f) with other terms and symbols.

TYPES OF MEASUREMENT SCALES

Recall that a big part of this course is learning when to use a particular statistical procedure. Which procedure to employ is determined by three things. First, decide what it is you want to know—what question about the characteristics of the sample or population do you want to answer? Then, your choice of procedures depends on the specific research design being employed, because different designs are analyzed differently. Finally, within a particular design, you'll measure a variable in such a way that the scores have certain underlying mathematical characteristics. The particular mathematical characteristics of scores also determine which statistics to use. Therefore, part of your job is to learn these characteristics. In other words, you must recognize the *scale of measurement* involved and whether the scale is *continuous* or *discrete*.

The Four Scales of Measurement

Numbers mean different things in different contexts. The number 1 on a license plate is different from a 1 in a race, which is different still from a 1 in a hockey score. The information that scores convey depends on the *scale of measurement* used to measure the variable. There are four types of measurement scales: Nominal, ordinal, interval, and ratio.

Nominal scales With a **nominal scale**, each score does not actually indicate an amount; rather, it is used simply for identification, as a name. (When you see *nominal*, think *name*.) License plate numbers and the numbers on the uniforms of football players reflect a nominal scale. In research, a nominal scale is used to identify the categories of a qualitative, or classification, variable. For example, we cannot perform any statistical operations on the words *male* and *female*. Therefore, we might assign each male participant a 1 and each female a 2. However, we could just as easily assign males a 2 and females a 1, or we could use any other two numbers. Because we assign the numbers arbitrarily, they do not have the mathematical properties normally associated with numbers. For example, here the number 1 does not indicate more than 0 yet less than 2, as it usually does.

Ordinal scales Sometimes, instead, a variable is measured using an **ordinal scale**: Here, the scores indicate rank order, so the score of 1 means the most or least of the variable, 2 means the second most or least, and so on. (For *ordinal,* think *ordered.*) In research, ordinal scales are used, for example, to rank participants in terms of their aggressiveness, or we might have participants rank the importance of certain attributes in their friends. Each score indicates an amount, but it is a relative amount. For example, relative to everyone else being ranked, you may be the number 1 student, but we do not know how good a student you actually are. Further, with an ordinal scale, there is not necessarily an equal unit of measurement separating each score. In a race, for example, first may be only slightly ahead of second, but second may be miles ahead of third. Also, there is no number 0 in ranks (no one can be "zero-th").

Interval scales When a variable is measured using an **interval scale**, however, each score indicates an actual amount, and there *is* an equal unit of measurement separating any two scores: The difference between 2 and 3 is the same as the difference between 3 and 4. (For *interval,* think *equal* interval.) Interval scales include the number 0, but it is not a "true" zero—it does not mean that zero amount of the variable is present. Therefore, even less of the variable can be present, so an interval scale allows negative numbers. Temperature measured in Celsius or Fahrenheit is an interval scale, because zero degrees does not mean that zero amount of heat is present—it means only that there is less than 1 degree and more than −1 degree. Interval scales are often used with psychological tests, such as intelligence or personality tests. Although a score of zero may be possible, it does not mean zero intelligence or zero personality.

Note that with an interval scale, it is incorrect to make "ratio statements" that compare the amount of a variable at one score relative to the amount at another score. For example, at first glance it seems that 4 degrees Celsius has twice as much heat as 2 degrees. However, if we convert these temperatures to the Fahrenheit scale, 2 and 4 degrees Celsius are about 35 and 39 degrees Fahrenheit, respectively, so the one temperature is not twice that of the other.

Ratio scales Only with a **ratio scale** do the scores reflect the true amount of a variable that is present, because the scores measure an actual amount, there is an equal unit of measurement, *and* 0 truly means that zero amount of the variable is present. Therefore, ratio scales do not allow negative numbers. Further, only with ratio scales can we make ratio statements, such as "4 is twice as much as 2." (So, for *ratio,* think *ratio*!) In research, ratio scales are used to measure such variables as the number of errors made on a test, the number of friends someone has, or the number of calories consumed in a day.

To help you remember the four scales of measurement, Table 6.1 summarizes their characteristics.

Discrete and Continuous Scales

The other important attribute of a measurement scale is whether it is continuous or discrete. A **continuous scale** allows for fractional amounts; it "continues" between the whole-number amounts, so decimals make sense. Age is a continuous variable because

TABLE 6.1 Summary of Types of Measurement Scales

Each column describes the characteristics of the scale.

	Type of measurement scale			
	Nominal	***Ordinal***	***Interval***	***Ratio***
What does the scale indicate?	Quality	Relative quantity	Quantity	Quantity
Is there an equal unit of measurement?	No	No	Yes	Yes
Is there a true zero?	No	No	No	Yes
How might the scale be used in research?	To identify males and females as 1 and 2	To judge who is 1st, 2nd, etc., in aggressiveness	To convey the results of intelligence and personality tests	To state the number of correct answers on a test
Additional examples	Telephone numbers Blood type Social security numbers	Military rank Letter grades Elementary school grade	Checkbook balance Winnings/losses at gambling Individual's standing relative to class average	Weight Height Distance traveled

it is possible to say that someone is 19.6879 years old. To be continuous, a variable must be at least theoretically continuous. For example, intelligence tests produce whole-number scores, so you cannot obtain an IQ score of, say, 95.6. But theoretically, an IQ of 95.6 makes sense, so intelligence is a theoretically continuous interval variable.

On the other hand, a **discrete scale** can be measured only in whole-number amounts. Here, decimals do not make sense. Usually, nominal and ordinal variables are discrete. In addition, some interval and ratio variables are discrete. For example, the number of cars someone owns and the number of children someone has are discrete ratio variables. It sounds strange when the government reports that the average family has 2.4 children and owns 1.78 cars, because these are discrete variables being treated as if they were continuous. (Imagine a .4 child driving a .78 car!)

There is a special type of a discrete variable. When there can be only two amounts or categories of the variable, it is a **dichotomous variable**; Pass/fail, male/female, and living/dead are examples of dichotomous variables.

The Impact of a Particular Scale

There are two important reasons to pay attention to the scale of measurement being employed. First, certain mathematical and statistical procedures make sense only with certain types of scores. It makes no sense to think that the football player with number 12 is bigger, faster, or has more of anything relative to player number 10, nor does calculating the average number make sense.

Second, different scales provide different degrees of precision and sensitivity. Recall that when developing scoring criteria or selecting the response scale for questionnaires, we seek the most sensitive, most discriminating measure. Nominal scales discriminate only grossly among participants, because scores essentially reflect only a yes/no classification. Ordinal scales, by measuring relative amounts, are more sensitive, but by being discrete and having no constant amount between scores, they still lack precision. Interval or ratio scales are the most sensitive measures, especially when they are continuous: Here, scores can reflect very small, subtle differences in behaviors. Thus, if possible, it is best to measure a behavior using a continuous interval or ratio scale.

> *REMEMBER* The sensitivity of measurements and which statistical procedure to apply to them depend on the type of measurement scale employed.

Regardless of the scale of measurement used to produce the raw scores, the first step is to summarize and organize them. The following sections show how to do this using either simple frequency, relative frequency, cumulative frequency, or percentile.

CREATING SIMPLE FREQUENCY DISTRIBUTIONS

The most common way to organize scores is to create a simple frequency distribution. A **simple frequency distribution** shows the number of times each score occurs in a set of data. The symbol for a score's frequency is f. To find f for a score, count how many times the score occurs. For example, if three participants scored 66, the frequency of 66 (its f) is 3. Creating a simple frequency distribution involves counting the frequency of every score in the data.

Presenting Simple Frequency in a Table

To see how to present a simple frequency distribution in a table, let's begin with the following raw scores. They might be from one of the variables in a correlational study, or they might be the dependent scores from an experiment.

14	14	13	15	11	15	13	10	12
13	14	13	14	15	17	14	14	15

In this disorganized arrangement, it's difficult to make sense out of the scores. Watch what happens, though, when they are arranged into the simple frequency table shown in Table 6.2 on the next page. The table consists of a score column and an f column. Notice that the score column begins with the highest score in the data at the *top* of the column. Below that are all *possible* whole-number scores in decreasing order, down to the lowest score that occurred. Thus, although no one obtained a score of 16, we still include it. Opposite each score in the f column is the score's frequency: In the sample, there is one 17, zero 16s, four 15s, and so on.

TABLE 6.2 Simple Frequency Distribution Table

The left-hand column identifies each score, and the right-hand column contains the frequency with which the score occurred.

Score	*f*
17	1
16	0
15	4
14	6
13	4
12	1
11	1
10	1

Now, we can easily see the frequency of each score and discern how the scores are distributed. We can also determine the combined frequency of several scores by adding together their *f*s. For example, the score of 13 has an *f* of 4, and the score of 14 has an *f* of 6, so the frequency of 13 and 14 is 4 + 6, or 10.

Note that even though there are 8 scores in the score column, *N* is not 8. There are 18 scores in the original sample, so *N* equals 18. If we add together all the values in the *f* column, the sum will equal 18: The 1 participant scoring 17, plus the 4 who scored 15, and so on, equals the *N* of 18.

REMEMBER The sum of all individual frequencies in a sample equals *N*.

That's how to create a simple frequency distribution. Such a distribution is also called a *regular frequency distribution* or a plain old *frequency distribution*.

Graphing a Simple Frequency Distribution

A graph of a simple frequency distribution essentially shows the relationship between each score and the frequency with which it occurs. We ask, "For a given score, what is its corresponding frequency?" Therefore, we place the scores on the *X* axis and the frequency of the scores on the *Y* axis. Then, we look for changes in frequency *as a function of* changes in the scores, looking at how the frequencies change as the scores increase.

REMEMBER A graph of a frequency distribution always shows the raw scores on the *X* axis.

A variable will involve one of the previous four types of measurement scales. The type of scale involved determines whether we create a bar graph, a histogram, or a polygon.

Bar graphs A frequency distribution of nominal or ordinal scores is graphed as a bar graph. A **bar graph** is a graph in which a vertical bar is centered over each score on the *X* axis. *In a bar graph, adjacent bars do not touch.*

Figure 6.1 shows two bar graphs of simple frequency distributions. (I've included the corresponding frequency tables so that you can see the data, but usually we do not include the table.) The upper graph shows the nominal variable of political affiliation of participants. The lower graph shows ordinal data involving military rank. In each, we've counted the number of people in each category. Then, the height of each bar corresponds to the score's frequency.

The reason we create bar graphs here is that both nominal and ordinal scales are usually discrete scales. The space between the bars indicates this fact. On the other hand,

FIGURE 6.1 Simple Frequency Bar Graph for Nominal and Ordinal Data

The height of each bar indicates the frequency of the corresponding score on the X axis.

Nominal variable of political affiliation	
Party	***f***
Communist	1
Socialist	3
Democrat	8
Republican	6

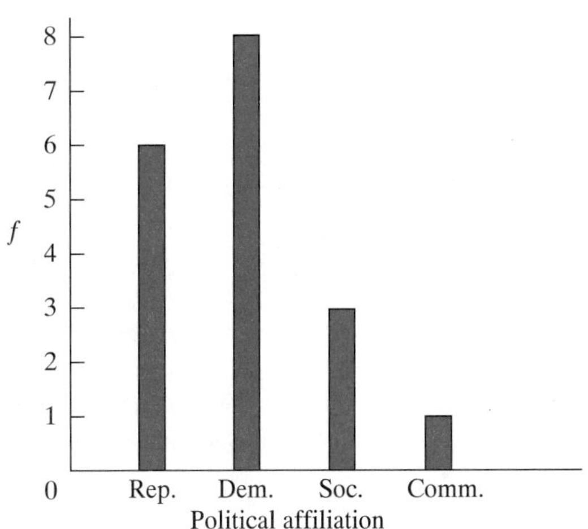

Ordinal variable of military rank	
Rank	***f***
General	3
Colonel	8
Lieutenant	4
Sergeant	5

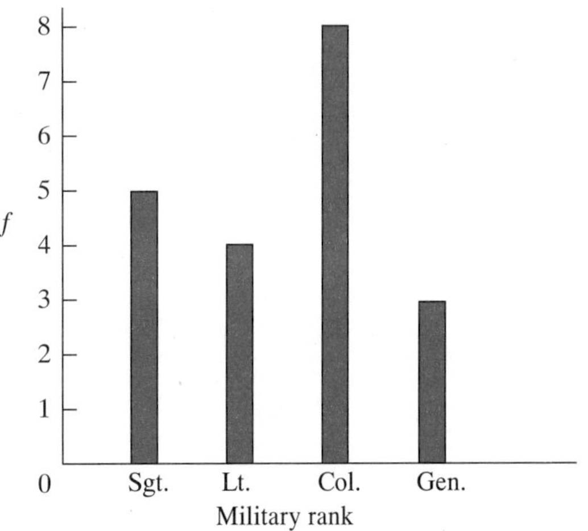

interval and ratio scales are usually at least theoretically continuous, so these scales are not usually plotted using bar graphs. Instead, we have two ways of graphing such scores, depending upon how many *different* scores the data include.

Histograms Create a histogram when plotting the frequency of a *small* range of interval or ratio scores. A **histogram** is similar to a bar graph except that *in a histogram, adjacent bars touch.* The absence of a space between the bars signals that the scale continues between scores. For example, say that we measured a sample of students on the ratio variable of the number of college courses they've taken, obtaining the data in Figure 6.2. Again, the height of each bar indicates the corresponding score's frequency.

Don't create a histogram when there is a large range of different scores (say if our students had taken from 1 to 50 courses). The 50 bars would need to be very skinny, so the graph would be difficult to read. Likewise, sometimes we plot more than one sample of scores on the same graph, and even with a small range of scores, overlapping histograms are hard to read. Instead, in such situations create a frequency polygon.

Frequency polygons To construct a **frequency polygon**, place a data point over each score on the X axis at the height on the Y axis that corresponds to the appropriate frequency. Then connect the data points using straight lines. Figure 6.3 shows the previous college course data plotted as a frequency polygon.

Notice that, unlike a bar graph or histogram, a simple frequency polygon includes on the X axis the next score *above* the highest score in the data and the next score *below* the lowest score (in Figure 6.3, scores of 0 and 8 are included). These added scores have a frequency of 0, so the polygon touches the X axis. In this way, we create a complete geometric figure—a polygon—with the X axis as its base.

Often you must read the frequency of a score directly from the polygon. To do this, locate the score on the X axis and then move upward until you reach the line forming the polygon. Then, moving horizontally, locate the frequency of the score. For example, as shown by the dashed line in Figure 6.3, the score of 4 has an f equal to 4.

FIGURE 6.2 Histogram Showing the Simple Frequency of College Courses Taken in a Sample

Score	*f*
7	1
6	4
5	5
4	4
3	6
2	7
1	9

FIGURE 6.3 Simple Frequency Polygon Showing the Frequencies of College Courses Taken in a Sample

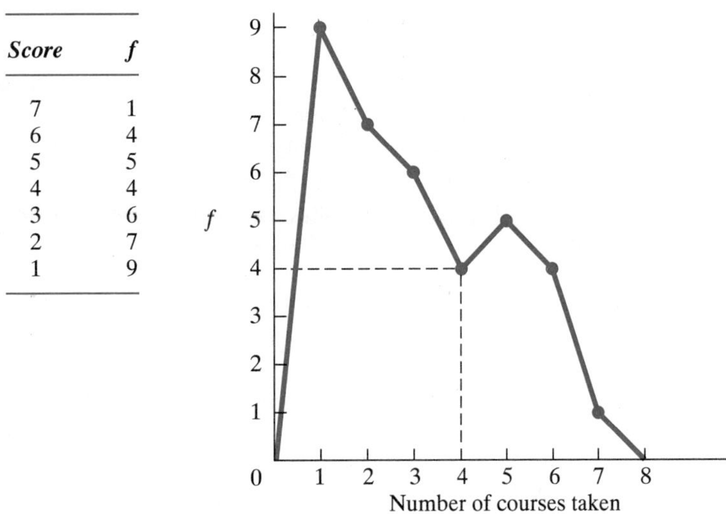

Score	*f*
7	1
6	4
5	5
4	4
3	6
2	7
1	9

> *REMEMBER* The height of the polygon above any score corresponds to the frequency of that score.

You will encounter bar graphs, histograms, and polygons often, so it is important to know the rules for constructing each. Remember that the type of graph you create depends on the scale of measurement used to measure the scores—the variable—plotted on the *X* axis. Then, consult Table 6.3.

TYPES OF SIMPLE FREQUENCY DISTRIBUTIONS

There are special names for common polygons having certain characteristic shapes. Each shape comes from an idealized frequency distribution of an infinite population of scores. By far the most important frequency distribution is the normal distribution. (This is the big one, folks.)

TABLE 6.3 When to Create a Bar Graph, Histogram, or Polygon

Always consider the scale of measurement used to measure the variable plotted on the X axis.

Graph	*When used*
Bar graph	With discrete scores, usually from a nominal or ordinal scale
Histogram	With a small range of continuous scores from an interval or ratio scale
Polygon	With a wide range of continuous scores from an interval or ratio scale

The Normal Distribution

Figure 6.4 shows the polygon of the ideal theoretical normal distribution. For reference, assume these are test scores from a population of college students. Although specific mathematical properties define such a polygon, in general it is a bell-shaped curve. But don't call it a bell curve! Call it a **normal curve** or a **normal distribution**, or say the scores are **normally distributed**.

To help you interpret the normal curve (or any polygon for that matter), imagine that you are flying in a helicopter over a parking lot. The *X* and *Y* axes are laid out on the ground, and an entire population is present. Those people who received a particular score stand in line in front of the marker for their score on the *X* axis. The lines of people are packed so tightly together that, from the air, all you see is a dark mass formed by the tops of many heads. If you painted a line that went behind the last person in line at each score, you would have the outline of the normal curve. This "parking lot view" is shown in Figure 6.5.

Thus, you can think of the normal curve as a solid geometric figure made up of all the participants at their different scores. The height of the curve above any score gives the corresponding *f* of the score on the *Y* axis, which is the same as counting the number of people in line at the score. Likewise, we might, for example, read off the frequencies on the *Y* axis for the scores between 30 and 35 and, by adding them together, obtain the *f* of scores between 30 and 35. We'd get the same answer by counting the number of people in line above each of these scores and adding them together. And, if we were to read off the frequencies on the *Y* axis for all scores and add them together, we would have the total number of scores (*N*). This is the same as counting the total number of people in the parking lot.

As you can see from Figures 6.4 and 6.5, the normal distribution has the following characteristics. The score with the highest frequency is the middle score between the highest and lowest scores (the longest line of people in the parking lot is at the score of 30). The normal curve is *symmetrical*, meaning that the left half below the middle score is a mirror image of the right half above the middle score. As we proceed away from the middle score toward the higher or lower scores, the frequencies at first decrease slightly. As we proceed farther from the middle score, the frequencies decrease more drastically, with the highest and lowest scores having relatively low frequency.

FIGURE 6.4 The Ideal Normal Curve

Scores farther above and below the middle scores occur with progressively lower frequencies.

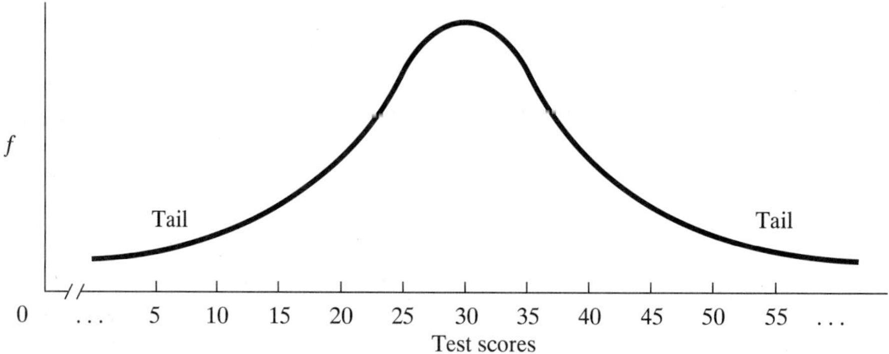

FIGURE 6.5 Parking Lot View of the Ideal Normal Curve

The height of the curve above any score reflects the number of people standing at that score.

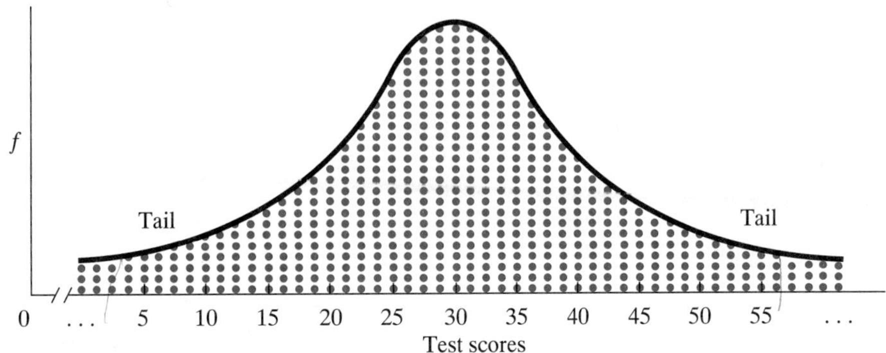

In statistics, the scores that are far above or below the middle score of any distribution are called the **extreme scores**. In a normal distribution, the extreme scores have a relatively low frequency. In the language of statistics, the far left and right portions of a normal curve containing the relatively low-frequency, extreme scores are called the **tails of the distribution**. In Figures 6.4 and 6.5, the tails are roughly below the score of 15 and above the score of 45.

The reason the normal distribution is important is because it is very common in statistics and psychological research: On most variables, most individuals score at or close to the middle score, with progressively fewer individuals scoring at more extreme higher and lower scores. Although real-world data never form a perfect normal curve, they usually come close enough for us to use the ideal normal curve as a "model"—it is our way of describing any approximately normal distribution.

Because the ideal normal curve represents a theoretical infinite population of scores, it has several characteristics that are not found with polygons created from actual data. First, with an infinite number of scores, we cannot label the *Y* axis with specific values of *f*. Simply remember that the higher the curve, the higher the frequency. Second, the theoretical normal curve is a smooth curved line. There are so many different whole-number and decimal scores that we do not need to connect the data points with straight lines. The individual data points form the solid curved line. Finally, regardless of how extreme a score might be, theoretically it will sometimes occur. Therefore, as we proceed into the tails of the distribution, there is never a frequency of zero, so the curve approaches, but never actually touches, the *X* axis.

Before you proceed, be sure that you are comfortable reading the normal curve. Can you see in Figure 6.4 that the most frequent scores are between 25 and 35? Do you see that a score of 15 has a relatively low frequency and a score of 45 has the same low frequency? Do you see that there are relatively few scores in the tail above 50 or in the tail below 10? Above all, you must be able to see this in your sleep:

> **On a normal distribution, the farther a score is from the central score, the less frequently the score occurs.**

Variations in the normal curve There are terms for describing variations in the normal curve. Consider the three curves in Figure 6.6. The word *kurtosis* refers to how flat or peaked—how fat or skinny—a distribution is. Curve A is generally what we think of as the ideal normal distribution, and it is called mesokurtic (*meso* means middle). Curve B is skinny relative to the ideal curve, and it is called leptokurtic (*lepto* means thin). In leptokurtic distributions, only a few scores around the middle score have a relatively high frequency. On the other hand, Curve C is fat relative to the ideal normal curve because there is a wide range of different scores around the middle score that each have a relatively high frequency. Such a curve is called platykurtic (*platy* means broad or flat).

These terms help us to describe various normal distributions. For statistical purposes, however, as long as we have a reasonably close approximation to the normal curve, these differences in shape are not all that critical.

Other Common Frequency Polygons

Not all variables form normal distributions. When a distribution does not fit the normal curve, it is a *nonnormal* distribution. The three most common nonnormal distributions are skewed, bimodal, and rectangular distributions.

Skewed distributions A **skewed distribution** is similar to a normal distribution except that it is not symmetrical: The left half of the polygon is not a mirror image of the right half. *A skewed distribution has only one pronounced tail.* As shown in Figure 6.7, a distribution may be either negatively skewed or positively skewed, and the skew is where the tail is.

A **negatively skewed distribution** contains extreme low scores that have low frequency, but does not contain extreme high scores that have low frequency. The left-hand polygon in Figure 6.7 shows an idealized negatively skewed distribution. This pattern might be found, for example, when measuring the running speed of professional football players. Most would tend to run at higher speeds, with a relatively few linemen lumbering in at the slower speeds. To remember that such a curve is negatively skewed, remember that the tail is over the lower scores, sloping toward zero, toward where *negative* scores would be.

On the other hand, a **positively skewed distribution** contains extreme high scores that have low frequency, but does not contain extreme low scores that have low frequency. The right-hand polygon in Figure 6.7 shows a positively skewed distribution. This pattern is common, for example, when measuring reaction time. Most frequently,

FIGURE 6.6 Variations of the Normal Curve

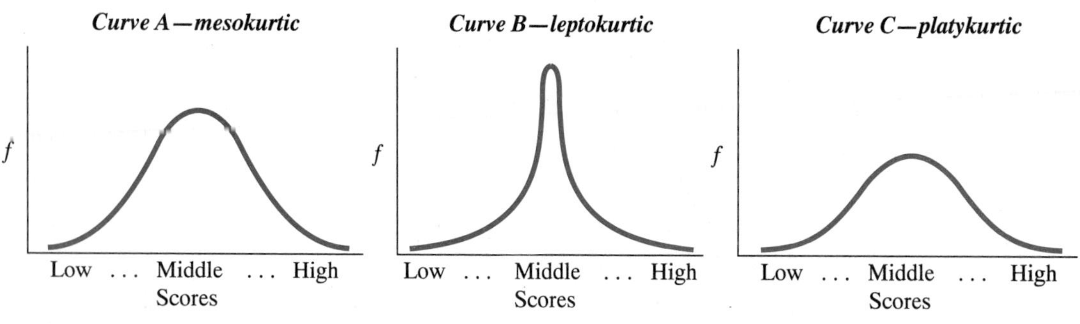

FIGURE 6.7 Idealized Skewed Distributions

The location of the distinctive tail determines whether the skew is positive or negative.

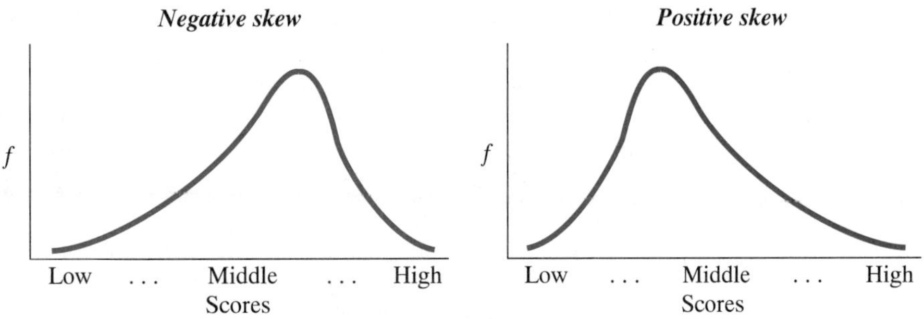

the scores will tend to be rather low (fast), but every once in while a participant "falls asleep at the switch," requiring a large amount of time and thus producing a high score. To remember that such a curve is positively skewed, remember that the tail is on the side away from zero, toward where the higher, *positive* scores are located.

> **REMEMBER** Whether a skewed distribution is negative or positive corresponds to whether the distinct tail is toward where the negative or positive scores would be.

Bimodal and rectangular distributions An idealized bimodal distribution is shown in the left-hand side of Figure 6.8. A **bimodal distribution** is a symmetrical distribution that contains two distinct humps. At the center of each hump is one score that occurs more frequently than the surrounding scores, and technically the center scores have the same frequency. Such a distribution would occur with test scores, for example, if most students scored at 60 or 80, with fewer students failing or scoring in the 70s or 90s.

The right-hand side of Figure 6.8 shows a rectangular distribution. A **rectangular distribution** is a symmetrical distribution shaped like a rectangle. There are no discernible tails because the extreme scores do not have relatively low frequencies. Such a distribution occurs whenever the frequency of all scores is the same.

FIGURE 6.8 Idealized Bimodal and Rectangular Distributions

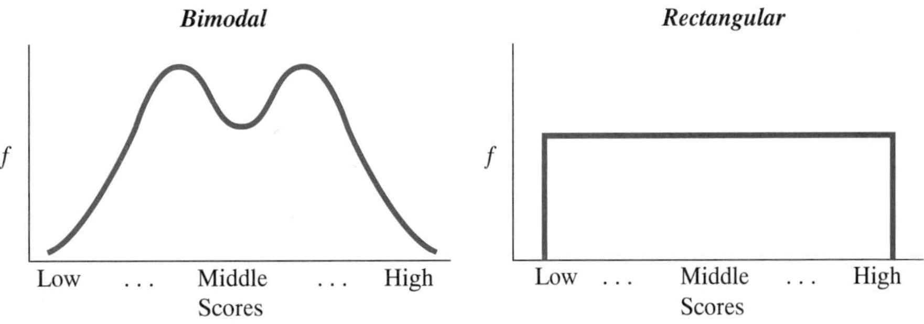

Real Data versus Ideal Distributions

If you're wondering why you need to know the names of the previous distributions, it's because we use descriptive statistics to describe the important characteristics of a sample of data. One important characteristic is the shape of the frequency distribution which the data form, so we apply the names of the previous distributions to sample data as well. Real data are never pretty, however, and the distribution in a sample will tend to be a bumpy, rough approximation of the smooth idealized curves we've discussed. For example, Figure 6.9 shows several frequency distributions of sample data, as well as the corresponding labels we might use. Notice we even apply these names to choppy histograms or bar graphs.

We generally assume that the sample represents a population that more closely fits the corresponding ideal polygon: We expect that if we measured the population, the additional scores and their corresponding frequencies would "fill in" the curve, smoothing it out to form the ideal curve.

We'll return to simple frequency distributions throughout the remainder of this book. However, counting each score's simple frequency is not the only thing we do in statistics.

CREATING RELATIVE FREQUENCY DISTRIBUTIONS

Another way to organize data is to transform each score's simple frequency into a relative frequency. **Relative frequency** is the proportion of N that is a score's simple fre-

FIGURE 6.9 Simple Frequency Distributions of Sample Data with Appropriate Labels

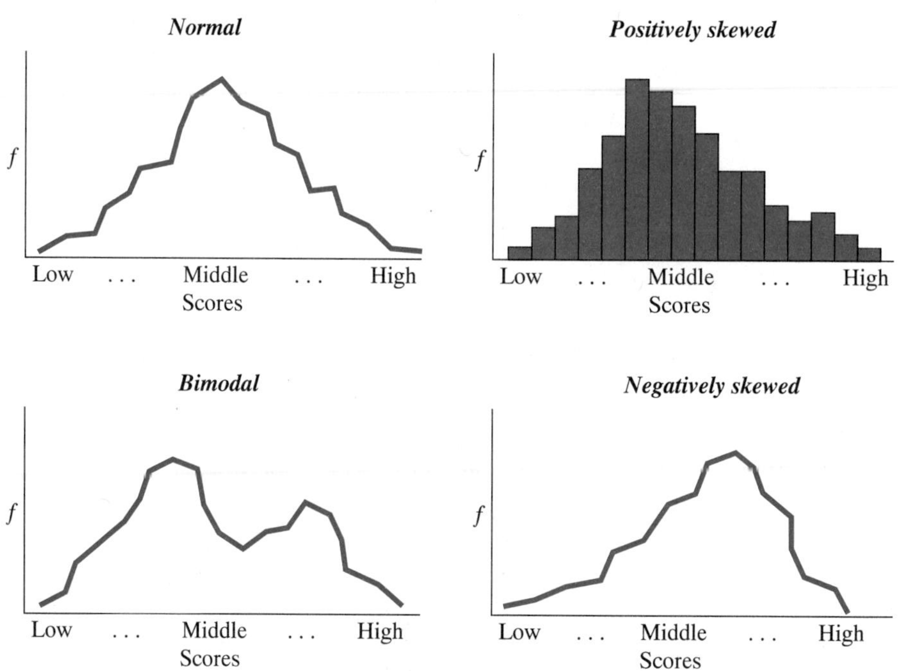

quency. While simple frequency is the *number* of times a score occurs in the data, relative frequency is the *proportion* of times the score occurs. (A proportion is a decimal number between 0 and 1 that indicates a fraction of the total.) The symbol for relative frequency is *rel. f.*

Why compute relative frequency? We are again asking how often certain scores occurred, but relative frequency is often easier to interpret than simple frequency. For example, the finding that a score has a simple frequency of 60 is difficult to interpret, because we have no frame of reference. However, we can easily interpret the finding that a score has a relative frequency of .20, because this means that the score's f is .20 of N; so, in other words, the score occurred .20 of the time in the sample.

Here is your first statistical formula.

THE FORMULA FOR COMPUTING A SCORE'S RELATIVE FREQUENCY IS

$$Rel.\, f = \frac{f}{N}$$

To compute the relative frequency of a score, divide the score's frequency by N. For example, say that out of 10 scores, the score of 7 has a simple frequency of 4. What is the relative frequency of 7? Using the formula, we have

$$Rel.\, f = \frac{f}{N} = \frac{4}{10} = .40$$

The score of 7 has a relative frequency of .40, meaning that 7 occurred .40 of the time in the sample.

Conversely, to compute the simple frequency that corresponds to a certain relative frequency, multiply the relative frequency times N. Thus, to find what simple frequency constitutes .4 out of an N of 10, multiply .4 times 10, and voilà, 4 is the simple frequency.

Presenting Relative Frequency in a Table

A distribution based on the relative frequency of the scores is called a **relative frequency distribution**. To create a relative frequency table, first create a simple frequency table as we did previously. Then add a third column labeled "*rel. f.*"

As an example, say that we asked a sample of mothers how many children they each have, obtaining the results shown in Table 6.4. To compute *rel. f*, we need N, the number of scores in the sample (here, $N = 20$). Then, the relative frequency for each score is the f for that score divided by N. The score of 1, for example, has $f = 4$, so its relative frequency is 4/20, or .20: In this sample, .20 of the participants have 1 child. And so on.

We can also use the table to determine the combined relative frequency of several scores by adding the individual frequencies together. For example, a score of 1 has a relative frequency of .20, and a score of 2 has a relative frequency of .50, so the relative frequency of 1 and 2 is .20 + .50, or .70: Mothers having 1 or 2 children compose .70 of this sample.

TABLE 6.4 Relative Frequency Distribution of Number of Children

The left-hand column identifies the score, the middle column shows each score's frequency, and the right-hand column shows each score's relative frequency.

Score	*f*	*rel. f*
6	1	.05
5	0	.00
4	2	.10
3	3	.15
2	10	.50
1	4	.20

You may find that working with relative frequency is easier if you transform it to a percentage. (Remember that, officially, relative frequency is a proportion.) By converting relative frequency to a percentage, you have the percent of the time that a score or scores occurred. To transform a proportion to percent, multiply the proportion times 100. Above, .20 of the scores were the score of 1, so (.20)(100) = 20% of the scores were 1. To transform a percent back to a relative frequency, divide the percent by 100.

To check your work, remember that the sum of all the relative frequencies in a distribution should equal 1.0: All scores together should constitute 1.0, or 100%, of the sample.

> ***REMEMBER*** Relative frequency indicates the proportion of time that a score occurred in the data.

Graphing a Relative Frequency Distribution

As with simple frequency, relative frequency is graphed as a bar graph if the scores are from a nominal or ordinal scale, and as a histogram or polygon if the scores are from an interval or ratio scale. Figure 6.10 presents examples using the data in Table 6.4. These graphs are drawn the same way as graphs of simple frequency except that here the *Y* axis reflects relative frequency, so it is labeled in increments between 0 and 1.0.

Finding Relative Frequency Using the Normal Curve

When data form a normal distribution, an extremely valuable procedure is to determine relative frequency directly from the normal curve. One reason for visualizing the normal curve as the outline of a parking lot full of people is so that you think of the normal curve as forming a solid geometric figure having an *area* underneath the curve. What we consider to be the total space occupied by people in the parking lot is, in statistical terms, the **total area under the curve**. This area represents the total frequency of all scores.

FIGURE 6.10 Examples of Relative Frequency Distributions (Using Data in Table 6.4)

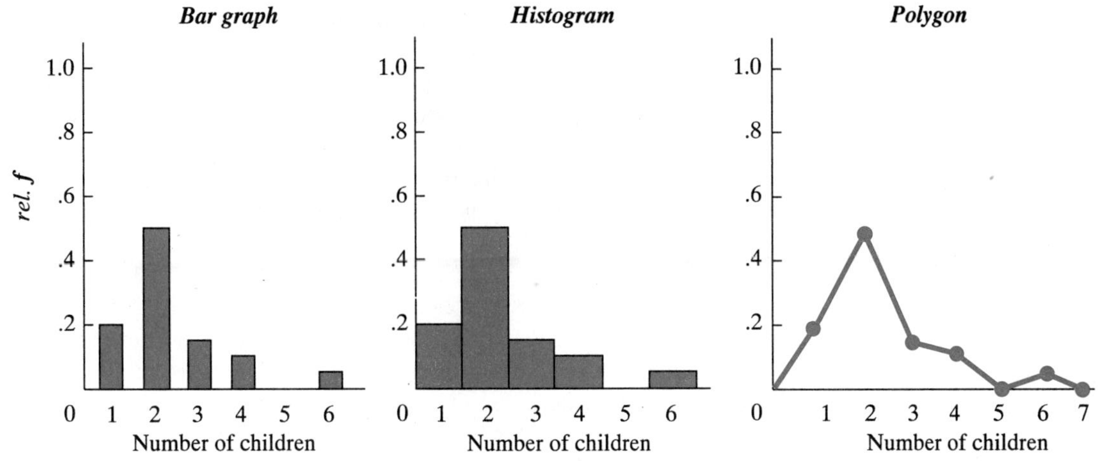

Bar graph *Histogram* *Polygon*

rel. f

Number of children Number of children Number of children

To find the relative frequency of scores in any portion of the distribution, we first find the area of that portion of the normal curve. We take a vertical slice of the polygon above the scores, and the area of this portion of the curve is the space occupied by the people obtaining those particular scores. We then compare this area to the total area, to determine the "proportion of the total area under the curve." Now, here's the important part:

> **The proportion of the total area under the normal curve at certain scores corresponds to the relative frequency of those scores.**

For example, Figure 6.11 shows a normal curve with the parking lot view. A vertical line is drawn through the middle score of 30, and so .50 of the parking lot is to the left of the line. Because the complete parking lot contains all participants, a slice that is .50 of it contains 50% of the participants. (We can ignore those relatively few people

FIGURE 6.11 Normal Curve Showing the Area Under the Normal Curve

The vertical line is through the middle score, so 50% of the distribution is to the left of the line and 50% is to the right of the line.

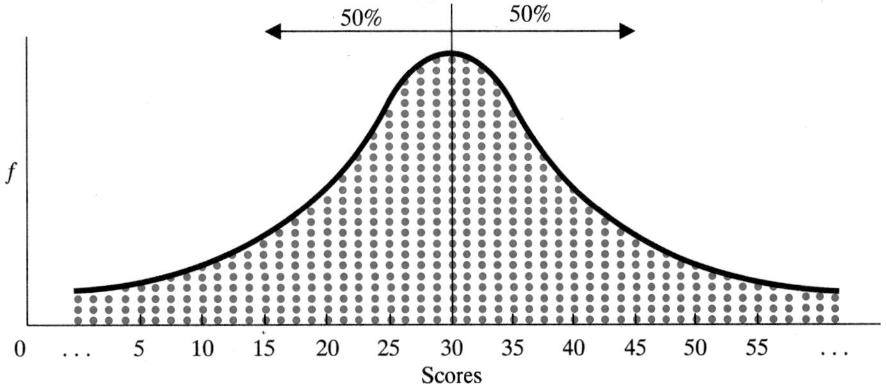

straddling the line.) People are standing in the left-hand part of the lot because they received scores of 29, 28, and so on, so in total, 50% of the participants obtained scores below 30. In other words, scores below 30 occurred 50% of the time. Thus, the scores below 30 have a relative frequency of .50.

In the same way, we can identify any proportion of the total area under the curve. Think of a proportion of the area under the curve as the proportion of the participants who are standing in that part of the parking lot. The proportion of people standing in that part of the parking lot is equal to the proportion of time that those scores occurred out of all the scores in the distribution. The proportion of time that certain scores occur out of all scores *is* relative frequency.

Of course, statisticians don't fly around in helicopters, eyeballing parking lots, but the same principle applies. Here's another example: Consider Figure 6.12. Say that by using a ruler and protractor, we determine that the total area under the curve—the entire polygon—occupies an area of 6 square inches on this page. This total area corresponds to the total of all frequencies for all scores, which is N. Say that we also determine that the shaded area under the curve between a score of 30 and 35 covers 2 square inches. This area corresponds to the frequencies of the scores found there. Therefore, the frequency of scores between 30 and 35 constitutes 2 out of the 6 square inches created by all scores, so these scores constitute two-sixths, or 33%, of the total distribution. Thus, the scores between 30 and 35 occur 33% of the time here, so they have a relative frequency of .33.

Because area corresponds to frequency, we would obtain the same answer if we used the formula for *rel. f.* First, we would add together the simple frequencies of every score between 30 and 35. Then, dividing the sum by N, we would again find that the relative frequency is .33. The advantage of using area under the curve, however, is that we can get the answer without knowing the N or the simple frequencies of any scores. In fact, whatever the variable might be, whatever the N might be, and whatever the frequency of each score is, we know that the area comprised by these scores is 33% of the total area, and that's all we need to know to determine their relative frequency. This is

FIGURE 6.12 Finding the Proportion of the Total Area Under the Curve

The complete curve occupies 6 square inches, with scores between 30 and 35 occupying 2 square inches.

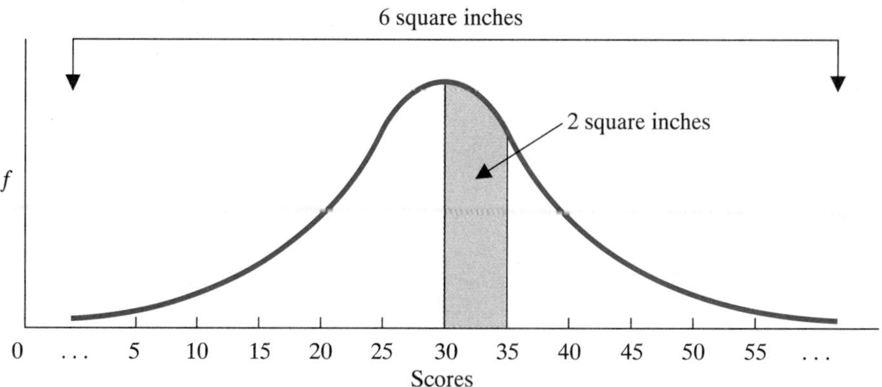

especially useful because, as we'll see in Chapter 9, statisticians have a system for finding the area under any part of the normal curve. This means we can easily determine the relative frequency for scores in any part of a normal distribution. (No, you won't need a ruler and a protractor.) Until then, simply remember this:

> ***REMEMBER*** Total area under the normal curve corresponds to the times that all scores occur, so a proportion of the total area corresponds to the proportion of time certain scores occur, which is their relative frequency.

CREATING CUMULATIVE FREQUENCY DISTRIBUTIONS

Another approach to summarizing data arises because sometimes we want to know not only how often a particular score occurred, but also its standing relative to other scores in the data. Knowing that 10 people received a score of 80 may not be as informative as knowing that 30 people scored above 80 or that 60 people scored below 80. When we seek such information, the convention is to count from *lower* scores, computing cumulative frequency. **Cumulative frequency** is the frequency of all scores at or below a particular score. The symbol for cumulative frequency is *cf.* The word *cumulative* implies accumulating: To compute a score's cumulative frequency, we accumulate, or add, the simple frequencies for scores below and at that score.

Presenting Cumulative Frequencies in a Table

To create a cumulative frequency table, first create a simple frequency table. Then add a column labeled "*cf.*" As an example, say that we've measured the ages of a sample of adolescents and then created Table 6.5.

TABLE 6.5 Cumulative Frequency Distribution of Age Scores

The left-hand column identifies the scores, the center column contains the simple frequency of each score, and the right-hand column contains the cumulative frequency of each score.

Score	*f*	*cf*
17	1	19
16	2	18
15	4	16
14	5	12
13	4	7
12	0	3
11	2	3
10	1	1

To compute cumulative frequency, begin with the *lowest* score. In Table 6.5, no one scored below 10 and 1 person scored 10, so we put 1 in the *cf* column opposite 10: One person is 10 years of age or younger. Next, there were two scores of 11. Adding this *f* to the *cf* for 10 gives the *cf* for 11: 3 participants are at or below the age of 11. Next, no one scored 12 and three children scored below 12, so the *cf* for 12 is also 3: There are 3 people at age 12 or below. In the same way, the *cf* of each score is the frequency for that score plus the cumulative frequency for the score immediately below it.

As a check on any cumulative frequency distribution you create, the *cf* for the highest score must equal *N*: All of the *N* participants obtained either the highest score or a score below it.

Graphing a Cumulative Frequency Distribution

Usually, it makes sense to compute cumulative frequency only for interval or ratio data, and the convention is always to create a *polygon*. Figure 6.13 shows the cumulative frequency polygon of the data from Table 6.5. In a cumulative frequency distribution, the *Y* axis is labeled "*cf*." On the *X* axis, as with previous polygons, include the next score *below* the lowest score in the data: 10 was the lowest age score, but 9 is included on the graph. Unlike previous polygons, however, do *not* include the next score above the highest score in the data. This is because we cannot tie the polygon back down to the *X* axis, because cumulative frequency never decreases. There cannot be fewer people having a score of 13 *or below* than received a score of 12 or below. Therefore, as the scores on the *X* axis increase, the height of the polygon must either remain constant or increase.

FIGURE 6.13 Cumulative Frequency Polygon Showing the Cumulative Frequencies of the Scores in Table 6.5.

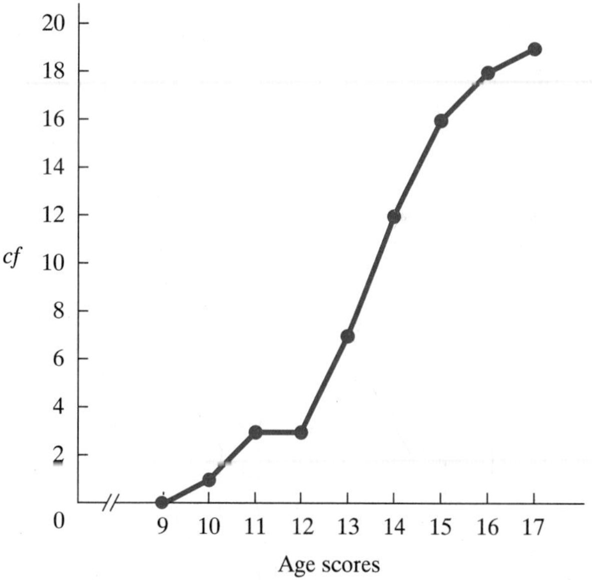

COMPUTING PERCENTILE

There is one other way to describe how often certain scores occurred in the data. Previously, we transformed simple frequency into relative frequency, because the proportion (or percent) of the time a score occurs is easier to interpret than the number of times it occurs. Likewise, cumulative frequency can be difficult to interpret because it is only the number of times scores at or below a score occur. Therefore, our final procedure is to transform cumulative frequency into a percent of the total. A **percentile** is the percent of all scores in the data that are at or below a certain score. While cumulative frequency indicates the *number* of participants who obtained a particular score or below, a percentile indicates the *percentage* of participants who obtained a particular score or below. Thus, for example, if a person scores at the 25th percentile, we know that 25% of all participants scored at or below that person's score.

When dealing with percentiles, you'll want either to determine the percentile for a particular score or to find the score that is at a particular percentile. There are several ways to compute these answers. A common way that we'll focus on is to use the area under the normal curve.

A percentile describes scores that are lower than a particular score, and on a normal curve, lower scores occur to the *left* of a particular score. Therefore, a percentile for a given score corresponds to the percent of the total curve that is to the *left* of the score. For example, on the distribution in Figure 6.14, 50% of the curve is to the left of the middle score of 30. Because scores to the left of 30 are below it, 50% of the distribution is below 30. (In the parking lot, 50% of the people are standing to the left of the line, and all of their scores are below 30.) Thus, the score of 30 is at the 50th percentile. Likewise, to find the percentile for a score of 20 in Figure 6.14, we would find the percent of the total curve that is to the left of 20. In Chapter 9, you'll learn how to determine this area, but for now, say that we find that 15% of the distribution is to the left of 20. Therefore, 20 is at the 15th percentile.

We can also work the other way to find the score at a given percentile. Say that we seek the score at the 85th percentile. We would measure over until 85% of the area under the curve is to the left of a certain point. If, as in Figure 6.14, the score of 45 is at that point, then 45 is at the 85th percentile.

Notice there's a slight change in the definition of percentile when using the normal curve. Technically, a percentile is the percent of scores *at* or below a certain score. However, the normal curve describes an infinite population, so we can treat those participants scoring *at* the score as a negligible portion of the total (remember we ignored those few people straddling the line). Then, a percentile is the percent of all scores that are *below* a certain score. Thus, in Figure 6.14, the score of 30 is at the 50th percentile, so this means that 50% of the scores are below 30 and 50% are above it.

When describing a *small* sample, however, we should *not* say that 50% of the scores are above the 50th percentile and 50% are below it. Those participants scoring *at* the 50th percentile might actually constitute a sizeable portion of a small sample—they might make up, say, 10% of the sample. Then, if we conclude that 50% are below, 50% are above, and 10% are at the score, we have the impossible total of 110% of the sample! Therefore, with small samples, percentile is defined as the percent of scores at or below a particular score.

FIGURE 6.14 Normal Distribution Showing the Area Under the Curve to the Left of Selected Scores

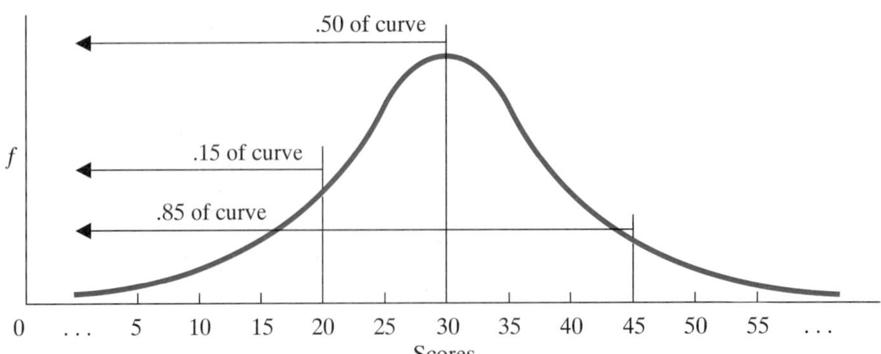

Using the normal curve to compute percentile is most accurate when you have a rather large sample or population that closely forms a normal distribution. If you have a small sample or a very nonnormal distribution, the easiest approach is to calculate percentiles using one of the statistical computer programs that are available. One other approach is to use the formulas presented in Appendix B.1.

A WORD ABOUT GROUPED FREQUENCY DISTRIBUTIONS

A rule of thumb in published research is that any of the previous frequency tables should contain between about 8 and 18 rows. Fewer than 8 scores tends to produce a small, often unnecessary, table, while more than 18 scores tends to produce a large, inefficient table. In the previous examples, we examined each score individually, creating **ungrouped distributions**. When there are too many scores to produce a manageable ungrouped distribution, we create a grouped distribution. In a **grouped distribution**, different scores are combined to form small groups, and then we report the total *f*, *rel. f*, or *cf* in each group.

For example, say that we measure how anxious 25 people each get when making a speech by giving them an anxiety questionnaire. Their scores span a wide range, so we create the grouped distribution shown in Table 6.6.

The group labeled 0–4 contains the scores 0, 1, 2, 3, and 4, while 5–9 contains scores 5 through 9, and so on. Each group is called a *class interval*, and the number of values spanned in each group is called the *interval size*. Here, we've used an interval size of 5, meaning that each group spans five scores.

To complete the table, find the *f* for each class interval by summing the frequencies for the individual scores in the interval. Thus, the scores between 0 and 4 have a total *f* of 7, while scores between 5 and 9 have an *f* of 4. Likewise, the relative frequency of scores between 0 and 4 is .28, while for 5–9, it is .16. The cumulative frequency for each interval indicates the number of scores that are at or below the *highest* score in the interval. Thus, there are 7 scores at 4 or below, with 11 scores at 9 or below. (For details on how to create and graph grouped distributions, consult Appendix B.1.)

TABLE 6.6 Grouped Distribution Showing *f*, *rel. f*, and *cf* for Each Group of Scores.

The left-hand column identifies the lowest and highest score in each class interval.

Scores	*f*	*rel. f*	*cf*
40–44	2	.08	25
35–39	2	.08	23
30–34	0	.00	21
25–29	3	.12	21
20–24	2	.08	18
15–19	4	.16	16
10–14	1	.04	12
5– 9	4	.16	11
0– 4	7	.28	7

PUTTING IT ALL TOGETHER

In this chapter, you've learned four procedures for describing how often certain scores in the data occur.

Simple frequency: the number of times a score occurs.

Relative frequency: the proportion of time a score occurs.

Cumulative frequency: the number of times scores at or below a score occur.

Percentile: the percent of the time scores at or below a score occur.

Regardless of whether you're summarizing an observational study or survey, the scores on a variable from a correlational study, or the dependent scores from an experiment, the procedure to use is simply the one that provides the most useful information. However, you may not automatically know which is the best technique. So, use the trial-and-error method: Try everything, and then choose the approach that most accurately summarizes the data for your purposes. Never be afraid to explore your data, using the techniques here or those you'll learn in future chapters.

As an aid to learning statistics, start drawing the normal curve. When you are working problems or taking tests, draw the curve and indicate where the low, middle, and high scores are located. Being able to see the problem will greatly simplify your task.

CHAPTER SUMMARY

1. A *transformation* converts one set of scores into a different set of scores. Transformations make scores easier to work with and make different kinds of scores comparable.

2. *Round off* the final answer in a calculation to two more decimal places than are in the original scores. If the digit in the next decimal place is equal to or greater than 5, round up; if the digit is less than 5, round down.

3. The symbol for the total number of scores in the data is N.

4. Which statistical procedure to use in a particular study depends on the *scale of measurement*: (1) In a *nominal scale*, numbers name or identify a quality or characteristic; (2) In an *ordinal scale*, numbers indicate rank order; (3) In an *interval scale*, numbers measure a specific amount, but with no true zero; and (4) In a *ratio scale*, numbers measure a specific amount, and 0 truly indicates zero amount.

5. In a *continuous* variable, decimals make sense. In a *discrete variable*, decimals do not make sense. A *dichotomous variable* is a discrete variable that has only two amounts or categories.

6. A *simple frequency distribution* shows the frequency with which each score occurred. The symbol for simple frequency is f.

7. When graphing simple frequency, if the variable involves a nominal or ordinal scale, create a *bar graph*. If the variable involves an interval or ratio scale and there are relatively few different scores, create a *histogram*. If there is a wide range of scores from an interval or ratio variable or there is more than one sample of scores, create a *polygon*.

8. In a *normal distribution* forming a *normal curve*, extreme high and low scores occur relatively infrequently, scores closer to the middle score occur more frequently, and the middle score occurs most frequently. The low-frequency, extreme low and extreme high scores are in the *tails* of the distribution.

9. A *negatively skewed distribution* is a nonsymmetrical distribution containing low-frequency, extreme low scores, but not containing low-frequency, extreme high scores. A *positively skewed distribution* is a nonsymmetrical distribution containing low-frequency, extreme high scores, but not containing low-frequency, extreme low scores.

10. A *bimodal distribution* is a symmetrical distribution containing two areas where there are relatively high-frequency scores. A *rectangular distribution* is a symmetrical distribution in which the extreme scores do not have relatively low frequencies.

11. The *relative frequency* of a score, symbolized by *rel. f*, is the proportion of time that the score occurred in a distribution.

12. The *proportion of the total area under the normal curve* above a score or scores equals the relative frequency of the score or scores.

13. The *cumulative frequency* of a score, symbolized by cf, is the frequency of all scores at or below the score.

14. *Percentile* indicates the percent of all scores at or below a given score. On the normal curve, the percentile of a score is the percent of the curve to the left of the score.

15. In an *ungrouped distribution*, individual scores are examined. In a *grouped distribution*, different scores are grouped together, and then the total f, *rel. f*, or cf for each group is computed.

KEY TERMS (with page references)

N *f* *rel. f* *cf*
bar graph (141)
bimodal distribution (147)
continuous scale (137)
cumulative frequency (153)
dichotomous variable (138)
discrete scale (138)
distribution (135)
extreme scores (145)
frequency (136)
frequency polygon (142)
histogram (142)
grouped distributions (156)
interval scale (137)
negatively skewed distribution (146)
nominal scale (136)
normal curve (144)
normal distribution (144)
ordinal scale (137)
percentile (155)
positively skewed distribution (146)
proportion of the area under the curve (151)
ratio scale (137)
rectangular distribution (147)
relative frequency (148)
relative frequency distribution (149)
simple frequency distribution (139)
skewed distribution (146)
tails of the distribution (145)
total area under the curve (150)
transformation (135)
ungrouped distributions (156)

REVIEW QUESTIONS

(Answers for odd-numbered questions and problems are provided in Appendix D.)

1. (a) What is a transformation? (b) Why do we transform data?
2. (a) To how many places do we round off a final answer? (b) What are the rules for rounding up or down when rounding to two decimal places?
3. What are the three things to consider when deciding on the particular statistical procedure you should employ?
4. (a) Define the four scales of measurement. (b) Rank order the four scales of measurement from most sensitive to least sensitive, and explain your answer.
5. What do each of the following mean? (a) *N* (b) *f* (c) *rel. f* (d) *cf*.
6. (a) What is the difference between a bar graph and a histogram? (b) With what kind of data is each used?
7. (a) What is the difference between a histogram and a polygon? (b) With what kind of data is each used?
8. What does it mean when a score is in a tail of the normal distribution?
9. What is the difference between (a) a skewed distribution and a normal distribution? (b) a bimodal distribution and a normal distribution? (c) a positively and negatively skewed distribution?
10. (a) What is a grouped frequency distribution? (b) To what score(s) does each *f* and *rel. f* in a grouped frequency table refer? (c) To what score(s) does each *cf* and percentile refer?
11. (a) Why must the *cf* for the highest score in a sample equal *N*? (b) Why must the sum of all *f*s in a sample equal *N*?

12. (a) How is percentile defined in a small sample? (b) How is percentile defined when calculated using the normal curve?

13. (a) What is the difference between a score's simple frequency and its relative frequency? (b) What is the difference between a score's cumulative frequency and its percentile?

14. What is the difference between how we use the proportion of the area under the normal curve to determine a score's relative frequency and how we use it to determine a score's percentile?

PRACTICE PROBLEMS

15. What type of frequency graph should you create when counting each of the following: (a) The males and females at a college? (b) The different body weights reported in a statewide survey? (c) The number of sergeants, lieutenants, captains, and majors in an army battalion? (d) The people falling into one of eight salary ranges?

16. The intermediate answers from some calculations based on whole-number scores are $X = 4.3467892$ and $Y = 3.3333$. We now want to find $X^2 + Y^2$. What values of X and Y do we use?

17. Round off the following numbers to two decimal places: (a) 13.7462 (b) 10.043 (c) 10.047 (d) .079 (e) 1.004.

18. A professor observes that a distribution of test scores is positively skewed. What does this indicate about the difficulty of the test?

19. Interpret each of the following: (a) In a small sample, you scored at the 35th percentile. (b) Your score has a *rel. f* of .40. (c) Your score is in the upper extreme scores of the normal curve. (d) Your score is in the left-hand tail of the normal curve. (e) Your score has a *cf* of 50. (f) From the normal curve, your score is at the 60th percentile.

20. In the chart below, identify the characteristics of each variable.

Variable	*Qualitative or quantitative*	*Continuous, discrete, or dichotomous*	*Type of measurement scale*
gender	________	________	________
academic major	________	________	________
amount of time before and after an event	________	________	________
restaurant ratings (best, next best, etc.)	________	________	________
speed	________	________	________
money in your pocket	________	________	________
position while standing in line	________	________	________
change in weight	________	________	________

21. From the data 1, 4, 5, 3, 2, 5, 7, 3, 4, 5, Poindexter created the following frequency table. What five things did he do wrong?

Score	*f*	*cf*
1	1	0
2	1	1
3	2	3
4	2	5
5	3	8
7	1	9
	$N = 6$	

22. Draw a normal curve and identify the approximate location of the following scores. (a) You have the most frequent score. (b) You have a low-frequency score, but the score is higher than most. (c) You have one of the lower scores, but it has a relatively high frequency. (d) Your score seldom occurred.

23. The following shows the distribution of final exam scores in a large introductory psychology class. The proportion of the total area under the curve is given for two segments.

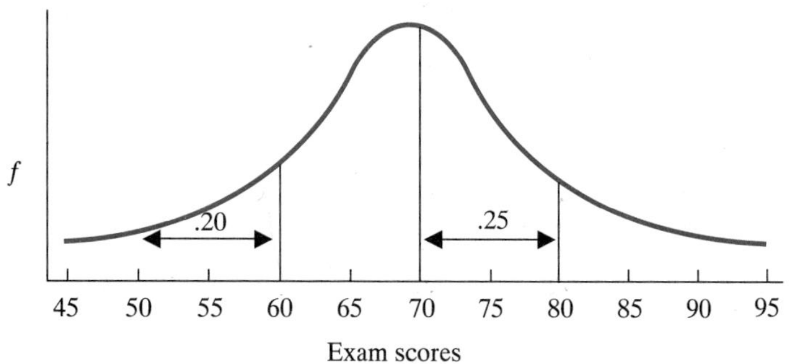

(a) Order the scores 45, 60, 70, 72, and 85 from most frequent to least frequent.
(b) What is the percentile of a score of 60?
(c) What proportion of the sample scored below 70?
(d) What proportion of students scored between 60 and 70?
(e) What proportion scored between 70 and 80?
(f) What is the percentile for a score of 80?

24. What is the advantage and disadvantage of creating a grouped frequency distribution?

25. Organize the scores below in a table showing simple frequency, relative frequency, and cumulative frequency.

49	52	47	52	52	47	49	47	50
51	50	49	50	50	50	53	51	49

26. Using the data in problem 25, draw (a) a simple frequency polygon; (b) a relative frequency histogram; (c) the appropriate graph showing the cumulative frequencies in these data.

27. Organize the scores below in a table showing simple frequency, cumulative frequency, and relative frequency.

16	11	13	12	11	16	12	16	15
16	11	13	16	12	11			

28. Using the data in question 27, draw the appropriate graph to show (a) simple frequency; (b) relative frequency; (c) cumulating frequency.

SUMMARY OF FORMULAS

1. *THE FORMULA FOR COMPUTING A SCORE'S RELATIVE FREQUENCY IS*

$$Rel.\ f = \frac{f}{N}$$

where f is the score's simple frequency and N is the number of scores in the sample.

7

Summarizing Research Using Measures of Central Tendency

Getting Started

To understand this chapter, recall the following:

- From Chapter 2, understand what a relationship is, what independent and dependent variables are, and what the logic of an experiment is.
- From Chapter 3, recall how systematic and unsystematic variables can weaken a relationship.
- From Chapter 4 recall the importance of consistent and "strong" manipulation of the independent variable, and consistency in measuring dependent scores.
- From Chapter 6, understand the four measurement scales and using the area under the curve to calculate percentile.

Your goals in this chapter are to learn:

- How measures of central tendency describe data.
- What the mean, median, and mode indicate and when each is appropriate.
- How a sample mean is used to describe both individual scores and the population of scores.
- What is meant by "deviations around the mean" and what they convey about each score's location and frequency in a normal distribution.
- How to interpret and graph the results of an experiment.

Recall that descriptive statistics describe the important characteristics of a set of data. The graphs and tables discussed in Chapter 6 are important because the type of distribution data form *is* one important characteristic. However, graphs and tables are not the most efficient way to summarize data. Instead, we compute individual numbers—*statistics*—that each communicate an important characteristic of the scores. This chapter discusses the important characteristic called central tendency. But first . . .

MORE STATISTICAL NOTATION

Recall that sample data are used to estimate the scores that are found in the population. So that we know when we're describing a sample and when we're describing a population, we use the following system. A number that describes a characteristic of a sample of scores is called a **statistic**, and the symbols for different statistics are letters from the English alphabet. A number that describes a characteristic of a population of scores is called a **parameter**, and the symbols for different parameters are letters from the Greek alphabet.

When calculating a statistic the formula is written so it can be applied to any data. Usually, the symbol X stands for each individual raw score in a study. When a formula says to do something to X, it means to do it to every score you're calling X.

A new symbol you'll see in conjunction with X is Σ, the Greek letter S, called sigma. Sigma means to sum, so ΣX is pronounced "**sum of X**" and literally means to add up all the X scores. For example, the sum of the scores 1, 2, and 3 is 6, so $\Sigma X = 6$. Notice that we do not care whether each X is a different score. If the scores are 4, 4, and 4, then $\Sigma X = 12$.

REMEMBER The symbol ΣX indicates to sum the X scores.

Finally, formulas often call for a series of mathematical steps that must be performed in the correct order. Sometimes, the steps are set apart by parentheses. Parentheses mean "the quantity," so always find the quantity inside the parentheses first and then perform the operations outside of the parentheses on that quantity. For example, $(2)(4 + 3)$ indicates to multiply 2 times "the quantity 4 plus 3." So first add, which gives $(2)(7)$, and then multiply to get 14.

Now, on to central tendency.

UNDERSTANDING CENTRAL TENDENCY

Measures of central tendency are important because they answer the most basic question about data: Are the scores generally high scores, generally low scores, or what? Without them, it is impossible to understand any large batch of scores. With them, we have one number that summarizes the sample or population, so that we know generally how the group performed. This also then provides a basis for determining how any individual performed relative to the group. Thus, in all research, the first step is always to shrink the data into one summary score, called a *measure of central tendency*.

FIGURE 7.1 Locations of Individual Scores on the Variable of Height

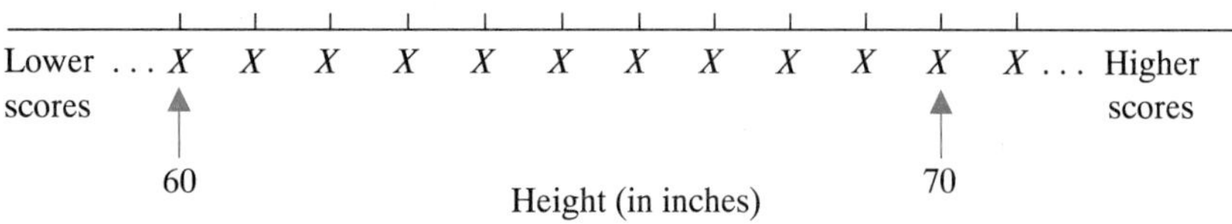

To understand central tendency, you need to first alter your perspective of what a score indicates. Think of a score as indicating a *location* on a variable. For example, if I am 70 inches tall, don't think of my score as indicating that I have 70 inches of height. Instead, think of me as being located on the variable of height at the point marked 70 inches. Think of any variable as an infinite continuum—a straight line—with each score indicating an individual's location on that line. Look at Figure 7.1: My score locates me at the address labeled 70 inches. If my brother is 60 inches tall, then he is located at the point marked 60 on the height variable. The idea is not so much that he is 10 inches shorter than I am, but rather that we are separated by a *distance* of 10 units—in this case, 10 "inch" units. In statistics, *scores are locations*, and the difference between any two scores is the distance between them.

From this perspective, a frequency polygon shows the location of all scores in a sample or population. For example, Figure 7.2 shows the polygons for two samples of height scores, one consisting of low scores and the other consisting of higher scores. In the "parking lot view" of the normal curve described in Chapter 6, participants' scores determine *where* they stand. A high score puts them on the right side of the distribution, a low score puts them on the left side, and a middle score puts them in the crowd in the middle. Further, when two distributions contain different scores, then the *distributions* have different locations on the variable.

Now you can see that whenever we ask, "Are the scores generally high scores or generally low scores?" we are actually asking, "*Where* on the variable is the distribution located?" A **measure of central tendency** is a statistic that summarizes the location of a distribution on a variable. Listen to its name: It is the score that indicates where the "center" of the distribution "tends" to be located. Thus, it is the score *around* where most of the scores are located and provides an "address" for the distribution. So, in Sample A in Figure 7.2, the most frequent scores are in the neighborhood of 59, 60, and 61 inches, so the measure of central tendency will indicate that the distribution is located around 60 inches. In Sample B, the scores tend to center around 70 inches.

Notice that the above example illustrates how to use descriptive statistics: From them we get an idea of what's in the data and we can *envision* the important aspects of the distribution *without* looking at every individual score. If a researcher said only that one normal distribution is centered at 60 and the other is centered around 70, you could envision the information presented in Figure 7.2. Although we lose some detail, we do answer the question of whether the scores in each sample are generally high or low scores. You'll see other statistics that add to this mental picture of a distribution, but measures of central tendency are at the core of summarizing a distribution.

REMEMBER The first step in summarizing any set of data is to compute the appropriate measure of central tendency.

FIGURE 7.2 Two Sample Polygons on the Variable of Height

Each polygon indicates the locations of the scores and their frequencies.

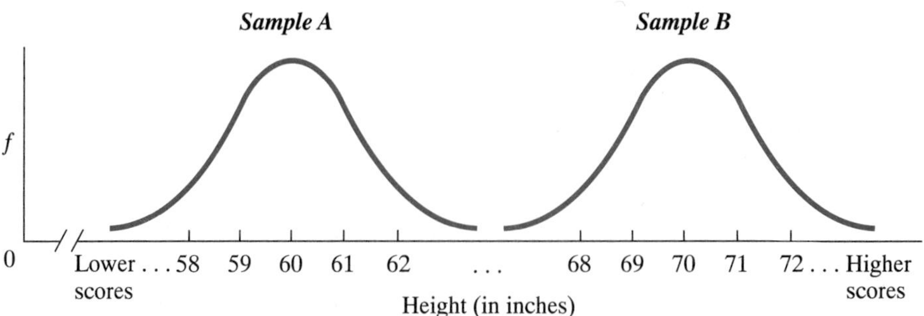

There are three common measures of central tendency and so the trick is to compute the correct one so that you *accurately* envision where most scores in the data are actually located. Which measure of central tendency to calculate depends on two factors:

1. The scale of measurement used, so that the summary makes sense, given the nature of the scores.
2. The shape of the frequency distribution the scores produce, so that the measure of central tendency accurately summarizes the distribution.

The following sections discuss the three measures of central tendency called the mode, the median, and the mean. Then, with this background, we'll see how measures of central tendency are used in research.

THE MODE

One way to describe where *most* of the scores are located in a distribution is to find the one score that occurs most. The most frequently occurring score is called the **modal score** or simply the **mode**. (There is no accepted symbol or abbreviation for the mode.) As an example, consider the scores 2, 3, 3, 4, 4, 4, 4, 5, 5, and 6. The score of 4 is the mode, because it occurs more frequently than any other score in the sample. You can see how the mode summarizes this distribution from Figure 7.3. Most of the scores *are* at or around 4. Also, notice that the distribution is roughly a normal curve, with the highest point over the mode. When a polygon has one hump, such as on a normal curve, the distribution is called **unimodal**, indicating that one score qualifies as the mode.

There may not always be a single mode in a set of data. For example, consider the scores: 2, 3, 4, 5, 5, 5, 6, 7, 8, 9, 9, 9, 10, 11, and 12. Here, 5 and 9 are tied for the most frequently occurring score. This sample is plotted in Figure 7.4. In Chapter 6, such a distribution was called **bimodal**, because it has two modes. Describing this distribution as bimodal and identifying the two modes summarizes where most of the scores tend to be located, because most scores are either around 5 or around 9.

FIGURE 7.3 A Unimodal Distribution

The vertical line marks the highest point on the distribution, thus indicating the most frequent score, which is the mode.

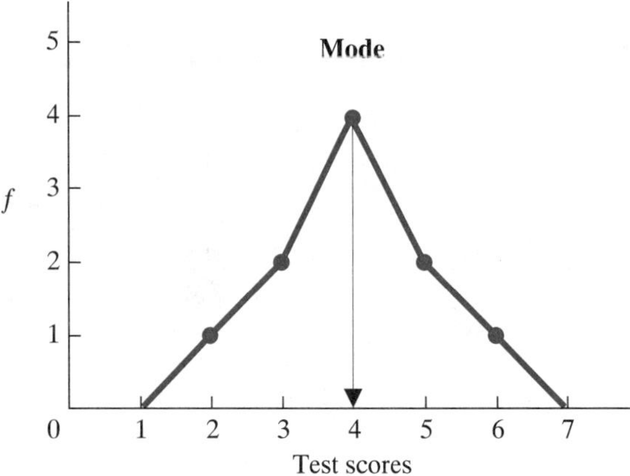

FIGURE 7.4 A Bimodal Distribution

Each vertical line marks one of the two equally high points on the distribution, indicating the location of one of the two modes.

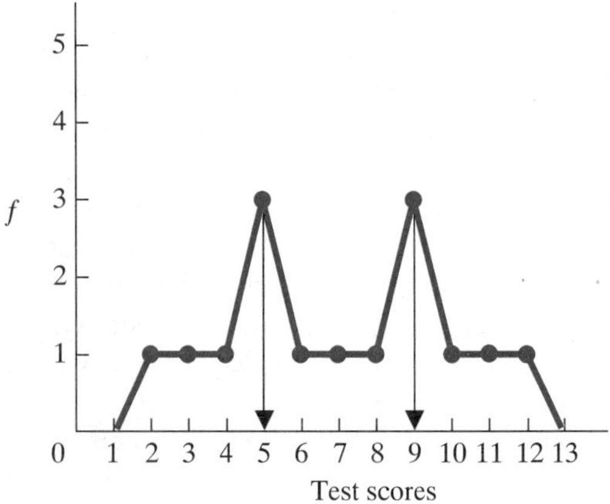

Uses of the Mode

The mode is typically used to describe scores from a nominal scale of measurement (when participants are classified using a qualitative variable). For example, say that we asked participants their favorite flavor of ice cream, and counting the number of responses in each category produced the bar graph in Figure 7.5. It makes sense to summarize such data by indicating the most frequently occurring category. Reporting that the modal response was a preference for category 5, "Goopy Chocolate," is very informative.

FIGURE 7.5 Bar Graph Showing the Frequencies of Preferred Ice Cream Flavors

The mode is flavor 5, "Goopy Chocolate."

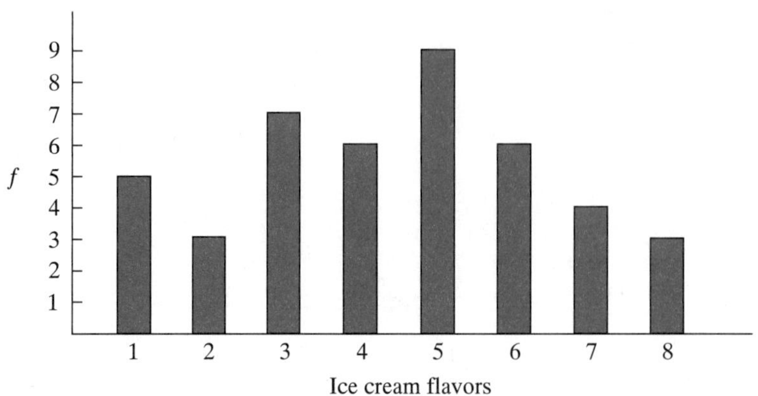

> *REMEMBER* The mode is the most frequently occurring score in the data, and is usually used to summarize nominal scores.

However, there are two potential problems with the mode. First, depending on the distribution, several scores may be tied for the highest frequency, and identifying many modes does not summarize the data. In the most extreme case, we might obtain a rectangular distribution with scores such as 4, 4, 5, 5, 6, 6, 7, 7. Either there is no mode, or all scores are the mode. Either way, the mode should not be determined.

A second problem is that the mode does not take into account any scores other than the most frequent score, so it ignores much of the information in the data. An *accurate* summary should reflect all scores so that we can accurately envision the entire distribution. For example, the mode is 7 in the skewed distribution containing the scores: 7, 7, 7, 20, 20, 21, 22, 22, 23, 24. The problem is that this gives you the wrong idea about the scores, because the majority of the data is not located *around* 7 (most scores are up there between 20 and 24). Thus, the mode may or may not accurately summarize where most scores in a distribution are located. Because of these problems, with ordinal, interval, or ratio scores we can usually compute a better measure of central tendency.

THE MEDIAN

Often, a better measure of central tendency is the median. The **median** is simply another name for the score at the 50th percentile. Recall that 50% of a distribution is at or below the 50th percentile. Thus, if the median is 10, 50% of the scores are at or below 10. The median is typically a better measure of central tendency than the mode because (1) only one score can be the median, and (2) the median will usually be around where most of the distribution is located. The symbol for the median is its abbreviation, *Mdn*.

Recall that, with a large sample or population, the 50th percentile is the score that separates the lower 50% of the distribution from the upper 50% of the distribution. For example, look at Graph A of Figure 7.6.

Because 50% of the area under the curve is to the left of the line, 50% of the scores are below the score at the line. Therefore, the score at the line is the 50th percentile, so that score is the median. In fact, the median is the score below which .50 of the area of *any* shaped polygon is located. For example, in the skewed distribution in Graph B of Figure 7.6, .50 of the area under the curve is to the left of the line, so 50% of the scores are to the left of the line, and so the score at the line is the median.

There are several ways to calculate the median. When scores form a perfect normal distribution as above, the median is also the most frequent score, so it always equals the mode. However, when data are not normally distributed, there is no easy way to determine where .50 of the area under the curve is located. However, the median can be *estimated* using the following system. Arrange the scores in order from lowest to highest. If there is an odd number of scores, the score in the middle position is the approximate median. For example, for the nine scores 1, 2, 3, 3, 4, 7, 9, 10, 11, the score in the middle position is the fifth score, so the median is the score of 4. If N is an even number, the average of the two scores in the middle is the approximate median. For example, for the ten scores 3, 8, 11, 11, 12, 13, 24, 24, 35, 46, the middle scores are at position 5 (the score of 12) and position 6 (the score of 13). The average of 12 and 13 is 12.5, so the median is approximately 12.5.

To calculate the median precisely, use the formula discussed in Part B.1 of Appendix B.1 to find the score at the 50th percentile. (Most computer programs employ this formula, providing the easiest solution.)

Uses of the Median

The median is not used to describe nominal data. For example, to say that 50% of a survey preferred "Goopy Chocolate" *or below* is confusing. On the other hand, the median is often the preferred measure of central tendency when the data are ordinal (rank-

FIGURE 7.6 Location of the Median in a Normal Distribution (A) and in a Skewed Distribution (B)

The vertical line indicates the location of the median, with one-half of the distribution on each side of it.

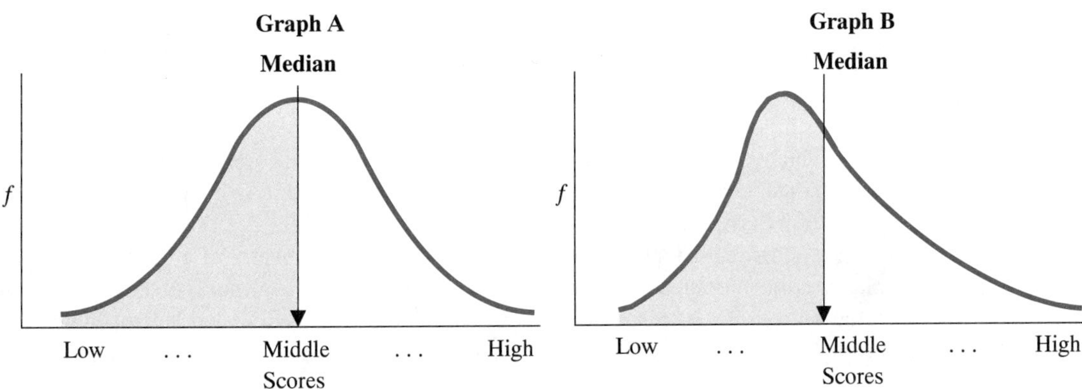

ordered) scores. For example, say that a group of students ranked how well a college professor teaches. If the professor's median ranking was 3, we know that 50% of the students rated the professor as number 1, 2, or 3. Also, as we shall see, the median is appropriate when interval or ratio scores form a very skewed distribution.

> ***REMEMBER*** The median (*Mdn*) is the score at the 50th percentile, and is used to summarize ordinal or highly skewed interval or ratio scores.

Computing the median still ignores some information in the data, however, because it reflects only the frequency of scores in the lower 50% of the distribution. It does not consider the mathematical values of these scores or the scores in the upper 50%. Therefore, the median is usually not our first choice for describing the central tendency of most distributions.

THE MEAN

The most common measure of central tendency in psychological research is the mean score, or simply the mean. The **mean** is the score located at the exact mathematical center of a distribution. The mean is what most people call the average and it is computed the same way you compute an average: Add up all the scores and then divide by the number of scores you added. Unlike the mode or the median, the mean includes every score, so it does not ignore any information in the data.

Let's first discuss the *sample* mean. Sample statistics use symbols from the English alphabet, and the symbol for a sample mean is $\overline{X}$. It is pronounced "the sample mean" (not "bar *X*," which sounds like the name of a ranch!). Get in the habit of thinking of $\overline{X}$ as a quantity itself, so that you understand statements such as "the size of $\overline{X}$" or "this $\overline{X}$ is larger than that $\overline{X}$."

To compute $\overline{X}$, recall that the symbol meaning "add up all the scores" is ΣX, and the symbol for the number of scores is *N*. Then,

THE FORMULA FOR COMPUTING A SAMPLE MEAN IS

$$\overline{X} = \frac{\Sigma X}{N}$$

As an example, take the scores 3, 4, 6, and 7. Adding the scores produces $\Sigma X = 20$, and N is 4. Thus, $\overline{X} = 20/4 = 5$. Saying that the mean of these scores is 5 indicates that the mathematical center of this distribution is at the score of 5. (As here, the center of the distribution may be a score that does not actually occur in the data.)

What is the mathematical center of a distribution? The center of a distribution is its balance point. Visualize a polygon as a teeter-totter on a playground. A score's location on the teeter-totter corresponds to its location on the *X* axis. The left side of Figure 7.7 shows the scores 3, 4, 6, and 7 sitting on the teeter-totter. The mean of 5 is the point that

FIGURE 7.7 The Mean as the Balance Point of a Distribution

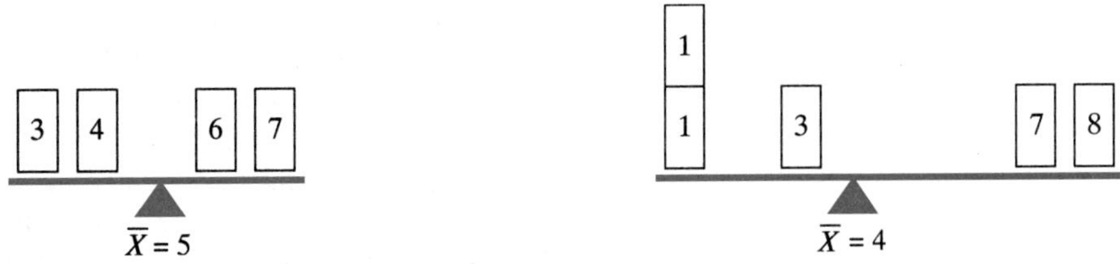

balances the distribution. The right side of Figure 7.7 shows how the mean is the balance point even when all scores do not have the same frequency (the score of 1 has an f of 2). Here the mean is 4, and it balances the distribution.

Uses of the Mean

Compute the mean whenever getting the "average" makes sense. Therefore, do not use the mean when describing nominal data. For example, say we are studying political affiliation, assigning a 1 to each Democrat, a 2 to Republicans and so on. It is meaningless to say that the average political affiliation was 2.3. The mode or percentages would be more informative. Likewise, the median is best when describing ordinal data (because it's strange to say, for example, that, on average, the runners in a race came in 5.7th). This leaves the mean to describe interval or ratio data, especially when the variable is continuous (when decimals make sense).

In addition, however, you must consider the shape of the distribution. The goal is to identify the point around which most of the scores tend to be located. The mean is simply the mathematical center of a distribution. Therefore, the mathematical center of the distribution must also be the point around which *most* scores are located. This will be the case when the distribution is *symmetrical* and *unimodal.* For example, say that we study the intelligence of cats by timing how long it takes them to escape from a maze. The data are 1, 2, 3, 3, 4, 4, 4, 5, 5, 6, and 7 minutes, which form the roughly normal distribution shown in Figure 7.8. The mean is appropriate here because it *is* that point around which most of the scores are located: Most of the cats did take around 4 minutes to escape.

The ultimate symmetrical distribution is the normal distribution, so always compute the mean to summarize a normal or approximately normal distribution. Notably, on a perfect normal distribution, all three measures of central tendency are located at the same score: In Figure 7.8, the score of 4 is the mean, it is the median, and it is the mode. If a distribution is only roughly normal, then the mean, median, and mode will be close to the same score. You might think that in such cases, any of the measures of central tendency would be good enough. Not true. Because the mean uses all of the information in the data, the mean is the preferred measure of central tendency.

> *REMEMBER* Describe the central tendency of a normal distribution of interval or ratio scores by computing the mean.

The mean does *not*, however, accurately describe a highly skewed distribution. For example, say that the previous cat subjects produced the escape-time scores of 1, 2, 2,

2, 3, and 14, forming the positively skewed distribution shown in Figure 7.9. Without the 14, the scores would form a symmetrical distribution with a mean of 2. However, because of that one extreme score of 14, the mean is pulled away from the low scores so that it can balance the distribution. Picture the distribution as a teeter-totter with a bunch of little guys—1s, 2s, and 3s—sitting at one end, trying to balance the big guy—the 14—sitting way at the other end. The balance point must now be located at 4. The problem is that a measure of central tendency is supposed to describe where most of the scores tend to be located. But in Figure 7.9, most scores are not around 4. As this illustrates, the mean is where the mathematical center is, but in a skewed distribution, the mathematical center is *not* where most of the scores are located.

The solution is to use the median to summarize very skewed distributions. Figure 7.10 shows the relative positions of the mean, median, and mode in such distributions. When the distribution is positively skewed, the mean is larger than the median. When the distribution is negatively skewed, the mean is less than the median. In both cases,

FIGURE 7.8 **Location of the Mean on a Distribution Formed by the Escape Times 1, 2, 3, 3, 4, 4, 4, 5, 5, 6, and 7**

The vertical line indicates the location of the mean score, which is the balance point of the distribution.

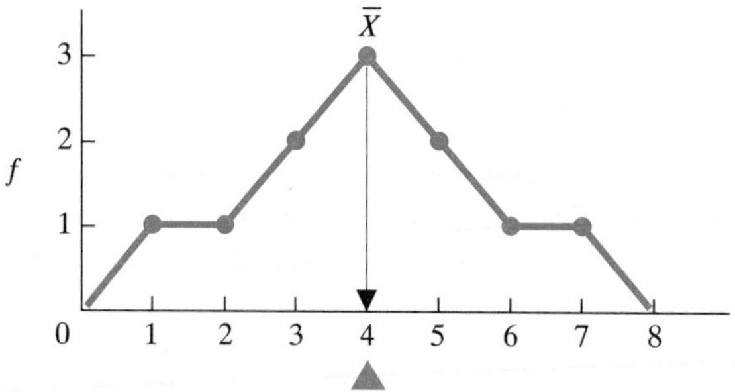

FIGURE 7.9 **Location of the Mean on a Skewed Distribution Formed by the Time Scores 1, 2, 2, 2, 3, 14**

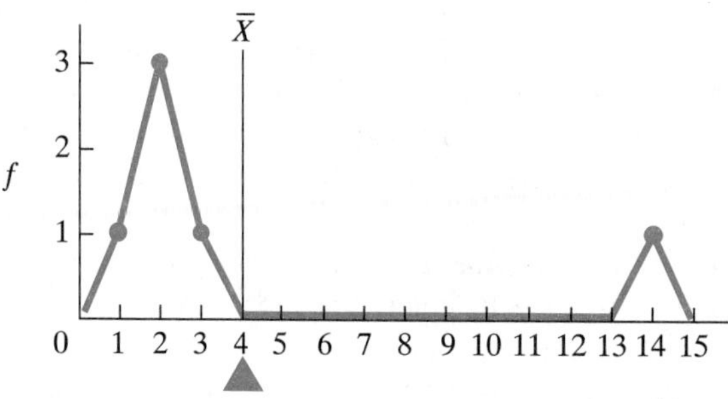

FIGURE 7.10 Measures of Central Tendency for Skewed Distributions

The vertical lines show the relative positions of the mean, median, and mode.

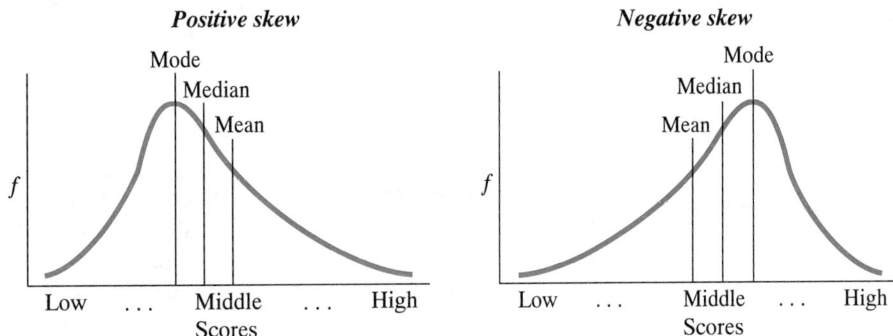

the mean is pulled toward an extreme tail and does not accurately summarize the distribution. Likewise, the mode tends to be toward the side away from the extreme tail, and most of the distribution is not centered here either. However, the median is not thrown off by extreme scores occurring in only one tail, because it does not take into account the actual values of the scores. Thus, of the three measures, the median most accurately reflects *around* where most of the scores tend to be located in a skewed distribution.

It is for the above reasons that the government uses the median to summarize such skewed distributions as that of yearly income or the price of houses. For example, the median income in the United States is about $39,000 a year. But there are a relatively small number of corporate executives, movie stars, professional athletes, and such who make millions! Averaging in these extreme high incomes would produce a mean income over $50,000. However, most incomes are not at or around $50,000, so the median is a better summary of the distribution.

Believe it or not, we've now covered measures of central tendency. In summary:

1. Use the mode with nominal (categorical) data or with a distinctly bimodal distribution of any type of scores.
2. Use the median with ordinal (ranked) scores or with a very skewed distribution of interval/ratio scores.
3. Use the mean with a symmetrical, unimodal distribution of interval/ratio scores.

Most often in psychological research, data are summarized using the mean. This is because most often psychologists measure variables using interval or ratio scores that, *simply because of the way nature works*, form at least a roughly normal distribution. Because the mean is used so extensively, we'll delve further into its characteristics and uses in the following sections.

Deviations Around the Mean

The mean forms the basis for several other procedures we'll see later, so it's important to understand why the mean is the balance point of a distribution. The mean is the mathematical center or balance point of a distribution because, *in total*, the mean is just as far from the scores above it as it is from the scores below it. The distance separating a score from the mean is called the score's **deviation**, indicating the amount the score deviates from the mean. A score's deviation is equal to the score minus the mean. In symbols, a deviation is the quantity $(X - \overline{X})$, which translates as "*X* minus the mean." Thus, if the sample mean is 47, a score of 50 deviates by +3, because 50 − 47 is +3. A score of 40 deviates from the mean of 47 by −7, because 40 − 47 = −7.

> *REMEMBER* Always subtract the mean *from* the raw score when computing a score's deviation.

When we determine the deviations of all scores in a sample, we find the *deviations around the mean.* Then the total distance all scores are from the mean is the **sum of the deviations around the mean**, which is the sum of all differences between the scores and the mean. And here's why the mean is the center or balance point of any distribution:

The sum of the deviations around the mean always equals zero.

For example, the scores 3, 4, 6, and 7 have a mean of 5. The upper portion of Table 7.1 shows how to compute the deviations around the mean for these scores. The lower portion of the table shows the deviations for a skewed distribution that has a mean of 4. In each sample, the sum of the deviations is zero. In fact, for *any* distribution of *any* shape, the sum of the deviations around the mean will always be zero. This is because the sum of the positive deviations always equals the sum of the negative deviations, so the sum of all deviations is zero.

TABLE 7.1 Computing Deviations Around the Mean for a Symmetrical and a Skewed Distribution

The mean is subtracted from each score, resulting in the score's deviation.

Symmetrical distribution

Score	*minus*	*Mean score*	*equals*	*Deviation*
3	−	5	=	−2
4	−	5	=	−1
6	−	5	=	+1
7	−	5	=	+2
			Sum =	0

Skewed distribution

Score	*minus*	*Mean score*	*equals*	*Deviation*
1	−	4	=	−3
2	−	4	=	−2
2	−	4	=	−2
2	−	4	=	−2
3	−	4	=	−1
14	−	4	=	+10
			Sum =	0

Many of the formulas we'll encounter involve something like the sum of the deviations around the mean. The code for finding the sum of the deviations around the mean is $\Sigma(X - \overline{X})$. Always start inside parentheses, so first find the deviation for each score: $(X - \overline{X})$. The Σ indicates to then sum these deviations. Thus, as in the upper portion of Table 7.1, $\Sigma(X - \overline{X}) = -2 + -1 + 1 + 2$, which equals zero.

USING THE MEAN IN RESEARCH

Because the sum of the deviations equals zero, the mean score is literally "more or less" the score that all participants obtained: Individual scores may be higher or lower than the mean, but those that are higher balance out with those that are lower. Because of this, the mean is a very useful tool. As you'll see in the following sections, a sample mean is used in three ways: To predict scores of individuals, to describe a score's relative location within a distribution, and to draw inferences about the population.

Using the Sample Mean to Predict Scores

The mean score is our best estimate—guess—about the score that any individual obtains in a sample. Because the mean is the central score, it is the *typical* score in the distribution. This implies that if all scores in the sample were the same, they would all be the mean score. Therefore, when in doubt, we treat all scores as if they are the mean score. For example, if your friends have a B average in college, they may not always get Bs, but you operate as if they do. If asked what you think they received in a particular course, you'd estimate B. For every other course, you'd also estimate B. Likewise, if the class average on an exam was 80, the best estimate for every student in the class is 80.

Notice that above you are using the mean to *predict* the score for an individual who is in the sample. We can also use the mean to predict any additional scores that are *not* in the original sample. Because the mean is typical of the scores already observed in a particular situation, it is the best prediction of any other scores that might be observed in that situation. Thus, your best guess is that your friends will continue to be B students, so for any future course you'd predict they'll get a B. Likewise, because the mean is the typical score of our participants, we assume that it also typifies the score of any similar individuals who might have participated. Thus, we'd predict that, like those students who averaged 80 on the exam, any similar students who missed the exam would have scored 80.

> ***REMEMBER*** Use the sample mean to predict the scores in the sample, or to predict additional scores we'd expect to find in the sample.

Of course, these predictions will sometimes be wrong. The amount of error in a prediction is the difference between what we say someone gets and what he or she actually gets. In symbols, this is the difference between someone's X and the $\overline{X}$ we predicted, or $(X - \overline{X})$. We've already seen that $(X - \overline{X})$ is a score's deviation, so expand your perspective here: A score's deviation is also the amount of error we have when using the mean to predict that score.

The reason we use the mean to predict scores is that then the *total* prediction error is the sum of these deviations, $\Sigma(X - \overline{X})$, and this *always* equals zero. For example, the exam scores of 70, 75, 85, and 90 have a $\overline{X}$ of 80. One student, Quasimodo, scored the 70. We would predict he scored 80, so we'd be wrong by -10. But another student, Attila, scored the 90. By estimating an 80 for him, we'd be off by $+10$. In the same way, our errors will cancel out so that the total error is zero. Likewise, we expect the differences between the mean and the scores that other students *would* have obtained to be about the same as the differences between the mean and the scores that the students in the sample *did* obtain. Thus, using the mean as the predicted score for anyone else should also result in a total prediction error equal to zero.

Predicting any single score other than the mean produces a total error *greater* than 0. If, for example, above we predict a score of 75 or 85 for everyone, the sum of the deviations would be $+20$ or -20, respectively. In statistics, a total prediction error of zero is best because it means that, *over the long run*, we overestimate by the same amount that we underestimate. (There is a joke about two statisticians shooting targets. One hits 1 foot to the left of the target, and the other hits 1 foot to the right. "Congratulations," one says. "We got it!") If we cannot perfectly describe every score, then we want our errors—the over- and underestimates—to cancel out to zero. Only the mean provides that capability.

Recognize, however, that although the *total* error in predictions will equal zero, any individual prediction may be off by a country mile. Later chapters will discuss how to reduce these errors in prediction. For now, simply remember that unless you have additional information about the scores, the mean is the best score to use when predicting or describing scores. This is because the over- and underestimates from all such predictions will cancel out to zero.

Using the Sample Mean to Describe a Score's Location

Another use of the mean is as the basis for describing the location of an individual score in a sample. A problem for science is that usually we do not know how to evaluate an individual score. If, for example, you score a 6 on a creativity test, we don't know whether *in nature*, your score is good, bad, or indifferent. Usually, the best we can do is to evaluate any raw score relative to the rest of the sample. Because the mean summarizes the sample, we examine a raw score by computing the amount it deviates from the mean. Then, the deviation score communicates the raw score's location relative to the mean, and indirectly, relative to the rest of the distribution.

For example, say that the creativity test produced the raw scores 1, 2, 3, 3, 4, 4, 4, 5, 5, 6, and 7, which form the approximately normal distribution in Figure 7.11. The X axis here is labeled using each creativity score, and underneath, the corresponding deviation, computed as $X - \overline{X}$. Each deviation consists of a number and a sign. A positive deviation indicates that the score is *greater* than the mean, and located to the *right* of the mean on the distribution. A negative deviation indicates that the score is *less* than, and thus falls to the *left* of, the mean. The size of the deviation (regardless of its sign) indicates the *distance* the score lies from the mean. A deviation of 0 indicates that the score is equal to and at the mean. The larger the deviation, the farther the score is above or below the mean.

Deviation scores in a normal distribution also communicate the *frequencies* of the corresponding raw scores. The larger a deviation (whether positive or negative), the

FIGURE 7.11 Frequency Polygon Showing Deviations from the Mean

The first row under the X axis indicates the original creativity scores, and the second row indicates the amounts the raw scores deviate from the mean.

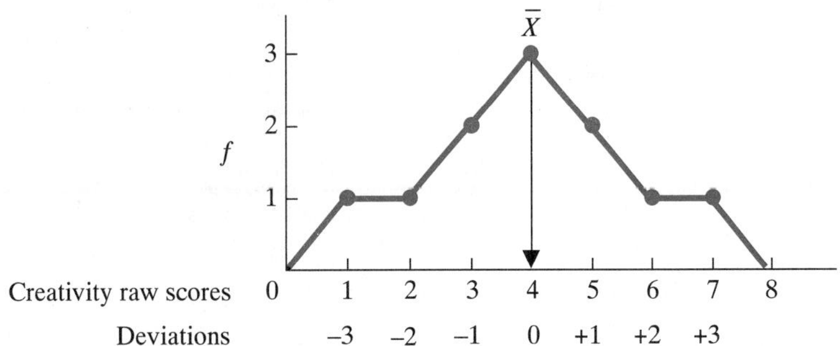

farther into the tail the corresponding raw score lies, and so the less frequently the raw score occurs. Also, the larger a deviation, the less frequently the *deviation* occurs. Above, the raw score of 7 produces the deviation of +3, and not only is 7 an extreme score that occurs only once, its deviation is also extreme and occurs only once. In fact, the frequency of any score's deviation will equal the frequency of that score, so as in Figure 7.11, whether we label the *X* axis using raw scores or deviations, we have the same frequency polygon.

The advantage of using deviation scores, however, comes when interpreting data, because deviation scores have a built-in frame of reference (the mean.) For example, by knowing that your creativity score of 6 transforms to a deviation score of +2, you can interpret your score *relative* to the rest of the distribution. By envisioning Figure 7.11, you know that a positive deviation of +2 indicates that you are above average (which with creativity is good), that you are to the right of and therefore above the 50th percentile (which is also good), and that you are out there in the direction of the less common scores, where the most creative people are (and that's good too). Conversely, if these scores reflected the number of blunders on a test, you'd know you were out there among those who made the highest number of blunders (and that's not so good). But either way, at least you'd have a better idea of how to interpret—*make sense of*—the score, and that is the purpose of statistics.

> ***REMEMBER*** A deviation score indicates a raw score's location and frequency relative to the rest of the distribution.

We'll elaborate on deviations around the mean in later chapters. For now, remember that on the normal curve, the larger the deviation (whether positive or negative), the farther the raw score is from the mean and thus the less frequently the score and its deviation occur.

Using the Sample Mean to Describe the Population Mean

The final use of a sample mean is to estimate the corresponding population mean. Recall that ultimately we seek to describe the entire population of scores we would find in a given situation. Populations are unwieldy, so we also summarize them using measures of central tendency. Here is what we want to know: If we examined the population, around which score would most of the scores be located?

Because we usually have interval or ratio scores that form at least an approximately normal distribution, we usually describe the population using the mean. The mean of a population is a parameter, symbolized by the Greek letter μ (pronounced "mew"). Thus, to indicate that the population mean is 143, we'd say $\mu = 143$. A mean is a mean, however, so a population mean has the same characteristics as a sample mean:

1. μ is the arithmetic average of all scores in the population.
2. μ is the score at the mathematical center of the distribution, so it is the "typical" score.
3. The sum of the deviations around μ, or $\Sigma(X - \mu)$, is zero.

Previously, these characteristics made the mean the best score to use when predicting any individual's score in a sample. For the same reasons, μ is the best score to use when predicting any individual's score in the population.

How do we determine the value of μ? If we know all of the scores in the population, then we compute μ using the same formula used to compute $\overline{X}$: $\mu = \Sigma X/N$. Usually, however, a population is infinitely large, so we cannot compute μ. Instead, we estimate μ based on the mean of a random sample. If, for example, a sample's mean in a particular situation is 99, then our best guess is that the population μ in that situation would also be 99. We make such an inference because it is a population with a mean of 99 that is most likely to produce a sample with a mean of 99. That is, we are very likely to obtain a sample of participants who score around 99 when most individuals in the population score around 99. On the other hand, we are very unlikely to obtain an entire sample that scores around 99 if, for example, the population mean is actually 4,000. Here, few participants should score around 99, but many should score around 4,000. Thus, wherever most scores in a sample are located should be where most scores in the population are located, so a random sample mean should be a good estimate of the population μ (assuming the sample is representative).

> ***REMEMBER*** The sample mean is used when describing or predicting the scores in a sample or in the corresponding population.

SUMMARIZING RESEARCH USING CENTRAL TENDENCY

Now you can understand how measures of central tendency are used in research. In descriptive research, we compute the mean any time we have a sample of normally distributed scores (or compute other measures of central tendency when appropriate). Thus, we might compute the mean number of times participants exhibit a particular behavior in an observational study, or compute the modal response in a survey. Based on such sample results, we can describe the typical participant and predict the scores of other individuals, including those of the entire population.

We perform similar steps when summarizing an experiment. For example, say that in studying memory, we predict that people will make more mistakes when recalling a long list of words than when recalling a short list. We conduct an overly simplistic experiment involving three conditions. In one condition participants read a list of 5 words and then recall it. In another condition, participants read a 10-item list and recall it, and in a third condition, they read a 15-item list and recall it. If the predicted relationship exists, then as the independent variable of list-length increases, scores on the dependent variable of recall errors also will tend to increase.

Say we obtain scores like those in Table 7.2. It appears there is the predicted relationship here, because a higher set of error scores tends to be associated with each condition. Most experiments involve many more participants, however, and with many scores it is often difficult to detect a relationship by looking at the raw scores. But that's what measures of central tendency are for: to summarize the scores and simplify the relationship. Thus, your first step is *always* to compute a measure of central tendency for the scores in each condition of an experiment.

Summarizing a Relationship

The measure of central tendency to compute in an experiment depends on the characteristics of the *dependent variable.* Therefore, compute the mean, median, or mode, depending upon (1) the scale of measurement used to measure the dependent variable, and (2) for interval or ratio scores, the shape of the distribution they form.

> *REMEMBER* The measure of central tendency used in an experiment is determined by the type of *dependent* scores.

In determining the shape of the distribution, consider how the scores are assumed to be distributed in the *population.* Obtain this information from the research literature, seeing how other researchers treat such scores. In our memory experiment, *recall errors* is a ratio variable that forms an approximately normal distribution, so we compute the mean for each condition (computing the mean in each column in Table 7.2). Here they are:

Condition 1: 5-item list	*Condition 2: 10-item list*	*Condition 3: 15-item list*
$\overline{X} = 3$	$\overline{X} = 6$	$\overline{X} = 9$

TABLE 7.2 Numbers of Errors Made by Participants when Recalling a 5-, 10-, or 15-Item List

Independent variable: Length of list

Condition 1: 5-item list	*Condition 2: 10-item list*	*Condition 3: 15-item list*
3	6	9
4	5	11
2	7	7

To interpret the means in an experiment (or in any study), simply envision the typical distribution of scores that would produce each mean. In our data, for example, a normal distribution producing a mean of 3 would contain scores above and below 3, with most of the scores close to 3. And so on for each condition, so that you envision something like the raw scores shown back in Table 7.2. Thus, recalling a 5-item list resulted in one distribution of scores located around 3, but recalling a 10-item list produced a different distribution located around 6, and recalling a 15-item list produced still another distribution located around 9. Thus, these means indicate that a relationship is present, because as the independent variable changes (from 5- to 10- to 15-item lists), the scores on the dependent variable also tend to change (from around 3, to around 6, to around 9, respectively).

Recall that one way to describe the relationship in an experiment is to say that "the scores on the dependent variable change *as a function of* changes in the independent variable." Because changes in the means reflect changes in the underlying raw scores, we also say "the *mean* dependent score changes as a function of changes in the independent variable." We can also say that this experiment "worked" because it demonstrates that list length is a variable that literally makes a "difference" in recall scores. Researchers often communicate that they have found a relationship by saying that they have found a difference (between the means). If no difference is found, then they have not found a relationship. Recognize, however, that not all of the means must differ for a relationship to be present. For example, we might find that only the mean (and raw scores) in the 5-item condition differs from the mean (and scores) in the 15-item condition. We still see a relationship if, *at least sometimes*, the dependent scores tend to change as the conditions of the independent variable change.

> *REMEMBER* A relationship is present when the mean scores on the dependent variable change as a function of changes in the independent variable.

The above logic also applies to the median or mode. For example, say that we study the dependent variable of political party affiliation, to see if it changes with a person's year in college. Political parties are categories involving nominal scores, so the mode is the appropriate measure of central tendency. We might see that freshmen most often claim to be Republican, but the mode for sophomores is Democrat, for juniors Socialist, and for seniors Communist. These data reflect a relationship because, as college level changes, political affiliation tends to change. Or, say we learn that the median income for freshmen is lower than the median income for sophomores, which is lower than that for juniors or seniors. This tells us that the location of the corresponding distribution on the variable of income is different for each class, so we know that the income "scores" of individuals must be changing as their year in college changes.

Finally, recall that for a reliable study, we often test participants over multiple trials within each condition. To summarize the trials, we often compute a measure of central tendency for each participant. For example, we would have had a better memory experiment by testing each participant's recall on several lists in a condition. Here, each person's "score" would actually be the *mean* number of errors he or she made over all lists in the condition. Then, we would again compute an overall mean for each condition, computing the mean of the participants' means. (That's right: In each condition, we compute the average of participants' individual average scores.)

Graphing the Results of an Experiment

Recall that on a graph, the "given" variable is placed on the *X* axis, and in an experiment, the given variable is the independent variable. Therefore, always place the independent variable on the *X* axis and the dependent variable on the *Y* axis. Instead of plotting the raw dependent scores on the *Y* axis, however, plot the measure of central tendency. Thus, each data point reflects either the mean, median, or modal dependent score for a condition of the independent variable.

The measure of central tendency to compute depends on the characteristics of the *dependent* variable. However, then you must select the type of graph to create. The type of graph to choose depends on the characteristics of the *independent* variable. Your choice is between creating a line graph or a bar graph.

Line graphs When the independent variable is an interval or ratio variable, create a line graph. In a **line graph**, plot individual data points and then connect adjacent points with straight lines. In our memory experiment, list length is a ratio variable, so we create the line graph shown on the left in Figure 7.12. Notice the label on the *Y* axis is *mean* recall errors, and the *X* axis is labeled with the conditions of the independent variable. Then, a data point above the 5-item condition is placed opposite the mean of 3 errors, a data point above the 10-item condition is at 6 errors, and a data point above the 15-item condition is at 9 errors.

We connect the adjacent data points with straight lines because we assume that, with interval or ratio data, the relationship *continues* in a straight line between the points shown on the *X* axis. Thus, if there had been a 6-item list, we assume its mean score would fall on the line connecting the means for the 5- and 10-item lists.

The line graph conveys the same information as the sample means did previously. For each mean, we envision the distribution that would produce it. As shown on the right in Figure 7.12, we envision a sample of raw scores and their corresponding data

FIGURE 7.12 Line Graphs Showing (A) The Relationship for Mean Errors in Recall as a Function of List Length and (B) The Data Points We Envision Around Each Mean

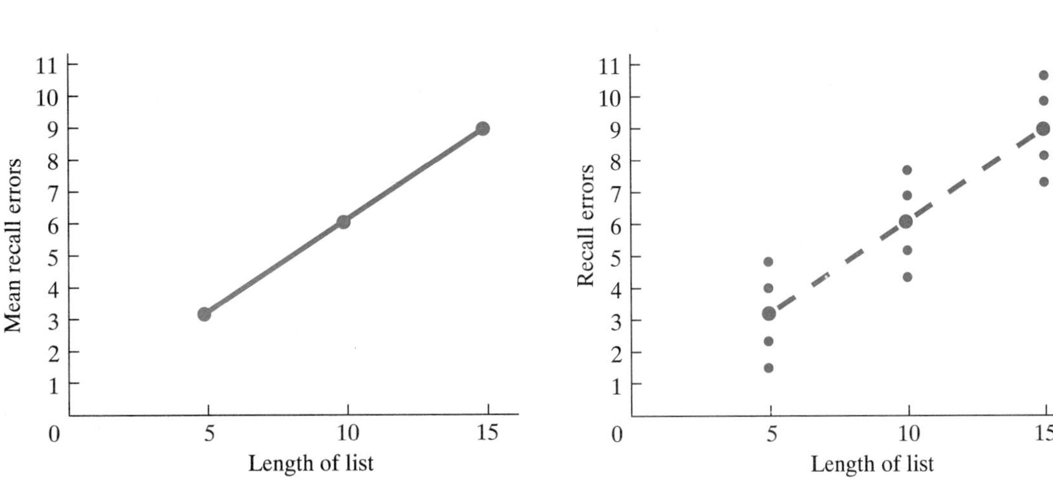

points that would occur *around*—above and below—the mean's data point. The different vertical locations of the means indicate that they have different values on the Y axis, and thus that there are different Y scores in each condition.

Notice that you can easily spot such a relationship, because the changing positions of the means on the Y axis produce a line graph that is *not* horizontal. On the other hand, say that each condition had produced a mean of 5. As shown on the left in Figure 7.13, this results in a horizontal line, which indicates that, as list length changes, the mean stays the same. This implies that (as on the right of the figure) the individual scores stay the same, regardless of the condition. Because the dependent scores stay the same when the independent variable changes, no relationship is present.

> *REMEMBER* On a graph, if the summary data points form a line that is not horizontal, then the individual Y scores are changing as the X scores change, and a relationship is present.

Bar graphs Create a **bar graph** when the independent variable is a nominal or ordinal variable. The rule here is the same as in Chapter 6: Create a bar graph *whenever* the X axis reflects a nominal or ordinal variable. Each bar is centered over a condition on the X axis, and the height of the bar corresponds to the mean (or median or mode) for the condition.

For example, say that in another experiment we compared the recall errors of psychology majors, English majors, and physics majors. Here, the independent variable of college major is a nominal variable, so we'd have the bar graph shown in Figure 7.14. This too shows a relationship: The tops of the bars do not form a horizontal line, so there are different means and thus different scores in each condition. The bars communicate that we arbitrarily placed psychology to the left of English. Therefore, if we inserted the additional category of sociology between psychology and English, we could not assume that the mean for sociology majors would fall on a line running between the means for psychology and English majors.

> *REMEMBER* The scale of measurement of the dependent variable determines the measure of central tendency to calculate; the scale of the independent variable determines the type of graph to create.

FIGURE 7.13 Line Graphs Showing (A) No Relationship for Mean Errors in Recall as a Function of List Length and (B) The Data Points We Envision Around Each Mean

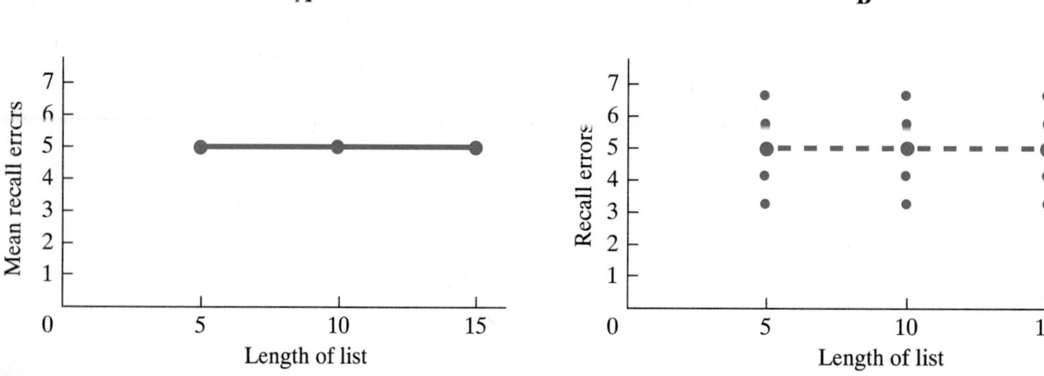

FIGURE 7.14 Bar Graphs Showing Mean Errors in Recall as a Function of College Major

The height of each bar corresponds to the mean score for the condition.

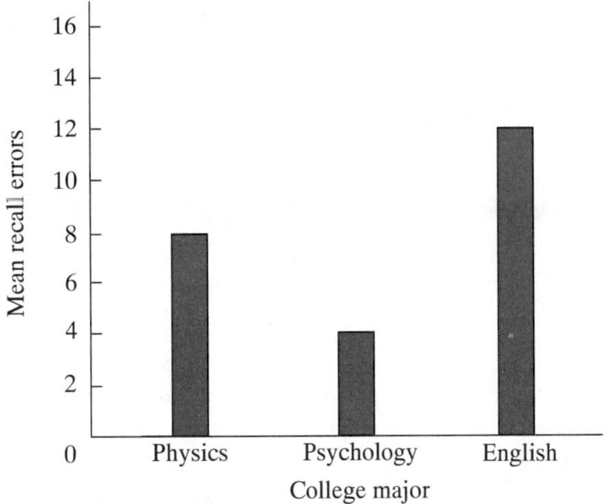

Inferring the Relationship in the Population

In the original memory experiment, we predicted that recall errors would increase as list length increased, and the sample data confirmed this. However, the big question remains: Is this how nature works? Do longer lists produce more errors for everyone in the population?

Recall that before making *any* inferences about the population, the sample data must pass our inferential procedures. If so, we use each sample mean to estimate the population mean that would be found for that condition. The mean for the 5-item condition was 3, so we infer that if the population were to recall a 5-item list, the mean in the population would be 3. In essence, we expect that everyone in this situation makes around 3 errors. Similarly, we infer that if the population recalled a 10-item list, μ would equal the sample mean of 6, and if the population recalled a 15-item list, μ would be 9.

We conceptualize the above populations in the following way. We've assumed that recall errors are normally distributed in the population, and we've estimated the location of the distribution of dependent scores for each condition. Thus, we envision the population of recall errors we would expect for each condition as shown in Figure 7.15. (Because these are frequency distributions, we plot the dependent scores of recall errors on the X axis.) Because the distributions have different values of μ, we can see the relationship that exists in the population: As the conditions of the independent variable change, the scores on the dependent variable tend to change so that there is a different population of scores for each condition. Essentially, for every 5 items in a list, everyone's score tends to increase by about 3 errors, and so the distribution slides 3 units to the right each time, going from around 3 to around 6 to around 9. (The overlap among the distributions simply shows that some people in one condition make the same number of errors as other people in an adjacent condition.)

Remember that the population of scores reflects everyone's behavior. If, as an independent variable changes, *everyone's* behavior tends to change, then we have learned

FIGURE 7.15 Locations of Populations of Error Scores as a Function of List Length

Each distribution contains the scores we would expect to find if the population were tested under each condition.

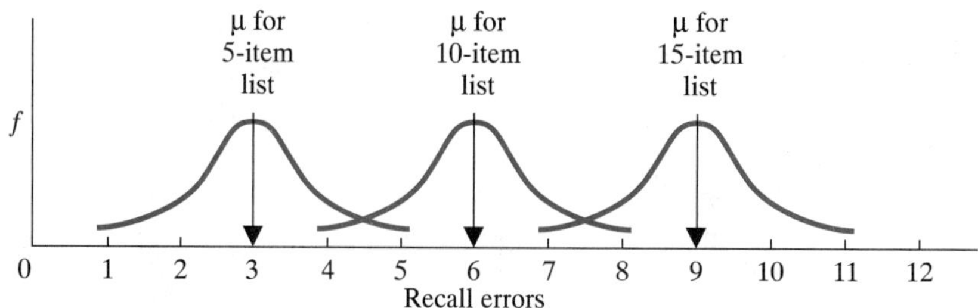

about a law of nature involving that behavior. Above, everyone's recall behavior tends to change as list length changes, so we have evidence of how human memory generally works in this situation. Now, we interpret the results "psychologically," generalizing to the theories, models, and hypothetical constructs that originally led to the study. At the same time, we try to understand and explain the relationship, answering such questions as why scores increase at this rate, what cognitive or physiological mechanism is responsible for such scores, and so on. And of course, don't forget that our confidence in these conclusions must be tempered by the usual concerns about construct and content validity, reliable and sensitive measurements, potential biases from demand characteristics, possible confoundings, and so on. Along these lines, its time to introduce an important consideration when designing a study, called power.

DESIGNING A POWERFUL EXPERIMENT

Previous chapters have touched on the idea that poor controls, individual differences, inconsistent manipulations, and unreliability all influence the dependent scores, so that we see a weaker, less consistent relationship than would otherwise be present. This is a serious problem, because any conclusion about a hypothesis hinges on first being convinced by the sample data that a relationship exists. Because of these flaws, however, it is possible to find an unconvincing relationship in the sample data, even when the variables are related in nature. For example, say that in the memory experiment, we obtained these unconvincing results:

5-item list	*10-item list*	*15-item list*
$\overline{X} = 3.11$	$\overline{X} = 3.12$	$\overline{X} = 3.13$

These means barely differ from each other, so the individual raw scores are barely changing as the conditions change, and the line graph will form close to a flat line. This pattern is close to the pattern we would see when there is no relationship. Therefore, we—and our statistical procedures—might misinterpret the data, deciding that the safest conclusion is that these variables are not related. Then, we would miss the relationship that really exists.

There is little we can do if the relationship in nature is really as weak as these data suggest. But, we certainly don't want to miss a substantial relationship that exists in nature, simply because through some flaw we obtained a very weak, unconvincing sample relationship. Therefore, we design a study so that if there is a relationship between the variables in nature, the data are likely to clearly and convincingly show it. The term that applies to this strategy is that we seek to maximize our "power." Power is actually an aspect of inferential statistics, so we'll wait until Chapter 13 for a precise statistical definition. For now, remember that a **powerful design** is more likely to show a convincing sample relationship.

Thus, your goal is create a powerful design. A powerful design might produce these results.

5-item list	*10-item list*	*15-item list*
$\overline{X} = 0$	$\overline{X} = 6$	$\overline{X} = 12$

Here, each change in the independent variable produces a relatively large difference in scores, and when graphed, these means will form a steeply slanted line graph. Therefore, these data present convincing evidence for a relationship, and so we are unlikely to miss the relationship in nature here.

There are several things that researchers do to maximize power. In particular, as we've just seen, large differences between the means of the conditions help to produce a convincing relationship, so one component of a powerful design is to produce large differences between the means. Large differences between the means of the conditions are produced by large differences between the scores. One way to do this is through *sensitive* measurements, which, you've seen, produce scores that reflect subtle differences in behavior. By being sensitive to small errors in memory, for example, we are more likely to detect differences in recall errors that are produced by changing list length. Another part of a powerful design is a *strong manipulation*. Recall that here, we create conditions that will produce large differences in behaviors so that we produce large differences in the scores between the conditions.

In later chapters, you'll see additional techniques for increasing power. All of them increase our chances of seeing a convincing relationship, and thus we are less likely to miss an independent variable that actually influences behavior. On the other hand, if we still don't see a relationship, we know we've done everything possible to find one, so we can be confident that the independent variable really does not work as predicted.

> *REMEMBER* One component of a powerful—convincing—design is to maximize the differences between the means of the conditions.

APA FORMAT FOR STATISTICAL NOTATION

Finally, recall that the American Psychological Association has developed the format and style that are used in most published reports of psychological research (described in Appendix A.) This includes defining the acceptable statistical symbols. Thus, as you saw, *Mdn* is the symbol for the median, and there is no symbol for the mode in APA format. Notably, in published research, the symbol for a sample mean is *M*, but the emphasis is on using the word "mean." (In our discussions, we need to identify the scores used to compute a mean, so we'll continue to use $\overline{X}$.) Although infrequent, the symbol for a population mean is μ.

PUTTING IT ALL TOGETHER

As you may have noticed, the mean is *the* measure of central tendency in psychological research, whether you are conducting a descriptive or experimental design. To be literate in research and statistics, you should understand the mode and the median, but the truly important topics in this chapter involve the mean and its characteristics, especially when applied to the normal distribution.

We will eventually discuss inferential statistical procedures, and they will tend to occupy all of your attention. Despite the emphasis such procedures receive, remember that the mean (or another central tendency measure) forms the basis for interpreting any study. You always want to say something like "the participants scored around 3" for a particular situation, because then you are describing their typical *behavior* in that situation. Thus, regardless of what other fancy procedures we discuss, remember to return to the measure of central tendency, so you can identify *around* where the scores in each condition are located.

CHAPTER SUMMARY

1. A *statistic* describes a characteristic of a sample of scores and is symbolized by a letter from the English alphabet. A *parameter* describes a characteristic of a population of scores and is symbolized by a letter from the Greek alphabet.

2. *Measures of central tendency* summarize the location of a distribution of scores on a variable, indicating around where the center of the distribution tends to be located. Which measure to compute depends on (a) the scale used to measure the variable, and (b) the shape of the distribution.

3. The *mode* is the most frequently occurring score(s) in a distribution, and is used primarily to summarize nominal data.

4. The *median*, (*Mdn*) is the score located at the 50th percentile. It is used primarily with ordinal data and with highly skewed interval or ratio data.

5. The *mean* is the average score, located at the mathematical center of a distribution. It is used with interval or ratio data that form a symmetrical, unimodal distribution. The symbol for a sample mean is $\overline{X}$, and the symbol for a population mean is μ.

6. The amount a score *deviates* from the mean is computed as $X - \overline{X}$. A deviation indicates the location of the raw score relative to the mean and relative to the distribution. In a normal distribution, the larger the deviation, the less frequently the score and the deviation occur.

7. The *sum of the deviations around the mean*, $\Sigma(X - \overline{X})$, always equals zero. In the absence of any other information, the mean is the best score to use when predicting an individual's score, because the total error across all such predictions will be the sum of the deviations around the mean, which will equal zero.

8. In graphing the results of an experiment, the independent variable is on the X axis and the dependent variable is on the Y axis. A *line graph* is created when the

independent variable involves a ratio or interval scale. A *bar graph* is created when the independent variable involves a nominal or ordinal scale.

9. On any graph, if the summary data points form a line that is not horizontal, then the individual Y scores change *as a function of* changes in the X scores, and a relationship is present. If the data points form a horizontal line, then a relationship is not present.

10. The *sample mean* in each condition of an experiment is the estimate of the population μ for that condition. When a relationship in the population is present, there will be different values of μ for two or more conditions of the independent variable.

11. A *powerful design* is more likely to show a clear and convincing sample relationship. One way to accomplish this is to produce large differences in dependent scores between the conditions.

KEY TERMS (with page references)

ΣX $\quad$ Mdn $\quad$ $\bar{X}$ $\quad$ $\Sigma(X - \bar{X})$ $\quad$ μ
bar graph (182)
bimodal (166)
deviation (174)
line graph (181)
mean (170)
measure of central tendency (165)
median (168)
mode (166)
parameter (164)
powerful design (185)
statistic (164)
sum of the deviations around the mean (174)
sum of X (164)
unimodal (166)

REVIEW QUESTIONS

(Answers for odd-numbered questions and problems are provided in Appendix D.)

1. (a) What is the difference between a statistic and a parameter? (b) What types of symbols are used for statistics and parameters?
2. (a) What does a measure of central tendency indicate? (b) What two aspects of the data determine which measure of central tendency to use?
3. (a) What is the mode, and with what type of data is it most appropriate? (b) What is the median, and with what type of data is it most appropriate? (c) What is the mean, and with what type of data is it most appropriate?
4. Why is it best to compute the mean for a normal distribution?
5. Which measure of central tendency is used most often in psychological research? Why?
6. Why is it inappropriate to compute the mean in a very skewed distribution?
7. What two pieces of information about the location of a score does a deviation score convey?

8. Why do we use the mean score in a sample to predict any score that might be found in that sample?
9. What is μ, and how do we usually determine its value?
10. (a) What is a powerful design? (b) Why do we seek a powerful design? (c) What are two ways to increase the power of a design?

PRACTICE PROBLEMS

11. For the following data, compute (a) the mean, and (b) the mode:

    55 57 59 58 60 57 56 58 61 58 59

12. (a) In problem 11, what is your estimate of the median (without computing it)? (b) Explain why you think your answer is correct. (c) Calculate the approximate median using the approach presented in this chapter.
13. After receiving many high grades, Foofy receives one low grade, resulting in an embarrassingly low grade average. (a) What has happened to her grade distribution to make it produce such a mean? (b) How could she summarize her grades to minimize the impact of that one low grade?
14. (a) For the data below, compute the mean:

    18 16 19 20 18 19 23 54 20 16
    18 19 18 19 18 40 30 19 18 38

    (b) What is the approximate median in these data?
15. A scientist collected the following sets of data. For each, indicate which measure of central tendency she should compute.
    (a) The following IQ scores:
    60, 72, 63, 83, 68, 74, 90, 86, 74, 80
    (b) The following anxiety scores:
    10, 15, 18, 15, 14, 13, 42, 15, 12, 14, 42
    (c) The following blood types:
    A−, A−, O, A+, AB−, A+, O, O, O, AB+
    (d) The following course grades:
    B, D, C, A, B, F, C, B, C, D, D
16. On a normal distribution, four participants obtained the following deviation scores: −5, 0, +3, and +1.
    (a) Which participant obtained the lowest raw score? How do you know?
    (b) Which participant's raw score had the lowest frequency? How do you know?
    (c) Which participant's raw score had the highest frequency? How do you know?
    (d) Which participant obtained the highest raw score? How do you know?
17. In a normal distribution of scores, four people obtained the following deviation scores: +1, −2, +5, and −10. (a) Which person obtained the highest raw score? (b) Which participant obtained the lowest raw score? (c) Rank-order the deviation scores in terms of their frequency, putting the score with the lowest frequency first.
18. Foofy says a deviation of +5 is always better than a deviation of −5. Why is she correct or incorrect?
19. For the following experimental results, specifically interpret the relationship between the independent and dependent variables:

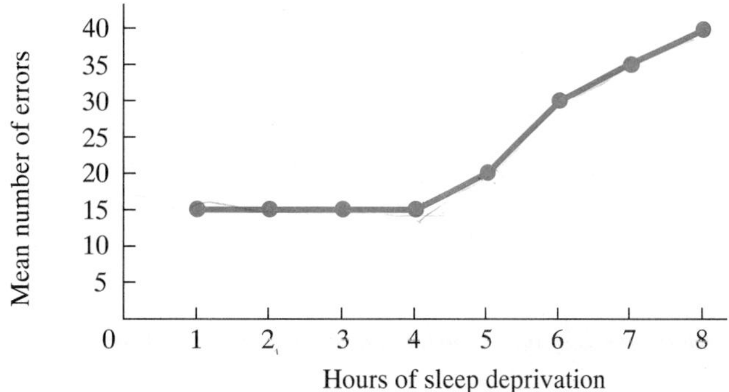

20. (a) In problem 19, give a title to the graph, using "as a function of." (b) If you participated in the above study and had been deprived of 5 hours of sleep, how many errors do we expect you would make? (c) If we tested all people in the world after 5 hours of sleep deprivation, how many errors would you expect each to make? (d) What symbol stands for your prediction in part (c)? (e) What issue of validity is raised by part (c)?

21. For each of the following experiments, determine which variable should be plotted on the Y axis and which on the X axis, whether a line graph or bar graph should be created, and how to summarize the dependent scores. (a) A study of income as a function of age (b) A study of politicians' number of positive votes on environmental issues as a function of the presence or absence of a wildlife refuge in their political districts (c) A study of running speed as a function of carbohydrates consumed (d) A study of rates of alcohol abuse as a function of ethnic group

22. Using the words "statistic" and "parameter," how do we learn about a relationship in a population?

23. Dr. Grumpy tested people on the Grumpy Emotionality Test as a function of increases in the amount of sunlight present when they were tested. The resulting line graph slants downward. What does this tell you about (a) the means for the conditions? (b) the raw scores for each condition? (c) the population μs? (d) the relationship between emotionality and sunlight in nature?

24. In problem 23, what would you do to ensure a powerful design?

25. You conduct a study to determine the impact that varying the amount of noise in an office has on worker productivity. You obtain the following productivity scores.

Condition 1: Low noise	*Condition 2: Medium noise*	*Condition 3: Loud noise*
15	13	12
19	11	9
13	14	7
13	10	8

(a) Assuming productivity scores are normally distributed ratio scores, summarize the results of this experiment. (b) Draw the appropriate graph for these data. (c) Assuming the data are representative, draw how to envision the populations produced by this experiment. (d) What conclusions can be drawn from this experiment?

26. Assume that the data in problem 25 reflect a highly skewed interval variable. (a) Summarize these scores. (b) What conclusion can be drawn from the sample data? (c) What conclusion can be drawn about the populations produced by this experiment?

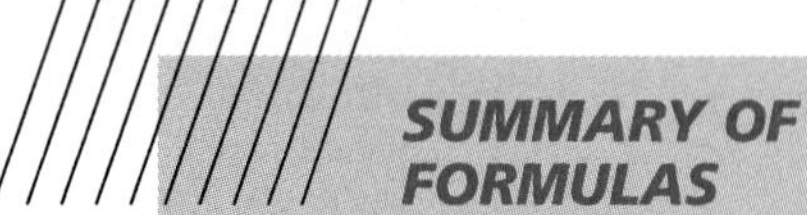

SUMMARY OF FORMULAS

1. *THE FORMULA FOR COMPUTING THE SAMPLE MEAN IS*

$$\bar{X} = \frac{\Sigma X}{N}$$

where ΣX stands for the sum of the scores and N is the number of scores.

2. To estimate the median, arrange the scores in rank order. If N is an odd number, the score in the middle position is approximately the median. If N is an even number, the average of the two scores in the middle positions is approximately the median.

8

Summarizing Research Using Measures of Variability

Getting Started

To understand this chapter, recall the following:

- From Chapter 2, understand what is meant by the strength of a relationship.
- From Chapter 3, recall how extraneous variables and threats to reliability and validity cause us to misinterpret a relationship.
- From Chapter 7, recall that the mean is the center of a distribution, what $\overline{X}$ and μ are, and why the sum of the deviations around the mean is zero.

Your goals in this chapter are to learn:

- What is meant by variability.
- When the range is used and how to interpret it.
- When the standard deviation and variance are used and how to interpret them.
- How to compute the variance and standard deviation for a sample, for a population, and as an estimate of the population based on a sample.
- How variance is used to measure errors in prediction.
- How for power, we control variability.

So far, you've learned that the first statistic to compute when describing *any* set of data is the appropriate measure of central tendency. This information simplifies the distribution and allows us to envision its typical score. But! Not all participants will behave in the same way, and so many scores may be very different from this typical score. Therefore, to completely describe a distribution, you must also answer the question "Are there large differences or small differences between the scores?" This chapter discusses procedures for describing the differences between scores, which are called *measures of variability*.

First, though, here are some new symbols and terms.

MORE STATISTICAL NOTATION

In this chapter, we'll see formulas involving several steps, so you must identify the quantity on which to perform the next operation. For example, a square root sign operates on "the quantity," so first, compute the quantity inside the square root sign. Thus, $\sqrt{2 + 7}$ becomes $\sqrt{9}$, which is 3. Likewise, the length of the dividing line in a fraction determines the quantity that is in the numerator (the number above the line) and in the denominator (the number below the line). First, complete fractions involving a short line. Thus, if we have

$$\frac{6 + \frac{12}{2}}{4}$$

First divide 12/2, then add 6, and then divide by 4 (the answer is 3). And note, if you become confused in the midst of a formula, there is an order of precedence to mathematical operations. Unless otherwise indicated, first perform squaring or finding a square root, then multiplication or division, and then addition or subtraction. Thus, $(2)(4) + 5$ is $8 + 5$, which is 13. Or, $2^2 + 3^2$ becomes $4 + 9$, which is 13.

A new symbol you'll see is ΣX^2, which is called the **sum of the squared *X*s**. It indicates to first square each score and then add up the squared scores. Thus, ΣX^2 for the scores 2, 2, and 3 first becomes $2^2 + 2^2 + 3^2$, which is $4 + 4 + 9$, which equals 17.

Learn right here to avoid confusing ΣX^2 with a similar-looking, but very different, operation symbolized by $(\Sigma X)^2$. This stands for the **squared sum of *X***. Here, first find the sum of the *X* scores and then square that sum. Thus, $(\Sigma X)^2$ for the scores 2, 2, and 3, is $(2 + 2 + 3)^2$, which is $(7)^2$, or 49. Notice that above, ΣX^2 gives 17, but $(\Sigma X)^2$ gives the very different answer of 49. Be careful with these terms.

> ***REMEMBER*** ΣX^2 indicates the sum of squared *X*s, and $(\Sigma X)^2$ indicates the squared sum of *X*.

This chapter also introduces *subscripts*. Pay attention to subscripts, because they are part of the symbols for certain statistics.

Finally, many statistics will have two different formulas. A "definitional formula" defines a statistic and shows you where the answer comes. However, a "computational formula" is used when actually computing a statistic. Trust me, computational formulas give exactly the same answers as definitional formulas, but they are much easier and faster to use.

UNDERSTANDING VARIABILITY

Computing a measure of variability is important because, without it, a measure of central tendency provides an incomplete description of a distribution. The mean, for example, indicates only the central score and where the most frequent scores are. It tells us little about scores that are not at the center of the distribution and/or that occur infrequently. You can see what's missing by looking at the three samples in Table 8.1. Each has a mean of 6, so if you didn't see the raw scores, you might think these were identical distributions. But, Sample A contains scores that differ greatly from each other and from the mean. Sample B contains scores that differ less from each other and from the mean. And Sample C shows no differences among the scores. Thus, to completely summarize data, we also need to know how much the scores differ from each other and from the center. This information is obtained by calculating a measure of variability.

Measures of variability summarize and describe the extent to which scores in a distribution *differ* from each other. Thus, when we ask whether there are large or small differences among the scores, we are asking the statistical question "How much variability is there in the data?" When there are many, relatively large differences among the scores, the data are said to be *variable* or to contain a large amount of *variability.*

In Chapter 7, you saw that a score indicates a participant's location on a variable and that the difference between two scores is the distance that separates them. From this perspective, measures of variability tell us how *spread out* the scores are. For example, Figure 8.1 on the next page shows the distances separating the scores in the previous samples. There are relatively large differences among the scores in Sample A, so this distribution is spread out. There are smaller differences in the scores in Sample B, so this distribution is not as spread out. There are no differences among the scores in Sample C, so there is no spread in this distribution. In statistical terms, the scores in Sample A show the greatest variability.

TABLE 8.1 Three Different Distributions Having the Same Mean Score

Sample A	*Sample B*	*Sample C*
0	8	6
2	7	6
6	6	6
10	5	6
12	4	6
$\overline{X} = 6$	$\overline{X} = 6$	$\overline{X} = 6$

FIGURE 8.1 Distance Between the Locations of Scores in Three Distributions

An X over a score indicates a participant who obtained that score. Each arrow indicates how spread out the scores are.

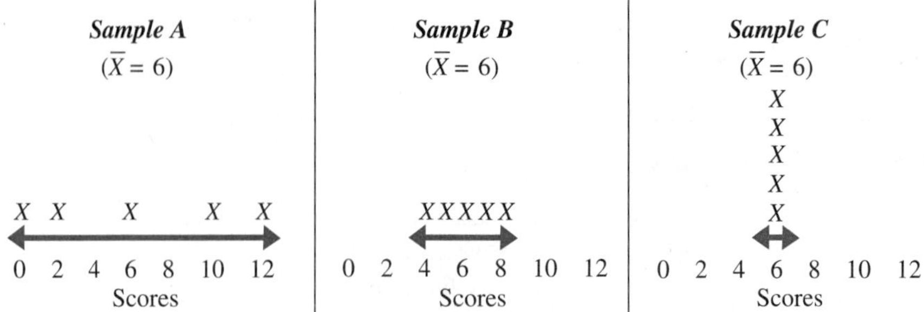

There is nothing magical about what produces variability. First, recall that participants will differ because of individual differences: Differences in genetics, physiology, experience, and so on, make individuals behave differently when in the same situation. Also, there are always momentary fluctuations in participant, researcher, environmental, and measurement variables that cause participants to behave differently. These differences in behaviors result in differences—variability—in scores.

You should always compute a measure of variability, because it shows two important and related aspects of the data. First, the opposite of variability is how *consistent* the scores are. Small variability indicates that the scores do not differ greatly, so they must be rather similar (and thus participants responded in a similar fashion). Conversely, large variability indicates that scores and behaviors were inconsistent, each being rather different from the next.

Second, a measure of variability indicates how accurately the measure of central tendency describes the distribution. The greater the variability, the more the scores are spread out, and so the less accurately they are represented by *one* central score. Conversely, the smaller the variability, the closer the scores are to each other and to the one central score. Thus, by knowing the amount of variability in each of the above samples, we know Sample C contains consistent scores (and so 6 very accurately represents it), Sample B contains less consistent scores (and so 6 is not so accurate a summary), and Sample A contains very inconsistent scores (and so 6 is not even close to most scores).

It is these same aspects of variability that produce differences in the shape of a normal distribution. For example, consider the three distributions in Figure 8.2. Distribution A is rather narrow or "skinny" because the high-frequency scores are close to the mean of 50, and relatively few scores were very far above or below the mean (e.g., few participants score at 40 or 60). Because scores are consistently near the mean, there are many small differences between the scores and few large ones. In other words, the variability here is small, and so the mean is a good summary of the scores.

Distribution B is a wider distribution because there are higher frequencies for scores farther above and below the middle (here, more participants score near 40 and 60). Thus, more often we'll find larger differences between the scores—the variability here is larger—and the mean is not such a good summary.

FIGURE 8.2 Three Variations of the normal curve

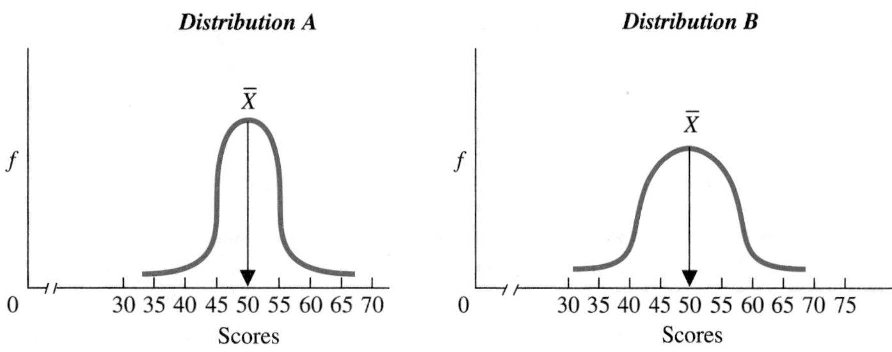

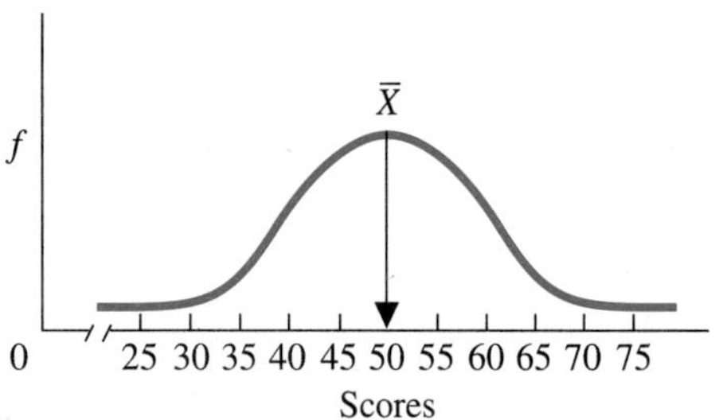

Distribution C is the "fattest" distribution, because here participants frequently scored way above or way below the mean, almost as often as they scored more central scores (here, scores near 40 and 60 have high frequencies). Therefore, because we'll find many large differences between the scores, the variability in this distribution is the largest of the three, and the mean is the poorest summary.

> *REMEMBER* Measures of variability indicate how much scores differ. While measures of central tendency indicate the location of a distribution, measures of variability indicate how spread out the distribution is.

As with previous procedures, the specific measure of variability you should compute depends on the scale of measurement involved and the shape of the distribution obtained. The following sections discuss three common measures of variability: the range, the variance, and the standard deviation.

The Range

One way to describe variability is to determine how far the lowest score is from the highest score. The descriptive statistic that indicates the distance between the two most extreme scores in a set of data is called the **range**.

THE FORMULA FOR COMPUTING THE RANGE IS

$$\text{Range} = \text{Highest score} - \text{Lowest score}$$

Thus, for example, the scores 0, 2, 6, 10, 12 have a range of $12 - 0 = 12$. The less variable scores of 4, 5, 6, 7, 8 have a range of $8 - 4 = 4$. And for the perfectly consistent scores of 6, 6, 6, 6, 6, the range is $6 - 6 = 0$. Thus, the range does communicate the spread in the data.

However, the range is a rather crude measure. Because it involves only the two most extreme scores, it is based on the least typical and often least frequent scores. Therefore, we usually compute the range as the *sole* measure of variability only with nominal or ordinal data. (For interval or ratio data forming a highly skewed distribution, we may compute a variation of the range called the "semi-interquartile range." As discussed in Part 2 of Appendix B, this statistic reflects the range between the scores at the 25th and 75th percentiles.)

For normally distributed interval or ratio scores, we calculate the variance and standard deviation.

Understanding the Variance and Standard Deviation

Most of the time psychological research involves interval or ratio data that more or less fit a normal or at least a symmetrical distribution, so the mean is the best measure of central tendency. When the mean is the appropriate measure of central tendency, we have two, similar measures of variability called variance and the standard deviation.

We *use* the variance and the standard deviation to describe and communicate how different the scores are from each other. We *calculate* them, however, by measuring how much the scores differ from the mean. The mean is our reference point because the mean is always the center of a distribution. Therefore, when scores are spread out from each other, they are also spread out from the mean. If scores are close to each other, they are also close to the mean.

The variance and standard deviation are appropriate with normal or other symmetrical distributions, because with them the mean is the point *around* which the distribution is located. *The variance and standard deviation allow us to quantify "around."* For example, if the grades in a statistics class form a normal distribution with a mean of 80, then most people scored *around* 80. But are most scores between 79 and 81, or between 60 and 100? By computing the variance and standard deviation, we can define "around."

> ***REMEMBER*** The variance and standard deviation are two measures of variability that indicate how much the scores are spread out around the mean.

Mathematically, the *distance* a score lies from the mean is computed as the *difference* between the score and the mean. Recall that this difference is symbolized as $(X - \overline{X})$ and is the amount the score *deviates* from the mean. Thus, a score's deviation indicates how much it is spread out from the mean. In a sample, some scores deviate from the mean by more than others, so to summarize the variability of all scores, we should determine the average amount that the scores deviate from the mean. We could call this the "average of the deviations." The larger the average of the deviations, the greater the variability between the scores and the mean.

To compute an average, we sum the scores and divide by N. We *might* find the average of the deviations by first computing $(X - \overline{X})$ for each participant, then summing these deviations to find $\Sigma(X - \overline{X})$, and finally dividing by N, the number of deviations. Altogether, the formula for the average of the deviations[1] would be

$$\text{Average of the deviations} = \frac{\Sigma(X - \overline{X})}{N}$$

We *might* compute the average of the deviations using this formula, except for a *big* problem. Recall that the sum of the deviations around the mean, $\Sigma(X - \overline{X})$, always equals zero, because the positive deviations cancel out the negative deviations. This means that the numerator in the above formula will always be zero, so the average of the deviations will always be zero. So much for the average of the deviations!

But remember our purpose here: We want a statistic *like* the average of the deviations, so that we know the average amount the scores are spread out or differ from the mean. But because mathematically, the average of the deviations is always zero, we calculate slightly more complicated statistics called the variance and standard deviation. But *think* of them as producing a number that, like an average, indicates the typical amount that the scores differ from the mean.

DESCRIBING THE SAMPLE VARIANCE

So, how do we compute something like the average of the deviations? If the problem is the positive and negative deviations, then the solution is to *square* the deviations: First, find the difference between each score and the mean, and then square that difference. This eliminates all negative deviations, so the sum of the squared deviations is not necessarily zero and neither is the average of the squared deviations. (This solution also results in statistics that have very useful characteristics.)

By finding the average of the squared deviations, we are computing the variance. The **variance** is the average of the squared deviations of scores around the mean. When we calculate this statistic for a sample of scores, we are computing the **sample variance**. The symbol for sample variance is S_X^2. Always include the squared sign (^{2}), because it is part of the symbol. The capital S indicates that we are describing a sample, and the subscript X indicates that it is computed for a sample of X scores.

REMEMBER S_X^2 stands for the sample variance.

Use this formula *only* when describing a sample of data (as distinct from the population).

THE DEFINITIONAL FORMULA FOR THE SAMPLE VARIANCE IS

$$S_X^2 = \frac{\Sigma(X - \overline{X})^2}{N}$$

[1] In advanced statistics, there is a very real statistic called the average deviation. This isn't it.

As an example, say that we measure the ages of some children and find scores of 2, 3, 4, 5, 6, 7, and 8, with a mean age of 5. To compute S_X^2 using the above formula, arrange the data as shown in Table 8.2. First, compute each deviation $(X - \overline{X})$ by subtracting the mean from each score. Next, as shown in the far right column, square each deviation to get $(X - \overline{X})^2$. Then, add the squared deviations to find $\Sigma(X - \overline{X})^2$, which here is 28. The N is 7. Filling in the formula for S_X^2 gives

$$S_X^2 = \frac{\Sigma(X - \overline{X})^2}{N} = \frac{28}{7} = 4.0$$

Thus, in this sample, the variance equals 4.0. In other words, the average squared deviation of the age scores around their mean is 4.0.

Computational Formula for the Sample Variance

To simplify the preceding formula, we have the following computational formula. Again, use this formula only when describing the *sample* variance.

THE COMPUTATIONAL FORMULA FOR THE SAMPLE VARIANCE IS

$$S_X^2 = \frac{\Sigma X^2 - \frac{(\Sigma X)^2}{N}}{N}$$

This formula says to first find the sum of the Xs, or ΣX; then, to square that sum; and then, divide the squared sum by N. Then, subtract that result from the sum of the squared Xs, or ΣX^2. Finally, divide that quantity by N.

For example, arrange the previous age scores as shown in Table 8.3. The ΣX is 35, ΣX^2 is 203, and N is 7. Putting these quantities into the computational formula, we have

$$S_X^2 = \frac{\Sigma X^2 - \frac{(\Sigma X)^2}{N}}{N} = \frac{203 - \frac{(35)^2}{7}}{7}$$

TABLE 8.2 Calculation of Variance Using the Definitional Formula

Subject	*Age Score*	−	$\overline{X}$	=	$(X - \overline{X})$	$(X - \overline{X})^2$
1	2	−	5	=	−3	9
2	3	−	5	=	−2	4
3	4	−	5	=	−1	1
4	5	−	5	=	0	0
5	6	−	5	=	1	1
6	7	−	5	=	2	4
7	8	−	5	=	3	9
	$N = 7$				$\Sigma(X - \overline{X})^2 = 28$	

TABLE 8.3 Calculation of Variance Using the Computational Formula

X score	X^2
2	4
3	9
4	16
5	25
6	36
7	49
8	64
$\Sigma X = 35$	$\Sigma X^2 = 203$

The squared sum of X, $(\Sigma X)^2$, is 35^2, which is 1225, so

$$S_X^2 = \frac{203 - \frac{1225}{7}}{7}$$

Now, 1225 divided by 7 equals 175, so

$$S_X^2 = \frac{203 - 175}{7}$$

Because 203 minus 175 equals 28, we have

$$S_X^2 = \frac{28}{7}$$

Finally, after dividing,

$$S_X^2 = 4.0$$

Thus, the sample variance for these age scores is again 4.0.

Do not read any further until you understand how to work this formula!

Interpreting Variance

The good news is that the variance is a legitimate measure of variability. Ideally, though, we want the average of the deviations, and the bad news is that the variance does not make much sense as an average deviation. There are two problems. First, because we square each deviation, the variance is always an unrealistically large number. For the age scores, the $\overline{X}$ is 5 and S_X^2 is 4. To say that the scores differ from the mean by an *average* of 4 is plain silly! Not one score actually deviates from the mean by as much as 4, so this is certainly not the average deviation. The second problem is that variance is bizarre because it measures in squared units: Above, we measured ages, so the variance indicates that the scores deviate from the mean by 4 *squared* years! (Whatever that means.)

Thus, it is difficult to interpret the variance as the "average" deviation. Is the variance therefore a waste of time? No, because variance is used extensively in the statistics we will discuss later. Also, variance does communicate the *relative* variability of scores. If someone reports that one sample has $S_X^2 = 1$ and another sample has $S_X^2 = 3$, you know that the second sample is more variable. Thus, think of variance as a number that generally communicates how variable the scores are: The larger the variance, the more the scores are spread out.

The measure of variability that more directly communicates the average deviation is called the standard deviation.

DESCRIBING THE SAMPLE STANDARD DEVIATION

The variance is always unrealistically large because we square each deviation. To solve this problem, we take the square root of the variance. The answer is called the standard deviation. The **standard deviation** is the square root of the variance, or the square root of the average squared deviation of scores around the mean.

To create the definitional formula for the **sample standard deviation**, we simply add the square root sign to the previous definitional formula for variance.

THE DEFINITIONAL FORMULA FOR THE SAMPLE STANDARD DEVIATION IS

$$S_X = \sqrt{\frac{\Sigma(X - \overline{X})^2}{N}}$$

Notice that the symbol for the sample standard deviation is S_X, which is the square root of the symbol for variance ($\sqrt{S_X^2}$ is S_X.) Conversely, squaring the standard deviation produces the variance.

REMEMBER S_X stands for the sample standard deviation.

To compute S_X using this formula, first compute the variance: Square each score's deviation, sum the squared deviations, and then divide that sum by N. In our previous age scores, the variance (S_X^2) was 4. Then, take the square root of the variance to find the standard deviation. In this case,

$$S_X = \sqrt{4.0}$$

so

$$S_X = 2.0$$

The standard deviation of the age scores is 2.0.

Computational Formula for the Sample Standard Deviation

To create the computational formula for the standard deviation, we merely add the square root symbol to the previous computational formula for the variance.

THE COMPUTATIONAL FORMULA FOR THE SAMPLE STANDARD DEVIATION IS

$$S_X = \sqrt{\frac{\Sigma X^2 - \frac{(\Sigma X)^2}{N}}{N}}$$

For example, using those age scores back in Table 8.3, ΣX is 35, ΣX^2 is 203, and N is 7. Putting these values into the formula gives

$$S_X = \sqrt{\frac{203 - \frac{(35)^2}{7}}{7}}$$

The computations inside the square root symbol produce the variance, which is 4.0. Then,

$$S_X = \sqrt{4.0}$$

Taking the square root, we again find that $S_X = 2.0$.

Be sure that your answer makes sense when computing S_X (and S_X^2). First, variability cannot be a negative number: You are measuring the *distance* scores are from the mean, and the formulas involve squaring each deviation. Second, the answer should fit the data. For example, raw scores that range from 0 to 50 cannot produce an "average" deviation of 50, nor is it likely that S_X is something like .80: With the mean in the middle, there would be at least one deviation of about +25 and −25, so think how many tiny deviations it would take to produce an "average" of .80. Strange answers may be correct for strange distributions, but:

> **For any roughly normal distribution, the standard deviation should equal about one-sixth of the range.**

Interpreting the Standard Deviation

There are three, related ways of interpreting the standard deviation. First, we interpret a S_X of 2.0 as indicating that our age scores deviate from the mean by an "average" of about 2. Some scores will deviate by more and some by less, but overall the scores deviate from the mean by something like an average of 2. Further, the standard deviation measures in the same units as the raw scores, so here the scores differ from the mean age by an "average" of 2 *years*.

Second, the standard deviation allows us to gauge how consistently close together the scores are, and correspondingly, how accurately they are summarized by the mean. Thus, if S_X is relatively large, we know that a relatively large proportion of the scores are rather far from the mean, with fewer scores close to it. If, S_X is small, however, then most scores are close to the mean, and relatively few are far from it.

Third, the standard deviation indicates how much the scores below the mean deviate from it, and how much the scores above the mean deviate from it, so S_X indicates how spread out the scores are *around* the mean. Therefore, we can further summarize a distribution by describing the scores that lie at "plus one standard deviation from the mean" ($+1S_X$) and "minus one standard deviation from the mean" ($-1S_X$). For example, the age scores of 2, 3, 4, 5, 6, 7, 8 produced a $\overline{X}$ of 5.0 and a S_X of 2.0. The score that is $+1S_X$ from the mean is the score at 5 + 2, or 7. The score that is $-1S_X$ from the mean is the score at 5 − 2, or 3. As you can see, a good way to summarize these scores is to say that the majority of the scores are between 3 and 7.

> ***REMEMBER*** The standard deviation indicates the "average deviation" from the mean, the consistency in the raw scores, and around where most scores in the distribution are located.

Applying the Standard Deviation to the Normal Curve

There is a mathematical relationship between the standard deviation and the normal curve, so that describing a distribution in terms of the scores that are between $-1S_X$ and $+1S_X$ is especially useful. For example, say that in a statistics class with a mean score of 80, the S_X is 5. The score at 80 − 5 ($-1S_X$) is 75, and the score at 80 + 5 ($+1S_X$) is 85. Figure 8.3 shows about where these scores are located on a normal distribution. First, notice that there is an easy way to determine where the scores at $-1S_X$ and $+1S_X$ are located on any normal curve. Over the scores that are close to the mean, the curve forms a downward convex shape (∩). As you travel away from the mean, at a certain point, the curve changes its pattern to an upward convex shape (∪). The points at which the curve changes its shape are called "inflection points." Because of the mathematical relationship between a normal curve and the standard deviation, the scores at the inflection points are always the scores that are one standard deviation away from the mean.

Now, Figure 8.3 shows how to summarize a distribution. First, saying that the mean is 80 implies that most scores are *around* 80. Then, finding the scores at $-1S_X$ and $+1S_X$ defines "around": Most of the scores are between 75 and 85. In fact, because of the relationship between the standard deviation and the normal distribution, approximately 34% of the scores in a perfect normal distribution are *always* between the mean and the score that is one standard deviation from the mean. Thus, as in Figure 8.3, 34% of the students have scores between 75 and 80, and 34% have scores between 80 and

FIGURE 8.3 Normal Distribution Showing Scores at Plus or Minus One Standard Deviation

With $S_X = 5$, the score of 75 is at $-1S_X$, and the score of 85 is at $+1S_X$. The percentages are the approximate percentages of the scores falling in each portion of the distribution.

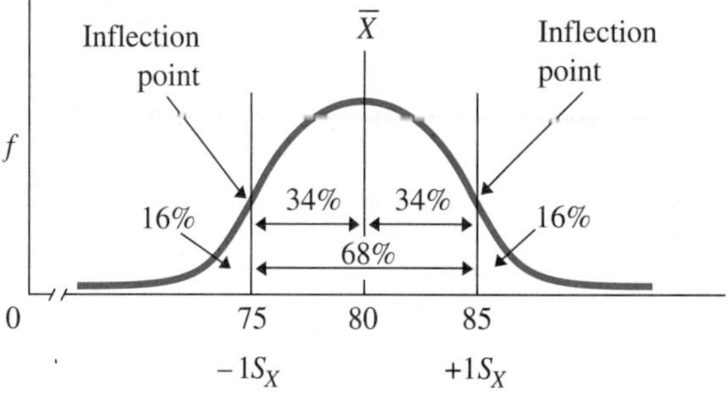

85. Altogether, approximately 68% of the scores are between the scores at $+1S_X$ and $-1S_X$ from the mean, so about 68% of the class has scores between 75 and 85. Conversely, only about 32% of the scores are outside this range, with about 16% below 75 and 16% above 85. Thus, saying that most scores are between 75 and 85 is an accurate summary, because the majority of scores (68%) are here.

Of course, it is unlikely that the scores from a small statistics class would produce an ideal normal distribution. However, if these scores are at least approximately normally distributed, we can operate as if the class formed the ideal normal distribution. Then, we *expect* about 68% of the scores in the class to fall between 75 and 85. The closer the distribution is to forming a perfect normal curve, the closer to precisely 68% of the scores will be between 75 and 85.

Recall that different samples of data will produce variations in the shape of a normal distribution. By finding the scores at $-1S_X$ and $+1S_X$ from the mean, we can envision and communicate these differences. For example, Figure 8.4 shows those three normal curves from the beginning of this chapter (for each, $\overline{X} = 50$). The size of the standard deviation (and variance) indicates how spread out a distribution is. For example, in Distribution A, the S_X is 4.0, so the most frequent scores are between 46 and 54 (between $+1S_X$ and $-1S_X$ from the mean). Essentially, the most frequent scores are bunched close to the mean, and so, most frequently, there are small deviations and thus a relatively small "average" or standard deviation. But in Distribution B, the relatively frequent scores are spread out over a wider range between about 43 and 57. Therefore the majority of the deviations are up to $+7$ and -7, so the "average" deviation is the S_X of 7. Finally, in Distribution C, the frequent scores are between about 38 and 62, and with

FIGURE 8.4 Three Variations of the Normal Curve

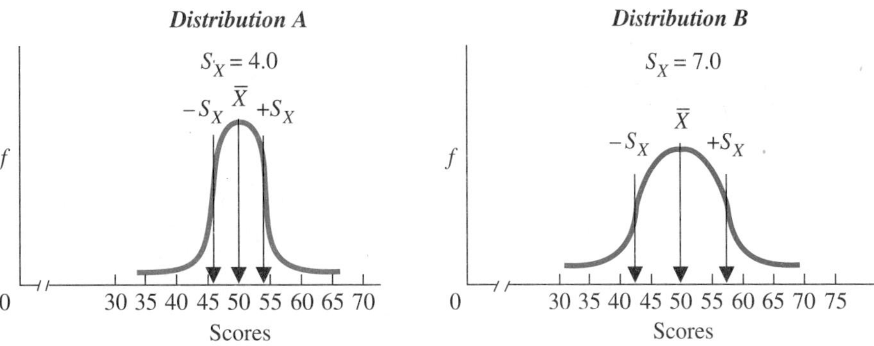

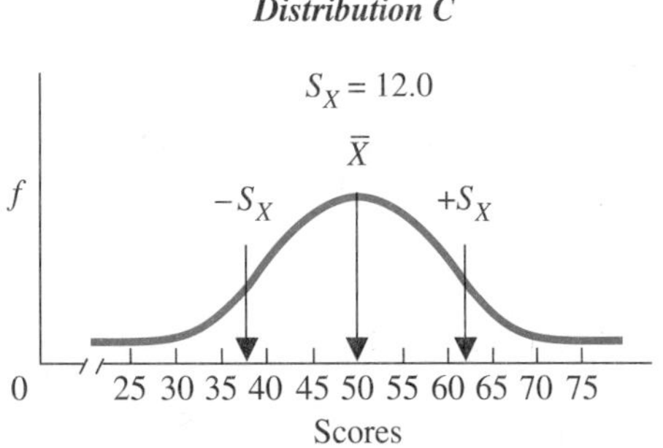

so many large deviations between $+12$ and -12, we have the large "average" deviation of S_X equal to 12. Thus, a larger standard deviation (or variance) indicates a wider distribution, because in a wider distribution, the more extreme scores occur more frequently. This produces more frequent large deviations and thus a larger "average" deviation.

REMEMBER The larger the value of S_X (or S_X^2), the more the scores are spread out around the mean, and the wider the distribution.

Despite differences in shape, any normal distribution will still have approximately 68% of the scores between the scores at $+1S_X$ and $-1S_X$ from the mean. This is because the "average" deviation from the mean will always lie at that inflection point, and with its characteristic bell shape, there will be about 34% of the total area between this point and the mean, beyond 16% of the area with this point in the tail. Thus, approximately 68% of the scores in Distribution A are between 46 and 54, while 68% of Distribution C is between 38 and 62.

In summary, then, here is how the standard deviation (and variance) add to our description of a distribution. If the data form a normal distribution, you can envision its shape. If the mean is 50, you know where the center of the distribution is and what the typical score is. And if, for example, $S_X = 4$, then you know that those participants who did not score 50 missed it by an "average" of 4 points, the distribution is relatively narrow, and most scores (68% of them) are between 46 and 54. Conversely, if you know that the $S_X = 12$, you know that participants who did not score 50 missed it by an "average" of 12 points, the distribution is relatively wide, and 68% of the scores are between 38 and 62.

THE POPULATION STANDARD DEVIATION AND THE POPULATION VARIANCE

Recall that our ultimate goal is to describe the population of scores. Once in a great while, psychologists will have a population of scores available to them, and then they can directly calculate the actual population variance and standard deviation. The symbol for the *true* or *known* population standard deviation is σ_X. (σ is the lowercase Greek letter sigma.) The symbol for the true population variance is σ_X^2. The definitional formulas for σ_X and σ_X^2 are similar to those we saw for a sample:

POPULATION STANDARD DEVIATION

$$\sigma_X = \sqrt{\frac{\Sigma(X - \mu)^2}{N}}$$

POPULATION VARIANCE

$$\sigma_X^2 = \frac{\Sigma(X - \mu)^2}{N}$$

The only novelty here is that we determine how far each score deviates from the population mean, (μ). Otherwise, the **population standard deviation** and **population**

variance indicate the same things about the population that we saw previously for the sample: Both are ways of measuring how much the scores differ from μ, indicating how much the scores are spread out in the population.

> *REMEMBER* The symbols σ_X and σ_X^2 are used when describing the true population variability.

These symbols (and formulas) are descriptive procedures for describing the population: They signal that we *know* the population standard deviation or variance. However, usually the population is infinitely large and/or unavailable, so we cannot use these formulas. Instead, we make an estimate, or inference, about the population based on a sample. Essentially, after we use $\overline{X}$ to estimate μ, we ask "What is our estimate of the variability of the scores around μ?"

Estimating the Population Variance and Population Standard Deviation

You might think that we could use the previous sample variance as our estimate of the population variance (and do likewise to estimate the standard deviation). If, for example, the sample variance is 4, should we then guess that the population variance is also 4? Nope! The sample variance and sample standard deviation are used to describe the variability of the scores in a sample *only*. They are *not* used to estimate the corresponding population parameters.

To understand why this is true, say that we measure a population of scores and compute its true variance (σ_X^2). We then draw a series of random samples from the population and compute the variance of each sample (S_X^2). Sometimes the sample variance will equal the population variance, but at other times the sample will not be perfectly representative of the population. Then, either the sample variance will be smaller than the population variance, or larger than the population variance. Over many random samples, however, more often than not the sample variance will *underestimate* the population variance. The same thing happens if we use the standard deviation.

In statistical terminology, the formulas for S_X^2 and S_X are called the **biased estimators**. Although the sample variance and standard deviation accurately describe a sample, they are biased toward underestimating the population parameters. This is a problem because, as in Chapter 7, if our estimates cannot be perfectly accurate, we at least want the underestimates and overestimates to cancel out over the long run. (Remember the two statisticians shooting targets?) With the biased estimators, the underestimates and overestimates do not cancel out. Instead, they are too often too small compared to the true population variance and standard deviation.

Why do S_X^2 and S_X produce biased estimates? Because their formulas are not designed for estimating the population. To estimate a population accurately, we should have a random sample, and so here, to estimate the variability, we should have a random sample of deviations. Yet, when we measure the variability of a sample, we use the mean as our reference point. In doing so, we encounter the restriction that the sum of the deviations, $\Sigma(X - \overline{X})$, always equals zero. Because of this, not all of the deviations in the sample are random. For example, say that the mean of five scores is 6, and that four of the scores are 1, 5, 7, and 9. Their deviations are −5, −1, +1, and +3, so the sum of their deviations is −2. Without even looking at the final score, we know it is 8, because it has a deviation of +2 and so then the sum of all deviations will be zero. Thus, this final deviation is determined by the other scores, so it is not random. Rather, only the deviations produced by the scores of 1, 5, 7, and 9 are random. The same would be true for any four of the five scores. Thus, when N is 5, only four of the scores actually reflect the random deviations of scores in the population. In general, out of N scores in a sample, only $N - 1$ of them actually reflect the random variability in the population.

The problem with the biased estimators (S_X and S_X^2) is that in them we divide by N. Because we divide by too large a number, the answer tends to be too small, underestimating the variability in the population. Instead, we should divide by the quantity $N - 1$. By doing so, we create the *unbiased* estimators. The **unbiased estimators** are procedures that provide the best estimate of the corresponding population's variance and standard deviation.

THE DEFINITIONAL FORMULAS FOR THE UNBIASED ESTIMATORS OF THE POPULATION VARIANCE AND STANDARD DEVIATION ARE

Estimated Population Variance

$$s_X^2 = \frac{\Sigma(X - \overline{X})^2}{N - 1}$$

Estimated Population Standard Deviation

$$s_X = \sqrt{\frac{\Sigma(X - \overline{X})^2}{N - 1}}$$

We are still computing a number that is analogous to the average of the deviations in the sample. Include all of the scores when computing the sum of the squared deviations in the numerator, *but* (and this is the big but), divide by $N - 1$, the number of scores in the sample minus one.

Notice that the symbol for the unbiased estimator of the standard deviation is s_X and the symbol for the unbiased estimator of the variance is s_X^2. To keep your symbols straight, remember that the *sample* variance and standard deviation use the capital or "big" S, and in their formulas you divide by the *big* value of N. The estimated *population* variance and standard deviation use the lowercase or *small s*, and you divide by the *smaller* $N - 1$. Further, think of s_X^2 and s_X as the inferential versions of the variance and standard deviation, because the *only* time you use them is to *infer* the variance or standard deviation of the population based on a sample. Think of S_X^2 and S_X as the descriptive versions, because they are used to *describe* the sample.

REMEMBER S_X^2 and S_X describe the variability in a sample; s_X^2 and s_X estimate the variability in the population.

For future reference, the quantity $N - 1$ is called the degrees of freedom. The **degrees of freedom** is the number of scores in a sample that reflect the random variability in the population. The symbol for degrees of freedom is df, so here, $df = N - 1$.

In the final analysis, you can think of $N - 1$ as simply a correction factor. Because $N - 1$ is a smaller number than N, dividing by $N - 1$ produces a slightly larger answer than does dividing by N. This larger answer will tend not to underestimate, so that over the long run we have a more accurate estimate of the population variability.

Computational Formulas for the Estimated Population Variance and Standard Deviation

The only difference between the computational formula for the estimated population variance and the previous computational formula for the sample variance is that here the final division is by $N - 1$.

THE COMPUTATIONAL FORMULA FOR THE ESTIMATED POPULATION VARIANCE IS

$$s_X^2 = \frac{\Sigma X^2 - \frac{(\Sigma X)^2}{N}}{N - 1}$$

In the previous examples using age scores, $N = 7$, $\Sigma X^2 = 203$, and $\Sigma X = 35$. Putting these quantities into the formula gives

$$s_X^2 = \frac{\Sigma X^2 - \frac{(\Sigma X)^2}{N}}{N - 1} = \frac{203 - \frac{(35)^2}{7}}{6}$$

Work through this formula the same way you did for the sample variance: 35^2 is 1225, and 1225 divided by 7 equals 175, so

$$s_X^2 = \frac{203 - 175}{6}$$

Now, 203 minus 175 equals 28, so

$$s_X^2 = \frac{28}{6}$$

and the final answer is

$$s_X^2 = 4.67$$

This answer is slightly larger than the sample variance for these age scores, which was $S_X^2 = 4.0$. Although 4.0 accurately describes the sample variance, it is likely to underestimate the variance of the population: 4.67 is more likely to be the population variance. In other words, if we could compute the true population variance, we would expect σ_X^2 to be 4.67.

A standard deviation is always the square root of the corresponding variance, so the formula for the estimated population standard deviation merely adds the square root sign to the above formula for the variance.

THE COMPUTATIONAL FORMULA FOR THE ESTIMATED POPULATION STANDARD DEVIATION IS

$$s_X = \sqrt{\frac{\Sigma X^2 - \frac{(\Sigma X)^2}{N}}{N - 1}}$$

Above, the estimated population variance for the age scores was $s_X^2 = 4.67$. Then, s_X is $\sqrt{4.67}$, or 2.16. Thus, if we could compute the standard deviation using the entire population of scores, we would expect σ_X to be 2.16.

Interpreting the Estimated Population Variance and Standard Deviation

Interpret the estimated variance and standard deviation in the same way as S_X^2 and S_X, except that now they indicate how much we *expect* the scores to be spread out in the population, how consistent or inconsistent we *expect* the scores to be, and how accurately we *expect* the population to be summarized by μ.

Notice that, assuming a sample is representative of the population, we have pretty much reached our goal of describing an unknown population of scores. If we can assume that the distribution is normal, we have described its overall shape. The sample mean ($\overline{X}$) provides a good estimate of the population mean (μ). The size of s_X (or s_X^2) is our estimate of how spread out the population is—an estimate of the "average amount" the scores deviate from μ. Further, we expect approximately 68% of the scores in the population to lie between the scores at $+1s_X$ and $-1s_X$ from μ. Then, because scores reflect behaviors, we have a good idea of how most individuals in the population behave in a given situation (which is why we conduct research in the first place).

A BRIEF REVIEW

To keep track of all of the symbols, names, and formulas for the different statistics you've seen, remember that variability refers to the differences between scores, and that the variance and standard deviation are two methods for describing variability. In every case, we are finding the difference between each score and the mean and then calculating something, more or less, like the average deviation.

Any standard deviation is merely the square root of the corresponding variance. For either measure, compute the descriptive versions when the scores are available: When describing how far the scores are spread out from the mean of a sample, calculate S_X^2 and S_X. When describing how far the scores are spread out from the mean of a population, calculate σ_X^2 and σ_X. When the population of scores is unavailable, infer the variability of the population based on a sample by computing the unbiased estimators, s_X^2 and s_X. The difference is that these inferential formulas require a final division by $N - 1$ instead of by N.

With the basics in hand, you can now apply the variance and standard deviation to research. The following sections discuss how they are used when we predict scores, and when we summarize a study.

VARIANCE AS THE ERROR IN PREDICTIONS

In Chapter 7, we saw that the sample mean is the best single score to use to predict unknown scores. However, not everyone will obtain the mean score, so sometimes our predictions will be wrong. It turns out that measures of variability describe the amount of error we have when using the mean to make predictions.

To estimate our error when predicting unknown scores, we determine our error when predicting the known scores in a sample: We pretend that we don't know the scores, predict them, and then see how close we came to the actual scores. For example, if that statistics class has a mean of 80, then our best guess is that any student in the class scored 80. Then, our error in a single prediction is the difference between the score someone received (X) and the score we predicted ($\overline{X}$), or the quantity ($X - \overline{X}$). We've already seen that ($X - \overline{X}$) is the amount that a score deviates from the mean. Because some predictions in a sample will contain more error than others, it makes sense to summarize the error by finding the average amount that participants' actual scores deviate from the mean score we predict for them. As we've seen, the way to find the "average" amount that scores deviate from the mean is to compute the variance and standard deviation.

Thus, here is a slightly novel way of thinking about measures of variability. Because they measure the difference between each score and the mean, they also measure the error in our predictions when we predict the mean for everyone in a sample. The larger the variability, the larger the differences between the mean and the scores, so the larger our error.

So, if the standard deviation in that statistics class is 5, then the actual scores differ from the mean of 80 by an "average" of 5 points. Therefore, if we predict 80 for everyone in the class, the actual scores will differ from the predicted score by an "average" of 5 points.

Similarly, the variance (S_X^2) is another way to measure the "average" deviation, so the variance also indicates the "average error" we have when predicting the mean score for everyone in a sample. In fact, in statistics, the proper way to describe the error in predictions is to compute the variance. For this reason, the variance is sometimes called "error variance." **Error variance** refers to the differences between the scores and the mean that produce the error in our predictions. The larger the variance, the larger the error, and the smaller the variance, the smaller the error. Thus, the sample variance shows the error variance when we use the sample mean to predict scores in a sample. Likewise, from the sample mean we can infer the population mean, and then, the estimated population variance reflects the error variance—differences—between the value of μ that we predict for everyone in the population and their actual scores.

> *REMEMBER* The sample variance (S_X^2) is the error variance in the sample, the "average" error when $\overline{X}$ is the predicted score for everyone in the sample. The estimated population variance (s_X^2) is the error variance we expect when μ (based on $\overline{X}$) is predicted for everyone in the population.

Researchers can always measure a sample of scores, compute the mean, and use it to predict scores. Therefore, the value of S_X^2 is the maximum error we are forced to accept when predicting scores in a sample (and s_X^2 is the maximum error when predicting scores in a population). As you'll see in later chapters, because the variance is the worst that we can do, it is our reference point. Anything that improves the accuracy of predictions is measured relative to the variance.

SUMMARIZING RESEARCH USING THE MEAN AND STANDARD DEVIATION

The standard deviation is usually preferred in published research, because it most directly indicates how consistently close the scores are to the mean. Thus, in an observational study, if the mean describes the number of times participants exhibited a particular behavior, the standard deviation indicates how consistently participants exhibited the behavior that often. Or, in summarizing a survey, if the mean rating from Likert-type questions describes the typical opinion held by participants, the standard deviation indicates the extent of disagreement among them.

The same approach is used in experiments. For example, in the previous chapter, we studied the effect of recalling either a 5-, 10-, or 15-item list. The mean summarized our dependent variable of recall scores, indicating *around* where participants in each condition scored. But, for the complete picture, we should also include the standard deviation in each condition, as in Table 8.4. Because normally there would be more scores per condition and a published report would not give the individual scores, get in the habit of using the $\overline{X}$ and S_X to envision the data that are present. Thus, as shown here, typically, a score of 3 was observed in the 5-item condition, with, on average, scores varying above or below this by about .82. In terms of error variance, squaring the S_X of .82 gives $S_X^2 = .67$. Thus, when we predict that people will score a 3 when recalling a 5-item list and we are wrong, we expect to be off by about .67. Likewise, we expect scores in the 10-item list to be around 6, but we'll be off by the S_X of 1.41, or by the S_X^2 of 1.99, and so on.

In addition, by knowing the S_X in each condition, we can gauge how consistent the relationship is. Remember that not all relationships are created equal, differing in their "strength" or "degree of association." The more consistently scores on the dependent variable change as conditions of the independent variable change, the stronger the relationship. Because the standard deviation (and variance) communicate the inconsistency of scores in each condition, they communicate the strength of a relationship.

For example, say that our experiment had produced either the strong or weak relationship shown in Table 8.5. Part A shows a perfectly consistent relationship because

TABLE 8.4 Mean and Standard Deviation in Each Condition of Recalling 5-, 10-, or 15-Item Lists

5-item list	*10-item list*	*15-item list*
3	5	9
4	5	11
2	8	7
$\overline{X} = 3$	$\overline{X} = 6$	$\overline{X} = 9$
$S_X = .82$	$S_X = 1.41$	$S_X = 1.63$

TABLE 8.5 Means and Standard Deviations in Recall Experiment with a Perfectly Strong or a Very Weak Relationship

(A) Perfectly strong relationship

5-item list	*10-item list*	*15-item list*
3	6	9
3	6	9
3	6	9
$\overline{X} = 3$	$\overline{X} = 6$	$\overline{X} = 9$
$S_X = 0$	$S_X = 0$	$S_X = 0$

(B) Very weak relationship

5-item list	*10-item list*	*15-item list*
3	0	2
6	4	4
0	8	9
$\overline{X} = 3$	$\overline{X} = 4$	$\overline{X} = 5$
$S_X = 2.45$	$S_X = 3.27$	$S_X = 2.94$

there is one dependent score associated with each condition. In other words, there is no difference or *variability* among the scores *within* each condition, and each S_X equals zero. In part B, however, the values of S_X are relatively large. This indicates that, as shown, the individual scores within the conditions are rather inconsistent and variable, so that overall this is a relatively weak and inconsistent relationship. In later chapters, we'll see more objective ways to determine the strength of a relationship, but, in essence, they consider the variability of the scores within each condition.

The strength of a relationship is an important component of interpreting an experiment, because it will suggest how much influence the independent variable has on the dependent variable. Above, the strength of the relationship suggests the extent to which recall scores are "caused" by list length. The perfectly consistent relationship would suggest that list length has a major, controlling effect on recall: It seems to be *the* variable that determines a score. Conversely, the weak relationship would suggest that there are other factors in addition to list length that cause or influence recall (perhaps intelligence or motivation is important). This is how we then begin to interpret results "psychologically": Above, we'd consider what the consistency and inconsistency in the relationship indicate about the influence of the amount of information in a list on its recall, and how this relates to theoretical explanations, models, and constructs involving memory storage and retrieval.

> ***REMEMBER*** Summarize an experiment by calculating the mean and standard deviation in each condition. Smaller values of S_X indicate a stronger relationship and thus a greater influence of the independent variable on dependent scores.

Variability and the Power of a Design

Before we get to interpreting the results psychologically, however, we must first find a relationship. Recall from the previous chapter that we may find such a weak, unconvincing relationship in the data that we *erroneously* decide that there really is no relationship present in nature. For example, the weak relationship back in Table 8.5 might cause us—and our statistics—to conclude that list length essentially has no influence on recall. Then, we may be missing a relationship that does exist in nature. To avoid this problem, recall that we seek a *powerful design*. With greater power, we are more likely to obtain clear and convincing evidence of a relationship, so that we don't miss relationships in nature.

Recall that one aspect of power is to use a *strong manipulation* that is likely to produce large differences in means *between* the conditions. (The weak relationship above is unconvincing partly because of the small differences between the means.) A second aspect of creating a powerful design is to aim for the strongest relationship possible. This is because the clearest, most convincing indication of a relationship in nature comes from the most consistent sample relationship. The perfectly strong relationship in Table 8.6 will be very difficult for us—and our statistics—to misinterpret as anything other than a relationship between list length and recall. However, the weak relationship is not so convincing: With much overlap in scores between the conditions, there is not a consistent pairing of one score with one list length. Therefore, we might erroneously conclude that there is not a relationship in nature here.

Whether we observe a weak or strong relationship depends on the amount of variability among scores *within* each condition or, in other words, the amount of *error variance*. Because we assume that nature is lawful, we assume that something causes error variance. Therefore, a key issue in creating a powerful design is to eliminate anything that might cause error variance—anything that might cause differences in scores *within* conditions. Then we will have the strongest relationship possible.

> ***REMEMBER*** For power, produce the strongest relationship possible. This occurs with large differences in scores *between* conditions, but with minimum differences in scores *within* conditions.

To minimize error variance, again focus on our old friends, the issues of reliability, *validity*, and *control*. For example, are the measurements unreliable, reflecting random error? If items in the above lists can sometimes be guessed, then even when participants actually remember the list in a condition to the same degree, we will see different scores. Or, do we lack *internal validity* because of fluctuating extraneous variables? If, for example, the physical environment changes unsystematically so that it differentially influences participants, they will have different scores within the same condition. In addition, *individual differences* produce error variance: Differences in participants' memory ability, motivation, or reactivity to being observed will produce different recall scores in the same condition.

As these examples illustrate, anything that influences participants can produce variability—*differences*—in scores within each condition, resulting in a weak relationship. Therefore, we have yet another reason for designing a study that accurately and exclusively measures the variables of interest, while controlling all other factors. Previously, we saw that avoiding design flaws was important for interpreting results *conceptually*:

We want to be correct regarding our interpretation of a behavior and the variables that cause it. Now, we've seen that these same design flaws are important for interpreting results *statistically*: We want to be correct regarding whether a relationship is really present. And, clearly, the statistical interpretations influence the conceptual interpretations, because we must find a statistical relationship before we can draw any inferences about the underlying behavior. Therefore, by dealing with the issues of reliability, validity, and control, we (1) create a powerful design so we draw the correct statistical interpretations that a relationship exists, and (2) eliminate design flaws so we draw the correct psychological interpretations about the variables involved in that relationship.

> ***REMEMBER*** By controlling threats to reliability and validity, we are more likely to produce a strong sample relationship and to interpret it correctly.

APA FORMAT FOR STATISTICAL NOTATION

As if you haven't seen enough symbols, research publications that follow the APA guidelines use the symbol "*SD*" for the sample standard deviation. If estimating any population parameter, the symbol " ^ " is placed above the parameter's symbol, so an estimated population standard deviation is $\hat{\sigma}$. Because the standard deviation is more easily interpreted, variance is usually not reported in published reports, although you will see the term "error variance."

PUTTING IT ALL TOGETHER

At this point, the three steps to analyzing any and all data should be like a reflex for you:

1. Consider the scale of measurement used and the shape of the distribution formed by the scores.
2. Describe *around* where most participants scored, usually by computing the $\overline{X}$ for the total sample or for each condition of an experiment.
3. Describe the *variability*—how spread out the scores are—around each mean, usually by computing the sample standard deviation.

With this information, you are largely finished with descriptive statistics, because you know the important characteristics of the sample data, and you'll be ready to draw inferences about the corresponding population. That's all there is to it.

CHAPTER SUMMARY

1. Unless otherwise indicated in a formula, the *order of mathematical operations* is to square or find the square root first, then multiply or divide, and then add or subtract.
2. *Measures of variability* describe how much the scores differ from each other, or how much the distribution is spread out.

3. The *range* is the difference between the highest and lowest scores.

4. The *variance* is the average of the squared deviations of scores around the mean.

5. The *standard deviation* is the square root of the variance. It can be thought of as the "average" amount that scores deviate from the mean.

6. There are three versions of the formula for variance: S_X^2 describes how far sample scores are spread out around the sample mean, σ_X^2 describes how far the population of scores is spread out around μ, and s_X^2 is computed using sample data, but is the unbiased estimate of how far the population is spread out around μ.

7. There are three versions of the formula for the standard deviation: S_X describes how far the sample scores are spread out around the sample mean, σ_X describes how far the population is spread out around μ, and s_X is computed using sample data, but is the unbiased estimate of how far the population is spread out around μ.

8. Formulas for descriptive measures of variability (for S_X^2 and S_X) use N as the final denominator, but the inferential formulas (for s_X^2 and s_X) use $N - 1$. The quantity $N - 1$ is the *degrees of freedom* in the sample.

9. The sample variance (S_X^2) also reflects the amount of *error* when the value of $\overline{X}$ is the predicted score for everyone in the sample. The estimated population variance (s_X^2,) is the expected error when the value of μ is the predicted score for everyone in the population.

10. The smaller the value of S_X (or S_X^2) in each condition of an experiment, the *stronger the relationship*.

11. *Error variance* is the variance in each condition, reflecting the error when using the mean of a condition to predict scores in that condition.

12. For *power*, researchers seek the strongest relationship possible. This occurs with large differences in scores *between* conditions, but small differences in scores *within* conditions.

13. Threats to reliability and validity and individual differences produce error variance. The greater the error variance, the weaker the relationship. Therefore, a *powerful design* minimizes error variance by controlling such threats and minimizing individual differences.

KEY TERMS (with page references)

ΣX^2 $(\Sigma X)^2$ S_X^2 s_X^2 σ_X^2 S_X s_X σ_X df
biased estimator (205)
degrees of freedom (206)
error variance (209)
estimated population standard deviation (206)
estimated population variance (206)
measures of variability (193)
population standard deviation (204)
population variance (204)
range (195)
sample standard deviation (200)
sample variance (197)
squared sum of X (192)
sum of the squared Xs (192)
unbiased estimator (206)

REVIEW QUESTIONS

(Answers for odd-numbered questions and problems are provided in Appendix D.)

1. If given no other information when completing a formula, what is the order in which to perform mathematical operations?
2. In any research, what three characteristics of a distribution must the researcher describe?
3. What do measures of variability communicate about (a) the size of the differences between the scores in a distribution? (b) how consistently participants behaved?
4. (a) What is the range? (b) Why is it not the most accurate measure of variability? (c) When is it used as the sole measure of variability?
5. (a) What do both the variance and standard deviation tell you about a distribution? (b) Which measure is usually computed? Why?
6. (a) What is the mathematical definition of the variance? (b) How is a sample's variance related to its standard deviation and vice versa?
7. (a) What do S_X, s_X, and σ_X have in common in terms of what they communicate? (b) How do they differ in terms of their use?
8. Why are estimates of the population variance and standard deviation always larger than the corresponding values for a sample from that population?
9. The variance of a distribution is $S_X^2 = 0$. What does this indicate about the distribution?
10. Why do the calculations for variance reflect the amount of error present when the mean is predicted for everyone in a sample?
11. (a) In an experiment, what is error variance? (b) What causes error variance?
12. (a) What are the two general aspects of producing a powerful design? (b) How do researchers minimize error variance? (c) Why is a more consistent relationship more powerful?

PRACTICE PROBLEMS

13. In a condition of an experiment, a researcher obtains the following creativity scores.

3	2	1	0	7	4	8	6	9	1
6	8	6	9	4	5	0	8	7	6

In terms of creativity, interpret the variability of these data using (a) the range (b) the variance (c) the standard deviation.

14. If you could test the entire population in problem 13, what would you expect each of the following to be: (a) The typical creativity score? (b) The variance? (c) The standard deviation? (d) The two scores between which about 68% of all creativity scores fall in this situation?
15. Say the sample in problem 13 had an N of 1000. How many people would you expect to score below 2.10? Why?
16. As part of studying the relationship between mental and physical health, you obtain the following heart rates.

73	72	67	74	78	84	79	71	76
78	76	79	81	75	80	78	76	

In terms of differences in heart rates, interpret these data using (a) the range (b) the variance (c) the standard deviation.

17. If you could test the population in problem 16, what would you expect each of the following to be: (a) The shape of the distribution? (b) The typical heart rate? (c) The variance? (d) The standard deviation? (e) The two scores between which about 68% of all heart rates fall?

18. Foofy has a normal distribution of scores ranging from 2 to 9. (a) She has computed the variance here to be −.06. What should you conclude from this answer, and why? (b) She recomputes the standard deviation to be 18. What should you conclude, and why? (c) She recomputes the variance to be 1.36. What should you conclude, and why?

19. For his test grades, Guchi has a $\overline{X}$ of 60 and $S_X = 20$. Pluto has a $\overline{X}$ of 60 and $S_X = 5$. (a) Who is the more consistent student, and why? (b) Who is more accurately described as a 60 student, and why?

20. (a) For which student in problem 19 can you more accurately predict the next test score, and why? (b) Who is more likely to do either extremely well or extremely poorly on the next exam, and why?

21. On a final exam, the $\overline{X} = 65$ and $S_X = 6$. What score would you predict for each student, and if you're wrong, what do you expect will be the error in your prediction?

22. In an experiment, how does the size of S_X in each condition suggest the strength of the relationship?

23. Consider the results of the following experiments.

Experiment 1

Condition 1	*Condition 2*	*Condition 3*
12	30	45
11	33	48
14	36	49
10	35	44

Experiment 2

Condition 1	*Condition 2*	*Condition 3*
18	8	3
13	11	9
9	6	5

(a) What should you do to summarize these experiments? (b) Using the means, summarize the relationship in each study. (c) Which experiment looks like it produced the stronger relationship? (d) Confirm your answer to part (c) mathematically. (e) Which experiment contains the greater amount of error variance? How do you know? (f) What does the amount of error variance suggest about the impact of the independent variable in each experiment?

24. A researcher finds a large degree of error variance in an experiment on children's ability to remember a passage they read as a function of the number of hours they have previously watched television. (a) What does this statement indicate about the scores in each condition? (b) What might cause such variability? (c) What impact will such variability have on the statistical results? (d) What impact will it have on the conceptual interpretation of the variable of television watching?

25. If you conducted Experiment 2 in problem 23 on the population, (a) what do you expect would be the most common, typical score per condition? (b) How consistently close to this score do you expect all participants to be?

SUMMARY OF FORMULAS

1. *The formula for the range is*

$$\text{Range} = \text{Highest score} - \text{Lowest score}$$

2. *The computational formula for the sample variance is*

$$S_X^2 = \frac{\Sigma X^2 - \frac{(\Sigma X)^2}{N}}{N}$$

3. *The computational formula for the sample standard deviation is*

$$S_X = \sqrt{\frac{\Sigma X^2 - \frac{(\Sigma X)^2}{N}}{N}}$$

4. *The computational formula for estimating the population variance is*

$$s_X^2 = \frac{\Sigma X^2 - \frac{(\Sigma X)^2}{N}}{N - 1}$$

5. *The computational formula for estimating the population standard deviation is*

$$s_X = \sqrt{\frac{\Sigma X^2 - \frac{(\Sigma X)^2}{N}}{N - 1}}$$

9

Summarizing Research Using *z*-Scores

Getting Started

To understand this chapter, recall the following:

- From Chapter 6, recall what relative frequency is, that it corresponds to the proportion of the total area under the curve, and that a percentile is the percentage of the curve to the left of a score.
- From Chapter 7, recall that the larger a score's deviation from the mean, the lower the score's frequency.
- From Chapter 8, recall that S_X and σ_X indicate the "average" deviation of scores around $\overline{X}$ and μ, respectively.

Your goals in this chapter are to learn:

- What a *z*-score is and what it tells you about a score's relative location.
- How the standard normal curve is used with *z*-scores to determine expected relative frequency, simple frequency, and percentile.
- The characteristics of a sampling distribution of means and what the standard error of the mean is.
- How a sampling distribution of means is used with *z*-scores to determine the expected relative frequency of sample means.

The techniques discussed in the preceding chapters for graphing, measuring central tendency, and measuring variability comprise the descriptive procedures used in most psychological research. In this chapter, we combine these procedures to answer another question about data: How does any one particular score compare to the other scores in a sample or population? We answer this question by transforming raw scores into "z-scores." Recall that transformations are for comparing scores on different variables and for making scores within the same distribution easier to interpret. The z-score transformation is the Rolls-Royce of transformations, because it allows us to interpret and compare scores from virtually *any* normal distribution of interval or ratio scores.

The following sections first examine the logic of z-scores and discuss how to compute them. Then we'll look at their uses, both in describing individual scores and in describing sample means.

MORE STATISTICAL NOTATION

The answers here will involve negative or positive numbers. However, sometimes we ignore a number's sign. The size of a number, regardless of its sign is the *absolute value* of the number.

Also, you'll encounter the symbol $\pm$, which means "plus or minus." It either describes two numbers or the range of numbers between them. Saying ± 1, means $+1$ and -1. Saying the scores "between ± 1," means all possible scores from -1, through 0, up to and including $+1$.

UNDERSTANDING z-SCORES

So far, we've used statistics to describe the performance of an entire sample. Now, we'll describe the performance of an *individual*. The problem is that psychologists usually don't know how to interpret someone's raw score: We don't know whether, in nature, a score is high or low, good or bad, or what. Instead, the best we can do is examine a score *relative* to the other scores in the distribution. **Relative standing** reflects the systematic evaluation of a score relative to the sample or population in which the score occurs. The way to calculate the relative standing of a score is to transform it into a z-score. Thus, a z-score indicates whether an individual's underlying raw score was relatively good, bad, or in-between.

To see how z-scores indicate relative standing, say that we conduct a study at Prunepit University in which we measure the attractiveness of a sample of males. We train several judges to evaluate participants on the variable of attractiveness, and each male's score is the total number of points assigned by the judges. The attractiveness scores form the normal curve shown in Figure 9.1. We want to interpret these scores, especially those of three men: Slug, who scored 35; Binky, who scored 65; and Biff, who scored 90. Using the statistics you've learned, you already know how to interpret each score in relative terms. Let's review.

What would we say to Slug? "Bad news, Slug. Your score is to the left of the mean, so you're below average in attractiveness in this sample. What's worse, you're *way*

FIGURE 9.1 Frequency Distribution of Attractiveness Scores at Prunepit U

Scores for three individuals are identified on the X axis.

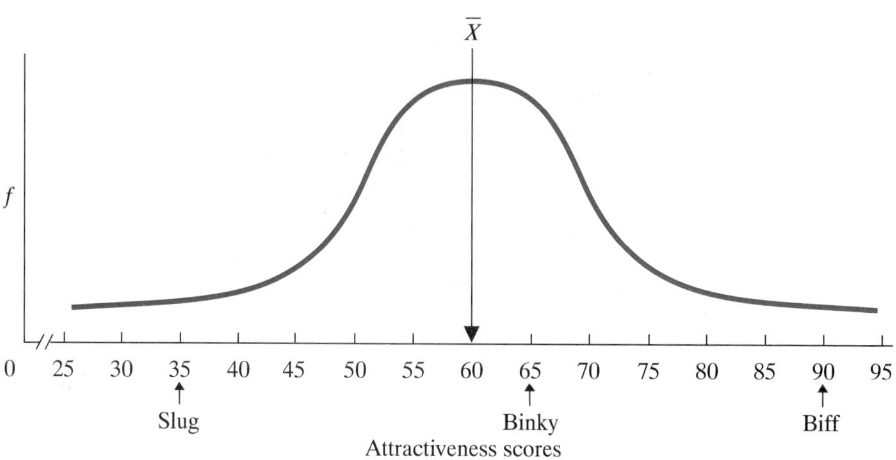

below the mean. Down in the tail of the distribution, the height of the curve above your score is not large, indicating a low *frequency*: Not many men received this low score. Also, the proportion of the total area under the curve at your score is small, so the *relative frequency*—the proportion of men receiving your score—is low. Finally, Slug, your *percentile* is low: A small percentage scored below your score, while a large percentage scored above it. So, Slug, scores like yours are relatively infrequent, and few scores are lower than yours. Relative to the others, you're ugly!"

What would we tell Binky? "Binky, there's good news and bad news. The good news is that your score of 65 is above the mean of 60, which is also the median, or 50th percentile: You are better looking than more than 50% of the sample. The bad news is that you are not *that* far above the mean. The area under the curve at your score is relatively large, and thus the relative frequency of your score is large: The proportion of equally attractive men is large. What's worse, there is a relatively large part of the distribution with higher scores."

And then there is Biff. "Yes, Biff, as you have repeatedly told everyone, you are one of the most attractive men around. The area under the curve at your score, and thus the relative frequency of your score, is quite small: Only a small proportion of the men are equally attractive. Also, the area under the curve to the left of your score is relatively large, so if we cared to figure it out, we'd find that you scored at a very high percentile: A large percentage of scores are below your score, while a small percentage are above your score."

The above interpretations reflect each man's relative standing within the distribution. To do this more precisely, we calculate their *z*-scores.

Describing a Score's Relative Location as a *z*-Score

The above descriptions of each man were determined by his score's location relative to the mean. Therefore, to quantify a score's relative standing, we begin by computing how far the score is above or below the mean. In other words, we first compute the score's deviation, which equals $(X - \bar{X})$. Thus, for example, Biff's raw score of 90 deviates from the mean of 60 by +30 (90 − 60 = +30). The + sign indicates that he is above the mean. A deviation of +30 *sounds* as if it might be a large deviation, but is it? As with a raw score, we do not necessarily know whether a particular deviation score should be considered large or small. Therefore, we need a frame of reference. When we examine the entire distribution, we see that only a few scores deviate by as much as Biff's score, and that is what makes his an impressively high score. Similarly, Slug's score of 35 deviates from the mean by −25 (35 − 60 = −25). This too is impressive, because only a few scores deviate below the mean by such an amount. Thus, a score is impressive if it is far from the mean, and "far" is determined by how frequently other scores deviate by that same amount.

To interpret a score's location, then, we need to compare its deviation to all deviations in the sample. To do this, we need a *standard* to compare to each *deviation*: We need a standard deviation! As in Chapter 8, the standard deviation is our way of computing the "average deviation" of the scores around the mean. By comparing an individual score's deviation to the standard deviation, we can describe the location of the score in terms of the average deviation. For example, say that our sample standard deviation is 10 (10 attractiveness points). Biff's deviation of +30 attractiveness points is equivalent to 3 standard deviations, so Biff's raw score is located 3 standard deviations above the mean. Thus, his raw score is impressive, because it is three times as far above the mean as the "average" amount scores were above the mean.

We have simply described Biff's score in terms of its distance from the mean, measured in standard deviation units. By doing so, we have performed a *z*-score transformation and computed Biff's *z*-score. A ***z*-score** is the distance a raw score deviates from the mean when measured in standard deviations. It is a single number that summarizes a raw score's relative standing: It describes the location of Biff's raw score relative to all scores in the sample.

Note that, like deviations, there are two components to a *z*-score: (1) a *z*-score will be either positive or negative, indicating whether the raw score is above or below the mean, and (2) the absolute value of the *z*-score (ignoring the sign) indicates how far the score lies from the mean when measured in standard deviations. Thus, because originally his deviation was +30, Biff is above the mean by plus 3 standard deviations, and so his *z*-score is +3. If he had been below the mean by this amount, his *z*-score would have been −3.

But, also note a fine distinction here: A *z*-score of +3 identifies a *location* on the distribution that is a *distance* of 3 standard deviations from the mean. (Keep location versus distance straight.)

> ***REMEMBER*** A *z*-score describes a raw score's location in terms of its distance above or below the mean when measured in standard deviations.

Computing *z*-Scores

Above, we performed two mathematical steps to compute Biff's *z*-score. First, we found his score's deviation by subtracting the mean from the raw score. Then we divided the score's deviation by the standard deviation. The symbol for a *z*-score is *z*.

THE FORMULA FOR TRANSFORMING A RAW SCORE IN A SAMPLE INTO A z-SCORE IS

$$z = \frac{X - \overline{X}}{S_X}$$

This is both the definitional and computational formula for z. When starting from scratch with a sample of raw scores, first compute $\overline{X}$ and S_X. Because we are computing a z-score from a *sample* of scores, we use the descriptive sample standard deviation, S_X, (the formula that involves dividing by N).

To find Biff's z-score, we substitute his raw score of 90, the $\overline{X}$ of 60, and the S_X of 10 into the formula:

$$z = \frac{X - \overline{X}}{S_X} = \frac{90 - 60}{10}$$

Find the deviation in the numerator first, and always subtract $\overline{X}$ *from* X. Then,

$$z = \frac{+30}{10}$$

After dividing,

$$z = +3.00$$

Likewise, Binky's raw score of 65 produces a z-score of

$$z = \frac{X - \overline{X}}{S_X} = \frac{65 - 60}{10} = \frac{+5}{10} = +.50$$

Binky's raw score is literally one-half of 1 standard deviation above the mean.

And finally, Slug's raw score is 35, so his z is

$$z = \frac{X - \overline{X}}{S_X} = \frac{35 - 60}{10} = \frac{-25}{10} = -2.50$$

Here, 35 minus 60 results in a deviation of *minus* 25, which, when divided by 10, results in a z-score of -2.50. Slug's raw score is 2.5 standard deviations *below* the mean. When working with z-scores, always pay attention to the positive or negative sign: It is part of the answer.

The previous formula is for describing the relative standing of a score within a *sample*. However, we can also compute a z-score for a score in a *population*, if we know the population mean (μ) and the true standard deviation of the population (σ_X).

THE FORMULA FOR TRANSFORMING A RAW SCORE IN A POPULATION INTO A z-SCORE IS

$$z = \frac{X - \mu}{\sigma_X}$$

This formula is identical to the previous formula except that now the answer indicates how far the raw score lies from the population mean, measured in units of the true population standard deviation. (*Note*: We *never* compute z-scores using the *estimated* population standard deviation, s_X.)

Computing a Raw Score when *z* Is Known

Sometimes we know a z-score and want to find the corresponding raw score. For example, in the Prunepit U. study, say that another student, Bucky, scored $z = +1.00$. What is his raw score? With $\overline{X} = 60$ and $S_X = 10$, his z-score indicates that he is 1 standard deviation above the mean, or, in other words, 10 points above 60. Therefore, his raw score is 70. What did we just do? We multiplied his z-score times S_X and then added the mean.

THE FORMULA FOR TRANSFORMING A z-SCORE IN A SAMPLE INTO A RAW SCORE IS

$$X = (z)(S_X) + \overline{X}$$

For Bucky's z-score of +1.00, we have

$$X = (+1.00)(10) + 60$$

so,

$$X = +10 + 60$$

so,

$$X = 70$$

To check this answer, compute the z-score for the raw score of 70. You should end up with the z-score you started with: +1.00.

Say that Fuzzy has a negative z-score of −1.30 (with $\overline{X} = 60$ and $S_X = 10$). Then,

$$X = (-1.30)(10) + 60$$

so,

$$X = -13 + 60$$

Adding a negative number is the same as subtracting its positive value, so,

$$X = 47$$

Fuzzy has a raw score of 47.

As usual, always check whether your answer makes sense. At the very least, negative z-scores must correspond to raw scores smaller than the mean, and positive z-scores must correspond to raw scores larger than the mean. Further, as you'll see, we seldom obtain z-scores greater than ±3 (plus or minus 3). Although they are possible, be very skeptical if you compute one and double-check your work.

INTERPRETING z-SCORES: THE z-DISTRIBUTION

The way to interpret z-scores is by creating a z-distribution. A ***z*-distribution** is the distribution produced by transforming an entire raw score distribution into z-scores. By transforming all attractiveness scores in the previous study to z-scores, we get the z-distribution shown in Figure 9.2.

Notice the three ways the X axis is labeled. This shows that by creating a z-distribution, we have only transformed the way in which we identify each score. Saying that Biff has a z of $+3$ is merely another way to say that he has a deviation of $+30$, or a raw score of 90. Recognize this very important fact: Because we are still looking at the same point on the distribution, Biff's z-score of $+3$ and his deviation of $+30$ have the same frequency, relative frequency, and percentile as his raw score of 90.

The advantage of looking at z-scores, however, is that they directly communicate a score's relative location in the distribution. The z-score of 0 here corresponds to the mean raw score of 60: A person having the mean score is zero distance from the mean. For any other score, the sign indicates the direction the score lies in relation to the mean. A "+" indicates that the score is above and graphed to the right of the mean. A "−" indicates that the score is below and graphed to the left of the mean. From this perspective, z-scores become increasingly larger numbers with a positive sign as you proceed to raw scores farther above and to the right of the mean, and such larger positive z-scores occur less frequently. Conversely, z-scores become increasingly larger numbers with a negative sign as you proceed to raw scores farther below and to the left of the mean, and such larger negative z-scores occur less frequently. However, do not be misled by negative z-scores: A raw score that is farther below the mean is a *smaller* raw score, but it has a *larger* negative z-score. Thus, for example, a z-score of -2 corresponds to a lower raw score than does a z-score of -1.

FIGURE 9.2 Distribution of Attractiveness Scores at Prunepit U

The labels on the X axis show first the raw scores, then the deviations, and then the z-scores.

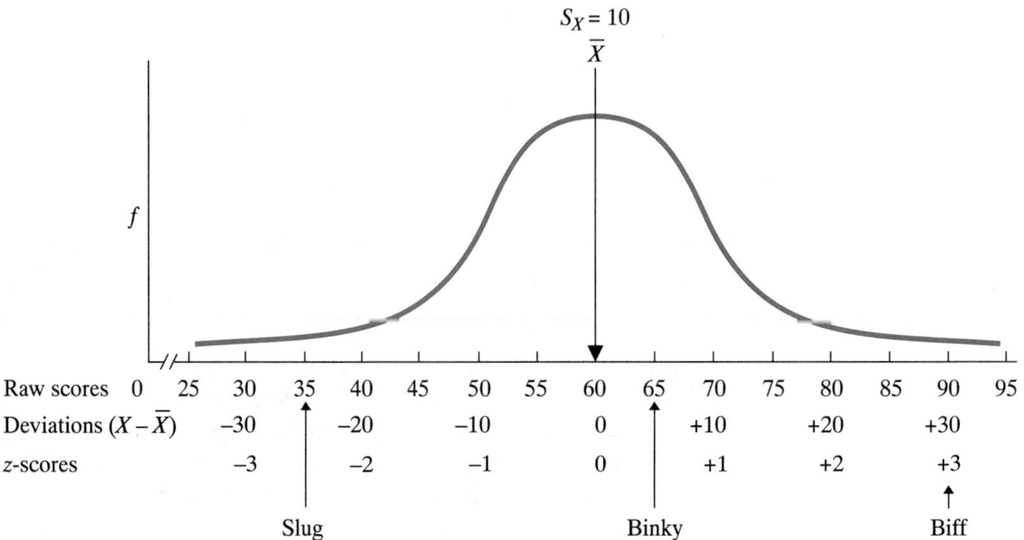

REMEMBER The farther a raw score is from the mean, the larger its corresponding z-score. On a normal distribution, the larger the z-score, whether positive or negative, the less frequently that z-score and the corresponding raw score occur.

Recognize that a negative z-score is not automatically a bad score. It depends on the nature of the variable being measured. For some variables, the goal is to have a low raw score that is below average (errors on a test, number of parking tickets, amount owed on a bill). With these variables, negative z-scores are best.

Characteristics of the z-Distribution

The previous graph illustrates three important characteristics of any z-distribution.

1. *A z-distribution always has the same shape as the raw score distribution.* A z-distribution forms a normal distribution only when the raw scores form a normal distribution.
2. *The mean of any z-distribution always equals 0.* The mean of the raw scores transforms into a z-score of 0. Or, if we compute the mean of the z-scores, the sum of the z-scores is the sum of the positive and negative deviations around the mean, which is 0, so the mean is 0.
3. *The standard deviation of any z-distribution always equals 1.* One standard deviation of the raw scores—regardless of its value—transforms into 1 z-score unit. Whether the standard deviation in the raw scores is 10 or 1, it is still one standard deviation, and one standard deviation is one z-score unit.

Because of these characteristics, all normal z-distributions are similar, so that a particular z-score will be at the same relative location on *any* distribution. Thus, for *any* variable, if $z = 0$, then the raw score equals the mean and is in the middle of the distribution. Or, for *any* variable, if a raw score produces a z of $+3$, it will, like Biff's, be a relatively infrequent score, located at the extreme high end. And so on.

As discussed in the following sections, these similarities provide us with three important uses for z-scores:

1. For comparing scores from different distributions.
2. For interpreting individual scores within a distribution.
3. For describing and interpreting sample means.

USING THE z-DISTRIBUTION TO COMPARE DIFFERENT DISTRIBUTIONS

In research, comparing a score on one variable to a score on a different variable is a problem. For example, say that Althea received a grade of 38 on a statistics quiz and a grade of 45 on an English paper. These grades reflect scores on different kinds of tasks, assigned by different instructors using different criteria, so it's like comparing apples to oranges. To avoid this problem, we transform the raw scores from each class into z-scores. This produces two z-distributions, each with a mean of 0, a standard deviation of 1, and a range of between about -3 and $+3$. Each z-score indicates an individual's relative standing in his or her respective class. Therefore, we can compare Althea's relative standing in English to her relative standing in statistics, and we are no longer comparing apples and oranges. (The z-transformation equates, or standardizes, the distributions, and so z-scores are often referred to as **standard scores**.)

Say that for the statistics quiz, the $\bar{X}$ was 30 and the S_X was 5. We transform all grades to z-scores, including Althea's grade of 38, which becomes $z = +1.60$. For the English paper, say the $\bar{X}$ was 40 and the S_X was 10, so Althea's grade of 45 becomes $z = +.50$. Figure 9.3 shows the locations of Althea's z-scores on the respective z-distributions. The different heights of the curves indicate that the English class contains more students than the statistics class. Regardless, a z-score of $+1.60$ is farther above the mean than a z of $+.50$. Thus, in terms of her relative standing in each class, Althea did better in statistics, because she is farther above the statistics mean than she is above the English mean.

Another student, Millie, obtained raw scores that produced zs of -2.00 in statistics and -1.00 in English. In which class did she do better? Her z-score of -1.00 in English is better, because it is less distance below the mean.

Of course, it would be easier to compare these two distributions if we plotted them on the same set of axes: z-scores enable us to do just that.

Plotting Different z-Distributions on the Same Graph

Transforming the statistics and English scores into z-scores establishes a common variable. Then, to see each student's relative location in each class, we can graph both distributions on one set of axes, as shown in Figure 9.4.

FIGURE 9.3 Comparison of Distributions for Statistics and English Grades, Showing Raw Scores and z-Scores

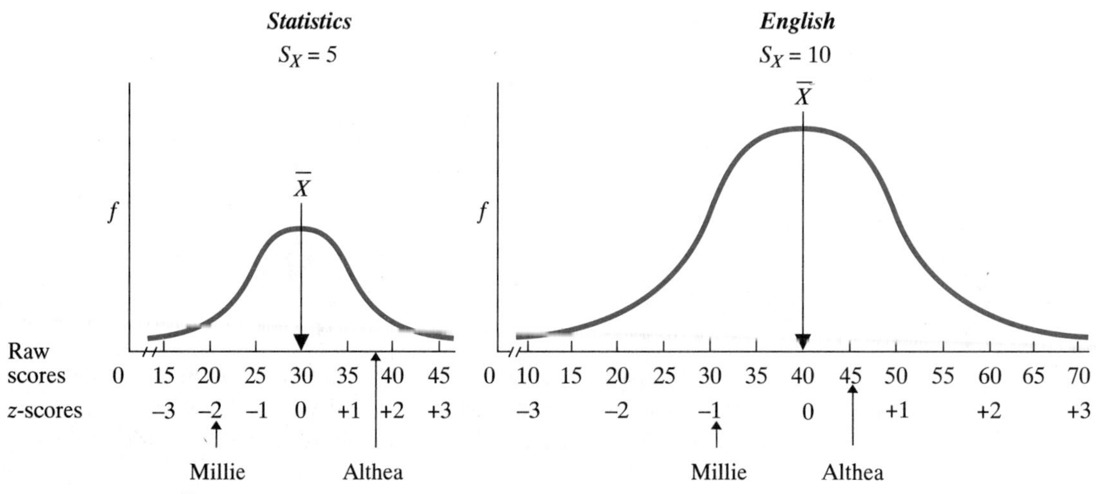

FIGURE 9.4 Comparison of Distributions for Statistics and English Grades, Plotted on the Same Set of Axes

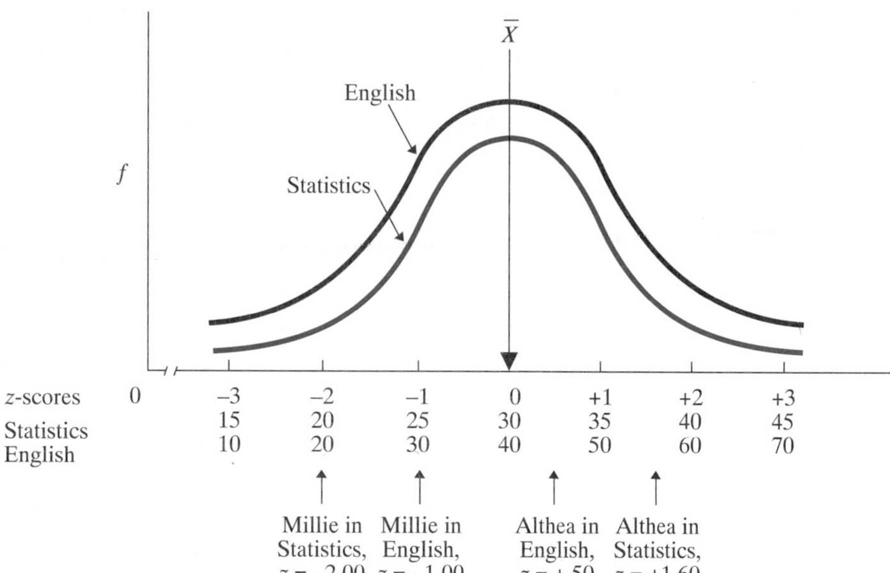

All normal *z*-distributions are similar, so there are only two minor differences between the curves. First, the classes have different standard deviations, so the raw scores for each class are spaced differently along the *X* axis. For example, going from the *z*-score of +1 to +2 corresponds to going from the raw scores of 35 to 40 in statistics, but from 50 to 60 in English. Second, the greater height of the English distribution reflects its larger *N*, so there is a higher *f* for each score. If the two raw score distributions had contained the same *N*, the curves would be identical. By plotting the two distributions on the same set of axes, we can easily compare anyone's scores: Althea scored better in statistics than in English, and Millie scored better in English than in statistics.

> ***REMEMBER*** To compare raw scores from two different variables, transform the scores into *z*-scores.

The fact that different *z*-distributions can be plotted on the same set of axes leads to our second use of the *z*-distribution: interpreting individual raw scores in any normal distribution.

USING THE *z*-DISTRIBUTION TO DESCRIBE INDIVIDUAL SCORES

An important statistical use of *z*-scores is computing the relative frequency of scores. Recall that relative frequency is the proportion of time that a score occurs. The *z*-distribution allows us to easily compute relative frequency, from which we can also compute simple frequency and percentile. Here's how:

Notice just how similar the two distributions are back in Figure 9.4: Any statistics or English raw score that produces the same *z*-score is at the same relative location in the distribution. And this will be true for the *z*-scores from any normally distributed variable. Thus, regardless of the variable, any raw score that equals the mean score has a *z*-score of 0 and is in the center of the *z*-distribution. Or, recall that the raw scores that are $\pm 1S_X$ from the mean are always located at the "inflection points," and now you know that such scores produce *z*-scores of ± 1. Therefore, for any variable, raw scores that produce a *z* of ± 1 are always at the inflection points. Likewise, any other *z*-score will always be in the same relative location on different distributions.

This is important because relative frequency can be computed using the proportion of the total area under the curve. If a particular *z*-score is always at the same location on the normal curve, then the proportion of the total area under the curve for that *z*-score is always the same. Therefore:

> **The relative frequency of a particular *z*-score will be the same on all normal *z*-distributions.**

For example, you already know that 50% of the scores on a normal curve are to the left of the mean. You also know that scores to the left of the mean produce negative *z*-scores, so in other words, negative *z*-scores make up 50% of a distribution. Thus, the students in each class with the negative *z*-scores in Figure 9.4 constitute 50% of their respective distributions. Further, 50% of a distribution corresponds to a relative frequency of .50. Thus, on *any* normal *z*-distribution, the relative frequency of the negative *z*-scores is .50.

Having determined the relative frequency of the *z*-scores, we can work backwards to find the relative frequency of the corresponding raw scores. In the statistics distribution in Figure 9.4, those students having negative *z*-scores have raw scores ranging between 15 and 30, so the relative frequency of scores from 15 to 30 here is .50. Likewise, English students having negative *z*-scores have raw scores ranging between 10 and 40, so the relative frequency of 10 to 40 here is .50.

Similarly, recall from Chapter 8 that approximately 68% of all scores in a normal distribution fall between the scores that are $\pm 1S_X$ from the mean (between the scores at the inflection points.) In other words, therefore, for *any* normal distribution, about 68% of the scores fall between the *z*-scores of $+1$ and -1. Thus, in Figure 9.4, students with *z*-scores between ± 1 constitute approximately 68% of their distributions. Having determined this, we can again work backwards to the raw scores: Statistics grades between 25 and 35 constitute approximately 68% of the statistics distribution, and English grades between 30 and 50 constitute approximately 68% of the English distribution.

In the same way, we can determine the relative frequencies for any set of scores once we envision it as a *z*-distribution. For example, in a normal distribution of IQ scores (whatever the $\overline{X}$ and S_X may be), we know that those IQ scores producing negative *z*-scores have a relative frequency of .50, and about 68% of all IQ scores fall between the two IQ scores corresponding to the *z*-scores of ± 1. The same will hold true for a distribution of running speeds, or a distribution of personality test scores, or for *any* normal distribution.

We can be even more precise and determine the relative frequency of scores in any portion of a distribution. To do so, we employ the standard normal curve.

The Standard Normal Curve

Because the relative frequency and location of a particular z-score is the same on any normal z-distribution, we conceptualize all normal z-distributions as conforming to one, standard curve. In fact, this curve is called the standard normal curve. The **standard normal curve** is a theoretical, perfect normal z-distribution. (Because it is a z-distribution, the mean of the standard normal curve is 0, and the standard deviation is 1.)

We use the standard normal curve to first determine the relative frequency of particular z-scores on a perfect normal curve. Once we know the relative frequency of certain z-scores, we work backwards, as we did above, to determine the relative frequency of the corresponding raw scores.

Thus, the first step is to find the relative frequency of the z-scores. To do this, statisticians have determined the proportion of the area under various parts of the normal curve. Look at Figure 9.5. The numbers above the *X* axis indicate the proportions of the total area between adjacent z-scores. The number on each arrow below the *X* axis, indicates the proportion of the total area between the mean and the z-score. (Don't worry: You don't need to memorize these proportions.)

The proportion of the total area under the curve is the same as relative frequency, so each proportion is the relative frequency of the z-scores located in that section of the curve. For example, .3413 of all z-scores are located between the z of 0 and the z of +1 on a perfect normal distribution. Or, multiplying the proportion times 100, 34.13% of all z-scores fall between the zs of 0 and +1. Similarly, z-scores between +1 and +2 occur 13.59% of the time, and z-scores between +2 and +3 occur 2.15% of the time. Because the distribution is symmetrical, the same proportions occur between the mean and the corresponding negative z-scores.

FIGURE 9.5 Proportions of Total Area Under the Standard Normal Curve

The curve is symmetrical: 50% of the scores fall below the mean, and 50% fall above the mean.

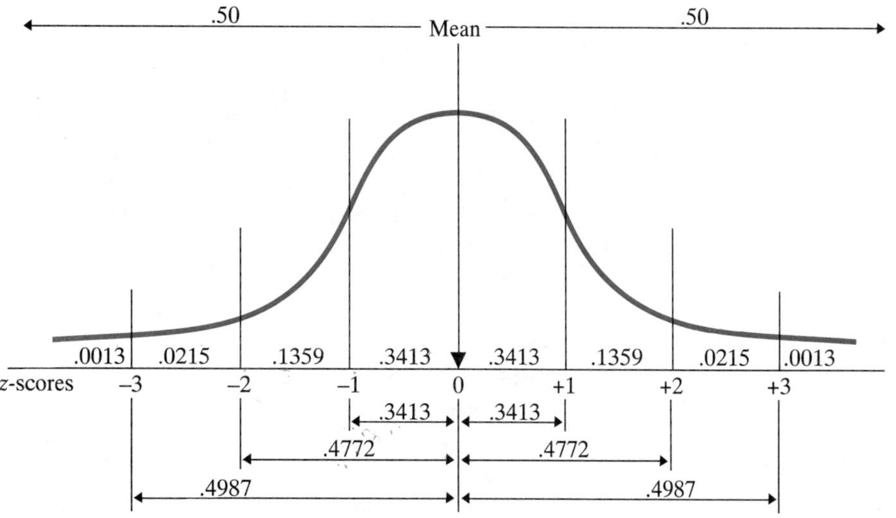

To determine the relative frequency for larger areas, add the above proportions. For example, .3413 of the distribution is located between $z = -1$ and the mean, and .3413 of the distribution is between the mean and $z = +1$. Thus, a total of .6826, or 68.26%, of the distribution is located between the zs of -1 and $+1$. (See, about 68% of the distribution really is between $\pm 1S_X$ from the mean.) We can also add together nonadjacent portions of the curve. For example, .0228, or 2.28%, of the distribution is in the tail of the distribution beyond $z = -2$, and 2.28% is beyond $z = +2$. Thus, a total of 4.56% of all scores fall in the tails beyond $z = \pm 2$.

Figure 9.5 shows why we seldom obtain z-scores greater than ± 3: Only .0013 of the scores are above $z = +3$, and only .0013 are below $z = -3$. In total, only .0026, (.26 of 1 percent) of the scores are beyond ± 3.00. Between $z = \pm 3$, however, is 99.74% of all scores (100% − .26% = 99.74%). Thus, for all practical purposes, the range of z is between ± 3. Also, now you can see why, in Chapter 8, I said that for normally distributed scores, the value of S_X should be about one-sixth of the range of the raw scores. The range for most raw scores is between $z = -3$ and $z = +3$, a distance of six times the standard deviation. If the range is six times the standard deviation, then the standard deviation is one-sixth of the range.

Applying the Standard Normal Curve Model

The above standard normal curve is especially useful in psychological research, because most variables are more or less normally distributed (at least in the population.) However, we do not draw a "more or less" normal curve to conceptualize each distribution. Instead, we greatly simplify nature by using the ideal normal curve as our "model" of the actual distribution, operating as if the raw scores form this curve. Essentially, the actual, roughly normal distribution is treated as coming "close enough" to the ideal that we assume the perfect normal curve is a reasonably accurate description of it. If we assume the raw scores form a perfect normal curve, then, by transforming the raw scores to z-scores, we'd have a perfect normal z-distribution. We envision any perfect normal z-distribution as the standard normal curve. Therefore, we can use the above procedures and the standard normal curve to describe any roughly normal distribution.

To find the relative frequency of raw scores in any part of the curve, first, transform the raw scores into z-scores. Then, from the standard normal curve, determine the proportion of the total area at these z-scores. This proportion is the relative frequency of the z-scores on a perfect normal curve. The relative frequency of the z-scores, however, equals the relative frequency of their corresponding raw scores on a perfect normal curve. Thus, the relative frequency obtained from the standard normal curve is the *expected* relative frequency of the raw scores in our data, if the data formed a perfect normal distribution.

> **REMEMBER** For any approximately normal distribution, transform the raw scores to z-scores and use the standard normal curve to find the expected relative frequency of the scores.

For example, the original attractiveness scores from Prunepit U. form an approximately normal distribution, so we can apply the standard normal curve model here. Say that Cubby has a raw score of 80, which, with $\overline{X} = 60$ and $S_X = 10$, is a z of $+2$. We can envision Cubby's location on the distribution as in Figure 9.6. We might first ask what

FIGURE 9.6 Location of Cubby's Score on the z-Distribution of Attractiveness Scores

Cubby is at approximately the 98th percentile.

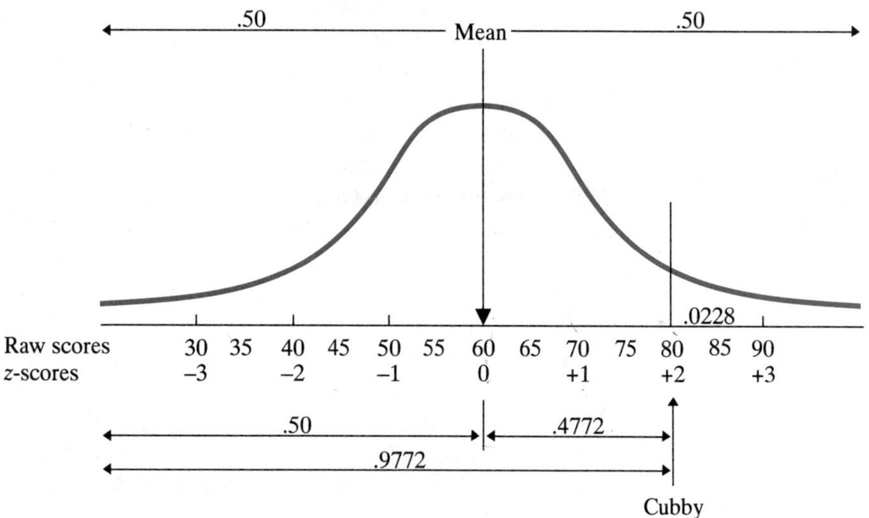

proportion of scores are expected to fall between the mean and Cubby's score. On the standard normal curve, .4772 of the total area falls between the mean and $z = +2$. Therefore, .4772 of all z-scores fall between the mean and a z of $+2$, so we expect .4772, or 47.72%, of all attractiveness scores at Prunepit U. to fall between the mean score of 60 and Cubby's score of 80.

We might also ask how *many* people scored between the mean and Cubby's score. Then we would convert the above relative frequency to simple frequency by multiplying the N of the sample times the relative frequency. Say that the N at Prunepit was 1000. If we expect .4772 of all scores to fall between the mean and a z of $+2$, then $(.4772)(1000) = 477.2$, so we expect about 477 scores to fall between the mean and Cubby's score.

How accurately the expected relative frequency from the model describes the actual scores depends on three aspects of the data:

1. The closer the raw scores are to forming a normal distribution, the more accurately the model describes the data. Therefore, use the standard normal curve model *only* if you can assume that the data are at least approximately normally distributed.
2. The larger the sample N, the more closely the sample tends to conform to a normal curve and, therefore, the more accurate the model will be. The model is most accurate when applied to very large samples or to populations.
3. The model is most appropriate when raw scores are theoretically continuous scores measured using ratio or interval scales.

The Prunepit data meet these requirements, so the expected results for Cubby should be fairly accurate.

Finding percentile for a given raw score We can also use the standard normal curve model to determine a score's expected percentile. Recall that a percentile is the percent of all scores below—graphed to the left of—a score. For example, to determine Cubby's percentile, look again back at Figure 9.6.

On a normal distribution, the mean is the median (the 50th percentile). Any positive z-score is above the mean, so Cubby's z-score of +2 is above the 50th percentile. In fact, as shown, Cubby's score is above the 47.72% of the scores that fall between the mean and his z-score. Thus, add the 50% of the scores below the mean to the 47.72% of the scores between the mean and his score. In total, 97.72% of all z-scores are below Cubby's z-score. In round numbers, Cubby's z-score is at the 98th percentile. Likewise, Cubby's raw score of 80 is at the 98th percentile. Conversely, if 97.72% of the curve is below a z of +2, then, as shown, only 2.28% of the curve is above a z of +2 (100% − 97.72% = 2.28%). Thus, anyone scoring above $z = +2$, or above the raw score of 80, would be in about the top 2% of all scores.

On the other hand, say that Elvis obtained an attractiveness score of 40, producing a z-score of −2. Find Elvis's percentile using Figure 9.7. Because .0215 of the distribution is between $z = -2$ and $z = -3$, and .0013 of the distribution is below $z = -3$, there is a total of .0228, or 2.28%, of the distribution below (to the left of) Elvis's score. With rounding, Elvis ranks at the 2nd percentile.

Finding a raw score at a given percentile We can also work in the opposite direction, finding a raw score at a particular relative frequency or percentile. Say that we want to find the raw score at the 16th percentile. Because the 16th percentile is below the 50th percentile, we are looking for a negative z-score. Consider Figure 9.8. If 16% of all scores are below the unknown score, then 34% of all scores are between it

FIGURE 9.7 Location of Elvis's Score on the z-Distribution of Attractiveness Scores

Elvis is at approximately the 2nd percentile.

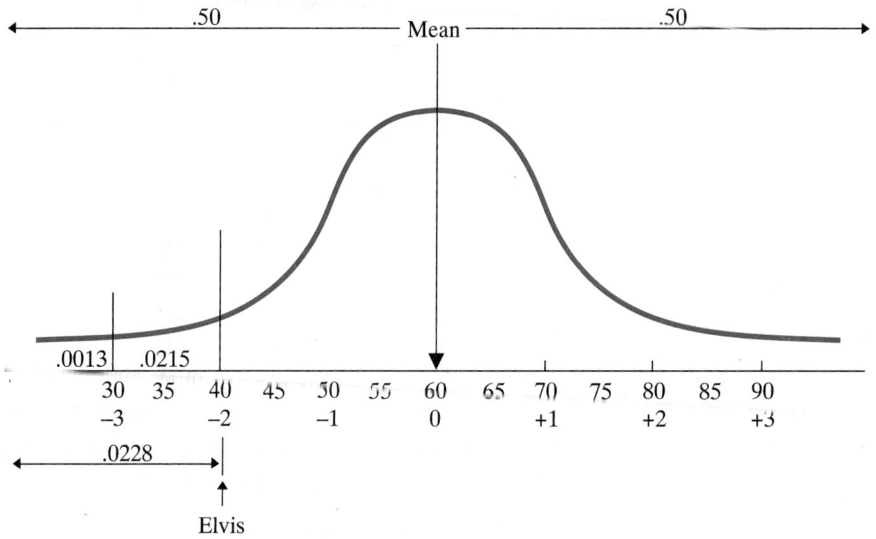

FIGURE 9.8 Proportions of the Standard Normal Curve at Approximately the 16th Percentile

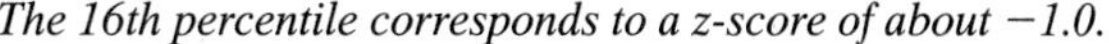
The 16th percentile corresponds to a z-score of about −1.0.

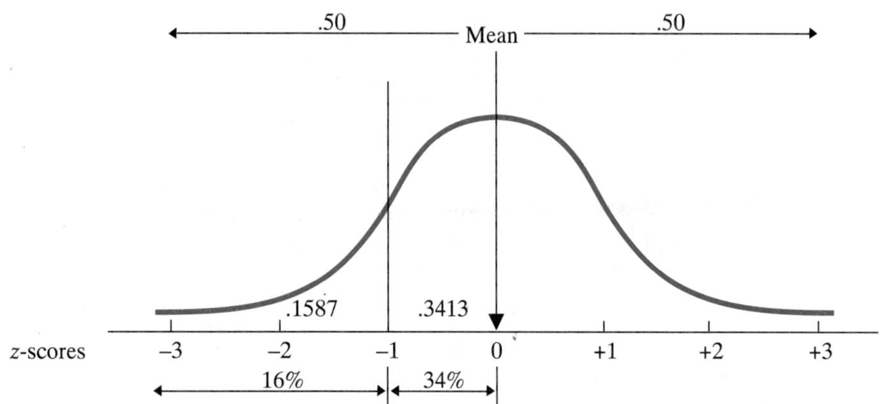

and the mean (50% − 16% = 34%). We have already seen that about 34% of a normal distribution is between a z of -1 and the mean, so that leaves about 16% of the distribution to the left of a z of -1 (although technically it is 50% − 34.13% = 15.87%). Thus, with rounding, a z of -1 is at approximately the 16th percentile.

We then use the formula $X = (z)(S_X) + \overline{X}$ to find the raw score at $z = -1$. For this sample, $\overline{X} = 60$ and $S_X = 10$, so $X = (-1)(10) + 60 = 50$. Thus, the raw score of 50 is expected to be at approximately the 16th percentile.

Using the z-Tables

So far, our examples have involved whole-number z-scores, although with real data, a z-score may contain decimals. However, fractions of z-scores do *not* result in proportional divisions of the previous areas. For example, the area between the mean and $z = +.5$ is *not* one-half of the area between the mean and $z = +1$. Instead, find the proportion of the total area under the standard normal curve by looking in Table 1 of Appendix C. This is called the *z-tables*, a portion of which is reproduced in Table 9.1 on the next page.

Say that you seek the proportions corresponding to $z = +1.63$. First, locate $z = 1.63$ in column A, labeled "z," and then move to the right. Column B, labeled "Area between the mean and z," contains the proportion of the area under the curve between the mean and the z identified in column A. Thus, .4484 of the curve, or 44.84% of all z-scores, is between the mean and $z = +1.63$. This is shown in Figure 9.9. Column C is labeled "Area beyond z in the tail" and contains the proportion of the curve that is in the tail beyond the z-score in column A. Thus, .0516 of the curve, or 5.16% of all z-scores, is in the tail of the distribution beyond $z = +1.63$ (also shown in Figure 9.9). If you get confused when using the z-tables, look at the normal distribution at the top of the tables. The shaded portion and arrows indicate the part of the curve described in each column.

TABLE 9.1 Sample Portion of the z-Tables

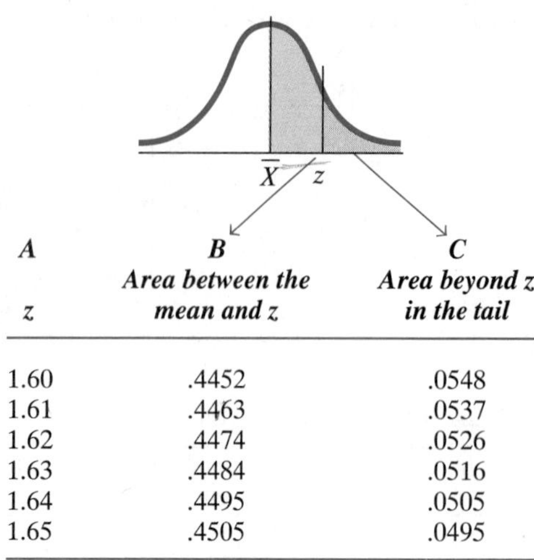

A z	B *Area between the mean and z*	C *Area beyond z in the tail*
1.60	.4452	.0548
1.61	.4463	.0537
1.62	.4474	.0526
1.63	.4484	.0516
1.64	.4495	.0505
1.65	.4505	.0495

To work in the opposite direction and find the z-score that corresponds to a particular proportion, read the columns in the opposite order. First, find the proportion in column B or C, depending on the area you seek, and then identify the corresponding z-score in column A. For example, say that you seek the z-score that demarcates 44.84% of the curve between the mean and z. In column B of the tables find .4484, which corresponds to the z-score of 1.63.

Notice that the z-tables contain no positive or negative signs. Because the normal distribution is symmetrical, only the proportions for one-half of the curve are given. *You* must decide whether z is positive or negative, based on the problem you're working.

Sometimes you will need a proportion not given in the z-tables, or you will need the proportion for a z-score that has three decimal places. In such cases, use the mathematical procedure called *linear interpolation* (described in Part 3 of Appendix B).

FIGURE 9.9 Distribution Showing the Area Under the Curve Above $z = +1.63$ and Between $z = +1.63$ and the Mean

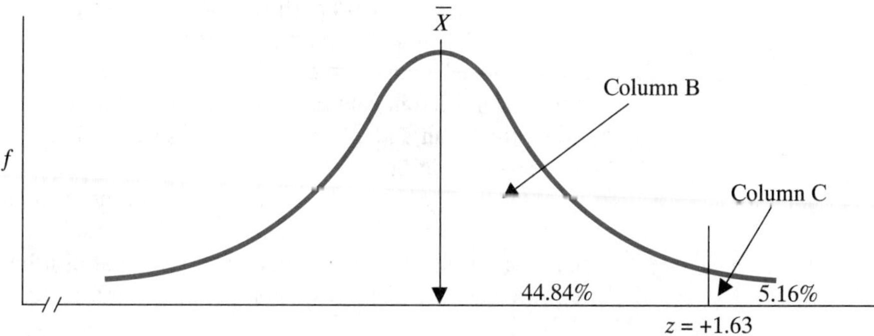

TABLE 9.2 Summary of Steps when Using the z-Tables

If you seek	*First you should*	*Then you*
Relative frequency of scores between $\bar{X}$ and X	transform X to z	find its area in column B*
Relative frequency of scores beyond X in tail	transform X to z	find its area in column C*
X that marks a given *rel. f* between X and $\bar{X}$	Find *rel. f* in column B	transform its z to X
X that marks a given *rel. f* beyond X in tail	find *rel. f* in column C	transform its z to X
Percentile of an X above $\bar{X}$	transform X to z	find area in column B and add .50
Percentile of an X below $\bar{X}$	transform X to z	find area in column C

*To find the simple frequency of the scores, multiply *rel. f* times N.

In summary, then, with the z-tables you can answer virtually any question about the relative standing of scores in any normal distribution. Table 9.2 summarizes the ways we have done this.

Don't lose sight of why it's important to know about these procedures. We use z-scores and the standard normal curve to describe relative standing because we can get a pretty good estimate of relative frequency, simple frequency, or percentile, *without* having to count up and examine the many individual scores that may be present. Instead, we simply need to know the mean and standard deviation and that the distribution is roughly normal. This simplifies the task when dealing with a sample, and it is the only way to deal with an infinitely large and thus unknown population.

Using z-Scores to Define Psychological Attributes

Z-scores often form the basis for defining a psychological attribute or characteristic. Because it is difficult to interpret the absolute value of any single raw score in the grand scheme of nature, it is also difficult to decide on the "cutoff" scores to use when classifying people based on these scores. What must someone do to be considered a genius? How do we define an abnormal personality? To answer such questions, psychologists often use a "statistical definition" based on relative standing. Essentially, this involves applying the normal curve model and defining an attribute in terms of a particular z-score. For example, we might statistically define the old-fashioned term "genius" as a person with a z-score of more than +2 on an intelligence test. Because a z greater than +2 falls in about the highest 2% of the distribution, we have defined a genius as anyone who scores in the top 2% of all IQ scores. Similarly, we might define as "abnormal" any person with a z-score beyond ±2 on a personality test. Such scores are "abnormal" in a statistical sense, because they are very infrequent in the population and are among the most extreme raw scores.

Instructors who "curve" grades generally do so using the normal curve and z-scores. They assume that grades are normally distributed, so they assign letter grades based on proportions of the area under the normal curve. If the instructor defines an A student as one who is in the top 2%, then students with z-scores greater than +2 receive As. If the instructor defines B students as those in the next 13%, then students having z-scores between +1 and +2 receive Bs, and so on.

USING z-SCORES TO DESCRIBE SAMPLE MEANS

So far, we've discussed using the standard normal curve model to describe the relative standing of any single raw score. Now, using the same logic, we'll determine the relative standing of an entire sample by evaluating its sample mean. This procedure is important, not only because it allows you to evaluate a sample, but also because it is the basis for inferential statistics (and you will be computing some of those in the very near future).

To see how the procedure works, say that we are investigating college entrance exams, and using the Scholastic Aptitude Test (SAT) we test a random sample of 25 students at Prunepit U. Their mean score is 520. Nationally the mean of *individual* SAT scores is 500 (and $\sigma_X = 100$), so it appears that at least some Prunepit students scored relatively high, pulling the overall mean to 520. But how do we interpret the performance of the sample as a whole? Is a sample mean of 520 impressively above average, or more mundane? By considering only the sample mean, we cannot answer this question, because we have the same problem we had when examining an individual raw score: Without a frame of reference, we don't know whether, in the grand scheme of things, a particular sample mean is good, bad, or indifferent.

The solution is to evaluate a sample mean in terms of its relative standing. Previously, we compared a particular raw score to all other possible scores that occur in this situation. Now, we'll compare a sample mean to the other sample means that might occur in this situation. As you'll see, we envision the possible sample means that might occur as a distribution of sample means. Then, by locating our sample mean on this distribution, we can determine whether the Prunepit sample is relatively impressive.

The first step, therefore, is to take a little detour and see how to create the distribution of all possible sample means. This distribution is called the sampling distribution of means.

The Sampling Distribution of Means

If the national average of SAT scores is 500, then, in the population of SAT scores, the mean (μ) is 500. Because we randomly selected a sample of 25 students and obtained their SAT scores, we essentially drew a random sample of 25 scores from this population. To evaluate our sample mean, we will first create a distribution showing the other means we might have obtained when randomly selecting a sample of 25 scores from this population.

One way to do this would be to record all SAT scores from the population on slips of paper and deposit them in a very large hat. We could then hire a statistician, and so that we can see *all* possible sample means that occur in this situation, have her sample the population an *infinite* number of times. (She'd get very bored, so the pay would have to be good.) She would randomly select a sample with the same size N as our's (25), compute the sample mean, replace the scores in the hat, draw another 25 scores, compute the mean, and so on. Because not all samples would contain the same scores, not all sample means would be the same. By constructing a frequency distribution of the different values of $\overline{X}$ she obtained, the statistician would create a sampling distribution of means. The **sampling distribution of means** is the frequency distribution of all possible sample means that occur when an infinite number of samples of the same size are randomly selected from one raw score population. Thus, the SAT sampling distribution of means is the population of all possible sample means that can occur when the SAT raw score population is exhaustively sampled using an N of 25. It is shown in Figure 9.10. A sampling distribution is similar to previous frequency distributions of raw scores, except that here each "score" on the X axis is a sample mean. Because this contains all possible SAT sample means, it contains the sample means we might have obtained with the Prunepit sample instead of our mean of 520. Therefore, by looking at this sampling distribution, we can determine the standing of our sample mean relative to all others and thus have a better idea of how to interpret it.

Notice that, as discussed in Chapter 5, the bored statistician used *simple* random sampling. We assume that this sampling technique generally produces the means that we might have obtained, even if in our actual study, we used some other sampling technique.

Think of the sampling distribution as something the bored statistician could create by infinitely sampling the underlying raw score population. In reality, however, we cannot "infinitely" sample a population, so Figure 9.10 shows a "theoretical sampling distribution." Nonetheless, we still know that the sampling distribution would look like this because of something called the central limit theorem. The **central limit theorem** is a statistical principle that defines (1) the shape of a theoretical sampling distribution, (2) the mean of the sampling distribution, and (3) the standard deviation of the sampling distribution.

FIGURE 9.10 Sampling Distribution of Random Sample Means of SAT Scores

The X axis shows the different values of $\overline{X}$ obtained when we sample the population of SAT scores where the mean is 500.

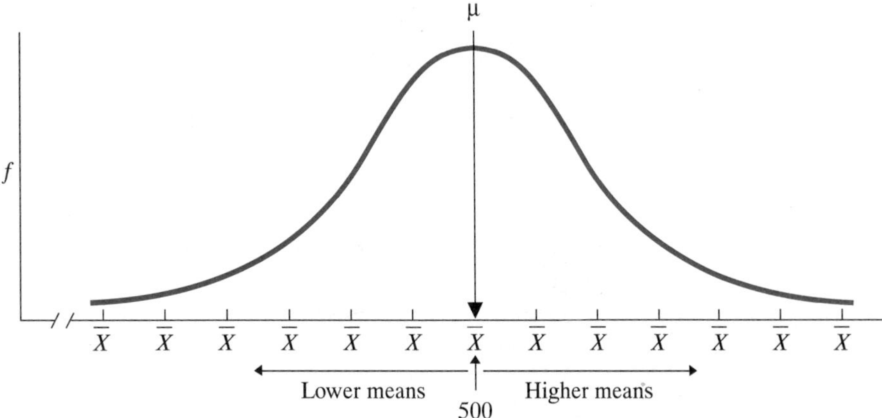

First, the central limit theorem says that the sampling distribution is always an approximately normal distribution, regardless of the shape of the underlying raw score distribution that we use to produce it. Thus, we know that the sampling distribution of SAT means forms an approximately normal distribution. Logically, this is because most often each $\overline{X}$ will equal the raw score population's μ. Sometimes, however, a sample will contain a few more high scores or low scores relative to the population, so the sample mean will be close to, but slightly above or below, μ. Less frequently, the statistician would obtain rather strange samples, producing $\overline{X}$s farther above or below μ. (The larger the N of the samples, the more closely the distribution conforms to the perfect normal curve.)

Second, the central limit theorem tells us that the mean of the sampling distribution always equals the mean of the underlying raw score population that we use to create the sampling distribution. The sampling distribution is the *population* of sample means, so its mean is called μ (and remember, it is the average sample mean.) Thus, back in Figure 9.10, the μ for individual SAT scores is 500, so the μ of the sampling distribution is 500. Logically, more often than not the bored statistician will select scores *around* 500 in each sample, so the $\overline{X}$s will average out to be 500.

Finally, although it's not shown in Figure 9.10, the sample means may be very different from one another and deviate greatly from the average sample mean (μ), or they may be very similar and deviate little from μ. The central limit theorem tells us that, as you'll see, the "standard deviation" of the sampling distribution can be calculated from the standard deviation of the underlying raw score population.

The importance of the central limit theorem is that we know the mean, standard deviation, and shape of the sampling distribution, *without* having to actually sample the infinite population of SAT scores. All we need to know is what the mean and standard deviation of the raw scores are, and that they are normally distributed. Likewise, the central limit theorem allows us to envision the sampling distribution that would be produced for *any* population of raw scores if we know these characteristics.

Why do we want to see the sampling distribution? Remember we took a small detour, but the original problem was to evaluate the Prunepit mean of 520. Once we envision the distribution in Figure 9.10, we have a model showing the frequency that different sample means occur simply by the luck of the draw when sampling the SAT population. Sometimes a sample mean higher than 500 occurs because, by chance, the statistician randomly selects a sample of predominantly high scores. At other times she might select mostly low scores, producing a mean below 500. And so on. Because our original Prunepit sample was a random sample obtained by chance from this population, this picture allows us to evaluate our sample mean relative to all other sample means that might occur in this situation.

To evaluate our sample, we simply need to determine where a mean of 520 falls on the X axis of the sampling distribution in Figure 9.10 and then interpret it accordingly. If 520 lies close to 500, then it is a frequent, common mean when sampling SAT scores. But if 520 lies far from 500 in the upper tail of the distribution, then it is a more unusual sample mean, because literally, such a mean seldom occurs in this situation. The sampling distribution is a normal distribution, and you already know how to determine the location of any "score" on a normal distribution—z-scores! That is, we determine how far the sample mean deviates from the mean of the sampling distribution, measured using the standard deviation of the distribution. Then, the z-score will tell us the sample mean's relative location within the sampling distribution, and thus indicate its relative standing among all means that occur in this situation.

To calculate the z-score for a sample mean, we need one more piece of information: The "standard deviation" of the sampling distribution.

The Standard Error of the Mean

The standard deviation of the sampling distribution of means is called the **standard error of the mean**. (The term "standard deviation" was already taken.) Recall that the terms *error* and *deviation* are synonymous. Therefore, like a standard deviation, the standard error of the mean can be thought of as the "average" amount that the sample means deviate from the μ of the sampling distribution.

For the moment, we'll discuss the *true* standard error of the mean, as if we had actually computed it using the entire sampling distribution. The symbol for the true standard error of the mean is $\sigma_{\overline{X}}$. The σ indicates that we are describing a population, but the subscript $\overline{X}$ indicates that we are describing the population of sample means—what we call the sampling distribution of means. The central limit theorem tells us that $\sigma_{\overline{X}}$ can be found using the following formula:

THE FORMULA FOR THE TRUE STANDARD ERROR OF THE MEAN IS

$$\sigma_{\overline{X}} = \frac{\sigma_X}{\sqrt{N}}$$

Notice that this formula involves σ_X: When we know the true standard deviation of the underlying raw score population, we can calculate the true "standard deviation" of the sampling distribution.

> ***REMEMBER*** The true standard error of the mean ($\sigma_{\overline{X}}$) is computed using the true standard deviation (σ_X) of the population of raw scores that is used to create the sampling distribution.

In the formula, the size of $\sigma_{\overline{X}}$ depends, first, on the size of σ_X. Logically, if the raw scores are highly variable, then each sample is likely to contain a very different set of scores and thus produce a very different mean each time (and so $\sigma_{\overline{X}}$ will be large). But, if the raw scores are not variable, then different samples will tend to contain the same scores, and so the means will be similar to one another (and $\sigma_{\overline{X}}$ will be small). Also, the size of $\sigma_{\overline{X}}$ depends on the size of N. With a very small N (say 2), it is easy for each sample to be very different from the next, so the sample means will differ (and $\sigma_{\overline{X}}$ will be large). However, with a large N, each sample will be more representative, so that all sample means will be closer to the population mean (and so $\sigma_{\overline{X}}$ will be small).

In our example, we can compute $\sigma_{\overline{X}}$ for the sampling distribution of SAT scores because we *know* that the true standard deviation of the population of SAT scores is 100. Because N was 25, the above formula says that the standard error of the mean is

$$\sigma_{\overline{X}} = \frac{100}{\sqrt{25}} = \frac{100}{5}$$

and so,

$$\sigma_{\bar{X}} = 20$$

A $\sigma_{\bar{X}} = 20$ indicates that in the SAT sampling distribution, the individual sample means differ from the μ of 500 by an "average" of 20 SAT points when the N of each sample is 25.

Now, at last, we can calculate a z-score for our sample mean.

Calculating a *z*-Score for a Sample Mean

Previously, you saw that when we know the population mean and the population standard deviation, the formula for transforming a raw score into a z-score is

$$z = \frac{X - \mu}{\sigma_X}$$

We transform a sample mean into a z-score using a similar formula.

THE FORMULA FOR TRANSFORMING A SAMPLE MEAN INTO A z-SCORE IS

$$z = \frac{\bar{X} - \mu}{\sigma_{\bar{X}}}$$

Don't be confused by the minor difference in symbols between the preceding formulas. In both, we are finding how far a score falls from the mean of a distribution, measured in standard deviations of that distribution. For a sample mean, we find how far the sample mean is from the mean of the sampling distribution (μ) measured in standard error units ($\sigma_{\bar{X}}$).

Using the above formula, we can calculate the z-score for the Prunepit sample. With $\bar{X} = 520$, $\mu = 500$, and $\sigma_{\bar{X}} = 20$, we have

$$z = \frac{\bar{X} - \mu}{\sigma_{\bar{X}}} = \frac{520 - 500}{20} = \frac{+20}{20} = +1.0$$

Thus, a sample mean of 520 has a z-score of $+1.0$ on the sampling distribution of means that occurs when N is 25, and the sampling distribution is created from the SAT raw score population, where $\mu = 500$ and $\sigma_X = 100$.

Using the Sampling Distribution to Determine the Relative Frequency of Sample Means

It is important to calculate a z-score for a sample mean, because then, everything we've said about a z-score for a raw score applies to the z-score for a sample mean. A z-score is a z-score! Thus, because our sample mean has a z-score of $+1$, we know that it's above the μ of the sampling distribution by an amount equal to the "average" amount that sample means deviate from μ. Therefore, we know that, although they were not stellar, the Prunepit students did outperform a substantial proportion of comparable samples. Likewise, if another sample of 25 SAT scores (say from Podunk U.) produced a mean of 440, we'd know how poorly these students performed: Here, $z = (440 - 500)/20 = -3.0$, so this sample mean would be among the lowest SAT means we'd ever expect to obtain.

To obtain a more precise description of a sample mean, we can go one step further: Because the sampling distribution of means is at least an approximately normal distribution, if we transformed *all* of the sample means in the sampling distribution into z-scores, we would have a roughly normal z-distribution. Recall that the standard normal curve is our model of *any* normal z-distribution. This is true even if it is a z-distribution of sample means! Therefore, as we did previously for raw scores, we can use the standard normal curve model and the z-tables to determine the expected relative frequency, simple frequency, or percentile for any sample mean.

Figure 9.11 shows the standard normal curve applied to the SAT sampling distribution. This is the same curve, with the same proportions, that we saw when describing raw scores. Once again, the farther a score (here a $\overline{X}$) is from the mean of the distribution (here μ), the larger the absolute value of the z-score. The larger the z-score, the smaller the relative frequency and simple frequency of the z-score and of the corresponding sample mean. Therefore, we again can use the z-tables to determine the proportion of the area under any part of the curve. This proportion is also the expected relative frequency of the corresponding sample means in that part of the sampling distribution.

For example, the sample from Prunepit U. has a z of $+1$ and, as you know, 34.13% of all scores fall between the mean and $z = +1$ on *any* normal distribution. Thus, 34.13% of all SAT sample means will fall between μ and the sample mean at a z of $+1$. Because, in our data, the μ is 500 and a z of $+1$ is at the sample mean of 520, we can also say that 34.13% of all SAT sample means are expected to fall between 500 and 520 (when N is 25). Further, by adding in the 50% of the distribution below μ, we see that about 84% of all means fall below—are to the left of—a z of $+1$. Therefore, our sample mean of 520 ranks at about the 84th percentile among all SAT sample means.

FIGURE 9.11 Proportions of the Standard Normal Curve Applied to the Sampling Distribution of SAT Means

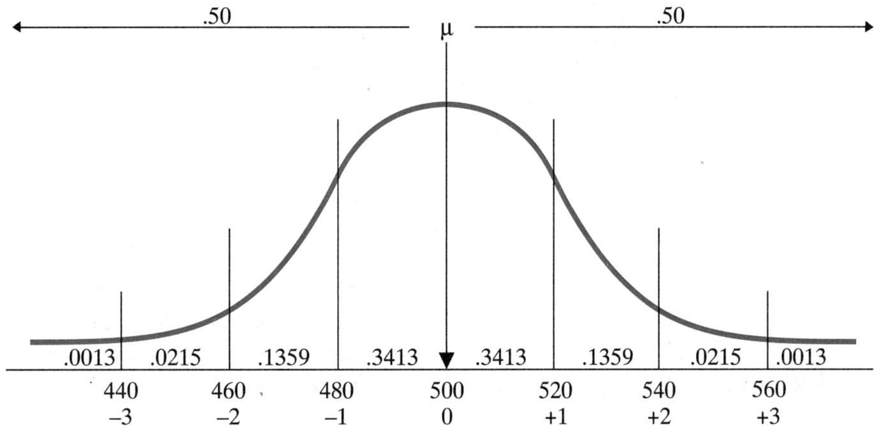

Similarly, a different sample mean of 540 would have a z of $+2$ on this sampling distribution. Because we know that about 2% of all z-scores are above a z of $+2$, we expect that only about 2% of all SAT sample means will be larger than 540. And, finally, say that we were about to test 500 samples: 2% of 500 is $(.02)(500) = 10$, so we would expect 10 of these samples to have a $\overline{X}$ above 540.

Thus, in summary, we can use this approach to describe a sample mean from any raw score population, if we know the population's μ and σ_X. First, using our sample's N and the σ_X, calculate the standard error of the mean ($\sigma_{\overline{X}}$.) Then, envision the sampling distribution (or better yet, draw it) as a normal distribution with a μ equal to the μ of the underlying raw score population. Then, using z-scores and the z-tables, you can determine relative frequency or describe the sample mean using any of the procedures we used for individual raw scores that were summarized back in Table 9.2.

> ***REMEMBER*** The way to describe and interpret a raw score or a sample mean is to transform it to a z-score and then apply the standard normal curve model.

APA FORMAT FOR STATISTICAL NOTATION

In published research, the symbol for a z-score is actually "z." The true standard error of the mean—what we've called $\sigma_{\overline{X}}$—is seldom reported, so there is no APA-approved symbol for it. In such situations, the term is described in words. There is, however, the symbol "*SE*," which is called the standard error, but because it uses English letters, it stands for an estimate, computed from sample data. We'll discuss this in Chapter 14.

PUTTING IT ALL TOGETHER

The most important concept for you to understand is that any normal distribution of scores can be described using the standard normal curve model and z-scores. To paraphrase a famous saying, a normal distribution is a normal distribution is a normal distribution. Any normal distribution contains the same proportions of the total area under the curve between z-scores. Therefore, picture a normal distribution and repeat after me: The larger the z-score, whether positive or negative, the farther the z-score and the corresponding raw score are from the mean of the distribution. The farther they are from the mean, the lower the relative frequency of the z-score and of the corresponding raw score. This is true whether the raw score is an individual's score or a sample mean.

By the way, what was Biff's percentile?

CHAPTER SUMMARY

1. The *relative standing* of a score reflects a systematic evaluation of the score relative to the sample or population. A *z-score* indicates a score's relative standing by indicating the distance the score is above or below the mean, measured in standard deviations.

2. The larger a positive z-score, the farther the raw score is above the mean. The larger the absolute value of a negative z-score, the farther the raw score is below the mean.

3. Transforming a raw score distribution into z-scores produces a *z-distribution*. The z-distribution has the same shape as the raw score distribution, but the mean of a z-distribution is always 0 and the standard deviation is always 1.

4. The *standard normal curve* is a perfect normal curve that is used as a model of any z-distribution when (a) the distribution is at least roughly normally distributed, and (b) the corresponding raw scores reflect an interval or ratio scale.

5. The *z-tables* give the proportion of the area under any part of the standard normal curve and this equals the relative frequency of z-scores falling in that part. This relative frequency leads to the *expected* relative frequency, simple frequency, and percentile of the corresponding raw scores.

6. The *sampling distribution of means* is the distribution of sample means obtained when samples of a particular N are randomly selected from a raw score population.

7. The *central limit theorem* shows that (a) the sampling distribution of means will be approximately normal, (b) the mean of the sampling distribution will equal the mean of the underlying raw score population, and (c) the variability of the sample means is related to the variability in the raw score population.

8. The true *standard error of the mean* ($\sigma_{\overline{X}}$) is the standard deviation of the sampling distribution of means. Computed when σ_X is known, $\sigma_{\overline{X}}$ indicates the average amount that sample means deviate from the μ of the sampling distribution.

9. The location of a sample mean on the sampling distribution of means can be described by calculating a z-score. It indicates the distance the sample mean ($\overline{X}$) is from the mean of the distribution (μ) measured in standard error units ($\sigma_{\overline{X}}$).

10. The z-tables give the proportion of the area under a part of the standard normal curve that is the expected relative frequency of sample means in that part of the sampling distribution of means.

11. Biff's percentile was 99.87.

KEY TERMS (with page references)

$\pm$ z $\sigma_{\overline{X}}$
central limit theorem (237)
relative standing (219)
sampling distribution of means (237)
standard error of the mean (239)
standard normal curve (229)
standard scores (226)
z-distribution (224)
z-score (221)

REVIEW QUESTIONS

(Answers for odd-numbered questions and problems are provided in Appendix D.)

1. (a) What does a z-score indicate? (b) What two factors influence the size of a particular z-score?
2. Why are z-scores beyond ± 3 seldom obtained?
3. What is a z-distribution?
4. What are the three uses of z-distributions when describing individual scores?
5. Why are z-scores referred to as standard scores?
6. Why is using z-scores and the standard normal curve model so useful?
7. (a) What is the standard normal curve model? (b) How is it applied to a set of data? (c) What criteria should be met for the model to give an accurate description of a sample?
8. (a) What is a sampling distribution of means? (b) When is it used? (c) Why is it useful?
9. (a) What three things does the central limit theorem tell us about a sampling distribution? (b) Why is this useful?
10. What does the standard error of the mean indicate?
11. (a) What are the steps for using the standard normal curve to find a raw score's relative frequency or percentile? (b) What are the steps for finding the raw score that cuts off a specified relative frequency or percentile? (c) What are the steps for finding a sample mean's relative frequency or percentile?

PRACTICE PROBLEMS

12. In freshman English last semester, Foofy earned a 76 ($\overline{X} = 85$, $S_X = 10$) and her friend Bubbles, in a different class, earned a 60 ($\overline{X} = 50$, $S_X = 4$). Should Foofy be bragging about how much better she did in the course? Why?
13. Poindexter received a grade of 55 on a biology test ($\overline{X} = 50$) and a grade of 45 on a philosophy test ($\overline{X} = 50$). He is considering whether to ask his professors to curve the grades using z-scores. (a) What other information should he consider before making his request? (b) Does he want the S_X to be large or small in biology? Why? (c) Does he want the S_X to be large or small in philosophy? Why?
14. Foofy computes z-scores for a set of normally distributed exam scores. She obtains a z-score of -3.96 for 8 (out of 20) of the students. What does this mean?
15. For the data:

    9 5 10 7 9 10 11 8 12 7 6 9

    (a) Compute the z-score for the raw score of 10. (b) Compute the z-score for the raw score of 6.
16. For the data in question 15, find the raw scores that correspond to the following: (a) $z = +1.22$ (b) $z = -0.48$.
17. Which z-score in each of the following pairs corresponds to the smaller raw score? (a) $z = +1.0$, $z = +2.3$ (b) $z = -2.8$, $z = -1.7$ (c) $z = -.70$, $z = +.20$ (d) $z = 0$, $z = -2.0$

18. For each pair in question 17, which z-score has the higher frequency?

19. In a normal distribution of scores, what proportion of all scores would you expect to fall in each of the following areas: (a) Between the mean and $z = +1.89$? (b) Below $z = -2.30$? (c) Between $z = -1.25$ and $z = +2.75$? (d) Above $z = +1.96$ and below $z = -1.96$?

20. For a distribution in which $\overline{X} = 100$, $S_X = 16$, and $N = 500$, answer the following: (a) What is the relative frequency of scores between 76 and the mean? (b) How many participants are expected to score between 76 and the mean? (c) What is the percentile of someone scoring 76? (d) How many participants are expected to score above 76?

21. Poindexter may be classified as having a math dysfunction—and thus not have to study statistics—if he scores below the 25th percentile on a national diagnostic test. The μ of the test is 75 and $\sigma_X = 10$. Approximately what raw score is the cutoff score for him to avoid statistics?

22. A test for selecting intellectually gifted children has a μ of 56 and σ_X of 8. (a) What percent of children are expected to score below 60? (b) What percent of scores will be above 54? (c) A gifted child is defined as being in the top 20%: Within rounding, what is the minimum test score needed to qualify as gifted?

23. Using the test in problem 22, you measure 64 children, obtaining a $\overline{X}$ of 57.28. (a) With $\mu = 56$, what statistical procedure can you use to determine if this sample should be considered gifted? (b) Compute the answer. (c) In what percent of the top scores is this sample mean?

24. For an IQ test, we know that $\mu = 100$ and $\sigma_X = 16$. We are interested in creating the sampling distribution when $N = 64$. (a) What does that sampling distribution of means reflect? (b) What is the shape of the distribution of IQ means and the mean of the distribution? (c) Calculate $\sigma_{\overline{X}}$ for this distribution. (d) What is your answer in (c) called, and what does it indicate?

25. A recent graduate has two job offers and must decide which to accept. The job in City A pays $27,000. The average cost of living there is $50,000, with a standard deviation of $15,000. The job in City B pays $12,000. The average cost of living there is $14,000, with a standard deviation of $1,000. Assuming the data are normally distributed, which is the better job offer? Why?

26. A researcher obtained a sample mean of 68.4 with $N = 49$. In the population, the mean is 65 and $\sigma_X = 10$. The researcher believes his sample mean is rather unusual. (a) Is he correct? (b) How often can he expect to obtain a sample mean that is higher than 68.4? (c) Why might he obtain such an unusual mean?

27. If you took 1,000 random samples of 50 participants each from a population where $\mu = 19.4$ and $\sigma_X = 6.0$, how many samples would you expect would produce a mean below 18?

28. Suppose you own shares of a company's stock, with its mean selling price at $14.89 based on the past 10 trading days. Over the years, the mean price of the stock has been $10.43 ($\sigma_X = \$5.60$). You wonder if the mean selling price over the next ten days can be expected to go higher. Should you wait to sell, or should you sell now?

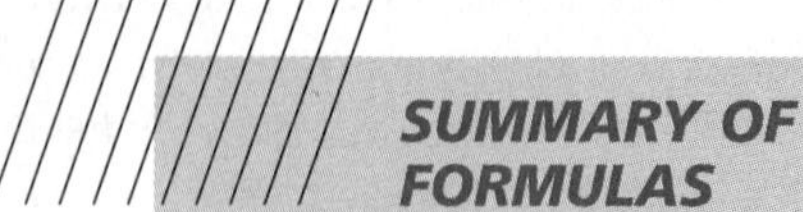

SUMMARY OF FORMULAS

1. *The formula for transforming a raw score in a sample into a z-score is*

$$z = \frac{X - \overline{X}}{S_X}$$

where X is the raw score, $\overline{X}$ is the sample mean, and S_X is the sample standard deviation.

2. *The formula for transforming a z-score in a sample into a raw score is*

$$X = (z)(S_X) + \overline{X}$$

3. *The formula for transforming a raw score in a population into a z-score is*

$$z = \frac{X - \mu}{\sigma_X}$$

4. *The formula for the true standard error of the mean is*

$$\sigma_{\overline{X}} = \frac{\sigma_X}{\sqrt{N}}$$

where σ_X is the true standard deviation of the raw score population, and N is the N of the sample.

5. *The formula for transforming a sample mean into a z-score on the sampling distribution of means is*

$$z = \frac{\overline{X} - \mu}{\sigma_{\overline{X}}}$$

where $\overline{X}$ is the sample mean, μ is the mean of the sampling distribution (which equals the μ of the underlying raw score distribution), and $\sigma_{\overline{X}}$ is the standard error of the mean of the sampling distribution.

Computing z-score for raw score

$$Z = \frac{X - \overline{X}}{Sx}$$

PART 3

CORRELATIONAL RESEARCH AND CORRELATIONAL STATISTICS

As you know, most psychological research examines a relationship between variables. Therefore, the final question to answer with descriptive statistics is "What is the nature of the relationship we have found?" There are two major approaches to answering this question covered in the next two chapters: Chapter 10 discusses "correlation," and Chapter 11 discusses "linear regression."

If it seems that the topics in the upcoming chapters are different from previous topics, it's because they *are* different. Although correlation and regression are major descriptive statistical procedures, they do not focus on means and standard deviations. Therefore, think of the upcoming chapters as somewhat of a detour. After we complete it, we'll return to describing a sample using the mean and standard deviation. In particular, we'll return to describing the location of a sample mean on a sampling distribution, so, don't forget that procedure.

10

Correlational Research and the Correlation Coefficient

GETTING STARTED

To understand this chapter, recall the following:

- From Chapter 2, recall what a data point is, and how to identify a strong relationship.
- From Chapter 3, recall what validity and reliability are, and why they are important.
- From Chapter 4, understand restriction of range, multiple raters, and inter-rater reliability.
- From Chapter 8, understand that greater variability indicates that scores are not close to each other.

Your goals in this chapter are to learn:

- The difference between analyzing correlational data and experimental data.
- How to read and interpret a scatterplot.
- How to interpret a correlation coefficient.
- How correlation is used to demonstrate different types of reliability and validity.
- When to use the Pearson r, the Spearman r_s, and the point-biserial r_{pb}.
- The logic of inferring a population correlation based on a sample correlation.

Recall that in a relationship, as the scores on one variable change, there is a consistent pattern of change in the scores on the other variable. Also, recall that a common approach for demonstrating a relationship is the "correlational design." This chapter discusses correlational research and the statistical procedures commonly used with it. We'll see when such procedures are used and what they tell us, and then we'll see how to calculate them. First, though, here are some more symbols.

MORE STATISTICAL NOTATION

Correlational analysis requires scores from two variables, some X scores and some Y scores. Usually, we obtain an X and a Y score from the same participant and then each participant's X is paired with the corresponding Y. If the X and Y scores are not from the same participant, there must be some other rational system for pairing the scores (for example, pairing the scores of roommates). Also, with pairs of scores, there must be the same number of X and Y scores.

The same conventions are used for Y that were previously used for X. Thus, ΣY is the sum of Y scores, ΣY^2 is the sum of squared Y scores, and $(\Sigma Y)^2$ is the squared sum of Y. The mean of the Y scores is $\overline{Y}$ and equals $\Sigma Y/N$. Similarly, the variance of a sample of Y scores is S_Y^2, and the sample standard deviation is S_Y. To find S_Y^2 or S_Y, use the same formulas for finding S_X^2 or S_X, except plug in Y scores instead of X scores.

You will also encounter three new notations. First, $(\Sigma X)(\Sigma Y)$ says to find the sum of the Xs and the sum of the Ys, and then multiply the two sums together. Second, ΣXY says to first multiply each X in a pair times its corresponding Y and then sum all of the resulting products.

> ***REMEMBER*** $(\Sigma X)(\Sigma Y)$ says to multiply the sum of X times the sum of Y. ΣXY says to multiply each X times its paired Y and then sum the products.

Finally, D indicates to find the *difference* between the X and Y scores in a pair, which you find by subtracting one from the other.

Now, on to correlation!

UNDERSTANDING CORRELATIONAL RESEARCH

The term *correlation* is synonymous with relationship, so in a correlational design we examine the relationship—examine the correlation—between variables. The relationship can involve scores from virtually any variables, regardless of how we obtain them. Often we measure the variables using a questionnaire or other observational technique, but we may also measure responses using any of the methods used in experiments. But recall that experimental and correlational designs differ in terms of how we demonstrate a relationship. For example, as people drink more coffee, they typically become more nervous. To demonstrate this in an experiment, we would manipulate the amount of coffee people consume: We might assign some participants to a condition where they drink 1 cup, while others drink 2 cups, and others drink 3 cups. Then, we would measure participants' nervousness (perhaps using physiological methods or a questionnaire). Our hypothesis implies the question, "For a given amount of coffee, what is a person's nervousness?" Recall that the "given" variable is always the *X* variable. The important thing to recognize about an experiment is that, by assigning participants to a condition, we, the researchers, determine each participant's *X* score: We decide whether their "score" is 1, 2, or 3 on the coffee variable. Then, we ask "For an *assigned X*, what *Y* score do participants tend to produce?"

In correlational research, however, we do not manipulate any variables. Instead, we simply measure two (or more) variables. Thus, we might simply ask participants the amount of coffee they consumed today, and then measure how nervous they are. The distinguishing aspect of a correlational design is that, by *not* assigning participants to an amount of the *X* variable, we do not determine their *X* scores. Rather, the scores on both variables reflect an amount or category of the variable that a participant has *already* experienced. Coffee is still the *X* variable, but here we ask "For a *reported X*, what *Y* score do people tend to produce?"

Note that, as the name implies, correlational research typically employs correlational statistics to summarize the relationship. However, computing a correlation does *not* automatically create a correlational design. As you'll see, correlational *statistics* can be applied to any design, including experiments. A correlational *design* occurs whenever we do not randomly assign participants to the levels of either variable, regardless of how the data are analyzed.

REMEMBER The distinguishing aspect of a correlational design is that we do not randomly assign participants to a specific level of either variable.

Drawing Conclusions from Correlational Research

Our confidence in the conclusions drawn from correlational designs is influenced by the same concerns we've raised previously about experiments. Thus, the procedures for measuring each variable should have construct and content validity, and they should be reliable and provide sensitive measurements that can detect subtle differences. Also, extraneous influences—such as demand characteristics, response sets, and the volunteer bias—should be eliminated. And, we seek consistency throughout by considering the four components of any study—the participants, environment, researcher, and measurement task.

In addition, recall from Chapter 3 that, compared to experiments, correlational designs have two flaws that severely reduce internal validity for concluding that differences in the *X* variable *cause* differences in *Y* scores: First, often we cannot be certain that *X* occurred before *Y*. For example, in the coffee study, perhaps participants were *first* more nervous and *then* drank more coffee. If so, then greater nervousness may actually cause greater coffee consumption. *In any correlational study, it is possible that Y causes X.* Second, correlational designs usually do not control extraneous variables, so there may be all sorts of confounding variables present. In particular, we don't randomly assign participants to a score on the *X* variable. Therefore, we do not control participant variables by randomizing and thus balancing them, so the *X* variable will be confounded by participant variables. For example, people who drink more coffee may all have a particular physiology, or all experience higher stress levels. Therefore, it may be that physiology or stress actually causes more nervousness. Or, perhaps some participants had less sleep than others the night before testing. Perhaps the lack of sleep caused these people to be *both* more nervous *and* to drink more coffee. In any correlational study, there is likely to be a hidden variable that causes *Y* to change.

Thus, the relationship found in a correlational study may mean that changes in *X* cause changes in *Y* as we think. But, changes in *Y* may cause changes in *X*, or some third variable may produce differences in both *X* and *Y*. Therefore, a single correlational study should *not* be interpreted as showing that changes in *X* cause changes in *Y*. (Recall that in a true experiment, we *do* randomly assign participants to conditions, and they experience a condition *before* the dependent variable. It is for these reasons that experiments are best for inferring the causes of behavior.)

> ***REMEMBER*** Causality is not inferred from a correlational design, because the order of occurrence of the variables is unknown, and potential confoundings are likely.

Reasons for Using the Correlational Approach

Though we must accept the limited evidence for causality found in a correlational design, it is still a legitimate research method. In fact, a correlational design may be preferable for several reasons.

First, because of ethical and practical considerations, some relationships can be studied only through a correlational design. For example, ethically we cannot study such variables as sexual abuse, accidents, or drug use by randomly assigning people to experience them in a true experiment. Likewise, it is impossible to manipulate such variables as a person's career, race, personality traits, or mental and physical illness. Yet, such variables can be studied through correlational methods. Thus, for example, we can measure the amount of abuse people have experienced and relate it to other behaviors or characteristics. Further, through replication, together with experimental studies of relevant constructs, researchers may eventually develop some degree of confidence in causal statements about such variables.

Second, correlational procedures are useful for discovering new relationships. For example, we might measure people on numerous variables that we suspect are related to nervousness (their health history, self-esteem level, physiology, diet, and so on) and then discover which variables actually form relationships. Such research is useful not only for describing the behavior but also for identifying possible causes to then study using experimental designs.

In addition, a laboratory experiment creates a rather artificial situation. A third advantage of correlational studies is that often they can be conducted outside of the laboratory, where potentially there is greater ecological and external validity. For example, if we are interested in a behavior of factory workers, studying employees while they work in a real factory is more valid than studying laboratory subjects in an artificial factory simulation.

And finally, recall that part of understanding a behavior is being able to predict when it will occur. Because of better external validity, the relationship found in a correlational study may be better for predicting behaviors than that found in an experiment.

REMEMBER Correlational designs are used to discover relationships, to solve ethical and practical problems, and to provide greater external validity.

DISTINGUISHING CHARACTERISTICS OF CORRELATIONAL ANALYSIS

There are four major differences between how we handle data in a correlational analysis versus in an experiment. First, if we conducted the coffee experiment, we would examine changes in each *mean* nervousness score (the *Y* scores) as a function of changes in the conditions of coffee consumed (the *X* scores). With correlational data, however, we typically have a rather large and unwieldy number of different *X* scores: People would probably report a wide range of coffee consumption beyond only 1, 2, or 3 cups. Comparing the mean nervousness scores from many groups would be difficult. Therefore, in correlational procedures, we do not compute a mean *Y* score at each *X*. Instead, we summarize the *entire* relationship formed by all pairs of *X*-*Y* scores in the data. This is the major advantage of using correlation, because it simplifies a complex relationship involving many scores into an easily interpreted statistic.

A second difference is that, because we examine all pairs of *X*-*Y* scores at once, we have *one* sample. Therefore, *N stands for the number of pairs of scores in the data.*

Third, either variable may be the *X* or *Y* variable. Above, we asked, "For a given amount of coffee, what are the nervousness scores?" so amount of coffee was the *X* variable and nervousness was the *Y* variable. Conversely, if we had asked, "For a given nervousness score, what is the amount of coffee consumed?" then nervousness would have been the *X* variable and amount of coffee the *Y* variable.

Finally, as we see in the next section, the data are graphed differently in correlational research than in an experiment. The individual pairs of scores are used to create a scatterplot.

Plotting Correlational Data: The Scatterplot

A **scatterplot** is a graph that shows the location of each data point formed by a pair of *X*-*Y* scores. The scatterplot in Figure 10.1 shows data that might occur if we actually studied nervousness and coffee consumption: People drinking 1 cup of coffee tend to have nervousness scores around 1, those drinking 2 cups have nervousness scores around 2, and so on. (*Note:* In the table on the left, two people scored 1 on coffee consumption and nervousness. As shown in the scatterplot, some researchers circle such a data point to indicate that points are plotted on top of each other.) *Always draw the scatterplot* of a set of correlational data. A scatterplot allows you to see the nature of the relationship that is present and to map out the best way to summarize it.

The shape of the scatterplot is an important indication of both the presence of a relationship and the nature of the relationship. We can summarize a scatterplot visually by drawing a line around its outer edges. A scatterplot may have any one of a number of shapes when a relationship is present. When no relationship is present, however, the scatterplot will be either circular or elliptical, oriented so that the ellipse is *parallel* to the *X* axis. The scatterplots in Figure 10.2 show what no relationship between coffee consumption and nervousness would look like. There is no relationship here because,

FIGURE 10.1 Scatterplot Showing Nervousness as a Function of Coffee Consumption

Each data point is created using participant's coffee consumption as the X score and nervousness as the Y score.

Cups of coffee: ***X***	*Nervousness scores:* ***Y***
1	1
1	1
1	2
2	2
2	3
3	4
3	5
4	5
4	6
5	8
5	9
6	9
6	10

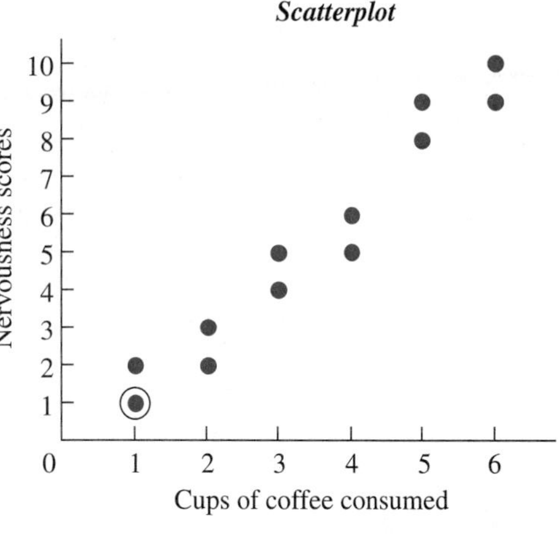

as the X scores increase, the Y scores do not consistently change, and no particular value of Y tends to be associated with a particular value of X. Instead, virtually the same batch of Y scores is associated with every value of X.

The scatterplots in Figure 10.2 are further summarized by a line that passes through the center of the scatterplot. This line is called the **regression line**. (Procedures for drawing the regression line are presented in the next chapter.) The orientation of the regression line matches the orientation of the scatterplot. Thus, when no relationship is present, the regression line is a horizontal straight line.

FIGURE 10.2 Scatterplots Showing No Relationship Between Coffee Consumption and Nervousness

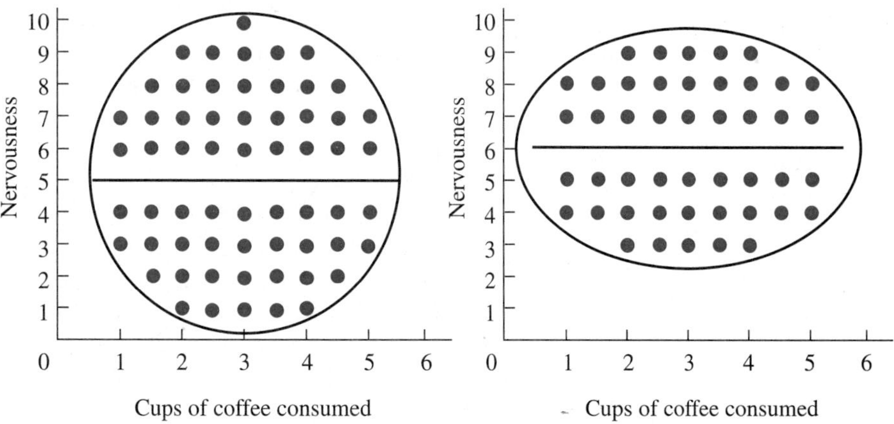

The Correlation Coefficient

When a relationship is present, the scatterplot forms a shape other than a circle or a horizontal ellipse, and the regression line is not horizontal. The shape and orientation of a particular scatterplot reflect the aspects of a relationship that we want to know about: What is the pattern that is formed? What direction do the scores change? How consistently do the scores change together? The way to answer such questions is to compute a correlation coefficient. The **correlation coefficient** is a statistic—a number—that describes the important characteristics of a relationship. Once you understand these characteristics, the coefficient summarizes the relationship so that you can envision the overall scatterplot, without needing to actually look at the individual data.

There are actually only two important characteristics of a relationship that the correlation coefficient communicates: the type of relationship that is present and the strength of the relationship. The following sections define these characteristics.

TYPES OF RELATIONSHIPS

The **type of relationship** that is present in a set of data is determined by the overall direction in which the *Y* scores change as the *X* scores change. There are two general types of relationships: Linear and nonlinear relationships.

Linear Relationships

The term *linear* means "straight line," and a linear relationship has a regression line that is a straight line. For example, the two scatterplots in Figure 10.3 show the linear relationships between the amount of time that students study and their test performance, and between the number of hours students spend watching television and the amount of time they spend sleeping. Both scatterplots show a linear relationship because (1) they do not form horizontal ellipses, and (2) they are best summarized by a straight line. We obtain such scatterplots because, in a **linear relationship**, as the *X* scores increase, the *Y* scores tend to change in only one direction. On the left, as students study longer, their grades tend only to increase. On the right, as students watch more television, their sleep tends only to decrease.

There are two subtypes of linear relationships, depending on the *direction* in which the *Y* scores change. The study-test relationship is a positive relationship. In a **positive linear relationship**, as the scores on the *X* variable increase, the scores on the *Y* variable also tend to increase. Thus, low *X* scores are paired with low *Y* scores, and high *X* scores are paired with high *Y* scores. Any relationship that fits the general pattern "the more *X*, the more *Y*" is a positive linear relationship. You can remember that such relationships are called positive by remembering that as the *X* scores increase, the *Y* scores change in the direction away from zero, toward higher *positive* scores.

On the other hand, the television-sleep relationship is a negative relationship. In a **negative linear relationship**, as the scores on the *X* variable increase, the scores on the

FIGURE 10.3 Scatterplots Showing Positive and Negative Linear Relationships

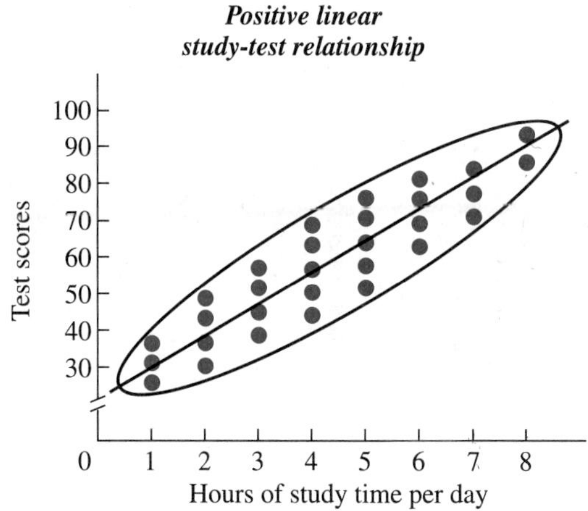

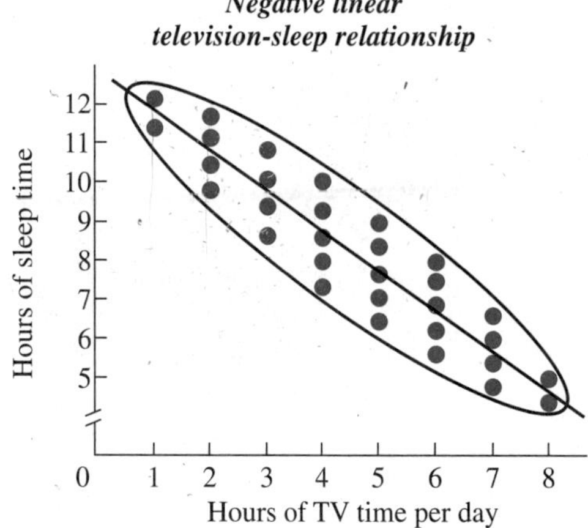

Y variable tend to decrease. Low X scores are paired with high Y scores, and high X scores are paired with low Y scores. Any relationship that fits the general pattern "the more X, the less Y" is a negative linear relationship. You can remember that such relationships are called negative by remembering that as the X scores increase, the Y scores change in the direction toward zero, toward the *negative* scores.

The term *negative* does not mean there is something wrong with the relationship. Negative relationships are no different from positive relationships *except* in terms of the direction in which the Y scores change as the X scores increase.

Nonlinear Relationships

If a relationship is not linear, then it is called nonlinear. *Nonlinear* means that the data cannot be summarized by a *straight* line. Thus, another name for a nonlinear relationship is a curvilinear relationship. In a **nonlinear**, or **curvilinear**, **relationship**, as the X scores change, the Y scores do not tend to *only* increase or *only* decrease: At some point, the Y scores change their direction of change.

Nonlinear relationships come in many different shapes, but Figure 10.4 shows two common ones. The scatterplot on the left shows the relationship between a person's age and the amount of time required to move from one place to another. Very young children move slowly, but as age increases, movement time decreases. Beyond a certain age, however, the time scores change direction so that now they increase. (Such a relationship is called *U-shaped.*) The scatterplot on the right shows the relationship between the number of alcoholic drinks people consume and their sense of feeling well. At first, people feel better as they drink, but beyond a certain point, more drinking makes them feel progressively worse. (This shape is called an *inverted U-shaped* relationship.) Curvilinear relationships may be even more complex than above, producing a wavy pattern that repeatedly changes direction.

FIGURE 10.4 Scatterplots Showing Nonlinear Relationships

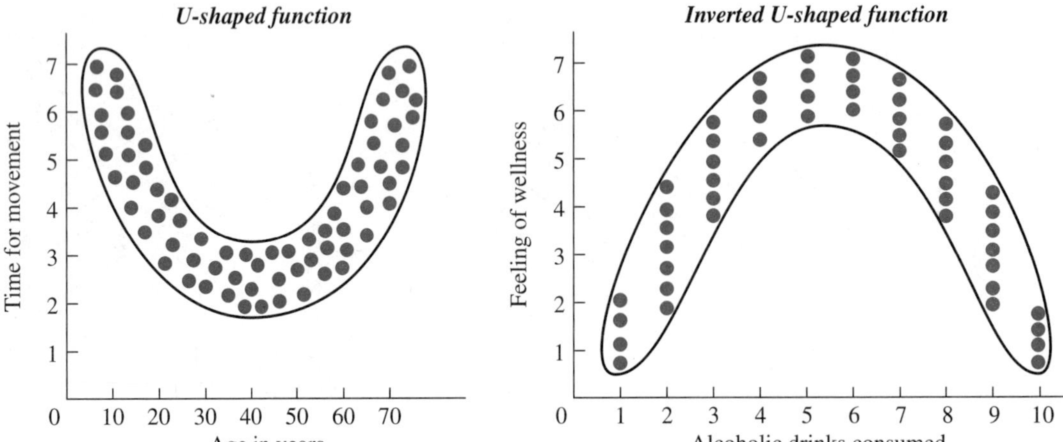

Note that the preceding terminology is also used to describe the type of relationship found in experiments. We have a positive relationship if, as the amount of the independent variable (X) increases, the dependent scores (Y) also increase. We have a negative relationship if the dependent scores decrease. We have a nonlinear relationship if the dependent scores change their direction of change.

How the Correlation Coefficient Describes the Type of Relationship

Correlational research in psychology focuses almost entirely on linear relationships, so we'll discuss only linear correlation. How do you know whether data form a linear relationship? Make a scatterplot! If the scatterplot is best summarized by a straight line, then linear correlation is appropriate. Also, sometimes you may want to describe the extent to which a nonlinear relationship has a linear component and somewhat fits a straight line. Here, too, linear correlation is appropriate. However, do not summarize a nonlinear relationship using a linear correlation coefficient. Describing a nonlinear relationship with a straight line is like putting a round peg into a square hole: The relationship will not fit the straight line very well, and the correlation coefficient will not accurately describe the relationship.

The correlation coefficient communicates two things about the type of relationship. First, merely by computing a linear correlation coefficient, we communicate that we are describing a linear relationship. Second, the coefficient itself communicates whether the linear relationship is positive or negative. If the coefficient—the number we compute—has a minus sign in front of it, then the relationship is negative. If the coefficient does not have a minus sign, then we put a plus sign in front of it, indicating a positive relationship.

The other characteristic of a relationship communicated by the correlation coefficient is the strength of the relationship.

STRENGTH OF THE RELATIONSHIP

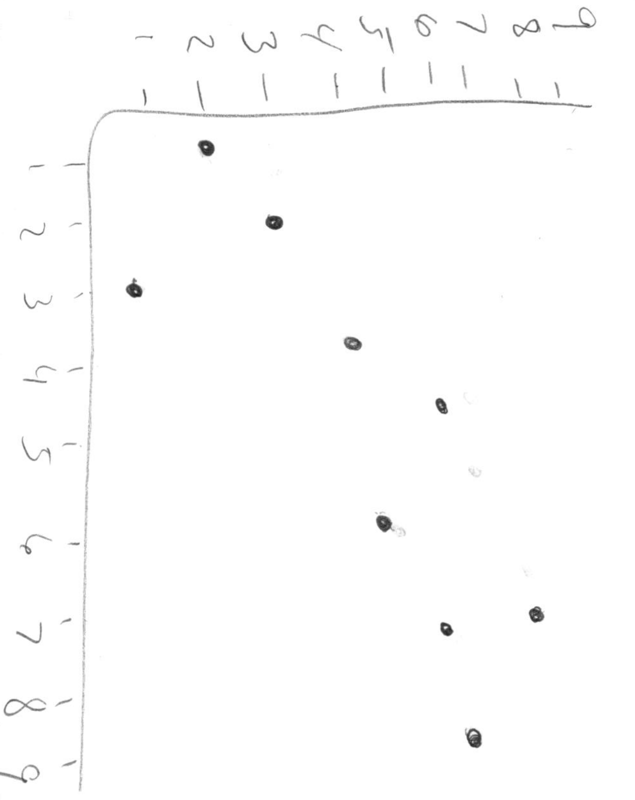

:an exhibit varying degrees of consistency, and the **strength** :tent to which one value of Y is consistently paired with one The strength of a relationship is also referred to as the *degree* ıte value of the correlation coefficient (the size of the number strength of the relationship. The largest value you can obtain ue is 0. (Thus, when we include the positive or negative sign, t may be any value from -1.0 to $+1.0$.) The *larger* the :fficient, the *stronger* the relationship. In other words, the ± 1.0, the more consistently one value of Y is paired with one

correlation coefficient has two components: the sign, :r a positive or negative relationship, and the absolute s the strength of the relationship.

ı coefficient is not difficult. The difficulty comes in interpret- s of the strength of the relationship. Therefore, we'll first dis- ·elation coefficient to envision the scatterplot that the data ıvision the nature of the relationship that is present. Our start- ıerfect relationship.

... of $+1.0$ or -1.0 describes a perfectly consistent linear relationship. Figure 10.5 shows an example of each.

There are four ways to think about what a correlation coefficient of ± 1.0 indicates about a relationship. First, it tells us that *every* participant who obtains a particular X score obtains one and only one value of Y. Every time X changes, the Y scores all change to one new value. Thus, ± 1.0 indicates a perfect one-to-one correspondence between the X and Y scores.

Second, a coefficient of ± 1.0 indicates that there are no differences among the Y scores associated with a particular X. Differences between scores is variability, so ± 1.0 indicates that there is no variability among the Y scores at each X.

Third, a coefficient of ± 1.0 ensures perfect predictability of Y scores. Pretend that we do not know someone's Y score. Because each X score is associated with only one Y score, if we know the person's X score, then we know his or her Y score. (You'll see how to predict Y scores in the next chapter.)

Fourth, because it indicates that there is no variability or differences among the Y scores at each X, a coefficient of ± 1.0 indicates that the data points at an X are all on top of one another. When we summarize the scatterplot with the regression line, all of the data points fall *on* the line, and so literally, the data form a perfect straight-line relationship.

FIGURE 10.5 Data and Scatterplots Reflecting Perfect Positive and Negative Correlations

Perfect positive coefficient = *+1.0*	
X	*Y*
1	2
1	2
1	2
3	5
3	5
5	8
5	8
5	8

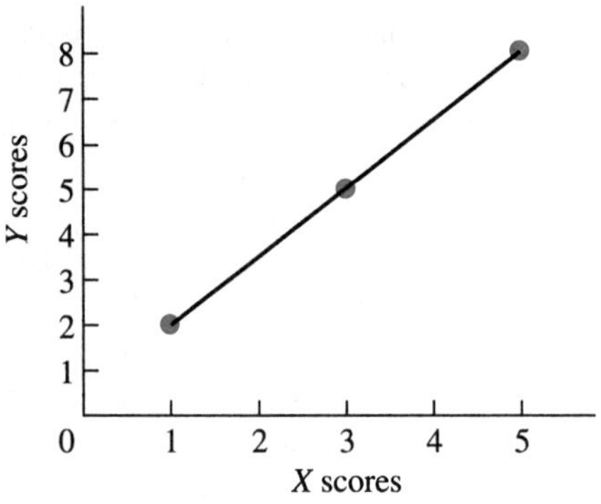

Perfect negative coefficient = *−1.0*	
X	*Y*
1	8
1	8
1	8
3	5
3	5
3	5
5	2
5	2
5	2

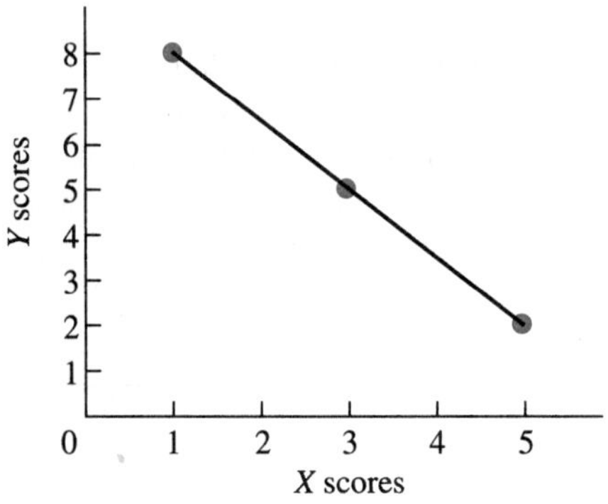

Intermediate Association

One way to think about a correlation coefficient is that it indicates how close the data come to forming a perfect linear relationship. With ± 1.0, the data do form a straight line. Interpret any other value in terms of how close it comes to ± 1.0, indicating how close the data come to forming a straight line.

For example, Figure 10.6 shows data and the resulting scatterplot that produce a correlation coefficient of +.98. Again, interpret the correlation coefficient in four ways. First, it indicates the degree of consistent association: Here, not every participant obtaining a particular *X* obtained the same *Y*. However, a coefficient of +.98 is close to ± 1.0, so there is "close" to perfect consistency between the *X* and *Y* scores.

Second, now there are *different* *Y* scores associated with a single *X* score, so there is variability among the *Y* scores at each *X* (e.g., participants with an *X* of 1 obtained *Y*s of 1 or 2). However, because with a coefficient of ±1.0, there is zero variability in *Y* scores at each *X*, so a coefficient of +.98 means there is close to zero variability:

FIGURE 10.6 Data and Scatterplot Reflecting a Correlation Coefficient of +.98

X	*Y*
1	1
1	2
1	2
3	4
3	5
3	5
5	7
5	8
5	8

The different *Y* scores at each *X* are relatively close to each other, so their variability is relatively small. The differences are "relatively" small when compared to the overall variability of all *Y* scores in the sample. Think of it this way: Over the entire sample, the above *Y* scores are between 1 and 8, so the overall range is 8. At each *X* score, however, the *Y*s span a range of only 1. It is this small variability in *Y* at each *X* relative to the overall variability in all *Y* scores that produces a correlation coefficient close to 1.

Third, when the correlation coefficient is not ±1.0, knowing each participant's *X* score allows us to predict only *around* what their *Y* scores will be: For an *X* of 1, for example, we'd predict a *Y* of around 1 or 2. There will be some error in our predictions here, and as in previous chapters, error in predictions because of variability is called "error variance." Here, the error variance is another name for the spread or variability in the *Y* scores at each *X*. A coefficient of +.98 indicates small error variance, because it indicates that everyone at an *X* has close to the same *Y* score. Therefore, our predictions for their *Y* will be close to their actual *Y* scores, so our errors will be small.

Fourth, because there is now variability in the *Y*s at each *X*, not all data points fall *on* the regression line: As in Figure 10.6, variability in *Y* results in vertical spread in the data points above and below the regression line at each *X*. But, a coefficient of +.98 is close to +1.0, indicating that the spread between the lowest and highest *Y* scores at each *X* is small. Therefore, the *Y* scores are close to, or hug, the regression line, resulting in a scatterplot that is a narrow, or skinny, ellipse. In fact, the correlation coefficient always tells us how skinny the scatterplot is. When the coefficient is ±1.0, the scatterplot forms a straight line, which is the skinniest ellipse possible. The closer the coefficient is to ±1.0, the skinnier the scatterplot, and vice versa.

The key to understanding the strength of any relationship is this:

> **As the variability—differences—in *Y* scores at each *X* becomes larger, the relationship becomes weaker.**

The correlation coefficient communicates this, because as the variability in the *Y*s at each *X* becomes larger, the absolute value of the coefficient becomes smaller.

Figure 10.7 shows data that produce a smaller correlation coefficient of −.28. The fact that this is a negative relationship has nothing to do with its strength. Rather, it is,

FIGURE 10.7 Data and Scatterplot Reflecting a Correlation Coefficient of −.28

X	*Y*
1	9
1	6
1	3
3	8
3	6
3	3
5	7
5	5
5	1

the large variability or spread in the *Y* scores at each *X* that makes this an inconsistent or "weak" relationship. This variability does two things that are contrary to what occurs in a consistent relationship. First, instead of the *Y* scores changing only when an *X* score changes, here, the *Y* scores change (differ) greatly even though the *X* score remains the same. Second, there is overlap between the *Y* scores at the different *X*s, so that instead of seeing one value of *Y* at one *X* and a different value of *Y* at a different *X*, here we see the same values of *Y* paired with different values of *X*. Thus, in contrast to a relationship, here the *Y* scores tend to change when *X* does not, and the *Y* scores tend to stay the same when *X* changes.

A coefficient of −.28 is not very close to ±1.0, indicating that this relationship is not very close to forming a perfectly consistent linear relationship. Therefore, we know this: (1) Only barely does one value or close to one value of *Y* tend to be associated with one value of *X*. (2) The variability in the *Y*s at each *X* is almost as large as the variability among all *Y* scores in the data. (3) Knowing participants' *X* scores will not produce a very accurate prediction of their actual *Y* scores. (4) The large variability in *Y* will produce a fat scatterplot that does not hug the regression line.

> ***REMEMBER*** Greater variability in the *Y* scores at each *X* results in a weaker relationship and thus a smaller correlation coefficient.

Although, theoretically, a correlation coefficient may be as large as ±1.0, in real research such values do not occur. Remember that scores reflect the behaviors of living organisms who seldom behave identically, even when in the same situation. Therefore, there will always be inconsistency in the *Y* scores at each *X*, so adjust your expectations about the relationships found in research accordingly. Generally, a coefficient between 0 and ±.20 is very weak and probably negligible. Coefficients in the neighborhood of ±.30 to ±.40 are common and they are considered respectable. A coefficient of around ±.50 is very substantial, and coefficients above ±.50 are downright impressive. A correlation of ±1.0 is so unlikely to occur that, if you ever obtain one, you should assume you've made a computational error. If you obtain a coefficient greater than ±1.0, you've definitely made an error, because ±1.0 indicates a perfect relationship, and you can't do better than that.

FIGURE 10.8 Data and Scatterplot Reflecting a Correlation Coefficient of 0

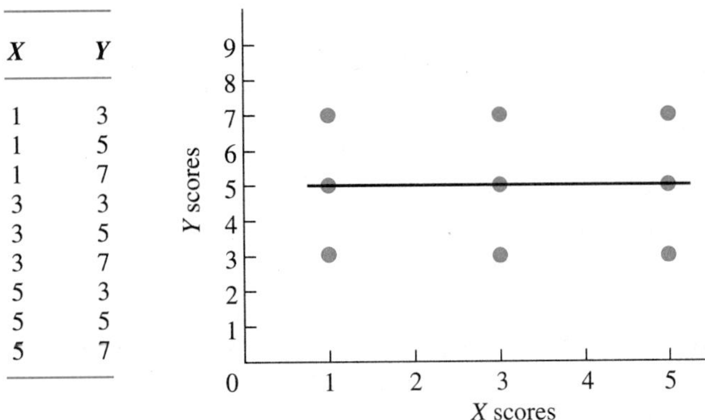

X	*Y*
1	3
1	5
1	7
3	3
3	5
3	7
5	3
5	5
5	7

Zero Association

The lowest possible value of the correlation coefficient is 0, indicating that no linear relationship is present. Figure 10.8 shows data that produce a correlation coefficient of 0. A scatterplot having this shape is as far from forming a slanted straight line as possible, and a correlation coefficient of 0 is as far from ± 1.0 as possible. Therefore, we know that no values of *Y* tend to be consistently associated with only one value of *X*. Instead, the *Y*s found at one *X* are largely the same as the *Y*s found at any other *X*. This also means that knowing someone's *X* score will not in any way help to predict the corresponding *Y* score. Finally, this indicates that the spread in *Y* at any *X* equals the overall spread in *Y* in the data, producing a scatterplot that is a circle or horizontal ellipse that in no way hugs the regression line.

> *REMEMBER* The larger the correlation coefficient (whether positive or negative), the stronger the relationship because the less the *Y*s are spread out at each *X* and the closer the data come to forming a straight line.

USING THE CORRELATION COEFFICIENT IN RESEARCH

To see how the correlation coefficient is used in research, say that we conducted the original coffee and nervousness study, and the data produce a correlation coefficient of +.55. The next step is to perform the appropriate inferential statistical procedures. If the correlation coefficient passes the inferential test, it is the basis for interpreting the study. For example, originally we predicted a positive linear relationship, with more coffee associated with more nervousness, so the positive coefficient of +.55 confirms our hypothesis. A negative coefficient would have contradicted the hypothesis. (In a different study, the hypothesis might lead us to predict only some kind of linear relationship, so that either a positive or negative coefficient would confirm the hypothesis.)

Further, we also know that a coefficient with an absolute value of .55 is a relatively strong, consistent relationship. The strength of the relationship is also important to our interpretation, because, as with experiments, it suggests the extent to which other variables are operating. If, for example, we had obtained a coefficient of +.90, this would suggest that few other variables are related to nervousness in addition to coffee consumed. Conversely, a coefficient of +.09 would suggest there are other more important variables related to nervousness that we have not considered. As usual, following this line of reasoning, we interpret the results "psychologically," considering what the particular relationship indicates about nervousness and coffee consumption, and how they relate to our theoretical explanations, models, and constructs involving emotions and physiology. This was a correlational design, however, so we do *not* infer that more coffee *causes* more nervousness!

Recognize that although a coefficient is *interpreted* as the degree of consistency in a relationship, it does not directly measure units of "consistency." Thus, for example, a coefficient of +.60 indicates a more consistent relationship than, say, a coefficient of +.30, but the relationship with a coefficient of .60 is not twice as consistent as that with .30. We'll discuss how to directly compare correlation coefficients in the next chapter. For now, stick to interpreting a coefficient in relative terms, based on how close it is to ± 1.0.

In addition to describing the overall results of a study, computing a correlation coefficient is the statistical technique for demonstrating the *reliability* and the *validity* of a measurement procedure in any experimental or correlational design.

Ascertaining Reliability

Recall that if a measurement procedure is reliable, then whenever a participant consistently exhibits a particular behavior, he or she should receive the same score. There are three ways a correlation coefficient is used to show reliability: It is used to show inter-rater reliability, test-retest reliability, and split-half reliability.

First, recall that often a measurement involves rating a participant's behavior, and for reliability, we employ multiple raters. To demonstrate that the behavior is judged reliably, we need to show high *inter-rater reliability*, the consistency of ratings by any two raters. For example, say that we are studying creativity and have two judges rate how creative participants are when "doodling." If the judges are reliable, then we should see a large positive correlation between their ratings: We should find that a low creativity score assigned to a participant by one rater was consistently matched by the other, while a high score given by one was also given by the other.

Second, a similar approach is used to show the reliability of any testing procedure that does not involve raters. **Test-retest reliability** indicates that participants tend to obtain the same score when tested at different times. For example, if a college exam has test-retest reliability, a student who produces a low score now should also produce a low score later, and a student scoring high now should also score high later. In other words, test-retest reliability is evident when there is a high, positive correlation between the scores obtained from the two testings. Likewise, a physiological measurement has test-retest reliability if scores from the same participants tested twice are positively correlated.

Test-retest reliability reflects the reliability of a participant's score over multiple testing *sessions*. The third approach is to determine whether the *trials* within one testing session are reliable. **Split-half reliability** indicates that participants' scores on some trials consistently match their scores on other trials. Typically, we first split a test in half by comparing the odd-numbered trials to the even-numbered trials. (This balances order effects due to fatigue or practice.) Then, we compute a summary score—such as a mean or the total number correct—for each participant on each half of the test. Then we correlate the summary scores. For example, if the questions on a college examination have split-half reliability, then students having a low mean on the odd questions should also have a low mean on the even questions, and so on. Likewise, we might determine the split-half reliability of a series of reaction-time trials by correlating the times from even- and odd-numbered trials.

REMEMBER Test-retest reliability is the correlation between repeated testings. Split-half reliability is the correlation between different trials within one testing.

For any of the above, a coefficient of +.80 or higher is usually required for the procedure to be considered reliable.

Ascertaining Validity

Recall that the issue of validity is whether a procedure actually measures what it is intended to measure. Believe it or not, one approach to demonstrating validity is simply a researcher's judgment that the procedure is valid. **Face validity** is the extent to which a measurement procedure appears to measure what it's intended to measure. Thus, if we judge that on its "face" a procedure looks reasonable, we have one, limited way of arguing the procedure is valid. For example, an intelligence test has face validity if it appears to measure intelligence.

REMEMBER Face validity means that a procedure is valid because it looks valid.

To produce more objective evidence of validity, however, we employ correlational procedures. One approach is to determine the convergent validity of a procedure. **Convergent validity** is the extent to which the scores obtained from one procedure are positively correlated with scores obtained from another procedure that is already accepted as valid. For example, say after developing a new test of creativity, we give the same people both our test and another accepted test. If our test is valid, then there should be a strong, positive correlation between the scores from the two tests. If so, we can argue that both procedures "converge" on and measure creativity.

Another approach is to look at **discriminant validity**, which is the extent to which scores obtained from one procedure are *not* correlated with scores from another procedure that measures other variables or constructs. Thus, our creativity test is valid if it does not correlate with accepted measures of intelligence or personality. In this case, we would argue that the procedure "discriminates" between what it is and is not intended to measure.

REMEMBER With convergent validity, a procedure correlates with other procedures that are valid. With discriminant validity, a procedure does not correlate with other, unintended measures.

TABLE 10.1 Summary of Methods for Ascertaining Reliability and Validity

Reliability	
Inter-rater reliability:	Ratings from two raters are positively correlated.
Test-retest:	Each participant's test and retest scores are positively correlated.
Split-half:	Participants' scores from half of the trials correlate positively with their scores from the other half of the trials.
Validity	
Face:	Procedure appears valid.
Convergent:	Procedure correlates with other accepted measures.
Discriminant:	Procedure does not correlate with other unintended measures.
Criterion	
Concurrent:	Procedure correlates with a present behavior.
Predictive:	Procedure correlates with a future behavior.

Even though two *procedures* correlate with each other, this does not necessarily mean that they reflect the intended *behaviors*. After all, it might be that neither our new creativity test nor the old accepted test actually reflects creativity. Therefore, another approach for demonstrating validity is to correlate the scores from a procedure with an observable behavior. **Criterion validity** is the extent to which a procedure correlates with a behavior. There are two subtypes of criterion validity.

Concurrent validity is the extent to which a procedure correlates with an individual's *present* behavior. For example, say that our definition of creativity is such that it should be negatively correlated with ability to follow directions. Concurrent validity would be demonstrated if people who scored high on the creativity test were poor at following directions, but those with low creativity scores followed directions well.

On the other hand, **predictive validity** is the extent to which a procedure correlates with an individual's *future* behavior. For example, say we used our creativity test to predict participants' future success at jobs requiring creative skills. The test has predictive validity if, when we later examine their job success, participants' actual success scores match their predicted scores.

> *REMEMBER* Criterion validity is the extent to which a procedure relates to a specific behavior, either distinguishing the behavior concurrently or predicting future behavior.

It's important to know the names of the various approaches to reliability and validity, so consult Table 10.1.

COMPUTING THE CORRELATION COEFFICIENT

The following sections discuss the three most common linear correlation coefficients: The *Pearson correlation coefficient*, the *Spearman rank-order correlation coefficient*, and the *point-biserial correlation coefficient*. In each case, the coefficient can be between 0 and ± 1.0, and everything you've seen previously about interpreting a coefficient applies to each one. The major difference among them is that they are calculated differently: as when selecting any other statistical procedure, the specific coefficient to compute in a particular situation depends on the *scale of measurement* used to measure the variables.

The Pearson Correlation Coefficient

By far the most common correlation coefficient in psychological research is the Pearson correlation coefficient. The **Pearson correlation coefficient** is used to describe the linear relationship between two interval or ratio variables. (Technically, this statistic is the Pearson Product Moment Correlation Coefficient, but it's usually called the Pearson coefficient. It was invented by Karl Pearson.) The symbol for the Pearson correlation coefficient is the lowercase r. When you see r, think "relationship." (All of the example coefficients in previous sections were rs.)

The statistical basis for r is that it compares how consistently each value of Y is paired with each value of X in a linear fashion. In Chapter 9, we saw that to compare scores from different variables, we transform the scores into z-scores. Essentially, calculating r involves transforming each Y score into a z-score (call it z_Y), transforming each X score into a z-score (call it z_X), and then determining the "average" amount of correspondence between the z_Ys and the z_Xs. The Pearson correlation coefficient is defined as

$$r = \frac{\Sigma(z_X z_Y)}{N}$$

Mathematically, multiplying each z_X times the corresponding z_Y of the pair, summing the products, and then dividing by N produces the average correspondence between the pairs.

Luckily, there's an easier way to compute r. The computational formula is derived from the above formula by replacing the symbols z_X and z_Y with their formulas, and then, for each z, replacing the symbols for the mean and standard deviation with their formulas. This produces a monster of a formula, but after reducing it, we have the smaller monster below.

THE COMPUTATIONAL FORMULA FOR THE PEARSON CORRELATION COEFFICIENT IS

$$r = \frac{N(\Sigma XY) - (\Sigma X)(\Sigma Y)}{\sqrt{[N(\Sigma X^2) - (\Sigma X)^2][N(\Sigma Y^2) - (\Sigma Y)^2]}}$$

Here's a new example: Say that when studying health-psychology, we collect scores from 10 people on the variables of the number of times they visited a doctor in the last year and the number of glasses of orange juice they drink daily. We want to describe the linear relationship between juice drinking and doctor visits, so, because we have ratio scores on both variables, we compute r. Table 10.2 shows a good way to set up the data. For the computational formula, we need to compute ΣX, ΣX^2, $(\Sigma X)^2$, ΣY, ΣY^2, $(\Sigma Y)^2$, ΣXY, and N. First, find each XY by multiplying each X times its corresponding Y, as shown in the far right column in Table 10.2. Then, sum the appropriate columns to get ΣX, ΣX^2, ΣY, ΣY^2, and ΣXY. Squaring ΣX and ΣY gives $(\Sigma X)^2$ and $(\Sigma Y)^2$.

TABLE 10.2 Sample Data for Computing the *r* Between Orange Juice Consumed (the *X* Variable) and Doctor Visits (the *Y* Variable)

	Glasses of juice per day		*Doctor visits per year*		
Participant	X	X^2	Y	Y^2	XY
1	0	0	8	64	0
2	0	0	7	49	0
3	1	1	7	49	7
4	1	1	6	36	6
5	1	1	5	25	5
6	2	4	4	16	8
7	2	4	4	16	8
8	3	9	4	16	12
9	3	9	2	4	6
10	4	16	0	0	0
$N = 10$	$\Sigma X = 17$ $(\Sigma X)^2 = 289$	$\Sigma X^2 = 45$	$\Sigma Y = 47$ $(\Sigma Y)^2 = 2209$	$\Sigma Y^2 = 275$	$\Sigma XY = 52$

Putting these quantities in the formula for *r*,

$$r = \frac{N(\Sigma XY) - (\Sigma X)(\Sigma Y)}{\sqrt{[N(\Sigma X^2) - (\Sigma X)^2][N(\Sigma Y^2) - (\Sigma Y)^2]}}$$

gives

$$r = \frac{10(52) - (17)(47)}{\sqrt{[10(45) - 289][10(275) - 2209]}}$$

To compute the numerator, multiplying 10 times 52 gives 520, and 17 times 47 is 799. Rewriting the formula, we have

$$r = \frac{520 - 799}{\sqrt{[10(45) - 289][10(275) - 2209]}}$$

Complete the numerator by subtracting 799 *from* 520, which is -279. (Note the negative sign.)

To compute the denominator, first perform the operations within each bracket. In the left bracket, 10 times 45 is 450, and from that subtract 289, obtaining 161. In the right bracket, 10 times 275 is 2750, and from that subtract 2209, obtaining 541. Rewriting one more time, gives

$$r = \frac{-279}{\sqrt{[161][541]}}$$

Multiplying the quantities in the brackets together is 161 times 541, which equals 87,101. After taking the square root of 87,101, we have

$$r = \frac{-279}{295.129}$$

We divide, and there you have it: $r = -.95$.

This r is not greater than ± 1, so our calculations *may* be correct. Also, this is a negative r, and in the raw scores there is a negative relationship: As orange juice scores increase, number of doctor visits decreases. (If you have any doubt, make a scatterplot.) Had this been a positive relationship, the numerator of the formula would not produce a negative number and r would not be negative.

Thus, we conclude that there is a negative linear relationship between juice-drinking and doctor visits. On a scale of 0 to ± 1, where 0 is no relationship and ± 1 is a perfect linear relationship, this relationship is a $-.95$. Relatively speaking, this is an extremely strong or consistant relationship: Each amount of orange juice is associated with one relatively small range of doctor visits, and as juice scores increase, doctor visits consistently decrease. Now, as usual, we proceed to interpret this astounding result psychologically.

> ***REMEMBER*** Compute the Pearson correlation coefficient when describing the linear relationship between two interval or ratio variables.

The Spearman Rank-Order Correlation Coefficient

Sometimes data involve ordinal or rank-order scores (first, second, third, etc.). The **Spearman rank-order correlation coefficient** describes the linear relationship between two variables measured using ranked scores. The symbol for the Spearman correlation coefficient is r_S (the s stands for Charles Spearman, who invented this one).

Recall that in psychological research, ranked scores often arise because a variable is difficult to measure quantitatively. Therefore, we evaluate each participant by making qualitative judgments, and then use these judgments to rank-order the participants. We use r_S to correlate the ranks on two such variables. Or, if we want to correlate one ranked variable with one interval or ratio variable, we transform the interval or ratio scores into ranked scores (we might rank participants with the highest interval score as 1, those with the second highest score as 2, and so on). Either way that we obtain the ranks, r_S tells us the extent to which participants' ranks on one variable consistently match the ranks on the other variable to form a linear relationship. If each participant has the same rank on both variables, r_S will equal $+1.0$. If everyone's rank on one variable is the opposite of the rank on the other variable, r_S will equal -1.0. If there is only some degree of consistent pairing of the ranks, r_S will be between 0 and ± 1.0, and if there is no consistent pairing, r_S will equal 0.

Because r_S describes the consistency with which rankings match, one use of r_S is to determine the extent to which two observers agree when they rank participants: that is, to determine the observers' inter-rater reliability. For example, say we employ two observers to determine the aggressiveness of a sample of children. After observing all of the children, each observer assigns the rank of 1 to his or her choice for most aggressive child, 2 to the second-most-aggressive child, and so on. Figure 10.9 shows data the two observers might produce for 9 children. In creating the scatterplot and computing r_S, we treat each observer as a variable: The scores on one variable are the rankings assigned by one observer to the children, and the scores on the other variable are the rankings assigned by the other observer. Judging from the scatterplot, it appears that there is a positive relationship here. To describe this relationship, we compute r_S.

FIGURE 10.9 Sample Data for Computing r_s Between Rankings Assigned to Children by Observer A and Observer B

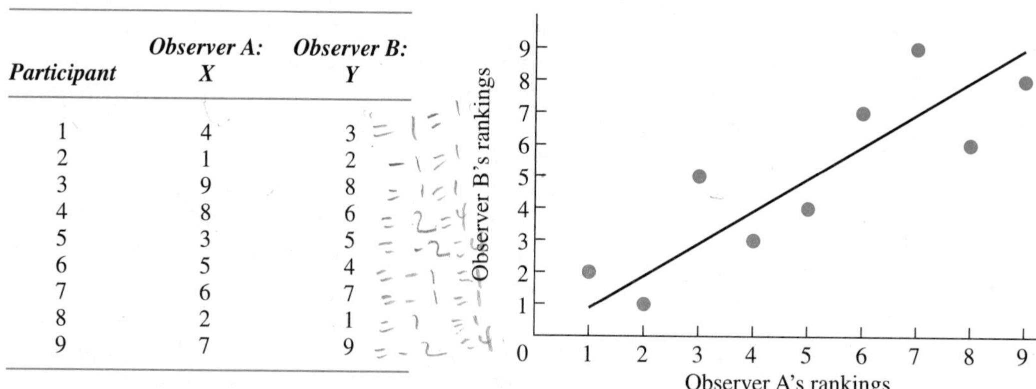

Participant	*Observer A:* *X*	*Observer B:* *Y*
1	4	3
2	1	2
3	9	8
4	8	6
5	3	5
6	5	4
7	6	7
8	2	1
9	7	9

THE COMPUTATIONAL FORMULA FOR THE SPEARMAN RANK-ORDER CORRELATION COEFFICIENT IS

$$r_s = 1 - \frac{6(\Sigma D^2)}{N(N^2 - 1)}$$

N is the number of pairs of ranks, and D is the difference between the two ranks in each pair. (Because of the mathematical properties of ranks, the formula *always* contains the 6 in the numerator.)

When using this formula, first arrange the data as shown in Table 10.3. For the column labeled D, you can either subtract each X from the corresponding Y, or, as shown here, subtract each Y from the corresponding X. After finding the Ds, compute D^2 by squaring each difference. Finally, determine the sum of the squared differences: Here, ΣD^2 is 18. To compute r_s, you also need N, the number of X-Y pairs (here, $N = 9$), and N^2 ($9^2 = 81$). Placing these quantities in the formula gives

$$r_s = 1 - \frac{6(\Sigma D^2)}{N(N^2 - 1)} = 1 - \frac{6(18)}{9(81 - 1)}$$

In the numerator, 6 times 18 equals 108. In the denominator, $81 - 1$ is 80, and 9 times 80 is 720. Now,

$$r_s = 1 - \frac{108}{720}$$

After dividing,

$$r_s = 1 - .15$$

Subtracting yields

$$r_s = +.85$$

TABLE 10.3 Data Arrangement for Computing r_s

Participant	Observer A: X	Observer B: Y	D	D^2
1	4	3	1	1
2	1	2	−1	1
3	9	8	1	1
4	8	6	2	4
5	3	5	−2	4
6	5	4	1	1
7	6	7	−1	1
8	2	1	1	1
9	7	9	−2	4
				$\Sigma D^2 = 18$

Thus, on a scale of 0 to ± 1.0, the rankings form a linear relationship to the extent that $r_S = +.85$. This indicates that a child receiving a particular ranking from one observer tended to receive close to the same ranking from the other observer, so the observers did demonstrate high inter-rater reliability. Notice, however, that a high negative r_S (such as $-.85$) would not indicate inter-rater reliability, because then low ranks by one observer would be paired with high ranks by the other observer, and vice versa.

REMEMBER Compute the Spearman correlation coefficient when describing the linear relationship between two ordinal variables.

Recognize that you cannot calculate r_S until after you have dealt with any tied ranks that occur in the data. A **tied rank** occurs when two participants receive the same rank-order score on the *same* variable. The problem with tied ranks is that they result in an incorrect value of r_S. Therefore, you must first resolve—correct—any tied ranks before computing r_S. As an example, say that we wish to correlate the finishing positions of the runners in two races. Table 10.4 shows such data with runners A and B tied for first place in race *Y*.

TABLE 10.4 Sample Data Containing Tied Ranks

Runner	Race X	Race Y		To resolve ties		New Y
A	4	1 }	. . . →	Tie uses up ranks 1 and 2,	. . . →	{1.5
B	3	1 }		becomes 1.5		{1.5
C	2	2}	. . . →	Becomes 3rd	. . . →	{3
D	1	3}	. . . →	Becomes 4th	. . . →	{4
.	.	.				.
.	.	.				.
.	.	.				.

Resolve tied ranks using the following logic: If runners A and B had not tied for first place, then one of them would have been first and one would have been second. Therefore, *assign to each participant at a tied rank the mean of the ranks that would have been used had there not been a tie*. The mean of 1 and 2 is 1.5, so, as in Table 10.4, Runners A and B are each assigned a new Y score of 1.5. Now, in a sense, you have used up first and second place (1 and 2), so runner C is assigned a new Y of 3. (After all, he was the third person to cross the finish line.) Likewise, assign runner D the new rank of 4. If there had been additional runners, we would assign them new ranks based on what we did above. For example, say there were four additional runners. If runners E, F, and G were originally tied for fourth place in race Y, they would now be tied for fifth. We'd resolve this tie by assigning them the mean of 5, 6, and 7 (i.e., each would be 6), and runner H would be ranked 8.

Once you have resolved all ties in the X and Y variables, compute r_s using the new ranks and the above formula.

The Point-Biserial Correlation Coefficient

Sometimes we want to correlate the scores from a continuous interval or ratio variable with the scores from a dichotomous variable (recall that this is a variable having only two categories). The **point-biserial correlation coefficient** describes the linear relationship between the scores from one continuous variable and one dichotomous variable. The symbol for the point-biserial correlation coefficient is r_{pb} (the pb stands for point-biserial, and no, Mr. Point and Mr. Biserial didn't invent this one). As usual, except for involving a different mix of variables, this describes a relationship in exactly the same way as previous coefficients have.

As an example, say that we correlate the dichotomous variable of gender (male/female) with the interval scores from a personality test. We cannot quantify "male" and "female," so first we arbitrarily assign numbers to represent these categories: Say we assign 1 to indicate male and 2 to indicate female. Think of each number as indicating whether a person scored "male" or "female." Then r_{pb} will describe how consistently certain personality test scores are paired with each gender score.

THE COMPUTATIONAL FORMULA FOR THE POINT-BISERIAL CORRELATION COEFFICIENT IS

$$r_{pb} = \left(\frac{\overline{Y}_2 - \overline{Y}_1}{S_Y}\right)(\sqrt{pq})$$

Always call the dichotomous variable the X variable and the interval or ratio variable the Y variable. Then, $\overline{Y}_1$ stands for the mean of the Y scores for one group on the dichotomous variable. (Here, $\overline{Y}_1$ will be the mean personality score for males.) The symbol $\overline{Y}_2$ stands for the mean of the Y scores for the other group. ($\overline{Y}_2$ will be the mean personality score for females.) The S_Y is the standard deviation of *all* Y scores in the data. The p stands for the proportion of the sample that is in one of the groups of the dichotomous variable. The q stands for the proportion of the sample in the other group.

Each proportion is equal to the number of individuals in the group divided by the total N of the study.

Say that we tested 10 people and obtained the data shown in Figure 10.10. First, compute S_Y, the standard deviation of Y. Substituting the data from Figure 10.10,

$$S_Y = \sqrt{\frac{\Sigma Y^2 - \frac{(\Sigma Y)^2}{N}}{N}} = \sqrt{\frac{26019 - \frac{(503)^2}{10}}{10}} = 8.474$$

Next, the first four people scored "male," and their mean $(\overline{Y}_1)$ is 45.50. The remaining six people scored "female," and their mean, $(\overline{Y}_2)$ is 53.50. Let's call p the proportion of the sample scoring "male," so p is 4/10, or .40. Then, q is the proportion of the sample scoring "female," which is 6/10, or .60.

Filling in the formula for r_{pb} gives

$$r_{pb} = \left(\frac{\overline{Y}_2 - \overline{Y}_1}{S_Y}\right)(\sqrt{pq}) = \left(\frac{53.50 - 45.50}{8.474}\right)(\sqrt{(.40)(.60)})$$

Subtracting 45.50 from 53.50 gives 8.00, so

$$r_{pb} = \left(\frac{8.00}{8.474}\right)(\sqrt{(.40)(.60)})$$

Dividing 8.00 by 8.474 gives .944. Also, .40 times .60 is .24, and the square root of .24 is .489. Thus,

$$r_{pb} = .944(.489)$$

After multiplying,

$$r_{pb} = +.462$$

FIGURE 10.10 Example Data for Computing r_{pb}

Participant	***Gender: X***	***Test: Y***	
	Males		
1	1	50	
2	1	38	$\overline{Y}_1 = 45.50$
3	1	41	
4	1	53	
	Females		
5	2	60	
6	2	50	
7	2	44	
8	2	68	$\overline{Y}_2 = 53.50$
9	2	53	
10	2	46	
$N = 10$	2	$\Sigma Y = 503$	

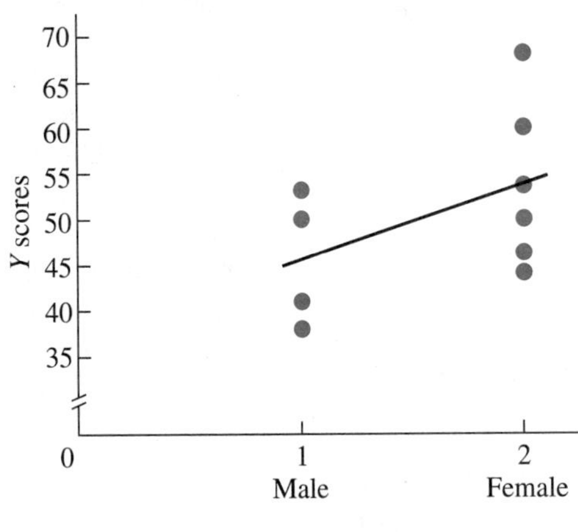

Thus, r_{pb} is $+.46$, so on a scale of 0 to ± 1.0, we have a moderately strong relationship: Somewhat close to one test score tends to be associated with one gender, and a different test score tends to be associated with the other gender.

Note that in this example the dichotomous variable is a qualitative variable, so the nominal scores of 1 and 2 do not actually reflect more or less of the gender variable. Therefore, the r_{pb} is positive only because we arbitrarily assigned a 1 to males and a 2 to females. Had we assigned females a 1 and males a 2, their locations on the X axis of the scatterplot would be reversed, producing a negative relationship. Likewise, had we chosen to call the female mean $\overline{Y}_1$ and the male mean $\overline{Y}_2$, we would have had $45.50 - 53.50$, which would have resulted in a negative r_{pb} of $-.46$. Thus, for any qualitative X variable, the absolute value of r_{pb} will accurately describe the strength of the relationship, but whether it is positive or negative depends on how you have arbitrarily arranged the data.

REMEMBER Compute the point-biserial correlation coefficient when describing the linear relationship between an interval/ratio variable and a dichotomous variable.

CREATING A POWERFUL CORRELATIONAL DESIGN

Recall that we always try to create a *powerful design*. This boils down to obtaining the strongest, most convincing relationship in our sample, so we won't miss a relationship that occurs in nature. This logic also applies to correlational research. Here, obtaining the most convincing relationship translates into obtaining the largest correlation coefficient possible.

As we've seen, the strength of a relationship and the size of the correlation coefficient depend on having minimum variability in Y scores at each X. There are two things that produce such error variance. First, individual differences will operate: Back in our coffee study, for example, some people will exhibit different nervousness scores for the same amount of coffee, because of *individual differences* in physiology, arousal levels, and so on. Second, any measurement will lack perfect *reliability* and *validity*, and there will be momentary fluctuations in variables that influence participants differently. Thus, our participants may incorrectly report their coffee consumption, the environment may differentially influence them, the researcher may behave inconsistently, or there may be inconsistency in measuring nervousness. Any of these factors can produce a less consistent relationship and lower the correlation coefficient. Thus, as with experiments, the key to obtaining a powerful correlational design is to obtain reliable and valid measurements, with a minimum of uncontrolled extraneous variables that may produce variability.

In addition, we increase power by avoiding the restriction of range problem.

The Restriction of Range Problem

Recall from Chapter 4 that a *restricted range* occurs when the range between the lowest and highest scores on one or both variables is small, or limited. A restricted range reduces the accuracy of the correlation coefficient, producing a coefficient *smaller* than it would be if the range were not restricted. Here's why.

Recall that the coefficient reflects the spread in *Y* at each *X* *relative* to the overall spread in all *Y*s. Look at Figure 10.11. When we consider the full range of *X* scores, the spread in the *Y* scores at each *X* is small relative to the overall variability in *Y*, and the data form a narrow ellipse that hugs the regression line. Therefore, *r* will be relatively large, and we will correctly conclude that there is a strong relationship between these variables.

If, however, we restrict the range of the *X* scores by collecting scores only between score A and score B in Figure 10.11, we'll have just the data in the shaded part of the scatterplot. Now, the spread in *Y*s at each *X* is large relative to the overall spread of all *Y*s in the shaded area. This makes the scatterplot more circular, with a relatively wide spread in the *Y*s at each *X*. Therefore, a coefficient using only the shaded portion will be relatively small, and we will conclude that there is a weak relationship here. This conclusion will be wrong, however, because we would have found a much stronger relationship if we had not restricted the range. (Because either variable can be called the *X* or *Y* variable, restricting the range of *Y* has the same effect as above.)

Thus, restriction of range leads to an erroneous *underestimate* of the degree of association between two variables. This is important because restricted range may result in such a small coefficient that we erroneously conclude the variables are not related in nature, when in fact they are. Therefore, to avoid missing a relationship, we seek a powerful design, and avoiding a restricted range is an aspect of increasing the power of a study.

How do you avoid restricting the range? Previously, you've seen that to produce a wider range of scores we avoid ceiling and floor effects (where scores are all very high or all very low). In addition, do not be too selective when obtaining participants. If we're interested in the relationship between a participant's high school grade average and subsequent salary, do not sample only honor students: Measure all students to get the entire range of grades. If we're correlating personality types with degree of emotional problems, don't restrict the study to only college students. People with severe

FIGURE 10.11 Scatterplot Showing Restriction of Range in *X* Scores

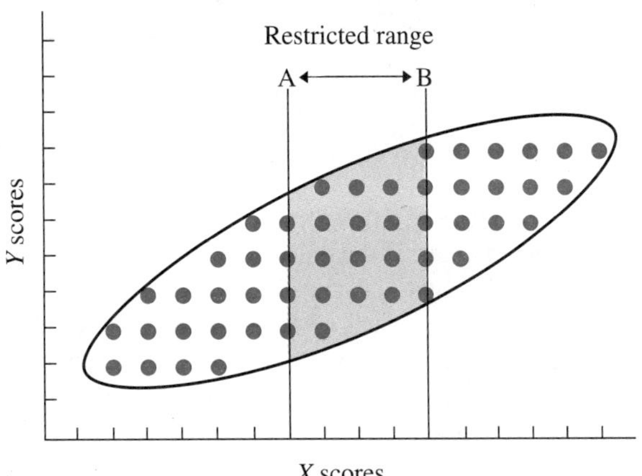

emotional problems tend not to be in college, so we won't have their scores. Instead, obtain the full range of scores by sampling from the general population. In all cases, the goal is to allow a wide range of scores to occur on both variables, so that we have a complete description of the relationship.

CORRELATIONS IN THE POPULATION

As you know, ultimately we use a sample to describe the population we would find if we could measure it. After we perform the appropriate inferential statistics, we use a sample correlation coefficient to estimate the correlation coefficient we would obtain if we could correlate the X and Y scores of everyone in the population.

The symbol for a population correlation coefficient is ρ. This is the Greek letter rho (the Greek r). Technically, ρ is the symbol for the population correlation coefficient when the Pearson r is used. Thus, we compute r for a random sample, which gives us an estimate of the value of ρ. However, if the data involve ranked scores, we compute r_s and have an estimate of the population coefficient symbolized by ρ_s. If the data involve one continuous variable and one dichotomous variable, we compute r_{pb} to estimate ρ_{pb}.

A population correlation coefficient is interpreted in the same way as a sample correlation coefficient. Thus, ρ is a number between 0 and ± 1.0, indicating either a positive or a negative linear relationship in the population. The larger the absolute value of ρ, the stronger the relationship: The more that one and only one value of Y tends to be associated with each X and the more closely the scatterplot for the population hugs the regression line. Interpret ρ_s and ρ_{pb} in the same manner.

APA FORMAT FOR STATISTICAL NOTATION

In published research, the symbols for sample correlation coefficients are those used in this chapter: r, r_s and r_{pb} stand for the Pearson, Spearman, and point-biserial correlations, respectively. However, the symbol for a population coefficient is not used, and rho (ρ) is used for a different type of correlation that is beyond this textbook.

PUTTING IT ALL TOGETHER

By far, the importance of a correlation coefficient is that it is one number that allows us to envision and summarize the important information in a scatterplot. If, for example, I say that a particular study produced an r equal to $+.70$, *without even seeing the data*, you know the essential aspects of the relationship in terms of its strength and direction. No other type of statistic so directly summarizes a relationship. Therefore, as we'll see in later chapters, even when conducting an experiment, you should always calculate the appropriate correlation coefficient to describe the strength and type of relationship you have observed.

CHAPTER SUMMARY

1. In a *correlational design*, the researcher does not manipulate either variable. The demonstrated relationship is not necessarily a causal relationship.

2. A *scatterplot* is a graph showing the location of each data point formed by a pair of *X*-*Y* scores.

3. A scatterplot is summarized by the *regression line*.

4. In a *positive linear relationship*, as the *X* scores increase, the *Y* scores tend to increase. In a *negative linear relationship*, as the *X* scores increase, the *Y* scores tend to decrease. In a *nonlinear relationship*, as the *X* scores increase, the *Y* scores do not only increase or only decrease.

5. A horizontal scatterplot, with a horizontal regression line, indicates *no relationship*. Sloping scatterplots with regression lines oriented so that *Y* increases as *X* increases indicate a *positive linear relationship*. Sloping scatterplots with regression lines oriented so that *Y* decreases as *X* increases indicate a *negative linear relationship*. Scatterplots producing curved regression lines indicate *nonlinear relationships*.

6. A *linear correlation coefficient* communicates the *type* of relationship (either positive or negative) and the *strength* of the relationship (the extent to which one value of *Y* is consistently paired with one and only one value of *X*).

7. The *smaller the absolute value of the coefficient*, the greater the variability in the *Y*s at each *X*, the greater the vertical width of the scatterplot, and the less accurately *Y* scores can be predicted from *X* scores.

8. *Test-retest reliability* indicates that participants tend to obtain the same score when repeatedly tested at different times. *Split-half reliability* indicates that participants' scores on some trials tend to match their scores on other trials.

9. With *face validity*, a measurement procedure appears valid. With *convergent validity*, a procedure is correlated with other procedures that are already accepted as valid. With *discriminant validity*, a procedure is not correlated with procedures that measure other things.

10. With *criterion validity*, the scores from a measurement procedure correlate with an observable behavior in one of two ways: With *concurrent validity*, a procedure correlates with a current behavior; with *predictive validity*, a procedure correlates with a future behavior.

11. The *Pearson correlation coefficient* (r) describes the linear relationship between two interval or ratio variables.

12. The *Spearman rank-order correlation coefficient* (r_s) describes the linear relationship between two variables measured using ranked scores.

13. The *point-biserial correlation coefficient* (r_{pb}) describes the linear relationship between scores from one interval or ratio variable and one dichotomous variable.

14. The *power* of a correlational design is increased by minimizing error variance and avoiding a restricted range, so that the largest possible coefficient is obtained.

15. When the range of scores on one or both variables is *restricted*, the correlation coefficient underestimates the strength of the relationship that would be found if the range were not restricted.

16. If it passes the appropriate inferential procedure, a sample correlation coefficient is used to estimate the corresponding *population correlation coefficient*: r estimates ρ, r_s estimates ρ_s, and r_{pb} estimates ρ_{pb}.

KEY TERMS (with page references)

ΣXY r r_s r_{pb} ρ ρ_s ρ_{pb}
concurrent validity (264)
convergent validity (263)
correlation coefficient (253)
criterion validity (264)
curvilinear relationship (255)
discriminant validity (263)
face validity (263)
linear relationship (254)
negative linear relationship (255)
nonlinear relationship (255)
Pearson correlation coefficient (265)
point-biserial correlation coefficient (270)
positive linear relationship (254)
predictive validity (264)
regression line (253)
scatterplot (252)
Spearman rank-order correlation coefficient (267)
split-half reliability (262)
strength of a relationship (257)
test-retest reliability (262)
tied rank (269)
type of relationship (254)

REVIEW QUESTIONS

(Answers for odd-numbered questions and problems are provided in Appendix D.)

1. What is the difference between an experiment and a correlational study in terms of how we (a) collect the data? (b) examine the relationship?

2. (a) You have collected data that you think show a relationship. What do you do next? (b) What is the advantage of computing a correlation coefficient?

3. What are the two reasons we can't conclude there is a causal relationship based on correlational research?

4. (a) When do you compute a Pearson correlation coefficient? (b) When do you compute a Spearman coefficient? (c) When do you compute a point-biserial coefficient?

5. (a) What is a scatterplot? (b) What is a regression line?

6. What two characteristics of a linear relationship are described by a correlation coefficient?
7. (a) Define a positive linear relationship. (b) Define a negative linear relationship. (c) Define a curvilinear relationship.
8. As the value of r approaches ± 1.0, what does it indicate about the following: (a) The shape of the scatterplot? (b) The variability of the Y scores at each X? (c) The closeness of Y scores to the regression line? (d) The accuracy with which we can predict Y if X is known?
9. What does a correlation coefficient equal to 0 indicate about the four characteristics in question 8?
10. What is the difference between test-retest reliability and split-half reliability?
11. (a) What is the difference between convergent and divergent validity? (b) How does criterion validity differ from the types of validity in part (a)? (c) What are the two types of criterion validity, and how is each determined?
12. (a) What does ρ stand for? (b) How is the value of ρ determined? (c) What does ρ tell you?

PRACTICE PROBLEMS

13. Why can't we obtain a correlation coefficient greater than ± 1?
14. For each of the following, indicate whether it is a positive linear, negative linear, or nonlinear relationship: (a) Quality of performance (Y) increases with increased arousal (X) up to an optimal level, then performance decreases with increased arousal. (b) Heavier jockeys (X) tend to win fewer horse races (Y). (c) As number of minutes of exercise per week (X) increases, dieting individuals lose more pounds (Y). (d) The number of bears in an area (Y) decreases as the area becomes increasingly populated by humans (X).
15. Poindexter sees the data in problem 14, part (d), and concludes, "To preserve the bear population, we should stop people from moving into bear country." What is the problem with his conclusion?
16. Why would a professor prefer to show the split-half reliability of a college exam instead of the test-retest reliability?
17. For each of the following, give the symbol for the correlation coefficient you should compute: (a) SAT scores and IQ scores. (b) The taste rankings of different types of tea by an expert and a novice. (c) Presence or absence of a head injury and scores on a vocabulary test. (d) Finishing position in a race and number of glasses of liquid consumed during the race.
18. In the correlation between orange juice consumed and number of doctor visits discussed in this chapter, does drinking more orange juice cause people to be healthier so that they don't have to go to the doctor?
19. In a correlational study, a researcher measured the number of boxes of tissue purchased per week and the number of vitamin tablets consumed per week for each participant. (a) Which is the independent and which is the dependent variable here? (b) Which variable is X? Which is Y?
20. (a) How do you maximize the power of a correlational design? (b) What produces a restricted range? (c) Why should it be avoided? (d) How is it avoided?

21. Foofy and Poindexter investigated the relationship between IQ score and high school grade average, studying students in a program for exceptionally smart students. They found an $r = +.03$, and concluded that there is virtually no relationship between IQ and grade average. Should you agree or disagree with this conclusion? (*Hint:* Is there a problem with their study?)

22. A researcher measures the following scores for a group of students where X is their number of errors on a math test, and Y is their satisfaction with their grades.

Pearsons Correlation coefficient

Participant	*Errors* *X*	*Satisfaction* *Y*
1	9	3
2	8	2
3	4	8
4	6	5
5	7	4
6	10	2
7	5	7

(a) With such ratio scores, summarize this relationship.
(b) How well will he be able to predict satisfaction scores using this relationship?

23. The data below reflect whether a participant is a college graduate (Y or N) and the score he or she obtained on a self-esteem test. To what extent is there a positive or negative linear relationship here?

Participant	*College Graduate* *X*	*Self-Esteem* *Y*
1	Y	8
2	Y	7
3	Y	12
4	Y	6
5	Y	10
6	N	2
7	N	8
8	N	6
9	N	1
10	N	9

24. In the data below, the X scores reflect students' academic rankings in their freshman class, and the Y scores reflect their rankings in their sophomore class. To what extent do these data form a linear relationship? (*Caution:* Think before you calculate.)

Participant	*Fresh.* X	*Soph.* Y
1	2	3
2	9	7
3	1	2
4	5	7
5	3	1
6	7	8
7	4	4
8	6	5
9	8	6

25. You want to know if a nurse's absences from work in one month (*Y*) can be predicted by knowing his or her score on a test of psychological "burnout" (*X*). What do you conclude from the following ratio data?

Participant	*Burnout* X	*Absences* Y
1	2	4
2	1	7
3	2	6
4	3	9
5	4	6
6	4	8
7	7	7
8	7	10
9	8	11

26. You hypothesize that students who sit toward the front of a classroom (those with a 0 on the *X* variable) perform better than those who sit toward the back of the classroom (1 on *X*) when given a brief quiz (the *Y* scores). Do these data support your hypothesis? (Call the group with 0s group 2.)

Participant	*Location* X	*Quiz* Y
1	0	4
2	0	6
3	0	11
4	0	5
5	1	8
6	1	5
7	1	8
8	1	11
9	1	7
10	1	4

27. A researcher observes the behavior of a group of monkeys in the jungle. She determines each monkey's relative position in the dominance hierarchy of the group (with an X of 1 being most dominant), and also notes each monkey's relative weight (with a Y of 1 being the lightest). What is the relationship between dominance and weight?

Participant	*Dominance* X	*Weight* Y
1	1	10
2	2	8
3	5	6
4	4	7
5	9	5
6	7	3
7	3	9
8	6	4
9	8	1
10	10	2

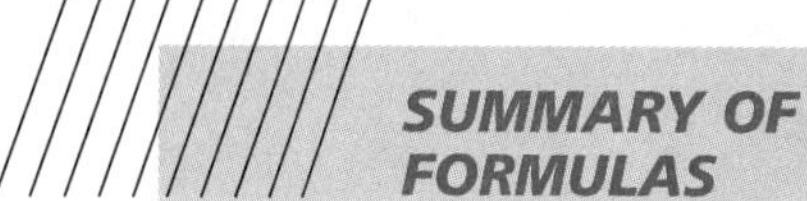

SUMMARY OF FORMULAS

1. *The computational formula for the Pearson correlation coefficient is*

$$r = \frac{N(\Sigma XY) - (\Sigma X)(\Sigma Y)}{\sqrt{[N(\Sigma X^2) - (\Sigma X)^2][N(\Sigma Y^2) - (\Sigma Y)^2]}}$$

where X and Y stand for the scores on the X and Y variables and N is the number of pairs in the sample.

2. *The computational formula for the Spearman rank-order correlation coefficient is*

$$r_s = 1 - \frac{6(\Sigma D^2)}{N(N^2 - 1)}$$

where N is the number of pairs of ranks and D is the difference between the two ranks in each pair.

3. *The computational formula for the point-biserial correlation coefficient is*

$$r_{pb} = \left(\frac{\overline{Y}_2 - \overline{Y}_1}{S_Y}\right)(\sqrt{pq})$$

where

$\overline{Y}_1$ is the mean of the scores on the continuous variable for one group of the dichotomous variable,

$\overline{Y}_2$ is the mean of the scores on the continuous variable for the other group of the dichotomous variable,

S_Y is the standard deviation of all Y scores,

p is the proportion of the sample in one dichotomous group and q is the proportion of the sample in the other dichotomous group. Each is found by dividing the number of participants in the group by N, the total number of X-Y pairs in the study.

11

Using Linear Regression to Predict Scores

Getting Started

To understand this chapter, recall the following:

- From Chapter 7, recall that without additional information, the $\overline{X}$ is used to predict all scores in a sample.
- From Chapter 8, understand that when using the mean to predict scores, variance is the "average error" in predictions.
- From Chapter 10, recall how r describes how much the scores hug the regression line.

Your goals in this chapter are to learn:

- How a regression line summarizes a scatterplot.
- How the regression equation is used to predict the Y scores at a given X.
- Which statistics measure errors in prediction when using regression.
- How the strength of the relationship determines how accurately Y scores can be predicted.
- What the term "proportion of variance accounted for" means.

When the laws of nature produce a relationship, certain Y scores are naturally paired with certain X scores. Therefore, if we know an individual's X score and the relationship between X and Y, we can predict the corresponding Y score. The statistical procedure used to make such predictions is called *linear regression*. In the following sections we examine the logic behind regression and see how to use it to predict scores. Then, we'll look at ways of measuring the errors in our predictions.

MORE STATISTICAL NOTATION

Be sure that you understand that the variance in Y scores (S_Y^2) and the standard deviation of Y (S_Y) are computed in the same ways that we compute these values for X scores. Also, recognize that, when graphed, the variability between any two Y scores is reflected by their different vertical locations along the Y axis. Therefore, the larger the values of S_Y^2 or S_Y, the more the Y scores are vertically spread out in the scatterplot.

UNDERSTANDING LINEAR REGRESSION

Recall that a goal of psychology is to predict when different behaviors will occur. This translates into predicting when someone has one score on a variable, and when they have a different score. We use relationships to make these predictions, and linear regression is the statistical procedure for using a relationship to predict scores. Regression procedures center around drawing the linear regression line, the summary line drawn through a scatterplot. Thus, technically, **linear regression** is the procedure for describing the best-fitting straight line that summarizes a linear relationship. We use this procedure in conjunction with the Pearson correlation. While r is the *statistic* that summarizes the linear relationship, regression produces the *line* that summarizes the relationship. Always compute r first to determine whether a relationship exists. If $r = 0$, then the regression line is unnecessary. If r is not 0, then linear regression helps to further describe and understand the relationship.

An easy way to understand the regression line is to compare it to a line graph. In Chapter 7, we created a line graph by plotting the mean of the Y scores at each X, and then connecting adjacent data points with straight lines. The left-hand scatterplot in Figure 11.1 shows the line graph of an experiment with four conditions. Thus, for

FIGURE 11.1 Comparison of a Line Graph and a Regression Line

Each data point is formed by an X-Y pair. Each asterisk (*) indicates the mean Y score at an X.

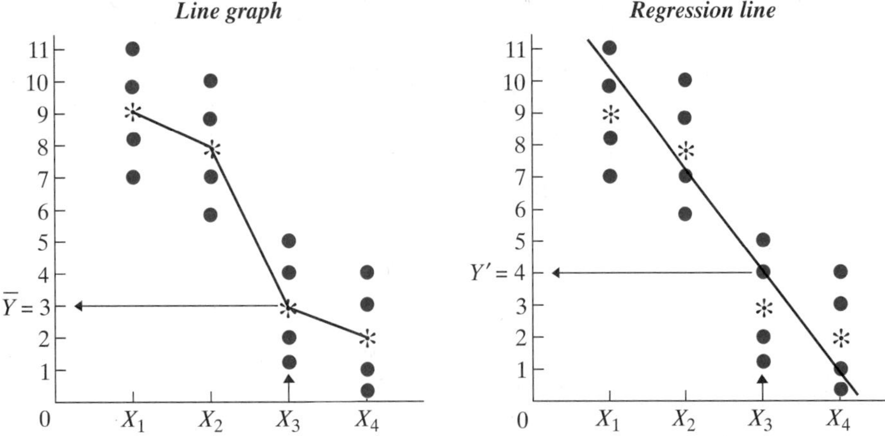

example, as the arrows indicate, the mean of Y at X_3 is 3. Because the mean is the central score, we assume that those participants scoring at X_3 all scored *around* a Y of 3, so (1) our best description of their scores is 3, and (2) our best prediction of Y for anyone else scoring at that X is also 3.

It is difficult, however, to see the linear (straight-line) relationship in these data, because the means do not fall in a straight line. Therefore, as in the right-hand graph in Figure 11.1, we summarize the linear relationship by drawing a regression line. Think of the regression line as a straightened-out version of the line graph: It is drawn so that it comes as close as possible to connecting the mean of Y at each X while still producing a straight line. Although not all means are on the line, the distance that some means are above the line averages out with the distance that others are below the line. Therefore, the regression line is the *best-fitting* line because, "on average," it passes through the center of the various Y means. Because each Y mean is in the center of the corresponding Y scores, by passing through the center of the means, the regression line passes through the center of the Y scores. Thus, the **linear regression line** is the straight line that summarizes the linear relationship in a scatterplot by, on average, passing through the center of the Y scores at each X. As usual, this is another descriptive procedure that allows us to summarize and envision data. Think of the regression line as reflecting the linear relationship hidden in the data. Because the actual Y scores fall above and below the line, the data only more or less form a straight line. But, we have no system for drawing a more or less linear relationship. Therefore, the regression line is how we envision what a perfect version of the linear relationship in our data would look like.

Read the regression line in the same way you read a line graph: Travel vertically from any X until intercepting the regression line, and then travel horizontally until intercepting the Y axis. For example, as indicated in the right-hand graph in Figure 11.1 the value of Y at X_3 is now 4. The symbol for this value is Y', which is pronounced "Y prime." Each Y' is a summary of the Y scores for that X based on the *entire* linear relationship formed across *all* X-Y pairs in the data. Because the Y scores are evenly spread out around (above and below) the regression line, they are evenly spread out around each value of Y'. Therefore, considering the entire linear relationship, participants at X_3 scored around 4, so 4 is our best description of their scores, and 4 is our best prediction of Y for anyone else scoring at that X. Thus, the symbol Y' stands for a **predicted Y score**: Each Y' is our best prediction of the Y scores at a corresponding X, based on the linear relationship that is summarized by the regression line.

Recognize that the Y' at any X is the value of Y falling *on* the regression line. The entire regression line, therefore, consists of the data points formed by pairing every possible value of X with its corresponding value of Y'. If we think of the line as reflecting the linear relationship hidden in the data, then each Y' is the Y score that everyone would have at each X if the perfect version of this relationship were present.

> *REMEMBER* The regression line summarizes the linear relationship in a sample and consists of the predicted Y score—the Y'—for every possible X.

Predicting Unknown Scores Using Regression

Now, you can see how regression techniques are used in psychological research. First, a relationship is established in a sample by computing r. Then, inferential procedures are performed to decide whether the sample is representative. If it is, we use the regression line to determine the Y' for any X. Each Y' is the score *around* which everyone at that X actually scored. We assume all potential participants are interchangeable, so for anyone else scoring that X, we'd predict that they too would score around that Y'. Therefore, we can measure the X scores of *new* participants who were not in the sample, and for their X, the corresponding Y' is our best prediction of their Y scores. Thus,

> **the importance of linear regression is that it is used to predict an individual's *unknown* Y score based on his or her X score from a correlated variable.**

Regression is common in correlational studies because the observed relationship is usually better for predicting behaviors than that found in an experiment: There is usually greater external validity and a more accurate description of the relationship. For this reason, regression techniques are common in applied research, especially when creating "selection tests." A selection test is for selecting people with certain qualifications or attributes. For example, students are taking a selection test when they take the Scholastic Aptitude Test (SAT) to be admitted to college. We know from previous students that SAT scores are somewhat positively correlated with college grades. Therefore, through regression techniques, the SAT scores of those students applying for college are used to predict their future college performance: A student's X score on the SAT leads to a predicted Y' of the student's college grade average. If the predicted grades are too low, the student is not admitted to the college. Similar selection tests are involved when people take a test when applying for a job so that the employer can predict who will be better workers, or when clinical patients take diagnostic tests for identifying those at risk of developing emotional problems. Not surprisingly, *predictive validity* (discussed in the previous chapter) is of paramount importance when creating selection tests.

> *REMEMBER* Linear regression is used to predict unknown Y scores based on an X score from a correlated variable.

The emphasis on prediction in correlation and regression leads to two important terms. We'll discuss using X scores to predict Y scores, but there are procedures out there for predicting X scores from Y. In statistical lingo, when X is used to predict Y scores, X is the **predictor variable** (it does the predicting). When the scores being predicted are on the Y variable, Y is the **criterion variable**. Thus, above, SAT scores are the predictor variable, and college grade average is the criterion variable. (To remember "criterion," remember that your predicted grades must meet a certain criterion for you to be admitted to the college.)

To use regression techniques, after establishing the relationship between X and Y, the first step is to create the regression line.

THE LINEAR REGRESSION EQUATION

To draw a regression line, we don't simply eyeball the scatterplot and sketch in something that looks good. Instead, we use the linear regression equation. The **linear regression equation** is the equation that produces the value of Y' at each X and thus defines the straight line that summarizes a relationship. When we plot the data points formed by the X-Y' pairs, and draw a line connecting them, we have the regression line. The regression equation describes two characteristics of the regression line: Its slope and its Y-intercept.

The **slope** of a line is a number that indicates how slanted the line is and the direction in which it slants. Figure 11.2 shows examples of regression lines that have different slopes. When there is no relationship, the regression line is horizontal—such as line A—and then the slope equals 0. A positive linear relationship—such as lines B and C—yields a slope that is a positive number. Because line C is steeper, its slope is a larger positive number. A negative linear relationship—such as line D—yields a slope that is a negative number.

The ***Y*-intercept** is the value of Y at the point where the regression line intercepts, or crosses, the Y axis. In other words, the Y-intercept is the value of Y' when X equals 0. In Figure 11.2, line B crosses the Y axis at 2, so its Y-intercept is 2. If we extended line C, it would intercept the Y axis at a point below the X axis, so its Y-intercept is a negative Y score. Because line D reflects a negative relationship, its Y-intercept is the relatively high Y score of 9. Finally, line A exhibits no relationship, and its Y-intercept equals 8. Notice that here the value of Y' for any value of X is always 8.

> **When there is no relationship, the regression line is flat and every value of Y' equals the Y-intercept.**

The regression equation works like this: The slope summarizes the *direction* in which Y scores change as X increases, and also the *rate* at which they change. In Figure 11.2, the steeply sloped line C reflects a relatively large change in Y scores for each increase in X, as compared to, say, line B, which reflects a smaller change in Y for each increase in X. The Y-intercept then indicates the starting point from which the Y scores change. Thus, together, the slope and intercept describe how, starting at a particular value, the Y scores change as X changes. Then, the summary of the Y scores at each X is Y'.

The symbol for the slope of the regression line is b. The symbol for the Y-intercept is a. Then:

FIGURE 11.2 Regression Lines That Have Different Slopes and *Y*-Intercepts

Line A indicates no relationship, lines B and C indicate positive relationships having different slopes and Y-intercepts, and line D indicates a negative relationship.

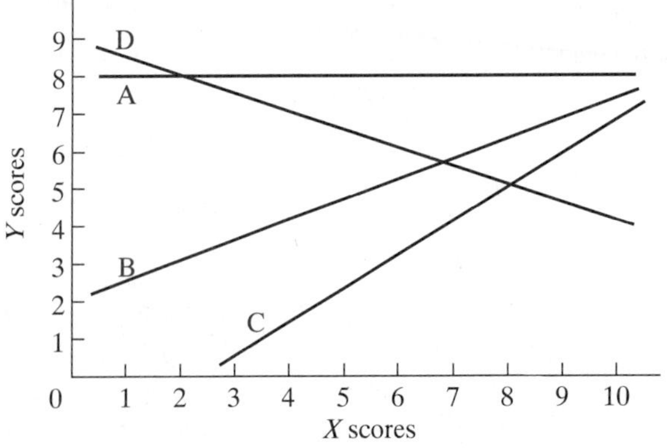

THE LINEAR REGRESSION EQUATION IS

$$Y' = bX + a$$

This formula says that to find the value of Y' for a given X, multiply the slope (b) times X and then add the Y-intercept (a.)

As an example, say that a researcher has developed a paper-and-pencil selection test to identify people who will be productive "widget-makers." To demonstrate that the test has predictive validity, the researcher examines whether test scores are correlated with widget-making ability. The researcher gives the test to a small N of 11 people and then, in a simulation of a factory setting, measures the number of widgets each participant makes in an hour. Figure 11.3 shows the resulting scatterplot, with test scores as the predictor (X) variable and number of widgets produced per hour as the criterion (Y) variable. The raw scores are also listed, arranged for computing r.

FIGURE 11.3 Scatterplot and Data for Widget-Making Study

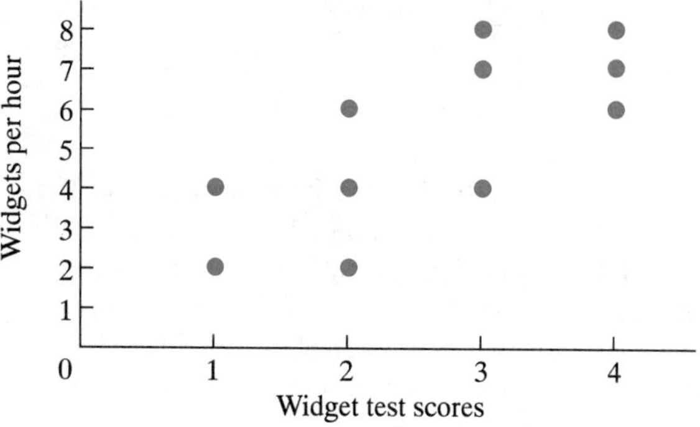

Participant	*Widget test score:* X	*Widgets per hour:* Y	XY
1	1	2	2
2	1	4	4
3	2	4	8
4	2	6	12
5	2	2	4
6	3	4	12
7	3	7	21
8	3	8	24
9	4	6	24
10	4	8	32
11	4	7	28
$N = 11$	$\Sigma X = 29$	$\Sigma Y = 58$	$\Sigma XY = 171$
	$\Sigma X^2 = 89$	$\Sigma Y^2 = 354$	
	$(\Sigma X)^2 = 841$	$(\Sigma Y)^2 = 3364$	
	$\bar{X} = 29/11 = 2.64$	$\bar{Y} = 58/11 = 5.27$	

The first step is to find r:

$$r = \frac{N(\Sigma XY) - (\Sigma X)(\Sigma Y)}{\sqrt{[N(\Sigma X^2) - (\Sigma X)^2][N(\Sigma Y^2) - (\Sigma Y)^2]}}$$

so

$$r = \frac{11(171) - (29)(58)}{\sqrt{[11(89) - 841][11(354) - 3364]}}$$

The result is $r = +.736$, which rounds to $r = +.74$. Thus, this is a quite strong positive linear relationship.

To predict widget-making scores, compute the linear regression equation. To do that, compute the slope and the Y-intercept. Compute the slope first.

Computing the Slope

THE FORMULA FOR THE SLOPE OF THE LINEAR REGRESSION LINE IS

$$b = \frac{N(\Sigma XY) - (\Sigma X)(\Sigma Y)}{N(\Sigma X^2) - (\Sigma X)^2}$$

N is the number of pairs of scores in the sample, and X and Y are the scores in the sample. This is not a difficult formula, because we typically compute the Pearson r first. The numerator in the formula for b is the same as the numerator in the formula for r. The denominator in the formula for b is the left-hand quantity in the denominator of the formula for r. [An alternative formula for the slope is $b = (r)\,(S_Y / S_X)$.]

Substituting the appropriate values from our computations of r in the widget study into the formula for b, we have

$$b = \frac{N(\Sigma XY) - (\Sigma X)(\Sigma Y)}{N(\Sigma X^2) - (\Sigma X)^2} = \frac{11(171) - (29)(58)}{11(89) - 841}$$

After multiplying and subtracting in the numerator,

$$b = \frac{199}{11(89) - 841}$$

After completing the denominator,

$$b = \frac{199}{138} = +1.44$$

Thus, the slope of the regression line for the widget-making data is $b = +1.44$. This positive slope indicates a positive relationship, which fits with the positive r of $+.74$. Had the relationship been negative, the formula would have produced a negative number for the slope.

We're not finished yet. Now compute the Y-intercept.

Computing the *Y*-Intercept

THE FORMULA FOR THE Y-INTERCEPT OF THE LINEAR REGRESSION LINE IS

$$a = \overline{Y} - (b)(\overline{X})$$

First, multiply the mean of all X scores ($\overline{X}$) times the slope of the regression line (b). Then, subtract that quantity from the mean of all Y scores ($\overline{Y}$). For the widget-making data, b is $+1.44$ and from Figure 11.3, $\overline{Y}$ is 5.27 and $\overline{X}$ is 2.64. Filling in the formula for a, we have

$$a = 5.27 - (+1.44)(2.64)$$

After multiplying,

$$a = 5.27 - (+3.80) = +1.47$$

Thus, the Y-intercept of the regression line for the widget-making study is $a = +1.47$.

We're still not finished!

Describing the Linear Regression Equation

Once you have computed the Y-intercept and the slope, rewrite the regression equation, substituting the computed values for a and b. Thus, for the widget-making study,

$$Y' = +1.44X + 1.47$$

This is the finished regression equation that describes the regression line for the relationship between widget test scores and widgets-per-hour scores.

Putting all of this together, the preceding computations are summarized in Table 11.1. We're still not finished! The final step is to graph the regression line.

Plotting the Regression Line

To plot the regression line, you need some pairs of X and Y' scores to use as data points. Therefore, choose some values of X, insert each into the finished regression equation,

TABLE 11.1 Summary of Computations for the Linear Regression Equation

1. Compute r.
2. Compute the slope, where $b = \dfrac{N(\Sigma XY) - (\Sigma X)(\Sigma Y)}{N(\Sigma X^2) - (\Sigma X)^2}$.
3. Compute the Y-intercept, where $a = \overline{Y} - (b)(\overline{X})$.
4. Substitute the values of a and b into the formula for the regression equation, $Y' = bX + a$.

and calculate the value of Y' for that X. Actually, you need only two data points to draw a straight line: One where X is low and one where X is high. (An easy low X to use is $X = 0$ because then Y' equals the Y-intercept, a.)

To see how the calculations work, we'll compute Y' for all X scores from the widget-making study. We begin with the finished regression equation:

$$Y' = +1.44X + 1.47$$

First, we find Y' for $X = 1$, so

$$Y' = +1.44(1) + 1.47$$

Multiplying 1 times +1.44 and adding 1.47 yields a Y' of 2.91. Thus, we predict that anyone scoring 1 on the widget-making test will make 2.91 widgets per hour. Using the same procedure, we obtain the values of Y' for the remaining X scores of 2, 3, and 4. These are shown in the table in Figure 11.4.

To graph the regression line, simply plot the data points for the X-Y' pairs and draw the line as in the graph in Figure 11.4. (*Note:* Published research reports typically do not include the scatterplot, nor is the regression line drawn through the Y-intercept.)

Now we're finished. (Really.)

Using the Regression Equation to Predict *Y* Scores

The Y' for a particular X is the predicted Y score for all participants having that X score. Above, for example, people scoring an X of 1 have a Y' of 2.91. Therefore, we predict that anyone else not in the sample who scores an X of 1 will also have a Y' of 2.91. Further, we can compute Y' for any value of X that falls *within* the range of Xs in the original sample, even if it's not an X that a participant originally obtained: No one originally scored an X of 1.5, but entering this value into the regression equation produces a Y' of 3.63. Do not, however, make predictions using X scores outside the range of the original X scores: Our regression equation is based on widget test scores between 1 and 4, so we shouldn't predict Y for an X of, say, 8. This is because we can't be sure what the relationship is like out there at 8—maybe its strength changes, maybe it has a steeper slope, or maybe its curvilinear!

FIGURE 11.4 Regression Line for Widget-Making Study

Widget test scores: X	*Predicted widgets per hour:* Y
1	2.91
2	4.25
3	5.79
4	7.23

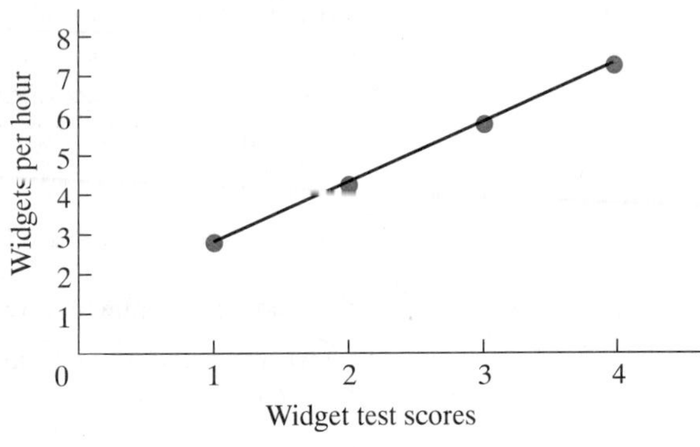

That's all there is to computing the regression line and predicting scores—except for the fact that any prediction we make may be wrong. Therefore, the remainder of this chapter deals with describing the amount of error in our predictions.

DESCRIBING ERRORS IN PREDICTION WHEN USING THE LINEAR REGRESSION EQUATION

A complete description of a relationship includes the descriptive statistics that summarize the error we have when we use the regression equation to predict Y scores. To describe the amount of error we expect in our predictions, we describe how well we can predict the actual Y scores in our sample: We pretend we don't know the scores, predict them, and then compare the predicted Y' scores to the actual Y scores. The predictions for some participants will be close to their actual Y scores, while for others there may be more error. Therefore, to summarize the error across the entire relationship, we compute something like the "average error" in predictions.

The error in a single prediction is the amount that a participant's actual Y score differs, or *deviates*, from the corresponding predicted Y' score: In symbols, this is $(Y - Y')$, and it is literally the difference between the actual Y score that participants got and the Y we predicted they'd get. To find the average error, we find something like the average of the deviations. First, we compute Y' for each individual in the data and subtract each Y' from its corresponding Y score. We would like to sum these differences, getting $\Sigma(Y - Y')$, and then find the average. But we can't. Recall that the regression line goes through the center of the scatterplot, so, like a mean, the Y' scores are in the center of the Y scores, with the Ys equally spread out above and below the Y' scores. Therefore, like a mean, the positive and negative deviations cancel out, and the sum of the deviations is always zero. Then the average error is always zero.

To solve this problem, we *square* each deviation. The sum of the squared deviations of $Y - Y'$ is not necessarily zero, so neither is the average squared deviation. (Does this sound familiar?) When we find the average of the squared deviations between the Y and corresponding Y' scores, we are computing a type of *variance* that describes the "average" spread of the actual Y scores around—above and below—their corresponding Y' scores.

Computing the Variance of the *Y* Scores Around *Y′*

The **variance of the *Y* scores around *Y′*** is the average squared difference between the actual Y scores at each X and the predicted Y' score for that X. The symbol for this *sample* variance is $S^2_{Y'}$. The S^2 indicates sample variance or error, and the subscript Y' indicates it is error associated with using Y' to predict Y scores.

THE DEFINITIONAL FORMULA FOR THE VARIANCE OF THE Y SCORES AROUND Y′ IS

$$S^2_{Y'} = \frac{\Sigma(Y - Y')^2}{N}$$

This formula says to subtract each Y' predicted for a participant from his or her corresponding actual Y score, square each deviation, sum the squared deviations, and then divide by N. The answer is one way to measure the amount of error we have when using regression and Y' to predict Y scores.

Remember the widget-making study? Table 11.2 shows the actual X and Y scores participants obtained, as well as the Y' scores we predicted for them using the regression equation. In the column labeled $Y - Y'$, each Y' is subtracted from the corresponding Y. In the column labeled $(Y - Y')^2$, each difference is squared. Then, summing the squared differences gives $\Sigma(Y - Y')^2$. Filling in the formula for $S^2_{Y'}$,

$$S^2_{Y'} = \frac{\Sigma(Y - Y')^2}{N} = \frac{22.096}{11}$$

After dividing,

$$S^2_{Y'} = 2.009$$

With rounding,

$$S^2_{Y'} = 2.01$$

Thus, the average squared difference between the actual Y scores and their corresponding values of Y' is 2.01. This indicates that, when using variance to measure error, we are "off" by something like an "average" of 2.01 when we predict participants' widget-making score (Y) based on their test score (X).

Recall that differences between a predicted score and the corresponding actual scores goes by the generic name of *error variance*. Therefore, $S^2_{Y'}$ describes the error variance when using regression to predict Y scores: It is literally a formula for variance that measures error in prediction. (The nongeneric name for error variance in regression is "the residual variance" or just "the residual.")

TABLE 11.2 Widget-Making Data with Computed Y' Scores

Participant	*Widget test score: X*	*Widgets per hour: Y*	*Predicted widgets: Y′*	$Y - Y'$	$(Y - Y')^2$
1	1	2	2.91	−.91	.828
2	1	4	2.91	1.09	1.188
3	2	4	4.35	−.35	.123
4	2	6	4.35	1.65	2.723
5	2	2	4.35	−2.35	5.523
6	3	4	5.79	−1.79	3.204
7	3	7	5.79	1.21	1.464
8	3	8	5.79	2.21	4.884
9	4	6	7.23	−1.23	1.513
10	4	8	7.23	.77	.593
11	4	7	7.23	−.23	.053
$N = 11$		$\Sigma Y = 58$ $\Sigma Y^2 = 354$ $(\Sigma Y)^2 = 3364$			$\Sigma(Y - Y')^2 = 22.096$

REMEMBER $S^2_{Y'}$ describes the "average error" when using Y' scores to predict Y scores.

In statistical language, the formulas for computing the regression line are called the *least-squares regression method.* This is because with them, the sum of the squared deviations $[\Sigma(Y - Y')^2]$ is zero, the least that it can be. The term "sum of squared deviations" is shortened to "squares." The least-squares method produces *squares* between Y and Y' that is the *least* that it can be. Any other method leads to greater error in predictions, resulting in larger differences between Y and Y' and a larger value of $S^2_{Y'}$.

Using the definitional formula for $S^2_{Y'}$ is very time-consuming. If in place of Y' in the definitional formula for $S^2_{Y'}$ we put in all of the formulas for finding Y' (for finding a, b, and so on) and then simplify that equation, we would find the components for the following.

THE COMPUTATIONAL FORMULA FOR THE VARIANCE OF Y SCORES AROUND Y′ IS

$$S^2_{Y'} = S^2_Y(1 - r^2)$$

This says to find the variance of all Y scores in the data (S^2_Y) and to square r. Subtract r^2 from 1 and then multiply the result times S^2_Y. The answer is $S^2_{Y'}$.

In the widget study, r was $+.736$. Using the data from Table 11.2, the S^2_Y is 4.38. Placing these numbers in the above formula gives

$$S^2_{Y'} = 4.38(1 - .736^2)$$

After squaring $+.736$ and subtracting the result from 1, we have

$$S^2_{Y'} = 4.38(.458)$$

so

$$S^2_{Y'} = 2.01$$

Again, we expect to be off by an "average" of about 2.01 when predicting participants' widget-making (Y) using their widget test score (X).

There are, however, the usual problems when interpreting a variance such as $S^2_{Y'}$. Squaring the difference between each Y and Y' produces an unrealistically large number. Also, the error is measured in squared units, so technically, above we were off by 2.01 *squared* widgets. (Sound familiar?) As usual, the solution is to find the square root of the variance, producing a type of standard deviation. To distinguish the standard deviation found in regression from other standard deviations, we call this one the *standard error of the estimate.*

Computing the Standard Error of the Estimate

The **standard error of the estimate** indicates the amount that the Y scores in a sample differ from their corresponding Y' scores. It is the clearest way to describe the "average" error when using Y' to predict Y scores. The symbol for the standard error of the estimate is $S_{Y'}$. (Remember, S measures the *error* in the sample, and Y' is our *estimate* of a participant's Y score.)

THE DEFINITIONAL FORMULA FOR THE STANDARD ERROR OF THE ESTIMATE IS

$$S_{Y'} = \sqrt{\frac{\Sigma(Y - Y')^2}{N}}$$

This is the same formula used previously for the variance of Y scores around Y', except with the added square root sign. Thus, to compute $S_{Y'}$, compute $S^2_{Y'}$ and then find its square root. In the widget-making study $S^2_{Y'} = 2.01$. Taking the square root produces an $S_{Y'} = 1.42$.

To create a computational formula, recall that the way to compute the variance of Y around Y' was

$$S^2_{Y'} = S^2_Y(1 - r^2)$$

Taking the square root of each component produces the computational formula.

THE COMPUTATIONAL FORMULA FOR THE STANDARD ERROR OF THE ESTIMATE IS

$$S_{Y'} = S_Y\sqrt{1 - r^2}$$

This says to find the square root of the quantity $1 - r^2$ and multiply it times the standard deviation of the Y score's (S_Y).

For the widget study, S^2_Y was 4.38, so S_Y is 2.093. r was +.736. Placing these numbers in the formula gives

$$S_{Y'} = 2.093\sqrt{1 - .736^2}$$

Squaring +.736 yields .542, which, when subtracted from 1, gives .458. The square root of .458 is .677. Thus,

$$S_{Y'} = 2.093(.677)$$

so

$$S_{Y'} = 1.42$$

Again, the standard error of the estimate is 1.42. Because the Y scores measure the variable of widgets per hour, the standard error of the estimate is 1.42 *widgets per hour*. Therefore, we conclude that when using the regression equation to predict the number of widgets produced per hour based on a person's widget test score, we will be wrong by an "average" of about 1.42 widgets per hour.

REMEMBER The standard error of the estimate ($S_{Y'}$) most clearly describes the "average" error when using the regression equation and Y' to predict Y scores.

It is appropriate to compute the standard error of the estimate anytime you compute a correlation coefficient, even if you do not perform regression—it's still important to know the average prediction error that using the regression procedure would produce.

Assumptions of Linear Regression

Because $S_{Y'}$ measures the differences between all Y and Y' scores, it indicates the amount the Y scores are spread out around—above and below—the Y' scores. In order for $S_{Y'}$ to accurately describe this spread, however, we must be able to make two assumptions about how the Y scores are distributed.

First, the Y scores should be equally spread out around Y' and the regression line *throughout* the relationship. This assumption is called homoscedasticity. **Homoscedasticity** occurs when the Y scores are spread out to the same degree at every X. The left-hand scatterplot in Figure 11.5 shows homoscedastic data from the widget study. Because the vertical distance separating the Y scores is the same at each X, the spread of the Y scores around the regression line—and around each Y'—is the same at each X. Therefore, $S_{Y'}$ will accurately describe this spread, at any X, so $S_{Y'}$ will accurately describe the error when predicting Y at any X. Conversely, the right-hand scatterplot shows an example of heteroscedastic data. **Heteroscedasticity** occurs when the spread in Y is not equal throughout the relationship. In such cases, $S_{Y'}$ will not accurately describe the "average" spread or error throughout the entire relationship. Here, for example, $S_{Y'}$ will be much larger than the actual average error when predicting Y scores associated with low test scores, and much less than the average error when predicting Y scores associated with high test scores.

The second assumption is that the Y scores at each X represents an approximately normal distribution. That is, if we constructed a frequency polygon of the Y scores at each X, we would expect to have a normal distribution centered around Y'. Figure 11.6 illustrates this assumption for the widget-making study. Meeting this assumption is

FIGURE 11.5 Illustrations of Homoscedastic and Heteroscedastic Data

The vertical width of the scatterplot above an X indicates how spread out the corresponding Y scores are. On the left, the Ys have the same spread at each X.

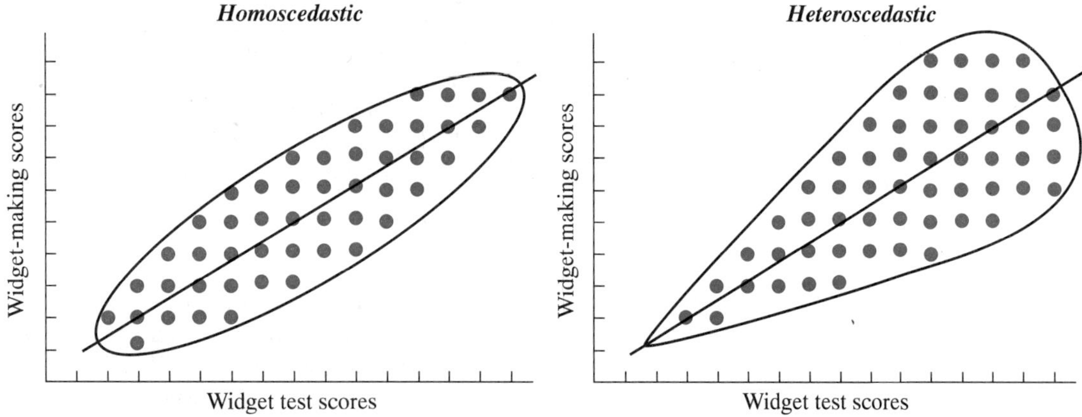

FIGURE 11.6 Scatterplot Showing Normal Distribution of *Y* Scores at each *X*

At each X, there is a normal distribution of different Y scores centered around Y′.

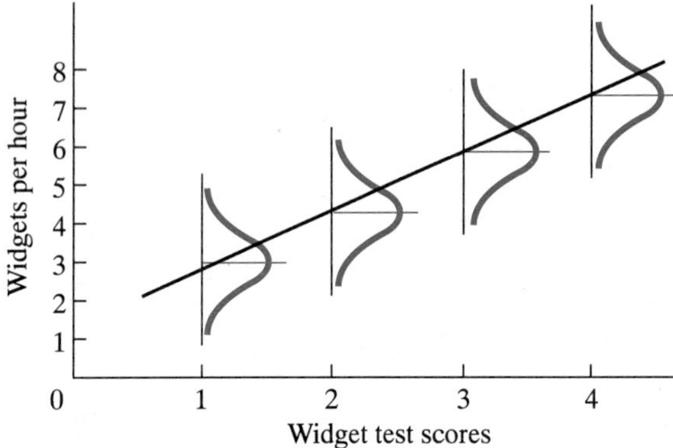

important because, recall, in a normal distribution, approximately 68% of all scores fall between ± 1 standard deviation from the mean. Because $S_{Y'}$ is like a standard deviation, if the *Y* scores are normally distributed around each Y', we expect approximately 68% of all *Y* scores to be between $\pm 1S_{Y'}$ from the regression line. Thus, in the widget-making study, the $S_{Y'}$ was 1.42, so we expect approximately 68% of the actual *Y* scores to fall within ± 1.42 of their respective Y' scores.

In summary, $S_{Y'}$ and $S^2_{Y'}$ indicate how much the *Y* scores are spread out around the Y' scores and thus indicate the amount of error we have when using Y' to predict the actual *Y* scores in a sample.

> *REMEMBER* The subscript Y' in $S_{Y'}$ and $S^2_{Y'}$ indicates that they measure the amount of error when using regression to predict *Y* scores.

Strength of the Relationship and Prediction Errors

The strength or consistency of a relationship determines the amount of error in our predictions. The stronger the relationship, the smaller the error. Therefore, the minimum error occurs when r is ± 1.0, because there is no spread or differences in the *Y* scores at each *X*, and the scatterplot *is* the regression line. The left-hand graph in Figure 11.7 shows such a perfect relationship. The Y' for each *X* equals the *Y* score every participant actually obtained for that *X*. Therefore, the difference between their *Y* scores and the Y' scores we predict for them is zero, our error is zero, and so $S_{Y'}$ equals 0 (as does $S^2_{Y'}$).

With a less consistent relationship, there are different *Y* scores at each *X*, so the scatterplot is vertically spread out around the regression line. The weaker the relationship, the greater the spread, and so the more frequently there are larger differences between participants' actual *Y* scores and their predicted Y' scores. Therefore, a weaker relationship produces greater error, resulting in larger values of $S_{Y'}$ and $S^2_{Y'}$.

The maximum errors occur when $r = 0$, as in the right-hand graph in Figure 11.7. Here, the regression line is horizontal, and all values of Y' equal the *Y*-intercept. Recognize that then the *Y*-intercept is the overall *mean* of all *Y* scores ($\overline{Y}$): The regression line

FIGURE 11.7 Scatterplots and Regression Lines when $r = +1$ and when $r = 0$

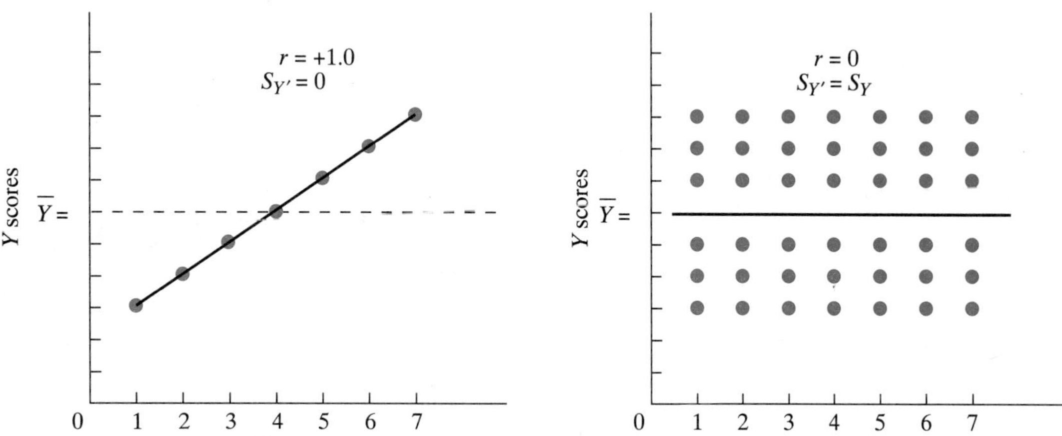

passes through the center of the Y scores, and when there is no relationship, that center is always at the sample's mean score. So, when there is no relationship, even if we use the regression equation to compute Y', we still end up predicting the value of $\overline{Y}$ for each participant.

When $r = 0$, the Y-intercept is equal to the mean of all Y scores, and this mean of Y is the predicted Y' for all participants.

When $r = 0$, the standard error of the estimate is at its maximum, and that is equal to the standard deviation of all Y scores in the sample (S_Y). Why? Because we predict the $\overline{Y}$ for everyone in the sample. We can call each prediction Y', or we can call it $\overline{Y}$, but it is the same score. Therefore, we can replace the symbol Y' with the symbol $\overline{Y}$ in the formula for the standard error of the estimate, as shown here:

$$S_{Y'} = \sqrt{\frac{\Sigma(Y - Y')^2}{N}} = \sqrt{\frac{\Sigma(Y - \overline{Y})^2}{N}} = S_Y$$

The resulting formula on the right is the formula for the standard deviation of all Y scores (S_Y). Thus, when $r = 0$, the standard error of the estimate ($S_{Y'}$) equals the total variability in the Y scores (S_Y). (Likewise, $S^2_{Y'}$ equals S^2_Y). This means that to whatever extent the Y scores are spread out around the $\overline{Y}$, to that extent we will be in error when predicting them using $\overline{Y}$ or Y'. This error can be seen as the vertical width of the scatterplot in the right-hand graph of Figure 11.7.

Thus, in sum, the size of $S_{Y'}$ and $S^2_{Y'}$ are *inversely* related to the absolute value of r, so that as r gets smaller, they get larger. When r is between 0 and ±1.0, $S_{Y'}$ or $S^2_{Y'}$ is between zero and the values of S_Y or S^2_Y, respectively. Figure 11.8 shows two such intermediate relationships. In the left-hand scatterplot, r is close to -1.0: The Y scores at each X are not spread out much around the regression line, so the actual Y scores are relatively close to their corresponding Y'. Therefore, the error ($S_{Y'}$ and $S^2_{Y'}$) will be relatively small. Conversely, in the right-hand scatterplot, r is much closer to 0: The Y scores at each X are spread out around the regression line, so many of the actual Y scores are relatively far from their corresponding Y'. Therefore, there will be more error, and $S_{Y'}$ and $S^2_{Y'}$ will be relatively large.

FIGURE 11.8 Scatterplots of Strong and Weak Relationships

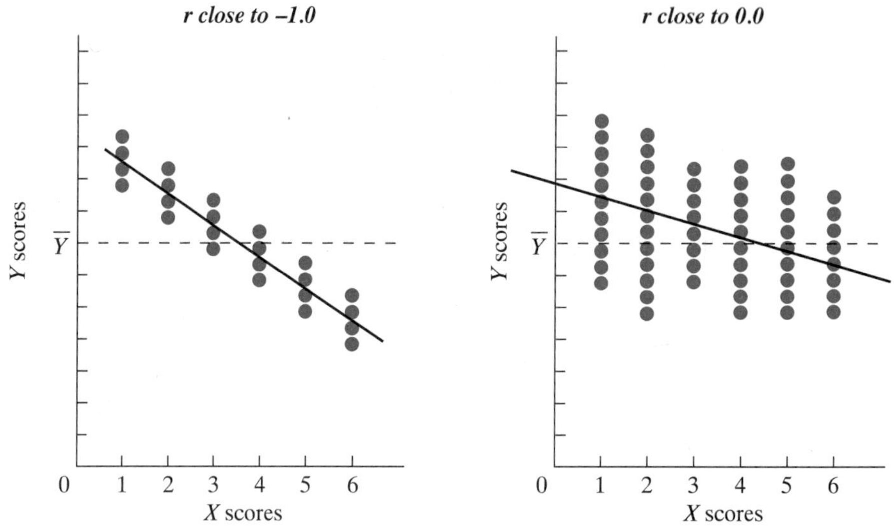

> ***REMEMBER*** As the strength of the relationship—and the size of r—increases, the Y scores are closer to their corresponding Y' scores, producing less error, so $S_{Y'}$ and $S^2_{Y'}$ are smaller.

Real research usually produces intermediate relationships, so there will be some amount of prediction error, and $S_{Y'}$ will be between 0 and S_Y (and $S^2_{Y'}$ will be between 0 and S^2_Y). However, notice that this indicates that we are *always* better at predicting Y when we use a relationship to produce Y' scores, compared to when we don't use the relationship. If we ignore the relationship (pretending r is 0), we end up predicting the $\overline{Y}$ for everyone, and our error will be at maximum, equal to the values of S^2_Y or S_Y. With even a weak relationship, however, we have somewhat less error, because $S_{Y'}$ or $S^2_{Y'}$ will be less than S_Y or S^2_Y, respectively. You can see this in Figure 11.8 above, because in both relationships, the actual Y scores are generally closer to the slanted regression line produced by the relationship than they are to the horizontal line running through the $\overline{Y}$ that we'd have if there were no relationship. Further, the stronger the relationship, the greater the difference in how well the Y scores hug the two lines. Thus, literally, the stronger the relationship, the closer the Y scores are to their respective Y' scores than they are to the $\overline{Y}$, so the better we are at predicting scores by using the relationship. We use this fact as the basis for evaluating a relationship. This evaluation process goes by the strange (and not quite grammatical) name of computing "the proportion of variance accounted for."

PREDICTING VARIABILITY: THE PROPORTION OF VARIANCE ACCOUNTED FOR

Computing "the proportion of variance accounted for" is the way to *quantitatively* evaluate how useful or important a relationship is. Without this statistic, we must be rather subjective when evaluating a relationship. In the widget study, for example, r was $+.74$, implying that we have reasonably accurate predictions of Y scores. The problem is that we cannot quantify this accuracy. Also, the $S_{Y'}$ indicates the predictions will be off by an "average" of 1.42, and using $S^2_{Y'}$, by an "average" of 2.01. But, we don't know if, in the grand scheme of things in nature, such errors are large or small. The *proportion of variance accounted for* solves these problems because it involves a frame of reference: The errors we have when using a relationship and regression to predict Y scores are compared to the errors in prediction we have if we don't use the relationship. This tells us how much the relationship reduces errors, so it tells us how useful and important the relationship is.

Statisticians tell us that the correct way to measure errors in prediction here is using *variance*. Notice, however, that the term "variance" has become somewhat generic because we've seen two different versions of it: When we use a relationship and regression to produce a Y' for each individual, the error in predictions is based on how much the Y scores differ from the Y' we predict. Then, the "average error" is $S^2_{Y'}$, the variance of Y scores around Y'.

Remember that the basis for calculating $S^2_{Y'}$ is finding each $Y - Y'$: Each difference between the Y score a participant actually obtained and the Y' we predict is obtained.

When there is *not* a relationship present, the $\overline{Y}$ is predicted for each individual, and the error in predictions is based on how much the Y scores differ from the $\overline{Y}$ we predict. The "average error" here is the variance in Y scores (S^2_Y). Essentially, using the above terminology, it is the "variance of Y scores around $\overline{Y}$."

Remember that the basis for calculating S^2_Y is to find each $Y - \overline{Y}$: Each difference between the Y score a participant actually obtained and the $\overline{Y}$ score we predict is obtained.

To calculate the proportion of variance accounted for, we compare these two variances. The proportion of variance accounted for indicates how much better off we are when using a relationship to predict scores compared to if we didn't know about the relationship. Therefore, first, we pretend that we don't know about the relationship: It's like $r = 0$, so we predict the mean of the Y scores for everyone in the sample. Here, based on $Y - \overline{Y}$, the "average" error is S^2_Y. Then, we compare this to the results if we do use the relationship and its regression equation to predict Y scores using Y'. Here, based on $Y - Y'$, the "average error" is $S^2_{Y'}$.

First, we'll use the definitional formula to calculate the proportion of variance accounted for.

THE DEFINITIONAL FORMULA FOR THE PROPORTION OF VARIANCE ACCOUNTED FOR BY

$$\text{Proportion of variance accounted for} = 1 - \left(\frac{S^2_{Y'}}{S^2_Y}\right)$$

As an example, in the widget-making data back in Table 11.2, $S^2_{Y'}$ was 2.01 and S^2_Y was 4.38. Thus, our "average error" is 4.38 when we don't use the relationship to predict scores and instead predict $\overline{Y}$ for everyone. But we're off by an average of only 2.01 when we do use the relationship to predict the appropriate Y' for everyone. The formula says to first make a ratio of $S^2_{Y'}/S^2_Y$, so we have

$$\frac{S^2_{Y'}}{S^2_Y} = \frac{2.01}{4.38} = .46$$

This ratio indicates the proportion of the error without the relationship that is still present with the relationship. Here, the error we have when we use the relationship is .46 of the error we have when we don't use the relationship.

But, if the error when using the relationship is only .46 of the error when not using the relationship, then with the relationship we can eliminate .54 of the error we'd have without the relationship. As in the formula, this proportion is found by subtracting the ratio from 1. Altogether,

$$1 - \frac{2.01}{4.38} = 1 - .46 = .54$$

Thus, using this relationship eliminates .54 or 54% of the error we'd have if we didn't use the relationship, so we are 54% more accurate with it. In other words, if we know participants' X scores and use this relationship and regression, we are, "on average," 54% closer to predicting their actual Y scores than if we don't use this relationship. In statistical terms, this relationship accounts for .54 of the variance in Y scores. The **proportion of variance accounted for** is the proportion of our prediction errors when we use the mean of Y to predict Y scores that is eliminated by using the relationship with X to predict the scores. In other words, it is the proportional improvement in predictions achieved by using a relationship to predict scores, compared to if we do not use the relationship.

Understand that the term "proportion of variance accounted for" is a shortened version of "the proportion of variance in Y scores that is accounted for by the relationship with X." The variance in Y we account for is S^2_Y, and it reflects all of the differences among the Y scores. When we do not use the relationship, we cannot predict any of these differences, because we continuously predict the same $\overline{Y}$ for everyone. Then, our error equals all of the differences between the Y and $\overline{Y}$, which is the variance in Y (S^2_Y). When using the relationship, however, we do predict different scores for different participants: We can, at least, predict a lower Y score for those who tend to score lower, a medium Y score for those scoring medium, and so on. Therefore, to some extent, we're closer to predicting when participants will have different Y scores. Therefore, of all the differences in Y measured by S^2_Y, using the relationship helps us to predict, or "account for," some proportion of them, so we say that we account for some proportion of the variance in Y.

> ***REMEMBER*** The proportion of variance accounted for is the proportional improvement in accuracy when using the relationship with X to predict Y scores, compared to the accuracy when using the $\overline{Y}$ to predict Y scores.

There is one other way to conceptualize the variance accounted for: It is the proportion of all variance in a sample that is *not* error variance. Error variance reflects those differences in Y scores that occur when X does not change, so essentially, it reflects those differences in Y that do not match up with changes in X. The proportion of variance accounted for reflects those differences in Y that *do* match—are correlated—with changes in X.

As we've seen, the stronger the relationship—and the larger the r—the better we are at predicting scores, and so the greater the proportion of variance accounted for. This is because with a stronger relationship, the error using the relationship ($S^2_{Y'}$) is even smaller relative to the error without using the relationship (S^2_Y). Essentially, we are even closer to predicting when someone has one Y score and when someone has a different Y score, so in other words, we are better at accounting for the variance in Y.

The fact that the size of r is related to the proportion of variance accounted for provides the basis for the world's easiest computational formula.

Using *r* to Compute the Proportion of Variance Accounted For

Using the above definitional formula is rather time-consuming. However, we saw that the size of r is related to the amount of error in our predictions ($S^2_{Y'}$) by the formula

$$S^2_{Y'} = S^2_Y(1 - r^2)$$

In fact, this formula contains all the components of the previous definitional formula, so solving for the proportion of variance accounted for, we have

$$1 - \frac{S^2_{Y'}}{S^2_Y} = r^2$$

Because 1 minus the ratio $S^2_{Y'}/S^2_Y$ is the definitional formula for the proportion of variance accounted for, we have the following computational formula:

THE COMPUTATIONAL FORMULA FOR THE PROPORTION OF VARIANCE ACCOUNTED FOR IS

$$\text{Proportion of variance accounted for} = r^2$$

Not too tough! To compute the proportion of variance accounted for, all you do is compute r (which you would do anyway) and square it. [Yes, it took a long time to get to such a simple method, but to understand r^2, you must understand $1 - (S^2_{Y'}/S^2_Y)$.]

Previously, the widget-making relationship accounted for .54 of the variance in Y scores. Because r for this study was $+.736$, we can compute the proportion of variance accounted for as $(.736)^2$, which also equals .54.

In statistical language, r^2 is called the **coefficient of determination**, which is merely another name for the proportion of variance accounted for. The proportion of variance *not* accounted for is called the **coefficient of alienation**, and equals $1 - r^2$. This value equals the ratio $S^2_{Y'}/S^2_Y$, which is the proportion of total error remaining (the proportion of all differences in Y that *is* error variance). In the widget-making study, r^2 was .54, so we still cannot account for $1 - .54$, or .46 of the variance in the Y scores.

Note that r^2 describes the proportion of *sample* variance that is accounted for by the relationship. If r passes the inferential statistical test, then r^2 is a *rough* estimate of the proportion of variance in Y that is accounted for by the relationship in the population.

Thus, we expect to be roughly 54% more accurate if we use the relationship and our widget test scores to predict any other, unknown widget-making scores in the population.

Uses of the Variance Accounted For

The reason we make such a big deal out of the proportion of variance accounted for is that it is *the* statistical measure of how "important" a particular relationship is. After all, it is variance and variability that lead to scientific inquiry in the first place. Thus, when researchers ask, "Why does a person do this instead of that?" they are trying to predict and explain differences in scores. In other words, they are trying to account for variance. The greater the proportion of variance accounted for by a relationship, the more accurately we can identify and predict differences in behavior, and thus the more scientifically useful the relationship is.

For example, at the beginning of this discussion, we wondered how to evaluate the widget-making study with an r of $+.74$ and a $S_{Y'}$ of 1.42. With r^2 equal to .54, we now know. We are .54 or 54% better off using this relationship than if we did not, and our error of 1.42 is 54% less than we'd have without this relationship. All in all then, this is a rather useful and thus important relationship, and the widget test should prove to be a valuable selection test.

This is especially so because, although theoretically a relationship may account for any proportion of the variance, in real research we get very excited when a relationship accounts for around 25% of the variance. Remember, this is an r of $\pm .50$, which is very good. Given the complexity of nature and the behaviors of living organisms, we are unlikely to find an r that is very close to ± 1.0, so we are also unlikely to find a relationship that accounts for close to 100% of the variance.

We also use r^2 when comparing different relationships to see which is more informative. Say that we find one relationship between the length of a person's hair and his or her creativity, but r is only $+.02$. Yes, this r indicates a relationship, but such a weak relationship is virtually useless. The fact that $r^2 = .0004$ indicates that knowing someone's hair length improves predictions about creativity by only four-hundredths of *1* percent! However, say that we also find another relationship between a person's age and his or her creativity, and here r is $-.40$. This relationship is more important, at least in a statistical sense, because $r^2 = .16$. Age is the more important variable for understanding differences in creativity, because knowing participants' ages gets us an average of 16% closer to predicting their creativity. Knowing their hair length gets us only .04% closer to predicting their creativity.

The proportion of variance accounted for is also an important consideration when interpreting a relationship "psychologically." Part of explaining a result is in terms of the impact or weight that nature gives to the X variable in the relationship with Y. For example, above, only .0004 of the changes in creativity scores are associated with changes in hair length. Thus, in nature, virtually everything that happens to creativity does so regardless of hair length, so hair length is basically irrelevant when it comes to creativity. However, about 16% of the changes in creativity scores are associated with age. It may be that age partly causes creativity, or it may be that age and creativity change together for some other reason. Regardless, age is somewhat relevant (it's about

TABLE 11.3 Summary of Computations in Linear Regression

1. Compute r.
2. Compute the slope, b, where $b = \dfrac{N(\Sigma XY) - (\Sigma X)(\Sigma Y)}{N(\Sigma X^2) - (\Sigma X)^2}$.
3. Compute the Y-intercept, where $a = \overline{Y} - (b)(\overline{X})$.
4. Substitute the values of a and b into the formula for the regression equation, $Y' = (b)(X) + a$.
5. Compute the standard error of the estimate ($S_{Y'}$) to describe the "average error" in prediction.
6. Compute r^2 to describe the proportion of variance in Y scores accounted for by the relationship.

16% of the entire picture) when it comes to creativity. Thus, literally, the greater the proportion of variance accounted for, the more important *in nature* the X variable is in the relationship with Y, so the more important it is to any psychological explanation.

It is for this reason that the logic of r^2 is applied to any relationship. For example, in the previous chapter, we discussed r_s and r_{pb}. Squaring these coefficients also indicates the proportion of variance accounted for. (It is as if we performed the appropriate regression analysis, computed $S^2_{Y'}$ and S^2_Y, and so on.) Likewise, as you'll see in later chapters, we also determine the proportion of variance accounted for in experiments: We describe the proportion of variance in the dependent variable (the Y scores) that is accounted for by using the relationship with the independent variable (the X scores). In all cases, the answer indicates how useful the relationship is.

> ***REMEMBER*** The proportion of variance accounted for is the basis for evaluating the scientific importance or usefulness of any relationship.

Computing r^2 goes hand in hand with computing the other components of correlation and regression. To help you remember them all, the procedures discussed in this chapter are summarized in Table 11.3.

A WORD ABOUT MULTIPLE CORRELATION AND REGRESSION

Researchers often examine relationships involving more than two variables, and then there are a number of advanced correlation and regression procedures to use. Although these procedures are appropriate regardless of how the variables are measured, they are frequently found in questionnaire and interview research. Usually, questions measuring several variables will be included in one test, from which we relate respondents' scores on each variable.

The most common procedure is to correlate several X variables with one Y variable. For example, there is a positive correlation between a person's height and his or her ability to play basketball: Taller people tend to make more baskets. There is also a positive correlation such that the more people practice basketball, the more baskets they tend to make. Obviously, to be as accurate as possible in predicting how well people shoot baskets, we should consider both how tall they are and how much they practice. In this example, there are two predictor variables (height and practice) that predict one criterion variable (basket shooting). When we simultaneously use multiple predictor variables for one criterion variable, we use the statistical procedures known as **multiple correlation** and **multiple regression**.

Although the computations involved in multiple correlation and multiple regression are beyond the scope of this text, the logic is the same as the logic of the procedures we've discussed. The multiple correlation coefficient, called R, indicates the strength of the relationship between the multiple predictors taken together and the criterion variable. The multiple regression equation allows us to predict someone's Y score by simultaneously considering his or her scores on all X variables. The squared multiple R is the proportion of variance in Y that is accounted for by using the relationship with the X variables to predict Y scores.

APA FORMAT FOR STATISTICAL NOTATION

In published research reports, R is the recognized symbol for the multiple correlation coefficient. However, you may encounter another symbol for the predicted Y score, which is $\hat{Y}$. Also, when discussing the regression equation for a population, instead of using b to stand for the slope, the term "beta" or "beta weight" may be used.

You will also encounter the term "covary" and "covariance" in discussions of the proportion of variance accounted for. This is simply another way of saying that the X and Y scores tend to change together, so that a particular Y tends to be paired with a particular X, and therefore we can use X to predict Y.

PUTTING IT ALL TOGETHER

This chapter and the previous one have introduced many new symbols and concepts. However, they boil down to three major topics:

1. *Correlation.* When there is a relationship between the X and Y variables, a particular value of Y tends to be paired with one value of X. The stronger the relationship, the more consistently one value of Y is paired with one value of X.
2. *Regression.* With a relationship, knowing each X score helps us to predict the corresponding Y score. We predict Y scores by calculating Y' scores using the linear regression equation, and graph these predictions as the linear regression line.
3. *Error in prediction.* The "average error" in predicting Y when using the relationship is the standard error of the estimate ($S_{Y'}$). The proportion of variance in Y that is accounted for by X is the amount we reduce errors in predicting Y scores when we use the relationship, compared to what they would be if we did not use the relationship. This proportion equals r^2.

CHAPTER SUMMARY

1. *Linear regression* is the procedure for predicting unknown Y scores based on a correlated X score. It produces the *linear regression line*, which is the best-fitting straight line that summarizes a linear relationship.

2. The *linear regression equation* includes the *slope (b)*, indicating how much and in what direction the regression line slants, and the *Y-intercept* (*a*), indicating the value of Y when the line crosses the Y axis.

3. For each X, the regression equation produces Y', which is the *predicted Y* score for that X. The regression line connects all X-Y' data points.

4. The *standard error of the estimate* ($S_{Y'}$), describes the "average" spread of the actual Y scores around the Y' scores, and thus the "average" error in predictions. The difference (and error) between Y and Y' is also summarized by the *variance of the Y scores around Y'* ($S^2_{Y'}$).

5. Regression requires the assumptions that (1) the Y scores are *homoscedastic*, meaning that the spread in the Y scores around all Y' scores is the same, and (2) the Y scores at each X are normally distributed around the corresponding value of Y'.

6. The stronger the relationship—the larger the r—the smaller the value of $S_{Y'}$ (and $S^2_{Y'}$), because the Y scores are closer to Y', and thus the smaller the difference between Y and Y'.

7. When r equals 0, $S_{Y'}$ equals S_Y. When r is between 0 and ± 1, the value of $S_{Y'}$ is between the value of S_Y and 0. When r equals ± 1, there is zero error in predictions, and $S_{Y'}$ equals zero.

8. The *proportion of variance accounted for* is the proportional improvement in accuracy achieved by using a relationship to predict Y scores, rather than using $\overline{Y}$ to predict Y scores. This *coefficient of determination* equals the squared correlation coefficient.

9. The proportion of variance not accounted for—*the coefficient of alienation*—equals $1 - r^2$. This is the proportion of the prediction error that is not eliminated when Y' is the predicted score instead of $\overline{Y}$.

10. The proportion of variance accounted for indicates the importance of a relationship.

11. *Multiple regression* and *multiple correlation* are procedures for describing the relationship when multiple predictor (X) variables are simultaneously used to predict scores on one criterion (Y) variable.

KEY TERMS (with page reference)

S^2_Y Y' b a $S^2_{Y'}$ $S_{Y'}$ r^2
coefficient of alienation (301)
coefficient of determination (301)
criterion variable (285)
heteroscedasticity (295)
homoscedasticity (295)
linear regression (283)
linear regression equation (285)
linear regression line (284)
multiple correlation (304)
multiple regression (304)
predicted Y score (284)
predictor variable (285)
proportion of variance accounted for (300)
slope (286)
standard error of the estimate (293)
variance of Y scores around Y' (291)
Y-intercept (286)

REVIEW QUESTIONS

(Answers for odd-numbered questions and problems are provided in Appendix D.)

1. What is the linear regression line?
2. What is the linear regression procedure used for?
3. (a) What is Y'? (b) How do you obtain it?
4. What is the general form of the linear regression equation? Identify its component symbols.
5. (a) What does the Y-intercept of the regression line indicate? (b) What does the slope of the regression line indicate?
6. (a) How do you decide which variable to call X in a correlation? (b) What other names are given to the X and Y variables?
7. (a) What is the name for $S_{Y'}$? (b) What does $S_{Y'}$ tell you about the spread in the Y scores? (c) What does $S_{Y'}$ tell you about your errors in prediction?
8. (a) What two assumptions must you make about the data in order for the standard error of the estimate to be accurate, and what does each mean? (b) How does heteroscedasticity lead to an inaccurate description of the data?
9. (a) How is the value of $S_{Y'}$ related to r? (b) When is $S_{Y'}$ at its maximum value? Why? (c) When is $S_{Y'}$ at its minimum value? Why?
10. (a) Conceptually, why is the proportion of variance accounted for equal to 1 with a perfect correlation? (b) Why is it 0 when there is no relationship?
11. How is r^2 interpreted?
12. What are the two statistical names for r^2?

PRACTICE PROBLEMS

13. What research steps must you go through to use the relationship between a person's IQ and grades in high school, so that if you know a person's IQ, you can more accurately predict the person's grades?
14. (a) Using the phrase "differences in Y scores" explain what the proportion of variance accounted for indicates (b) Why do most relationships in psychological research account for between 16% and 25% of the variance?
15. In analyzing a correlational study, what statistical result will you produce to (a) summarize the strength of relationship? (b) describe the characteristics of the relationship? (c) see the relationship hidden in the data? (d) determine the amount of error in predictions? (e) determine the importance of the relationship?
16. A researcher determined that the correlation between statistics grades and scores on an admissions test to graduate school in psychology is $r = +.41$. (a) With $S_Y = 3.90$, compute the standard error of the estimate for these data. (b) If the researcher predicts the overall mean score on the admissions test for each student, using variance, on average, how much error can she expect? (c) If she predicts admissions test scores using the regression equation and statistics grades, using variance, on average, how much error can she expect? (d) What proportion of the error in (b) remains even after using the regression equation? (e) What proportion of the error in (b) is eliminated by using the regression equation? (f) What is your answer to part (e) called?

17. Bubbles has a statistics grade of 70, and Foofy has a grade of 98. (a) Based on the data in problem 16, who is predicted to have a higher grade on the admissions test? Why? (b) Subsequently, Bubbles received the higher test score. Explain how this can occur.

18. Poindexter conducted a correlational study measuring participants' ability to concentrate and their ability to remember, finding $r = +.30$. He also correlated their ability to visualize information and their memory ability, obtaining an $r = +.60$. He concludes that there is twice as consistent, and therefore twice as informative, a relationship between visualization and memory ability as there is between concentration and memory ability. Why do you agree or disagree?

19. (a) In problem 18, what advanced statistical procedures can Poindexter employ to improve his predictions about memory ability even more? (b) Say that the resulting correlation coefficient is .67. Using the proportion of variance accounted for, explain what this means.

20. A researcher finds that variable A accounts for 25% of the variance in variable B. Another researcher finds that variable C accounts for 50% of the variance in variable B. Why is variable C considered to produce a relationship that is scientifically more important?

21. A student complains that it is unfair to use scores from the Scholastic Aptitude Test (SAT) to determine college admission because she might do much better in college than predicted. (a) What statistic(s) will indicate whether her complaint is correct? (b) What concern about the test's validity is she actually addressing?

22. What do you know about a research project when you see that multiple correlation and regression procedures were performed?

23. In a study, you measure how much participants are initially attracted to a person of the opposite sex (X) and how anxious they become during their first meeting with him or her (Y). For the following ratio data:

Participant	X	Y
1	2	8
2	6	14
3	1	5
4	3	8
5	6	10
6	9	15
7	6	8
8	6	8
9	4	7
10	2	6

(a) Compute the statistic that describes the nature of the relationship formed by the data. (b) Compute the linear regression equation. (c) What anxiety score do you predict for any subject who produces an attraction score of 9? (d) When using this data, what is the "average" amount of error you should expect in your predictions?

24. (a) For the relationship in problem 23, what is the proportion of variance in Y that is accounted for by X? (b) What is the proportion of variance not accounted for?

(c) Why is or is not this a valuable relationship? (d) Is how much people are attracted to others a major cause of how nervous they become during their initial meeting?

25. A researcher computes a Spearman r_S of $+.20$ when correlating the rankings of students in their research class (X) with their rankings in terms of how studious they are (Y). Another researcher computes a point-biserial correlation of $-.20$ when correlating a participant's gender (X) with his or her studiousness. Using the proportion of variance accounted for, interpret each result.

26. Using two questionnaires, a researcher measures how positive a participant's mood is (X) and how creative he or she is (Y), obtaining the following interval scores.

Participant	*X*	*Y*
1	10	7
2	8	6
3	9	11
4	6	4
5	5	5
6	3	7
7	7	4
8	2	5
9	4	6
10	1	4

(a) Compute the statistic that summarizes this relationship. (b) What is the predicted creativity score for anyone scoring 3 on the mood questionnaire? (c) Assuming that your prediction is in error, what is the amount of error you expect to have? (d) How much smaller will your error be if you use the regression equation than if you merely use the overall mean creativity score as the predicted score for everyone?

27. Foofy borrows the linear regression equation in a published study involving adolescent children that relates the variables of age (X) and depression scores (Y). She enters the ages of some senior citizens to predict how depressed they will be? Why is this a mistake?

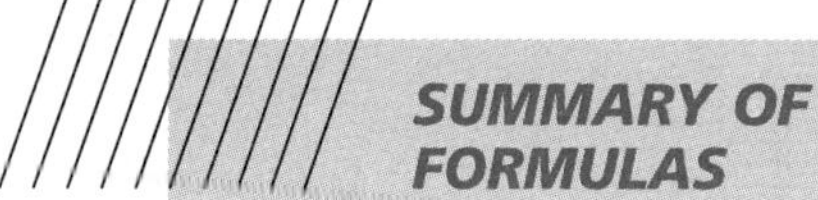

SUMMARY OF FORMULAS

1. *The formula for the linear regression equation is*

$$Y' = bX + a$$

where b stands for the slope of the line, X stands for an X score, and a stands for the Y intercept.

2. *The formula for the slope of the linear regression line is*

$$b = \frac{N(\Sigma XY) - (\Sigma X)(\Sigma Y)}{N(\Sigma X^2) - (\Sigma X)^2}$$

where N is the number of pairs of scores in the sample and X and Y are the scores in the sample.

3. *The formula for the Y-intercept of the linear regression line is*

$$a = \overline{Y} - (b)(\overline{X})$$

where $\overline{Y}$ is the mean of all Y scores, b is the slope of the regression line, and $\overline{X}$ is the mean of all X scores.

4. *The computational formula for the variance of Y scores around Y′ is*

$$S^2_{Y'} = S^2_Y(1 - r^2)$$

where S^2_Y is the variance of all Y scores in the sample.

5. *The computational formula for the standard error of the estimate is*

$$S_{Y'} = S_Y\sqrt{1 - r^2}$$

where S_Y is the standard deviation of all Y scores in the sample.

6. *The computational formula for the proportion of variance in Y that is accounted for by a linear relationship with X is*

$$\text{Proportion of variance accounted for} = r^2$$

7. *The computational formula for the proportion of variance not accounted for is*

$$\text{Proportion of variance not accounted for} = 1 - r^2$$

PART 4

INTRODUCTION TO INFERENTIAL STATISTICS

Believe it or not, you now know the common descriptive statistics used in psychological research: In experiments, we describe central tendency (usually with the mean) and variability (usually with the standard deviation.) In correlational studies, we describe the relationship (usually using the Pearson r) and summarize and use the relationship (with regression techniques.)

Now, we are ready to discuss how *inferential* statistics are used in psychological research. Recall that the goal of research is to describe the relationship in the population, but we cannot actually observe the population. Inferential procedures tell us what we would *expect* to find if we could perform this study on the entire population: Would the population have the same mean as our sample? If we observe different samples that produce different means, would we find the same difference between the population means? Would the correlation coefficient in the population be the same as in the sample?

Because we cannot *know* what the population contains, however, the best we can do is to place an intelligent bet. In essence, inferential procedures are ways to make bets about the population that have a high probability of being correct. The first step in understanding this process is to understand probability. Chapter 12 discusses the concept of probability and how it is used to make statistical decisions. Subsequent chapters then deal with the inferential procedures used with different designs. As you read each chapter, however, remember to keep one eye on the big picture: All inferential procedures involve making decisions about the scores and relationship we would find in the population, if we could study it.

12

Probability and Making Decisions About Chance Events

Getting Started

To understand this chapter, recall the following:

- From Chapter 6, recall what relative frequency is, and that it is computed as f/N.
- From Chapter 8, understand that with a z-score for a raw score or a sample mean, we obtain the proportion of the area under a part of the normal curve that equals the relative frequency of the scores or means in that part of the curve.

Your goals in this chapter are to learn:

- What probability communicates.
- How probability is an event's relative frequency in the population.
- How the probability of raw scores is computed using z-scores and the standard normal curve.
- How the probability of sample means is computed using z-scores and the standard normal curve.
- How to set up and use a sampling distribution of means to determine whether a sample is likely to represent a particular population.

This chapter sets the foundation for understanding inferential procedures. Therefore, there is little in the way of how to conduct research and there are few statistical formulas. Instead, the chapter introduces you to the wonderful world of probability. As you'll see, psychologists use probability in conjunction with the standard normal curve model to make decisions about their data. We'll keep the discussion simple because you do not need to be an expert in probability. However, you do need to understand the basic logic of chance.

MORE STATISTICAL NOTATION

In daily conversation, the words *chances*, *odds*, and *probability* are used interchangeably. In statistics, however, there are differences among them. Odds are expressed as fractions or ratios ("The odds of winning are 1 in 2"). Chance is expressed as a percentage ("There is a 50% chance of winning"). Probability is expressed as a decimal ("The probability of winning is .50"). In statistics, always express the answer as a probability.

The symbol for probability is the lowercase p. The probability of a particular event—such as event A—is written as $p(\text{A})$, which is pronounced "p of A" or "the probability of A."

THE LOGIC OF PROBABILITY

Probability is used to describe random, chance events. Such events occur when nature is being fair—when there is no bias toward one event over another (no rigged roulette wheels or loaded dice). Thus, a chance event occurs or does not occur merely because of the luck of the draw. In statistical work, chance is a very important concept, and probability is our way of mathematically describing how chance operates to produce an event.

How can we describe an event that happens only by chance? By paying attention to how often chance produces the event. The probability of any event is based on how often the event occurs *over the long run*. Intuitively, we use this logic all the time: If event A happens frequently over the long run, then we tend to think that it is likely to happen at any moment, and we say that A has a high probability. If event B happens infrequently, then we tend to think that it is unlikely to happen, and we say that B has a low probability.

When we decide that event A happens frequently, we are making a relative judgment. Compared to anything else that might happen in this situation, event A happens frequently. That is, we determine the *relative frequency* of A: The proportion of time that A occurs out of all possible events that might occur in this situation. In statistical terminology, all possible events that can occur in a given situation form the *population* of events. Thus, the **probability** of an event is equal to the relative frequency of the event in the population of all possible events that can occur.

> ***REMEMBER*** The probability of an event equals the event's relative frequency in the population.

If a population contains all possible events that might occur, then the event or events that *do* occur make up a *sample* from that population. Thus, probability describes our expectation that a sample will contain a particular event when we randomly sample from a particular population. Essentially, we assume that an event's past relative frequency in the population will continue in the future. To indicate our *confidence* that the event will occur in any future sample, we express this relative frequency as probability. For example, I am a rotten typist, and while typing the manuscript for this book, say I randomly made typos 80% of the time. This means that in the population of my typing, typos have a relative frequency of .80. We expect the relative frequency of typos to continue at a rate of .80 in anything else I type. This expected relative frequency is expressed as a probability, so the probability is .80 that I will make a typo when I type the next woid.

As this illustrates, a probability is a mathematical statement indicating the likelihood of an event when a particular population is randomly sampled. It is how we express our confidence that a particular event will occur. Thus, if event A has a relative frequency of zero in a particular situation, then the probability of event A is zero. This means that we do not expect A to occur in this situation because it never does. But if event A has a relative frequency of .10 in this situation, then A has a probability of .10. Because it occurs only 10% of the time in the population, we expect it to occur in only 10% of our samples, so we have some—but not much—confidence that the event will occur in the next sample. On the other hand, if A has a probability of .95, we are confident that it will occur: A occurs 95% of the time in the population, so we expect it in 95% of our samples. At the most extreme, event A may occur 100% of the time (it is 100% of the population), and so its probability is 1. Here, we are positive it will occur in this situation because it always does.

An event cannot happen less than 0% of the time nor more than 100% of the time, so a probability can *never* be less than 0 or greater than 1. Also, all events in a population together constitute 100% of the time, so the relative frequencies of all events must add up to 1, and the probabilities of all events must add up to 1. Thus, if the probability of my making a typo at any moment is .80, then because $1 - .80 = .20$, the probability is .20 that any word I type will be error free.

Understand that except when p equals either 0 or 1, we are never certain that an event will or will not occur in a particular situation. The probability of an event is its relative frequency *over the long run* (in the infinite population), so it is up to chance whether a particular sample contains the event. For example, even though I make typos at a rate of .80, I may go for quite a while without making a typo. That 20% of the time I make no typos has to occur sometime. Thus, although the probability is .80 that I will make a typo in each word, it is only over the long run that we truly expect to see precisely 80% typos.

People who fail to understand that probability implies over the long run fall victim to the "gambler's fallacy." For example, say we observe my typing for a while, and it is error-free. The fallacy is believing that errors "must" occur now, essentially thinking that errors have become more likely. Or, say we flip a coin and get 7 heads in a row. The fallacy is thinking that a head is now less likely to occur, because it's already occurred too often (as if the coin says, "Hold it. That's enough heads for a while!"). The mistake of the gambler's fallacy is failing to recognize that the probability of an event is not altered by whether it has recently occurred or not, because probability is determined by the event's relative frequency *over the long run in the population.*

COMPUTING PROBABILITY

Computing the probability of an event is simple: We need only determine its relative frequency in the population. When we know the relative frequency of every event in a population, we have a probability distribution. A **probability distribution** indicates the probability of all possible events in a population.

Creating Probability Distributions

There are two ways to create a probability distribution. One way is to measure the relative frequency of events in the population, creating an **empirical probability distribution**. Typically, however, we cannot observe the entire population, so we create the distribution by observing a random sample from the population. We assume that the relative frequency of events in the sample represents the relative frequency of events in the population. For example, say that Dr. Fraud is sometimes very cranky, and apparently, his crankiness is random. We observe him on 18 days and determine that he is cranky on 6 of them. Relative frequency equals f/N, so the relative frequency of Dr. Fraud's crankiness is 6/18, or .33. We expect that in the population, he will continue to be cranky 33% of the time, so the probability that he will be cranky today is $p = .33$. Conversely, he was not cranky on 12 of the 18 days, which is 12/18, or .67. Thus, $f = .67$ that he will not be cranky today. Because his cranky days plus his noncranky days constitute all possible events, we have the complete probability distribution for his crankiness.

Statistical procedures usually rely on the other way to create a probability distribution: A **theoretical probability distribution** is a theoretical model of the relative frequencies of events in a population. We devise theoretical probability distributions based on how we assume nature distributes events in the population. Then from the model, we determine the relative frequency of each event in the population. This relative frequency is then the probability of the event in any random sample. For example, consider the probabilities when tossing a coin. On any one toss, there are two possible outcomes: a head or a tail. We assume that nature has no bias toward heads or tails, so over the long run, we expect 50% heads and 50% tails. In other words, we expect the relative frequency of heads to be .50 and the relative frequency of tails to be .50. Because relative frequency in the population *is* probability, we have the theoretical probability distribution: For a head, $p = .50$, and for a tail, $p = .50$.

Likewise, consider when we draw a playing card from a deck of 52 cards. We assume that there is no bias favoring any one card, so over the long run, we expect each card to occur at a rate of once out of every 52 draws, so each card has a relative frequency of 1/52, or .0192. Therefore, the probability of drawing any specific card on a single random draw is $p = .0192$.

And that is the logic of probability. First, we either theoretically or empirically devise a model of how events are distributed in the population (called a probability distribution). This gives the expected relative frequency of each event in the population. Then, an event's expected relative frequency equals its probability of occurring in a particular sample.

General Formula for Computing Probability

Hidden in the above examples is a method for computing probability. When all events in a population have the same frequency then the events are *equally likely*. Then:

THE FORMULA FOR COMPUTING PROBABILITY WHEN EVENTS ARE EQUALLY LIKELY IS

$$p(\text{event}) = \frac{\text{Number of outcomes that satisfy event}}{\text{Total number of possible outcomes}}$$

The numerator is the number of possible outcomes that satisfy the requirements of the event we are describing. When flipping a coin, for example, there is one outcome that satisfies the condition of showing a head. The denominator is the total number of possible outcomes that can occur. Two possible outcomes can occur with a coin: either head or tail. Therefore, the probability of a head is 1/2, which equals .5.

Likewise, we might define the event as drawing a king from a deck of cards. There are four kings in a deck, and any one would satisfy us. With a total of 52 possible outcomes, the probability of randomly drawing a king on one draw is 4/52, or .0769.

You can even apply this formula to real life! For example, raffle tickets are sometimes sold one for a dollar and sometimes sold three for a dollar. Many people think they have a better chance of winning when everyone gets three tickets for a dollar. They're wrong! Say that 100 people each spend a dollar and get one ticket. Then each person's probability of winning is 1/100, or .01. If 100 people each buy 3 tickets for a dollar, then each person's probability of winning is 3/300. But 3/300 equals 1/100, so for each person, the probability of winning is still .01.

The above formula is rather tedious when the event being described is a complex sequence of alternatives. Therefore, shortcut formulas for some common complex events are provided in Appendix B.4.

Factors Affecting the Probability of an Event

Not all random events are the same, and their characteristics influence their probability. First, events may be either independent or dependent. Two events are **independent events** when the probability of one is *not* influenced by the occurrence of the other event. For example, contrary to popular belief, washing your car does *not* make it rain. These are independent events, so the probability of rain does not increase when you wash your car. On the other hand, two events are **dependent events** when the probability of one *is* influenced by the occurrence of the other event. For example, whether you pass an exam usually depends on whether you study: The probability of passing increases or decreases, depending on whether studying occurs, so these are dependent events.

The probability of an event is also affected by the type of sampling we perform. Not in terms of the type of sampling discussed back in Chapter 5 (e.g, simple, systematic, or stratified sampling,) but in terms of whether the sampling alters the population and thus affects any probability. On the one hand, when **sampling with replacement**, any previously selected samples are replaced back into the population before drawing additional samples. For example, sampling with replacement occurs if, after drawing a playing card, we return it to the deck before drawing a second card. Notice that the population on both the first and second draw is based on 52 possible outcomes, so the probability of a card being selected either time is constant. Likewise, flipping a coin is treated as sampling with replacement, because a head or tail does not diminish the number of possible heads or tails remaining in the population, so the probabilities remain constant. On the other hand, when **sampling without replacement**, we do not replace any previously selected samples in the population before selecting again. Thus, sampling without replacement occurs if, after a card is drawn, it is then discarded. Now, the probability of drawing a particular card on the first draw is based on 52 possible outcomes, but the probability of drawing a card on the second draw is based on only 51 outcomes. With fewer possible outcomes, the probability is slightly larger on the second draw.

The reason we discuss probability is not that we have an uncontrollable urge to flip coins and draw cards. In research and statistics, the "events" we're interested in are *scores*. We usually assume that scores are independent (whether your friend scores high or low on a test does not influence the p that you'll score high or low), and sampled with replacement (like when flipping a coin, the occurrence of a particular score does not diminish its occurrence in the population, so its p remains constant).

Researchers use probability to make decisions about scores and samples of scores. To do that, they use the standard normal curve.

OBTAINING PROBABILITY FROM THE STANDARD NORMAL CURVE

In most psychological research, we usually assume that the scores form a normal distribution. Then our "theoretical probability distribution" is based on the standard normal curve. Here's how it works.

Determining the Probability of Individual Scores

In Chapter 8, we used z-scores to find the proportion of the total area under the normal curve in any part of a distribution. This proportion corresponds to the relative frequency of the scores in an ideal population. But, we've just seen that the relative frequency of scores in the population equals the probability of those scores. Thus,

> **The proportion of the area under the curve for scores in any part of the distribution equals the probability of those scores.**

For example, the normal curve in Figure 12.1 provides the complete probability distribution for a set of scores. Say that we seek the probability of randomly selecting a

FIGURE 12.1 *z*-Distribution Showing the Area for Scores Below the Mean and Between 0 and 1

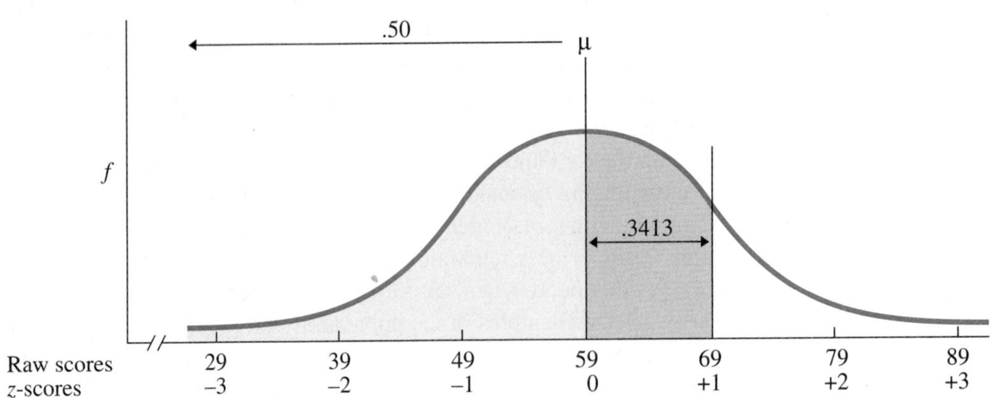

score from below the mean of 59 (from the lightly shaded area in Figure 12.1). This is the same as asking about selecting a *person* who has a score below 59. To answer this, first think in terms of *z*-scores. Raw scores below the mean produce negative *z*-scores. Therefore, the question can be restated as "What is the probability of randomly selecting a negative *z*-score?" Negative *z*-scores constitute 50% of the curve and thus have a relative frequency of .50. Therefore, the probability is .50 that we will select a negative *z*-score. Because negative *z*-scores correspond to raw scores below 59, the probability is also .50 that an individual we select will have a raw score below 59.

Likewise, all of the techniques you learned for finding the area under the curve using *z*-scores and the *z*-tables correspond to finding probability. Let's review.

Say that we seek the probability of selecting a raw score between 59 and 69 (from the dark shaded area in Figure 12.1). The formula for a *z*-score in the population is

$$z = \frac{X - \mu}{\sigma_X}$$

Say that in these data, a raw score of 69 has a z of $+1.0$. From column B of the *z*-tables in Appendix C, *z*-scores between the mean and a z of $+1.0$ occur .3413 of the time. Thus, the probability is .3413 of randomly selecting any one of these *z*-scores. Because these *z*-scores correspond to raw scores between 59 and 69, the probability is also .3413 that we will select a raw score between 59 and 69.

Similarly, the probability of randomly selecting a raw score between 49 and 69 is found by first converting the raw scores to *z*-scores: We seek the probability and thus the area between the *z*-scores of $+1$ and -1. Doubling the .3413 above, we see that, in total, *z*-scores between ± 1 constitute .6826 of the curve, so their probability (and that of raw scores between 49 and 69) is .6826.

Or, we can determine the probability of selecting a score greater than a particular *z*-score. For example, what is the probability of selecting a *z*-score larger than $+2.0$? In Figure 12.2, *z*-scores above $+2.0$ are in the shaded area on the right. The *z*-tables indicate that scores above $z = +2.0$ constitute .0228 of the distribution and thus occur .0228 of the time. Therefore, the probability of randomly selecting a *z*-score above $+2.0$ is .0228. Then, to find the raw score at this z, we use the formula

$$X = (z)(\sigma_X) + \mu$$

This would indicate that, as in Figure 12.2, .0228 is the probability of selecting a raw score above 79.

And finally, what is the probability of selecting a z-score that is beyond a z of ± 2.0? The phrase "beyond ± 2.0" means that we seek scores above $+2.0$ or below -2.0, so we seek the probability of drawing a score from either of the shaded areas shown in Figure 12.2. Scores above $z = +2.0$ constitute .0228 of the curve, and scores below $z = -2.0$ constitute an additional .0228 of the curve. The word "or" indicates we don't distinguish between the two tails, so we *add* the shaded areas and their *p*s together. In total, .0228 + .0228, or .0456, of the curve contains scores that will satisfy us. Because z-scores beyond ± 2.0 occur a total of .0456 of the time, the probability of randomly selecting a z beyond ± 2.0 is .0456. In Figure 12.2, a raw score of 39 corresponds to a z of -2.0, and a raw score of 79 corresponds to a z of $+2.0$. Therefore, the probability is .0456 that we will randomly select a raw score below 39 or above 79.

> ***REMEMBER*** When we use the word "or" when describing events, it means to *add* their individual areas or probabilities together.

Determining the Probability of Sample Means

We can also use the normal curve to find the probability of sample means by looking at the sampling distribution of means. In Chapter 9, we conceptualized the sampling distribution as the frequency distribution of all possible sample means that would result if a "bored statistician" randomly sampled a raw score population an infinite number of times using a particular N. Because the sampling distribution shows how sample means are distributed in the population, it forms a theoretical probability distribution. Here's how it works.

In Chapter 9, we found a sample mean's location on a sampling distribution by first computing the standard error of the mean (the standard deviation of the sampling distribution) using the formula

$$\sigma_{\overline{X}} = \frac{\sigma_X}{\sqrt{N}}$$

FIGURE 12.2 Area Under the Curve Beyond $z = +2.0$

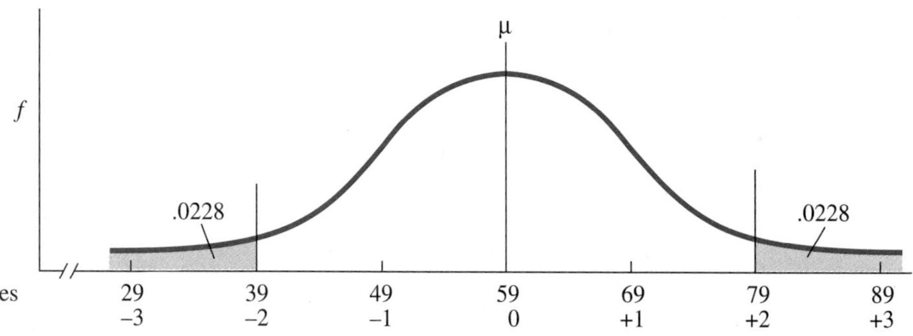

Then, we computed the z-score for a sample mean using the formula:

$$z = \frac{\overline{X} - \mu}{\sigma_{\overline{X}}}$$

Then, by applying the standard normal curve model, we determined the relative frequency of sample means falling above or below that z-score. Now, as we just did with raw scores, we can use this relative frequency to determine the probability of randomly selecting particular sample means.

For example, look again at our old sampling distribution of SAT means shown in Figure 12.3. The population mean (μ) of this distribution is 500; and when N is 25, the standard error of the mean is 20. Say we're interested in those means with z-scores between 0 and +1.0. The relative frequency of such z-scores is .3413, so the relative frequency of sample means that produce these z-scores is also .3413. Therefore, the probability of randomly selecting a sample mean with a z-score between 0 and +1.0 is $p = .3413$. And, therefore, the probability is .3413 that we will select a sample mean between 500 and 520 from this population.

Think about this: Randomly selecting a sample mean is the same as randomly selecting a sample of raw scores that produce that mean. Likewise, randomly selecting a sample of raw scores is the same as randomly selecting a sample of participants and then measuring their raw scores. Therefore, the probability of selecting certain sample means is also the probability of selecting the corresponding samples that produce those means. Thus, we can rephrase our finding above: When we randomly select 25 students from this SAT population, the probability of selecting a sample that produces a mean between 500 and 520 is .3413.

Here's another example. Previously, we determined that z-scores beyond ±2.0 have a probability of .0456. Thus, the probability of selecting a sample mean having a z-score beyond ±2.0 is also .0456. On our SAT sampling distribution, z-scores of ±2.0 correspond to means of 540 and 460, respectively. Therefore, when we sample this SAT population, the probability is .0456 that we will randomly select a sample of 25 scores that produces a mean below 460 or above 540.

Why would anyone want to do this? Recall that we are discussing probability because we will eventually perform inferential statistics. The beauty of the above procedure is that, as you saw in Chapter 9, the central limit theorem tells us the characteristics of the sampling distribution we'd have for *any* raw score population. Therefore, we

FIGURE 12.3 Sampling Distribution of SAT Means when $N = 25$

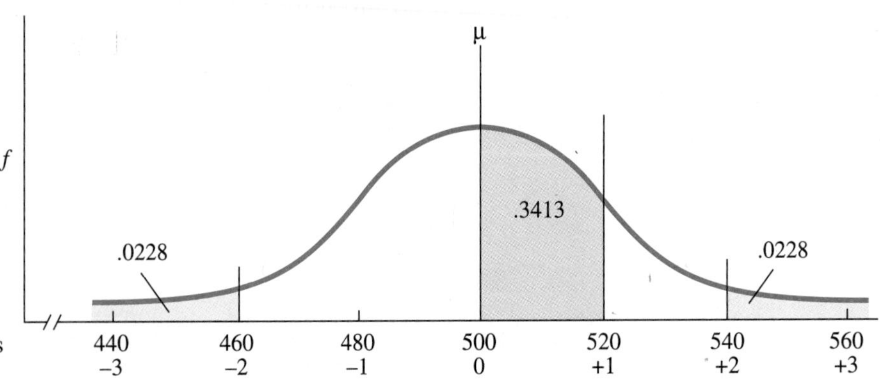

can determine the probability of obtaining particular sample means from *any* raw score population. Determining the probability of a particular result is the basis for all inferential statistics.

The next step is to understand how to use probability to make decisions.

MAKING DECISIONS BASED ON PROBABILITY

To begin, let's make a decision about my typing. Recall that $p = .80$ that I'll make a typo at any moment. Should you decide that my next word will contain a typo? Yes, it's a good bet. Why? Because you are likely to win the bet. How do we know this? The probability that you've correctly decided about an event equals the probability that chance will produce the event. To see this, look at the bet over the long run: Assume that 100% of the time that you're in this situation you'll bet that I'll make a typo. On 80% of the time I do make typos, so you will be correct 80% of the time. Thus, the relative frequency of winning the bet over the long run is .80, so the probability of winning any single bet is .80. I do not make typos 20% of the time, so you will lose the bet 20% of the time. Thus, the probability is .20 that you will lose any single bet. Conversely, if you bet that I will not make a typo, $p = .20$ that you'll win the bet, and $p = .80$ that you'll lose the bet.

As this illustrates, we bet in favor of high-probability events because then we are likely to win the bet. We bet against low-probability events, because then too, the probability of winning is high. In statistics, we also make bets and again, we make the decision that is most likely to be correct. The bet we make involves deciding whether a sample represents a particular population.

Deciding Whether a Sample Represents a Population

Recall that in any experiment or descriptive study, we want to say that the way in which a random sample behaves indicates the way in which the population would behave if we could observe it. However, we can never be certain how the population would behave, because there is no guarantee that the sample accurately reflects the population. In other words, we are never certain that a sample is *representative* of the population.

Back in Chapter 2 you saw that a representative sample is a mini-version of the population, having the same characteristics as the population. However, representativeness is not all or nothing. A sample can be more or less representative, having more or less of the characteristics in the population. This is because how representative a sample is depends on random chance—the luck of the draw of which scores are selected. By chance, the sample may be somewhat different from the population from which it is selected, and thereby represent that population somewhat poorly.

Here, then, is the central problem for researchers (and the reason for inferential statistics): A sample can be different from the population it actually represents, so that it appears to represent some *other* population. Thus, although a sample always represents a population, we are never sure which population it represents: The sample may poorly represent one population, or it may represent another population altogether.

REMEMBER Any sample may poorly represent one population, or it may accurately represent a different population.

For example, say someone flips a coin 7 times and obtains 7 heads in a row. On the one hand, it's possible that this unusual sample occurs simply by chance: We've merely shown up at a time when chance produced a sample that is unrepresentative of normal coin tosses. But on the other hand, we might suspect that the coin is "rigged." That is, instead of the sample poorly representing the population of tosses produced by a fair coin, it may be that the sample represents the population of tosses produced by a rigged coin.

We can make a decision here using this logic: If there were, say, 55% heads and 45% tails, we could accept that the sample represents the population of fair coin tosses—it's close enough to the ideal 50-50 split between heads and tails that we'd expect. Even 60% heads and 40% tails is somewhat representative of this population. Such outcomes are reasonably likely to occur when tossing a fair coin, so it's reasonable—a good bet—that chance produced a less than perfectly representative sample of the population of fair tosses.

Beyond a certain point, however, we begin to doubt that only random chance is at work. For example, obtaining 70% heads and 30% tails is rather unlikely, which literally means that chance is unlikely to produce such an unrepresentative sample from the population of fair coin tosses. And with 100% heads (7 in a row), we begin to seriously doubt the honesty of the coin: A fair coin—and the population of fair coin tosses—is extremely unlikely to produce a sample containing 7 heads in a row. In fact, it turns out that the probability of this event equals 1/128, or about .008. (This p can be calculated using the "binomial expansion" presented in Appendix B.4.) Thus, random chance and a fair coin produce such an unusual sample only about .8 of 1% of the time! It is silly to bet on such an unlikely event, so we should reject the idea that our sample is a sample of—and represents—fair coin tosses. Instead, it's more sensible to conclude that the coin is rigged, because a rigged coin would be more likely to produce so many heads in a row. (That's what "rigged" means!)

Here's another example. You obtain a mysterious paragraph of someone's typing, but you don't know whose. Is it mine? Does this sample represent the population of my typing? Say there are zero typos in the paragraph. It's possible that by some quirk I produced such an unrepresentative paragraph, but it's not likely: I type errorless words only 20% of the time, so the probability that I could produce an entire errorless paragraph is extremely small. Thus, because chance is *too unlikely* to produce such a sample from the population of my typing, we should decide against this low-probability event. Instead, we should conclude that the sample represents the population of another, competent typist where this sample is more likely.

On the other hand, say that there are typos in 75% of the words in the mystery paragraph. This is reasonably consistent with what you would expect if the sample represents my typing. Although we expect 80% typos from me over the long run, we don't really expect *precisely* 80% typos in every sample. Rather, a sample with 75% errors seems likely to occur simply by chance when the population of my typing is sampled. Thus, you can accept that this paragraph represents my typing, but does so somewhat poorly: Through random chance, there are slightly fewer typos in the sample than in the population, but it's close enough to be one of mine.

We use this same logic in research to decide whether a sample of scores is representative of a particular population. This is the basis of all inferential statistical procedures: Using the probability of obtaining a particular sample from a particular population, we can decide whether the sample represents that population. If the sample is likely to occur when the population is sampled, then it is likely that the sample represents that population. If the sample is unlikely to occur when that population is sampled, then the sample probably represents some other population.

> *REMEMBER* Inferential statistics are used to decide whether a sample is likely or unlikely to occur in a particular population of scores.

The next chapter puts all of this into a research context. In the final sections of this chapter, we'll examine the mechanics of formally deciding whether a sample of scores represents a particular population.

MAKING DECISIONS ABOUT A SAMPLE MEAN

To see how we decide if a sample from an experiment represents a particular population, say that we return to Prunepit University and obtain a random sample of SAT scores that produces a mean of 550. This is surprising because we think that students at Prunepit U. are terminally average. Because the ordinary, national population of SAT scores has a μ of 500, we should have obtained a sample mean of 500 if our sample was perfectly representative of this population. How do we explain a sample mean of 550? On the one hand, the simplest explanation is that we obtained a sample of relatively high SAT scores merely because of random chance—the luck of the draw of who was selected to be in the sample. Thus, it is possible that chance produced a less than perfectly representative sample of the population where μ is 500. On the other hand, perhaps the sample does not come from or represent the ordinary, national population of SAT scores: After all, these *are* Prunepit students, so they may belong to a very different population of students, having some other μ.

To decide whether the sample represents the population of SAT scores where μ is 500, we'll determine the probability of obtaining a sample mean of 550 from this population. As we've seen, we determine the probability of a sample mean by computing its *z*-score on the appropriate sampling distribution of means. For the Prunepit problem, we envision the sampling distribution shown in Figure 12.4, showing the frequencies of all the different means that the bored statistician would obtain if, using our *N*, she randomly sampled the ordinary SAT population an infinite number of times. Because she was always representing the ordinary SAT population where μ is 500, whether she obtained a particular mean that was high, low, or in-between depends purely on the luck of the draw of which scores she happened to select for that sample. Therefore, think of a sampling distribution as a "picture of chance," showing how often random chance produces various sample means when we sample a particular raw score population. Here, the sampling distribution shows how often chance will produce a particular sample mean when the sample represents the underlying population where μ is 500.

By calculating our sample mean's *z*-score, we can locate the mean on the sampling distribution, and thus determine its likelihood. For example, say that we find that the *z*-score places our sample mean at location A in Figure 12.4. Read what the frequency distribution indicates by following the dotted line: This mean has a very high frequency. Thus, when someone draws a sample from the ordinary SAT population, selecting one with a mean of 550 is a very frequent, common, and *likely* event. Anytime

FIGURE 12.4 Sampling Distribution of SAT Means Showing Two Possible Locations of Our Sample Mean

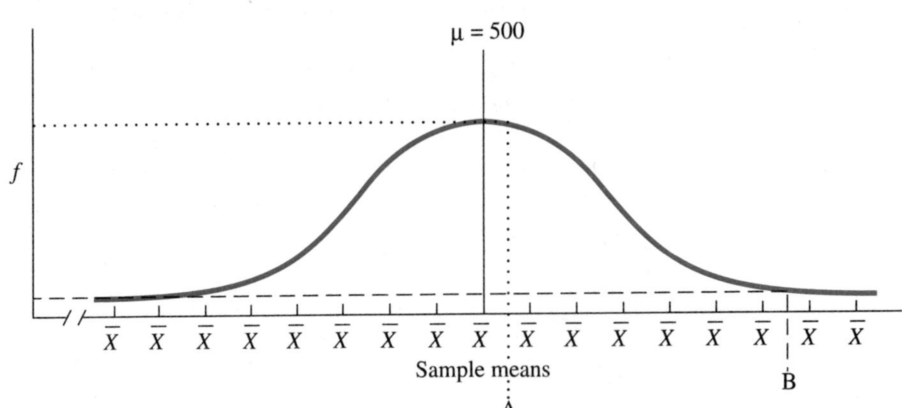

you deal with this population, this is a mean you'd expect. Therefore, if *we* were dealing with the ordinary SAT population when drawing the Prunepit sample, we'd be likely—we'd expect—to get the mean of 550. Thus, because our sample would be likely to come from the ordinary SAT population, we would accept that the sample represents it.

However, say that instead, the *z*-score for our sample mean places it at location B on Figure 12.4: Following the dashed line here shows that this is a very low frequency mean. This indicates that when someone samples the ordinary SAT population, getting a sample that is so unrepresentative that it has a mean of 550 is a very *in*frequent, *un*common, and *un*likely event. Anytime you deal with this population, you'll almost never find such a mean. Therefore, if *we* were dealing with the ordinary SAT population when drawing the Prunepit sample, we would not expect such a mean, because they almost never happen. Thus, because our sample mean would be so unlikely to come from the ordinary SAT population, we would reject that the sample represents it. Instead, it makes more sense to conclude that the sample represents some other population (having some other μ) where a sample mean of 550 would be more likely to occur.

Be sure you understand the above logic. If you do, you're ready to perform the mechanics of the procedure. Notice that we must perform two tasks: (1) determine the probability of obtaining our sample from the original population, and (2) decide whether the sample is too unlikely to be representing this population. We perform both tasks simultaneously, once we have set up the sampling distribution and identified the critical value.

Setting Up the Sampling Distribution

As you saw above, if our sample mean is "close" to the mean of the sampling distribution (close to 500,) then we can accept that we have a slightly unrepresentative sample but are still representing this population. Thus, any sample means around location A in Figure 12.4, or those that are close to but below the μ of 500 would all lead to this conclusion. But, if our sample mean is far enough out into the tail of the sampling distribution (not "close" to 500), then we reject the idea that chance produced a slightly unrepresentative sample. Instead, we conclude that the reason our sample mean is so far from 500 is because it does not represent the population where μ is 500. Thus, any sample means around location B in Figure 12.4, or those that are far out but in the opposite tail of the distribution, would all lead to this conclusion.

But how close is close enough, and how far is far enough to make these decisions? To formalize the decision process, we do this: At some point, a sample mean is so far above or below 500 that it is unbelievable that chance produced such an unrepresentative sample. AND, any means beyond this point—farther into the tail—are also unbelievable. To identify this point, we literally draw a line in each tail of the distribution, as shown in Figure 12.5. In statistical terms, the shaded areas beyond the lines make up the *region of rejection*. As shown, very infrequently are samples so poor at representing the SAT population that they have means lying in the region of rejection. In fact:

> **Means in the region of rejection are so unrepresentative of the underlying raw score population that it's a better bet they represent some other population.**

Thus, the **region of rejection** is the part of a sampling distribution containing values that are so unlikely to occur that we "reject" that they represent the underlying raw score population. Essentially, in the example, we "shouldn't" get a sample mean that lies in the region of rejection if we're representing the ordinary SAT population, because such means almost never occur with this population. Therefore, if we do get such a mean, we probably aren't representing this population: We reject that the sample represents the underlying raw score population and decide that the sample represents some other population.

Conversely, if the Prunepit mean is not in the region of rejection, then it's not unlikely to be representing the ordinary SAT population. In fact, by our definition, sample means not in the region of rejection are likely to occur when this population is sampled and thus likely to represent it. In such cases, we "retain" the idea that because of chance, the sample is simply poorly representing this population of SAT scores.

(*Note:* By placing part of the region of rejection in *both* tails of the sampling distribution, we are employing what is called a **two-tailed test**. As you'll see in the next chapter, two-tailed procedures are used when we simultaneously test whether a sample mean is either too far above or too far below μ to be representing that μ.

FIGURE 12.5 Setup of Sampling Distribution of SAT Means Showing the Region of Rejection

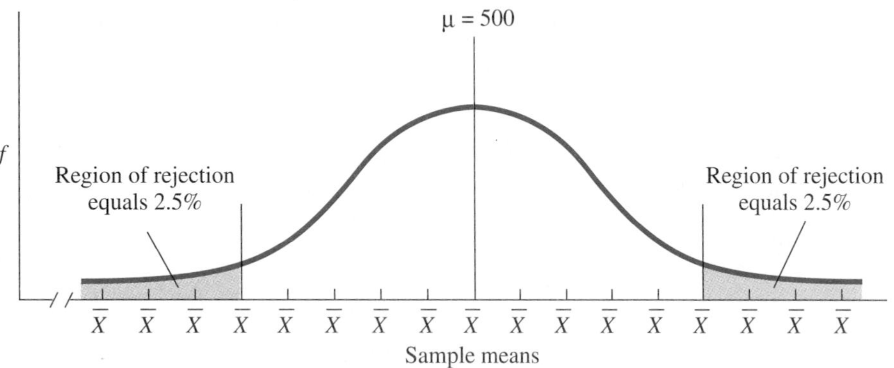

How do we know where to draw the line that starts the region of rejection? By defining our criterion. The **criterion** is the probability that defines samples as too unlikely to accept as representing a particular population. Psychologists usually set .05 as their criterion probability. Thus, by this criterion, sample means that occur less than 5% of the time when representing the ordinary SAT population are so unlikely that if we get such a mean, we'll reject that our sample represents this population.

The criterion determines the size of the region of rejection. Back in Figure 12.5, the sample means that occur 5% of the time are those that make up the extreme 5% of the sampling distribution. Because we're talking about the means above *or* below 500, we are saying that *together*, they make up a *total* of 5% of the curve. Therefore, dividing 5% in half, the region of rejection in each tail is the extreme 2.5% of the sampling distribution.

> ***REMEMBER*** The criterion probability that defines samples as unlikely—and also determines the size of the region of rejection—is usually $p = .05$.

Now, to make a decision about our sample, the task boils down to determining if our sample mean falls in the region of rejection. To do this, we compare the sample's z-score to the critical value.

Identifying the Critical Value

There is a specific z-score at the spot on the sampling distribution where we drew the line to mark the beginning of the region of rejection. Because the absolute value of z-scores gets larger as we go farther into the tails, if the z-score for our sample is *larger* than the z-score at the line, then our sample mean lies *in* the region of rejection. The z-score at the line is called the critical value. The **critical value** marks the edge of the region of rejection and thus defines the value required for a sample to fall in the region of rejection. Essentially, it is the z-score that defines a sample as "too unlikely."

How do we determine the critical value of z? By considering our criterion. With a criterion of .05, we've set up the region of rejection so that each tail contains the extreme 2.5% or .025 of the total area under the curve. From the z-tables (column C), the extreme .025 of the curve lies beyond the z-score of 1.96. Therefore, in each tail, the region of rejection begins at 1.96, so ± 1.96 is the critical value of z. Thus, as shown in Figure 12.6, labeling the inner edges of the region of rejection with ± 1.96 completes how you should set up the sampling distribution.

Then, we will use Figure 12.6 to determine whether our Prunepit sample mean lies in the region of rejection by comparing the sample's z-score to the critical value of z. It simply involves this:

> **A sample mean lies in the region of rejection if its z-score lies beyond the critical value.**

Thus, if our Prunepit mean has a z-score with an absolute value that is *larger* than ± 1.96, then the sample lies in the region of rejection. If our mean has a z-score that is *smaller than or equal to* the critical value, then the sample is *not* in the region of rejection.

> ***REMEMBER*** The critical value defines the minimum value of z a sample must have in order to lie in the region of rejection.

FIGURE 12.6 Completed Sampling Distribution of SAT Means Showing Region of Rejection and Critical Values

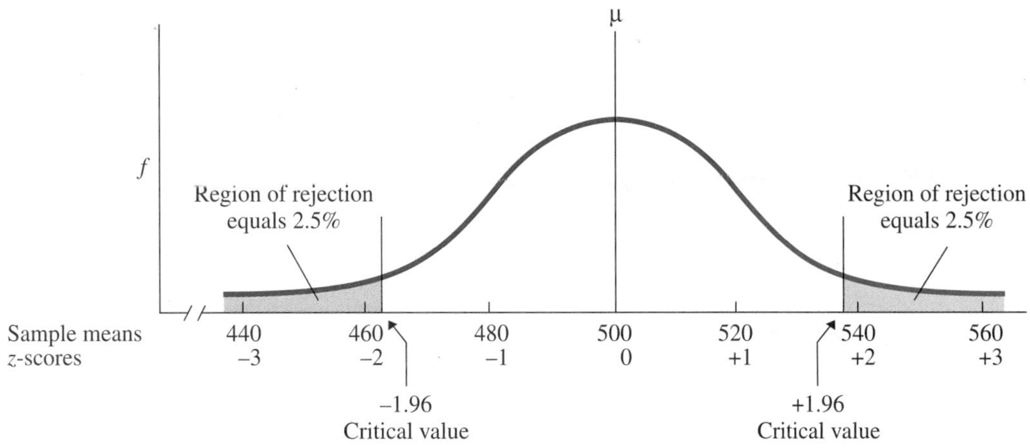

Deciding Whether the Sample Represents the Population

At long last, we can evaluate our sample mean of 550 from Prunepit U. First, we compute the sample's *z*-score on the sampling distribution created from the ordinary SAT population. The, σ_X for SAT scores is 100, and our N was 25, so the standard error of the mean is

$$\sigma_{\overline{X}} = \frac{\sigma_X}{\sqrt{N}} = \frac{100}{\sqrt{25}} = 20$$

The *z*-score is:

$$z = \frac{\overline{X} - \mu}{\sigma_{\overline{X}}} = \frac{550 - 500}{20} = +2.5$$

Think about this *z*-score. If our sample represents the ordinary SAT population, it's doing a very poor job of it: A perfectly representative sample would have a mean of 500 and thus a *z*-score of 0. Good old Prunepit produced a *z*-score of +2.5!

To confirm our suspicions, compare the sample's *z*-score to the critical value. Locating the sample's *z*-score on the sampling distribution gives us the complete picture, shown on the next page in Figure 12.7. (When performing this procedure, you should draw the complete picture too.) The sample's *z* of +2.5—and the underlying sample mean of 550—lie in the region of rejection. This tells us that a sample mean of 550 is among those means that we consider to be extremely unlikely to occur when someone is representing the ordinary population of SAT scores. In other words, very seldom does chance produce such samples from this population, so it is not a good bet that chance produced our sample from this population. Therefore, we reject that our sample represents the population of SAT scores where μ is 500.

Notice that we make a definitive yes or no decision. Because our sample would be unlikely to occur if it were representing the SAT population where μ is 500, we decide that no, it definitely does not represent that population.

FIGURE 12.7 Sampling Distribution of SAT Means Showing Location of the Prunepit U. Sample Relative to the Critical Value

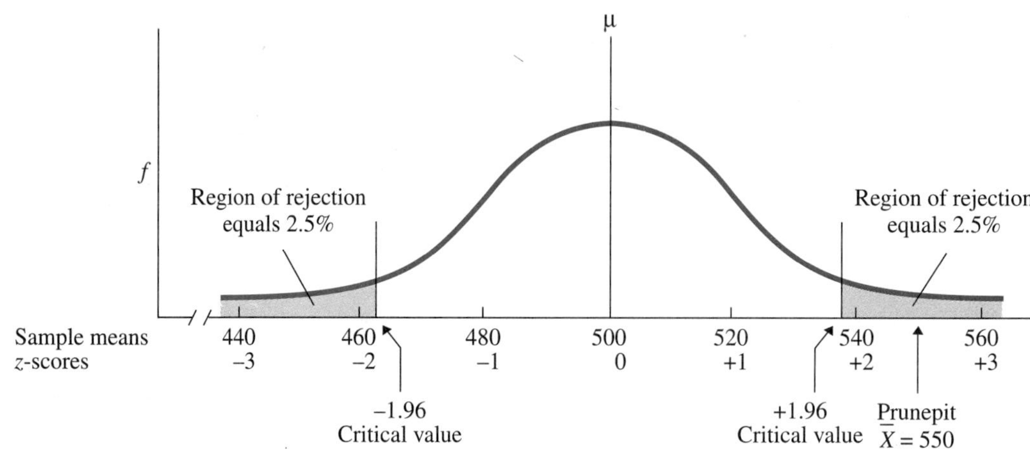

We wrap up our conclusions in this way: If the sample does not represent the ordinary SAT population, then it must represent some other population. For example, perhaps the Prunepit students obtained the high mean of 550 because they lied about their scores, so they may represent the population of students who lie about the SAT. Or, perhaps they are more intelligent or motivated than ordinary students, and thus represent the population of overachievers. Or, maybe Prunepit U. is located on a toxic waste dump, and the sample represents the population of SAT scores for those living on toxic waste dumps.

Finally, having rejected that the sample represents the population where μ is 500, we use the sample mean to estimate the μ of the population that the sample *does* represent. A sample having a mean of 550 is most likely to come from a population having a μ of 550. Therefore, our best guess is that the Prunepit sample represents an SAT population that, for whatever reason, has a μ of 550.

Thus, in sum, as we did with previous bets, we decide against the low-probability event that the sample represents the SAT population where μ is 500, and decide in favor of the high-probability event that the sample represents a population where μ is 550.

On the other hand, say that our sample mean had been 480, resulting in a z-score of $(480 - 500)/20 = -1.00$. Because -1.00 does not lie beyond the critical value of ± 1.96, our sample mean is not in the region of rejection. Look back at Figure 12.7, to see where a mean of 480 is located: When the bored statistician sampled the population, this sample mean was relatively frequent and thus likely. Because of this, we can accept that random chance produced a less than perfectly representative sample for us but that the sample probably still represents the ordinary SAT population where μ is 500.

REMEMBER When a sample's z-score lies beyond the critical value, *reject* the idea that the sample represents the underlying raw score population reflected by the sampling distribution. When the z-score does not lie beyond the critical value, *retain* the idea that the sample may represent that raw score population.

Other Ways to Set Up the Sampling Distribution

In the above example, the region of rejection was in both tails of the distribution because we wanted to make a decision about any sample mean that was either too far above or too far below 500. Instead, however, we can place the entire region of rejection in only one tail of the distribution. (The next chapter discusses why we would do this.) By placing the entire region of rejection in one tail of the sampling distribution only, we are employing a **one-tailed test**. One-tailed procedures are used when we test only whether a sample mean is too far above μ, or only whether the mean is too far below μ, to be representing that μ.

Say that we had been interested only in SAT sample means *less than* 500. Means below μ have negative z-scores, so the entire region of rejection constituting 5% of the curve, is in the lower tail of the sampling distribution, as in Figure 12.8. Notice that we have a different critical value. From the z-tables (and using the interpolation procedures described in Appendix B.3), the extreme 5% of a distribution lies beyond a z-score of 1.645. Therefore, our sample's z-score must lie beyond *minus* 1.645 for the sample mean to be in the region of rejection. If it does, we will again conclude that such a sample mean is too unlikely to occur when sampling the SAT raw score population where $\mu = 500$, so we'll reject the idea that the sample represents this population.

On the other hand, say that we had been interested only in sample means *greater* than 500. Then we'd place the entire region of rejection (the entire 5%) in the upper tail of the sampling distribution, as in Figure 12.9. Now the critical value is *plus* 1.645. If our sample's z-score is beyond +1.645, then the sample mean lies in the region of rejection. Then, we again reject the idea that the sample represents the underlying raw score population.

FIGURE 12.8 Setup of SAT Sampling Distribution to Test Negative z-Scores

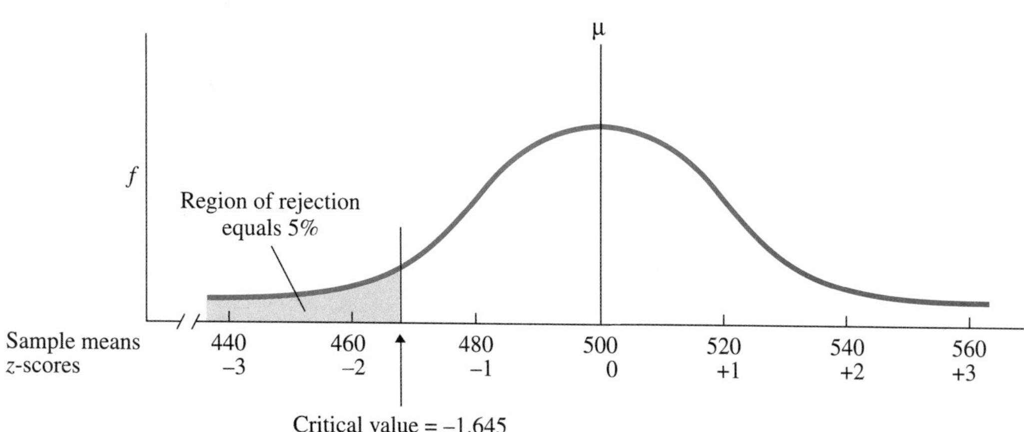

FIGURE 12.9 Setup of SAT Sampling Distribution to Test Positive *z*-Scores

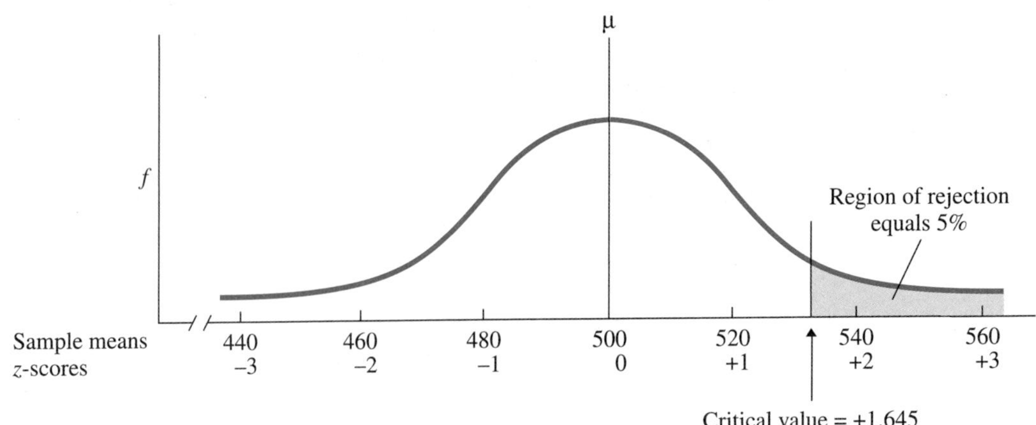

On Being Wrong when We Decide about a Sample

Unlikely events are just that: They are unlikely, not impossible. Thus, it's possible that I might type an errorless paragraph or that we'd get seven heads in a row. And, it's possible that the sample mean of 550 actually represents the ordinary SAT population where μ is 500. The sampling distribution shows that when we *are* representing the ordinary SAT population, sample means out in the region of rejection do occur sometimes (the bored statistician sometimes did obtain such means from this population). Maybe our Prunepit mean was one of those means. Thus, *anytime* we reject that a sample represents a particular population, we may be wrong.

We can also be wrong when we retain the idea that the sample represents the ordinary SAT population. Consider the most extreme case, in which we obtain a sample mean of 500! This sample certainly appears to represent the ordinary population of SAT scores where μ is 500. Using the above procedures, we'd compute a *z*-score of 0, so we would retain this idea. But it is possible that this sample actually represents some other population. Perhaps, for example, the sample is actually a very unrepresentative sample from the population where μ is 550! Maybe, simply by the luck of the draw, our sample contains too many low scores, so the mean is 500 instead of 550, and so it appears to represent the population where μ is 500. In the same way, *anytime* we retain the idea that a sample represents a particular population, we may be wrong.

Thus, regardless of which population we decide a sample represents, there is the possibility that we have made an incorrect decision. Such errors are not likely, however, and that's why we perform inferential statistical procedures. By incorporating probability into our decision making, we have greater confidence that we have correctly identified the population that a sample represents. Then, we have greater confidence that we are correctly interpreting and generalizing the results of our research.

PUTTING IT ALL TOGETHER

The decision-making process discussed in this chapter is used in all inferential statistics. The basic question is always "Does our sample data represent a particular raw score population?" If the sample mean is different from the population μ we expect, then either (1) through the luck of the draw, we have a slightly unrepresentative sample of that population, or (2) we are representing a different population. To answer this question, we always perform the following steps:

1. Create a sampling distribution from the underlying raw score population we think the sample may represent.

2. Select the criterion probability that defines a sample as "too unlikely" and also defines the size of the region of rejection.

3. Based on the criterion and region of rejection, determine the critical value.

4. Compute a statistic, such as a z-score, to describe the results of our study.

5. If the z-score lies beyond the critical value, then our sample is in the region of rejection. Therefore, the sample is unlikely to be representing the underlying raw score population, so we reject that it does, and conclude that the sample represents some other population that is more likely to produce such data.

6. If the z-score does not lie beyond the critical value, then our sample is not in the region of rejection. Therefore, the sample is likely to be representing the underlying raw score population, so we retain the idea that the sample represents this population, although somewhat poorly.

CHAPTER SUMMARY

1. *Probability* (p), indicates the likelihood of an event when random chance is operating. The probability of an event is its relative frequency in the population.

2. The probability of *equally likely events* equals the number of outcomes that can satisfy the event out of the total number of possible outcomes that can occur.

3. The probability of correctly predicting a chance event equals the probability that the event will occur. The probability of incorrectly predicting a chance event equals the probability that the event will not occur.

4. Events are *independent* if the probability of one event is not influenced by the occurrence of the other event. Events are *dependent* if the probability of one event is influenced by the occurrence of the other.

5. *Sampling with replacement* is replacing a sample in the population before another sample is selected. *Sampling without replacement* is *not* replacing a sample in the population before another is selected.

6. A *theoretical probability distribution* is a theoretical model of the relative frequencies of all possible events in a population when random chance is operating.

7. The standard normal curve model is a theoretical probability distribution that can be applied to any normal raw score distribution. Raw scores are transformed to z-scores, and the proportion of the area under the curve is the probability of

randomly selecting those z-scores. This is also the probability of selecting the corresponding raw scores.

8. A sampling distribution of means is also a theoretical probability distribution. Sample means are transformed to z-scores, and the proportion of the area under the curve is the probability of randomly selecting those z-scores. This is also the probability of selecting the corresponding sample means.

9. The probability of randomly selecting a particular sample mean is the same as the probability of randomly selecting a sample of participants whose scores produce that sample mean.

10. The *region of rejection* is located in the tail or tails of a sampling distribution. A z-score in the region of rejection indicates the sample mean is unlikely to be representing the underlying raw score population reflected by the sampling distribution.

11. In a *two-tailed test*, part of the region of rejection is in each tail of the sampling distribution. In a *one-tailed test*, either the region of rejection is in the upper tail only, or is in the lower tail only.

12. The edge of the region of rejection closest to the μ of the sampling distribution is at the *critical value*. A sample mean is in the region of rejection if the sample's z-score is beyond the critical value.

13. The size of the region of rejection is determined by the *criterion*, which is the probability that defines a sample as too unlikely. Usually, the criterion is .05. This produces a region of rejection that constitutes the extreme .05 of the sampling distribution.

KEY TERMS (with page references)

criterion (325)
critical value (326)
dependent events (316)
empirical probability distribution (315)
independent events (316)
one-tailed test (329)
probability (313)
probability distribution (315)
region of rejection (325)
sampling with replacement (317)
sampling without replacement (317)
theoretical probability distribution (315)
two-tailed test (325)

REVIEW QUESTIONS

(Answers for odd-numbered questions and problems are provided in Appendix D.)

1. (a) What does a probability convey about a random event in a sample? (b) What is the probability of a random event based on?

2. (a) What is the difference between an empirical probability distribution and a theoretical probability distribution? (b) Why is the proportion of the area under the normal curve equal to probability?
3. (a) What is sampling with replacement? (b) What is sampling without replacement? (c) How does sampling without replacement affect the probability of events, compared to sampling with replacement?
4. (a) When are events independent? (b) When are they dependent?
5. A sample produces a mean that is different from the μ of the population that we think the sample represents. What are the two possible reasons for this difference?
6. When testing the representativeness of a sample mean, (a) what is the criterion? (b) what is the region of rejection? (c) what is the critical value?
7. What does comparing the critical value to a sample's z-score indicate?
8. What is the difference between how a two-tailed test is set up and how a one-tailed test is set up?

PRACTICE PROBLEMS

9. What is the probability of (a) getting a six when rolling a die? (b) selecting a diamond when cutting a deck of cards? (c) randomly guessing the correct answer to a multiple-choice question with four choices? (d) selecting the ace of diamonds twice in a row when sampling a deck of cards without replacement?
10. The p of obtaining 7 heads in a row with a fair coin is .008, so we reject that our coin is fair (that only chance produced this result). (a) What is the p that we are incorrect? (b) What is the p that we are correct?
11. A couple with eight children, all girls, decides to have one more baby, because the next one is bound to be a boy! Is this reasoning accurate?
12. Foofy read in the newspaper that there is a .05% chance of swallowing a spider while you sleep. She subsequently developed insomnia. (a) What is the probability of swallowing a spider? (b) Why isn't her insomnia justified on the basis of this probability? (c) Why is her insomnia justified on the basis of this probability?
13. Poindexter's uncle is planning to build a house on land that has been devastated by hurricanes 160 times in the past 200 years. Because there hasn't been a major storm there in 13 years, his uncle is certain this is a safe investment. His nephew argues that there definitely will be a hurricane in the next year or so. What are the fallacies in the reasoning of both men?
14. Four airplanes from different airlines have crashed in the past two weeks. Bubbles must travel on a plane, but she is terrified that it will crash. Her travel agent claims that the probability of a plane crash is minuscule. Who is correctly interpreting the situation? Why?
15. For each of the following, indicate whether the first event is dependent on, or is independent of, the second event: (a) Playing golf; the weather. (b) Buying new shoes; buying a new car. (c) Losing weight; eating fewer calories. (d) Winning the lottery; playing the same numbers each time.
16. What is the probability of randomly selecting a participant who scores the following: (a) $z = +2.03$ or above? (b) $z = -2.8$ or above? (c) z between -1.5 and $+1.5$? (d) z beyond ± 1.72?

17. For a distribution in which $\overline{X} = 43$ and $S_X = 8$, what is the probability of randomly selecting the following: (a) A score of 27 or below? (b) A score of 51 or above? (c) A score between 42 and 44? (d) A score below 33 or above 49?
18. You are shopping for a used car. Over the life of the car you are thinking of buying, the probability of engine trouble is .65. (a) If you conclude that the engine will malfunction, what is the probability that you are correct? What is the probability that you are incorrect? (b) If you conclude that the engine will not malfunction, what is the probability that you are correct? What is the probability that you are incorrect? (c) Should you purchase this car? Why?
19. The mean of a population of raw scores is 18 ($\sigma_X = 12$). What is the probability of randomly selecting a sample of 30 scores having a mean above 24?
20. The mean of a population of raw scores is 50 ($\sigma_X = 18$). What is the probability of randomly selecting a sample of 40 scores having a mean below 46?
21. How do researchers use probability in inferential statistics?
22. (a) Why do we conclude that a low-probability sample does not represent a particular population? (b) Why do we conclude that a high-probability sample does represent a particular population? (c) Why is it possible that each conclusion above may be wrong? (d) Why is it unlikely that we're wrong?
23. Suppose that for the data in problem 19, you obtained a sample mean of 24. Using the .05 criterion with the region of rejection in both tails of the sampling distribution, should you consider the sample to be representative of the population in which $\mu = 18$? Why?
24. Suppose that for the data in problem 20, you obtained a sample mean of 46. Using the .05 criterion with the region of rejection in both tails of the distribution, should you consider the sample to be representative of the population in which $\mu = 50$? Why?
25. In a study, you use a questionnaire and obtain the following data representing the aggressive tendencies of some football players:

    40 30 39 40 41 39 31 28 33

    (a) Researchers have found that in the population of nonfootball players, μ is 30 ($\sigma_X = 5$). Using both tails of the sampling distribution, determine whether your football players represent a different population. (b) What do you conclude about the population of football players and its μ?
26. On a standard test of motor coordination, the population of average bowlers has a mean score of 24, with a standard deviation of 6. A random sample of 30 bowlers at Fred's Bowling Alley had a mean of 26. A sample of 30 bowlers at Ethel's Bowling Alley had a mean of 18. Using the criterion of $p = .05$ and both tails of the sampling distribution, what should we conclude about each sample's representativeness of the population of average bowlers?
27. (a) In problem 26, if each sample did not represent the population of average bowlers, what would be your best estimate of the μ of the population it does represent? (b) Explain the logic behind this conclusion.
28. Foofy computes the $\overline{X}$ from data that her professor says is a random sample drawn from population Q. She determines that this sample mean has a z-score of +41 on the sampling distribution for population Q (and she computed it correctly!). She claims she has proven that this could not be a random sample from population Q. Do you agree or disagree? Why?

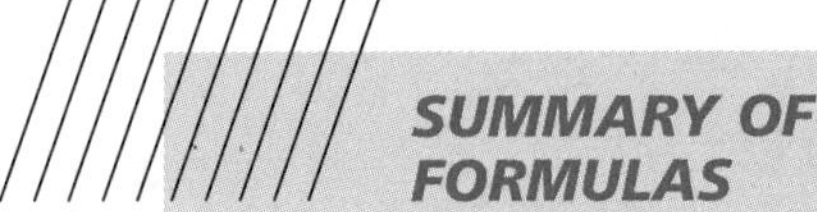

SUMMARY OF FORMULAS

1. *The formula for computing probability for equally likely events is*

$$p(\text{event}) = \frac{\text{Number of outcomes that satisfy event}}{\text{Total number of possible outcomes}}$$

2. *The formula for the true standard error of the mean is*

$$\sigma_{\overline{X}} = \frac{\sigma_X}{\sqrt{N}}$$

where σ_X is the true standard deviation of the raw score population.

3. *The formula for transforming a sample mean into a z-score on the sampling distribution of means is*

$$z = \frac{\overline{X} - \mu}{\sigma_{\overline{X}}}$$

where $\overline{X}$ is the sample mean, μ is the mean of the sampling distribution (which is also equal to the μ of the underlying raw score distribution), and $\sigma_{\overline{X}}$ is the standard error of the mean of the sampling distribution of means.

13

Overview of Statistical Hypothesis Testing: The *z*-Test

Getting Started

To understand this chapter, recall the following:

- From Chapter 7, recall that a relationship in the population occurs when different means from the conditions of an independent variable reflect different distributions of dependent scores.
- From Chapter 12, recall that when a sample's *z*-score falls in the region of rejection, the sample is unlikely to be representing the underlying raw score population.

Your goals in this chapter are to learn:

- Why the possibility of sampling error leads to performing inferential statistical procedures.
- When experimental hypotheses lead to either a one-tailed or two-tailed statistical test.
- How to set up a sampling distribution for one- and two-tailed tests.
- How to interpret significant and nonsignificant results.
- What Type I errors, Type II errors, and power are.

From the previous chapter, you know the basics involved in inferential statistics. In this chapter, we'll put these procedures into a research context and present the statistical language and symbols used to describe them. The discussion will introduce the formal system psychologists use in *all* inferential procedures. Therefore, be alert to the pattern here, and understand the general steps and terminology involved. Until further notice, we'll be talking about experiments. We'll start with the "*z*-test," but first . . .

MORE STATISTICAL NOTATION

Five new symbols will be used in stating mathematical relationships:

1. The symbol for *greater than* is $>$. We read from left to right, so $A > B$ means that A is greater than B. (The large opening in "$>$" is always on the side of the larger quantity, and the symbol points toward the smaller quantity.)
2. The symbol for *less than* is $<$, so $B < A$ means that B is less than A.
3. The symbol for *greater than or equal to* is $\geq$, so $B \geq A$ indicates that B is greater than or equal to A.
4. The symbol for *less than or equal to* is $\leq$, so $B \leq A$ indicates that B is less than or equal to A.
5. The symbol for *not equal to* is $\neq$, so $A \neq B$ indicates that A is different from B.

THE ROLE OF INFERENTIAL STATISTICS IN RESEARCH

As you saw in the previous chapter, a random sample may be more or less representative of a population because, just by the luck of the draw, the sample contains too many high scores or too many low scores relative to the population. Because the sample is not perfectly representative, the sample mean does not equal the population mean.

The shorthand term for communicating the idea that chance produced an unrepresentative sample is to say that the sample reflects sampling error. **Sampling error** results when chance produces a sample statistic (such as $\overline{X}$) that is not equal to the population parameter it represents (such as μ). Because of the luck of the draw, the *sample* is in *error* to some degree in representing the population.

> *REMEMBER* Sampling error results when, by chance, the scores that are selected produce a sample statistic that is different from the population parameter it represents.

It is because of sampling error that researchers perform inferential statistics. Recall that in an experiment, we change the conditions of the independent variable in hopes of changing the dependent scores. If the means for the conditions change, we want to infer that if we performed the experiment on the entire population, we would find a different population of scores—located at a different μ—under each condition. But here is where sampling error comes in. Maybe the sample means for the conditions differ because of the luck of the draw, and they are actually poorly representing the *same* population. If so, then testing everyone in the population under each condition would not produce a relationship: We'd find the same population of scores, having the same μ, in each condition. Or, perhaps there is a relationship in the population, but because of sampling error, the relationship in our sample data is different from it.

For example, say we compare men and women on the dependent variable of creativity. In nature, men and women don't really differ on this variable, but through sampling error—the luck of the draw—we might end up with some female participants who are more creative than our male participants. Thus, sampling error will mislead us into thinking there is a relationship between gender and creativity, although really there is not. Or, say that we measure the heights of some men and women, and, by chance, our participants are some relatively short men and tall women. If we didn't already know that the population of men is taller, sampling error would mislead us into concluding that women are taller.

In any research situation, there is always the possibility we are being misled by sampling error as in the above examples. Therefore, to deal with the possibility of sampling error, we apply inferential statistics. **Inferential statistics** are used to decide whether sample data represent a relationship in the population. Using the process discussed in the previous chapter, we decide whether it is likely that the samples represent populations that form a particular relationship or whether it is likely we are being misled by sampling error and the samples actually represent populations that do not form the relationship. The specific inferential procedure employed in a given research situation depends on the research design and on the scale of measurement used when measuring the *dependent variable*. There are two general categories of inferential statistics: Parametric and nonparametric.

Parametric statistics are procedures that require certain assumptions about the raw score populations being represented. Recall that parameters describe the characteristics of a population, so parametric procedures are used when we can assume the population has certain characteristics. The assumptions of a procedure are the rules for using it, so think of them as a checklist for selecting a procedure. There are specific assumptions for each parametric procedure, but two assumptions are common to them all: (1) The population of dependent scores forms a normal distribution, and (2) The scores are interval or ratio scores. Thus, parametric procedures are used when it's appropriate to calculate the mean in each condition. (In this and upcoming chapters, we'll focus on parametric procedures.)

Nonparametric statistics are inferential procedures that do not require stringent assumptions about the populations represented by the samples. These procedures are used with nominal or ordinal dependent scores or with skewed distributions of interval or ratio scores (when it is appropriate to calculate the median or mode). The common nonparametric procedures are discussed in Chapter 21.

We use nonparametric procedures whenever the data clearly violate the assumptions of parametric procedures. However, we can use a parametric procedure if the data come close to meeting its assumptions. This is because parametric procedures are robust. With a **robust procedure**, if we do not meet the assumptions of the procedure perfectly, we will have only a negligible amount of error in the inferences we draw. So, for example, if data represent a population that is approximately normally distributed, we can still use a parametric procedure.

Regardless, both parametric and nonparametric procedures have the same use: They are for deciding whether the data reflect a relationship found in nature or whether sampling error is misleading us into thinking a relationship is present when really it is not. A study is *never* completed until you have performed inferential statistics and made this decision. The first step is to set up the problem correctly.

SETTING UP INFERENTIAL PROCEDURES

It's not appropriate to think about a statistical analysis only after you have collected data. There are several decisions to make beforehand to be sure the data will be "analyzable." It's possible to collect data and then find out that there are no appropriate statistical procedures to apply.

To set up a statistical analysis, first examine your experimental hypotheses. **Experimental hypotheses** describe the predicted outcome we may or may not find in an experiment. Thus, from our constructs and operational definitions we have one experimental hypothesis that says we *will* demonstrate the predicted relationship—manipulating the independent variable will work as expected. We also have the other, opposite hypothesis that says we will *not* demonstrate the predicted relationship—manipulating the independent variable will not work as expected.

We may predict a relationship in one of two ways. The simplest prediction is that there is some kind of relationship, but we are not sure whether scores will increase or decrease as we change the independent variable (essentially we're unsure whether it's a positive or negative linear relationship). This leads to the "two-tailed" test introduced in Chapter 12. A **two-tailed test** is used when we predict there is a relationship, but do not predict the direction in which scores will change.

The other, more complicated prediction not only predicts a relationship, but also predicts the *direction* in which the scores will change: We may predict that as we change the independent variable, the dependent scores will increase (producing a positive relationship), or we may predict that they will decrease (producing a negative relationship). This leads to the one-tailed test introduced in Chapter 12. A **one-tailed test** is used when we predict the specific direction in which scores will change.

> ***REMEMBER*** A two-tailed test is used when you do not predict the direction that dependent scores will change. A one-tailed test is used when you do predict the direction that scores will change.

Let's first examine a study involving a two-tailed test. Say that we're interested in brain physiology, and have discovered a neural substance that is related to learning ability and intelligence. After several successful replications with animal subjects, we are ready to test this substance with humans in an "IQ pill." The amount of the pill is our independent variable, and the person's IQ is our dependent variable. For the moment, say that we believe the pill will affect IQ, but we're unsure whether it will make people smarter or dumber. Therefore, we predict a relationship where the more of the pill a person consumes, the more his or her IQ will change. In a nutshell, the possible outcomes are (1) we will demonstrate that the pill works by either increasing or decreasing IQ scores, or (2) we will not demonstrate that the pill works, because IQ scores will not change. Once we know the hypotheses and predictions, we design the study.

Designing a Single-Sample Experiment

Although there are many ways to design the IQ pill study, the simplest approach is a single-sample experiment. In a **single-sample experiment**, the mean from a sample tested under one condition is used to infer the corresponding μ, and this is compared to a *known* μ for another condition to determine if a relationship exists. For example, say we will randomly select one sample of participants and give each one pill. After waiting for the pill to work, we'll test the participants using a standard IQ test. Then the sample's $\overline{X}$ will represent the population μ of IQ scores of all people when they have taken one pill. To demonstrate a relationship, however, we must compare the population represented by our sample to another population that has received some other amount of the pill. *To perform any single-sample experiment, we must already know the population mean under some other condition of the independent variable.* One amount of the pill is zero pills. The IQ test we are using has been given to many people over the years who have not taken the pill, and say this population of IQ scores has a μ of 100. We will compare this population without the pill to the population with the pill represented by our sample. (Essentially, the population that has taken the IQ test is equivalent to a control group). If the population represented by the sample with the pill has a different μ than the population without the pill, then we will have demonstrated a relationship in the population.

After designing the study, the next step is to create the statistical hypotheses.

Creating the Statistical Hypotheses

In order to apply statistical procedures, we must translate the experimental hypotheses into statistical hypotheses. To do so, we redefine the experimental hypotheses in terms of the μ we'd find if we could test the entire population, and the experiment either "works" or "does not work." Thus, **statistical hypotheses** are proposals about the population parameters that sample data represent if the predicted relationship does or does not exist in nature. There are always two statistical hypotheses, the alternative hypothesis and the null hypothesis.

The alternative hypothesis Although you can create the hypotheses in either order, it is easier to create the alternative hypothesis first, because it corresponds to the experimental hypothesis that the experiment *does* work as predicted. The **alternative hypothesis** describes the population parameters that the sample data represent if the predicted relationship exists in nature. The alternative hypothesis is always the hypothesis of a difference; it says that changing the independent variable produces the predicted *difference* in the population of scores. Therefore, it is the hypothesis that the sample data represent a relationship in nature.

For example, if the IQ pill works as predicted and we tested the entire population, then we would find one of two outcomes. Figure 13.1 shows the populations if the pill *increases* IQ scores. This shows a relationship because, by changing the conditions, everyone's IQ is increased so that the distribution moves to the right, over to the higher

FIGURE 13.1 Relationship in the Population if the IQ Pill Increases IQ Scores

As the amount of the pill changes from 0 to 1, the IQ scores in the population tend to increase.

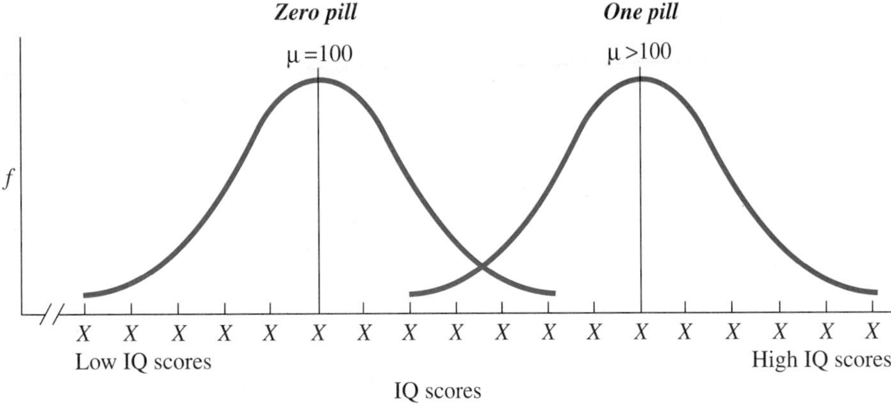

IQ scores. We don't know how much IQ scores will increase, so we don't know the specific value of μ with the pill. But we do know that if the pill increases IQ, then the μ of the population with the pill will be *greater than 100*, because 100 is the μ of the population without the pill.

On the other hand, Figure 13.2 shows the populations if the pill *decreases* IQ scores. With the pill, everyone's IQ decreases, so the distribution is moved to the left, over to the lower IQ scores. Again, the specific value of μ with the pill is unknown, but if the pill decreases IQ, then the μ of the population with the pill will be *less than 100* (because 100 is the μ of the population without the pill).

FIGURE 13.2 Relationship in the Population If the IQ Pill Decreases IQ Scores

As the amount of the pill changes from 0 to 1, the IQ scores in the population tend to decrease.

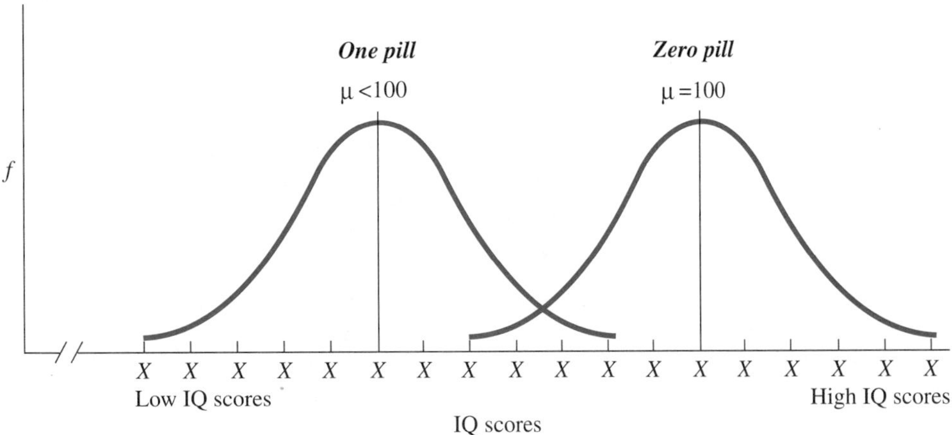

The alternative hypothesis is a shorthand way of communicating all of the above. If the pill works as predicted, then the population with the pill will have a μ that is either greater than or less than 100. In other words, the population mean with the pill will *not equal 100*. The symbol for the alternative hypothesis is H_a. (The H stands for hypothesis, and the subscript a stands for alternative.) For the IQ pill experiment, the alternative hypothesis is

$$H_a\text{: } \mu \neq 100$$

H_a implies that our sample mean produced with the pill represents a population mean not equal to 100. If, with the pill, μ is not 100, then there is a relationship in the population. Thus, we can interpret H_a as implying that our independent variable works as predicted.

The null hypothesis The statistical hypothesis corresponding to the experimental hypothesis that the independent variable does *not* work as predicted is called the null hypothesis. The **null hypothesis** describes the population parameters that the sample data represent if the predicted relationship does *not* exist in nature. The null hypothesis is the hypothesis of "no difference," saying that changing the independent variable does *not* produce the predicted difference in the population. Instead, it implies that the data poorly represent the situation where the predicted relationship does *not* exist: the sample data may form a relationship, but this is due to sampling error, and there is not really this relationship in the population (in nature).

If the IQ pill does nothing, then it would be as if the pill were not present. We already know that the population of IQ scores without the pill has a μ of 100. Therefore, if the pill does not work, then after everyone has taken the pill, IQ scores will be unchanged and μ will still be 100. Thus, if we measured the population with and without the pill, we would have one population of scores, located at the μ of 100, as shown in Figure 13.3.

FIGURE 13.3 Population of Scores if the IQ Pill Does Not Affect IQ Scores

Here, there is no relationship.

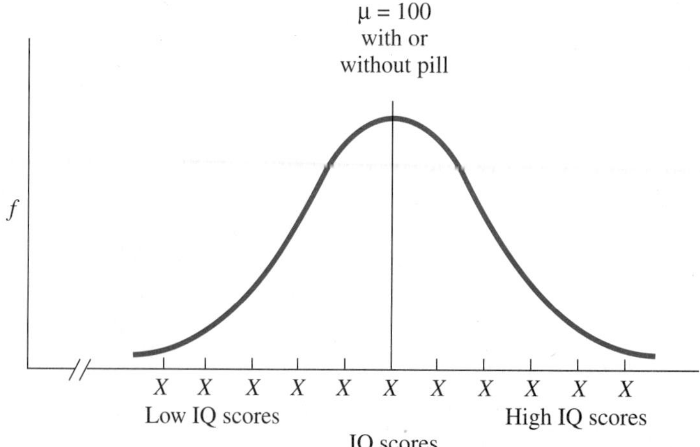

The null hypothesis is a shorthand way of communicating the above. The symbol for the null hypothesis is H_0. (The subscript is 0 because *null* means zero, as in zero relationship.) The null hypothesis for the IQ pill study is

$$H_0: \mu = 100$$

H_0 implies that the sample mean produced with the pill represents a population mean equal to 100. If μ is still 100 with the pill, then there is not the predicted relationship. Thus, H_0 implies that the independent variable really does not work as predicted.

> ***REMEMBER*** The alternative hypothesis (H_a) says that the sample data represent a μ that reflects the predicted relationship. The null hypothesis (H_0) says that the sample data poorly represent the μ that's found when the predicted relationship is not present.

Here's another example: Say we'll measure the creativity of a sample of men to see if they differ from women, and we know that women have a μ of 75 on the creativity test. The two-tailed alternative hypothesis is that men are different from women, so the men's population mean should be different from the women's μ of 75, so H_a: $\mu \neq 75$. The null hypothesis is that, regardless of how the sample of men score, the population of scores for men is the same as for women, so their means are the same, so H_0: $\mu = 75$.

The final step prior to collecting data is to select and set up the appropriate statistical procedure. We'll violate the order of things, however, and go directly to some data so that you can understand what it is we're setting up.

The Logic of Statistical Hypothesis Testing

The statistical hypotheses for the IQ pill study are

$$H_0: \mu = 100$$

$$H_a: \mu \neq 100$$

Notice that, together, H_0 and H_a always include all possibilities, so one or the other must be true: Our sample mean represents either a μ equal to 100 or a μ not equal to 100. Each is a hypothesis—a guess—that may or may not be correct. We use inferential procedures to test (choose between) the hypotheses. To see why we need "statistical hypothesis testing," say that we randomly selected a sample of 36 people, gave them the IQ pill, measured their IQ, and found that the mean IQ score was 105. Can we conclude that the IQ pill works?

We would *like* to say this: People who have not taken the pill have a mean IQ of 100. If the pill did not work, then the sample mean should have been 100. Therefore, a sample mean of 105 suggests that the pill does work, raising IQ scores about 5 points. If the pill does this for the sample, it should do this for the population. Therefore, we expect that a population that received the pill would have a μ of 105. Our results appear to be consistent with our alternative hypothesis, which says that the sample represents a population mean not equal to 100. Thus, it seems that if we measured everyone in the population with and without the pill, we would have the distributions shown previously in Figure 13.1, with the population that received the pill located at a μ of 105.

Conclusion: We have demonstrated a relationship such that increasing the amount of the pill from 0 to 1 is associated with increasing IQ scores.

But hold on! Not so fast! Remember sampling error? We just assumed that the sample is *perfectly* representative of the population it represents. But what if there *was* sampling error? Maybe we obtained a mean of 105, not because the pill works, but because we inaccurately represented the situation where the pill does *not* work. Maybe the pill does nothing, but, by chance, we happened to select participants who already had a high IQ. Thus, maybe the null hypothesis is correct: Even though it does not look like it, maybe the sample represents the population where μ is still 100. Maybe we have not demonstrated that the pill works.

In fact, we can never *know* whether the IQ pill works based on the results of one study. Whether the sample mean is 105, 1050, or 105,000, it is still possible that the null hypothesis is true: The pill doesn't work, the sample actually represents the population where μ is 100, and the sample mean is different from 100 because of sampling error.

> ***REMEMBER*** The null hypothesis always maintains that the sample data reflect sampling error and thus that there is not really the predicted relationship in the population.

Thus, whenever we obtain sample data that show the predicted relationship, we cannot automatically generalize to the population, because there are always two things that can produce such data: sampling error or a real relationship in nature. Essentially, H_0 says that sampling error produced the sample relationship, and so we should not believe there is a corresponding relationship in nature. The H_a says that there is a relationship in nature that produced the sample relationship, so that we can believe that nature operates as the sample data suggest.

The only way to resolve this dilemma for certain is to measure the population and see if the relationship exists. Thus, to know whether the pill actually works, we would have to give it to the entire population and see whether μ was 100 or 105. We cannot do that. But, although we can never *prove* whether the null hypothesis is true, we can determine how *likely* it is to be true. That is, we can determine the probability that sampling error would produce a sample mean of 105 when the sample actually comes from the population where μ is 100. If such a mean is "too unlikely," then we'll reject H_0, rejecting the idea that the sample poorly represents this population.

If this sounds familiar, it's because it is the procedure discussed in the previous chapter. In fact, all parametric and nonparametric statistics involve this same logic: inferential statistics always test the null hypothesis by determining how likely it is for chance (sampling error) to produce our sample data from the population described by the null hypothesis. If the data are too unlikely, then we conclude that the null hypothesis is the incorrect hypothesis.

The only differences among the different inferential procedures is in their calculations. Therefore, to select the correct procedure, consider whether the experiment's design and the scale of measurement of the dependent variable are appropriate for the procedure. In statistical lingo, consider whether the study meets the *assumptions* of the procedure.

The IQ pill study meets the assumptions of the parametric inferential procedure known as the *z*-test.

TESTING A MEAN WHEN σ_X IS KNOWN: THE z-TEST

You already know how to perform the z-test. The **z-test** is the procedure for computing a z-score for a sample mean on the sampling distribution of means that we've discussed in previous chapters. The formula for the z-test is the formula used in Chapter 9 and again in Chapter 12 (and we'll see it again in a moment). The assumptions of the z-test are

1. We have randomly selected one sample.
2. The dependent variable is at least approximately normally distributed in the population, and it involves an interval or ratio scale.
3. We *know* the mean of the population of raw scores under some other condition of the independent variable.
4. We *know* the true standard deviation of this population (σ_X). (It is *not* estimated using the sample.)

The z-test is appropriate for the IQ pill study because our one sample of IQ scores are from an interval variable, the population of IQ scores without the pill is normally distributed, and we know its σ_X. Say that, from the research literature, we know that in the population where μ is 100, the standard deviation is 15.

> *REMEMBER* The z-test is used in a single-sample experiment if the raw score population's σ_X is known.

After choosing the statistical procedure, we can set up the sampling distribution.

Setting Up the Sampling Distribution for a Two-Tailed Test

In the IQ pill study, H_0 says that the pill does not work, so the sample represents the population without the pill where μ is 100. If H_0 is correct, we "should" have obtained a sample mean of 100. Why did we get a $\overline{X} = 105$? According to H_0, because of chance—a little bit of sampling error. Thus, if H_0 is true, it should be likely for sampling error to produce a sample mean of 105 when we are representing the population where μ is 100. Therefore, to test H_0 we determine how likely a sample mean of 105 is to occur when we are sampling from the raw score population where μ is 100 (and σ_X is 15.) For this, we envision the sampling distribution of means created from this raw score population. It is as if we have again hired the (very) bored statistician. Using our N of 36, she infinitely samples the IQ raw score population without the pill, where μ is 100. This will produce a sampling distribution of means with a μ of 100. Notice, the μ of the sampling distribution always equals the value of μ given in the null hypothesis. Here, H_0 says our sample represents the population where $\mu = 100$, so we examine the sampling distribution of all means we might get from this population, and there the average sample mean (the sampling distribution μ) is also 100.

> *REMEMBER* The μ of the sampling distribution always equals the value described by H_0.

You can call the sampling distribution the H_0 sampling distribution, because it describes the situation *when null is true*: Here it describes all possible random samples from a population where μ *is* 100. Any sample mean not equal to 100 occurs *solely* because of sampling error—the luck of the draw that determined who was selected for that particular sample. In the pill study, the sampling distribution essentially shows the frequency distribution of all of the $\overline{X}$s we might get when the pill doesn't work. (Always add the phrase "when null is true" to any information you get from a sampling distribution.)

Once you envision the sampling distribution, set up the statistical test in the same way as in the previous chapter: Determine the size and location of the region of rejection, and identify the critical value. The finished distribution is shown in Figure 13.4. To get there, however, we have some new symbols and terms.

1. *Choosing alpha*: Recall from Chapter 12 that the *criterion* is the probability that defines sample means as "too unlikely" to be representing the underlying raw score population, which in turn defines the size of the region of rejection. The symbol for the criterion is α, the Greek letter **alpha**. Psychologists usually set their criterion at .05, so in code they say $\alpha = .05$, meaning that the region of rejection is the extreme 5% of the curve.

2. *Locating the region of rejection in the two-tailed test*: Recall that the region of rejection may involve either both tails or only one tail of the sampling distribution. Our pill study involves two-tailed hypotheses, so we have a two-tailed test. This is because we predicted that the pill would make people either smarter or dumber than those without the pill. Those without the pill have a $\mu = 100$, so we would be happy if our $\overline{X}$ is either larger than 100 or smaller than 100 and, in either case, unlikely to be representing the population in which $\mu = 100$. On the sampling distribution, the sample means above or below 100 that are unlikely are those in the tail. Therefore, as shown in Figure 13.4, we place part of the region of rejection in each tail. (Anytime we have two-tailed hypotheses and a two-tailed test, part of the region of rejection is in each tail of the sampling distribution.)

3. *Determining the critical value*: The critical value of z is abbreviated as z_{crit}. Recall that with $\alpha = .05$, the two tails together make up 5% of the distribution, so the region of rejection in each tail is 2.5% of the distribution. From the z-tables, a z of 1.96 demarcates this region, and so we complete Figure 13.4 by adding that z_{crit} is ± 1.96.

The next step is to calculate the z-score for our sample mean.

Computing the z-Test

Here is some more code. The z-score we compute is "obtained" from the data, so it is called *z obtained*, which we abbreviate as z_{obt}. You know how to compute this from previous chapters.

THE COMPUTATIONAL FORMULA FOR THE z-TEST IS

$$z_{obt} = \frac{\overline{X} - \mu}{\sigma_{\overline{X}}}$$

FIGURE 13.4 H_0 Sampling Distribution of IQ Means for a Two-Tailed Test

There is a region of rejection in each tail of the distribution, marked by the critical values of ± 1.96.

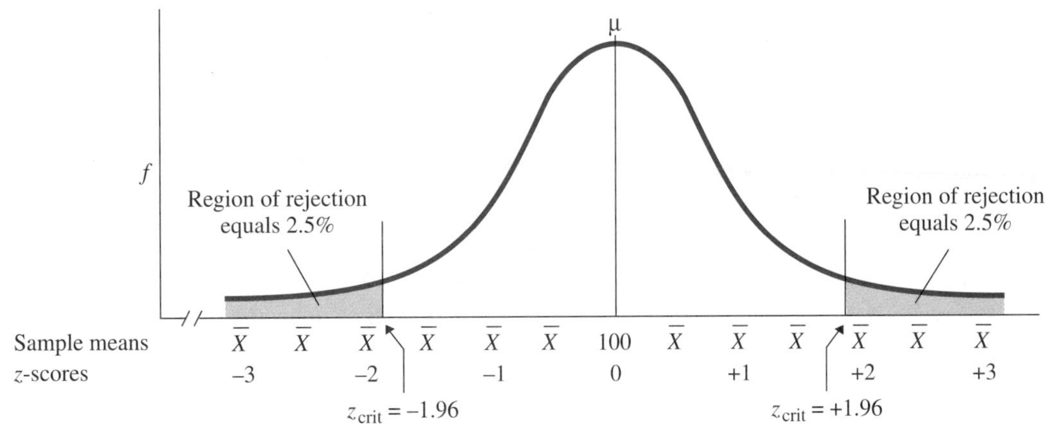

In the formula, $\overline{X}$ is the value of our sample mean, μ is the mean of the sampling distribution when H_0 is true (the μ of the raw score population that H_0 says the sample represents), and $\sigma_{\overline{X}}$ is the standard error of the mean, which is computed as

$$\sigma_{\overline{X}} = \frac{\sigma_X}{\sqrt{N}}$$

where N is the N of the sample and σ_X is the true population standard deviation.

For the IQ pill study, the population standard deviation (σ_X) is 15, and N is 36. Thus,

$$\sigma_{\overline{X}} = \frac{\sigma_X}{\sqrt{N}} = \frac{15}{\sqrt{36}} = \frac{15}{6} = 2.5$$

Then, the z-score for our sample mean of 105 is

$$z_{obt} = \frac{\overline{X} - \mu}{\sigma_{\overline{X}}} = \frac{105 - 100}{2.5} = \frac{+5}{2.5} = +2.0$$

Thus, on the sampling distribution from the population where $\mu = 100$ (and $\sigma_{\overline{X}} = 2.5$), our sample mean has a z-score of +2.0.

The final step is to interpret this z_{obt} by comparing it to z_{crit}.

INTERPRETING z_{obt}

Remember that H_0 implied that the pill does not work and that our sample actually represents the raw score population where μ is 100. If we are to believe H_0, then a mean of 105 should be relatively frequent and thus likely to occur when sampling from the raw score population where μ is 100. However, the sampling distribution in Figure 13.5 shows just the opposite. Use the same logic as we used in the previous chapter. A z_{obt} of +2.0 tells us that the bored statistician would very infrequently obtain a sample mean

FIGURE 13.5 Sampling Distribution of IQ Means

The sample mean of 105 is located at $z_{obt} = +2.0$.

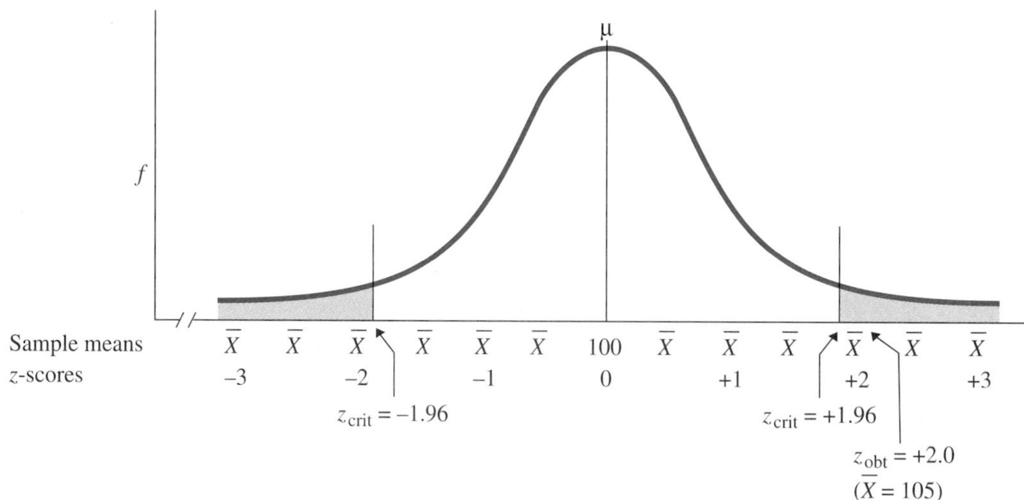

of 105 when she was drawing samples that represent the population where μ is 100. This makes it difficult to believe that we obtained our sample mean by drawing it from the population where μ is 100. In fact, because a z_{obt} of $+2.0$ is beyond the z_{crit} of ± 1.96, the sample mean is in the region of rejection. Therefore, we conclude that our mean of 105 is "too unlikely" to accept as representing the population where $\mu = 100$. That is, the idea that our sample is merely a poor representation of the population where $\mu = 100$ is not reasonable: Samples are seldom *that* poor at representing this population. Therefore, we reject the idea that our sample poorly represents this population.

In statistical terms, we say that we have rejected the null hypothesis. H_0 states that our sample represents the population where μ is 100, and we have found that this is not a reasonable hypothesis. Essentially, if H_0 were true, we "shouldn't" have gotten a sample mean of 105, because a mean of 105 is so unlikely when H_0 is true. Because we did get a mean of 105, it is unlikely that H_0 is true. If we reject H_0, then we are left with H_a, and we also say that we "accept H_a." Here, H_a is $\mu \neq 100$, so we accept that the sample represents a population where μ is not 100. Thus, in sum, we have determined that our sample is unlikely to represent the population where μ is 100, so we conclude that it is likely to represent a population where μ is not 100.

REMEMBER When a sample statistic falls beyond the critical value, the statistic lies in the region of rejection, so we reject H_0 and accept H_a.

Reporting Significant Results

The shorthand way of communicating that we have rejected H_0 and accepted H_a is to use the term *significant*. (Statistical hypothesis testing is sometimes called "significance testing.") *Significant* does *not* mean important or impressive. **Significant** indicates that our results are too unlikely to occur if the predicted relationship does not exist in the population. Therefore, it implies that the relationship found in a study is "believable," representing a "real" relationship found in nature, and that we are not being misled by sampling error.

> ***REMEMBER*** The term *significant* indicates that we have rejected the null hypothesis and believe that our data reflect a real relationship found in nature.

The term *significant* is used in several ways. We might say that the pill produced a "significant difference" in IQ scores. This indicates that the difference between the sample mean and the μ found without the pill is too large to accept as being due to sampling error. Or, we might say that we obtained a "significant z": Our sample mean has too large a z-score to accept that the sample represents the μ described by H_0. Or, we can say that there is a "significant effect of the pill": The change in IQ scores reflected by the sample mean is unlikely to be caused by sampling error, so presumably it is the effect of—caused by—changing the conditions of the independent variable.

It is important to remember that your decision is simply either yes, to reject H_0, or no, to not reject H_0. All z-scores in the region of rejection are treated the same, so one z_{obt} cannot be "more significant" than another. Likewise, there is no such thing as "very significant" or "highly significant." (That's like saying "very yes" or "highly yes.") If z_{obt} is beyond z_{crit}, regardless of how far it is beyond, you completely and fully reject H_0, and the results are simply significant, period!

But, also, recognize that whether a result is significant depends on how you define "unlikely." *Significant* implicitly means that *given your* α and therefore the size of your region of rejection, you have decided that the data are unlikely to represent the population described by the null hypothesis. Therefore, anytime you report the results of a statistical test, indicate the statistic computed, the obtained value, and the α used. Thus, to report our significant z_{obt} of +2.0, we would write

$$z_{obt} = +2.0, \ p < .05$$

Notice that instead of indicating that α equals .05, we indicate that the probability (p) is less than .05, or $p < .05$. We'll discuss the reason for this shortly.

Interpreting Significant Results

By accepting H_a, we also accept the corresponding experimental hypothesis that the independent variable works as predicted: Apparently, the IQ pill study demonstrated that the pill works. However, there are three very important restrictions on how far we can go in claiming that the pill works.

First, we did not *prove* that H_0 is false. All we have "proven" is that a sample of 36 scores is unlikely to produce a mean of 105 if the scores represent or come from a population where $\mu = 100$ (and σ_X is 15.) However, as the sampling distribution shows, means of 105 do occur once in a while when we *are* representing this population. Maybe the pill did not work, and our sample was simply very unrepresentative. There is *always* that possibility.

Second, the term "significant" indicates only that the *numbers* in the data are unlikely to occur if the sample represents a population of *numbers* in which the relationship does not exist. It does not mean that these numbers accurately reflect our variables, or that the behaviors and constructs are related in the way that we've hypothesized. Thus, by saying we have demonstrated a relationship, we're saying that the sample data reflect *some* variable in nature that is associated with the higher scores we call IQ scores. But that variable may *not* be the pill. In other words, we might have had a confounding: The higher IQ scores in our sample might actually have occurred because participants cheated on the IQ test, or because there was something in the air that made them smarter, or because there were sunspots, or who-knows-what! Only a well-controlled design can eliminate such factors, so as usual, we still must *argue* that it is the pill that produced higher IQ scores.

Finally, assuming that the pill increased IQ scores and produced the mean of 105, then it is logical to assume that if we gave the pill to everyone in the population, the resulting μ would be 105. However, even if the pill works, the μ is probably not *exactly* 105. Our sample may reflect (you guessed it) sampling error! That is, the sample may accurately indicate that the pill influences IQ, but it may not perfectly represent *how much* the pill influences scores. Therefore, if we gave the pill to the population, we might find a μ of 104, or 106, or *any* other value. However, a sample mean of 105 is most likely when the population μ is close to 105, so we would conclude that the μ resulting from our pill is probably *around* 105.

Bearing these qualifications in mind, we can return to our sample mean of 105 and interpret it the way we wanted to several pages back: It looks as if the pill increases IQ scores by about 5 points. But now, we have much greater confidence in this conclusion, because we have determined it is unlikely that we are being misled by sampling error. Therefore, we are more confident that a relationship exists in the population and that we have discovered something about how nature operates. Therefore, we now proceed to interpret and explain the relationship "psychologically," generalizing the results back to the hypothetical constructs, theories, or models that generated the study.

Retaining H_0

For the sake of illustration, let's say that the IQ pill had instead produced a sample mean of 99. Should we conclude that the pill decreases IQ scores, or should we conclude that these data reflect sampling error from the population that occurs with no pill, where μ is 100? Using the z-test, we compute the z-score for the sample as

$$z_{\text{obt}} = \frac{\overline{X} - \mu}{\sigma_{\overline{X}}} = \frac{99 - 100}{2.5} = \frac{-1.0}{2.5} = -.40$$

Thus, this sample mean has a z_{obt} of $-.40$. As usual, we examine the sampling distribution, shown in Figure 13.6. A z_{obt} of $-.40$ is *not* beyond the z_{crit} of ± 1.96, so the sample mean does not lie in the region of rejection. As the figure shows, when the bored statistician sampled the population where μ is 100, she frequently obtained a mean of 99. Thus, a sample mean of 99 was likely to have occurred through sampling error if we were representing this population. Therefore, the null hypothesis—that our sample is merely a poor representation of a population where μ is 100—is a reasonable hypothesis. In other words, our sample mean of 99 was likely to have occurred if the pill does not work, so we will not conclude that the pill works. Likewise, we *never* conclude that

FIGURE 13.6 Sampling Distribution of IQ Means

The sample mean of 99 has a z_{obt} of −.40.

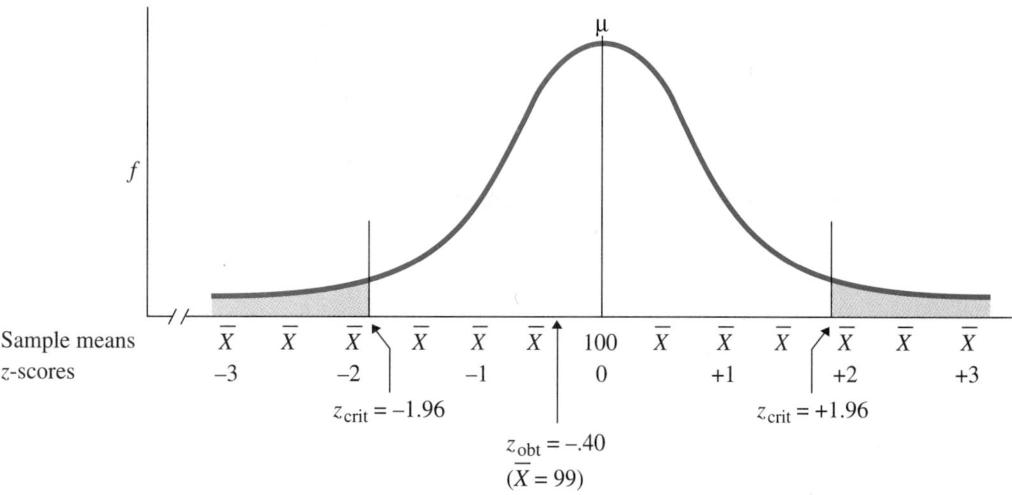

an independent variable works if the results are likely to be due to sampling error. So, we say that we have "failed to reject H_0" or that we "retain H_0." This conveys that using the idea of a little sampling error from the population where μ is 100 can explain these results just fine, thank you, so we will not reject this explanation.

The shorthand way to communicate all of this is to say that we have nonsignificant results. (Don't say *insignificant.*) **Nonsignificant** indicates that results are *not* too unlikely to accept as being due to sampling error. In other words, the differences reflected by the results were likely to have occurred by chance, without there being a relationship in the population.

> ***REMEMBER*** Nonsignificant means that we have failed to reject H_0 because the results are not in the region of rejection, so they are likely to occur when there is no relationship in nature.

When a result is not significant, we again report the α level used in making the decision. Thus, to report our nonsignificant z_{obt} when $\alpha = .05$, we would write

$$z_{obt} = -0.40, \ p > .05$$

Notice that with nonsignificant results, we indicate that *p* is *greater* than .05.

Interpreting Nonsignificant Results

When we retain H_0, we also retain the corresponding experimental hypothesis that the independent variable did not work as expected. However, we have not proven that the pill does *not* work. We have simply failed to find convincing evidence that the pill *does* work. The only thing we are sure of is that sampling error *could* have produced our data if there was no relationship. Thus, by failing to reject H_0, we still have two contradictory hypotheses that are both viable: (1) H_0, that the data only reflect sampling error and do not really represent a relationship, and (2) H_a, that the data do represent a real relationship. Thus, we simply don't know if the pill works or not. Maybe, in fact, the pill did not work. Or maybe the pill did work, but it changed scores so little that we were not convinced that it worked. Or maybe the pill would normally change IQ scores greatly, but we did not see this because we have sampling error in representing the different population that would be created.

Thus, when we do not reject H_0, we cannot say anything about whether the independent variable actually influences behavior or not, and we do not even begin to interpret the results psychologically. All that we can say is that we have failed to find a significant difference, and thus we have failed convincingly to demonstrate that the predicted relationship exists.

> ***REMEMBER*** Nonsignificant results provide no convincing evidence—one way or the other—as to whether a relationship exists in nature.

You cannot design a study that is intended to show that no relationship exists. For example, you could not run a study to demonstrate that the pill does not work. At best, you'll end up retaining both H_0 and H_a, and at worst, you'll end up rejecting H_0, showing that it does work.

SUMMARY OF STATISTICAL HYPOTHESIS TESTING

The steps and logic we've discussed are used in all inferential procedures, so it's worthwhile to review them. In any experiment, after creating the experimental hypotheses and designing the study to demonstrate the predicted relationship, you then

1. Create the statistical hypotheses: H_0 describes the population mean that the sample mean represents if the predicted relationship does *not* exist. H_a describes the population mean that the sample mean represents if the predicted relationship *does* exist.
2. Select the appropriate parametric or nonparametric procedure by matching the assumptions of the procedure to the study.
3. Select the value of α, which determines the size of the region of rejection.
4. Collect the data and compute the obtained value of the inferential statistic. This is analogous to finding a *z*-score for the sample data on the sampling distribution.
5. Set up the sampling distribution for a one- or two-tailed test, and, based on α, determine the critical value.
6. Compare the obtained value to the critical value.
7. If the obtained value lies beyond the critical value and so is in the region of rejection, reject H_0, accept H_a, and describe the results as significant. Then, describe and interpret the relationship in the population based on the sample data.
8. If the obtained value does not lie beyond the critical value and so is not in the region of rejection, do not reject H_0, and describe the results as nonsignificant. Do *not* draw any conclusions about the relationship.

THE ONE-TAILED TEST

Sometimes, we predict that scores will only increase or only decrease, and then we perform a one-tailed test. Recall, a *one-tailed test* is used when we predict the *direction* in which scores will change. The statistical hypotheses and the sampling distribution are different in a one-tailed test.

The One-Tailed Test for Increasing Scores

Say that we had developed a "smart" pill. Then, the experimental hypotheses are (1) the pill makes people smarter by increasing IQ scores, or (2) the pill does not make people smarter.

For the statistical hypotheses, start with the alternative hypothesis, which again follows the experimental hypothesis that the independent variable works as predicted. Here, people without the pill have a μ of 100, so if the pill worked for everyone, it would *increase* the population of IQ scores so that μ would be greater than 100. In symbols, this alternative hypothesis is H_a: $\mu > 100$. On the other hand, H_0 implies that the independent variable does not work as predicted. A "smart pill" does not work if it either leaves IQ scores unchanged or *decreases* them (making people dumber). Then, μ will either equal 100 or be less than 100. Therefore, H_0: $\mu \leq 100$.

As usual, we test H_0 by examining the sampling distribution that describes the sample means that occur when H_0 is true. The population of raw scores we will use to create the sampling distribution is the one in which $\mu = 100$. This is because, if the population μ with the pill is above 100, then it is automatically above any value less than 100.

> ***REMEMBER*** A one-tailed null hypothesis always includes a population parameter *equal* to some value. Test H_0 by testing whether the sample data represent that population.

We again set $\alpha = .05$, but because we have a one-tailed test, the entire region of rejection is in *one tail* of the sampling distribution. You can identify which tail to put it in by identifying the result you must see in order to claim that your independent variable works as predicted. To say that the smart pill works, we must conclude that the sample mean represents a μ larger than 100. To do that, first, the sample mean itself must be larger than 100 (if not, then not even the people in the sample are smarter than people not given the pill). Second, the sample mean must be *significantly* larger than 100. Means that are significant and larger than 100 are in the region of rejection in the upper tail of the sampling distribution. Therefore, we place the entire region of rejection in the upper tail, to form the sampling distribution shown in Figure 13.7. We don't place anything in the lower tail, because for this study, sample means down there are not different from means close to 100: All show that the smart pill doesn't work, and we are not interested in distinguishing between whether it doesn't work because it has no influence on IQ or because it makes people dumber. Finally, we identify the critical value. As in the previous chapter, the region of rejection in the upper tail of the distribution that constitutes 5% of the curve is marked by a z_{crit} of $+1.645$.

Say that after testing the pill on a sample ($N = 36$), we find $\overline{X} = 106.58$. The sampling distribution is still based on the population where $\mu = 100$ and $\sigma_X = 15$, so using

FIGURE 13.7 Sampling Distribution of IQ Means for a One-Tailed Test of Whether Scores Increase

The region of rejection is entirely in the upper tail.

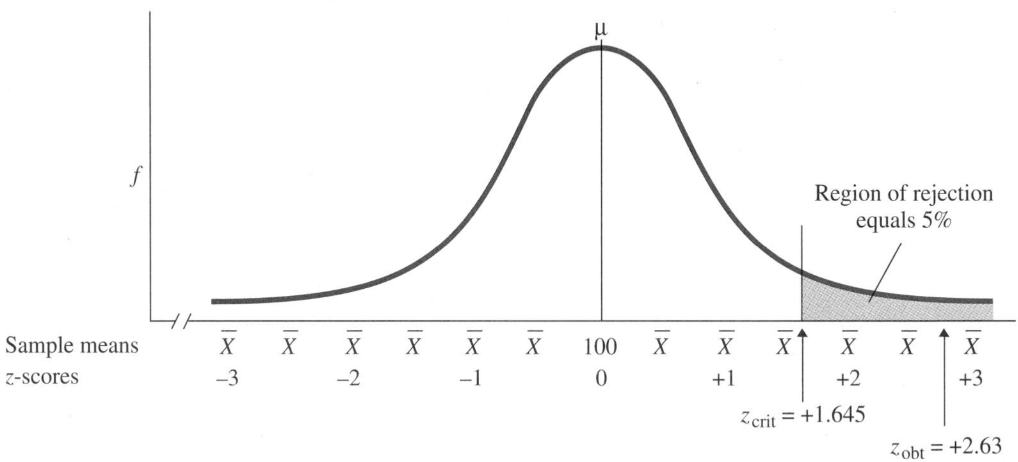

the previous data and formula for the z-test, this sample mean has a z-score of (106.58 − 100)/2.5, which is +2.63. As shown in Figure 13.7, this z_{obt} is beyond the z_{crit}, so it is in the region of rejection. Therefore, the sample mean is unlikely to be representing the population where $\mu = 100$. If the sample is unlikely to represent the population where μ is 100, then it is even more unlikely to represent a population where μ is *less than* 100. Therefore, we reject the null hypothesis that $\mu \leq 100$, and accept the alternative hypothesis that $\mu > 100$. We conclude that the pill produces a significant increase in IQ scores, and estimate that with the pill, μ would equal about 106.58 (keeping in mind all of the cautions and qualifications for interpreting significant results that we discussed previously).

If the z_{obt} had not been in the region of rejection, we would have retained H_0, and we would have no evidence as to whether the smart pill works or not.

The One-Tailed Test for Decreasing Scores

Say instead that we had created a pill to lower IQ scores. If the pill works and we gave it to the entire population, the population μ would be *less than* 100, so H_a: $\mu < 100$. On the other hand, if the pill does not work, it would produce the same population as no pill (with $\mu = 100$), or it would make people smarter (with $\mu > 100$), so H_0: $\mu \geq 100$.

Again, we test the null hypothesis, using the sampling distribution where μ is 100. But the only way to conclude that the pill lowers IQ is if our sample mean is significantly *less* than 100. Therefore, the region of rejection is in the lower tail of the distribution, as shown in Figure 13.8

With $\alpha = .05$, the z_{crit} is now *minus* 1.645. If the sample mean produces a *negative* z_{obt} beyond −1.645 (for example, $z_{obt} = -1.69$), then we reject the H_0 that the sample mean represents a μ equal to or greater than 100, and we accept the H_a that the sample represents a μ less than 100. However, if z_{obt} does not fall in the region of rejection (for example, if $z_{obt} = -1.25$), we do not reject H_0, and we have no evidence as to whether the pill works or not.

FIGURE 13.8 Sampling Distribution of IQ Means for a One-Tailed Test of Whether Scores Decrease

The region of rejection is entirely in the lower tail.

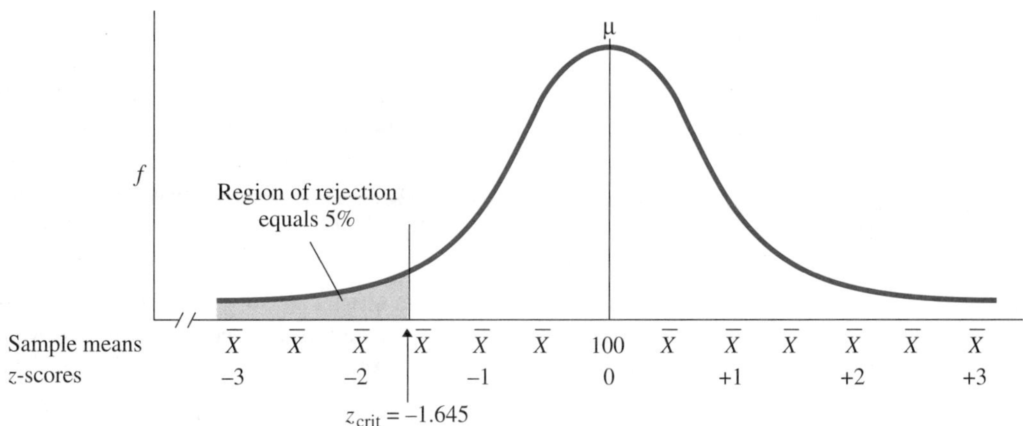

Choosing One-Tailed versus Two-Tailed Tests

In the previous one-tailed tests, there is a region of rejection in only one tail, so z_{obt} is significant only if it lies beyond z_{crit} *and* has the same sign as z_{crit}. This means that, technically, you could not reject H_0 if the pills worked opposite to the way you predicted they would work. And, you cannot move the region of rejection after the results are in to make them significant. If the smart pill actually lowered scores, you would not switch and say, "Whoops, I meant to say it decreased scores." The tail you use is determined by your hypothesis, and, after years of developing the theoretical and biochemical basis for a "smart pill," it would make no sense to suddenly say that the same basis leads you to predict it's a "dumb pill." Likewise, it makes no sense to switch between a one-tailed and a two-tailed test after the fact.

Therefore, use a one-tailed test *only* if you have a *convincing* reason for predicting the direction in which the independent variable will change the dependent scores. Otherwise, use a two-tailed test. This is safer, because it allows you to conclude that the independent variable produced a change, even if you could not accurately predict whether it would increase or decrease scores.

> ***REMEMBER*** Use a two-tailed test unless you have a good reason for predicting the direction in which scores will change.

ERRORS IN STATISTICAL DECISION MAKING

There is one other issue to consider when performing hypothesis testing, and it involves potential errors. These are not errors in our calculations, but rather they are errors in our decisions: Regardless of whether we conclude that sample data do or do not represent the predicted relationship, we may be wrong.

Type I Errors: Rejecting H_0 when H_0 Is True

Sometimes, the variables we investigate really are not related in nature, and so H_0 is really true. It's possible that when in this situation, we will obtain data that cause us to reject H_0. If so, we will make what is called a Type I error. A **Type I error** is rejecting H_0 when H_0 is true. In practical terms, it is concluding that the independent variable works when it really doesn't.

Thus, previously, when we rejected H_0 with our IQ pill, it is possible that the pill did not work and we made a Type I error. How could this happen? Because our sample was exactly what the sampling distribution indicated it was: a very unlikely and unrepresentative sample from the population where μ is 100. Essentially, the sample so poorly represented the situation where the pill did not work that we mistakenly thought the pill did work.

In a Type I error, there is so much sampling error that we—and the statistical procedures—are fooled into concluding that the predicted relationship exists when it really does not.

Any time researchers discuss Type I errors, it is a given that H_0 is true. Thus, think of it as sometimes we are in the "Type I situation" where the predicted relationship does not exist. In this situation, you may or may not make a mistake. If you reject H_0 in this situation, then you've *made* a Type I error: You rejected H_0 when you shouldn't have. If you retain H_0 in this situation, then you've *avoided* making a Type I error: You've made the correct decision by concluding there is no evidence that the pill works, and the pill really doesn't work.

We never know if we're making a Type I error, because only nature knows if our variables are related or not. The best we can do is determine the *probability* of making a Type I error. The probability of a Type I error is the probability of saying "reject" *on those times when H_0 is true*. This probability is determined by the size of the region of rejection, so the theoretical probability of a Type I error is α. Here's why.

For the IQ pill, for example, Figure 13.9 shows the sampling distribution of all of the means that can happen when H_0 is true—100% of the time when we are in the Type I situation. With $\alpha = .05$, the total region of rejection is 5% of the distribution, so sample

FIGURE 13.9 Sampling Distribution of Sample Means Showing That 5% of All Sample Means Fall in the Region of Rejection when H_0 Is True

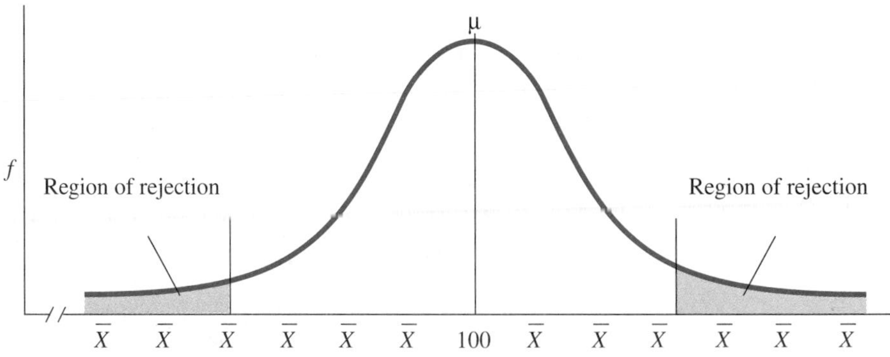

means that are in the region of rejection occur 5% of the time. But, H_0 is true, so these means will cause us to *erroneously* reject H_0, and they occur 5% of the time. In other words, over the long run, the relative frequency of Type I errors is .05. Therefore, when we reject H_0, the theoretical probability is .05 that we've made a Type I error. (The same is true in a one-tailed test.)

You either will or will not make the correct decision in the situation where H_0 is true. If α is the probability of making a Type I error, then $1 - \alpha$ is the probability of avoiding a Type I error by retaining H_0 when it is true. That's because, if samples are in the region of rejection on 5% of the time when H_0 is true, then 95% of the time they are not in the region of rejection when H_0 is true. Thus, over the long run, 95% of the time we will not obtain sample means that cause us to erroneously reject H_0. Therefore, anytime we retain H_0 when $\alpha = .05$, the theoretical probability is .95 that we've avoided a Type I error.

> ***REMEMBER*** Sometimes H_0 is true. If we then reject H_0 we've made a Type I error. Its theoretical probability is α. Avoiding a Type I error is retaining H_0 when H_0 is true, and its theoretical probability is $1 - \alpha$.

Here is an important distinction: Although the *theoretical* probability of a Type I error equals α, its *actual* probability is slightly less than α. This is because in figuring the size of the region of rejection, we include the critical value. Yet, to reject H_0, z_{obt} must be *larger* than the critical value. We cannot determine the precise area under the curve for the infinitely small point located at z_{crit}, so we can't remove it from the 5%. All that we can say is that when α is .05, any z_{obt} that falls in the region of rejection is in less than 5% of the curve. Because the actual region of rejection is less than α, the actual probability of a Type I error is also less than α.

Now, you can understand the reason that psychologists typically set α at .05: We want to minimize the probability of making a Type I error. The problem with an α greater than .05 is that, then, we are too likely to conclude there is a relationship in nature when actually there is not. This may not sound like a big deal, but the next time you're in an airplane, consider that the designer's belief that the wings will stay on may actually be a Type I error: He's been misled by sampling error into *erroneously* thinking the wings will stay on. A 5% chance of this is scary enough—we certainly don't want a larger chance that the wings will fall off. In science, we are skeptical and careful, so we make decisions like a jury: We want to be convinced "beyond a reasonable doubt" that sampling error did not produce our results, and having only a 5% chance that it did is reasonably convincing.

And consider this: With $\alpha = .05$, 5% of all conclusions drawn in psychological research are wrong! Over the long run, we expect to make Type I errors 5% of the time, mistakenly concluding that nature is related in a particular way when, in fact, sampling error produced our results. The trouble is, we don't know which conclusions are wrong. However, recall from Chapter 1 that science requires *replication*—in particular, *literal* (or *exact*) replication. Nature is consistent, so we assume that over repeated studies, erroneous, chance outcomes will not be replicated. Thus, the sampling error needed to erroneously conclude there is a real relationship is unlikely to appear consistently in other studies. Therefore, over time, we will identify those supposed relationships that are actually Type I errors.

In the mean time, in each of the previous examples when we rejected H_0, the probability of a Type I error was slightly less than .05. That is why we reported a significant result using the symbols "$p < .05$." Think of this as a shortened form of "p(Type I error) $< .05$," indicating that the probability of making a Type I error here is less than .05, and that's why the results are significant. In reporting research, always include this p, so that others will know the probability of a Type I error in your study.

On the other hand, we reported a nonsignificant result using "$p > .05$." Think of this as indicating that we'd need a region of rejection having an area *greater* than the one being used in order for our results to lie in the region. A bigger region would mean a bigger alpha ("greater than .05"). However, that's not allowed, because then the probability of a Type I error would be too great. Instead, because the results are not in the region defined by our α, they are not significant.

Type I errors are the reason a study must meet the assumptions of a statistical procedure. If we violate the assumptions, then the actual probability of a Type I error will be larger than α. If, for example, $\alpha = .05$, but we severely violate a procedure's assumptions, the actual probability of a Type I error may turn out to be, say, .20! But recall that parametric tests are "robust." This means that we can violate the assumptions of a procedure somewhat, and the probability of a Type I error will still be close to α (it will be only, say, .051 when we think it is .050).

Sometimes making a Type I error is so dangerous that we want to reduce its probability even further. Then, we usually set alpha at .01. For example, we might make $\alpha = .01$ if the smart pill had some dangerous side effects. We would be especially concerned about needlessly exposing the public to such dangers if the pill is actually worthless, so we would want to decrease the likelihood of concluding the pill works when it really does not. When α is .01, the region of rejection is the extreme 1% of the sampling distribution and we have a larger absolute critical value. Then, we will reject H_0 only 1% of the time when it is true, so the probability of making a Type I error is now $p < .01$.

Remember, however, that we use the term significant in an all-or-nothing fashion: A result is not "more" significant when α is .01 than when it is .05. If z_{obt} falls in any region of rejection, then the result is significant, period! The only difference is that, when α is .01, there is a smaller probability we've made a Type I error.

Finally, many computer programs indicate the exact probability of a Type I error for a result. For example, "$p = .02$" indicates that the z_{obt} falls in the extreme 2% of the sampling distribution, and thus, the probability of a Type I error here is .02. If our α is .05, then this result would fall in the region of rejection, so it is significant. However, the computer might produce "$p = .07$," which indicates that to call this result significant, we'd need a region of rejection that is the extreme 7% of the sampling distribution. Because this implies an α of .07, which is greater than .05 and thus too big, this result is not significant.

Type II Errors: Retaining H_0 when H_0 Is False

In addition to Type I errors, it is possible to make a totally different kind of error. Sometimes, the variables we investigate really are related in nature, and so H_0 is really false. When in this situation, if we obtain data that cause us to retain H_0, then we make a Type II error. A **Type II error** is retaining H_0 when H_0 is false (and H_a is true). With a Type II error, we conclude that we have no evidence for the predicted relationship in the population, when, in fact, the relationship exists. In practical terms, we fail to identify that the independent variable really does work.

Thus, when we retained H_0 with the sample mean of 99 and did not claim the pill worked, it is possible that the pill *did* work and that we made a Type II error. How could this happen? Because the sample mean of 99 was so close to the μ without the pill of 100 that the difference could be easily explained as sampling error, so we were not convinced a relationship was really present. But! Perhaps what we missed is that the pill only slightly decreases IQ, dropping everyone's score about 1 point to a μ of only 99. Or perhaps the pill actually increases IQ greatly, say to a μ of 105, but we obtained an unrepresentative sample of this. Either way:

> **in a Type II error, the sample mean is so close to the μ described by H_0 that we—and our statistics—are fooled into concluding that sampling error produced the results when, in fact, the predicted relationship exists.**

Anytime we discuss Type II errors, it is a given that H_0 is false and H_a is true. Thus, we are in the "Type II situation" whenever we discuss those times that the predicted relationship does exist. In this situation, we may or may not make a mistake. If we retain H_0, we make a Type II error. If we reject H_0, we *avoid* making a Type II error: We've made the correct decision by concluding that the pill works when the pill really does work.

The computation of the probability of Type II errors is beyond the scope of this discussion, but you should know that the symbol for the theoretical probability of a Type II error is β, (the Greek letter **beta**). Thus, when we retain H_0, β is the probability that we have just made a Type II error. On the other hand, $1 - \beta$ is the probability of avoiding a Type II error. Thus, when we reject H_0, the probability is $1 - \beta$ that we have made a correct decision and rejected a false H_0.

> ***REMEMBER*** When H_0 is false, a Type II error is retaining H_0, and its theoretical probability is β. Avoiding a Type II error is rejecting H_0 when H_0 is false, and its theoretical probability is $1 - \beta$.

Comparing Type I and Type II Errors

There's no doubt that Type I and Type II errors are two of the most confusing inventions ever devised. So, first recognize that Type I and Type II errors are mutually exclusive: If there's a possibility we've made one type of error, then there is no chance of making the other type of error. A Type I error is saying "reject" when we shouldn't, so if we reject, then maybe we've made this error. But then there is no chance of a Type II error, because this is saying "retain" when we shouldn't, and we did not say retain. Likewise, saying "retain" makes it impossible to make a Type I error.

Second, if you don't make one type of error, then you are not automatically making the other error. Remember: In the Type I *situation*, H_0 is really true (the variables are not related). In the Type II *situation*, H_0 is really false (the variables are related). You can't be in both situations simultaneously, because variables can't be both related and not related at the same time. Therefore, the type of error you can *potentially* make is determined by your situation—what nature "says" about the relationship. Then, whether you make the error depends on whether you agree or disagree with nature.

Thus, there are actually four possible outcomes in any study. Look at Table 13.1.

TABLE 13.1 Possible Results of Rejecting or Retaining H_0

		Our decision	
		We reject H_0 (claim H_a is true)	***We retain H_0 (claim H_0 may be true)***
The truth about H_0	***H_0 is true (H_a is false: no relationship exists)***	We make a Type I error ($p = \alpha$)	We are correct, avoiding a Type I error ($p = 1 - \alpha$)
	H_0 is false (H_a is true: a relationship exists)	We are correct, avoiding a Type II error ($p = 1 - \beta$)	We make a Type II error ($p = \beta$)

As in the upper row of the table, sometimes (though we never know when) H_0 really is true. Then, our decision to reject H_0 is a Type I error (with a $p = \alpha$). But, if we retain H_0, we avoid a Type I error and make the correct decision (with $p = 1 - \alpha$). Conversely, as in the lower row of the table, sometimes (we also never know when) H_0 is really false. Then, deciding to retain H_0 is a Type II error (with $p = \beta$). But, if we reject H_0, we avoid a Type II error and make the correct decision (with $p = 1 - \beta$).

In any experiment, the results of the inferential procedure will place us in one of the two columns. If we reject H_0, either we've made a Type I error or we've made the correct decision and avoided a Type II error. If we retain H_0, either we've made a Type II error or we've made the correct decision and avoided a Type I error.

Statistical procedures are designed to minimize the probability of Type I errors because the most serious mistake is to conclude that an independent variable works when really it does not. Basing scientific "facts" on what are actually Type I errors can cause untold damage. On the other hand, Type II errors are also important. In order for us to learn about nature, we must avoid Type II errors and conclude that an independent variable works when it really does. This brings us back to the idea of "power."

The Power of a Statistical Test

The goal of scientific research is to reject H_0 when H_0 is false: We conclude that the pill works, and the truth is that the pill does work. Not only have we avoided making an error, but we have also learned about a relationship in nature. This ability is so important that it has a special name: **Power** is the probability that we will reject H_0 when it is false, correctly concluding that the sample data reflect a real relationship. Essentially, power is the probability that we will not miss a real relationship in nature. Missing the relationship is a Type II error, so power is the probability that we will not make a Type II error. Thus, power equals $1 - \beta$.

Power is important because, after all, why bother to conduct a study if we are unlikely to reject the null hypothesis even when the predicted relationship really *does* exist? Therefore, whether we have sufficient power is crucial whenever we decide to *retain* H_0. For example, previously, when we failed to find a significant effect of the pill, we would worry that the problem was that we lacked power: Maybe the probability was not high that we would reject H_0, *even if the pill really worked.* Therefore, we always want to maximize the power of a study, so that we'll have confidence in our decision if we ultimately retain H_0. Essentially, the idea is this: We do everything we can to ensure that, in case we end up in the Type II situation where there *is* a relationship in nature, we—and our statistics—will be unlikely to miss it. If we still end up retaining H_0, we know it's not for lack of trying. We're confident that if a relationship was out there, we would have found it. Therefore, we are confident in the decision to retain H_0, and in statistical lingo, we say that we're confident we have avoided a Type II error.

> *REMEMBER* We seek to maximize power so that if we retain H_0, we are confident we are not making a Type II error.

The time to build in power is when designing a study. We are talking about those times we are in the Type II situation, so H_0 is false and we should reject it. In other words, our results should be *significant*. Therefore, anything that increases the likelihood that results are significant increases power. Results are significant if z_{obt} is larger than z_{crit}, so anything that increases the size of the obtained value relative to the critical value increases the probability that the results will be significant and thus increases power.

> *REMEMBER* The larger the obtained value, the more likely it is to be significant and thus the greater the power.

If it sounds like we're rigging the decision to reject H_0, remember this: With α at .05 or less, we minimize the probability of making the *wrong* decision when H_0 is true (not making a Type I error). At the same time, by maximizing power, we maximize the probability of making the *correct* decision when H_0 is false (not making a Type II error).

There are two approaches to maximizing power. First, previous chapters have discussed designing a *powerful study* by using a *strong manipulation*, eliminating *error variance* within the conditions, and so on. The goal was to produce a more dramatic and more consistent relationship. Intuitively, we are less likely to mistake a strong relationship as resulting from sampling error, because chance is so unlikely to produce stronger ones. (For example, its impossible to believe that chance could produce a relationship where the correlation coefficient is ± 1, so we won't make a mistake here!) Inferential statistics reflect the strength of the relationship in that a stronger relationship translates into a larger obtained value that is more likely to be significant.

The second approach for maximizing power is to employ *powerful statistics*. For example, previously, I said we use nonparametric procedures only if we cannot use parametric procedures. This is because parametric tests are more powerful than nonparametric tests: If we analyze data using a parametric test, we are more likely to reject H_0 than if we analyze the same data using a nonparametric test. Therefore, we try to design research that incorporates parametric procedures.

In addition, a one-tailed test is more powerful than a two-tailed test. This is because the z_{crit} for a one-tailed test is smaller than the z_{crit} for a two-tailed test. Previously, we used a z_{crit} of 1.645 for a one-tailed test and 1.96 for a two-tailed test. All other things being equal, any z_{obt} is more likely to be beyond 1.645 than beyond 1.96. Thus, we are more likely to conclude that results are significant with a one-tailed test than with a two-tailed test. (But remember that here we can reject H_0 only if z_{obt} has the same sign as z_{crit}.)

In later chapters we'll see additional ways to maximize power.

APA FORMAT FOR STATISTICAL NOTATION

The latest APA rules require that a research report explicitly state the alpha level being used, saying something like "I set alpha at .05." Then, report the results of each inferential test as shown in this chapter: Give the symbol for the test (e.g., z), the obtained value, and then indicate whether p is greater than or less than alpha (e.g., $p < .05$ if the results are significant, or $p > .05$ if they are not). In addition to this code, however, always also clearly say whether you consider a result to be significant or not significant.

PUTTING IT ALL TOGETHER

Essentially, the purpose of inferential statistics is to minimize the probability of making Type I errors. If we had not performed the z-test for the studies in this chapter, we might have concluded that the IQ pills worked, even though we were actually being misled by sampling error. We would have no idea if this occurred, nor even the chances that it occurred. After finding a significant result, however, we can be confident that we have not made a Type I error, because we know the probability of doing so is less than .05. (Similarly, if results are not significant, through the concept of power we can be confident that we have not missed a pill that works.)

There is a rhythm to all inferential procedures that goes like this:

1. Based on the predictions of the study, create the H_0 that describes the populations being represented if the predicted relationship does not exist, and the H_a that describes the populations being represented if the predicted relationship does exist.
2. Envision the sampling distribution showing the sample means that occur when representing the underlying raw score population that H_0 says the data represent.
3. Select alpha and identify the one- or two-tailed critical value that defines the region of rejection.
4. Compute the obtained statistic that, like a z-score, locates the results of the study on the sampling distribution when H_0 is true.
5. If the obtained value is larger than the critical value, it is unlikely that the results represent the populations described by H_0, so reject H_0 and accept H_a, call the results significant, and describe and interpret the relationship we believe exists in nature (but recognize that possibly we've made a Type I error).
6. If the obtained value does not lie beyond the critical value, it is not unlikely that the results represent the populations described by H_0, so retain H_0, call the results nonsignificant, and we are not convinced the relationship exists in nature (but possibly we've made a Type II error).

That's it! That's inferential statistics (well, not quite).

CHAPTER SUMMARY

1. *Sampling error* occurs when random chance produces a sample statistic that is not equal to the population parameter it represents.
2. *Inferential statistics* are for deciding whether sample data represent a particular relationship in the population.
3. *Parametric statistics* are inferential procedures that require assumptions about the parameters of the underlying raw score populations the data represent. They are performed with normally distributed, interval or ratio scores.
4. *Nonparametric statistics* are inferential procedures that do not require assumptions about the population parameters represented by a sample. They are performed when interval or ratio scores are not normally distributed, or when nominal or ordinal scores are being measured.
5. In a *single-sample experiment*, the mean from a sample tested under one condition is used to infer the corresponding μ, and this μ is compared to a known μ for another condition to determine if a relationship exists.
6. The *alternative hypothesis* (H_a) is the statistical hypothesis that describes the population μs being represented if the predicted relationship exists in the population.
7. The *null hypothesis* (H_0) is the statistical hypothesis that describes the population μs being represented if the predicted relationship does not exist.
8. A *two-tailed test* is used when the direction in which the dependent scores will change is not predicted. A *one-tailed test* is used when the direction of the relationship is predicted.
9. *Alpha* (α) is the theoretical size of the region of rejection. Typically, α equals .05.
10. The *z-test* is the parametric procedure used in a single-sample experiment if (a) the population contains interval or ratio scores that are normally distributed and (b) the standard deviation of the raw score population is known.
11. If z_{obt} lies beyond z_{crit}, then the corresponding sample mean lies in the region of rejection. This indicates that the mean is unlikely to occur when sampling from the population described by H_0. Therefore, *reject* H_0 and *accept* H_a. This is called a *significant* result and is taken as evidence that the predicted relationship exists in the population.
12. If z_{obt} does not lie beyond z_{crit}, then the corresponding sample mean is *not* located in the region of rejection. This indicates that the mean is likely to occur when sampling from the population described by H_0. Therefore, we *fail to reject* or we *retain* H_0. This is called a *nonsignificant* result and is taken as a failure to obtain evidence that the predicted relationship exists in the population.
13. A *Type I error* occurs when a true H_0 is rejected. The theoretical probability of a Type I error equals α. If a result is significant, the actual probability of a Type I error is $p < \alpha$. The theoretical probability of avoiding a Type I error by retaining a true H_0 is $1 - \alpha$.

14. A *Type II error* occurs when a false H_0 is retained. The theoretical probability of making a Type II error is β. The theoretical probability of avoiding a Type II error by rejecting a false H_0 is $1 - \beta$.

15. When we reject H_0, we have either made a Type I error or avoided a Type II error. When we retain H_0, we have either made a Type II error or avoided a Type I error.

16. *Power* is the probability of rejecting a false H_0, and it equals $1 - \beta$. When used appropriately, parametric procedures are more powerful than nonparametric procedures, and one-tailed tests are more powerful than two-tailed tests. The manner in which a study is designed and conducted also influences power.

KEY TERMS (with page references)

$\geq$ $\leq$ $\neq$ H_0 H_a α z_{crit} z_{obt} β
alpha (346)
alternative hypothesis (340)
beta (359)
experimental hypotheses (339)
inferential statistics (338)
nonparametric statistics (338)
nonsignificant (351)
null hypothesis (342)
one-tailed test (339)
parametric statistics (338)
power (360)
robust procedure (338)
sampling error (337)
significant (348)
single-sample experiment (340)
statistical hypotheses (340)
two-tailed test (339)
Type I error (356)
Type II error (358)
z-test (345)

REVIEW QUESTIONS

(Answers for odd-numbered questions and problems are provided in Appendix D.)

1. (a) What is sampling error? (b) Why does the possibility of sampling error present a problem to researchers when inferring a population μ from a sample $\overline{X}$?

2. What are inferential statistics used for?

3. What is the difference between a real relationship and one in a sample that results from sampling error?

4. What four things must a researcher do prior to collecting data for a study?

5. (a) What does α stand for, and what two things does it determine? (b) How does the size of α affect whether a result is significant or nonsignificant?

6. (a) What does the term *significant* convey about the results of an experiment? What is a significant result in terms of (b) the obtained and critical value? (c) the region of rejection of the sampling distribution? (d) our likelihood of obtaining our sample mean when H_0 is true? (e) α?

7. (a) Why do researchers prefer parametric procedures? (b) Why can we use parametric procedures even if we cannot perfectly meet their assumptions?

8. (a) What are experimental hypotheses? (b) What are statistical hypotheses? (c) What does H_0 communicate? (d) What does H_a communicate?

9. (a) When do you use a one-tailed test? (b) When do you use a two-tailed test?

10. (a) What are the advantage and the disadvantage of two-tailed tests? (b) What are the advantage and the disadvantage of one-tailed tests?

PRACTICE PROBLEMS

11. For each of the following experiments, describe the experimental hypotheses (identifying the independent and dependent variables): (a) Studying whether the amount of pizza consumed by college students during finals week increases relative to the rest of the semester. (b) Studying whether performing breathing exercises alters blood pressure. (c) Studying whether sensitivity to pain is affected by increased levels of hormones. (d) Studying whether frequency of dreaming decreases as a function of more light in the room while sleeping.

12. For each study in problem 11, indicate whether a one-tailed or a two-tailed test should be used, and state the H_0 and H_a. Assume that $\mu = 50$ when the amount of the independent variable is zero.

13. Listening to music while taking a test may be relaxing, or it may be distracting. To determine which, 49 participants are tested while listening to music, and they produce a $\overline{X} = 54.63$. The μ for students who have taken this test without music is 50 ($\sigma_X = 12$). (a) Should we use a one-tailed or two-tailed test? Why? (b) What are H_0 and H_a for this study? (c) Compute z_{obt}. (d) With $\alpha = .05$, what is z_{crit}? (e) Do we have evidence of a relationship in the population? If so, describe the relationship.

14. A researcher wonders whether attending a private high school leads to higher or lower performance on a test of social skills. A random sample of 100 students from a private school produces a mean score of 71.30 on the test, and the national mean score for students from public schools is 75.62 ($\sigma_X = 28$). (a) Should she use a one-tailed or a two-tailed test? Why? (b) What are H_a and H_0 for this study? (c) Compute z_{obt}. (d) With $\alpha = .05$, what is z_{crit}? (e) What should the researcher conclude about this relationship in the population?

15. (a) What is the probability that the researcher in problem 13 made a Type I error? Describe what the error would be using her independent and dependent variables. (b) What is the probability that the researcher in problem 13 made a Type II error? What would the error be in terms of the independent and dependent variables?

16. (a) What is the probability that the researcher in problem 14 made a Type I error? Describe what the error would be using her independent and dependent variables. (b) What is the probability that the researcher in problem 14 made a Type II error? What would the error be in terms of the independent and dependent variables?

17. A researcher hypothesizes that males and females are the same when it comes to intelligence. Why is this hypothesis impossible to test?

18. Researcher A finds a significant negative relationship between increasing stress level and ability to concentrate. Researcher B replicates this study but finds a nonsignificant relationship. Identify the statistical error that each researcher may have made.

19. (a) What is power? (b) Why do researchers want to maximize power? (c) Why is a one-tailed test more powerful than a two-tailed test?

20. A report indicates that Brand X toothpaste significantly reduced tooth decay relative to other brands, with $p < .44$. (a) What does this indicate about the researcher's decision about Brand X? (b) What might make you suspicious of the claim that Brand X works better than other brands?

21. Foofy claims that using a one-tailed test is cheating, because a one-tailed test produces a smaller absolute value of z_{crit}, and therefore it is easier to reject H_0 than it is with a two-tailed test. If the independent variable doesn't work, she claims, we are more likely to make a Type I error. Why is she correct or incorrect?

22. Poindexter claims that the real cheating occurs when we increase power. He reasons that we are more likely to reject H_0 when H_0 is true, and therefore we are more likely to make a Type I error. Why is he correct or incorrect?

23. Bubbles reads a report of Study A, in which the results are significant: $z_{obt} = +1.97, p < .05$. She also reads about Study B, in which $z_{obt} = +14.21$, $p < .0001$. (a) She concludes that the results of Study B are way beyond the critical value used in Study A, falling in a region of rejection containing only .0001 of the sampling distribution. Is she correct or incorrect? (b) She concludes that the results of Study B are more significant than those of Study A. Why is she correct or incorrect? (c) In terms of their conclusions, what is the difference between the two studies?

24. A researcher measures the self-esteem scores of a sample of statistics students, reasoning that their frustration with this topic may lower their self-esteem relative to that of the typical college student (where $\mu = 55$ and $\sigma_X = 11.35$). He obtains the following scores.

44 55 39 17 27 38 36 24 36

(a) Should he use a one-tailed or two-tailed test? Why? (b) What are H_0 and H_a for this study? (c) Compute z_{obt}. (d) With $\alpha = .05$, what is z_{crit}? (e) What should the researcher conclude about the relationship between the self-esteem of statistics students and that of other students?

25. (a) Why is obtaining a significant result the goal of research? (b) Why is declaring the results significant not the final step in conducting a study?

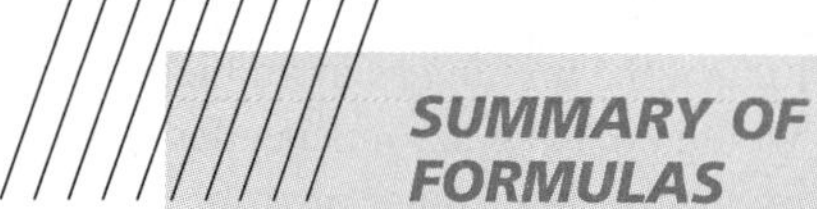

SUMMARY OF FORMULAS

1. *The computational formula for the z-test is*

$$z_{obt} = \frac{\overline{X} - \mu}{\sigma_{\overline{X}}}$$

where $\overline{X}$ is our sample mean and μ is the mean of the sampling distribution when H_0 is true (the μ of the raw score population described by H_0).

2. *The computational formula for the standard error of the mean is*

$$\sigma_{\bar{X}} = \frac{\sigma_X}{\sqrt{N}}$$

where N is our sample N and σ_X is the true population standard deviation.

14

The Single-Sample Study: Testing a Sample Mean or Correlation Coefficient

Getting Started

To understand this chapter, recall the following:

- From Chapter 2, recall the difference between a true and quasi-independent variable.
- From Chapter 8, recall that s_X is the *estimated population standard deviation*, that s_X^2 is the *estimated population variance*, and that both involve degrees of freedom (df) which equals $N - 1$.
- From Chapter 10, recall the uses and interpretation of r, r_s, and r_{pb}.
- From Chapter 13, remember the basics of significance testing.

Your goals in this chapter are to learn:

- The difference between the z-test and the t-test.
- How to perform hypothesis testing using the t-test.
- What the confidence interval for μ is.
- How to perform significance testing of r, r_s, and r_{pb}.
- How to increase the power of a t-test or correlation coefficient.

The statistical hypothesis testing you learned in the previous chapter is second nature to behavioral researchers, whether they're conducting descriptive or experimental research, in the laboratory or in the field. Therefore, the thing for you to learn now is how the procedure is applied to different types of research designs. This chapter begins the process by introducing the "t-test." Like the z-test, the t-test is for a single-sample experiment. You'll also see that the t-test forms the basis for significance testing of a correlation coefficient. Finally, this chapter introduces the confidence interval, a new procedure for describing a population μ. However, the calculations and interpretation of these procedures are extremely similar to those of the z-test. Therefore, much of this chapter contains more of a variation on a theme than brand-new material.

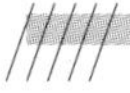

MORE STATISTICAL NOTATION

Officially, the t-test (with a lowercase t) is Student's t-test (although it was developed by a statistician named W. S. Gosset). The answer obtained from the t-test is symbolized by t_{obt}. The critical value of t is symbolized by t_{crit}.

We will again be computing s_X—the estimated population standard deviation—and s_X^2—the estimated population variance. Remember that the formula for s_X was

$$s_X = \sqrt{\frac{\Sigma X^2 - \frac{(\Sigma X)^2}{N}}{N - 1}}$$

To calculate s_X^2, simply don't take the square root.

UNDERSTANDING THE *t*-TEST FOR A SINGLE-SAMPLE MEAN

Recall that an assumption of the z-test is that we know the true standard deviation of the raw score population (σ_X), so that we can compute the true standard error of the mean of the sampling distribution, ($\sigma_{\bar{X}}$). In most actual research, however, we do *not* know the standard deviation of the raw score population. That's because researchers explore unknown and uncharted areas of behavior ("To boldly go where no one has gone . . ." and all that), so usually we know little about the population. Instead, in such situations, we *estimate* the value of σ_X by computing s_X. Then, we use this estimated population standard deviation to compute an *estimate* of the standard error of the mean. Then, we compute something *like* a z-score to locate the sample mean on the H_0 sampling distribution. However, because we are estimating, we are not computing a z-score. Instead, we are computing t_{obt} and performing the single-sample t-test. The **single-sample *t*-test** is the parametric procedure used to test the null hypothesis for a single-sample experiment when the standard deviation of the raw score population must be estimated.

REMEMBER With a one-sample experiment, use the z-test when σ_X is known; use the t-test when σ_X is estimated from s_X.

We are still asking the same question here that we asked in Chapter 13, but the characteristics of our design simply dictate that we use a slightly different procedure to answer it. Here is an example. Say that in one of those "home-and-gardening/good-housekeeper" magazines, there is a test of one's housekeeping abilities. The magazine is targeted at women, and it reports that nationally, the average test score for women is 75 (so their μ is 75), but it does not bother to report the standard deviation. Our question is "How do men score on this test?" To answer it, we'll give the test to a random sample of men (perhaps even using stratified sampling for representativeness), and use their $\overline{X}$ test to estimate the μ of the population of men. Then, we can compare this μ to the μ of 75 for the population of women. If men score differently from women, then we have found a relationship, whereas the (quasi-) independent variable of gender changes, the population of test scores changes.

However! As usual, there are two things that could produce sample data that show such a relationship. First, the men's $\overline{X}$ may be different from 75 because of sampling error while, in fact, men and women actually belong to the one, same population where μ is 75. Or second, it may be that there really is a relationship in nature that causes the men's $\overline{X}$ to be different from 75. To determine the best explanation, we perform the *t*-test. The first step is to set up the test:

1. *The statistical hypotheses*: For the moment, let's be open-minded and look for any kind of difference, so we have a two-tailed test. If men are different from women, then the μ for men will not equal the μ for women of 75, so H_a is $\mu \neq 75$. If men are not different, however, then their μ will equal that of women, so H_0 is $\mu = 75$.
2. *Alpha*: We must select an alpha level: .05 sounds good.
3. *Check the assumptions*: For the single-sample *t*-test, you should be able to assume the following about the *dependent* variable:
    1. There is one random sample of interval or ratio scores.
    2. The raw score population forms a normal distribution.
    3. The standard deviation of the raw score population is estimated by the s_X.

It is acceptable if the data are only somewhat normally distributed, because like all parametric tests, the *t*-test is robust—it produces minimal error even if we violate its assumptions somewhat. This is especially true if N is at least 30.

From reading similar research, we see that the housekeeping study meets these assumptions, so we collect the data. For simplicity, say that we test 9 men. (For maximum power, we never collect so few scores in an actual experiment.) The sample mean turns out to be $\overline{X} = 65.67$, so we'd expect the population of men to score around a μ of 65.67. Because females score around a μ of 75, maybe we have demonstrated a relationship in which changing gender from female to male results in lower housekeeping scores. This would be consistent with H_a. On the other hand, H_0 says that gender is not related to test scores, and we are being misled by sampling error: We selected some exceptionally sloppy men, so the sample poorly represents the male population where $\mu = 75$.

We test this H_0 using exactly the same logic as in the *z*-test. By computing t_{obt}, we locate our sample mean on the sampling distribution of means that occurs when representing the population where μ is 75. If t_{obt} is beyond t_{crit}, our sample mean lies in the region of rejection, so we will reject the idea that the sample represents this population.

The only differences between the *z*-test and the *t*-test are that t_{obt} is not calculated in the same way as z_{obt}, and t_{crit} comes from the *t*-distribution.

CALCULATING THE SINGLE-SAMPLE *t*-TEST

The computation of t_{obt} consists of three steps that parallel the three steps in the *z*-test as shown in Table 14.1.

The first step in the *z*-test was to describe the variability of the raw score population with the true standard deviation (σ_X). For the *t*-test, we compute the estimated standard deviation (s_X) using the formula provided at the beginning of this chapter.

The second step of the *z*-test was to compute the true standard error of the mean ($\sigma_{\overline{X}}$) by dividing σ_X by $\sqrt{N}$. For the *t*-test, we compute the *estimated* standard error of the mean by dividing s_X by $\sqrt{N}$.

THE DEFINITIONAL FORMULA FOR THE ESTIMATED STANDARD ERROR OF THE MEAN IS

$$s_{\overline{X}} = \frac{s_X}{\sqrt{N}}$$

As with $\sigma_{\overline{X}}$, we are finding the standard deviation of the sampling distribution of means. But, because it involves s_X, the **estimated standard error of the mean** is an estimate of the standard deviation of the sampling distribution of means. Notice that the symbol here is $s_{\overline{X}}$: The *s* stands for an estimate of the standard deviation, and the subscript $\overline{X}$ indicates that it is for a distribution of means.

The third step in the *z*-test was to compute z_{obt}, using the formula: $z_{obt} = (\overline{X} - \mu)/\sigma_{\overline{X}}$. The final step in the *t*-test is to compute t_{obt}.

THE DEFINITIONAL FORMULA FOR THE t-TEST FOR A SINGLE-SAMPLE MEAN IS

$$t_{obt} = \frac{\overline{X} - \mu}{s_{\overline{X}}}$$

TABLE 14.1 Comparison of the Steps in Computing the *z*-Test and *t*-Test

Steps	***z-test***	***t-test***
1. Variability of raw scores	true σ_X	estimated s_X
2. Standard error of the mean	$\sigma_{\overline{X}} = \frac{\sigma_X}{\sqrt{N}}$	$s_{\overline{X}} = \frac{s_X}{\sqrt{N}}$
3. Locate $\overline{X}$ on sampling distribution	$z_{obt} = \frac{\overline{X} - \mu}{\sigma_{\overline{X}}}$	$t_{obt} = \frac{\overline{X} - \mu}{s_{\overline{X}}}$

In the formula, $\overline{X}$ is the sample mean, μ is the mean of the H_0 sampling distribution (which equals the value of μ described in the null hypothesis), and $s_{\overline{X}}$ is the estimated standard error of the mean.

Notice the similarity between the formulas for z_{obt} and t_{obt}. The z_{obt} indicates the distance that the sample mean is from the μ of the sampling distribution, measured in units called the standard error of the mean. The t_{obt} measures this distance in estimated standard error units.

Computational Formulas for the Single-Sample *t*-Test

You can compute t_{obt} using the three steps given above, or you can use one of the following computational formulas. First, replacing the symbol $s_{\overline{X}}$ with the formula for computing it gives

$$t_{obt} = \frac{\overline{X} - \mu}{\frac{s_X}{\sqrt{N}}}$$

To shorten the computations, you can avoid taking the square root when computing s_X. Instead, replace the standard deviation with the estimated variance (s_X^2) and take the square root of the entire denominator. Thus,

THE COMPUTATIONAL FORMULAS FOR THE SINGLE-SAMPLE t-TEST ARE

$$t_{obt} = \frac{\overline{X} - \mu}{\sqrt{\frac{s_X^2}{N}}} \quad \text{or} \quad t_{obt} = \frac{\overline{X} - \mu}{\sqrt{(s_X^2)\left(\frac{1}{N}\right)}}$$

You can use either of these formulas. The formula on the left computes $s_{\overline{X}}$ by first dividing s_X^2 by N, and then finding the square root. But, dividing by N is the same as multiplying by $1/N$, so the formula on the right computes $s_{\overline{X}}$ by multiplying s_X^2 times the quantity $1/N$. The final number in the denominator of any of these formulas is still the estimated standard error ($s_{\overline{X}}$).

For our housekeeping study, say we obtained the data in Table 14.2. First, compute s_X^2. Substituting the data into the formula gives

$$s_X^2 = \frac{\Sigma X^2 - \frac{(\Sigma X)^2}{N}}{N - 1} = \frac{39289 - \frac{349281}{9}}{9 - 1} = 60.00$$

Thus, the estimated variance of the population of test scores is 60.

Now, compute t_{obt} for the mean of 65.67 when the population μ is 75, s_X^2 is 60, and N is 9. Filling in a computational formula, we have

$$t_{obt} = \frac{\overline{X} - \mu}{\sqrt{(s_X^2)\left(\frac{1}{N}\right)}} = \frac{65.67 - 75}{\sqrt{(60)\left(\frac{1}{9}\right)}}$$

TABLE 14.2 Test Scores of Nine Participants

Participant	*Scores (X)*	X^2
1	50	2500
2	75	5625
3	65	4225
4	72	5184
5	68	4624
6	65	4225
7	73	5329
8	59	3481
9	64	4096
$N = 9$	$\Sigma X = 591$	$\Sigma X^2 = 39289$
	$(\Sigma X)^2 = 349281$	
	$\overline{X} = 65.67$	

In the denominator, 1/9 is .11, which multiplied times 60 is 6.667. So

$$t_{\text{obt}} = \frac{65.67 - 75}{\sqrt{6.667}} = \frac{-9.33}{2.582} = -3.61$$

The square root of 6.667 is 2.582, so the estimated standard error of the mean ($s_{\overline{X}}$) is 2.582. Dividing -9.33 by 2.582 gives the t_{obt} of -3.61.

Thus, our sample mean produced a t_{obt} of -3.61 on the sampling distribution of means where $\mu = 75$. This is very similar to a z-score of -3.61. According to H_0, our sample represents the population where μ is 75, so ideally, the sample mean "should" be 75, producing a t_{obt} equal to 0. However, a t_{obt} of -3.61 suggests we have a sample that is unlikely to be representing this population. The question is, "Is a t_{obt} of -3.61 significant?" To answer this, the final step is to compare t_{obt} to the appropriate t_{crit}, and for that we examine the t-distribution.

The *t*-Distribution

In previous chapters, we described the sampling distribution of means using z-scores, because the z-distribution is the appropriate model of the sampling distribution when σ_X is *known*. The t-distribution is the appropriate model when σ_X is *estimated*. Think of the t-distribution in the following way. One last time, we hire our *very* bored statistician. She infinitely draws samples of the same size N from the raw score population described by H_0. For each sample, she computes $\overline{X}$, s_X, and t_{obt}. She then plots the frequency distribution of the different means, labeling the X axis with the corresponding values of t_{obt} as well. This is the ***t*-distribution**, the distribution of all possible values of t_{obt} computed for random sample means selected from the raw score population described by H_0.

You can envision a t-distribution as shown in Figure 14.1. As with z-scores, a sample mean equal to μ has a t equal to zero. Means greater than μ have positive values of t, and means less than μ have negative values of t. The larger the absolute value of t, the farther it and the corresponding sample mean are from the μ of the distribution. Therefore, the larger the t, the lower a mean's relative frequency and thus the lower its probability.

FIGURE 14.1 Example of a *t*-Distribution of Random Sample Means

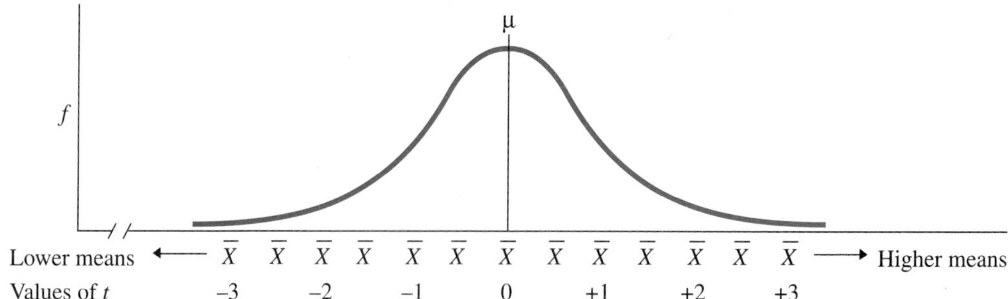

The t_{obt} locates our sample mean on this model, telling us the probability of obtaining the mean when H_0 is true. To complete the *t*-test, we find t_{crit} and create the region of rejection. If t_{obt} is beyond t_{crit}, then our sample mean is too unlikely a mean to accept as representing the population described by H_0.

But, there is one important novelty here: There are actually *many* versions of the *t*-distribution, each having a slightly different shape. The shape of a particular distribution depends on the size of the *N* that is used when creating the *t*-distribution. When *N* is small, the *t*-distribution will be a very rough approximation to the normal curve. This is because each sample will often contain large sampling error, so often s_X will be very different from σ_X, and this inconsistency produces a *t*-distribution that is only roughly normal. Larger samples however, tend to represent the population more accurately, so s_X will be close to the true value of σ_X. As with the *z*-test, using the true value of σ_X produces a sampling distribution that conforms to the normal distribution. In between, as sample size increases, each *t*-distribution will be a successively closer approximation to the true normal curve.

The fact that there are differently shaped *t*-distributions is important for one reason: When we set up the region of rejection, we want it to contain precisely that portion of the curve defined by our α. If $\alpha = .05$, then we want to mark off precisely the extreme 5% of the curve. On distributions that are shaped differently, we mark off that 5% at different locations. Because the size of the region of rejection is marked off by the critical value, *differently shaped t-distributions will have different critical values.* For example, Figure 14.2 shows a one-tailed region of rejection in two *t*-distributions. Say that the extreme 5% of Distribution A is beyond a t_{crit} of +2.5 (the shaded area in Figure 14.2). If we also use +2.5 as t_{crit} on Distribution B, however, the region of rejection will contain *more* than 5% of the distribution. Conversely, the t_{crit} marking off 5% of Distribution B will mark off *less* than 5% of Distribution A. (The same problem also exists for a two-tailed test.)

This issue is important because α and the size of the region of rejection determine the probability of a Type I error. Unless we use the t_{crit} that marks off the correct region of rejection, the actual probability of a Type I error will not equal our α (and that's not supposed to happen!). Thus, there is only one version of the *t*-distribution that we should use when testing a particular t_{obt}: the one that the bored statistician would have created when using the *same N* as in our sample.

FIGURE 14.2 Comparison of Two t-Distributions Based on Different Sample *N*s

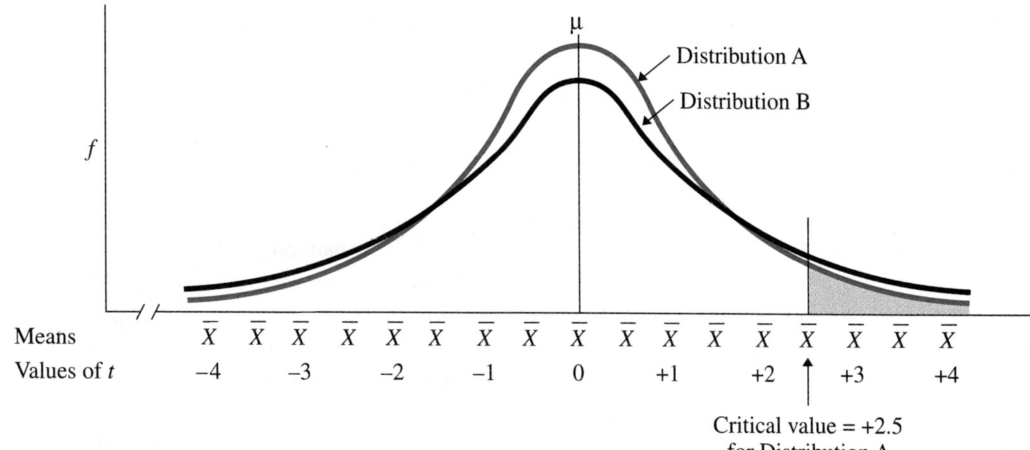

The Degrees of Freedom

To be precise, it's not N that determines the appropriate t-distribution for a study. Instead, the shape of a particular t-distribution is determined by the size of $N - 1$, what we call the degrees of freedom, or *df*. Because we compute s_X using $N - 1$, it is *df* that determines how consistently s_X estimates the true σ_X. Therefore, the larger the *df*, the closer the t-distribution is to forming a normal curve.

It does not take a tremendously large *df*, however, to produce a truly normal t-distribution. When *df* is greater than 120, the t-distribution is virtually identical to the standard normal curve, and t is the same as z. But when *dfs* are between 1 and 120, there are differently shaped t-distributions having different critical values. Therefore, when our *df* is between 1 and 120, we use the *df* to first identify the appropriate t-distribution. Then the t_{crit} on that distribution will demarcate a region of rejection that matches the α we have selected, so that the probability of a Type I error truly equals α.

> ***REMEMBER*** The appropriate t_{crit} for the single-sample t-test comes from the t-distribution that has *df* equal to $N - 1$, where N is the number of scores in our sample.

The *t*-Tables

We identify the t_{crit} on the appropriate t-distribution by using Table 2 in Appendix C, titled "Critical Values of t." Take a look at these "t-tables." There are separate tables for two-tailed and one-tailed tests. In each, identify the appropriate column for α. Then, find the value of t_{crit} in the row opposite the *df* in your sample. For example, in the housekeeping study, N is 9, so *df* is $N - 1 = 8$. For a two-tailed test with $\alpha = .05$ and $df = 8$, t_{crit} is ± 2.306.

The tables contain no positive or negative signs. In a two-tailed test, you must add the "±," and in a one-tailed test, depending on your hypothesis, you supply either "+"

or "−." Also, notice that the table uses the symbol for infinity (∞) for *df* greater than 120. This means that when a sample has *df* greater than 120, using the sample to estimate the population's standard deviation is virtually the same as using the infinite population to calculate the true standard deviation. Then, the *t*-distribution matches the standard normal curve, and the critical values are those we saw with the *z*-test.

Interpreting the Single-Sample *t*-Test

After calculating t_{obt} and identifying t_{crit}, we are ready to make a decision about the results of a study. Remember in the housekeeping study, we must decide whether or not the men's mean of 65.67 represents the same population of scores that women have, where μ is 75. Once we have the values of t_{obt} and t_{crit}, the single-sample *t*-test is identical to the *z*-test. Our t_{obt} is -3.61, and the two-tailed t_{crit} is ± 2.306. With this information, we envision the sampling distribution shown in Figure 14.3. This is the sampling distribution when H_0 is true and the samples *do* represent the population where μ is 75. However, the t_{obt} lies beyond the t_{crit}, so the results are significant: Our $\overline{X}$ of 65.67 is so unlikely to occur if H_0 is true (if men and women are really the same here), that we reject H_0, rejecting that we were representing the population where $\mu = 75$. As usual, however, there is a chance, equal to α, that we have just made a Type I error (rejecting H_0 when it is really true).

The rules for interpreting significant results here are exactly the same as in the previous chapter. By rejecting that the sample mean of 65.67 represents the μ of 75, we accept the alternative hypothesis that the sample mean represents a μ not equal to 75. Because a sample mean of 65.67 is most likely to occur in the population where μ is 65.67, our best estimate is that the sample represents a population of scores for men located at around 65.67. Thus, we expect one population of scores for men located at around 65.67 and a different population of scores for women located at a μ of 75. We conclude that the results demonstrate a relationship in the population between the independent variable (gender) and the dependent variable (test scores).

FIGURE 14.3 Two-Tailed *t*-Distribution for $df = 8$ when H_0 Is True and $\mu = 75$

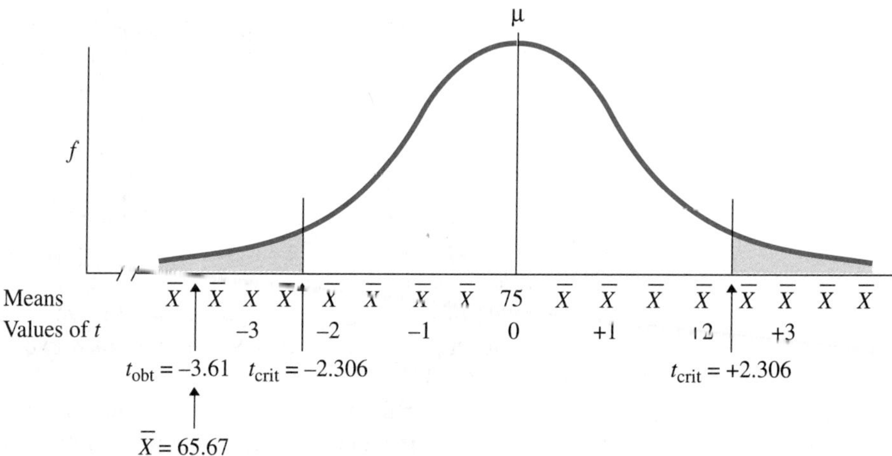

Then, as always, we proceed to interpret the relationship psychologically, generalizing to relevant behaviors and constructs. Did our results occur because men are more ignorant about housekeeping, and if so, why? Or, are they pretending to be ignorant so they can avoid housework, and if so, why? And so on. (Regardless of the interpretation, be especially cautious about concluding that gender *causes* differences in test scores. As we saw in Chapter 2, this *quasi-independent variable* is probably confounded by all sorts of participant variables—like differences in peer pressure, stereotyping, or social desirability—that may cause men to have lower test scores.

If the t_{obt} had not fallen beyond t_{crit} (for example, if $t_{obt} = +1.32$), then it would not lie in the region of rejection and we would not reject H_0. We would conclude that the sample was likely to occur if we were representing the population where μ is 75, so we would have no convincing evidence—one way or the other—regarding a relationship between gender and test scores. As usual, however, then there is a chance, equal to β, that we have just made a Type II error (retaining H_0 when it is really false).

Testing One-Tailed Hypotheses with the Single-Sample *t*-Test

We would perform a one-tailed test if, for example, we had predicted that men score *higher* than women. Then H_a would be that the sample represents a population μ greater than 75 (H_a: $\mu > 75$). The H_0 would be that the sample represents a population μ less than or equal to 75 (H_0: $\mu \leq 75$). For the sample to represent the predicted population of higher scores, the sample mean must be *significant* and *larger* than 75. Those means that are significantly larger than 75 are in the region of rejection in the upper tail of the sampling distribution, and so t_{crit} is positive, as in the graph on the left in Figure 14.4.

We would also perform a one-tailed test if we had predicted that men score *lower* than women, using the sampling distribution on the right in Figure 14.4. Now, H_a is that μ is less than 75, and H_0 is that μ is greater than or equal to 75. Because we seek a sample mean that is less than 75 and significant, the region of rejection is in the lower tail and t_{crit} is negative.

FIGURE 14.4 H_0 Sampling Distributions of *t* for a One-Tailed Test

On the left, we predict an increase in scores. On the right, we predict a decrease in scores.

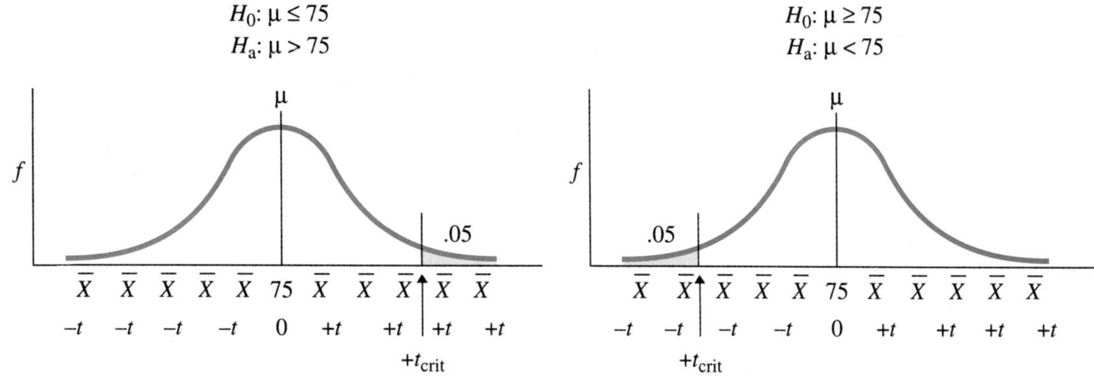

In either case, calculate t_{obt} using the previous formulas. If t_{obt} is larger than t_{crit} and has the same sign, then the sample mean is in the region of rejection, so the $\overline{X}$ is unlikely to be representing a μ described by H_0. Therefore, reject H_0, accept H_a, the results are significant, and interpret the relationship psychologically.

Some Help when Using the *t*-Tables

If you peruse the *t*-tables (a little light reading for the terminally bored), you will *not* find a critical value for every *df* between 1 and 120. When the *df* of your sample does not appear in the table, there are two approaches you can take.

First, remember that all we need to know is whether t_{obt} lies in the region of rejection. Often, you can determine this by examining the critical values for the *df* above and below the *df* of your sample. For example, say that we perform a one-tailed *t*-test at $\alpha = .05$ with 49 *df*. The *t*-tables give t_{crit} for 40 *df* (+1.684) and for 60 *df* (+1.671). Because 49 *df* lies between 40 *df* and 60 *df*, the critical value we seek is between +1.671 and +1.684. It's a good idea to draw a picture of this, as shown in Figure 14.5.

Our actual region of rejection starts at a point between these two critical values. Therefore, if t_{obt} lies beyond the t_{crit} of +1.684, then it is already in the region of rejection for 49 *df*, and so it is significant. On the other hand, if t_{obt} is *not* beyond the t_{crit} of +1.671, then it is way short of the region of rejection we'd have for 49 *df*, and so it is not significant.

In the same way, you can evaluate any obtained value that falls *outside* of the bracketing critical values given in the tables. But, if t_{obt} falls *between* the bracketing values of t_{crit} given in the tables, then you should use the second approach, which is to perform the interpolation procedure described in Appendix B.3.

FIGURE 14.5 One *t*-Distribution Showing the Location of Three Values of t_{crit}

The t_{crit} of +1.684 is for 40 df (dashed line), the t_{crit} of +1.671 is for 60 df (dotted line), and the t_{crit} for 49 (solid line) is between them.

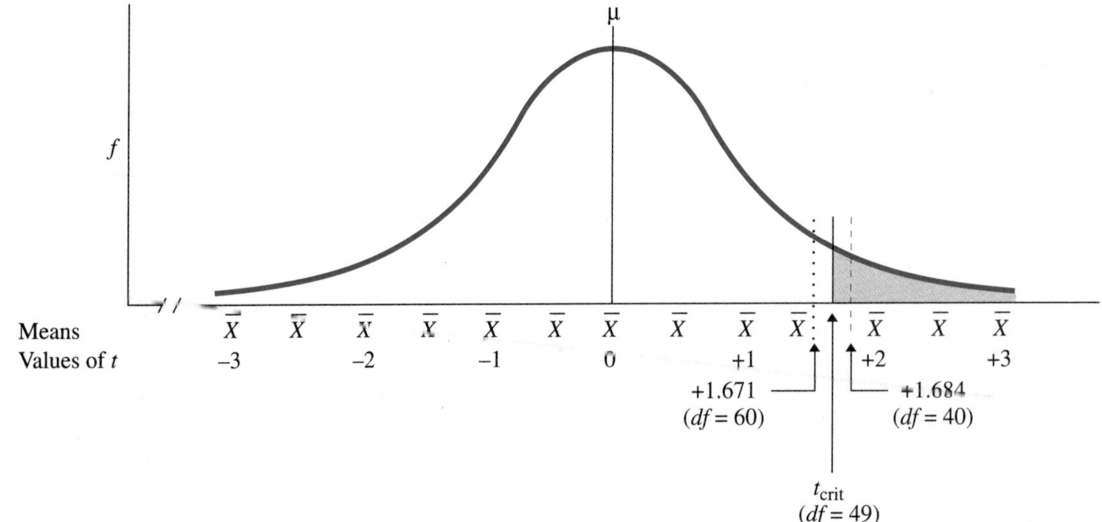

ESTIMATING THE POPULATION μ BY COMPUTING A CONFIDENCE INTERVAL

As we've seen, after rejecting H_0, we estimate the population μ that the sample mean represents. There are, however, two ways to estimate the value of μ. One way is **point estimation**, in which we describe a point on the variable at which the population μ is expected to fall. For example, we estimated that the μ for men is located on the variable of housekeeping scores at the *point* identified as 65.67. However, no one really believes that if we actually tested the entire population, μ would be *exactly* 65.67. The problem with point estimation is that it is extremely vulnerable to sampling error. Our sample of men probably does not *perfectly* represent the population of men. Realistically, therefore, we can say only that the population μ for men is probably *around* 65.67.

The other, better way to estimate μ is to include the possibility of sampling error and perform interval estimation. With **interval estimation**, we specify an interval—a range of values—within which we expect the population parameter to fall. You often encounter such intervals in real life, and they are usually phrased in terms of "plus or minus" some amount, called the **margin of error**. For example, when the evening news reports that a sample survey showed that 45% of the voters support the president, the margin of error may be plus or minus 3%. This means that the pollsters created an interval around 45%. They expect that if they actually surveyed the entire population, the μ would be within ±3% of 45%. In other words, they believe that between 42% and 48% of all voters in the population support the president.

We perform interval estimation by creating a confidence interval. Confidence intervals can be used to describe various population parameters, but the most common is the confidence interval for a single μ. The **confidence interval for a single μ** describes a range of values of μ, any one of which our sample mean is likely to represent. Thus, instead of saying the sample mean represents a μ *around* 65.67, a confidence interval is the way to statistically define "around." Thus, for our study, a confidence interval will identify those values of μ above and below 65.67 that our sample mean is likely to represent, as shown here:

$$\underbrace{\mu_{\text{low}} \; \ldots \; \mu \quad \mu \quad \mu \quad \mu \quad 65.67 \quad \mu \quad \mu \quad \mu \quad \mu \; \ldots \; \mu_{\text{high}}}_{\text{values of } \mu \text{, one of which is likely to be represented by our sample mean}}$$

The symbol μ_{low} stands for the lowest value of μ that the sample mean is likely to represent, and μ_{high} stands for the highest value of μ that the mean is likely to represent. When we compute these two values, we have the confidence interval.

When is a sample mean likely to represent a particular μ? It depends on sampling error. For example, we intuitively know that sampling error is unlikely to produce a sample mean of 65.67 if μ is, say, 500. In other words, 65.67 is *significantly different* from 500. But, sampling error *is* likely to produce a sample mean of 65.67 if, for example, μ is 65. In other words, a mean of 65.67 is not significantly different from 65. Thus, a sample mean is likely to represent a particular value of μ if the sample mean is *not* significantly different from that μ. The logic behind computing a confidence interval is to compute the highest and lowest values of μ that are not significantly different from the sample mean. All μs between these two values are also not significantly different from the sample mean, so the mean is likely to represent one of them.

REMEMBER A confidence interval describes the highest and lowest values of μ that are not significantly different from our sample mean.

Computing the Confidence Interval for μ

Because the *t*-test was appropriate for testing the significance of our sample mean, it also forms the basis for the confidence interval. Here is what's behind the formula for the confidence interval: We seek the highest and lowest values of μ that are not significantly different from the sample mean. For a $\overline{X}$ to differ significantly from μ, its t_{obt} must be *beyond* t_{crit}. Therefore, the most a sample mean can differ from μ and still not differ significantly is when its t_{obt} *equals* t_{crit}. We can state this using the formula for the *t*-test:

$$t_{obt} = \frac{\overline{X} - \mu}{s_{\overline{X}}} = t_{crit}$$

To find the largest and smallest values of μ that do not differ significantly from our sample mean, we determine the values of μ to put into this formula. Because we are describing values above and below the sample mean, we use the *two-tailed* value of t_{crit}. Thus, we first find the value of μ that produces a $-t_{obt}$ equal to $-t_{crit}$. Rearranging the above formula, we have:

$$\mu = (s_{\overline{X}})(+t_{crit}) + \overline{X}$$

To find the value of μ that produces a $+t_{obt}$ equal to $+t_{crit}$, the formula is

$$\mu = (s_{\overline{X}})(-t_{crit}) + \overline{X}$$

Our sample mean represents a μ *between* these two values of μ, so we put the above formulas together into one formula.

THE COMPUTATIONAL FORMULA FOR THE CONFIDENCE INTERVAL FOR A SINGLE μ IS

$$(s_{\overline{X}})(-t_{crit}) + \overline{X} \leq \mu \leq (s_{\overline{X}})(+t_{crit}) + \overline{X}$$

The symbol μ stands for the unknown value represented by our sample mean. The values of $\overline{X}$ and $s_{\overline{X}}$ are computed from the sample data. Find the two-tailed t_{crit} in the *t*-tables at α for $df = N - 1$, where *N* is the sample *N*.

REMEMBER In computing a confidence interval, use the two-tailed critical value, even if you performed one-tailed hypothesis testing.

Let's compute the confidence interval for our sample of housekeeping scores. There, $\overline{X} = 65.67$ and $s_{\overline{X}} = 2.582$. The two-tailed t_{crit} for $df = 8$ and $\alpha = .05$ is ± 2.306. Filling in the formula for the confidence interval, we have

$$(2.582)(-2.306) + 65.67 \leq \mu \leq (2.582)(+2.306) + 65.67$$

After multiplying 2.582 times −2.306 and +2.306, we have

$$-5.954 + 65.67 \leq \mu \leq +5.954 + 65.67$$

Adding −5.954 is the same as subtracting 5.954, so the formula at this point indicates that the sample mean represents a μ of 65.67, plus or minus 5.954.

After adding ±5.954 to 65.67, we have

$$59.72 \leq \mu \leq 71.62$$

This is the finished confidence interval. We can return to the previous diagram of the confidence interval and replace the symbols μ_{low} and μ_{high} with the numbers 59.72 and 71.62, respectively.

$$\underbrace{59.72 \;\ldots\; \mu \;\; \mu \;\; \mu \;\; \mu \;\; 65.67 \;\; \mu \;\; \mu \;\; \mu \;\; \mu \;\ldots\; 71.62}$$

values of μ, one of which is likely to be represented by our sample mean

As shown, our sample mean probably represents a μ that is greater than or equal to 59.72, but less than or equal to 71.62.

Confidence Intervals and the Size of Alpha

Why do we call this a "confidence" interval? We defined this interval using $\alpha = .05$, so .05 is the theoretical probability of making a Type I error. Thus, 5% of the time the interval will be in error and will not contain the μ represented by our $\overline{X}$. Recall, however, that the quantity $1 - \alpha$ is the probability of avoiding a Type I error. Thus, $1 - .05$, or 95%, of the time the interval will contain the μ represented by our $\overline{X}$. Therefore, the probability is .95 that the interval contains the μ. Recall that probability is our way of expressing confidence in an event. Thus, we are 95% confident that the interval between 59.72 and 71.62 contains the μ represented by our sample of men. The amount of confidence we have (e.g., 95%) is part of the formal name for a confidence interval, so always include it. Officially, here we computed the "95% confidence interval."

The smaller the α, the smaller the probability of an error, so the greater our confidence. Had we set α at .01, we would have the 99% confidence interval. With $df = 8$, t_{crit} would be ±3.355, and the 99% confidence interval would be

$$57.01 \leq \mu \leq 74.33$$

Note that the 99% confidence interval spans a wider range of values than did the 95% confidence interval. That's because the wider the interval, the greater our confidence that it contains the μ we seek. (Think of a confidence interval as a fishing net. The larger the net, the greater our confidence that we'll catch the μ being represented.) There is, however, an inevitable trade-off: A wider range will less precisely identify the specific value of μ represented by a sample. Usually, we compromise between sufficient confidence and sufficient precision by creating the 95% confidence interval.

If the original *t*-test in the housekeeping study had not been significant, then we would not compute the confidence interval (because one μ it would include would be 75, the μ for women.) However, given our results, we conclude our single-sample *t*-test by saying, with 95% confidence, that the sample of men represents a μ between 59.72 and 71.62. Because the center of the interval is at 65.67, we still communicate that μ is *around* 65.67, but much more precisely than if we merely said that μ is somewhere around 65.67. Therefore, anytime you are describing the μ represented by a sample mean, you should compute a confidence interval.[1]

SUMMARY OF THE *t*-TEST

All of the preceding procedures boil down to the following steps:

1. Check that the experiment meets the assumptions of the *t*-test.
2. Create either the two-tailed or one-tailed H_0 and H_a.
3. From the sample data, compute s_X^2 (or s_X); then compute $s_{\bar{X}}$, and then compute t_{obt}.
4. For the *df* in the study $(N - 1)$, find the appropriate t_{crit}.
5. If t_{obt} is beyond t_{crit}, reject H_0, the results are significant, and interpret the relationship psychologically. If t_{obt} is not beyond t_{crit}, the results are not significant.
6. For significant results, use the two-tailed t_{crit} to compute the confidence interval for the μ represented by the $\bar{X}$.

SIGNIFICANCE TESTS FOR CORRELATION COEFFICIENTS

It's time to shift mental gears and consider another type of single-sample study—a correlational study in which a correlation coefficient is computed. For example, here's a new study: Say that we had chosen to examine the relationship between a man's age and his housekeeping score in a correlational design. We measure the test scores and ages of 25 men, and determine that for such data, the Pearson correlation coefficient is appropriate. Using the formula from Chapter 10, we compute an $r = -.45$, indicating that the older a man, the lower his housekeeping score.

Remember, though, that this correlation coefficient describes the relationship in the sample. Ultimately, we want to describe the relationship in the population. Therefore, we use the sample coefficient to estimate the population parameter we would expect to find if we computed the correlation for the entire population. Recall that the population correlation coefficient is called rho, and its symbol is ρ. Thus, in our study, we would estimate that ρ would equal $-.45$ if we measured the entire population of men.

But hold on, there's a problem here: That's right, sampling error. The problem of sampling error applies to *all* statistics. Here, the idea is that only because of the luck of the draw of who was selected for the sample do their scores form a relationship, but in nature, there is either no relationship or a different relationship. Therefore, here we go again. For any correlation coefficient, you must determine whether it is significant.

[1] To compute a confidence interval when performing the *z*-test, use the formula given above, except use the critical values from the *z*-tables. If $\alpha = .05$, then $z_{crit} = \pm 1.96$. If $\alpha = .01$, then $z_{crit} = \pm 2.575$.

REMEMBER Never accept that a sample correlation coefficient represents a real relationship in nature unless it is significant.

Statistical Hypotheses for the Correlation Coefficient

As usual, we should create the experimental and statistical hypotheses before collecting the data, and we can perform either a one-tailed or a two-tailed test. Use a two-tailed test if the direction of the relationship is not predicted. For example, in the housekeeping study, we might predict that the study demonstrates either that older men produce higher test scores (a positive correlation), or that older men produce lower scores (a negative correlation). Then, the other hypothesis is that the study will not demonstrate any kind of relationship.

This latter hypothesis translates into the null hypothesis, because H_0 always implies that the predicted relationship does not exist. If there is not a positive or negative correlation, then there is zero correlation. Most of the time, behavioral researchers test the null hypothesis involving zero correlation in the population. Therefore, in this book,

THE TWO-TAILED NULL HYPOTHESIS FOR SIGNIFICANCE TESTING OF A CORRELATION COEFFICIENT IS

$$H_0\text{: } \rho = 0$$

H_0 implies that our r represents a ρ equal to zero. If r does not equal zero, the difference is because of sampling error. You can understand how such sampling error can occur by looking at the hypothetical scatterplot in Figure 14.6. Assume this shows the population of X and Y scores when H_0 is true: There is no relationship, and so ρ is 0. Recall that a circular scatterplot reflects zero correlation, while a slanting elliptical scatterplot reflects an r not equal to zero. The null hypothesis implies that, by chance, we selected an elliptical sample scatterplot from the circular population plot. Therefore, r may not equal 0, but this is because it poorly represents a population where ρ equals 0. (Thus, H_0 says that age and housekeeping scores are not really related, but the scores in the sample by chance happen to pair up so that it looks like they're related.)

On the other hand, the alternative hypothesis always implies that the predicted relationship exists in the population. If we predict that there is either a positive or a negative relationship, we predict that ρ does *not* equal zero.

THE TWO-TAILED ALTERNATIVE HYPOTHESIS FOR SIGNIFICANCE TESTING OF A CORRELATION COEFFICIENT IS

$$H_a\text{: } \rho \neq 0$$

H_a implies that r represents a population where ρ is not zero and thus reflects a real relationship in the population. If so, we assume that the population's scatterplot would be similar to the sample's scatterplot.

FIGURE 14.6 Scatterplot of a Population for Which $\rho = 0$, as Described by H_0

Any r is a result of sampling error when selecting a sample scatterplot from this scatterplot.

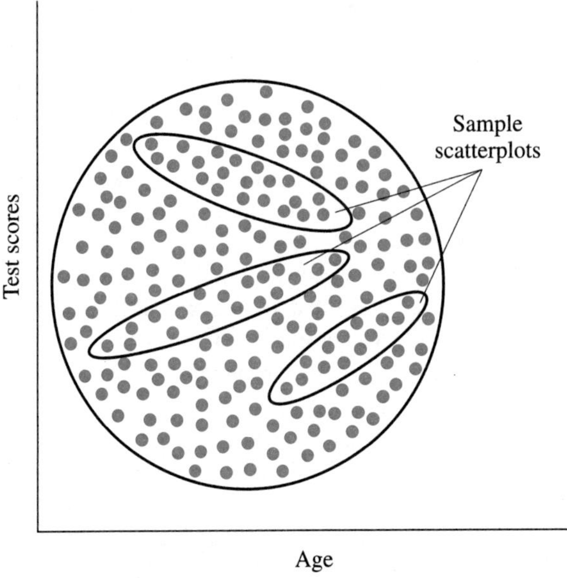

As usual, we test H_0, so here we test whether the sample correlation represents a ρ of 0. If r is unlikely to occur if we are representing a ρ of 0, then we reject H_0 and accept H_a (that the sample represents a population where $\rho \neq 0$).

Recall from Chapter 10 that there are three types of correlation coefficients: The Pearson r, the Spearman r_s, and the point-biserial r_{pb}. The logic and format of the above statistical hypotheses are used regardless of which coefficient you compute (merely change the subscripts). The following sections discuss the particulars of hypothesis testing for each type of coefficient.

The Significance Test for the Pearson *r*

As usual, the first step is to make sure the study meets the assumptions of the statistical procedure. The assumptions for hypothesis testing of the Pearson correlation coefficient are

1. There is a random sample of X-Y pairs, and each variable is an interval or ratio variable.
2. The Y scores and the X scores in the sample each represent a normal distribution. Further, they represent a *bivariate* normal distribution. This means that the Y scores at each value of X form a normal distribution and that the X scores at each value of Y form a normal distribution. (If N is larger than 25, however, violating this assumption is of little consequence.)
3. The null hypothesis states that the population correlation is zero. (When H_0 states that ρ is some other value, a different procedure is used.)

Our housekeeping and age data meet these assumptions, so we set α at .05 and test r. To do that, we examine the sampling distribution.

The sampling distribution of *r* The H_0 sampling distribution of r shows the different values of r that occur when H_0 is true and we are sampling the population where ρ is 0. The bored statistician quit! But, by now, you could create this sampling distribution yourself. Using our N, you would select an infinite number of samples of X-Y pairs from the population where $\rho = 0$ (as if you pulled each sample of data points from the circular scatterplot in Figure 14.6). Each time, you would compute r. If you then plotted the frequency of the various values of r, you would have the sampling distribution of r. The **sampling distribution of a correlation coefficient** is a frequency distribution that shows all possible values of the coefficient that can occur when samples of size N are drawn from a population where ρ is zero. Such a sampling distribution is shown in Figure 14.7. The only novelty here is that instead of showing different sample means along the X axis, different values of r are plotted. As shown, when ρ is 0, most frequently r will also equal zero, so the mean of the sampling distribution—the average r—is 0. Because of sampling error, however, sometimes r will not equal zero. The larger the r (whether positive or negative), the less frequent and thus the less likely it is when the sample represents a population where ρ is zero.

To test H_0, we simply determine where on this distribution our r lies. To do so, we could perform a variation of the t-test, but luckily that is not necessary. Instead, the value of r directly communicates its location on the sampling distribution. The mean of the sampling distribution is always 0. So, for example, our r of $-.45$ is a distance of .45 below the mean. Therefore, we test H_0 simply by examining the value of the obtained r. The symbol for an obtained r is r_{obt}. To determine whether r_{obt} lies in the region of rejection, we compare it to the critical value of r, which is symbolized as r_{crit}.

Testing the Pearson *r* As with the t-distribution, the shape of the sampling distribution of r is slightly different for each df, so there is a different value of r_{crit} for each df.

FIGURE 14.7 Distribution of Random Sample *r*s when $\rho = 0$

It is an approximately normal distribution, with values of r plotted along the X axis.

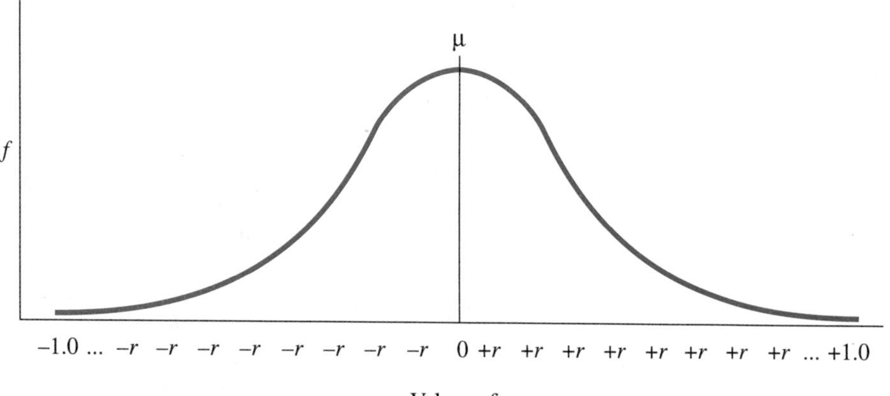

Table 3 in Appendix C gives the critical values of r. To use these "r-tables," we first need the appropriate degrees of freedom. But, here's a new one: With the Pearson correlation coefficient, the degrees of freedom equals $N - 2$, where N is the number of *pairs* of scores in the sample. (Recall that $N - 1$ was a correction factor. Different statistics require different correction factors, so the computation of their df will change.)

> ***REMEMBER*** For the Pearson r, the degrees of freedom equals $N - 2$, where N is the number of pairs of scores.

To find r_{crit}, enter Table 3 for either a one-tailed or two-tailed test at the appropriate α and df. For the housekeeping correlation, N was 25, so $df = 23$. For a two-tailed test with $\alpha = .05$ and $df = 23$, r_{crit} is $\pm.396$. Armed with this information, we set up the sampling distribution as in Figure 14.8. An r_{obt} of $-.45$ is beyond the r_{crit} of $\pm.396$, so r_{obt} is in the region of rejection. As usual, this means that we reject H_0. To see why, look at the low frequency that the sampling distribution shows for such an r. This r is so unlikely to occur, if we had been representing the population where ρ is 0, that we reject the H_0 that we were representing this population. We conclude that r_{obt} is "significantly different from zero."

Interpreting a significant *r* The rules for interpreting a significant result here are the same as before. In particular, α is again the theoretical probability of a Type I error. Now, a Type I error is rejecting the H_0 that there is zero correlation in the population, when in fact there is zero correlation in the population. With $\alpha = .05$, when H_0 is true, we'll obtain values of r_{obt} that cause us to erroneously reject H_0 a total of 5% of the time. Thus, the probability that we've made a Type I error this time is slightly less than .05.

Remember that by rejecting H_0, we have not proven anything. In particular, this was a correlational study, so we have not proven that changes in age *cause* test scores to change. In fact, we have not even proven that there is a relationship in nature (we may

FIGURE 14.8 H_0 Sampling Distribution of r when H_0: $\rho = 0$

For the two-tailed test, there is a region of rejection for positive values of r_{obt} and for negative values of r_{obt}.

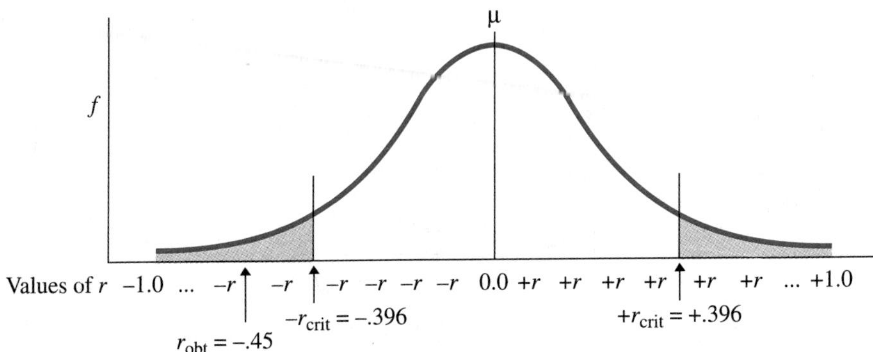

have made a Type I error). Instead, we are simply more confident that the r_{obt} does not merely reflect some quirk of sampling error, it appears to represent a real relationship in nature.

Because the sample r_{obt} is $-.45$, our best estimate is that in the population, ρ equals $-.45$. However, recognizing that the sample may contain sampling error, we expect that ρ is probably *around* $-.45$. (We could more precisely identify the value of ρ by computing a confidence interval for the values of ρ that r_{obt} is likely to represent. Confidence intervals for ρ, however, are computed using a different formula than the one discussed previously.)

In Chapter 11, we saw that we further describe such a relationship by computing the linear regression equation and the proportion of variance accounted for, or r^2. However, we do this only when r_{obt} is significant! Only then are we confident that we're describing a "real" relationship. Therefore, we would now compute the linear regression equation for predicting housekeeping scores if we know a man's age. We also compute r^2, which equals $-.45^2$ or .20. Recall that this is the proportion of variance in Y scores that is accounted for by the relationship with X. Here, it indicates that we are, on average, 20% more accurate when we use the relationship with age to predict test scores than we are when we do not use the relationship.

Recognize that it is r^2 and not "significance" that determines how important and useful a relationship is. The term *significant* indicates only that the relationship is unlikely to be a fluke of chance. But it still may be a weak and thus unimportant relationship. The r^2 indicates the importance of a relationship, because the larger it is, the more that knowing participants' X scores improves our accuracy in predicting and understanding differences in their Y scores—in their behavior.

Thus, a relationship must be significant to be even potentially important, because first we must believe it is real. But, a significant relationship is not necessarily useful. For example, in certain circumstances, an r of $+.10$ may be significant. Such a relationship, however, is *not* statistically important: $.10^2$ is only .01, so this relationship accounts for only 1% of the variance. Thus, it is virtually useless in explaining differences in Y scores. (We're only 1% better off with it than without it.) Therefore, although this relationship is not likely to occur through sampling error, at the same time, it is a statistically unimportant and not very useful relationship.

After describing the relationship, as usual the final step is to interpret it psychologically, generalizing to the relevant hypothetical constructs. For example, perhaps the above data reflect socialization processes, with older men scoring lower on the housekeeping test because they come from generations where typically wives did the housekeeping, while men were the "breadwinners."

Of course, if r_{obt} had not fallen beyond r_{crit}, we would retain H_0 and conclude that the sample may represent a population where $\rho = 0$. As usual, here we have not proven that there is *not* a relationship in the population—we have simply failed to demonstrate convincingly that there *is* a relationship. Therefore, make no claims about the relationship that may or may not exist in the population, and do not describe it using the regression equation or r^2.

One-tailed tests of *r* If our experimental hypothesis had predicted only a positive correlation or only a negative correlation, then we would perform one of these one-tailed tests.

THE ONE-TAILED HYPOTHESES FOR SIGNIFICANCE TESTING OF A CORRELATION COEFFICIENT ARE

Predicting positive correlation	***Predicting negative correlation***
H_0: $\rho \leq 0$	H_0: $\rho \geq 0$
H_a: $\rho > 0$	H_a: $\rho < 0$

Test each H_0 by again testing whether r_{obt} represents a population where there is zero relationship—so again examine the sampling distribution for $\rho = 0$. From the r-tables in Appendix C, find the one-tailed critical value for *df* and α, and set up one of the sampling distributions shown in Figure 14.9. When predicting a positive correlation, use the sampling distribution on the left. The r_{obt} is significant if it is positive and falls beyond the positive r_{crit}. When predicting a negative correlation, use the distribution on the right. The r_{obt} is significant if it is negative and falls beyond the negative r_{crit}.

In either situation, if r_{obt} is not beyond the appropriate r_{crit}, then r_{obt} is not significant, and the study has failed to demonstrate the predicted relationship.

Significance Testing of the Spearman r_s and the Point-Biserial r_{pb}

The Spearman correlation coefficient (r_s) and the point-biserial correlation coefficient (r_{pb}) are tested using procedures similar to that of r. These correlations describe sample relationships, but perhaps they merely reflect sampling error. Perhaps if we computed the correlation in the population, we would find that our r_s actually represents a population correlation, symbolized by ρ_s, that is 0. Likewise, perhaps our r_{pb} actually represents a population correlation, symbolized by ρ_{pb}, that is 0. Therefore, before we can

FIGURE 14.9 H_0 Sampling Distribution of r Where $\rho = 0$ for One-Tailed Test

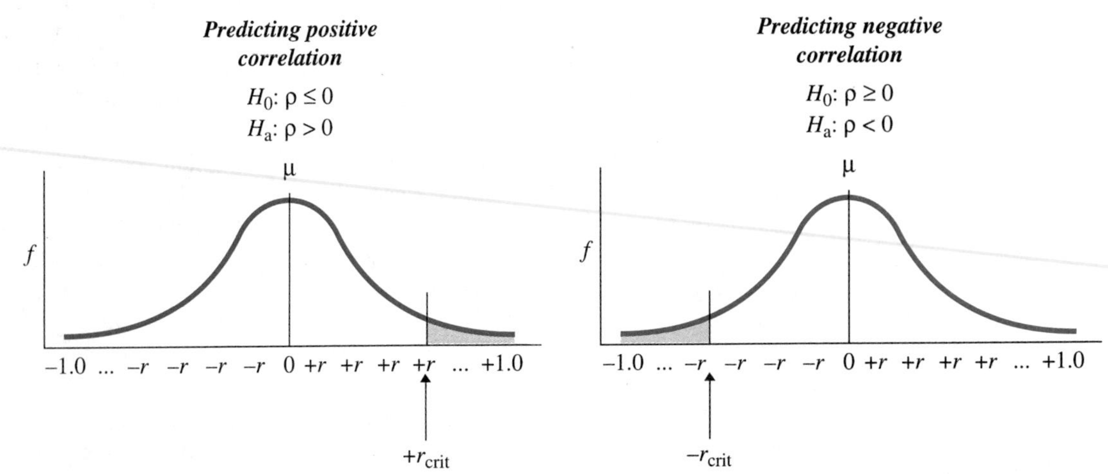

conclude that these correlations represent a relationship in nature, we must perform the appropriate hypothesis testing.

To test each sample correlation coefficient, perform the following steps:

1. Set alpha: How about .05?
2. Consider the assumptions of the test. The r_S requires a random sample of pairs of *ranked* (ordinal) scores. The r_{pb} requires random scores from one dichotomous variable and one interval or ratio variable. (Because of the type of data involved and the lack of parametric assumptions, r_S and r_{pb} are technically nonparametric procedures.)
3. Create the statistical hypotheses. You can test either the one- or two-tailed hypotheses we had with ρ, except substitute ρ_S or ρ_{pb}.

The only new aspect in testing r_S or r_{pb} is in their respective sampling distributions.

Significance testing of r_S To test r_S, we use a new family of sampling distributions and a different table of critical values. Table 4 in Appendix C, contains the critical values of r_S. Obtain the critical value from this table as in previous tables, except here use N, *not* degrees of freedom.

> ***REMEMBER*** The critical value of r_S is obtained using N, the number of pairs of scores in the sample.

Here's an example. In Chapter 10, we determined the inter-rater reliability of two observers by correlating their rankings of the aggressiveness of 9 children. We found $r_S = +.85$. To believe that the observers are reliable, however, we must believe that this is a real relationship, and not that their rankings happened to pair up by chance. In other words, this r_S must be significant. We assumed the observers' rankings would agree, so we predicted a positive correlation. Therefore, we have a one-tailed test with these hypotheses H_0: $\rho_S \leq 0$ and H_a: $\rho_S > 0$. From Table 4 in Appendix C, with $\alpha = .05$ and $N = 9$, the critical value for the one-tailed test is $+.600$. Thus, we envision the H_0 sampling distribution of r_S when $N = 9$ as shown in Figure 14.10.

FIGURE 14.10 One-Tailed H_0 Sampling Distribution of Values of r_S when H_0 is $\rho_S = 0$

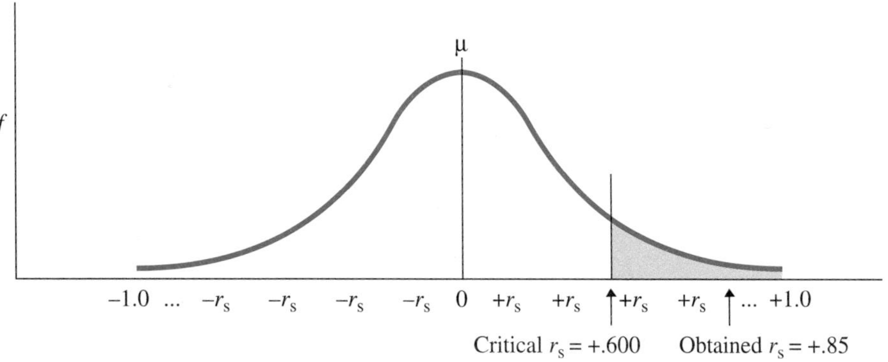

The obtained r_S of +.85 is beyond the critical value of +.600, so we reject H_0: An r_S of +.85 is too unlikely to occur for us to accept as representing the population where ρ_S is zero or less than zero. Therefore, we accept H_a (that $\rho_S > 0$). We have a significant r_S, and we estimate that the correlation in the population of such rankings (ρ_S) is around +.85.

Because it is significant, we would also compute the squared r_S to determine the usefulness of this relationship. Then, interpret the results psychologically. (With different predictions, we might have performed the other one-tailed test or a two-tailed test and proceeded accordingly.)

Significance testing of r_{pb} Test r_{pb} using the same logic as above. The sampling distributions of r_{pb} are identical to the distributions for the Pearson r, so critical values of r_{pb} are obtained from the "r-tables" in Table 3 in Appendix C. Again, the degrees of freedom equals $N - 2$.

REMEMBER The critical values for r_{pb} are the same as those for r.

As an example, in Chapter 10, we computed the r_{pb} of +.46 for 10 participants using the dichotomous variable of gender (male or female) and the continuous variable of scores on a personality test. Say we perform a two-tailed test with the hypotheses, H_0: $\rho_{pb} = 0$ and H_a: $\rho_{pb} \neq 0$. From Table 3 in Appendix C, with $\alpha = .05$ and $df = 8$, the critical value is $\pm.632$. You can envision the sampling distribution as shown in Figure 14.11. The obtained r_{pb} of +.46 is *not* beyond the critical value, so we do not reject H_0. We conclude that our sample may represent the population where ρ_{pb} equals zero. Thus, we have no evidence—one way or the other—that gender and personality scores are related.

In a different study, predicting only a positive or only a negative correlation would lead to a one-tailed test. Remember, though, as discussed in Chapter 10, *we* determine whether r_{pb} is positive or negative by how we arrange the categories of the dichotomous variable, so be sure the predictions in a one-tailed test match your arrangement.

FIGURE 14.11 H_0 Sampling Distribution of r_{pb} when H_0 is $\rho_{pb} = 0$

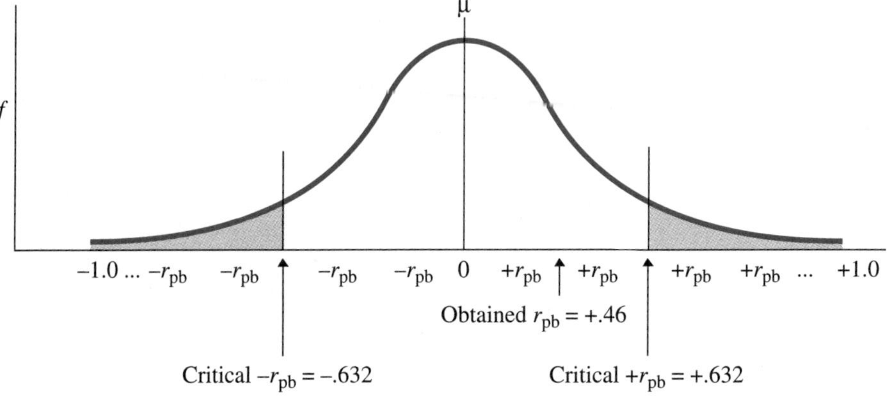

SUMMARY OF TESTING A CORRELATION COEFFICIENT

All of the preceding procedures boil down to the following steps:

1. Check that the study meets the assumptions of r, r_s, or r_{pb}.
2. Create either the two-tailed or one-tailed H_0 and H_a.
3. From the sample data, compute the correlation coefficient.
4. Obtain the critical value:
   The critical value for r or for r_{pb} is in Table 3 using $df = N - 2$.
   The critical value for r_s is in Table 4 using $df = N$.
5. If the obtained coefficient is beyond the critical value, reject H_0, the results are significant, and interpret the relationship psychologically. If the coefficient is not beyond the critical value, the results are not significant.
6. For significant results, compute the proportion of variance accounted for by squaring the obtained coefficient, and perform linear regression.

MAXIMIZING THE POWER OF THE *t*-TEST AND CORRELATION COEFFICIENT

Recall that a goal when designing a study is to maximize power. *Power* is the probability of not committing a Type II error—not retaining H_0 when it is false. Having sufficient power becomes an issue whenever we retain H_0, because we want to be confident that we did not make the wrong decision and miss a relationship in nature. Recall that the logic is that we're talking about those times when H_0 is false, and so we should reject it. Therefore, we maximize power by maximizing the probability of obtaining significant results. To do that, we maximize the absolute size of the obtained statistic relative to the critical value. The larger the obtained value, the more likely it is to fall beyond the critical value and thus the more likely it is to be significant.

Previously, we've seen that a powerful design provides convincing evidence of a relationship. For the t-test, such a relationship will increase the size of the obtained value relative to the critical value. Look at the formula for t_{obt}:

$$t_{obt} = \frac{\overline{X} - \mu}{\frac{s_X}{\sqrt{N}}}$$

There are three aspects of a study that increase power here:

1. *Larger differences produced by changing the independent variable increase power.* Recall that we seek a *strong manipulation* of the independent variable that produces large differences in scores between the conditions. In the single-sample experiment, this translates into a larger difference between $\overline{X}$ and μ. Mathematically, a larger difference between $\overline{X}$ and μ produces a larger numerator. All other things (N and s_X) being equal, dividing into a larger numerator results in a larger t_{obt}.

2. *Smaller variability in the raw scores increases power.* Recall that we seek to minimize the variability of scores within each condition (minimizing the *error variance*). This is because the *t*-test measures the difference between $\overline{X}$ and μ relative to the standard error of the mean ($s_{\overline{X}}$). The size of the standard error is influenced by the variability in the raw scores (s_X). Therefore, the smaller the variability of the raw scores, the smaller the denominator. Dividing by a smaller denominator produces a larger t_{obt}.
3. *For small samples, a larger N increases power.* The size of *N* influences the results in two ways. First, in the formula, dividing by a larger *N* produces a smaller denominator, which results in a larger t_{obt}. Second, a larger *N* produces larger *df*, which produces a smaller t_{crit}. The smaller the t_{crit}, the more likely that t_{obt} lies beyond it, so the more likely that t_{obt} is significant. However, this is for *small* samples. Generally, an *N* of 30 is needed for minimal power, and increasing *N* up to 121 increases power substantially. However, an *N* such as 500 is not substantially more powerful than an *N* of, say, 450.

REMEMBER Increase power in an experiment by maximizing differences in dependent scores between conditions, minimizing differences among scores within conditions, and testing a large *N*.

Likewise, we seek to maximize the power of a correlational study. We do so by maximizing the size of the obtained coefficient. A larger coefficient is more likely to fall beyond the critical value, so in case there really is a relationship present, we are more likely to have significant results and thus avoid a Type II error. The following are ways to maximize the power of a correlation coefficient.

1. *Avoiding a restricted range increases power.* Recall that a restricted range occurs when there is a small range of scores on the *X* or *Y* variable. This produces a smaller coefficient than would be found without a restricted range. Thus, we seek to measure the full range of possible *X* and *Y* scores.
2. *Minimizing the variability of the Y scores at each X increases power.* The smaller the variability in *Y* scores at each *X*, the stronger the relationship and the larger the coefficient. Therefore, we seek to minimize inconsistency that might produce variability in *Y* scores at each *X*.
3. *Describing linear relationships with linear correlations increases power.* The coefficients we've used describe the extent to which the data form a linear relationship. If the relationship is nonlinear, then the coefficient will be small and possibly not significant. We lose power because we conclude that there is no relationship when, in fact, a nonlinear relationship exists.
4. *Increasing the N of small samples maximizes power.* Because of lessened control, correlational designs frequently produce substantial error variance and a relatively weak relationship. Therefore, we compensate by employing a large *N*, often in the range of several hundred participants. If a given relationship occurs for a larger *N*, the coefficient is larger. Also, a larger *N* produces larger *df*, so the critical value is smaller and therefore the coefficient is more likely to be significant.

REMEMBER Increase the power of a correlation coefficient by avoiding a restricted range, minimizing the variability in *Y* scores, and increasing *N*.

APA FORMAT FOR STATISTICAL NOTATION

In published research, the results of a *t*-test are reported as follows. For the housekeeping study, our t_{obt} of -3.61 was significant, so we would report: $t(8) = -3.61, p < .05$. Notice the *df* in parentheses. Also, the probability is less than .05 that we have made a Type I error. However, the *t*-tables show that when α is .01, t_{crit} is only ± 3.355, and so our t_{obt} would be significant if we had used the .01 level. Therefore, it would be better to say $p < .01$, because then we would know that the probability of a Type I error is not in the neighborhood of .04, .03, or .02. Conversely, we discussed a nonsignificant t_{obt} of -1.32, which would be reported as $t(8) = -1.32, p > .05$. (Notice the ">".)

Report a correlation coefficient in the same way. For example, our significant *r* of $-.45$ would be reported as $r(23) = -.45, p < .05$. Notice the *df* in parentheses. Use the same format for the Spearman r_s except, instead of *df*, report *N*: in our example, $r_s(9) = +.85, p < .05$. Report r_{pb} using the same rules: In our example, r_{pb} was not significant, so $r_{pb}(8) = +.46, p > .05$.

Confidence intervals are usually reported in words, either describing the interval (e.g., "the mean is between the values of . . ."), or as a margin of error (e.g., ". . . with an expected error of plus or minus . . ."). Either way, always indicate whether it is a 95% or 99% confidence interval.

PUTTING IT ALL TOGETHER

Notice that for each statistic discussed in this chapter, we performed virtually the same operations. In testing *any* statistic, we ultimately do and say the same things. In all cases, if the obtained statistic is out there far enough on the H_0 sampling distribution, it is too unlikely to occur for us to accept as representing the H_0 situation, so we reject H_0. Any H_0 implies that the sample data do not represent the predicted relationship, so rejecting H_0 increases our confidence that the data *do* represent the predicted relationship. We are confident in this decision, because the probability is less than α that we've made an error. Conversely, if we fail to reject H_0, then hopefully we have sufficient power, so that error here is unlikely too. These are the fundamentals of *all* inferential procedures.

CHAPTER SUMMARY

1. The *t-test* is for testing a single-sample mean when (a) there is one random sample of interval or ratio data, (b) the raw score population is normally distributed, and (c) the standard deviation of the raw score population is estimated by computing s_X from the sample data.

2. In the *t*-test, compute the *estimated standard error of the mean* ($s_{\overline{X}}$), which is an estimate of the standard deviation of the sampling distribution.

3. A *t-distribution* is a theoretical sampling distribution of all possible values of t_{obt} when a raw score population is infinitely sampled using a particular *N*. The appropriate *t*-distribution to use in a study is the one identified by $N - 1$ degrees of freedom (*df*).

4. In *point estimation*, a μ is assumed to be at the point on the variable equal to $\overline{X}$. Because the sample probably contains sampling error, a point estimate is likely to

be incorrect. In *interval estimation*, a μ is assumed to lie within a specified interval. Interval estimation is performed by computing a confidence interval.

5. The *confidence interval for a single* μ describes a range of μs, any one of which the sample mean is likely to represent. The interval contains the highest and lowest values of μ that are not significantly different from the sample mean. Our confidence that the interval contains the value of μ is equal to $(1 - \alpha)100$.
6. The *sampling distribution of a correlation coefficient* is a frequency distribution showing all possible values of the coefficient that occur when samples of size N are drawn from a population where the correlation coefficient is zero.
7. Significance testing of the *Pearson r* assumes (a) a random sample of pairs of scores from two interval or ratio variables and (b) the Y scores are normally distributed at each value of X, and the X scores are normally distributed at each value of Y.
8. Significance testing of the *Spearman* r_s assumes a random sample of pairs of ranked-order (ordinal) scores.
9. Significance testing of the *point-biserial* r_{pb} assumes a random sample of pairs of scores where one score is from a dichotomous variable and one score is from an interval or ratio variable.
10. Only when a correlation coefficient is significant is it appropriate to compute the linear regression equation and the proportion of variance accounted for.
11. To maximize the power of the t-test, (a) create large differences between the conditions of the independent variable, (b) minimize the variability in the sample, and (c) increase the N of small samples.
12. To maximize the power of a correlation coefficient, (a) avoid a restricted range, (b) minimize the variability in Y at each X, (c) use the appropriate coefficient, and (d) increase the N of small samples.

KEY TERMS (with page references)

$s_{\bar{X}}$ t_{obt} t_{crit} df H_0 H_a r_{obt} r_{crit}
confidence interval for a single μ (379)
estimated standard error of the mean (371)
interval estimation (379)
margin of error (379)
point estimation (379)
sampling distribution of a correlation coefficient (385)
single sample t-test (369)
t-distribution (373)

REVIEW QUESTIONS

(Answers for odd-numbered questions and problems are provided in Appendix D.)

1. A scientist has conducted a single-sample experiment. (a) What two parametric procedures are available to her? (b) What is the deciding factor for selecting between them? (c) What are the other assumptions of the t-test?

2. In this chapter, we discussed 5 different statistical procedures (plus power). List them.
3. (a) What is the difference between $s_{\bar{X}}$ and $\sigma_{\bar{X}}$? (b) How is their use the same?
4. (a) Why are there different values of t_{crit} when samples have different Ns? (b) What must you determine in order to find t_{crit}?
5. (a) Summarize the steps involved in analyzing the results of a single-sample experiment. (b) Summarize the steps involved in analyzing the results of a correlational study.
6. Say you have a sample mean of 44 in a study. (a) Estimate the corresponding μ using point estimation. (b) What does a confidence interval computed for this μ tell you? (c) Why is computing a confidence interval a better approach than using a point estimate?
7. (a) What is power? (b) Why does power become important when we fail to reject H_0? (c) What do researchers do to avoid this dilemma?
8. What are the three aspects of maximizing the power of a *t*-test?
9. What are the four aspects of maximizing the power of a correlation coefficient?
10. (a) Why must a relationship be significant in order to be important? (b) Why can a relationship be significant and still be unimportant?
11. What is always the final step in examining the data in any study?

PRACTICE PROBLEMS

12. Poindexter performed a two-tailed experiment in which $N = 20$. He couldn't find his *t*-tables, but he remembered the t_{crit} at $df = 10$. He decided to compare his t_{obt} to this t_{crit}. Why is this a correct or incorrect approach? (*Hint:* Consider whether t_{obt} turns out to be significant or nonsignificant at this t_{crit}.)
13. You wish to determine whether this textbook is beneficial or detrimental to students learning research methods and statistics. On a national exam, $\mu = 68.5$ for students who have used other textbooks. A random sample of students who have used this book has the following scores:

    64 69 92 77 71 99 82 74 69 88

    (a) What are H_0 and H_a for this study? (b) Compute t_{obt}. (c) With $\alpha = .05$, what is t_{crit}? (d) What do you conclude about the use of this book? (e) Compute the confidence interval for μ.
14. A researcher predicts that smoking cigarettes degrades a person's sense of smell. On a standard test of olfactory sensitivity, the μ for nonsmokers is 18.4. By giving this test to a random sample of people who smoke a pack a day, the researcher obtains the following scores:

    16 14 19 17 16 18 17 15 18 19 12 14

    (a) What are H_0 and H_a for this study? (b) Compute t_{obt}. (c) With $\alpha = .05$, what is t_{crit}? (d) What should the researcher conclude about this relationship? (e) Compute the confidence interval for μ.
15. Foofy conducts a study to determine if hearing an argument in favor of an issue alters participants' attitudes toward the issue one way or the other. She presents a thirty-second speech in favor of an issue to 8 participants. In a national survey,

the mean attitude score in favor of the issue was $\mu = 50$. With this survey, she obtains the following scores.

10 33 86 55 67 60 44 71

(a) What are H_0 and H_a? (b) What is the value of t_{obt}? (c) With $\alpha = .05$, what is the value of t_{crit}? (d) What are the statistical results? (e) If appropriate, compute the confidence interval for μ. (f) Using the preceding statistics, what conclusions should Foofy draw about the relationship between such arguments and their impact on attitudes?

16. For the study in problem 15, (a) What statistical principle should Foofy be concerned with? (b) Identify three problems with her study from a statistical perspective. (c) Why would correcting the problems identified in (b) improve her study?

17. Poindexter examined the relationship between the quality of sneakers worn by volleyball players and their average number of points scored per game. Studying 20 people who owned sneakers of good to excellent quality, he computed $r = +.41$. He immediately claimed to have support for the notion that better-quality sneakers are related to better performance on a somewhat consistent basis. He then computed r^2 and the regression equation. Do you agree or disagree with his approach? Why?

18. Eventually, for the study in problem 17, Poindexter reported that $r(18) = +.41$, $p > .05$. (a) What should he conclude about this relationship? (b) What other computations should he perform to describe the relationship in these data? (c) What statistical principle should he be concerned with? (d) What aspects of the study can he improve to deal better with this principle? (e) What will correcting these things from (d) do in regard to his finding significant results?

19. A scientist suspects that as stress level changes, so does the amount of impulse buying. He collects data from 72 participants and obtains an r of $+.38$. (a) What are H_0 and H_a? (b) With $\alpha = .05$, what is r_{crit}? (c) What are the statistical results of this study? (d) What conclusions should be drawn about the relationship in the population? (e) What other calculations should be performed to describe the relationship in these data?

20. Foofy examines the relationship between an individual's physical strength and his or her college grade point average. She computes the correlation for a sample of 2,000 participants and obtains $r(1998) = +.08$, $p < .0001$. She claims she has uncovered a useful tool for predicting which college applicants are likely to succeed academically. Do you agree or disagree? Why?

21. A researcher investigates the relationship between handedness and strength of personality. She tests 42 participants, assigning left-handers a score of 1 and right-handers a score of 2. She obtains a correlation coefficient of $+.33$ between subjects' handedness and their scores on a personality test. (a) Which type of correlation coefficient did she compute? (b) What are H_0 and H_a? (c) With $\alpha = .05$, what is the critical value? (d) What should the researcher conclude about this relationship in the population? (e) What should she conclude about the direction of the relationship in the population? (f) Are the results of this study relatively useful?

22. A newspaper article claims that for all U.S. colleges, the academic rank of the college is related to the rank of its football team. You examine the accuracy of this claim. From a sample of 28 colleges, you obtain a correlation coefficient of $-.32$. (a) Which type of correlation coefficient did you compute? (b) What are H_0 and H_a? (c) With $\alpha = .05$, what is the critical value? (d) What are the statistical results? (e) What should you conclude about the accuracy of the newspaper claim for all colleges in the United States? (f) In trying to determine a particular school's academic ranking in your sample, how important is it that you look at the school's football ranking?
23. To predict a person's sense of humor from their mathematical ability, a researcher measures participants' math skills and how funny they find three puns to be. He tests 10 math majors and finds a nonsignificant *r*. (a) What characteristic of his participants may account for this result? (b) What problem with his criterion variable may account for this result? (c) What other obvious improvement in power can he achieve?
24. In question 23, say that previous research has shown that people with very high or very low math skills tend to find puns humorous, but those with intermediate skills do not. How can this finding account for the nonsignificant *r*?
25. You wish to compute the 95% confidence interval for a sample with $df = 80$. Using interpolation (described in Appendix B.3), determine t_{crit}.
26. A published research report includes one of the following statements. For each, identify *N*, the procedure performed and the outcome, the relationship, and the error possibly being made. (a) "When we examined the perceptual skills data, the mean of 55 for the sample of adolescents differed significantly from the population mean of 70 for adults, $t(45) = +3.76$, $p < .01$." (b) "The correlation between personality type and emotionality, however, was not significantly different from zero, with $r(25) = +.22$, $p > .05$."

SUMMARY OF FORMULAS

1. *The definitional formula for the single sample t-test is*

$$t_{obt} = \frac{\overline{X} - \mu}{s_{\overline{X}}}$$

$s_{\overline{X}}$ is computed as

$$s_{\overline{X}} = \frac{s_X}{\sqrt{N}}$$

s_X is computed as

$$s_X = \sqrt{\frac{\Sigma X^2 - \frac{(\Sigma X)^2}{N}}{N - 1}}$$

2. *The computational formulas for the single sample t-test are*

$$t_{obt} = \frac{\overline{X} - \mu}{\sqrt{\frac{s_X^2}{N}}} \quad \text{and} \quad t_{obt} = \frac{\overline{X} - \mu}{\sqrt{(s_X^2)\left(\frac{1}{N}\right)}}$$

where s_X^2 is the estimated variance computed for the sample.
Values of t_{crit} are found in Table 2 of Appendix C for $df = N - 1$.

3. *The computational formula for the confidence interval for a single* μ *is*

$$(s_{\overline{X}})(-t_{crit}) + \overline{X} \leq \mu \leq (s_{\overline{X}})(+t_{crit}) + \overline{X}$$

where t_{crit} is the two-tailed value for $df = N - 1$, and $\overline{X}$ and $s_{\overline{X}}$ are computed using the sample data.

4. *To test a correlation coefficient*, compare the obtained correlation coefficient to the critical value.
   (a) *Critical values of r* are found in Appendix C, Table 3, for $df = N - 2$, where N is the number of pairs of scores in the sample.
   (b) *Critical values of* r_s are found in Appendix C, Table 4, for N, the number of pairs in the sample.
   (c) *Critical values of* r_{pb} are found in Appendix C, Table 3, for $df = N - 2$, where N is the number of pairs in the sample.

PART 5

DESIGNING AND ANALYZING TWO-SAMPLE EXPERIMENTS

So far, we've discussed statistical procedures for a single-sample experiment, which compares the $\overline{X}$ measured under one condition of the independent variable to a known value of μ under another condition. Now we will discuss the two-sample experiment: We measure dependent scores under two conditions of the independent variable, estimate the population μ for each, and determine if they reflect a relationship. In the next two chapters, we discuss the major design issues as well as the parametric statistics of two-sample experiments.

15

The Two-Sample Between-Subjects Experiment and the Independent-Samples *t*-Test

Getting Started

To understand this chapter, recall the following:

- From Chapter 3, recall what reliability and internal and external validity are. Also, review what a confounding is.
- From Chapter 10, understand the point-biserial correlation coefficient, r_{pb}.
- From Chapter 11, recall how to conceptualize the proportion of variance accounted for.
- And remember what you've learned about inferential statistics.

Your goals in this chapter are to learn:

- What constitutes a between-subjects design and independent samples.
- How to control participant variables in a between-subjects design.
- How to perform the independent-samples *t*-test.
- How to compute a confidence interval for the difference between two μs.
- How r_{pb} describes the effect size in a two-sample experiment.

In this chapter, we discuss how to design a two-sample experiment, including how to deal with the issue of participant variables. Then, we discuss how to analyze such research using the two-sample *t*-test, a test similar to the *t*-test in the previous chapter. Also, we'll discuss additional procedures for describing a significant relationship.

MORE STATISTICAL NOTATION

It's time to pay close attention to subscripts. We will compute the mean of each of two conditions, identifying one as $\overline{X}_1$ and the other as $\overline{X}_2$. Likewise, we'll compute an estimate of the variance of the raw score population represented by each condition, identifying one as s_1^2 and the other as s_2^2.

And here's a new one: So far, the uppercase N has stood for the number of scores in a sample. However, N actually indicates the total number of scores in the study, but with only one sample, it was also the number of scores in the study. Now, we will discuss experiments with two samples—two *conditions.* The lowercase n stands for the number of scores in a condition. Thus, n_1 is the number of scores in condition 1, and n_2 is the number of scores in condition 2.

DESIGNING THE TWO-SAMPLE EXPERIMENT

To perform the single-sample experiment discussed in previous chapters, we must already know the value of μ for a population of raw scores under one condition of the independent variable. Usually, however, research focuses on unknown psychological processes, so we do not know any μs. Instead, we estimate the μ that would be found in a condition by testing a sample under that condition and computing $\overline{X}$. The simplest approach then, is a two-sample experiment. In a **two-sample experiment**, participants' scores are measured under two conditions of the independent variable. Condition 1 produces $\overline{X}_1$ that we use to estimate μ_1, the μ for the population if everyone was tested under condition 1. Condition 2 produces $\overline{X}_2$ that represents μ_2, the μ for the population if everyone was tested under condition 2. If each condition would produce a different population of scores, then we have demonstrated a relationship in nature: As we change the conditions of the independent variable, the scores in the population also tend to change.

For example, say we are interested in the notion that people who witness a crime or other event may recall the event better when they are hypnotized. We will create two samples of participants who each watch a videotape of a supposed robbery. Later, one group will be hypnotized and then answer 30 questions about the details of the event. The other group—the control condition—will answer the questions without benefit of hypnosis. Thus, the conditions of the independent variable are the presence or absence of hypnosis, and the dependent variable is the number of questions answered correctly. You can envision this design as shown in Table 15.1. The recall scores are normally distributed ratio scores, so we compute the mean of each condition, summing vertically in each column. If the means differ, we'll have evidence of a relationship where, as the amount of hypnosis changes, recall accuracy also changes.

TABLE 15.1 Diagram of Hypnosis Study

The independent variable is degree of hypnosis, and the dependent variable is recall

	No hypnosis	*Hypnosis*
Recall scores →	*X*	*X*
	X	*X*
	X	*X*
	X	*X*
	X	*X*
	$\overline{X}$	$\overline{X}$

As usual, to allow a clear interpretation of the variables and behaviors under study, we apply all of the controls discussed previously. Thus, we seek a *reliable manipulation* of hypnosis so that when under hypnosis, all participants are consistently hypnotized to the same degree. We seek *reliable* and *valid* questions so that we actually and only measure memory for the robbery. We seek *internal validity* so that differences in recall scores between the conditions are really due to differences in hypnosis. And we seek *external validity* so that the way the samples operate is really the way the general population operates. Essentially, we accomplish these goals by controlling all *extraneous variables* that may fluctuate *within* a condition or *between* the conditions.

At the same time, we cannot claim to have demonstrated anything about a behavior unless there is a *significant* relationship in the sample data. But our statistical decisions are only as good as the data we collect (garbage in, garbage out!). Therefore, we also seek a *powerful design* that produces likely-to-be-significant data. For example, compare the powerful and unpowerful examples in Table 15.2. The powerful data provide a much more convincing demonstration that hypnosis improves memory: Hypnosis makes a relatively big difference in recall scores between conditions, and there is perfect consistency—no *error variance*—within each condition because no differences between scores occur. To achieve such data, recall that we seek a *strong manipulation* so that the hypnotized group is deeply hypnotized, and so we will see large differences in recall scores between the groups. Also, we seek to eliminate fluctuating extraneous variables so that we minimize differences in recall scores within each condition, making the relationship more consistent.

TABLE 15.2 Possible Data from Hypnosis Study Showing Little Power and Maximum Power

Unpowerful		*Powerful*	
No hypnosis	*Hypnosis*	*No hypnosis*	*Hypnosis*
30	20	10	30
10	8	10	30
23	29	10	30
15	23	10	30
17	20	10	30
$\overline{X} = 19$	$\overline{X} = 20$	$\overline{X} = 10$	$\overline{X} = 30$

After we collect the data, the parametric statistical procedure to apply in a two-sample experiment is the two-sample t-test. However, there are two distinctly different ways to select the participants for our samples and, for each, there is a very different version of the t-test. One version, called the *independent samples t*-test, is discussed here. (The other version, called the *dependent samples t*-test, is discussed in the next chapter.)

> *REMEMBER* There are two versions of the two-sample t-test, depending on how the samples are created.

The **independent samples *t*-test** is used to analyze a two-sample experiment that consists of independent samples. With **independent samples**, participants are selected for each condition without regard for those selected in the other condition, and each participant serves in only one condition. You can recognize this design by the *absence* of anything fancy used to create the samples: We do not match up participants between the different conditions, nor do we test the same participants in different conditions. Instead, in this design, we have one random sample of participants in one condition, and another, separate, and "independent" sample in the other condition.

Note that another name for a design having independent samples is *between-subjects*. Thus, also in a **between-subjects design**, participants are selected for a condition without regard for who is selected in another condition, and each participant serves in only one condition.

Therefore, we have a new and major design decision to make: Should we create a between-subjects design? Whether a between-subjects design is appropriate depends first on whether it is appropriate to compare participants in one condition to an entirely different batch of subjects in the other condition. For example, in the hypnosis study, we do not want participants to have practice with the different conditions and answer the memory questions more than once, so we should choose a separate sample for each condition, producing a between-subjects design.

> *REMEMBER* Part of designing a two-sample experiment is deciding whether to create a between-subjects design.

This decision involves more than just whether it is appropriate to have two independent samples. Whether a between-subjects design is appropriate also depends on whether we can still adequately control important participant variables.

CONTROLLING PARTICIPANT VARIABLES IN A BETWEEN-SUBJECTS DESIGN

So far, we've taken the participants in a study pretty much for granted. But participants are thinking, feeling and behaving organisms who can modify any measurement procedure. Therefore, an important aspect of designing a study is to consider participant variables that may unduly influence the results. Recall that **participant variables** are inherent, personal characteristics that distinguish one individual from another. These are the variables that produce *individual differences*, and include differences in physical and mental ability, attitudes and emotions, personal history and experiences, and social or economic level.

Remember, we want to control any extraneous variable that may fluctuate *within* a condition or *between* the conditions. Participant variables that fluctuate *within conditions* threaten reliability because differences between participants cause them to respond differently and inconsistently, resulting in error variance. Participant variables that fluctuate *between conditions* threaten internal validity, because we cannot know whether differences in scores between the conditions are due to our manipulation or to the participant variable. Ideally, therefore, we seek to control all such variables so that all participants are equivalent on any variable that may influence the results.

> *REMEMBER* Whether a between-subjects design is appropriate depends on whether it allows for adequate control of important participant variables.

To identify participant variables to control, look for any characteristic that is substantially correlated with the independent and dependent variables. Such a correlation *may* indicate that the extraneous variable has a causal influence. First, look for differences among participants that may influence the impact of the independent variable. In the hypnosis study, for example, people differ in how easily they are hypnotized, how long they remain "under," and so on. If our participants differ greatly along this variable, then not everyone in the hypnosis condition will experience the same hypnosis, and so we may not produce consistent, significant differences in recall between the conditions.

Second, look for differences among participants that may influence responses on the dependent variable. For example, when measuring recall of the videotaped robbery, a person's inherent memory ability will influence his or her retention of the details. This can produce differences in recall scores between or within our conditions, although they will have nothing to do with the effect of hypnosis.

Generally, when the stimulus is rather concrete and elicits a physical response, look for participant variables that influence physical responses. These may be physiological, such as participants' height or degree of coordination, or psychological, such as their cognitive abilities or motivation. For stimuli and responses that involve social behaviors or attitudes, look for variables that influence social processes, such as personality or cultural differences. As usual, the research literature is helpful in identifying important participant variables to control. Research specifically related to your study will indicate variables that others believed needed controlling. General research investigating individual differences will indicate variables that can influence the behavior you are studying.

> *REMEMBER* A participant variable that is correlated with the influence of the independent variable or with performance on the dependent variable is a potential variable to control.

With a between-subjects design, our first line of defense for controlling participant variables is random assignment.

Random Assignment

In a between-subjects design involving a true independent variable, we use **random assignment** of participants to each condition. This controls participant variables by randomly mixing them, so that differences in a variable are balanced out in each condition. For example, by randomly assigning people to our hypnosis conditions, some who have a good memory and some who do not should end up in each condition. Overall, differences in recall scores between the conditions should not be due to differences in the memory ability of participants, so this potential confounding should be eliminated.

Be careful, however, to assign participants in a truly random way, avoiding any hidden variable that determines their assignment. For example, we wouldn't assign students who sit in the front of a class all to one condition and those sitting in the back to the other. Where students sit is not random, so we might confound the conditions with various personal characteristics. Similarly, do not assign to the same condition all people who first volunteer for a study. Those who participate early in a study may be more prompt, compulsive, or ambitious than later subjects. Instead, randomly assign participants to different conditions as they arrive so that such characteristics are spread out between conditions.

Pros and cons of random assignment Given how frequently research findings can be replicated, random assignment—and random selection—are powerful tools for producing balanced, representative samples in each condition. This is especially heartening because we often cannot identify the important participant variables to be controlled. With random assignment, we don't need to know the variables that are being controlled, because whatever they are in the population, they occur in a balanced way in each condition.

There are, however, three potential problems with random assignment. First, random assignment is not guaranteed to balance participant variables within each condition. Thus, for example, by chance we may still have people in one hypnosis condition who all have a much better memory than those in the other, so that the independent variable is confounded. Second, random assignment works less well with small samples, so with small *ns* we are likely to have groups that differ along important participant variables. Third, when random assignment does balance out a variable effectively, the variable then fluctuates *within* each condition. But then this fluctuation can produce differences in *scores* within each condition. After all, the reason we control a variable is because we think that more or less of it makes a *difference* in scores. Therefore, random assignment can produce potentially larger differences—larger error variance—among the scores within each condition, resulting in a weaker relationship. For example, we should end up with participants in each hypnosis condition having various memory abilities. But this may then produce a wide range in recall scores within each condition, resulting in the weaker, less powerful relationship shown back in Table 15.2.

Because of these potential problems, researchers sometimes actively control participant variables. One approach is to balance such variables.

Balancing Participant Variables

We do not leave the balancing of a critical participant variable to random chance, because the possibility of a serious confounding is too great. Instead, we control the variable by systematically balancing or *counterbalancing* its influence within each condition.

To balance a participant variable, we first make the variable part of our *selection criteria*. For obvious physical or personal characteristics (e.g. gender or age), we merely solicit participants who meet the criteria. For less obvious characteristics, we

pretest participants, in which, prior to conducting the study, we measure potential participants on the variable to be controlled. For example, we may measure a physical attribute (strength), a cognitive skill (reading ability), or a personality trait (anxiety level). Recognize that conducting a pretest is no different from measuring participants on a dependent variable, so we need a valid and reliable measurement technique that takes into account such issues as scoring criteria, sensitivity, demand characteristics, order effects, and so on.

Using the pretest information, we create a separate subject "pool" for each aspect of the variable we wish to balance. For example, in the hypnosis study, we could control participants' gender by creating a pool of males and a pool of females. To control for memory ability, we could identify those males and females who have good and poor memory using an appropriate pretest. Then, we assign participants so that each pool is represented in each condition in a balanced way. For example, we could randomly select and randomly assign participants so that 25% of those assigned to each condition are from the male-good memory pool, 25% are from the female-good memory pool, and so on. This design is shown in Table 15.3. The *X*s in each row represent participants' scores from the corresponding pool. To determine the effect of the conditions of hypnosis, we ignore gender and memory ability and average all scores vertically in a condition. Then, the mean score in each condition should be equally influenced by differences in memory ability and gender, so that any differences between conditions cannot be confounded by these variables.

This procedure introduces an important new term: Above, when we ignore the gender and memory ability of participants and obtain an overall mean score in each column, we are "collapsing" across the participant variables. **Collapsing across a variable** means that we combine scores from the different amounts or categories of that variable. Above, we collapsed across gender and memory ability. If we used a male experimenter with half the participants in each condition and a female experimenter with the other half, we would collapse across experimenter gender by combining the scores of people tested by both experimenters, computing one overall mean for each condition. Likewise, when we test participants on multiple trials in a condition, we average them together, so we collapse across trials.

> ***REMEMBER*** Collapsing across a variable means that we combine the scores from the different levels of the variable.

TABLE 15.3 Diagram of the Hypnosis Experiment Showing Balancing of Gender and Memory Ability

	No hypnosis	*Hypnosis*
Male-Good memory	X X X X	X X X X
Female-Good memory	X X X X	X X X X
Male-Poor memory	X X X X	X X X X
Female-Poor memory	X X X X	X X X X
	$\overline{X}$	$\overline{X}$

Pros and cons of balancing The benefit here is that if we find a significant relationship, then, because we've balanced the participant variable, we can be sure that it was not a confounding, so we have greater internal validity. We also have greater external validity, because we demonstrate the relationship even with the different levels of the variable present. Above, we are sure gender and memory ability do not confound the results, and we demonstrate a more general relationship because different genders and memory abilities are present.

The drawback is that we are less likely to find a significant relationship. As with random assignment, counterbalancing involves changing a variable *within* conditions, resulting in greater variability in the scores within each condition. Above, by including males and females who have good and poor memories, we are likely to see larger variability in recall scores than if we tested only males or only people with a good memory. Thus, counterbalancing may produce a relatively large error variance, so we obtain a less consistent relationship that has less power and is less likely to be significant.

Also, if you think about it long enough, you can identify any number of variables to counterbalance in any study. The drawback is that extensive balancing schemes greatly complicate the design of a study. Further, because different participants must be tested with each level of a balanced variable, this may dramatically increase the number of individuals required in each condition. And finally, a pretest may alert participants to the variables under study or to the purpose and predictions of the research. This knowledge may communicate *demand characteristics* that participants respond to during the experiment proper. (To avoid such problems, some form of deception in the pretest may be necessary.)

> *REMEMBER* Balancing a participant variable ensures that it cannot confound the results, but it may produce increased error variance, and pretesting may communicate demand characteristics.

Limiting the Population

An alternative to counterbalancing a participant variable is to limit the population based on that variable, so that we keep the variable constant. Then, the variable cannot influence the results. For example, if we expect males and females to differ greatly in how hypnosis influences their memory, we might limit the population to males only or to females only.

We limit the population through selection criteria. We pretest participants to identify those who meet the criteria and are approximately the same on the participant variable. For example, we might create a pool of males who have a very good eyewitness memory. Then, from this pool, we would randomly select and assign participants to each condition.

Pros and cons of limiting the population There are two advantages to selecting participants from a more limited population. First, this increases internal validity by eliminating a potential confounding that might occur with random assignment: By testing only males, for example, gender cannot possibly confound the results. Second, this increases power by reducing the error variance: The more similar the participants, the less variable the scores are likely to be within each condition. Above, differences in scores within a condition that might occur between males and females will not occur when all participants are males. Therefore, the relationship will be stronger and more likely to be significant.

There are also two drawbacks to limiting the population. First, if we become too selective, we may create a *restriction of range problem*. For example, by limiting the study to just men with a very good memory, we might see little or no difference in recall scores *between* the hypnosis conditions. Second, because we are more selective in choosing participants, they represent a more limited population, and so external validity is reduced. Thus, if we test only males, we will have no basis for generalizing to females.

Researchers usually opt for increased power and internal validity, even at the expense of external validity. Therefore, the advantages of limiting the population usually outweigh the disadvantages.

> ***REMEMBER*** Limiting the population eliminates potential confounding by a participant variable and reduces error variance, but at the possible cost of restricted range and reduced external validity.

Selecting the Approach for Dealing with Participant Variables

Random assignment, counterbalancing, and limiting the population are not mutually exclusive procedures. We could, for example, limit the population to only one gender and then balance memory ability. And regardless of the extent to which we counterbalance or limit the population, we still rely on random selection and random assignment to balance any other participant variables within and between conditions.

There are two considerations when selecting a procedure or combination of procedures to control a variable. First, how important is the variable? The more likely it is to influence the results, the more it must be actively controlled. Never leave the control of a highly influential variable to random assignment: Either counterbalance it or limit the population to keep it constant.

Second, weigh the goal of having the statistical power to find a significant relationship with the goal of making internally and externally valid inferences about the relationship. The larger the number of variables that are counterbalanced, the more that scores within each condition may change, so the greater the error variance may be. Conversely, keeping a variable constant by limiting the population minimizes error variance, but at the cost of reduced external validity because a more unique type of participant is being tested.

The same problems arise when counterbalancing *any* environmental, researcher, or measurement variable as well. For example, we could balance experimenter gender, employing a male experimenter with half of the people in each hypnosis condition and a female experimenter with the other half. This would produce greater generalizability, because we demonstrate the relationship with both types of experimenter. But we would balance this variable because we expect that whether a male or female experimenter is present *makes a difference* to participants and to their scores. Therefore, counterbalancing will produce greater variability in scores within the conditions. If only a male or only a female experimenter were present throughout, however, we would see less error variance, but we would also demonstrate the relationship in a more limited situation.

There is no easy solution to this predicament. We strive for a happy medium, but, if pushed, researchers generally risk producing a unique situation. So, counterbalance only those few variables that are *likely* to confound the independent variable or that *seriously* bias dependent scores. Control other, more minor variables by keeping them constant.

> *REMEMBER* Whether to counterbalance an extraneous variable depends on how much it threatens internal validity.

If any of the above approaches do not solve a problem with a participant variable, we may instead employ the "within-subjects designs" discussed in the next chapter. However, if it is appropriate to use a between-subjects design and we have two conditions, the results are analyzed using the independent-samples *t*-test.

THE INDEPENDENT-SAMPLES *t*-TEST

Remember that with independent samples—with a between-subjects design—we randomly select and assign a participant to one condition, without regard to those selected for either condition. The samples then consist of *independent events*, which, as we saw in Chapter 12, means that the probability of a particular score occurring in one sample is not influenced by a particular score occurring in the other sample. Then, the data have the correct characteristics for this procedure.

As an example of this *t*-test, say that we conduct the hypnosis study using a between-subjects design, comparing the recall scores for a sample tested under hypnosis to those from a control condition that was not hypnotized. By now you know the routine: (1) Check the assumptions of the statistical procedure and create the statistical hypotheses. (2) Set up and perform the statistical test. (3) If the results are significant, describe the relationship.

Assumptions of the Independent-Samples *t*-Test

In addition to requiring two independent samples, this *t*-test requires that

1. The dependent variable measures interval or ratio scores.
2. The population of raw scores represented by each sample forms a normal distribution. (If each sample n is greater than 30, the populations need form only roughly normal distributions.)
3. And here's a new one: The populations represented by the samples have homogeneous variance. **Homogeneity of variance** means that the true variance (σ_X^2) of the populations represented by the samples is the same.
4. It is not required that each condition have the same n. (The more the ns differ from each other, however, the more important it is to have homogeneity of variance.)

Chapter 19 introduces a test for determining whether we can assume homogeneity of variance. For the moment, let's say that from the research literature, we find that the hypnosis study meets the above assumptions. Now for the statistical hypotheses.

Statistical Hypotheses for the Independent-Samples *t*-Test

Depending on the experimental hypotheses, we may have a one-tailed or a two-tailed test. For now, say that we don't specifically predict the *direction* of the difference that hypnosis will make between the two conditions, so we have a two-tailed test: We merely predict that the samples will be different, representing different populations that have different μs.

First, the alternative hypothesis: In general terms, we expect condition 1 to produce $\overline{X}_1$ which represents μ_1, the μ for the population under condition 1. Condition 2 should produce a different $\overline{X}_2$, representing μ_2, the μ for the population under condition 2. A possible outcome from such an experiment is shown in Figure 15.1. For statistical purposes, the specific values of μ_1 and μ_2 are not important. What *is* important is that μ_1 and μ_2 are *different* from each other. If the sample means represent a different population for each condition, then the experiment has demonstrated a relationship in nature: Changing the independent variable produces a change in the population of dependent scores.

Because we do not predict which μ will be larger, the predicted relationship exists if one μ is larger or smaller than the other. That is, μ_1 should not equal μ_2. We could state the alternative hypothesis as H_a: $\mu_1 \neq \mu_2$, but there is a better way. If the two μs are not equal, then their *difference* does not equal zero. Thus, the two-tailed alternative hypothesis is

$$H_a\text{: } \mu_1 - \mu_2 \neq 0$$

H_a implies that the means from our conditions each represent a different population of recall scores, having a different μ.

Of course, there's our old nemesis, the null hypothesis. Perhaps there is no relationship, so if we tested everyone under the two conditions, we would find the same population and μ. In Figure 15.1, for example, we might find only the lower or only the upper distribution, or we might find one in the middle. Then, the conditions of the independent variable literally would not make a difference in the population, and there

FIGURE 15.1 Relationship in the Population in a Two-Sample Experiment

As the conditions change, the population tends to change in a consistent fashion.

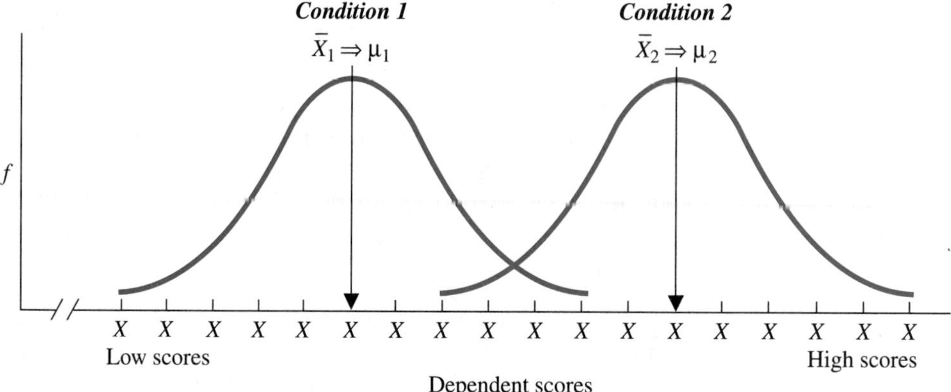

would be only one value of μ: Call it μ_1 or μ_2, it wouldn't matter, because μ_1 *equals* μ_2. We could state this as H_0: $\mu_1 = \mu_2$, but again there is a better way. If the two μs are equal, then their difference is zero. Thus, the two-tailed null hypothesis is

$$H_0: \mu_1 - \mu_2 = 0$$

H_0 implies that both sample means represent the same population of recall scores, having the same μ. If the sample means differ, it is because of sampling error in representing that one μ.

Notice that we derived these hypotheses without specifying the value of either μ, so we have the same hypotheses regardless of the dependent variable being measured. Therefore, the above hypotheses are the two-tailed hypotheses for *any* independent-samples *t*-test when testing whether there is no relationship in the population.

As usual, we test the null hypothesis, and to do so, we examine the sampling distribution.

The Sampling Distribution for the Independent-Samples *t*-Test

To understand the logic of the sampling distribution here, say that in the hypnosis study, we find a mean recall score of 20 in the no-hypnosis condition, and a mean of 23 in the hypnosis condition. We summarize these results by looking at the *difference* between the means: Changing from no hypnosis to hypnosis results in a difference in mean recall of 3 points. We always test H_0 by finding the probability of obtaining our results when H_0 is true. Here, we will determine the probability of obtaining a difference of 3 between two $\overline{X}$s when they both represent the same μ.

> ***REMEMBER*** The independent-samples *t*-test determines the probability of obtaining our difference between $\overline{X}$s when H_0 is true.

Think of the sampling distribution as follows. Using the same *n*s as in our study, we select *two* random samples from one raw score population. (Just like H_0 says happened in our study.) We compute the two sample means and arbitrarily subtract one from the other. The result is the *difference between the means*, symbolized by $\overline{X}_1 - \overline{X}_2$. We do this an infinite number of times and plot a frequency distribution of these differences. We have the **sampling distribution of differences between the means**, which is the distribution of all possible differences between two means when they are drawn from the raw score population described by H_0. You can envision this sampling distribution as shown in Figure 15.2. This is just like any other sampling distribution except that along the *X* axis are the *differences* between two sample means, each labeled $\overline{X}_1 - \overline{X}_2$. As usual, the mean of the sampling distribution is the value stated in H_0, and here it is 0. The mean is zero because most often both sample means will equal the μ of the population of raw scores, so the difference between them will be zero. However, sometimes by chance, both sample means will not equal μ or each other. Depending on whether $\overline{X}_1$ or $\overline{X}_2$ is larger, the difference will be greater than zero (positive) or less than zero (negative). The larger the absolute difference between the means, the farther into a tail of the distribution the difference falls, so the less likely such a difference is when H_0 is true.

FIGURE 15.2 Sampling Distribution of Differences Between Means when H_0: $\mu_1 - \mu_2 = 0$

The mean of this distribution is zero. Larger positive differences are to the right, and larger negative differences are to the left.

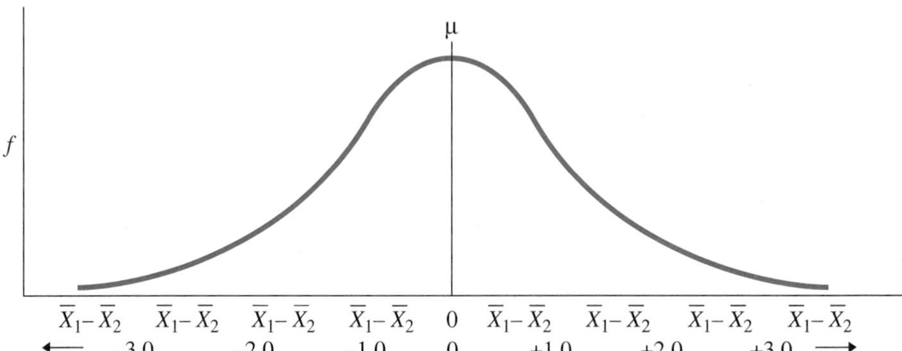

To test H_0, we simply determine where the difference between our sample means lies on this sampling distribution. Our model of this sampling distribution is the t-distribution, so we locate the difference by computing t_{obt}.

Computing the Independent-Samples *t*-Test

In the previous chapter, we computed t_{obt} by performing three steps: first computing the estimated variance of the raw score population, then computing the estimated standard error of the sampling distribution, and then computing t_{obt}. We complete the same three steps to perform the two-sample t-test.

Estimating the population variance First, compute s_X^2 for each sample, using the formula

$$s_X^2 = \frac{\Sigma X^2 - \frac{(\Sigma X)^2}{n}}{n - 1}$$

Each time, use the Xs from only one condition, and n is the number of scores in that condition.

Let's label the hypnosis condition as Sample 1, so its mean, variance, and n are $\overline{X}_1$, s_1^2 and n_1, respectively. For the no-hypnosis condition, we have $\overline{X}_2$, s_2^2 and n_2. Say that we obtain the results shown in Table 15.4.

Each s_X^2 estimates the population variance, but each may contain sampling error. (Because of this, if s_1^2 does not equal s_2^2, we have not necessarily violated the assumption of homogeneity of variance in the population.) To obtain the best estimate of the population variance, we'll compute a weighted average of the two values of s_X^2. Each variance is weighted based on the size of df in the sample. The weighted average of the sample variances is called the **pooled variance**, and its symbol is s_{pool}^2.

TABLE 15.4 Data from the Hypnosis Study

	Condition 1: hypnosis	*Condition 2: no hypnosis*
Mean details recalled	$\overline{X}_1 = 23$	$\overline{X}_2 = 20$
Number of subjects	$n_1 = 17$	$n_2 = 15$
Sample variance	$s_1^2 = 9.0$	$s_2^2 = 7.5$

THE COMPUTATIONAL FORMULA FOR THE POOLED VARIANCE IS

$$s^2_{pool} = \frac{(n_1 - 1)s_1^2 + (n_2 - 1)s_2^2}{(n_1 - 1) + (n_2 - 1)}$$

This formula says to multiply the s_X^2 from each sample times $n - 1$ for that sample, then add the results together and divide by the sum of $(n_1 - 1) + (n_2 - 1)$.

Placing the data in Table 15.4 in the above formula, we have

$$s^2_{pool} = \frac{(17 - 1)9.0 + (15 - 1)7.5}{(17 - 1) + (15 - 1)}$$

In the numerator, 16 times 9 is 144, and 14 times 7.5 is 105. In the denominator, 16 plus 14 is 30, so

$$s^2_{pool} = \frac{144 + 105}{30} = \frac{249}{30} = 8.30$$

Thus, we estimate that the variance of any of the populations of recall scores represented by our samples is 8.30.

Next, we use s^2_{pool} to compute the standard error of the sampling distribution.

Computing the standard error of the difference The standard error of the sampling distribution of differences between the means is called the standard error of the difference. The **standard error of the difference** is the estimated standard deviation of the sampling distribution of differences between the means. It indicates how spread out the values of $\overline{X}_1 - \overline{X}_2$ are when the distribution is created using samples having our n and our value of s^2_{pool}. The symbol for the standard error of the difference is $s_{\overline{X}_1 - \overline{X}_2}$. (The subscript indicates we are dealing with differences between pairs of means.)

In the previous chapter, for the single-sample t-test, a formula for the standard error of the mean was

$$s_{\overline{X}} = \sqrt{(s_X^2)\left(\frac{1}{N}\right)}$$

The formula for the standard error of the difference is very similar.

THE DEFINITIONAL FORMULA FOR THE STANDARD ERROR OF THE DIFFERENCE IS

$$s_{\bar{X}_1 - \bar{X}_2} = \sqrt{(s^2_{\text{pool}})\left(\frac{1}{n_1} + \frac{1}{n_2}\right)}$$

To compute $s_{\bar{X}_1 - \bar{X}_2}$, first reduce the fractions $1/n_1$ and $1/n_2$ to decimals. Then, add them together and multiply the sum times s^2_{pool}. Then, find the square root.

For the hypnosis study, s^2_{pool} is 8.3, n_1 is 17, and n_2 is 15. Filling in the above formula gives

$$s_{\bar{X}_1 - \bar{X}_2} = \sqrt{8.3\left(\frac{1}{17} + \frac{1}{15}\right)}$$

Because 1/17 is .059 and 1/15 is .067, their sum is .126. Then

$$s_{\bar{X}_1 - \bar{X}_2} = \sqrt{8.3(.126)} = \sqrt{1.046} = 1.023$$

Thus, our standard error of the difference equals 1.023.

After computing the standard error of the difference, we compute t_{obt}.

Computing t_{obt} In previous inferential procedures, we have found how far "off" our study's results were from the value in the population that H_0 says the results represent, measured in standard error units. We again perform this task, but now our results are the *difference* between our means. Also, the value in the population that H_0 says the results represent is now the *difference* between the μs. Thus, in the hypnosis study, we will measure how far 3 (the difference between our means) is from 0 (the difference between μs that H_0 says our means represent) when measured using the standard error of the difference. In symbols, we have

THE DEFINITIONAL FORMULA FOR THE INDEPENDENT-SAMPLES t-TEST IS

$$t_{\text{obt}} = \frac{(\bar{X}_1 - \bar{X}_2) - (\mu_1 - \mu_2)}{s_{\bar{X}_1 - \bar{X}_2}}$$

$\bar{X}_1$ and $\bar{X}_2$ are the sample means, $s_{\bar{X}_1 - \bar{X}_2}$ is computed as above, and $\mu_1 - \mu_2$ is the difference specified by the null hypothesis. (The reason for writing H_0 as $\mu_1 - \mu_2 = 0$ is that it indicates the mean of the sampling distribution and thus the value of $\mu_1 - \mu_2$ to put in this formula.)

For the hypnosis study, the sample means were 23 and 20, the difference between μ_1 and μ_2 specified by H_0 is 0, and $s_{\bar{X}_1 - \bar{X}_2}$ is 1.023. Putting these values into the above formula gives

$$t_{\text{obt}} = \frac{(23 - 20) - 0}{1.023}$$

Then,

$$t_{obt} = \frac{(+3) - 0}{1.023} = \frac{+3}{1.023} = +2.93$$

Our t_{obt} is +2.93. Thus, the difference of +3 between our sample means is located at something like a *z*-score of +2.93 on the sampling distribution of differences when H_0 is true and both samples represent the same population.

Computational formulas for the independent-samples *t*-test We can save a little paper by combining some of the previous steps. First, in the formula for $s_{\bar{X}_1 - \bar{X}_2}$, we replace the symbol for s^2_{pool} with the formula for s^2_{pool}. Then,

THE COMPUTATIONAL FORMULA FOR THE STANDARD ERROR OF THE DIFFERENCE IS

$$s_{\bar{X}_1 - \bar{X}_2} = \sqrt{\left(\frac{(n_1 - 1)s_1^2 + (n_2 - 1)s_2^2}{(n_1 - 1) + (n_2 - 1)}\right)\left(\frac{1}{n_1} + \frac{1}{n_2}\right)}$$

In the left-hand parentheses, compute s^2_{pool}, and by multiplying it times the value in the right-hand parentheses, and then taking the square root, we have $s_{\bar{X}_1 - \bar{X}_2}$.

We can also combine the steps of computing s^2_{pool}, $s_{\bar{X}_1 - \bar{X}_2}$, and t_{obt} into one formula.

THE COMPUTATIONAL FORMULA FOR THE INDEPENDENT-SAMPLES t-TEST IS

$$t_{obt} = \frac{(\bar{X}_1 - \bar{X}_2) - (\mu_1 - \mu_2)}{\sqrt{\left(\frac{(n_1 - 1)s_1^2 + (n_2 - 1)s_2^2}{(n_1 - 1) + (n_2 - 1)}\right)\left(\frac{1}{n_1} + \frac{1}{n_2}\right)}}$$

Compared to the previous definitional formula, here, in the denominator, the symbol for the standard error has been replaced by its above computational formula.

Thus, for the hypnosis study, we have

$$t_{obt} = \frac{(23 - 20) - 0}{\sqrt{\left(\frac{(17 - 1)9.0 + (15 - 1)7.5}{(17 - 1) + (15 - 1)}\right)\left(\frac{1}{17} + \frac{1}{15}\right)}}$$

which becomes

$$t_{obt} = \frac{+3}{\sqrt{(8.3)(.126)}} = \frac{+3}{1.023} = +2.93$$

Again, $t_{obt} = +2.93$.

Interpreting the Independent-Samples *t*-test

To determine if t_{obt} is significant, compare it to t_{crit}, which is found in Table 2 in Appendix C. As usual, obtain t_{crit} using degrees of freedom, but with two samples, the *df* are computed differently: Now, $df = (n_1 - 1) + (n_2 - 1)$.

> *REMEMBER* Critical values of t for the independent samples t-test are found using $df = (n_1 - 1) + (n_2 - 1)$.

Another way of expressing *df* is $(n_1 + n_2) - 2$.

For the hypnosis study, $n_1 = 17$ and $n_2 = 15$, so *df* equals $(17 - 1) + (15 - 1)$, which is 30. With alpha at .05, the two-tailed t_{crit} is ± 2.042. Figure 15.3 locates these values on the sampling distribution of differences. The interpretation here is the same as for previous inferential tests: H_0 says that the difference between our sample means is merely a poor representation of no difference between the μs. However, samples are seldom *that* poor at representing no difference. Essentially, the sampling distribution shows the differences between our conditions that sampling error would produce if the hypnosis and no-hypnosis conditions do not really differ in nature. But then, a difference of +3 hardly ever happens. Because t_{obt} (and a difference of +3) is in the region of rejection, we reject H_0 and conclude that the difference of +3 is unlikely to be representing zero difference in the population. In other words, the difference between our means is significantly different from zero. Because $\alpha = .05$, the probability is less than .05 that we have made a Type I error (rejected a true H_0).

We now accept the alternative hypothesis that the difference between the sample means represents a difference between the μs that is not zero. Then, we work backwards to the individual populations. Saying that the difference between the means is significantly different from zero is the same as saying that the two means differ significantly from each other. Here, the mean for hypnosis (23) is larger than the mean for no hypnosis (20). Thus, we have evidence of a relationship in the population where

FIGURE 15.3 H_0 Sampling Distribution of Differences Between Means when $\mu_1 - \mu_2 = 0$

The t_{obt} shows the location of $\overline{X}_1 - \overline{X}_2 = +3.0$.

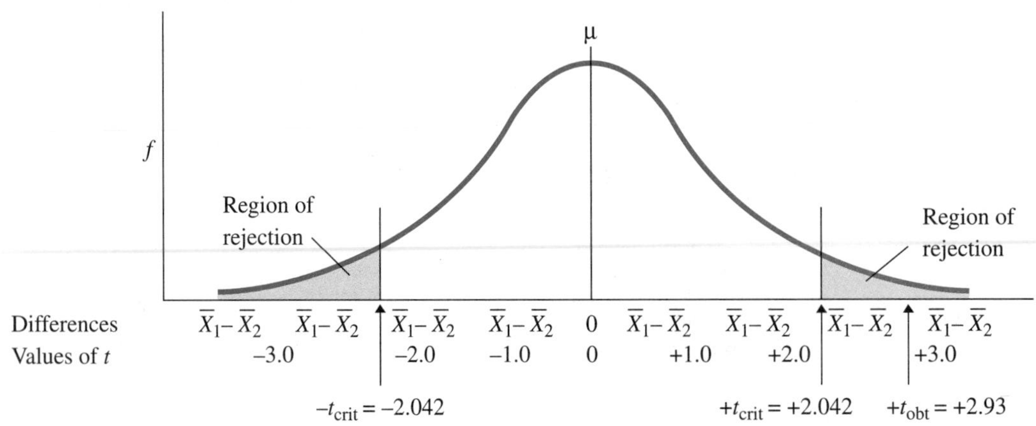

increasing the amount of hypnosis produces higher recall scores. So, to be precise, we conclude that hypnosis leads to significantly higher recall scores than no hypnosis.

If t_{obt} were not beyond t_{crit}, we would not reject H_0, and we would have no evidence—on way or the other— about a relationship between hypnosis and recall.

Because we did find a significant difference, we now proceed to interpret the relationship psychologically. To do that, we first want to describe and understand the characteristics of the relationship. From the previous chapter, you already know that one step would be to compute the confidence interval for a single μ for each condition. To do so, look at only one condition at a time, using its $\overline{X}$ and s_X^2, and compute a new standard error and t_{crit} as shown in Chapter 14. For each condition, the confidence interval will indicate the range of values of μ that the mean of the condition is likely to represent.

However, there is also another way to describe the populations represented by the conditions—by creating a confidence interval for the *difference* between their μs.

Confidence Interval for the Difference Between Two μs

The **confidence interval for the difference between two μs** describes a range of *differences* between two μs, any one of which is likely to be representated by the *difference* between our two sample means. For example, above, we found a difference of +3 between the sample means, so if we could examine the corresponding populations, we would expect their difference would also be *around* +3. The confidence interval will contain the highest and lowest values around +3 that the difference between our sample means is likely to represent.

THE COMPUTATIONAL FORMULA FOR THE CONFIDENCE INTERVAL FOR THE DIFFERENCE BETWEEN TWO μS IS

$$(s_{\overline{X}_1-\overline{X}_2})(-t_{crit}) + (\overline{X}_1 - \overline{X}_2) \leq \mu_1 - \mu_2 \leq (s_{\overline{X}_1-\overline{X}_2})(+t_{crit}) + (\overline{X}_1 - \overline{X}_2)$$

Here, $\mu_1 - \mu_2$ stands for the unknown difference we are estimating, t_{crit} is the *two-tailed* value found for the appropriate α at $df = (n_1 - 1) + (n_2 - 1)$, and the values of $s_{\overline{X}_1-\overline{X}_2}$ and $(\overline{X}_1 - \overline{X}_2)$ are computed in the *t*-test from the sample data.

In the hypnosis study, the two-tailed t_{crit} for $df = 30$, and $\alpha = .05$ is ± 2.042. We computed that $s_{\overline{X}_1-\overline{X}_2}$ is 1.023 and $\overline{X}_1 - \overline{X}_2$ is +3. Filling in the formula gives

$$(1.023)(-2.042) + (+3) \leq \mu_1 - \mu_2 \leq (1.023)(+2.042) + (+3)$$

Multiplying 1.023 times ± 2.042 gives

$$-2.089 + (+3) \leq \mu_1 - \mu_2 \leq +2.089 + (+3)$$

So finally,

$$.0911 \leq \mu_1 - \mu_2 \leq 5.089$$

Because $\alpha = .05$, this is the 95% confidence interval: We are 95% confident that the difference between our means represents a difference between μs that falls within this interval. In essence, if someone asked us how big a difference hypnosis makes for everyone when answering questions about an event, we'd answer that we are 95% confident that the difference is, on average, between about .09 and 5.09 correct answers.

Performing One-Tailed Tests on Independent Samples

We could have performed a one-tailed test if we had predicted the *direction* of the difference between the two conditions. Say that we predicted a positive relationship where the greater the degree of hypnosis, the higher the recall scores. Everything discussed above applies here, but beware: We *arbitrarily* call one mean $\overline{X}_1$ and one mean $\overline{X}_2$ and then subtract $\overline{X}_1 - \overline{X}_2$. How we assign the subscripts determines whether the difference is positive or negative, and thus whether t_{obt} is positive or negative. As you know, the sign of t_{obt} is very important in a one-tailed test.

To prevent confusion, use more meaningful subscripts than 1 and 2. For example, we could use h for the hypnosis condition and n for the no-hypnosis condition. Then, follow these steps:

1. Decide which $\overline{X}$ and corresponding μ is expected to be larger. (Say we think the μ for hypnosis (μ_{h}) is larger.)
2. Arbitrarily decide which condition to subtract from the other. (We'll subtract no-hypnosis *from* hypnosis.)
3. Decide whether the difference will be positive or negative. (By subtracting the smaller μ_{n} from the larger μ_{h}, the difference should be positive, or *greater* than zero.)
4. Create H_{a} and H_0 to match this prediction. (Our H_{a} is that $\mu_{\text{h}} - \mu_{\text{n}} > 0$; H_0 is that $\mu_{\text{h}} - \mu_{\text{n}} \leq 0$.)
5. Use the previous formulas for t_{obt}, but be sure to subtract the $\overline{X}$s in the same way the μs are subtracted. (We used $\mu_{\text{h}} - \mu_{\text{n}}$, so we'd compute $\overline{X}_{\text{h}} - \overline{X}_{\text{n}}$.)
6. Locate the region of rejection based on our predictions and subtraction. (Our $\overline{X}_{\text{h}} - \overline{X}_{\text{n}}$ must produce a positive and significant t_{obt}, so the region of rejection is in the right-hand tail of the sampling distribution, and t_{crit} is positive.

One-tailed tests are confusing because, while *still predicting a larger* μ_h, we could have reversed H_{a}, saying H_{a}: $\mu_{\text{n}} - \mu_{\text{h}} < 0$. Here, subtracting the larger μ_{h} from the smaller μ_{n} produces a difference that is less than zero, and subtracting the sample means this way should produce a negative t_{obt}. Now, the region of rejection is in the negative tail of the distribution and t_{crit} is negative.

Notice that if you subtract the $\overline{X}$s when calculating t_{obt} opposite to how you subtract the μs in H_0 and H_{a}, then the sign of t_{obt} will be opposite to the sign of t_{crit}, so the results cannot be significant.

DESCRIBING THE RELATIONSHIP IN A TWO-SAMPLE EXPERIMENT

The fact that a t_{obt} is significant is not the end of the story. If you stop after hypothesis testing, then you've *found* a relationship, but you have not *described* it. It's like saying,

"I've computed a correlation coefficient, but I'm not telling what it is." Therefore, you're not finished until you've fully described the relationship.

The starting point is always the sample mean for each condition, so that we understand the behavior by summarizing the typical score—and typical behavior—found in each condition. Also, pay attention to the *direction* of the difference between the means, because this indicates how the scores—and the behaviors—change as the independent variable changes. And then, confidence intervals generalize the findings, describing the range of typical scores—and typical behaviors—we expect in the population (in nature).

In addition, always describe the relationship by graphing it. Recall that we plot the mean of each condition on the Y axis and the conditions of the independent variable on the X axis. Thus, we would plot the results of the hypnosis study as shown in Figure 15.4.

Interpret the graph and relationship by, in essence, applying *correlational* statistics. We performed the t-test because it is the more powerful way to test H_0 in a two-sample experiment. However, recall that the advantage of correlational procedures is that only they describe the type and strength of a relationship. Thus, look at the graph as showing the relationship between participants' Y score (their dependent score) and their X score (their condition on the independent variable). First, the slanting line graph shows a positive relationship. By knowing the *type* of relationship present, we have more information when we try to understand the behaviors reflected by the variables.

Next, envision the *scatterplot* that the data would form: Because the mean is the center of the scores, the data points would be above and below the mean of 20 in the no-hypnosis condition and "around" the mean of 23 in the hypnosis condition. Also, recall from Chapter 11 that the *regression line* is the line that summarizes the scatterplot by running through its center. With only two conditions, the line graph connecting the means of the two conditions *is* the regression line. Thus, using it, we predict the mean score of 20 or 23, respectively, for any other people we might test under these hypnosis conditions.

What's missing is the *strength* of the relationship. Therefore, the next step is to think in terms of a *correlation coefficient*. Compute a correlation coefficient, however, *only* when t_{obt} is significant: It makes sense to describe a relationship only when we're first

FIGURE 15.4 Line Graph of the Results of the Hypnosis Study

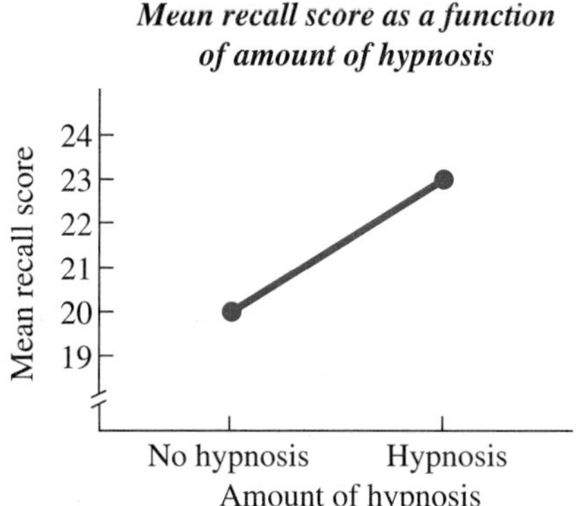

confident there *is* a relationship. Then, we correlate the scores from the dependent variable with the conditions of the independent variable.

> ***REMEMBER*** Whenever the results of an experiment are significant, think in terms of correlational procedures to describe and interpret the relationship.

Describing the Strength of the Relationship in a Two-Sample Experiment Using r_{pb}

The point-biserial correlation coefficient (r_{pb}) is the appropriate coefficient for describing a parametric two-sample experiment. This is because r_{pb} is used with one dichotomous X variable (that is, consisting of two categories) and one continuous interval or ratio Y variable. In a two-sample experiment, the conditions of the independent variable form a dichotomous X variable, and scores on the dependent variable are a continuous interval or ratio Y variable.

We could compute r_{pb} using the formula in Chapter 10, but instead we can compute it using t_{obt}.

THE FORMULA FOR COMPUTING r_{pb} FROM t_{obt} IS

$$r_{pb} = \sqrt{\frac{(t_{obt})^2}{(t_{obt})^2 + df}}$$

Insert the value of the significant t_{obt} and the df used in the t-test.

In the hypnosis study, $t_{obt} = +2.94$ with $df = 30$, so

$$r_{pb} = \sqrt{\frac{(2.94)^2}{(2.94)^2 + 30}} = \sqrt{\frac{8.64}{8.64 + 30}} = \sqrt{\frac{8.64}{38.64}} = \sqrt{.224} = .47$$

Thus, the relationship between amount of hypnosis and recall scores can be summarized as $r_{pb} = .47$. But, notice that the final step in the formula is to find the square root, so the answer will always be positive. Therefore, depending on the data, you must decide whether r_{pb} is positive or negative. The hypnosis study produced a positive relationship, so $r_{pb} = +.47$.

The r_{pb} here is interpreted as any other correlation coefficient: It describes how consistently participants scored at or close to the mean of their condition, and thus whether we should envision a "skinny" or "fat" scatterplot. Thus, a larger r_{pb} indicates a stronger, more consistent relationship. On a scale of 0 to ± 1, the hypnosis data produced a reasonably strong, consistent relationship.

Recall, however, that a problem with a correlation coefficient is that it can be difficult to interpret because we can only subjectively evaluate it relative to 0 and ± 1. Instead, the most direct way to evaluate a relationship is to square the correlation coefficient, computing the proportion of variance accounted for. In experiments, we do that by computing "effect size."

Describing Effect Size in a Two-Sample Experiment

To compute the proportion of variance accounted for in a two-sample experiment, square the value of r_{pb} (or simply don't find the square root in the previous formula). The answer is interpreted in the same way that it was back in Chapter 11. Essentially, r^2_{pb} indicates how much more accurately we can predict dependent (Y) scores when we know the condition under which participants were tested (their X score), compared to when we are unaware of the relationship and instead predict the overall mean of all Y scores in the study. For the hypnosis study, squaring r_{pb} is $.47^2 = .22$. Thus, on average, we are 22% closer to participants' actual recall score when we predict they scored at the mean of their condition, compared to when we predict they scored at the overall mean recall score in the experiment.

> *REMEMBER* In a two-sample experiment, r^2_{pb} equals the proportion of the variance in dependent scores accounted for by the relationship with the independent variable.

In an experiment, the proportion of variance accounted for goes by a different name: It is called the *effect size*. This is because when an experiment demonstrates a significant relationship, our explanation is that the independent variable has an *effect* on the dependent variable, "causing" dependent scores to change. (The quotation marks are there to remind you that we never *prove* it is the independent variable that causes the scores to change.) Thus, we explain the variability in recall scores, for example, as being caused by changing the conditions of hypnosis, and how consistently hypnosis does this is its effect size. The **effect size** indicates how consistently differences in the dependent scores are caused by changes in the independent variable. The larger the effect size, the more consistently the scores in each condition are located at or close to the mean for that condition, so the more consistent is the influence of the independent variable. (*Note:* There are actually several ways to measure effect size, but computing r^2_{pb} is a good way to do it in a two-sample experiment.)

The greater the effect size, the more that knowing the condition of the independent variable improves our accuracy in describing and predicting participants' dependent scores—their behavior—so the greater the scientific importance of the relationship. For example, we found that only 22% of the differences in recall scores are accounted for by hypnosis. We assume that everything has a cause, so there must be *other* variables that are causing the substantial unaccounted-for differences in recall scores (for example, perhaps a participant's attention to detail or concentration ability plays an important role). Therefore, hypnosis is only modestly important in determining recall scores in this study. A larger effect size would indicate that the scores are more similar within each condition. This would mean that the independent variable *alone* plays a greater role in determining each person's score, and so the variable is more important.

Although a large effect size indicates an important relationship in a statistical sense, it does not indicate importance in a practical sense. For example, the conclusion that memory is improved by hypnosis has limited practical importance. (To improve my memory, should I walk around under hypnosis all the time?) Statistical importance addresses a different issue: If we want to understand how nature works when it comes to hypnosis and memory, *then* this relationship is relevant and important. It is relevant because the results were significant, so we are confident that there really is a relationship found in nature. It is important to the extent that hypnosis accounts for 22% of the differences in recall scores.

> ***REMEMBER*** Effect size indicates how big a role the conditions of the independent variable play in determining scores on the dependent variable.

POWER AND THE INDEPENDENT-SAMPLES *t*-TEST

Remember that we always seek to maximize *power*, which is the probability of rejecting H_0 when it is false. We have seen that this boils down to producing as consistent and convincing a relationship as possible. In the *t*-test, a more convincing relationship translates into a larger t_{obt}, so the results are more likely to be significant. Then, in case we're in the situation where null is really false, we are less likely to retain it, and so we are less likely to miss a real relationship and make a Type II error.

Looking at the formula, there are three ways to create a more powerful design that increases the size of t_{obt}.

$$t_{obt} = \frac{(\overline{X}_1 - \overline{X}_2) - (\mu_1 - \mu_2)}{\sqrt{\left(\frac{(n_1 - 1)s_1^2 + (n_2 - 1)s_2^2}{(n_1 - 1) + (n_2 - 1)}\right)\left(\frac{1}{n_1} + \frac{1}{n_2}\right)}}$$

1. *Maximize the difference between the conditions.* Employ a strong manipulation that is likely to produce large differences in dependent scores *between* the conditions. This produces a larger value of $(\overline{X}_1 - \overline{X}_2)$, producing a larger t_{obt}.
2. *Minimize the variability within each condition.* Eliminate any fluctuating extraneous variable that might produce differences in scores *within* a condition. This minimizes each s_X^2, which results in a smaller s_{pool}^2. Then, the overall denominator is smaller, which produces a larger t_{obt}.
3. *Maximize the sample* ns. A larger n_1 and n_2 also results in a smaller denominator and thus a larger t_{obt}. In addition, larger *ns* give a larger *df*, resulting in a smaller t_{crit}. Then, t_{obt} is more likely to be significant.

Generally, for minimum power, at least 15 to 30 participants per condition are needed. Increasing the *ns* beyond this tends to substantially increase power, until *n* is 60 per condition. Increasing *n* beyond this number only modestly increases power. Of course, if more participants can easily be tested, this will increase external validity, which is also good. Further, if we cannot produce relatively large differences between conditions and/or we expect large error variance, we compensate by testing even larger *ns*. Reading the literature related to a study will show what other researchers find acceptable here. Also, for help in making decisions regarding power, there are advanced statistical procedures called "power analysis" (e.g., Cohen, 1988).

> ***REMEMBER*** The power of an experiment is increased by larger differences between conditions, reduced variability within conditions, and larger *ns*.

It is especially important to keep an eye on the *n*s, because sometimes participants must be dropped from the study.

ELIMINATING PARTICIPANTS FROM THE DATA

Even with all our precautions, research never runs as smoothly as planned (Murphy's Law always applies). Some participants will behave strangely. (I've had people go to sleep!) Through debriefing, you may find some participants were biased by a demand characteristic or discover others who were told the details of the study by a previous participant. A fire drill may occur while testing someone, or your tape recorder may blow a fuse.

In such situations, participants are not participating in the study that you designed: They are not being exposed to the independent variable reliably, they are not responding as directed, or they are being influenced by extraneous variables. Therefore, you may exclude their data from the analysis. Be very sure that these participants do not belong in the study, and you cannot exclude them just because their scores do not confirm the prediction. (That's rigging the results and committing fraud: You might as well make up the data.) When in doubt, therefore, include a participant's data. But, if scores are clearly inappropriate, you can exclude them. Then, for the proper *n*, test additional participants to fill in for those excluded. (Any study that produces many excluded participants, however, is a problem, because it contains a consistent hidden factor that is selecting a biased sample.)

APA FORMAT FOR STATISTICAL NOTATION

Two-sample experiments are fairly common in psychological research, so you are likely to use two-sample *t*-tests in your own research, and you'll need to understand them when reading the research of others. The significant t_{obt} from the hypnosis study would be reported as $t(30) = +2.94, p < .05$. (Note the *df* in parentheses.)

Effect size is another procedure you'll frequently encounter. In fact, as of 1994, the American Psychological Association now requests that all published research include a measure of effect size.[1] It is better to directly report the effect size than the correlation coefficient, and remember that r^2_{pb} is one of several ways to measure effect size. Thus, we might say something like "The effect size, as measured by r^2_{pb}, was .22."

PUTTING IT ALL TOGETHER

Everything we've said about the independent-samples *t*-test boils down to the following: Design a well-controlled study by identifying potentially troubling participant variables and deciding on the best way to either balance them or keep them constant. Design a powerful study by testing sufficient *n*s, minimizing differences in scores within conditions, and maximizing differences between conditions. If the design meets the assumptions, create two-tailed or one-tailed hypotheses. From the sample data,

[1] See the fourth edition of the *Publication Manual of the American Psychological Association*, 1994, published by the American Psychological Association, Washington, D.C.

compute the $\overline{X}$ and s_X^2 for each condition, then compute s_{pool}^2, $s_{\overline{X}_1 - \overline{X}_2}$ and t_{obt}. Determine the appropriate t_{crit}. The t_{obt} is significant if it is beyond t_{crit}. If so, we are confident the results reflect a real relationship in nature (with $p < \alpha$ that we're wrong). Consider computing the confidence interval for the μ represented by the $\overline{X}$ of each condition or computing the confidence interval for the difference between the μs. Also, graph the results and compute the effect size using r_{pb}^2. Then, interpret the relationship psychologically.

CHAPTER SUMMARY

1. A *between-subjects design* contains *independent samples*. Two samples are independent when participants are randomly selected for a condition, without regard for who else has been selected for either condition, and each participant is in only one condition.
2. Researchers control participant variables that are correlated with the influence of the independent variable or with performance on the dependent variable.
3. In a between-subjects design, participant variables are controlled by balancing them through *random assignment*, by *counterbalancing* them, and by keeping them constant through *limiting the population* being sampled.
4. Counterbalancing participant variables tends to increase internal and external validity, but it may increase error variance and reduce power. Limiting the population reduces error variance and increases power, but it may reduce external validity.
5. A *pretest* is used to identify participants who meet certain selection criteria.
6. *Collapsing across a variable* means to combine scores from the different amounts or categories of that variable.
7. The *independent-samples t-test* assumes that (a) two independent samples of scores measure an interval or ratio variable; (b) the populations of raw scores form a normal distribution; and (c) the populations have homogeneous variance.
8. *Homogeneity of variance* means that the values of σ_X^2 in the populations being represented are equal.
9. A significant t_{obt} from the independent-samples t-test indicates that the difference between $\overline{X}_1 - \overline{X}_2$ is unlikely to represent the difference between μ_1 and μ_2 described by H_0. Therefore, the results are assumed to represent the predicted relationship in the population.
10. The *confidence interval for the difference between the two μs* contains a range of differences between two μs, any one of which is likely to be represented by the difference between two sample means.
11. The strength of a significant relationship between the independent and dependent variables in a two-sample experiment is described by computing the point-biserial correlation coefficient (r_{pb}).

12. The *squared point-biserial coefficient* (r^2_{pb}) measures the proportion of variance in the dependent scores that is accounted for by changing the conditions of the independent variable.

13. The proportion of variance accounted for in an experiment is called the *effect size*. The larger the effect size, the more consistently the dependent scores change as the conditions of the independent variable change.

14. The power of the two-sample *t*-test increases with (a) larger differences in scores between the conditions, (b) smaller variability of scores within conditions, and (c) larger *n*.

KEY TERMS (with page references)

s^2_{pool} n_1 n_2 $s_{\bar{X}_1 - \bar{X}_2}$ r_{pb} r^2_{pb}
between-subjects design (403)
collapsing across a variable (406)
confidence interval for the difference between two μs (417)
effect size (421)
homogeneity of variance (409)
independent samples (403)
independent-samples *t*-test (403)
participant variables (403)
pooled variance (412)
pretest (406)
random assignment (404)
sampling distribution of differences between the means (411)
standard error of the difference (413)
two-sample experiment (401)

REVIEW QUESTIONS

(Answers for odd-numbered questions and problems are provided in Appendix D.)

1. A scientist has conducted a two-sample experiment. (a) What two versions of a parametric procedure are available to him? (b) What is the deciding factor for selecting between them?

2. (a) How do you create independent samples? (b) How do you create a between-subjects design?

3. How do you identify participant variables that may confound a study?

4. (a) How does random assignment to conditions control participant variables? (b) When is counterbalancing participant variables more appropriate than random assignment? Why?

5. (a) What positive impact does counterbalancing participant variables have on internal and external validity? (b) What negative impact does it have on the data?

6. (a) What positive impact does limiting the population have on the results of a study? (b) What negative impact does it have?

7. What problems arise from pretesting participants?

8. (a) What are the assumptions for the independent-samples *t*-test? (b) What is homogeneity of variance?

9. What does it mean to collapse across a variable?

10. (a) When is it acceptable to exclude a participant's data? (b) How might you reduce external validity by doing so?

11. After obtaining a significant two-sample t_{obt}, what three things should we do to complete the analysis?

12. (a) What does a measure of effect size indicate? (b) How is it computed in a two-sample experiment?

13. What three statistical procedures did you learn in this chapter?

14. (a) What does the confidence interval for the difference between two μs indicate? (b) How is this different from the confidence interval for a single μ?

PRACTICE PROBLEMS

15. In an experiment, a researcher seeks to demonstrate a relationship between hot or cold baths (the independent variable) and the amount of relaxation they produce (the dependent variable). He obtains the following relaxation scores:

Sample 1 (hot): $\overline{X} = 43$, $s_X^2 = 22.79$, $n = 15$

Sample 2 (cold): $\overline{X} = 39$, $s_X^2 = 24.6$, $n = 15$

(a) What are H_0 and H_a for this study? (b) Compute t_{obt}. (c) With $\alpha = .05$, what is t_{crit}? (d) What should the researcher conclude about this relationship? (e) Compute the confidence interval for the difference between the μs. (f) How big of an effect does bath temperature have on relaxation? (g) Describe how you would graph these results.

16. A researcher investigates whether a period of time feels longer or shorter when people are bored than when they are not bored. The researcher obtains the following estimates of the time period (in minutes):

Sample 1 (bored): $\overline{X} = 14.5$, $s_X^2 = 10.22$, $n = 28$

Sample 2 (not bored): $\overline{X} = 9.0$, $s_X^2 = 14.6$, $n = 34$

(a) What are H_0 and H_a for this study? (b) Compute t_{obt}. (c) With $\alpha = .05$, what is t_{crit}? (d) What should the researcher conclude about this relationship? (e) Compute the confidence interval for the difference between the μs. (f) How important is boredom in determining how quickly time seems to pass?

17. Foofy predicts that students who use a computer program that corrects spelling errors will receive higher grades on a term paper. She uses an independent-samples design in which Group A uses a spelling checker and Group B does not. She tests H_0: $\mu_A - \mu_B \leq 0$ and H_a: $\mu_A - \mu_B > 0$. She obtains a negative value of t_{obt}. (a) What should she conclude about this outcome? (b) Assuming that her sample means actually support her predictions, what miscalculation is she likely to have made?

18. To increase the power of the hypnosis study in this chapter, (a) How can we maximize differences between the conditions? (b) How can we minimize error variance? (c) What else should we do?

19. A researcher investigates whether classical background music is more or less soothing to air-traffic controllers than Top-40 background music. He plays classical background music to one group and Top-40 music to another. At the end of the day, he gives each subject an irritability questionnaire and obtains the following data:

$$\text{Sample 1 (classical): } \overline{X} = 14.69, s_X^2 = 8.4, n = 6$$

$$\text{Sample 2 (Top-40): } \overline{X} = 17.21, s_X^2 = 11.6, n = 6$$

After computing the independent-samples t-test, he finds $t_{\text{obt}} = +1.38$. (a) With $\alpha = .05$, report the statistical results. (b) What should the researcher conclude about these results? (c) What other statistics should be computed? (d) What statistical flaw is likely in the experiment? (e) What could the researcher do to improve the experiment? (f) What effect might this have?

20. An experimenter investigated the effects of sensitivity training on police effectiveness at resolving domestic disputes. He randomly sampled a group of police officers who had completed a sensitivity course and a group who had not. Participants were tested on their ability to successfully resolve a simulated domestic dispute. The following success scores were obtained:

No course	*Course*
11	13
14	16
10	14
12	17
8	11
15	14
12	15
13	18
9	12
11	11

(a) Should a one-tailed or a two-tailed test be used? (b) Subtracting *course from no course*, what are the null and alternative hypotheses? (c) Compute t_{obt} and determine whether it is significant. (d) Compute the confidence interval for the difference between μs. (e) What conclusions can the experimenter draw from these results? (f) Compute the effect size and interpret it.

21. If the results of problem 20 are not significant, what three things can the researcher consider to increase power?

22. (a) What is the final step when completing an experiment? (b) Why is r_{pb}^2 useful at this stage?

23. Someone proposes that a person's ability to become "absorbed" in a fantasy situation is an important variable we should control in the hypnosis study discussed in this chapter. How would we know if this proposal is correct?

24. It turns out that the proposal in problem 23 is correct. (a) What are three ways we might control this participant variable? (b) What is the best way, and why?

25. When reading a research article, you encounter the following: Identify the design, the N, the statistical procedure, the resulting relationship, and whether a Type I or Type II error is possibly being made. "The between-subjects t-test indicated a significant difference between the mean for men (5.4) and for women (9.3), with $t(58) = +7.93, p < .01$. However, the effect size was only .08."

SUMMARY OF FORMULAS

1. *The formula for computing the independent-samples t-test is*

$$t_{obt} = \frac{(\overline{X}_1 - \overline{X}_2) - (\mu_1 - \mu_2)}{\sqrt{\left(\frac{(n_1 - 1)s_1^2 + (n_2 - 1)s_2^2}{(n_1 - 1) + (n_2 - 1)}\right)\left(\frac{1}{n_1} + \frac{1}{n_2}\right)}}$$

Values of t_{crit} are found in Table 2 in Appendix C for $df = (n_1 - 1) + (n_2 - 1)$.

In the formula, $(\overline{X}_1 - \overline{X}_2)$ is the difference between the sample means, $(\mu_1 - \mu_2)$ is the difference described in H_0, s_1^2 and n_1 are from one sample, and s_2^2 and n_2 are from the other sample. Values of s_1^2 and s_2^2 are found using the formula

$$s_X^2 = \frac{\Sigma X^2 - \frac{(\Sigma X)^2}{n}}{n - 1}$$

2. *The computational formula for the confidence interval for the difference between two μs is*

$$(s_{\overline{X}_1 - \overline{X}_2})(-t_{crit}) + (\overline{X}_1 - \overline{X}_2) \leq \mu_1 - \mu_2 \leq (s_{\overline{X}_1 - \overline{X}_2})(+t_{crit}) + (\overline{X}_1 - \overline{X}_2)$$

where t_{crit} is the two-tailed value for $df = (n_1 + n_2) - 2$, the quantity $(\overline{X}_1 - \overline{X}_2)$ is the difference between the sample means, and $s_{\overline{X}_1 - \overline{X}_2}$ is the standard error of the difference found using the formula

$$s_{\overline{X}_1 - \overline{X}_2} = \sqrt{\left(\frac{(n_1 - 1)s_1^2 + (n_2 - 1)s_2^2}{(n_1 - 1) + (n_2 - 1)}\right)\left(\frac{1}{n_1} + \frac{1}{n_2}\right)}$$

3. *The formula for computing r_{pb} from t_{obt} is*

$$r_{pb} = \sqrt{\frac{(t_{obt})^2}{(t_{obt})^2 + df}}$$

With independent samples, $df = (n_1 - 1) + (n_2 - 1)$, where each n is the number of scores in a sample.

4. *The proportion of variance accounted for* in a two-sample experiment equals r_{pb}^2.

16

The Two-Sample Within-Subjects Experiment and the Dependent-Samples *t*-Test

Getting Started

To understand this chapter, recall the following:

- From Chapter 4, recall why we employ multiple trials and what order effects are.
- From Chapter 15, recall the reasons for controlling participant variables and how counterbalancing increases internal validity but also increases error variance. Also, recall the logic of two-sample experiments, how to graph the results, and how r^2_{pb} measures effect size.

Your goals in this chapter are to learn:

- The difference between matched-groups and repeated-measures designs.
- How subject history, subject maturation, and subject mortality can confound a study.
- What counterbalancing of order effects is.
- The pros and cons of matched-groups and repeated-measures designs.
- How to perform the dependent-samples *t*-test.
- How to compute a confidence interval for the μ of difference scores.
- How to compute effect size in a two-sample, within-subjects experiment.

In the previous chapter, we discussed one version of the two-sample t-test—the *independent-samples t-test* that is used with a *between-subjects design*. In this chapter, we discuss the other version of the two-sample t-test—the "dependent-samples" t-test that is used with a "within-subjects" design. In the following sections, we'll first see the logic and methods used for creating within-subjects designs and deal with some special problems they create. Then, we'll discuss the mechanics of performing the t-test, which you'll be happy to know is very similar to previous procedures.

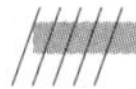

MORE STATISTICAL NOTATION

The major novelty in this chapter is that we will compute *difference* scores: the symbol D stands for the difference score produced when we subtract one *raw* score from another. We'll also compute the mean of the difference scores, symbolized as $\overline{D}$. When we compute the variance of the difference scores, we'll use the symbol s_D^2. And, when we discuss the population of difference scores, the mean of the population is μ_D.

DESIGNS THAT DIRECTLY CONTROL PARTICIPANT VARIABLES

In the between-subjects designs discussed previously, the approach was to control participant variables through random assignment and counterbalancing (for example, 50% of the participants in a condition are male and 50% are female, or participants who are tall are mixed in with those who are short). Then our *hope* is that the different levels of the variables cancel each other out, so that overall, the group in one condition is comparable to the group in the other condition. The problem is that this balancing act may not work. Then, if the participants in one condition are different from those in the other condition, the independent variable is confounded by the participant variable. Also, we saw that by intentionally changing a participant variable within a condition, we will produce different scores *within* the conditions, producing greater error variance and a weaker relationship.

Instead, to gain greater control of participant variables and to reduce error variance, we can more directly ensure that the individuals in one condition are comparable to those in the other conditions. We employ this approach when there is one or more *crucial* participant variable that must be controlled. As usual, such variables are correlated with the impact of the independent variable, or with the behavior measured by the dependent variable. To control such variables, unlike in the between-subjects design, we use somewhat fancy procedures for selecting participants and creating the samples. There are two types of designs we may use: matched-groups designs and repeated-measures designs.

Matched-Groups Designs

One way to guarantee we have comparable participants in each condition is to create a matched-groups design. In a **matched-groups design**, each participant in one condition "matches" a participant in the other condition(s) on one or more extraneous variable. Here is a simple example.

Say that we want to measure how well people in two samples shoot baskets in basketball, with one sample using a standard ball and the other using a new type of ball (with handles). Think of all the variables that we would want participants to be comparable on (e.g., physical size, skill level, amount of practice at basketball, motivation etc.). Consider the participants' heights. By the luck of random assignment, it is possible that one sample might end up with only tall participants, while the other contains only short participants. If this occurs, then any *apparent* differences in basket shooting produced by the independent variable could actually be due to differences in participants' height. In other words, height is *confounded* with the independent variable. Therefore, because height is so crucial in this setting, we won't leave its control up to the luck of random assignment. Instead, we will create two samples containing participants who are the same—have "matching"—height.

To create matched samples, first, identify pairs of participants who have the same score on the variable to be controlled (using a pretest if necessary). Notice, we match participants on an *extraneous* variable and *not* the independent or dependent variable! Then, randomly assign each member of the pair to one condition. Thus, above, we would identify pairs of people who are the same height, and assign one member of each pair to a condition. If we select two people who are 72" tall, we randomly assign one to each condition. Likewise, a 60" person in one condition is matched with a 60" person in the other condition, and so on.

If necessary, we can match participants on more than one variable. For example, we might want to match gender as well as height. This would produce the design shown in Table 16.1. Each row contains the scores of a matched pair of participants: the first pair consists of two males, both 72" tall, the second pair is two females, both 72" tall, and so on. (For *power* we'd test considerably more participants than four.) Think of a row as representing a very small experiment with one participant per condition. Any difference in basket shooting in the row cannot be due to differences in height or gender, because these variables are constant. Then, because an experiment with one participant per condition is not reliable, we replicate this study with other pairs.

TABLE 16.1 Diagram of the Basketball Experiment

Each row represents two people who are matched on gender and height. Each X represents a person's basket-shooting score.

	Standard basketball	***New basketball***
Pair 1: Male, 72"	*X*	*X*
Pair 2: Female, 72"	*X*	*X*
Pair 3: Male, 60"	*X*	*X*
Pair 4: Female, 60"	*X*	*X*
	$\overline{X}$	$\overline{X}$

In all other ways, the experiment is like any other, with all of the controls we've discussed previously. Thus, for example, for *reliability*, we'd test participants on *multiple trials*, having them shoot baskets with their particular ball a number of times. Then, we assume that random differences in their motivation, anxiety, or skill on different trials balance out. Here, each person's score would actually be a summary score, *collapsing* across trials. Then, we collapse the data by averaging vertically in a column, and the overall mean becomes a reliable estimate of the typical basket-shooting score in each condition. And, because the potential influence of different heights and gender is equally represented in each condition, any differences between conditions cannot be due to these variables.

Participants can be matched using any relevant extraneous variable, such as weight, age, physical ability, or the school they attend. We may also rely on natural pairs to match participants. For example, roommates or husband-and-wife teams are already matched in terms of having the same housing arrangements. Another common approach is to test identical twins, assigning one of each pair to a condition. Because genetic influences are equated, any differences in a behavior between the conditions must be due to environmental causes. Likewise, in animal research, pairs may be created from litter mates to match them on variables related to their experiences.

If it is difficult to find participants who have identical scores on the matching variable, you can rank-order participants and create pairs using adjacent ranked scores. Thus, above, the two males whose heights rank as 1st and 2nd would form one pair, the next two tallest men would form the next pair, and so on.

> ***REMEMBER*** In a matched-groups design, each participant in one condition matches a participant in every other condition in terms of one or more extraneous variables.

Pros and cons of matched groups The advantage to matching is that it ensures that in every condition there is a participant with virtually the same score on the participant variable(s) we wish to control. Then, these variables are constant across the conditions, eliminating these potential confoundings. By controlling height and gender in the above experiment, for example, we have greater internal validity for inferring that differences between the conditions are due to our treatment.

There are, however, limitations to a matched-groups design. Again, we have the problem that pretesting may communicate a study's hypothesis and thus increase *demand characteristics*. In addition, to find matching participants, we may have to pretest many individuals and/or settle for a very small *N*. Finally, with a design that involves several conditions of the independent variable, matching triplets or larger numbers can be very difficult.

The biggest problem, however, is in measuring and matching important participant variables. First, we may not know the important variables that need to be matched. Second, we may not have a valid and reliable method for measuring the matching variable. And finally, if there are many variables to control, it may be almost impossible to find individuals who match on them all.

When matching is unworkable but the study still calls for tightly controlling participant variables, we can instead employ a repeated-measures design.

Repeated-Measures Designs

The more variables on which participants match, the more potential confoundings that are eliminated. In fact, the ideal would be to have participants who are identical in every respect. The way to have identical participants is to test the *same* individual in each condition. This technique is called repeated measures. In a **repeated-measures design**, each participant is tested under all conditions of an independent variable.

Repeated measures are different from the "multiple trials" discussed previously. In multiple trials, the same participant is repeatedly observed in *one* condition. With repeated measures, the same participant is repeatedly observed under *all* conditions, regardless of the number of trials per condition.

Here's a different example for a repeated measures design, a classic called the "Stroop interference task" (Stroop, 1935). In this study, participants were presented colored ink patches, and the researcher measured their reaction time to identify the color present. In the control condition, only color patches were presented. In the experimental condition, the word name for a color was superimposed on a patch of a different color. To see how this works, quickly identify the color of the ink used to print the word below.

red

Identification of the ink color is interfered with by processing the word, so that reaction times are slowed.

Say that we wish to perform this type of study, with an experimental condition where color names are presented with colored inks, and a control condition where nonsense words (such as BJB) are presented with the colored inks. However, performance on this task depends on complex cognitive and perceptual processes, so potentially, the same problem exists as with the basketball study. If, by luck, one condition contains participants who are all better at these processes than those in the other condition, there is the possibility of confounding. However, we do not understand these processes sufficiently to know precisely which variables to directly control, and even if we did, counterbalancing in a between-subjects design would be unworkable, limiting the population would limit generalizability, and finding participants who match on so many variables would be impossible. The solution is to test the same people under every condition, thus keeping these variables constant. Therefore, we will measure participants' reaction time when presented the nonsense words and also measure the same people when presented the color names. This design is shown in Table 16.2. Each row represents the scores from one participant tested under both conditions, so although we have one sample of participants, we have two samples of scores. Again think of a row as representing a small experiment with the same participant in both conditions. Any difference in reaction time cannot be due to differences in participant variables because they are all constant. Then, for greater reliability, we replicate this study with other participants. (Again, we'd test more participants than those shown.)

All of the usual design requirements apply, so, for example, participants' gender is also counterbalanced. For reliability, we test multiple trials (say 50), using different word and color combinations (such as "yellow" printed in green ink, "blue" printed in red ink, and so on.) Then, each participant's score in a condition is actually the mean

TABLE 16.2 Diagram of Repeated Measures Design of Stroop Experiment

Each row represents one person tested under both conditions. Each X represents a person's mean reaction time for the trials in the condition.

	Nonsense word (e.g., BJB)	***Color name (e.g., RED)***
Participant 1 (male, order1)	*X*	*X*
Participant 2 (male, order2)	*X*	*X*
Participant 3 (female, order1)	*X*	*X*
Participant 4 (female, order2)	*X*	*X*
	$\overline{X}$	$\overline{X}$

reaction time for all trials in that condition. Recall that one problem with multiple trials, however, is *order effects*, the influence of experiencing a series of trials. Any one order—with its peculiar effects—could bias scores so that they are especially high or low. Therefore, we might control order effects by testing each half of our participants under one of two orders (indicated in Table 16.2 as order1 and order2).

Collapsing vertically in each column, the mean score for each condition is the typical reaction time per condition. Because the same people are being observed, any differences in mean reaction time between the conditions cannot be due to differences in participants' cognitive abilities, physical quickness, and so on, because such variables are represented equally in both conditions.

Note: a special type of repeated-measures design is employed when participants are measured before and after some event or treatment. This is called a **pretest-posttest design**. For example, to test whether meditation reduces physical stress, we might measure the same person's blood pressure before and after a period of meditation. Or, to determine the effectiveness of a weight-loss diet, we would measure each person's weight before and after a period of dieting.

> *REMEMBER* A repeated-measures design matches participants along all participant variables by testing each participant under all conditions of an independent variable.

Pros and cons of repeated measures The strength of a repeated measures design is that it should eliminate potential confounding from virtually any participant variable: Differences between the conditions should not be due to differences in such variables because the same participant is in every condition.

On the other hand, repeated measures have several drawbacks. First, repeated measures "should" keep participant variables constant, but individuals change from moment to moment, so they will be different from one condition to the next. In particular, there is the problem that participants eventually experience all of the conditions.

Therefore, participants may identify what they think is the purpose and hypothesis of the study, creating demand characteristics that lead to unnatural behavior. In the Stroop study, for example, people may erroneously decide they are supposed to respond slower to the nonsense words.

There is also a problem because we must test the various conditions in a sequence that occurs over time, and so scores will be influenced by several factors. **Subject history** refers to the fact that participants continue to have a life and experience things that can change them and influence their responses. Similarly, scores are influenced by **subject maturation**: As someone grows older and more mature, he or she changes in ways that influence responses. Such factors may *severely* reduce internal validity: A response to one condition measured now and a response to another condition measured later may be confounded by changes in a participant due to history and maturation.

Another weakness of repeated measures is that they produce greater "subject mortality." This doesn't mean that participants literally die (usually). Rather, **subject mortality** refers to the loss of participants because their participation "dies out" before the study is completed. This can occur in a between-subjects design or anytime that participants refuse to continue in a condition. It is most prominent when repeated testing requires a considerable amount of time per participant, so to reduce fatigue and overload, we spread out testing over several days. People show up for the initial session but do not return for later ones. The problem is, mortality effects are selective: People who continue to participate may find the study more interesting, perform better at the task, be more committed to helping science, or be more desperate for college credit or money. In any case, the results are biased. For example, in testing a new diet, the people who give up on dieting are likely to disappear. Those who stay may be so motivated that *any* diet would work well. Then, the success of the test diet may actually be due to a characteristic of the participants. Likewise, in any type of design, subject mortality results in only a certain type of participant, and so we lose external validity for generalizing to the broader population.

To counter these influences, try to obtain repeated measures (and multiple trials) within a short time span. Also, attempt to make the mechanics of participating in the study easy, with a task that is interesting and brief, so that its completion does not require extremely dedicated volunteers. And, pay attention to the degree of subject mortality, and during debriefing ask participants about their reasons for participating, so that you can gauge how biased the sample is.

> ***REMEMBER*** A repeated-measures design may be confounded by subject history, subject maturation, subject mortality, and demand characteristics.

Finally, a major problem with repeated measures is that they produce a new kind of order effects.

Controlling Order Effects in a Repeated-Measures Design

Recall that order effects are the influence of performing a series of trials. These effects include: (1) *Practice effects*—getting better at the task over trials; (2) *Fatigue effects*—getting worse at the task over trials; (3) *Carry-over effects*—the experience of any one trial that influences scores on subsequent trials; and (4) *Response sets*—from previous trials, developing a habitual response for subsequent trials.

Previously, we discussed order effects as they occur over multiple trials *within* a particular condition. With repeated measures, however, these effects also occur *between* conditions. After all, from a participant's perspective, changing from one condition to another largely involves an additional sequence of trials—more of the same. So, for example, in the Stroop study above, by the time participants get to the second condition, they may be tired and inattentive, or they may be very good at identifying ink color, or they may be very reactive to having the experimenter around. If the second condition were performed first, however, these influences might not be present. Further, order effects interact with the previous problems of subject maturation, history, and mortality. If a particular condition was performed at a different point in the sequence, maturation and history might not have changed participants so much. Or, perhaps subject mortality would have selected a different type of participant. Thus, performance in one condition may be higher or lower than in another, just because of the order effects operating on each condition. We cannot prevent order effects, but we can attempt to balance their influence.

To control for order effects in a repeated-measures design with two conditions, we *counterbalance* the order in which participants perform the conditions: Half the participants perform condition 1 followed by condition 2, and the remaining participants perform condition 2 followed by condition 1. Thus, in the Stroop study, half the participants will be tested first with the control condition, and half will start with the experimental condition, as shown in Table 16.3. All other design requirements still apply, so (1) the participants' gender is counterbalanced and (2) because we're testing multiple trials, we also control for order effects within conditions by testing different participants under different orders (indicated as order1 and order2). Collapsing vertically in each column, the mean score for each condition is the typical reaction time per condition. Because the same person is being observed, however, virtually all participant variables should be constant. Further, any difference between the two conditions is not due to a particular order in which the conditions were performed, because both possible orders of conditions are present. (The counterbalancing schemes used in more complex repeated-measures designs are discussed in Chapter 19.)

> *REMEMBER* Repeated-measures designs require counterbalancing of the order in which participants perform the conditions.

CHOOSING A DESIGN

There is much to consider when deciding whether to conduct the between-subjects (independent-samples) design discussed in the previous chapter or the matched-groups or repeated-measure designs discussed in this chapter. Usually, the choice is between repeated-measures and between-subjects designs. Matched groups are typically used for controlling only one participant variable, but when participant variables are an issue, there are usually many to be controlled.

A repeated-measures design is preferred when participants' responses are likely to be strongly influenced by individual differences in cognitive strategies, physical abilities, or experiences. Essentially, this design is used when it makes sense to compare a

TABLE 16.3 Diagram of Stroop Experiment Showing Counterbalancing of Order of Conditions

The top half of the diagram shows participants tested with one order, and the bottom half shows subjects tested in the reverse order.

		Nonsense word (e.g. BJB)	*Color name (e.g. RED)*
Participants tested in control condition first	*Participant 1 (male, order1)*	*X*	*X*
	Participant 2 (male, order2)	*X*	*X*
	Participant 3 (female, order1)	*X*	*X*
	Participant 4 (female, order2)	*X*	*X*
Participants tested in experimental condition first	*Participant 5 (male, order1)*	*X*	*X*
	Participant 6 (male, order2)	*X*	*X*
	Participant 7 (female, order1)	*X*	*X*
	Participant 8 (female, order2)	*X*	*X*
		$\bar{X}$	$\bar{X}$

participant in one condition to the same participant in the other conditions. Thus, studies involving memory and learning are usually conducted this way, as are studies that examine a sequence, as when studying the effects of practice or maturation. (As always, reading the research literature will help you to make this decision.) Further, we select such designs because repeated measures (and matched groups) are analyzed in a way that results in reduced error variance, producing a more powerful design than a comparable between-subjects design.

Other design considerations, however, may prevent the use of repeated measures: First, sometimes a particular condition may produce rather permanent changes in behavior so that one order of conditions has unique carry-over effects. If so, we have **nonsymmetrical carry-over effects**, which occur when the carry-over effects from one order of conditions do not balance out those of another order. Such effects occur whenever performing task A and then task B is not the same as performing task B and then task A. For example, we would not want to test the same participants in more than one condition if each involved some sort of surprise: You can surprise someone only once. Likewise, once you have taught participants something in one condition, you cannot "unteach" them in a subsequent condition. Or, as is often the case in animal research, a condition may involve some surgical technique that cannot be undone. In such situations, counterbalancing will not effectively balance out the bias produced by a particular order of conditions. Instead, use a between-subjects design, because no carry-over effects are possible.

Also, do not underestimate the influence of subject history, maturation, and mortality. These may be more detrimental to a study than the lessened control occurring in a between-subjects design. In addition, a repeated-measures design often places greater demands on our ability to create stimuli. Typically, we need many more different yet comparable stimuli when participants are exposed to all conditions than when they are exposed to only one condition.

Finally, consider the advantages of repeated measures versus the disadvantages of counterbalancing. As we saw in the previous chapter, controlling a variable through counterbalancing changes the variable within a condition, and thus tends to produce greater variability among scores within the conditions. Repeated measures almost always require extensive counterbalancing, and so including the influence of many changing variables tends to increase error variance, reducing the strength of the relationship.

The key to selecting a design is the number and importance of participant variables that must be controlled. If numerous uncontrolled participant variables could seriously reduce reliability and validity, then a repeated-measures design is preferred despite the difficulties it presents. If there are only a few crucial participant variables, however, a repeated-measures design may create more problems than it solves. Then, a better choice may be to identify the most serious participant variable and control it by matching participants on that variable in a matched-groups design. Or, we can obtain valid and reliable results from a between-subjects design, especially by balancing participant variables and/or limiting the population.

> ***REMEMBER*** Between-subjects designs are preferred if carry-over effects are nonsymmetrical, if the task does not allow repeated testing, or if extensive counterbalancing is unwise.

With either a matched-groups or repeated-measures design that involves two conditions, the results are analyzed using the dependent-samples *t*-test.

THE DEPENDENT-SAMPLES *t*-TEST

From a statistical point of view, there are only two major types of designs. On the one hand, recall that in a *between-subjects design*, we randomly select a different group of participants to serve in each condition, without considering those selected in the other conditions. On the other hand, in a **within-subjects design**, for each participant in one condition there is a comparable participant in the other conditions. Because this occurs in either a matched-groups or a repeated-measures design, in statistical terms, both are within-subjects design. (There's a bit of confusion here, because in research terms, a matched-groups design is sometimes called between-subjects, because it does involve different groups of participants. We'll call both matched groups and repeated measures within-subjects designs, because we analyze both in the same way.)

Matched-groups and repeated-measures designs are statistically similar, because both involve dependent samples. **Dependent samples** occur when each score in one sample is paired with a particular score in the other sample. The term "dependent" is used here as it was back in Chapter 12, when we described dependent events: They occur when the probability of one event is influenced by the occurrence of the other event. With dependent samples, the probability that a particular score will occur in one sample is influenced by the paired score that occurs in the other sample. For example, if a five-foot-tall male shooting baskets scored close to 0 in one sample, the probability is high that the matching five-footer also will score close to 0. This is not the case with independent samples. There, the fact that someone has a particular score in one condition does not influence the probability of someone else having that score in the other condition.

The distinction between independent or dependent samples is important because all previous inferential procedures have assumed we have *independent* samples. That is, when creating the sampling distribution and computing the probability of a particular mean or means, we computed the probability assuming we were describing independent events. With dependent samples, however, this probability must be computed differently. Therefore, when a design involves dependent samples, we employ the dependent-samples *t*-test. The ***t*-test for dependent samples** is the parametric procedure used for testing the sample means from two dependent samples.

> *REMEMBER* Perform the dependent-samples *t*-test when an experiment involves two conditions and is either a matched-groups or repeated-measures design.

Assumptions of the Dependent-Samples *t*-Test

Except for requiring dependent samples, the assumptions of the dependent-samples *t*-test are the same as those for the independent-samples *t*-test: (1) The dependent variable involves an interval or ratio scale; (2) It is normally distributed; (3) The raw score populations represented by the data have homogeneous variance; and (4) Because related samples form pairs of scores, the *n*s in the two conditions must be equal.

If the data meet the assumptions, then, as usual, create the statistical hypotheses, set up and perform the statistical test, and if the results are significant, describe and interpret the relationship.

The Logic of the Dependent-Samples *t*-Test

Enough about basketball and colored ink! Let's say we are interested in phobias (irrational fears of objects or events). We have a new therapy to test on spider-phobics. From the local phobia club, we randomly select a decidedly unpowerful N of five spider-phobics, and test the therapy using repeated measures of two conditions—before therapy and after therapy. That is, before the therapy, we measure each person's fear to a picture of a spider, measuring heart rate, breathing rate, etc., and then compute a "fear" score between 0 and 20. After providing the therapy, we again measure the person's fear response to the picture. (A pretest-posttest design such as this always calls for the dependent-samples *t*-test.) From reading related research, we can assume the study meets the assumptions of the dependent-samples *t*-test, and we set alpha at .05.

We expect to demonstrate that the therapy will decrease a person's fear, so our hypotheses are one-tailed: If we tested the therapy on the population of spider-phobics, we'd expect to find a relationship in which the μ of fear scores before therapy is *higher* than the μ of fear scores after therapy.

So far, this is similar to the one-tailed independent-samples t-test. However, instead of directly comparing the means from each condition, we must first transform the data. Then, we test the hypotheses using the transformed scores.

We transform the raw scores by finding the *difference score* (D) between the two raw scores in each pair. Say that in the phobia study we collected the data shown in Table 16.4. We find each difference score by arbitrarily subtracting each phobic's after-therapy score from the corresponding before-therapy score. (We could subtract the before scores from the after scores, but subtract all scores in the same way.)

The sample of difference scores is summarized by computing the mean difference score ($\overline{D}$). To do so, add the positive and negative differences to find the sum of the differences, (ΣD), and then divide by N, the number of difference scores. For the phobia data, $\overline{D}$ equals 18/5, which is +3.6. Thus, the before scores were, on average, 3.6 points higher than the after scores.

Now, here's the strange part: Forget about the before and after scores for the moment, and consider *only* the difference scores. From a statistical standpoint, we have *one* sample mean from *one* independent random sample of scores. As in Chapter 14, with one sample mean, we perform the single-sample t-test! The fact that we have difference scores in no way violates this t-test, so we will create the statistical hypotheses and then test them in virtually the same way we did with the single-sample t-test.

> ***REMEMBER*** The t-test for two dependent samples is performed by converting the raw scores to difference scores, and then applying the single-sample t-test to the difference scores.

Statistical Hypotheses for the Dependent-Samples *t*-Test

Our sample of difference scores represents the population of difference scores that would result if we could measure the population of raw scores under each condition and then subtract the scores in one population from the corresponding scores in the other population. The mean of the population of difference scores is μ_D. To create our statistical hypotheses, we simply determine the predicted values of μ_D in H_0 and H_a.

TABLE 16.4 Scores for the Before-Therapy and After-Therapy Conditions

Each D equals (Before − After).

Subject	*Before therapy*	−	*After therapy*	=	*Difference D*
1. (Foofy)	11	−	8	=	+3
2. (Biff)	16	−	11	=	+5
3. (Millie)	20	−	15	=	+5
4. (Attila)	17	−	11	=	+6
5. (Slug)	10	−	11	=	−1
					$\Sigma D = 18$

Start with H_a. In the one-tailed phobia study, we predict that the population of fear scores after therapy will contain lower scores than the population of fear scores before therapy. If we subtract the lower after scores from the higher before scores (as we did in the sample), then we should have a population of difference scores containing positive numbers. The resulting μ_D should also be a positive number. The alternative hypothesis always implies that the predicted relationship exists, so here,

$$H_a: \mu_D > 0$$

H_a implies that our sample represents a population of differences having a μ_D greater than zero, and thus that after-therapy scores are lower than before-therapy scores in the population.

On the other hand, there are two ways we may fail to demonstrate the predicted relationship. First, the therapy may do nothing to fear scores, so that the population of before scores contains the same fear scores as the population of after scores. Then, if we subtract the after scores from the before scores, the population of difference scores will have a μ_D of zero. Note that *not* every difference score in the population must equal zero. Because of chance fluctuations in physiological or psychological factors, not all participants will produce exactly the same fear score on two observations, and thus their difference scores will not be zero. On average, however, the positive and negative differences should cancel out to produce a μ_D of zero.

Second, the therapy can fail if, afterwards, people are *more* frightened. Then, subtracting larger after scores from smaller before scores produces a population of negative difference scores, with a μ_D that is less than zero. Thus, given the way we are subtracting to produce difference scores, our null hypothesis is

$$H_0: \mu_D \leq 0$$

H_0 implies that the sample represents such a population, and thus that the predicted relationship between therapy and fear scores does not exist.

As usual, we test H_0 by testing whether our sample mean is likely to represent the μ described by H_0. Here, H_0 says that the sample mean represents the population of difference scores where μ_D at most equals zero. If the sample perfectly represents this population, then $\overline{D}$ should equal zero. However, because of those chance fluctuations in fear scores, all of the difference scores in the sample may not equal zero, and then neither will $\overline{D}$. Thus, H_0 says that $\overline{D}$ represents a population where μ_D is zero, and if $\overline{D}$ is not zero, it's because of sampling error.

We always test H_0 by examining the sampling distribution of means, so here we examine the sampling distribution of $\overline{D}$. This is the frequency distribution of the different values of $\overline{D}$ that occur by chance when H_0 is true. Then, we locate our $\overline{D}$ on this sampling distribution by computing t_{obt}.

Computing the Dependent-Samples *t*-Test

Computing t_{obt} here is identical to computing the single-sample *t*-test discussed in Chapter 14, except that whenever a formula had the symbol X, it now has the symbol D. To compute t_{obt}, perform the following three steps.

1. First, find s_D^2, which is the estimated variance of the population of difference scores.

THE FORMULA FOR s_D^2 IS

$$s_D^2 = \frac{\Sigma D^2 - \frac{(\Sigma D)^2}{N}}{N - 1}$$

For example, the data from the phobia study are presented in Table 16.5. First, calculate N, ΣD, $\overline{D}$, and ΣD^2. Then:

$$s_D^2 = \frac{\Sigma D^2 - \frac{(\Sigma D)^2}{N}}{N - 1} = \frac{96 - \frac{(18)^2}{5}}{4} = 7.80$$

Essentially, if we could create the population of difference scores for the phobia study, we estimate that its standard deviation would be 7.80.

2. The second step is to find $s_{\overline{D}}$. This is the **standard error of the mean difference**, or the "standard deviation" of the sampling distribution of $\overline{D}$. (Just like $s_{\overline{X}}$ was the standard deviation of the sampling distribution when we called the mean $\overline{X}$.)

THE FORMULA FOR THE STANDARD ERROR OF THE MEAN DIFFERENCE IS

$$s_{\overline{D}} = \sqrt{(s_D^2)\left(\frac{1}{N}\right)}$$

For the phobia study, $s_D^2 = 7.8$ and $N = 5$, so

$$s_{\overline{D}} = \sqrt{(s_D^2)\left(\frac{1}{N}\right)} = \sqrt{(7.8)\left(\frac{1}{5}\right)} = \sqrt{1.56} = 1.25$$

Thus, if therapy really does not work, the sampling distribution of the different values of $\overline{D}$ that would occur has a "standard deviation" of 1.25.

TABLE 16.5 Summary of Data from Phobia Study

Subject	*Before therapy*	−	*After therapy*	=	*Difference D*	D^2
1	11		8		+3	9
2	16		11		+5	25
3	20		15		+5	25
4	17		11		+6	36
5	10		11		−1	1
	$\overline{X} = 14.80$		$\overline{X} = 11.20$		$\Sigma D = +18$	$\Sigma D^2 = 96$
$N = 5$					$\overline{D} = +3.6$	

3. The third step is to compute t_{obt}.

THE DEFINITIONAL FORMULA FOR THE DEPENDENT-SAMPLES t-TEST IS

$$t_{obt} = \frac{\overline{D} - \mu_D}{s_{\overline{D}}}$$

For the phobia study, $\overline{D}$ is $+3.6$, $s_{\overline{D}}$ is 1.25, and H_0 says that μ_D equals 0. Filling in the formula, we have

$$t_{obt} = \frac{\overline{D} - \mu_D}{s_{\overline{D}}} = \frac{+3.6 - 0}{1.25} = +2.88$$

This tells us that our sample $\overline{D}$ is located at a t_{obt} of $+2.88$ on the sampling distribution of $\overline{D}$ when $\mu_D = 0$.

Computational Formula for the Dependent-Samples *t*-Test We can combine the above steps of computing $s_{\overline{D}}$ and t_{obt} into one formula.

THE COMPUTATIONAL FORMULA FOR THE DEPENDENT-SAMPLES t-TEST IS

$$t_{obt} = \frac{\overline{D} - \mu_D}{\sqrt{(s_D^2)\left(\frac{1}{N}\right)}}$$

The numerator is the same as in the definitional formula. The denominator simply contains the formula for the standard error of the mean difference instead of its symbol.

For the phobia study, the formula gives

$$t_{obt} = \frac{+3.6 - 0}{\sqrt{(7.8)\frac{1}{5}}} = \frac{+3.6}{\sqrt{1.56}} = \frac{+3.6}{1.25} = +2.88$$

so t_{obt} is again $+2.88$.

Interpreting the Dependent-Samples *t*-Test

Figure 16.1 shows the sampling distribution for interpreting t_{obt}. This is another sampling distribution of means, except that each mean is from a sample of difference scores drawn from the population of difference scores where μ_D equals zero. For the phobia study, it essentially shows all values of $\overline{D}$ we'd expect to get because of chance fluctuations in participants' before and after scores if H_0 is true and the therapy really does not work. Because of these fluctuations, sometimes $\overline{D}$ will be positive and sometimes it will be negative. But, over the long run, the $\overline{D}$s will average out to be 0, so the μ of the distribution is zero. The values of $\overline{D}$ that are farther above or below zero are less likely

FIGURE 16.1 One-Tailed Sampling Distribution of $\overline{D}$s when $\mu_D = 0$

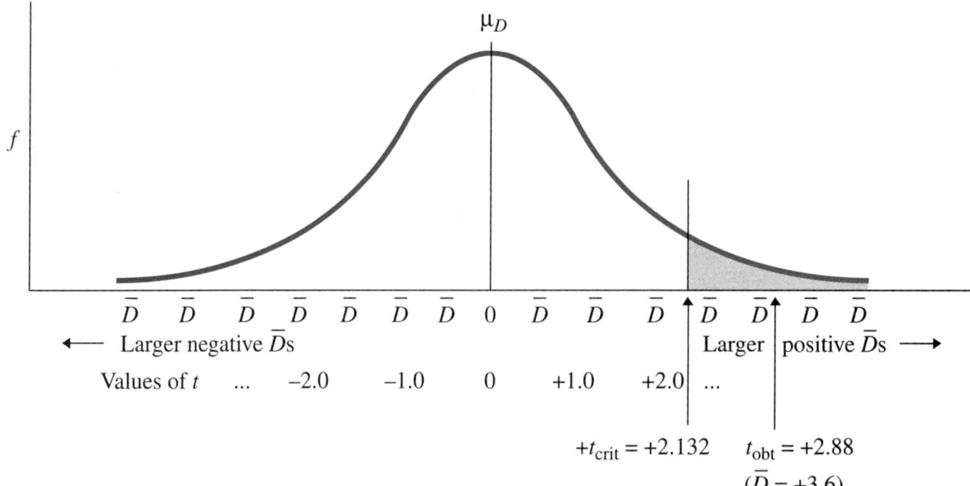

to occur when H_0 is true. Therefore, if our $\overline{D}$ (and its t_{obt}) is out there far enough into the tail of the sampling distribution, it is unlikely that H_0 is true.

We interpret t_{obt} by comparing it to t_{crit}. Find t_{crit} in the *t*-tables (Table 2 in Appendix C). Here, again, $df = N - 1$, but N is the number of *difference* scores.

> ***REMEMBER*** For the dependent-samples *t*-test, $df = N - 1$, where N is the number of *difference* scores.

For the phobia study, with $\alpha = .05$ and $df = 4$, the one-tailed t_{crit} is $+2.132$. It is *positive* because when we subtract the (hopefully) smaller after scores from the larger before scores, we should obtain a positive value of $\overline{D}$ that is significant. Such means are in the region of rejection in the upper tail, where t_{crit} is positive. Then, as shown in Figure 16.1 our t_{obt} of $+2.88$ is in the region of rejection, so our $\overline{D}$ of $+3.6$ is unlikely to be representing the population where $\mu_D \leq 0$. Therefore, we reject H_0, the results are significant, and we conclude that the $\overline{D}$ of $+3.6$ is significantly different from zero. (And we hope we haven't made a Type I error, whose $p < .05$.)

By rejecting H_0, we accept H_a that the sample represents a μ_D that is greater than zero. We would see such a population of difference scores only if the population of before-therapy scores contained scores that were higher than those in the population of after-therapy scores. Therefore, our results reflect two populations of scores, one for before therapy and a different, lower one for after therapy. This provides evidence of a relationship in the population so that changing the conditions of the independent variable (from before therapy to after therapy) results in different populations of dependent (fear) scores. In fact, looking at the original fear scores, the mean of the before scores was 14.80 and the mean of the after scores was 11.20. The difference between these means is also $+3.6$, and it too is significant. Essentially, a difference of $+3.6$ is significant here, regardless if it is calculated as the mean difference ($\overline{D}$) or as the difference between the raw score means ($\overline{X}_1 - \overline{X}_2$).

Thus, we conclude that the before-therapy and after-therapy scores represent a relationship in the population, so we are confident that the therapy works. As usual, we now interpret the results psychologically, using relevant hypothetical constructs, models, and theories to explain why these particular fear scores were observed in each condition and how the therapy works to decrease a person's spider-phobia. (If t_{obt} had not been beyond t_{crit}, then we would retain H_0, we would not have convincing evidence that the therapy reduces fear scores, and we'd worry whether we had made a Type II error.)

Above, we could have reversed how we computed the difference scores, subtracting the predicted larger before scores from the smaller after scores. Then, if the therapy did not work, we would expect a $\overline{D}$ of zero or greater, so we'd have H_0: $\mu_D \geq 0$. If the therapy worked, we would expect a negative $\overline{D}$ representing a μ_D less than zero, and we'd have H_a: $\mu_D < 0$. Or, if we could not predict the direction of the relationship, we'd create two-tailed hypotheses: The difference scores either do or do not reflect differences between the raw score populations. If the populations do not differ, then μ_D is zero, so H_0: $\mu_D = 0$. If the populations of raw scores differ, then μ_D is not zero, so H_a: $\mu_D \neq 0$. We would test any of these hypotheses using the same approach as in the hypnosis study.

As usual, for any significant result, we want to describe the relationship we have found. The procedures applied here are the same as those used previously with the independent-samples *t*-test. As shown in the following sections, we compute confidence intervals, graph the results, and compute the effect size.

> *REMEMBER* The three procedures to perform with *any* significant relationship are computing confidence intervals, graphing the relationship, and computing effect size.

Computing the Confidence Interval for μ_D

Based on our samples, our best estimate is that in the population, before therapy the μ would be *around* 14.80, and after therapy the μ would be *around* 11.20. It would be nice to compute a confidence interval here, but we *cannot* compute a confidence interval for each μ (as in Chapter 14), nor can we compute the confidence interval for the difference between two μs (as in Chapter 15): Our sample means are from *dependent samples*, and this violates the assumptions of these procedures. Instead, we must deal with the difference scores, because only they do not violate any assumptions. Because our $\overline{D}$ is $+3.6$, it probably represents a population of difference scores where μ_D is "around" $+3.6$. We compute a confidence interval to describe this μ_D. The **confidence interval for μ_D** describes a range of values of μ_D, one of which our $\overline{D}$ is likely to represent. We compute the interval by computing the highest and lowest values of μ_D that are not significantly different from $\overline{D}$.

THE COMPUTATIONAL FORMULA FOR THE CONFIDENCE INTERVAL FOR μ_D IS

$$(s_{\overline{D}})(-t_{crit}) + \overline{D} \leq \mu_D \leq (s_{\overline{D}})(+t_{crit}) + \overline{D}$$

(This is the same as the formula for the confidence interval for μ presented in Chapter 14, except the symbol $\overline{X}$ has been replaced with $\overline{D}$.) The value of t_{crit} is the *two-tailed* value for $df = N - 1$, where N is the number of difference scores. From the *t*-test, $s_{\overline{D}}$ is the standard error of the mean difference, and $\overline{D}$ is the mean difference score.

For the phobia study, $s_{\overline{D}} = 1.25$ and $\overline{D} = +3.6$, and with $\alpha = .05$ and $df = 4$, t_{crit} is ± 2.776. Filling in the formula, we have

$$(1.25)(-2.776) + 3.6 \leq \mu_D \leq (1.25)(+2.776) + 3.6$$

which becomes

$$0.13 \leq \mu_D \leq 7.07$$

Thus, we are 95% confident that our sample mean difference of +3.6 represents a population μ_D within this interval. In other words, if we performed this study on the entire population, we would expect the average difference in before and after scores to be between 0.13 and 7.07.

Graphing the Relationship

Graph the relationship from the dependent-samples *t*-test using the original *raw scores*. Plot the mean of the raw scores in each condition on the *Y* axis and the conditions of the independent variable on the *X* axis. For the phobia study, the mean fear score before therapy was 14.80, and the mean fear score after therapy was 11.20. They result in the line graph shown in Figure 16.2. Thus, we have summarized the typical score—and typical behavior—found in each condition, and the slanting line indicates a negative linear relationship here. Also, envision the scatterplot formed by the individual fear scores in each condition. Because the data points are around—above and below—the mean *Y* score at each *X*, the best prediction of someone's *Y* score in a particular condition would be the mean of that condition.

Computing Effect Size

What's missing is the *strength* of the relationship. As in the previous chapter, when the results of a two-sample experiment are significant, we can calculate the point-biserial correlation coefficient (r_{pb}). It is appropriate regardless of whether we have a within-subjects or between-subjects design. The only difference is that here the *df* equal $N - 1$, where *N* is the number of *difference* scores.

THE FORMULA FOR COMPUTING r_{pb} FROM t_{obt} IS

$$r_{pb} = \sqrt{\frac{(t_{obt})^2}{(t_{obt})^2 + df}}$$

Recall that the more informative statistic is the effect size (the proportion of variance accounted for). Again, it is the squared correlation coefficient, or r^2_{pb}. For the phobia study with $t_{obt} = +2.88$ and $df = 4$, $r_{pb} = -.82$, so, $r^2_{pb} = .67$. Thus, we can

FIGURE 16.2 Line Graph of the Results of the Phobia Study

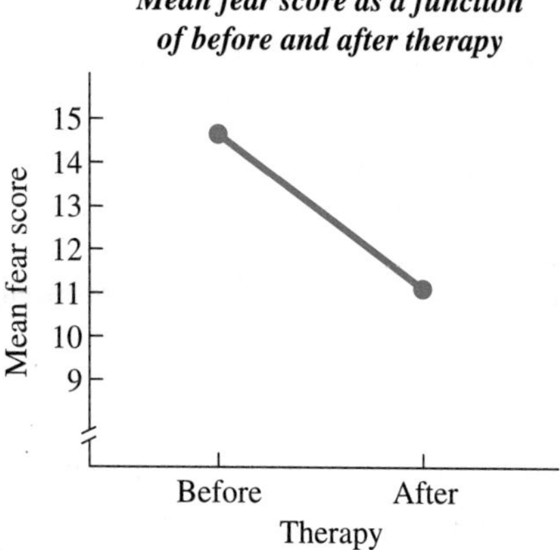

account for 67% of the variance in fear scores by knowing whether participants have undergone the therapy. In other words, on average we are 67% closer to predicting participants' actual fear scores when we predict the mean score of each condition for them, rather than when we predict the overall mean fear score of the experiment. Recall that the greater the effect size, the greater the scientific importance of a relationship. Thus, we have stumbled upon a rather important therapy, because so much of the changes in fear scores can be attributed to whether or not participants have experienced it.

> *REMEMBER* Always determine the effect size in the significant results of any between-subjects or within-subjects design.

POWER AND THE DEPENDENT-SAMPLES *t*-TEST

Remember power? Power is the probability of *not* making a Type II error, or the probability of rejecting H_0 when it is false. Recall that we maximize power by designing a powerful study, which in turn maximizes the size of t_{obt} relative to t_{crit}. Look again at the formula for t_{obt}:

$$t_{obt} = \frac{\overline{D} - \mu_D}{\sqrt{(s_D^2)\left(\frac{1}{N}\right)}}$$

Producing a powerful design and powerful data translates into a larger t_{obt} in the following ways:

1. A strong manipulation maximizes the difference between the two conditions, maximizing the size of $\overline{D}$. Then, the numerator in the formula is larger, so t_{obt} will be larger.

2. Controlling extraneous variables minimizes the variability of the raw scores in each condition. This minimizes the differences between the D scores, producing a smaller s_D^2 and thus a smaller denominator, resulting in a larger t_{obt}.
3. Maximizing N produces a smaller denominator and thus a larger t_{obt}. Also, a larger N gives a larger df, resulting in a smaller value of t_{crit}.

Recognize that the dependent-samples t-test is intrinsically more powerful than the independent-samples t-test. This is because dependent samples result in less variability among the scores. For example, say that we (incorrectly) reanalyzed the phobia study, pretending we had independent samples. The variability of the raw fear scores would be larger than the variability of the difference scores. Table 16.6 shows this for the scores of Participants 2 and 3 from the phobia study. Although there is variability (differences) in their before scores or in their after scores, there is no variability in their difference scores. Reduced variability produces a larger t_{obt}, so the t_{obt} for dependent samples will be larger than for independent samples. A larger t_{obt} is more likely to be significant, so a dependent samples design has greater power.

The increased power of a within-subjects design helps to compensate if, for any reason, we can test only a small number of participants using repeated measures. For comparable power in a between-subjects design, we need a larger N. In essence, the strategy is either to observe a few participants many times or to observe many participants on fewer occasions.

APA FORMAT FOR STATISTICAL NOTATION

In published research, the dependent-samples t-test is also called the *related*-samples or the *correlated*-samples t-test. Regardless, to report significant results, as from our phobia study, we report $t(4) = +2.88, p < .05$. The confidence interval for μ_D is usually described in words, and if we calculate the effect size using the point-biserial correlation coefficient, it is reported using the symbol r_{pb}^2.

PUTTING IT ALL TOGETHER

Recognize that when you start to counterbalance order and other extraneous variables, the process of designing a study may seem overwhelming. As a friend once remarked, "First, you have to consider *everything*!" This is true, but you don't have to *control* everything. Although we want data from a well-controlled experiment, we must actu-

TABLE 16.6 Scores of Participants 2 and 3 from Phobia Study

Participant	*Before therapy*	−	*After therapy*	=	*Difference D*
2	16		11		+5
3	20		15		+5

ally get the data! Don't try to control so many variables that you can't conduct the study. Instead, control those variables that seriously confound the results or severely reduce reliability. Keep in mind that when you institute a control to eliminate one problem, you often produce other problems. Therefore, you are never going to produce the perfect study, so produce the best study you can within practical limits.

Also, recognize that it is not a coincidence that all of the previous procedures seem to follow a repetitious sequence: In *all* inferential statistics, we locate a study's results on a sampling distribution by computing the obtained statistic. If the obtained value is beyond the critical value, the results are significant—the sample relationship is likely to reflect a real relationship in nature. Then, by looking at (usually) the means of the conditions, and using confidence intervals, a graph of the relationship and measures of effect size, we try to interpret what the relationship indicates about the underlying psychological processes that produced it. This is the pattern to expect in any study in the research literature, or in any study that you conduct.

CHAPTER SUMMARY

1. In a *within-subjects* design, for each participant in one condition there is a comparable participant in the other condition(s). In a *matched-groups design*, each participant in one condition is matched with a participant in every other condition along an extraneous variable. In a *repeated-measures* design, each participant is measured under all conditions of an independent variable.
2. A repeated-measures design that entails measuring participants before and after an event is called a *pretest-posttest design*.
3. Repeated measures are especially prone to confounding by *subject history*, *subject maturation*, *subject mortality*, and *order effects*.
4. *Subject history* refers to the fact that participants continue to have experiences that can change them and influence their responses.
5. *Subject maturation* refers to the fact that as an individual grows older and more mature, he or she changes in ways that influence responses.
6. *Subject mortality* refers to the loss of participants because their participation dies out before the study is completed.
7. To *counterbalance order effects* between two conditions in a repeated-measures design, half of the participants perform condition 1 and then condition 2, and the remaining participants complete the conditions in the reverse order.
8. *Nonsymmetrical carry-over effects* occur when the carry-over effects from one order of conditions do not balance out those of another order.
9. The *dependent-samples t-test* is the parametric inferential procedure used to test either a matched-groups or repeated-measures design. A significant t_{obt} indicates that the mean of the difference scores between the conditions ($\overline{D}$) is significantly

different from the μ_D described by H_0. Then, the means of the raw scores in each condition also differ significantly.

10. The *confidence interval* for μ_D contains a range of values of μ_D, any one of which is likely to be represented by the sample mean difference ($\overline{D}$).

11. The strength of a significant relationship between the independent and dependent variables in a two-sample experiment is described by the *point-biserial correlation coefficient* (r_{pb}).

12. The *effect size* in a two-sample experiment is the squared value of r_{pb}. The larger the effect size, the more consistently the dependent scores change as the conditions of the independent variable change, so (1) the greater the role of the independent variable in determining scores, and (2) the greater the accuracy in predicting scores (and understanding the behavior) when using the relationship.

13. The power of the dependent-samples *t*-test increases with (a) larger differences in scores between the conditions, (b) smaller variability of scores within each condition, and (c) larger *N*. All other things being equal, the *t*-test for dependent samples is more powerful than the *t*-test for independent samples.

KEY TERMS (with page references)

$\overline{D}$ s_D^2 $s_{\overline{D}}$ μ_D
confidence interval for μ_D (445)
dependent samples (439)
matched-groups design (430)
nonsymmetrical carry-over effects (437)
pretest-posttest design (434)
repeated-measures design (433)
standard error of the mean difference (442)
subject history (435)
subject maturation (435)
subject mortality (435)
t-test for dependent samples (439)
within-subjects design (438)

REVIEW QUESTIONS

(Answers for odd-numbered questions and problems are provided in Appendix D.)

1. A scientist has conducted a two-sample experiment. (a) What two versions of a parametric procedure are available to her? (b) What is the deciding factor for selecting between them?

2. (a) What is the difference between independent and dependent samples? (b) What are the two ways to create dependent samples? (c) What other assumptions must be met before using the dependent-samples *t*-test?

3. Which is more powerful, a dependent-samples or an independent-samples design? Why?

4. How do you identify participant variables that may confound a study?
5. (a) How can participant variables influence external validity? (b) How can they influence internal validity?
6. What is meant by (a) subject mortality? (b) subject history? (c) subject maturation?
7. How do each of the influences in question 6 bias your results?
8. (a) How is a matched-groups design created? (b) How does it control participant variables?
9. (a) How is a repeated-measures design created? (b) How does it control subject variables?
10. What problems are associated with a matched-groups design?
11. What problems are associated with a repeated-measures design?
12. What does the confidence interval for μ_D indicate?
13. A researcher has obtained a statistically significant two-sample t_{obt}. What additional procedures are needed to complete the analysis?
14. (a) What are nonsymmetrical carry-over effects? (b) Why won't counterbalancing the order of conditions be effective when such effects are present?
15. (a) What type of design is present in a pretest-posttest design? (b) How is it analyzed?
16. (a) Designs with independent samples also go by what other name? (b) Repeated-measures or matched-groups designs are also referred to using what two names?

PRACTICE PROBLEMS

17. A rather dim student proposes testing the conditions of "male" and "female" as a repeated-measures study. (a) What's wrong with this idea? (b) What control techniques can be applied instead?
18. For each of the following, identify the type of design and the type of *t*-test that is required: (a) An investigation of the effects of a new memory-enhancing drug on the memory of Alzheimer's patients, testing a group of patients before and after administration of the drug. (b) An investigation of the effects of alcohol on motor coordination, comparing one group of participants given a moderate dose of alcohol to the population μ for people given no alcohol. (c) An investigation of whether males and females rate differently the persuasiveness of an argument delivered by a female speaker. (d) The study described in (c) but with the added requirement that for each male of a particular age, there is a female of the same age.
19. You conduct a repeated-measures design, comparing a condition in which you train people to improve their memory to a control condition. (a) What problem will counterbalancing the order of conditions not solve? (b) What is the technical name for this problem?
20. You conduct a study in which the dependent variable is the degree of a participant's helpfulness in aiding a confederate to study for an exam in psychology. In each condition, participants are tested on five consecutive days. (a) What characteristics of the people who complete the study may bias the results? (b) What is the technical name for this problem?

21. In a repeated-measures design, a participant fails to return on the second testing. (a) Foofy says she won't bother about the score she'd have there, leaves it blank, and performs the dependent-samples t-test anyway. What's wrong with this idea? (b) To correct this problem, she decides to analyze the data using the independent-samples t-test. What's wrong with this idea?

22. A repeated-measures study of the effects of a motivational message compares the effects of the message to a control group on performance of 30 trials of a manual dexterity task. (a) Specify the scheme for dealing with order effects for both multiple trials and repeated measures. (b) Why should we counterbalance the order of conditions? (c) Why should we not counterbalance the order of conditions? (d) What alternative would eliminate the problems in (b) and (c)?

23. A researcher asks whether participants score higher or lower on a questionnaire measuring their emotional well-being after exposure to either high or low levels of sunshine. The same 8 participants are first measured after low-level exposure and then again after high-level exposure. The resulting well-being scores are

Low:	14	13	17	15	18	17	14	16
High:	18	12	20	19	22	19	19	16

(a) Subtracting low from high, what are H_0 and H_a? (b) Compute the appropriate t-test. (c) With $\alpha = .05$, report your results. (d) Compute the appropriate confidence interval. (e) What is the predicted well-being score for a participant tested under low sunshine? Under high sunshine? (f) On average, how much more accurate are these predictions than if we did not know how much sunshine participants experience? (g) What should the researcher conclude about these results?

24. A researcher investigates whether children exhibit a higher number of aggressive acts after watching a violent television show. The number of aggressive acts for the same ten children before and after watching the show are as follows:

Sample 1 (after)	*Sample 2 (before)*
5	4
6	6
4	3
4	2
7	4
3	1
2	0
1	0
4	5
3	2

(a) Subtracting before scores from after scores, what are H_0 and H_a for this study? (b) Compute t_{obt}. (c) With $\alpha = .05$, what is t_{crit}? (d) What should the researcher conclude about this relationship? (e) Compute the confidence interval for μ_D. (f) If you want to understand children's aggression, how important is it to consider whether they watch violent television shows?

25. You investigate whether the older or younger male in pairs of brothers tends to be more extroverted. You obtain the following extroversion scores:

Sample 1 (younger)	*Sample 2 (older)*
10	18
11	17
18	19
12	16
15	15
13	19
19	13
15	20

(a) What are H_0 and H_a for this study? (b) Compute t_{obt}. (c) With $\alpha = .05$, what is t_{crit}? (d) What should you conclude about this relationship? (e) Is this a scientifically informative relationship?

26. What would you do to increase the power of the phobia study discussed in this chapter?

SUMMARY OF FORMULAS

1. *The computational formula for the dependent-samples t-test is*

$$t_{obt} = \frac{\overline{D} - \mu_D}{\sqrt{(s_D^2)\left(\frac{1}{N}\right)}}$$

Values of t_{crit} are found in Table 2 in Appendix C for $df = N - 1$, where N is the number of difference scores.

In the formula, $\overline{D}$ is the mean of the difference scores, μ_D is the value described by H_0, and s_D^2 is the variance of the difference scores, found using the formula

$$s_D^2 = \frac{\Sigma D^2 - \frac{(\Sigma D)^2}{N}}{N - 1}$$

where D is each difference score and N is the number of difference scores.

2. *The computational formula for the confidence interval for* μ_D *is*

$$(s_{\bar{D}})(-t_{\text{crit}}) + \bar{D} \leq \mu_D \leq (s_{\bar{D}})(+t_{\text{crit}}) + \bar{D}$$

where t_{crit} is the two-tailed value for $df = N - 1$ where N is the number of difference scores, and $s_{\bar{D}}$ is the standard error of the mean difference, found using the formula

$$s_{\bar{D}} = \sqrt{(s_D^2)\left(\frac{1}{N}\right)}$$

where s_D^2 is the variance of difference scores and N is the number of difference scores.

3. *The formula for computing* r_{pb} *from* t_{obt} *is*

$$r_{\text{pb}} = \sqrt{\frac{(t_{\text{obt}})^2}{(t_{\text{obt}})^2 + df}}$$

where $df = N - 1$, where N is the number of difference scores.

4. *The proportion of variance accounted for* in a dependent-samples experiment equals r_{pb}^2.

PART 6

DESIGNING AND ANALYZING COMPLEX EXPERIMENTS

Each new type of experiment and its statistical procedure that we discuss is more complex than the previous one. So far, we are up to two-sample experiments involving two conditions of an independent variable. However, researchers often conduct experiments that involve more than two conditions. In fact, they often conduct experiments that involve more than one independent variable, with each involving more than two conditions. In the following three chapters, we will discuss such designs. We'll also see how they are analyzed using the procedure called the analysis of variance. This procedure can be applied to an almost limitless number of different designs, and it is by far the most common statistical procedure found in psychological research.

17

The One-Way Between-Subjects Experiment and the One-Way Analysis of Variance

Getting Started

To understand this chapter, recall the following:

- From Chapter 7, recall that variance measures the differences between scores by measuring their distance from the mean.
- From Chapter 13, understand why we limit the probability of a Type I error to .05.
- From Chapter 15, recall why we compute the effect size to describe significant results.
- And from our various discussions, understand that all inferential procedures involve testing H_0 by calculating a statistic that locates our data on the sampling distribution.

Your goals in this chapter are to learn:

- The terminology of analysis of variance.
- Why we compute the ANOVA and then post hoc tests.
- What is meant by treatment variance and error variance.
- Why F_{obt} should equal 1 if H_0 is true, and why F_{obt} is greater than 1 if H_0 is false.
- When to compute Fisher's protected *t*-test or Tukey's *HSD*.
- How "eta squared" describes effect size.

In this chapter, we'll discuss experiments that involve more than two conditions from one independent variable. However, the design issues concerning *any* experiment are largely the same and you already know them. Therefore, our focus will be on the statistical procedure used with such experiments, called *analysis of variance*.

MORE STATISTICAL NOTATION

The analysis of variance has its own language:

1. Analysis of variance is abbreviated as **ANOVA**.
2. An independent variable is called a **factor**.
3. Each condition of the independent variable is also called a **level** or **treatment**, and differences produced by the independent variable are a **treatment effect**.
4. The symbol for the number of levels in a factor is **k**.
5. There are different versions of ANOVA: When an experiment contains conditions from one independent variable it is a **one-way design** analyzed using a **one-way ANOVA**.
6. When the independent variable is tested using independent samples in all conditions, it is a **between-subjects factor** and we perform the **between-subjects ANOVA**. When the independent variable involves dependent samples, it is a **within-subjects factor** and requires different formulas, called the **within-subjects ANOVA**.

In this chapter, we'll discuss the one-way, between-subjects ANOVA.

DESIGNING MULTILEVEL EXPERIMENTS

Analysis of variance is the parametric procedure for determining whether significant differences exist in an experiment that contains two or more conditions. There's a bit of confusion here, because when you have two conditions of the independent variable, you can use either a two-sample *t*-test or ANOVA: You'll reach exactly the same conclusions about the null hypothesis with each procedure, and both have the same probability of making Type I and Type II errors. You *must* use ANOVA, however, when you have more than two conditions of an independent variable.

Why would we want to conduct a study that involves more than two conditions of an independent variable? There are three reasons. Sometimes researchers examine more than two conditions because of the logic of their study: For example, we would need three levels of the factor of mood if we attempted to either elevate participants' moods by reading them a positive story, depress their moods by reading them a negative story, or have no influence on mood by presenting them a neutral control condition. As usual, the goal here is to demonstrate a relationship between the independent and dependent variables. The only novelty is that now we have three samples of scores. (Adding a control condition often leads to 3 levels of a factor.)

A second reason for testing more than two conditions is to more accurately describe the *type* of relationship that is present. Recall that a relationship may be either linear (following a straight line) or nonlinear (following a line that changes direction). In a study with just two conditions, one group's mean can be only higher or lower than the other group's mean, so the data can show only a linear relationship, even if the relationship in nature is nonlinear. At least three conditions are needed to see a nonlinear relationship. For example, earlier we discussed a study in which we manipulated room temperature to influence participants' aggressiveness. Figure 17.1 shows the graphs we might obtain with two or four temperature conditions. With the two conditions in graph A, we assume that aggression scores at other, untested temperatures (such as at 80 and 100 degrees) would change in the same way as they did at the observed temperatures of 70 and 90 degrees, so that all means would fall on the straight line. But this is an assumption! By testing the additional temperature conditions, we might confirm this linear relationship, or we might instead find a nonlinear relationship, as in graph B. We wouldn't know that the relationship is like this with only two conditions. Therefore, researchers often include three conditions, in case the relationship is nonlinear. The maximum tends to be six to eight conditions, which is more than adequate for describing most relationships.

Finally, one other reason for including multiple levels of a factor is that after going to all the effort of creating the materials and setting up testing for two conditions, often little additional effort is needed to test additional conditions. Usually, it requires little work to alter stimuli, instructions, or the measurement task, so that additional conditions can be studied in a very cost-effective way. After all, the reason for conducting research is to get data that describe behaviors, and so the more data we can get, the more we learn.

> ***REMEMBER*** Researchers study multiple conditions of an independent variable to test their hypothesis adequately, to demonstrate a nonlinear relationship, and to obtain the maximum information from a study.

FIGURE 17.1 Two-Condition and Four-Condition Temperature-Study Results

(A) The inferred linear relationship with two conditions, and (B) the demonstrated nonlinear relationship with four conditions.

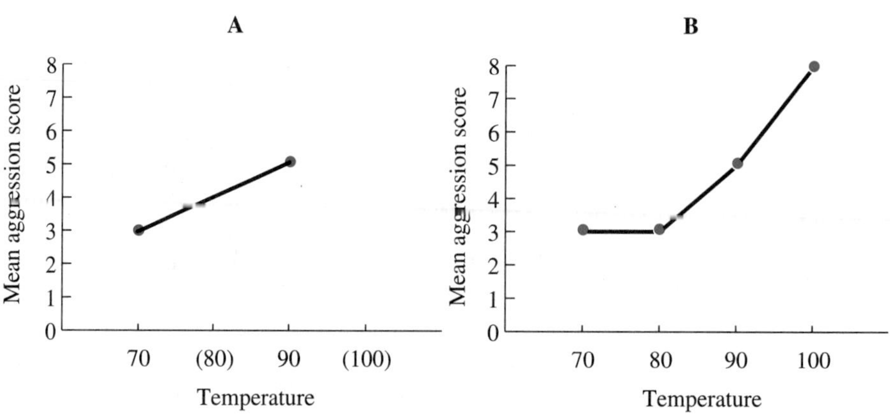

OVERVIEW OF ANOVA

Here is an example study. Let's examine how well people perform a task depending on how difficult they believe the task will be (the "perceived difficulty" of the task). We randomly select three samples containing the unpowerful n of 5 participants each and provide them with the same 10 easy math problems. However, to influence their perceptions, we tell participants in Level 1 that the problems are easy, in Level 2 that the problems are of medium difficulty, and in Level 3 that the problems are difficult. The dependent measure is the number of problems that participants correctly solve within an allotted time. If participants are tested under only one condition, and we do not match them, then this is a one-way, between-subjects design. You can see this design in Table 17.1. Each column is a level of the factor, containing the scores of participants tested under that condition. The mean of each level—the "level mean"—is the mean of the scores in each column. The overall mean is the mean of all scores in the experiment. Because there are three levels in this factor, $k = 3$. (Notice that the general format is to label the factor as Factor A, with levels A_1, A_2, A_3, and so on.) Further, the symbol n stands for the number of scores in a condition, and here $n = 5$ per level. The total number of scores in the experiment is N, and here $N = 15$.

Notice that it is not required that the number of participants in each condition—the *ns*—be equal (e.g, we could have tested an n of 6 in one condition, an n of 8 in another, etc.). However, the *ns* should not be wildly unequal: Do not have 60 participants in one condition and 5 in another. On the other hand, when possible, try to have "equal *ns*" in all conditions. The easiest computer programs require equal *ns* and some statistical procedures are *much* easier to perform with equal *ns*.

REMEMBER Although it is not required, try to have equal *ns* in all conditions.

All of the usual design considerations apply for creating a strong and reliable manipulation of the independent variable, and a valid and reliable measurement of the

TABLE 17.1 Diagram of a Study Having Three Levels of One Factor

	Factor A: independent variable of perceived difficulty			
	Level A_1: easy	***Level A_2: medium***	***Level A_3: difficult***	← *Conditions* $k = 3$
Dependent Scores →	X	X	X	
	X	X	X	
	X	X	X	
	X	X	X	
	X	X	X	
	$\overline{X}_1$	$\overline{X}_2$	$\overline{X}_3$	
	$n_1 = 5$	$n_2 = 5$	$n_3 = 5$	$N = 15$

dependent variable (considering a sensitive measure, demand characteristics, construct validity, etc.). Thus, we would attempt to convince participants that under "easy," the problems are *very* easy, but under "difficult," the problems are *very* difficult. We would also counterbalance the order in which different participants within each condition perform the math problems, and we might limit the population or counterbalance important participant variables (such as their math ability or their "math phobia").

Ideally, we will find a different mean for each condition. Then, we want to conclude that if the entire population was tested under each level of difficulty, we would find three different populations of scores located at three different μs. But, there's the usual problem: Differences between the sample means may reflect sampling error, while we would actually find the same population of scores, having the same μ, for each difficulty level. Therefore, as usual, before we can conclude that a relationship exists, we must eliminate the idea that the differences among the sample means merely reflect sampling error in representing that no relationship is present.

How ANOVA Controls for Experiment-Wise Error Rate

You might think that we could use the independent-samples *t*-test to test for significant differences between the three means above. That is, we might perform "multiple *t*-tests," testing whether $\overline{X}_1$ differs from $\overline{X}_2$, then whether $\overline{X}_2$ differs from $\overline{X}_3$, and finally whether $\overline{X}_1$ differs from $\overline{X}_3$. We *cannot* use this approach because of the resulting probability of making a Type I error (rejecting a true H_0). With $\alpha = .05$, the theoretical probability of a Type I error in a *single* *t*-test is .05. However, we can make a Type I error when comparing $\overline{X}_1$ to $\overline{X}_2$, or when comparing $\overline{X}_2$ to $\overline{X}_3$, or when comparing $\overline{X}_1$ to $\overline{X}_3$. Therefore, the *overall* probability of making a Type I error *somewhere* in the experiment is considerably greater than .05. This overall probability of making a Type I error is called the **experiment-wise error rate**.

We can use the *t*-test when comparing only two means because, with only one comparison, the experiment-wise error rate equals α. When there are more than two levels in a factor, however, performing multiple *t*-tests results in an error rate that is greater than the α we selected. Because of the importance of avoiding Type I errors, we cannot afford to have the actual α greater than we think it is. Therefore, we *must* perform ANOVA. The ANOVA simultaneously compares the means from all conditions while keeping the experiment-wise error rate equal to the α we have chosen.

> ***REMEMBER*** The reason for performing ANOVA is because it keeps the experiment-wise error rate equal to the α we select.

As with any statistical test, we next check the assumptions, set up the hypotheses, and then perform the test.

Assumptions of the One-Way Between-Subjects ANOVA

Perform the one-way between-subjects ANOVA when:

1. The experiment has only one independent variable, and all conditions contain independent samples.

2. Each condition contains a random sample of interval or ratio scores.
3. The population represented by the scores in each condition forms a normal distribution.
4. The variances of all populations represented in the study are homogeneous.

If the study meets these assumptions, set α (usually at .05) and create the statistical hypotheses.

Statistical Hypotheses of ANOVA

ANOVA tests only two-tailed hypotheses. The null hypothesis is that there are no differences among the populations represented by the conditions. Thus, for the perceived difficulty study with the three levels of easy, medium, and difficult, we have

$$H_0: \mu_1 = \mu_2 = \mu_3$$

As usual, H_0 implies that changing the independent variable does not make a difference in the population, and so any differences between our sample means occur because they poorly represent that one μ that would be found for all conditions.

In general, for a factor with k levels, the null hypothesis is

$$H_0: \mu_1 = \mu_2 = \ldots = \mu_k$$

The "$\ldots = \mu_k$" indicates that there are as many μs as there are levels.

You might think that the alternative hypothesis would be that the μs are not equal, or $\mu_1 \neq \mu_2 \neq \mu_3$. However, a study may demonstrate a relationship in which only *some* but not *all* conditions differ. Thus, perhaps our data represent a difference between μ_1 and μ_2, but not between μ_1 and μ_3, or perhaps only μ_2 and μ_3 differ. To communicate this idea, the alternative hypothesis is

$$H_a\text{: not all } \mu\text{s are equal}$$

H_a implies that there is a relationship in the population such that the population mean represented by one of our levels will be different from the population mean represented by at least one other level.

We always test H_0, so in ANOVA, we test whether all sample means represent the same population mean.

The Order of Operations in ANOVA: The *F*-Statistic and Post Hoc Comparisons

The statistic that forms the basis for ANOVA is F. First, we compute F to determine whether two or more sample means represent different μs. The F we calculate is the F_{obt}, which we compare to the critical value, the F_{crit}.

When F_{obt} is not significant, it indicates that there are no significant differences between any of the level means and that all means are likely to represent the same μ. When this occurs, the experiment has failed to demonstrate a relationship, we are finished with the statistical analysis, and it's back to the drawing board.

When F_{obt} is significant, however, it indicates that *somewhere* among the level means *at least two* means are likely to represent different μs. The problem is that F_{obt}

does not indicate *which* specific means differ significantly and perhaps more than two means are significantly different, or maybe all of them are. Thus, for example, if F_{obt} for the perceived difficulty study is significant, it will indicate only that there is at least one significant difference somewhere among the means for the easy, medium, and difficult levels, but we won't know where.

Therefore, the next step is to determine which level means actually differ significantly. To do this, we perform a second statistical procedure, called post hoc comparisons. (*Post hoc* means "after the fact," which here is after F_{obt} is significant.) **Post hoc comparisons** are like *t*-tests, in which we compare all possible *pairs* of sample means from a factor. Thus, for the perceived difficulty study, we'll compare the means from easy and medium, from easy and difficult, and from medium and difficult. Together, these comparisons will indicate which means differ significantly from each other.

Note that we perform post hoc comparisons *only* when F_{obt} is significant. This two-step procedure ensures that the experiment-wise probability of a Type I error will be less than .05 (or whatever alpha we selected).

> ***REMEMBER*** If F_{obt} is significant, perform post hoc comparisons to determine which specific means differ significantly.

There is one exception to this rule. When there are only two levels in the factor, the significant difference indicated by F_{obt} must be between the only two means in the study, so it is unnecessary to perform post hoc comparisons.

The first step is to compute F_{obt}. Therefore, the following sections present the statistical basis for ANOVA and the logic of its computation.

COMPONENTS OF THE *F*-STATISTIC

Analysis of variance does just that: It analyzes variance. That is, we take the total variability of the scores in an experiment and break it up, or "partition" it, in terms of its source. There are two potential sources of variance. First, scores may differ from each other even when participants are in the same condition. We call this variability the **variance within groups**. Second, scores may differ from each other because they are from different conditions. We call this variability the **variance between groups**.

Using the sample data, we estimate the value that each of these variances would have in the population. But we do not *call* each an estimated variance. Instead, we call each a *mean square*. This is because, when calculating the estimated population variance, we find $\Sigma(X - \bar{X})^2$, which is the sum of squared deviations around the mean. Then, by dividing by $N - 1$, we compute something like the average (or *mean*) of the squared deviations. In ANOVA, we shorten "mean of the squared deviations" to "mean square." The symbol for a mean square is *MS*. Because we estimate the variance within groups and the variance between groups, we compute two mean squares, the mean square within groups and the mean square between groups.

The Mean Square Within Groups

The **mean square within groups** is an estimate of the variability of scores in the population as measured by differences *within* the conditions of an experiment. The symbol for the mean square within groups is MS_{wn}. Think of MS_{wn} as the "average variability" of the scores within each condition around the mean of that condition. Table 17.2 illustrates how to conceptualize the computation of MS_{wn}. Essentially, we find the variance in level 1 (finding the squared differences between the scores in level 1 and $\overline{X}_1$), then we find the variance of scores in level 2 around $\overline{X}_2$, and then we find the variance of scores in level 3 around $\overline{X}_3$. Then, we "pool"—average together—the variances, just like we did in the independent-samples *t*-test back in Chapter 15. Thus, the MS_{wn} is the "average" variability of the scores in each condition around the mean of that condition.

The MS_{wn} reflects the inherent variability in scores that arises from individual differences or from other random factors when participants are all treated the same. We've seen in previous chapters that such variance is called error variance. Thus, the MS_{wn} estimates the **error variance** in the population, which we'll symbolize as σ^2_{error} (MS_{wn} is also known as the *error term*). In symbols,

Sample	***Estimates***	***Population***
MS_{wn}	$\rightarrow$	σ^2_{error}

Because we assume homogeneity of variance, σ^2_{error} has one value—and MS_{wn} estimates that value—regardless of whether H_0 is true or false. If H_0 is true, each condition is a sample from the same population, so each provides an estimate of that population's σ^2_{error}. Pooling them simply provides a better estimate. If H_0 is false, each condition may come from a different population, but homogeneity of variance means that σ^2_{error} in each population is the same. Therefore, each condition still provides an estimate of this σ^2_{error}, but pooling them provides the better estimate. So, for example, if we calculate MS_{wn} to be 4, then we estimate that the variance equals 4 in the population(s) being represented by our conditions.

> *REMEMBER* The MS_{wn} is an estimate of the error variance, the inherent variability within any population represented by the samples.

TABLE 17.2 How to Conceptualize the Computation of MS_{wn}

	Factor A	
Level A_1:	***Level A_2:***	***Level A_3:***
X	X	X
X	X	X
X	X	X
X	X	X
X	X	X
$\overline{X}_1$	$\overline{X}_2$	$\overline{X}_3$

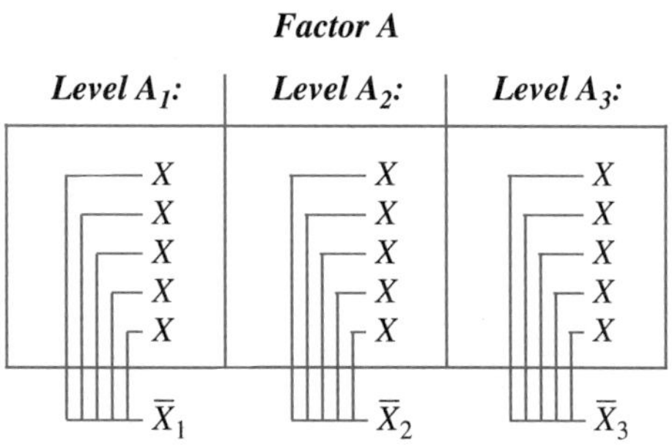

The Mean Square Between Groups

The other variance we compute is the mean square between groups. The **mean square between groups** is an estimate of the variability in scores that occurs *between* the levels in a factor. The mean square between groups is symbolized by MS_{bn}. Table 17.3 shows how to conceptualize the computation of MS_{bn}. Here we determine how much each level mean deviates from the overall mean of the experiment. In the same way that the deviations of raw scores around their mean describe how different the scores are from each other, the deviations of the level means around the overall mean indicate how different the level means are from each other. *Thus, MS_{bn} is our way of measuring how much the means differ from each other.*

The key to understanding ANOVA is to understand what MS_{bn} represents when H_0 is true and when it is false. First, when H_0 is true, MS_{bn} is just another way to estimate σ^2_{error}, another estimate of the inherent variability of the raw scores in the population. This is because when H_0 is true, the scores in the different conditions all come from the same population. However, not all scores will equal μ or each other. Instead, simply by chance, we may get one batch of scores that differs from another batch, so that their means differ. But, pretend for the moment that in the population, the individual scores differ by very little, so that everyone has close to the same score (close to μ). Here, in each sample we'll get essentially the same scores as in the next sample. Therefore, each sample mean will be very close to the next, so that all means are close to the same score (and close to μ). On the other hand, pretend that the population contains great variability, so that the scores are very different from each other (spread out around μ). Now, the scores in one sample are likely to be very different from the scores in the next sample. Therefore, the sample means will also be very different from each other (and also spread out around μ). The point is that to whatever degree the individual raw scores in a population differ (the size of σ^2_{error}), random sample means from that population will also differ to that same degree, and this will be reflected by MS_{bn}.

So, when H_0 is true and we're dealing with only one population, MS_{bn} estimates the population's inherent variability. But, remember that MS_{wn} also estimates the population's inherent variability. Therefore, because both reflect the same variability, both

TABLE 17.3 How to Conceptualize the Computation of MS_{bn}

	Factor A		
Level A_1	*Level* A_2	*Level* A_3	
X	X	X	
X	X	X	
X	X	X	
X	X	X	
X	X	X	
$\overline{X}_1$	$\overline{X}_2$	$\overline{X}_3$	Overall $\overline{X}$

produce a number that estimates the one value of σ^2_{error}, and most important, *they should be equal.*

> REMEMBER When H_0 is true, MS_{bn} estimates the variability among the individual scores in the population—the σ^2_{error}—just like MS_{wn} does, and so MS_{bn} should equal MS_{wn}.

Now, consider when H_0 is false and the scores from different conditions do not all come from the same population. Now, MS_{bn} estimates two things. First, the sample means differ because we have a *treatment effect*: A relationship exists in the population so that at least two of the conditions represent different populations. Differences between the populations due to treatment are called treatment variance, which is symbolized as σ^2_{treat}. **Treatment variance** reflects differences between scores that occur because the scores are from different populations. We estimate these differences using the differences between the level means, which we determine by calculating MS_{bn}. Therefore, MS_{bn} contains an estimate of the treatment variance.

The second thing MS_{bn} estimates when H_0 is false is the same as when H_0 is true: To some extent MS_{bn} reflects the inherent variability among the scores in each population, so it estimates σ^2_{error}. This is because any sample won't be perfectly representative of its population, so its $\overline{X}$ will differ from its μ. Then, the level $\overline{X}$s differ from each other, not only because they come from different populations, but also because each $\overline{X}$ differs from its μ. How much each $\overline{X}$ differs from its μ depends on the inherent variability of the scores: The more that the individual scores are spread out from μ, the more extreme the scores in the sample may be, so the more that the $\overline{X}$ may differ from μ.

Regardless of how big the variability is, the important idea here is that MS_{bn} will still, in part, reflect the inherent variability in the scores, so in part it reflects σ^2_{error}. But, recall that MS_{bn} also reflects the differences between the conditions. Therefore, in sum, MS_{bn} contains estimates of *both* error variance and treatment variance. In symbols, this is

Sample	***Estimates***	***Population***
MS_{bn}	$\rightarrow$	$\sigma^2_{\text{error}} + \sigma^2_{\text{treat}}$

The σ^2_{error} component is the same value as estimated by MS_{wn}. But with the added σ^2_{treat} component, MS_{bn} will now be *larger* than MS_{wn}. Thus, for example, say that when MS_{wn} equals 4, the MS_{bn} equals 10. Think of this MS_{bn} as indicating that, in addition to an error variance of 4, there is an "average difference" of 6 between the populations.

> REMEMBER If H_0 is false, then MS_{bn} contains estimates of both *error* variance (which measures differences *within* each population) and *treatment* variance (which measures differences *between* the populations).

As it turns out, the actual size of MS_{wn} or MS_{bn} is not all that informative. Instead, we are interested in their ratio, called the *F*-ratio.

Comparing the Mean Squares: The Logic of the *F*-Ratio

The ***F*-ratio** equals the mean square between groups divided by the mean square within groups. Forming this ratio produces F_{obt}.

THE COMPUTATIONAL FORMULA FOR THE F-RATIO IS

$$F_{\text{obt}} = \frac{MS_{\text{bn}}}{MS_{\text{wn}}}$$

MS_{bn} is always on top!

We conceptualize the F-ratio as representing this:

$$\begin{array}{cccc} & \textbf{\textit{Sample}} & \textbf{\textit{Estimates}} & \textbf{\textit{Population}} \\ F_{\text{obt}} = & \dfrac{MS_{\text{bn}}}{MS_{\text{wn}}} & \begin{array}{c}\rightarrow\\ \rightarrow\end{array} & \dfrac{\sigma^2_{\text{error}} + \sigma^2_{\text{treat}}}{\sigma^2_{\text{error}}} \end{array}$$

The MS_{bn} represents the inherent differences among scores in any population (σ^2_{error}), *plus* whatever differences there are between the populations represented by the conditions (σ^2_{treat}). This value is divided by the MS_{wn}, which only estimates the error variance in the populations (σ^2_{error}).

Now, you can understand what the F-ratio indicates about the null hypothesis. If H_0 is true and all conditions represent the same population, then MS_{bn} contains solely σ^2_{error}, and the σ^2_{treat} component equals zero. In symbols, when H_0 is true,

$$\begin{array}{cccc} & \textbf{\textit{Sample}} & \textbf{\textit{Estimates}} & \textbf{\textit{Population}} \\ F_{\text{obt}} = & \dfrac{MS_{\text{bn}}}{MS_{\text{wn}}} & \begin{array}{c}\rightarrow\\ \rightarrow\end{array} & \dfrac{\sigma^2_{\text{error}} + 0}{\sigma^2_{\text{error}}} = \dfrac{\sigma^2_{\text{error}}}{\sigma^2_{\text{error}}} = 1 \end{array}$$

Both mean squares estimate the one value of σ^2_{error}. Therefore, the mean square between groups should *equal* the mean square within groups. When two numbers are equal, their ratio equals 1. Thus:

When H_0 is true, MS_{bn} should equal MS_{wn}, and so F_{obt} should equal 1.

We can then turn this around to make a decision about H_0 in a study. For example, say that when MS_{wn} equals 4, the MS_{bn} also equals 4. This produces an $F_{\text{obt}} = 1$, which is the ideal result we'd expect if H_0 were true for our study.

On the other hand, if H_0 is false, then at least two conditions represent different populations, and there are differences due to treatment. Therefore, the σ^2_{treat} component of MS_{bn} does not equal zero, so

$$\begin{array}{cccc} & \textbf{\textit{Sample}} & \textbf{\textit{Estimates}} & \textbf{\textit{Population}} \\ F_{\text{obt}} = & \dfrac{MS_{\text{bn}}}{MS_{\text{wn}}} & \begin{array}{c}\rightarrow\\ \rightarrow\end{array} & \dfrac{\sigma^2_{\text{error}} + \text{some amount of } \sigma^2_{\text{treat}}}{\sigma^2_{\text{error}}} = F > 1 \end{array}$$

Here, MS_{bn} contains error variance *plus* some amount of treatment variance, so MS_{bn} will be *larger* than MS_{wn}, which always contains only error variance. Placing a larger numerator over a smaller denominator in the F ratio produces an F_{obt} greater than 1. Thus:

When H_0 is false, MS_{bn} is larger than MS_{wn}, and so F_{obt} is greater than 1.

Here, too, we can make a decision about H_0 in a study. For example, say that when our MS_{wn} equals 4, the MS_{bn} equals 10. This produces an F_{obt} of 2.5, which is greater than 1: This is the type of result we'd expect if H_0 were false in our experiment.

The larger the difference between the level means, the larger MS_{bn} will be. Regardless, however, the size of MS_{wn} remains constant, so the larger the differences, the larger the F_{obt}. This will be true for a positive or negative linear relationship or for a curvilinear relationship, because in each case, MS_{bn} will simply be larger than MS_{wn}, and so F_{obt} will be greater than 1. (This is why we have only two-tailed hypotheses in ANOVA.) Conversely, an F_{obt} between 0 and 1 is possible, but it occurs when the MS_{wn} is larger than the MS_{bn}. Here, we assume that H_0 is true and that MS_{bn} and/or MS_{wn} are merely poor estimates of the error variance and therefore not equal. F_{obt} cannot be less than zero, because the mean squares are variances, which cannot be negative numbers.

Thus, F_{obt} should equal 1 if the level means represent the same μ, and F_{obt} should be greater than 1 if the level means represent different μs. But hold on! There's one other reason F_{obt} might be greater than 1, and that is (here we go again) sampling error! When H_0 is true, F_{obt} "should" equal 1 *if* the mean squares are perfectly representative. *But*, through sampling error with *one* population, we might obtain differences between the level means that are larger than the differences between the individual scores. This will produce an MS_{bn} that is larger than MS_{wn}, so F_{obt} will be greater than 1 simply because of sampling error.

This all boils down to the same old problem of significance testing. An F_{obt} greater than 1 may accurately reflect the situation where two or more conditions represent different populations of raw scores. Or, because of sampling error, an F_{obt} greater than 1 may inaccurately reflect the situation where all conditions represent the same population. Therefore, whenever F_{obt} is greater than 1, we must test H_0: We determine the probability of obtaining such an F_{obt} when H_0 is true. To do this, we examine the *F*-distribution.

The *F*-Distribution

The ***F*-distribution** is the sampling distribution that shows the various values of *F* that occur when H_0 is true and all conditions represent one population. We could create a sampling distribution in the following way: Using the same number of levels and the same *n*s as in our study, we would randomly sample one raw score population, and then compute MS_{bn}, MS_{wn}, and F_{obt}. After doing this an infinite number of times, we would plot the various values of F_{obt}. The resulting distribution can be envisioned as in Figure 17.2. It shows the different values of *F* that occur by chance when all level means *do* represent the same μ. The *F*-distribution is skewed because there is no limit to how large F_{obt} can be, but it cannot be less than zero. The mean of the distribution is 1 because, most often when H_0 is true, MS_{bn} will equal MS_{wn} and *F* will equal 1.

We are concerned with the upper tail, which shows that sometimes the data are unrepresentative, and by chance produce an MS_{bn} that is larger than MS_{wn} and thus an *F* greater than 1. As shown, however, the larger the *F*, the farther to the right it is, and thus the less frequent and less likely it is to occur when H_0 is true. To identify how far to the right is far enough, we create the region of rejection using F_{crit}. (Because the F_{obt} can reflect a relationship only when it is greater than 1, the entire region of rejection is in the upper tail of the *F*-distribution. Thus, with ANOVA, we always have two-tailed hypotheses, but we test them using a one-tailed test.) If F_{obt} is larger than F_{crit}, then F_{obt}—and the differences between the conditions that produced it—are unlikely to occur when H_0 is true. Therefore, we reject H_0 and have a significant F_{obt}.

FIGURE 17.2 Sampling Distribution of F When H_0 Is True

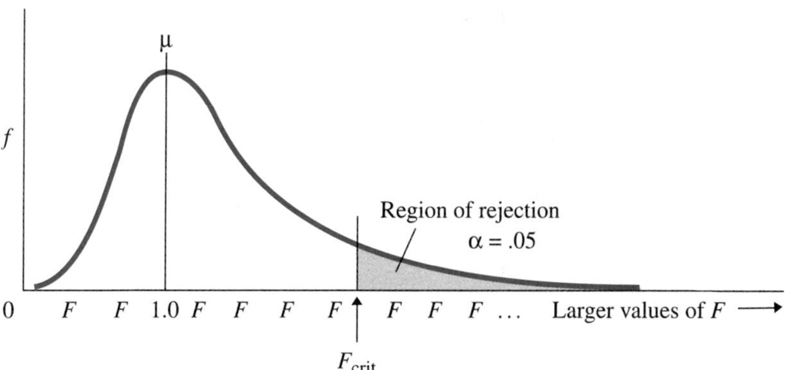

Degrees of Freedom and the Critical Value

Like the t-distribution, the F-distribution is a family of curves. Each distribution has a slightly different shape, depending on the degrees of freedom in the data, and thus there is a different value of F_{crit} for each *df*. However, *two* values of *df* determine the shape of each F-distribution: the *df* for the mean square between groups and the *df* for the mean square within groups. The symbol for the *df* between groups is df_{bn}, and the symbol for the *df* within groups is df_{wn}. We use both df_{bn} and df_{wn} when finding F_{crit}.

To obtain F_{crit}, turn to Table 5 in Appendix C, entitled "Critical Values of F." Across the top of these "F-tables," the columns are labeled "*df* between groups," and along the left side, the rows are labeled "*df* within groups." Locate the appropriate column and row using the *dfs* from your study. The critical values of F in dark type are for $\alpha = .05$, and the values in light type are for $\alpha = .01$. For example, say we eventually determine that $df_{bn} = 2$ and $df_{wn} = 12$. Then, for $\alpha = .05$, F_{crit} is 3.88.

Be careful to keep your "withins" and "betweens" straight: $df_{bn} = 2$ and $df_{wn} = 12$ is very different from $df_{bn} = 12$ and $df_{wn} = 2$.

Don't be overwhelmed by the details of ANOVA. Buried in here is the simple idea that the larger the differences between the means for the conditions, the larger the MS_{bn} and thus the larger the F_{obt}. If the F_{obt} is larger than F_{crit}, then the F_{obt} is unlikely to occur if the means from the conditions represent the same population μ. In such cases, we reject H_0 and confidently conclude that the data represent a relationship in nature.

Now all we need to do is the computations, so hold on, here we go.

COMPUTING THE F-RATIO

The computations require one more new term. When we computed the estimated variance in Chapter 8, the quantity $\Sigma(X - \overline{X})^2$ was called the sum of the squared deviations. In ANOVA, this is shortened to the **sum of squares**. The symbol for the sum of squares is *SS*, so in the numerator of the formula for variance, we can replace the sum of the squared deviations with *SS*:

$$s_X^2 = \frac{\Sigma(X - \overline{X})^2}{N - 1} = \frac{SS}{df} = MS$$

In the denominator, $N - 1$ is the degrees of freedom, so we replace $N - 1$ with *df*. Because variance is called a mean square in ANOVA, the fraction formed by the *SS* divided by the *df* is the general formula for a mean square.

Adding subscripts, we will compute the mean square between groups (MS_{bn}) by computing the sum of squares between groups (SS_{bn}), and then dividing by the degrees of freedom between groups (df_{bn}). We will compute the mean square within groups (MS_{wn}) by computing the sum of squares within groups (SS_{wn}), and then dividing by the degrees of freedom within groups (df_{wn}). Once we have MS_{bn} and MS_{wn}, we compute F_{obt}.

If all this strikes you as the most confusing thing ever devised by humans, you'll find it helpful to create an ANOVA summary table. (Computer programs often print the results of ANOVA in a summary table, so you'll need to understand this, or it'll all be gibberish.) Here is the general format of the summary table for a one-way ANOVA:

Summary Table of One-Way ANOVA

Source	*Sum of squares*	*df*	*Mean square*	*F*
Between	SS_{bn}	df_{bn}	MS_{bn}	F_{obt}
Within	SS_{wn}	df_{wn}	MS_{wn}	
Total	SS_{tot}	df_{tot}		

The source column identifies each component. Along the way, we also compute the total sum of squares (SS_{tot}), and the total *df* (df_{tot}). The F_{obt} is always placed in the row labeled "Between." In place of the word "Between," you can use the name of the independent variable. Also, in place of the word "Within," you will sometimes see "Error."

Computational Formulas for the One-Way, Between-Subjects ANOVA

Say that we performed the perceived difficulty study discussed earlier: We told three conditions of five participants each that some math problems were easy, of medium difficulty, or difficult, and we measured the number of problems they solved correctly. The data are presented in Table 17.4.

The first step is to compute ΣX, ΣX^2, and $\overline{X}$ for each level. Adding the ΣX from each level gives the total ΣX (ΣX_{tot}). Adding the ΣX^2 from each level gives the total ΣX^2, (ΣX^2_{tot}). Then, as shown in the following sections, there are four steps in the computations, finding: (1) the sum of squares, (2) the degrees of freedom, (3) the mean squares, and (4) F_{obt}. So that you don't get lost, fill in the ANOVA summary table as you complete each step. (There *will* be a test later.)

TABLE 17.4 Data from Perceived Difficulty Experiment

Factor A: perceived difficulty			
Level A_1: easy	*Level A_2: medium*	*Level A_3: difficult*	
9	4	1	
12	6	3	
4	8	4	
8	2	5	
7	10	2	
			Totals
$\Sigma X = 40$	$\Sigma X = 30$	$\Sigma X = 15$	$\Sigma X_{tot} = 85$
$\Sigma X^2 = 354$	$\Sigma X^2 = 220$	$\Sigma X^2 = 55$	$\Sigma X^2_{tot} = 629$
$n_1 = 5$	$n_2 = 5$	$n_3 = 5$	$N = 15$
$\overline{X}_1 = 8$	$\overline{X}_2 = 6$	$\overline{X}_3 = 3$	$k = 3$

Computing the sums of squares First compute the sum of squares. Do this in three steps.

Step 1 Compute the total sum of squares (SS_{tot}).

THE COMPUTATIONAL FORMULA FOR THE TOTAL SUM OF SQUARES IS

$$SS_{tot} = \Sigma X^2_{tot} - \left(\frac{(\Sigma X_{tot})^2}{N}\right)$$

Treat the entire experiment as if it were one big sample. Then, ΣX_{tot} is the sum of all Xs, and ΣX^2_{tot} is the sum of all squared Xs. N is the total N in the study.

Using the data from Table 13.4, $\Sigma X^2_{tot} = 629$, $\Sigma X_{tot} = 85$, and $N = 15$, so

$$SS_{tot} = 629 - \frac{(85)^2}{15}$$

$$SS_{tot} = 629 - \frac{7225}{15}$$

$$SS_{tot} = 629 - 481.67$$

Thus, $SS_{tot} = 147.33$.

Step 2 Compute the sum of squares between groups (SS_{bn}).

THE COMPUTATIONAL FORMULA FOR THE SUM OF SQUARES BETWEEN GROUPS IS

$$SS_{bn} = \Sigma\left(\frac{(\text{sum of scores in the column})^2}{n \text{ of scores in the column}}\right) - \left(\frac{(\Sigma X_{tot})^2}{N}\right)$$

When we diagram the study, each column represents a level of the factor. Thus, find the ΣX for each level, square ΣX, and then divide by the n in that level. After doing this for all levels, add the results together and subtract the quantity $(\Sigma X_{tot})^2/N$. Thus,

$$SS_{bn} = \left(\frac{(40)^2}{5} + \frac{(30)^2}{5} + \frac{(15)^2}{5}\right) - \left(\frac{(85)^2}{15}\right)$$

so

$$SS_{bn} = (320 + 180 + 45) - 481.67$$

and

$$SS_{bn} = 545 - 481.67$$

Thus, $SS_{bn} = 63.33$.

Step 3 Compute the sum of squares within groups (SS_{wn}). Mathematically, SS_{tot} equals SS_{bn} plus SS_{wn}. Therefore, the total minus the between leaves the within.

THE COMPUTATIONAL FORMULA FOR THE SUM OF SQUARES WITHIN GROUPS IS

$$SS_{wn} = SS_{tot} - SS_{bn}$$

Above, SS_{tot} is 147.33 and SS_{bn} is 63.33, so

$$SS_{wn} = 147.33 - 63.33 = 84.00$$

Thus, $SS_{wn} = 84.00$.

Filling in the first column of the ANOVA summary table, we have

Summary Table of One-Way ANOVA

Source	*Sum of squares*	*df*	*Mean square*	*F*
Between	63.33	df_{bn}	MS_{bn}	F_{obt}
Within	84.00	df_{wn}	MS_{wn}	
Total	147.33	df_{tot}		

As a double check, make sure that the total equals the sum of the between plus the within.

Now compute the degrees of freedom.

Computing the degrees of freedom Compute df_{bn}, df_{wn}, and df_{tot}. Again, there are three steps.

1. *The degrees of freedom between groups equals* $k - 1$, where k is the number of levels in the factor. In the example, there are three levels of perceived difficulty (easy, medium, and difficult), so $k = 3$. Thus, $df_{bn} = 2$.

2. *The degrees of freedom within groups equals $N - k$,* where N is the total N of the study and k is the number of levels in the factor. In the example, N is 15 and k is 3, so df_{wn} equals 12.
3. *The degrees of freedom total equals $N - 1$,* where N is the total N in the experiment. In the example, N is 15, so $df_{tot} = 14$.

To check your answers, be sure that the df_{tot} equals the sum of the df_{bn} plus the df_{wn}. After adding the *df* to the summary table, it looks like this:

Summary Table of One-Way ANOVA

Source	*Sum of squares*	*df*	*Mean square*	*F*
Between	63.33	2	MS_{bn}	F_{obt}
Within	84.00	12	MS_{wn}	
Total	147.33	14		

Now find each mean square

Computing the mean squares Work directly from the summary table to compute the mean squares. Any mean square equals the appropriate sum of squares divided by the corresponding *df.*

THE COMPUTATIONAL FORMULA FOR THE MEAN SQUARE BETWEEN GROUPS IS

$$MS_{bn} = \frac{SS_{bn}}{df_{bn}}$$

From the summary table for our example,

$$MS_{bn} = \frac{63.33}{2} = 31.67$$

THE COMPUTATIONAL FORMULA FOR THE MEAN SQUARE WITHIN GROUPS IS

$$MS_{wn} = \frac{SS_{wn}}{df_{wn}}$$

For the example,

$$MS_{wn} = \frac{84}{12} = 7.00$$

Do *not* compute the mean square for SS_{tot}. Now, in the summary table, we have

Summary Table of One-Way ANOVA

Source	*Sum of squares*	*df*	*Mean square*	*F*
Between	63.33	2	31.67	F_{obt}
Within	84.00	12	7.00	
Total	147.33	14		

Computing the F_{obt} Last, but not least, compute F_{obt}.

THE COMPUTATIONAL FORMULA FOR F IS

$$F_{obt} = \frac{MS_{bn}}{MS_{wn}}$$

In the example, MS_{bn} is 31.67 and MS_{wn} is 7.00, so

$$F_{obt} = \frac{MS_{bn}}{MS_{wn}} = \frac{31.67}{7.00} = 4.52$$

Now the completed ANOVA summary table is

Summary Table of One-Way ANOVA

Source	*Sum of squares*	*df*	*Mean square*	*F*
Between	63.33	2	31.67	4.52
Within	84.00	12	7.00	
Total	147.33	14		

Interpreting F_{obt} in a One-Way ANOVA

To interpret F_{obt}, we must have F_{crit}, so turn to the *F*-tables in Appendix C. In the example, df_{bn} is 2 and df_{wn} is 12. With $\alpha = .05$, F_{crit} is 3.88.

Thus, F_{obt} is 4.52 and F_{crit} is 3.88. Lo and behold, as shown in Figure 17.3, F_{obt} is significant. The null hypothesis says that the differences between our level means are due to sampling error and that all means poorly represent one μ. However, the F_{obt} is out there in the region of rejection, telling us that such differences between $\overline{X}$s hardly ever happen when H_0 is true. Because F_{obt} is larger than F_{crit}, we reject H_0, concluding that our different level means are unlikely to be representing one population μ. Thus, we conclude that the F_{obt} is significant and that the factor of perceived difficulty produced a significant difference in mean performance scores. As usual, because $\alpha = .05$, the probability that we just made a Type I error is $p < .05$.

FIGURE 17.3 Sampling Distribution of F when H_0 Is True for $df_{bn} = 2$ and $df_{wn} = 12$

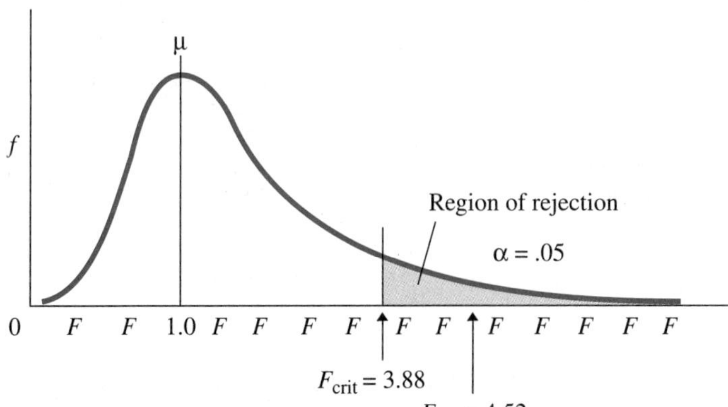

Of course, had F_{obt} been less than F_{crit}, then the corresponding differences between the level means would *not* be unlikely to occur when H_0 is true, so we would not reject H_0.

Because we rejected H_0 and accepted H_a, we have a "treatment effect." To understand the nature of this effect—to see how our manipulation influenced scores—we examine the level means.

Perceived difficulty		
Easy	***Medium***	***Difficult***
$\overline{X}_1 = 8$	$\overline{X}_2 = 6$	$\overline{X}_3 = 3$

We are confident that these means represent a relationship in the population: It appears that increasing perceived difficulty is associated with fewer problems solved. However, we do not know whether *every* increase in difficulty always produces a different population of scores having a different μ. Remember, a significant F_{obt} merely indicates that there is *at least one* significant difference somewhere between the means. Now, we must determine which specific means differ significantly, and to do that we perform post hoc comparisons.

PERFORMING POST HOC COMPARISONS

There are several versions of post hoc tests (each named after its developer). Different procedures differ in how likely they are to produce Type I or Type II errors. For example, one procedure—the Scheffe Test—is very conservative, meaning it is biased toward avoiding Type I errors, even at the risk of making Type II errors. Other common procedures—the Newman-Keuls or Duncan tests—are rather liberal, meaning they are biased toward avoiding Type II errors, even at the risk of making Type I errors. Two in-between procedures that give good protection from both types of errors are Fisher's protected t-test and Tukey's *HSD* test.[1] Which test you should use depends on whether or not your *ns* are equal.

Fisher's Protected *t*-Test

Perform **Fisher's protected *t*-test** when the *ns* are *not* equal in all levels of the factor.

THE COMPUTATIONAL FORMULA FOR THE PROTECTED t-TEST IS

$$t_{obt} = \frac{\bar{X}_1 - \bar{X}_2}{\sqrt{MS_{wn}\left(\frac{1}{n_1} + \frac{1}{n_2}\right)}}$$

This is basically the formula for the independent-samples t-test, except that MS_{wn} has replaced the pooled variance (s^2_{pool}) used in the t-test. We are testing H_0: $\mu_1 - \mu_2 = 0$, where $\bar{X}_1$ and $\bar{X}_2$ are the means for any two levels of the factor, and n_1 and n_2 are the corresponding *ns* in those levels. The t_{crit} is the two-tailed value found in Appendix C, Table 2, for $df = df_{wn}$.

It is not incorrect to perform the protected t-test even when all *ns* are equal. For example, let's compare the mean from our easy level ($\bar{X} = 8.0$) to the mean from the difficult level ($\bar{X} = 3.0$). Each n is 5, and from the ANOVA, MS_{wn} is 7.0. Filling in the formula gives

$$t_{obt} = \frac{8.0 - 3.0}{\sqrt{7.0\left(\frac{1}{5} + \frac{1}{5}\right)}}$$

Then,

$$t_{obt} = \frac{+5.0}{\sqrt{7.0(.4)}}$$

which becomes

$$t_{obt} = \frac{+5.0}{\sqrt{2.8}} = \frac{+5.0}{1.67} = +2.99$$

Now, compare t_{obt} to the *two-tailed* value of t_{crit} found in the t-tables. For the example, $\alpha = .05$ and in our ANOVA $df_{wn} = 12$, so t_{crit} is ± 2.179. Because the t_{obt} of $+2.99$ is beyond the t_{crit} of ± 2.179, the means from the easy and difficult levels differ significantly (they do not represent the same μ).

To complete the post hoc comparisons, perform the protected t-test on all possible pairs of means in the factor. Thus, after comparing the means from easy and difficult, compare the means from easy and medium, and then the means from medium and difficult. When you're finished, the experiment-wise error rate will be *protected*, so that the probability of a Type I error for all of these comparisons together is $p < .05$.

[1] S. G. Carmer and M. R. Swanson (1973). An evaluation of ten multiple comparison procedures by Monte Carlo methods. *Journal of the American Statistical Association*, 68, 66–74.

If a factor contains many levels, then the protected *t*-test becomes very tedious. If you're thinking there *must* be an easier way, you're right.

Tukey's *HSD* Multiple Comparisons Test

Perform **Tukey's *HSD* multiple comparisons test** when the *n*s in all levels of the factor are equal. The *HSD* is a variation of the *t*-test that computes the minimum difference between two means that is required for them to differ significantly (*HSD* stands for the Honestly Significant Difference). There are four steps in performing the *HSD* test.

Step 1: Find q_k. Using the appropriate q_k in the computations is what protects the experiment-wise error rate. The value of q_k is found in Table 6 in Appendix C, entitled "Values of the Studentized Range Statistic, q_k." In the table, locate the column labeled with the k that corresponds to the number of means in the factor. Next, find the row labeled with the df_{wn} from the ANOVA. Then, find the value of q_k for the appropriate α. For our study above, $k = 3$, $df_{wn} = 12$, and $\alpha = .05$, so $q_k = 3.77$.

Step 2: Compute the *HSD*.

THE COMPUTATIONAL FORMULA FOR THE TUKEY HSD TEST IS

$$HSD = (q_k)\left(\sqrt{\frac{MS_{wn}}{n}}\right)$$

MS_{wn} is the denominator from the *F*-ratio, and *n* is the number of scores in each level of the factor.

In the example, MS_{wn} was 7.0 and n was 5, so

$$HSD = (q_k)\left(\sqrt{\frac{MS_{wn}}{n}}\right) = (3.77)\left(\sqrt{\frac{7.0}{5}}\right) = 4.46$$

Step 3: Determine the differences between all means. Subtract each mean from every other mean. Ignore whether differences are positive or negative (this is a two-tailed test of H_0: $\mu_1 - \mu_2 = 0$).

The differences for the perceived difficulty study are shown below:

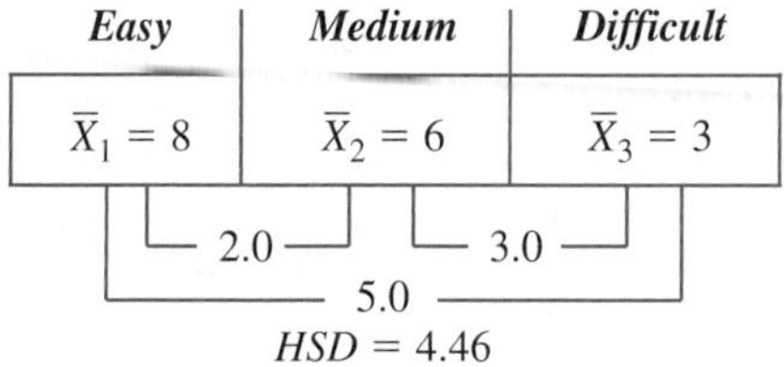

On the line connecting any two levels is the absolute difference between their means.

Step 4: Compare each difference to the *HSD*. If the absolute difference between two means is *greater than* the *HSD*, then these means differ significantly. If the absolute difference between the two means is less than or equal to the *HSD*, then it is *not* a significant difference.

Above, the *HSD* was 4.46. The means from the easy level (8) and the difficult level (3) differ by more than 4.46, so they differ significantly. The mean from the medium level (6) differs from the other means by less than 4.46, however, so it does not differ significantly from them.

Thus, our final conclusion about this study is that it demonstrated a relationship between participants' scores and perceived difficulty, but only for the easy and difficult conditions. If these two conditions were each given to the population, we would expect to find two different populations of scores, having two different μs. We cannot say anything about whether the medium level would produce a different population, however, because we failed to find that it produced a significant difference. Now, as usual, we begin to interpret the results in psychological terms, explaining why this manipulation worked as it did, and what underlying constructs, models, or behaviors are involved.

REMEMBER Post hoc comparisons are required whenever F_{obt} is significant and there are more than two conditions, so that we know which conditions differ.

SUMMARY OF THE STEPS IN PERFORMING A ONE-WAY ANOVA

It has been a long haul, but here is everything involved when performing a one-way ANOVA:

1. The null hypothesis is H_0: $\mu_1 = \mu_2 = \ldots = \mu_k$, and the alternative hypothesis is H_a: not all μs are equal. Choose α, check the assumptions, and collect the data.
2. First, compute the sum of squares between groups (SS_{bn}) and the sum of squares within groups (SS_{wn}). Then, compute the degrees of freedom between groups (df_{bn}) and the degrees of freedom within groups (df_{wn}). Dividing SS_{bn} by df_{bn} gives the mean square between groups (MS_{bn}), and dividing SS_{wn} by df_{wn} gives the mean square within groups (MS_{wn}). Finally, dividing MS_{bn} by MS_{wn} gives F_{obt}.
3. Find F_{crit} in Appendix C, Table 5, using the df_{bn} and the df_{wn}. If H_0 is true, F_{obt} "should" equal 1. The larger the value of F_{obt}, the less likely that H_0 is true. If F_{obt} is larger than F_{crit}, then F_{obt} is significant, indicating that the means in at least two conditions differ significantly.
4. If F_{obt} is significant and there are more than two levels of the factor, determine which specific levels differ significantly by performing post hoc comparisons. Perform the protected t-test if the ns are not equal in all levels, or perform the *HSD* procedure if all ns are equal.

If you followed all of that, then congratulations, you're getting *good* at this stuff. Of course, all of this merely determines whether there is a relationship. Now we must describe that relationship.

DESCRIBING THE RELATIONSHIP IN A ONE-WAY ANOVA

As in previous chapters, you are not finished after demonstrating a significant relationship. Ultimately, you must understand the relationship, and to help, you should describe the relationship by (1) computing confidence intervals, (2) graphing the relationship, and (3) computing the effect size.

The Confidence Interval for Each Population μ

In our example, the mean from the easy condition was 8.0, so we expect that the population mean represented by this condition would be "around" 8. As usual, to more clearly define "around," we compute a confidence interval for the μ represented by the sample mean. This is the same confidence interval that was discussed in Chapter 14, except that here it is computed using the components of ANOVA.

THE COMPUTATIONAL FORMULA FOR THE CONFIDENCE INTERVAL FOR A SINGLE μ IS

$$\left(\sqrt{\frac{MS_{\text{wn}}}{n}}\right)(-t_{\text{crit}}) + \overline{X} \leq \mu \leq \left(\sqrt{\frac{MS_{\text{wn}}}{n}}\right)(+t_{\text{crit}}) + \overline{X}$$

The value of t_{crit} is the *two-tailed* value found in the t-tables, using the appropriate α and using df_{wn} as the df. The MS_{wn} is from the ANOVA, and $\overline{X}$ and n are from the level we are describing.

For example, in the easy condition, $\overline{X} = 8.0$, $MS_{\text{wn}} = 7.0$, $df_{\text{wn}} = 12$, and $n = 5$. The two-tailed t_{crit} (at $df = 12$ and $\alpha = .05$) is ± 2.179. Placing these values in the formula gives

$$\left(\sqrt{\frac{7.0}{5}}\right)(-2.179) + 8.0 \leq \mu \leq \left(\sqrt{\frac{7.0}{5}}\right)(+2.179) + 8.0$$

This becomes

$$(-2.578) + 8.0 \leq \mu \leq (+2.578) + 8.0$$

And finally,

$$5.42 \leq \mu \leq 10.58$$

Because $\alpha = .05$, this is the 95% confidence interval: If we were to test the entire population under our easy condition, we are 95% confident that their μ would fall between 5.42 and 10.58.

Follow the same procedure to describe the μ from any other significant level of a factor.

Graphing the Results in ANOVA

As usual, graph the results by placing the mean dependent score for each condition on the Y axis and the conditions of the independent variable (the levels of the factor) on the X axis. Figure 17.4 shows the line graph for the perceived difficulty study. Notice that

FIGURE 17.4 Mean Number of Problems Correctly Solved as a Function of Perceived Difficulty

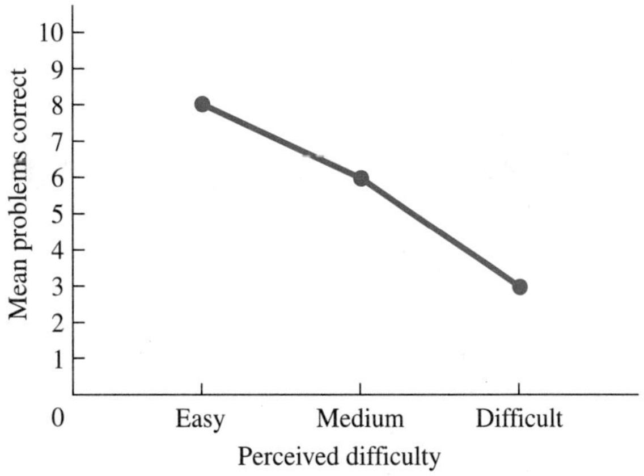

we include all levels of the factor: Here, we included the medium level of difficulty, even though it did not produce significant differences.

As usual, the line graph summarizes the relationship that is present, and here it indicates a largely negative linear relationship. Now, we need to describe the strength of this relationship.

Eta Squared: The Effect Size in the Sample Data

So far, we know only that we have some degree of consistent relationship that is significant. Therefore, the first step is to think "correlation coefficient" to describe the strength of the relationship between the independent and dependent variables. However, here a new correlation coefficient is computed, called eta (pronounced "ay-tah"). **Eta** is analogous to r_{pb}, except that eta can be used to describe any linear or nonlinear relationship containing two or more levels of a factor.

But, remember that to get to the heart of describing a relationship, we compute the "squared correlation coefficient." This is the *effect size* of the independent variable—the proportion of variance in dependent scores that is associated with changing the conditions. With ANOVA, effect size is computed by squaring eta: **eta squared** indicates the proportion of variance in the dependent variable that is accounted for by changing the levels of a factor. The symbol for eta squared is η^2.

THE COMPUTATIONAL FORMULA FOR η^2 IS

$$\eta^2 = \frac{SS_{bn}}{SS_{tot}}$$

The SS_{bn} reflects the differences between the conditions. The SS_{tot} reflects the total differences between all scores in the experiment. Thus, η^2 reflects the proportion of the total differences in the scores that is associated with differences between the conditions.

For example, in the perceived difficulty study, SS_{bn} was 63.33 and SS_{tot} was 147.33, so

$$\eta^2 = \frac{SS_{\text{bn}}}{SS_{\text{tot}}} = \frac{63.33}{147.33} = .43$$

This is interpreted in the same way that we previously interpreted r^2_{pb}. The larger the value of η^2, the more consistently the factor "caused" participants to have a particular score, and thus the more scientifically important the factor is for explaining and predicting differences in the underlying behavior. Thus, here an η^2 of .43 indicates that we are 43%, more accurate at predicting participants' scores when we predict for them the mean from the particular difficulty level they were tested under, rather than predicting the overall mean of the study. In other words, 43% of the variance in these scores is accounted for, or explained, as resulting from changing the level of perceived difficulty. Because 43% is a substantial amount, we conclude that perceived difficulty plays a substantial role in determining a person's score.

The η^2 can be used with either equal or unequal *ns*. But, it is a *descriptive* statistic, and only describes the effect size in sample data. Usually, this is adequate, but other procedures are needed to estimate the effect size in the population.

POWER AND THE ANOVA

Recall that we always want to maximize *power*, the probability of rejecting H_0 when it is false. Here, we do so by maximizing the size of F_{obt}. Look at the F-ratio:

$$F_{\text{obt}} = \frac{MS_{\text{bn}}}{MS_{\text{wn}}}$$

A more powerful design will increase the size of the numerator or decrease the size of the denominator, producing a larger F_{obt}. As in previous chapters, we seek (1) a strong manipulation that maximizes the size of the differences between the level means, thus increasing the size of MS_{bn}; (2) added control that minimizes the variability—error variance—of scores within conditions, thus reducing the size of MS_{wn}; and (3) larger *ns*, thus increasing df_{wn} and also minimizing MS_{wn}. A larger df_{wn} also results in a smaller F_{crit}. Any of the above increases the probability that F_{obt} is significant, producing greater power. The same considerations also increase the power of post hoc comparisons.

In addition, all of the other issues of power from previous chapters apply to experiments involving ANOVA, except that now you simply have more levels. Thus, on the one hand, you must be careful when counterbalancing variables because you may increase error variance and thus decrease power. On the other hand, such techniques can increase internal and external validity.

APA FORMAT FOR STATISTICAL NOTATION

In current published research, the entire ANOVA summary table is usually not included. Instead, as part of a sentence, the F_{obt} is reported in the same way as previous results have been. Thus, the results of the perceived difficulty study would be reported as: $F(2,12) = 4.52, p < .05$. Notice, in the parentheses are both the df_{bn} and df_{wn}, and in that order: Get in the habit of always saying df_{bn} first and then df_{wn}. MS_{wn} may also be reported, but recall that it estimates the error term, so its symbol is *MSE*—standing for "mean square error."

When reporting a post hoc test, indicate the name of the test and the alpha level employed. Then, indicate which conditions produced significant differences. If there are many conditions, create a table to present these results. (To save space, each *HSD* or t_{obt} is often not reported.) The accepted symbol for eta squared is η^2.

PUTTING IT ALL TOGETHER

When all is said and done, the *F*-ratio is a convoluted way of measuring the differences between the means of our conditions and then fitting those differences to a sampling distribution. The larger the F_{obt}, the less likely that the differences between the means are the result of sampling error. A significant F_{obt} indicates that your means are unlikely to all represent one population mean. Perform a post hoc test to determine which level means differ significantly. Then, graph the relationship and compute η^2. That's all there is to it.

CHAPTER SUMMARY

1. The general terms used previously and their corresponding ANOVA terms are

General term	=	*ANOVA term*
independent variable	=	factor
condition	=	level
sum of squared deviations	=	sum of squares (*SS*)
variance (s^2_X)	=	mean square (*MS*)
effect of independent variable	=	treatment effect

2. Researchers study three or more conditions of an independent variable because their hypothesis requires it, to demonstrate a nonlinear relationship, and to obtain the maximum information from a study.

3. The *one-way* ANOVA tests for significant differences between the means from two or more levels of one factor. A *between-subjects factor* consists of independent samples tested under all levels. A *within-subjects* factor consists of dependent samples (created either by matching or by repeated measures).

4. The *experiment-wise error rate* is the probability of a Type I error somewhere in the experiment. ANOVA is used instead of multiple *t*-tests because ANOVA keeps the experiment-wise error rate equal to α.

5. The assumptions of the one-way between-subjects ANOVA are (a) the scores in each condition are independent random samples, (b) each sample represents a

normally distributed population of interval or ratio scores, and (c) all populations represented have homogeneous variance.

6. ANOVA tests *two-tailed hypotheses*. H_0 is that the means from all conditions represent the same μ. H_a is that *not* all μs are equal.

7. The *mean square within groups* (MS_{wn}) estimates the *error variance*, the inherent variability among scores within each population. The *mean square between groups* (MS_{bn}) estimates the error variance plus the treatment variance. *Treatment variance* reflects differences in scores between the populations that are produced by the levels of the factor.

8. F_{obt} is computed from the *F-ratio*, which equals the mean square between groups divided by the mean square within groups.

9. F_{obt} may be greater than 1 because either (a) there is no treatment effect, but the sample means poorly represent this; or (b) two or more sample means represent different population means.

10. The *F-distribution* is the sampling distribution of all possible values of F_{obt} when H_0 is true.

11. The larger the F_{obt}, the less likely it is that all level means represent one population mean. If F_{obt} is significant, then level means are unlikely to all represent the same population mean.

12. If F_{obt} is significant, and there are more than two levels of the factor, then perform *post hoc comparisons* to determine which means differ significantly. When the *n*s are *not* equal, perform *Fisher's protected t-test* on all pairs of means. If all *n*s are equal, perform *Tukey's HSD test.*

13. In ANOVA, *eta squared* (η^2) describes the effect size—the proportion of variance accounted for by the factor.

14. The power of ANOVA increases with increased differences between the conditions, decreased variability of scores within each condition, and increased *n*.

KEY TERMS (with page references)

k F_{obt} F_{crit} MS_{wn} σ^2_{error} MS_{bn} σ^2_{treat} df_{bn} df_{wn} η^2 SS_{bn} SS_{wn} HSD

analysis of variance (457)
ANOVA (457)
between-subjects ANOVA (457)
between-subjects factor (457)
error variance (463)
eta (479)
eta squared (479)
experiment-wise error rate (460)
F-distribution (467)
F-ratio (465)
factor (457)
Fisher's protected *t*-test (475)
level (457)
mean square between groups (464)
mean square within groups (463)
one-way ANOVA (457)
one-way design (457)
post hoc comparisons (462)
sum of squares (468)

treatment (457)
treatment effect (457)
treatment variance (465)
Tukey's *HSD* Multiple Comparisons Test (476)
variance between groups (462)
variance within groups (462)
within-subjects ANOVA (457)
within-subjects factor (457)

REVIEW QUESTIONS

(Answers for odd-numbered questions and problems are provided in Appendix D.)

1. What does each of the following terms mean: (a) ANOVA? (b) One-way design? (c) Factor? (d) Level? (e) Between-subjects factor? (f) Within-subjects factor?

2. A researcher conducts an experiment in which scores are measured under two conditions of an independent variable. (a) How will the researcher know whether to perform a parametric or nonparametric statistical procedure? (b) Which parametric procedures are available to her? (c) If the researcher conducts an experiment with three levels of the independent variable, which two versions of a parametric procedure are available to her? (d) How can she select between the choices in (c)?

3. What are three reasons for conducting a study with three or more levels of a factor?

4. (a) What are error variance and treatment variance? (b) What are the two types of mean squares, and what does each estimate?

5. (a) What is the experiment-wise error rate? (b) Why does performing ANOVA solve the problem of experiment-wise error rates created by performing multiple *t*-tests?

6. Summarize the steps involved in analyzing a multilevel experiment.

7. (a) In a study comparing the effects of four conditions of the independent variable, what is H_0? (b) What is H_a in the same study? (c) Describe in words what H_0 and H_a say for the study.

8. (a) Why should F_{obt} equal 1 if the data represent the H_0 situation? (b) Why is F_{obt} greater than 1 when the data represent the H_a situation? (c) What does a significant F_{obt} indicate about differences between the levels of a factor?

9. (a) When is it necessary to perform post hoc comparisons? Why? (b) When is it unnecessary to perform post hoc comparisons? Why?

10. When do you use each of the two types of post hoc tests discussed in this chapter?

11. What does η^2 indicate?

PRACTICE PROBLEMS

12. (a) Why must the relationship in a one-way ANOVA be significant in order to be potentially important? (b) What does "significant" tell you about the relationship? (c) Why can the relationship be significant yet unimportant?

13. (a) Poindexter computes an F_{obt} of .63. How should this be interpreted? (b) He computes another F_{obt} of 21.7. How should this be interpreted?

14. Foofy obtained a significant F_{obt} from an experiment with five levels. She concludes that changing each condition of the independent variable results in a significant change in dependent scores. (a) Why is she incorrect? (b) What must she do before making this claim?

15. (a) What is the difference between n and N? (b) What does k stand for? (c) What is another name for an independent variable? (d) What are two other names for a condition? (e) If a study involves independent samples, what type of ANOVA is performed? (f) If a study involves dependent samples, what type of ANOVA is performed?

16. A researcher finds a treatment effect for different amounts of a drug on participants' health. (a) What does she mean by "treatment effect"? (b) How does the researcher determine if there's a treatment effect? (c) How does she determine the nature of the treatment effect?

17. A researcher reports that the one-way between-subjects factor of participants' salary ($k = 3$) had a significant effect on participants' self-esteem. In general terms: (a) Describe this design. (b) Interpret the results.

18. In problem 17, if the researcher has instead described a one-way, within-subjects factor (with $k = 3$), what would this indicate about the design?

19. In problem 17, the level means for low, medium, and high salaries were 12, 12, and 18, respectively. Interpret these results.

20. This chapter discussed how to complete four statistical procedures. What are they?

21. Here are data from a between-subjects experiment studying the effect of age on creativity scores:

Age 4	*Age 6*	*Age 8*	*Age 10*
3	9	9	7
5	11	12	7
7	14	9	6
4	10	8	4
3	10	9	5

(a) Compute F_{obt} and create an ANOVA summary table. (b) With $\alpha = .05$, what do you conclude about F_{obt}? (c) Perform the appropriate post hoc comparisons. (d) What should you conclude about this relationship? (e) Statistically, how important is the relationship in this study? (f) Describe how to graph these results.

22. In a study where $k = 3$, $n = 16$, $\overline{X}_1 = 45.3$, $\overline{X}_2 = 16.9$, and $\overline{X}_3 = 8.2$, you compute the following sums of squares.

Source	*Sum of squares*	*df*	*Mean square*	*F*
Between	147.32	___	___	___
Within	862.99	___	___	
Total	1010.31	___		

(a) Complete the ANOVA summary table. (b) With $\alpha = .05$, what do you conclude about F_{obt}? (c) Perform the appropriate post hoc comparisons. What do you conclude about this relationship? (d) What is the effect size in this study, and what does this tell you about the influence of the independent variable?

23. A researcher investigated the number of viral infections people contracted as a function of the amount of stress they experienced during a six-month period. She obtained the following data:

Negligible stress	*Minimal stress*	*Moderate stress*	*Severe stress*
2	4	6	5
1	3	5	7
4	2	7	8
1	3	5	4

(a) What are H_0 and H_a? (b) Compute F_{obt} and complete the ANOVA summary table. (c) At $\alpha = .05$, what is F_{crit}? (d) Report the result in the proper format. (e) Perform the appropriate post hoc comparisons. (f) What can you conclude about this study? (g) Describe the effect size and interpret it. (h) Estimate the range of μ that is likely to be found in the severe stress condition.

24. A researcher investigated the effect of volume of background noise on participants' error rates while performing a boring task. He tested three groups of randomly selected students and obtained the following error data and sums of squares:

	Low volume	*Moderate volume*	*High volume*
$\overline{X}$	61.5	65.5	48.25
n	4	5	7

Summary Table of One-Way ANOVA

Source	*Sum of squares*	*df*	*Mean square*	*F*
Between	652.16			
Within	612.75			
Total	1264.92			

(a) Complete the ANOVA. (b) At $\alpha = .05$, what is F_{crit}? (c) Report the result in the proper format. (d) Perform the appropriate post hoc tests. (e) What can you conclude about this study? (f) What other procedures should you perform?

25. (a) In the perceived difficulty study discussed in this chapter, how could you increase power? (b) How do these strategies increase the power of F_{obt}? (c) What do they do to the post hoc tests?

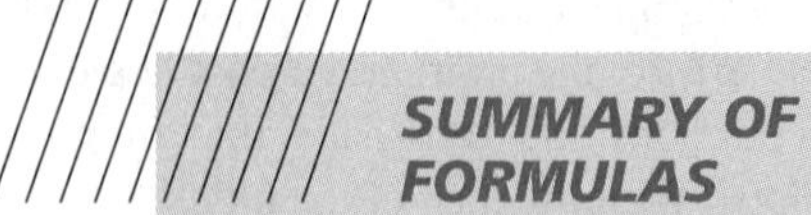

SUMMARY OF FORMULAS

1. *The format for the summary table for a one-way ANOVA is as follows:*

Summary Table of One-Way ANOVA

Source	*Sum of squares*	*df*	*Mean square*	*F*
Between	SS_{bn}	df_{bn}	MS_{bn}	F_{obt}
Within	SS_{wn}	df_{wn}	MS_{wn}	
Total	SS_{tot}	df_{tot}		

2. Computing the sum of squares

(a) *The computational formula for* SS_{tot} *is*

$$SS_{tot} = \Sigma X^2_{tot} - \left(\frac{(\Sigma X_{tot})^2}{N}\right)$$

All scores in the experiment are included, and N is the total number of scores.

(b) *The computational formula for* SS_{bn} *is*

$$SS_{bn} = \Sigma\left(\frac{(\text{Sum of scores in the column})^2}{n \text{ of scores in the column}}\right) - \left(\frac{(\Sigma X_{tot})^2}{N}\right)$$

where each column contains the scores from one level of the factor.

(c) *The computational formula for* SS_{wn} *is*

$$SS_{wn} = SS_{tot} - SS_{bn}$$

3. Computing the mean squares

(a) *The computational formula for* MS_{bn} *is*

$$MS_{bn} = \frac{SS_{bn}}{df_{bn}}$$

with $df_{bn} = k - 1$, where k is the number of levels in the factor.

(b) *The computational formula for* MS_{wn} *is*

$$MS_{wn} = \frac{SS_{wn}}{df_{wn}}$$

with $df_{wn} = N - k$, where N is the total N of the study and k is the number of levels in the factor.

4. *The computational formula for the F-ratio is*

$$F_{\text{obt}} = \frac{MS_{\text{bn}}}{MS_{\text{wn}}}$$

Critical values of F are found in Table 5 in Appendix C for df_{bn} and df_{wn}.

5. *The computational formula for the protected t-test is*

$$t_{\text{obt}} = \frac{\overline{X}_1 - \overline{X}_2}{\sqrt{MS_{\text{wn}}\left(\frac{1}{n_1} + \frac{1}{n_2}\right)}}$$

Values of t_{crit} are the two-tailed values found in the t-tables for $df = df_{\text{wn}}$.

6. *The computational formula for the HSD is*

$$HSD = (q_k)\left(\sqrt{\frac{MS_{\text{wn}}}{n}}\right)$$

Values of q_k are found in Table 6 of Appendix C for df_{wn} and k, where k equals the number of levels of the factor.

7. *The computational formula for the confidence interval for a single* μ *is*

$$\left(\sqrt{\frac{MS_{\text{wn}}}{n}}\right)(-t_{\text{crit}}) + \overline{X} \leq \mu \leq \left(\sqrt{\frac{MS_{\text{wn}}}{n}}\right)(+t_{\text{crit}}) + \overline{X}$$

$\overline{X}$ and n are from the level being described, and t_{crit} is the two-tailed value of t_{crit} at the appropriate α for df_{wn}.

8. *The computational formula for eta squared is*

$$\eta^2 = \frac{SS_{\text{bn}}}{SS_{\text{tot}}}$$

18

The Two-Way Between-Subjects Experiment and the Two-Way Analysis of Variance

GETTING STARTED

To understand this chapter, recall the following:

- From Chapter 17, understand the terms *factor* and *level*, what a significant F indicates, when to perform post hoc tests, and what η^2 indicates.

Your goals in this chapter are to learn:

- What two-way factorial designs are and why researchers conduct them.
- What a significant main effect indicates.
- What a significant interaction indicates.
- How to compute the Fs in a two-way ANOVA, perform post hoc tests, compute η^2, and draw the graph for main and interaction effects.
- How to interpret the results of a two-way experiment.

Researchers often create even larger studies than those discussed in the previous chapter, often testing the influence of multiple factors. An experiment that contains more than one factor requires a multifactor ANOVA. To introduce multifactor experiments and multifactor ANOVA, this chapter discusses experiments with two factors, which are analyzed using a two-way, between-subjects ANOVA. This is like the ANOVA of the previous chapter, except that we compute several values of F. Therefore, be forewarned that the procedure is rather involved (although it is more tedious than it is difficult).

MORE STATISTICAL NOTATION

As with all experiments, the purpose of a two-factor experiment is to determine whether there is a relationship between the independent variable and the dependent variable. The only novelty is that, in a **two-way design**, there are two independent variables—two factors. Such designs are analyzed by performing a two-way ANOVA. The **two-way ANOVA** is the parametric inferential procedure performed on an experiment containing two independent variables. However, there are again different formulas, depending on whether the study involves independent or dependent samples. For now, we'll discuss designs in which both independent variables are tested using independent samples, in which case we perform the **two-way between-subjects ANOVA**.

Each factor may contain any number of levels, so we have a code for describing a specific design. The generic format is to label one independent variable as factor A and the other independent variable as factor B. To describe a particular design, we use the number of levels in each factor. If, for example, factor A has two levels and factor B has two levels, we have a "two-by-two" design and perform a "two-by-two ANOVA," which is written as 2×2. If one factor has four levels and the other factor has three levels, we have a 4×3 ANOVA, and so on.

To understand a two-way design, say that we are again interested in the effects of a "smart pill" on a person's IQ. We'll call the number of smart pills given to participants factor A, and test two levels, 1 or 2 pills. The design of this factor is shown in Table 18.1. Each column represents a level of factor A and, within a column, the *X*s represent IQ scores. Averaging the scores vertically in each column yields the mean IQ for each pill level, showing the effect of factor A: how IQ changes as a function of increasing dosage.

Say that from a totally different perspective, we're also interested in the relationship between age and IQ. We'll call age factor B, and test two levels, 10- and 20-year-olds. Envision this factor as in Table 18.2. Here the two conditions are arranged horizontally, so that each *row* represents a different level of the factor. Then averaging the scores horizontally in each row yields the mean IQ for each age level, showing the effect of factor B: how IQ changes as a function of increasing age.

TABLE 18.1 Diagram of Factor of Number of Smart Pills

Each X represents a participant's IQ score, and each $\overline{X}$ is the mean for a level of factor A.

Factor A: Number of pills	
Level A_1: one pill	*Level A_2: two pills*
X	X
X	X
X	X
X	X
X	X
X	X
$\overline{X}$	$\overline{X}$

TABLE 18.2 Diagram of Factor of Age

Each row represents a level of age. Each X represents a participant's IQ score, and each $\overline{X}$ is the mean for a level of factor B.

Factor B: age			
	Level B_1: 10-year-olds	X X X X X X	$\overline{X}$
	Level B_2: 20-year-olds	X X X X X X	$\overline{X}$

To create a two-way design, we simultaneously manipulate both participants' age and number of pills. Visualize this design as in Table 18.3. Each column is still a level of factor A (number of pills). Each row is still a level of factor B (age). But now we have a new term: Each small square produced by a particular combination of a level of factor A with a level of factor B is called a **cell**. Here, there are four cells, each containing a sample of participants who are one age and are given one amount of the pill. For example, the highlighted cell contains the scores of 20-year-olds who receive one pill.

Most computer programs identify each cell using the levels of the two factors. In Table 18.3, the levels of factor A are A_1 and A_2 and the levels of factor B are B_1 and B_2. Then, for example, the cell formed by combining level 1 of factor A and level 1 of factor B is cell A_1B_1. Also, we identify the mean and *n* from each cell in the same way, so, for example, in cell A_1B_1 is $\overline{X}_{A_1B_1}$.

One final point: Combining all levels of one factor with all levels of another factor produces a **complete factorial design**. The design in Table 18.3 is a complete factorial, because all levels of drug dose are combined with all age levels. On the other hand, in

TABLE 18.3 Two-Way Design for Studying the Factors of Number of Smart Pills and Participants' Age

		Factor A: Number of pills	
		Level A_1: 1 pill	*Level A_2: 2 pills*
Factor B: age	*Level B_1: 10-year-olds*	X X X $\overline{X}_{A_1B_1}$	X X X $\overline{X}_{A_2B_1}$
	Level B_2: 20-year-olds	X X X $\overline{X}_{A_1B_2}$	X X X $\overline{X}_{A_2B_2}$

scores

one of the four cells

an **incomplete factorial design**, not all levels of the two factors are combined. If, for example, we did not collect data for 20-year-olds given one smart pill, we would have an incomplete factorial design. Incomplete factorial designs require elaborate procedures not discussed here.

THE REASON FOR MULTIFACTOR STUDIES

Why study two factors in one experiment? After all, we could perform two separate studies, one testing the effect of factor A and one testing the effect of factor B. The answer is that a multifactor design has three major advantages over a single-factor design.

First, in a multifactor design, we can learn everything about the influence of each factor that we would learn if it were the only independent variable. But, we can also study something with a multifactor design that would otherwise be missed—the *interaction effect*. For now, think of an interaction as the influence of combining the levels from the two factors: It shows how the effect of one independent variable *depends* on the level of the other independent variable that is present. Thus, above, the interaction would indicate the influence of a particular dose of smart pill depending on the age of participants. Interactions are important because, in nature, there are always varying amounts of many variables present that combine to influence a behavior. The primary reason for conducting multifactor studies is to examine such interactions.

A second reason, however, for multifactor experiments is that often, once we have created a design for studying one independent variable, only a minimum of additional effort is required to study additional factors. Thus, multifactor studies can be an efficient and cost-effective way of determining the effects of—and interactions among—several independent variables.

Finally, multifactor experiments often are produced because we set out to study one variable, but additional factors are created through counterbalancing of extraneous variables. For example, let's say that we had set out to study only the influence of the smart pills. But, to prevent confounding, we counterbalanced participants' age, with half 10-year-olds and half 20-year-olds in each condition. Instead of collapsing across and ignoring age, however, we can treat age as a second factor to create the above 2×2 design. Then we can examine the influence of age, as well as its interaction with the pill factor. Thus, by *analyzing* the study as a two-way design, we obtain much more information from an experiment that, regardless, we are going to conduct in the same way. Therefore, always consider whether to analyze any single-factor study as a multifactor design involving counterbalanced variables.

> *REMEMBER* Two-way designs are used (1) to examine the interaction between two independent variables, (2) to maximize the information obtained from a study, and (3) to examine the influence of counterbalanced extraneous variables.

OVERVIEW OF THE TWO-WAY ANOVA

As usual, regardless of whether we're talking about each factor separately or their interaction, we want to conclude that, if we tested the entire population under the various conditions, we'd find different populations of scores located at different μs. But there is the usual problem: Differences between our sample means may simply reflect sampling error, so we might actually find the same population, having the same μ, for all conditions. Therefore, once again we must eliminate the idea that the differences between the sample means merely reflect sampling error. To do this, we perform ANOVA. As usual, we first set alpha (usually $\alpha = .05$) and then check the assumptions.

Assumptions of the Two-Way Between-Subjects ANOVA

Perform the two-way between-subjects ANOVA on a two-way design if it is a complete factorial design and

1. All cells contain independent samples of participants.
2. The dependent variable measures interval or ratio scores that are approximately normally distributed.
3. The populations all have homogeneous variance.

Logic of the Two-Way ANOVA

Enough about smart pills. Here's a semi-fascinating idea for a study. Have you ever noticed that television commercials are much louder than the programs themselves? Advertisers seem to believe that increased volume creates increased viewer attention and so makes the commercial more persuasive. To test whether louder messages are more persuasive, we'll play a recording of an advertising message to participants at each of three volumes. Volume is measured in decibels, but to simplify things we'll call the three levels of volume soft, medium, and loud. Say that we're also interested in the differences between how males and females are persuaded, so our other factor is the gender of the listener. If, in one study, we examine both the volume of the message and the gender of the listener, we have a two-factor experiment involving three levels of volume and two levels of gender. We'll test all conditions with independent samples, so we have a 3×2 between-subjects, factorial ANOVA. The dependent variable indicates how persuasive a person believes the message to be on a scale of 0 (not at all) to 25 (totally convincing).

We collect the scores and organize them as in Table 18.4. For simplicity, we have a distinctly unpowerful N: Nine men and nine women were randomly selected, and then three men and three women were randomly assigned to hear the message at each volume. Thus, three persuasiveness scores are in each cell.

But now what? How do we make sense out of it all? We want to determine the effect on persuasiveness scores when we change (1) the levels of the volume factor, (2) the levels of the gender factor, and (3) the combination, or interaction, of volume and gender. Because we view each of these effects separately, we view the means from each separately: We examine the means produced by changing volume, the means for male versus female, and the means from the interaction. For each, we want to determine whether the effect is significant, so we look at the means in a way that is very similar to a one-way ANOVA. You already understand a one-way ANOVA, so the rest of this chapter is simply a guide for computing the various Fs. In a nutshell, here is where we're going:

> **Any two-way ANOVA breaks down into computing the *F*s for the two main effects and for the interaction effect.**

TABLE 18.4 A 3 × 2 ANOVA for the Factors of Volume of Message and Gender of Subject

		Factor A: volume		
		Level A_1: soft	*Level A_2: medium*	*Level A_3: loud*
Factor B: gender	*Level B_1: male*	9 4 11	8 12 13	18 17 15
	Level B_2: female	2 6 4	9 10 17	6 8 4

$N = 18$

Main Effects

The **main effect** of a factor is the effect that changing the levels of the factor has on the dependent scores, while ignoring all other factors in the study. In the persuasiveness study, to find the main effect of factor A (volume) we simply ignore the levels of factor B (gender.) Literally erase the horizontal line that separates the rows of males and females back in Table 18.4, and treat the experiment as if it were this:

Factor A: volume			
Level A_1: soft	*Level A_2: medium*	*Level A_3: loud*	
9	8	18	
4	12	17	
11	13	15	$k_A = 3$
2	9	6	
6	10	8	
4	17	4	
$\overline{X}_{A_1} = 6$ $n_{A_1} = 6$	$\overline{X}_{A_2} = 11.5$ $n_{A_2} = 6$	$\overline{X}_{A_3} = 11.33$ $n_{A_3} = 6$	

By ignoring whether there are males and females in each level, we have *collapsed* across gender. For now, we simply have six people tested under each volume. Then, in this diagram, there is one factor, with three means from the three levels of volume. Thus, k_A—the number of levels in factor A—is 3, with $n = 6$ in each level.

When we collapse across one factor, we have the **main effect means** for the remaining factor. Thus, collapsing across gender produces the main effect means for the three levels of volume ($\overline{X}_{A_1} = 6$, $\overline{X}_{A_2} = 11.5$, and $\overline{X}_{A_3} = 11.33$).

After collapsing, we essentially perform a one-way ANOVA on the above diagram. We ask "Do these main effect means represent different μs that would be found if we tested the entire population under each of the three volumes?" To answer this question, first create the statistical hypotheses for factor A. The null hypothesis is

$$H_0: \mu_{A_1} = \mu_{A_2} = \mu_{A_3}$$

For our study, this says that changing volume has no effect, so the main effect means from all levels of volume represent the same population of persuasiveness scores. If we can reject H_0, then we will accept the alternative hypothesis, which is

$$H_a\text{: not all } \mu_A \text{ are equal}$$

For our study, this says that at least two main effect means from the volume factor represent different populations of persuasiveness scores, having different μs.

To test H_0, we compute an F_{obt} called F_A. If F_A is significant, it indicates that at least two main effect means differ significantly. Then, we describe this relationship by graphing the main effect means, performing post hoc comparisons to determine which specific means from factor A differ significantly, and determining the effect size of factor A.

After examining the main effect of factor A, we move on to the main effect of factor B. To do this, collapse across factor A (volume). That is, erase the vertical lines separating the levels of volume shown back in Table 18.4, producing the following diagram of the main effect of factor B:

Factor B: gender					
	Level B_1: male	9 4 11	8 12 13	18 17 15	$\overline{X}_{B_1} = 11.89$ $n_{B_1} = 9$
	Level B_2: female	2 6 4	9 10 17	6 8 4	$\overline{X}_{B_2} = 7.33$ $n_{B_2} = 9$

Now, we simply have the persuasiveness scores of males and females, ignoring the fact that some of each heard the message at different volumes. In this diagram, there is one factor with two levels. We treat this as a one-way ANOVA to see if there are significant differences between the main effect means for males ($\overline{X}_{B_1} = 11.89$) and females ($\overline{X}_{B_2} = 7.33$). Notice that with two levels of gender, k_B is 2 and the n of each level is 9. (For factor A, k was 3 and n was 6.)

> ***REMEMBER*** In a two-way ANOVA, the values of n and k may be different for each factor.

For the main effect of factor B, the null hypothesis is

$$H_0\text{: } \mu_{B_1} = \mu_{B_2}$$

For our study, this says that changing gender has no effect, so the mean for males represents the same μ as the mean for females. The alternative hypothesis is

$$H_a\text{: not all } \mu_B \text{ are equal}$$

For our study, this says that our samples of males and females represent different populations of persuasiveness scores, having different μs.

To test H_0 for factor B, we compute a separate F_{obt}, called F_B. If F_B is significant, it indicates that the main effect means for factor B differ significantly. Then, we graph the main effect means for factor B, perform the post hoc comparisons on these main effect means, and compute the effect size of factor B.

Interaction Effects

After examining the main effects of factors A and B, we turn to the interaction. The interaction of two factors is called a two-way interaction. The **two-way interaction** is the influence on scores that results from combining the levels of factor A with the levels of factor B. In our example, the interaction is the effect of each volume when combined with each gender. An interaction is identified as A × B. Here, factor A has 3 levels and factor B has 2 levels, so we have a 3 × 2 interaction. (This is pronounced the "3 by 2" interaction, which here is the "volume by gender" interaction.)

Because an interaction examines the combination of both factors, we do not collapse across, or ignore, either factor. Instead, each *cell* is a level of the interaction and so by examining the **cell means**, we examine the **interaction means**.

> *REMEMBER* When looking at the interaction effect, compare the cell means. When looking at a main effect, compare the level means.

The interaction between volume and gender is shown in Table 18.5. These are the means from the original six cells, each containing three scores, that were back in Table 18.4, so $k_{A \times B}$ is 6 and n is 3.

These interaction means may or may not actually reflect an *interaction effect*: there may or may not be a relationship present. The relationship is complicated, because both independent variables are changing, as well as the dependent variable. **Therefore, to recognize when an interaction effect is present:**

1. First, look at the relationship between factor A and the dependent scores under *one* level of factor B.
2. Then, see if this relationship *is different* for the other levels of factor B.
3. An interaction effect is present if the relationship between factor A and the dependent scores *changes* as the levels of factor B change. (The effect is also present if the relationship between factor B and scores changes as the levels of factor A change.)

TABLE 18.5 The Volume by Gender Interaction

		Factor A: volume		
		Soft	*Medium*	*Loud*
Factor B: gender	*Male*	$\bar{X} = 8$	$\bar{X} = 11$	$\bar{X} = 16.67$
	Female	$\bar{X} = 4$	$\bar{X} = 12$	$\bar{X} = 6$

$k = 6$
$n = 3$

It is easier to see this when the cell means are laid out as a one-way design.

A × B interaction effect

Male soft	*Male medium*	*Male loud*	*Female soft*	*Female medium*	*Female loud*
9	8	18	2	9	6
4	12	17	6	10	8
11	13	15	4	17	4
$\overline{X} = 8$	$\overline{X} = 11$	$\overline{X} = 16.67$	$\overline{X} = 4$	$\overline{X} = 12$	$\overline{X} = 6$

$k_{A \times B} = 6$
$n = 3$

The means are grouped so that on the left are the three means for males as volume changes. On the right are the means for females as volume changes. For males, each increase in volume apparently results in an increase in the mean score (going from 8 to 11 to 16.67). Thus, there is a somewhat positive linear relationship between volume and scores for males. However, a *different* relationship is found between volume and scores for females. Here, increasing volume from soft to medium apparently increases the mean (from 4 to 12), but increasing volume from medium to loud apparently decreases the mean (down to 6). Thus, for females there is apparently a nonlinear relationship, where as volume increases, persuasiveness scores first increase but then decrease.

For an interaction effect to be present, the specific nature of the relationship for males and females is not important, as long as volume and scores form a different relationship for each gender. An **interaction effect** is present when the relationship between one factor and dependent scores changes as the levels of the other factor change. In other words, an interaction occurs when the influence of changing one factor is not the same under each level of the other factor: Increasing volume does not have the same effect for males as it does for females. Therefore, you can always recognize that an interaction is present because you must use the word *depends* when interpreting the overall influence of one independent variable: What is the overall effect of increasing volume? The answer *depends* on whether we're talking about males or females.

You can also see the interaction by looking at the relationship between gender and dependent scores at each level of volume. Sometimes males score higher, sometimes females do—it *depends* on which level of volume is present.

Conversely, an interaction effect would not be present if the means showed the same pattern for males and females. For example, say the cell means had been as follows:

		Factor A: volume		
		Soft	*Medium*	*Loud*
Factor B: gender	*Male*	$\overline{X} = 5$	$\overline{X} = 10$	$\overline{X} = 15$
	Female	$\overline{X} = 20$	$\overline{X} = 25$	$\overline{X} = 30$

Here, increasing the volume increases scores by about 5 points, *regardless* of whether it's for males or females. (Or, females always score higher, regardless of volume.) Thus, an interaction effect is not present when the influence of changing the levels of one factor does not depend on which level of the other variable is present. Or, in other words, there is no interaction when there is the same relationship between the scores and one factor for each level of the other factor.

> *REMEMBER* A two-way interaction effect occurs when the influence that one factor has on scores depends on which level of the other factor is present.

As with other effects, the data may appear to represent an interaction, but this may be an illusion created by sampling error. Therefore, we determine whether there is a significant interaction by performing a procedure similar to performing a one-way ANOVA on the cell means. However, this is not merely finding whether the cell means differ significantly. Instead, we test the extent to which the cell means differ *after* we've removed those differences that are due to the main effects of factors A and B.

First we create the statistical hypotheses. In symbols, the null hypothesis is rather complex[1]. In words, H_0 is that there is not an interaction effect in the population and any appearance of one in the cell means is the result of sampling error. The alternative hypothesis is that at least two of the cell means do represent an interaction in the population.

To test H_0, we compute another F_{obt}, called $F_{A \times B}$. If $F_{A \times B}$ is significant, it indicates that at least two of the cell means differ significantly in a way that produces an interaction effect. Then, we graph the interaction (cell) means, perform post hoc comparisons to determine which means differ significantly, and compute the effect size of the interaction.

Overview of the Computations of the Two-Way ANOVA

Thus, to review, in a two-way ANOVA we compute three *F*s: one for the main effect of factor A, one for the main effect of factor B, and one for the interaction of A $\times$ B. Table 18.6 summarizes all of the means from the persuasiveness study that these *F*s compare. First, we collapse across factor B (ignoring gender), and F_A tests the difference between the main effect means of factor A, volume (the column means of 6, 11.5, and 11.33). Next, we collapse across factor A (ignoring volume), and F_B examines the difference between the main effect means for factor B, gender (the row means of 11.89 and 7.33.) Finally, we do not collapse across either factor, and $F_{A \times B}$ tests for an interaction between volume and gender (comparing the six cell means of 8, 4, 11, etc.). The logic and calculations for each of these are the same as in the one-way ANOVA, because any F_{obt} is the ratio formed by dividing the mean square between groups by the mean square within groups.

Recall that MS_{wn} is the variance within groups. In a two-way ANOVA it is computed by finding the "average" variability in the cells. All participants in a cell are treated identically, so any differences among their scores are due to the inherent variability of scores. Thus, the MS_{wn} again estimates the error variance in any of the raw score populations. This is the *one* estimate of the error variance used as the denominator in computing all three *F* ratios.

[1] Technically, H_0 says that differences between scores due to A at one level of B equal the differences between scores due to A at the other level of B. Thus, we have H_0: $\mu_{A_1B_1} - \mu_{A_2B_1} = \mu_{A_1B_2} - \mu_{A_2B_2} = \mu_{A_2B_1} - \mu_{A_3B_1} = \mu_{A_2B_2} - \mu_{A_3B_2}$. H_a is that not all differences are equal.

TABLE 18.6 Summary of Persuasiveness Study Showing the Means That Are Tested by Each F_{obt}.

		Factor A: volume			
		A_1: soft	A_2: medium	A_3: loud	
Factor B: gender	B_1: male	$\overline{X} = 8$	$\overline{X} = 11$	$\overline{X} = 16.67$	$\overline{X}_{male} = 11.89$
	B_2: female	$\overline{X} = 4$	$\overline{X} = 12$	$\overline{X} = 6$	$\overline{X}_{fem} = 7.33$
		$\overline{X}_{soft} = 6$	$\overline{X}_{med} = 11.5$	$\overline{X}_{loud} = 11.33$	

(F_B tests $\overline{X}_{male}$ and $\overline{X}_{fem}$; F_A tests $\overline{X}_{soft}$, $\overline{X}_{med}$, and $\overline{X}_{loud}$.)

The $F_{A \times B}$ tests the six cell means.

Also recall that the variance between groups indicates the differences between the means, which provides an estimate of the treatment effect in the population. Because we have two factors and the interaction, however, we partition the between-groups variance into (1) variance between groups due to factor A, (2) variance between groups due to factor B, and (3) variance between groups due to the interaction. We compute a separate mean square between groups for each of these as an estimate of the treatment variance each produces in the population.

All of the components of the two-way ANOVA are shown in Table 18.7. As usual, any mean square is equal to the appropriate sum of squares divided by the corresponding degrees of freedom. Therefore, for factor A (volume), we first compute the sum of squares between groups for factor A (called SS_A), and then, after dividing by the degrees of freedom for factor A (called df_A), we have the mean square between groups for factor A (called MS_A).

Likewise, for factor B (gender), we compute the sum of squares between groups for factor B (SS_B), and then divide by the degrees of freedom between groups for factor B (df_B), to get the mean square between groups for factor B (MS_B).

For the interaction, we compute the sum of squares between groups for A × B ($SS_{A \times B}$), and divide by the degrees of freedom for A × B ($df_{A \times B}$), to get the mean square between groups for the interaction ($MS_{A \times B}$). We also compute MS_{wn} by computing SS_{wn} and then dividing by df_{wn}.

To complete the summary table, for factor A, we divide MS_A by MS_{wn} to produce F_A. For factor B, dividing MS_B by MS_{wn} produces F_B. For the interaction, dividing $MS_{A \times B}$ by MS_{wn} produces $F_{A \times B}$.

Each F_{obt} is tested as in the previous chapter. F_{obt} may be larger than 1 because (1) H_0 is true, but we have sampling error in representing this, or (2) H_0 is false. The larger the value of F_{obt}, the less likely it is that H_0 is true. If any F_{obt} is larger than F_{crit}, then it is significant, and we reject the corresponding H_0.

TABLE 18.7 Summary Table of Two-Way ANOVA

Source	*Sum of squares*	*df*	*Mean square*	*F*
Between				
Factor A (volume)	SS_A	df_A	MS_A	F_A
Factor B (gender)	SS_B	df_B	MS_B	F_B
Interaction (vol × gen)	$SS_{A \times B}$	$df_{A \times B}$	$MS_{A \times B}$	$F_{A \times B}$
Within	SS_{wn}	df_{wn}	MS_{wn}	
Total	SS_{tot}	df_{tot}		

COMPUTING THE TWO-WAY ANOVA

Having a computer perform the calculations is the best way to perform this ANOVA. Regardless, first organize the data in each cell as in Table 18.8. Then, compute ΣX and ΣX^2 for each cell and note the n of each cell. Thus, for the male-soft cell, $\Sigma X = 4 + 9 + 11 = 24$, $\Sigma X^2 = 4^2 + 9^2 + 11^2 = 218$, and $n = 3$. Also, compute the mean for each cell (e.g., for male-soft, $\overline{X} = 24/3 = 8$). These are the means that are tested in the interaction.

To look at the volume means, collapse across gender. Compute ΣX in each column, which equals the sum of the ΣXs from the cells in that column (for soft, $\Sigma X = 24 + 12$). Note the n in each column (here, $n = 6$) and compute the sample mean for each column (e.g., $\overline{X}_{soft} = 6$). These are the means that are tested in the main effect of factor A.

To look at the gender means, collapse across volume. Compute ΣX in each row, which equals the sum of the ΣXs from the cells in that row (for males, $\Sigma X = 24 + 33 + 50 = 107$). Note the n in each row (here, $n = 9$) and compute the sample mean for each row (e.g., $\overline{X}_{male} = 11.89$). These are the means that are tested in the main effect of factor B.

Finally, compute the total ΣX (called ΣX_{tot}) by adding the ΣX from all columns (so $\Sigma X_{tot} = 36 + 69 + 68 = 173$). Alternatively, you can add the ΣX from all rows. Also, find the total ΣX^2 (called ΣX^2_{tot}) by adding the ΣX^2 from each cell (so $\Sigma X^2_{tot} = 218 + 377 + 838 + 56 + 470 + 116 = 2075$. Note that the total N is 18.

As you'll see in the following sections, the above components are used to complete the ANOVA. To keep track of your computations, fill in the ANOVA summary table as you go along.

Computing the Sums of Squares

First, compute the sums of squares.

Step 1: Compute the total sum of squares.

THE COMPUTATIONAL FORMULA FOR THE TOTAL SUM OF SQUARES IS

$$SS_{tot} = \Sigma X^2_{tot} - \left(\frac{(\Sigma X_{tot})^2}{N} \right)$$

TABLE 18.8 Summary Data for 3 × 2 ANOVA

		Factor A: volume			
		A_1: *soft*	A_2: *medium*	A_3: *loud*	
Factor B: gender	B_1: *male*	4 9 11 $\bar{X} = 8$ $\Sigma X = 24$ $\Sigma X^2 = 218$ $n = 3$	8 12 13 $\bar{X} = 11$ $\Sigma X = 33$ $\Sigma X^2 = 377$ $n = 3$	18 17 15 $\bar{X} = 16.67$ $\Sigma X = 50$ $\Sigma X^2 = 838$ $n = 3$	$\bar{X}_{male} = 11.89$ $\Sigma X = 107$ $n = 9$
	B_2: *female*	2 6 4 $\bar{X} = 4$ $\Sigma X = 12$ $\Sigma X^2 = 56$ $n = 3$	9 10 17 $\bar{X} = 12$ $\Sigma X = 36$ $\Sigma X^2 = 470$ $n = 3$	6 8 4 $\bar{X} = 6$ $\Sigma X = 18$ $\Sigma X^2 = 116$ $n = 3$	$\bar{X}_{fem} = 7.33$ $\Sigma X = 66$ $n = 9$
		$\bar{X}_{soft} = 6$ $\Sigma X = 36$ $n = 6$	$\bar{X}_{med} = 11.5$ $\Sigma X = 69$ $n = 6$	$\bar{X}_{loud} = 11.33$ $\Sigma X = 68$ $n = 6$	$\Sigma X_{tot} = 173$ $\Sigma X^2_{tot} = 2075$ $N = 18$

This says to divide $(\Sigma X_{tot})^2$ by N and then subtract the answer from ΣX^2_{tot}.

From Table 18.8, $\Sigma X_{tot} = 173$, $\Sigma X^2_{tot} = 2075$, and $N = 18$. Filling in the formula gives

$$SS_{tot} = 2075 - \left(\frac{(173)^2}{18}\right)$$

which becomes

$$SS_{tot} = 2075 - 1662.72$$

so $SS_{tot} = 412.28$.

Note that the quantity $(\Sigma X_{tot})^2/N$ above is also used when computing other sums of squares. It is called the *correction* (here, the correction equals 1662.72).

Step 2: Compute the sum of squares for factor A. In the diagram of the two-way ANOVA, always have factor A form the *columns*.

THE COMPUTATIONAL FORMULA FOR THE SUM OF SQUARES BETWEEN GROUPS FOR COLUMN FACTOR A IS

$$SS_A = \Sigma\left(\frac{(\text{sum of scores in the column})^2}{n \text{ of scores in the column}}\right) - \left(\frac{(\Sigma X_{tot})^2}{N}\right)$$

This says to square ΣX for each column of factor A and divide by the n in the column. Then, add the answers together and then subtract the correction.

From Table 18.8, the three column sums were 36, 69, and 68, and n was 6. Filling in the formula gives

$$SS_{\text{A}} = \left(\frac{(36)^2}{6} + \frac{(69)^2}{6} + \frac{(68)^2}{6}\right) - \left(\frac{(173)^2}{18}\right)$$

$$SS_{\text{A}} = (216 + 793.5 + 770.67) - 1662.72$$

$$SS_{\text{A}} = 1780.17 - 1662.72$$

so $SS_{\text{A}} = 117.45$.

Step 3: Compute the sum of squares between groups of factor B. In the diagram, of the two-way ANOVA, the levels of factor B should form the *rows*.

THE COMPUTATIONAL FORMULA FOR THE SUM OF SQUARES BETWEEN GROUPS FOR ROW FACTOR B IS

$$SS_{\text{B}} = \Sigma\left(\frac{(\text{sum of scores in the row})^2}{n \text{ of scores in the row}}\right) - \left(\frac{(\Sigma X_{\text{tot}})^2}{N}\right)$$

This says to square ΣX for each level of factor B and divide by the n in the level. Then, add the answers and then subtract the correction.

In Table 18.8, the row sums were 107 and 66, and n was 9. Filling in the formula gives

$$SS_{\text{B}} = \left(\frac{(107)^2}{9} + \frac{(66)^2}{9}\right) - 1662.72$$

$$SS_{\text{B}} = 1756.11 - 1662.72$$

so $SS_{\text{B}} = 93.39$.

Step 4: Compute the sum of squares between groups for the interaction. First, compute something called the overall sum of squares between groups, identified as SS_{bn}.

THE COMPUTATIONAL FORMULA FOR SS_{bn} IS

$$SS_{\text{bn}} = \Sigma\left(\frac{(\text{sum of scores in the cell})^2}{n \text{ of scores in the cell}}\right) - \left(\frac{(\Sigma X_{\text{tot}})^2}{N}\right)$$

Find $(\Sigma X)^2$ for each cell, divide by the n of the cell, add the answers from all cells together, and subtract the correction.

From Table 18.8

$$SS_{bn} = \left(\frac{(24)^2}{3} + \frac{(33)^2}{3} + \frac{(50)^2}{3} + \frac{(12)^2}{3} + \frac{(36)^2}{3} + \frac{(18)^2}{3}\right) - 1662.72$$

$$SS_{bn} = 1976.33 - 1662.72$$

so $SS_{bn} = 313.61$.

The SS_{bn} equals the sum of squares for factor A plus the sum of squares for factor B plus the sum of squares for the interaction. Therefore, to find $SS_{A \times B}$, subtract the sum of squares for the main effects (in steps 2 and 3) from SS_{bn}. Thus,

THE COMPUTATIONAL FORMULA FOR THE SUM OF SQUARES BETWEEN GROUPS FOR THE INTERACTION IS

$$SS_{A \times B} = SS_{bn} - SS_A - SS_B$$

In the example, $SS_{bn} = 313.61$, $SS_A = 117.45$, and $SS_B = 93.39$, so

$$SS_{A \times B} = 313.61 - 117.45 - 93.39$$

so, $SS_{A \times B} = 102.77$.

Step 5: Compute the sum of squares within groups. The sum of squares within groups plus the overall sum of squares between groups equals the total sum of squares. Therefore, subtracting the overall SS_{bn} in step 4 from SS_{tot} in step 1 gives the SS_{wn}.

THE COMPUTATIONAL FORMULA FOR THE SUM OF SQUARES WITHIN GROUPS IS

$$SS_{wn} = SS_{tot} - SS_{bn}$$

In our example, $SS_{tot} = 412.28$ and $SS_{bn} = 313.61$, so

$$SS_{wn} = 412.28 - 313.61$$

Thus, $SS_{wn} = 98.67$.

Computing the Degrees of Freedom

Now, compute the various values of df.

1. *The degrees of freedom between groups for factor A is* $k_A - 1$, where k_A is the number of levels in factor A. (In our example, k_A is the three levels of volume, so $df_A = 2$.)
2. *The degrees of freedom between groups for factor B is* $k_B - 1$, where k_B is the number of levels in factor B. (In the example, k_B is the two levels of gender, so $df_B = 1$.)

3. *The degrees of freedom between groups for the interaction is the df for factor A multiplied times the df for factor B.* (Above, $df_A = 2$ and $df_B = 1$, so $df_{A \times B} = 2$.)
4. *The degrees of freedom within groups equals $N - k_{A \times B}$*, where N is the total N of the study and $k_{A \times B}$ is the number of cells in the study. (In our example, N is 18 and we have six cells, so $df_{wn} = 18 - 6 = 12$.)
5. *The degrees of freedom total equals $N - 1$.* Also, the sum of the above *df*s should equal df_{tot}. (In the example, $N = 18$, so $df_{tot} = 17$.)

Computing the Mean Squares

Perform the remainder of the computations by working directly from the summary table. So far, the sums of squares and degrees of freedom produce Table 18.9.

Now, compute the mean squares. Any mean square equals the appropriate sum of squares divided by the appropriate *df*. Therefore,

THE COMPUTATIONAL FORMULA FOR THE MEAN SQUARE FOR FACTOR A IS

$$MS_A = \frac{SS_A}{df_A}$$

In the example,

$$MS_A = \frac{117.45}{2} = 58.73$$

THE COMPUTATIONAL FORMULA FOR THE MEAN SQUARE FOR FACTOR B IS

$$MS_B = \frac{SS_B}{df_B}$$

TABLE 18.9 Summary Table of Two-Way ANOVA

Source	*Sum of squares*	*df*	*Mean square*	*F*
Between				
Factor A (volume)	117.45	2	MS_A	F_A
Factor B (gender)	93.39	1	MS_B	F_B
Interaction (vol × gen)	102.77	2	$MS_{A \times B}$	$F_{A \times B}$
Within	98.67	12	MS_{wn}	
Total	412.28	17		

In the example,

$$MS_{\text{B}} = \frac{93.39}{1} = 93.39$$

THE COMPUTATIONAL FORMULA FOR THE MEAN SQUARE FOR THE INTERACTION IS

$$MS_{\text{A}\times\text{B}} = \frac{SS_{\text{A}\times\text{B}}}{df_{\text{A}\times\text{B}}}$$

Thus,

$$MS_{\text{A}\times\text{B}} = \frac{102.77}{2} = 51.39$$

THE COMPUTATIONAL FORMULA FOR THE MEAN SQUARE WITHIN GROUPS IS

$$MS_{\text{wn}} = \frac{SS_{\text{wn}}}{df_{\text{wn}}}$$

Therefore,

$$MS_{\text{wn}} = \frac{98.67}{12} = 8.22$$

Putting these values in the summary table produces Table 18.10.

Now, finally, compute the *F*s.

Computing F_{obt}

Any F_{obt} equals the appropriate *MS* between groups divided by the MS_{wn}. Therefore,

THE COMPUTATIONAL FORMULA FOR F_{A} IS

$$F_{\text{A}} = \frac{MS_{\text{A}}}{MS_{\text{wn}}}$$

In our example,

$$F_{\text{A}} = \frac{58.73}{8.22} = 7.14$$

TABLE 18.10 Summary Table of Two-Way ANOVA

Source	*Sum of squares*	*df*	*Mean square*	*F*
Between				
Factor A (volume)	117.45	2	58.73	F_A
Factor B (gender)	93.39	1	93.39	F_B
Interaction (vol × gen)	102.77	2	51.39	$F_{A \times B}$
Within	98.67	12	8.22	
Total	412.28	17		

THE COMPUTATIONAL FORMULA FOR F_B IS

$$F_B = \frac{MS_B}{MS_{wn}}$$

Thus,

$$F_B = \frac{93.39}{8.22} = 11.36$$

THE COMPUTATIONAL FORMULA FOR $F_{A \times B}$ IS

$$F_{A \times B} = \frac{MS_{A \times B}}{MS_{wn}}$$

Thus,

$$F_{A \times B} = \frac{51.39}{8.22} = 6.25$$

And now, the finished summary table is shown in Table 18.11.

Interpreting Each F_{obt}

Determine whether each F_{obt} is significant by comparing it to the appropriate F_{crit}. Find each F_{crit} in the F-tables (Table 5 in Appendix C) using the df_{bn} and the df_{wn} used in computing the F_{obt}.

1. To find F_{crit} for testing F_A, use df_A as the df between groups and df_{wn}. In the example, $df_A = 2$ and $df_{wn} = 12$, so for $\alpha = .05$, the F_{crit} is 3.88.

TABLE 18.11 Summary Table of Two-Way ANOVA

Source	Sum of squares	df	Mean square	F
Between				
Factor A (volume)	117.45	2	58.73	7.14
Factor B (gender)	93.39	1	93.39	11.36
Interaction (vol × gen)	102.77	2	51.39	6.25
Within	98.67	12	8.22	
Total	412.28	17		

2. To find F_{crit} for testing F_B, use df_B as the *df* between groups and df_{wn}. In the example, $df_B = 1$ and $df_{wn} = 12$, so for $\alpha = .05$, the F_{crit} is 4.75.
3. To find F_{crit} for the interaction, use $df_{A \times B}$ as the *df* between groups and df_{wn}. In the example, $df_{A \times B} = 2$ and $df_{wn} = 12$, so for $\alpha = .05$, the F_{crit} is 3.88.

Note that because factors A and B have different *dfs* for between groups, they have different critical values.

> *REMEMBER* Each F_{crit} will be different if the degrees of freedom between groups are different.

Thus, we end up comparing each F_{obt} from the ANOVA summary table with the F_{crit}, as follows:

	F_{obt}	F_{crit}
Main effect of volume (A)	7.14	3.88
Main effect of gender (B)	11.36	4.75
Interaction (A × B)	6.25	3.88

By now you can do this in your sleep. Imagine a sampling distribution with a region of rejection and F_{crit} in the positive tail. (If you can't imagine this, look back in Chapter 17 at Figure 17.2.) First, the F_A of 7.14 is larger than its F_{crit}, so F_A falls in the region of rejection. Therefore we conclude there is a significant main effect of volume. The APA format for reporting this is like that of previous *F*s, so this result is $F(2,12) = 7.14$, $p < 05$. To interpret any effect, examine the *pattern* formed by the *means* of the factor—the ANOVA summary table is no help whatsoever. Table 18.12 again shows the means from the persuasiveness study that we saw in Table 18.6. The significant F_A indicates that increasing volume produced significant differences somewhere among the means of 6, 11.5, and 11.33. Likewise, the F_B is significant, so the mean for males (11.89) differs significantly from the mean for females (7.33). Report this as $F(1,12) = 11.36$, $p < .05$. Finally, the $F_{A \times B}$ is significant, so there is a signifi-

TABLE 18.12 Summary of Means for Persuasiveness Study

		Factor A: volume			
		A_1: *soft*	A_2: *medium*	A_3: *loud*	
Factor B: gender	B_1: *male*	$\bar{X} = 8$	$\bar{X} = 11$	$\bar{X} = 16.67$	$\bar{X}_{male} = 11.89$
	B_2: *female*	$\bar{X} = 4$	$\bar{X} = 12$	$\bar{X} = 6$	$\bar{X}_{fem} = 7.33$
		$\bar{X}_{soft} = 6$	$\bar{X}_{med} = 11.5$	$\bar{X}_{loud} = 11.33$	

F_A (column means); F_B (row means)

The $F_{A \times B}$ tests the six cell means.

cant interaction effect among the six cell means: The influence of changing volume depends on whether participants are males or females (and vice versa.) Report this result as $F(2,12) = 6.25, p < .05$.

Recognize that it is just a coincidence of the particular data in this example that all three values of F_{obt} were significant. Whether any one F_{obt} is significant does not influence whether any other F_{obt} is significant. With different data, any combination of the main effects and/or the interaction may or may not be significant.

At this point, we have completed the ANOVA, but we are not yet finished with the analysis. Because each significant F_{obt} indicates only that a difference exists somewhere among the corresponding means, the next step is to examine those means.

INTERPRETING THE TWO-WAY EXPERIMENT

First, examine each significant main effect and interaction by graphing their respective means and performing the post hoc comparisons on those means.

Graphing the Main Effects

As usual, plot the dependent variable along the Y axis and the levels of a factor along the X axis. Graph the main effect of factor A by plotting the main effect means from each level of factor A (the column means in Table 18.12). Graph the main effect of factor B separately, plotting the main effect means from each level of factor B (the row means in Table 18.12). Figure 18.1 shows these graphs. (Because volume is measured in decibels, the X axis of the volume factor should be labeled in decibels.) Note that the main effect of gender is plotted as a bar graph because this is a nominal independent variable.

Such simple graphs probably would not appear in a publication, but always draw them so you can see the pattern formed by the means. The graph on the right shows that

FIGURE 18.1 Graphs Showing Main Effects of Volume and Gender

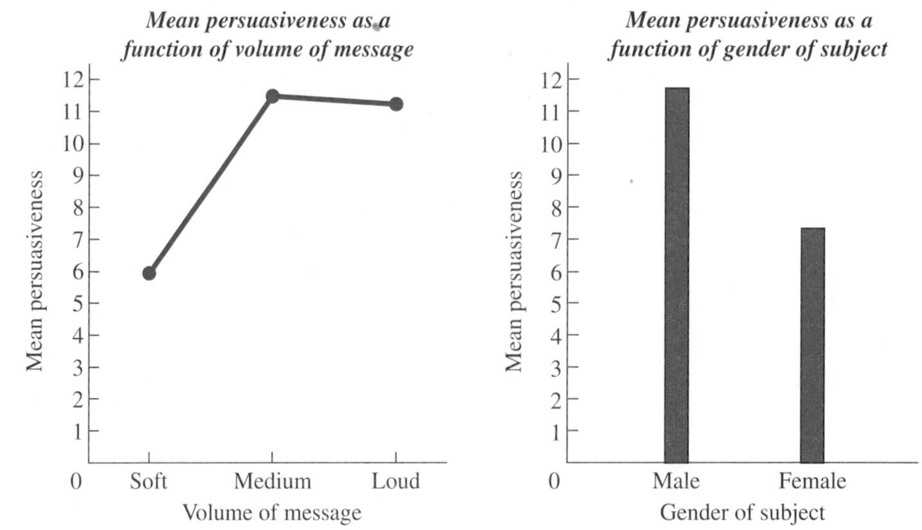

males scored higher than females. In the graph on the left, the slanting line between soft and medium volume suggests a large, possibly significant, difference between those means. The line between medium and loud volume is close to horizontal, however, so these means are close to equal, and there may not be a significant difference here.

Graphing the Interaction Effect

An interaction can be a beast to interpret, so always graph it. Graph the interaction by plotting all *cell means* on a *single* graph. As usual, place the dependent variable along the Y axis. Place the levels of one factor along the X axis. Show the second factor by drawing a separate line on the graph that connects the means for each level of that factor. (Because there's a line for each level of the second factor, place the factor with the most levels on the X axis so that there are as few lines as possible.) For the persuasiveness study, the X axis is labeled with the three volume levels, and the finished graph is in Figure 18.2. As in any graph, we're showing the relationship between the X variable and the Y scores, but we show this relationship as it occurs under each level of the other factor. Here, we show the relationship between volume and persuasiveness scores first for males, and then for females. Thus, approach this in the same way as when looking at the means of the interaction. First, examine the relationship between volume and persuasiveness scores for males using the upper half of Table 18.12:

	Factor A: volume		
	Soft	***Medium***	***Loud***
Male	$\bar{X} = 8$	$\bar{X} = 11$	$\bar{X} = 16.67$

FIGURE 18.2 Graph of Cell Means, Showing Mean Persuasiveness as a Function of Volume of Message and Subject Gender

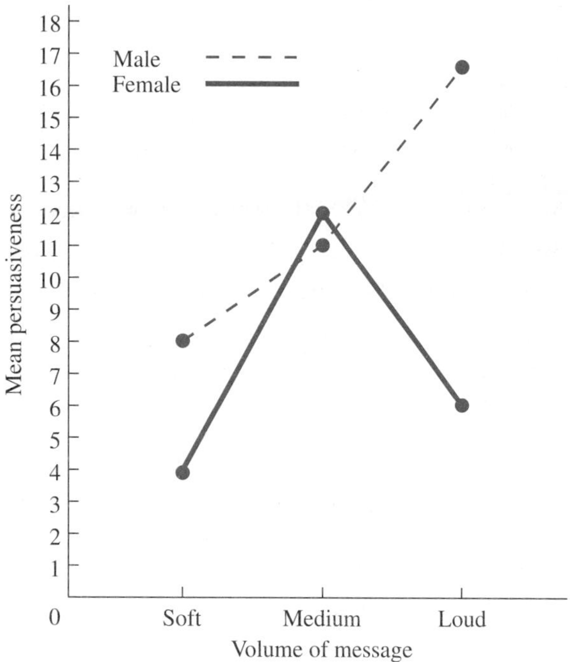

Plot these cell means and connect the adjacent data points with straight lines. As when graphing main effects, include all cell means here, even if the post hoc tests indicate some do not differ significantly.

Next, look at the relationship between volume and scores for females, or

	Factor A: volume		
	Soft	***Medium***	***Loud***
Female	$\overline{X} = 4$	$\overline{X} = 12$	$\overline{X} = 6$

Also plot these three means and connect the adjacent data points.

> ***REMEMBER*** The graph of an interaction contains a separate line to show the relationship between *X* and *Y* that occurs for each level of the other factor.

Notice that we identify each condition by using different symbols for the data points or different kinds of lines. Also notice that we always provide a key to indicate the conditions that each line represents.

Interpret the graph of an interaction by looking at one line at a time. Thus, for males (the dashed line), as volume increased, mean persuasiveness scores increased. For females (the solid line), as volume increased, persuasiveness scores first increased but then decreased. Overall, the relationship between increasing volume and scores was not the same for males and females. In other words, the effect or influence that increasing volume has on persuasiveness scores depends on whether the participants are male or female.

Of course, if the interaction were not significant, then we would have no reason to believe that changing the volume had different effects on males and females, regardless of what the graph suggested. Further, we do not know which of these cell means actually differ significantly, because we haven't performed the post hoc comparisons yet.

Before we do, however, note one final aspect of an interaction. An interaction can produce an infinite variety of different graphs, but

when an interaction effect is present, it produces lines that are *not* parallel.

Remember that each line summarizes a relationship and that a line that is shaped or oriented differently from another line indicates a different relationship. Therefore, when the lines in the interaction graph are not parallel, each line depicts a *different* relationship. This indicates that the relationship between X and Y depends on the second factor, so an interaction is present. Conversely, when an interaction is not present, the lines will be parallel, with each line depicting essentially the same relationship. To see this, say that our data had produced one of the two graphs in Figure 18.3. The graph on the left is the ultimate in nonparallel lines. Here, as the levels of A change, the mean scores either increase or decrease, *depending* on the level of B we're talking about. Therefore, an interaction effect is present. In the graph on the right, however, the lines are parallel. Here, as the levels of A change, the scores increase, regardless of which level of factor B we're talking about. Therefore, this graph does not depict an interaction effect. (The fact that the scores are higher in B_1 than in B_2 is the main effect of factor B.)

Think of significance testing for the interaction as testing whether the lines are significantly different from parallel. When $F_{A \times B}$ is *not* significant, the lines on the graph are not significantly different from parallel, so they may represent parallel lines that would be found if we graphed the means of the populations. When $F_{A \times B}$ is significant, somewhere in the graph the lines *do* differ significantly from parallel. Therefore, if we could graph the means of the populations, the lines probably would not be parallel, and there would be an interaction in the population.

FIGURE 18.3 Two Graphs Showing when an Interaction Is and Is Not Present

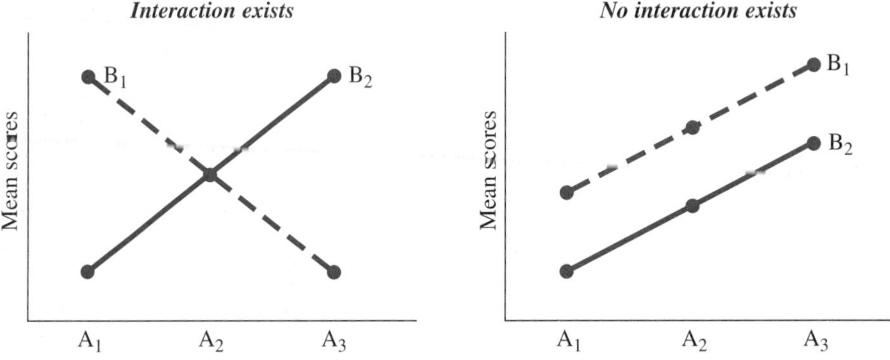

REMEMBER When graphed, interaction effects produce nonparallel lines.

Seeing Main Effects in a Graph of the Interaction

In published research articles, often only a graph of the interaction is provided, and you are expected to visualize the main effects from it. Because cell means are averaged together to obtain main effect means, you can envision the data points for the main effect of a factor as the average of the appropriate data points in the interaction graph. For example, say we had obtained the data in Figure 18.4. On the graph at the left, the asterisks show where, on the *Y* axis, the overall mean for each level of volume is located after we collapse across gender (averaging the two data points in each circle). Plotting the line formed by the asterisks on a separate graph (with the *X* axis labeled for volume level) would show the main effect of volume. On the graph at the right, the asterisks show where the mean for each gender level is located after collapsing across volume (averaging the three data points in each circle). Plotting the line formed by these asterisks on a graph (with the *X* axis labeled male and female) would show the main effect of gender.

Performing the Post Hoc Comparisons

As usual, perform post hoc comparisons on the means from any *significant* F_{obt}. If there are unequal *n*s in a factor, perform Fisher's protected *t*-test from Chapter 17. If the *n*s are equal, perform Tukey's *HSD* procedure, also from Chapter 17. However, the HDS for an interaction effect is computed differently than for a main effect.

Performing Tukey's *HSD* for main effects Perform post hoc comparisons on the main effect means for each significant main effect. Recall that the computational formula for the *HSD* is

$$HSD = (q_k)\left(\sqrt{\frac{MS_{wn}}{n}}\right)$$

FIGURE 18.4 Main Effects Seen in the Graph of an Interaction

The dots are cell means and the asterisks are visualized main effect means.

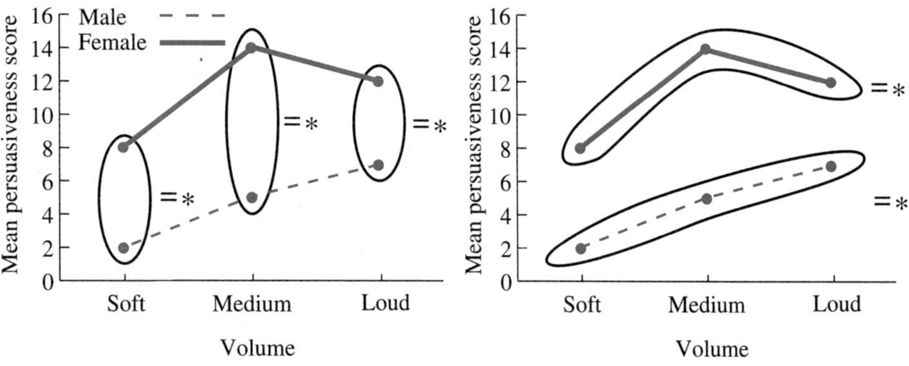

where MS_{wn} is the denominator of the F_{obt}, q_k is found in Table 6 of Appendix C for df_{wn} and k (where k is the number of levels in the factor), and n is the number of scores in a level. But, beware: First, for each factor, there may be a different value of n! Here is a diagram of the persuasiveness study showing the n in each cell and each main effect:

		Factor A: volume			
		Soft	*Medium*	*Loud*	
Factor B: gender	*male*	$n = 3$	$n = 3$	$n = 3$	$n = 9$
	female	$n = 3$	$n = 3$	$n = 3$	$n = 9$
		$n = 6$	$n = 6$	$n = 6$	

With 3 scores per cell, there are 6 scores per column, so $n = 6$ when computing the *HSD* for the main effect means for volume. But, in each row is a total of 9 scores, so $n = 9$ when computing the *HSD* for the main effect means for gender. And, when comparing the cell means of the interaction, $n = 3$. Thus,

> ***n* is the number of scores used to compute each mean that you are presently examining.**

Also, beware because q_k depends on k. When factors have a different k, they have different values of q_k.

> REMEMBER The *HSD* for each main effect may involve a different value of k or n.

In the persuasiveness study, the volume factor has three main effect means, so $k = 3$, and n is 6. In the ANOVA, $MS_{wn} = 8.22$ and $df_{wn} = 12$. From Table 6, for $\alpha = .05$, $q_k = 3.77$. Placing these values in the formula gives

$$HSD = (q_k)\left(\sqrt{\frac{MS_{wn}}{n}}\right) = (3.77)\left(\sqrt{\frac{8.22}{6}}\right) = 4.41$$

Thus, the *HSD* for factor A is 4.41.

Finding the differences between all pairs of factor A means, we have

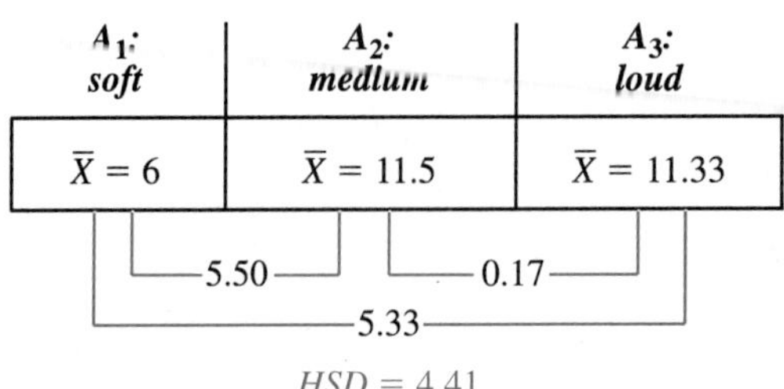

In the middle of each line connecting two means is the absolute difference between them. The mean for soft volume differs from the means for medium and loud by more than 4.41, so soft volume produces a significant difference from the other volumes. But, the means for medium and loud volume differ by less than 4.41, so these conditions do not differ significantly.

When a factor contains only two levels (like gender), do not bother to perform post hoc comparisons (it must be that the males differ significantly from the females). If, however, there are more than two levels in a significant factor B, compute the appropriate *HSD* for the *n* and *k* in that factor and compare the main effect means as above.

Performing Tukey's *HSD* for the interaction The post hoc comparisons for a significant interaction involve the cell means. However, do not compare every cell mean to every other cell mean. Look at Table 18.13. We would not, for example, compare the mean for males at the loud volume to the mean for females at the soft volume. This is because even if the means do differ significantly, we would not know what caused the difference, because the two cells differ in terms of both gender *and* volume. In other words, gender is *confounded* by volume and vice versa, producing a confounded comparison. A **confounded comparison** occurs when two cells differ along more than one factor. When performing post hoc comparisons, we perform only **unconfounded comparisons**, in which two cells differ along only one factor. Therefore, compare only cell means within the same column because these differences result from factor B. Also, compare means within the same row, because these differences result from factor A. Do not, however, make any diagonal comparisons, because these are confounded comparisons.

> *REMEMBER* Make only unconfounded comparisons when performing post hoc comparisons on an interaction.

With equal *ns* in all cells, we compare the means in the interaction using a slight variation of the Tukey *HSD*.[2] Previously, we found q_k in Table 6 using k, the number of means being compared. To do this for an interaction, we first determine the **adjusted *k***.

TABLE 18.13 Summary of Interaction Means for Persuasiveness Study

Solid lines connecting two cells show examples of unconfounded comparisons; dashed lines connecting two cells show examples of confounded comparisons.

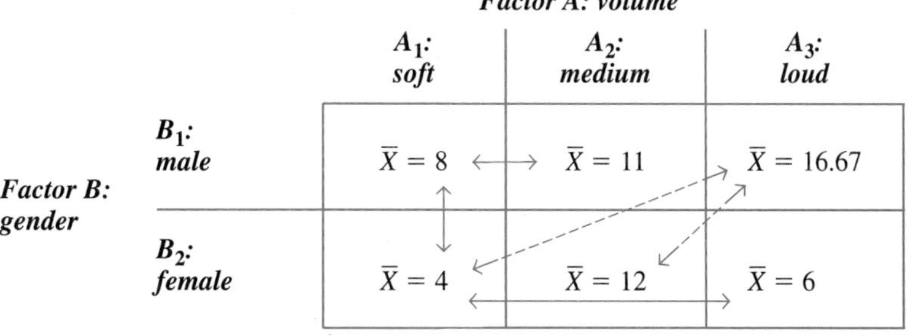

		Factor A: volume		
		A_1: *soft*	A_2: *medium*	A_3: *loud*
Factor B: gender	B_1: *male*	$\bar{X} = 8$	$\bar{X} = 11$	$\bar{X} = 16.67$
	B_2: *female*	$\bar{X} = 4$	$\bar{X} = 12$	$\bar{X} = 6$

[2]Adapted from Cicchetti, 1972.

TABLE 18.14 Values of Adjusted *k*

Design of study	*Number of cell means in study*	*Adjusted value of k*
2 × 2	4	3
2 × 3	6	5
2 × 4	8	6
3 × 3	9	7
3 × 4	12	8
4 × 4	16	10
4 × 5	20	12

This value adjusts for the actual number of unconfounded comparisons being made. Obtain the adjusted *k* from Table 18.14 shown here (and at the beginning of Table 6 of Appendix C). In the left column, locate the design of your study. Ignore the order of the numbers. We called the persuasiveness study a 3 × 2 design, but look at the row labeled "2 × 3." For that row, as a double-check confirm that the middle column contains the number of cells in the interaction (we have 6). In the right-hand column is the *adjusted k* (for this example, it's 5).

The *adjusted k* is the value of *k* to use in obtaining q_k from Table 6 of Appendix C. Thus, for the persuasiveness study, with $\alpha = .05$, $df_{wn} = 12$, and adjusted $k = 5$, the $q_k = 4.51$. Now, compute the *HSD* using the same formula used previously. Our MS_{wn} is 8.22, but now *n* is 3, the number of scores in each *cell*. We have

$$HSD = (q_k)\left(\sqrt{\frac{MS_{wn}}{n}}\right) = (4.51)\left(\sqrt{\frac{8.22}{3}}\right) = 7.47$$

Thus, the *HSD* for the interaction is 7.47.

Now, determine the differences between all cell means within each column and within each row. To see these differences, arrange them as shown in Table 18.15. On the line connecting two cells is the absolute difference between their means. Any dif-

TABLE 18.15 Table of Interaction Means

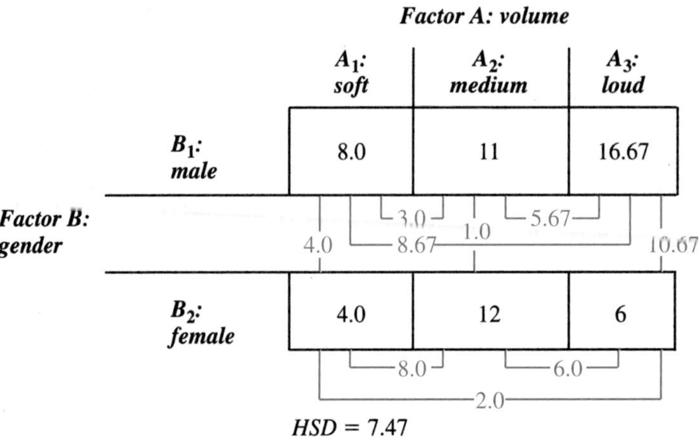

ference between two means that is larger than the *HSD* is a significant difference. There are only three significant differences here: (1) between the mean for females at the soft volume and the mean for females at the medium volume; (2) between the mean for males at the soft volume and the mean for males at the loud volume; and (3) between the mean for males at the loud volume and the mean for females at the loud volume.

Interpreting the Overall Results of the Experiment

There is no *one* way to interpret all experiments, because each experiment indicates something different. The goal is to come up with a complete, honest, and simplified description of the results of the study. To do that, look at the *pattern formed by the means that the post hoc tests indicate differ significantly* within the significant main effects and interaction effects. All of the differences found in the persuasiveness study are summarized in Table 18.16. Outside of the diagram are the main effect means, and any two means connected by a line differ significantly. Inside the diagram, each line connecting two cell means indicates a significant difference within the interaction.

When interpreting the results of a two-way design, of course, ignore any effects that are not significant. But then, however, the focus must be on the *interaction* when it is significant, even if there are significant main effects. This is because the conclusions about significant main effects often must be qualified (or are downright untrue) because of the interaction. For example, there is a significant main effect of gender, so we might conclude that, overall, males score higher than females. However, the cell means of the interaction show a different picture, because here gender differences *depend* on the volume: Only in the loud condition is there a significant difference between males and females. (This difference is so large that it produced an overall mean for males that is larger than the overall mean for females.) Therefore, because the interaction contradicts the overall pattern suggested by the main effect, we *cannot* make a general conclusion about differences between males and females.

Likewise, we cannot make an overall conclusion based on the main effect of volume, which showed that soft volume was significantly different from both the medium and loud volumes. The interaction indicates that increasing the volume from soft to medium

TABLE 18.16 Summary of Significant Differences in Our Persuasiveness Study

Each line connects two means that differ significantly.

		Factor A: volume			
		Level A_1: soft	*Level A_2: medium*	*Level A_3: loud*	
Factor B: gender	*Level B_1: male*	8.0	11	16.67	$\overline{X} = 11.89$
	Level B_2: female	4.0	12	6	$\overline{X} = 7.33$
		$\overline{X}_{soft} = 6$	$\overline{X}_{med} = 11.5$	$\overline{X}_{loud} = 11.33$	

produced a significant difference *only* for females, and increasing the volume from soft to loud produced a significant difference *only* for males.

Thus, as above, usually we cannot draw any conclusions about significant main effects when the interaction is significant. After all, the interaction indicates that the influence of one factor *depends* on the level of the other factor that is present, so we cannot turn around and act as though either factor has a consistent overall effect. Therefore, in such situations, the interpretation of a study is usually limited to the interaction. When the interaction is not significant, then focus on any significant main effects.

> ***REMEMBER*** The primary interpretation of a two-way ANOVA rests on the interpretation of the significant interaction.

Thus, we conclude that increasing the volume of a message beyond soft does tend to increase persuasiveness scores in the population, but this increase occurs for females with medium volume and for males with loud volume. Further, differences in persuasiveness scores between males and females do occur in the population, but only if the volume of the message is loud.

Remember experiment-wise error, the probability of a Type I error somewhere in our conclusions? Well, after all of the above shenanigans, the experiment-wise error is protected so that for all of these conclusions together, the probability of a Type I error is still $p < .05$. Also, remember power—the probability of not making a Type II error? All that was said in previous chapters about power applies to the two-way ANOVA as well. Thus, for any differences that are not significant, we worry whether we have maximized power by maximizing the difference between the means, minimizing the variability within each cell, and having a large enough n.

Also, remember confidence intervals? We can compute the confidence interval for the population μ represented by each significant main effect mean or cell mean. This is the same confidence interval for μ presented in the previous chapter, and it's formula is reproduced in this chapter's Summary of Formulas.

As usual, after finding significant results, we would now turn to interpreting the results in psychological terms. And, as usual, for help in interpreting each relationship, we compute its effect size.

Describing the Effect Size: Eta Squared

Recall that we always think "squared correlation coefficient" to describe a significant relationship. Therefore, in the two-way ANOVA, again compute eta squared (η^2) to describe effect size—the proportion of variance in the dependent scores that is accounted for by a manipulation. Compute a separate eta squared for each *significant* main and interaction effect. The formula for eta squared here is

$$\eta^2 = \frac{\text{Sum of squares between groups for the effect}}{SS_{\text{tot}}}$$

To compute each eta squared, divide the sum of squares for the factor (either SS_{A}, SS_{B}, or $SS_{\text{A}\times\text{B}}$) by SS_{tot}. For example, for our factor A (volume), SS_{A} was 117.45 and SS_{tot} was 412.28. Therefore,

$$\eta^2_{\text{A}} = \frac{SS_{\text{A}}}{SS_{\text{tot}}} = \frac{117.45}{412.28} = .28$$

Thus, if we predict participants' scores using the main effect mean of the volume condition they were tested under, we can account for 28% of the total variance in persuasiveness scores. Following the same procedure for the gender factor, SS_B is 93.39, so η^2_B is .23: Predicting the mean of a gender condition for male and female participants, respectively, will account for an additional 23% of the variance in scores. Finally, $SS_{A \times B}$ is 102.77, so $\eta^2_{A \times B}$ is .25: Using the mean of the cell to predict participants' scores, we can account for an additional 25% of the variance.

Recall that the greater the effect size, the more important the factor is in determining participants' scores. Because each of the above effects has about the same effect size, they are all of equal importance in understanding differences in persuasiveness scores in this experiment. Suppose, however, that one effect accounted for only .01, or 1%, of the total variance. Such a small η^2 indicates that this relationship is very inconsistent. Therefore, it is not a very useful or informative relationship, and we are better served by emphasizing the other, larger significant effects. In essence, if eta squared indicates that an effect was not a big deal in the experiment, then we should not make a big deal out of it when interpreting the experiment.

The effect size is especially important to consider when dealing with interactions. The one exception to the rule of always focusing on the significant interaction is when it has a very small effect size. If the interaction has a very small effect size (say, only .02), then although the interaction contradicts the pattern in a main effect, it is only slightly and inconsistently contradictory. In such cases, we focus the interpretation on any significant main effects that had a more substantial effect size.

REMEMBER Consider effect size when determining which factors to focus on when interpreting a two-way ANOVA.

SUMMARY OF THE STEPS IN PERFORMING A TWO-WAY ANOVA

The following summarizes the steps for performing a two-way ANOVA:

1. Design the experiment, check the assumptions, and collect the data.
2. Compute the sums of squares between groups for each main effect and for the interaction, and compute the sum of squares within groups. Dividing each sum of squares by the appropriate *df* produces the corresponding mean square. Dividing each mean square between groups by the mean square within groups produces each F_{obt}.
3. Find F_{crit} in Table 5 of Appendix C, using the *df* between groups for each factor or interaction and the df_{wn}. If the F_{obt} is larger than F_{crit}, then there is a significant difference between two or more of the means for that factor or interaction.
4. Graph the main effects by plotting the level means of a factor, with the dependent variable on the *Y* axis and the levels of the factor on the *X* axis. Graph the interaction by plotting the cell means. Label the *X* axis with the levels of one factor, and in the body of the graph use a separate line to connect the cell means produced at each level of the other factor.
5. Perform post hoc comparisons for each significant main effect or interaction.
6. Compute eta squared to describe the proportion of variance in dependent scores accounted for by each significant main effect or interaction.

7. Based on the significant main and/or interaction effects and their values of η^2, develop an overall conclusion regarding the relationships formed by the means from cells and levels that differ significantly.
8. Compute the confidence interval for the value of μ represented by the mean in any relevant level or cell.

Congratulations, you're getting *very* good at this stuff.

APA FORMAT FOR STATISTICAL NOTATION

In APA publications, each F_{obt} is reported as shown previously. However, avoid using subscripts or letters, and instead identify a factor or interaction using words. (Thus, we might say, "The gender by volume interaction was significant, $F(2,12) = 6.25$, $p < .05$.") For completeness, all *F*s from the ANOVA are reported, whether significant or not, and the results of all post hoc tests are reported, even if the focus is then only on the interaction.

Create graphs as discussed here. Never use different colors of ink to identify the different lines in an interaction graph. Instead, always provide a key.

PUTTING IT ALL TOGETHER

Throughout previous chapters, you may have been misled into thinking that you should perform only the primary analyses that test your predictions directly. Your goal as a researcher, however, is not only to demonstrate the predicted relationship but also to understand it. Therefore, after you have performed your primary analyses, explore the data. You can group scores along any potentially relevant variables. (For example, did the time of day during which participants were tested produce differences?) Or, you may correlate scores with personal information collected from participants. (Does their age relate to their performance?) The more precisely you examine your data and participants, the more precisely you'll be able to explain how a behavior operates and to describe the variables that influence it.

CHAPTER SUMMARY

1. In a *two-way between-subjects ANOVA*, there are two independent variables, and all of the conditions of both factors contain independent samples. In a *complete factorial design*, all levels of one factor are combined with all levels of the other factor. Each *cell* is formed by a combination of a level from each factor.
2. The ANOVA examines the *main effect* of manipulating each variable separately, as well as the *interaction effect* of manipulating both variables simultaneously.
3. The assumptions of the two-way between-subjects *ANOVA* are that (a) each cell is a random independent sample of interval or ratio scores, (b) the populations represented in the study are normally distributed, and (c) the variances of all populations are homogeneous.

4. In a two-way ANOVA, an F_{obt} is computed for each main effect and for the interaction. The means in each main effect result from *collapsing* across the levels of the other factor. In the interaction, the cell means are examined without collapsing.

5. A *significant* F_{obt} *for a main effect* indicates that changing the levels of the factor produce significant differences in scores.

6. A significant F_{obt} for an interaction indicates that the effect of changing the levels of one factor *depends on* which level of the other factor is present. Therefore, the relationship between one factor and the dependent variable changes as the levels of the other factor change. When graphed, an interaction produces *nonparallel lines*.

7. Post hoc comparisons are performed on each significant effect that has more than two levels. Post hoc comparisons on the interaction are performed for *unconfounded* comparisons only. The means from two cells are unconfounded if the cells differ along only one factor.

8. Conclusions from a two-way ANOVA are based on the significant main and interaction effects and which level or cell means differ significantly. The primary interpretation of a two-way ANOVA usually rests on the *significant interaction*.

9. Eta squared describes the effect size of each significant main effect and interaction. A confidence *interval* can be computed for the μ represented by any $\overline{X}$ in the study.

KEY TERMS (with page references)

F_A F_B $F_{A\times B}$ SS_A df_A k_A MS_A SS_B df_B k_B MS_B $SS_{A\times B}$ $df_{A\times B}$ $k_{A\times B}$ $MS_{A\times B}$
adjusted *k* (513)
cell (490)
complete factorial design (490)
confounded comparison (513)
incomplete factorial design (491)
interaction effect (496)
interaction (cell) means (495)
main effect (493)
main effect means (493)
two-way ANOVA (489)
two-way between-subjects ANOVA (489)
two-way design (489)
two-way interaction (495)
unconfounded comparison (513)

REVIEW QUESTIONS

(Answers for odd-numbered questions and problems are provided in Appendix D.)

1. Identify the following terms: (a) Two-way design, (b) Complete factorial, (c) Cell, (d) Two-way between-subjects design.
2. What are three reasons for conducting two-factor experiments?

3. For a 2 × 2 ANOVA, describe the following in words: (a) The statistical hypotheses for factor A. (b) The statistical hypotheses for factor B. (c) The statistical hypotheses for A × B.
4. Identify the *F*s that are computed in a two-way ANOVA involving factors A and B.
5. (a) What is the difference between a main effect mean and a cell mean? (b) A significant main effect indicates what about your manipulation? (c) A significant interaction indicates what about your manipulation? (d) Why do we usually base the interpretation of a two-way design on the interaction when it is significant?
6. What does it mean to collapse across a factor?
7. Say that in a 3 × 4 ANOVA with equal *n*s, all *F*s are significant. What other procedures should be performed?
8. (a) When is it appropriate to compute the effect size in a two-way ANOVA? (b) How many times might you do this in one design? (c) For each effect, what does the effect size indicate?
9. (a) What is a confounded comparison, and when does it occur? (b) What is an unconfounded comparison, and when does it occur? (c) Why don't we perform post hoc tests on confounded comparisons?
10. Why is a two-way ANOVA similar to three one-way ANOVAs?

PRACTICE PROBLEMS

11. In a study, factor A has 3 levels and factor B has 4 levels. In each cell, $n = 5$. What is the n when examining (a) the means from the main effect of A? (b) the means from the main effect of B? (c) the means in the interaction?
12. Assuming your results are significant, what does each of the following questions mean, and how do you answer it? (a) What is the main effect of factor A? (b) What is the main effect of factor B? (c) What is the interaction effect?
13. Below are the cell means of three experiments. For each experiment, compute the main effect means and indicate whether there appears to be an effect of A, B, and/or A × B.

Study 1

	A_1	A_2
B_1	2	4
B_2	12	14

Study 2

	A_1	A_2
B_1	10	5
B_2	5	10

Study 3

	A_1	A_2
B_1	8	14
B_2	8	2

14. In problem 13, if you graph the cell means (labeling the X axis with factor A), what pattern will you see for each interaction?
15. (a) How can you increase the power of a two-way ANOVA? (b) Doing so will also increase the power of what other procedure? (c) Why is having more power a good idea?
16. A researcher studies participants' frustration levels when solving problems both as a function of the difficulty of the problem and as a function of whether they are

math or logic problems. She finds that logic problems produce significantly more frustration than math problems, that greater difficulty leads to significantly greater frustration, but that more difficult math problems produce significantly greater frustration than more difficult logic problems. In the ANOVA performed for this study, what effects are significant?

17. In question 16, say the researcher instead found no difference between math and logic problems, but that frustration significantly increases with greater difficulty, and that this is true for both math and logic problems. In the ANOVA, what effects are significant?

18. In an experiment, you measure the popularity of two brands of soft drinks (factor A), and for each brand you test males and females (factor B). The following table shows the main effect and cell means from the study:

		Factor A		
		Level A_1: brand X	*Level A_2: brand Y*	
Factor B:	*Level B_1: male*	14	23	18.5
	Level B_2: female	25	12	18.5
		19.5	17.5	

(a) Describe the graph of the interaction means when factor A is on the *X* axis. (b) Does there appear to be an interaction? Why? (c) Why will a significant interaction prohibit you from making conclusions based on the main effects?

19. When should a study be analyzed using the two-way between-subjects ANOVA?

20. A researcher examines performance on an eye-hand coordination task as a function of three levels of reward and three levels of practice, obtaining the following cell means.

		Reward		
		Low	*Medium*	*High*
Practice	*Low*	4	10	7
	Medium	5	5	14
	High	15	15	15

(a) What are the main effect means for reward, and what do they indicate about this factor? (b) What are the main effect means for practice, and what do they indicate? (c) Is an interaction likely? (d) How would you perform unconfounded post hoc comparisons of the cell means?

21. (a) In question 20, why does the interaction contradict your conclusions about the effect of reward? (b) Why does the interaction contradict your conclusions about practice?
22. In question 20, the researcher reports that the effect size of reward is .14, that the effect size of practice is .31, and that the interaction accounts for .01 of the variance. What does each value indicate about the influence of these effects?
23. A study compared the performance scores of males and females tested either early or late in the day. Here are the data:

		Factor A	
		Level A_1: males	Level A_2: females
Factor B	Level B_1: early	6 11 9 10 9	8 14 17 16 19
	Level B_2: late	8 10 9 7 10	4 6 5 5 7

(a) Using $\alpha = .05$, perform an ANOVA and complete the summary table. (b) Compute the main effect means and interaction means. (c) Perform the appropriate post hoc comparisons. (d) What do you conclude about the relationships this study demonstrates? (e) Compute the effect size where appropriate.

24. A researcher investigated the effects of (1) whether participants meditate, and (2) the degree of introversion they exhibit, on the dependent variable of hypnotic suggestibility. She collected the following data:

		Factor A		
		Low introversion	Medium introversion	High introversion
Factor B	Meditation	5 6 2 2 5	7 5 6 9 5	9 8 10 10 10
	No meditation	10 10 9 10 10	2 5 4 3 2	5 6 5 7 6

(a) Complete the ANOVA and create a summary table. (b) Determine which effects are significant. (c) For each significant effect, compute the means and perform the appropriate post hoc comparisons. (d) Compute the effect size where appropriate. (e) What conclusions can be drawn from this study?

25. You conduct an experiment involving two levels of self-confidence (A_1 is low, and A_2 is high) and examine participants' anxiety scores after they speak to one of four groups of differing sizes (B_1 through B_4 represent speaking to a small, medium, large, or extremely large group, respectively). You compute the following sums of squares ($n = 5$ and $N = 40$):

Source	*Sum of squares*	*df*	*Mean square*	*F*
Between				
Factor A	8.42	___	___	___
Factor B	76.79	___	___	___
Interaction	23.71	___	___	___
Within	110.72	___	___	
Total	219.64	___		

(a) Complete the ANOVA summary table. (b) With $\alpha = .05$, what do you conclude about each F_{obt}? (c) Compute the appropriate values of *HSD*. (d) For the levels of factor B, the means are $\overline{X}_1 = 18.36$, $\overline{X}_2 = 20.02$, $\overline{X}_3 = 24.6$, and $\overline{X}_4 = 27.3$. What should you conclude about the main effect of B? (e) How important is the size of the audience in determining a participant's anxiety score? (f) How important is the participant's self-confidence?

26. A researcher investigates the effects of 5 levels of frustration (Factor A) and low and high amounts of sleep deprivation (Factor B) on depression scores ($n = 5$ and $N = 50$). He obtains the following sums of squares.

Source	*Sum of squares*	*df*	*Mean square*	*F*
Between				
Factor A	22.69	___	___	___
Factor B	46.02	___	___	___
Interaction	6.13	___	___	___
Within	109.25	___	___	
Total	184.09	___		

(a) Complete the ANOVA summary table. (b) Which effects are significant? (c) Which post hoc comparisons are appropriate? (d) Compute the effect size where appropriate. (e) What conclusions can be drawn from this study?

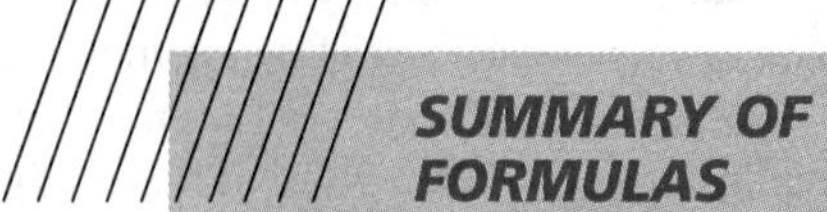

SUMMARY OF FORMULAS

The general format for the summary table for a two-way between-subjects ANOVA is

Summary Table of Two-Way ANOVA

Source	*Sum of squares*	*df*	*Mean square*	*F*
Between				
Factor A	SS_A	df_A	MS_A	F_A
Factor B	SS_B	df_B	MS_B	F_B
Interaction	$SS_{A\times B}$	$df_{A\times B}$	$MS_{A\times B}$	$F_{A\times B}$
Within	SS_{wn}	df_{wn}	MS_{wn}	
Total	SS_{tot}	df_{tot}		

1. Computing the sums of squares

(a) The computational formula for SS_{tot} is

$$SS_{tot} = \Sigma X^2_{tot} - \left(\frac{(\Sigma X_{tot})^2}{N}\right)$$

(b) The computational formula for the sum of squares between groups for the column factor A is

$$SS_A = \Sigma\left(\frac{(\text{Sum of scores in the column})^2}{n \text{ of scores in the column}}\right) - \left(\frac{(\Sigma X_{tot})^2}{N}\right)$$

(c) The computational formula for the sum of squares between groups for the row factor B is

$$SS_B = \Sigma\left(\frac{(\text{Sum of scores in the row})^2}{n \text{ of scores in the row}}\right) - \left(\frac{(\Sigma X_{tot})^2}{N}\right)$$

(d) The computational formula for the sum of squares between groups for the interaction is

$$SS_{A\times B} = SS_{bn} - SS_A - SS_B$$

where SS_{bn} is found using the formula

$$SS_{bn} = \Sigma\left(\frac{(\text{Sum of scores in the cell})^2}{n \text{ of scores in the cell}}\right) - \left(\frac{(\Sigma X_{tot})^2}{N}\right)$$

(e) The computational formula for the sum of squares within groups is

$$SS_{\text{wn}} = SS_{\text{tot}} - SS_{\text{bn}}$$

2. Computing the degrees of freedom

(a) The degrees of freedom between groups for factor A (df_{A}) equals $k_{\text{A}} - 1$, where k_{A} is the number of levels in factor A.

(b) The degrees of freedom between groups for factor B (df_{B}) equals $k_{\text{B}} - 1$, where k_{B} is the number of levels in factor B.

(c) The degrees of freedom between groups for the interaction ($df_{\text{A}\times\text{B}}$) equals df_{A} multiplied times df_{B}.

(d) The degrees of freedom within groups (df_{wn}) equals $N - k_{\text{A}\times\text{B}}$, where N is the total N of the study and $k_{\text{A}\times\text{B}}$ is the total number of cells in the study.

3. Computing the mean square

(a) The formula for MS_{A} is

$$MS_{\text{A}} = \frac{SS_{\text{A}}}{df_{\text{A}}}$$

(b) The formula for MS_{B} is

$$MS_{\text{B}} = \frac{SS_{\text{B}}}{df_{\text{B}}}$$

(c) The formula for $MS_{\text{A}\times\text{B}}$ is

$$MS_{\text{A}\times\text{B}} = \frac{SS_{\text{A}\times\text{B}}}{df_{\text{A}\times\text{B}}}$$

(d) The formula for MS_{wn} is

$$MS_{\text{wn}} = \frac{SS_{\text{wn}}}{df_{\text{wn}}}$$

4. Computing F_{obt}

(a) The formula for F_{A} is

$$F_{\text{A}} = \frac{MS_{\text{A}}}{MS_{\text{wn}}}$$

(b) The formula for F_{B} is

$$F_{\text{B}} = \frac{MS_{\text{B}}}{MS_{\text{wn}}}$$

(c) The formula for $F_{A\times B}$ is

$$F_{A\times B} = \frac{MS_{A\times B}}{MS_{wn}}$$

5. The critical values of F are found in Table 5 of Appendix C.
   (a) To find F_{crit} to test F_A, use df_A and df_{wn}.
   (b) To find F_{crit} to test F_B, use df_B and df_{wn}.
   (c) To find F_{crit} to test $F_{A\times B}$, use $df_{A\times B}$ and df_{wn}.

6. Performing Tukey's *HSD* post hoc comparisons
   (a) For a significant main effect, the computational formula for the HSD is

$$HSD = (q_k)\left(\sqrt{\frac{MS_{wn}}{n}}\right)$$

where q_k is found in Table 6 in Appendix C for k equal to the number of levels in the factor, MS_{wn} is the denominator of F_{obt}, and n is the number of scores used to compute each mean in the factor. Any means that differ by more than the *HSD* are significantly different.

(b) For a significant interaction, the HSD is computed as follows.

(1) Enter the following table for the design (or number of cells), and obtain the adjusted value of k.

Values of Adjusted *k*

Design of study	***Number of cell means in study***	***Adjusted value of k***
2 × 2	4	3
2 × 3	6	5
2 × 4	8	6
3 × 3	9	7
3 × 4	12	8
4 × 4	16	10
4 × 5	20	12

(2) Enter Table 6 in Appendix C for the value of q_k, using the adjusted k and df_{wn}.
(3) Compute the value of *HSD* as described in step 6*(a)* above.
(4) Any unconfounded cell means that differ by more than the *HSD* are significantly different.

7. *The computational formula for eta squared is*

$$\eta^2 = \frac{\text{Sum of squares between groups for the factor}}{SS_{tot}}$$

When η^2 is computed for factor A, factor B, or the A × B interaction, the sum of squares between groups for the factor is SS_A, SS_B, or $SS_{A\times B}$, respectively.

8. *The computational formula for the confidence interval for a single* μ, *is*

$$\left(\sqrt{\frac{MS_{\text{wn}}}{n}}\right)(-t_{\text{crit}}) + \overline{X} \leq \mu \leq \left(\sqrt{\frac{MS_{\text{wn}}}{n}}\right)(+t_{\text{crit}}) + \overline{X}$$

where t_{crit} is the two-tailed value at the appropriate α with $df = df_{\text{wn}}$, MS_{wn} is from the ANOVA, and $\overline{X}$ and n are from the level or cell being described.

19

Within-Subjects Experiments and Other Multifactor Designs

Getting Started

To understand this chapter, recall the following:

- From Chapters 15 and 16, understand how to create a between-subjects or a within-subjects factor.
- From Chapter 16, recall why we counterbalance the order of conditions in a repeated-measures design.
- From Chapter 18, understand how a two-way ANOVA involves the two main effects and the interaction, and be sure you can interpret an interaction.

Your goals in this chapter are to learn:

- The logic of a one-way within-subjects ANOVA.
- The logic of a two-way within-subjects ANOVA.
- How mixed designs are created and analyzed.
- The logic and analysis of experiments having three or more factors.
- What planned comparisons, simple main effects, and the F_{max} test are.
- What a multivariate analysis and a meta-analysis are.

This chapter first explores one-way and two-way designs that involve within-subjects factors. The logic and calculations here are simply variations on designs you've seen in previous chapters. (We won't focus on the calculations, but their formulas are provided in Appendix B, beginning with Part B.5.) We'll also briefly discuss the logic of a three-way design and a few other topics that you may encounter in the literature.

There is no section called More Statistical Notation here because you already know the symbols from previous ANOVAs. The reason we even discuss additional ANOVAs is because they result from the design problem of controlling participant variables.

CONTROLLING PARTICIPANT VARIABLES IN COMPLEX DESIGNS

Recall that we control participant variables that are correlated with the influence of the independent variable or with responses on the dependent variable. If we don't, then just by luck, one condition may end up containing participants who all score high on the participant variable, while another condition scores low on it. Then, this variable may *confound* the results, so that differences in dependent scores between the conditions are due to the participant variable and not the independent variable.

For a two-sample design, Chapter 15 discussed how to prevent such confounding in a *between-subjects* design by either limiting the population or counterbalancing such variables. Chapter 16 discussed how, instead, we may create a *within-subjects* design by creating either (1) a *matched-groups design* by pairing participants who match on the participant variable, placing one member of each pair in each condition, or (2) a *repeated-measures design* by testing the same participants under all levels of a factor.

Matched-groups designs work best when there is only one major participant variable to control. However, when participant variables are a concern, usually many variables are at issue. Then, the repeated-measures design is best, because a participant matches himself or herself on virtually all participant variables. Also, we may need to test a factor having several levels, or we may have a multifactor design. To find matching participants for many levels or cells is virtually impossible. Therefore, repeated measures is the much more common approach in complex designs.

> ***REMEMBER*** Repeated measures are the primary method for controlling participant variables in a complex design.

As an example, let's first discuss a one-way repeated-measures design: Say we are interested in how the manner in which people are dressed influences how comfortable they feel in a social setting. However, there are probably great differences in participant variables that influence how people react in this situation (e.g., how shy or self-conscious they are, or their past social experiences). To have these participant variables constant across our different conditions, we'll conduct a repeated-measures design. Then, we can see how a self-assured and comfortable person reacts with different forms of dress, as well as how a nervous and shy person reacts.

Say that on three consecutive days we have each participant act as a "greeter" for people participating in another experiment. One day participants dress very casually, another day they dress semiformally, and on another they dress formally. At the end of each session, participants answer a brief questionnaire describing how comfortable they felt (with higher scores indicating greater comfort). Labeling the independent variable of type of dress as factor A, we have the design in Table 19.1.

This is just like previous one-way designs, except that the *same* participants are tested in each condition: Each row in the diagram is one person's three scores. Thus, we will test participants under level A_1 (casual) and obtain their comfort scores, test them again under level A_2 (semiformal), obtaining their scores, and test them under level A_3 (formal). Collapsing vertically in each column, each mean score is the typical comfort score per condition. Hopefully, we'll see a relationship such that as manner of dress changes, comfort scores change. However, because the same person is being observed in each condition, virtually all participant variables should be constant. Therefore, we have greater confidence that it is manner of dress—and not a participant variable—that is causing the different comfort scores.

All of the usual design issues apply here, so we seek a reliable, valid, and strong manipulation of the factor without confoundings, and a reliable and valid measurement of the dependent variable. In particular, recall that a major concern with repeated measures is to control *order effects.*

Order Effects in Repeated-Measures Designs

Recall that order effects are the influence on scores that arises from completing a particular order. This may be from a particular order of trials when multiple trials occur within a condition, or, with repeated measures, order effects are produced by a particular order of conditions. Participants may change over the course of the experiment because of *practice, fatigue, carry-over effects*, or *response sets.* (In our study, participants are likely to be more comfortable on the second day of greeting because of practice, regardless of how they are dressed.) Also, individuals change over time because of *subject history* and *subject maturation*, so each participant will not remain the same from one session to the next. (Between the conditions, our participants grow one day older and may experience things that make them more or less comfortable when tested next.) These factors can *severely* reduce internal validity: If a response to a condition

TABLE 19.1 Diagram of One-Way Repeated-Measures Study of the Influence of Type of Dress on Participants' Comfort Levels

		Factor A: type of dress		
		Level A_1: casual	*Level A_2: semiformal*	*Level A_3: formal*
	1	*X*	*X*	*X*
	2	*X*	*X*	*X*
Participants	*3*	*X*	*X*	*X*
	4	*X*	*X*	*X*
	5	*X*	*X*	*X*
		$\overline{X}_{A_1}$	$\overline{X}_{A_2}$	$\overline{X}_{A_3}$

measured now is different than if it were measured later, then responses to each condition are due to *when* it occurs in the sequence, and not because of our independent variable.

We cannot prevent such order effects, so instead, we balance their influence. There are three methods for controlling order effects: complete counterbalancing, partial counterbalancing, or randomization.

Complete Counterbalancing between Conditions

Complete counterbalancing is the process of balancing order effects by testing different participants with different orders, so that all possible orders are present. For example, calling the three conditions of our greeting study conditions A, B, and C, produces these six possible orders:

ABC ACB BCA BAC CAB CBA

Notice two things about these orders. First, each condition appears in every position within the sequence: A appears twice as the first condition, twice as the second condition, and twice as the third condition (likewise for B and C). Second, every possible sequence is included: For the sequence beginning with A, the two possible orders ABC and ACB are included (and so on). Thus, complete counterbalancing balances a condition's position both in the sequence and in the order of the conditions coming before and after it. Applying this technique to the greeting study, we have the diagram shown in Table 19.2.

Now, one-third of the participants experience condition A first, so performance under this condition may be biased because of its location in the sequence. However, condition B also occurs first for one-third of the subjects, as does condition C, so these conditions are equally biased. Likewise, each condition occurs second at times, and third at times.

TABLE 19.2 Diagram of Completely Counterbalanced Greeting Experiment

Each row represents participants tested under a particular sequence of the three conditions.

		Conditions	
Orders	***A*** ***casual***	***B*** ***semiformal***	***C*** ***formal***
Participants tested using ABC	X X X	X X X	X X X
Participants tested using ACB	X X X	X X X	X X X
Participants tested using BCA	X X X	X X X	X X X
Participants tested using BAC	X X X	X X X	X X X
Participants tested using CAB	X X X	X X X	X X X
Participants tested using CBA	X X X	X X X	X X X
	$\overline{X}$	$\overline{X}$	$\overline{X}$

All other design issues still apply, so we might counterbalance having both male and female participants. Or, to control order effects resulting from the order in which participants answer the questions about their comfort level, we'd give different participants different orders of questions. The only novelty here is that we do all of this balancing *within each order of conditions*. For example, for those participants having order ABC, half would be male and half female, and some of each would answer the questions in different orders.

Then, collapsing vertically in each column, each mean is the typical comfort score per condition, with no confounding (1) by gender of participants or other participant variables, (2) by order effects of the trials within each condition, or (3) by history, maturation, or order effects occurring because of when in the sequence each condition was performed.

Note that the term *complete counterbalancing* is also applied when counterbalancing the order of trials *within* a condition. If above, for example, all possible orders of the questions were given within each condition, we'd have complete counterbalancing of the order of questions.

The advantage of complete counterbalancing is that all possible orders are present, so no bias due to order is possible. However, as you may have noticed, the major drawback to complete counterbalancing is that it creates a very complex design. This is especially so if there is also extensive counterbalancing of other variables. Further, the resulting design may require many more participants so that we can test some under each order.

When complete counterbalancing is unworkable, an alternative approach is partial counterbalancing.

Partial Counterbalancing

Partial counterbalancing is balancing order effects by using only some of the possible orders. For example, with three conditions, it is common to use the orders ABC, BCA, and CAB. As here, usually a partial counterbalancing scheme balances the position at which a condition occurs in the sequence, but does not balance the conditions coming before or after it. (This type of counterbalancing scheme is called a "Latin square design.") When applied to the greeting study, it produces the diagram in Table 19.3.

Much simpler! And that is the advantage of partial counterbalancing: Sometimes all we want is to prevent confounding by one particular order, so all we need to do is have several orders present. The disadvantage of this technique, however, is that it balances only practice effects or other biases that occur because of *where* in the sequence a condition occurs (first, second, or third). Partial counterbalancing does not control for *carry-over effects* (the influence on one condition resulting from having performed a previous condition). In Table 19.3, for example, carry-over effects are not balanced, because B follows A and C follows B in two-thirds of the sequences, but C never immediately follows A. Therefore, when carry-over effects are likely to occur between conditions, we instead include all orders and completely counterbalance.

REMEMBER Partial counterbalancing presents some of the possible orders of conditions to control practice effects. Complete counterbalancing includes all possible orders to control practice and carry-over effects.

TABLE 19.3 Diagram of Partially Counterbalanced Greeting Experiment

Each row represents those participants tested under a particular sequence of the three conditions.

		Conditions		
		A *casual*	*B* *semiformal*	*C* *formal*
	Participants tested using ABC	*X X X*	*X X X*	*X X X*
Orders	***Participants tested using BCA***	*X X X*	*X X X*	*X X X*
	Participants tested using CAB	*X X X*	*X X X*	*X X X*
		$\overline{X}$	$\overline{X}$	$\overline{X}$

The term *partial counterbalancing* can also be applied to multiple trials within each condition. If, in the above design, half the participants per row answer questions in one order and the remaining half per row answer them in the reverse order, we have partially counterbalanced the order of questions within conditions.

The third approach to controlling order effects is randomization.

Randomizing the Order of Conditions

With **randomization**, we randomly create different orders under which different participants are tested. For example, we could randomize the order of the three dress-style conditions by randomly creating a sequence for each participant (e.g., writing the three conditions on slips of paper and drawing a sequence for each participant). Likewise, we could randomize the order in which multiple trials are performed *within* a condition. (e.g., we could randomize the order in which our questions are answered by each participant within each condition).

Randomization works best when there are many conditions or trials, and the goal is simply to include some different orders in an unsystematic way. With only a few conditions, we may, by chance, fail to produce balancing orders. Above, we may often get orders with A-B, but few with B-A, and with only three conditions, this is a critical omission. Therefore, partial or complete counterbalancing is usually employed when there are only a few conditions, so that order effects can be treated systematically.

> ***REMEMBER*** In a repeated-measures design, use complete or partial counterbalancing or randomization to control order effects due to the order of conditions.

As usual, after we design and conduct the study, we must analyze it.

THE ONE-WAY WITHIN-SUBJECTS ANALYSIS OF VARIANCE

In a one-way within-subjects ANOVA, there is one independent variable in which we either match different participants across the conditions or repeatedly measure the same participants under all conditions. The other assumptions here are the same as with previous ANOVAs: (1) The dependent variable is a normally distributed ratio or interval variable, and (2) the populations of scores represented by the data have homogeneous variance.

As a simple example, say that the greeting study produced the data shown in Table 19.4. Collapsing vertically, we obtain the mean in each column to see the effect of factor A. Notice that the *ns* and *N* are based on the number of *scores*: There is an *n* of 5 scores in each level, and with three levels, a total *N* of 15. As usual, we're testing whether the means from the different levels represent different population μs. Therefore, as usual, H_0 is $\mu_1 = \mu_2 = \mu_3$ and H_a is that not all μs are equal. The only novelty here is in how to calculate F_{obt}.

A Word about Calculating the Within-Subjects F_{obt}

To understand the calculations, begin by viewing Table 19.4 as a *two-way* ANOVA: Factor A—the column factor—is the factor we've manipulated. But the different subjects we've tested—the rows—form a second factor, here with five levels. The interaction is between the subjects factor and the type-of-dress factor.

We view the design this way, because previously when computing F_{obt} we needed a mean square within groups (MS_{wn}). This is an estimate of the error variance (σ^2_{error}) the inherent variability in any population being represented. We computed MS_{wn} using the differences between the scores in each cell and the mean of the cell. However, in a within-subjects factor as above, each cell contains only one score. Therefore, the mean of a cell *is* the score in the cell, and differences within a cell are always zero. Obviously, we cannot compute MS_{wn} in the usual way.

However, in a repeated-measures ANOVA, the mean square for the *interaction* between factor A and subjects (abbreviated $MS_{A \times S}$) does reflect the inherent variability of scores. Recall that an interaction indicates that the influence of one factor changes, depending on which level of the other factor is present. It is because of the inherent

TABLE 19.4 Data for One-Way Repeated-Measures Study

		Factor A: type of dress			
		Level A_1: casual	*Level A_2: semiformal*	*Level A_3: formal*	
Participants	*1*	4	9	1	
	2	6	12	3	
	3	8	4	4	
	4	2	8	5	
	5	10	7	2	
		$\overline{X}_1 = 6$	$\overline{X}_2 = 8$	$\overline{X}_3 = 3$	$N = 15$ $k = 3$

variability between participants that the influence of a particular dress condition will change, depending on which participant is present. Therefore, $MS_{A \times S}$ is the estimate of error variance (σ^2_{error}) between scores, and so it is the denominator of the F-ratio.

Otherwise, the ANOVA here is similar to previous ones. As usual, the numerator of the F-ratio (MS_A) describes the differences between the means in factor A, and it estimates the variability due to error plus the variability due to treatment. Thus, the F-ratio for a repeated-measures factor is

$$\begin{array}{cccc} & \textit{Sample} & \textit{Estimates} & \textit{Population} \\ F_{obt} = & \dfrac{MS_A}{MS_{A \times S}} & \begin{array}{c}\rightarrow \\ \rightarrow\end{array} & \dfrac{\sigma^2_{error} + \sigma^2_{treat}}{\sigma^2_{error}} \end{array}$$

> ***REMEMBER*** When computing the F_{obt} for a within-subjects factor, the denominator of the F-ratio is the mean square for the interaction between the factor and subjects.

If H_0 is true and all μs are equal, then both the numerator and denominator will contain only σ^2_{error}, so F_{obt} will equal 1. However, the larger the F_{obt}, the more likely that different μs are being represented. If F_{obt} is significant, then at least two of the means from factor A represent different μs.

To calculate F_{obt}, we need the mean squares, and to calculate them, we need the sums of squares and *df*. Therefore, using the formulas in Appendix B.5, the previous data would produce the results shown in Table 19.5. The sum of squares for A and for the interaction are each divided by their corresponding *df* to produce the mean square. Then, the mean square for factor A (MS_A) is divided by the error term ($MS_{A \times Subs}$) to produce the F_{obt} for factor A. We don't bother to calculate an F_{obt} for the subjects factor or the interaction because, at most, they would indicate that participants differ from each other, which is not surprising or informative.

Interpreting the Within-Subjects F_{obt}

Interpret the above F_{obt} exactly as you would in a between-subjects ANOVA. First, find the critical value in Table 5 of Appendix C. Use df_A as the degrees of freedom between groups. The table also requires the degrees of freedom within groups, but recall that we replaced the mean square for within groups with the interaction between factor A and subjects. Therefore, anytime we need df_{wn}, here, use $df_{A \times Subs}$ instead. In the example, for $\alpha = .05$, $df_A = 2$, and $df_{A \times Subs} = 8$, so F_{crit} is 4.46.

TABLE 19.5 ANOVA Summary Table for the One-Way Within-Subjects Greeting Study.

Source	*Sum of squares*	*df*	*Mean square*	*F*
Factor A (Dress)	63.33	2	31.67	3.49
Subjects	11.33	4		
Interaction (A × Subs)	72.67	8	9.08	
Total	147.33	14		

Because the F_{obt} here is not larger than F_{crit}, it is not significant. Thus, we do not have evidence that our level means represent different populations, so we have no evidence of a relationship between type of dress and comfort scores. Had F_{obt} been significant, it would have indicated that at least two of the level means differ significantly. Then, to further describe and understand the relationship, we would graph the results and compute eta squared (dividing SS_A by SS_{tot}), as discussed in Chapter 17. We would also compute post hoc comparisons and confidence intervals as discussed below. Then, as in every study, we'd interpret the results psychologically, generalizing the relationship in the sample to relevant hypothetical constructs, models, and so on.

Recall from Chapter 16 that the dependent-samples *t*-test is more powerful than the independent-samples *t*-test, because the variability in the scores is less. For the same reason, the within-subjects ANOVA is more powerful than the between-subjects ANOVA. Here, some variability in the raw scores is removed, producing an $MS_{A \times Subs}$ that is smaller than the MS_{wn} would be if a between-subjects ANOVA had been computed. Therefore, a larger F_{obt} is produced, which is more likely to be significant, so we have greater power. Thus, the above example was not significant because there was a small *N* and the level means did not differ drastically, especially in light of the relatively large variability in the scores. However, this design was still more powerful—more likely to produce significant results—than a comparable between-subjects design.

Computing Tukey Post Hoc Tests and Confidence Intervals for a Within-Subjects Factor

Repeated measures must produce equal *n*s in all levels, so perform Tukey's *HSD* instead of Fisher's protected *t*-test (from Chapter 17). However, the formula for Tukey's *HSD* previously involved MS_{wn}, the denominator when calculating a between-subjects *F*-ratio. In a within-subjects factor, $MS_{A \times Subs}$ is used instead of MS_{wn} as the denominator. In fact, as we'll see, other types of within-subjects ANOVAs use various components (with different symbols) as the denominator of the *F*-ratio. Therefore, to create a general formula, the term "Denominator of *F*-ratio" has been put into the formula for *HSD*.

THE FORMULA FOR TUKEY'S HSD INVOLVING A WITHIN-SUBJECTS FACTOR IS

$$HSD = (q_k)\left(\sqrt{\frac{\text{Denominator of } F\text{-ratio}}{n}}\right)$$

Thus, if the previous one-way within-subjects ANOVA had produced significant results, then $MS_{A \times S}$ would be the denominator of our *F*-ratio, so the value of $MS_{A \times Subs}$ would be the numerator in the above formula. Find q_k in Table 6 of Appendix C as usual, but when you need df_{wn}, use the *df* used to compute the denominator of the *F*-ratio being examined. (For the above example, this was $df_{A \times Subs}$.) As always, *n* is the number of scores in each level. Then, as usual, find the difference between each pair of level means. Here, we'd compare the means from the casual and semiformal conditions, the casual and formal conditions, and the semiformal and formal conditions. Any difference that is larger than the *HSD* would be a significant difference.

We can also compute a confidence interval for the μ estimated by each $\overline{X}$: Use the formula from Chapter 17, but where it asks for MS_{wn} instead use the denominator of the F-ratio (here, $MS_{A \times Subs}$.) Also, when finding t_{crit}, in place of df_{wn}, use $df_{A \times Subs}$.

REMEMBER For any within-subjects factor, replace MS_{wn} or df_{wn} in a previous formula with the mean square or *df* used in the denominator of the *F*-ratio.

THE TWO-WAY WITHIN-SUBJECTS DESIGN

Sometimes we create a *two*-factor design and, because there are participant variables to control, *both* factors are within-subjects factors. In a **two-way within-subjects design** either (1) the same group of participants is repeatedly measured in all conditions of two factors, (2) matched participants are in all cells, or (3) there are matched groups on one variable and repeated measures on the other. If the data fit the criteria for parametric statistics, the results are analyzed using the **two-way within-subjects ANOVA**. The logic and interpretation for this procedure are identical to that of a two-way between-subjects design.

Here's an example: In our previous study, we might have lacked *ecological validity* by having participants wear formal clothes in the daytime. Therefore, let's add the factor of time of day. We'll again have participants greet people, but we'll test them on only two days—once in the condition of formal dress and once in the condition of casual dress. As the second factor, we'll test them twice during the day—once in the morning (the AM condition) and once in the evening (the PM condition). The dependent variable is again participants' comfort rating (with higher scores indicating greater comfort). We'll test each person in all conditions of this 2×2 factorial repeated-measures design. All of the usual controls apply, such as balancing gender, counterbalancing order effects of trials within conditions, counterbalancing the order of conditions, and so on. However, collapsing across these controls, the mean comfort rating for the interaction cells and for the main effects are shown in Table 19.6. The computational formulas for the two-way within-subjects ANOVA are different from those for the between-subjects design, and are presented in Appendix B.5. (The example is a 2×2, but there can be more levels in either factor.) Essentially, though, we

TABLE 19.6 Mean Comfort Ratings in the 2×2 Repeated-Measures Study of Style of Dress and Time of Testing.

		Factor A: style of dress		
		Casual	***Formal***	
Factor B: time of testing	***PM***	$\overline{X} = 11.00$	$\overline{X} = 16.70$	$\overline{X} = 13.85$
	AM	$\overline{X} = 12.00$	$\overline{X} = 6.00$	$\overline{X} = 9.00$
		$\overline{X} = 11.50$	$\overline{X} = 11.33$	

FIGURE 19.1 Graph of Mean Comfort Ratings as a Function of the Interaction Between Style of Dress and Time of Testing.

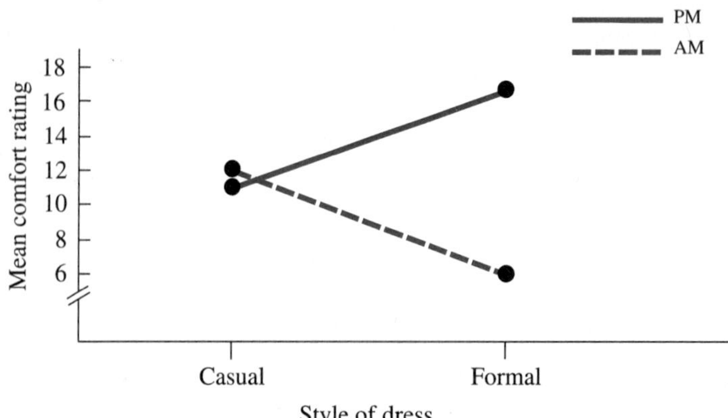

again view this as a series of one-way ANOVAs. First, collapsing vertically across time of testing, we examine the main effect (column) means for factor A, style of dress: Here, casual dress produced slightly higher comfort scores (11.50) than formal dress (11.33). Testing F_A will indicate whether these means differ significantly.

Next, collapsing horizontally across style of dress, we examine the main effect (row) means for time of testing: Apparently, participants were more comfortable when greeting in the PM (13.85) than in the AM (9.00). Testing F_B will indicate whether these means differ significantly.

Finally, we examine the interaction by comparing the cell means. To see the pattern more clearly, graph the four means. Placing style of dress on the *X* axis produces Figure 19.1. As usual, read the graph by looking at the relationship between *X* and *Y*: What happens to comfort ratings when dress changes from casual to formal? Well, that depends. For AM, comfort scores decrease, producing the negatively sloped dashed line. But for PM, scores increase, producing the positively sloped solid line. Although there appears to be an interaction effect here, the $F_{A \times B}$ will indicate whether it is significant.

For each effect, perform the Tukey *HSD* post hoc test if (1) the F_{obt} is significant, and (2) there are more than two levels. Use the formula discussed earlier in this chapter that involves the "Denominator of *F*-ratio." This is important because in the two-way within-subjects ANOVA, there is a different denominator in the *F*-ratio for each main effect and for the interaction. Also, find the *adjusted k* when testing the interaction, as discussed in Chapter 18.

Finally, compute eta squared (η^2) for each significant main effect or interaction, dividing the *SS* for the factor by the total *SS*. Then, interpret the results psychologically, focusing on the interaction if it's significant. If the interaction is not significant, focus on any significant main effects.

THE TWO-WAY MIXED DESIGN

Recall that, in a matched-groups design, it can be difficult to find sufficient numbers of matching participants, and that with repeated measures we may have an unwieldy counterbalancing scheme. These problems can be overwhelming in a two-way design. Therefore, it may be better to create a within-subjects factor only when it critically requires control of participant variables, and to test any other factor as a between-subjects factor. When a design features a "mix" of within-subjects and between-subjects factors, it is called a "mixed design." With two factors, it is a **two-way mixed design**.

> *REMEMBER* A two-way mixed design has one within-subjects factor and one between-subjects factor.

Such a two-way design may arise because we are primarily interested in two variables, one of which is best suited to a within-subjects design, while the other is best suited to a between-subjects design. Or, we may begin with only one within-subjects factor, but then examine the effects of counterbalancing a second, between-subjects variable. Likewise, one common mixed design arises because we start with one between-subjects variable, but we also include the within-subjects factor of multiple trials so that we can examine practice effects. And, finally, a mixed design commonly arises when we begin with one factor set up as a pretest-posttest design—measuring the same participants both before and after a treatment—and create a between-subjects factor by adding a control group.

Here's an example involving a control group from real research on "subliminal perception." Typically, this research involves presenting a stimulus that is visible very briefly—say, for about 5 milliseconds. (It takes about 150 milliseconds to blink.) The hypothesis is that the stimulus is somehow processed, even though people do not consciously recognize that it was present. There are many misconceptions regarding subliminal perception. (There is no accepted evidence that brief messages hidden in advertisements make you buy a product, or that hidden messages in music turn you into a dangerous psychopath.) There is, however, well-controlled experimental evidence that a subliminal stimulus can register. For example, in social research, flashing words that describe honesty or meanness produce a corresponding bias in participants' later description of a confederate (Erdley & D'Agostino, 1988). Or, clinical research has shown an influence of soothing types of subliminal messages (see Silverman & Weinberger, 1985, for a review).

Let's consider the study conducted by Silverman, Ross, Adler, and Lustig (1978). They tested the ability of men at dart-throwing before and after presentation of the subliminal message "Beating Dad is OK." The message was hypothesized to reduce residual guilt developed from childhood feelings of competition with father figures.

A *poor* way to set up this study is as the one-way design shown in Table 19.7. After collapsing vertically in each condition, if the mean dart scores are significantly higher after the message, we'd like to conclude that the message improved performance. But! There is something very wrong here in terms of potential confoundings! Here's a hint: Remember *maturation*, *history*, *reactivity*, and *practice effects*? Perhaps the After-message scores improved because of the influence of these variables. That is, maybe the men acclimated to being tested, or their brains matured and developed better eye-hand coordination, or they got better at dart-throwing because of the practice they received during the earlier condition. For any of these reasons, participants may be better at dart throwing after the message, but not because of the message.

To eliminate these competing hypotheses, we need a control group that does everything the experimental group does but, instead of seeing the message "Beating Dad is

TABLE 19.7 Diagram of a One-Way Dart-Throwing Experiment

Xs represent each subject's dart score before and after the message.

Before message	*After message*
X X X	X X X
Low $\overline{X}$	High $\overline{X}$

OK," sees a *placebo* message that does not alleviate guilt. Adding a control group creates a between-subjects factor, with some individuals tested before and after the experimental message, and others tested before and after the control message. Now, we have the much-better, two-way mixed design shown in Table 19.8. If the dependent variable meets the criteria for parametric procedures, we compute the **two-way mixed-design ANOVA**. The computational formulas for this design are presented in Appendix B.6 (and again, the design need not be a 2 × 2). The logic here is the same as in previous examples, however, because *all* multifactor ANOVAs are treated as a series of one-way ANOVAs. Therefore, as usual, we'll compute and test an F_{A} to compare the Before-After means, an F_{B}, which indicates whether the "Dad" versus the control message produced significant differences, and an $F_{A \times B}$, indicating whether the cell means differ significantly.

In this example, however, the main effects are not likely to indicate anything interesting. Collapsing vertically in Table 19.8, the main effect means for Before and After include both the "Dad" and control messages. Therefore, difference between these means shows only that scores change between the two testings. The difference may be due to the experimental message or to maturation and practice effects. We cannot tell.

TABLE 19.8 Diagram of the Two-Way Mixed-Design Dart-Throwing Experiment

In each cell are the individual dart-throwing scores and the cell mean. Also shown are the main effect means for the column and row factors.

		Repeated-measures factor		
		Before message	***After message***	
Between-subjects factor	***Participants with "Dad" message***	X X X X $\overline{X}$	X X X X $\overline{X}$	$\overline{X}$
	Participants with control message	X X X X $\overline{X}$	X X X X $\overline{X}$	$\overline{X}$
		$\overline{X}$	$\overline{X}$	

FIGURE 19.2 Ideal Interaction Between Pretest vs. Posttest and Control vs. Experimental Cells

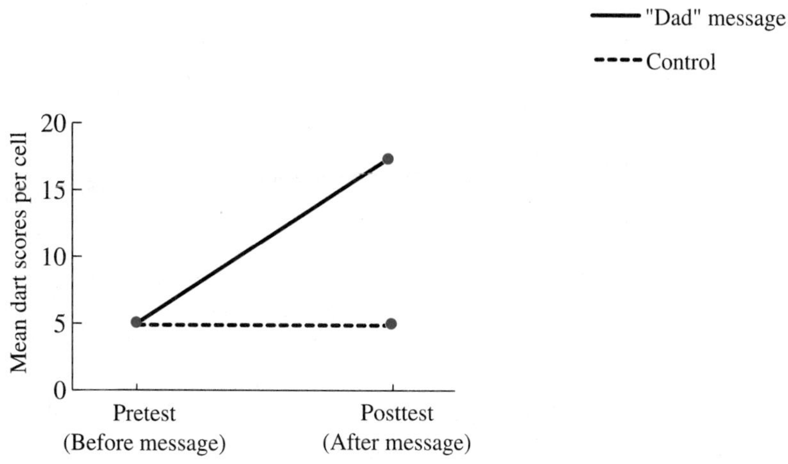

Likewise, collapsing horizontally across Before and After gives the main effect means for the two types of messages. If the "Dad" message produces a higher mean than the control message, we will not know whether this occurred because the Before-message scores were higher and/or because the After-message scores were higher.

The specific test of the hypothesis that the "Dad" message increases performance comes from the interaction of the four cell means. Ideally, we would predict a significant interaction that produces the graph shown in Figure 19.2. We know these data produce an interaction because the lines are not parallel. Then, ideally, the post hoc comparisons will confirm the following: (1) There is no difference in the Before-message scores for the two groups, suggesting that the study is not contaminated by initial differences in dart-throwing skills between the two groups of participants. (2) There is no change in scores from Before-message to After-message for the control group, suggesting that maturation, acclimation to testing, practice, and so on, are not producing a Before-After difference in the experimental group. (3) The After-message scores of men receiving the "Dad" message are significantly higher than those receiving the control message. This combination of findings would convincingly support the hypothesis that the "Dad" message does improve dart-throwing. (As this example illustrates, with a little thought you can predict and understand interaction effects, so regardless of the type of design, don't think solely in terms of main effects.)

In a mixed design, again perform the Tukey *HSD* test for any significant effects with more than two means. Once again, however, computing each of the above *F*s involves a different denominator in the *F*-ratio. Therefore, as before, be sure to use the appropriate *MS* when computing the *HSD* for each *F*.

THE THREE-WAY DESIGN

The beauty of ANOVA is that it can be applied to even more complex experiments with as many factors as you wish, regardless of whether the design is all between-subjects,

TABLE 19.9 Diagram of a Three-Way Design for the Factors of Before and After Messages, Type of Messages, and Participant Gender

Each mean is the mean dart score of participants in that cell.

	Males		*Females*	
	Before message	*After message*	*Before message*	*After message*
"Dad" message	$\bar{X} = 10$	$\bar{X} = 20$	$\bar{X} = 8$	$\bar{X} = 12$
Control message	$\bar{X} = 10$	$\bar{X} = 10$	$\bar{X} = 8$	$\bar{X} = 10$

all within-subjects, or mixed. You may add more independent variables, or analyze more counterbalanced control factors.

For example, say that we add the variable of participants' gender (male versus female) to the above two-way dart study. With three factors, we have a **three-way design**, which here happens to have two levels of each factor, so it is a $2 \times 2 \times 2$ design. Say that we obtained the data for this mixed design shown in Table 19.9. The previous 2×2 design for males is on the left. On the right, that design is replicated, but with females. If the data fit the criteria of a parametric procedure, then a three-way mixed-design ANOVA is appropriate. In the following sections, we'll discuss how to interpret such a study (but not how to calculate the *F*s: You really need a computer for that).

Main Effects

Because there are three independent variables, the ANOVA produces a separate F_{obt} for three main effects. As usual, to find a main effect, we collapse across the other factors. Thus, to find the main effect of gender, we average all of the males' scores together (for the box on the left, in Table 19.9, $\bar{X} = 12.5$), and all of the females' scores together (in the box on the right, $\bar{X} = 9.5$). Apparently, overall, males were better at throwing darts than females. To find the main effect of Before-message versus After-message, we average together the columns containing Before scores, regardless of gender ($\bar{X} = 9.0$), and the columns containing After scores ($\bar{X} = 13.0$). Apparently, overall, participants scored higher on the posttest than on the pretest. Finally, the main effect of type of message is the average of scores in the rows of the "Dad" message ($\bar{X} = 12.5$), and in the rows of the control message ($\bar{X} = 9.5$). Apparently, people who saw the "Dad" message scored higher than those who saw the control message.

Two-Way Interactions

Three factors produce *three* two-way interactions, and each has a separate F_{obt}. To examine each two-way interaction, we collapse across the third factor. Thus, collapsing across gender produces the interaction of Before-After and "Dad"-control messages, shown below:

	Before	*After*
"Dad"	$\overline{X} = 9$	$\overline{X} = 14$
Control	$\overline{X} = 9$	$\overline{X} = 10$

The mean in each cell is based on both males' and females' scores. The difference between the "Dad" and control messages is greater in the After-message condition. (To put it another way, the difference between Before-message and After-message depends on the type of message.) Apparently, therefore, there is an interaction between these two factors.

To produce the other two-way interactions, we collapse across the third factor.

Gender and type of message interaction

	Male	*Female*
"Dad"	$\overline{X} = 15$	$\overline{X} = 10$
Control	$\overline{X} = 10$	$\overline{X} = 9$

Gender and before-after interaction

	Male	*Female*
Before	$\overline{X} = 10$	$\overline{X} = 8$
After	$\overline{X} = 15$	$\overline{X} = 11$

On the left, collapsing across Before-After produces the interaction between gender and type of message. Note that the difference between the "Dad" and control messages is greater for males than it is for females. (To put it another way, the difference between males and females depends on which message they receive.) Thus, there is an apparent interaction between gender and type of message.

On the right, collapsing across type of message produces the interaction between gender and Before-After. Here, males show a greater increase from Before to After than do females. (In other words, the difference between males and females depends on whether we examine the Before scores or the After scores.) Thus, apparently there is also a two-way interaction here.

The Three-Way Interaction

Finally, we do not collapse across any factor, computing an F_{obt} for the *three-way interaction*: This is the effect of simultaneously changing the levels of all three factors. Previously, we saw that in a two-way interaction, the effect of one variable changes, depending on the level of the second factor that is present. In a **three-way interaction**, the two-way interaction between any two variables changes, depending on which level of the third factor is present. (Conversely, if the three-way interaction is not significant, then we have basically the same two-way interaction regardless of the level of the third factor that is present.)

The only way to interpret a three-way interaction is to first graph it. Graphing the original cell means from Table 19.9, produces the three-way interaction in Figure 19.3. As this shows, the interaction between Before-After and "Dad"-control depends on whether participants are male or female. For males, there is a dramatic change from pretest to posttest scores with the "Dad" message, but control males show no change. For females, there is a different two-way interaction: There is slight improvement in dart-throwing following the control message, suggesting that the control females benefited from practice at throwing darts. Following the "Dad" message, however, experimental females showed a slight, additional improvement beyond the practice effects of the control females. Thus, the "Dad" message had a minimal positive influence on females, so maybe they aren't intensely guilty about competing with their fathers to begin with. There is dramatic improvement after the "Dad" message among males, however, so maybe they do feel guilty about this competition, so that the message reduces an otherwise serious restriction on their performance.

> ***REMEMBER*** A three-way interaction shows that the interaction between any two factors depends on which level of the third factor is present.

Note: In a published report, this interaction would be graphed on *one* set of *X-Y* axes (see the APA format section at the end of this chapter).

Of course, we would not believe any of the previous interpretations unless the main effects and interactions were significant, and for each, we'd perform post hoc comparisons to determine which specific means differ significantly. Then, as usual, we would interpret the results by first focusing on significant interactions, because they contradict main effects. A significant three-way interaction, however, contradicts any two-way interactions: Above, we saw that the two-way interaction between Dad-control and

FIGURE 19.3 Graphs Showing How the Two-Way Interaction Between Pretest and Posttest and "Dad"-Control Message Changes as a Function of Subject's Gender

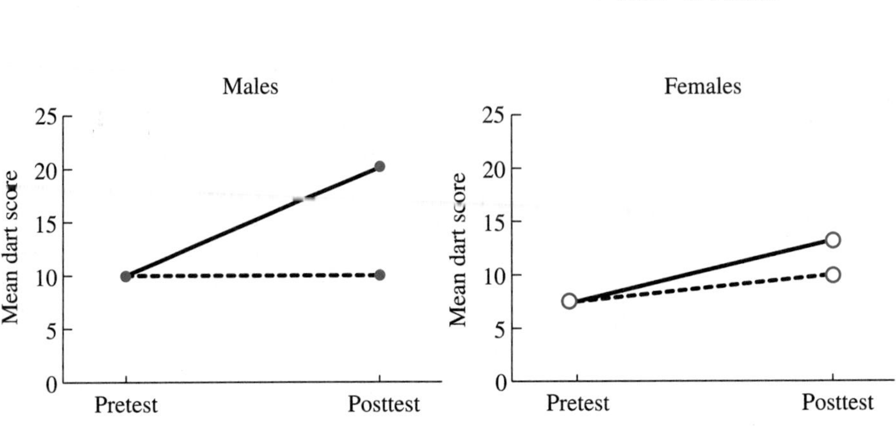

Before-After *depends on* whether it involves males or females. Therefore, the interpretation of a three-way design focuses on the significant three-way interaction. Thus, based on Figure 19.3, we would attempt to explain the psychological reasons behind why the "Dad" message produced a dramatic improvement in scores for males, but produced a small improvement for females. If the three-way interaction is not significant, we focus on significant two-way interactions. If these interactions are not significant, then we focus on significant main effects.

In sum, the logic and interpretation of all multifactor ANOVAs is pretty much the same, with the only difference being the details of how the *F*s are computed. Therefore, you're ready for virtually any ANOVA found in the literature. Before leaving this topic, however, there are several related procedures to briefly discuss.

THE TEST FOR HOMOGENEITY OF VARIANCE: THE F_{max} TEST

Throughout the discussion of *t*-tests and ANOVA, we have assumed that the populations represented by the data have *homogeneous variance*: The value of σ^2_X is the same for each population. This is important, because violating this assumption results in a situation where the actual probability of a Type I error will be greater than our α. Therefore, if we are unsure whether the data meet this assumption, we can perform a homogeneity of variance test. A **homogeneity of variance test** determines whether the population variances are likely to be homogeneous. Although there are several tests of homogeneity, a simple version is Hartley's F_{max} test. It is used for any between-subjects design when all *n*s are equal.

To perform the F_{max} test, first compute the estimated population variance (s^2_X) for each condition. Then, select the largest and smallest values of s^2_X. Then,

THE COMPUTATIONAL FORMULA FOR THE F_{max} TEST IS

$$F_{max} = \frac{\text{Largest } s^2_X}{\text{Smallest } s^2_X}$$

Critical values for F_{max} are found in Table 7 in Appendix C, where *k* is the number of levels in the factor, and *n* is the number of scores in each level.

The logic of the F_{max} test is the same as the logic of the *F*-ratio. As usual, the null hypothesis says there is no difference, so here it says that the two sample variances represent the same, homogeneous σ^2_X. If both values of s^2_X perfectly represent the same σ^2_X, then they should be equal, so their ratio should equal 1. If F_{max} is greater than 1, H_0 says this is due to sampling error. However, the larger the F_{max}, the greater the difference between the variances, so the less likely it is that they represent the same σ^2_X. If the F_{max} is larger than the critical value, it is significant, and the two s^2_X differ significantly. Then, we *cannot* assume that the population variances are homogeneous, and we should *not* perform the parametric procedure. Instead, we perform the appropriate nonparametric procedure (discussed in Chapter 21).

If F_{max} is not significant, then we do not have evidence that the sample variances represent different population variances. In other words, we can assume there is homogeneous variance, so it is acceptable to perform the ANOVA or *t*-test.

OTHER WAYS TO COMPARE THE MEANS IN A FACTORIAL DESIGN

There are two variations of post hoc comparisons that will crop up when reading the psychological literature. They are "planned comparisons" and "simple main effects."

Planned Comparisons

Instead of computing an F_{obt} and then performing post hoc tests, you may find research that only performs planned comparisons. With post hoc tests, all means in a factor are compared to each other, but with planned comparisons, the hypotheses lead us to compare the means in certain conditions only: We "plan ahead" which of the conditions should differ, and those are the ones we compare. **Planned comparisons** are procedures for comparing only some levels in a factor. For example, say we conduct a study of stress levels as a function of listening to various types of music—classical, jazz, rock and roll—or to a control condition of silence. After presenting participants with each condition, we measure their stress levels using a questionnaire. We might use planned comparisons to compare only the control condition to each of the other conditions: comparing control to classical, control to jazz, and so on, without comparing jazz to classical, jazz to rock, etc. This allows us to see how each type of music operates compared to nothing.

Planned comparisons are also called *a priori comparisons*, and formulas for computing them can be found in advanced statistics texts.

Simple Main Effects

There is also another approach for comparing the cell means in an interaction that you may encounter, called simple main effects. A **simple main effect** is the effect of one independent variable at *one level* of a second independent variable. For example, say that we add the second factor of the time of day of testing (either AM or PM) to the above music and stress design, producing this experiment.

		Type of music			
		Classical	*Jazz*	*Rock and roll*	*Silence*
Time	*AM*	$\overline{X}$	$\overline{X}$	$\overline{X}$	$\overline{X}$
	PM	$\overline{X}$	$\overline{X}$	$\overline{X}$	$\overline{X}$

While post hoc comparisons compare all unconfounded pairs of cell means in the diagram, a simple main effect is similar to calculating an F for one row or column. For example, we might examine the simple main effect of changing type of music within the AM only, looking only at the upper row of cell means in the above diagram. The simple main effect is analyzed as a one-way ANOVA on these cell means, but with somewhat different computations. (See, for example, Hinkle, Wiersma & Jurs, 1994.) If the simple main effect is significant, it indicates that for AM, changing type of music produces a significant relationship, and that somewhere among these four means there are significant differences. This information is helpful if, for example, there is not a significant simple main effect for type of music when testing in the PM. Then, we'd know that the overall interaction reflects a relationship for AM but no relationship for PM.

GOING BEYOND THE ANALYSIS OF VARIANCE

In the literature, you'll also encounter two types of research approaches that expand upon the type of ANOVA we have discussed, including more variables and taking a broader perspective. These approaches are called "multivariate statistics" and "meta-analysis."

Multivariate Analysis

Everything in our discussions so far has involved *one* dependent variable, and the statistics we have performed are called **univariate statistics**. We can, however, measure participants on two or more dependent variables in one experiment. For example, in the music study above, we might have measured the same participants' stress, their happiness, and their self-esteem. Statistics for multiple dependent variables are called **multivariate statistics**. These include the multivariate *t*-test and the multivariate analysis of variance (MANOVA). Even though these are very complex procedures, the basic logic still holds: The larger the t_{obt} or F_{obt}, the less likely it is that the samples represent the same population. If the results are significant, the observed relationship between the independent variables and dependent variables is unlikely to be the result of sampling error. Given these significant results, the researcher then examines the influence of the independent variables on each individual dependent variable at a time, using the *t*-tests or ANOVAs we've discussed.

Meta-Analysis

Recall that ultimately, confidence in the external validity of research is developed through repeated studies that literally and conceptually replicate a finding. Rather than subjectively evaluating the extent to which several studies support a particular hypothesis, however, researchers analyze the studies using meta-analysis. **Meta-analysis** is a statistical procedure for combining, testing, and describing the results from different studies. Researchers generally take one of two approaches: Either they determine whether the experiments taken together consistently show a significant effect of a particular variable, or they estimate the effect size of a variable based on all of the studies.

On the one hand, a meta-analysis provides objective methods for generalizing a variable's effect, and because the results are based on many participants tested under varying procedures, we have a high degree of confidence in the conclusions. On the other hand, a meta-analysis glosses over many differences in operational definitions, controls, and measurement procedures, glossing over the quality of the studies as well. Therefore, although a meta-analysis adds to our understanding of a behavior, we must necessarily speak in *very* general terms.

APA FORMAT FOR STATISTICAL NOTATION

In a published report of a design having three or more factors, the interaction is graphed on *one* set of *X*-*Y* axes. For example, the 2 × 2 × 2 interaction from the dart-throwing study back in Figure 19.3 would appear on one set of axes using four different lines as shown in Figure 19.4. Note the legend (or key) in the figure. We combine solid lines for experimental groups and dashed lines for controls with solid dots for males and open dots for females. Thus, •————• connects the means of the male experimental group, ○————○ connects the means of the female experimental group, •- - - - - - - - -• connects those of the male control group, and ○- - - - - - - - -○ connects those of the female control group.

PUTTING IT ALL TOGETHER

There is no limit to the number of factors you can have in a study or test in an ANOVA. You can study four independent variables in the same study (using a between-subjects, within-subjects, or mixed design) and perform a four-way ANOVA, or you can create a five-way design, and so on. There are, however, practical limits to such designs. The number of participants needed becomes quite large, and the counterbalancing scheme or stimulus requirements may be impossibly complex. Although with effort these problems can be solved, researchers are also limited by their ability to interpret such studies. In a "simple" four-way study—a (2 × 2 × 2 × 2) design—the ANOVA provides separate *F*s for four main effects, six two-way interactions, four three-way interactions, and

FIGURE 19.4 Mean Dart-Throwing Scores as a Function of the Three-Way Interaction Between Pretest-Posttest, Dad vs Control Message, and Gender.

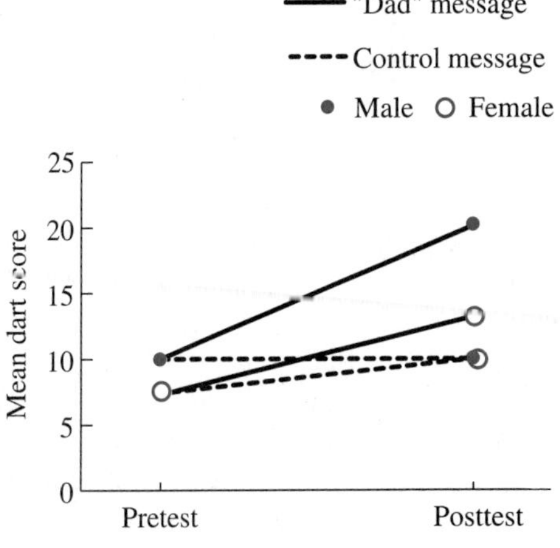

one monster four-way interaction (there would be eight lines on its graph!). If this sounds very complicated, it's because it *is* very complicated. Three-way interactions are difficult to interpret, and interactions that contain more than three factors are practically impossible to interpret. (The three-way interaction in this chapter was clear and easy to interpret because I made it up! Real data tend to produce a confusing pattern of overlapping line graphs that is *much* more difficult to interpret.)

Remember that a major concern of science is to simplify the complexity found in nature. Duplicating this complexity in a study is counterproductive. Therefore, unless you have a very good reason for including many factors in one experiment, it is best to examine only two, or at most three, factors at a time. Conduct additional experiments to investigate the influence of other variables. In each, you can perform a literal replication of portions of your previous studies, thus greatly increasing their internal and external validity. And, although you will not learn of the simultaneous interactions of many variables, you will understand what you do learn.

CHAPTER SUMMARY

1. With *complete counterbalancing*, different participants are tested with different orders so that all possible orders of conditions or trials are present. With *partial counterbalancing*, participants are tested using only some of the possible orders of conditions or trials. With *randomization*, different subjects are tested using different random orders of conditions or trials.
2. Partial counterbalancing balances the influence of *only practice effects*. Complete counterbalancing balances *practice and carry-over effects.*
3. A *one-way within-subjects ANOVA* is applied to a study having one factor in which the same participants are tested under all conditions, or there are matched subjects in each condition.
4. In a *two-way within-subjects design*, matched groups or the same repeatedly measured participants are tested in all conditions of two independent variables.
5. In a *two-way mixed design*, one within-subjects and one between-subjects factor are examined.
6. Any within-subjects factor is more *powerful* than if it were tested as a between-subjects factor.
7. A *three-way design* produces three main effects, three two-way interactions, and one three-way interaction. In a *three-way interaction*, the two-way interaction between two factors changes as the levels of the third factor change.
8. The differences between particular ANOVAs are in how F_{obt} is computed, particularly in the denominator of the F-ratio. When performing Tukey's post hoc test on a factor, use the denominator of the F-ratio for that factor.
9. The F_{max} *test* tests whether the variances from the levels in an experiment differ significantly. If they do not, then the data meet the assumption of *homogeneity of variance*.

10. *Planned comparisons* compare only some specified pairs of conditions in a factor.

11. A *simple main effect* is the effect of one factor within the interaction at one level of a second factor.

12. *Univariate statistics* are performed when a study investigates one dependent variable. *Multivariate statistics* are the inferential procedures performed when participants are measured on two or more dependent variables.

13. *Meta-analysis* involves statistical procedures for combining, testing, and describing the results from different studies.

KEY TERMS (with page references)

F_{max}
complete counterbalancing (531)
homogeneity of variance test (545)
meta-analysis (547)
multivariate statistics (547)
partial counterbalancing (532)
planned comparisons (546)
randomization (533)
simple main effect (546)
three-way design (542)
three-way interaction (543)
two-way mixed-design ANOVA (540)
two-way mixed design (539)
two-way within-subjects ANOVA (537)
two-way within-subjects design (537)
univariate statistics (547)

REVIEW QUESTIONS

(Answers for odd-numbered questions and problems are provided in Appendix D.)

1. (a) A researcher conducts a study involving one independent variable. (a) What are the two general types of parametric procedures available to her? (b) She next conducts a study involving two independent variables. What are the three versions of a parametric procedure available to her? (c) In (b), what aspect of her design determines which version she should perform?

2. (a) How do you identify participant variables that may confound a study? (b) How can such variables influence the external validity of a study? (c) How can they influence its internal validity?

3. (a) What is the reason for creating a within-subjects factor? (b) What are the two ways to create a within-subjects factor? (c) How does each eliminate possible confounding?

4. What is the possible confounding due to order that is produced by a repeated-measures factor? (b) What changes in participants occur that can influence the results? (c) How do these changes potentially confound the results?

5. (a) What are the three ways to control order effects? (b) When is each most appropriate?

6. What is the difference between a two-way within-subjects design and (a) a two-way between-subjects design? (b) a two-way mixed design?

7. (a) What is the major difficulty in creating a complex design using matched groups? (b) What is the major difficulty in creating a complex design using repeated measures?

8. What are three reasons researchers create a mixed design?

9. Compared to a between-subjects factor, what is the major difference in the one-way within-subjects ANOVA when (a) calculating the *F*-ratio? (b) calculating *HSD*? (c) finding F_{crit} or q_k in the tables?

10. When do we create (a) a two-way between-subjects design? (b) a two-way within-subjects design? (c) a two-way mixed design?

11. (a) When do researchers create a three-way design? (b) How many *F*s are produced in such a design? (c) What does a three-way interaction effect indicate?

12. (a) What is the F_{max} test used for? (b) What does a significant F_{max} indicate, and what should you do? (c) What does a nonsignificant F_{max} indicate, and what should you do?

13. (a) What is the difference between post hoc comparisons and planned comparisons? (b) What does a simple main effect examine?

14. What is the difference between univariate and multivariate statistics?

15. (a) What is a meta-analysis? (b) What two approaches may it involve?

PRACTICE PROBLEMS

16. Which of these relationships suggests using a repeated-measures design? (a) Examining the improvement in language ability as children grow older. (b) Measuring participants' reaction when the experimenter surprises them by unexpectedly shouting, using one of three levels of volume. (c) Comparing the dating strategies of males and females. (d) Comparing memory ability as a function of amount of alcoholic beverage consumed.

17. We conduct a repeated-measures study of the effects of three types of motivational messages. Participants listen to a message every day for one week, then they complete a 20-question test of well-being, then they begin listening to the next message, and so on. (a) Name three potential confoundings due to participants that might arise over the three weeks of testing. (b) Calling the three messages A, B, and C, how would you completely counterbalance the order of conditions? (c) How would you partially counterbalance order of conditions? (d) What other order effects are present, and how would you control them? (e) What problem is likely to be created by any one message that makes repeated measures a problem?

18. We decide to conduct the study in problem 17 as a between-subjects design instead. (a) Describe this design. (b) How does it eliminate the problems in 17(a) and 17(e)? (c) What new problems does it create?

19. You measure the dependent variable of participants' hypnotic suggestibility as a function of whether or not they meditate before being tested, and whether they were shown a film containing a low, medium, or high amount of fantasy. The fantasy-level factor is repeated measures, the meditation factor is between-subjects. (a) What is the name for this type of design? (b) Identify the *F*s you would obtain (without actually calculating them) and indicate what each will tell you. (c) For the following data, compute the means for each main effect and interaction. Which effects appear likely to be significant? (d) What will you conclude about this study?

	Amount of fantasy		
	Low	***Medium***	***High***
Meditation	5	7	9
	6	5	8
	2	6	10
	2	9	10
	5	5	10
No meditation	10	2	5
	10	5	6
	9	4	5
	10	3	7
	10	2	6

(To perform the complete ANOVA, see Practice Problem 1 in Appendix B.7.)

20. In problem 19, say that instead, both meditation and fantasy level are repeated-measures factors. (a) What is the name for this design? (b) Identify the *F*s you will obtain (without actually calculating them) and indicate what each will tell you. (c) Will the power of this design be larger or smaller than in problem 19? Why? (To perform the complete ANOVA, see Practice Problem 1 in Appendix B.6.)

21. In problem 19, what does the simple main effect appear to indicate for the effect of amount of fantasy when participants meditate?

22. Chapter 16 described a study that tested a new therapy on spiderphobics by measuring their fear of a spider in a Before-therapy condition and again in an After-therapy condition. (a) What major design flaw was present in this study? (b) How would you fix it? (c) Identify the type of analysis you would apply to the improved study. (d) Let Before/After be factor A and Therapy/No-therapy be factor B. If significant, what will F_A, F_B, and $F_{A \times B}$ each indicate?

23. Below are the cell means from a study comparing the performance of young boys and girls who are given candy or money as a reward, and who are tested either in the early morning or early afternoon.

	Boys		***Girls***	
	Candy	***Money***	***Candy***	***Money***
Morning	$\overline{X} = 10$	$\overline{X} = 20$	$\overline{X} = 8$	$\overline{X} = 12$
Afternoon	$\overline{X} = 20$	$\overline{X} = 10$	$\overline{X} = 8$	$\overline{X} = 12$

(a) Compute the means for each main effect and interaction. (b) Assuming that any difference between means of at least 10 is a significant difference, which main effects and interactions are significant? (c) What is your overall conclusion about the effect of the variables in this study?

24. You study whether alcohol affects performance on a simple eye-hand coordination task and whether the time of year of testing affects performance. Each participant performed the task immediately after drinking 0 or 3 drinks and each did so once during the summer and once during the winter. With $n = 3$ in each cell, the following cell means were obtained.

		Drinks prior to task performance	
		A_1: 0 drinks	*A_2: 3 drinks*
Time of year	*B1: summer*	16	6
	B2: winter	11	12

(a) What is the name for this type of design? (b) Identify the Fs you would obtain (without actually calculating them) and indicate what each will tell you. (c) Compute the means for each main effect. (d) Which effects appear likely to be significant? (e) What will you conclude about this study? (To complete the ANOVA summary table of this study, see Practice Problem 2 in Appendix B.6.)

25. A researcher studies the influence of four doses of a new drug to reduce depression in adult women who either do or do not have the AIDs virus (are HIV+ or HIV−). Dosage is a repeated-measures factor and HIV status is a between-subjects factor. With $n = 3$ in each cell, the following overall mean mood improvement scores were obtained.

		Factor B: dose of antidepressant			
		B_1: control	*B_2: low*	*B_3: med.*	*B_4: high*
Factor A: HIV status	*A_1: HIV−*	4	5	13	17
	A_2: HIV+	3	6	12	19

(a) What is the name for this type of design? (b) Identify the Fs you would obtain (without actually calculating them) and indicate what each will tell you. (c) Compute the means for each main effect. (d) Which effects appear likely to be significant? (e) What will you conclude about this study? (To complete the ANOVA summary table of this study, see Practice Problem 2 in Appendix B.7.)

26. You measure 21 students' degree of positive attitude toward their statistics course at four equally spaced intervals during the semester. The mean score for each level is as follows: Time 1, 62.50; Time 2, 64.68; Time 3, 69.32; Time 4, 72.00. You obtain the following sums of squares:

Source	*Sum of squares*	*df*	*Mean square*	*F*
Factor A	189.30	3		
Subjects	402.79	20		
A × Subjects	688.32	60		
Total	1280.41	83		

(a) What are H_0 and H_a? (b) Complete the ANOVA summary table. (c) With $\alpha = .05$, what do you conclude about F_{obt}? (d) Perform the appropriate post hoc comparisons. (e) What is the effect size in this study? (f) What do you conclude about this relationship?

27. In a study on the influence of practice on a task requiring eye-hand coordination, participants are tested after no practice, after 1 hour of practice, and again after 2 hours of practice. You obtain the following data, with higher scores indicating better performance.

	Amount of practice		
Participants	*Zero*	*One hour*	*Two hours*
S1	4	3	6
S2	3	5	5
S3	1	4	3
S4	3	4	6
S5	1	5	6
S6	2	6	7
S7	2	4	5
S8	1	3	8

(a) What are H_0 and H_a? (b) Complete the ANOVA summary table. (c) With $\alpha = .05$, what do you conclude about F_{obt}? (d) Perform the appropriate post hoc comparisons. (e) What is the effect size in this study? (f) What should you conclude about this relationship?

SUMMARY OF FORMULAS

1. *The formulas for the one-way within-subjects ANOVA are found in Part B.5 of Appendix B.*

   The format of the Summary Table of One-Way Within-Subjects ANOVA is

Source	***Sum of squares***	***df***	***Mean square***	***F***
Factor A (Between Groups)	SS_A	df_A	MS_A	F_{obt}
Subjects	SS_{subs}			
A × Subjects	$SS_{A \times Subs}$	$df_{A \times Subs}$	$MS_{A \times Subs}$	
Total	SS_{tot}	df_{tot}		

   The formula for F_{obt} is

$$F_{obt} = \frac{MS_A}{MS_{A \times S}}$$

   Critical values of F are found in Table 5 in Appendix C, for df_A as the degrees of freedom between groups, and $df_{A \times Subs}$ as the degrees of freedom within groups.

2. *The formula for Tukey's HSD involving a within-subjects factor is*

$$\text{HSD} = (q_k)\left(\sqrt{\frac{\text{Denominator of } F\text{-ratio}}{n}}\right)$$

   Values of q_k are found in Table 6 in Appendix C using k, the number of levels of the factor, and df_{wn}, the degrees of freedom used when computing the denominator of the F-ratio being tested. n is the number of scores in each mean being tested.

3. *Formulas for the two-way, within-subjects ANOVA are in Part 5 of Appendix B.*

4. *Formulas for the two-way, mixed-design ANOVA are in Part 6 of Appendix B.*

5. *To compute eta squared (η^2) in any of these designs:*

   Divide the SS between groups for the factor by the SS_{tot}.

6. *The computational formula for the homogeneity of variance test is*

$$F_{max} = \frac{\text{Largest } s_X^2}{\text{Smallest } s_X^2}$$

Critical values of F_{max} are found in Table 7 in Appendix C using k, the number of levels in the factor, and $n - 1$, where n is the number of scores in each level.

PART 7

ALTERNATIVE APPROACHES TO DESIGN AND ANALYSIS

Believe it or not, you now understand the vast majority of the designs and analyses used in psychological research. Most often, studies involve parametric data in a two- or three-way factorial experiment using ANOVA or in a correlational design using the Pearson correlation coefficient. Sometimes, however, researchers do not conduct the typical factorial experiment, and sometimes they don't obtain data that are appropriate for parametric statistics. In the next chapter, we discuss some alternative types of designs. Then, in the following chapter, we discuss statistical procedures that are used with nonparametric data.

20

Quasi-Experiments and Single-Subject Designs

Getting Started

To understand this chapter, recall the following:

- From Chapter 2, recall why participants are randomly assigned to conditions and the difference between a true and quasi-independent variable.
- From Chapter 3, recall the definition of a correlational design, and its internal and external validity.
- From Chapter 18, understand how to interpret an interaction.

Your goals in this chapter are to learn:

- The common types of quasi-experimental designs and their pitfalls.
- The types of single-subject designs.
- The pros and cons of conducting small *N* research.

This chapter focuses on design issues rather than statistical procedures. First, we'll discuss the common ways to design quasi-experiments. Then, we'll discuss an entirely different approach, in which an experiment involves only one participant. Finally, we'll introduce research conducted on a grand scale, called program evaluation. None of these topics is especially difficult, but there are a number of variations—each with its own name—so pay attention to the terminology.

UNDERSTANDING QUASI-EXPERIMENTS

Recall that in a *true experiment*, the researcher randomly assigns participants to the conditions of the independent variable, so it is the researcher who determines each individual's "score" on the *X* variable. Sometimes, however, the nature of the variable is such that participants cannot be randomly assigned to conditions. For example, say we think that personality type influences creative ability. We cannot randomly assign people to a certain personality, so, instead, we would compare the creative abilities of a group of people already having one type of personality to a group having another type, and so on. Such a design is a quasi-experiment. As discussed in Chapter 2, the participants in a **quasi-experiment** are assigned to a particular condition because they have already experienced or currently exhibit that condition of the variable. The term *quasi* means "seemingly," so this design has the appearance of a true experiment. But, we do not truly manipulate the independent variable, so a quasi-experiment involves a **quasi-independent variable**: We lay out the design and compare the scores between conditions as in a true experiment, but we only appear to administer the independent variable.

Quasi-experiments bear a remarkable resemblance to correlational designs. In both, participants have a score on the *X* variable because they have already experienced or exhibit that level of the variable. Thus, whether we call it an experiment or not, the above example is equivalent to a study in which we merely approach a number of people, measure their personality and their creativity, and then look at the relationship between their scores. Thus, technically, a quasi-experiment is a correlational design that tests the hypothesis that a relationship exists.

The name "quasi-experiment," however, communicates two important differences from a correlational design. First, in a correlational design, participants determine the range of *X* scores obtained, and the researcher examines the relationship across this full range. In a quasi-experiment, the researcher chooses a few, specific values of the *X* variable to examine. Thus, we might identify only three personality types as the conditions of our quasi-independent variable, while in a truly correlational design, participants might demonstrate many more personality types.

The second distinction is that a correlational design usually implies that there is little control of extraneous variables. A quasi-experiment usually implies more control of researcher, environmental, and task variables than the correlational version. Ideally, such controls yield a more reliable and internally valid study.

Thus, a quasi-experiment is essentially a more controlled version of a correlational design. Because it *is* a correlational design, however, a quasi-experiment has the same problem of limited *internal validity*: It is difficult to draw the correct inferences about what was involved in the relationship *in* ("internal" to) the study. In particular, there is the problem of inferring the causes of a behavior. Because participants are not randomly assigned to conditions, participant variables are not balanced between the conditions. Therefore, the conditions may be confounded by participant variables. For example, people differing in personality type might also differ in physiology, genetics, or history, any one of which can actually be the cause of differences in their creativity. Thus, we could not conclude that personality type causes creativity level.

Also, as with correlational designs, often we cannot eliminate the influence of other potential confounding variables, nor can we always identify which variable occurs first. Because of these restrictions, a quasi-experiment—even when conducted under highly controlled laboratory conditions—provides little confidence that differences in the independent variable cause differences in the dependent variable.

Still, a quasi-experiment is a legitimate research approach. In fact, some of the most interesting and informative relationships in psychology involve quasi-independent variables. However, we simply accept that, at most, the results of a single study *suggest* the causal variable and that, as usual, we build confidence in a conclusion only through replication.

> *REMEMBER* Do not infer the cause of a behavior in a quasi-experiment, because the lack of random assignment allows for potential confounding by participant variables.

Quasi-experiments generally occur in one of three situations: when the independent variable is a participant variable (e.g., personality type), when it is an environmental event (e.g., having a particular teacher), and when it is the passage of time (e.g., comparing different age groups). We'll discuss each type separately in the following sections.

QUASI-INDEPENDENT VARIABLES INVOLVING PARTICIPANT VARIABLES

Researchers are studying a quasi-independent variable whenever they study a participant variable. Such variables include differences in participants' anxiety, depression, self-esteem, attitudes, cognitive or physical characteristics, history and experiences, or social or work classifications. We "manipulate" such variables to the extent that we select the different types of participants that are present in the experiment. Thus, for example, researchers have compared the conditions of male versus female using a host of dependent variables (usually finding gender differences). Likewise, research has examined differences in how left- and right-handers perform various cognitive and artistic tasks. In field research, researchers use quasi-independent variables when they examine factory workers whose jobs differ in level of responsibility, pay rate, and so on. And, quasi-independent variables also occur in animal research that compares the behaviors of different species or compares animals who differ in innate aggressiveness or dominance. Also, a quasi-independent variable is involved any time the conditions compare "normal" to "abnormal" participants, as in clinical research.

Creating the Conditions of a Quasi-Independent Participant Variable

Identifying the participants for each condition requires first measuring individuals on the quasi-independent variable. Often pretesting is needed, either observing potential participants' overt behavior or administering a questionnaire that measures their characteristics. Using the scores from the pretest, we then *operationally define* each condition.

For example, let's say we hypothesize a relationship between a person's having low, medium, or high self-esteem and his or her willingness to take risks. From the research literature we can obtain any number of existing self-esteem tests, and one classic measure of risk-taking is the distance at which people stand from the target in a ring-toss game. After administering the self-esteem test to a large pool of people, we use their scores to select participants for each condition. Because few people are likely to exhibit an identical level of self-esteem, however, we can define "low self-esteem" as a test score of between 0 and 10, "medium self-esteem" as a score between 45 and 55, and "high self-esteem" as a score between 90 and 100. The design for this study is shown in Table 20.1.

Except for the absence of random assignment to conditions, this design is the same as in a true experiment. We face all of the usual concerns, such as *ethics*, *standardized procedures*, *demand characteristics*, *reliable scoring*, and so on. Also, we can combine the factor of self-esteem with other variables in a factorial design, and we may employ any combination of true and quasi-independent variables. We analyze the results of quasi-experiments using the same procedures as in previous true experiments. Thus, compute the mean (or other summary measure) for each condition and perform the *t*-test, ANOVA, or other appropriate procedures to determine if the conditions differ significantly. (Unless it is a matched-groups or a pretest-posttest design, a quasi-independent variable involving a participant variable will always require a between-subjects analysis.)

Recall that a key issue in any experiment is to create a reliable and strong manipulation of the independent variable. How effectively the conditions of a quasi-independent variable are manipulated hinges on the selection pretest. (Because this test is itself a measurement procedure, it has the usual design concerns, such as *scoring criteria*, *sensitivity*, *reliability*, and *demand characteristics*.) Then, as always, we seek a valid manipulation of the independent variable, so for example, the above pretest must validly identify differences in self-esteem. Also, we seek a reliable, consistent manipulation, so the self-esteem scores should reliably reflect differences in self-esteem.

Finally, we seek to maximize statistical power by, first, creating a *strong manipulation*. Therefore, participants should have *very* distinctly low, medium, and high self-esteem scores so that the conditions are very different from one another. Second, we want to minimize error variance by eliminating differences *within* each group. The more that participants differ on the independent variable within a condition, the greater the variability in dependent scores that we may see. Therefore, the range of selection scores that create each condition should be narrowly defined. Thus, we will try to select very similar people within each condition in terms of self-esteem, because then they should score consistently in terms of risk-taking. And, finally, recall that when we have lessened control and a potentially large error variance, we compensate by testing a relatively large *N*. Then, hopefully, we will see large, significant differences in risk-taking scores.

TABLE 20.1 Diagram of a One-Way Experiment with a Quasi-Independent Variable

Each X represents a participant's risk-taking score.

Self-esteem level		
Low (0–10)	*Medium (45–55)*	*High (90–100)*
X	X	X
X	X	X
X	X	X
X	X	X
X	X	X
$\overline{X}$	$\overline{X}$	$\overline{X}$

If we still do not find differences, one reason may be because of "regression toward the mean."

The Problem of Regression Toward the Mean

There is a potential flaw in reliability that can occur whenever we seek to identify participants who are relatively extreme on a variable. Recall that any measurement technique can be unreliable to some extent, containing measurement error because of random distractions and flukes. Simply by chance, these influences can conspire in such a way that some participants obtain extreme scores: Some people will be particularly lucky or unlucky at guessing answers, some may feel particularly good while others are having a bad day, or there may be quirks in the measurement procedure that cause some to score especially well or especially poorly. Such random, momentary influences will not always be present, however, and they have a way of averaging out. Therefore, if we measure these same individuals again, their scores will tend to be less extreme, simply by chance. This time, the high scores aren't so high and the lows aren't so low, but tend more toward the middle. Because the mean falls in the middle, another way to say this is that a participant's score will tend to be closer to the mean. This outcome is known as regression toward the mean. **Regression toward the mean** occurs when, because of inconsistent random factors, extreme scores tend to change in the direction of moving closer to the mean.

The problem with regression toward the mean is that, with it, we do not have a strong manipulation. For example, people identified by the pretest as having very high or very low self-esteem scores are likely to exhibit a more average level of self-esteem. Therefore, our three conditions may not actually differ in self-esteem as much as we think. Even if self-esteem does cause risk-taking, with smaller differences between the levels of self-esteem, we may find small, possibly nonsignificant differences in risk-taking.

An additional problem is that regression toward the mean also threatens internal validity, because what appears to be a change in scores due to the treatment may actually be nothing more than a change in random measurement error. For example, say that in a different study we test a counseling technique for raising a person's low self-esteem, using a pretest-posttest design. We measure and select people having very low self-esteem, then apply the treatment, and then measure their self-esteem again. To some extent the peculiarities that produced very low self-esteem when we tested participants the first time will not be present the second time. Therefore, their second score will tend to be higher (closer to the mean), *regardless* of whether the treatment works or not.

We try to counteract regression toward the mean by using multiple trials from the most reliable selection tests possible. Also, we can include a control group—another group that is measured at the same times as the experimental group but does not experience the treatment. The extent to which the control group's scores change will show the extent of extraneous influences, including that of regression toward the mean.

> ***REMEMBER*** Regression toward the mean is a change in extreme scores toward less extreme scores that occurs because random influences are not consistently present.

Other Factors Influencing Our Interpretation

Even in a quasi-experiment, we can attempt to control extraneous participant variables. We can test from a limited population or match participants on relevant variables (e.g., we might limit age and/or match participants on their ring-tossing ability). Or, we can balance participant variables (e.g., we can test an equal number of males and females in each condition). And, we use random sampling to balance out other variables: We randomly select individuals to pretest, and from those who meet the criteria for a condition, we randomly select those who will actually participate. However, such controls do not eliminate the problem that a quasi-independent variable is still likely to be confounded by extraneous participant variables.

Also, another problem of correlational studies is especially relevant to quasi-experiments involving participant variables: Often, we cannot confidently identify the temporal order in which the variables occur. For example, someone's self-esteem level might cause their risk-taking level as we've implied, but it is also possible that one's risk-taking level might cause a certain self-esteem level to develop. Knowing which variable occurs first is necessary for identifying the causal variable.

Finally, our interpretation must consider whether the pretest has created *demand characteristics* that alerted participants to our variables and caused them to behave differently than they otherwise would. To counter this, we might use deception to disguise both the pretest and the purpose of the study. Also, recognize that in correlational study, we can test the variables in the order that is least biasing to participants, capitalizing on the fact that one variable does not truly precede the other anyway. Thus, we might first measure many people on the dependent variable of risk-taking, and then give them the selection test to determine who will be placed in each condition when we analyze the data.

> *REMEMBER* Do not infer causality in quasi-experiments involving participant variables, because regression toward the mean may be operating, there may be confounding by participant variables, the order of the independent and dependent variables is uncertain, and the selection device may produce demand characteristics.

Bearing these restrictions in mind, if the results are significant, then, as usual, the final step is to explain psychologically how and why the independent and dependent variables are related in nature. For help, graph the relationship and, despite the problems of causality, compute the *effect size* of any significant quasi-independent variable.

QUASI-INDEPENDENT VARIABLES INVOLVING ENVIRONMENTAL EVENTS: THE TIME-SERIES DESIGN

A second type of quasi-experiment arises when investigating the effect that an uncontrollable environmental event has on behavior. Natural disasters (such as floods, hurricanes, and earthquakes) can dramatically affect an individual's mental health. Governments, schools, and industries institute programs that can influence a person's productivity and satisfaction. And societal events, such as wars, riots, and economic recessions, can alter individuals' expectations and attitudes.

Usually such variables cannot be validly studied in the laboratory (how do you create a war?). Instead, researchers study such events using the general quasi-experimental approach known as a time-series design. A **time-series design** is a repeated-measures design in which participants' behavior is measured prior to the occurrence of an event and again after it has occurred. Although this sounds like the typical pretest-posttest design, it is a quasi-experiment because participants cannot be randomly assigned to receive the treatment: We cannot randomly select those people who will experience an earthquake or who will have their school adopt a new program. We also have difficulty in creating control groups, and we cannot control the occurrence of the independent variable (in a city hit by a hurricane, not everybody experiences the same ferocity). We therefore have considerably less internal validity for concluding that the independent variable causes the dependent behavior, as well as less external validity for concluding that the same relationship is found with other participants and settings.

> ***REMEMBER*** Do not infer causality in a quasi-experiment involving environmental events because of confounding by participant variables and because of inadequate controls.

While there are numerous approaches to time-series designs, the four major types are discussed below. (See Campbell & Stanley, 1963, for the definitive brief text on such designs.)

One-Group Pretest-Posttest Designs

In the **one-group pretest-posttest design**, we obtain a single pretest measure on a group and then, after the event, obtain a single posttest measure of the group. For example, Nolen-Hoeksema and Morrow (1991) examined the mental stress of people before and after an earthquake. Or, Frank and Gilovich (1988) hypothesized that wearing black uniforms leads to more aggressive behavior, so they examined the number of penalty minutes incurred by a National Hockey League team before and after it changed to black uniforms.

Note that such designs provide extremely weak internal validity for inferring the causes of a behavioral change. The overwhelming problem is that they lack a control group. For example, without knowing the penalty scores of a control hockey team that is repeatedly measured, we have no idea whether the penalty scores might have changed in the experimental group, even if the uniforms had not been changed. To see this, look at the two graphs in Figure 20.1.

On the left, the one-group design appears to show that changing uniforms produced an increase in penalties. However, with a control group, we might have obtained the data on the right, showing that with or without the uniform change, penalty minutes increased. This outcome would suggest that some confounding factor had changed that actually produced the increase in penalties in the experimental group. Maybe all teams became more aggressive, or the referees began calling more penalties than previously. Or, perhaps scores changed because of the players' ongoing history and maturation (maybe aggressiveness naturally increases as players become older). Or, maybe the results reflect mortality effects (with less aggressive players leaving the team between

FIGURE 20.1 Graphs Showing the Potentially Missing Information when a Control Group Is Not Present in a Pretest-Posttest Design

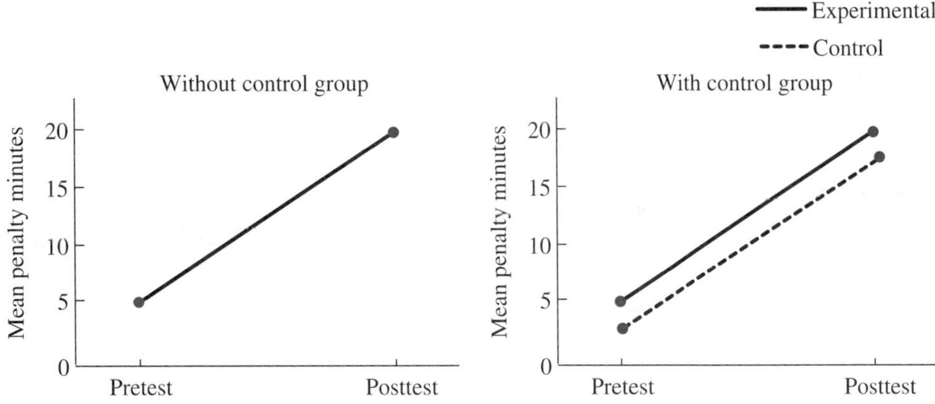

measurements). Or, maybe the results reflect regression toward the mean (perhaps at the pretest, players were coincidentally experiencing very low penalty rates, and the increase at the posttest merely reflects natural fluctuations in scores).

When a study involves a simple one-group pretest-posttest design, there is no way to eliminate these possibilities. Therefore, because the conclusions from such a study are so weak, this design is typically used only when no alternative design is possible.

> ***REMEMBER*** In the one-group pretest-posttest design, the absence of a control group means that we cannot eliminate the possibility that extraneous variables caused the dependent scores to change.

Nonequivalent Control Group Designs

You might think that the solution to the above problem is simply to add a control group. Implicitly, however, we always seek an *equivalent* control group. By equivalent we mean that the control group is similar to the experimental group in terms of participant variables and in terms of experiences between the pretest and the posttest. In true experiments, we attempt to obtain an equivalent control group by (1) randomly assigning participants to conditions so that we balance participant variables, and (2) keeping all experiences the same for both groups. Thus, the ideal would be to randomly select half of a team to change uniforms and the other half not to. Or to select half of a city to experience an earthquake and the other half not. Then the experimental and control groups would have similar characteristics and similar experiences between the pretest and posttest. Then, any differences in their posttest scores could be attributed to the treatment.

The problem, of course, is that we cannot create such an equivalent control group. In most cases, all members of the relevant participant pool automatically experience the treatment. The best we can do is to obtain a **nonequivalent control group**—a group that has different characteristics and different experiences during the study. For example, we might also observe another hockey team that did not change to black uniforms during the same season in which we observe our experimental team. This would be a nonequivalent control group because different teams have players with different styles of play, different coaches, different game strategies, and different experiences during the season. Likewise, if we selected people who live in a different city as the control group for people who experience an earthquake, this too would be a nonequivalent group, because people living in another city may be intrinsically different and have different daily experiences. Nonetheless, a nonequivalent control group is better than nothing.

To analyze such results, we should not simply compare the posttest scores of the experimental and control groups. Any difference here is confounded by initial differences between the groups and by differences in experiences during the study. Instead, we can examine the *difference* between the pretest and posttest scores in each group. To illustrate, let's say the hockey teams produced the penalty data shown in Figure 20.2. Computing the difference for each group indicates the *relative* change that occurs from pretest to posttest. The experimental team showed an increase in penalty minutes from a mean of 4 to a mean of 10 minutes, a *difference* of 6. The control team showed an increase from 10 to 12, a difference of only 2. Regardless of the actual number of penalties in each group, the important finding is that, over the same time period, there was a larger increase for the team that changed uniforms.

To determine whether this difference is significant, we could first compute a pretest-posttest difference score for each player in the control group and in the experimental group. Then, because these form two independent samples of difference scores, we would perform the independent samples *t*-test, comparing the mean difference score for the control group with that of the experimental group. Alternatively, we could perform a two-way ANOVA on the raw penalty scores and examine the *interaction*. As Figure 20.2 shows, the relationship between pretest-posttest scores and penalty minutes *depends* on whether we are talking about the control group or the experimental group,

FIGURE 20.2 Data for a Nonequivalent Control Group Design

These data show penalties for both experimental and control teams over the same pretest and posttest period.

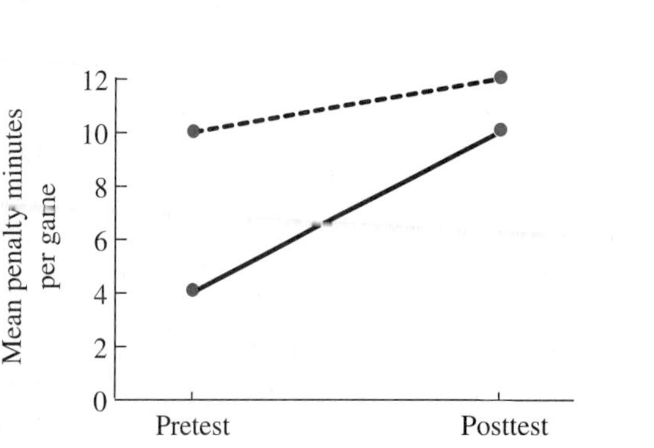

so there is apparently an interaction effect here. If the interaction is not significant, then the data essentially form the pattern shown back in the right-hand graph of Figure 20.1: Here, the change in penalty scores does not depend on whether a team changed uniforms.

When interpreting such results, recognize that a nonequivalent control group design provides only some degree of improvement in internal validity compared to the previous one-group design. The nonequivalent control group helps to eliminate potential confounding, but *only* from factors that are *common* to both groups. In the hockey study, for example, Figure 20.2 suggests that there was no confounding factor common to both teams that produced the increase in penalties. If any maturation, history, or environmental effects common to all hockey players had been operating, then the difference between pretest and posttest would have been the same for both teams. Because the experimental group exhibited a larger change, something else was present for only that team which produced the change. However, it is possible that this "something else" was not the change in uniforms. A nonequivalent groups design does not eliminate the possibility of a unique confounding or a random fluctuation that occurred only for the experimental group. Thus, it might have been some event specific to only the experimental team that actually brought about the increase in penalties (maybe a new coach was hired who actively promoted more aggressive play).

> ***REMEMBER*** A nonequivalent control group design eliminates only confounding by variables that are common to both the experimental and control groups.

Interrupted Time-Series Designs

Sometimes, we do not have access to a control group that is even approximately equivalent. For example, it is difficult to imagine the control group for survivors of an airplane crash or for those who have served as president of the United States. In such cases, we can test whether the pretest-to-posttest changes in scores would have occurred without the treatment by examining the scores of the experimental group at other times before and after the treatment. In an **interrupted time-series design**, we make observations at several spaced times prior to the occurrence of the independent variable and at several times after it. In fact, this was the approach taken by Frank and Gilovich (1988), who examined the penalty records for 10 years before and 6 years after the hockey team changed to black uniforms. Their results were similar to those shown in Figure 20.3. The researchers also incorporated the idea of a nonequivalent control group by comparing the team to the entire league. To do this, they transformed the team's yearly total penalty minutes to a z-score based on the average penalty time for the entire league. Recall that z-scores describe relative standing, so here a below-average score produces a negative z and an above-average score produces a positive z. Figure 20.3 shows that, before the uniform change, the team was consistently below the league average in penalties, but after the change, it was consistently above average.

From such a pattern we see two things. First, the many pretest and posttest observations demonstrate the normal random fluctuations in scores from year to year. These are not as large as the change from before to after the uniform change, so the apparent effect of changing uniforms cannot be dismissed as a random fluctuation. Second, because we see a long-term stable level of responding before the treatment and a long-term stable

FIGURE 20.3 Data for Interrupted Time-Series Design

Shown here are the yearly penalty records (in z-scores) of the hockey team before and after changing to black uniforms.

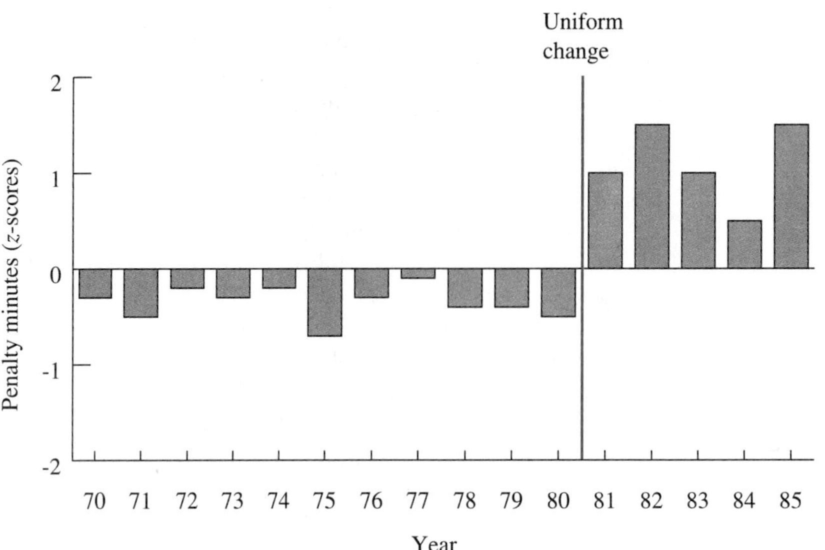

level after the treatment, it is unlikely that history, maturation, or environmental variables produced the observed change. These variables would be expected to operate over the entire 16-year period, producing similar changes at other points in time. Yet, the change occurred *only* when the treatment was introduced. (Advanced statistical procedures are available for determining whether this is a significant change; see Cook and Campbell, 1979.)

Thus, the interrupted time-series design allows us to conclude that the pretest-to-posttest change in dependent scores did not result from a random fluctuation in scores or from a repeatedly occurring confounding variable. The one weakness in the design is that some variable might have coincidentally changed *once*, at the same time the treatment was introduced. For example, hockey teams change players yearly, and perhaps, by chance, more penalty-prone players were acquired during the same year as the uniform change. However, such an explanation would require a rather exceptional coincidence, considering all of the changes in the makeup and experiences of the team over this 16-year period. Therefore, we have substantial confidence that the change in behavior is due to the treatment. (Frank and Gilovich, 1988, provided additional confidence by also reporting a laboratory study demonstrating that wearing black does increase aggressiveness.)

REMEMBER The numerous pretest and posttest observations of an interrupted time-series design reduce, but do not eliminate, the possibility that the treatment is confounded with some other event.

Multiple Time-Series Designs

To further increase confidence in the conclusions from a quasi-experiment, we can combine the interrupted time-series design and the nonequivalent control group design, creating a **multiple time-series design**. Here, we observe an experimental group and a nonequivalent control group, obtaining several spaced pretest scores and several spaced posttest scores for each. Thus, for example, we might examine several years of penalty records both for the team that changes uniforms and for another team that does not, as shown in Figure 20.4. This shows the effect of the treatment in two ways. First, with the experimental group, the change in behavior occurs only after the treatment has been introduced, with one stable behavior before and a different stable behavior after the treatment. Second, the change from pretest to posttest scores in the experimental group is larger than that in the control group.

Although there might still be some factor that occurred simultaneously with the treatment, the fact that it does not produce the same results in the control group means that it is specific to the experimental group. Further, the fact that throughout all these years it occurs only once and simultaneously with the treatment means that it would have to be an extreme coincidence. Together, therefore, these findings make it very unlikely that a confounding variable produced the change in the experimental group.

> ***REMEMBER*** A multiple time-series design examines numerous pretest and posttest observations for both an experimental and nonequivalent control group.

In addition to the previous designs, there is one other way to create a quasi-experiment.

FIGURE 20.4 Data for a Multiple Time-Series Design

The yearly penalty record of a hockey team before and after changing to black uniforms, and of a nonequivalent control team.

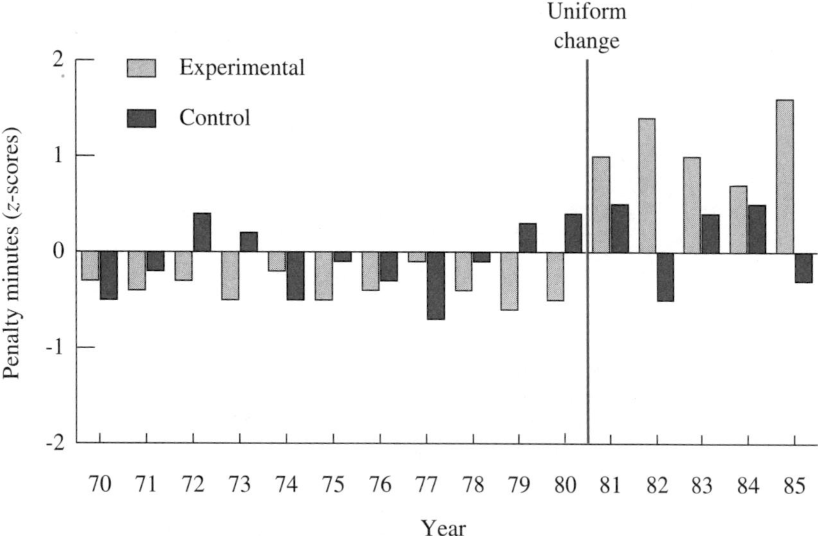

THE QUASI-INDEPENDENT VARIABLE OF THE PASSAGE OF TIME

Another important quasi-independent variable in psychology is the passage of time. The entire field of developmental psychology is built around the variable of age, focusing on how it relates to changes in social, emotional, and cognitive behavior. Researchers also study the passage of time in other settings, as when comparing experienced workers with inexperienced workers. These are quasi-independent variables, because we cannot randomly assign people to be a certain age or to experience only a certain amount of work. Therefore, such studies are like the previous time-series designs, in that we sample participants' behavior at different points, before and after the passage of a certain amount of time. However, they differ from time-series designs in one important way. In time-series designs, an environmental event was the variable of interest, while the accompanying passage of time between measurements allowed for potential confoundings from maturation and history. In the present designs, the passage of time—with the accompanying maturation and history—is the variable of interest, while environmental events are potential confoundings.

There are three general approaches to studying the passage of time: Longitudinal designs, cross-sectional designs, and cohort designs.

Longitudinal Designs

In a **longitudinal design**, we observe the effect of the passage of time by repeatedly measuring a group of participants. For example, let's say we want to study vocabulary development in a group of children. To do so, we'll test them yearly from ages four to eight. As in Table 20.2, such a design is set up and analyzed in the same way as any other repeated-measures experiment. Collapsing vertically, any differences between the mean scores for the conditions will reflect changes in vocabulary skills as a function of age. As usual, this factor may be part of a multifactor design, in which other true or quasi-independent variables are examined.

Researchers also study briefer periods of time. For example, Nelson and Sutton (1990) examined white-collar workers over a nine-month period to determine how they coped with work-related stress. And here's an interesting twist: Gladue and Delaney

TABLE 20.2 Diagram of a One-Way Longitudinal Study, Showing Repeated Observations of Each Participant at Different Ages

Xs represent vocabulary scores.

	Age (in years)				
	4	*5*	*6*	*7*	*8*
Participant 1	X	X	X	X	X
Participant 2	X	X	X	X	X
Participant 3	X	X	X	X	X
Participant 4	X	X	X	X	X
Participant 5	X	X	X	X	X
	$\overline{X}$	$\overline{X}$	$\overline{X}$	$\overline{X}$	$\overline{X}$

(1990) investigated whether men and women become more attractive to one another as the closing time of a bar approaches. Using a repeated-measures design, they asked bar patrons to rate the attractiveness of the other patrons on several occasions during the evening. They found that attractiveness increased as time wore on. (Surprisingly, the ratings were not positively correlated with alcohol consumption, so alcohol was not the reason for increased attractiveness.)

The overriding advantage of longitudinal studies like these is that, as a repeated-measures design, they keep participant variables reasonably constant between the conditions. Thus, observing the same children as they age keeps constant such variables as their genetic makeup, their parents, the environments they're raised in, and so on.

There are, however, several disadvantages to longitudinal designs. First, just keeping in touch with participants over a lengthy period can be difficult, so these studies often involve a small *N*, and the results may be biased by subject mortality. Second, the design is repeated measures and so successive conditions may be confounded by order effects (which cannot be counterbalanced). Third, and most important, a longitudinal study is inherently confounded by any extraneous variable that participants experience during the study. For example, an increase in a boy's vocabulary between ages four and five might appear to reflect normal development but may actually be due to his learning to read or watching certain television shows. Finally, a longitudinal study may not generalize well to future generations, because the society and culture are constantly changing. A study of language development in the 1950s, for example, may not generalize to children in the 1990s, because of such recent innovations as educational television and preschool education.

REMEMBER Longitudinal designs are confounded by extraneous events that occur during the course of the study, and they may not generalize over time.

Cross-Sectional Designs

We can also study the passage of time using a **cross-sectional design**. This is a between-subjects quasi-experiment in which participants are observed at different ages or at different points in a temporal sequence. Thus, for example, we might select a cross section of ages, testing the vocabulary of a group of four-year-olds, a different group of five-year-olds, and so on, as shown in Table 20.3. Basically, this is an example of the design we examined earlier in which the researcher selects participants for each condition using a participant variable—except that the variable here is based on time. (Again, this factor may be part of a multifactor design, which also examines other true or quasi-independent variables.)

The major advantage of a cross-sectional design is that the study can be conducted rather quickly. The major disadvantage is that the conditions may differ in terms of many confounding variables. For example, our five-year-old participants will differ from the four-year-olds in genetic makeup, family environment, and other variables that may cause the differences in their vocabulary scores.

REMEMBER A cross-sectional design involves a between-subjects comparison of different age groups. It may be confounded by any other variable that also distinguishes the groups.

TABLE 20.3 Diagram of a One-Way Cross-Sectional Study, Showing Observations of a Different Group of Participants at Each Age

Xs represent vocabulary scores.

		Age (in years)		
4	*5*	*6*	*7*	*8*
X	*X*	*X*	*X*	*X*
X	*X*	*X*	*X*	*X*
X	*X*	*X*	*X*	*X*
X	*X*	*X*	*X*	*X*
X	*X*	*X*	*X*	*X*
$\overline{X}$	$\overline{X}$	$\overline{X}$	$\overline{X}$	$\overline{X}$

In fact, a special confounding can occur in cross-sectional studies because of differences in subject history. It is called a cohort effect. **Cohort effects** occur when age differences are confounded by differences in subject history. The larger the differences in age, the greater the potential for cohort effects. For example, say we study memory ability as a function of age by testing people born in the United States in 1930, 1950, and 1970. These groups differ not only in age but also in that each group grew up during a different era. Therefore, their backgrounds differ in terms of health and nutritional care, educational programs, and cultural experiences: One group reached adolescence during World War II, another during the birth of television, and the third when drugs and "disco" were common. Thus, any observed differences in memory ability may actually be due to these differences in history. Further, if each group's unique background influences performance, then the results will generalize poorly to other generations that have different backgrounds.

> ***REMEMBER*** Cohort effects are the confounding of age differences with generational history differences.

Because of the greater likelihood of confoundings, cross-sectional designs are generally considered to be less effective than longitudinal designs. However, especially if participants are matched across conditions on relevant variables, such designs do provide an immediate comparison of individuals who differ in age or time-related experiences.

Cohort Designs

We cannot completely prevent cohort effects, but we can identify when they are present by employing a cohort design. A **cohort design** is a longitudinal study of several groups, each from a different generation. For example, let's say we repeatedly study the vocabulary development in one generation of children beginning when they were four years old in 1990 and in another generation of children beginning when they were four in 1994. As shown in Table 20.4, this design is set up and analyzed in the same way as any other two-way mixed-design experiment.

TABLE 20.4 Diagram of a Two-Way Cohort Study

Xs represent vocabulary scores.

		Repeated measures over age 4	5	6	7	8		
1990 participants	*1*	X	X	X	X	X		
	2	X	X	X	X	X	$\overline{X}$ ←	Generation main effect
	3	X	X	X	X	X		
	4	X	X	X	X	X		
1994 participants	*1*	X	X	X	X	X		
	2	X	X	X	X	X	$\overline{X}$ ←	
	3	X	X	X	X	X		
	4	X	X	X	X	X		
Age main effect →		$\overline{X}$	$\overline{X}$	$\overline{X}$	$\overline{X}$	$\overline{X}$		

Collapsing over scores vertically produces the mean score for each age, and differences between the means show the main effect of age. This factor provides the longitudinal, developmental information. Collapsing scores horizontally produces the main effect mean of each generation. If there is no significant difference between these means, then there is no evidence that the scores differ on the basis of a child's generation. If there is a difference between the two groups, however, then cohort effects may be present, and the developmental results are less likely to generalize to other generations. Likewise, the absence of a significant interaction between generation and age would suggest that changes in scores with age are basically similar—parallel—regardless of each generation's history. A significant interaction, however, would indicate that the changes with age that we see *depend* on which generation we examine—in which case there is a cohort effect.

> ***REMEMBER*** A cohort design is the longitudinal study of several groups, each from a different generation.

To help you remember the names and procedures of all the preceding quasi-experimental designs, they are summarized in Table 20.5.

UNDERSTANDING SMALL *N* RESEARCH AND THE SINGLE-SUBJECT DESIGN

So far, we have focused on experiments involving *groups* of people or animals. However, there is an entirely different kind of experiment, in which only one participant is studied. A **single-subject design** is a repeated-measures experiment conducted on one participant. Typically, the experiment (with an *N* of 1) is then replicated on a few more participants, so this research is also known as **small *N* research**. A single-subject

TABLE 20.5 Summary of Quasi-Experimental Designs

Type of design	*Procedure*
Designs involving participant variables	Create conditions on the basis of a participant's characteristic.
Time-series designs	
One-group pretest-posttest design	Measure one group once before and once after the event.
Nonequivalent control group design	Conduct pretest and posttest on both an experimental and a nonequivalent control group.
Interrupted time-series design	Obtain repeated measurements of one group, both before and after event.
Multiple time-series design	Conduct interrupted time-series measurements on both an experimental and a control group.
Designs involving temporal variables	
Longitudinal design	Obtain repeated measures as a function of age or experience.
Cross-sectional design	Use a between-subjects design based on age or experience.
Cohort design	Examine repeated-measures factor based on age and a between-subjects factor based on generation.

design is different from a case study, discussed in Chapter 5. A case study is a descriptive study. A single-subject design is an experiment that manipulates an independent variable.

Before considering the particulars of such designs, let's discuss why we would want to use them.

The Argument for Small *N* Designs

Some researchers argue that there are three unacceptable flaws in experiments involving groups of participants (Sidman, 1960). The first pertains to error variance, the random differences between scores found within the conditions. Typically, with group designs, we use random assignment of participants and counterbalancing of extraneous variables. Because we therefore include the influence of fluctuating variables within each condition, the design itself produces much of the error variance. The inconsistency in scores then makes it difficult to see a relationship hidden in the data (so that we must rely on obtuse statistics). Further, researchers then ignore the differences in behavior reflected by error variance and the variables that cause them. We ignore differences in behavior between participants (*intersubject* differences), and different behaviors in the same participant from moment to moment (*intrasubject* differences). Yet, these variables are potentially important aspects of the behavior under study.

The second flaw is that, because of the variability in individual scores, we must compute the mean (or similar measures) in each condition. Yet, a mean score may misrepresent the behavior of any and all individuals (how often does the mean score accurately describe your performance on an exam?). Then, incredibly, after using group means to describe a relationship, we turn around and generalize the findings to individuals! Psychology is supposed to study the laws of behavior as they apply to the individual, but in group designs, we never examine a relationship in terms of the individual.

The third flaw involves the problem of demonstrating a consistent, reliable effect of the independent variable. Usually, we demonstrate a relationship only once in a particular study, typically testing participants only briefly under the various conditions. Then, we rely on inferential statistics to conclude that the study is reliable. That is, if the results are significant, the relationship is unlikely to be due to random chance. Instead, it is likely to be caused by something that makes it reproducible, so a significant relationship is also described as a reliable relationship. We do not, however, have any *empirical* evidence that the relationship is reproducible. Other researchers may replicate a study, but their situation and participants inevitably will differ from ours. And, in their replication, researchers also seldom demonstrate empirically that the relationship is reliable.

> ***REMEMBER*** Group designs ignore the causes of error variance, they rely on mean scores to describe individuals, and they do not empirically show that an effect is reliable.

Small N designs address these problems in the following ways:

1. They control participant variables and individual differences, not by balancing them, but by keeping them constant. With only one participant, there can be no intersubject differences in scores. And, if we see an inconsistency in the participant's response, we know that some extraneous variable is responsible, so we can attempt to identify and understand it.
2. Our "analysis" of the data is usually accomplished by visual inspection. (That's right, we don't perform statistics when $N = 1$!) Instead, we look at a graph of the data to see whether there is a relationship between the independent and dependent variables. Because we rely on visual inspection, we accept that there is an effect only when it is obvious. The size of the effect, then, is the obvious amount that the participant's response changes between conditions.
3. To be sure that the effect of the independent variable is reliable, we perform the manipulation repeatedly on the same participant, or we perform a replication of the experiment on a few additional participants. Each replication is treated as a separate study, however, so we don't gloss over individuals by combining their results. Ultimately, then, because the relationship is based on individuals, we are studying reliable relationships in the psychology of individuals.

The most common type of single-subject design involves a baseline.

The Logic of Baseline Designs

If an experiment contains only one participant, then, of course, it must be a repeated-measures design. Typically, the study involves only two levels of the independent variable: a control condition with zero amount of the variable present and a treatment condition with some nonzero amount of the variable present. The independent variable usually involves a type of reward, punishment, or environmental stimulus. The dependent variable usually reflects the participant's quantity of responding, such as the number of responses made or the magnitude of the responses. For example, counting the number of times a rat presses a lever under the presence/absence of a reward fits this design. In fact, this approach has been the mainstay of B. F. Skinner and others who have studied "instrumental" or "operant" conditioning in animals. However, the design is also used with humans, especially in the area of "behavior modification," where researchers study how rewards and punishments influence the occurrence of anxiety attacks, eating disorders, and so on.

Observing a participant under a control condition establishes a baseline. A **baseline** is the level of performance on the dependent variable when the independent variable is not present. It is used for comparison to the level of performance when the variable is present. (The general name for this type of design is a **baseline design**.) To establish the baseline, the participant is observed for a substantial period of time, observing numerous responses. Once the participant has habituated to the procedure so that the baseline is stable, we have the typical response rate when the treatment is not present. Then, we introduce the experimental treatment condition and establish the participant's response rate in this situation. If the response rate with the treatment is different from that without the treatment, we have demonstrated an effect of the independent variable. The procedure is then replicated with several other participants, and the results from all are published as one report.

The fundamental logic of baseline designs is to compare the baseline response rate to the treatment response rate, but as the following sections show, there are two general approaches we may take.

Reversal Designs

The simplest approach would be to test a participant first when the independent variable is not present, in order to obtain the baseline (call this condition A). Then, we could observe the participant after the variable is present (call this condition B). This simple "AB" design could be used to show that rats, for example, will press a lever more often when food is dispensed as a reward than in an earlier baseline condition when food is not dispensed.

By showing that responding is different when the treatment is present, we may be tempted to conclude that the treatment has an effect. If this is all we do, however, we are open to the rival hypothesis that some confounding factor produced the change in responding. Maybe some confounding environmental stimulus led to the increased lever-pressing. Or, perhaps changes in the rat's ongoing history or maturation coincidentally caused the increased lever-pressing (or maybe the rat got bored and started pressing to entertain itself).

To demonstrate that it is the presence of the treatment and not some other variable that is controlling the participant's behavior, the strategy is to return the participant to the control condition after the treatment condition is over. If responding "reverses" to the baseline rate, we have evidence that the behavior is controlled by the treatment. This approach is called a reversal design. In a **reversal design**, the researcher repeatedly alternates between the baseline condition and the treatment condition. When we present the baseline phase, the treatment phase, and then the baseline phase again, the design is described as an ABA reversal design. For even more convincing evidence, we may reintroduce the treatment condition again, employing an ABAB design (or any extended sequence, such as an ABABAB design).

To see the effects of the manipulation, we graph the results, as shown in Figure 20.5. Going from testing under condition A to testing under condition B, we see that the introduction of food leads to increased responding. Then, after removing the reward and returning to condition A, the response "extinguishes," eventually returning to its

FIGURE 20.5 Ideal Results from an ABAB Reversal Design

Lever-pressing rate is shown to be a function of the presence or absence of a food reinforcer.

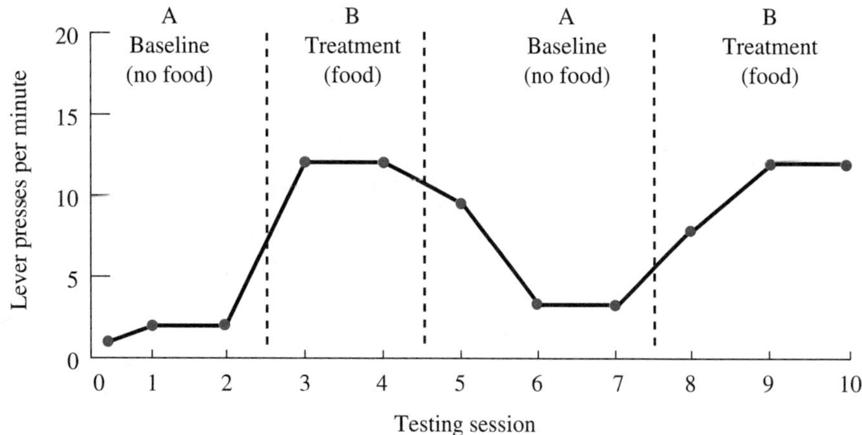

original baseline rate. Reintroducing the reward reinstates the response rate, and so on. Because it is unlikely that a confounding variable would repeatedly and simultaneously change with each of the conditions, we are confident that the treatment caused the behavioral change. Then, replicating this study on a few other participants further reduces the possibility that the behavioral change was due to a confounding variable that coincidentally changed with the treatment.

> ***REMEMBER*** A reversal design demonstrates the effect of a variable by repeatedly alternating between testing with and without the treatment condition.

Multiple-Baseline Designs

Recall that any repeated-measures design may introduce the problem of carry-over effects from one condition to the other. If the above reversal designs are to work, the carry-over effect of the treatment must be reversible. Many treatments, however, involve a permanent, irrevocable change. For example, once a rat has learned to respond to a stimulus, some learning may remain, so that the animal's responding never returns to the original baseline rate. Further, some clinical treatments are not reversible for ethical reasons. For example, it may be unethical for a researcher to discontinue a treatment that reduces a person's phobic reactions, just for the sake of the research.

If we do not reverse the treatment in such situations, we do not eliminate the possibility that the change in behavior is due to maturation, to history, or to an environmental influence that occurred coincidentally with the treatment. The solution is to employ a multiple-baseline design. A **multiple-baseline design** reduces the possibility of confounding factors by examining more than one baseline. The logic is that we eliminate potential confoundings by demonstrating that a behavior changes only when the treatment is introduced, regardless of when it is introduced. There are three general variations of the multiple-baseline design.

One approach is to establish **multiple baselines across participants**. Here, we measure a baseline for several individuals on the same behavior, but we introduce the treatment for each at a different time. For example, the argument that maturation, history, or some other variable might cause a rat to increase lever-pressing relies on the idea that the variable changed at the precise moment that we introduced the treatment. To counter this argument, we might obtain the baselines for several rats, but for each we introduce the food reward at a different point in time. Let's say we obtain the data shown in Figure 20.6. This eliminates the argument that some other variable produced

FIGURE 20.6 Idealized Data from a Multiple-Baseline Design Across Participants

Note the different points in time at which a food reward was introduced.

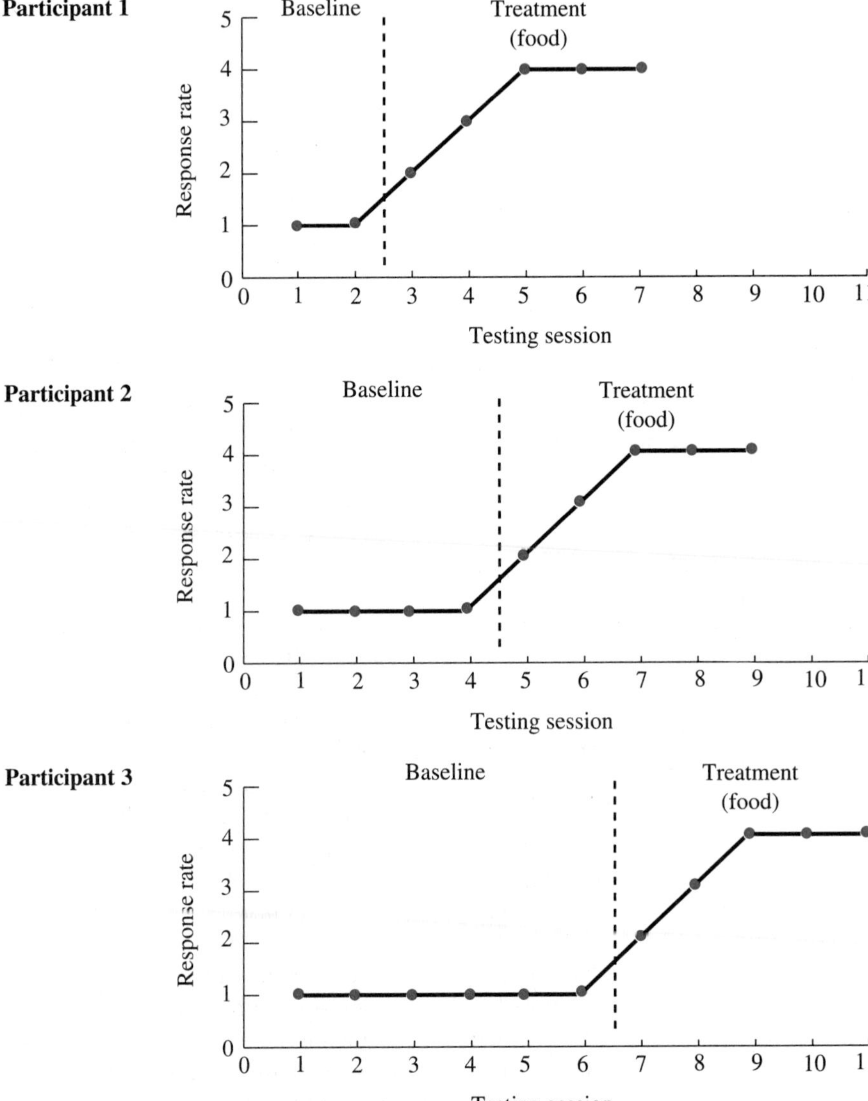

the results, because we start the treatment at a different time for each rat, and the behavior changes *only* with the treatment. An incredible coincidence would be required for a confounding variable to change simultaneously with the onset of treatment for each rat. (This approach is also used when replicating the previous reversal design with different participants, by varying the time at which the ABA conditions are instituted for each participant.)

A second approach is to collect **multiple baselines across behaviors**. Here, we measure a baseline for several behaviors from one participant and apply the treatment to each behavior at a different time. For example, say we are concerned with a child who is disruptive in school, and we establish baselines for aggressive acts, for temper tantrums, and for attention-seeking behavior. We develop a treatment involving verbal feedback that should reduce all of these behaviors. The treatment is applied first to one behavior, later to the second behavior, and still later to the third. If the incidence of each type of behavior drops only when the treatment is introduced, it is implausible that an extraneous confounding variable coincidentally caused the change in each behavior.

Alternatively, we might hypothesize that the treatment will affect only one of the above behaviors. After introducing the treatment, we should find that the target behavior changes but that the other behaviors remain at their baseline rate. If so, we can be confident that it was not changes in some extraneous variable that produced the change, because it should have changed all of the behaviors.

The third approach is to establish **multiple baselines across situations**. Here, we establish baselines for one behavior on the same participant, but in different situations. For example, we might establish a baseline for a child's temper tantrums when at school and also when at home. Then, at different points in time, we apply a treatment phase to a type of tantrum. It is unlikely that an extraneous variable that decreases tantrums would coincidentally occur with the treatment at different times, *and* at school and at home.

> ***REMEMBER*** A multiple-baseline design shows the effect of a variable by demonstrating a change in the target behavior only when the treatment is introduced.

For a summary of the layout of the different baseline designs, consult Table 20.6.

TABLE 20.6 Summary of the Different Types of Baseline Designs Commonly Used in Single-Subject Research

Design	*Layout*
Reversal design (ABA)	Alternates between control and treatment conditions
Multiple baseline	Compares influence of treatment with baseline under different situations
Across participants	Examines treatment effect after different-length baseline for one behavior from different participants
Across behaviors	Examines treatment effect on different behaviors from one participant
Across situations	Examines treatment effect on one behavior from one participant in different situations

Other Approaches to Single-Subject Designs

There are many variations to the single-subject approach. We can, for example, study the effects of several levels of a variable: First, we observe the control baseline condition (A), then observe one treatment level (B), then observe a different treatment level (C), and so on. To reverse the effects of each treatment, we insert a control condition between each treatment, producing an ABACAD design. We can even study an interaction effect by combining two treatments.

In addition to the baseline designs we've discussed, the term *single-subject design* can also refer to the kinds of repeated-measures experiments described in previous chapters. We test only one participant, but still measure a typical dependent variable, compute a mean or other summary score for multiple trials per condition, and so on. This approach is common when studying a person with an extraordinary attribute, such as when someone has an exceptional memory, an unusual physiological characteristic, or a unique set of symptoms.

Choosing Between Single-Subject and Group Designs

The major advantage of single-subject designs is that they allow us to examine a relationship between variables in a single individual. Further, sometimes they are necessary because the behavior of interest is found in an extremely small percentage of the population, and a researcher can find only a few participants to study. Sometimes, too, a design entails so much time and effort per participant that a small N is required. And, single-subject designs are useful for initially exploring a behavior or for studying variables that cause error variance in group studies.

The disadvantages of these designs stem from, first, the fact that they involve repeated measures. They become less feasible the more that carry-over effects occur. In addition, they are not commonly used for studying an interaction involving several levels of each factor, because they create impossibly complex schemes. Finally, any single-subject design is wiped out by mortality effects: Rats may die during a study, and humans require extreme patience and motivation for long-term participation. The solution to such problems may be a between-subjects group design. Such designs can be conducted more quickly, and they allow for the use of deception and other procedures that are not feasible with repeated measures.

As usual, selecting a design depends on the hypothesis and variables being studied, as well as all of the concerns about potential flaws that we've discussed. Of particular importance is finding a balance between internal and external validity. On the one hand, the potentially great control of variables in a single-subject design achieves a high degree of internal validity. So, we may prefer a single-subject design when the possible influence of fluctuating participant variables is of primary concern. On the other hand, a major drawback of single-subject research is its limited external validity for generalizing to other individuals and situations. Because results are tied to one or a few participants, the results may be very different from those we would find with other participants. (Remember, random sampling does not work so well at balancing participant variables with very small samples.) At the same time, results are tied to a highly controlled and individualized setting, so generalizability is limited to similar settings. A group design, however, provides greater confidence that the conclusions generalize to other individuals and settings.

The pros and cons of a single-subject design are listed in Table 20.7.

TABLE 20.7 Pros and Cons of a Single-Subject Design

Pros	*Cons*
High internal validity	Limited external validity
Eliminates intersubject variance and examines intrasubject variance	Repeated measures influenced by morality and carry-over effects
Describes relationship for an individual	Biased by characteristics of individual studied
Empirically demonstrates reliability of effect	Not practical for studying interactions

REMEMBER Single-subject designs provide substantial internal validity but have limited external validity.

A WORD ABOUT PROGRAM EVALUATION

There is one other type of design that you should be familiar with, which incorporates a combination of the various procedures already discussed. It is most common when researchers conduct studies on community human services programs, such as government programs for preventing or treating drug and alcohol abuse, or social or educational programs (e.g., school lunch programs.) **Program evaluation** refers to a variety of procedures for developing and evaluating social programs. Think of the social program as essentially an applied experiment in social change: We employ the experimental principle that providing some form of treatment to participants—to society—will result in a corresponding change in behavior. Program evaluation is used to set up and evaluate the experiment: It provides feedback to administrators and service providers, as well as providing scientific information about how the program works as a quasi-independent variable.

Although this research encompasses many procedures (see Posavac & Carey, 1989), it usually consists of four basic phases:

1. *Need assessment*: Before designing a particular program, researchers identify the services that are needed and determine whether potential users of the program will use it.
2. *Program planning*: When designing the program, researchers consider the behavior and situation being addressed and apply findings from the literature that suggest the best approach to use.
3. *Program monitoring*: Once the program is implemented, researchers monitor it to ensure that it provides the intended services and that clients are using them.
4. *Outcome evaluation*: Eventually, researchers determine whether the program is having its intended effect, by using a time-series study that compares behaviors before and after the program's implementation.

The data in each of these phases come from such sources as field surveys of the community; archival studies of hospital, school, and police records; and interviews, unobtrusive observations, and case studies of service providers and clients. On the one hand, such procedures suffer from all of the flaws we have discussed, especially because they are quasi-experiments. On the other hand, program evaluation addresses a very real societal need and so flawed data are generally considered better than no data (as long as the flaws are recognized and considered).

REMEMBER Program evaluation involves procedures for creating and evaluating social programs.

PUTTING IT ALL TOGETHER

The typical, true laboratory experiment involving groups of participants is most common in psychology, because it's practical and efficient, it provides a relatively high degree of internal validity, and it provides some external validity for generalizing to other situations and participants. However, quasi-experiments and small *N* designs are also important approaches. Quasi-experiments greatly expand the types of influences on behavior that can be studied, and small *N* designs eliminate error variance, especially variability due to individual differences that group designs incorporate.

Perhaps the most important thing to remember about quasi-experiments is that they often look like true experiments, especially when a quasi-independent participant variable is studied in a laboratory setting. When evaluating your own research or that of others, however, you won't see a red flag signaling the nature of the design. Instead, always carefully examine whether random assignment to conditions truly occurs. If not, remember that the results only *suggest* the causes of the behavior under study.

CHAPTER SUMMARY

1. In a *quasi-experiment* involving a *quasi-independent variable*, participants cannot be randomly assigned to conditions. Instead, they are assigned to a condition based upon some inherent characteristic. Because the independent variable may be confounded by participant variables, quasi-experiments have much less internal validity than true experiments.
2. Effective manipulation of a quasi-independent variable involving a participant variable hinges on the selection of participants for each condition who are similar to each other, but very different from those in other conditions. The problems here are confounding by participant variables, and uncertainty about the order of the independent and dependent variables.
3. *Regression toward the mean* occurs when, because of inconsistent random factors, extreme scores tend to change in the direction of coming closer to the mean.
4. A *time-series design* is a quasi-experimental repeated-measures design in which a behavior is sampled at different times. The problems here are confounding by participant variables—including history and maturation—and inadequate controls.
5. A *one-group pretest-posttest* design has no control group.

6. In a *nonequivalent control group design*, the control and experimental groups have different characteristics and different experiences during the study.

7. In an *interrupted time-series design*, observations are made at several spaced times prior to the treatment and at several times after it.

8. In a *multiple time-series design*, both an experimental group and a nonequivalent control group are observed at several times before the treatment and at several times after it.

9. In a *longitudinal design*, participants are repeatedly measured to observe the effect of the passage of time. The problems here are confounding by participant variables and by extraneous environmental variables.

10. A *cross-sectional design* is a between-subjects experiment in which participants are observed at different ages or at different points in a temporal sequence.

11. *Cohort effects* occur when differences in age are confounded by differences in subject history.

12. A *cohort design* is a factorial design consisting of a longitudinal study of several groups, each from a different generation.

13. Group designs have been criticized because they (a) ignore the variables that cause error variance, (b) rely on mean scores that may barely show an effect and are inaccurate for describing individuals, and (c) do not empirically show that an effect is reliable.

14. A *single-subject* or *small N design* involves a repeated-measures experiment conducted on one participant that is replicated with a few other participants. The advantages of this design are that it (a) keeps participant variables constant, (b) provides a clear indication of the effect size of a variable, and (c) empirically demonstrates the reliability of the effect.

15. A *baseline* is the level of performance on the dependent variable when the independent variable is not present. It is used as a comparison to performance when the variable is present.

16. A *reversal design* (such as an ABA design) repeatedly alternates between the baseline and the treatment conditions.

17. When the influence of a manipulation cannot be reversed, a *multiple-baseline design* is used, in which a baseline is established for one behavior from several participants, for several behaviors from one participant, or for one behavior from one participant in several situations.

18. Single-subject designs are appropriate when studying a detailed description of one participant, when the treatment does not produce large carry-over effects, and when many observations per participant are necessary. Otherwise, a group design may be preferable.

19. *Program evaluation* involves procedures for developing and evaluating applied social programs.

KEY TERMS (with page references)

baseline (576)
baseline design (576)
cohort design (572)
cohort effects (572)
cross-sectional design (571)
interrupted time-series design (567)
longitudinal design (570)
multiple baselines across behaviors (579)
multiple baselines across participants (578)
multiple baselines across situations (579)
multiple-baseline design (577)
multiple time-series design (569)
nonequivalent control group (565)
one-group pretest-posttest design (564)
program evaluation (581)
quasi-experiment (559)
quasi-independent variable (559)
regression toward the mean (562)
reversal design (576)
single-subject design (573)
small *N* research (573)
time-series design (564)

REVIEW QUESTIONS

(Answers for odd-numbered questions and problems are provided in Appendix D.)

1. (a) What is the difference between a true experiment and a quasi-experiment? (b) In what ways are quasi-experiments and correlational designs similar? (c) In what way(s) are they different?

2. What three types of variables are studied as quasi-independent variables?

3. (a) How do you design a quasi-independent variable to study a participant variable? (b) What is the goal when using the scores from a selection pretest to create conditions? (c) What four problems reduce internal validity here?

4. (a) What produces confoundings in a quasi-experiment involving a participant variable? (b) What other causes of confoundings occur with other types of quasi-experiments?

5. (a) What is a one-group pretest-posttest design? (b) What is missing from this design? (c) What extraneous variables may confound this design?

6. (a) What is a nonequivalent control group design? (b) What potential confounding variables does it eliminate? (c) What potential confounding variables are not eliminated?

7. (a) What is an interrupted time-series design? (b) What potential confounding variables does it eliminate? (c) What potential confoundings does it not eliminate?

8. (a) What is a multiple time-series design? (b) What potential confounding variables does it eliminate? (c) What potential confoundings does it not eliminate?

9. (a) What is a longitudinal design? (b) What is the major advantage of this design? (c) What is the major flaw in this design?

10. (a) What is a cross-sectional design? (b) What is its major strength? (c) What is its major weakness?
11. (a) What are cohort effects? (b) What is a cohort design? (c) What is the advantage of this design? (d) How do you determine whether cohort effects are present?
12. What is program evaluation?
13. (a) What is a reversal design? (b) What is the logic for eliminating confoundings in this design? (c) What is the major factor that prohibits its use?
14. (a) What is a multiple-baseline design involving one behavior from several participants? (b) What is the logic for eliminating confoundings in this design?
15. What is a multiple-baseline design (a) involving several behaviors from one participant? (b) involving one behavior for one participant in several situations?
16. What is regression toward the mean?

PRACTICE PROBLEMS

17. Why will a quasi-independent variable involving a participant variable usually require a between-subjects analysis?
18. Poindexter wants to perform a longitudinal study, measuring yearly the same group of students as they pass through their freshman, sophomore, junior, and senior years in college. To control order effects between conditions, he will counterbalance the order in which participants are tested. Is this a good idea? Why?
19. At the beginning of the semester, you obtain the highest score on a physical-fitness test in a gym class. During the semester, your scores get worse, while students who were initially very unfit tend to score higher. You conclude that the gym class helps unfit people but harms those who are most fit. (a) What rival explanation involving random factors might explain these results? (b) How would it cause the changes in scores? (c) How would you test this hypothesis?
20. You conduct a study of the influence of relaxation training on participants' momentary anxiety (measured using heart rate). (a) Should this study involve an ABA reversal design or a multiple-baseline design? (b) Describe the specific design to use.
21. (a) What are three advantages to using a single-subject design in question 20? (b) What are two disadvantages?
22. Foofy tests the happiness of a group of sorority pledges at the beginning of the semester and again at the end of the semester after being admitted to the sorority. She finds that the latter scores are higher, and so she concludes that joining a sorority increases a woman's happiness. (a) What is the name of this design? (b) What major flaw is present? (c) What rival hypotheses can you suggest to explain her results? (d) What would you do to improve the study?
23. You study the maturity levels of students at four times during the college year (factor A). You also compare freshmen from 10 years ago with present-day freshmen (factor B). (a) What type of variable is factor A? (b) What type of variable is factor B? (c) What type of design have you created?

24. In question 23, you obtain the following cell means. What should you conclude about (a) the presence of cohort effects? (b) how maturity changes during a college student's year?

	Time 1	*Time 2*	*Time 3*	*Time 4*
10 years ago	10	20	30	40
Present-day	25	25	25	25

25. In two nonequivalent control group designs, you obtain the following mean stress scores for people before and after an earthquake. (a) What should you conclude about whether the treatment caused the change in scores in the experimental group in Study A? (b) What other hypotheses are plausible? (c) What should you conclude in Study B? (d) What hypotheses are eliminated in Study B? (e) What possible confounding still might occur in Study B?

Study A	*Before*	*After*
Control	20	50
Experimental	30	60

Study B	*Before*	*After*
Control	60	70
Experimental	50	85

21

Chi Square and Other Nonparametric Statistical Procedures

GETTING STARTED

To understand this chapter, recall the following:

- From Chapter 5, recall the various observational and descriptive methods researchers use.
- From Chapter 6, recall the four types of measurement scales (nominal, ordinal, interval, and ratio).
- From Chapters 15 and 16, remember why we create within-subjects or between-subjects designs, the independent- and the dependent-samples t-test, and homogeneity of variance.
- From Chapters 17 and 19, recall the uses of the within-subjects and between-subjects ANOVA, post hoc tests, and eta squared.

Your goals in this chapter are to learn:

- When to use nonparametric statistics.
- The logic and use of the one-way chi square.
- The logic and use of the two-way chi square.
- The nonparametric procedures corresponding to the independent- and dependent-samples t-test, and to the one-way between-subjects and within-subjects ANOVA.

The one remaining topic in research methods and statistics to discuss is nonparametric statistics. Don't despair, though, because they are very similar to previous statistics we've seen: Nonparametric procedures are still inferential statistics for deciding whether the differences between samples are likely to represent a relationship in the population. Therefore, H_0 and H_a, Type I and Type II errors, alpha levels, critical values, and maximizing power all apply. And, as usual, these procedures can be applied to descriptive or experimental designs, from the laboratory or the field.

In the following sections, we'll first discuss the most common nonparametric procedure, called chi square, and see how it is calculated for a one-way and a two-way design. Then, we'll introduce the nonparametric procedures that are analogous to *t*-tests and ANOVAs, except that they are used with rank-order scores. (Their calculations are presented in Appendix B.8.)

THE REASONS FOR USING NONPARAMETRIC PROCEDURES

Previous parametric procedures (e.g., *t*-tests and ANOVA) required that dependent scores involve an interval or ratio scale, that samples represent normally distributed populations, and that the population variances are homogeneous. However, sometimes data will not fit a parametric procedure. We cannot insist on using a parametric procedure when the data seriously violate its assumptions, because doing so results in an *increased* probability of a *Type I error*. Recall that the whole purpose of inferential statistics is to avoid rejecting H_0 when it is true, but here the actual probability of a Type I error will be unacceptably larger than the alpha level we have set. Instead, in such cases, we use nonparametric procedures. **Nonparametric statistics** are inferential procedures that do not require a normal distribution or homogeneous variance, and the data may be nominal (categorical) or ordinal (rank-ordered). Regardless, however, the probability of a Type I error will still equal our alpha.

Understand that whether to use a nonparametric procedure depends solely on the characteristics of the *dependent variable* selected for the study. However, nonparametric procedures are never our first choice. First, they are less *powerful* than parametric procedures. Second, we try to avoid nominal and ordinal scales, because they are less *precise* and *sensitive* for measuring differences in behavior, and even their measures of central tendency (the *mode* or *median*) are less precise. Therefore, in most laboratory studies, we try to choose an interval or ratio variable that is normally distributed and has homogeneous variance. (When in doubt, check the literature to see how others treat a variable.) However, sometimes the dependent variable involves an interval or ratio scale, but the populations are severely skewed and/or do not have homogeneous variance. Then, we are forced to use nonparametric procedures.

More commonly, nonparametric procedures occur in descriptive research or in field experiments, where we are forced to use a nominal or ordinal dependent variable. For example, often a survey measures a nominal variable (e.g., whether someone is male or female), and so we count the frequency in each category. Or, in observational research, we may be forced to rank-order different behaviors (e.g., rating one participant as showing the most of the variable, another the second-most, and so on). In field experiments, we may need to count the frequency of different behaviors. And, in archival research, we may simply note the presence/absence of a behavior.

REMEMBER Use nonparametric statistics when dependent scores form skewed or otherwise nonnormal distributions, when the population variance is not homogeneous, or when scores are measured using ordinal or nominal scales.

The most common nonparametric procedure is called chi square.

CHI SQUARE PROCEDURES

Chi square procedures are used when participants are measured using a *nominal variable*. Unlike with previous dependent variables we've discussed, with nominal variables a response does not indicate an amount, but rather it indicates the *category* that a participant falls into. Thus, we have nominal or categorical variables when we count how many individuals answer yes, no, or maybe to a question; how many indicate that they are male or female or claim to vote Republican, Democratic, or Communist; how many say that they were or were not abused as children; and so on. In each case, we count the number or *frequency*, of participants who fall into each category.

The next step is to determine what the data represent. For example, we might find that out of 100 people, 40 say yes to a particular question and 60 say no. These numbers indicate how the *frequencies are distributed* across the categories of yes/no. As usual, we want to draw inferences about the population: If we asked everyone in the population this question, can we infer that 40% would say yes and 60% would say no? Or would the frequencies be distributed in a different manner? To make inferences about the frequencies in the population, we perform chi square (pronounced "kigh square"). The **chi square procedure** is the nonparametric inferential procedure for testing whether the frequencies in each category in a sample represent those frequencies in the population.

REMEMBER Use the chi square procedure for significance testing when you measure the number of participants that are in different categories.

The symbol for the chi square statistic is χ^2. Theoretically, there is no limit to the number of categories—levels—we may have in a variable and no limit to the number of variables we may have. Therefore, a chi square design is described in the same way as ANOVAs: When a study has only one variable, perform the one-way chi square; when a study has two variables, use the two-way chi square; and so on.

THE ONE-WAY CHI SQUARE: THE GOODNESS OF FIT TEST

The **one-way chi square** is used when data consist of the frequencies with which participants belong to the different categories of *one* variable. As usual, we're examining a relationship, but here it's a relationship between the different categories and the frequency with which individuals fall in each. We ask, "As the categories change, do the frequencies with which participants fall into the categories also change?"

Here is an example that calls for a one-way chi square: Being right-handed or left-handed is apparently related to brain organization, and, interestingly, many of history's great geniuses were left-handed. To explore the relationship between the frequencies of left- and right-handedness in geniuses, say that, using an IQ test, we identify a random sample of 50 geniuses. Then, we ask them whether they're left-handed or right-handed (ambidextrous is not an option). We count the total number of left-handers and right-handers, and the results are shown here:

Handedness	
Left-handers	*Right-handers*
$f_o = 10$	$f_o = 40$

$k = 2$
$N = \text{total } f_o = 50$

Each column contains the frequency with which participants fall into that category. We call this value the **observed frequency**, symbolized by f_o. The sum of the f_o from all categories equals N, the total number of participants in the study. Notice that k again stands for the number of levels, or categories, (here $k = 2$).

The above results seem pretty straightforward: 10 of the 50 geniuses, or 20%, are left-handers, and 40 of them, or 80%, are right-handers. Therefore, we might conclude that the same distribution of 20% left-handers and 80% right-handers would occur in the population of all geniuses. But, there is the usual problem: Sampling error. Maybe, by luck, the people in this sample are unrepresentative, so in the population of all geniuses, we would not find this distribution of right- and left-handers. Maybe these results poorly represent some *other* distribution. As usual, this is the null hypothesis, implying that we are being misled by sampling error.

What is that "other distribution" of frequencies that the sample poorly represents? To answer this, we create a *model* of the distribution of the frequencies we expect to find in the population if H_0 is *true*. Recall that H_0 always implies that the study failed to demonstrate the predicted relationship. Therefore, the H_0 model describes the distribution of frequencies in the population if there is not the predicted relationship.

Notice that another name for the chi square procedure is the **goodness of fit test**. This is because the one-way χ^2 procedure tests how "good" the "fit" is between our data and the H_0 model. Thus, goodness of fit is merely another way of asking whether sample data represent the distribution of frequencies in the population described by H_0.

Creating the Statistical Hypotheses for Chi Square

Usually, we test the H_0 that there is no difference between the frequencies in the categories in the population, meaning that H_0 says there is no relationship in the population. For the handedness study, say that, for the moment, we ignore that there are more right-handers than left-handers in the world. Therefore, if there is no relationship in the population, then there is no difference between the frequencies of left- and right-handers. Thus, our H_0 model is that the frequencies of left-handed and right-handed geniuses in the population are equal. There is no conventional way to write the hypothesis in symbols, so simply write

H_0: all frequencies in the population are equal

This implies that if the observed frequencies (f_o) in the sample are not equal, it's because of sampling error.

The alternative hypothesis always implies that the study did demonstrate the predicted relationship, so here,

H_a: not all frequencies in the population are equal

H_a implies that the observed frequencies represent different frequencies of left- and right-handers in the population of geniuses.

Note: the one-way χ^2 tests only two-tailed hypotheses.

Computing the Expected Frequencies

To compute the χ^2 statistic, we translate the H_0 model into the expected frequency for each category. The **expected frequency** is the frequency we would find in a category if the sample data perfectly represented the distribution of frequencies in the population described by the null hypothesis. The symbol for an expected frequency is f_e.

In our study, H_0 is that the frequencies of left- and right-handers are equal. If the sample perfectly represents this, then out of our 50 participants, 25 should be right-handed and 25 should be left-handed. Thus, the expected frequency in each category is $f_e = 25$.

For future reference, notice that f_e is actually based on a probability. If the frequencies in the population are equal, then the probability of someone's being left-handed equals the probability of someone's being right-handed. With only two possible categories, the probability of being in a category is .5. Recall that probability is the same as relative frequency, so we expect .5 of all geniuses to be left-handed and .5 of all geniuses to be right-handed. Therefore, out of the 50 geniuses in our study, we expect to have a frequency of (.5)(50), or 25, in each category. *Thus, the expected frequency in a category is equal to the probability of being in that category multiplied times the N of the study.*

Whenever H_0 is that the frequencies in the categories are equal, the f_e will be the same in all categories, and there's a shortcut for computing it.

THE COMPUTATIONAL FORMULA FOR EACH EXPECTED FREQUENCY WHEN TESTING AN H_0 OF NO DIFFERENCE IS

$$f_e \text{ in each category} = \frac{N}{k}$$

Thus, in the handedness study, with an N of 50 and $k = 2$,

$$f_e \text{ in each category} = \frac{50}{2} = 25$$

Note: Sometimes f_e may contain a decimal. For example, if we included the third category of ambidextrous, then $k = 3$, and each f_e would be 16.67.

As in any statistical test, we must check that the study meets the assumptions of the test.

Assumptions of the One-Way Chi Square

The assumptions of the one-way χ^2 are

1. Participants are categorized along one variable having two or more categories, and the frequency in each category is counted.
2. Each participant can be in only one category (i.e., you cannot have repeated measures).
3. Category membership is *independent*: The fact that an individual is in one category does not influence the probability that another participant is in any other category.
4. The computations include the responses of *all* participants in the study (i.e., you would not count only the number of right-handers. In a different study, if you counted the number of people who agreed with some statement, you would also include a second category of those who disagreed).
5. So that the data meet certain theoretical rules, the f_e in any category should be at least 5.

Computing Chi Square

If the sample perfectly represents the situation where H_0 is true, then every f_o should equal its f_e. If they are not equal, H_0 says that the difference is due to sampling error. But, the greater the difference between the observed and expected frequency, the less likely it is that the difference is due to sampling error. Therefore, the greater the difference between f_o and f_e, the less likely it is that H_0 is true and that the sample represents an equal distribution of frequencies in the population.

The χ^2 is a way to measure the differences between f_o and f_e in all categories in a study. We compute an obtained χ^2, which we'll call χ^2_{obt}:

THE COMPUTATIONAL FORMULA FOR CHI SQUARE IS

$$\chi^2_{obt} = \Sigma\left(\frac{(f_o - f_e)^2}{f_e}\right)$$

Find the difference between f_o and f_e in each category, square that difference, and then divide it by the f_e for that category. After doing this for all categories, sum the quantities, and the answer is χ^2_{obt}. (*Note:* Because each difference is squared, χ^2 can never be a negative number.)

For the handedness study, we have these frequencies:

Handedness	
Left-handers	***Right-handers***
$f_o = 10$ $f_e = 25$	$f_o = 40$ $f_e = 25$

Filling in the formula gives

$$\chi^2_{\text{obt}} = \Sigma\left(\frac{(f_o - f_e)^2}{f_e}\right) = \left(\frac{(10 - 25)^2}{25}\right) + \left(\frac{(40 - 25)^2}{25}\right)$$

After subtracting,

$$\chi^2_{\text{obt}} = \left(\frac{(-15)^2}{25}\right) + \left(\frac{(15)^2}{25}\right)$$

Squaring then gives

$$\chi^2_{\text{obt}} = \left(\frac{225}{25}\right) + \left(\frac{225}{25}\right)$$

After dividing,

$$\chi^2_{\text{obt}} = 9 + 9$$

so $\chi^2_{\text{obt}} = 18.0$.

Interpreting Chi Squared

As always, we interpret this statistic by determining its location on the H_0 sampling distribution. Here, the H_0 sampling distribution contains all possible values of χ^2 that occur due to sampling error when H_0 is true. Thus, for the handedness study, the χ^2-distribution shows all possible values of χ^2 that occur when the frequency of membership in two categories are equal in the population. This distribution is shown in Figure 21.1.

Even though the χ^2-distribution is not at all normal, it is used in the same way as previous sampling distributions. When H_0 is true, more often than not each f_o equals its f_e, so their differences and χ^2 equal zero. However, sometimes, by chance, the observed frequencies differ from the expected frequencies, producing a χ^2 greater than zero. The

FIGURE 21.1 Sampling Distribution of χ^2 when H_0 Is True

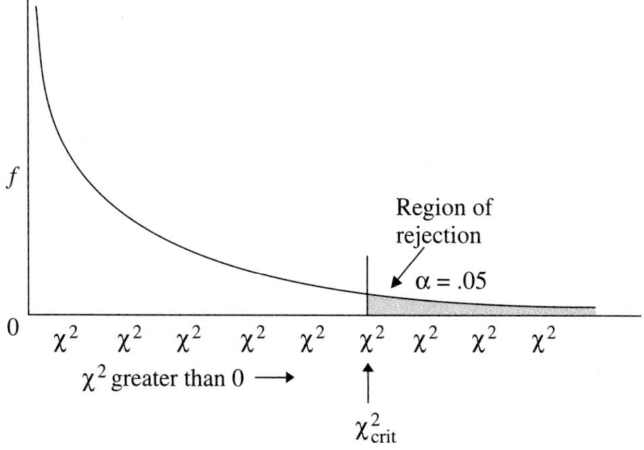

larger the value of χ^2, the larger the differences between the observed and expected frequencies and the less frequently such differences occur by chance. At some point, χ^2 is so large that we think something else must be causing the differences between each f_o and f_e: It is because the observed frequencies do *not* represent the H_0 model. Thus, if χ^2_{obt} is larger than the critical value, then it is in the region of rejection and is significant: The observed frequencies are unlikely to represent the distribution of frequencies in the population that is described by H_0.

With chi square we again have two-tailed hypotheses but one region of rejection. The symbol for the critical value of χ^2 is χ^2_{crit}. As with previous statistics, the χ^2-distribution changes shape as the degrees of freedom change, so to find the appropriate value of χ^2_{crit} we must first have the degrees of freedom.

> **In a one-way χ^2, the degrees of freedom equals $k - 1$, where k is the number of categories.**

Find the critical value of χ^2 in Table 8 in Appendix C, entitled "Critical Values of Chi Square." For the handedness study, $k = 2$, so $df = 1$, and with $\alpha = .05$, $\chi^2_{crit} = 3.84$. Our χ^2_{obt} of 18.0 is larger than the χ^2_{crit} of 3.84, so these results are significant. Thus, we reject the H_0 that each f_o represents an equal frequency in the population. We also accept the H_a that the sample represents frequencies in the population that are not equal. In fact, as in our samples, we would expect to find about 20% left-handers and 80% right-handers in the population of geniuses. We conclude there is evidence of a relationship between the categories of handedness and the frequency with which geniuses fall into each. Then, as usual, we interpret this relationship psychologically, attempting to explain what aspects of being left-handed and a genius are related (this is a *quasi-experiment*, however, so we cannot infer the cause of anything).

If χ^2_{obt} had not been significant, we would have failed to reject H_0 and would have no evidence—one way or the other—regarding how handedness is distributed among geniuses.

Other Uses of the Goodness of Fit Test

Instead of testing an H_0 that the frequencies in all categories are distributed equally, we can also test other H_0 models, which say that the frequencies are distributed in some other way. For example, we should not have ignored the fact that only about 10% of the general population is left-handed. The better test is to determine whether the distribution of handedness among our geniuses fits this distribution of handedness in the general population. Now we have H_0: 10% left-handed, 90% right-handed. For simplicity, we can write the alternative as H_a: not H_0—our data represent a population of geniuses that is not 10% left-handed and 90% right-handed.

As usual, we compute each f_e based on H_0. If H_0 is true and the sample perfectly represents it, then left-handed geniuses should occur 10% of the time. For our 50 geniuses, 10% is 5, so for left-handers $f_e = 5$. Right-handed geniuses should occur 90% of the time, and 90% of 50 is 45, so here, $f_e = 45$. As usual, according to H_0, any differences between the observed and expected frequencies are due to sampling error in representing this model.

We should *not* perform two χ^2 procedures on the same data, but for the sake of illustration, we'll compare the previous handedness data and our new expected frequencies. We have

Handedness	
Left-handers	***Right-handers***
$f_o = 10$ $f_e = 5$	$f_o = 40$ $f_e = 45$

$$k = 2$$
$$\text{Total } f_o = 50$$

Compute χ^2 using the same formula as in the previous section. Thus,

$$\chi^2_{obt} = \Sigma\left(\frac{(f_o - f_e)^2}{f_e}\right) = \left(\frac{(10 - 5)^2}{5}\right) + \left(\frac{(40 - 45)^2}{45}\right)$$

(Notice there is a different value of f_e in each fraction.) Working through the formula gives

$$\chi^2_{obt} = 5.0 + .56$$

so, $\chi^2_{obt} = 5.56$.

With $\alpha = .05$ and $k = 2$, the critical value of χ^2 for $df = 1$ is again 3.84. Because the χ^2_{obt} of 5.56 is larger than χ^2_{crit}, we reject H_0 and conclude that the observed frequencies are significantly different from what we would expect if handedness in the population of geniuses was distributed as it is in the general population. Instead, our best guess is that the population of geniuses would be distributed as in our sample data, with 20% left-handers and 80% right-handers.

Graphing the Results in a One-Way Chi Square

As usual, a graph is a useful way to summarize data, especially if there are more than two categories. Label the Y axis with the frequencies and the X axis with the categories, and then plot the f_o in each category. Figure 21.2 shows the results of the handedness study. Handedness is a nominal variable, and recall that when the X variable is a nominal variable, we create a *bar graph*.

Unlike ANOVA, the one-way chi square usually is not followed by post hoc comparisons. A significant χ^2_{obt} indicates that *all* frequencies are distributed in a manner that is significantly different from that described by H_0. Thus, we use the observed frequency in each category to estimate the frequencies that would be found in the population. Also, there is no measure of effect size.

FIGURE 21.2 Frequencies of Left- and Right-Handed Geniuses

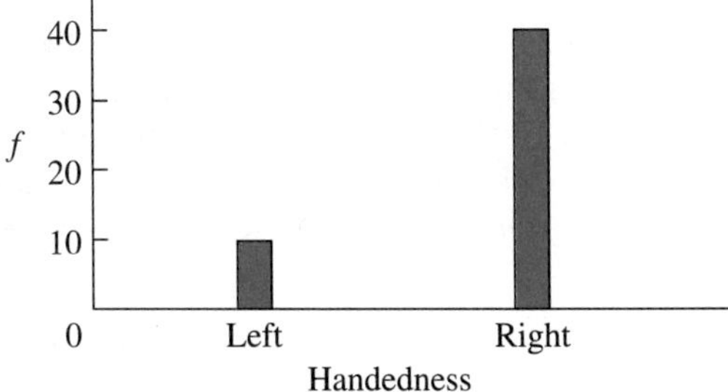

THE TWO-WAY CHI SQUARE: THE TEST OF INDEPENDENCE

The **two-way chi square procedure** is used when we count the frequencies with which participants belong to the categories of *two* variables. This is similar to the two-way factorial design we saw in previous chapters. Depending on the number of categories in each variable, the design can be a 2 × 2, a 2 × 3, a 4 × 3, and so on. The procedure for computing χ^2 is the same regardless of the design.

The assumptions of the two-way chi square are the same as for the one-way chi square. (If an f_e is less than 5, do not compute χ^2. Instead, perform Fisher's exact test.[1])

Logic of the Two-Way Chi Square

Here is a study that calls for a two-way chi square: At one time, psychologists claimed there were two personality types: Type A and Type B. The Type A person tends to be a very pressured, hostile individual who never seems to have enough time. The Type B person tends not to be so time-pressured, being more relaxed and mellow. A controversy developed over whether people with Type A personalities are less healthy, especially when it comes to the big one—having heart attacks. Say that we enter this controversy by randomly selecting a sample of 80 people. Using the appropriate test, we determine how many are Type A and how many Type B. We then count the frequency with which Type A and Type B people have had heart attacks. We must also count the frequency with which Type A and Type B people have *not* had heart attacks (see item 4 in "Assumptions of the One-Way Chi Square"). Therefore, we have two categorical variables: Personality type (A or B) and health (heart attack or no heart attack). We can diagram this study as

		Personality type	
		Type A	*Type B*
Health	*Heart attack*	f_o	f_o
	No heart attack	f_o	f_o

Although this looks like a two-way ANOVA, it is not analyzed like one. Instead of testing for main effects and an interaction, *the two-way χ^2 procedure tests only what is essentially the interaction*. That is, it tests whether the distribution of the frequencies in the categories of one variable *depends* on which category of the other variable we examine. Because of this, the two-way χ^2 is called a **test of independence**: It determines whether the frequency of participants falling into a particular category of one variable is independent of the frequency of their falling into a particular category of the other variable. Thus, our study will test whether the frequencies for having or not having a heart attack are independent of the frequencies for being Type A or Type B. To

[1]Described in S. Siegel and N. J. Castellan (1988), *Nonparametric Statistics for the Behavioral Sciences*, 2nd ed. (New York: McGraw Hill).

TABLE 21.1 An Example of Observed Frequencies when Personality Type and Heart Attacks Are Independent of Each Other

		Personality type	
		Type A	*Type B*
Health	*Heart attack*	$f_o = 20$	$f_o = 20$
	No heart attack	$f_o = 20$	$f_o = 20$

understand "independence," Table 21.1 shows an ideal example of data when two variables are independent. Here, the frequency of having or not having a heart attack does not depend on the frequency of being Type A or Type B or vice versa. Another way to view the two-way χ^2 is as a test of whether a correlation exists between the variables. When variables are independent, there is no correlation. Then, using the categories from one variable is no help in predicting the frequencies for the other variable. In Table 21.1, knowing if people are Type A or Type B does not help to predict how frequently they have or do not have a heart attack (and vice versa).

On the other hand, Table 21.2 shows an ideal example of data when two variables are not independent, but are dependent. Here, the frequency of a heart attack or no heart attack *depends* on personality type. Also, a correlation exists, because whether people are Type A or Type B is a very good predictor of whether they have or have not had a heart attack (and vice versa).

The null hypothesis always says that there is zero correlation in the population, so the null hypothesis in the two-way χ^2 always says that the variables are *independent* in the population. If, in the sample data, the variables appear to be dependent and correlated, H_0 says that this is due to sampling error. The alternative hypothesis is that the variables are dependent (correlated).

Computing the Expected Frequencies in the Two-Way Chi Square

As usual, the expected frequencies are based on the model described by H_0, so here we compute the f_e in each category based on the idea that the variables are independent. To see how to do this, say that the heart attack study produced the data in Table 21.3.

TABLE 21.2 An Example of Observed Frequencies when Personality Type and Heart Attacks Are Dependent on Each Other

		Personality type	
		Type A	*Type B*
Health	*Heart attack*	$f_o = 40$	$f_o = 0$
	No heart attack	$f_o = 0$	$f_o = 40$

TABLE 21.3 Frequencies as a Function of Personality Type and Participant's Health

		Personality type		
		Type A	*Type B*	
Health	*Heart attack*	$f_o = 25$	$f_o = 10$	Row total = 35
	No heart attack	$f_o = 5$	$f_o = 40$	Row total = 45
		Column total = 30	Column total = 50	Total = 80 $N = 80$

After recording the f_o for each cell, first compute the total of the observed frequencies in each column and in each row. Also, compute the total of all frequencies, which equals N. (As a check, the sum of the row totals should equal the sum of the column totals, which equals N.)

Now, compute the expected frequency in each cell. Here is the logic that we will use. Let's begin with the cell labeled Heart attack and Type A. As with the one-way χ^2, an f_e is based on the probability of falling into the category when H_0 is true. Therefore, we'll determine the probability of someone having a heart attack and being Type A, if these characteristics are independent. Independent of everything else, 35 people had a heart attack (the row total) out of our 80 participants. Thus, the probability of a heart attack is 35/80, or .438. Likewise, the probability of someone being Type A is 30 (the column total) out of 80, or 30/80, which is .375. The probability of two independent events occurring together equals their respective probabilities multiplied together. (This "multiplication rule" is discussed in Appendix B.4.) Multiplying .438 times .375 gives .164. Thus, the probability of someone having a heart attack and being Type A is .164, if the two variables are independent. Because probability is also relative frequency, out of our 80 participants, we expect .164 times 80, or 13.125 people to be in this cell if the variables are independent. Therefore, the expected frequency for this cell is $f_e = 13.125$.

Luckily, there is a shortcut formula for calculating each f_e. Above, we multiplied 35/80 times 30/80 and then multiplied the answer times 80. The 35 is the total f_o of the *row* that contains the cell, 30 is the total f_o of the *column* that contains the cell, and 80 is the total N of the study. Using these components, we construct a formula.

THE COMPUTATIONAL FORMULA FOR COMPUTING THE EXPECTED FREQUENCY IN A CELL OF A TWO-WAY CHI SQUARE IS

$$f_e = \frac{(\text{Cell's row total } f_o)(\text{Cell's column total } f_o)}{N}$$

For each cell, multiply the total observed frequencies for the row containing the cell times the total observed frequencies for the column containing the cell, and then divide by the N of the study.

Table 21.4 shows the f_e for each cell in our study. To check your work, confirm that the sum of the f_es in each column or row equals the column or row total.

If H_0 is true and the variables are independent, then, except for some sampling error, each observed frequency should equal each corresponding expected frequency. The larger the difference between f_o and f_e, however, the less likely it is that the data represent variables that are independent. And, the larger the difference between each f_o and f_e, the larger the value of χ^2_{obt}.

Computing the Two-Way Chi Square

Compute the two-way χ^2_{obt} using the same formula used in the one-way design, which is

$$\chi^2_{obt} = \Sigma\left(\frac{(f_o - f_e)^2}{f_e}\right)$$

With the data in Table 21.4, we have

$$\chi^2_{obt} = \left(\frac{(25 - 13.125)^2}{13.125}\right) + \left(\frac{(10 - 21.875)^2}{21.875}\right) + \left(\frac{(5 - 16.875)^2}{16.875}\right) + \left(\frac{(40 - 28.125)^2}{28.125}\right)$$

In the numerator of each fraction is the observed frequency minus the expected frequency for a cell, and in the denominator is the expected frequency for that cell. Solving each fraction gives

$$\chi^2_{obt} = 10.74 + 6.45 + 8.36 + 5.01$$

so $\chi^2_{obt} = 30.56$.

To evaluate χ^2_{obt}, compare it to the appropriate χ^2_{crit}. First, determine the degrees of freedom.

> **The degrees of freedom in a two-way chi square is**
> ***df* = (Number of rows − 1)(Number of columns − 1)**

TABLE 21.4 Diagram Containing f_o and f_e for Each Cell

Each f_e equals the row total times the column total, divided by N.

		Personality type		
		Type A	***Type B***	
Participant's health	***Heart attack***	$f_o = 25$ $f_e = 13.125$ (35)(30)/80	$f_o = 10$ $f_e = 21.875$ (35)(50)/80	Row total = 35
	No heart attack	$f_o = 5$ $f_e = 16.875$ (45)(30)/80	$f_o = 40$ $f_e = 28.125$ (45)(50)/80	Row total = 45
		Column total = 30	Column total = 50	Total = 80

For our study, *df* is (2 − 1)(2 − 1), or 1. Again, find the critical value of χ^2 in Table 8 in Appendix C. At $\alpha = .05$ and $df = 1$, χ^2_{crit} is 3.84.

Our χ^2_{obt} of 30.56 is larger than χ^2_{crit}, so the obtained χ^2 is significant. When the two-way χ^2 is significant, the observed frequencies are unlikely to be representing frequencies from variables that are independent. Therefore, we reject H_0 that the variables are independent and accept the alternative hypothesis: We are confident that the sample represents frequencies from two variables that are dependent in the population. In other words, we conclude that there is a significant correlation such that the frequency of having or not having a heart attack depends on the frequency of being Type A or Type B (and vice versa).

If χ^2_{obt} had not been larger than the critical value, we would not have rejected H_0. Then, we could not say whether these variables are independent or not.

> ***REMEMBER*** A significant two-way χ^2 indicates that the sample data are likely to represent two variables that are dependent (or correlated) in the population.

Additional Procedures in the Two-Way Chi Square

As usual, when we find a significant two-way χ^2_{obt}, we then want to understand the relationship in the data and interpret it psychologically. Therefore, as always, graph the data and describe the strength of the relationship.

Graphing the two-way Chi Square We graph the data in a two-way chi square in the same way that we graphed a two-way interaction in previous chapters, except that here we create a bar graph. Observed frequency is plotted along the *Y* axis, and one of the categorical variables is plotted along the *X* axis. The other categorical variable is indicated in the body of the graph. Figure 21.3 shows a bar graph for the heart attack study. Mentally draw one line connecting the tops of the solid bars and one connecting the tops of the open bars—if the lines are not parallel, an interaction effect is indicated. Then, interpret it accordingly: Whether there is a high or low frequency for each personality type depends on whether participants have or have not had a heart attack; or, whether there is a high or low frequency of heart attacks depends on whether we're talking about Type A or Type B personalities.

FIGURE 21.3 Frequency of Heart Attacks and Personality Type

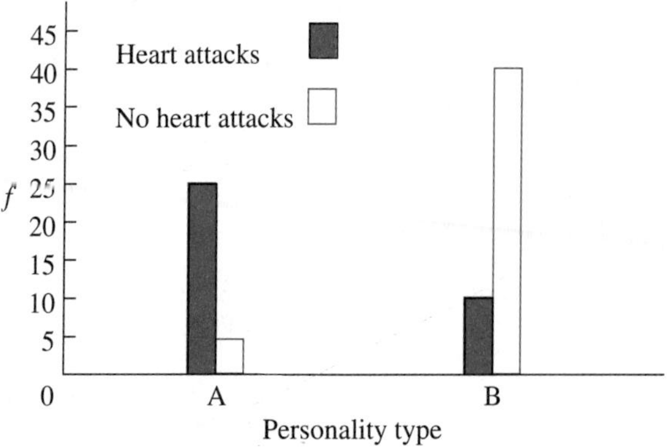

Describing the Relationship in a Two-Way chi square A significant two-way chi square indicates that there is a significant correlation between the two variables. Therefore, to describe the relationship, first think "correlation coefficient."

In a 2×2 chi square (that is significant), describe the strength of the relationship by computing a new correlation coefficient known as the **phi coefficient**. The symbol for the phi coefficient is ϕ and its value can be between 0 and $+1$. Think of phi as comparing our data to the ideal situations when the variables are or are not perfectly dependent. A value of 0 would indicate that the data are independent, producing a pattern such as back in Table 21.1. The larger the value of phi, however, the closer the data come to fitting an ideal pattern of dependent data, such as in Table 21.2.

THE COMPUTATIONAL FORMULA FOR THE PHI COEFFICIENT IS

$$\phi = \sqrt{\frac{\chi^2_{\text{obt}}}{N}}$$

N equals the total number of participants in the study.

For the heart attack study, χ^2_{obt} was 30.56 and N was 80, so ϕ is

$$\phi = \sqrt{\frac{\chi^2_{\text{obt}}}{N}} = \sqrt{\frac{30.56}{80}} = \sqrt{.382} = .62$$

Thus, on a scale of 0 to $+1$, where $+1$ indicates that the variables are perfectly dependent, we found a correlation of .62 between the frequency of heart attacks and the frequency of personality types.

But, remember that the best way to describe a relationship is to square the correlation coefficient, computing the proportion of variance accounted for. If we did not take the square root in the above formula, we would have ϕ^2 (phi squared). This is analogous to r^2 or η^2, indicating how much more accurately we can predict scores by using the relationship. Above, $\phi^2 = .38$, so we are 38% more accurate in predicting the frequency of heart attacks/no heart attacks when we know personality type (or vice versa).

In a significant two-way chi square that is *not* a 2×2 design, do *not* compute the phi coefficient. Instead, compute the **contingency coefficient**, symbolized by C.

THE COMPUTATIONAL FORMULA FOR THE CONTINGENCY COEFFICIENT IS

$$C = \sqrt{\frac{\chi^2_{\text{obt}}}{N + \chi^2_{\text{obt}}}}$$

N is the number of participants in the study. Interpret C the same way you interpret ϕ. Likewise, C^2 is analogous to ϕ^2.

REMEMBER When a two-way χ^2 is significant, describe the strength of the correlation (dependency) by computing ϕ or C.

NONPARAMETRIC PROCEDURES FOR RANKED DATA

In addition to chi square, there is one other category of nonparametric procedures, those used with rank-ordered (ordinal) scores. We obtain ranked scores in a study for one of two reasons. First, sometimes participants' scores on the dependent variable are initially measured using ranked scores (where participants are assigned a score of 1st, 2nd, etc.). Second, sometimes the dependent variable is initially measured using interval or ratio scores, but they violate the assumptions of parametric procedures by not being normally distributed or not having homogeneous variance. Therefore, we transform the scores by assigning them ranks: The highest raw score is ranked 1, the next highest score is ranked 2, and so on. Either way, we then compute one of the following nonparametric inferential statistics to determine whether there are significant differences in the ranked scores for the different conditions of the independent variable.

The Logic of Nonparametric Procedures for Ranked Data

Instead of computing the mean of each condition in the experiment, with nonparametric procedures we add the ranked scores in each condition and then examine these sums of ranks. The symbol for a sum of ranks is ΣR. (First, always handle tied ranks as described in Chapter 10.) Then, we compare the observed sum of ranks to an expected sum of ranks. To see the logic of this, say we have ranked the performance of a small college class, and then separated the participants into males and females as follows:

Female	*Male*
1	2
4	3
5	6
8	7
$\Sigma R = 18$	$\Sigma R = 18$

First, look at the individual scores: There is no difference between the groups, with each group containing both high and low ranks. Now, look at the sum of the ranks for each group: When the individual ranks are distributed equally between the groups, the sums of ranks are equal (here, each ΣR is 18). Because there is no difference between the samples, they represent the same population, containing both low ranks and high ranks. The null hypothesis always states that the populations are the same, so the fact that each ΣR is 18 supports the H_0 that we have the same population of ranks for each condition. Turning this around, we could have first determined the *expected sum of ranks* in each condition when H_0 is true (we would expect 18 here). Then, if the actual *observed sum of ranks* equals the expected, we would have evidence that H_0 is true.

But, say the data had turned out differently, as below:

Female	*Male*
1	5
2	6
3	7
4	8
$\Sigma R = 10$	$\Sigma R = 26$

The female group contains all of the low ranks, and the male group contains all of the high ranks. Because these samples are different, they may represent two different populations. The alternative hypothesis is always that the populations are different, so here H_a says that one population contains predominantly low ranks and the other contains predominantly high ranks. Notice that when the data support H_a, the observed sum of ranks in each condition is different from the expected sum of ranks: Here, each ΣR is not equal to 18.

Thus, the observed sum of ranks in each condition should equal the expected sum if H_0 is true, and each observed sum will *not* equal the expected sum if H_a is true. But, as usual, there is another reason that each observed sum does not equal the expected sum: It may be that H_0 is true, but the data reflect sampling error in representing this. However, the larger the difference between the expected and observed sum of ranks, the less likely it is that this difference is due to sampling error, and the more likely it is that each condition represents a different distribution of ranks in the population.

Each of the following nonparametric procedures involves a statistic that measures the difference between the expected and the observed sum of ranks. If the statistic is a certain size, then we reject H_0 and accept H_a: We are confident that the reason the observed sum of ranks is different from the expected sum of ranks is that the conditions represent different populations of ranks. And if the ranks reflect underlying interval or ratio scores, a significant difference in ranks indicates that the conditions also represent different populations of interval/ratio scores as well.

Choosing a Nonparametric Procedure

The parametric *t*-tests and one-way ANOVAs found in previous chapters each have a corresponding nonparametric version used for ranked data. Your first task is to know which nonparametric procedure to choose for the type of research design you are testing. The nonparametric versions of the parametric procedures we have previously discussed are presented in Table 21.5.

The following sections briefly describe when and how each procedure is applied. Their very straightforward calculations, however, are presented in Appendix B.8.

TABLE 21.5 Parametric Procedures and Their Nonparametric Counterparts

Type of design	*Parametric test*	*Nonparametric test*
Two independent samples	Independent-samples *t*-test	Mann-Whitney *U* or Rank Sums test
Two dependent samples	Dependent-samples *t*-test	Wilcoxon *T*-test
Three or more independent samples	Between-subjects ANOVA (Post hoc test: protected *t*-test)	Kruskal-Wallis *H* test (Post hoc test: Rank Sums test)
Three or more dependent samples	Within-subjects ANOVA (Post hoc test: Tukey's *HSD*)	Friedman χ^2 test (Post hoc test: Nemenyi's test)

Test for Two Independent Samples: The Mann-Whitney *U* Test and the Rank Sums Test

There are two nonparametric procedures that are analogous to the *t*-test for two independent samples: The Mann-Whitney *U* test and the Rank Sums test. Both are used to test for significant differences between ranked scores measured under two between-subjects conditions of an independent variable. Which test to use depends on the *n* in each condition.

The Mann-Whitney *U* test The **Mann-Whitney *U* test** is used when the *n* in each condition is equal to or less than 20 and you have two independent samples of ranks. For example, say we measure the reaction times of two groups of people to different symbols. For one group, the symbols are printed in black ink, and for the other, they are printed in red ink. We wish to know whether there is a significant difference between reaction times for each colored symbol. With two independent samples, this looks like the typical *t*-test situation. However, a raw score population of reaction times tends to be highly positively skewed, so we cannot perform the *t*-test. Instead, we transform the reaction-time scores to ranked scores and compute the Mann-Whitney *U*.

Say that the *n* in each condition is 5 (but we can perform this procedure when the *n*s are not equal). Table 21.6 gives the reaction times (measured in milliseconds) and their corresponding ranks for this study. As shown, first, we assign the rank of 1 to the lowest score in the experiment, regardless of which group it is in. We assign the rank of 2 to the second lowest score in the experiment, and so on. Then, we compute ΣR for each group. The sums of ranks (17 and 38, respectively) are different from each other, so it appears there is a different sample of ranks in each condition, representing a different population of ranks.

To test whether this is a significant difference, we calculate U_{obt}, as described in Appendix B.8.1. Then, we compare U_{obt} to U_{crit}, which is found in Table 9 of Appendix C, entitled "Critical Values of the Mann-Whitney *U*." We can perform either a one-tailed or two-tailed test.

Watch out when comparing U_{obt} to U_{crit}: The U_{obt} is significant if it is *equal to or less than* U_{crit}. Think of U_{obt} as a transformation in which a larger difference between the ΣR of the conditions results in a *smaller* U_{obt}. If U_{obt} is small enough, then the difference is so large that H_0 is unlikely to be true, and instead, it is likely that each group represents a different population of ranks. In the example, a significant U_{obt} will indicate that, as in Table 21.6, the red-symbol condition produces lower-ranked scores (e.g, 1, 2, and 3) than the black-symbol condition. Further, if the conditions differ significantly in terms of the ranked scores, then they also differ significantly in terms of the original reaction-time scores. Thus, here, we would conclude that the red-symbol condition produced significantly faster reaction times. Then, as usual, we interpret the relationship psychologically. (And, with $\alpha = .05$, the probability that we've made a Type I error is $p < .05$.) If the results are not significant, we would have no evidence of a relationship between symbol color and speed, either in terms of the ranked scores or the original reaction times. (And we'd worry whether we had sufficient power or had made a Type II error.)

Recall that we compute the *effect size* of the independent variable when results are significant. The only way to do this here is to ignore the rule about *n* and reanalyze the data using the following Rank Sums test.

TABLE 21.6 Example Ranked Data from Two Independent Samples

Red symbols		*Black symbols*	
Reaction time	*Ranked score*	*Reaction time*	*Ranked score*
540	2	760	7
480	1	890	8
600	5	1105	10
590	3	595	4
605	6	940	9
	$\Sigma R = 17$		$\Sigma R = 38$

The rank sums test The **rank sums test** is used to test two independent samples of ranks when the n in either condition is *greater* than 20. As an example, however, we'll violate this rule and use the previous ranked scores from the reaction-time study.

Again, as shown back in Table 21.6, we rank-order all scores in the experiment. Then, the calculations are described in Part 8.2 of Appendix B. In these calculations, we select one condition and essentially perform the z-test discussed in Chapter 13. However, instead of comparing the difference between $\overline{X}$ and μ, we compare the difference between the observed and expected sums of ranks. A larger difference produces a larger z_{obt}. Then, we obtain either the one-tailed or two-tailed z_{crit} from the z-tables (Table 1 in Appendix C.) If z_{obt} is larger than the corresponding z_{crit}, then H_0 is unlikely to be true for that condition. Because the size of ΣR in one condition is inversely related to ΣR in the other condition, if sampling error is unlikely to produce the ranks in one condition, it is unlikely to produce them in the other. Therefore, a significant z_{obt} indicates a significant difference between the two conditions. If the ranked scores differ significantly, then we conclude that the original reaction-time scores also differ significantly ($p < .05$).

If z_{obt} is significant, describe the effect size using the formula in Appendix B.8.5 to compute eta squared. With only two conditions, eta squared is analogous to r^2_{pb}, indicating the proportion of variance in ranked scores accounted for by the relationship with the independent variable. It is also approximately the proportion of the variance in the underlying raw (reaction-time) scores that is accounted for.

> ***REMEMBER*** The Mann-Whitney U and the rank sums test are the nonparametric versions of the independent-samples t-test.

The Wilcoxon *T*-Test for Two Dependent Samples

The **Wilcoxon *T*-test** is analogous to the dependent-samples t-test for ranked data. Recall that dependent samples are produced by matched samples or by repeated measures. For example, say we perform a study similar to the previous reaction-time study, but this time we measure the reaction times of the *same* participants to both the red and black symbols. Table 21.7 gives the data we might obtain.

TABLE 21.7 Example Data for the Wilcoxon Test for Two Dependent Samples

Participant	*Reaction time to red symbols*	*Reaction time to black symbols*	*Difference, D*	*Ranked scores*	*R−*	*R+*
1	540	760	−220	6	6	
2	580	710	−130	4	4	
3	600	1105	−505	9	9	
4	680	880	−200	5	5	
5	430	500	−70	3	3	
6	740	990	−250	7	7	
7	600	1050	−450	8	8	
8	690	640	+50	2		2
9	605	595	+10	1		1
10	520	520	0			
					$\Sigma R = 42$	$\Sigma R = 3$

Notice that this begins like the dependent-samples t-test back in Chapter 16: We find the difference between each pair of reaction-time scores, so that we have one sample of difference scores. Here, we've subtracted each reaction time to the black symbol from the reaction time to the red symbol. However, we then assign a rank based on the size of the difference.

The steps for calculating the Wilcoxon T are presented in Part 8.3 of Appendix B. Essentially, we separate out the ranked scores for positive differences (labeled $R+$) from those for negative differences (labeled $R-$). The H_0 says that there should be the same number of positive and negative differences, as well as the same number of large and small differences, so the ΣR for positive differences should equal the ΣR for negative differences. However, if the conditions differ, then there will be a preponderance of only large negative differences (as in our data), or large positive differences, and then the two sums of ranks are not equal. (Here, we have $\Sigma R = 42$ and 3, respectively.)

To test whether this difference is significant, we compute T_{obt} (notice the uppercase T.) We find the one- or two-tailed T_{crit} in Table 10 of Appendix C, entitled "Critical Values of the Wilcoxon T." Again, **watch out:** The T_{obt} is significant if it is *equal to or less than* T_{crit}. If so, then, as in previous procedures, we conclude that each condition represents a different distribution of ranks and thus a different population of reaction-time scores ($p < .05$).

There is no way to compute eta squared for this design.

> *REMEMBER* The Wilcoxon T is the nonparametric version of the dependent-samples t-test.

The Kruskal-Wallis *H* Test

The **Kruskal-Wallis *H* test** is analogous to a one-way between-subjects ANOVA for ranked data. It assumes that the study involves one independent variable with at least three conditions, each of which involves an independent sample with at least 5 participants per condition.

Here's a new example. Say we examine the relationship between a golfer's height (using the conditions of short, medium, and tall) and how far he or she hits the ball (measured in meters). However, say that based on the F_{max} test (from Chapter 19), we cannot assume that the distance scores have homogeneous variance, so we cannot use the parametric ANOVA. Instead, we rank the distance scores and perform the Kruskal-Wallis *H*-test on these ranks, as shown in Table 21.8.

The steps for calculating the Kruskal-Wallis *H* are presented in Part 8.4 of Appendix B. Essentially, we first rank the scores in the experiment (assigning 1 to the lowest score, 2 to the second lowest score, and so on). Then, we calculate the sum of the ranks (ΣR) in each condition. The H_0 is that all conditions represent the same population of ranks, so the three sums should be equal. Calculating H_{obt} indicates how much the sums differ. The more that they differ, the larger the H_{obt}, and the less likely that H_0 is true. The *H* statistic produces the same sampling distribution as χ^2, so we find H_{crit} in the χ^2 tables (Table 8 in Appendix C). If H_{obt} is larger than H_{crit}, then H_{obt} is significant, indicating that two or more of the conditions differ significantly. Then, as with ANOVA, we perform post hoc comparisons to determine which specific conditions differ significantly. These comparisons are performed using the previous rank sums test. This is analogous to Fisher's protected *t*-test (discussed in Chapter 17), and it is used regardless of the *n* in each group. Here, we would perform three rank sums tests, comparing short to medium, short to tall, and medium to tall. Any significant rank sums test indicates that the two conditions of ranks—as well as their underlying distance scores—differ significantly.

> ***REMEMBER*** The Kruskal-Wallis *H* is the equivalent of the one-way between-subjects ANOVA for ranked scores. The post hoc procedure is the *rank sums test*.

Finally, for a significant *H*, we describe the effect size by calculating a version of eta squared (see Appendix B.8.4).

The Friedman χ^2 Test

The **Friedman χ^2 test** is analogous to a one-way within-subjects ANOVA for ranks. It assumes that the study involves one factor, with either a matched-groups or a

TABLE 21.8 Example Data for the Kruskal-Wallis *H*-Test

		Height			
Short		*Medium*		*Tall*	
Score	*Rank*	*Score*	*Rank*	*Score*	*Rank*
10	2	24	3	68	14
28	6	27	5	71	15
26	4	35	7	57	10
39	8	44	9	60	12
6	1	58	11	62	13
	$\Sigma R_1 = 21$		$\Sigma R_2 = 35$		$\Sigma R_3 = 64$

repeated-measures design with *three* or more conditions. With only three levels of the factor, there must be at least 10 scores per condition. With only four levels, there must be at least five scores per condition.

As an example, consider a study in which the initial scores are already ranked. The three levels of the independent variable are the teaching styles of Dr. Highman, Dr. Shyman, and Dr. Whyman. The same group of students who have taken courses from all three instructors rank-order their effectiveness, producing the data in Table 21.9.

If the scores are not already ranks, we first assign the rank of 1 to the lowest score received by participant 1, assign the rank of 2 to the second lowest score received by participant 1, and so on. Repeat the process for each participant. Then, compute the sum of the ranks in each condition. The H_0 is that all conditions represent the same population of ranks, so the three sums should be equal. To determine how much the sums differ, we compute a version of chi square (instead of comparing the observed and expected frequency in each group, this compares the observed and expected sums of ranks). The more that they differ, the larger the χ^2, and the less likely that H_0 is true. We compare χ^2_{obt} to χ^2_{crit} (from Table 8 in Appendix C). If χ^2_{obt} is larger than χ^2_{crit}, the results are significant, and as with previous ANOVAs, at least two of the conditions represent different populations.

When the Friedman χ^2 is significant, perform post hoc comparisons using **Nemenyi's procedure**. This procedure is analogous to Tukey's *HSD* test (in Chapter 17.) In it, we compute one *critical difference*. Then, we find the mean of the ranks in each condition, and then find the difference between each pair of means. In the example, we'll find the difference between the mean ranks for Highman, Shyman, and Whyman. Any two conditions that differ by more than the critical difference are significantly different.

> ***REMEMBER*** The Friedman χ^2 is the equivalent of the one-way within-subjects ANOVA for ranked scores. The post hoc procedure is called *Nemenyi's procedure*.

We can also describe the effect size by calculating a version of eta squared.

TABLE 21.9 Example Data for the Friedman Test

	Rankings for three instructors		
Participant	*Dr. Highman*	*Dr. Shyman*	*Dr. Whyman*
1	1	2	3
2	1	3	2
3	1	2	3
4	1	3	2
5	2	1	3
6	1	3	2
7	1	2	3
8	1	3	2
9	1	3	2
10	2	1	3
$N = 10$	$\Sigma R_1 = 12$	$\Sigma R_2 = 23$	$\Sigma R_3 = 25$

APA FORMAT FOR STATISTICAL NOTATION

In the example of a one-way χ^2, we calculated an obtained value that was significant. In a published report, this result would be reported as $\chi^2(1, N = 50) = 18.0, p < .05$. Notice that, in addition to the *df* in parentheses, the total *N* of the study is also included. The results from the two-way χ^2, the Kruskal-Wallis *H*, and the Friedman χ^2 are reported in the same way. Other statistics in this chapter are reported as in previous chapters.

PUTTING IT ALL TOGETHER

Congratulations. You are now familiar with the basic statistical and research procedures used in psychology and other behavioral sciences. Even if you someday go to graduate school, you'll find that there is little in the way of basics for you to learn.

CHAPTER SUMMARY

1. *Nonparametric procedures* are used when data do not meet the assumptions of parametric procedures.
2. *Chi square* (χ^2) is used when the data are the frequencies with which participants fall into different categories.
3. The *one-way* χ^2 (or *goodness of fit test*) is used when categorizing participants along one variable. A significant χ^2_{obt} indicates that the observed frequencies are unlikely to represent the distribution of frequencies in the population described by H_0.
4. The *two-way* χ^2 (or *test of independence*) is used when simultaneously categorizing participants along two variables. The H_0 is that the variables are independent (not correlated). A significant χ^2 indicates that the data are unlikely to represent variables that are independent in the population, so the two variables are dependent, or correlated.
5. In a significant 2×2 χ^2, describe the relationship with the *phi correlation coefficient* (ϕ). In a significant two-way χ^2 that is not 2×2, describe the relationship using the *contingency coefficient* (*C*). The larger these coefficients are, the closer the variables are to being perfectly dependent or correlated. Squaring ϕ or *C* gives the proportion of variance accounted for, indicating how much more accurately the frequencies of category membership on one variable can be predicted by knowing participants' category membership on the other variable.
6. The two nonparametric versions of the independent-samples *t*-test for ranks are the *Mann-Whitney U test* (performed when the *n* in each condition is less than 20), and the *rank sums test* (performed when the *n* in either condition is greater than 20).
7. The *Wilcoxon T-test* is the nonparametric equivalent of the dependent-samples *t*-test for ranks.

8. The *Kruskal-Wallis H test* is the nonparametric equivalent of the one-way between-subjects ANOVA for ranks. The rank sums test is used as the post hoc test to determine which conditions differ.

9. The *Friedman χ^2 test* is the nonparametric equivalent of the one-way, within-subjects ANOVA for ranks. *Nemenyi's procedure* is the post hoc test to determine which conditions differ.

10. *Eta squared* describes the relationship found in experiments involving ranked data.

KEY TERMS (with page references)

f_o f_e χ^2_{obt} χ^2_{crit} ϕ C
chi square procedure (589)
contingency coefficient (601)
expected frequency (591)
Friedman χ^2 test (607)
goodness of fit test (590)
Kruskal-Wallis H test (606)
Mann-Whitney U test (604)
Nemenyi's procedure (608)
nonparametric statistics (588)
observed frequency (590)
one-way chi square (589)
phi coefficient (601)
rank sums test (605)
test of independence (596)
two-way chi square procedure (596)
Wilcoxon T-test (605)

REVIEW QUESTIONS

(Answers for odd-numbered questions and problems are provided in Appendix D.)

1. What do all nonparametric procedures have in common with all parametric procedures?
2. (a) Which variable in an experiment determines whether to use parametric or nonparametric procedures? (b) When are nonparametric procedures used?
3. Thinking back on the previous six chapters, what three aspects of the independent variable(s) and one aspect of the dependent variable determine the inferential procedure to perform in a particular experiment?
4. Why shouldn't we use parametric procedures when the data clearly violate their assumptions?
5. How does designing a study so that the data meet the assumptions of parametric procedures allow us to (a) have a better design? (b) use better statistics?
6. (a) Nonparametric procedures are used with which two scales of measurement? (b) What two things can be "wrong" with interval or ratio scores so that parametric procedures are not appropriate? (c) How do we "fix" interval/ratio scores so that nonparametric procedures can be applied?
7. (a) What is the symbol for observed frequency? What does it mean? (b) What is the symbol for expected frequency? What does it mean?

8. (a) When do you use chi square? (b) When do you compute the one-way χ^2? (c) When do you compute the two-way χ^2?

9. (a) What does a significant one-way chi square indicate? (b) What does a significant two-way chi square indicate?

10. (a) When is the phi coefficient used, and what does it indicate? (b) What does ϕ^2 indicate? (c) When is the contingency coefficient used, and what does it indicate? (d) What does C^2 indicate?

11. What is the basic logic underlying the testing of H_0 in all nonparametric procedures for ranked data?

12. What is the nonparametric version of each of the following: (a) A one-way, between-subjects ANOVA? (b) An independent-samples t-test ($n < 20$)? (c) A dependent-samples t-test? (d) An independent-samples t-test ($n > 20$)? (e) A one-way, within-subjects ANOVA? (f) Fisher's protected t-test? (g) Tukey's *HSD* test?

PRACTICE PROBLEMS

13. A survey finds that, given the choice, 34 females prefer males much taller than themselves, and 55 females prefer males only slightly taller than themselves. (a) What are H_0 and H_a for this survey? (b) With $\alpha = .05$, what would you conclude about the preference of females in the population? (c) Describe how you would graph these results.

14. Foofy counts the students who say they like Professor Demented and those who say they like Professor Randomsampler. She then performs a one-way χ^2 to determine if there is a significant difference between the frequency with which students like each professor. (a) Why is this approach incorrect? (b) How should she analyze the data?

15. In the general population, political party affiliation is 30% Republican, 55% Democratic, and 15% other. To determine whether this distribution is also found among the elderly, in a sample of 100 senior citizens, we find 18 Republicans, 64 Democrats, and 18 other. (a) What are H_0 and H_a? (b) What is f_e for each group? (c) Compute χ^2_{obt}. (d) With $\alpha = .05$, what do you conclude about party affiliation in the population of senior citizens?

16. A study similar to the one in problem 15 determines the frequency of the different political party affiliations for male and female senior citizens.

		Affiliation		
		Republican	*Democrat*	*Other*
Gender	*Male*	18	43	14
	Female	39	23	18

(a) What are H_0 and H_a? (b) What is f_e in each cell? (c) Compute χ^2_{obt}. (d) With $\alpha = .05$, what should we conclude about gender and party affiliation in the population of senior citizens? (e) How consistent is this relationship?

17. The following data reflect the frequency with which people voted in the last election and were satisfied with the officials elected:

		Satisfied	
		Yes	*No*
Vote	*Yes*	48	35
	No	33	52

(a) What are H_0 and H_a? (b) What is f_e in each cell? (c) Compute χ^2_{obt}. (d) With $\alpha = .05$, what should we conclude about the correlation here? (e) How consistent is the relationship for these data?

18. We show participants a picture of a person either smiling, frowning, or smirking. For each condition, participants indicate whether the pictured person was either happy or sad. (a) Describe the factor(s) and level(s) in this design and how to analyze the results. (b) What flaws are there in terms of the scores we obtain? (c) What flaws are there in terms of the statistics used? (d) How can we improve the study?

19. Select the statistical procedure that should be used to analyze the data from each of the following studies: (a) An investigation of the effects of a new pain reliever on rankings of the emotional content of words describing pain. A randomly selected group of participants is tested before and after administration of the drug. (b) An investigation of the effects of eight different colors of spaghetti sauce on tastiness scores. A different random sample of participants tastes each color of sauce, and then the tastiness scores are ranked. (c) An investigation of the effects of increasing amounts of alcohol consumption on reaction-time scores. The scores are ranked, and the same group of participants is tested after 1, 3, and 5 drinks. (d) An investigation of two levels of the variable of family income. In two random samples, we rank-order the percentage of participants' income spent on new clothing last year.

20. A study compares the maturity level of a group of students who have completed a research course to a group of students who have not. Maturity scores for college students are skewed interval scores. How would you determine if there is a significant difference between the two conditions? (To analyze data from this problem, see Practice Problem 2 in Appendix B.8.)

21. We wish to compare the attitude scores of people when tested in the morning to their attitude scores when tested in the afternoon. From a morning and an afternoon attitude test, we obtain interval data that have significantly heterogeneous variance. How should we determine if there is a significant difference in scores as a function of testing times. (To analyze data from this problem, see Practice Problem 1 in Appendix B.8.)

22. An investigator evaluated the effectiveness of a therapy on three types of patients, testing those who are either depressed, manic, or schizophrenic. After the therapy, she determined an improvement score. These interval scores, however, form very skewed distributions. What procedure(s) would you use to determine significant differences between the three conditions? (To analyze data from this problem, see Practice Problem 4 in Appendix B.8.)

23. A therapist evaluates the progress of a sample of clients in a new treatment program after one month, after two months, and again after three months. Such progress data don't have homogeneous variance. What statistical procedure(s) should be used to analyze the data? (To analyze data from this problem, see Practice Problem 3 in Appendix B.8.)

24. A research article specifies that a Wilcoxon test was performed. (a) What does this test indicate about the design and scores used in the study? (b) What would be indicated if a Friedman test had been performed?

25. (a) In the example study for chi square involving handedness in this chapter, how would you compute central tendency? (b) In the example study for the Mann-Whitney U and rank sums test involving colored symbols, how would you compute central tendency for the ranks and for the reaction times?

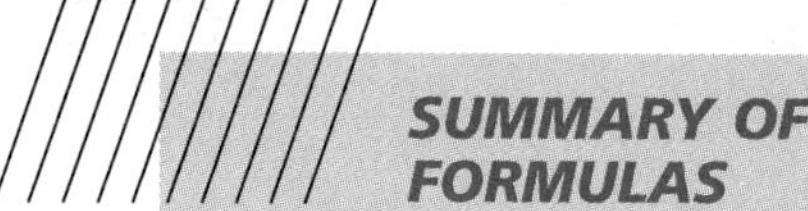

SUMMARY OF FORMULAS

1. *The computational formula for chi square is*

$$\chi^2_{\text{obt}} = \Sigma\left(\frac{(f_o - f_e)^2}{f_e}\right)$$

where f_o is the observed frequency and f_e is the expected frequency.

(a) Computing expected frequency

(1) *In a one-way chi square, when testing an H_0 of no difference, each expected frequency is*

$$f_e = \frac{N}{k}$$

where N is the total N in the study and k is the number of categories.

(2) *In a two-way chi square, the expected frequency in each cell is*

$$f_e = \frac{(\text{Cell's row total } f_o)(\text{Cell's column total } f_o)}{N}$$

(b) *Critical values of χ^2 are found in Table 8 of Appendix C.*

(1) In a one-way chi square, the degrees of freedom are

$$df = k - 1$$

where k is the number of categories in the variable.

(2) In a two-way chi square, the degrees of freedom are

$$df = (\text{Number of rows} - 1)(\text{Number of columns} - 1)$$

2. *The computational formula for the phi coefficient is*

$$\phi = \sqrt{\frac{\chi^2_{obt}}{N}}$$

where *N* is the total number of participants in the study.

3. *The computational formula for the contingency coefficient is*

$$C = \sqrt{\frac{\chi^2_{obt}}{N + \chi^2_{obt}}}$$

where *N* is the total number of participants in the study.

ORGANIZING AND COMMUNICATING RESEARCH USING APA FORMAT

GETTING STARTED

To understand this appendix, recall the following:

- From Chapter 1, recall that a research hypothesis must be testable, falsifiable, rational, and parsimonious.
- From Chapter 2, recall that research begins with broad constructs, is "whittled down" to precise operational definitions, and is then generalized back to the broad constructs.
- From Chapter 3, recall the requirements for designing the independent and dependent variables in an experiment.
- From Chapter 7, recall the uses and interpretation of the mean score in each condition, and how to graph an experiment's results.
- From Chapter 15, recall the independent-samples *t*-test.

Your goals here are to learn

- The basic components of the psychological literature and how to search it.
- How to organize the needed information when reporting a study.
- The parts of an APA-style report and the purpose of each.
- What information should and should not be reported in a research report.
- The style and tone that a research report should have.

Recall that science is a community effort in which we try to correct each other's errors by skeptically evaluating each study. Also, recall that scientific facts are ultimately built through replication of findings. To allow critical evaluation and to build evidence for a hypothesis through replication, researchers share the results of their studies by publishing them and thus contributing to the research literature. This appendix discusses the literature and describes how a research article is created. By knowing the process an author uses in writing an article, you can read the literature more effectively. Also, as a psychology student, you'll probably be reporting your own study sooner or later.

In the following sections, we'll first design an experiment and then see what goes into preparing a manuscript for reporting it in the literature. (The final section of this appendix shows a completed sample report of the study.) Be forewarned that the study here is very simple and does not incorporate all of the design or statistical issues discussed in this textbook. The idea is to show you the basics. However, the same rules and logic apply to a more elaborate experiment. Likewise, this format is used when reporting other types of designs, whether descriptive, correlational, single-subject, and so on.

AN EXAMPLE STUDY

Let's say that in a cognitive psychology course, you read the study by Bower, Karlin, and Dueck (1975). They studied short-term memory by presenting participants with 28 simple cartoons called "droodles." Each droodle is a meaningless geometric shape, but it becomes meaningful when a verbal interpretation is provided. Two examples of droodles are shown in Figure A.1. Some participants were told that droodle A shows a "midget playing a trombone in a telephone booth" and that droodle B shows "an early bird that caught a very strong worm." Other participants were not given an interpretation. Bower et al. found that those participants given interpretations could recall (sketch) more of the droodles than those who had not. The authors concluded that the interpretations made the droodles more "meaningful," allowing participants to integrate the droodles with their knowledge in memory. Then, when participants tried to recall the droodles, this knowledge provided useful "retrieval cues."

However, there is a potential problem here: The interpretations not only make the droodles meaningful but do so in a humorous way. By using interpretations that are both humorous and meaningful, this study may have been confounded: On the one

FIGURE A.1 Examples of "Droodles"

These droodles were accompanied by the following interpretations: (a) "A midget playing a trombone in a telephone booth," and (b) "An early bird that caught a very strong worm."

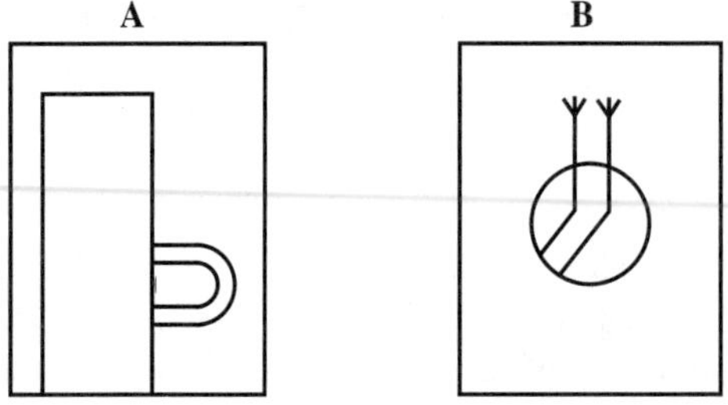

From G. H. Bower, M. B. Karlin & A. Dueck (1975), "Comprehension and Memory for Pictures," *Memory and Cognition*, 3(2), 216–222. Reprinted by permission of the Psychonomic Society, Inc. and the authors.

hand, the interpretations might make the droodles meaningful and thus more memorable, as the authors suggested. On the other hand, the interpretations make the droodles humorous, and their humor might make the droodles more memorable. This second idea leads to a rival hypothesis: When the contexts in which stimuli occur differ in humor, differences in memory for the stimuli are produced. Say that we decide to test this hypothesis.

The hypothesis suggests that greater humor *causes* improved memory, so a well-controlled, internally valid laboratory experiment is in order. In fact, the design of Bower et al. seems appropriate. They compared the effects of an interpretation versus the absence of an interpretation on memory for the droodles. We can test our hypothesis by presenting humorous and nonhumorous interpretations. The prediction is that droodles with humorous interpretations will be better recalled.

Before proceeding, we need to be sure the study is rational, ethical, and practical. Rationally speaking, the idea that humor acts as a cue for recalling information seems to fit known memory processes (but we'll check), and understanding memory is a worthwhile psychological study. Ethically, asking participants to remember droodles does not appear to cause any major harm (but we'll check). And practically speaking, such a study seems doable and does not require inordinate time, expense, or hard-to-find participants or equipment.

As we begin creating the design for the study, we find that we don't know very much about this topic, so—to the literature!

THE RESEARCH LITERATURE

Previous research is the ultimate source for learning about a particular psychological topic. Published research provides background on the issues that pertain to a research question so that a hypothesis fits with existing constructs and with the results of previous studies. The literature also suggests numerous ideas for interesting studies and describes established procedures to incorporate into a study.

Recall that defining the target population early in the design process helps to develop a more precise hypothesis as well as directing us to the most relevant portions of the literature. The Bower et al. experiment studied memory in normal adults. Therefore, we need to find past research on adults regarding (1) how the constructs of "humor" and "meaningfulness" are defined and how they may influence "memory," (2) whether humorous stimuli are better retained than nonhumorous stimuli, and (3) whether other studies using the Bower et al. design have identified flaws in it, have replicated it, or (heaven forbid) have already tested the effects of humorous and nonhumorous interpretations as we will do.

What Constitutes the Research Literature?

The term *research literature* does not mean books or newspapers found in the supermarket or popular magazines such as *Time* or *Psychology Today*. At best, these contain synopses of research articles that most likely omit necessary details. Therefore, go to professional books and psychological journals. Books provide useful background, but because of the time required to create them, even new books may be a few years behind the latest developments. Therefore, focus on journals for the most current developments in a topic, because they are published once or more a year.

Not all professional journals, however, are of the same quality. In some, the primary requirement for publishing an article is that the author(s) pay the publication costs. These journals have less stringent requirements for quality research. Other journals are "refereed," meaning that each article undergoes "peer review" by several psychologists who have expertise in the topic being studied. To gauge the quality of a journal, check the section that describes its editorial policies. Also, look for journals published by professional organizations of psychologists such as the American Psychological Association, the American Psychological Society, or the Psychonomic Society. One function of these organizations is to disseminate quality research. (However, you still should approach each study with a critical eye.)

Searching the Literature

To search the literature, begin with a topic in mind. Most journals are organized around a subarea of psychology (e.g., social, cognitive, abnormal) identified by the journal's title (such as *Cognitive Psychology* or the *Journal of Personality and Social Psychology*). If you have only a vague idea for a study, perusing the journals may provide articles with more specific ideas to explore. If you have a specific research idea, however, consult reference tools that search the literature in a more systematic fashion.

During a search, remember that, eventually, the goal of any study is to explain the results "psychologically," so this is the focus when searching the literature. However, begin by trying to find *all* published research that *might* relate to the topic. Then, whittle it down to those that actually do.

Psychological Abstracts The ***Psychological Abstracts*** is a monthly publication that describes studies recently published in other psychology journals. Its index is organized using the variables and hypothetical constructs commonly studied by psychologists. Therefore, when using this index, try to select specific terms that might be used in the titles of relevant articles. For the droodle study, we would first look in the index of recent issues under such terms as humor, meaningfulness, and short-term memory. The *Abstracts* also provide a separate author index, so we would also look up the authors of the original droodle study to see if they have reported other similar research. For each article listed, an "abstract"—a brief synopsis—of the study is presented. By reading the abstract, we determine whether to read the entire article.

Computerized literature searches Many college libraries provide a user-friendly computer program that searches the literature for you. These programs incorporate a large database covering years of research literature. You simply enter the names of your constructs and variables, and the computer provides abstracts and the references for studies filed under those terms. In fact, the computer will call up many references for a general term, so carefully cross-reference your terms to produce a more selective search. For example, merely entering "memory" as a search term will produce hundreds of irrelevant studies for us. But entering "memory and humor" will call up references more directly related to our study.

Bibliographies of research articles When you find an article on a topic of interest, its bibliography contains references to related studies. By reading the articles it cites, and then reading the references in those articles, you can work backward in time and learn about research that came *before* the original study. Sometimes, there will also be references to psychological conventions and meetings at which researchers orally presented their research. For a copy of such a presentation, contact the first author cited in the reference. (For assistance, the American Psychological Association provides a directory of its members' addresses.)

Social Science Citation Index When you find a relevant article that is several years old, search for more recent articles that came *after* the original study by using the ***Social Science Citation Index***. This publication identifies a research article by authors and date, and then lists articles published in a given year that have cited it. Thus, for example, we could look up the original 1975 droodle study in the index for 1996, 1997, and so on, hoping to find more recent related articles.

Review articles A review article surveys and summarizes a large body of theoretical and empirical literature dealing with a particular topic. Such articles provide a useful overview as well as references to many studies. The title of a review article usually contains the word *review*, and some books and journals specialize in review articles, such as *Psychological Bulletin* and *Annual Review of Psychology*.

References on testing materials Often a design employs a paper-and-pencil test to measure intelligence, personality, creativity, attitudes, emotions, motivations, and so on. Instead of creating the test and being uncertain of its reliability or its content and construct validity, look for acceptable tests that already exist. To find them, consult reference books that describe common psychological tests. Such books usually have titles indicating that they describe tests (such as *The Mental Measurements Yearbook* or *Measures of Personality and Social Psychological Attitudes*).

A computerized literature search is also useful for finding research articles that have employed such tests. To be efficient, cross-reference the name of the attribute to be measured with the term "assessment." For example, if in a different study we wanted to measure depression, using the terms "depression" and "assessment" would limit the search to studies that involve the measurement of depression.

Completing the Droodle Study

The literature search would provide no studies that cause us to question the original Bower et al. (1975) procedure of presenting droodles as to-be-remembered stimuli. Also, there are no ethical or practical concerns, and because this procedure produced informative and powerful results (they were significant), we can adopt it for our study. In fact, it is desirable to use the procedure from previous studies because (1) we replicate their findings, and (2) our results more easily and directly integrate with other findings.

The literature contains many studies that replicate the finding that, for a variety of stimuli, the more meaningful a stimulus is, the better it is retained. For example, when learning a list of words, participants who use each word in a sentence will recall the words better than if they merely think of a rhyme for each word (Lockhart & Craik, 1990).

Surprisingly, however, the literature search produces little research that directly studies how and why humor improves memory (but see McAninch, Austin & Derks, 1992, and Dixon, Willingham, Strano & Chandler, 1989). Numerous studies, however, show that more *distinctive* stimuli are better retained than less distinctive stimuli (e.g., Schmidt, 1985). For example, in a list of words, a word printed in a different style of print is retained better than the other words that are visually similar (Hunt & Elliott, 1980).

The literature will not always address an issue from exactly our perspective, so often we must generalize from previous findings and constructs to fit them to the hypothesis. Thus, in suggesting that humor influences memory, we can propose that a humorous interpretation makes a droodle more distinctive in memory, thereby making it more memorable. Essentially, then, we propose that humor is one component of the construct of distinctiveness—one way to make a stimulus distinctive.

Although the meaningfulness of a stimulus may appear to be the same as its distinctiveness, researchers distinguish between the two concepts. Desrochers and Begg (1987), for example, suggest that distinctiveness is the extent to which unique cues are associated with the particular context in which the stimulus was encountered. Essentially, a distinctive event is notable and thus stands out in memory. Therefore, greater distinctiveness enhances access to the stimulus, allowing us to "find" it in memory. Meaningfulness, on the other hand, is the extent to which the components of the stimulus are organized and integrated. A meaningful event is tied together, so that we know all of its "parts." Therefore, once we access a memory of a stimulus, greater meaningfulness enhances recall of the components of the stimulus (see also Einstein, McDaniel & Lackey, 1989).

Although the preceding discussion greatly simplifies the debate about the hypothetical constructs of distinctiveness and meaningfulness, for our study it boils down to this: On the one hand, the importance of the interpretations in the original droodle study may be that they were humorous, and thus made the droodles more distinctive and in turn more memorable. On the other hand, the importance of the interpretations may have nothing to do with the humor involved. Perhaps they simply made the droodles more meaningful and thus more memorable. Our task is to design a study that clearly shows the influence of humor, separate from the influence of meaningfulness.

By discussing the constructs of memory, humor, and meaningfulness, we have begun to create their *operational definitions*. Now we "whittle down" these constructs, completing the design by defining the specific variables and procedures.

Defining the variables Our independent variable involves changing the amount of humor given to the droodles by their interpretations. The challenge, however, is to manipulate the amount of humor while producing equally meaningful interpretations. If the droodles are not always made equally meaningful, humor and meaningfulness will be confounded. Then, we will be unable to tell whether more humor or more meaningfulness improves retention of a droodle.

What seems to make an interpretation in Bower et al. humorous is that it provides an unusual explanation involving unexpected objects, people, or animals. So, if we revise the original interpretations to provide common explanations involving predictable objects, people, and animals, they should be less humorous (and less distinctive) but just as meaningful as the originals. For example, from the humorous interpretation "This is a midget playing the trombone in a telephone booth," we can derive the less humorous interpretation "This is a telephone booth with a technician inside, repairing the broken door handle." In both cases the droodle features a telephone booth, so if a telephone booth is particularly meaningful and memorable, it is equally so in both the humorous and nonhumorous conditions. Also, both interpretations involve the meaningful integration of a person, a telephone booth, and an object (either a trombone or a door handle).

Thus, we will have two conditions of the independent variable: In one we provide participants with nonhumorous interpretations (as defined above), and in the other we provide humorous interpretations (also, as defined above). If humor is an attribute that aids memory, then the humorous interpretations should produce better recall of the droodles. If humor is not psychologically important in this way, then there should be no difference in retention between the two conditions.

Now, consider all of the details involved in devising a reliable and valid study. First, if there is only one droodle per condition, participants might forget or remember it because of some hidden peculiarity in it. Instead, the original Bower et al. study presented 28 droodles per condition, so we'll use the same number of droodles. The easiest way to obtain the droodles is to use the ones from Bower et al. (To borrow stimuli not fully presented in an article, write to the first author of the article.) If, instead, we decided to create the stimuli, then we must control extraneous variables so that all stimuli are comparable. Thus, we would specify rules for creating stimuli so that they all have equal complexity and memorability: All are of equal size, all are drawn in black ink, all contain only two basic geometric shapes, and so on. Although Bower et al. handed each drawing of a droodle to participants, for better control, we can present the droodles using a slide projector with an electronic timer, or have participants sit at a computer-controlled video monitor.

Also, for consistency, all interpretations will contain roughly the same number and type of words, and all will begin with the phrase "This is a . . . ." As in the original study, we will test participants one at a time, reading them the interpretation as they first view a droodle. We'll read all interpretations at the same speed and volume, with the same tone of voice and expressiveness. (To further ensure consistency, we might record the interpretations and time the playback to occur when participants view each droodle.) In addition, the humorous interpretations should all be consistently humorous for a wide range of participants, the nonhumorous interpretations should be consistently nonhumorous, and, as a group, the humorous interpretations should be consistently more humorous than the nonhumorous interpretations.

The dependent variable is recall of the droodles, but we must also decide how to define and measure it. As in Bower et al. (1975), the participants will study each droodle for 10 seconds, so that everyone has the same amount of study time and the same retention period. Immediately after all droodles have been presented, participants will sketch all droodles on sheets of paper containing a grid of approximately 3-by-3-inch squares. They will place each droodle in a square, so that we can tell what shapes a participant believes go together to form one droodle.

Completing the design We—the researchers—could score the sketches as correct or incorrect ourselves, but our judgment may not be reliable. Instead, therefore, we'll enlist two other people as scorers who are "blind" to the purposes of the study. A response is correct if both scorers agree that it matches an original droodle.

We must also create clear and precise instructions for participants so that they know exactly what to do at each step, and so that we can control their extraneous behaviors. If possible, the instructions should be worded identically, consistently read or recorded, be of the same duration, and so on for all conditions. Further, the researcher must attempt to behave identically when testing all participants, and the environment must be constant for them all.

We must also decide on the specific participants to be examined. Variables such as age, gender, and cultural background may influence what material people consider to be humorous. And, we want them all to see the droodles clearly and to understand the interpretations that accompany them. To keep such variables constant, we will randomly select as participants, Introductory Psychology students who are similar in age and background, with good eyesight, hearing, and English abilities. To avoid practice effects from showing the same people both conditions of droodles, we'll test a separate, independent sample of participants in each condition, and we'll balance gender. To have a powerful *N*, we'll test 40 people per condition, selecting 20 males and 20 females for each.

Finally, we plan out the statistical analysis. Each person's score will be the total number of correctly recalled droodles. These are ratio scores that meet the requirements of parametric statistics, so the inferential statistical procedure to use is the independent-samples *t*-test. Because we predict that humor will improve recall scores, we have a one-tailed test. (Instead, we could perform the one-way between-subjects ANOVA on the factor of humorous/nonhumorous interpretations.)

Although there are other designs we might create, let's assume we conducted the above study and found that the average number of droodles recalled was 15.2 with non-humorous interpretations and 20.5 with humorous interpretations. The *t*-test indicated a significant difference, so this is a believable relationship. Therefore, we interpret the results psychologically, first inferring that humor does influence recall, and then working back to the broader hypothetical constructs of how humor and distinctiveness operate on memory.

To share the results with other researchers, we'll prepare a written report.

ORGANIZATION OF A RESEARCH ARTICLE

Most psychological research articles follow the rules set down in the *Publication Manual of the American Psychological Association* (1994). Now in its fourth edition, this is the reference source for answering *any* question regarding the organization, content, and style of a research report. Although "APA format" or "APA style" may at first appear to be a very rigid, arbitrary set of rules, it is necessary. This format minimizes publishing costs by defining precisely the space and effort that a publication requires. It also specifies the information that any report should contain, how the information should be organized, and how it should be reported.

Especially for beginning researchers, APA format is a very useful organizational scheme. As a reader, it tells you where to look in an article to find certain information and how to understand the shorthand codes used to present it. As an author, it tells you how to organize a paper, what to say, and how to say it. And as a researcher, it provides a framework for remembering the many design aspects of a study that must be considered. Asking yourself the question "What will I say in each section of a report of this study?" is a cue for remembering the issues to deal with.

The sections of an article describe the various aspects of a study in the order in which they logically occur. In Chapter 2, we saw that the flow of a study can be depicted using the diagram on the left in Figure A.2, where we work from the general to the specific and then back to the general. Likewise, on the right, an APA-style report is organized following these same steps, with four major sections:

- The *Introduction* presents the hypothetical constructs as they are used in past research, develops the hypothesized relationship between the variables for the target population, and provides the specific predictions of the study.
- The *Method* section describes the specifics of the design and how the data were collected.
- The *Results* section reports the descriptive and inferential statistics performed and describes the statistical relationship found.
- The *Discussion* section interprets the results first in terms of the variables, and then generalizes to the broader relationship between the hypothetical constructs with which we began.

REMEMBER The organization of a research report follows the logical order of the steps performed in conducting the research.

FIGURE A.2 The Parallels Between Research Activity and APA Format

The flow of a research study is from a general hypothesis to the specifics of the study, and then back to the general hypothesis. The APA format also follows this pattern.

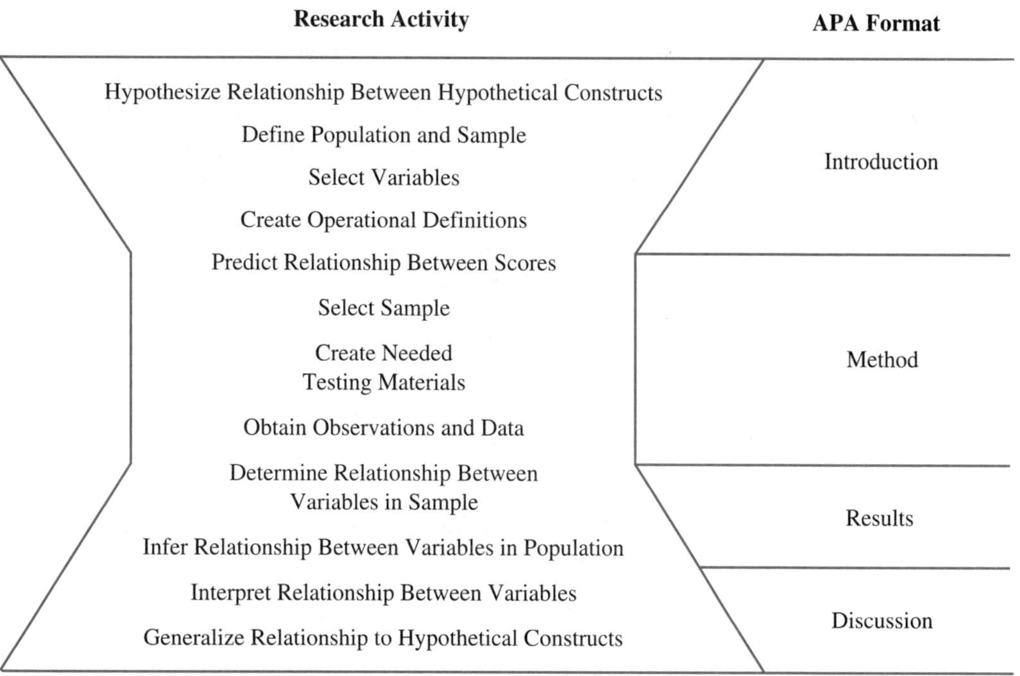

The ultimate goal of APA format is precision in communication. At the same time, we need to conserve space and avoid redundancy. Thus, strive to state each idea clearly, to say it once, and to report only the necessary information. To meet the goal of precise yet concise communication, both the author and the reader make certain implicit assumptions.

The Assumptions of the Author and Reader

The reader assumes that the author understands statistics and research methods, that the author has described any unusual or unexpected events, and that he or she is a reasonable, ethical, and competent researcher. Many things are left unsaid in a research article, because the reader can assume that commonly accepted procedures were used and that omitted details are unimportant. Thus, for example, do not say, "I compared the obtained statistic to the critical value" because all researchers know this must be done. Stating this would be superfluous.

The author assumes that the reader is also a competent psychologist. Therefore, a report does not give a detailed background of the topic under study, because the assumption is that the reader already knows something about it, or will read the references provided. The author also assumes that the reader understands statistics and research methods. *Do not teach statistics and design principles to the reader.* Do not say "Reliable data were important because . . ." or "A *t*-test was performed because . . . " The reader should already know why reliability is important and why a *t*-test is performed. Finally, always use common terminology (such as reliable, valid, confounding), but without providing definitions. The author assumes that the reader either understands them or will find out what they mean.

As the author, you should focus on providing readers with the information they cannot get elsewhere—*your thoughts and actions as a researcher*. What conclusions did *you* draw from a previous article? What do *you* mean when using certain hypothetical constructs? What logic did *you* use in deriving a hypothesis or prediction? And what do *you* think a result indicates about the behavior under study? As the author, you are the expert, so give the reader the benefit of your wisdom. Your job is to describe clearly and concisely all of the important mental and physical activities you performed in creating, conducting, and interpreting the study. The goal is to provide readers the information necessary to (1) understand the study, (2) evaluate the study, and (3) perform a literal replication of the study.

REMEMBER A good report allows the study to be fully understood, scientifically evaluated, and literally replicated.

Some Rules of Style

There are many specific rules for preparing a research article, so refer to the *Publication Manual* for complete instructions. Below are some general rules for preparing a research article that conforms to APA style:

1. A report describes a completed study, so it is written in the past tense ("I predicted that . . ."). The exception is to state in the present tense any general conclusions that apply to present or future situations ("Humor influences recall by . . .").

2. Cite all sources from which you obtained information, using only the last names of the author(s) and the date. You may use the reference as the subject of a sentence: "Smith and Jones (1992) defined distinctiveness as . . ." Or you may state an idea and provide the reference in parentheses: "Distinctiveness is defined as . . . (Smith & Jones, 1992)." (In a parenthetical citation, "&" is used instead of "and.") When citing an article with three to six authors, include all names the first time you cite it, but thereafter refer to it using only the first author and the Latin phrase *et al*. Thus, first we say "Bower, Karlin, and Dueck (1975)," but subsequently we say "Bower et al. (1975)." When citing an article with more than six authors, even the first time it is cited, use only the first author and et al.
3. Refrain from directly quoting an article. Instead, paraphrase and summarize the idea, so that *you* tell the readers what they should understand about the idea. Also, address a study itself, not its authors. For example, the phrase "Bower et al." refers primarily to a reported experiment, not to the people who conducted it. Thus, we write "The results are reported *in* Bower et al. (1975)" instead of "The results are reported *by* Bower et al. (1975)."
4. To distinguish your study from other studies, refer to it as "this study" or "the present study." However, do not use these phrases in a way that attributes human actions to nonhuman sources, as in "This study attempted to demonstrate that. . . ." Instead, use "I" as the subject of these verbs. (Use "we" *only* if you have a coauthor.)
5. Use accepted psychological terminology when possible. When you use a nonstandard term or name a variable, define the word the first time it is used and then use that word consistently. In the droodle study, we'll define "humorous" and use only this term, rather than mixing in related terms such as "funny" or "entertaining." This prevents confusion about whether we mean something slightly different by "funny" or "entertaining." In addition, do not use contractions or slang terms. A reader from a different part of the country or another country may not understand such terms.
6. Avoid abbreviations. They are justified only if (a) a term consists of several words, (b) it appears *very* frequently throughout the report, and (c) you are not using many different abbreviations. If you must abbreviate, do so by creating an acronym, using the first letter of each word of the term. Define the complete term the first time it is used, with its acronym in parentheses. Thus, you might say "Short-term Memory (STM) is . . . ." Then use *only* the acronym, *except* as the first word of a sentence: There, always use the complete term.
7. Use words for numbers between zero and nine, and digits for numbers that are 10 and larger. However, use digits for any size number if (a) you are writing a series of numbers in which at least one is 10 or larger, or (b) the number contains a decimal or refers to a statistical result or to a precise measurement (such as a specific score or the number of participants). Thus, you would say "The three conditions, with 5 individuals per condition . . . ." Never begin a sentence with a number expressed in digits.
8. In research published before 1994, the generic term "subjects" refers to the individuals that researchers study. A post-1994 change in APA style now requires the use of less impersonal and more precise terms. The generic term to use is

"participants," but where appropriate use more descriptive terms such as students, children, men, women, rats, and so on. In addition, avoid gender-biased language. Thus, refer to the gender of participants using the equivalent terms "male" and "female" and to individuals as "he" or "she." When possible, use neutral terms such as "Chairperson."

9. Finally, use precise wording. In the droodle study, we won't say that participants "saw" or "looked at" a droodle, or that they "forgot" a droodle, because we don't *know* that these events occurred. We know only that participants were presented a droodle or failed to recall it.

THE COMPONENTS OF AN APA-STYLE RESEARCH ARTICLE

The rules presented here (and in the APA's *Publication Manual*) describe how to prepare a *manuscript* that is ready for delivery to a publisher who then prepares it for print. Therefore, your job is to follow the prescribed format, *not* to produce a pretty, final copy that looks like the journal version.

The components of an APA-style manuscript, in the order in which they occur, are

- Title page
- Abstract page
- Introduction
- Methods
    - Participants
    - Materials (or Apparatus)
    - Procedure
- Results
- Discussion
- References
- Tables and Figures

All parts are typed, double-spaced, and without "justifying" the right-hand margin. The following sections examine each component in detail, using examples from a manuscript of the droodle study. (The complete manuscript is presented at the end of this appendix.) Throughout this discussion, compare the previous steps we went through when designing the study—and all that was said—to what is actually reported. Translating and summarizing your thoughts and activities are the keys to creating a research report.

The Title

The **Title** allows readers to determine whether they want to read the article. It should clearly communicate the variables and relationship being studied, but it should consist of no more than 12 words. Titles often contain the phrase "as a function of." For example, "Helping Behavior as a Function of Self-Esteem" indicates that the researcher examined the relationship between participants' helping behavior and different levels of their self-esteem. A title such as "Decreased Errors in Depth Perception as a Function of Increased Illumination Levels" provides the added information that the observed relationship is negative, such that greater illumination is associated with fewer errors. Because illumination level can be manipulated easily, this title probably describes an experiment in which "illumination level" was the independent variable and "errors," the dependent variable.

Titles also often begin with the phrase "Effect of," as in "Effect of Alcohol Consumption on Use of Sexist Language." The word *effect* means "influence." Such a title is a causal statement, implying that an experiment was conducted and that changes in the independent variable (amount of alcohol consumed) caused a change in the dependent variable (amount of sexist language used by participants). Note the difference between effect (usually a noun) and affect (usually a verb). If *X affects Y*, then there is an *effect* of *X* on *Y*. (Here's a trick for remembering this distinction: *Effect* means *end result*, and both begin with *e*. *Affect* means *alter*, and both begin with *a*.)

The title should provide sufficient information for readers to determine whether the article is relevant to their literature search. Choose terms that are specific, and never use abbreviations or terms that need to be defined. Thus, for our study, we will not include "droodles" because most people won't know what they are. Instead, we might use the title "Effect of Humorous Interpretations on Immediate Recall of Nonsense Figures." This wording identifies the variables, specifying that we are studying short-term memory of drawings. Contrast this with such terrible titles as: "A Study of Humor and Memory" (of course it's a study!), or "When Does Memory Work Better?" (what does "work" mean?). Either of these are useless for determining whether the article is relevant to a specific research topic.

In an APA-style manuscript, the **title page** is a separate page containing the title, your name, and the formal title of your college or university. A sample title page appears in Figure A.3. The title page is page number 1, with the number placed in the upper right corner of the page, as it is on *all* other pages. The minimum margin all around is 1 inch.

The title page also contains two other components. First, left of the page number is the **manuscript page header**, consisting of the first two or three words from *your* title. The header appears on all subsequent pages, so if any pages become separated, the publisher can identify them as belonging to your manuscript. (This is another reason for all researchers not to use titles beginning "A Study of.") Second, on the first line below the header are typed the words "Running head:" followed by a different, abbreviated title. This **running head** will be printed at the top of each page in the published article. (On this page of your textbook, the running head is "The Components of an APA-Style Research Article.")

The Abstract

The title page is followed by the **Abstract**, which is a brief summary of the study. The abstract describes the specific variables used, important participant characteristics, a brief description of the overall design, and the key relationship obtained. It also indicates the theoretical approach taken in interpreting the results, though often without giving the actual interpretation.

Although the abstract accompanies the article, it is also reproduced in *Psychological Abstracts*, so it must be able to stand alone, containing no abbreviations or uncommon terms (no "droodles"). It should include only details that answer the reader's question:

FIGURE A.3 Sample Title Page of a Research Manuscript

Notice the location and spacing of the various components.

Effect of Humorous 1

Running head: EFFECT OF HUMOROUS INTERPRETATIONS ON RECALL

Effect of Humorous Interpretations on

Immediate Recall of Nonsense Figures

Gary W. Heiman

Podunk University

"Is this article relevant to my literature search?" Most authors write the abstract after writing the report, so they can summarize the key points easily. If you find it difficult to compress a lengthy paper into 100–120 words, think of the abstract as an elaboration of the title. Given the title, what else would you say to communicate the gist of the article? The abstract for the droodle study is in Figure A.4.

FIGURE A.4 Sample Abstract Page

The abstract page is page number 2, with a centered heading reading "Abstract." The abstract itself is one paragraph long. Note that the first line is not indented.

Effect of Humorous 2

Abstract

The effect of humor on the immediate recall of simple visual stimuli was investigated. Eighty college students (20 men and 20 women per condition) viewed 28 nonsensical line drawings that were each accompanied by either a humorous or nonhumorous verbal interpretation. Although the interpretations were comparable in the meaningfulness they conveyed, those participants presented with humorous interpretations correctly recalled significantly more drawings than those presented nonhumorous interpretations. The results suggest that a meaningful and humorous context provides additional retrieval cues beyond those cues provided by a meaningful yet nonhumorous context. The effect of the cues produced by humor is interpreted as creating a more distinctive and thus more accessible memory trace.

REMEMBER The *title* describes the relationship under investigation. The *abstract* summarizes the report. Together, they allow readers to determine whether the article is relevant to their literature search.

The Introduction

The **Introduction** should reproduce the logic you used to derive the hypothesis and to design the study to test it. It is the Introduction that shows the "whittling down" process, beginning with broad descriptions of behaviors and hypothetical constructs and translating them into the specific variables of a study. It then describes the predicted relationship between scores that will be measured using the operational definitions.

Researchers read an introduction with two goals in mind. First, a reader wants to understand the hypothesis and logic of the study. Thus, the author should introduce the hypothesis and the psychological explanations being tested, the general design (e.g., whether correlational or experimental), the reasons that certain operational definitions are employed, and why a particular result will support the predictions and hypothesis of the study. Both the purpose of the study and the population under study should be clear. (Unless specified, we assume that the relationship between variables applies to the broadest population.) Readers also evaluate the hypothesis to be sure there are no circular *pseudo-explanations*, and that rival hypotheses and extraneous variables have been considered.

The reader's second goal is to look for empirical evidence that supports the hypothesis. The Introduction is where virtually all references to past research occur, including those studies that do and do not support the hypothesis. Further, if the study is successful, the author will attempt to interpret and explain the findings "psychologically," so the Introduction also contains the conceptual and theoretical issues to be discussed later.

The reader assumes that, unless otherwise noted, a study cited in support of a hypothesis is reasonably convincing. Previous studies are reported very briefly, usually with the author merely citing them by name (rather than explaining them in detail) to indicate that they provide support. If discussed at all, previous studies are described in terms of the specific information the author judged to be important when deriving his or her hypotheses. The details of a study are provided only when (1) they are necessary for the reader to understand the author's comments about the study, or (2) they are necessary for showing support for the author's position. Usually, however, we do not report such details as the number of participants, the statistics used, or the specifics of the design.

A portion of the Introduction for the droodle study appears in Figure A.5. Although we know how the study turns out, the Introduction is written as if we do not, describing the process we went through *before* collecting the data. Thus, our Introduction begins within the larger context of the hypothetical constructs of meaningfulness and its influence on memory. Then, we work from the broad ideas to the specifics of the study. However, we immediately focus on the perspective taken to study the hypothetical constructs. We orient the reader, providing the major relevant conclusions from past research and their references. We also identify when we are merely speculating. Notice that the purpose of the study is stated *early* in the Introduction—in this case, at the end of the first paragraph. Subsequent paragraphs further retrace our logic, defining the

FIGURE A.5 Sample Portion of the Introduction

Note that the title is repeated, and that we do not label this section as the Introduction.

Effect of Humorous 3

Effect of Humorous Interpretations

on Immediate Recall of Nonsense Figures

Researchers have consistently demonstrated that retention of to-be-learned material improves when the material is presented in a context that leads to meaningful processing (Lockhart & Craik, 1990). In particular, Bower, Karlin, and Dueck (1975) presented college students with a series of "droodles," which are each a meaningless line drawing that can be made meaningful by presentation of an accompanying verbal interpretation. Those individuals who were provided the interpretations correctly recalled (sketched) significantly more of the droodles immediately following their presentation than did those individuals given no interpretations. However, each interpretation in Bower et al. (1975) defined a droodle in a humorous fashion, using unexpected and incongruent actors and actions. Thus, differences in the meaningfulness attributed to

constructs of meaningfulness and distinctiveness and explaining how humor might influence memory. Then, we describe how we define and manipulate humor while keeping meaningfulness constant.

It is important to always state the connection between past research and the present study. Usually, after describing previous findings, you can point out a question or flaw that has not been addressed. You might say something like "However, this interpretation does not consider . . . ." or "However, this variable was not studied . . . ." Then, address the problem you have raised.

The overall flow of the *Introduction* should be such that it leads to a final paragraph that begins with something like "Therefore, in the present study . . . ." Then, state the specific hypothesis and relationship being studied, indicate the general approach for defining and manipulating the variables, and specify the prediction. The details of how the data were collected are then described in the next section.

REMEMBER The Introduction presents all information that will be used to interpret the results including the conceptual and theoretical logic of the study, relevant past research, and the predictions of the study.

The Method

Next comes the **Method** section which contains the information needed to understand, critique, and literally replicate the data-collection procedures. To collect data we need participants, testing materials and equipment, and a specific testing procedure and design. APA format requires that these topics be presented in three separate subsections, in this order: (1) Participants, (2) Materials (or Apparatus), and (3) Procedure. The beginning of our Method section is shown in Figure A.6.

Participants The **Participants** section describes the participants so that other researchers can obtain comparable individuals and look for uncontrolled participant variables. Thus, identify important characteristics (e.g., gender, age, school affiliation) and specify any criteria used when selecting participants. If animals are tested, identify their species, genus, and strain, and the commercial supplier. Always report the number of individuals tested. Because their motivation is important, describe any form of reimbursement that was used. Also, in this section or in a letter sent to the journal editor, an author must certify that participants were treated in accordance with the ethical principles of the APA.

Materials (or Apparatus) This section immediately follows the Participants section (see Figure A.6). Usually it is called **Materials** because most studies involve mainly testing *materials* such as stimulus objects, tests and printed material, slides, drawings, and so on. However, call this section **Apparatus** if testing mainly involves *equipment* such as computers, recording devices, and the like. (If extensive discussion is required, you can create two sections and use both titles.) Regardless of its title, describe the relevant materials and apparatus, but without explaining how they are used. Again, organize the information according to the logical order in which the components occur: In our study, we present a droodle, give an interpretation, and then measure retention.

Supplies must be described so that the reader can understand, evaluate, and reproduce them. Therefore, if supplies are purchased, indicate the manufacturer and model, or the edition or version. If materials are borrowed from previous research, briefly describe them and provide the citation. If you build equipment, describe it so a researcher can reproduce it. If you create visual stimuli, describe the rules used to create them in terms of their dimensions, their color, and so on. If you create verbal stimuli, describe the rules used to select them, such as the length of words or sentences, their meaning and content, their difficulty level, and so on. For any paper-and-pencil tests, describe the number of questions, the format of each question, and the way in which participants indicate their responses. Also, report information about the reliability and validity of a procedure. For example, the speed and error rates of equipment should be indicated because such rates affect reliability. With paper-and-pencil tests, either note their previously demonstrated validity and reliability or briefly report any procedures you performed to determine this.

Note that all physical dimensions are reported using the metric system, and that common units of measurement are abbreviated. Table A.1 provides the most common abbreviations used in psychological research. If you measure in nonmetric units, report the measurement both in nonmetric and in converted metric units.

Keep in mind that only *important* elements are reported. Readers know the necessary steps in designing a study, and generally understand why and how each component is

FIGURE A.6 Sample Portion of the Method Section

Notice the placement of the headings, as well as the use of capital letters and underlining.

humorous interpretations should be more frequently recalled than those accompanied by nonhumorous interpretations.

Method

Participants

Forty female and 40 male undergraduate students from an introductory psychology course at Podunk University each received $3.00 for their voluntary participation. All were between 20 and 22 years of age (mean age = 20.7 years), were born in the United States, were raised in English speaking families, and had normal or corrected eyesight and hearing. Participants were randomly assigned to either the humorous or nonhumorous condition, with 20 males and 20 females in each condition.

Materials

The 28 droodles from Bower et al. (1975) were reproduced, each consisting of a black-ink line drawing involving two

chosen. (They've taken this course!) Therefore, do not specify such things as how participants were randomly selected or how you determined their age. Likewise, do not describe obvious equipment (e.g., whether participants used a pencil or a pen to complete a questionnaire, or what furniture was present in the room where testing took place). Note a detail only if it (1) would not be expected by a reasonable researcher, or (2) would seriously influence the reliability or validity of the measurements.

Procedure Next, the **Procedure** describes how you brought the participants, materials, and apparatus together to perform the actual study. A portion of this section for the droodle study is in Figure A.7.

TABLE A.1 Common Abbreviations Used in APA Format

Notice that abbreviations do not take periods.

Unit	*Symbol*	*Unit*	*Symbol*
centimeters	cm	meters	m
grams	g	milliliters	mL
hours	hr	millimeters	mm
kilograms	kg	minutes	min
liters	L	seconds	s

FIGURE A.7 Sample Portion of the Procedure Section

with a loop attached to the lower right side. The humorous interpretation was "This shows a midget playing a trombone in a telephone booth." The nonhumorous interpretation was "This shows a telephone booth with a technician inside fixing the broken door handle."

Response forms for recalling the droodles consisted of a grid of 3 by 3 in. (7.62 cm by 7.62 cm) squares printed on standard sheets of paper.

Procedure

Participants were tested individually and viewed all 28 droodles accompanied by either the humorous or nonhumorous interpretations. Participants were instructed to study each droodle during its presentation for later recall and were told that the accompanying interpretation would be helpful in remembering it. A timer in the slide projector presented each

The best way to organize this section is to follow the temporal sequence that occurred in the study. The first thing we do is give participants their instructions, so first summarize the instructions. Then, describe the tasks performed by the participants in the order in which they were performed, as well as any controls you included, such as counterbalancing groups or randomizing trials. A useful strategy is to describe first those aspects of the procedure that are common to all participants and then to distinguish one condition from another. (Always work from the general to the specific.) (*Note:* Briefly report the outcome of any pilot study here or in the above Materials section, wherever it most directly applies.)

At this point, the various parts of the Method section should communicate the complete design of the study. If not, an optional *Design* section may be added. This describes the layout of the study in terms of the conditions, participants, and variables used, so that essentially a reader can diagram the study as we have in previous chapters. But note that this section should be necessary only with a complicated study, involving numerous groups or variables, or elaborate steps in testing.

In some instances, additional sections can be created—but, again, only if they are truly necessary. For example, if we took extensive steps to determine the reliability of a procedure, and this element was central to the study, we might describe these steps in a *Reliability of Measures* section.

REMEMBER The Method section contains the *Participants* section (describing the characteristics of participants). *Materials* or *Apparatus* section (describing the testing materials and equipment), and the *Procedure* section (describing the testing situation and design).

The Results

The next section is the **Results**, which reports the statistical procedures performed and the statistical outcomes obtained. However, *don't* interpret the results here, only report them. A portion of the Results section for the droodle study appears in Figure A.8.

Describe the results in the same order in which you perform the steps of the analysis. First, there must be some scores to analyze, so first describe how you operationally defined and tabulated each participant's score. (We described how each droodle was scored as correct or incorrect.) Also, describe any transformations performed, such as when converting each participant's number correct to a percentage. It is at this point that any information regarding the reliability of the data is noted (such as the *inter-rater reliability* of the scorers).

Any analysis then involves first computing the descriptive statistics that summarize the scores and relationship. We usually report the mean and standard deviation for each

FIGURE A.8 Sample Portion of the Results Section

Notice that the heading is centered.

instructed to recall the droodles in any order, sketching each droodle within one grid on the response sheet.

Results

Two assistants who were unaware of the purposes of the study scored the participants' sketches. A sketch was considered to indicate correct recall if both scorers agreed that it depicted a droodle. (On only 2% of the responses did the scorers disagree.) Each participant's score was then the total number of correctly recalled droodles.

The mean number of droodles correctly recalled was 20.50 in the humorous interpretation condition (SD = 3.25) and 15.20 in the nonhumorous interpretation condition (SD = 4.19). With an alpha level of .05, a one-tailed independent samples t-test indicated a significant difference between the conditions, t(78) = 6.32, p <.05. The relationship between amount of humor condition. Recall that the symbol for a mean is "*M*" and for a standard deviation is "*SD*." However, use symbols in parenthetical statements or tables, and use words in regular sentences. Thus, say "The mean score was . . .", instead of "The *M* was . . . ."

The next step is to perform the appropriate inferential procedure, so next provide the formal name for the procedure and describe how it was applied to the data. Then, report the results of the analysis. Always indicate the alpha level employed, report all significant *and* nonsignificant outcomes, (e.g., report all *F*s in an ANOVA), and for each, the term *significant* or *nonsignificant* must appear. As in previous chapters, report the symbol for the obtained value (e.g., *r*, *t*, or *F*), the degrees of freedom in parentheses, the obtained value, and the probability of a Type I error. In the droodle study, for example, we reported

t(78) = 6.32, p < .05.

Note that when published, statistical symbols are italicized. To indicate this in the manuscript, they are underlined. (Additional rules apply for symbols from the Greek alphabet; see the *Publication Manual*.)

If the results of the inferential procedure are significant, we perform secondary analyses that describe the relationship. As in Chapter 11, for example, with a correlation, we compute the regression line. Or, as in Chapter 17, with a significant *F*, we perform post hoc comparisons. Also, as in Chapter 15, always indicate the *effect size* of each independent variable. (For the droodle study, we could include that the squared point-biserial correlation coefficient (r^2_{pb}) is .34, indicating that the humor factor accounts for 34% of the differences in recall scores.) For each of these secondary analyses, again identify the procedure and then report the results. (The results from a manipulation check are usually reported here also.)

Remember that one result cannot be "more significant" than another, and there is no such thing as a "very significant" or "highly significant" result. Also, do not attribute human actions to statistical procedures, saying such things as "according to the ANOVA . . ." or "the *t* gave significance." Instead, say "there were significant differences between the means" or "there was a significant effect of the independent variable."

Figures Because of cost and space considerations, include graphs, tables, or other artwork only when the information is so complicated that the reader will benefit from a visual presentation. Usually, graphs—called **Figures**—provide the clearest way to summarize the *pattern* in a relationship. However, you should also have something to say about each figure, telling readers what they should see in it. (For illustrative purposes, a figure is included in the droodle manuscript, although the relationship is so simple that a figure is unnecessary.)

Every figure is numbered, even if there is only one. At the point in the narrative where readers should look at the figure, direct their attention to it by saying something like "As can be seen in Figure 1 . . . ." *Do not*, however, physically place the figure here (the publisher will do that). The graph is drawn on a separate page and placed after the references at the *end* of the manuscript. In the droodle study, Figure A.9 shows how we refer to the figure, which is shown in Figure A.10. (There are numerous rules for preparing a figure, so check the *Publication Manual*.) Fully label each axis with the names of the variables and their amounts. Use black ink, because color is expensive to

FIGURE A.9 Sample Portion of the Results Section Showing Reference to a Figure

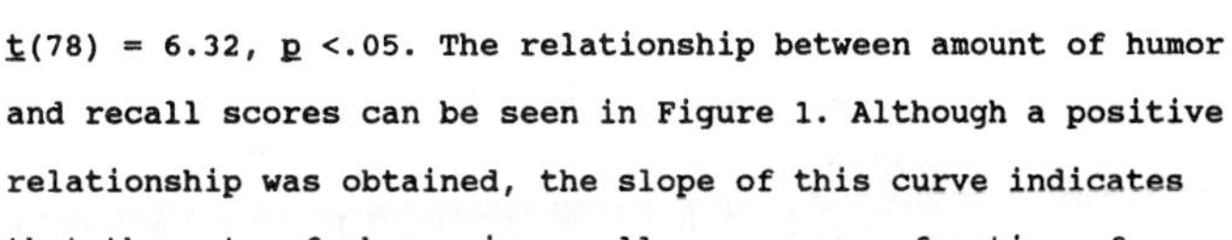

$t(78) = 6.32$, $p < .05$. The relationship between amount of humor and recall scores can be seen in Figure 1. Although a positive relationship was obtained, the slope of this curve indicates that the rate of change in recall scores as a function of increased humor was not large.

Discussion

The results of the present study indicate that humorous interpretations lead to greater retention of droodles than do

publish (and a reader might be color blind!). If a figure shows more than one relationship (more than one line or set of bar graphs), use different symbols for each (e.g., one solid line and one dashed). Then, provide a key to the symbols. (See Figure 18.2 in Chapter 18 and Figure 21.3 in Chapter 21.)

Every figure has an explanatory title, called the **figure caption**, which briefly identifies the variables and relationship depicted. (See Figure A.10.) *Do not*, however, actually put the figure caption on the figure (the publisher does that). Instead, list the figure captions from all figures on one **Figure Caption page**, which is another separate page at the end of the manuscript.

FIGURE A.10 Sample Figure for the Droodle Study

The caption for the graph reads: "Mean number of droodles correctly recalled as a function of nonhumorous and humorous interpretations."

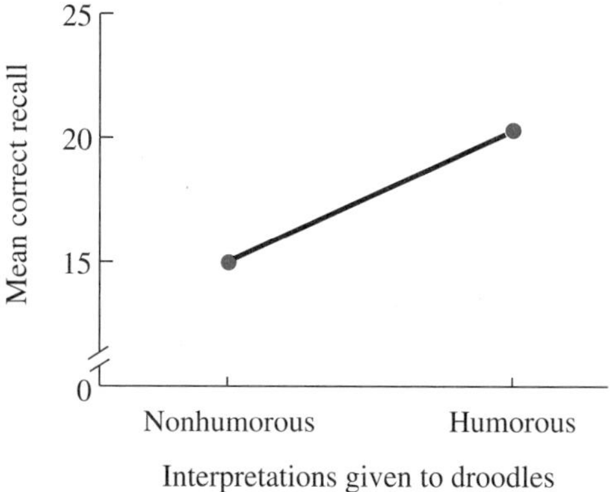

Tables Create a **table** when it is important for the reader to see the precise numerical values of means, percentages, and so on, but there are too many numbers to list in a sentence. All tables are numbered consecutively, and, as with figures, the reader is directed to them at appropriate points in the Results section. The actual tables are placed at the end of the manuscript. Note that you *do* place the title for a table on the table itself.

For example, say that we compared the recall of our male and female participants, depending on whether the interpretation referred to humans, animals, plants, or objects. If we presented this information, using sentences, it would be very dense and difficult to follow. Instead, we create the table in Table A.2 shown in manuscript form. (The *Publication Manual* provides detailed instructions for various tables.)

The title should clearly yet concisely summarize the table, all headings should be brief yet clear, and the layout should be easily understood. Use horizontal lines only when they are truly necessary (vertical lines are almost never needed). Report the data using digits, centered under the headings.

REMEMBER The *Results* section summarizes the data and the relationship obtained, and reports the statistical procedures performed.

The Discussion

In the **Discussion** section you interpret the results and draw your conclusions. Here the questions originally posed in the Introduction are answered. Begin at the point *after* you have *already* reported a significant relationship (do not report any statistics here),

TABLE A.2 Example of APA-Style Table in Manuscript Form

Notice the table's title is underlined, and the table is double spaced.

Table 1

Recall of Droodle Types for Males and Females

	Gender			
	Males		Females	
Type	M	SD	M	SD
Human	2.33	0.68	3.55	1.01
Animal	2.14	0.46	4.21	0.98
Plant	5.70	1.86	3.23	2.79
Object	4.99	2.30	1.45	0.99

so the question is, "Do the results confirm (1) the predictions, and thus (2) the hypothesis?" You can almost always answer this question by beginning the discussion with the phrase "The results of the present study . . . ." See Figure A.9 again.

As the term Discussion implies, however, do not merely state the conclusions—*discuss* them. That is, after answering the original research question, explain what the answer tells us about the behavior. Recall from the funnel diagram back in Figure A.2 that, in the Discussion section, we work backwards from the specific to the general. Thus, beginning with the narrowly defined relationship in the study, generalize to the relationship between the variables that might be found with other individuals or situations. Then generalize the findings based on the variables to the constructs you originally set out to study.

Begin by focusing on the descriptive statistics (inferential statistics are no help here). Throughout this book, I've said that after finding a significant relationship, we interpret it "psychologically." Here is where we do that. So, become a psychologist again, translating the numbers and statistics into descriptions of behaviors and the variables that influence them. For example, in the droodle study, the humorous interpretations produced higher recall scores. Higher recall scores indicates better retention, a mental *behavior* that is different from what occurred when nonhumorous interpretations were given. Thus, based on the scores in each condition, the discussion proposes how manipulating humor influences the memory system. (See Figure A.11.) On the other hand, we must not ignore those droodles given nonhumorous interpretations, because they were frequently recalled, and the addition of humor had no great effect. Thus, as here, factor into the conclusions what the direction and rate of change in scores indicate, what the consistency or inconsistency in the relationship indicates, and what the proportion of variance accounted for indicates. Also, in studies with more than two conditions, only

FIGURE A.11 Sample Portion of the Discussion Section

Effect of Humorous 8

nonhumorous interpretations. Because the meaningfulness of the droodles provided by the interpretations was presumably constant in both conditions, it appears that humor provides an additional source of retrieval cues. This conclusion is consistent with the proposal that humor increases the distinctiveness of a stimulus, thereby facilitating recall by increasing the accessibility of the stimulus in memory.

The improvement in recall produced by humor, however, was relatively small. This result may be due to the fact that all droodles were made meaningful, although sometimes by a nonhumorous interpretation. As in other research (Lockhart &

some conditions may represent a relationship. In such cases, also consider why and how this result occurs.

Recall that all explanations must rationally fit with previous findings and theoretical explanations. Thus, the goal is to provide an integrated and consistent explanation, answering the question, "Given our findings and past findings, what is the present state of knowledge about the behavior or construct?" In the droodle study, for example, we relate our findings to current explanations of the role of distinctiveness and meaningfulness in memory. Notice, however, the use of such words as *presumably*, *probably*, and *apparently*. Do not say "prove," or provide explanations as if they are fact. And although you may say *causes* or *influences*, the difficulty in identifying causal variables should lead you to use these words cautiously.

At the same time, always consider any major flaws in the design that limit confidence in a conclusion. When looking for flaws, however, do not use the argument that the data may be unrepresentative or that a larger sample is needed. The significant inferential statistics have eliminated these arguments. Instead, raise questions based on these important design issues:

1. *Reliability*: Did changing the interpretations given to the droodles consistently manipulate the variable of humor? Did we consistently and only measure a person's recall of the droodles?
2. *Internal validity*: Were the humorous and nonhumorous interpretations equal in meaningfulness, or did the unusual, humorous interpretation yield a broader meaning? If by manipulating humor we also manipulated meaningfulness, then maybe greater meaningfulness produced the higher recall scores. If it is likely that this (or another) confounding occurred, then we have reduced internal validity for saying that amount of humor influenced recall.
3. *External validity*: Is it appropriate to generalize this relationship to other people and situations, or did our participants have an unusual sense of humor, so that the results are unique? Also, droodles are simple visual stimuli, so can we generalize the influence of humor to verbal material or to complex visual material?
4. *Content and construct validity*: Do the recall scores actually reflect "memory" for the droodles? Have we correctly defined "meaningfulness" and "humor" as they operate in nature? Also, we rather arbitrarily speculated that humor produces "distinctiveness," but we have no empirical evidence of this.

Do not try to hide or ignore any flaws you find—we all know that it is impossible to conduct a perfect study. Instead, either provide counterarguments to explain why a potential flaw does not seriously reduce confidence in a conclusion, or qualify and limit the conclusions in light of the troubling flaw.

Researchers often conclude the Discussion section by pointing out the next steps to be taken in the research area. Remember, as the author you are the expert, so indicate what hypotheses should be tested next. (For example, we would note the lack of evidence that humor makes a stimulus more distinctive, and suggest that researchers attempt to confirm this hypothesis.)

REMEMBER The *Discussion* section answers the questions posed by the study, interpreting the results in terms of what is now known about the underlying behavior.

The Reference Page

The final section following the Discussion is the **Reference page**(s). This lists alphabetically the complete references for all sources cited in the article. *Each source should be one that you have read.* If, for example, you learn about Jones' article from reading Smith's report, you should read Jones too (because Smith may be misleading). If you do not, then the reference to Jones should indicate that it is "as cited in" Smith.

As shown in Figure A.12, each reference is typed as a paragraph. (The publisher will convert it to the normal hanging-indent format, as in the References in this book.) For a journal article, provide the last name and first initials of each author, listed in the same order as they appear in the article. Next, give the year of publication, the article's title, and the title of the journal, its volume number, and the page numbers of the article. The *Publication Manual* provides slightly different rules for referencing books, book chapters, monthly magazines, and so on.

PUTTING IT ALL TOGETHER

Most research ideas come from the literature. Authors may suggest rival explanations for their results, or point out untested hypotheses. Also, no study is perfect, so you may find flaws that suggest a research hypothesis. Or, you may discover two published studies that contradict each other, so you can design a study to resolve the debate. You may

FIGURE A.12 Sample Portion of Reference Page

Notice the punctuation and underlining.

Effect of Humorous 10

References

Bower, G. H., Karlin, M. B., & Dueck, A. (1975). Comprehension and memory for pictures. Memory and Cognition, 3, 216-220.

Desrochers, A., & Begg, I. (1987). A theoretical account of encoding and retrieval processes in the use of imagery-based mnemonic techniques: The special case of the keyword method. In M. A. McDaniel & M. Pressley (Eds.), Imagery and related mnemonic processes: Theories, individual differences, and applications (pp. 56-77). New York: Springer-Verlag.

Einstein, G. O., McDaniel, M. A., & Lackey, S. (1989). Bizarre imagery, interference, and distinctiveness. Journal of Experimental Psychology: Learning, Memory, and Cognition, 15, 137-146.

Hunt, R. R., & Elliott, J. M. (1980). The role of

also literally replicate a study, but it is more interesting and informative to also include a new twist or perspective to the design that simultaneously expands our knowledge. For example, in replicating the above droodle study, we might add a third, no-interpretation, control condition.

Developing a research idea will be easier if you recognize that any published article makes the study *sound like* it was a smooth-running, perfectly planned, well-organized process. In reality, it wasn't. An article will not report all the people who volunteered for the study but never showed up. It will gloss over the difficulty the researcher had in finding an artist who could draw droodles or the hours it took to invent their interpretations. And it will not mention the number of prior attempts, using different stimuli or procedures, that failed to produce interpretable results. Thus, although an article may give the impression that the researcher was omniscient and that the study ran like clockwork, don't be fooled. Research is much more challenging—and more fun—than that.

CHAPTER SUMMARY

1. A research report is organized based on the sequence in which the various aspects of the study occur.
2. Most psychological articles follow the rules set down in the *Publication Manual of the American Psychological Association*, so that they conform to "APA format."
3. The *Psychological Abstracts* contains the abstracts of articles published in psychological journals.
4. The *Social Science Citation Index* is used to identify recent articles that cite a previous article.
5. A report should not present information that is redundant with a reader's knowledge or other reference sources. Rather, it should provide the necessary information for (a) *understanding the study*, (b) *evaluating it*, and (c) *literally replicating it.*
6. The *Title* should clearly communicate the variables and relationship being studied. The *Abstract* should summarize the report. Together, these elements allow readers to determine whether they want to read the article.
7. The *Introduction* presents all information that will be used to interpret the results. It reconstructs the logic and cites the literature the researcher used in working from the hypothetical constructs to the specific predicted relationship of the study.
8. The *Method* section provides the information needed to understand, critique, and literally replicate the data-collection procedures. It consists of three subsections: *Participants*, *Materials* (or *Apparatus*), and *Procedure*.
9. The *Participants* section defines the participants of a study in terms of their characteristics, their selection, their number, and their reimbursement.

10. The *Materials* (or *Apparatus*) section describes the characteristics of the stimuli, the response materials, and the equipment used to test participants. Information about the reliability and validity of the material and apparatus is also included here.

11. The *Procedure* section describes the situation(s) in which participants were tested. It should summarize the instructions and the task(s), and complete the description of the design.

12. The *Results* section describes the statistical procedures performed and the outcomes obtained. In this order, it (a) describes the scores, (b) reports the descriptive statistics, (c) identifies each inferential procedure performed, and (d) reports the results of the procedure. Report primary analyses first, then secondary analyses.

13. In the *Discussion* section, the results are interpreted and the conclusions are drawn. The initial questions posed by the study are answered and the findings are related to past findings, providing an integrated description of a behavior or construct. It is here that major potential flaws in the study are evaluated.

14. In a manuscript, after the Discussion come the *References*, the *Tables*, the *Figure Caption Page*, and the *Figures*.

KEY TERMS (with page references)

Abstract (627)
Apparatus section (632)
Discussion section (638)
Figures (636)
Figure caption (636)
Figure Caption page (637)
Introduction (630)
manuscript page header (627)
Materials section (632)
Method section (632)
Participants section (632)
Procedure section (633)
Psychological Abstracts (618)
Reference page (641)
Results section (635)
running head (627)
Social Science Citation Index (619)
Table (637)
Title (626)
Title page (627)

REVIEW QUESTIONS

(Answers for odd-numbered questions and problems are provided in Appendix D.)

1. (a) What are two reasons for conducting a literature search prior to conducting a study? (b) What constitutes the "research literature"?
2. (a) What information do *Psychological Abstracts* contain? (b) What information does the *Social Science Citation Index* provide? (c) What is a "review article"?
3. What are the three goals of a research report in terms of the information provided to the reader?

4. What is the source for the rules for creating a psychological research report?
5. What are the six major sections in a report prior to the references?
6. What are the three major subsections of the *Method* section?
7. In a research report, (a) what does the author assume about the reader? (b) what does the reader assume about the author? (c) how does an author decide whether to include a piece of information?
8. (a) What are the two goals of the reader when reading the *Introduction*? (b) The information provided in the *Method* should allow the reader to do what three things?
9. (a) When should you use abbreviations? (b) How are abbreviations created? (c) When do you use digits or words when presenting numbers? (d) What is the rule regarding abbreviations and numbers at the beginning of a sentence?
10. What information should you include in the title of a research article?
11. What information should you include in the abstract of a research article?
12. From the reader's perspective, what is the purpose of reading your title and abstract?
13. (a) How do you create the manuscript page header that appears at the top of each page of a manuscript? (b) What is the running head, and where does it appear?

PRACTICE PROBLEMS

14. (a) What is the basis for organizing the *Introduction*? (b) What is the basis for organizing the *Procedure* section?
15. (a) What determines whether to have a *Materials* or an *Apparatus* section? (b) What determines whether to create additional sections in the *Method* section?
16. (a) Summarize the information that is presented in the Introduction. (b) In general terms, what remaining information about a study is not included here?
17. (a) What information is contained in each subsection of the *Method* section? (b) In general terms, what remaining information about a study is not reported in the Method section?
18. (a) How is the Results section organized? (b) In general terms, what remaining information about a study is not reported here?
19. (a) When should you include a figure in a research report? (b) When should you include a table in a research report?
20. (a) How is the Discussion section related to the Introduction? (b) In addition to drawing a conclusion about your specific prediction, what other issues are addressed in the Discussion section?
21. For each of the following statements, indicate two reasons that its format is incorrect: (a) "40 students will hear the music and be tested." (b) "Because the critical value is 2.45 and the obtained value is 24.7, the results are very significant." (c) "The mean scores in the respective conditions for men were 1.4, 3.0, 2.7, 6.9, 11.8, 14.77, 22.31, 25.6, 33.7, and 41.2. For girls, the mean scores were . . . ." (d) "To create the groups, the participants were split in half, with five individuals in each." (e) "The results were significant, indicating the null hypothesis should be rejected. Therefore, I conclude that the relationship demonstrates . . . ." (f) Title: "Type of Interpretation as a Function of Remembering Funny Droodles."
22. In problem 21, revise each statement so that it employs correct APA style.

23. We wish to measure the aggressiveness of a sample of adolescents. Other than creating the test, what two approaches can we take to obtain a valid and reliable test of aggressiveness?

24. How would you go about finding literature that investigates the possible connection between violence on television and heightened aggressiveness in adolescents?

25. You find an article related to the topic of television and aggressiveness in adolescents. How is this article used to find relevant research that occurred prior to it?

26. The article you find in problem 25 was published in 1980. How is this article used to find more recent related research?

Sample APA-Style Research Report

Running head: EFFECT OF HUMOROUS INTERPRETATIONS ON RECALL

Effect of Humorous Interpretations on
Immediate Recall of Nonsense Figures

Gary W. Heiman
Podunk University

Abstract

The effect of humor on the immediate recall of simple visual stimuli was investigated. Eighty college students (20 men and 20 women per condition) viewed 28 nonsensical line drawings that were each accompanied by either a humorous or nonhumorous verbal interpretation. Although the interpretations were comparable in the meaningfulness they conveyed, those participants presented with humorous interpretations correctly recalled significantly more drawings than those presented nonhumorous interpretations. The results suggest that a meaningful and humorous context provides additional retrieval cues beyond those cues provided by a meaningful yet nonhumorous context. The effect of the cues produced by humor is interpreted as creating a more distinctive and thus more accessible memory trace.

Effect of Humorous Interpretations

on Immediate Recall of Nonsense Figures

Researchers have consistently demonstrated that retention of to-be-learned material improves when the material is presented in a context that leads to meaningful processing (Lockhart & Craik, 1990). In particular, Bower, Karlin, and Dueck (1975) presented college students with a series of "droodles," which are each a meaningless line drawing that can be made meaningful by presentation of an accompanying verbal interpretation. Those individuals who were provided the interpretations correctly recalled (sketched) significantly more of the droodles immediately following their presentation than did those individuals given no interpretations. However, each interpretation in Bower et al. (1975) defined a droodle in a humorous fashion, using unexpected and incongruent actors and actions. Thus, differences in the meaningfulness attributed to the droodles may have been confounded by differences in the humor associated with the droodles. The purpose of the present study was to investigate the effect of humorous interpretations when the meaningfulness of the droodles is kept constant.

Few studies can be found that directly examine how the humor associated with a stimulus influences recall of the stimulus. However, it is reasonable to speculate that the relevant dimension of humor may be that it is simply one type of context that makes a stimulus meaningful. Desrochers and Begg (1987) defined the meaningfulness of a stimulus as the extent to which the components of the stimulus are organized and integrated. Therefore, meaningfulness provides retrieval cues that enhance recall of the components of the stimulus, once the stimulus has been accessed in memory. From this perspective, either a humorous or a nonhumorous context should produce equivalent recall of stimuli, as long as both contexts provide an equivalent level of meaningful organization.

On the other hand, humor may play a different role than that of only providing a meaningful context. Because it provides an unusual and unexpected interpretation, humor may make a stimulus more distinctive in memory. The distinctiveness of a stimulus is defined as the number of novel attributes that it can be assigned (Schmidt, 1985). Research has shown that greater distinctiveness does improve retrieval (Hunt & Elliott, 1980). Desrochers and Begg (1987) and Einstein, McDaniel, and Lackey (1989) suggest that distinctiveness is created by unique cues that are associated with the particular context in which the stimulus was encountered. Therefore, distinctiveness enhances access to the overall memory trace for a stimulus. From this perspective, a humorous context should facilitate recall of a stimulus to a greater extent than a nonhumorous context, because, in addition to organizing the components of a stimulus through its meaning, humor provides additional retrieval cues that make the memory trace for the stimulus more distinctive and thus more accessible.

In this study, I tested the above proposals by determining

whether droodles accompanied by humorous interpretations are better retained than when they are accompanied by nonhumorous interpretations. For each of the humorous interpretations of Bower et al. (1975), I produced a non-humorous version that would provide an equally meaningful interpretation of the droodle. If humor adds retrieval cues over and above those produced by meaningful processing, then droodles accompanied by humorous interpretations should be more frequently recalled than those accompanied by nonhumorous interpretations.

Method

Participants

Forty female and 40 male undergraduate students from an introductory psychology course at Podunk University each received $3.00 for their voluntary participation. All were between 20 and 22 years of age (mean age = 20.7 years), were born in the United States, were raised in English speaking families, and had normal or corrected eyesight and hearing. Participants were randomly assigned to either the humorous or nonhumorous condition, with 20 males and 20 females in each condition.

Materials

The 28 droodles from Bower et al. (1975) were reproduced, each consisting of a black-ink line drawing involving two interconnected geometric shapes. Droodles were copied to film slides for presentation by a standard Kodak carousel projector (model 28-b).

For each humorous interpretation in Bower et al. (1975), a non-humorous version was created. Each interpretation consisted of a 10 to 14 word sentence, beginning with the phrase "This shows a. . . ." A humorous interpretation referred to an unusual action by unexpected people or animals using incongruent objects. A nonhumorous interpretation was derived by changing the humorous interpretation so that it described common actions by predictable actors using congruent objects. The meaning of each droodle was altered as little as possible, with only the humorous components being replaced with comparable, nonhumorous components. For example, one droodle consisted of a rectangle with a loop attached to the lower right side. The humorous interpretation was "This shows a midget playing a trombone in a telephone booth." The nonhumorous interpretation was "This shows a telephone booth with a technician inside fixing the broken door handle."

Response forms for recalling the droodles consisted of a grid of 3 by 3 in. (7.62 cm by 7.62 cm) squares printed on standard sheets of paper.

Procedure

Participants were tested individually and viewed all 28 droodles accompanied by either the humorous or nonhumorous interpretations. Participants were instructed to study each droodle during its presentation for later recall and were told that the accompanying interpretation would be helpful in remembering it. A timer in the slide projector presented each slide containing a droodle for 10 s, with approximately 2 s between slides. As each slide was presented, I recited the appropriate interpretation. The recall task began immediately after the final droodle was presented. Participants were instructed to recall the droodles in any order, sketching each droodle within one grid on the response sheet.

Results

Two assistants who were unaware of the purposes of the study scored the participants' sketches. A sketch was considered to indicate correct recall if both scorers agreed that it depicted a droodle. (On only 2% of the responses did the scorers disagree.) Each participant's score was then the total number of correctly recalled droodles.

The mean number of droodles correctly recalled was 20.50 in the humorous interpretation condition ($\underline{SD}$ = 3.25) and 15.20 in the nonhumorous interpretation condition ($\underline{SD}$ = 4.19). With an alpha level of .05, a one-tailed independent samples $\underline{t}$-test indicated a significant difference between the conditions, $\underline{t}(78) = 6.32$, $\underline{p} < .05$. The relationship between amount of humor and recall scores can be seen in Figure 1. Although a positive relationship was obtained, the slope of this curve indicates that the rate of change in recall scores as a function of increased humor was not large.

Discussion

The results of the present study indicate that humorous interpretations lead to greater retention of droodles than do nonhumorous interpretations. Because the meaningfulness of the droodles provided by the interpretations was presumably constant in both conditions, it appears that humor provides an additional source of retrieval cues. This conclusion is consistent with the proposal that humor increases the distinctiveness of a stimulus, thereby facilitating recall by increasing the accessibility of the stimulus in memory.

The improvement in recall produced by humor, however, was relatively small. This result may be due to the fact that all droodles were made meaningful, although sometimes by a nonhumorous interpretation. As in other research (Lockhart & Craik, 1990), the meaningful processing produced by a nonhumorous interpretation may have provided relatively effective retrieval cues. Then the additional retrieval cues produced by the distinctiveness of a humorous interpretation would only moderately improve the retrievability of the droodles. In addition, these results may have occurred because a nonhumorous interpretation given to such a simple visual stimulus produced a reasonably distinctive trace. Additional unique cues provided by a humorous interpretation would then only moderately increase a droodle's distinctiveness, resulting in only a moderate improvement in recall.

It is possible, of course, that humor added to the meaningfulness of a droodle, instead of to its distinctiveness. Desrochers and Begg (1987) suggested that increased meaningfulness results in increased organization of a stimulus in memory. Humor may have added to the meaningfulness of a droodle by providing additional ways to organize it, so that its components were better retrieved. Further research is needed to determine whether humor produces a more distinctive or a more meaningful stimulus, especially when the stimulus is more complex than a simple droodle.

References

Bower, G. H., Karlin, M. B., & Dueck, A. (1975). Comprehension and memory for pictures. Memory and Cognition, 3, 216-220.

Desrochers, A., & Begg, I. (1987). A theoretical account of encoding and retrieval processes in the use of imagery-based mnemonic techniques: The special case of the keyword method. In M. A. McDaniel & M. Pressley (Eds.), Imagery and related mnemonic processes: Theories, individual differences, and applications (pp. 56-77). New York: Springer-Verlag.

Einstein, G. O., McDaniel, M. A., & Lackey, S. (1989). Bizarre imagery, interference, and distinctiveness. Journal of Experimental Psychology: Learning, Memory, and Cognition, 15, 137-146.

Hunt, R. R., & Elliott, J. M. (1980). The role of nonsemantic information in memory: Orthographic distinctiveness effects on retention. Journal of Experimental Psychology: General, 109, 49-74.

Lockhart, R. S., & Craik, F. I. M. (1990). Levels of processing: A retrospective commentary on framework for memory research. Canadian Journal of Psychology, 44, 87-112.

Schmidt, S. R. (1985). Encoding and retrieval processes in the memory for conceptually distinctive events. Journal of Experimental Psychology: Learning, Memory, and Cognition, 11, 565-578.

Figure Caption

Figure 1. Mean number of droodles correctly recalled as a function of nonhumorous and humorous interpretations.

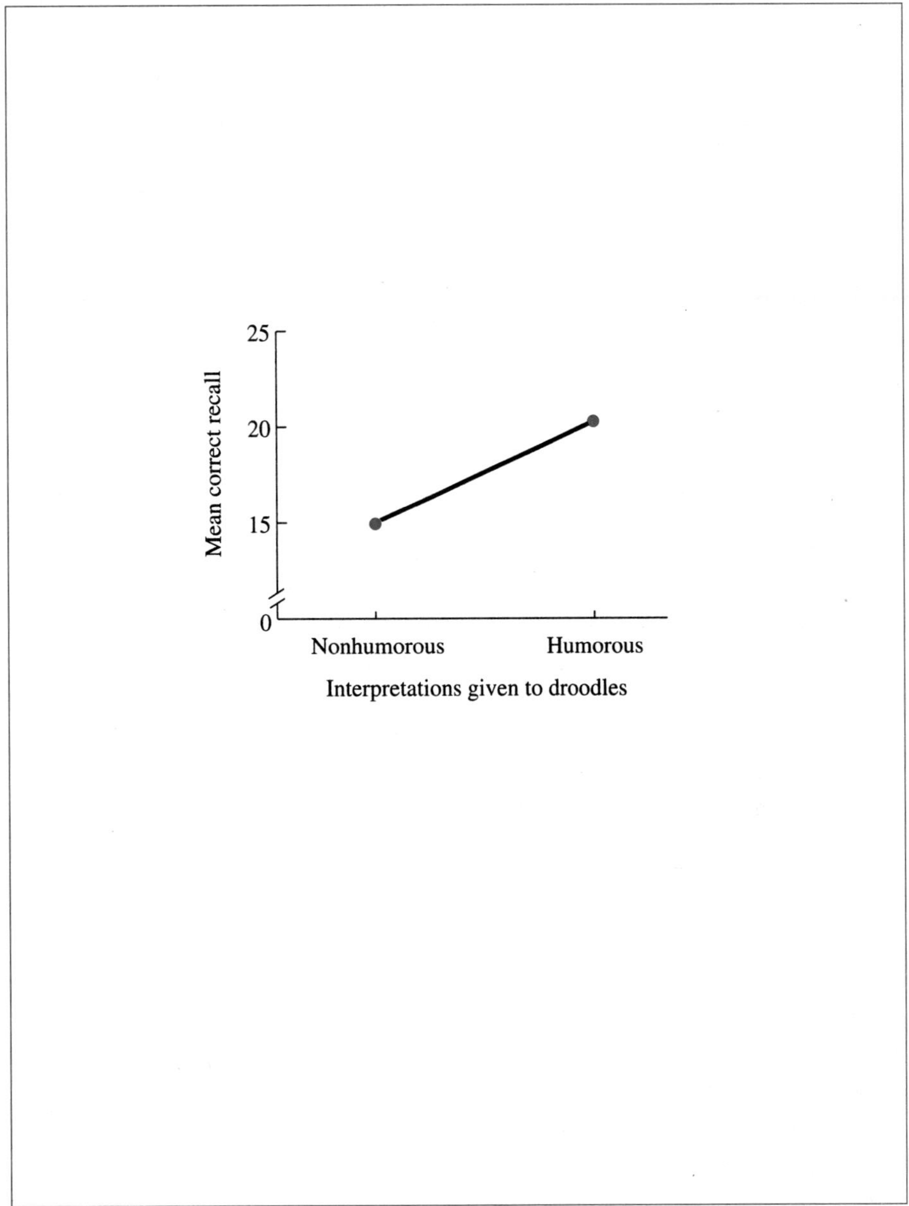
25
20
15
0
Mean correct recall
Nonhumorous
Humorous
Interpretations given to droodles

ADDITIONAL STATISTICAL FORMULAS

B.1. Computing Percentiles

B.2. Computing the Semi-Interquartile Range

B.3. Performing Linear Interpolation

B.4. Additional Formulas for Computing Probability

B.5. The One-Way Within-Subjects Analysis of Variance

B.6. The Two-Way Within-Subjects Analysis of Variance

B.7. The Two-Way Mixed-Design Analysis of Variance

B.8. Nonparametric Procedures for Ranked Data

- B.8.1 The Mann-Whitney *U* Test
- B.8.2 The Rank Sums Test
- B.8.3 The Wilcoxon *T*-Test
- B.8.4 The Kruskal-Wallis *H* Test
- B.8.5 The Friedman χ^2 Test

B.1: COMPUTING PERCENTILES

The following shows how to calculate either the percentile of a particular score, or the score at a particular percentile. These formulas first require creating grouped frequency distributions.

CREATING GROUPED FREQUENCY DISTRIBUTIONS

In a **grouped distribution** different scores are grouped together, and then the total *f*, *rel. f*, or *cf* of each group is reported. Say that we have the following 25 scores:

3	4	4	18	4	28	26	41	5	40	4	6	5
18	22	3	17	12	26	4	20	8	15	38	36	

First, determine the number of scores the data span (their "range"). Use the formula:

$$\text{Number of values} = (\text{High score} - \text{Low score}) + 1$$

Thus, there is a span of 39 values between 41 and 3, inclusive.

Next, decide how many scores to put in each group, with the same range of scores in each group. You can operate as if the sample contained a wider range of scores than was actually in the data. For example, we'll operate as if our scores were from 0 to 44, spanning 45 scores. This allows nine groups, each spanning 5 scores, resulting in the grouped distribution shown in Table B.1.

TABLE B.1 **Grouped Distribution Showing *f*, *rel. f*, and *cf* for Each Group of Scores**

The column on the left identifies the lowest and highest score in each class interval.

Scores	*f*	*rel. f*	*cf*
40–44	2	.08	25
35–39	2	.08	23
30–34	0	.00	21
25–29	3	.12	21
20–24	2	.08	18
15–19	4	.16	16
10–14	1	.04	12
5– 9	4	.16	11
0– 4	7	.28	7

The group labeled "0–4" contains the scores 0, 1, 2, 3, and 4, while "5–9" contains 5 through 9, and so on. Each group is called a *class interval*, and the number of values spanned in each is the *interval size*. Here, the interval size is 5. Choose an interval size that is easy to work with (such as 2, 5, 10, or 20), and that results in between 8 and 18 intervals.

Notice several things about the score column in Table B.1. First, each interval is labeled with the low score on the left. Second, the low score in each interval is a whole-number multiple of the interval size of 5. Third, every class interval is the same size. (Even though the highest score in the data is only 41, we have the complete highest interval of 40–44.) Finally, the intervals are arranged so that higher scores are located toward the top of the column.

To complete the table, find the *f* for each class interval by summing the individual frequencies of all scores in the group. In our data, there were no scores of 0, 1, or 2, but there were two 3s and five 4s. Thus, the 0–4 interval has a total *f* of 7. For the 5–9 interval, there were two 5s, one 6, no 7s, one 8, and no 9s, so the 5–9 interval has a total *f* of 4. And so on.

Compute the relative frequency for each interval by dividing the *f* for the interval by *N*. Remember, *N* is the total number of raw scores (here 25), not the number of class intervals. Thus, for the 0–4 interval, *rel. f* equals 7/25 or .28.

Compute the cumulative frequency for each interval by counting the number of scores that are at or below the *highest* score in the interval. Begin with the lowest interval. There are 7 scores at 4 or below, so the *cf* for interval 0–4 is 7. Next, *f* is 4 for the scores between 5 and 9, and adding the 7 scores below the interval produces a *cf* of 11 for the interval 5–9. And so on.

Real versus Apparent Limits

What if one of the scores in the above example were 4.6? This score seems too large to be in the 0–4 interval, but too small to be in the 5–9 interval. To allow for such scores, we consider the "real limits" of each interval. These are different from the upper and lower numbers of each interval seen in the frequency table, which are called the *apparent upper limit* and the *apparent lower limit*, respectively. As shown in Table B.2, however, the apparent limits for each interval imply corresponding real limits.

TABLE B.2 Real and Apparent Limits

The apparent limits in the column on the left imply the real limits in the column on the right.

Apparent limits (lower–upper)	***imply***	***Real limits (lower–upper)***
40–44	→	39.5–44.5
35–39	→	34.5–39.5
30–34	→	29.5–34.5
25–29	→	24.5–29.5
20–24	→	19.5–24.5
15–19	→	14.5–19.5
10–14	→	9.5–14.5
5– 9	→	4.5– 9.5
0– 4	→	−0.5– 4.5

Note that (1) each real limit is halfway between the lower apparent limit of one interval and the upper apparent limit of the interval below it, and (2) the lower real limit of one interval is always the same number as the upper real limit of the interval below it. Thus, 4.5 is halfway between 4 and 5, so 4.5 is the lower real limit of the 5–9 interval and the upper real limit of the 0–4 interval. Also, the difference between the lower real limit and the upper real limit equals the interval size $(9.5 - 4.5 = 5)$.

Real limits eliminate the gaps between intervals, so now a score such as 4.6 falls into the interval 5–9, because it falls between 4.5 and 9.5. If scores equal a real limit (such as two scores of 4.5), put half in the lower interval (between -0.5 and 4.5) and half in the upper interval (4.5–9.5). If one such score is left over, flip a coin to pick the interval.

Real limits also apply to ungrouped data. An individual score is actually a class interval with an interval size of 1. Thus, when a score in an ungrouped distribution is labeled 6, this is both the upper and the lower apparent limits. However, the lower and upper real limits are 5.5 and 6.5, respectively.

Graphing Grouped Distributions

Grouped distributions are graphed in the same way as ungrouped distributions, *except* that the X axis is labeled differently. To graph grouped simple frequency or grouped relative frequency, label the X axis using the *midpoint* of each class interval. To find the midpoint, multiply .5 times the interval size, and add the result to the lower real limit. For example, above, the interval size of 5 multiplied times .5 is 2.5. For the 0–4 interval, the lower real limit was $-.5$. Adding 2.5 to $-.5$ yields 2. Thus, 2 on the X axis identifies the class interval of 0–4. And so on.

As usual, for nominal or ordinal scores, create a bar graph, and for interval or ratio scores, create a histogram or polygon. Figure B.1 presents a histogram and polygon for

FIGURE B.1 Grouped Frequency Polygon and Histogram

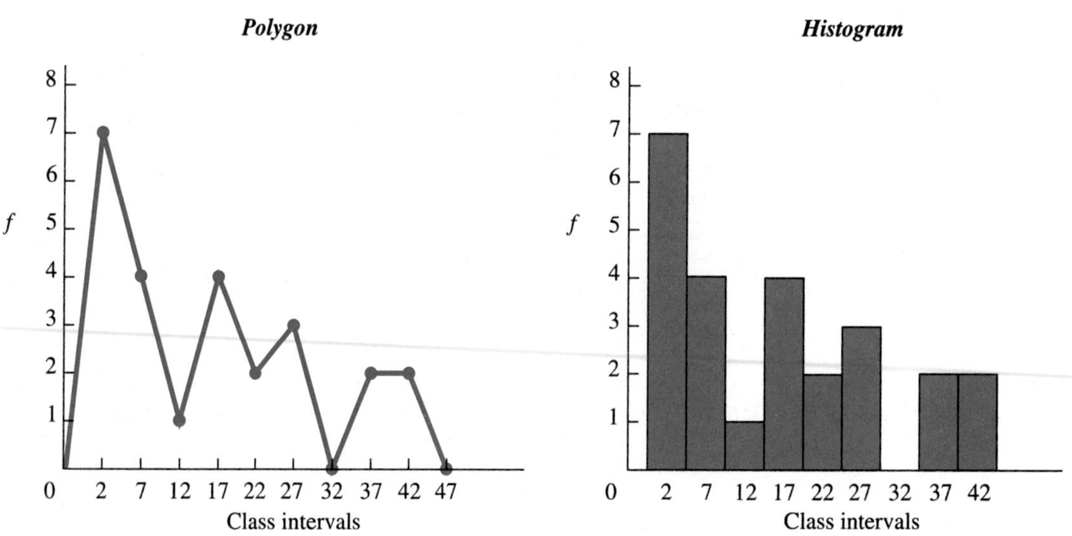

FIGURE B.2 Grouped Cumulative Frequency Polygon

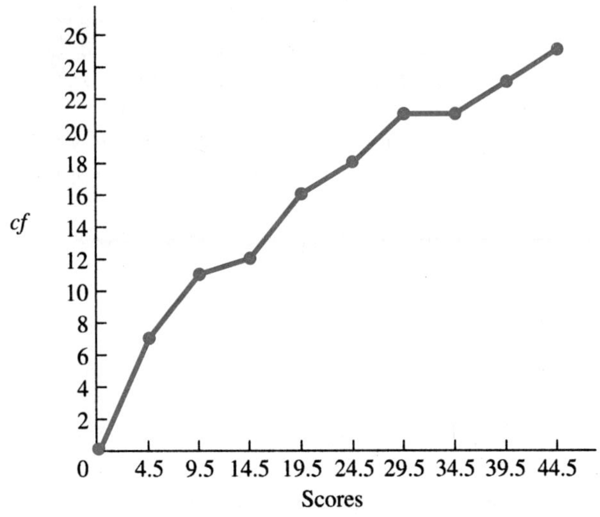

the frequency data back in Table B.1. The height of each data point or bar corresponds to the total simple frequency of all scores in the class interval. Plot a relative frequency distribution in the same way, except label the Y axis accordingly.

Figure B.2 presents the cumulative frequency polygon for these data. Here, the X axis is labeled using the *upper real limit* of each interval. Thus, the 0–4 interval is represented at 4.5 on the X axis, and the 5–9 interval is at 9.5. Then, each data point is the *cf* for the group.

DETERMINING THE SCORE AT A GIVEN PERCENTILE

Percentiles are computed from a cumulative frequency distribution. As an example, say that our scores reflect the number of minutes required for a rat to run a maze. The cumulative frequency distribution for these data is in Table B.3.

TABLE B.3 Cumulative Frequency Distribution of Maze-Running Times for Laboratory Rats

Score	*f*	*cf*
5	1	10
4	1	9
3	2	8
2	3	6
1	3	3
	$N = 10$	

Say that we seek the score at the 50th percentile. To find the score at a particular percentile, find the score that has a *cf* that corresponds to that particular percentage of *N*. Here, we are looking for the score with a *cf* that is 50% of *N*. Because *N* is 10, the score at the 50th percentile is the score having a *cf* of 5. But, the score of 1 has a *cf* of only 3, and the score of 2 has a *cf* of 6. Therefore, the score that has a *cf* of 5 is somewhere between 1 and 2.

To compute a percentile, treat the scores as if they were from a continuous variable that allows decimals. Then, look at the real limits. For the scores of 1 and 2, we see

Scores	*f*	*cf*
1.5–2.5	3	6
.5–1.5	3	3

Because the score we seek has a *cf* of 5, the score is above 1.5 (which has a *cf* of only 3), so the score is in the interval 1.5–2.5. Thus, we'll proceed into this interval far enough beyond 1.5 to accumulate a *cf* of 5. We assume that the frequency in an interval is evenly spread throughout the interval, so that, for example, if we go to a score that is halfway between the upper and lower limits, we accumulate one-half of the frequency in the interval. Conversely, if we accumulate one-half of the frequency in an interval, we're at the score that is halfway between the upper and lower limits. Above, the score we seek has a *cf* of 5, so we want the score above 1.5 that increases the *cf* by 2. If we went to a score of 2.5, we would accumulate an additional *f* of 3, increasing the *cf* by 3, which is too much. We want an *f* of 2 out of the 3, so we want two-thirds of the total frequency in the interval. To accumulate two-thirds of the frequency in the interval, we go to the score that is two-thirds of the way between the lower and upper limits. To find the score that is two-thirds of the way between 1.5 and 2.5, multiply two-thirds, or .667, times the interval size of 1, which gives .667. Then, adding .667 to 1.5 takes us to the score of 2.17. Thus, 2.17 is two-thirds of the way through this interval, so it has a *cf* of 5. Therefore, 2.17 is at the 50th percentile, so 50% of the rats completed the maze in 2.17 minutes or less.

Luckily, there's a formula that accomplishes all of the above at once.

THE FORMULA FOR FINDING THE SCORE AT A GIVEN PERCENTILE IS

$$\text{Score} = \text{LRL} + \left(\frac{\text{Target } cf - cf \text{ below interval}}{f \text{ within interval}}\right)(\text{Interval size})$$

The formula requires the following:

1. Target *cf*: The cumulative frequency of the score you seek. To find it, transform the percentile into a proportion and then multiply it by *N*. The interval containing this *cf* contains the score you seek. (In the example, the target *cf* is 5.)

2. LRL: The lower real limit of the interval that contains the score you seek. (In the example above, it is 1.5.)
3. *cf* below interval: The cumulative frequency for the interval below the interval containing the score you seek. (In the example, it is 3.)
4. *f* within interval: The frequency in the interval that contains the score. (In the example, it is 3.)
5. Interval size: The interval size used to create the frequency distribution. (Above, it is 1.)

Putting these numbers into the formula gives

$$\text{Score} = 1.5 + \left(\frac{5 - 3}{3}\right)(1)$$

First, (5 − 3)/3 gives 2/3, which is .667. So

$$\text{Score} = 1.5 + (.667)(1)$$

After multiplying,

$$\text{Score} = 1.5 + .667$$

So finally,

$$\text{Score} = 2.17$$

Again, the score at the 50th percentile for these data is 2.17.

Although we had an interval size of 1, you can use this formula for any interval size.

Finding a Percentile for a Given Score

You can also work from the opposite direction when you have a score in mind and wish to find its percentile. For example, say in the rat data back in Table B.3, we seek the percentile for the score of 4. First, we find the *cf* of the score within the interval and add it to the *cf* below the interval. Then, determine the percent of scores that are at or below the score. You accomplish this using the following formula.

THE FORMULA FOR FINDING THE PERCENTILE OF A GIVEN SCORE IS

$$\text{Percentile} = \left(\frac{cf \text{ below interval} + \left(\dfrac{\text{Score} - \text{LRL}}{\text{Interval size}}\right)\left(\begin{matrix} f \text{ within} \\ \text{interval}\end{matrix}\right)}{N}\right)(100)$$

This formula requires the following:

1. Score: The score for which you are computing the percentile. (Here, it is 4.)
2. *cf* below interval: The cumulative frequency of the interval below the interval containing the score. (In the example, it is 8.)

3. LRL: The lower real limit of the interval containing the score. (In the example, it is 3.5.)
4. f within interval: The frequency in the interval containing the score. (Here, it is 1.)
5. Interval size: The interval size used to create the grouped distribution. (Here, it is 1.)
6. N: The total number of scores in the sample. (Here, $N = 10$.)

Putting these numbers into the formula gives

$$\text{Percentile} = \left(\frac{8 + \left(\frac{4.0 - 3.5}{1} \right)(1)}{10} \right)(100)$$

In the numerator, 4.0 − 3.5 divided by 1 is .5, so

$$\text{Percentile} = \left(\frac{8 + (.5)(1)}{10} \right)(100)$$

Multiplying .5 by 1 gives .5, so

$$\text{Percentile} = \left(\frac{8 + .5}{10} \right)(100)$$

After adding,

$$\text{Percentile} = \left(\frac{8.5}{10} \right)(100)$$

and after dividing,

$$\text{Percentile} = (.85)(100)$$

Finally, the answer is

$$\text{Percentile} = 85$$

Thus, the score of 4.0 in the above distribution is at the 85th percentile.

PRACTICE PROBLEMS

(Answers for odd-numbered problems are provided in Appendix D.)

1. Organize the scores below in an ungrouped distribution showing simple frequency, cumulative frequency, and relative frequency.

49	52	47	52	52	47	49	47	50
51	50	49	50	50	50	53	51	49

(a) What is the percentile for the score of 51? (b) What score is at the 50th percentile?

2. A group of students received the following grades on a test of typing ability. Using an interval size of 5, group the scores and construct a table that shows simple, relative, and cumulative frequency.

76	66	80	82	76	80	84	86	80	86
85	87	74	90	92	87	91	94	94	91
94	93	57	82	76	76	82	90	87	91
66	80	57	66	74	76	80	84	94	66

(a) Find the score that corresponds to the 70th percentile. (b) What is the percentile for a score of 91?

3. Below are the weights (in pounds) of 28 high school students. Using an interval size of 4, group the scores and construct a table showing simple, relative, and cumulative frequency. The lowest apparent limit is 100.

122	117	116	114	110	109	107
105	103	102	129	126	123	123
122	122	119	118	117	112	108
117	117	126	123	118	113	112

(a) What is the percentile for a student who weighs 117 pounds? (b) What weight corresponds to the 80th percentile?

B.2: COMPUTING THE SEMI-INTERQUARTILE RANGE

This part presents the procedures for computing the semi-interquartile range discussed in Chapter 8. The **semi-interquartile range** is one-half of the distance between the scores at the 25th and 75th percentiles.

THE FORMULA FOR COMPUTING THE SEMI-INTERQUARTILE RANGE IS

$$\frac{\text{Score at 75th percentile} - \text{Score at 25th percentile}}{2}$$

First determine the scores at the 25th and 75th percentiles using the formula given in Part B.1 for finding the score at a given percentile. Then subtract the score at the 25th percentile from the score at the 75th percentile and divide by 2.

For example, say that in some data the score of 12 is at the 25th percentile and the score of 17 is at the 75th percentile. The semi-interquartile range is (17 − 12)/2, which is 5/2, or 2.5. Essentially, we've determined that the average distance between the median and the scores at the 25th and 75th percentile is 2.5. In other words, the 25% of the distribution immediately below or above the median is, on average, within 2.5 points of the median.

B.3: PERFORMING LINEAR INTERPOLATION

This section presents the procedures for linear interpolation of z-scores as discussed in Chapter 9, and of values of t_{crit} as discussed in Chapter 14.

INTERPOLATING FROM THE *z*-TABLES

We interpolate to find a proportion not shown in the *z*-tables or when dealing with a *z*-score that has three decimal places (carry all computations to four decimal places).

Finding an Unknown *z*-Score

Say that we seek a *z*-score that corresponds to exactly .45 (.4500) of the curve between the mean and *z*. First, from the *z*-tables, identify the two bracketing proportions—the closest proportions above and below the target proportion. Note their corresponding *z*-scores. For .4500, the bracketing proportions are .4505 at $z = 1.6500$ and .4495 at $z = 1.6400$. Arrange the values this way:

	Known proportion under curve	*Unknown z-score*
Upper bracket	.4505	1.6500
Target	.4500	?
Lower bracket	.4495	1.6400

Because the "known" target proportion of .4500 is bracketed by .4505 and .4495, the unknown target *z*-score falls between 1.6500 and 1.6400.

First, deal with the known side: the target of .4500 is halfway between .4495 and .4505. That is, the difference between the lower known proportion and the target proportion is one-half of the difference between the two known proportions. Therefore, the *z*-score corresponding to .4500 is also halfway between the two bracketing *z*-scores of 1.6400 and 1.6500. The difference between these *z*-scores is .010, and one-half of that is .005. Thus, to go to halfway between 1.6400 and 1.6500, we add .005 to 1.6400. Therefore, a *z*-score of 1.6450 corresponds to .4500 of the curve between the mean and *z*.

The answer will not always be so obvious, so follow these steps:

Step 1: Determine the difference between the upper and lower known brackets. In the example, $.4505 - .4495 = .0010$. This is the total distance between the two proportions.

Step 2: Determine the difference between the known target and the lower known bracket. Above, $.4500 - .4495 = .0005$.

Step 3: Form a fraction dividing the answer from step 2 by the answer from step 1. Above, the fraction is .0005/.0010 or .5. Thus, .4500 is .5 of the distance from .4495 to .4505.

Step 4: Find the difference between the two brackets in the unknown column. Above, $1.6500 - 1.6400 = .010$. This is the total distance between the *z*-scores that bracket the unknown *z*-score.

Step 5: Multiply the proportion found in step 3 by the answer found in step 4. Above, $(.5)(.010) = .005$. The unknown target *z*-score is .005 larger than the lower bracketing *z*-score.

Step 6: Add the answer in step 5 to the lower bracketing z-score. Above, $.005 + 1.640 = 1.645$. Thus, .4500 of the normal curve lies between the mean and $z = 1.645$.

Finding an Unknown Proportion

Also apply the above steps to find an unknown proportion for a known three-decimal z-score. For example, say we seek the proportion between the mean and a z of 1.382. From the z-tables, the upper and lower brackets around this z are 1.390 and 1.380. Arrange the z-scores and corresponding proportions as shown below.

	Known z-score	*Unknown proportion under curve*
Upper bracket	1.390	.4177
Target	1.382	?
Lower bracket	1.380	.4162

To find the target proportion, use the above steps.

Step 1: $1.390 - 1.380 = .010$
This is the total difference between the known bracketing z-scores.
Step 2: $1.382 - 1.380 = .002$
This is the distance between the lower known bracketing z-score and the target z-score.
Step 3: $\frac{.002}{.010} = .20$
This is the proportion of the distance that the target z-score lies from the lower bracket. A z of 1.382 is .20 of the distance from 1.380 to 1.390.
Step 4: $.4177 - .4162 = .0015$
The total distance between the brackets of .4177 and .4162 in the unknown column is .0015.

The known target z-score is .20 of the distance from the lower bracketing z-score to the higher bracketing z-score. Therefore, the proportion we seek is .20 of the distance from the lower bracketing proportion to the upper bracketing proportion.
Step 5: $(0.20)(0.0015) = .0003$
Thus, .20 of the distance separating the bracketing proportions in the unknown column is .0003.
Step 6: $.4162 + .0003 = .4165$
Increasing the lower proportion in the unknown column by .0003 takes us to the point corresponding to .20 of the distance between the bracketing proportions. This point is .4165, which is the proportion that corresponds to $z = 1.382$.

INTERPOLATING CRITICAL VALUES

Sometimes, you must interpolate between the critical values in a table. Apply the same steps described above, except now use degrees of freedom and critical values.

For example, say that we seek the t_{crit} corresponding to 35 *df* (with $\alpha = .05$, two-tailed test). The *t*-tables have values only for 30 *df* and 40 *df*, giving the following:

	Known df	***Unknown critical value***
Upper bracket	30	2.042
Target	35	?
Lower bracket	40	2.021

Because 35 *df* is halfway between 30 *df* and 40 *df*, the critical value for 35 *df* is halfway between 2.042 and 2.021. Following the steps described for *z*-scores we have

Step 1: $40 - 30 = 10$
This is the total distance between the known bracketing *df*s.
Step 2: $35 - 30 = 5$
This is the distance between the *upper* bracketing *df* and the target *df*.
Step 3: $\frac{5}{10} = .50$
This is the proportion of the distance that the target *df* lies from the upper known bracket: 35 is .50 of the distance from 30 to 40.
Step 4: $2.042 - 2.021 = .021$
The total distance between the bracketing critical values in the unknown column is .021.

The *df* of 35 is .50 of the distance between the bracketing *df*s, so the critical value we seek is .50 of the distance between 2.042 and 2.021, or .50 of .021.
Step 5: $(.050)(.021) = .0105$
Thus, .50 of the distance between the bracketing critical values is .0105. Because critical values decrease as *df* increases, and we are going from 30 *df* to 35 *df*, we *subtract* .0105 from 2.042.
Step 6: $2.042 - .0105 = 2.0315$
Thus, $t = 2.0315$ is the critical value associated with 35 *df* at $\alpha = .05$ for a two-tailed test.

The same logic can be applied to find critical values for any other statistic.

PRACTICE PROBLEMS

(Answers for odd-numbered problems are provided in Appendix D.)

1. What is the *z*-score you must score above to be in the top 25% of scores?
2. Foofy obtains a *z*-score of 1.909. What proportion of scores are between her score and the mean?
3. For $\alpha = .05$, what is the two-tailed t_{crit} for $df = 50$?
4. For $\alpha = .05$, what is the two-tailed t_{crit} for $df = 55$?

B.4: ADDITIONAL FORMULAS FOR COMPUTING PROBABILITY

The following extends the discussion of computing probability found in Chapter 12.

THE MULTIPLICATION RULE

When computing the probability of complex events, sometimes we are "satisfied" only if several events occur. Use the multiplication rule when the word "and" links the events that must *all* occur for us to be satisfied. *The following multiplication rule is used with independent events.* (For dependent events, a different, more complex rule is needed.)

THE MULTIPLICATION RULE FOR INDEPENDENT EVENTS IS

$$p(\text{A and B}) = p(\text{A}) \times p(\text{B})$$

This says that the probability of several independent events is equal to their individual probabilities *multiplied* together. Thus, the probability of having both A and B occur is equal to the probability of A multiplied times the probability of B. (If there were three events, then all three probabilities would be multiplied together, and so on.)

The multiplication rule is appropriate when describing a *series* of independent events. Say that we want to know the probability of obtaining 3 heads on 3 coin tosses. In other words, what is the probability of obtaining a head *and* then a head *and* then a head? Thus, by the multiplication rule,

$$p(\text{head}) \times p(\text{head}) \times p(\text{head}) = .5 \times .5 \times .5 = .125$$

Also use the multiplication rule when two or more independent events occur *simultaneously*. For example, the probability of drawing the king of hearts can be restated as the probability of drawing a king *and* a heart simultaneously. With 4 kings, the probability of a king is 4/52, or .0769. With 13 hearts, the probability of drawing a heart is 13/52, or .25. The probability of drawing a king and a heart is (.0769 × .25) or .0192.

THE ADDITION RULE

Sometimes we seek any *one* of a number of outcomes that may occur. Use the addition rule when the word "or" links the events that will satisfy us. There are two versions of the addition rule, however, depending on whether these are mutually exclusive or mutually inclusive events. **Mutually exclusive events** are events that cannot occur together. Heads and tails, for example, are mutually exclusive on any *one* flip of a coin. Conversely, **mutually inclusive events** can occur together. For example, drawing a king from a deck is mutually inclusive with drawing a heart, because we can draw the king of hearts.

THE ADDITION RULE FOR MUTUALLY EXCLUSIVE EVENTS IS

$$p(\text{A or B}) = p(\text{A}) + p(\text{B})$$

Here, the probability of being satisfied by having either A or B occur is equal to the probability of A plus the probability of B. For example, the probability of randomly drawing a queen or a king equals the probability of a king (4/52 or .0769) added to the probability of a queen (also .0769). Thus, $p(\text{king or queen}) = .0769 + .0769 = .1538$.

When events are mutually *inclusive*, we may obtain A, or B, or A and B simultaneously. For example, say that we seek the probability of drawing either a king *or* a heart on one draw. We *might* think that with 4 kings and 13 hearts, there are a total of 17 cards that will satisfy us. Wrong! There are only 16. The problem is that we counted the king of hearts twice, once as a king and once as a heart. To correct this, we must subtract the "extra" king of hearts.

THE ADDITION RULE FOR MUTUALLY INCLUSIVE EVENTS IS

$$p(\text{A or B}) = p(\text{A}) + p(\text{B}) - [p(\text{A}) \times p(\text{B})]$$

This says that the probability of any one of several events is equal to the sum of the probabilities of the individual events *minus* the probability of the events' occurring simultaneously (minus the probability of A and B). Compute the probability of A and B using the multiplication rule, where $p(\text{A and B}) = p(\text{A}) \times p(\text{B})$. For example, the probability of a king is .0769, and the probability of a heart is 13/52, or .25. The probability of a king and a heart is 1/52, or .0192. Altogether,

$$p(\text{king or heart}) = .0769 + .25 - .0192 = .3077$$

You can combine the addition and multiplication rules. For example, what is the probability of drawing either the jack of diamonds *or* the king of spades on one draw, *and* then drawing either the 5 *or* the 6 of diamonds on a second draw? In symbols, this is

$$p[(\text{A or B}) \text{ and } (\text{C or D})]$$

Because these events are all mutually exclusive, we have

$$p[(\text{A or B}) \text{ and } (\text{C or D})] = [p(\text{A}) + p(\text{B})] \times [p(\text{C}) + p(\text{D})]$$

When sampling with replacement, the answer is .00148. When sampling without replacement, the answer is .00151.

THE BINOMIAL EXPANSION

Sometimes, we seek the probability of obtaining a subset of outcomes out of a series of tries. For example, we might seek the probability of obtaining one head out of three coin tosses or the probability of having certain numbers selected for the lottery. To answer such questions, we use a formula called the **binomial expansion**.

A "binomial" situation exists when one of only two possible outcomes occurs on each occasion and the two outcomes are mutually exclusive. Then the binomial expansion is used to compute the probability of obtaining a certain number of one of the outcomes in some total number of tries. In statistical terms, we find the probability of a certain *combination* of N events taken r at a time. Because either a head or a tail occurs on each toss of the coin, the binomial expansion can be used to determine the probability of obtaining some number of heads in a certain number of tosses. We'll use the symbol p_C to stand for the probability of the particular combination that satisfies us.

THE FORMULA FOR THE BINOMIAL EXPANSION IS

$$p_C = \left(\frac{N!}{r!(N - r)!}\right)(p^r)(q^{N-r})$$

N stands for the total number of tries, and r stands for the number of events that satisfy us. Thus, to find the probability of obtaining 1 head in 3 tries, $N = 3$ and $r = 1$. The p stands for the probability of the desired event, and we raise it to the r power. Here, heads is the desired event, so $p = .5$. With $r = 1$, we have $.5^1$. The q stands for the probability of the event that is not desired, and it is raised to the $N - r$ power. Tails is the undesirable event, so $q = .5$. Because $N - r$ equals 2, we have $.5^2$. Thus,

$$p_C = \left(\frac{3!}{1!(3 - 1)!}\right)(.5^1)(.5^2)$$

The exclamation point (!) is the symbol for *factorial*, meaning to multiply the number times all whole numbers less than it down to 1. Thus, 3! equals 3 times 2 times 1, for an answer of 6. Also, 1! is (1)(1), or 1, and (3 − 1)! is (2)!, which is 2. So, now

$$p_C = \left(\frac{6}{1(2)}\right)(.5^1)(.5^2)$$

A number raised to the first power is that number, so $.5^1$ equals .5. (A number raised to the zero power equals 1.) Because $.5^2$ is .25, we have

$$p_C = \left(\frac{6}{1(2)}\right)(.5)(.25)$$

And then,

$$p_C = 3(.125)$$

and so, $p_C = .375$: the probability of obtaining 1 head in 3 coin tosses is .375. Notice that this is not the probability of obtaining at least 1 head. Rather, it is the probability of obtaining precisely 1 head (and 2 tails) in 3 coin tosses.

We also use the binomial expansion when we can classify events as either "yes" or "no." For example, say we seek the probability of showing a two on 4 out of 6 rolls of one die. The desired two is the "yes," and we want it to happen 4 times, so $r = 4$. Its probability on any single roll is p, which is 1/6, or .167. Any other number on the die is a "no," the probability of which is q, which equals 5/6, or .83. Thus, we have

$$p_C = \left(\frac{N!}{r!(N - r)!}\right)(p^r)(q^{N-r}) = \left(\frac{6!}{4!(6 - 4)!}\right)(.167^4)(.83^2)$$

which becomes

$$p_C = 15(.00054) = .0081$$

The probability of rolling a die 6 times and showing a two on 4 rolls is .0081.

PRACTICE PROBLEMS

(Answers for odd-numbered problems are provided in Appendix D.)

1. (a) When a question is in terms of the probability of this "and" that, what mathematical procedure is employed? (b) When the question is in terms of the probability of this "or" that, what do you do? (c) When a question uses "or," what characteristics of the events must be considered?
2. Which of the following events are mutually inclusive and which are mutually exclusive: (a) Being male or female? (b) Being sunny and rainy? (c) Being tall and weighing a lot? (d) Being age 16 and being a registered voter?
3. Say that for every 100 people, 34 have an IQ above 116 and the rest are below 116, and 40 are introverted, 35 are extroverted, and 25 are in-between. (a) What is the probability of randomly selecting two people with an IQ above 116? (b) What is the probability of selecting either an introverted or an extroverted person? (c) What is the probability of selecting someone with an IQ above 116 who is introverted? (d) What is the probability of selecting either someone with an IQ above 116 or someone who is introverted? (e) What is the probability of selecting someone in-between, and then selecting either someone who has an IQ above 116 or who is introverted?
4. We seek the probability of obtaining three heads in a row with 3 coin tosses. Determine this probability using the multiplication rule.
5. (a) When do you use the binomial expansion? (b) Out of 5 coin tosses, what is the probability of obtaining 4 heads? (c) What is the probability of obtaining 1 head in 5 coin tosses? (d) Why is the answer in (c) the same as in (b)?
6. When rolling dice, what is the probability of each of the following? (a) Getting a 4 or a 5 rolling one die; (b) Getting a 4 twice in a row rolling one die; (c) Getting a 5 on only one die when rolling two dice at once; (d) Getting three 1s in 5 rolls of one die.

B.5: THE ONE-WAY WITHIN-SUBJECTS ANALYSIS OF VARIANCE

This section contains the formulas for the one-way within-subjects ANOVA discussed in Chapter 19. In that chapter, we studied how participants' style of dress influences their comfort level in a social setting. In a repeated-measures design, participants greeted people when dressed casually, semiformally, or formally, and each time indicated their comfort level. Say that 5 participants produced the data shown in Table B.4.

The first step is to compute the ΣX, the $\overline{X}$, and the ΣX^2 for each level of factor A (each column). Then compute ΣX_{tot} and ΣX^2_{tot}. Also compute ΣX_{sub}, which is the ΣX for each participant's scores (each horizontal row). Notice that the *n*s and *N* are based on the number of *scores*, not the number of participants.

TABLE B.4 Data and Initial Computations for Example One-Way Repeated Measures Study

		Factor A: type of dress			
		Level A_1: casual	*Level A_2: semiformal*	*Level A_3: formal*	
Participants	*1*	4	9	1	$\Sigma X_{sub} = 14$
	2	6	12	3	$\Sigma X_{sub} = 21$
	3	8	4	4	$\Sigma X_{sub} = 16$
	4	2	8	5	$\Sigma X_{sub} = 15$
	5	10	7	2	$\Sigma X_{sub} = 19$
		$\Sigma X = 30$ $\Sigma X^2 = 220$ $n_1 = 5$ $\bar{X}_1 = 6$	$\Sigma X = 40$ $\Sigma X^2 = 354$ $n_2 = 5$ $\bar{X}_2 = 8$	$\Sigma X = 15$ $\Sigma X^2 = 55$ $n_3 = 5$ $\bar{X}_3 = 3$	Total: $\Sigma X_{tot} = 30 + 40 + 15 = 85$ $\Sigma X^2_{tot} = 220 + 354 + 55 = 629$ $N = 15$ $k = 3$

As you perform the following calculations, create the ANOVA summary table as shown later in Table B.5.

Step 1: Compute the total sum of squares using the formula

$$SS_{tot} = \Sigma X^2_{tot} - \left(\frac{(\Sigma X_{tot})^2}{N}\right)$$

From the example

$$SS_{tot} = 629 - \left(\frac{85^2}{15}\right)$$

$$SS_{tot} = 629 - 481.67$$

$$SS_{tot} = 147.33$$

(*Note:* The $(\Sigma X_{tot})^2/N$ is the *correction term* in the following computations. Here, the correction is 481.67.)

Step 2: Compute the sum of squares for factor A using the formula

$$SS_A = \Sigma\left(\frac{(\text{Sum of scores in the column})^2}{n \text{ of scores in the column}}\right) - \left(\frac{(\Sigma X_{tot})^2}{N}\right)$$

For the example

$$SS_A = \left(\frac{(30)^2}{5} + \frac{(40)^2}{5} + \frac{(15)^2}{5}\right) - 481.67$$

$$SS_A = 545 - 481.67$$

$$SS_A = 63.33$$

Step 3: Find the sum of squares for subjects using the formula

$$SS_S = \frac{(\Sigma X_{sub1})^2 - (\Sigma X_{sub2})^2 + \cdots + (\Sigma X_n)^2}{k} - \frac{(\Sigma X_{tot})^2}{N}$$

In the example,

$$SS_S = \frac{(14)^2 + (21)^2 + (16)^2 + (15)^2 + (19)^2}{3} - 481.67$$

$$SS_S = 493 - 481.67$$

$$SS_S = 11.33$$

Step 4: Find the sum of squares for the interaction using the formula

$$SS_{A \times S} = SS_{tot} - SS_A - SS_S$$

Thus,

$$SS_{A \times S} = 147.33 - 63.33 - 11.33$$

$$SS_{A \times S} = 72.67$$

Step 5: Determine the degrees of freedom.

(a) For Factor A:

$$df_A = k_A - 1$$

so here,

$$df_A = 3 - 1 = 2$$

(b) For the interaction of A × Subjects:

$$df_{A \times S} = (k_A - 1)(k_{subs} - 1)$$

so here,

$$df_{A \times S} = (2)(4) = 8$$

Step 6: Compute the mean square for Factor A using the formula

$$MS_A = \frac{SS_A}{df_A}$$

or

$$MS_A = \frac{\text{Step 2}}{\text{Step 5(a)}}$$

so here,

$$MS_A = \frac{63.33}{2} = 31.67$$

Step 7: Compute the mean square for the interaction using the formula

$$MS_{A \times S} = \frac{SS_{A \times S}}{df_{A \times S}}$$

or

$$MS_{A \times S} = \frac{\text{Step 4}}{\text{Step 5(b)}}$$

so here,

$$MS_{A \times S} = \frac{72.67}{8} = 9.08$$

Step 8: Find F_{obt} using the formula

$$F_{obt} = \frac{MS_A}{MS_{A \times S}}$$

or

$$F_{obt} = \frac{\text{Step 6}}{\text{Step 7}}$$

so here,

$$F_{obt} = \frac{31.67}{9.08} = 3.49$$

The finished ANOVA summary table is shown in Table B.5.

Step 9: Find F_{crit} in Table 5 of Appendix C. Use df_A as the degrees of freedom between groups and $df_{A \times S}$ as the degrees of freedom within groups. In the example, for $\alpha = .05$, $df_A = 2$, and $df_{A \times S} = 8$, so F_{crit} is 4.46, so the results are not significant.

Step 10: For a significant factor with more than two levels, compute Tukey's *HSD*, using the formula

$$HSD = (q_k)\left(\sqrt{\frac{\text{Denominator of } F_{obt}}{n}}\right)$$

q_k is found in Table 6 in Appendix C using $df_{A \times S}$ as the df_{wn}. The "denominator of F_{obt}" is the $MS_{A \times S}$, and n is the number of scores per condition.

Step 11: For a significant F, compute eta squared using the formula

$$\eta^2 = \frac{SS_A}{SS_{tot}}$$

TABLE B.5 Summary Table of One-Way Within-Subjects ANOVA

Source	*Sum of squares*	*df*	*Mean square*	*F*
Factor A (dress)	63.33	2	31.67	3.49
Subjects	11.33	4		
Interaction				
(A × subjects)	72.67	8	9.08	
Total	147.33	14		

Step 12: Compute the confidence interval for any condition using the formula

$$\left(\sqrt{\frac{\text{Denominator of } F_{\text{obt}}}{n}}\right)(-t_{\text{crit}}) + \overline{X} \leq \mu \leq \left(\sqrt{\frac{\text{Denominator of } F_{\text{obt}}}{n}}\right)(+t_{\text{crit}}) + \overline{X}$$

where "the denominator of F_{obt}" is the *MS* used in calculating F_{obt}; *n* is the number of scores per condition and $\overline{X}$ is the mean of the condition. The t_{crit} is the two-tailed value from Table 2 in Appendix C, using as *df*, the *df* used in computing the denominator of F_{obt}.

PRACTICE PROBLEMS

(Answers for odd-numbered problems are provided in Appendix D.)

1. In a study of the influence of practice on an eye-hand coordination task, participants are tested prior to any practice, after 1 hour of practice, and again after 2 hours of practice. In the following data, higher scores indicate better performance.

	Amount of practice		
Participants	***Zero***	***One hour***	***Two hours***
S1	4	3	6
S2	3	5	5
S3	1	4	3
S4	3	4	6
S5	1	5	6
S6	2	6	7
S7	2	4	5
S8	1	3	8

(a) What are H_0 and H_a? (b) Complete the ANOVA summary table. (c) With $\alpha = .05$, what do you conclude about F_{obt}? (d) Perform the appropriate post hoc comparisons. (e) What is the effect size in this study? (f) What should you conclude about this relationship?

2. You measure 21 students' degree of positive attitude toward statistics at four equally spaced intervals during the semester. The mean score for each level is: Time 1, 62.50; Time 2, 64.68; Time 3, 69.32; Time 4, 72.00. You obtain the following sums of squares:

Source	*Sum of squares*	*df*	*Mean square*	*F*
Factor A	189.30			
Subjects	402.79			
A × subjects	688.32			
Total	1280.41			

(a) What are H_0 and H_a? (b) Complete the ANOVA summary table. (c) With $\alpha = .05$, what do you conclude about F_{obt}? (d) Perform the appropriate post hoc comparisons. (e) What is the effect size in this study? (f) What do you conclude about this relationship?

B.6: THE TWO-WAY WITHIN-SUBJECTS ANALYSIS OF VARIANCE

As discussed in Chapter 19, Table B.6 shows example data from a 2 × 2 within-subjects design, with three scores per cell.

TABLE B.6 Data from 2 × 2 Within-Subjects Design

		Factor A		
Factor B		A_1	A_2	
B_1	*Subject 1*	8	18	
	Subject 2	12	17	
	Subject 3	13	15	
		$\overline{X} = 11$ $\Sigma X = 33$ $\Sigma X^2 = 377$ $n = 3$	$\overline{X} = 16.7$ $\Sigma X = 50$ $\Sigma X^2 = 838$ $n = 3$	$\overline{X} = 13.85$ $\Sigma X = 83$ $n = 6$
B_2	*Subject 1*	9	6	
	Subject 2	10	8	
	Subject 3	17	4	
		$\overline{X} = 12$ $\Sigma X = 36$ $\Sigma X^2 = 470$ $n = 3$	$\overline{X} = 6$ $\Sigma X = 18$ $\Sigma X^2 = 116$ $n = 3$	$\overline{X} = 9$ $\Sigma X = 54$ $n = 6$
		$\Sigma X = 69$ $n = 6$ $\overline{X} = 11.5$	$\Sigma X = 68$ $n = 6$ $\overline{X} = 11.33$	$\Sigma X_{total} = 137$ $\Sigma X^2_{total} = 1801$ $N = 12$ $k_A = 2$ $k_B = 2$

TABLE B.7 A × Subject Table after Collapsing Across Factor B

	Factor A A_1	A_2	ΣX_{sub}
Subject 1	17	24	41
Subject 2	22	25	47
Subject 3	30	19	49

Step 1: In each cell, compute the sum of scores (ΣX), the sum of the squared scores (ΣX^2), n, and the mean (the interaction means). Determine k_A (the number of levels of factor A), and for each column, compute ΣX, n, and the mean (the main effect means of factor A). Determine k_B (the number of levels of factor B), and for each row, compute ΣX, n, and the mean (the main effect means of factor B).
Step 2: Also, determine

$$\Sigma X_{total} = 69 + 68 = 137$$

$$\Sigma X^2_{total} = 377 + 838 + 470 + 116 = 1801$$

$$N = 3 + 3 + 3 + 3 = 12$$

Create a table in which you collapse across factor B (as in Table B.7). Create another table in which you collapse across factor A (as in Table B.8).
(*Note:* The ΣX_{sub} for each subject must be the same in each table.)

Step 3: Compute the correction term.

$$\text{Correction term} = \left(\frac{(\Sigma X_{total})^2}{N}\right) = \frac{137^2}{12} = 1564.08$$

Step 4: As you perform the following calculations, create the ANOVA summary table shown in Table B.9. (Note that the table has components due to each factor and due to the interaction of factors and subjects.)

Step 5: Compute the total sum of squares.

$$SS_{tot} = \Sigma X^2_{total} - \text{Step 3}$$
$$SS_{tot} = 1801 - 1564.08 = 236.92$$

TABLE B.8 B × Subject Table after Collapsing Across Factor A

	Factor B B_1	B_2	ΣX_{sub}
Subject 1	26	15	41
Subject 2	29	18	47
Subject 3	28	21	49

TABLE B.9 Summary Table of Two-Way Within-Subjects ANOVA

Source	*Sum of squares*	*df*	*Mean square*	*F*
Factor				
A	.09	1	.09	.004
B	70.09	1	70.09	52.70
A×B	102.07	1	102.07	23.52
Subjects				
A×S	44.66	2	22.33	
B×S	2.66	2	1.33	
A×B×S	8.68	2	4.34	
Total	236.92	11	(not computed)	

Step 6: Compute the sum of squares for the column factor A.

$$SS_{\text{A}} = \Sigma\left(\frac{(\text{Sum of scores in each column})^2}{n \text{ of scores in the column}}\right) - \text{Step 3}$$

$$SS_{\text{A}} = \left(\frac{(69)^2}{6} + \frac{(68)^2}{6}\right) - 1564.08 = .09$$

Step 7: Compute the sum of squares for the row factor B.

$$SS_{\text{B}} = \Sigma\left(\frac{(\text{Sum of scores in each row})^2}{n \text{ of scores in the row}}\right) - \text{Step 3}$$

$$SS_{\text{B}} = \left(\frac{(83)^2}{6} + \frac{(54)^2}{6}\right) - 1564.08 = 70.09$$

Step 8: Compute the total sum of squares between groups (not reported in the summary table).

$$SS_{\text{bn}} = \Sigma\left(\frac{(\text{Sum of scores in each cell})^2}{n \text{ of scores in the cell}}\right) - \text{Step 3}$$

$$SS_{\text{bn}} = \left(\frac{(33)^2}{3} + \frac{(50)^2}{3} + \frac{(36)^2}{3} + \frac{(18)^2}{3}\right) - 1564.08$$

$$SS_{\text{bn}} = 172.25$$

Step 9: Compute the sum of squares for the A × B interaction.

$$SS_{\text{A}\times\text{B}} = SS_{\text{bn}} - SS_{\text{A}} - SS_{\text{B}}$$

$$SS_{\text{A}\times\text{B}} = \text{Step 8} - \text{Step 6} - \text{Step 7}$$

$$SS_{\text{A}\times\text{B}} = 172.25 - .09 - 70.09 = 102.07$$

Step 10: Compute the sum of squares for subjects (not reported in the summary table).

$$SS_S = \frac{(\Sigma X_{sub1})^2 + (\Sigma X_{sub2})^2 \ldots + (\Sigma X_n)^2}{(k_A)(k_B)} - \text{Step 3}$$

$$SS_S = \frac{(41)^2 + (47)^2 + (49)^2}{(2)(2)} - 1564.08$$

$$SS_S = 8.67$$

Step 11: Compute the sum of squares for the A × Subjects interaction (using Table B.7).

$$SS_{A\times S} = \Sigma\frac{(\text{Sum of each A} \times \text{Subject score})^2}{k_B} - \text{Step 3} - SS_A - SS_{subs}$$

$$SS_{A\times S} = \Sigma\frac{(\text{Sum of each A} \times \text{Subject score})^2}{k_B} - \text{Step 3} - \text{Step 6} - \text{Step 10}$$

$$SS_{A\times S} = \frac{(17)^2 + (24)^2 + (22)^2 + (25)^2 + (30)^2 + (19)^2}{2} - 1564.08 - .09 - 8.67$$

$$SS_{A\times S} = 44.66$$

Step 12: Compute the sum of squares for the B × Subjects interaction (using Table B.8).

$$SS_{B\times S} = \Sigma\frac{(\text{Sum of each B} \times \text{Subject score})^2}{k_A} - \text{Step 3} - SS_B - SS_{subs}$$

$$SS_{B\times S} = \Sigma\frac{(\text{Sum of each B} \times \text{Subject score})^2}{k_A} - \text{Step 3} - \text{Step 7} - \text{Step 10}$$

$$SS_{B\times S} = \frac{(26)^2 + (15)^2 + (29)^2 + (18)^2 + (28)^2 + (21)^2}{2} - 1564.08 - 70.09 - 8.67$$

$$SS_{B\times S} = 2.66$$

Step 13: Compute the sum of squares for the A × B × Subjects interaction.

$$SS_{A\times B\times S} = SS_{tot} - SS_A - SS_B - SS_{A\times B} - SS_{subs} - SS_{A\times S} - SS_{B\times S}$$

$$SS_{A\times B\times S} = \text{Step 5} - \text{Step 6} - \text{Step 7} - \text{Step 9} - \text{Step 10} - \text{Step 11} - \text{Step 12}$$

$$SS_{A\times B\times S} = 236.92 - .09 - 70.09 - 102.07 - 8.67 - 44.66 - 2.66$$

$$SS_{A\times B\times S} = 8.68$$

Step 14: Compute the degrees of freedom.
(a) Factor A:

$$df_A = k_A - 1$$
$$df_A = 2 - 1 = 1$$

(b) Factor B:

$$df_B = k_B - 1$$
$$df_B = 2 - 1 = 1$$

(c) A × B interaction:

$$df_{A\times B} = (df_A)(df_B)$$
$$df_{A\times B} = (1)(1) = 1$$

(d) Subjects:

$$df_S = \text{Number of subjects} - 1$$
$$df_S = 3 - 1 = 2$$

(e) A × Subjects interaction:

$$df_{A\times S} = (df_A)(df_S)$$
$$df_{A\times S} = (1)(2) = 2$$

(f) B × Subjects interaction:

$$df_{B\times S} = (df_B)(df_S)$$
$$df_{B\times S} = (1)(2) = 2$$

(g) A × B × Subjects interaction:

$$df_{A\times B\times S} = (df_A)(df_B)(df_S)$$
$$df_{A\times B\times S} = (1)(1)(2) = 2$$

(h) Total:

$$df_{tot} = N - 1$$
$$df_{tot} = 12 - 1 = 11$$

Step 15: Compute the mean square for factor A.

$$MS_A = \frac{SS_A}{df_A}$$

$$MS_A = \frac{\text{Step 6}}{\text{Step 14a}}$$

$$MS_A = \frac{.09}{1} = .09$$

Step 16: Compute the mean square for factor B.

$$MS_B = \frac{SS_B}{df_B}$$

$$MS_B = \frac{\text{Step 7}}{\text{Step 14b}}$$

$$MS_B = \frac{70.09}{1} = 70.09$$

Step 17: Compute the mean square for the A × B interaction.

$$MS_{A\times B} = \frac{SS_{A\times B}}{df_{A\times B}}$$

$$MS_{A \times B} = \frac{\text{Step 9}}{\text{Step 14c}}$$

$$MS_{A \times B} = \frac{102.07}{1} = 102.07$$

Step 18: Compute the mean square for the A × Subjects interaction.

$$MS_{A \times S} = \frac{SS_{A \times S}}{df_{A \times S}}$$

$$MS_{A \times S} = \frac{\text{Step 11}}{\text{Step 14e}}$$

$$MS_{A \times S} = \frac{44.66}{2} = 22.33$$

Step 19: Compute the mean square for the B × Subjects interaction.

$$MS_{B \times S} = \frac{SS_{B \times S}}{df_{B \times S}}$$

$$MS_{B \times S} = \frac{\text{Step 12}}{\text{Step 14f}}$$

$$MS_{B \times S} = \frac{2.66}{2} = 1.33$$

Step 20: Compute the mean square for the A × B × Subjects interaction.

$$MS_{A \times B \times S} = \frac{SS_{A \times B \times S}}{df_{A \times B \times S}}$$

$$MS_{A \times B \times S} = \frac{\text{Step 13}}{\text{Step 14g}}$$

$$MS_{A \times B \times S} = \frac{8.68}{2} = 4.34$$

Step 21: Compute the *F* for the main effect of factor A.

$$F_A = \frac{MS_A}{MS_{A \times S}}$$

$$F_A = \frac{\text{Step 15}}{\text{Step 18}}$$

$$F_A = \frac{.09}{22.33} = .004$$

Step 22: Compute the *F* for the main effect of factor B.

$$F_B = \frac{MS_B}{MS_{B \times S}}$$

$$F_B = \frac{\text{Step 16}}{\text{Step 19}}$$

$$F_B = \frac{70.09}{1.33} = 52.70$$

Step 23: Compute the F for the A × B interaction.

$$F_{A \times B} = \frac{MS_{A \times B}}{MS_{A \times B \times S}}$$

$$F_{A \times B} = \frac{\text{Step 17}}{\text{Step 20}}$$

$$F_{A \times B} = \frac{102.07}{4.34} = 23.52$$

Step 24: For each obtained F above, find the appropriate critical value in Table 5 in Appendix C, using the appropriate degrees of freedom.

- For Factor A: df_A is the df between and $df_{A \times S}$ is the df within. Above, for $\alpha = .05$ and $df_A = 1$ and $df_{A \times S} = 2$, F_{crit} is 18.51, so F_{obt} of .004 is not significant.
- For Factor B: df_B is the df between and $df_{B \times S}$ is the df within. Above, for $\alpha = .05$ and $df_B = 1$ and $df_{B \times S} = 2$, the F_{crit} is 18.51, so F_{obt} of 52.70 is significant.
- For A × B: $df_{A \times B}$ is the df between and $df_{A \times B \times S}$ is the df within. Above, for $\alpha = .05$ and $df_{A \times B} = 1$ and $df_{A \times B \times S} = 2$, the F_{crit} is 18.51, so F_{obt} of 23.52 is significant.

Step 25: For each significant F with more than two levels, compute Tukey's HSD using the formula

$$HSD = (q_k)\left(\sqrt{\frac{\text{Denominator in } F_{obt}}{n}}\right)$$

where "Denominator in F_{obt}" is the MS used as the denominator when calculating the F_{obt}. n is the number of scores that each mean being compared is based on. The q_k is found in Table 6 in Appendix C, using k and the df used in calculating the MS in the denominator of F_{obt} as the df_{wn}. For the interaction, first determine the *adjusted* k as described in Chapter 18.

Step 26: For each significant F, compute η^2 using the formula

$$\eta^2 = \frac{\text{Sum of squares for the effect}}{SS_{tot}}$$

where "Sum of squares for the effect" is the SS used in calculating the numerator of the F_{obt}, whether SS_A, SS_B, or $SS_{A \times B}$. The SS_{tot} is the total sum of squares in the ANOVA.

Step 27: Compute the confidence interval for the population μ represented by the mean of any level or cell using the formula presented in Step 12 in the previous section (B.5) of this appendix.

PRACTICE PROBLEMS

(Answers for odd-numbered problems are provided in Appendix D.)

1. You measure the dependent variable of participants' hypnotic suggestibility as a function of whether they meditate before being tested, and whether they were shown a film containing a low, medium, or high amount of fantasy. The same participants are tested under all conditions. Perform all appropriate statistical analyses, and determine what you should conclude about this study.

	Amount of fantasy		
	Low	***Medium***	***High***
Meditation	5 6 2 2 5	7 5 6 9 5	9 8 10 10 10
No meditation	10 10 9 10 10	2 5 4 3 2	5 6 5 7 6

2. You study whether alcohol and whether the time of year the alcohol is consumed affects performance on an eye-hand coordination task. Each participant performed the task either before drinking 0 or 3 drinks, and each was tested during the summer and during the winter. With $n = 3$ in each cell, the following cell means were obtained.

		Drinks prior to task performance	
		A_1: 0 drinks	***A_2: 3 drinks***
Time of year	***B1: summer***	16	6
	B2: winter	11	12

Summary Table

Source	*Sum of squares*	*df*	*Mean square*	*F*
Factor				
A	90.75	_____	_____	_____
B	6.75	_____	_____	_____
A×B	47.50	_____	_____	_____
Subjects				
A×S	8.00	_____	_____	
B×S	2.00	_____	_____	
A×B×S	4.25	_____	_____	
Total	236.92	_____	(not computed)	

(a) Complete the ANOVA summary table. (b) With an $\alpha = .05$, what do you conclude about each F_{obt}? (c) Perform the appropriate post hoc comparisons. What do you conclude about the relationships in this study? (d) Determine the effect size where appropriate and interpret it.

B.7: THE TWO-WAY MIXED-DESIGN ANALYSIS OF VARIANCE

This design is diagrammed differently than previous designs. Arrange the data so that the row factor is Factor A and is the between-subjects factor. Factor B is the column factor and is the within-subjects factor. Table B.10 shows example data from a 2 × 2 mixed design.

TABLE B.10 Data from Two-Way Mixed Design

Factor A is the between-subjects factor and Factor B is the within-subjects factor.

Factor A		Factor B: B_1	Factor B: B_2	ΣX_{sub}
A_1	*Subject 1*	3	10	13
	Subject 2	5	16	21
	Subject 3	7	13	20
		$\bar{X} = 5$ $\Sigma X = 15$ $\Sigma X^2 = 83$ $n = 3$	$\bar{X} = 13$ $\Sigma X = 39$ $\Sigma X^2 = 525$ $n = 3$	$\bar{X} = 9$ $\Sigma X = 54$ $n = 6$
A_2	*Subject 4*	8	7	15
	Subject 5	6	7	13
	Subject 6	4	4	8
		$\bar{X} = 6$ $\Sigma X = 18$ $\Sigma X^2 = 116$ $n = 3$	$\bar{X} = 6$ $\Sigma X = 18$ $\Sigma X^2 = 114$ $n = 3$	$\bar{X} = 6$ $\Sigma X = 36$ $n = 6$
		$\Sigma X = 33$ $n = 6$ $\bar{X} = 5.5$	$\Sigma X = 57$ $n = 6$ $\bar{X} = 12.5$	$\Sigma X_{total} = 90$ $\Sigma X^2_{total} = 838$ $N = 12$ $k_A = 2$ $k_B = 2$

Step 1: In each cell, compute the sum of scores (ΣX), the sum of the squared scores (ΣX^2), n, and the mean (the interaction means). Determine k_A (the number of levels of factor A), and, for each level, compute ΣX, n, and the mean (the main effect means of factor A). Determine k_B (the number of levels of factor B), and for each column, compute ΣX, n, and the mean (the main effect means of factor B).

Also, calculate the sum of the scores obtained by each participant (ΣX_{sub}).

Step 2: Determine

$$\Sigma X_{total} = 54 + 36 = 90$$

$$\Sigma X^2_{total} = 83 + 525 + 116 + 114 = 838$$

$$N = 3 + 3 + 3 + 3 = 12$$

Step 3: Compute the correction term.

$$\text{Correction term} = \left(\frac{(\Sigma X_{total})^2}{N}\right) = \frac{90^2}{12} = 675$$

Step 4: As you perform the following calculations, create the ANOVA summary table shown in Table B.11. (This table is organized differently from previous two-way summary tables. Here, the components of the between-subjects factor A are placed together, and then the components of the within-subjects factor and the interaction are placed together.)

Step 5: Compute the total sum of squares.

$$SS_{tot} = \Sigma X^2_{total} - \text{Step 3}$$

$$SS_{tot} = 838 - 675 = 163$$

Step 6: Compute the sum of squares for subjects (not reported in the summary table).

$$SS_{subs} = \frac{(\Sigma X_{sub1})^2 + (\Sigma X_{sub2})^2 \ldots + (\Sigma X_n)^2}{k_B} - \text{Step 3}$$

$$SS_{subs} = \frac{(13)^2 + (21)^2 + (20)^2 + (15)^2 + (13)^2 + (8)^2}{2} - 675$$

$$SS_{subs} = 59$$

TABLE B.11 Summary Table of Two-Way Mixed-Design ANOVA

Source	*Sum of squares*	*df*	*Mean square*	*F*
Between groups				
Factor A	27.00	1	27.00	3.38
Error between	32.00	4	8.00	
Within groups				
Factor B	48.00	1	48.00	24.00
A×B interaction	48.00	1	48.00	24.00
Error within	8.00	4	2.00	
Total	163.00	11		

Step 7: Compute the sum of squares for the between-subjects, row factor A.

$$SS_{\text{A}} = \Sigma\left(\frac{(\text{Sum of scores in each row})^2}{n \text{ of scores in the row}}\right) - \text{Step 3}$$

$$SS_{\text{A}} = \left(\frac{(54)^2}{6} + \frac{(36)^2}{6}\right) - 675 = 27$$

Step 8: Compute the sum of squares for the within-subjects, column factor B.

$$SS_{\text{B}} = \Sigma\left(\frac{(\text{Sum of scores in each column})^2}{n \text{ of scores in the column}}\right) - \text{Step 3}$$

$$SS_{\text{B}} = \left(\frac{(33)^2}{6} + \frac{(57)^2}{6}\right) - 675 = 48$$

Step 9: Compute the sum of squares for the "error between."

$$SS_{\text{e:bn}} = SS_{\text{subs}} - SS_{\text{A}}$$

$$SS_{\text{e:bn}} = \text{Step 6} - \text{Step 7}$$

$$SS_{\text{e:bn}} = 59 - 27 = 32$$

Step 10: Compute the total sum of squares between groups (not reported in the summary table).

$$SS_{\text{bn}} = \Sigma\left(\frac{(\text{Sum of scores in each cell})^2}{n \text{ of scores in the cell}}\right) - \text{Step 3}$$

$$SS_{\text{bn}} = \left(\frac{(15)^2}{3} + \frac{(39)^2}{3} + \frac{(18)^2}{3} + \frac{(18)^2}{3}\right) - 675$$

$$SS_{\text{bn}} = 123$$

Step 11: Compute the sum of squares for the A × B interaction.

$$SS_{\text{A}\times\text{B}} = SS_{\text{bn}} - SS_{\text{A}} - SS_{\text{B}}$$

$$SS_{\text{A}\times\text{B}} = \text{Step 10} - \text{Step 7} - \text{Step 8}$$

$$SS_{\text{A}\times\text{B}} = 123 - 27 - 48 = 48$$

Step 12: Compute the sum of squares for the "error within."

$$SS_{\text{e:wn}} = SS_{\text{tot}} - SS_{\text{subs}} - SS_{\text{B}} - SS_{\text{A}\times\text{B}}$$

$$SS_{\text{e:wn}} = \text{Step 5} - \text{Step 6} - \text{Step 8} - \text{Step 11}$$

$$SS_{\text{e:wn}} = 163 - 59 - 48 - 48 = 8$$

Step 13: Compute the degrees of freedom.
(a) Factor A:

$$df_{\text{A}} = k_{\text{A}} - 1$$

$$df_{\text{A}} = 2 - 1 = 1$$

(b) Factor B:

$$df_B = k_B - 1$$

$$df_B = 2 - 1 = 1$$

(c) A × B interaction:

$$df_{A\times B} = (df_A)(df_B)$$

$$df_{A\times B} = \text{(Step 13a)(Step 13b)}$$

$$df_{A\times B} = (1)(1) = 1$$

(d) Error between groups:

$$df_{e:bn} = (k_A)(n - 1)$$

$$df_{e:bn} = (2)(3 - 1) = 4$$

(e) Error within subjects:

$$df_{e:wn} = (k_B - 1)(k_A)(n - 1)$$

$$df_{e:wn} = (2 - 1)(2)(3 - 1) = 4$$

(f) Total:

$$df_{tot} = N - 1$$

$$df_{tot} = 12 - 1 = 11$$

Step 14: Compute the mean square for factor A.

$$MS_A = \frac{SS_A}{df_A}$$

$$MS_A = \frac{\text{Step 7}}{\text{Step 13a}}$$

$$MS_A = \frac{27}{1} = 27$$

Step 15: Compute the mean square for factor B.

$$MS_B = \frac{SS_B}{df_B}$$

$$MS_B = \frac{\text{Step 8}}{\text{Step 13b}}$$

$$MS_B = \frac{48}{1} = 48$$

Step 16: Compute the mean square for the A × B interaction.

$$MS_{A\times B} = \frac{SS_{A\times B}}{df_{A\times B}}$$

$$MS_{A \times B} = \frac{\text{Step 11}}{\text{Step 13c}}$$

$$MS_{A \times B} = \frac{48}{1} = 48$$

Step 17: Compute the mean square for error between.

$$MS_{e:bn} = \frac{SS_{e:bn}}{df_{e:bn}}$$

$$MS_{e:bn} = \frac{\text{Step 9}}{\text{Step 13d}}$$

$$MS_{e:bn} = \frac{32}{4} = 8$$

Step 18: Compute the mean square for error within.

$$MS_{e:wn} = \frac{SS_{e:wn}}{df_{e:wn}}$$

$$MS_{e:wn} = \frac{\text{Step 12}}{\text{Step 13e}}$$

$$MS_{e:wn} = \frac{8}{4} = 2$$

Step 19: Compute the F for the main effect of A.

$$F_A = \frac{MS_A}{MS_{e:bn}}$$

$$F_A = \frac{\text{Step 14}}{\text{Step 17}}$$

$$F_A = \frac{27}{8} = 3.38$$

Step 20: Compute the F for the main effect of B.

$$F_B = \frac{MS_B}{MS_{e:wn}}$$

$$F_B = \frac{\text{Step 15}}{\text{Step 18}}$$

$$F_B = \frac{48}{2} = 24$$

Step 21: Compute the F for the A × B interaction.

$$F_{A \times B} = \frac{MS_{A \times B}}{MS_{e:wn}}$$

$$F_{A \times B} = \frac{\text{Step 16}}{\text{Step 18}}$$

$$F_{A \times B} = \frac{48}{2} = 24$$

Step 22: For each obtained F above, find the appropriate critical value in Table 5 in Appendix C, using the appropriate degrees of freedom.

- For Factor A: df_A is the df between and $df_{e:bn}$ is the df within. Above, for $\alpha = .05$ and $df_A = 1$ and $df_{e:bn} = 4$, the F_{crit} is 7.71, so the main effect of Factor A is not significant.
- For Factor B: df_B is the df between and $df_{e:wn}$ is the df within. Above, for $\alpha = .05$ and $df_B = 1$ and $df_{e:wn} = 4$, the F_{crit} is 7.71, so the main effect of Factor B is significant.
- For A × B: $df_{A \times B}$ is the df between and $df_{e:wn}$ is the df within. Above, for $\alpha = .05$ and $df_{A \times B} = 1$ and $df_{e:wn} = 4$, the F_{crit} is 7.71, so the interaction effect is significant.

Step 23: For each significant F with more than two levels, compute Tukey's *HSD* using the formula given in Step 25 in section B.6.

Step 24: For each significant F, compute eta squared using the formula given in Step 26 in section B.6.

Step 25: Compute the confidence interval for the population μ represented by the mean of any level or cell using the formula given in Step 12 in section B.5.

PRACTICE PROBLEMS

(Answers for odd-numbered problems are provided in Appendix D.)

1. You measure the dependent variable of participants' hypnotic suggestibility as a function of whether they meditate before being tested, and whether they were shown a film containing a low, medium, or high amount of fantasy. The meditation factor is between subjects, the fantasy-level factor is repeated measures.

	Amount of fantasy		
	Low	***Medium***	***High***
Meditation	5	7	9
	6	5	8
	2	6	10
	2	9	10
	5	5	10
No meditation	10	2	5
	10	5	6
	9	4	5
	10	3	7
	10	2	6

Perform all appropriate statistical analyses, and determine what to conclude about this study.

2. A researcher studies the influence of four doses of a new drug to reduce depression in adult women who either have the AIDs virus (are HIV+) or do not have it (are HIV−). Dosage is a repeated-measures factor and HIV status is a between-subjects factor. With $n = 3$ in each cell, the following overall mean mood improvement scores were obtained.

		Factor B: dose of antidepressant			
		B_1: *control*	B_2: *Low*	B_3: *Med.*	B_4: *High*
Factor A: HIV status	A_1: *HIV−*	4	5	13	17
	A_2: *HIV+*	3	6	12	19

Summary Table

Source	*Sum of squares*	*df*	*Mean square*	*F*
Between groups				
Factor A	21.00	____	____	____
Error between	20.50	____	____	____
Within groups				
Factor B	67.75	____	____	____
A×B interaction	30.00	____	____	____
Error within	34.50	____	____	
Total	173.75	____		

(a) Complete the ANOVA summary table. (b) With an $\alpha = .05$, what do you conclude about each F_{obt}? (c) Perform the appropriate post hoc comparisons. What do you conclude about the relationships in this study? (d) Determine the effect size where appropriate. What does it indicate about the observed effects?

B.8: NONPARAMETRIC PROCEDURES FOR RANKED DATA

This section presents the nonparametric inferential procedures for ranked (ordinal) scores that were described in Chapter 21.

B.8.1: The Mann-Whitney *U* test

The Mann-Whitney test is appropriate when the n in each condition is equal to or less than 20 and you have two independent samples of ranks. For example, as in Chapter 21, say we measure the reaction times of two groups of people to symbols when printed in black ink or red ink. Table B.12 gives the reaction times (in milliseconds) and their corresponding ranks for this study.

TABLE B.12 Example Ranked Data from Two Independent Samples

Red symbols		*Black symbols*	
Reaction time	*Ranked score*	*Reaction time*	*Ranked score*
540	2	760	7
480	1	890	8
600	5	1105	10
590	3	595	4
605	6	940	9
	$\Sigma R = 17$		$\Sigma R = 38$
	$n = 5$		$n = 5$

Step 1: *Assign ranks to all scores in the experiment.* Assign the rank of 1 to the lowest score in the experiment, the rank of 2 to the second lowest score, and so on.

Step 2: *Compute the sum of the ranks for each group.* Compute ΣR for each group, and note its n, the number of scores in the group.

Step 3: *Compute two versions of the Mann-Whitney U.* Compute U_1 for Group 1, using the formula

$$U_1 = (n_1)(n_2) + \frac{n_1(n_1 + 1)}{2} - \Sigma R_1$$

where n_1 is the n of Group 1, n_2 is the n of Group 2, and ΣR_1 is the sum of ranks from Group 1. Let's call the red symbol group Group 1 so

$$U_1 = (5)(5) + \frac{5(5 + 1)}{2} - 17 = 40 - 17 = 23.0$$

Step 4: *Compute U_2 for Group 2*

$$U_2 = (n_1)(n_2) + \frac{n_2(n_2 + 1)}{2} - \Sigma R_2$$

where ΣR_2 is the sum of ranks from Group 2. For the black symbol group,

$$U_2 = (5)(5) + \frac{5(5 + 1)}{2} - 38 = 40 - 38 = 2.0$$

Step 5: *Determine the Mann-Whitney U_{obt}.* In a two-tailed test, U_{obt} is the *smaller* of U_1 or U_2. Here $U_{obt} = 2.0$. In a one-tailed test, we predict that one of the groups has the larger sum of ranks, and then this group's U is U_{obt}.

Step 6: *Find the critical value of U in Table 9 of Appendix C entitled "Critical Values of the Mann-Whitney U."* For either a one- or two-tailed test, locate U_{crit} using n_1 and n_2. For the example, with a two-tailed test, U_{crit} is 2.0.

Step 7: *Compare U_{obt} to U_{crit}.* U_{obt} is significant if it is *equal to or less than* U_{crit}. With $U_{obt} = 2.0$, the two conditions differ significantly.

Step 8: *To describe the effect size, compute eta squared.* To do this, ignore the rule about n and reanalyze the data using the rank sums test.

B.8.2: The Rank Sums Test

The rank sums test is used with two independent samples of ranks when the n in either condition is *greater* than 20. As an illustration, however, we'll use the scores from the previous study in Table B.12.

Step 1: *Assign ranks to the scores in the experiment.* Rank-order all scores in the experiment.

Step 2: *Choose one group and compute the sum of the ranks.* Compute ΣR for one group.

Step 3: *Compute the expected sum of ranks, ΣR_{exp}, for the chosen group.*

$$\Sigma R_{\text{exp}} = \frac{n(N + 1)}{2}$$

where n is the n of the chosen group and N is the total N of the study. For the red-symbol group

$$\Sigma R_{\text{exp}} = \frac{5(10 + 1)}{2} = \frac{55}{2} = 27.5$$

Step 4: *Compute the rank sums statistic.*

$$z_{\text{obt}} = \frac{\Sigma R - \Sigma R_{\text{exp}}}{\sqrt{\dfrac{(n_1)(n_2)(N + 1)}{12}}}$$

where ΣR is the sum of the ranks for the chosen group, ΣR_{exp} is the expected sum of ranks for the chosen group, n_1 and n_2 are the ns of the two groups, and N is the total N.

$$z_{\text{obt}} = \frac{17 - 27.5}{\sqrt{\dfrac{(5)(5)(10 + 1)}{12}}}$$

$$z_{\text{obt}} = \frac{-10.5}{\sqrt{22.92}} = \frac{-10.5}{4.79} = -2.19$$

Step 5: *Find the critical value of z in the z-tables (Table 1 in Appendix C).* At $\alpha = .05$, the two-tailed $z_{\text{crit}} = \pm 1.96$. In a one-tailed test, predict whether the ΣR of the chosen group will be greater than or less than the expected sum of ranks, and use the one-tailed value of either $+1.645$ or -1.645.

Step 6: *Compare z_{obt} to z_{crit}.* If the absolute value of z_{obt} is larger than z_{crit}, there is a significant difference between the samples. In the example, $z_{\text{obt}} = -2.19$ and $z_{\text{crit}} = \pm 1.96$, so the samples differ significantly.

Step 7: *Describe a significant relationship using eta squared.* Here, eta squared is analogous to r^2_{pb} (discussed in Chapter 15).

$$\eta^2 = \frac{(z_{\text{obt}})^2}{N - 1}$$

where z_{obt} is computed in the above rank sums test and N is the total number of participants. In the example, η^2 is .53.

B.8.3: The Wilcoxon *T* Test

The Wilcoxon test is analogous to the dependent-samples *t*-test for ranked data. For example, as in Chapter 21, say in the above reaction-time study, we measure the reaction times of the same participants to both the red and black symbols, producing the data in Table B.13.

Step 1: *Determine the difference score (D) for each pair of scores.* For each pair, subtract the score in one condition from the score in the other. It makes no difference which score is subtracted from which, but subtract all scores in the same way.

Step 2: *Determine the N of the nonzero difference scores.* Ignore all difference scores equal to zero and count the number of nonzero differences. In the example, $N = 9$.

Step 3: *Assign ranks to the nonzero difference scores.* Ignore the sign (+ or −) and assign the rank of 1 to the smallest difference, the rank of 2 to the second smallest difference, and so on.

Step 4: *Separate the ranks, using the sign of the difference scores.* Create two columns of ranks. The $R-$ column contains the ranks assigned to negative differences in Step 3. The $R+$ column contains the ranks assigned to positive differences.

Step 5: *Compute each sum of ranks.* Compute ΣR for the column labeled "$R+$" and for the column labeled "$R-$."

Step 6: *Determine the Wilcoxon T_{obt}.* In the two-tailed test, T_{obt} is the smaller ΣR in Step 5. In the example, $T_{obt} = 3$. In the one-tailed test, we predict whether most differences are positive or negative, so we predict whether the $R+$ or $R-$ column contains the smaller ΣR. The ΣR predicted to be smallest is T_{obt}.

Step 7: *Find the critical value of T in Table 10 of Appendix C, entitled "Critical Values of the Wilcoxon T."* Use the appropriate alpha level and *N*, the number of nonzero difference scores. Above, for $\alpha = .05$, T_{crit} is 5.0.

TABLE B.13 Example Data for the Wilcoxon Test for Two Dependent Samples

Participant	*Reaction time to red symbols*	*Reaction time to black symbols*	*Difference, D*	*Ranked scores*	*R−*	*R+*
1	540	760	−220	6	6	
2	580	710	−130	4	4	
3	600	1105	−505	9	9	
4	680	880	−200	5	5	
5	430	500	−70	3	3	
6	740	990	−250	7	7	
7	600	1050	−450	8	8	
8	690	640	+50	2		2
9	605	595	+10	1		1
10	520	520	0			
			$N = 9$		$\Sigma R = 42$	$\Sigma R = 3$

Step 8: *Compare T_{obt} to T_{crit}.* The T_{obt} is significant if it is *equal to or less than* T_{crit}. In the example, $T_{obt} = 3.0$ and $T_{crit} = 5.0$, so the samples differ significantly.

There is no recognized way to compute η^2 for this procedure.

B.8.4: The Kruskal-Wallis H Test

The Kruskal-Wallis H test is analogous to a one-way between-subjects ANOVA for ranked data. It assumes that there are *three* or more conditions with at least five participants in each.

For example, as in Chapter 21, say we examine how far golfers hit the ball as a function of their height (short, medium, or tall). The raw scores and their ranks are shown in Table B.14.

Step 1: *Assign ranks, using all scores in the experiment.* Assign the rank of 1 to the lowest score in the experiment, the rank of 2 to the second lowest score, and so on.

Step 2: *Compute the sum of the ranks in each condition.* Compute ΣR in each column.

Step 3: *Compute the sum of squares between groups.*

$$SS_{bn} = \frac{(\Sigma R_1)^2}{n_1} + \frac{(\Sigma R_2)^2}{n_2} + \ldots + \frac{(\Sigma R_k)^2}{n_k}$$

For each level, square the sum of the ranks and then divide by n. Then, add the amounts together. For the example,

$$SS_{bn} = \frac{(21)^2}{5} + \frac{(35)^2}{5} + \frac{(64)^2}{5} = 88.2 + 245 + 819.2$$

$$SS_{bn} = 1152.4.$$

Step 4: *Compute the H_{obt}.*

$$H_{obt} = \left(\frac{12}{N(N+1)}\right)(SS_{bn}) - 3(N+1)$$

where N is the N of the study.

TABLE B.14 Example Data for the Kruskal-Wallis *H* Test

		Height				
Short		***Medium***		***Tall***		
Score	***Rank***	***Score***	***Rank***	***Score***	***Rank***	
10	2	24	3	68	14	
28	6	27	5	71	15	
26	4	35	7	57	10	
39	8	44	9	60	12	
6	1	58	11	62	13	
	$\Sigma R_1 = 21$ $n_1 = 5$		$\Sigma R_2 = 35$ $n_2 = 5$		$\Sigma R_3 = 64$ $n_3 = 5$	$N = 15$

In the example,

$$H_{obt} = \left(\frac{12}{15(15 + 1)}\right)(1152.4) - 3(15 + 1) = (.05)(1152.4) - 48$$

$$H_{obt} = 57.62 - 48 = 9.62$$

Step 5: *Find the critical value of H in the χ^2 tables (Table 8 in Appendix C).* The $df = k - 1$, where k is the number of levels in the factor. In the example, for $\alpha = .05$ and $df = 2$, χ^2_{crit} is 5.99.

Step 6: *Compare H_{obt} to the critical value of χ^2.* If H_{obt} is *larger* than H_{crit}, then H_{obt} is significant. Above, the H_{obt} of 9.62 is significant, indicating that at least two of the conditions represent different populations of ranks (and distance scores).

Step 7: *Perform post hoc comparisons using the rank sums test.* When H_{obt} is significant, determine which conditions differ by performing the rank sums test on every pair of conditions, regardless of the n in each group. Treat each pair of conditions being compared as if they comprised the entire study, and perform the rank sums test described in Part B.8.2. In the example, short versus medium produces $z_{obt} = 1.36$, short versus tall produces $z_{obt} = 2.62$, and medium versus tall produces $z_{obt} = 2.40$. With $\alpha = .05$, z_{crit} is ± 1.96. Therefore, the short and medium conditions are not significantly different, but they both differ significantly from the tall condition.

Step 8: *Describe a significant relationship using eta squared.*

$$\eta^2 = \frac{H_{obt}}{N - 1}$$

where H_{obt} is computed in the Kruskal-Wallis test and N is the total number of participants. In the example, $\eta^2 = .69$.

B.8.5: The Friedman χ^2 Test

The Friedman χ^2 test is analogous to a one-way within-subjects ANOVA for ranks. With only three levels of the factor, there must be at least 10 scores per condition. With only four levels, there must be at least five scores per condition. For example, as in Chapter 21, say we examine the rankings of three instructors, as shown in Table B.15.

Step 1: *Assign ranks within the scores of each participant.* If the scores are not already ranks, assign the rank of 1 to the lowest score received by Participant 1, the rank of 2 to the second lowest score received by Participant 1, and so on. Repeat the process for each participant.

Step 2: *Compute ΣR in each condition.* Compute the sum of the ranks in each column.

Step 3: *Compute the sum of squares between groups.*

$$SS_{bn} = (\Sigma R_1)^2 + (\Sigma R_2)^2 + \ldots + (\Sigma R_k)^2$$

In the example,

$$SS_{bn} = (12)^2 + (23)^2 + (25)^2 = 1298$$

TABLE B.15 Example Data for the Friedman χ^2 Test

	Rankings for three instructors		
Participant	***Dr. Highman***	***Dr. Shyman***	***Dr. Whyman***
1	1	2	3
2	1	3	2
3	1	2	3
4	1	3	2
5	2	1	3
6	1	3	2
7	1	2	3
8	1	3	2
9	1	3	2
10	2	1	3
$N = 10$	$\Sigma R_1 = 12$	$\Sigma R_2 = 23$	$\Sigma R_3 = 25$

Step 4: *Compute* χ^2_{obt}.

$$\chi^2_{obt} = \left(\frac{12}{(k)(N)(k + 1)}\right)(SS_{bn}) - 3(N)(k + 1)$$

where N is the number of participants and k is the number of levels of the factor.

Thus,

$$\chi^2_{obt} = \left(\frac{12}{(3)(10)(3 + 1)}\right)(1298) - 3(10)(3 + 1)$$

$$\chi^2_{obt} = (.10)(1298) - 120 = 129.8 - 120$$

$$\chi^2_{obt} = 9.80.$$

Step 5: *Find the critical value of* χ^2. Use the χ^2-tables (Table 8 in Appendix C). The $df = k - 1$, where k is the number of levels in the factor. For the example, for $df = 2$ and $\alpha = .05$, the χ^2_{crit} is 5.99.

Step 6: *Compare* χ^2_{obt} *to* χ^2_{crit}. If χ^2_{obt} is larger than χ^2_{crit}, the results are significant. Above, χ^2_{obt} of 9.80 is larger than χ^2_{crit} of 5.99, so the results are significant: At least two of the conditions differ significantly.

Step 7: *When the* χ^2_{obt} *is significant, perform post hoc comparisons using Nemenyi's procedure.*

(a) *Compute the critical difference.*

$$\text{Critical difference} = \sqrt{\left(\frac{k(k + 1)}{6(N)}\right)(\chi^2_{crit})}$$

where k is the number of levels of the factor, N is the number of participants, and χ^2_{crit} is the critical value used in the Friedman χ^2.

In the example,

$$\text{Critical difference} = \sqrt{\left(\frac{3(3 + 1)}{6(10)}\right)(5.99)}$$

$$\text{Critical difference} = \sqrt{(.2)(5.99)} = \sqrt{1.198} = 1.09$$

(b) *Compute the mean rank for each condition.* For each condition, divide the ΣR by the number of participants. In the example, the mean ranks are 1.2, 2.3, and 2.5 for Highman, Shyman, and Whyman, respectively.

(c) *Compute the differences between all pairs of mean ranks.* Subtract each mean rank from the other mean ranks. Any absolute difference that is larger than the critical difference is a significant difference. In the example, Highman differs from the other two instructors by 1.10 and 1.30, which are significant, but the others differ by .20, which is not significant.

Step 8: *Describe a significant relationship using eta squared.*

$$\eta^2 = \frac{\chi^2_{\text{obt}}}{(N)(k) - 1}$$

where χ^2_{obt} is the Friedman χ^2, N is the number of participants, and k is the number of levels of the factor. For the example, $\eta^2 = .34$.

PRACTICE PROBLEMS

(Answers for odd-numbered problems are provided in Appendix D.)

1. We wish to compare the attitude scores of people when tested in the morning to their attitude scores when tested in the afternoon. From a morning and an afternoon attitude test, we obtain the following interval data, but they have significantly heterogeneous variance. With $\alpha = .05$, determine if there is a significant difference in scores as a function of testing times.

Morning	*Afternoon*
14	36
18	31
20	19
28	48
3	10
34	49
20	20
24	29

2. A study compares the maturity level of a group of students who have completed a research course to a group of students who have not. Maturity scores for college students tend to be skewed. For the following interval scores, answer the questions below.

No research	*Research*
43	51
52	58
65	72
23	81
31	92
36	64

(a) Do the groups differ significantly ($\alpha = .05$)? (b) What do you conclude about maturity scores you expect to find in the population of students who have taken research and in the population that hasn't?

3. A therapist evaluates the progress of a sample of clients in a new treatment program after one month, two months, and again after three months. Such progress scores have heterogeneous variance. For the following data, (a) Determine whether overall there are significant differences as a function of time of testing ($\alpha = .05$). (b) Specifically, which times differ significantly? (c) What is the effect size of the factor?

Participants	*1 month*	*2 months*	*3 months*
1	12	23	33
2	14	25	18
3	20	29	30
4	15	18	29
5	26	20	30
6	26	29	34
7	11	19	22
8	20	26	27
9	25	20	35
10	14	30	35

4. An investigator evaluated the effectiveness of activity therapy on three types of patients. She collected the following improvement ratings. (In the population, these data form highly skewed distributions.)

Depressed	*Manic*	*Schizophrenic*
16	7	13
11	9	6
12	5	10
20	4	15
21	8	14

(a) Determine whether overall there are significant differences as a function of type of disorder ($\alpha = .05$). (b) Specifically, which types of patients differ significantly? (c) What is the effect size of the factor?

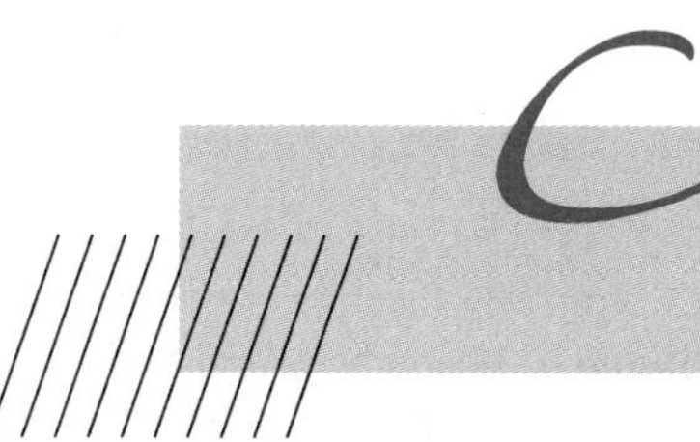

STATISTICAL TABLES

Table 1 Proportions of Area Under the Standard Normal Curve

Table 2 Critical Values of t

Table 3 Critical Values of the Pearson Correlation Coefficient

Table 4 Critical Values of the Spearman Rank-Order Correlation Coefficient

Table 5 Critical Values of F

Table 6 Values of Studentized Range Statistic, q_k

Table 7 Critical Values of the F_{max} Test

Table 8 Critical Values of Chi Square

Table 9 Critical Values of the Mann-Whitney U

Table 10 Critical Values of the Wilcoxon T

Table 1 Proportions of Area Under the Standard Normal Curve: The z-Tables

Column (A) lists z-score values. Column (B) lists the proportion of the area between the mean and the z-score value. Column (C) lists the proportion of the area beyond the z-score in the tail of the distribution. (*Note:* Because the normal distribution is symmetrical, areas for negative z-scores are the same as those for positive z-scores.)

(A)	(B)	(C)	(A)	(B)	(C)	(A)	(B)	(C)
z	*Area between mean and z*	*Area beyond z in tail*	z	*Area between mean and z*	*Area beyond z in tail*	z	*Area between mean and z*	*Area beyond z in tail*
0.00	.0000	.5000	0.30	.1179	.3821	0.60	.2257	.2743
0.01	.0040	.4960	0.31	.1217	.3783	0.61	.2291	.2709
0.02	.0080	.4920	0.32	.1255	.3745	0.62	.2324	.2676
0.03	.0120	.4880	0.33	.1293	.3707	0.63	.2357	.2643
0.04	.0160	.4840	0.34	.1331	.3669	0.64	.2389	.2611
0.05	.0199	.4801	0.35	.1368	.3632	0.65	.2422	.2578
0.06	.0239	.4761	0.36	.1406	.3594	0.66	.2454	.2546
0.07	.0279	.4721	0.37	.1443	.3557	0.67	.2486	.2514
0.08	.0319	.4681	0.38	.1480	.3520	0.68	.2517	.2483
0.09	.0359	.4641	0.39	.1517	.3483	0.69	.2549	.2451
0.10	.0398	.4602	0.40	.1554	.3446	0.70	.2580	.2420
0.11	.0438	.4562	0.41	.1591	.3409	0.71	.2611	.2389
0.12	.0478	.4522	0.42	.1628	.3372	0.72	.2642	.2358
0.13	.0517	.4483	0.43	.1664	.3336	0.73	.2673	.2327
0.14	.0557	.4443	0.44	.1700	.3300	0.74	.2704	.2296
0.15	.0596	.4404	0.45	.1736	.3264	0.75	.2734	.2266
0.16	.0636	.4364	0.46	.1772	.3228	0.76	.2764	.2236
0.17	.0675	.4325	0.47	.1808	.3192	0.77	.2794	.2206
0.18	.0714	.4286	0.48	.1844	.3156	0.78	.2823	.2177
0.19	.0753	.4247	0.49	.1879	.3121	0.79	.2852	.2148
0.20	.0793	.4207	0.50	.1915	.3085	0.80	.2881	.2119
0.21	.0832	.4168	0.51	.1950	.3050	0.81	.2910	.2090
0.22	.0871	.4129	0.52	.1985	.3015	0.82	.2939	.2061
0.23	.0910	.4090	0.53	.2019	.2981	0.83	.2967	.2033
0.24	.0948	.4052	0.54	.2054	.2946	0.84	.2995	.2005
0.25	.0987	.4013	0.55	.2088	.2912	0.85	.3023	.1977
0.26	.1026	.3974	0.56	.2123	.2877	0.86	.3051	.1949
0.27	.1064	.3936	0.57	.2157	.2843	0.87	.3078	.1922
0.28	.1103	.3897	0.58	.2190	.2810	0.88	.3106	.1894
0.29	.1141	.3859	0.59	.2224	.2776	0.89	.3133	.1867

Table 1 (cont.) Proportions of Area Under the Standard Normal Curve: The *z*-Tables

(A)	*(B)*	*(C)*	*(A)*	*(B)*	*(C)*	*(A)*	*(B)*	*(C)*
z	*Area between mean and z*	*Area beyond z in tail*	*z*	*Area between mean and z*	*Area beyond z in tail*	*z*	*Area between mean and z*	*Area beyond z in tail*
0.90	.3159	.1841	1.25	.3944	.1056	1.60	.4452	.0548
0.91	.3186	.1814	1.26	.3962	.1038	1.61	.4463	.0537
0.92	.3212	.1788	1.27	.3980	.1020	1.62	.4474	.0526
0.93	.3238	.1762	1.28	.3997	.1003	1.63	.4484	.0516
0.94	.3264	.1736	1.29	.4015	.0985	1.64	.4495	.0505
0.95	.3289	.1711	1.30	.4032	.0968	1.65	.4505	.0495
0.96	.3315	.1685	1.31	.4049	.0951	1.66	.4515	.0485
0.97	.3340	.1660	1.32	.4066	.0934	1.67	.4525	.0475
0.98	.3365	.1635	1.33	.4082	.0918	1.68	.4535	.0465
0.99	.3389	.1611	1.34	.4099	.0901	1.69	.4545	.0455
1.00	.3413	.1587	1.35	.4115	.0885	1.70	.4554	.0446
1.01	.3438	.1562	1.36	.4131	.0869	1.71	.4564	.0436
1.02	.3461	.1539	1.37	.4147	.0853	1.72	.4573	.0427
1.03	.3485	.1515	1.38	.4162	.0838	1.73	.4582	.0418
1.04	.3508	.1492	1.39	.4177	.0823	1.74	.4591	.0409
1.05	.3531	.1469	1.40	.4192	.0808	1.75	.4599	.0401
1.06	.3554	.1446	1.41	.4207	.0793	1.76	.4608	.0392
1.07	.3577	.1423	1.42	.4222	.0778	1.77	.4616	.0384
1.08	.3599	.1401	1.43	.4236	.0764	1.78	.4625	.0375
1.09	.3621	.1379	1.44	.4251	.0749	1.79	.4633	.0367
1.10	.3643	.1357	1.45	.4265	.0735	1.80	.4641	.0359
1.11	.3665	.1335	1.46	.4279	.0721	1.81	.4649	.0351
1.12	.3686	.1314	1.47	.4292	.0708	1.82	.4656	.0344
1.13	.3708	.1292	1.48	.4306	.0694	1.83	.4664	.0336
1.14	.3729	.1271	1.49	.4319	.0681	1.84	.4671	.0329
1.15	.3749	.1251	1.50	.4332	.0668	1.85	.4678	.0322
1.16	.3770	.1230	1.51	.4345	.0655	1.86	.4686	.0314
1.17	.3790	.1210	1.52	.4357	.0643	1.87	.4693	.0307
1.18	.3810	.1190	1.53	.4370	.0630	1.88	.4699	.0301
1.19	.3830	.1170	1.54	.4382	.0618	1.89	.4706	.0294
1.20	.3849	.1151	1.55	.4394	.0606	1.90	.4713	.0287
1.21	.3869	.1131	1.56	.4406	.0594	1.91	.4719	.0281
1.22	.3888	.1112	1.57	.4418	.0582	1.92	.4726	.0274
1.23	.3907	.1093	1.58	.4429	.0571	1.93	.4732	.0268
1.24	.3925	.1075	1.59	.4441	.0559	1.94	.4738	.0262

Table 1 (cont.) Proportions of Area Under the Standard Normal Curve: The *z*-Tables

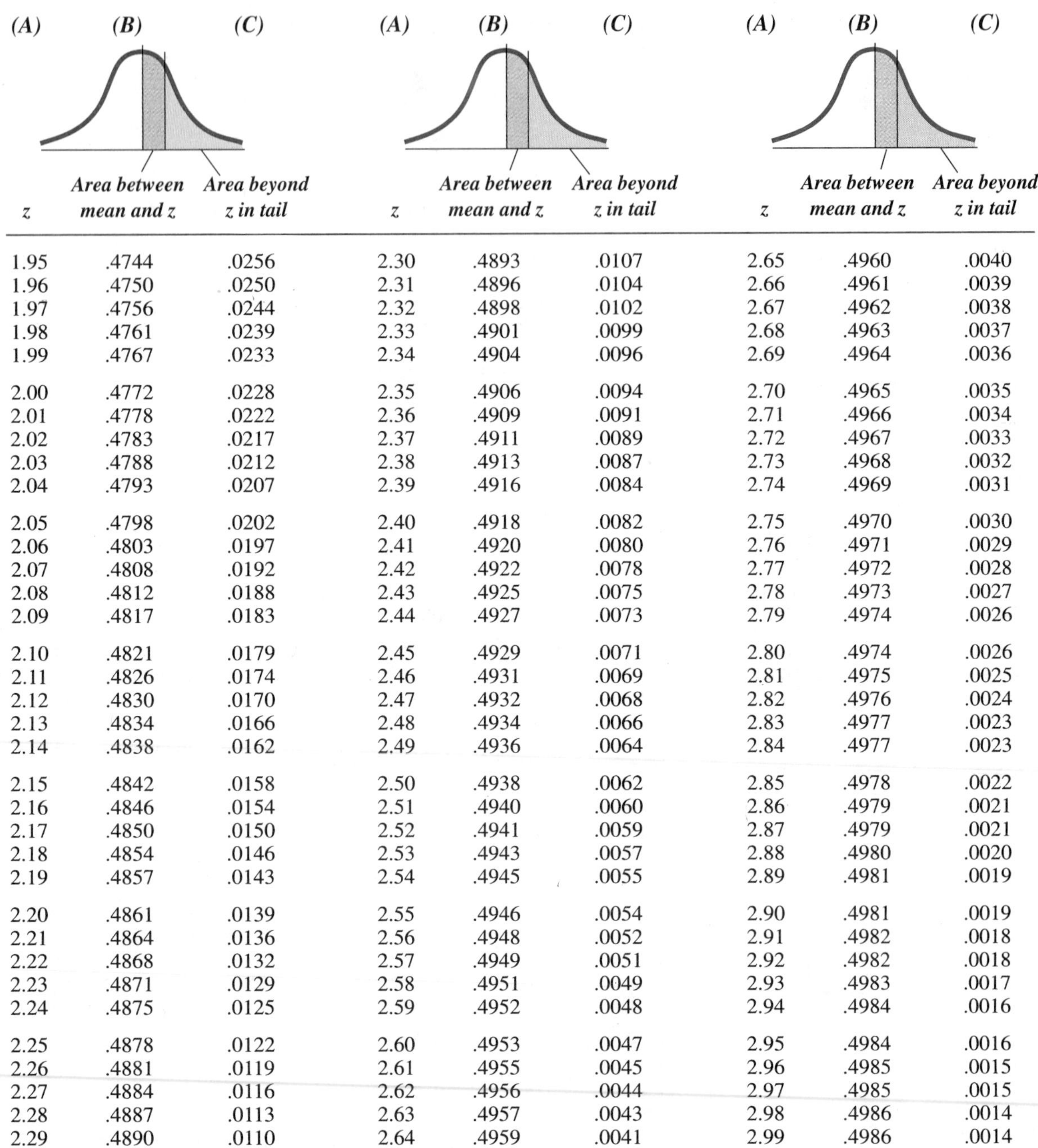

(A) *z*	(B) *Area between mean and z*	(C) *Area beyond z in tail*	(A) *z*	(B) *Area between mean and z*	(C) *Area beyond z in tail*	(A) *z*	(B) *Area between mean and z*	(C) *Area beyond z in tail*
1.95	.4744	.0256	2.30	.4893	.0107	2.65	.4960	.0040
1.96	.4750	.0250	2.31	.4896	.0104	2.66	.4961	.0039
1.97	.4756	.0244	2.32	.4898	.0102	2.67	.4962	.0038
1.98	.4761	.0239	2.33	.4901	.0099	2.68	.4963	.0037
1.99	.4767	.0233	2.34	.4904	.0096	2.69	.4964	.0036
2.00	.4772	.0228	2.35	.4906	.0094	2.70	.4965	.0035
2.01	.4778	.0222	2.36	.4909	.0091	2.71	.4966	.0034
2.02	.4783	.0217	2.37	.4911	.0089	2.72	.4967	.0033
2.03	.4788	.0212	2.38	.4913	.0087	2.73	.4968	.0032
2.04	.4793	.0207	2.39	.4916	.0084	2.74	.4969	.0031
2.05	.4798	.0202	2.40	.4918	.0082	2.75	.4970	.0030
2.06	.4803	.0197	2.41	.4920	.0080	2.76	.4971	.0029
2.07	.4808	.0192	2.42	.4922	.0078	2.77	.4972	.0028
2.08	.4812	.0188	2.43	.4925	.0075	2.78	.4973	.0027
2.09	.4817	.0183	2.44	.4927	.0073	2.79	.4974	.0026
2.10	.4821	.0179	2.45	.4929	.0071	2.80	.4974	.0026
2.11	.4826	.0174	2.46	.4931	.0069	2.81	.4975	.0025
2.12	.4830	.0170	2.47	.4932	.0068	2.82	.4976	.0024
2.13	.4834	.0166	2.48	.4934	.0066	2.83	.4977	.0023
2.14	.4838	.0162	2.49	.4936	.0064	2.84	.4977	.0023
2.15	.4842	.0158	2.50	.4938	.0062	2.85	.4978	.0022
2.16	.4846	.0154	2.51	.4940	.0060	2.86	.4979	.0021
2.17	.4850	.0150	2.52	.4941	.0059	2.87	.4979	.0021
2.18	.4854	.0146	2.53	.4943	.0057	2.88	.4980	.0020
2.19	.4857	.0143	2.54	.4945	.0055	2.89	.4981	.0019
2.20	.4861	.0139	2.55	.4946	.0054	2.90	.4981	.0019
2.21	.4864	.0136	2.56	.4948	.0052	2.91	.4982	.0018
2.22	.4868	.0132	2.57	.4949	.0051	2.92	.4982	.0018
2.23	.4871	.0129	2.58	.4951	.0049	2.93	.4983	.0017
2.24	.4875	.0125	2.59	.4952	.0048	2.94	.4984	.0016
2.25	.4878	.0122	2.60	.4953	.0047	2.95	.4984	.0016
2.26	.4881	.0119	2.61	.4955	.0045	2.96	.4985	.0015
2.27	.4884	.0116	2.62	.4956	.0044	2.97	.4985	.0015
2.28	.4887	.0113	2.63	.4957	.0043	2.98	.4986	.0014
2.29	.4890	.0110	2.64	.4959	.0041	2.99	.4986	.0014

Table 1 (cont.) Proportions of Area Under the Standard Normal Curve: The *z*-Tables

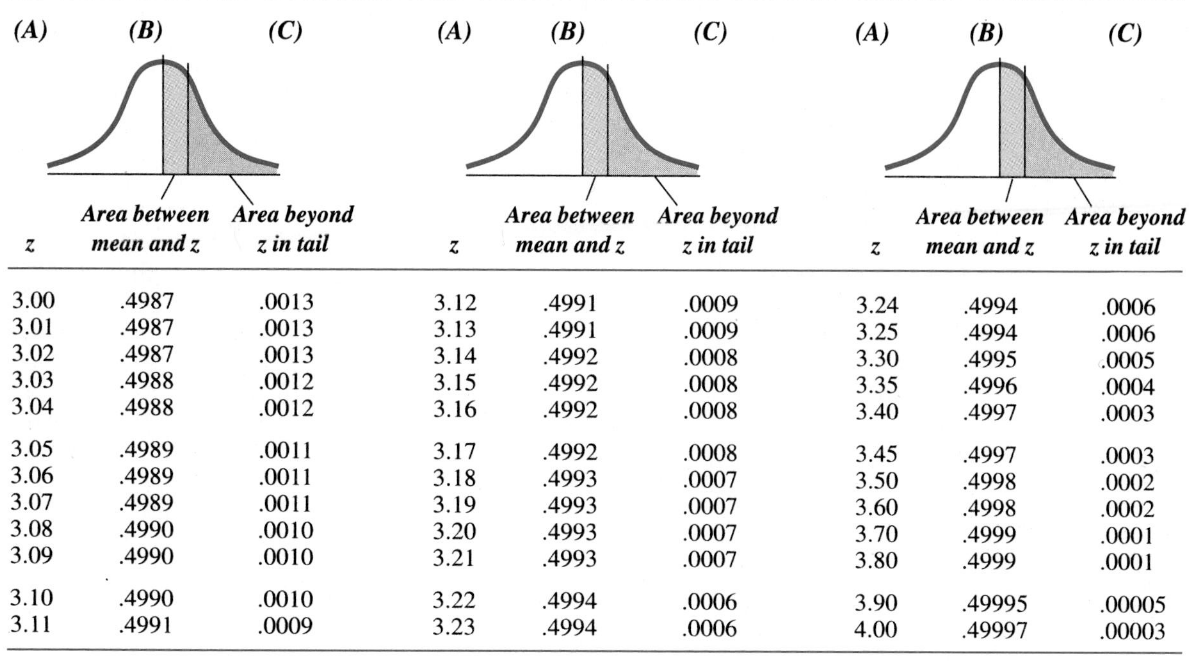

(A) z	(B) Area between mean and z	(C) Area beyond z in tail	(A) z	(B) Area between mean and z	(C) Area beyond z in tail	(A) z	(B) Area between mean and z	(C) Area beyond z in tail
3.00	.4987	.0013	3.12	.4991	.0009	3.24	.4994	.0006
3.01	.4987	.0013	3.13	.4991	.0009	3.25	.4994	.0006
3.02	.4987	.0013	3.14	.4992	.0008	3.30	.4995	.0005
3.03	.4988	.0012	3.15	.4992	.0008	3.35	.4996	.0004
3.04	.4988	.0012	3.16	.4992	.0008	3.40	.4997	.0003
3.05	.4989	.0011	3.17	.4992	.0008	3.45	.4997	.0003
3.06	.4989	.0011	3.18	.4993	.0007	3.50	.4998	.0002
3.07	.4989	.0011	3.19	.4993	.0007	3.60	.4998	.0002
3.08	.4990	.0010	3.20	.4993	.0007	3.70	.4999	.0001
3.09	.4990	.0010	3.21	.4993	.0007	3.80	.4999	.0001
3.10	.4990	.0010	3.22	.4994	.0006	3.90	.49995	.00005
3.11	.4991	.0009	3.23	.4994	.0006	4.00	.49997	.00003

Table 2 Critical Values of t: The t-Tables

(*Note:* Values of $-t_{\text{crit}}$ = values of $+t_{\text{crit}}$.)

Two-tailed test

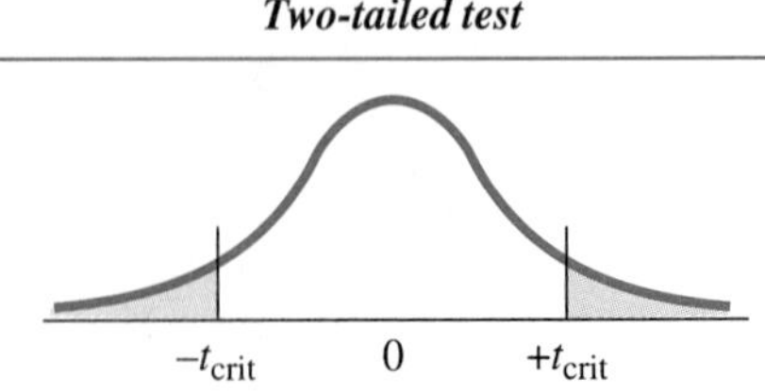

One-tailed test

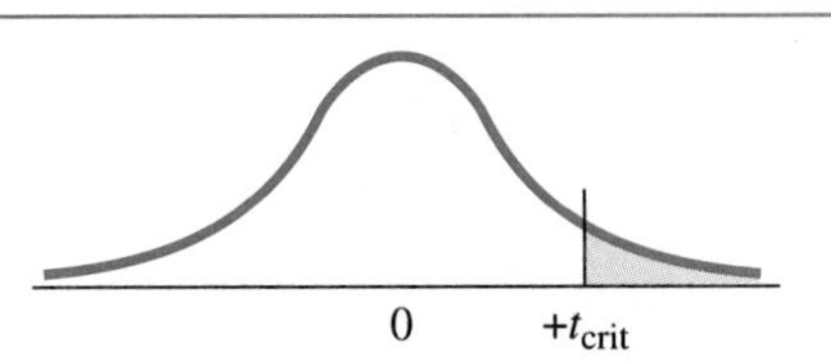

	Two-tailed test: Level of significance			One-tailed test: Level of significance	
df	α = .05	α = .01	*df*	α = .05	α = .01
1	12.706	63.657	1	6.314	31.821
2	4.303	9.925	2	2.920	6.965
3	3.182	5.841	3	2.353	4.541
4	2.776	4.604	4	2.132	3.747
5	2.571	4.032	5	2.015	3.365
6	2.447	3.707	6	1.943	3.143
7	2.365	3.499	7	1.895	2.998
8	2.306	3.355	8	1.860	2.896
9	2.262	3.250	9	1.833	2.821
10	2.228	3.169	10	1.812	2.764
11	2.201	3.106	11	1.796	2.718
12	2.179	3.055	12	1.782	2.681
13	2.160	3.012	13	1.771	2.650
14	2.145	2.977	14	1.761	2.624
15	2.131	2.947	15	1.753	2.602
16	2.120	2.921	16	1.746	2.583
17	2.110	2.898	17	1.740	2.567
18	2.101	2.878	18	1.734	2.552
19	2.093	2.861	19	1.729	2.539
20	2.086	2.845	20	1.725	2.528
21	2.080	2.831	21	1.721	2.518
22	2.074	2.819	22	1.717	2.508
23	2.069	2.807	23	1.714	2.500
24	2.064	2.797	24	1.711	2.492
25	2.060	2.787	25	1.708	2.485
26	2.056	2.779	26	1.706	2.479
27	2.052	2.771	27	1.703	2.473
28	2.048	2.763	28	1.701	2.467
29	2.045	2.756	29	1.699	2.462
30	2.042	2.750	30	1.697	2.457
40	2.021	2.704	40	1.684	2.423
60	2.000	2.660	60	1.671	2.390
120	1.980	2.617	120	1.658	2.358
∞	1.960	2.576	∞	1.645	2.326

From Table 12 of E. Pearson and H. Hartley, *Biometrika Tables for Statisticians*, Vol 1, 3rd ed. Cambridge: Cambridge University Press, 1966. Reprinted with permission of the Biometrika trustees.

Table 3 Critical Values of the Pearson Correlation Coefficient and the Point-Biserial Correlation Coefficient: The r and r_{pb} Tables

Two-tailed test

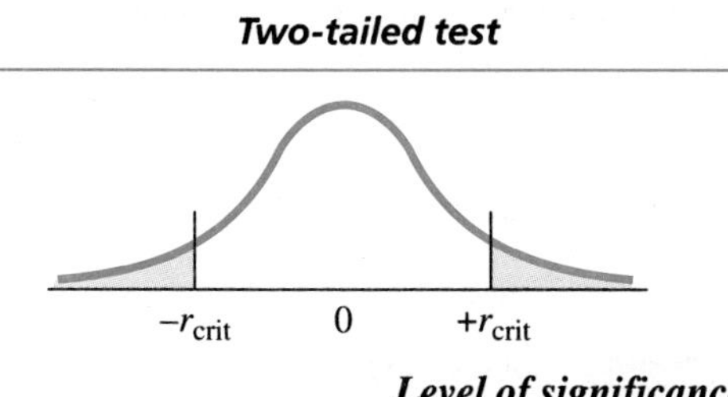

df (*no. of pairs* − 2)	*Level of significance* α = .05	α = .01
1	.997	.9999
2	.950	.990
3	.878	.959
4	.811	.917
5	.754	.874
6	.707	.834
7	.666	.798
8	.632	.765
9	.602	.735
10	.576	.708
11	.553	.684
12	.532	.661
13	.514	.641
14	.497	.623
15	.482	.606
16	.468	.590
17	.456	.575
18	.444	.561
19	.433	.549
20	.423	.537
21	.413	.526
22	.404	.515
23	.396	.505
24	.388	.496
25	.381	.487
26	.374	.479
27	.367	.471
28	.361	.463
29	.355	.456
30	.349	.449
35	.325	.418
40	.304	.393
45	.288	.372
50	.273	.354
60	.250	.325
70	.232	.302
80	.217	.283
90	.205	.267
100	.195	.254

One-tailed test

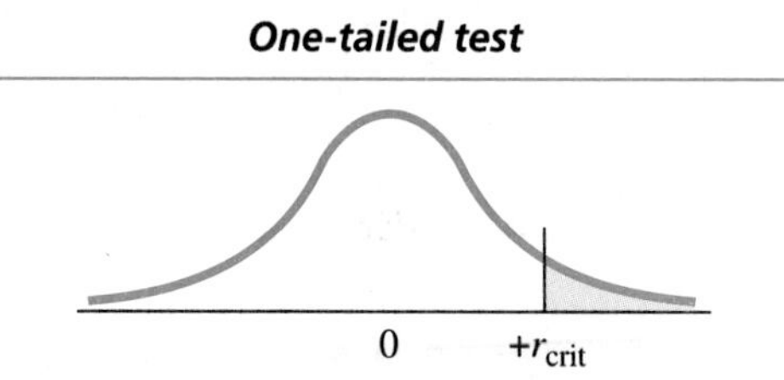

df (*no. of pairs* − 2)	*Level of significance* α = .05	α = .01
1	.988	.9995
2	.900	.980
3	.805	.934
4	.729	.882
5	.669	.833
6	.622	.789
7	.582	.750
8	.549	.716
9	.521	.685
10	.497	.658
11	.476	.634
12	.458	.612
13	.441	.592
14	.426	.574
15	.412	.558
16	.400	.542
17	.389	.528
18	.378	.516
19	.369	.503
20	.360	.492
21	.352	.482
22	.344	.472
23	.337	.462
24	.330	.453
25	.323	.445
26	.317	.437
27	.311	.430
28	.306	.423
29	.301	.416
30	.296	.409
35	.275	.381
40	.257	.358
45	.243	.338
50	.231	.322
60	.211	.295
70	.195	.274
80	.183	.256
90	.173	.242
100	.164	.230

From Table IV of R. A. Fisher and F. Yates, *Statistical Tables for Biological, Agricultural and Medical Research*, 6th ed. London: Longman Group Ltd., 1974. Reprinted by permission of Addison-Wesley Longman, Ltd.

Table 4 Critical Values of the Spearman Rank-Order Correlation Coefficient: The r_s-Tables

(*Note:* To interpolate the critical value for an N not given, find the critical values for the N above and below your N, add them together, and then divide the sum by 2.) When N is greater than 30, transform r_s to a z-score, using the formula $z_{obt} = (r_s)(\sqrt{N-1})$. For $\alpha = .05$, the two-tailed z_{crit} is 1.96, and the one-tailed z_{crit} is 1.645.

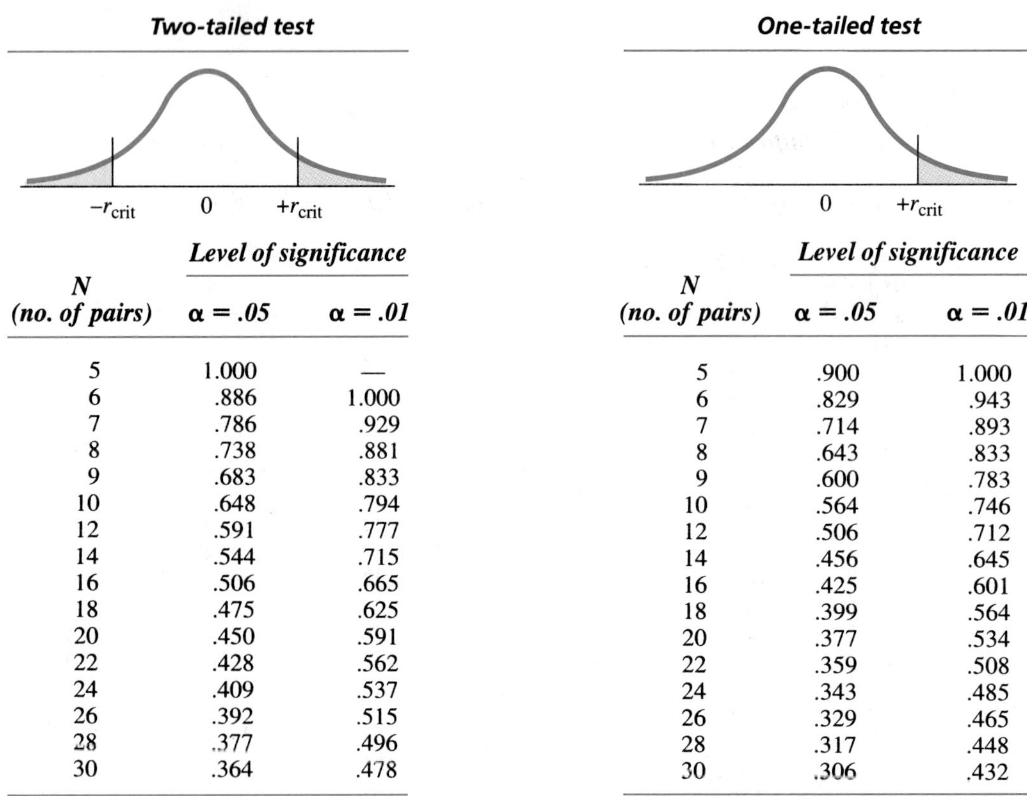

	Two-tailed test: Level of significance			One-tailed test: Level of significance	
***N* (no. of pairs)**	***α* = .05**	***α* = .01**	***N* (no. of pairs)**	***α* = .05**	***α* = .01**
5	1.000	—	5	.900	1.000
6	.886	1.000	6	.829	.943
7	.786	.929	7	.714	.893
8	.738	.881	8	.643	.833
9	.683	.833	9	.600	.783
10	.648	.794	10	.564	.746
12	.591	.777	12	.506	.712
14	.544	.715	14	.456	.645
16	.506	.665	16	.425	.601
18	.475	.625	18	.399	.564
20	.450	.591	20	.377	.534
22	.428	.562	22	.359	.508
24	.409	.537	24	.343	.485
26	.392	.515	26	.329	.465
28	.377	.496	28	.317	.448
30	.364	.478	30	.306	.432

From E. G. Olds (1949), The 5 Percent Significance Levels of Sums of Squares of Rank Differences and a Correction, *Ann. Math. Statist.*, **20**, 117–118, and E. G. Olds (1938), Distribution of Sums of Squares of Rank Differences for Small Numbers of Individuals, *Ann. Math. Statist.*, **9**, 133–148.

Table 5 Critical Values of *F*: The *F*-Tables

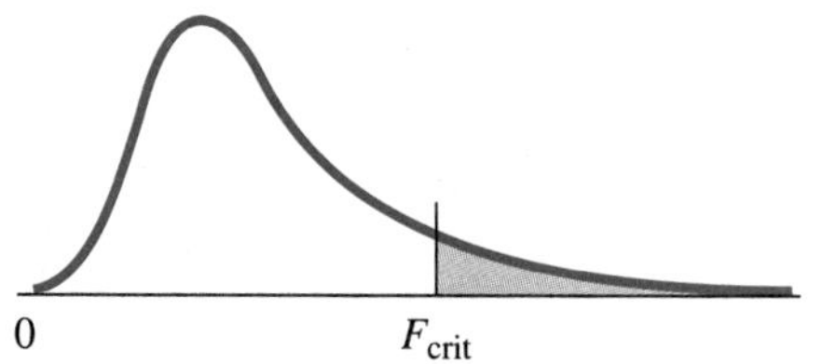

Critical values for α = .05 are in **dark numbers**.
Critical values for α = .01 are in light numbers.

Degrees of freedom within groups (degrees of freedom in denominator of F ratio)	α	*Degrees of freedom between groups (degrees of freedom in numerator of F ratio)* 1	2	3	4	5	6	7	8	9	10	11	12	14	16	20
1	**.05**	**161**	**200**	**216**	**225**	**230**	**234**	**237**	**239**	**241**	**242**	**243**	**244**	**245**	**246**	**248**
	.01	4,052	4,999	5,403	5,625	5,764	5,859	5,928	5,981	6,022	6,056	6,082	6,106	6,142	6,169	6,208
2	**.05**	**18.51**	**19.00**	**19.16**	**19.25**	**19.30**	**19.33**	**19.36**	**19.37**	**19.38**	**19.39**	**19.40**	**19.41**	**19.42**	**19.43**	**19.44**
	.01	98.49	99.00	99.17	99.25	99.30	99.33	99.34	99.36	99.38	99.40	99.41	99.42	99.43	99.44	99.45
3	**.05**	**10.13**	**9.55**	**9.28**	**9.12**	**9.01**	**8.94**	**8.88**	**8.84**	**8.81**	**8.78**	**8.76**	**8.74**	**8.71**	**8.69**	**8.66**
	.01	34.12	30.82	29.46	28.71	28.24	27.91	27.67	27.49	27.34	27.23	27.13	27.05	26.92	26.83	26.69
4	**.05**	**7.71**	**6.94**	**6.59**	**6.39**	**6.26**	**6.16**	**6.09**	**6.04**	**6.00**	**5.96**	**5.93**	**5.91**	**5.87**	**5.84**	**5.80**
	.01	21.20	18.00	16.69	15.98	15.52	15.21	14.98	14.80	14.66	14.54	14.45	14.37	14.24	14.15	14.02
5	**.05**	**6.61**	**5.79**	**5.41**	**5.19**	**5.05**	**4.95**	**4.88**	**4.82**	**4.78**	**4.74**	**4.70**	**4.68**	**4.64**	**4.60**	**4.56**
	.01	16.26	13.27	12.06	11.39	10.97	10.67	10.45	10.27	10.15	10.05	9.96	9.89	9.77	9.68	9.55
6	**.05**	**5.99**	**5.14**	**4.76**	**4.53**	**4.39**	**4.28**	**4.21**	**4.15**	**4.10**	**4.06**	**4.03**	**4.00**	**3.96**	**3.92**	**3.87**
	.01	13.74	10.92	9.78	9.15	8.75	8.47	8.26	8.10	7.98	7.87	7.79	7.72	7.60	7.52	7.39
7	**.05**	**5.59**	**4.47**	**4.35**	**4.12**	**3.97**	**3.87**	**3.79**	**3.73**	**3.68**	**3.63**	**3.60**	**3.57**	**3.52**	**3.49**	**3.44**
	.01	12.25	9.55	8.45	7.85	7.46	7.19	7.00	6.84	6.71	6.62	6.54	6.47	6.35	6.27	6.15
8	**.05**	**5.32**	**4.46**	**4.07**	**3.84**	**3.69**	**3.58**	**3.50**	**3.44**	**3.39**	**3.34**	**3.31**	**3.28**	**3.23**	**3.20**	**3.15**
	.01	11.26	8.65	7.59	7.01	6.63	6.37	6.19	6.03	5.91	5.82	5.74	5.67	5.56	5.48	5.36
9	**.05**	**5.12**	**4.26**	**3.86**	**3.63**	**3.48**	**3.37**	**3.29**	**3.23**	**3.18**	**3.13**	**3.10**	**3.07**	**3.02**	**2.98**	**2.93**
	.01	10.56	8.02	6.99	6.42	6.06	5.80	5.62	5.47	5.35	5.26	5.18	5.11	5.00	4.92	4.80
10	**.05**	**4.96**	**4.10**	**3.71**	**3.48**	**3.33**	**3.22**	**3.14**	**3.07**	**3.02**	**2.97**	**2.94**	**2.91**	**2.86**	**2.82**	**2.77**
	.01	10.04	7.56	6.55	5.99	5.64	5.39	5.21	5.06	4.95	4.85	4.78	4.71	4.60	4.52	4.41
11	**.05**	**4.84**	**3.98**	**3.59**	**3.36**	**3.20**	**3.09**	**3.01**	**2.95**	**2.90**	**2.86**	**2.82**	**2.79**	**2.74**	**2.70**	**2.65**
	.01	9.65	7.20	6.22	5.67	5.32	5.07	4.88	4.74	4.63	4.54	4.46	4.40	4.29	4.21	4.10
12	**.05**	**4.75**	**3.88**	**3.49**	**3.26**	**3.11**	**3.00**	**2.92**	**2.85**	**2.80**	**2.76**	**2.72**	**2.69**	**2.64**	**2.60**	**2.54**
	.01	9.33	6.93	5.95	5.41	5.06	4.82	4.65	4.50	4.39	4.30	4.22	4.16	4.05	3.98	3.86
13	**.05**	**4.67**	**3.80**	**3.41**	**3.18**	**3.02**	**2.92**	**2.84**	**2.77**	**2.72**	**2.67**	**2.63**	**2.60**	**2.55**	**2.51**	**2.46**
	.01	9.07	6.70	5.74	5.20	4.86	4.62	4.44	4.30	4.19	4.10	4.02	3.96	3.85	3.78	3.67
14	**.05**	**4.60**	**3.74**	**3.34**	**3.11**	**2.96**	**2.85**	**2.77**	**2.70**	**2.65**	**2.60**	**2.56**	**2.53**	**2.48**	**2.44**	**2.39**
	.01	8.86	6.51	5.56	5.03	4.69	4.46	4.28	4.14	4.03	3.94	3.86	3.80	3.70	3.62	3.51
15	**.05**	**4.54**	**3.68**	**3.29**	**3.06**	**2.90**	**2.79**	**2.70**	**2.64**	**2.59**	**2.55**	**2.51**	**2.48**	**2.43**	**2.39**	**2.33**
	.01	8.68	6.36	5.42	4.89	4.56	4.32	4.14	4.00	3.89	3.80	3.73	3.67	3.56	3.48	3.36
16	**.05**	**4.49**	**3.63**	**3.24**	**3.01**	**2.85**	**2.74**	**2.66**	**2.59**	**2.54**	**2.49**	**2.45**	**2.42**	**2.37**	**2.33**	**2.28**
	.01	8.53	6.23	5.29	4.77	4.44	4.20	4.03	3.89	3.78	3.69	3.61	3.55	3.45	3.37	3.25

Table 5 (cont.) Critical Values of *F*: The *F*-Tables

Degrees of freedom within groups (degrees of freedom in denominator of F ratio)	α	*Degrees of freedom between groups (degrees of freedom in numerator of F ratio)*														
		1	*2*	*3*	*4*	*5*	*6*	*7*	*8*	*9*	*10*	*11*	*12*	*14*	*16*	*20*
17	.05	4.45	3.59	3.20	2.96	2.81	2.70	2.62	2.55	2.50	2.45	2.41	2.38	2.33	2.29	2.23
	.01	8.40	6.11	5.18	4.67	4.34	4.10	3.93	3.79	3.68	3.59	3.52	3.45	3.35	3.27	3.16
18	.05	4.41	3.55	3.16	2.93	2.77	2.66	2.58	2.51	2.46	2.41	2.37	2.34	2.29	2.25	2.19
	.01	8.28	6.01	5.09	4.58	4.25	4.01	3.85	3.71	3.60	3.51	3.44	3.37	3.27	3.19	3.07
19	.05	4.38	3.52	3.13	2.90	2.74	2.63	2.55	2.48	2.43	2.38	2.34	2.31	2.26	2.21	2.15
	.01	8.18	5.93	5.01	4.50	4.17	3.94	3.77	3.63	3.52	3.43	3.36	3.30	3.19	3.12	3.00
20	.05	4.35	3.49	3.10	2.87	2.71	2.60	2.52	2.45	2.40	2.35	2.31	2.28	2.23	2.18	2.12
	.01	8.10	5.85	4.94	4.43	4.10	3.87	3.71	3.56	3.45	3.37	3.30	3.23	3.13	3.05	2.94
21	.05	4.32	3.47	3.07	2.84	2.68	2.57	2.49	2.42	2.37	2.32	2.28	2.25	2.20	2.15	2.09
	.01	8.02	5.78	4.87	4.37	4.04	3.81	3.65	3.51	3.40	3.31	3.24	3.17	3.07	2.99	2.88
22	.05	4.30	3.44	3.05	2.82	2.66	2.55	2.47	2.40	2.35	2.30	2.26	2.23	2.18	2.13	2.07
	.01	7.94	5.72	4.82	4.31	3.99	3.76	3.59	3.45	3.35	3.26	3.18	3.12	3.02	2.94	2.83
23	.05	4.28	3.42	3.03	2.80	2.64	2.53	2.45	2.38	2.32	2.28	2.24	2.20	2.14	2.10	2.04
	.01	7.88	5.66	4.76	4.26	3.94	3.71	3.54	3.41	3.30	3.21	3.14	3.07	2.97	2.89	2.78
24	.05	4.26	3.40	3.01	2.78	2.62	2.51	2.43	2.36	2.30	2.26	2.22	2.18	2.13	2.09	2.02
	.01	7.82	5.61	4.72	4.22	3.90	3.67	3.50	3.36	3.25	3.17	3.09	3.03	2.93	2.85	2.74
25	.05	4.24	3.38	2.99	2.76	2.60	2.49	2.41	2.34	2.28	2.24	2.20	2.16	2.11	2.06	2.00
	.01	7.77	5.57	4.68	4.18	3.86	3.63	3.46	3.32	3.21	3.13	3.05	2.99	2.89	2.81	2.70
26	.05	4.22	3.37	2.98	2.74	2.59	2.47	2.39	2.32	2.27	2.22	2.18	2.15	2.10	2.05	1.99
	.01	7.72	5.53	4.64	4.14	3.82	3.59	3.42	3.29	3.17	3.09	3.02	2.96	2.86	2.77	2.66
27	.05	4.21	3.35	2.96	2.73	2.57	2.46	2.37	2.30	2.25	2.20	2.16	2.13	2.08	2.03	1.97
	.01	7.68	5.49	4.60	4.11	3.79	3.56	3.39	3.26	3.14	3.06	2.98	2.93	2.83	2.74	2.63
28	.05	4.20	3.34	2.95	2.71	2.56	2.44	2.36	2.29	2.24	2.19	2.15	2.12	2.06	2.02	1.96
	.01	7.64	5.45	4.57	4.07	3.76	3.53	3.36	3.23	3.11	3.03	2.95	2.90	2.80	2.71	2.60
29	.05	4.18	3.33	2.93	2.70	2.54	2.43	2.35	2.28	2.22	2.18	2.14	2.10	2.05	2.00	1.94
	.01	7.60	5.42	4.54	4.04	3.73	3.50	3.33	3.20	3.08	3.00	2.92	2.87	2.77	2.68	2.57
30	.05	4.17	3.32	2.92	2.69	2.53	2.42	2.34	2.27	2.21	2.16	2.12	2.09	2.04	1.99	1.93
	.01	7.56	5.39	4.51	4.02	3.70	3.47	3.30	3.17	3.06	2.98	2.90	2.84	2.74	2.66	2.55
32	.05	4.15	3.30	2.90	2.67	2.51	2.40	2.32	2.25	2.19	2.14	2.10	2.07	2.02	1.97	1.91
	.01	7.50	5.34	4.46	3.97	3.66	3.42	3.25	3.12	3.01	2.94	2.86	2.80	2.70	2.62	2.51
34	.05	4.13	3.28	2.88	2.65	2.49	2.38	2.30	2.23	2.17	2.12	2.08	2.05	2.00	1.95	1.89
	.01	7.44	5.29	4.42	3.93	3.61	3.38	3.21	3.08	2.97	2.89	2.82	2.76	2.66	2.58	2.47
36	.05	4.11	3.26	2.86	2.63	2.48	2.36	2.28	2.21	2.15	2.10	2.06	2.03	1.98	1.93	1.87
	.01	7.39	5.25	4.38	3.89	3.58	3.35	3.18	3.04	2.94	2.86	2.78	2.72	2.62	2.54	2.43
38	.05	4.10	3.25	2.85	2.62	2.46	2.35	2.26	2.19	2.14	2.09	2.05	2.02	1.96	1.92	1.85
	.01	7.35	5.21	4.34	3.86	3.54	3.32	3.15	3.02	2.91	2.82	2.75	2.69	2.59	2.51	2.40
40	.05	4.08	3.23	2.84	2.61	2.45	2.34	2.25	2.18	2.12	2.07	2.04	2.00	1.95	1.90	1.84
	.01	7.31	5.18	4.31	3.83	3.51	3.29	3.12	2.99	2.88	2.80	2.73	2.66	2.56	2.49	2.37
42	.05	4.07	3.22	2.83	2.59	2.44	2.32	2.24	2.17	2.11	2.06	2.02	1.99	1.94	1.89	1.82
	.01	7.27	5.15	4.29	3.80	3.49	3.26	3.10	2.96	2.86	2.77	2.70	2.64	2.54	2.46	2.35

Table 5 (cont.) Critical Values of F: The F-Tables

Degrees of freedom within groups (degrees of freedom in denominator of F ratio)		*Degrees of freedom between groups (degrees of freedom in numerator of F ratio)*														
	α	*1*	*2*	*3*	*4*	*5*	*6*	*7*	*8*	*9*	*10*	*11*	*12*	*14*	*16*	*20*
44	**.05**	**4.06**	**3.21**	**2.82**	**2.58**	**2.43**	**2.31**	**2.23**	**2.16**	**2.10**	**2.05**	**2.01**	**1.98**	**1.92**	**1.88**	**1.81**
	.01	7.24	5.12	4.26	3.78	3.46	3.24	3.07	2.94	2.84	2.75	2.68	2.62	2.52	2.44	2.32
46	**.05**	**4.05**	**3.20**	**2.81**	**2.57**	**2.42**	**2.30**	**2.22**	**2.14**	**2.09**	**2.04**	**2.00**	**1.97**	**1.91**	**1.87**	**1.80**
	.01	7.21	5.10	4.24	3.76	3.44	3.22	3.05	2.92	2.82	2.73	2.66	2.60	2.50	2.42	2.30
48	**.05**	**4.04**	**3.19**	**2.80**	**2.56**	**2.41**	**2.30**	**2.21**	**2.14**	**2.08**	**2.03**	**1.99**	**1.96**	**1.90**	**1.86**	**1.79**
	.01	7.19	5.08	4.22	3.74	3.42	3.20	3.04	2.90	2.80	2.71	2.64	2.58	2.48	2.40	2.28
50	**.05**	**4.03**	**3.18**	**2.79**	**2.56**	**2.40**	**2.29**	**2.20**	**2.13**	**2.07**	**2.02**	**1.98**	**1.95**	**1.90**	**1.85**	**1.78**
	.01	7.17	5.06	4.20	3.72	3.41	3.18	3.02	2.88	2.78	2.70	2.62	2.56	2.46	2.39	2.26
55	**.05**	**4.02**	**3.17**	**2.78**	**2.54**	**2.38**	**2.27**	**2.18**	**2.11**	**2.05**	**2.00**	**1.97**	**1.93**	**1.88**	**1.83**	**1.76**
	.01	7.12	5.01	4.16	3.68	3.37	3.15	2.98	2.85	2.75	2.66	2.59	2.53	2.43	2.35	2.23
60	**.05**	**4.00**	**3.15**	**2.76**	**2.52**	**2.37**	**2.25**	**2.17**	**2.10**	**2.04**	**1.99**	**1.95**	**1.92**	**1.86**	**1.81**	**1.75**
	.01	7.08	4.98	4.13	3.65	3.34	3.12	2.95	2.82	2.72	2.63	2.56	2.50	2.40	2.32	2.20
65	**.05**	**3.99**	**3.14**	**2.75**	**2.51**	**2.36**	**2.24**	**2.15**	**2.08**	**2.02**	**1.98**	**1.94**	**1.90**	**1.85**	**1.80**	**1.73**
	.01	7.04	4.95	4.10	3.62	3.31	3.09	2.93	2.79	2.70	2.61	2.54	2.47	2.37	2.30	2.18
70	**.05**	**3.98**	**3.13**	**2.74**	**2.50**	**2.35**	**2.23**	**2.14**	**2.07**	**2.01**	**1.97**	**1.93**	**1.89**	**1.84**	**1.79**	**1.72**
	.01	7.01	4.92	4.08	3.60	3.29	3.07	2.91	2.77	2.67	2.59	2.51	2.45	2.35	2.28	2.15
80	**.05**	**3.96**	**3.11**	**2.72**	**2.48**	**2.33**	**2.21**	**2.12**	**2.05**	**1.99**	**1.95**	**1.91**	**1.88**	**1.82**	**1.77**	**1.70**
	.01	6.96	4.88	4.04	3.56	3.25	3.04	2.87	2.74	2.64	2.55	2.48	2.41	2.32	2.24	2.11
100	**.05**	**3.94**	**3.09**	**2.70**	**2.46**	**2.30**	**2.19**	**2.10**	**2.03**	**1.97**	**1.92**	**1.88**	**1.85**	**1.79**	**1.75**	**1.68**
	.01	6.90	4.82	3.98	3.51	3.20	2.99	2.82	2.69	2.59	2.51	2.43	2.36	2.26	2.19	2.06
125	**.05**	**3.92**	**3.07**	**2.68**	**2.44**	**2.29**	**2.17**	**2.08**	**2.01**	**1.95**	**1.90**	**1.86**	**1.83**	**1.77**	**1.72**	**1.65**
	.01	6.84	4.78	3.94	3.47	3.17	2.95	2.79	2.65	2.56	2.47	2.40	2.33	2.23	2.15	2.03
150	**.05**	**3.91**	**3.06**	**2.67**	**2.43**	**2.27**	**2.16**	**2.07**	**2.00**	**1.94**	**1.89**	**1.85**	**1.82**	**1.76**	**1.71**	**1.64**
	.01	6.81	4.75	3.91	3.44	3.14	2.92	2.76	2.62	2.53	2.44	2.37	2.30	2.20	2.12	2.00
200	**.05**	**3.89**	**3.04**	**2.65**	**2.41**	**2.26**	**2.14**	**2.05**	**1.98**	**1.92**	**1.87**	**1.83**	**1.80**	**1.74**	**1.69**	**1.62**
	.01	6.76	4.71	3.88	3.41	3.11	2.90	2.73	2.60	2.50	2.41	2.34	2.28	2.17	2.09	1.97
400	**.05**	**3.86**	**3.02**	**2.62**	**2.39**	**2.23**	**2.12**	**2.03**	**1.96**	**1.90**	**1.85**	**1.81**	**1.78**	**1.72**	**1.67**	**1.60**
	.01	6.70	4.66	3.83	3.36	3.06	2.85	2.69	2.55	2.46	2.37	2.29	2.23	2.12	2.04	1.92
1000	**.05**	**3.85**	**3.00**	**2.61**	**2.38**	**2.22**	**2.10**	**2.02**	**1.95**	**1.89**	**1.84**	**1.80**	**1.76**	**1.70**	**1.65**	**1.58**
	.01	6.66	4.62	3.80	3.34	3.04	2.82	2.66	2.53	2.43	2.34	2.26	2.20	2.09	2.01	1.89
∞	**.05**	**3.84**	**2.99**	**2.60**	**2.37**	**2.21**	**2.09**	**2.01**	**1.94**	**1.88**	**1.83**	**1.79**	**1.75**	**1.69**	**1.64**	**1.57**
	.01	6.64	4.60	3.78	3.32	3.02	2.80	2.64	2.51	2.41	2.32	2.24	2.18	2.07	1.99	1.87

Reprinted by permission from *Statistical Methods*, by George W. Snedecor and William G. Cochran, Eighth Edition, © 1989 by The Iowa State University Press, 2121 South State Avenue, Ames, Iowa 50010.

Table 6 Values of Studentized Range Statistic, q_k

For a one-way ANOVA, or a comparison of the means from a main effect, the value of k is the number of means in the factor.

To compare the means from an interaction, find the appropriate design (or number of cell means) in the table below and obtain the adjusted value of k. Then, use adjusted k as k to find the value of q_k.

Values of Adjusted k

Design of study	*Number of cell means in study*	*Adjusted value of k*
2 × 2	4	3
2 × 3	6	5
2 × 4	8	6
3 × 3	9	7
3 × 4	12	8
4 × 4	16	10
4 × 5	20	12

Values of q_k for $\alpha = .05$ are **dark numbers** and for $\alpha = .01$ are light numbers.

Degrees of freedom within groups (degrees of freedom in denominator of F ratio)	α	*k = number of means being compared*										
		2	*3*	*4*	*5*	*6*	*7*	*8*	*9*	*10*	*11*	*12*
1	**.05**	**18.00**	**27.00**	**32.80**	**37.10**	**40.40**	**43.10**	**45.40**	**47.40**	**49.10**	**50.60**	**52.00**
	.01	90.00	135.00	164.00	186.00	202.00	216.00	227.00	237.00	246.00	253.00	260.00
2	**.05**	**6.09**	**8.30**	**9.80**	**10.90**	**11.70**	**12.40**	**13.00**	**13.50**	**14.00**	**14.40**	**14.70**
	.01	14.00	19.00	22.30	24.70	26.60	28.20	29.50	30.70	31.70	32.60	33.40
3	**.05**	**4.50**	**5.91**	**6.82**	**7.50**	**8.04**	**8.48**	**8.85**	**9.18**	**9.46**	**9.72**	**9.95**
	.01	8.26	10.60	12.20	13.30	14.20	15.00	15.60	16.20	16.70	17.10	17.50
4	**.05**	**3.93**	**5.04**	**5.76**	**6.29**	**6.71**	**7.05**	**7.35**	**7.60**	**7.83**	**8.03**	**8.21**
	.01	6.51	8.12	9.17	9.96	10.60	11.10	11.50	11.90	12.30	12.60	12.80
5	**.05**	**3.64**	**4.60**	**5.22**	**5.67**	**6.03**	**6.33**	**6.58**	**6.80**	**6.99**	**7.17**	**7.32**
	.01	5.70	6.97	7.80	8.42	8.91	9.32	9.67	9.97	10.20	10.50	10.70
6	**.05**	**3.46**	**4.34**	**4.90**	**5.31**	**5.63**	**5.89**	**6.12**	**6.32**	**6.49**	**6.65**	**6.79**
	.01	5.24	6.33	7.03	7.56	7.97	8.32	8.61	8.87	9.10	9.30	9.49
7	**.05**	**3.34**	**4.16**	**4.69**	**5.06**	**5.36**	**5.61**	**5.82**	**6.00**	**6.16**	**6.30**	**6.43**
	.01	4.95	5.92	6.54	7.01	7.37	7.68	7.94	8.17	8.37	8.55	8.71
8	**.05**	**3.26**	**4.04**	**4.53**	**4.89**	**5.17**	**5.40**	**5.60**	**5.77**	**5.92**	**6.05**	**6.18**
	.01	4.74	5.63	6.20	6.63	6.96	7.24	7.47	7.68	7.87	8.03	8.18
9	**.05**	**3.20**	**3.95**	**4.42**	**4.76**	**5.02**	**5.24**	**5.43**	**5.60**	**5.74**	**5.87**	**5.98**
	.01	4.60	5.43	5.96	6.35	6.66	6.91	7.13	7.32	7.49	7.65	7.78

Table 6 (cont.) Values of Studentized Range Statistic, q_k

Degrees of freedom within groups (degrees of freedom in denominator of F ratio)	α	*k = number of means being compared*										
		2	*3*	*4*	*5*	*6*	*7*	*8*	*9*	*10*	*11*	*12*
10	.05	3.15	3.88	4.33	4.65	4.91	5.12	5.30	5.46	5.60	5.72	5.83
	.01	4.48	5.27	5.77	6.14	6.43	6.67	6.87	7.05	7.21	7.36	7.48
11	.05	3.11	3.82	4.26	4.57	4.82	5.03	5.20	5.35	5.49	5.61	5.71
	.01	4.39	5.14	5.62	5.97	6.25	6.48	6.67	6.84	6.99	7.13	7.26
12	.05	3.08	3.77	4.20	4.51	4.75	4.95	5.12	5.27	5.40	5.51	5.62
	.01	4.32	5.04	5.50	5.84	6.10	6.32	6.51	6.67	6.81	6.94	7.06
13	.05	3.06	3.73	4.15	4.45	4.69	4.88	5.05	5.19	5.32	5.43	5.53
	.01	4.26	4.96	5.40	5.73	5.98	6.19	6.37	6.53	6.67	6.79	6.90
14	.05	3.03	3.70	4.11	4.41	4.64	4.83	4.99	5.13	5.25	5.36	5.46
	.01	4.21	4.89	5.32	5.63	5.88	6.08	6.26	6.41	6.54	6.66	6.77
16	.05	3.00	3.65	4.05	4.33	4.56	4.74	4.90	5.03	5.15	5.26	5.35
	.01	4.13	4.78	5.19	5.49	5.72	5.92	6.08	6.22	6.35	6.46	6.56
18	.05	2.97	3.61	4.00	4.28	4.49	4.67	4.82	4.96	5.07	5.17	5.27
	.01	4.07	4.70	5.09	5.38	5.60	5.79	5.94	6.08	6.20	6.31	6.41
20	.05	2.95	3.58	3.96	4.23	4.45	4.62	4.77	4.90	5.01	5.11	5.20
	.01	4.02	4.64	5.02	5.29	5.51	5.69	5.84	5.97	6.09	6.19	6.29
24	.05	2.92	3.53	3.90	4.17	4.37	4.54	4.68	4.81	4.92	5.01	5.10
	.01	3.96	4.54	4.91	5.17	5.37	5.54	5.69	5.81	5.92	6.02	6.11
30	.05	2.89	3.49	3.84	4.10	4.30	4.46	4.60	4.72	4.83	4.92	5.00
	.01	3.89	4.45	4.80	5.05	5.24	5.40	5.54	5.56	5.76	5.85	5.93
40	.05	2.86	3.44	3.79	4.04	4.23	4.39	4.52	4.63	4.74	4.82	4.91
	.01	3.82	4.37	4.70	4.93	5.11	5.27	5.39	5.50	5.60	5.69	5.77
60	.05	2.83	3.40	3.74	3.98	4.16	4.31	4.44	4.55	4.65	4.73	4.81
	.01	3.76	4.28	4.60	4.82	4.99	5.13	5.25	5.36	5.45	5.53	5.60
120	.05	2.80	3.36	3.69	3.92	4.10	4.24	4.36	4.48	4.56	4.64	4.72
	.01	3.70	4.20	4.50	4.71	4.87	5.01	5.12	5.21	5.30	5.38	5.44
∞	.05	2.77	3.31	3.63	3.86	4.03	4.17	4.29	4.39	4.47	4.55	4.62
	.01	3.64	4.12	4.40	4.60	4.76	4.88	4.99	5.08	5.16	5.23	5.29

From B. J. Winer, *Statistical Principles in Experimental Design,* McGraw-Hill, 1962; abridged from H. L. Harter, D. S. Clemm, and E. H. Guthrie, The probability integrals of the range and of the studentized range, WADC Tech. Rep. 58–484, Vol. 2, 1959, Wright Air Development Center, Table II.2, pp. 243–281. Reproduced with permission of The McGraw-Hill Companies, Inc.

Table 7 Critical Values of the F_{max} Test

Critical values for α = .05 are **dark numbers** and for α = .01 are light numbers.

(*Note: n* = number of scores in each condition or cell.)

		k = number of samples in the study										
n − 1	α	*2*	*3*	*4*	*5*	*6*	*7*	*8*	*9*	*10*	*11*	*12*
4	**.05**	**9.60**	**15.50**	**20.60**	**25.20**	**29.50**	**33.60**	**37.50**	**41.40**	**44.60**	**48.00**	**51.40**
	.01	23.20	37.00	49.00	59.00	69.00	79.00	89.00	97.00	106.00	113.00	120.00
5	**.05**	**7.15**	**10.80**	**13.70**	**16.30**	**18.70**	**20.80**	**22.90**	**24.70**	**26.50**	**28.20**	**29.90**
	.01	14.90	22.00	28.00	33.00	38.00	42.00	46.00	50.00	54.00	57.00	60.00
6	**.05**	**5.82**	**8.38**	**10.40**	**12.10**	**13.70**	**15.00**	**16.30**	**17.50**	**18.60**	**19.70**	**20.70**
	.01	11.10	15.50	19.10	22.00	25.00	27.00	30.00	32.00	34.00	36.00	37.00
7	**.05**	**4.99**	**6.94**	**8.44**	**9.70**	**10.80**	**11.80**	**12.70**	**13.50**	**14.30**	**15.10**	**15.80**
	.01	8.89	12.10	14.50	16.50	18.40	20.00	22.00	23.00	24.00	26.00	27.00
8	**.05**	**4.43**	**6.00**	**7.18**	**8.12**	**9.03**	**9.78**	**10.50**	**11.10**	**11.70**	**12.20**	**12.70**
	.01	7.50	9.90	11.70	13.20	14.50	15.80	16.90	17.90	18.90	19.80	21.00
9	**.05**	**4.03**	**5.34**	**6.31**	**7.11**	**7.80**	**8.41**	**8.95**	**9.45**	**9.91**	**10.30**	**10.70**
	.01	6.54	8.50	9.90	11.10	12.10	13.10	13.90	14.70	15.30	16.00	16.60
10	**.05**	**3.72**	**4.85**	**5.67**	**6.34**	**6.92**	**7.42**	**7.87**	**8.28**	**8.66**	**9.01**	**9.34**
	.01	5.85	7.40	8.60	9.60	10.40	11.10	11.80	12.40	12.90	13.40	13.90
12	**.05**	**3.28**	**4.16**	**4.79**	**5.30**	**5.72**	**6.09**	**6.42**	**6.72**	**7.00**	**7.25**	**7.48**
	.01	4.91	6.10	6.90	7.60	8.20	8.70	9.10	9.50	9.90	10.20	10.60
15	**.05**	**2.86**	**3.54**	**4.01**	**4.37**	**4.68**	**4.95**	**5.19**	**5.40**	**5.59**	**5.77**	**5.93**
	.01	4.07	4.90	5.50	6.00	6.40	6.70	7.10	7.30	7.50	7.80	8.00
20	**.05**	**2.46**	**2.95**	**3.29**	**3.54**	**3.76**	**3.94**	**4.10**	**4.24**	**4.37**	**4.49**	**4.59**
	.01	3.32	3.80	4.30	4.60	4.90	5.10	5.30	5.50	5.60	5.80	5.90
30	**.05**	**2.07**	**2.40**	**2.61**	**2.78**	**2.91**	**3.02**	**3.12**	**3.21**	**3.29**	**3.36**	**3.39**
	.01	2.63	3.00	3.30	3.40	3.60	3.70	3.80	3.90	4.00	4.10	4.20
60	**.05**	**1.67**	**1.85**	**1.96**	**2.04**	**2.11**	**2.17**	**2.22**	**2.26**	**2.30**	**2.33**	**2.36**
	.01	1.96	2.20	2.30	2.40	2.40	2.50	2.50	2.60	2.60	2.70	2.70

Table 8 Critical Values of Chi Square: The χ^2-Tables

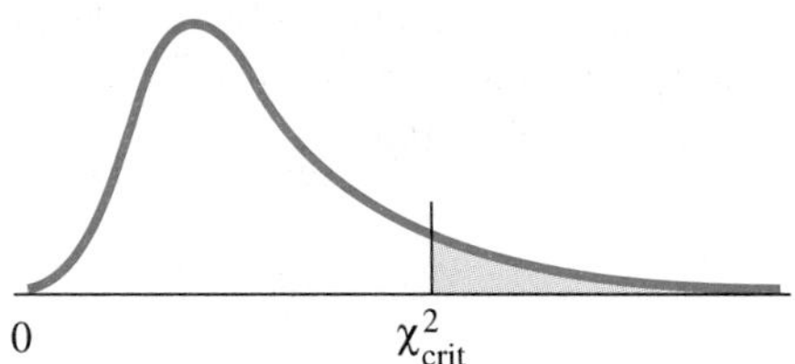

	Level of significance	
df	$\alpha = .05$	$\alpha = .01$
1	3.84	6.64
2	5.99	9.21
3	7.81	11.34
4	9.49	13.28
5	11.07	15.09
6	12.59	16.81
7	14.07	18.48
8	15.51	20.09
9	16.92	21.67
10	18.31	23.21
11	19.68	24.72
12	21.03	26.22
13	22.36	27.69
14	23.68	29.14
15	25.00	30.58
16	26.30	32.00
17	27.59	33.41
18	28.87	34.80
19	30.14	36.19
20	31.41	37.57
21	32.67	38.93
22	33.92	40.29
23	35.17	41.64
24	36.42	42.98
25	37.65	44.31
26	38.88	45.64
27	40.11	46.96
28	41.34	48.28
29	42.56	49.59
30	43.77	50.89
40	55.76	63.69
50	67.50	76.15
60	79.08	88.38
70	90.53	100.42

From Table IV of R. A. Fisher and F. Yates, *Statistical Tables for Biological, Agricultural, and Medical Research*, 6th ed. London: Longman Group Ltd., 1974. Reprinted by permission of Addison-Wesley Longman, Ltd.

Table 9 Critical Values of the Mann-Whitney *U*

To be significant, the U_{obt} must be equal to or be *less than* the critical value. (Dashes in the table indicate that no decision is possible.) Critical values for $\alpha = .05$ are **dark numbers** and for $\alpha = .01$ are light numbers.

Two-tailed test

n_2 (no. of scores in Group 2)	α	*n*₁ (no. of scores in Group 1) 1	2	3	4	5	6	7	8	9
1	**.05**	**—**	**—**	**—**	**—**	**—**	**—**	**—**	**—**	**—**
	.01	—	—	—	—	—	—	—	—	—
2	**.05**	**—**	**—**	**—**	**—**	**—**	**—**	**—**	**0**	**0**
	.01	—	—	—	—	—	—	—	—	—
3	**.05**	**—**	**—**	**—**	**—**	**0**	**1**	**1**	**2**	**2**
	.01	—	—	—	—	—	—	—	—	0
4	**.05**	**—**	**—**	**—**	**0**	**1**	**2**	**3**	**4**	**4**
	.01	—	—	—	—	—	0	0	1	1
5	**.05**	**—**	**—**	**0**	**1**	**2**	**3**	**5**	**6**	**7**
	.01	—	—	—	—	0	1	1	2	3
6	**.05**	**—**	**—**	**1**	**2**	**3**	**5**	**6**	**8**	**10**
	.01	—	—	—	0	1	2	3	4	5
7	**.05**	**—**	**—**	**1**	**3**	**5**	**6**	**8**	**10**	**12**
	.01	—	—	—	0	1	3	4	6	7
8	**.05**	**—**	**0**	**2**	**4**	**6**	**8**	**10**	**13**	**15**
	.01	—	—	—	1	2	4	6	7	9
9	**.05**	**—**	**0**	**2**	**4**	**7**	**10**	**12**	**15**	**17**
	.01	—	—	0	1	3	5	7	9	11
10	**.05**	**—**	**0**	**3**	**5**	**8**	**11**	**14**	**17**	**20**
	.01	—	—	0	2	4	6	9	11	13
11	**.05**	**—**	**0**	**3**	**6**	**9**	**13**	**16**	**19**	**23**
	.01	—	—	0	2	5	7	10	13	16
12	**.05**	**—**	**1**	**4**	**7**	**11**	**14**	**18**	**22**	**26**
	.01	—	—	1	3	6	9	12	15	18
13	**.05**	**—**	**1**	**4**	**8**	**12**	**16**	**20**	**24**	**28**
	.01	—	—	1	3	7	10	13	17	20
14	**.05**	**—**	**1**	**5**	**9**	**13**	**17**	**22**	**26**	**31**
	.01	—	—	1	4	7	11	15	18	22
15	**.05**	**—**	**1**	**5**	**10**	**14**	**19**	**24**	**29**	**34**
	.01	—	—	2	5	8	12	16	20	24
16	**.05**	**—**	**1**	**6**	**11**	**15**	**21**	**26**	**31**	**37**
	.01	—	—	2	5	9	13	18	22	27
17	**.05**	**—**	**2**	**6**	**11**	**17**	**22**	**28**	**34**	**39**
	.01	—	—	2	6	10	15	19	24	29
18	**.05**	**—**	**2**	**7**	**12**	**18**	**24**	**30**	**36**	**42**
	.01	—	—	2	6	11	16	21	26	31
19	**.05**	**—**	**2**	**7**	**13**	**19**	**25**	**32**	**38**	**45**
	.01	—	0	3	7	12	17	22	28	33
20	**.05**	**—**	**2**	**8**	**13**	**20**	**27**	**34**	**41**	**48**
	.01	—	0	3	8	13	18	24	30	36

Table 9 (cont.) Critical Values of the Mann-Whitney *U*

n_1 (no. of scores in Group 1)										
10	*11*	*12*	*13*	*14*	*15*	*16*	*17*	*18*	*19*	*20*
—	**—**	**—**	**—**	**—**	**—**	**—**	**—**	**—**	**—**	**—**
—	—	—	—	—	—	—	—	—	—	—
0	**0**	**1**	**1**	**1**	**1**	**1**	**2**	**2**	**2**	**2**
—	—	—	—	—	—	—	—	—	0	0
3	**3**	**4**	**4**	**5**	**5**	**6**	**6**	**7**	**7**	**8**
0	0	1	1	1	2	2	2	2	3	3
5	**6**	**7**	**8**	**9**	**10**	**11**	**11**	**12**	**13**	**13**
2	2	3	3	4	5	5	6	6	7	8
8	**9**	**11**	**12**	**13**	**14**	**15**	**17**	**18**	**19**	**20**
4	5	6	7	7	8	9	10	11	12	13
11	**13**	**14**	**16**	**17**	**19**	**21**	**22**	**24**	**25**	**27**
6	7	9	10	11	12	13	15	16	17	18
14	**16**	**18**	**20**	**22**	**24**	**26**	**28**	**30**	**32**	**34**
9	10	12	13	15	16	18	19	21	22	24
17	**19**	**22**	**24**	**26**	**29**	**31**	**34**	**36**	**38**	**41**
11	13	15	17	18	20	22	24	26	28	30
20	**23**	**26**	**28**	**31**	**34**	**37**	**39**	**42**	**45**	**48**
13	16	18	20	22	24	27	29	31	33	36
23	**26**	**29**	**33**	**36**	**39**	**42**	**45**	**48**	**52**	**55**
16	18	21	24	26	29	31	34	37	39	42
26	**30**	**33**	**37**	**40**	**44**	**47**	**51**	**55**	**58**	**62**
18	21	24	27	30	33	36	39	42	45	48
29	**33**	**37**	**41**	**45**	**49**	**53**	**57**	**61**	**65**	**69**
21	24	27	31	34	37	41	44	47	51	54
33	**37**	**41**	**45**	**50**	**54**	**59**	**63**	**67**	**72**	**76**
24	27	31	34	38	42	45	49	53	56	60
36	**40**	**45**	**50**	**55**	**59**	**64**	**67**	**74**	**78**	**83**
26	30	34	38	42	46	50	54	58	63	67
39	**44**	**49**	**54**	**59**	**64**	**70**	**75**	**80**	**85**	**90**
29	33	37	42	46	51	55	60	64	69	73
42	**47**	**53**	**59**	**64**	**70**	**75**	**81**	**86**	**92**	**98**
31	36	41	45	50	55	60	65	70	74	79
45	**51**	**57**	**63**	**67**	**75**	**81**	**87**	**93**	**99**	**105**
34	39	44	49	54	60	65	70	75	81	86
48	**55**	**61**	**67**	**74**	**80**	**86**	**93**	**99**	**106**	**112**
37	42	47	53	58	64	70	75	81	87	92
52	**58**	**65**	**72**	**78**	**85**	**92**	**99**	**106**	**113**	**119**
39	45	51	56	63	69	74	81	87	93	99
55	**62**	**69**	**76**	**83**	**90**	**98**	**105**	**112**	**119**	**127**
42	48	54	60	67	73	79	86	92	99	105

Table 9 (cont.) Critical Values of the Mann-Whitney *U*

One-tailed test

n_2 (no. of scores in Group 2)	α	n_1 (no. of scores in Group 1) 1	2	3	4	5	6	7	8	9
1	**.05**	**—**	**—**	**—**	**—**	**—**	**—**	**—**	**—**	**—**
	.01	—	—	—	—	—	—	—	—	—
2	**.05**	**—**	**—**	**—**	**—**	**0**	**0**	**0**	**1**	**1**
	.01	—	—	—	—	—	—	—	—	—
3	**.05**	**—**	**—**	**0**	**0**	**1**	**2**	**2**	**3**	**3**
	.01	—	—	—	—	—	—	0	0	1
4	**.05**	**—**	**—**	**0**	**1**	**2**	**3**	**4**	**5**	**6**
	.01	—	—	—	—	0	1	1	2	3
5	**.05**	**—**	**0**	**1**	**2**	**4**	**5**	**6**	**8**	**9**
	.01	—	—	—	0	1	2	3	4	5
6	**.05**	**—**	**0**	**2**	**3**	**5**	**7**	**8**	**10**	**12**
	.01	—	—	—	1	2	3	4	6	7
7	**.05**	**—**	**0**	**2**	**4**	**6**	**8**	**11**	**13**	**15**
	.01	—	—	0	1	3	4	6	7	9
8	**.05**	**—**	**1**	**3**	**5**	**8**	**10**	**13**	**15**	**18**
	.01	—	—	0	2	4	6	7	9	11
9	**.05**	**—**	**1**	**3**	**6**	**9**	**12**	**15**	**18**	**21**
	.01	—	—	1	3	5	7	9	11	14
10	**.05**	**—**	**1**	**4**	**7**	**11**	**14**	**17**	**20**	**24**
	.01	—	—	1	3	6	8	11	13	16
11	**.05**	**—**	**1**	**5**	**8**	**12**	**16**	**19**	**23**	**27**
	.01	—	—	1	4	7	9	12	15	18
12	**.05**	**—**	**2**	**5**	**9**	**13**	**17**	**21**	**26**	**30**
	.01	—	—	2	5	8	11	14	17	21
13	**.05**	**—**	**2**	**6**	**10**	**15**	**19**	**24**	**28**	**33**
	.01	—	0	2	5	9	12	16	20	23
14	**.05**	**—**	**2**	**7**	**11**	**16**	**21**	**26**	**31**	**36**
	.01	—	0	2	6	10	13	17	22	26
15	**.05**	**—**	**3**	**7**	**12**	**18**	**23**	**28**	**33**	**39**
	.01	—	0	3	7	11	15	19	24	28
16	**.05**	**—**	**3**	**8**	**14**	**19**	**25**	**30**	**36**	**42**
	.01	—	0	3	7	12	16	21	26	31
17	**.05**	**—**	**3**	**9**	**15**	**20**	**26**	**33**	**39**	**45**
	.01	—	0	4	8	13	18	23	28	33
18	**.05**	**—**	**4**	**9**	**16**	**22**	**28**	**35**	**41**	**48**
	.01	—	0	4	9	14	19	24	30	36
19	**.05**	**0**	**4**	**10**	**17**	**23**	**30**	**37**	**44**	**51**
	.01	—	1	4	9	15	20	26	32	38
20	**.05**	**0**	**4**	**11**	**18**	**25**	**32**	**39**	**47**	**54**
	.01	—	1	5	10	16	22	28	34	40

n_1 (no. of scores in Group 1)										
10	*11*	*12*	*13*	*14*	*15*	*16*	*17*	*18*	*19*	*20*
—	—	—	—	—	—	—	—	—	**0**	**0**
—	—	—	—	—	—	—	—	—	—	—
1	**1**	**2**	**2**	**2**	**3**	**3**	**3**	**4**	**4**	**4**
—	—	—	0	0	0	0	0	0	1	1
4	**5**	**5**	**6**	**7**	**7**	**8**	**9**	**9**	**10**	**11**
1	1	2	2	2	3	3	4	4	4	5
7	**8**	**9**	**10**	**11**	**12**	**14**	**15**	**16**	**17**	**18**
3	4	5	5	6	7	7	8	9	9	10
11	**12**	**13**	**15**	**16**	**18**	**19**	**20**	**22**	**23**	**25**
6	7	8	9	10	11	12	13	14	15	16
14	**16**	**17**	**19**	**21**	**23**	**25**	**26**	**28**	**30**	**32**
8	9	11	12	13	15	16	18	19	20	22
17	**19**	**21**	**24**	**26**	**28**	**30**	**33**	**35**	**37**	**39**
11	12	14	16	17	19	21	23	24	26	28
20	**23**	**26**	**28**	**31**	**33**	**36**	**39**	**41**	**44**	**47**
13	15	17	20	22	24	26	28	30	32	34
24	**27**	**30**	**33**	**36**	**39**	**42**	**45**	**48**	**51**	**54**
16	18	21	23	26	28	31	33	36	38	40
27	**31**	**34**	**37**	**41**	**44**	**48**	**51**	**55**	**58**	**62**
19	22	24	27	30	33	36	38	41	44	47
31	**34**	**38**	**42**	**46**	**50**	**54**	**57**	**61**	**65**	**69**
22	25	28	31	34	37	41	44	47	50	53
34	**38**	**42**	**47**	**51**	**55**	**60**	**64**	**68**	**72**	**77**
24	28	31	35	38	42	46	49	53	56	60
37	**42**	**47**	**51**	**56**	**61**	**65**	**70**	**75**	**80**	**84**
27	31	35	39	43	47	51	55	59	63	67
41	**46**	**51**	**56**	**61**	**66**	**71**	**77**	**82**	**87**	**92**
30	34	38	43	47	51	56	60	65	69	73
44	**50**	**55**	**61**	**66**	**72**	**77**	**83**	**88**	**94**	**100**
33	37	42	47	51	56	61	66	70	75	80
48	**54**	**60**	**65**	**71**	**77**	**83**	**89**	**95**	**101**	**107**
36	41	46	51	56	61	66	71	76	82	87
51	**57**	**64**	**70**	**77**	**83**	**89**	**96**	**102**	**109**	**115**
38	44	49	55	60	66	71	77	82	88	93
55	**61**	**68**	**75**	**82**	**88**	**95**	**102**	**109**	**116**	**123**
41	47	53	59	65	70	76	82	88	94	100
58	**65**	**72**	**80**	**87**	**94**	**101**	**109**	**116**	**123**	**130**
44	50	56	63	69	75	82	88	94	101	107
62	**69**	**77**	**84**	**92**	**100**	**107**	**115**	**123**	**130**	**138**
47	53	60	67	73	80	87	93	100	107	114

From the *Bulletin of the Institute of Educational Research*, 1, No. 2, Indiana University, with permission of the publishers.

Table 10 Critical Values of the Wilcoxon T

To be significant, the T_{obt} must be equal to or *less than* the critical value. (Dashes in the table indicate that no decision is possible.) In the table, N is the number of nonzero differences that occurred when T_{obt} was calculated.

Two-tailed test

N	$\alpha = .05$	$\alpha = .01$	N	$\alpha = .05$	$\alpha = .01$
5	—	—	28	116	91
6	0	—	29	126	100
7	2	—	30	137	109
8	3	0	31	147	118
9	5	1	32	159	128
10	8	3	33	170	138
11	10	5	34	182	148
12	13	7	35	195	159
13	17	9	36	208	171
14	21	12	37	221	182
15	25	15	38	235	194
16	29	19	39	249	207
17	34	23	40	264	220
18	40	27	41	279	233
19	46	32	42	294	247
20	52	37	43	310	261
21	58	42	44	327	276
22	65	48	45	343	291
23	73	54	46	361	307
24	81	61	47	378	322
25	89	68	48	396	339
26	98	75	49	415	355
27	107	83	50	434	373

Table 10 (cont.) Critical Values of the Wilcoxon *T*

One-tailed test

N	α = .05	α = .01	*N*	α = .05	α = .01
5	0	—	28	130	101
6	2	—	29	140	110
7	3	0	30	151	120
8	5	1	31	163	130
9	8	3	32	175	140
10	10	5	33	187	151
11	13	7	34	200	162
12	17	9	35	213	173
13	21	12	36	227	185
14	25	15	37	241	198
15	30	19	38	256	211
16	35	23	39	271	224
17	41	27	40	286	238
18	47	32	41	302	252
19	53	37	42	319	266
20	60	43	43	336	281
21	67	49	44	353	296
22	75	55	45	371	312
23	83	62	46	389	328
24	91	69	47	407	345
25	100	76	48	426	362
26	110	84	49	446	379
27	119	92	50	466	397

From F. Wilcoxon and R. A. Wilcox, *Some Rapid Approximate Statistical Procedures, Revised Edition* (Pearl River, NY: Lederle Laboratories, 1964).

APPENDIX D

ANSWERS TO ODD-NUMBERED REVIEW QUESTIONS AND PRACTICE PROBLEMS

This appendix provides answers to the odd-numbered items in the "Review Questions" and "Practice Problems" sections found at the end of each chapter.

Chapter 1

1. To conduct their own research and to understand that of others.

3. To organize, summarize, and communicate the IQ scores, and to draw conclusions about what the scores indicate about intelligence.

5. (a) Scientists are uncertain, open-minded, skeptical, cautious, and ethical.
(b) To protect science from misleading information.

7. To describe, explain, predict, and control behavior.

9. A hypothesis should be *testable* (a test of the hypothesis is possible); *falsifiable* (the hypothesis potentially may be shown to be false); *precise* (the hypothesis involves specific terms and applies to a specific situation); *rational* (the hypothesis fits what is known about nature); *parsimonious* (the hypothesis is as simple an explanation as possible).

11. A causal hypothesis postulates a particular cause of a behavior. A descriptive hypothesis postulates particular characteristics of a behavior or provides a goal of observations.

13. Because the design may contain flaws that reduce confidence in its conclusions.

15. Replication is repeatedly conducting studies to build confidence in a hypothesis. It eliminates coincidental influences in one study that may mislead us.

17. Ask what empirical, objective, systematic, and controlled evidence there is. How is the research flawed, has it been replicated, and what confidence is there in the conclusions?

19. The researcher's, because your observations are unlikely to be objective, systematic, and controlled.

21. It is unscientific to require faith in the events and explanations being studied.

23. (a) To confirm it, you must find people who don't wake up and then die. If they're dead, you can't determine what they were dreaming about.
(b) By looking for disconfirmation: Finding people who dreamt they hit the bottom of the cliff but did not die would disconfirm this hypothesis.
(c) The data are not very objective or empirical: Maybe participants didn't really dream of falling off a cliff, or maybe they woke up briefly prior to hitting bottom, but they forgot.

25. It is not a science because creationism requires religious faith; science excludes faith because we can't know which is the "correct" one.

27. This statement is not a theory; it is a hypothesis; and "adequate," "necessary," and "balance" must be defined precisely.

Chapter 2

1. (a) In a relationship, certain scores on one variable are associated with certain scores on the other variable, and as the scores on one variable change, the scores on the other variable also tend consistently to change.
(b) Relationships reflect the operation of a law of nature, so by understanding relationships, we understand nature.

3. (a) A population is all members of a specific group for which a law of nature applies; a sample is a subset of the population.
(b) The behaviors or scores from the sample are used to infer the scores or behaviors that would be found in the population if it could be studied.

5. A data point is a dot plotted on a graph to represent a pair of X and Y scores.

7. (a) A representative sample occurs because, by chance, the scores selected have the same characteristics as those in the population.

(b) An unrepresentative sample occurs because, by chance, the scores do not have the same characteristics as those in the population.

9. Inferential statistics are used to decide whether the sample data represent a particular relationship in the population.

11. (a) The independent variable is the overall variable assumed to be the causal variable; conditions are the amounts or categories of the independent variable under which participants are tested.
(b) The dependent variable measures participants' behavior and is assumed to be influenced by the independent variable.

13. With a true independent variable, participants can be randomly assigned to any condition. With a quasi-independent variable, participants must be assigned to a particular condition because of an inherent characteristic.

15. In experiments, we change one variable and measure the other to *produce* a relationship; in descriptive designs, we measure two variables to *observe* a relationship.

17. Study A is an experiment, because the researcher manipulates the amount of alcohol participants consume. Study B is a correlational study, because the researcher merely measures, without manipulating, the amount of alcohol participants consume.

19. Parts (a), (d), and (e) describe experiments; parts (b) and (c) describe quasi-experiments.

21. Samples A and D.

23. A relationship is in Study A and Study C because, as the scores on one variable change, the scores on the other variable tend to change.

25. Because each relationship suggests there is something about the way nature operates so that as the amount of the *X* variable changes, the amount of the *Y* variable also changes.

27. (a) Wall color is the independent variable.
(b) Test grades is the dependent variable.
(c) Mood is an intervening variable.

Chapter 3

1. We ask if the data reflect what we think they reflect (i.e., are they reliable and valid?).

3. (a) An extraneous variable potentially influences results, but is not a variable we wish to study.
(b) An unsystematic extraneous variable changes inconsistently; a systematic extraneous variable changes along with the variables of interest.
(c) They may reduce the strength of the relationship.
(d) They lead to errors because the variables we think are operating are not, and we miss those that are.

5. (a) Content validity is the degree to which a measurement reflects the intended variable or behavior.
(b) Construct validity is the degree to which a measurement reflects the intended hypothetical construct.
(c) Internal validity is the degree to which there are no unintended variables reflected in the relationship observed in the study.
(d) External validity is the degree to which results generalize to other individuals and settings.

7. (a) Control the situation so that the variable does not occur.
(b) Have the same amount or category of the variable present throughout all conditions.
(c) Produce equal and opposite amounts of the variable in every condition to balance out any biases.

9. Whether the experimental situation generalizes to natural settings and natural behaviors.

11. (a) Greater control of extraneous variables increases internal validity, but produces a more unique situation that does not generalize well.
(b) A natural setting that generalizes well tends to be uncontrolled, allowing potential confoundings that reduce internal validity.

13. (a) The advantage is that experimental methods tend to have high internal validity. The disadvantage is that they tend to have reduced external validity.
(b) We have greater confidence in identifying the causes of the behavior, but less confidence that a natural behavior is being observed.

15. (a) With a true independent variable, participants can be randomly assigned to conditions. With a quasi-independent variable, subjects must be assigned to a condition because of an inherent characteristic.
(b) Quasi-independent variables are likely to be confounded by extraneous participant variables, so there are many differences between the conditions that may cause differences in dependent scores.

17. (a) A confounding variable.
(b) Keep your mood constant throughout the study or balance it by testing each type of model while you are in both moods.

19. (a) A quasi-experiment.
(b) Quasi-independent variable.
(c) Conditions (or levels).

(d) Dependent variable.
(e) Little confidence, because amount of wine may be confounded by other differences in participants (e.g., their fitness or diet).

21. (a) Amount of aspirin is a confounding variable.
(b) Because reduced heart disease may be caused by greater amounts of aspirin, this confounding reduces internal validity for concluding that red wine reduces heart disease.

23. Conduct either a quasi-experiment (conditions of the independent variable are the amount of participants' inherent fear of disease and dependent scores reflect number of partners) or a correlational study (measuring each person's fear and number of partners). Either design is flawed because we cannot conclude that greater fear causes fewer sexual partners. Confounding variables may actually determine the number of partners (e.g., their age, attractiveness, marital status).

25. (a) A correlational design.
(b) No, this type of design has little internal validity for inferring causality.
(c) The age and personality of drivers of brightly colored cars (young, liberal, less cautious) may make them more accident-prone compared with drivers of muted-colored cars (older, conservative, cautious).
(d) A true experiment: Randomly assign participants to conditions where they are given a car of a certain color to drive for a time, during which we measure their accident rates.

Chapter 4

1. (a) A strong manipulation is likely to produce large differences in scores between conditions.
(b) To avoid a weak relationship that causes us to erroneously conclude there is not one in nature.
(c) Select conditions that are substantially different from each other, and have participants experience a condition sufficiently for it to influence them.

3 (a) It is a measurement, in addition to the dependent variable, that determines whether the treatment had its intended effect.
(b) A manipulation check is performed during the study; a pilot study is performed prior to the study to validate stimuli and debug procedures.

5. (a) Practice effects are the influence on trials resulting from practicing trials.
(b) Carry-over effects are the influence on trials from experiencing previous trials.
(c) A response set is a bias toward responding in a particular way because of previous responses made.

7. A sensitive measure produces different scores for small differences in behavior.

9. (a) Automation is using electronic or mechanical devices to present stimuli and/or to measure and record responses.
(b) It increases reliability.
(c) It may heighten reactivity and, over time, instrumentation effects may actually decrease reliability.

11. (a) Experimental realism is the extent to which a measurement task engages participants. We seek it so that participants ignore demand characteristics.
(b) Ecological validity occurs if the task reflects natural behaviors; experimental realism occurs if the task actively engages participants.

13. Research ethics deal with balancing a researcher's right to study a behavior with the right of participants to be protected from abuse.

15. Obtain informed consent and provide a debriefing.

17. (a) In role playing, subjects pretend they are in a particular situation.
(b) It minimizes risks to participants.
(c) Participants may not provide realistic or accurate responses.

19. (a) You cannot read the lists consistently for all participants, and differences may influence their memory.
(b) You expect the conditions to influence memory in a certain way, and inconsistency in your pronunciation, voice, inflection, and so on can make a list more or less memorable and produce the expected results.
(c) Through automation: Play a tape recording of the lists to all participants.
(d) Instrumentation effects may occur, with the recording becoming distorted and unclear with use. (Several copies of the original recording are needed.)

21. (a) By selecting stimulus words such that for the similar condition they are very similar, and for the dissimilar condition, they are very dissimilar.
(b) Provide practice trials.
(c) Provide several lists per condition, and compute a summary score from these multiple trials.
(d) Order effects may result from multiple trials.
(e) Counterbalance the order of the lists presented to different participants in each condition.

23. (a) To improve reliability, because only one film might be particularly arousing or not arousing.

(b) Order effects due to the order in which films are presented.
(c) Counterbalance so that different participants in a condition view the films in different orders.

25. By adding to reactivity and communicating experimenter expectancies that decrease internal validity, and that reduce generalizability or external validity.

27. (a) Participants may respond to demand characteristics and provide the expected response, even though their views remain the same.
(b) Participants may not reveal their private feelings, so they may all behave in the same, neutral fashion, producing no differences between conditions.
(c) Employ a manipulation check (e.g., a questionnaire) to directly assess participants' sexist views.

Chapter 5

1. That the researcher observes and describes participants or their behavior, usually in natural settings, without manipulating or controlling any variables.

3. (a) Behaviors are observed in a natural setting that is not influenced by the researcher or by participants reacting to demand characteristics.
(b) The results may be biased by researcher expectations, we may not have random sampling, and we obtain qualitative data that may lack precision, accuracy, and sensitivity.

5. (a) A case study involves a description of one individual, organization, or event.
(b) It provides an in-depth, complete description of a subject or event.
(c) A single case provides little external validity for generalizing to other cases.

7. (a) Simple random sampling is randomly selecting subjects from a list of the population. Systematic random sampling is randomly selecting a starting point and then selecting every *n*th participant on the list.
(b) Stratified random sampling is proportionate random selection from each important subgroup in the population.
(c) Cluster sampling is randomly selecting certain groups and then observing all subjects in each group.

9. (a) Quota sampling proportionately samples from the population but relies on convenience sampling to obtain each proportion.
(b) Snowball sampling is identifying potential subjects through previously tested subjects.

11. (a) When mailing is the best method for reaching participants, a lengthy survey is required, and the researcher is not in a hurry to obtain the data.
(b) When the appropriate sample can be reached by telephone, the survey is not lengthy, and it is necessary to obtain the data rapidly.
(c) So that the sample is representative.

13. Measure *quantitative* behaviors, such as physical actions, and count their frequency, measure their duration, or determine whether they occur in a given interval. Eliminate experimenter biases using multiple raters.

15. (a) They are differently worded versions of the same questionnaire.
(b) When repeatedly testing the same participants.

17. (a) For greater internal validity; select a mild, safe and ethical independent variable that will produce different levels of participants' anxiety, and in each, measure their problem-solving ability.
(b) For greater external validity and to be more ethical; measure participants' existing anxiety level (using a questionnaire) and their problem-solving ability, and see if they relate.

19. (a) Including "dorm" and "roommate" make it double-barreled, delete the "very," and provide more points on the scale.
(b) Both "much" and "poorly" are undefined, "frequently" and "seldom" do not fit the question, and use an even-numbered scale.

21. It is probably a catch trial for identifying inconsistent responders.

23. Obtain informed consent prior to entering the restroom; solicit volunteers who are told they'll be secretly observed throughout the day; have the observer be visible to participants; select a behavior that would be considered less private.

25. (a) The judgments and their scoring may not be reliable.
(b) Train the judges to use explicit rules for evaluating and assigning scores for aggressiveness.
(c) Employ multiple raters who are blind to the study's goals.
(d) Determine that there is high inter-rater reliability.

Chapter 6

1. (a) A transformation is a mathematical procedure for systematically converting a set of scores into different scores.
(b) To make scores easier to work with and to make different kinds of scores comparable.

3. Consider what you wish to know about the data, the specific design employed, and the scale of measurement used to measure the scores.
5. (a) *N* is the total number of scores in a sample.
   (b) *f* is frequency, the number of times a score occurs.
   (c) *rel. f* is relative frequency, the proportion of time certain scores occur.
   (d) *cf* is cumulative frequency, the number of times scores at or below a certain score occur.
7. (a) A histogram has a discrete bar above each score; a polygon has data points above the scores that are connected by straight lines.
   (b) Histograms are used with a few interval or ratio scores; polygons are used with a wide range of interval or ratio scores.
9. (a) A normal distribution is symmetrical, with a tail at each side; a skewed distribution is nonsymmetrical, with only one distinct tail.
   (b) A normal distribution has only one "hump" showing one score having the highest frequency; a bimodal distribution has two humps, showing two scores with the same highest frequency.
   (c) A negatively skewed distribution has a tail at the lowest scores; a positively skewed distribution has a tail at the highest scores.
11. (a) Because all *N* scores are either at or below the highest score.
   (b) Because the number of all individual scores added together equals the total number of scores.
13. (a) Simple frequency is the number of times a score occurs in a sample; relative frequency is the proportion of time the score occurs.
   (b) Cumulative frequency is the number of times that scores at or below the score occur; percentile is the percent of the time that scores at or below the score occur.
15. (a) Bar graph.
   (b) Polygon.
   (c) Bar graph.
   (d) Histogram.
17. (a) 13.75
   (b) 10.04
   (c) 10.05
   (d) .08
   (e) 1.00
19. (a) 35% of the sample scored at or below the score.
   (b) The score occurred 40% of the time in the sample.
   (c) It is one of the highest and least frequent scores.
   (d) It is one of the lowest and least frequent scores.
   (e) 50 participants had either your score or one below it.
   (f) 60% of the distribution is to the left of (below) your score.
21. The *N* should be 10; the scores should be listed in descending order; a row containing the score of 6 should be included; the *cf* for the score of 1 should be 1; and the *cf* for all other scores should be corrected so that at the score of 7 the *cf* is 10.
23. (a) 70, 72, 60, 85, 45.
   (b) The 20th percentile, because .20 of the scores are below 60.
   (c) With .50 of the curve to the left of 70, .50 of the sample scored below 70.
   (d) With .50 of the curve to the left of 70, and .20 of the curve below 60, .50 − .20 = .30 of the curve (sample) is between 60 and 70.
   (e) .25.
   (f) With .25 of scores between 70 and 80, and .50 of scores below 70, a total of .75 of scores are below 80, so 80 is the 75th percentile.

25.

Score	*f*	*rel. f*	*cf*
53	1	.05	18
52	3	.17	17
51	2	.11	14
50	5	.28	12
49	4	.22	7
48	0	.00	3
47	3	.17	3

27.

Score	*f*	*rel. f*	*cf*
16	5	.33	15
15	1	.07	10
14	0	.00	9
13	2	.13	9
12	3	.20	7
11	4	.27	4

Chapter 7

1. (a) A statistic describes a characteristic of a sample. A parameter describes a characteristic of a population.
   (b) Symbols for statistics are letters from the English alphabet. Symbols for population parameters are letters from the Greek alphabet.
3. (a) The mode is the most frequently occurring score, used with nominal scores.

(b) The median is the score at the 50th percentile (50% of the scores are at or below the median), used with ordinal scores or highly skewed interval or ratio scores.
(c) The mean is the average of the scores, used with symmetrical, unimodal distributions of interval or ratio scores.

5. The mean; psychological variables usually form a normal distribution, which are best summarized by the mean.

7. It indicates whether the score is above or below the mean, and how far from the mean it is.

9. It is the Greek "mu," the symbol for the population mean, and is usually estimated based on the mean of a random sample.

11. (a) $\Sigma X = 638$, $N = 11$, $\overline{X} = 58$.
(b) The mode is 58.

13. (a) The low grade produced a negatively skewed distribution.
(b) Compute her median grade.

15. (a) Mean.
(b) Median (these ratio scores are skewed).
(c) Mode (this is a nominal variable).
(d) Median (this is an ordinal variable).

17. (a) The subject scoring +5.
(b) The subject scoring −10.
(c) −10, +5, −2, +1.

19. Mean errors do not change until 5 hours of sleep deprivation, and then increase with increasing sleep deprivation.

21. (a) Income on *Y* axis, age on *X* axis; line graph; find median income per age group (income is skewed).
(b) Positive votes on *Y* axis, presence or absence of a wildlife refuge on *X* axis; bar graph; find mean number of votes per *X* group.
(c) Running speed on *Y* axis, amount of carbohydrates consumed on *X* axis; line graph; find mean running speed per amount if normally distributed.
(d) Alcohol abuse on *Y* axis, ethnic group on *X* axis; bar graph; find mean rate of alcohol abuse per group.

23. (a) The mean score on the test decreases as amount of sunlight increases.
(b) Raw scores tend to decrease as amount of sunlight increases.
(c) If the data pass the inferential test, then the populations of scores and their μs tend to decrease as the conditions increase.
(d) The data provide evidence of a relationship in nature.

25. (a) The means for Conditions 1, 2, and 3 are 15, 12, and 9, respectively.
(b)

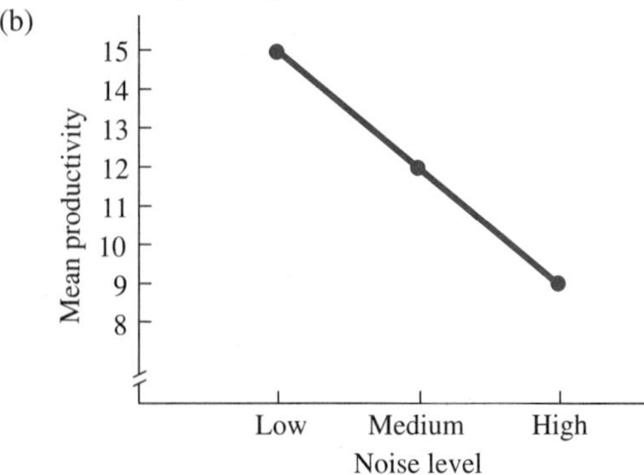

(c)

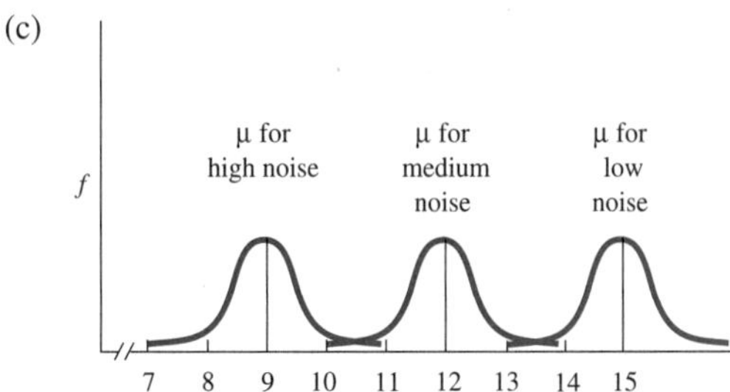

(d) Apparently, the relationship is that as noise level increases, the typical productivity score decreases from around 15 to around 12 to around 9.

Chapter 8

1. Perform squaring and taking a square root first, then multiplication and division, then addition and subtraction.

3. (a) The larger the variability, the more the scores differ or are spread out.
(b) The smaller the variability, the more consistent their scores and behavior.

5. (a) They both communicate how much the scores are spread out around the mean.
(b) The standard deviation, because it can be more directly interpreted as the "average" distance the scores are from the mean.

7. (a) All are forms of the standard deviation, communicating the "average" amount scores differ from the mean.
(b) S_X is a sample's standard deviation; s_X is an estimate of the population's standard deviation based on a sample, and σ_X is the population's true standard deviation.

9. This S_X^2 indicates no differences between the scores and the mean, so all participants obtained the same score, equal to the mean.

11. (a) Error variance is the differences between the scores in each condition and the mean of the condition.
    (b) It is caused by unreliability and fluctuating extraneous variables.

13. (a) Range $= 9 - 0 = 9$, so the data spanned 9 different creativity scores.
    (b) $\Sigma_X = 100$, $\Sigma X^2 = 668$, and $N = 20$, so $S_X^2 = (668 - 500)/20 = 8.40$: The average squared deviation of creativity scores from the mean is 8.40.
    (c) Because $S_X = 2.90$, on average the creativity scores differed from the mean by about 2.90.

15. About 160 people. The score of 2.10 is a distance of 2.90 or one standard deviation below the $\overline{X}$ of 5. About 34% of the scores are between 2.10 and the mean, so 16% of the scores are below 2.1: 16% of 1000 is $(.16)(1000) = 160$.

17. (a) The sample tends to be normally distributed, so we'd expect the population to be normal.
    (b) Because $\overline{X} = 1297/17 = 76.29$, we expect the typical score (μ) to be 76.29.
    (c) $s_X^2 = (99{,}223 - 98{,}953.47)/16 = 16.85$.
    (d) $s_X = 4.10$.
    (e) Between 72.19 $(76.29 - 4.10)$ and 80.39 $(76.29 + 4.10)$.

19. (a) Pluto, because his S_X is smaller.
    (b) Pluto, because his scores are closer to 60.

21. Predict the $\overline{X}$ of 65 for each student. Error is measured as variance, so $S_X^2 = 6^2 = 36$.

23. (a) Compute the mean and standard deviation of each condition.
    (b) Experiment 1: As the conditions change, dependent scores tend to increase from around 11.75 to 33.5 to 46.5. Experiment 2: As the conditions change, dependent scores tend to decrease from 13.33 to 8.33 to 5.67.
    (c) Experiment 1.
    (d) In Experiment 1, for conditions 1, 2, and 3 the $S_X = 1.48$, 2.29, 2.06, respectively. In Experiment 2, for conditions 1, 2, and 3, the $S_X = 3.68$, 2.05, and 2.49, respectively.
    (e) Experiment 2, because it produces larger values of S_X, which, when squared, indicate larger error variance.
    (f) With more consistency and less variability, the independent variable in Experiment 1 apparently has a greater influence in determining scores. Greater variability in Experiment 2 suggests other variables were influencing scores.

25 (a) In each condition, it would be the $\overline{X}$ of 11.33, 8.33, and 5.67, respectively.
    (b) Rather close: As each s_X indicates, "on average" scores will differ from their mean by 4.51, 2.52, and 3.06, respectively.

Chapter 9

1. (a) A z-score indicates the distance, measured in standard deviation units, that a score is above or below the mean.
   (b) The size of the score's deviation and the size of the standard deviation.

3. A z-distribution is the distribution that results when a distribution of raw scores is transformed into z-scores.

5. Because z-scores standardize or equate different distributions so that they can be compared and graphed on the same set of axes.

7. (a) It is our model of the perfect normal z-distribution.
   (b) It is used as a model of any normal distribution of raw scores after being transformed to z-scores.
   (c) The raw scores should be at least approximately normally distributed, they should be from a continuous interval or ratio variable, and the sample should be large.

9. (a) That it is normally distributed, that μ equals the μ of the raw score population, and that the standard error of the mean equals the raw score population standard deviation divided by the square root of N.
   (b) With this information, we can compute a z-score to evaluate a sample mean from *any* normally distributed variable.

11. (a) Convert the raw score to z, use z with the z-tables to find the proportion of the area under the appropriate part of the normal curve, and that proportion is the *rel. f*; or use it to determine percentile.
    (b) In column B or C of the z-tables, find the specified *rel. f* or the *rel. f* converted from the percentile, identify the corresponding z at that proportion, transform the z into its raw score, and that score is the cutoff score.
    (c) Compute the standard error of the mean, transform the sample mean into a z-score, and follow the steps in part (a).

13. (a) He should consider the size of each class's standard deviation.

APPENDIX D

(b) Small. A small S_X will give him a large positive z-score, placing him far above the mean.
(c) Large. With a large S_X, he will have a small negative z and still be close to the mean.

15. $\Sigma X = 103$, $\Sigma X^2 = 931$, and $N = 12$, so $S_X = 1.98$ and $\overline{X} = 8.58$.
(a) For $X = 10$, $z = (10 - 8.58)/1.98 = +.72$.
(b) For $X = 6$, $z = (6 - 8.58)/1.98 = -1.30$.

17. (a) $z = +1.0$
(b) $z = -2.8$
(c) $z = -.70$
(d) $z = -2.0$

19. (a) .4706
(b) .0107
(c) .3944 + .4970 = .8914
(d) .0250 + .0250 = .05

21. From the z-table, the 25th percentile is at approximately $z = -.67$. The cutoff score is then $X = (-.67)(10) + 75 = 68.3$.

23. (a) Evaluate any $\overline{X}$ by computing its z-score.
(b) $\sigma_{\overline{X}} = 8/\sqrt{64} = 1.0$; $z = (57.28 - 56)/1.0 = +1.28$, so it is a rather high, extreme mean.
(c) Only .1003 of the curve is above this mean, so it is among the top 10% of all means.

25. For City A, her salary has a z of $(27{,}000 - 50{,}000)/15{,}000 = -1.53$. For City B, her salary has a z of $(12{,}000 - 14{,}000)/1000 = -2.0$. City A is the better offer, because her income will be closer to the average cost of living in that city.

27. Convert $\overline{X}$ to a z-score. First, compute $\sigma_{\overline{X}} = 6/\sqrt{50} = .849$. Then, $z = (18 - 19.4)/.849 = -1.65$. From the z-tables, .0495 of the curve is below this score. Out of 1,000 samples, you would expect $(.0495)(1000) = 49.5$ sample means to be below 18.

Chapter 10

1. (a) In experiments, the researcher manipulates one variable and measures participants' responses on another variable; in correlational studies, the researcher merely measures participants' responses on two variables.
(b) In experiments, the researcher computes the mean of the dependent scores (Y scores) for each condition of the independent variable (each X score); in correlational studies, the researcher examines the relationship over all X-Y pairs simultaneously by computing a correlation coefficient.

3. In correlational research, we don't necessarily know which variable occurred first, nor are confounding variables controlled that might be the cause.

5. (a) A scatterplot is a graph of the individual data points formed from a set of X-Y pairs.
(b) A regression line is the summary straight line that best fits through the scatterplot.

7. (a) As the X scores increase, the Y scores tend to increase.
(b) As the X scores increase, the Y scores tend to decrease.
(c) As the X scores increase, the Y scores do not tend to only increase or only decrease.

9. (a) The scatterplot has a circular or horizontal elliptical shape.
(b) The variability in Y at each X is equal to the overall variability across all Y scores in the data.
(c) The Y scores are not at all relatively close to the regression line.
(d) Knowing X does not improve accuracy in predicting Y.

11. (a) Convergent validity is the extent a procedure correlates with other procedures that are valid. Discriminant validity is the extent a procedure is not correlated with procedures that measure other unintended variables or constructs.
(b) Convergent and discriminant validity involve correlating the scores from two tests. Criterion validity correlates scores from a test with a behavior.
(c) Concurrent validity is the extent a procedure correlates with a present behavior; predictive validity is the extent a procedure correlates with a future behavior.

13. A correlation coefficient of ± 1 indicates perfect consistency, and a relationship cannot be more consistent than that.

15. He is incorrectly inferring that more people cause fewer bears. The real cause may be the number of hunters, or the amount of pesticides used, or the noise level associated with more people.

17. (a) r.
(b) r_S.
(c) r_{pb}.
(d) r_S (after the liquid-consumed scores are transformed to rank-order scores).

19. (a) There is no independent or dependent variable in a correlational study.
(b) The researcher will implicitly ask what scores on one variable occur for a "given" amount of the other variable: X is the given variable, Y is the other variable.

21. Disagree. The problem is a restricted range, because exceptionally smart subjects produce a small range of IQ scores and grade averages. With an unrestricted range, there may be a much larger r.

23. First, compute r_{pb}. For those with degrees, $\overline{Y}_2 = 8.6$; for those without degrees, $\overline{Y}_1 = 5.2$; $S_Y = 3.208$, $p = .50$, and $q = .50$. $r_{pb} = (1.06)(.50) = .53$. Looking at those without college degrees and then at those with degrees, this is a positive linear relationship with an intermediate degree of association.

25. To answer this question, compute r. $\Sigma X = 38$, $\Sigma X^2 = 212$, $(\Sigma X)^2 = 1444$, $\Sigma Y = 68$, $\Sigma Y^2 = 552$, $(\Sigma Y)^2 = 4624$, $\Sigma XY = 317$, and $N = 9$. $r = (2853 - 2584)/\sqrt{(464)(344)} = +.67$. This is a positive linear relationship of intermediate strength, so a nurse's "burnout" score will allow reasonably accurate prediction of the individual's absenteeism.

27. Compute r_s: $\Sigma D^2 = 312$; $r_s = 1 - (1872/990) = -.89$. There is a strong negative relationship between these variables, so that the most dominant tend to weigh the most, and less dominant weigh less.

Chapter 11

1. It is the line that summarizes a scatterplot by, on average, passing through the center of the Y scores at each X.

3. (a) Y' is the predicted Y score for a given X.
(b) It is computed from the linear regression equation.

5. (a) The Y intercept indicates the value of Y when the regression line crosses the Y axis.
(b) The slope indicates the direction of the regression line and the degree to which it slants.

7. (a) It is the standard error of the estimate.
(b) It is a standard deviation, indicating the "average" amount that the Y scores at each X deviate from their corresponding values of Y'.
(c) It indicates the "average" amount that the actual scores differ from the Y' scores, so it is the "average" error.

9. (a) $S_{Y'}$ is inversely related to the absolute value of r.
(b) $S_{Y'}$ is at its maximum (equal to S_Y) when $r = 0$, because with no relationship the amount that the Y scores deviate from the Y' scores equals the overall spread in the data.
(c) $S_{Y'}$ is at its minimum (equal to 0) when $r = \pm 1.0$, because with a perfect relationship there are no differences between Y scores and the corresponding Y' scores.

11. r^2 can be interpreted as the proportional improvement when using the relationship with X to predict Y scores, compared to using the overall mean of Y to predict Y scores.

13. Select a random sample and measure their IQ and high school average. Compute the correlation coefficient and (after inferential procedures) compute the regression equation. Enter anyone's IQ (X) in the equation to find the predicted high school average (Y').

15. (a) r.
(b) The regression equation.
(c) The regression line graph.
(d) $S_{Y'}$.
(e) r^2.

17. (a) Foofy. The positive r indicates that the higher the statistics grade, the higher the test score.
(b) The relationship does not account for 83% of the variance, and $S_{Y'}$ is large, so predictions will not be very accurate, as with Bubbles and Foofy.

19. (a) He should use multiple correlation and multiple regression procedures, considering both a subject's concentration and visualization abilities when predicting memory ability.
(b) With a multiple R of $+.67$, R^2 is $.45$: He is 45% more accurate in predicting memory ability by considering both concentration and visualization abilities than if these predictors are not considered.

21. (a) The standard error of the estimate most directly communicates how much better (or worse) than predicted she is likely to perform.
(b) Its predictive validity.

23. (a) Compute r: $\Sigma X = 45$, $\Sigma X^2 = 259$, $(\Sigma X)^2 = 2025$, $\Sigma Y = 89$, $\Sigma Y^2 = 887$, $(\Sigma Y)^2 = 7921$, $\Sigma XY = 460$, and $N = 10$, so $r = (4600 - 4005)/\sqrt{(565)(949)} = +.81$.
(b) $b = (4600 - 4005)/565 = +1.05$ and $a = 8.9 - (1.05)(4.5) = 4.18$, so $Y' = (+1.05)X + 4.18$.
(c) Using the completed regression equation, for participants with an attraction score of 9, the predicted anxiety score is $Y' = (+1.05)9 + 4.18 = 13.63$.
(d) Compute $S_{Y'}$; $S_Y = 3.081$, so, $S_{Y'} = (3.081)\sqrt{1 - .81^2} = 1.81$. Our "average error" is 1.81 when we use Y' to predict each anxiety score.

25. Square each coefficient: $.20^2 = .04$. Knowing students' class rankings or knowing a student's gender each results in 4% more accuracy in predicting studiousness scores.

27. The relationship was established only on adolescents, and it may not be the same for the elderly: the r, slope, Y intercept, or type (linear or nonlinear) may be different.

Chapter 12

1. (a) It is the expected relative frequency of the event.
(b) It is based on the event's relative frequency in the population.

3. (a) Sampling with replacement is replacing a sample in the population before another sample is selected.
   (b) Sampling without replacement is not replacing a sample before another is selected.
   (c) Over successive samples, sampling without replacement increases the probability of an event, because there are fewer events that can occur; with replacement, each probability remains constant.
5. Either the sample poorly represents that population, or it represents some other population.
7. It indicates whether or not the sample's z-score (and $\overline{X}$) lies in the region of rejection.
9. (a) $p = 1/6 = .167$.
   (b) $p = 13/52 = .25$.
   (c) $p = 1/4 = .25$.
   (d) $p = 0$. After selecting the ace the first time, it cannot be selected again.
11. No. Sex of a child is an independent event, so previous children do not influence whether this child is a boy or girl.
13. The p of a hurricane is $160/200 = .80$. The uncle is looking at an unrepresentative sample from the past 13 years. Poindexter uses the gambler's fallacy, failing to realize that this p is based on the long run, and in the next few years there may not be a hurricane.
15. (a) Dependent: You're less likely to golf in rain, snow, and so on.
   (b) The answer depends on how much money you have. If you're poor, they're probably dependent—after buying a car, you're less able to buy shoes. If you're rich, the events are independent.
   (c) Dependent: Weight loss depends on calories consumed.
   (d) Independent: Your chances of winning are the same, whether you use the same or different numbers.
17. (a) $z = (27 - 43)/8 = -2.0$; $p = .0228$.
   (b) $z = (51 - 43)/8 = +1.0$; $p = .1587$.
   (c) $z = (42 - 43)/8 = -.13$; $z = (44 - 43)/8 = +.13$; $p = .0517 + .0517 = .1034$.
   (d) $z = (33 - 43)/8 = -1.25$; $z = (49 - 43)/8 = +.75$; $p = .1056 + .2266 = .3322$.
19. Transform 24 to z: $\sigma_{\overline{X}} = 12/\sqrt{30} = 2.19$; $z = (24 - 18)/2.19 = +2.74$; $p = .0031$
21. They use it to determine whether a sample is likely to represent a particular population. The poorer the sample is at representing the population, the less likely that the sample represents it.
23. No. With a $z = +2.74$, this mean falls beyond the critical value of $+1.96$. It is too unlikely to be accepted as representing this population.
25. (a) The $\overline{X} = 321/9 = 35.67$; $\sigma_{\overline{X}} = 5/\sqrt{9} = 1.67$. Then, $z = (35.67 - 30)/1.67 = +3.40$. With a critical value of ± 1.96, conclude that the football players do not represent this population.
   (b) Football players form a population different from nonfootball players, having a μ of about 35.67.
27. (a) For Fred's sample, we'd estimate $\mu = 26$, and for Ethel's, $\mu = 18$.
   (b) The population with $\mu = 26$ is most likely to produce a sample with $\overline{X} = 26$; the population with $\mu = 18$ is most likely to produce a sample with $\overline{X} = 18$.

Chapter 13

1. (a) Sampling error occurs when, by luck, a sample statistic is different from the population parameter it represents.
   (b) A sample may poorly represent one population, or it may represent some other population.
3. In a real relationship, nature pairs certain X and Y scores to form a relationship. Sampling error, by chance, pairs up scores to produce the appearance of a relationship.
5. (a) α stands for the criterion probability; it determines the size of the region of rejection and the theoretical probability of a Type I error.
   (b) The smaller the α, the larger the absolute value of z_{crit}, and the larger z_{obt} must be to be significant.
7. (a) They are more powerful than nonparametric procedures.
   (b) Parametric procedures are robust, meaning that violating their assumptions somewhat does not result in a large increase in the probability of a Type I error.
9. (a) A one-tailed test is used when predicting the direction in which the scores will change.
   (b) A two-tailed test is used when predicting a relationship but not the direction in which scores will change.
11. (a) Changing the independent variable from a week other than finals week to finals week increases the dependent variable of amount of pizza consumed; the experiment will not demonstrate an increase.
   (b) Changing the independent variable from not performing breathing exercises to performing them changes the dependent variable of blood pressure; the experiment will not demonstrate a change.

(c) Changing the independent variable by increasing hormone levels changes the dependent variable of pain sensitivity; the experiment will not demonstrate a change.
(d) Changing the independent variable by increasing amount of light will decrease the dependent variable of frequency of dreams; the experiment will not demonstrate a decrease.

13. (a) A one-tailed test: *beneficial* implies only higher scores.
(b) H_0: $\mu \leq 50$, H_a: $\mu > 50$.
(c) $\sigma_{\bar{X}} = 12/\sqrt{49} = 1.71$; $z_{obt} = (54.63 - 50)/1.71 = +2.71$.
(d) $z_{crit} = +1.645$.
(e) Because z_{obt} is beyond z_{crit}, his results are significant: There's a relationship in the population, where changing from no music to music results in test scores' changing from a μ of 50 to a μ of around 54.63.

15. (a) The probability of a Type I error is $p < .05$; concluding that music influences scores, when really it does not. (b) The probability of a Type II error is 0 (he rejected H_0); concluding that music does not influence scores, when really it does.

17. Because confirming the hypothesis rests on not rejecting H_0, in which case the researcher is still confronted by H_0 and H_a—that there may or may not be a difference.

19. (a) Power is the probability of rejecting a false H_0 (the probability of not making a Type II error).
(b) So that if they fail to reject H_0, they are confident that they would have rejected it if it were false.
(c) In a one-tailed test, the critical value is smaller than in a two-tailed test; so the obtained value is more likely to be larger than the critical value, and thus is more likely to be significant.

21. She is correct about it being easier to reject H_0, but she is incorrect about Type I errors. For a given α, the total size of the region of rejection is the same regardless of whether a one- or a two-tailed test is used, and α is the probability of making a Type I error.

23. (a) She is correct.
(b) She is incorrect. In both studies, the researchers decided the results were too unlikely to reflect sampling error from the H_0 population; they merely defined *too unlikely* differently.
(c) The probability of a Type I error is less in Study B.

25. (a) Because only a significant result is believed to represent a relationship in nature, and the goal is to describe nature.
(b) Because a significant relationship must then be described and understood, so that we can interpret it psychologically.

Chapter 14

1. (a) The t-test and the z-test.
(b) Compute z if the true standard deviation of the raw score population (σ_X) is known; compute t if σ_X must be estimated by s_X.
(c) A random sample of interval/ratio dependent scores that form at least an approximately normal distribution.

3. (a) $s_{\bar{X}}$ is the estimated standard error of the mean; $\sigma_{\bar{X}}$ is the true standard error of the mean.
(b) Both are used as a standard deviation to locate a sample mean on the sampling distribution of means.

5. (a) Compare $\bar{X}$ from one condition to a known μ under another condition by computing t_{obt} and comparing it to t_{crit}. If t_{obt} is significant, compute a confidence interval for the μ being represented and interpret the relationship psychologically.
(b) Compare the obtained coefficient to the appropriate critical value; if the coefficient is significant, compute the regression equation and graph it, compute the proportion of variance accounted for, and interpret the relationship psychologically.

7. (a) Power is the probability of rejecting H_0 when it really is false (the probability of not making a Type II error).
(b) Because we want to know that we were likely to reject H_0, even if it really was false.
(c) They initially design the study to maximize power.

9. Avoid a restricted range, minimize the variability in Y at each X, compute the coefficient appropriate for the type of data, and test a large N.

11. To describe the characteristics of the relationship, so that we can interpret it psychologically.

13. (a) H_0: $\mu = 68.5$; H_a: $\mu \neq 68.5$
(b) $s^2_X = 130.5$; $s_{\bar{X}} = \sqrt{130.5/10} = 3.61$; $t_{obt} = (78.5 - 68.5)/3.61 = +2.77$
(c) With $df = 9$, $t_{crit} = \pm 2.262$.
(d) Using this book rather than other books produces a significant improvement in exam scores: $t_{obt}(9) = 2.77, p < .05$.
(e) $(3.61)(-2.262) + 78.5 \leq \mu \leq (3.61)(+2.262) + 78.5 = 70.33 \leq \mu \leq 86.67$

15. (a) H_0: $\mu = 50$; H_a: $\mu \neq 50$.
(b) $t_{obt} = (53.25 - 50)/8.44 = +.39$.
(c) For $df = 7$, $t_{crit} = \pm 2.365$.

(d) $t(7) = +.39, p > .05$.
(e) The results are not significant, so do not compute the confidence interval.
(f) She has no evidence that strong arguments change people's attitudes toward this issue.

17. Disagree. He did not perform significance testing to eliminate the possibility that his correlation was merely a fluke resulting from sampling error.

19. (a) H_0: $\rho = 0$; H_a: $\rho \neq 0$.
(b) With $df = 70$, $r_{crit} = \pm.232$.
(c) $r(70) = +.38, p < .05$.
(d) The correlation is significant, so he should conclude that the relationship exists in the population, with ρ approximately +.38.
(e) Compute the regression equation and r^2.

21. (a) r_{pb}.
(b) H_0: $\rho_{pb} = 0$; H_a: $\rho_{pb} \neq 0$.
(c) For $df = 40$, $r_{crit} = \pm.304$.
(d) The r_{pb} is significant, so she expects the ρ_{pb} to be approximately .33.
(e) It is a positive relationship if left-handers are assigned a lower score than right-handers on the variable of handedness.
(f) $(r_{pb})^2 = .11$. The relationship accounts for only 11% of the variance in personality scores, so the results are not very useful.

23. (a) Math majors are likely to produce a restricted range of scores—a ceiling effect—when measured on mathematical ability, resulting in a small r.
(b) Using only three puns may be an insensitive procedure that produces a restricted range—perhaps a floor effect if no one thinks any of the puns are funny.
(c) Test a larger N.

25. The df of 80 are .33 of the distance between the dfs at 60 and 120, so the target t_{crit} is .33 of the distance from 2.000 to 1.980: 2.000 − 1.980 = .020, so (.020)(.33) = .0066. Thus, 2.000 − .0066 equals the target t_{crit} of 1.993.

Chapter 15

1. (a) The independent-samples t-test and the dependent-samples t-test.
(b) Whether the design involves independent samples or not.

3. By identifying variables that are strongly correlated with the independent or dependent variable.

5. (a) It improves internal validity by eliminating a potential confounding. It improves external validity by including a wider variety of participants.
(b) It can increase error variance and decrease the strength of the relationship and power.

7. A pretest may alert subjects to the variables being studied and communicate demand characteristics.

9. Collapsing across a variable is combining scores from the different amounts or categories of that variable.

11. Graph the results, compute the appropriate confidence interval, and compute the effect size.

13. The independent-samples t-test, the confidence interval for the difference between two μs, and computing effect size using r^2_{pb}.

15. (a) H_0: $\mu_1 - \mu_2 = 0$; $H_a = \mu_1 - \mu_2 \neq 0$.
(b) $s^2_{pool} = 23.695$; $s_{\bar{X}_1-\bar{X}_2} = 1.78$; $t_{obt} = (43 - 39)/1.78 = +2.25$.
(c) With $df = (15 - 1) + (15 - 1) = 28$, $t_{crit} = \pm 2.048$.
(d) The results are significant: in the population, hot baths (with μ about 43) produce different relaxation scores than cold baths (with μ about 39).
(e) $(1.78)(-2.048) + 4 \leq \mu_1 - \mu_2 \leq (1.78)(+2.048) + 4 = .35 \leq \mu_1 - \mu_2 \leq 7.65$
(f) $r^2_{pb} = (2.25)^2/[(2.25)^2 + 28] = .15$, so bath temperatures do not have a very large effect.
(g) Label the X axis bath temperature; label the Y axis mean relaxation score; plot the data point for cold baths at a Y of 39 and for hot baths at a Y of 43; connect the data points with a straight line.

17. (a) She should retain H_0, because in her one-tailed test the signs of t_{obt} and t_{crit} are different.
(b) She probably did not subtract the sample means in the same way that she subtracted the μs in her hypotheses.

19. (a) With $df = 10$, $t_{crit} = \pm 2.228$, so $t(10) = +1.38, p > .05$.
(b) The results are not significant. There is no evidence that changing the type of background music affects the irritability of air-traffic controllers.
(c) No other statistics are computed.
(d) The experiment is likely to have insufficient power.
(e) He could use larger samples, design and give the test so as to reduce variability in each group, and select and define the type of music so as to obtain larger differences between the means.
(f) It would increase the likelihood of rejecting H_0 if the relationship exists.

21. Alter the training to produce larger differences in success scores; test participants more consistently to reduce variability in the conditions; increase N.

23. Read the literature or conduct a pilot study to determine if "absorption" is substantially correlated with

participants' ability to recall a situation or with how hypnotized they become.

25. Independent-samples design; $N = 60$; independent-samples t-test; a significant relationship (with $\alpha = .01$) where changing from male to female increased scores from around 5.4 to 9.3, but it accounts for only 8% of the variance in dependent scores; a Type I error.

Chapter 16

1. (a) The independent-samples t-test and the dependent-samples t-test.
   (b) Whether the scientist employed a between-subjects or a within-subjects design, respectively.
3. A within-subjects design, because the dependent-samples t-test is more powerful.
5. (a) They reduce external validity when the participants in the samples are unrepresentative of the population.
   (b) They reduce internal validity when participants differ between conditions so that a confounding exists.
7. They reduce internal validity because differences in responses between conditions may result from these factors instead of the conditions of the independent variable. They reduce external validity because the behaviors and participants do not represent those found in other situations where these factors are different or not present.
9. (a) By testing the same participants under all conditions of the independent variable.
   (b) It provides participants who have virtually identical participant variables in all conditions.
11. Conditions are prone to confounding by participants' history and maturation, by demand characteristics resulting from experiencing all conditions, by subject mortality, and by order effects between conditions.
13. Graph the results, compute the appropriate confidence interval, and compute the effect size.
15. (a) A repeated-measures (within-subjects) design.
    (b) Use the dependent-samples t-test.
17. (a) It is impossible to test people when they are male and again when they are female.
    (b) Match each male with a corresponding female on relevant participant variables.
19. (a) Testing people after training them to improve their memory and then testing them under the control condition will be very different from first testing them under the control condition and then after training.
    (b) A nonsymmetrical carry-over effect.
21. (a) This t-test requires the same number of scores (paired) in each condition.
    (b) The data violate the assumptions of the independent-samples t-test, and so it should not be performed.
23. (a) H_0: $\mu_D = 0$, H_a: $\mu_D \neq 0$.
    (b) $t_{obt} = (2.63 - 0)/.75 = +3.51$.
    (c) With $df = 7$, $t_{crit} = \pm 2.365$, so $t(7) = +3.51$, $p < .05$
    (d) $.86 \leq \mu_D \leq 4.40$.
    (e) The $\overline{X}$ of 15.5; the $\overline{X}$ of 18.13.
    (f) $r^2_{pb} = (3.51)^2/[(3.51)^2 + 7] = .64$; they are, on average, about 64% more accurate.
    (g) High amounts of sunshine produce significantly higher well-being scores than low amounts, with the μ of the difference scores between .86 and 4.40.
25. (a) H_0: $\mu_D = 0$; H_a: $\mu_D \neq 0$.
    (b) $t_{obt} = (3.0 - 0)/1.592 = +1.88$.
    (c) With $df = 7$, $t_{crit} = \pm 2.365$, $p < .05$.
    (d The results are not significant. We have no evidence of a relationship.
    (e) We cannot determine effect size with a nonsignificant result, because we do not know if a relationship exists or not.

Chapter 17

1. (a) Analysis of variance.
   (b) A study that contains one independent variable.
   (c) An independent variable.
   (d) A condition of the independent variable.
   (e) All samples are independent.
   (f) All samples are related, because either a repeated-measures or a matched-samples design is used.
3. To test the hypothesis adequately, to demonstrate a nonlinear relationship, and to obtain the maximum information from a study.
5. (a) It is the overall probability of a Type I error after comparing all pairs of means in an experiment.
   (b) Multiple t-tests result in an experiment-wise error rate larger than α. Performing ANOVA and then post hoc tests, produces an experiment-wise error rate equal to α.
7. (a) H_0: $\mu_1 = \mu_2 = \mu_3 = \mu_4$
   (b) H_a: not all μs are equal.
   (c) H_0 is that all μs represented by the levels are the same; H_a is that not all μs represented by the levels are the same.
9. (a) When F_{obt} is significant and k is greater than 2. The F_{obt} indicates only that two or more sample means differ significantly; post hoc tests determine which specific levels produced significant differences.

(b) When F_{obt} is not significant, because we are not convinced there are any differences to be found, or when $k = 2$, because there is only one possible difference between means in the study.

11. It describes the effect size in the sample—the proportion of variance in dependent scores accounted for by changing the levels of the independent variable.

13. (a) This occurs when MS_{bn} is less than MS_{wn}; then, either term is a poor estimate of σ^2_{error}, and H_0 is assumed to be true.
(b) He made a computational error: F_{obt} cannot be a negative number.

15. (a) n is the number of scores in a condition; N is the number of scores in the experiment.
(b) k is the number of conditions in an experiment.
(c) Factor.
(d) Level and treatment.
(e) A between-subjects ANOVA
(f) A within-subjects ANOVA.

17. (a) Self-esteem was measured in three groups that each receive a particular salary.
(b) The between-subjects F was significant, indicating significant differences somewhere among the three mean self-esteem scores for the conditions.

19. Low and medium salaries do not produce significant differences in self-esteem scores, but both produce significantly lower scores than high salaries.

21. (a)

Source	*Sum of squares*	*df*	*Mean square*	*F*
Between	134.80	3	44.93	17.08
Within	42.00	16	2.63	
Total	176.80	19		

(b) With $df = 3$ and 16, $F_{crit} = 3.24$, so F_{obt} is significant, $p < .05$.
(c) For $k = 4$ and $df_{wn} = 16$, $q_k = 4.05$, so $HSD = (4.05)(\sqrt{2.63/5}) = 2.94$; $\bar{X}_4 = 4.4$, $\bar{X}_6 = 10.8$, $\bar{X}_8 = 9.40$, $\bar{X}_{10} = 5.8$.
(d) This is an inverted U-shaped function, in which only ages 4 and 10 and ages 6 and 8 do not differ significantly.
(e) Because $\eta^2 = 134.8/176.8 = .76$; this relationship accounts for 76% of the variance, so it is a very important relationship.
(f) Label the X axis with the independent variable of age and the Y axis with the mean creativity score. Plot the mean score for each condition, and connect adjacent data points with straight lines.

23. (a) H_0: $\mu_1 = \mu_2 = \mu_3 = \mu_4$; H_a: not all μs are equal.
(b)

Source	*Sum of squares*	*df*	*Mean square*	*F*
Between groups	47.69	3	15.90	9.19
Within groups	20.75	12	1.73	
Total	68.44	15		

(c) For $df = 3, 12$, $F_{crit} = 3.49$.
(d) $F(3,12) = 9.19, p < .05$.
(e) $\bar{X}_1 = 2.0$, $\bar{X}_2 = 3.0$, $\bar{X}_3 = 5.75$, $\bar{X}_4 = 6.0$. $q_k = 4.20$, $HSD = (4.20)(\sqrt{1.73/4}) = 2.76$, significant differences are between negligible and moderate, negligible and severe, and minimal and severe.
(f) Increasing stress levels significantly increases infection rate, although only differences in nonadjacent stress conditions produced significant differences in number of infections.
(g) $\eta^2 = 47.69/68.44 = .70$; changing stress levels accounts for 70% of the variance in infection scores in the sample data.
(h) $(\sqrt{1.73/4})(-2.179) + 6.0 \leq \mu \leq (\sqrt{1.73/4})(+2.179) + 6.0 = 4.57 \leq \mu \leq 7.43$.

25. (a) Create a strong manipulation by convincing participants that the problems differ greatly in difficulty; test consistently to minimize the variability within conditions; increase the ns.
(b) Larger differences between means increase MS_{bn}; reduced variability and larger ns reduce MS_{wn}; together these produce a larger F_{obt} that is more likely to be significant.
(c) They increase the power of post hoc tests.

Chapter 18

1. (a) The study contains two independent variables.
(b) All levels of one factor are combined with all levels of the other factor.
(c) The combination of a level of factor A with a level of factor B.
(d) A two-factor design where all cells contain independent samples.

3. (a) H_0: the μs represented by the level means of factor A are equal; H_a: not all μs are equal.
(b) H_0: the μs represented by the level means from factor B are equal; H_a: not all μs are equal.
(c) H_0: the μs represented by the cell means do not form an interaction; H_a: they do form an interaction.

5. (a) A main effect mean is based on scores in a level of one factor while collapsing across the other

factor. A cell mean is the mean of scores from a particular combination of a level of A with a level of B without collapsing.

(b) That changing the levels of the factor produced a significant difference somewhere among the level means.

(c) That changing the levels of both factors produced a significant difference somewhere among the cell means such that an interaction is formed.

(d) Because the interaction indicates that the effect of either factor depends on the level of the other factor that is present, so overall conclusions about a main effect of A or B are inaccurate.

7. Perform Tukey's *HSD* on each main effect and the interaction, graph the main effects and interaction, and compute each η^2; where appropriate, compute confidence intervals for the μ represented by a cell or level mean.

9. (a) When two cells differ along more than one factor; when comparing cell means that are diagonally positioned.

(b) When two cells differ along only one factor; when comparing cell means within the same column or row.

(c) Because we cannot determine which factor produced the difference.

11. (a) 20.

(b) 15.

(c) 5.

13. Study 1: For A, means are 7 and 9; for B, means are 3 and 13. There are effects for A and B but not for A × B. Study 2: For A, means are 7.5 and 7.5; for B, means are 7.5 and 7.5. There is no effect for A or B, but there is an effect for A × B. Study 3: For A, means are 8 and 8; for B, means are 11 and 5. There is no effect for A, but there are effects for B and A × B.

15. (a) By using a strong manipulation of each factor, minimizing error variance through consistency, and testing large *n*s.

(b) The post hoc tests.

(c) Then, if a result is not significant, we are confident we did not miss a relationship that really exists.

17. Only the main effect for difficulty level is significant.

19. When the study has two factors; all cells involve independent samples; and the dependent scores are normally distributed, interval/ratio scores.

21. (a) Because as the amount of reward increases, performance does not first increase and then decrease under every level of practice as indicated by the main effect means.

(b) Because increasing the amount of practice does not increase performance under every level of reward as indicated by the main effect means.

23. (a)

Source	*Sum of squares*	*df*	*Mean square*	*F*
Between groups				
Factor A	7.20	1	7.20	1.19
Factor B	115.20	1	115.20	19.04
Interaction	105.80	1	105.80	17.49
Within groups	96.80	16	6.05	
Total	325.00			

For each factor, $df = 1$ and 16, so $F_{crit} = 4.49$: factor B and the interaction are significant, $p < .05$.

(b) For factor A, $\overline{X}_1 = 8.9$, $\overline{X}_2 = 10.1$; for factor B, $\overline{X}_1 = 11.9$, $\overline{X}_2 = 7.1$; for the interaction, $\overline{X}_{A_1B_1} = 9.0$, $\overline{X}_{A_1B_2} = 8.8$, $\overline{X}_{A_2B_1} = 14.8$, $\overline{X}_{A_2B_2} = 5.4$.

(c) Factor A is not significant and factor B contains only two levels, so such tests are unnecessary. For A × B, adjusted $k = 3$, so $q_k = 3.65$, $HSD = (3.65)(\sqrt{6.05/5}) = 4.02$: the only significant differences are between males and females tested early, and between females tested early and females tested late.

(d) Conclude that a relationship exists between gender and test scores when testing is early, and that early and late testing produce a relationship with test scores for females, $p < .05$.

(e) For B, $\eta^2 = 115.2/325 = .35$; for A × B, $\eta^2 = 105.8/325 = .33$.

25. (a)

Source	*Sum of squares*	*df*	*Mean square*	*F*
Between				
Factor A	8.42	1	8.42	2.43
Factor B	76.79	3	25.60	7.40
Interaction	23.71	3	7.90	2.28
Within	110.72	32	3.46	
Total	219.64	39		

(b) For, 1 and 32 *df*, $F_{crit} = 4.15$; for 3 and 32 *df*, $F_{crit} = 2.90$. Only the F_{obt} for factor B is significant.

APPENDIX D

(c) For factor B, $n = 10$, $df_{wn} = 32$, $q_k = 3.83$, and $HSD = 2.25$.
(d) Except for between B_1 and B_2, changing each level of B results in a significant increase in scores.
(e) For audience size, $\eta^2 = .35$, so it is a reasonably important variable in determining anxiety.
(f) The self-confidence factor was not significant, so do not compute η^2.

Chapter 19

1. (a) A *t*-test or a one-way ANOVA.
(b) A two-way between-subjects, within-subjects, or mixed-design ANOVA.
(c) Whether both factors are tested using independent samples; both factors are tested using dependent samples (usually with repeated measures); or one factor involves independent samples and one involves dependent samples.

3. (a) To control participant variables.
(b) By creating matched groups or by using repeated measures.
(c) Matching provides similar participants in all conditions in terms of the matching variable; repeated measures provides similar participants in all conditions in terms of virtually all participant variables.

5. (a) Complete counterbalancing, partial counterbalancing, and randomization.
(b) Use complete counterbalancing to control practice effects and carry-over effects, use partial counterbalancing to control practice effects alone, and use randomization to provide some degree of balancing of practice and carry-over effects.

7. (a) The difficulty is finding several participants at a time who all match in order to place one in each cell.
(b) The difficulty is in the complex counterbalancing schemes, which require a larger *N*.

9. (a) The estimate of σ^2_{error} in the denominator comes from $MS_{A \times subs}$ instead of MS_{wn}.
(b) The formula also involves $MS_{A \times subs}$ instead of MS_{wn}.
(c) The *df*s used in the tables are those from $MS_{A \times subs}$ instead of MS_{wn}.

11. (a) To study the main effects and interactions of three factors.
(b) Seven: for A, B, C, A × B, A × C, B × C, and A × B × C.
(c) The interaction between two factors does not remain constant under each level of the third factor.

13. (a) In post hoc comparisons, all pairs of means from a factor are compared; in planned comparisons, only some specified means are compared.
(b) It examines the main effect of one factor for only one level of the other factor within the interaction.

15. (a) It combines the results from numerous separate studies.
(b) To determine whether a factor consistently produces a significant effect, or to determine its effect size.

17. (a) Subject history, subject maturation, and order effects.
(b) Each of six groups of participants will hear the messages in one order, either ABC, ACB, BCA, BAC, CAB, or CBA.
(c) A third of the participants will hear the messages in one order, either ABC, BCA, or CAB.
(d) Order effects among the 20 questions: At a minimum have half of each of the above groups answer using order 1–20, and the other half answer using order 20–1.
(e) Nonsymmetrical carry-over effects.

19. (a) Two-way, mixed design.
(b) One *F* for Factor A indicating whether, overall, fantasy level produced a significant difference; one *F* for Factor B indicating whether, overall, meditation level produced a significant difference; and one *F* for the interaction indicating whether the influence of meditation level depends on fantasy level (or vice versa).
(c) The means are

	Low	*Med*	*High*	
Meditation	4.0	6.4	9.4	6.6
No meditation	9.8	3.2	5.8	6.3
	6.9	4.8	7.6	

The main effect of fantasy level and the interaction probably are significant, but the main effect of meditation probably is not.
(d) Based on the interaction, the relationship between increasing fantasy levels and hypnotic suggestibility is essentially a positive linear relationship for subjects who meditate, but it is a nonlinear, U-shaped relationship for those who do not meditate.

21. There appears to be a positive linear relationship where increasing fantasy levels produce increased suggestibility.
23. (a) The main effect means for boys = 15 and girls = 10; for candy = 11.5 and money = 13.5; and for morning = 12.5 and afternoon = 12.5. The means for the two-way interactions are

	Boys	*Girls*
Morning	$\overline{X} = 15$	$\overline{X} = 10$
Afternoon	$\overline{X} = 15$	$\overline{X} = 10$

	Candy	*Money*
Morning	$\overline{X} = 9$	$\overline{X} = 16$
Afternoon	$\overline{X} = 14$	$\overline{X} = 11$

	Boys	*Girls*
Candy	$\overline{X} = 15$	$\overline{X} = 8$
Money	$\overline{X} = 15$	$\overline{X} = 12$

The three-way interaction is diagrammed in problem 23.
(b) Only the three-way interaction is significant.
(c) Using money significantly improves performance for boys only in the morning but decreases their performance in the afternoon.
25. (a) A two-way mixed design.
(b) F_B will indicate the overall difference between depression for the four doses, F_A will indicate the overall difference between scores for positive-negative status, and $F_{A \times B}$ will indicate whether the difference between scores for HIV+ and HIV− depends on drug dose (and vice versa).
(c) For the four doses, the means are 3.5, 5.5, 12.5, and 18. For HIV−, the mean is 9.75, and for HIV+, the mean is 10.
(d) Probably only the main effect for dose and the interaction are significant.
(e) From the interaction, only the low and high drug doses produced an increase in mood scores of HIV+ participants relative to those who are HIV−.
27. (a) H_0: $\mu_1 = \mu_2 = \mu_3$; H_a: not all μs are equal.
(b) $SS_{tot} = 477 - 392.04$; $SS_A = 445.125 - 392.04$; and $SS_{subs} = 1205/3 - 392.04$.

Source	*Sum of squares*	*df*	*Mean square*	*F*
Subjects	9.63	7		
Factor A	53.08	2	26.54	16.69
A × subjects	22.25	14	1.59	
Total	84.96	23		

(c) With $df_A = 2$ and $df_{A \times subs} = 14$, the F_{crit} is 3.74. The F_{obt} is significant.
(d) The $q_k = 3.70$ and $HSD = 1.65$. The means for zero, one, and two hours are 2.13, 4.25, and 5.75, respectively. Significant differences occurred between zero and one hour and between zero and two hours, but not between one and two hours.
(e) Eta squared $(\eta^2) = 53.08/84.96 = .62$.
(f) The variable of amount of practice is important in determining performance scores, but although 1 or 2 hours of practice significantly improved performance compared to no practice, 2 hours was not significantly better than 1 hour.

Chapter 20

1. (a) In a true experiment, participants are randomly assigned to conditions; in a quasi-experiment, participants are assigned to a condition because of an inherent characteristic or past experience.
(b) In both, participants' score on the *X* variable is determined by an inherent characteristic or past experience.
(c) Quasi-experiments tend to be more controlled, and only some levels of the *X* variable are investigated.
3. (a) For each condition, select participants who demonstrate the desired level of the quasi-independent variable.
(b) To select participants for a condition who are very similar on the independent variable but very different from those in other conditions.
(c) Confounding by participant variables; the pretest may produce demand characteristics; regression toward the mean; and the order of the independent and dependent variables may be in question.
5. (a) The design where a group is measured once before and once after a treatment.
(b) A control group.

APPENDIX D

(c) Participants' history, maturation, and mortality; confounding environmental effects; experimenter effects; or regression toward the mean.

7. (a) The design where a group is measured at several spaced times prior to and after the treatment.
(b) Confounding variables that continuously fluctuate and thus would cause scores to change prior to or after the treatment.
(c) Confounding variables that change only with the onset of the treatment.

9. (a) The design where a group is repeatedly measured to observe the effect of the passage of time.
(b) As a repeated-measures design, it eliminates confounding due to participant variables by keeping them constant.
(c) Any changing environmental variables may confound the independent variable.

11. (a) Cohort effects occur when differences in age are confounded by differences in subject history.
(b) A design consisting of a longitudinal study of several groups, each from a different generation.
(c) It allows us to determine whether cohort effects are present.
(d) They are present if there are significant differences between the generations tested, or if there is a significant interaction between age and generation.

13. (a) A design that alternates testing between the baseline condition and the experimental condition.
(b) It is unlikely that a confounding variable would repeatedly change at the same time that we change the conditions.
(c) Carry-over effects that cannot be reversed.

15. (a) A design that measures a baseline for several behaviors from a participant but applies the treatment to each behavior at a different time.
(b) A design that measures baselines for one behavior on the same participant but in different situations, and then institutes the treatment in each situation at different times.

17. The different conditions usually contain different and unmatched participants, producing independent samples and a between-subjects analysis.

19. (a) The results may reflect regression toward the mean.
(b) If, by chance, your score was higher than usual, or if those most unfit were lower than usual, then when the chance factors are not present, the scores would be closer to the mean. This would make you appear to become less fit, and the others more fit.
(c) Test a control group at the beginning and end of the semester and see if they show regression toward the mean.

21. (a) It will keep participant variables constant, clearly show the effect size of the variable, and empirically demonstrates the reliability of the effect.
(b) It has the problems of any repeated-measures design, and external validity is limited.

23. (a) Longitudinal; repeated measures.
(b) Cohort; between subjects.
(c) Cohort design.

25. (a) The before-after difference of 30 occurred for both the control and experimental groups, so there is no influence of the earthquake.
(b) Some experience common to both groups increased stress scores.
(c) The before-after difference for the control group is 10, but for the experimental group it is 35, so there is an influence of the earthquake.
(d) No confounding variable common to both groups could be responsible for the experimental group's data.
(e) A confounding variable unique to the experimental group could have produced the results.

Chapter 21

1. They are all inferential procedures for determining whether sample data are likely to represent a relationship in the population.

3. The number of conditions when testing one independent variable, the number of independent variables being tested, whether the design involves independent or dependent samples, and whether the dependent variable requires a parametric or nonparametric procedure.

5. (a) Parametric procedures involve interval or ratio dependent scores, which tend to be more sensitive and precise than nominal or ordinal scores.
(b) Parametric statistics are more powerful than nonparametric statistics.

7. (a) Observed frequency (f_o) is the number of participants that are in a category.
(b) Expected frequency (f_e) is the number of participants expected to be in a category if the data perfectly represent the distribution described by H_0.

9. (a) That the sample frequencies are unlikely to represent the distribution of frequencies in the population described by H_0.
(b) That category membership on one variable depends on, or is correlated with, category membership on the other variable.

11. If the sample data represent the populations of ranks described by H_0, then the sum of ranks in a group should equal the expected sum of ranks. The more they differ, the less likely it is that the sample represents the populations described by H_0. If the results are significant, the data are likely to represent some other distribution of ranks.

13. (a) H_0: the frequencies of females preferring slightly taller or much taller men are equal in the population; H_a: the frequencies are not equal in the population.
(b) With $N = 89$, $f_e = 89/2 = 44.5$ for each group. The $\chi^2 = 2.48 + 2.48 = 4.96$. With $df = 1$, $\chi^2_{crit} = 3.84$, so the results are significant. Conclude in the population of females, about 55/89, or 62%, prefer slightly taller males, and about 38% prefer much taller males, $p < .05$.
(c) Label the Y axis "frequency" and the X axis with each type of female. For each, draw a bar graph to the height of their frequencies.

15. (a) H_0: the elderly population is 30% Republican, 55% Democrat, and 15% other; H_a: affiliations in the elderly population are not distributed this way.
(b) For Republicans, $f_e = (.30)(100) = 30$; for Democrats, $f_e = (.55)(100) = 55$; and for others, $f_e = (.15)(100) = 15$.
(c) $\chi^2_{obt} = 4.80 + 1.47 + .60 = 6.87$.
(d) For $df = 2$, $\chi^2_{crit} = 5.99$, so the results are significant: Party membership in the population of senior citizens is different from that in the general population, and is distributed as in our samples, $p < .05$.

17. (a) H_0: in the population, the frequency with which people did or did not vote is independent of the frequency of whether they were satisfied with the outcome and vice versa. H_a: the frequencies are dependent.
(b) For voters, satisfied $f_e = 40.02$, dissatisfied $f_e = 42.98$; for nonvoters, satisfied $f_e = 40.98$, dissatisfied $f_e = 44.02$.
(c) $\chi^2_{obt} = 6.07$.
(d) $\chi^2_{crit} = 3.84$. The results are significant; therefore, in the population, whether people are satisfied with the election results depends on whether they voted, $p < .05$.
(e) The phi coefficient = .19, so it is not a very consistent relationship.

19. (a) The Wilcoxon T-test.
(b) The Kruskal-Wallis H-test.
(c) The Friedman χ^2 test.
(d) The Mann-Whitney U test or the rank sums test, depending on the size of n.

21. By performing the Wilcoxin T test.

23. By performing the Friedman χ^2 test to find overall differences, and then Nemenyi's post hoc procedure to identify specific conditions that differ.

25. (a) For such a nominal variable, compute the mode (most frequent) handedness, or the percentage for each.
(b) For ranked scores, compute the median rank in each condition. Because the reaction times are skewed, also compute the median reaction time in each condition.

Appendix A

1. (a) To learn how the constructs and behaviors are conceptualized, and to learn of useful procedures and designs for studying them.
(b) Professional-level journals (and books.)

3. To provide the information needed to understand the study, evaluate it, and literally replicate it.

5. The Title page, Abstract, Introduction, Methods, Results and Discussion.

7. (a) That the reader is knowledgeable about research methods, statistics, and the topic being discussed.
(b) That the author is a knowledgeable and reasonable researcher who understands research and statistics, and who will report any unusual aspects of the study.
(c) Information is included if it is not otherwise available to the reader.

9. (a) When the term consists of several words, it is used frequently, and there are not many abbreviations.
(b) Create an acronym when the term first appears using the first letter of each word in the term.
(c) Use digits if the quantity is 10 or larger, contains a decimal, is a result or a measurement, or the number is one in a series that includes digits.
(d) Never begin a sentence using an abbreviation or digits.

11. A brief overview of the hypothesis, method, results and conclusions of the study.

13. (a) It is the first two or three words of the article's title.
(b) It is a different, brief title typed at the bottom of the manuscript's title page that will appear at the top of each page of the published article.

15. (a) Use Apparatus with predominantly hardware and equipment; use Materials with predominantly paper materials.
(b) They must be necessary.

17. (a) In Participants, describe the number and type of participants tested; in Material/Apparatus, describe the stimuli and equipment used in testing; and in Procedure, describe the steps involved in testing.

(b) The results and conclusions of the study.

19. (a) When the reader should see the overall pattern in the obtained relationship.

(b) When the reader should see the precise values of means, etc., and there are too many to include in the narrative.

21. (a) The sentence begins with the numeral 40; it is written in future tense. (And "hear" is inappropriate.)

(b) This teaches statistics; a result is never "very" significant.

(c) So many numbers should be presented in a table or figure; the words "men" and "girls" imply different ages and may be construed as sexist.

(d) "Split in half" cannot be what the author truly means, implying that participants were sliced up; the number of participants should be in digits, not words.

(e) This teaches statistics; conclusions are not reported in the Results, nor are statistics given in the Discussion.

(f) The name of each variable will not be understood; the order of the variables reverses the independent and dependent variables; "funny" is inappropriate.

23. Search for an existing test in specialized books of tests or in previous studies that might have used such a test.

25. By reading the articles in its reference section, and then reading the articles in their reference sections.

Appendix B

Part B.1: Computing Percentiles

1.

Score	*f*	*rel. f*	*cf*
53	1	.05	18
52	3	.17	17
51	2	.11	14
50	5	.28	12
49	4	.22	7
48	0	.00	3
47	3	.17	3

(a) The score of 51 is at the 72nd percentile.

(b) The score at the 50th percentile is

$$\text{Score} = 49.5 + \left(\frac{9-7}{5}\right)(1) = 49.90$$

3.

Score	*f*	*rel. f*	*cf*
128 − 131	1	.04	28
124 − 127	2	.07	27
120 − 123	6	.21	25
116 − 119	8	.29	19
112 − 115	4	.14	11
108 − 111	3	.11	7
104 − 107	2	.07	4
100 − 103	2	.07	2

(a) $\text{Percentile} = \left(\dfrac{11 + \dfrac{117 - 115.5}{4}(8)}{28}\right)(100) =$

$$\left(\frac{11 + .375(8)}{28}\right)(100) = \left(\frac{11+3}{28}\right)(100) =$$

50th percentile

(b) $\text{Score} = 119.5 + \left(\dfrac{22.4 - 19}{6}\right)(4) = 119.5 + .567(4)$

$\text{Score} = 119.5 + 2.268 = 121.768 = 121.77$

Part B.3: Performing Linear Interpolation

1. The target z-score is between $z = .670$ at .2514 of the curve and $z = .680$ at .2483. With .2500 at .0014/.0031 of the distance between .2514 and .2483, the corresponding z-score is .00452 above .67, at .67452.

3. The df of 50 is bracketed by $df = 40$ with $t_{crit} = 2.021$, and $df = 60$ with $t_{crit} = 2.000$. Because 50 is at .5 of the distance between 40 and 60, the target t_{crit} is .5 of the .021 between the brackets, which is 2.0105.

Part B.4: Additional Formulas for Computing Probability

1. (a) Multiply the individual probabilities times each other.

(b) Add the individual probabilities together.

(c) Consider whether the events are mutually inclusive or mutually exclusive.

3. (a) The probability is the same as that of first selecting one person and then selecting another. The p(above 116) = .34, so p(two people above 116) = (.34)(.34) = .1156.

(b) These are mutually exclusive events, so with p(introverted) = .40 and p(extroverted) = .35, p(introverted or extroverted) = .40 + .35 = .75.

(c) With p(above 116) = .34 and p(introverted) = .40, p(above 116 and introverted) = (.34)(.40) = .136.

(d) These are mutually inclusive events, so with p(above 116) = .34, p(introverted) = .40, and p(above 116 and introverted) = .136, p(above 116 or introverted) = (.34 + .40) − .136 = .604.

(e) The p(in-between) = .25, and from part (d), p(above 116 or introverted) = .604. Therefore, p(in-between and then above 116 or introverted) = (.25)(.604) = .151.

5. (a) When we want to find the probability of obtaining a sequence of events in which each event involves one of two mutually exclusive possibilities.

(b) p(4 heads) = (5!/4!(1)) $(.5^4)(.5^1)$ = (120/24)(.03125) = .15625.

(c) p(1 head) = (5!/(1!(4!)) $(.5^1)(.5^4)$ = (120/24)(.03125) = .15625.

(d) Obtaining 1 head in 5 tosses is equivalent to obtaining 4 tails; since p(4 tails) = p(4 heads), the answer in (c) is the same as in (b).

Part B.5: The One-Way Within-Subjects Analysis of Variance

1. (a) H_0: $\mu_1 = \mu_2 = \mu_3$; H_a: not all μs are equal.

(b) SS_{tot} = 477 − 392.04; SS_A = 445.125 − 392.04; and SS_{subs} = 1205/3 − 392.04.

Source	*Sum of squares*	*df*	*Mean square*	*F*
Factor A	53.08	2	26.54	16.69
Subjects	9.63	7		
A × subjects	22.25	14	1.59	
Total	84.96	23		

(c) With $df_A = 2$ and $df_{A\times subs} = 14$, the F_{crit} is 3.74. The F_{obt} is significant.

(d) The $q_k = 3.70$ and $HSD = 1.65$. The means for zero, one, and two hours are 2.13, 4.25, and 5.75, respectively. Significant differences occurred between zero and one hour and between zero and two hours, but not between one and two hours.

(e) Eta squared (η^2) = 53.08/84.96 = .62.

(f) The variable of amount of practice is important in determining performance scores, but although 1 or 2 hours of practice significantly improved performance compared to no practice, 2 hours was not significantly better than 1 hour.

Part B.6: The Two-way Within-Subjects Analysis of Variance

1.

Factor B: amount of fantasy

Factor A		**B_1: low**	**B_2: med**	**B_3: high**	
	Sub 1	5	7	9	
	Sub 2	6	5	8	
	Sub 3	2	6	10	
	Sub 4	2	9	10	
	Sub 5	5	5	10	
A_1: meditation		$\overline{X} = 4$ $\Sigma X = 20$ $\Sigma X^2 = 94$ $n = 5$	$\overline{X} = 6.4$ $\Sigma X = 32$ $\Sigma X^2 = 216$ $n = 5$	$\overline{X} = 9.4$ $\Sigma X = 47$ $\Sigma X^2 = 445$ $n = 5$	$\overline{X} = 6.6$ $\Sigma X = 99$ $n = 15$
	Sub 1	10	2	5	
	Sub 2	10	5	6	
	Sub 3	9	4	5	
	Sub 4	10	3	7	
	Sub 5	10	2	6	
A_2: no meditation		$\overline{X} = 9.8$ $\Sigma X = 49$ $\Sigma X^2 = 481$ $n = 5$	$\overline{X} = 3.2$ $\Sigma X = 16$ $\Sigma X^2 = 58$ $n = 5$	$\overline{X} = 5.8$ $\Sigma X = 29$ $\Sigma X^2 = 171$ $n = 5$	$\overline{X} = 6.09$ $\Sigma X = 94$ $n = 15$
		$\Sigma X = 69$ $\overline{X} = 6.9$ $n = 10$	$\Sigma X = 48$ $\overline{X} = 4.8$ $n = 10$	$\Sigma X = 76$ $\overline{X} = 7.6$ $n = 10$	$\Sigma X_{total} = 193$ $\Sigma X^2_{total} = 1465$

$N = 30$ $k_A = 2$ $k_B = 3$

A × Subject Table after Collapsing Across Factor B:

Factor A

	A_1	A_2	A_2	ΣX_{Sub}
Subject 1	15	9	14	38
Subject 2	16	10	14	40
Subject 3	11	10	15	36
Subject 4	12	12	17	41
Subject 5	15	7	16	38

B × Subject Table after Collapsing Across Factor A

Factor B

	B_1	B_2	ΣX_{Sub}
Subject 1	21	17	38
Subject 2	19	21	40
Subject 3	18	18	36
Subject 4	21	20	41
Subject 5	20	18	38

$$\text{Correction term} = \left(\frac{(\Sigma X_{\text{total}})^2}{N}\right) = \frac{193^2}{30} = 1241.63$$

$$SS_{\text{tot}} = 1465 - 1241.63 = 223.37$$

$$SS_{\text{A}} = \left(\frac{(69)^2 + (68)^2 + (68)^2}{10}\right) - 1241.63 = 42.47$$

$$SS_{\text{B}} = \left(\frac{(99)^2 + (94)^2}{15}\right) - 1241.63 = .84$$

$$SS_{\text{bn}} = \left(\frac{(33)^2 + (50)^2 + (36)^2 + (18)^2 + (36)^2 + (18)^2}{5}\right) - 1241.63 = 184.57$$

$$SS_{\text{A}\times\text{B}} = 184.57 - 42.47 - .84 = 141.26$$

$$SS_{\text{subs}} = \frac{(38)^2 + (40)^2 + (36)^2 + (41)^2 + (38)^2}{(2)(3)} - 1241.63$$

$$SS_{\text{subs}} = 2.54$$

$$SS_{\text{A}\times\text{S}} = \frac{(15)^2 + (9)^2 + (14)^2 + (16)^2 + (10)^2 + (14)^2 + (11)^2 + (10)^2}{2} + \frac{(15)^2 + (12)^2 + (12)^2 + (17)^2 + (15)^2 + (7)^2 + (16)^2}{2} - 1241.63 - 42.47 - 2.54$$

$$SS_{\text{A}\times\text{S}} = 16.86$$

$$SS_{\text{B}\times\text{S}} = \frac{(21)^2 + (17)^2 + (19)^2 + (21)^2 + (18)^2 + (18)^2 + (21)^2 + (20)^2}{2} + \frac{(20)^2 + (18)^2}{3} - 1241.63 - .84 - 2.54 = 3.32$$

$$SS_{\text{A}\times\text{B}\times\text{S}} = 223.37 - 42.47 - .84 - 141.26 - 2.54 - 16.86 - 3.32 = 16.08$$

Source	*Sum of squares*	*df*	*Mean square*	*F*
Factor				
A	42.47	2	21.35	10.12
B	.84	1	.84	1.01
A×B	141.26	2	70.63	35.14
Subjects				
A×S	16.86	8	2.11	
B×S	3.32	4	.83	
A×B×S	16.08	8	2.01	
Total	223.37	29		

For $\alpha = .05$ and $df_{\text{A}} = 2$ and $df_{\text{A}\times\text{S}} = 8$, $F_{\text{crit}} = 4.46$, so A is significant. For $df_{\text{B}} = 1$ and $df_{\text{B}\times\text{S}} = 4$, $F_{\text{crit}} = 7.71$, so B is not significant. For $df_{\text{A}\times\text{B}} = 2$ and $df_{\text{A}\times\text{B}\times\text{S}} = 8$, $F_{\text{crit}} = 4.46$, so A × B is significant.

For Factor A, $k = 3$ and $df = 8$, so $q_k = 4.04$. $HSD = (4.04)(\sqrt{2.11/10}) = (4.04)(0.46) = 1.86$. All levels differ significantly. For the interaction, $k = 5$ and $df = 8$, so $q_k = 4.89$. $HSD = (4.89)(\sqrt{2.01/5}) = (4.89)(0.63) = 3.1$. Meditation and no meditation differ at each level of fantasy. With meditation, low versus high differ; with no meditation, low versus medium and low versus high differ.

For Factor A, $\eta^2 = 42.47 / 223.37 = .19$. For A × B, $\eta^2 = 141.26 / 223.37 = .63$.

Part B.7: The Two-Way Mixed-Design Analysis of Variance

1. (a)

		Level of fantasy: factor A			
Factor A: meditation		***B_1: low***	***B_2: med***	***B_3: high***	ΣX_{sub}
	Sub 1	5	7	9	21
	Sub 2	6	5	8	19
	Sub 3	2	6	10	18
	Sub 4	2	9	10	21
	Sub 5	5	5	10	20
A_1: meditation		$\bar{X} = 4$ $\Sigma X = 20$ $\Sigma X^2 = 94$ $n = 5$	$\bar{X} = 6.4$ $\Sigma X = 32$ $\Sigma X^2 = 216$ $n = 5$	$\bar{X} = 9.4$ $\Sigma X = 47$ $\Sigma X^2 = 445$ $n = 5$	$\bar{X} = 6.6$ $\Sigma X = 99$ $n = 15$
	Sub 6	10	2	5	17
	Sub 7	10	5	6	21
	Sub 8	9	4	5	18
	Sub 9	10	3	7	20
	Sub 10	10	2	6	18
A_2: no meditation		$\bar{X} = 9.8$ $\Sigma X = 49$ $\Sigma X^2 = 481$ $n = 5$	$\bar{X} = 3.2$ $\Sigma X = 16$ $\Sigma X^2 = 58$ $n = 5$	$\bar{X} = 5.8$ $\Sigma X = 29$ $\Sigma X^2 = 171$ $n = 5$	$\bar{X} = 6.09$ $\Sigma X = 94$ $n = 15$
		$\Sigma X = 69$ $\bar{X} = 6.9$ $n = 10$ $N = 30$	$\Sigma X = 48$ $\bar{X} = 4.8$ $n = 10$ $k_A = 2$	$\Sigma X = 76$ $\bar{X} = 7.6$ $n = 10$ $k_B = 3$	$\Sigma X_{total} = 193$ $\Sigma X^2_{total} = 1465$

$$\text{Correction term} = \left(\frac{193^2}{30}\right) = 1241.63$$

$$SS_{tot} = \Sigma X^2_{total} - \text{Step 3} = 1465 - 1241.63 = 223.37$$

$SS_{subs} =$

$$\frac{(21)^2 + (19)^2 + (18)^2 + (21)^2 + (20)^2 + (17)^2 + (21)^2}{3}$$

$$+ \frac{(18)^2 + (20)^2 + (18)^2}{3} - 1241.63 = 6.70$$

$$SS_A = \left(\frac{(99)^2 + (94)^2}{15}\right) - 1241.63 = .84$$

$$SS_B = \left(\frac{(69)^2 + (48)^2 + (76)^2}{10}\right) - 1241.63 = 42.47$$

$$SS_{e:bn} = 6.70 - .84 = 5.86$$

$$SS_{bn} = \left(\frac{(20)^2 + (32)^2 + (47)^2 + (49)^2 + (16)^2 + (29)^2}{5}\right) - 1241.63 = 184.57$$

$$SS_{A \times B} = 184.57 - .84 - 42.47 = 141.26$$

$$SS_{e:wn} = 223.37 - 6.70 - 42.47 - 141.26 = 32.94$$

Source	*Sum of squares*	*df*	*Mean square*	*F*
Between groups				
A (meditation)	.84	1	.84	1.15
Error between	5.86	8	.73	
Within groups				
B (fantasy)	42.47	2	21.24	10.31
A×B	141.26	2	70.63	34.29
Error within	32.94	16	2.06	
Total	223.37	29		

For $\alpha = .05$ and $df_A = 1$ and $df_{e:bn} = 8$, $F_{crit} = 5.32$, so A is not significant. For $df_B = 2$ and $df_{e:wn} = 16$, $F_{crit} = 3.63$, so B is significant. For $df_{A \times B} = 2$ and $df_{e:wn} = 16$, $F_{crit} = 3.63$, so A × B is significant.

For the B main effect, $k = 3$ and the $df = 12$, so $q_k = 3.65$. $HSD = (3.65)(\sqrt{2.06/10}) = (3.65)(0.45) = 1.66$. Only low versus medium and medium versus high differ significantly. For the interaction, $k = 5$ and $df = 16$, so $q_k = 4.33$. $HSD = (4.33)(\sqrt{2.06/5}) = (4.33)(0.64) = 2.78$. There is a significant difference between meditation versus no meditation for each fantasy level. With meditation, only low and medium fantasy don't differ. With no meditation, only medium and high fantasy don't differ.

For the fantasy main effect, $\eta^2 = 42.47/223.37 = .19$. For the interaction, $\eta^2 = 141.26/223.37 = .63$.

Part B.8: Nonparametric Procedures for Ranked Data

1. (a) Sum of positive ranks = 1, sum of negative ranks = 27, so $T_{obt} = 1$. $T_{crit} = 2$. The conditions differ in terms of ranks, and in terms of the underlying attitude scores.

3. (a) $\Sigma R_1 = 12$, $\Sigma R_2 = 19$, $\Sigma R_3 = 29$; $N = 10$, $k = 3$, $SS_{bn} = 1346$, $\chi^2_{obt} = 14.6$; $df = 2$, $\chi^2_{crit} = 5.99$; there are significant differences somewhere among the conditions.

(b) For Nemenyi's procedure, critical difference = 1.09 and mean ranks = 1.2, 1.9, and 2.9; only the one- and three-month testings differ significantly.

(c) $\eta^2 = 14.6/29 = .50$.

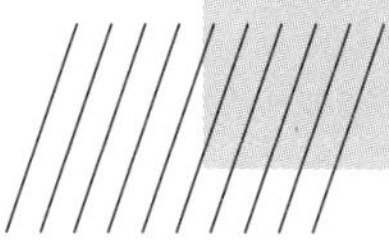

GLOSSARY

Adjusted *k* The value of *k* used to find q_k when performing the Tukey *HSD* test on the cell means of an interaction.

Alpha The Greek letter α, which symbolizes the criterion, the size of the region of rejection of a sampling distribution, and the theoretical probability of making a Type I error

Alternate forms Different versions of the same questionnaire

Alternative hypothesis The statistical hypothesis that describes the population parameters that the sample data represent if the predicted relationship does exist; symbolized by H_a

Analysis of variance The parametric procedure for determining whether significant differences exist in an experiment that involves two or more sample means; abbreviated ANOVA

ANOVA Abbreviation of *Analysis of variance*

Applied research Research conducted primarily for the purpose of solving an existing problem

Archival research Research for which written records constitute the source of data

As a function of A way to describe a relationship using the format "changes in *Y* as a function of changes in *X*"

Automation The use of equipment to present stimuli or to measure and record scores

Bar graph A graph in which a free-standing vertical bar is centered over each score on the *X* axis; used with nominal or ordinal scores for the independent variable, which represent discrete categories

Barnum statements Questions or statements that are so global and vague that everyone would agree with them or select the same response for them

Baseline The level of performance on the dependent variable when the independent variable is not present

Baseline design A single-subject design in which performance on the dependent variable when the independent variable is not present is compared to performance when the variable is present

Basic research Research conducted primarily for the purpose of simply obtaining knowledge

Beta The Greek letter β, which symbolizes the theoretical probability of making a Type II error

Between-subjects ANOVA The type of ANOVA that is performed when a study involves between-subjects factors

Between-subjects design A design in which all factors are between-subjects factors

Between-subjects factor The type of factor created when an independent variable is studied using independent samples in all conditions

Biased estimators The name applied to the sample variance and standard deviation when used to estimate the population variance and population standard deviation

Bimodal distribution A symmetrical frequency polygon with two distinct humps; each hump represents high frequency scores and the center scores of each hump technically have the same frequency

Carry-over effects The influence that a participant's experience of a trial has on his or her performance of subsequent trials

Case study An in-depth description of one participant, organization, or event

Causal hypothesis A hypothesis that tentatively explains a particular influence on, or cause of, a behavior

Ceiling effects A restriction of range that occurs when a task is too easy, causing most scores to be near the highest possible score

Cell In a multi-factor ANOVA, the combination of one level of one factor with one level of the other factor(s)

Central limit theorem A statistical principle that defines the mean, standard deviation, and shape of a theoretical sampling distribution

χ^2-distribution The sampling distribution of all possible values of χ^2 that occur when the samples represent the distribution of frequencies described by the null hypothesis

Chi square procedure The nonparametric inferential procedure for testing whether the frequencies of category membership in the sample represent the predicted frequencies in the population; used with nominal data

Closed-ended question In a questionnaire or interview, a question accompanied by several answers from which a participant must select his or her response

Classification variable See *Qualitative variable*

Cluster sampling A sampling technique in which certain groups are randomly selected and all participants in each group are observed

Coefficient of alienation The proportion of variance not accounted for by a relationship; computed by subtracting the squared correlation coefficient from 1

Coefficient of determination The proportion of variance accounted for by a relationship; computed by squaring the correlation coefficient

Cohort design A factorial design consisting of a longitudinal study of several groups, each from a different generation

Cohort effects The situation that occurs when age differences are confounded by differences in subject history

Collapsing across a variable To combine scores from the different amounts or categories of that variable

Complete counterbalancing Testing different participants with different orders so that all possible orders of conditions or trials occur in a study

Complete factorial design A design in which all levels of one factor are combined with all levels of the other factors

Conceptual replication The repeated test or confirmation of a hypothesis using a design different from that of the original study

Concurrent validity The extent to which a procedure correlates with the present behavior of participants

Condition An amount or category of the independent variable that creates the specific situation under which participants' scores on the dependent variable are measured

Confederates People enlisted by a researcher to act as other participants or "accidental" passers-by, thus creating a social situation to which "real" participants then respond

Confidence interval A statistically defined range of values of the population parameter, one of which the sample statistic is likely to represent

Confidence interval for a single μ A statistically defined range of values of μ, one of which is likely to be represented by the sample mean

Confidence interval for the difference between two μs A statistically defined range of differences between two population μs, one of which is likely to be represented by the difference between the two sample means

Confidence interval for μ_D An interval containing a range of values of μ_D, one of which is likely to be represented by the sample mean ($\overline{D}$) in a related samples *t*-test

Confounded comparison In ANOVA, a comparison of two cells that differ along more than one factor

Confounded variables See *Confounding*

Confounding A situation that occurs when an extraneous variable systematically changes along with the variable hypothesized to be a causal variable

Construct validity The extent to which a measurement reflects the hypothetical construct of interest

Content analysis A scoring procedure for open-ended questions in which the researcher counts specific words or themes in a participant's responses

Content validity The extent to which a measurement reflects the variable or behavior of interest

Contingency coefficient The statistic that describes the strength of the relationship in a two-way chi square when there are more than two categories of either variable; symbolized by *C*

Continuous scale A measurement scale that allows for fractional amounts of the variable being measured

Control The elimination of unintended, extraneous factors that might influence the behavior being studied

Control group A group of participants who are measured on the dependent variable but receive zero amount of the independent variable, thus providing a baseline for comparison to the experimental group

Convenience sampling A sampling approach in which the researcher studies the participants who are conveniently available

Convergent validity The extent to which the scores obtained from one procedure are positively correlated with the scores obtained from another procedure that is already accepted as valid

Correlation coefficient A number, computed from the pairs of *X* scores and *Y* scores in a set of data, that summarizes and describes the type of relationship present and the strength of that relationship

Correlational design A design in which scores on two or more variables are measured to determine whether they form the predicted relationship

Counterbalancing The process of systematically changing the order of trials for different participants in a balanced way, so as to counter the biasing influence of any one order

Criterion The probability that provides the basis for deciding whether a sample is too unlikely to have occurred by chance and thus is unrepresentative of a particular population

Criterion validity The extent to which the scores obtained from a procedure correlate with an observable behavior

Criterion variable The variable in a relationship whose unknown scores are predicted through use of the known scores on the predictor variable

Critical value The value of the sample statistic that marks the edge of the region of rejection in a sampling distribution; values that fall beyond it fall in the region of rejection

Cross-sectional design A quasi-experimental between-subjects design in which participants are observed at different ages or at different points in a temporal sequence

Cumulative frequency The frequency of those scores at or below a particular score; symbolized by *cf*

Cumulative frequency distribution A distribution of scores organized to show the frequency of the scores at or below each score

Curvilinear relationship See *Nonlinear relationship*

Data The scores of participants in psychological research that reflect a behavior

Data point A dot plotted on a graph to represent a pair of *X* and *Y* scores

Debriefing The procedure by which researchers inform participants about all aspects of a study after they have participated in it, in order to remove any negative consequences of the procedure

Deception Any false information given to participants in order to disguise the procedure or design

Degree of association See *Strength of a relationship*

Degrees of freedom The number of scores in a sample that are free to vary, and thus the number that is used to calculate an estimate of the population variability; symbolized by *df*

Demand characteristics Cues within the research context that guide or bias a participant's behavior

Dependent events Events for which the probability of one event is influenced by the occurrence of the other

Dependent measure See *Dependent variable*

Dependent samples Samples created by matching each subject in one sample with a subject in the other sample or by repeatedly measuring the same subject under all conditions; also called *Related samples*

Dependent samples *t*-test The statistical procedure that is appropriate for significance testing when the scores meet the requirements of a parametric test, the design involves matched groups or repeated measures, and there are only two conditions of the independent variable

Dependent variable In an experiment, the variable that is measured under each condition of the independent variable

Descriptive design See *Descriptive research*

Descriptive hypothesis A hypothesis that tentatively describes a behavior in terms of its characteristics or the situation in which it occurs

Descriptive methods The research methods used to test descriptive hypotheses

Descriptive research The observation and description of a behavior, the situation it occurs in, or the individuals exhibiting it.

Descriptive statistics Mathematical procedures for organizing, summarizing, and describing the important characteristics of a sample of data

Design The specific manner in which a research study is conducted

Determinism The assumption that behavior is solely influenced by natural causes and does not depend on free will

Deviation The distance that separates a score from the mean and thus indicates how much the score differs from the mean

Dichotomous variable A discrete variable that has only two possible amounts or categories

Disconfirmation The process of rejecting a hypothesis because evidence disproves it

Discrete scale A measurement scale that allows for measurement only in whole-number amounts

Discriminant validity The extent to which the scores obtained from one procedure are not correlated with the scores obtained from another procedure that measures other variables or constructs

Distribution An organized set of data

Double-barreled questions Questions that have more than one component

Double-blind procedure The procedure in which both the researcher who interacts with the participants and the participants themselves are unaware of the treatment being presented

Ecological validity The extent to which an experimental situation can be generalized to natural settings and behaviors

Effect size The proportion of variance accounted for in an experiment, which indicates how consistently differences in the dependent scores are influenced by changes in the independent variable

Empirical The requirement of science that the basis for conclusions about nature be through observation of it

Empirical probability distribution A probability distribution based on observations of the relative frequency of events

Environmental variables The aspects of the environment that can influence scores

Error variance The variability in *Y* scores at each *X* score, or the inherent variability within a population, estimated in ANOVA by the mean square within groups

Estimated population standard deviation The unbiased estimate of the population standard deviation, symbolized by s_X

Estimated population variance The unbiased estimate of the population variance, symbolized by s_X^2

Estimated standard error of the mean An estimate of the standard deviation of the sampling distribution of means, used in calculating the single-sample *t*-test; symbolized by $s_{\bar{X}}$

Eta The correlation coefficient used to describe a linear or nonlinear relationship containing two or more levels of a factor; symbolized by η

Eta squared The proportion of variance in the dependent variable that is accounted for by changing the levels of a factor; the effect size of a factor in a sample; symbolized by η^2

***Ex post facto* research** Research conducted after a phenomenon has occurred

Expected frequency In chi square, the frequency expected in a category if the sample data perfectly represent the distribution of frequencies in the population described by the null hypothesis; symbolized by f_e

Experiment A design in which one variable is actively changed or manipulated and scores on another variable are measured to determine whether there is a relationship

Experiment-wise error rate The probability of making a Type I error when comparing all means in an experiment

Experimental group(s) Those participants who receive a nonzero amount of the independent variable and are then measured on the dependent variable

Experimental hypotheses Two statements made before a study is begun, describing the predicted relationship that the study may or may not demonstrate

Experimental methods The research methods used to test causal hypotheses

Experimental realism The extent to which the experimental task engages participants psychologically, such that they become less concerned with demand characteristics

Experimenter expectancies Subtle cues provided by the experimenter about the responses that participants should give in a particular condition

External validity The extent to which results generalize to other participants and other situations

Extraneous variables Variables that may influence the results of a study but are not the variables of interest

Extreme scores The scores that are relatively far above and below the middle score of a distribution

***F*-distribution** The sampling distribution of all possible values of *F* that occur when the null hypothesis is true and all conditions represent one population μ

***F*-ratio** In ANOVA, the ratio of the mean square between groups to the mean square within groups

***F* statistic** See *F-ratio*

Face validity The extent to which a measurement procedure appears to measure what it is intended to measure

Factor In ANOVA, an independent variable

Factorial design See *Complete factorial design*

Falsifiable The requirement of a scientific hypothesis that it be possible for a test to show that the hypothesis is false

Field experiment An experiment conducted in a natural setting

Field research Any type of study conducted in a natural setting instead of in a laboratory

Field survey A procedure in which participants complete a questionnaire or interview in a natural setting

Fisher's protected *t*-test The post hoc procedure performed with ANOVA to compare means from a factor in which all levels do not have equal *n*

Floor effects A restriction of range that occurs when a task is too difficult, causing most or all scores to be near the lowest possible score

Forced-choice procedure A measure in which participants must select from a limited set of choices, such as a multiple-choice test

Frequency The number of times each score occurs within a set of data; also called simple frequency; symbolized by *f*

Frequency polygon A graph that shows interval or ratio scores (*X* axis) and their frequencies (*Y* axis), using data points connected by straight lines

Friedman Chi Square test The one-way within-subjects ANOVA for ranked scores, performed when there are more than two levels of one factor

Generalize To apply the conclusions of a study to other participants or situations

Goodness of fit test See one-way chi square procedure

Grouped distribution A distribution formed by combining different scores to make small groups whose total frequencies, relative frequencies, or cumulative frequencies can then be manageably reported

Habituation The process by which participants are familiarized with a procedure before actual data collection is commenced, in order to reduce reactivity

Hawthorne effect A bias in participants' behavior—usually an improvement in performance—that results from the special treatment and interest shown by a researcher

Heterogeneity of variance A characteristic of populations when they do not have the same variance

Heteroscedasticity An unequal spread of *Y* scores around the regression line (that is, around the values of Y')

Histogram A graph similar to a bar graph but with adjacent bars touching, used to plot the frequency distribution of a small range of interval or ratio scores

Homogeneity of variance A characteristic of populations when they have the same variance

Homogeneity of variance test A test performed before a *t*-test or ANOVA is conducted to determine whether populations can be assumed to have homogeneity of variance; also called the F_{max} test

Homoscedasticity An equal spread of Y scores around the regression line (that is, around the values of Y')

Human Subjects Review Committee A committee at colleges and research institutions that is charged with the responsibility of reviewing all prospective research procedures to ensure the ethical and safe treatment of participants

Hypothesis A formally stated expectation about a behavior that defines the purpose and goals of a research study

Hypothetical construct An abstract concept used in a particular theoretical manner to relate different behaviors according to their underlying features or causes

Incomplete factorial design An ANOVA design in which not all levels of all factors are combined

Independent events Events for which the probability of one event is not influenced by the occurrence of the other

Independent samples Samples created by selecting each participant for one sample without regard to the participants selected for any other sample

Independent samples *t*-test The statistical procedure used for significance testing that is appropriate when the scores meet the requirements of a parametric test, the design involves independent samples, and there are only two conditions of the independent variable

Independent variable In an experiment, the variable that is hypothesized to cause a change in the dependent variable and is systematically changed or manipulated by the researcher; also called a *factor*

Individual differences Variations in individuals' traits, backgrounds, genetic make-up, and other characteristics that make individuals different from one another and produce different responses to the same situation thus influencing the strength of a relationship

Inferential statistics Mathematical procedures for deciding whether a sample relationship represents a relationship that actually exists in the population

Informed consent The procedure by which researchers inform participants about a study prior to their participation in it, and obtain participants' explicit consent to participate

Instrumentation effects Changes in measurement procedures that occur through use of equipment over time, making the measurements less reliable

Inter-rater reliability The extent to which raters agree on the scores they assign to a participant's behavior

Interaction effect The effect produced by the concurrent manipulation of two independent variables such that the influence of changing the levels of one factor depends on which level of the other factor is present

Interaction means The cell means from a multifactor design that are examined to find an interaction effect

Internal validity The extent to which the observed relationship reflects the relationship between the variables in a study

Interrupted time-series design A quasi-experimental repeated-measures design in which observations are made at several spaced times before and then after a treatment

Interval estimation An estimation technique where the value of a population parameter is assumed to lie within a specified interval

Interval scale A measurement scale in which each score indicates an actual amount, an equal unit of measurement separates consecutive scores, zero is not a true zero value, and negative scores are possible

Intervening variable An internal subject characteristic that is influenced by the independent variable and, in turn, influences the dependent variable

Kruskal-Wallis *H* test The nonparametric version of the one-way between-subjects ANOVA for ranked scores

Lawful The assumption that events in nature can be understood as a predictable sequence of natural causes and effects

Leading questions Questions that are so loaded with social desirability or experimenter expectancies that there is one obvious response

Level In ANOVA, each condition of the factor (independent variable); also called *treatment*

Likert-type questions A measure in which participants rate statements, such as when using a scale of 1 to 5 where 1 indicates "strongly agree" and 5 indicates "strongly disagree"

Line graph A graph in which X scores from an interval or ratio variable are plotted by connecting adjacent data points with straight lines; used when the independent variable implies a continuous, ordered amount

Linear regression The procedure for predicting participants' scores on one variable based on the linear relationship with participants' scores on another variable

Linear regression equation The equation that defines the straight line summarizing a linear relationship by describing the value of Y' at each X

Linear regression line The best-fitting straight line that summarizes the scatterplot of a linear relationship by, on average, passing through the center of all Y scores

Linear relationship A correlation between the X scores and Y scores in a set of data in which the Y scores tend to change in only one direction as the X scores increase, forming a slanted straight regression line on a scatterplot

Literal replication The precise duplication of the specific design and results of a previous study

Longitudinal design A quasi-experimental design in which a researcher repeatedly measures a group of participants in order to observe the effect of the passage of time

Main effect In a multifactor ANOVA, the effect on the dependent scores of changing the levels of one factor while collapsing over other factors in the study

Main effect means In a multifactor design, the means from the levels of one factor, after collapsing across the other factor(s), that are examined to find a main effect

Manipulation check A measurement of participants, in addition to the dependent variable, that is used to check that they were influenced as intended

Mann-Whitney *U* test The nonparametric version of the independent samples *t*-test for ranked scores when *n* is less than or equal to 20

Margin of error The confidence interval that is computed when estimating the population's responses to a field survey

Matched-groups design A research design in which each participant in one condition is matched with a subject in every other condition along an extraneous subject variable

Mean The average of a group of scores, interpreted as the score around which the scores in a distribution tend to be clustered

Mean square In ANOVA, an estimated population variance, symbolized by *MS*

Mean square between groups In ANOVA, the variability in scores that occurs between the levels in a factor or the cells in an interaction

Mean square within groups In ANOVA, the variability in scores that occurs in the conditions, or cells; also known as the *error term*

Measure of central tendency A score that summarizes the location of a distribution on a variable by indicating where the center of the distribution tends to be located

Measurement variables The aspects of the stimuli presented or the measurement procedure employed that may influence scores

Measures of variability Measures that summarize and describe the extent to which scores in a distribution differ from one another

Median The score located at the 50th percentile; symbolized by *Mdn*; also called the median score

Meta-analysis Statistical procedures for combining, testing, and describing the results from different studies

Modal score See *Mode*

Mode The most frequently occurring score in a sample; also called the *modal score*

Model A generalized, hypothetical description that, by analogy, explains the process underlying a set of common behaviors

Multifactor experiment An experiment in which the researcher examines several independent variables and their interactions

Multiple-baseline design A design in which a baseline is established for one behavior from several participants, for several behaviors from one participant, or for one behavior from one participant in several situations

Multiple baselines across behaviors A design in which a baseline for each of several different behaviors from one participant is measured, and then the treatment is applied to each behavior at a different time

Multiple baselines across participants A design in which a baseline on the same behavior for each of several individuals is measured, and then the treatment is introduced for each at a different time

Multiple baselines across situations A design in which baselines for one behavior in each of several different situations are established on the same participant, and then the treatment is applied to each behavior at a different time

Multiple correlation and regression Statistical procedures performed when multiple predictor (*X*) variables are used to predict one criterion (*Y*) variable

Multiple raters The term referring to the use of several judges to subjectively evaluate participants, so as to balance out the biases of any one judge

Multiple time-series design A quasi-experimental repeated-measures design in which an experimental group and a nonequivalent control group are observed at several spaced times before and then after a treatment

Multiple trials The repeated testing of participants within a condition

Multivariate statistics The inferential statistical procedures used when a study involves multiple dependent variables

Naturalistic observation The unobtrusive observation of participants' behaviors in an unstructured fashion

Negative linear relationship A linear relationship in which the *Y* scores tend to decrease as the *X* scores increase

Negatively skewed distribution A frequency polygon with low frequency, extreme low scores but without corresponding low frequency, extreme high ones, so that its only pronounced tail is in the direction of the lower scores

Nemenyi's procedure The post hoc procedure performed with the Friedman χ^2 test

Nominal scale A measurement scale in which each score identifies a quality or category and does not indicate an amount

Nonequivalent control group In a quasi-experiment, a control group whose subject characteristics and experiences are different from those of the experimental group

Nonexperimental methods See *Descriptive methods*

Nonlinear relationship A relationship in which the Y scores change their direction or change as the X scores change, forming a curved regression line; also called a *curvilinear relationship*

Nonparametric statistics Inferential procedures that do not require stringent assumptions about the parameters of the raw score population represented by the sample data; usually used with scores most appropriately described by the median or the mode

Nonprobability sampling Any sampling technique in which every potential participant in the population does not have an equal likelihood of being selected for a study

Nonsignificant Describes results that are considered likely to result from sampling error when the predicted relationship does not exist; it indicates failure to reject the null hypothesis

Nonsymmetrical carry-over effects Order effects that occur from one order of conditions or trials that cannot be balanced out by another order

Normal curve model The most common model of how nature operates; it is based on the normal curve and describes a normal distribution of a population of scores

Normal distribution A frequency distribution forming a bell-shaped curve that is symmetrical about the mean

Null hypothesis The statistical hypothesis that describes the population parameters the sample data represent if the predicted relationship does not exist; symbolized by H_0

Objectivity The requirement of science that a researcher's personal biases do not influence observations or conclusions

Observational research Research where participants are observed in an unobtrusive manner; see also *Naturalistic observation*; *Systematic naturalistic observation*; and *Participant observation*

Observed frequency In chi square, the frequency with which subjects fall in a category of a variable; symbolized by f_o

One-group pretest-posttest design A quasi-experimental pretest-posttest design for which there is no control group

One-tailed test The test used to evaluate a statistical hypothesis that predicts that scores will only increase or only decrease

One-way ANOVA The analysis of variance performed when an experiment has only one independent variable

One-way chi square The chi square procedure performed when a study examines category membership along one variable

One-way design A research design involving the manipulation of one independent variable

Open-ended question In a questionnaire or interview, a question for which the participant determines both the alternatives to choose from and the response

Operational definition The definition of a construct or variable in terms of the operations used to measure it

Order effects The influence on a particular trial that arises from its position in a sequence of trials

Ordinal scale A measurement scale in which scores indicate rank order or a relative amount

Parameter See *Population parameter*

Parametric statistics Inferential procedures that require certain assumptions about the parameters of the raw score population represented by the sample data; usually used with scores most appropriately described by the mean

Partial counterbalancing Balancing order effects by testing different participants using only some of the possible orders

Participants The individuals in a sample

Participant observation The unobtrusive observation of a group in which the researcher is an active member

Participant variables The personal characteristics that distinguish one participant from another

Pearson correlation coefficient The correlation coefficient that describes the strength and type of a linear relationship between two interval or ratio variables; symbolized by r

Percent A proportion multiplied times 100

Percentile A cumulative percentage; the percentage of all scores in the sample that are at or below a particular score

Phi coefficient The statistic that describes the strength of the relationship in a two-way chi square when there are only two categories for each variable; symbolized by ϕ

Pilot study A miniature version of a study used to test a procedure prior to the actual study

Placebo An inactive substance that provides the demand characteristics of a manipulation while presenting zero amount of the independent variable

Planned comparisons In ANOVA, statistical procedures for comparing only some conditions in an experiment

Point-biserial correlation coefficient The correlation coefficient that describes the strength of the linear relationship between scores from one continuous interval or ratio variable and one dichotomous variable; symbolized by r_{pb}

Point estimation The estimation procedure where the value of the population parameter is assumed to equal the value of the corresponding sample statistic

Pooled variance The weighted average of the sample variances in a two-sample experiment; symbolized by s^2_{pool}

Population The large group of all possible scores that would be obtained if the behavior of every individual of interest in a particular situation could be measured

Population parameter A number that describes a characteristic of a population of scores, symbolized by a letter from the Greek alphabet; also called a *parameter*

Population standard deviation The square root of the population variance, or the square root of the average squared deviation of scores around the population mean; symbolized by σ_X

Population variance The average squared deviation of scores around the population mean; symbolized as σ_X^2

Positive linear relationship A linear relationship in which the *Y* scores tend to increase as the *X* scores increase

Positively skewed distribution A frequency polygon with low frequency, extreme high scores but without corresponding low frequency, extreme low ones, so that its only pronounced tail is in the direction of the higher scores

Post hoc comparisons In ANOVA, statistical procedures used to compare all possible pairs of conditions to determine which ones differ significantly from each other

Power The probability that a statistical test will allow the rejection of a false null hypothesis

Powerful design A design that is more likely to clearly show a convincing sample relationship

Practice trials The testing of participants as in the real study, but the data from these trials are not included when analyzing the results

Practice effects The influence on performance that arises from practicing a task

Predicted *Y* score In linear regression, the best description and prediction of the *Y* scores at a particular *X*, based on the linear relationship summarized by the regression line; symbolized by Y'

Prediction A statement as to how a behavior will be manifested in a research situation, describing the specific results that will be found

Predictive validity The extent to which a procedure allows for accurate predictions about a participant's future behavior

Predictor variable The variable for which known scores in a relationship are used to predict unknown scores on another variable

Pretest A measure used to identify and select potential participants, prior to conducting a study

Pretest-posttest design A research design in which participants are measured before and after a treatment

Probability A mathematical statement indicating the likelihood that an event will occur when a particular population is randomly sampled; symbolized by p

Probability distribution The probability of every possible event in a population, derived from the relative frequency of every possible event in that population

Probability sampling Any sampling technique in which every potential participant in the population has an equal likelihood of being selected for a study

Program evaluation The procedures undertaken to evaluate the goals, activities, and outcomes of social programs

Proportion A decimal number between 0 and 1 that indicates a fraction of a total

Proportion of the area under the curve The proportion of the total area beneath the normal curve at certain scores, which represents the relative frequency of those scores

Proportion of variance accounted for The proportion of the error in predicting scores that is eliminated when, instead of using the mean of *Y*, the relationship with the *X* variable is used to predict *Y* scores; the proportional improvement in predicting *Y* scores thus achieved

Pseudo-explanation A circular statement that explains an event by renaming it

Psychological Abstracts A monthly publication that describes studies recently published in psychology journals

Publication Manual of the American Psychological Association The reference source regarding the organization, content, and style of a research manuscript

Qualitative variable A variable that reflects a quality or category

Quantitative variable A variable that reflects a quantity or amount

Quasi-experiment A study in which participants cannot be randomly assigned to conditions but, instead, are assigned to a particular condition on the basis of some inherent characteristic

Quasi-independent variable The independent variable in a quasi-experiment

Quota sampling A sampling technique in which, using convenience sampling, the sample has the same percentage of each subgroup as is found in the population

Random assignment A method of selecting a sample for an experiment such that the condition each participant experiences is determined in a random and unbiased manner

Random sampling A method of selecting samples whereby all members of the population have the same chance of being selected for a sample and all samples have the same chance of being selected

Randomization The creation of different random orders of trials under which different participants are tested

Range The difference between the highest and lowest scores in a set of data

Rank sums test The nonparametric version of the independent samples t-test for ranked scores when n is greater than 20; also the post hoc procedure performed with the Kruskal-Wallis H test

Ratio scale A measurement scale in which each score indicates an actual amount, an equal unit of measurement separates consecutive scores, zero means zero amount, and negative scores are not possible

Reactivity The bias in responses that occurs when participants know they are being observed

Reaction time The amount of time a participant takes to respond to a stimulus

Rectangular distribution A symmetrical frequency polygon shaped like a rectangle; it has no discernible tails because extreme scores do not have relatively low frequencies

Region of rejection That portion of a sampling distribution that contains values considered too unlikely to occur by chance, found in the tail or tails of the distribution

Regression line The line drawn through the long dimension of a scatterplot that best fits the center of the scatterplot and thus visually summarizes the scatterplot and indicates the type of relationship that is present

Regression toward the mean The tendency of extreme scores to become less extreme; this occurs because random influences are not consistently present

Relationship A correlation between two variables so that a change in one variable is accompanied by a consistent change in the other variable

Relative frequency The proportion of time a score occurs in a distribution, equal to the proportion of the total number of scores that the score's simple frequency represents; symbolized by *rel. f*

Relative frequency distribution A distribution of scores, organized to show the proportion of time each score occurs in the data

Relative standing A description of a particular score derived from a systematic evaluation of the score using the characteristics of the sample or population in which it occurs

Reliability The extent to which a measurement is consistent, can be reproduced, and avoids error

Repeated-measures design A design in which each participant is measured repeatedly under all conditions of an independent variable

Replication The process of repeatedly conducting studies that test and confirm a hypothesis so that confidence in its truth can be developed

Representative sample A sample whose characteristics and behaviors accurately reflect those of the population from which it is drawn

Research design The way in which a study is laid out so as to demonstrate a relationship

Research ethics The question of how to balance the rights of a researcher to study a behavior with the rights of participants to be protected from abuse

Researcher variables The behaviors and characteristics of the researcher that may influence the reactions of subjects

Response scale The number and type of choices provided for each question in a questionnaire or interview

Response set A bias toward responding in a particular way because of previous responses made

Restriction of range Improper limitation of the range of scores obtained on a variable

Reversal design A design in which the researcher alternates between the baseline condition and the treatment condition

Robust procedure A procedure that alters the probability of a Type I error only a negligible amount, even if the assumptions of the procedure are not perfectly met; describes parametric procedures

Role playing A way to study a behavior by having participants pretend they are in a particular situation

Sample A relatively small subset of a population that is selected to represent or stand in for the population; a subset of the complete group of scores found in any particular situation

Sample standard deviation The square root of the sample variance

Sample statistic A number that describes a characteristic of a sample of scores, symbolized by a letter from the English alphabet; also called a statistic

Sample variance The average of the squared deviations of the scores around the mean

Sampling distribution of a correlation coefficient A frequency distribution showing all possible values of the coefficient that occur when samples of a particular size are drawn from a population whose correlation coefficient is zero

Sampling distribution of differences between the means A frequency distribution showing all possible differences between two means that occur when two independent samples of a particular size are drawn from the population of scores described by the null hypothesis

Sampling distribution of mean differences A frequency distribution showing all possible mean differences that occur when the difference scores from two dependent samples of a particular size are drawn from the population of difference scores described by the null hypothesis

Sampling distribution of means A frequency distribution showing all possible sample means that occur when samples of a particular size are drawn from the raw score population described by the null hypothesis

Sampling error The difference, due to random chance, between a sample statistic and the population parameter it represents

Sampling with replacement A sampling procedure in which a previously selected sample is returned to the population before additional samples are selected

Sampling without replacement A sampling procedure in which previously selected samples are not returned to the population before additional samples are selected

Scatterplot A graph of the individual data points from a set of *X*-*Y* pairs

Scientific method The assumptions, attitudes, goals, and procedures for creating and answering questions about nature in a scientific manner

Scoring criteria The system for assigning scores to different responses

Self-report A measure in which participants describe their feelings or thoughts

Semi-interquartile range The average distance between the median and the scores at the 25th and 75th percentiles (the quartiles), used to describe highly skewed distributions

Sensitive measure A procedure for measuring the dependent variable that produces different scores for small or subtle differences in behavior

Significant Describes results that are considered too unlikely to result from chance sampling error if the predicted relationship does not exist; it indicates rejection of the null hypothesis

Simple frequency distribution A distribution of scores, organized to show the number of times each score occurs in a set of data

Simple main effect The effect of one factor at one level of a second factor

Simple random sampling A sampling technique in which participants are randomly selected from a list of the members of the population

Single-blind procedure The procedure in which participants are unaware of the treatment they are receiving

Single-sample *t*-test The parametric procedure used to test the null hypothesis for a single-sample experiment when the standard deviation of the raw score population must be estimated

Single-subject design A repeated-measures experiment conducted on one participant

Skewed distribution A frequency polygon similar in shape to a normal distribution except that it is not symmetrical and it has only one pronounced tail

Slope A number that indicates how much a linear regression line slants and in which direction it slants; symbolized by b

Small *N* research A study in which a single-subject experiment is replicated on a few participants

Snowball sampling A sampling technique in which the researcher contacts potential participants who have been identified by previously tested participants

Social desirability The demand characteristic that causes participants to provide what they consider to be the socially acceptable response

Social Science Citation Index A reference source that identifies a given research article by authors and date, and then lists subsequent articles that have cited it

Sorting task A measure in which participants sort stimuli into different groups

Spearman rank-order correlation coefficient The correlation coefficient that describes the linear relationship between pairs of ranked scores; symbolized by r_s

Split-half reliability The consistency with which participants' scores on some trials match their scores on other trials

Squared correlation coefficient The proportion of total variance in *Y* scores that is systematically associated with changing *X* scores

Squared sum of *X* A result calculated by adding all scores and then squaring their sum; symbolized by $(\Sigma X)^2$

Standard deviation The statistic that communicates the average of the deviations of the scores from the mean in a set of data, computed by obtaining the square root of the variance; see also *Sample standard deviation*

Standard error of the difference The estimated standard deviation of the sampling distribution of differences between the means of independent samples in a two-sample experiment; symbolized by $S_{\bar{X}_1-\bar{X}_2}$

Standard error of the estimate A standard deviation that indicates the amount that actual *Y* scores in a sample differ from their corresponding Y' scores; symbolized as $S_{Y'}$

Standard error of the mean The standard deviation of the sampling distribution of means; used in the *z*-test (symbolized by $\sigma_{\bar{X}}$) and in the single-sample *t*-test (symbolized by $s_{\bar{X}}$)

Standard error of the mean difference The standard deviation of the sampling distribution of mean differences between dependent samples in a two-sample experiment; symbolized by $s_{\bar{D}}$

Standard normal curve A theoretical perfect normal curve, which serves as a model of the perfect normal *z*-distribution

Standard scores See *z-score*

Statistic See *Sample statistic*

Statistical hypotheses Two statements (H_0 and H_a) that describe the population parameters the sample statistics will represent if the predicted relationship exists or does not exist

Statistical notation The standardized code for the mathematical operations performed in formulas, for the order in which operations are performed, and for the answers obtained

Stratified random sampling A sampling technique involving the identification of important subgroups in the population, followed by the proportionate random selection of participants from each subgroup

Strength of a relationship The extent to which one value of Y within a relationship is consistently associated with one and only one value of X; also called the degree of association

Strong manipulation Manipulation of the independent variable in such a way that participants' behavior is greatly differentiated, thus producing large differences in dependent scores between the conditions

Structured interview An interview in which participants are asked a specific set of predetermined questions in a controlled manner

Subject history The bias that arises due to participants' experiences that influence repeated measures

Subject maturation The bias that arises due to the changes that occur as an individual grows older and more mature that influence repeated measures

Subject mortality effects The bias that arises when participants fail to show up for a study or discontinue their participation before the study is completed

Subjects See *Participants*

Sum of squares The sum of the squared deviations of a set of scores around a statistic

Sum of the deviations around the mean The sum of all differences between the scores and the mean; symbolized as $\Sigma(X - \overline{X})$

Sum of X The sum of the scores in a sample; symbolized by ΣX

Sum of the squared Xs The sum after squaring each score in a sample; symbolized by ΣX^2

Systematic Refers to variable that changes consistently

Systematic naturalistic observation The unobtrusive observation of a particular behavior or situation in a structured fashion

Systematic random sampling A sampling technique in which every *n*th participant is selected from a list of the members of the population

***t*-distribution** The sampling distribution of all possible values of t that occur when samples of a particular size represent the raw score population(s) described by the null hypothesis

***t*-test for dependent samples** See *Dependent samples t-test*

***t*-test for independent samples** See *Independent samples t-test*

***t*-test** See *Dependent samples t-test*; *Independent samples t-test*

Tail (of a distribution) The far-left or far-right portion of a normal distribution, containing relatively low frequency, extreme scores

Testable A requirement of a scientific hypothesis that it be possible to devise a test of the hypothesis

Test of independence See *Two-way chi square procedure*

Test-retest reliability The consistency with which participants obtain the same overall score when tested at different times

Theoretical probability distribution A probability distribution based on a theoretical model of the relative frequencies of events in a population

Theory A logically organized set of proposals that defines, explains, organizes, and interrelates knowledge about many behaviors

Three-way design A three-way design involving three main effects, three two-way interactions, and one three-way interaction

Three-way interaction The interaction of three factors such that the two-way interaction between two factors changes as the levels of the third factor change

Tied rank The situation that occurs when two subjects in a sample receive the same rank-order score on a variable

Time-series design A quasi-experimental repeated-measures design in which participants' behavior is sampled before and then after the occurrence of an event

Total area under the curve The area beneath the normal curve, which represents the total frequency of all scores

Transformation A systematic procedure for converting a set of scores into a different but equivalent set of scores

Treatment effect The result of changing the conditions of an independent variable so that different populations of scores having different μs are produced

Treatments The conditions of the independent variable; also called levels

Treatment variance In ANOVA, the variability between scores from different populations that would be created by the different levels of a factor

Trial A single complete instance of testing in an experimental series

True experiment A study in which the researcher actively changes or manipulates the independent variable, and in which participants can be randomly assigned to conditions

True independent variable The independent variable in a true experiment

Tukey's *HSD* test The post hoc procedure performed with ANOVA to compare means from a factor in which all levels have equal n

Two-sample experiment A design that compares two conditions of one independent variable

Two-tailed test The test used to evaluate a statistical hypothesis that predicts a relationship, but not whether scores will increase or decrease

Two-way ANOVA The parametric inferential procedure performed when an experiment contains two independent variables

Two-way between-subjects design A design in which an independent sample of participants is tested under each condition of two independent variables

Two-way chi square procedure The chi square procedure performed in testing whether, in the population, frequency of category membership on one variable is independent of frequency of category membership on another variable

Two-way design A design involving the manipulation of two independent variables

Two-way interaction The interaction of two factors such that the relationship between one factor and the dependent scores is different for and depends on each level of the other factor; also called two-way interaction effect

Two-way mixed design A design that involves one within-subjects factor and one between-subjects factor

Two-way mixed-design ANOVA The parametric inferential procedure performed when an experiment involves one within-subjects factor and one between-subjects factor

Two-way within-subjects ANOVA The parametric inferential procedure performed when an experiment involves two within-subjects factors

Two-way within-subjects design A design in which matched groups or the same repeatedly measured participants are tested in all conditions of two independent variables

Type I error A statistical error in which a large amount of sampling error causes rejection of the null hypothesis even though the null hypothesis is true (that is, when the predicted relationship does not exist)

Type II error A statistical error in which the closeness of the sample statistic to the population parameter described by the null hypothesis causes the null hypothesis to be retained even though it is false (that is, when the predicted relationship does exist)

Type of relationship The form of the pattern between the X scores and the Y scores in a set of data, determined by the overall direction in which the Y scores change as the X scores change

Unbiased estimators The formulas for using the sample data to estimate the population variance and standard deviation that involve dividing by $N - 1$

Unconfounded comparisons In an ANOVA, comparisons of cell means that differ along only one factor

Undefined terms Components of questions whose meaning is unclear, and thus the meaning of participants' responses to them is also unclear

Ungrouped distribution A distribution showing the frequency, relative frequency, or cumulative frequency of each individual score in the data

Unimodal distribution A distribution whose frequency polygon has only one hump and thus has only one score that qualifies as the mode

Univariate statistics Statistics that involve one dependent variable

Unobtrusive measures Procedures by which participants' behavior is measured without their being aware that measurements are being made

Unstructured interview An interview in which the questions are not rigidly predetermined, thus allowing for substantial discussion and interaction between participant and interviewer

Unsystematic Refers to a variable that changes with no consistent pattern

Validity The extent to which a procedure measures what it is intended to measure

Variable Any measurable aspect of a behavior or influence on behavior that may change so that, when measured, can produce two or more different scores

Variance A measure of the variability of the scores in a set of data, computed as the average of the squared deviations of the scores around the mean; see also *Sample variance*; *Error variance*

Variance between groups In ANOVA, the differences between scores that occur between participants who are in different conditions or populations

Variance of Y scores around Y' In regression, the average squared deviation between the actual Y scores and corresponding Y' scores, symbolized by $S_{Y'}$

Variance within groups In ANOVA, the inherent differences between scores that occur between participants who are in the same condition or population

Volunteer bias The bias that arises from the fact that a given sample contains only those participants who are willing to participate in the study

Wilcoxon t-test The nonparametric version of the dependent samples t-test for ranked scores

Within-subjects ANOVA The ANOVA performed when a study involves within-subjects factors

Within-subjects design A design in which all factors are within-subjects factors

Within-subjects factor The type of factor created when an independent variable is studied using dependent samples in all conditions, either because participants are matched or repeatedly measured

Y-intercept The value of Y at the point where the linear regression line intercepts the Y axis; symbolized by a

Y prime The value of Y that falls on the regression line above any X; symbolized as Y'

z-distribution The distribution produced by transforming all raw scores in a distribution into z-scores

z-score The statistic that describes the location of a raw score in terms of its distance from the mean when measured in standard deviation units; symbolized by z; also known as a standard score because it allows comparison of scores on different kinds of variables by equating, or standardizing, the distributions

z-table The table that gives the proportion of the total area under the standard normal curve for any two-decimal z-score

z-test The parametric procedure used to test the null hypothesis for a single-sample experiment when the true standard deviation of the raw score population is known

REFERENCES

American Psychological Association. (1994). *Publication manual of the American Psychological Association* (4th ed.). Washington, DC: Author.

American Psychological Association. (1992). Ethical principles of psychologists and code of conduct. *American Psychologist, 47*, 1597–1611.

Anderson, C. A., & Anderson, D. C. (1984). Ambient temperature and violent crime: Tests of the linear and curvilinear hypotheses. *Journal of Personality and Social Psychology, 46*, 91–97.

Anderson, P. (1983). Decision making by objection and the Cuban missile crisis. *Administrative Science Quarterly, 28*, 201–222.

Barefoot, J. C., Hoople, H., & McClay, D. (1972). Avoidance of an act which would violate personal space. *Psychonomic Science, 28*, 205–206.

Barlow, D. H., & Hernsen, M. (1984). *Single case experimental designs: Strategies for studying behavior change* (2nd ed.). New York: Pergamon Press.

Bell, P. A. (1980). Effects of heat, noise, and provocation on retaliatory evaluative behavior. *Journal of Social Psychology, 110*, 97–100.

Bell, P. A., & Baron, R. A. (1976). Aggression and heat: The mediating role of negative affect. *Journal of Applied Social Psychology, 6*, 18–30.

Boesch-Acherman, H., & Boesch, C. (1993). Tool use in wild chimpanzees: New light from dark forests. *Current Directions in Psychological Science, 2*, 18–21.

Bower, G. H., Karlin, M. B., & Dueck, A. (1975). Comprehension and memory for pictures. *Memory and Cognition, 3*(2), 216–220.

Bramel, D., & Friend, R. (1981). Hawthorne, the myth of the docile worker, and class bias in psychology. *American Psychologist, 36*, 867–878.

Campbell, D. T., & Stanley, J. C. (1963). *Experimental and quasi-experimental designs for research.* Boston: Houghton Mifflin.

Carlson, M., Marcus-Newhall, A., and Miller, N. (1990). Effects of situational aggression cues: A quantitative review. *Journal of Personality and Social Psychology, 58*, 622–633.

Christensen, L. (1988). Deception in psychological research: When is it justified? *Personality and Social Psychology Bulletin, 14*, 664–675.

Cicchetti, D. V. (1972). Extension of multiple range tests to interaction tables in the analysis of variance. *Psychological Bulletin, 77*, 405–408.

Cohen, J. (1988). *Statistical power analysis for the behavioral sciences.* Hillsdale, NJ: Lawrence Erlbaum Associates.

Connors, J. G., & Alpher, V. S. (1989). Alcohol themes within country-western songs. *International Journal of the Addictions, 24*, 445–451.

Cook, T. D., & Campbell, D. T. (1979). *Quasi-experimentation: Design and analysis issues for field settings.* Chicago: Rand McNally.

Crusco, A. H., & Wetzel, C. G. (1984). The Midas touch: The effect of interpersonal touch on restaurant tipping. *Personality and Social Psychology Bulletin, 10*, 512–517.

Cunningham, M. R., Shaffer, D. R., Barbee, A. P., Wolff, P. L., & Kelley, D. J. (1990). Separate processes in the relation of elation and depression to helping: Social versus personal concerns. *Journal of Abnormal and Social Psychology, 26*, 13–33.

Desrochers, A., & Begg, I. (1987). A theoretical account of encoding and retrieval processes in the use of imagery-based mnemonic techniques: The special case of the keyword method. In M. A. McDaniel & M. Pressley (Eds.), *Imagery and related mnemonic processes: Theories, individual differences, and applications* (pp. 56–77). New York: Springer Verlag.

Dixon, P. N., Willingham, W., Strano, D. A., & Chandler, C. K. (1989). Sense of humor as a mediator during incidental learning of humor-related material. *Psychological Reports, 64*, 851–855.

Eagly, A. H., Ashmore, R. D., MaKijani, M. G., & Longo, L. C. (1991). What is beautiful is good but . . . : A meta-analytic review of research on the physical attractiveness stereotype. *Psychological Bulletin, 110*, 109–128.

Einstein, G. O., McDaniel, M. A., & Lackey, S. (1989). Bizarre imagery, interference, and distinctiveness. *Journal of Experimental Psychology: Learning, Memory, and Cognition, 15*, 137–146.

Ellsworth, P. C., Carlsmith, J. M., & Henson, A. (1972). The stare as stimulus to flight in human subjects: A series of field experiments. *Journal of Personality and Social Psychology, 21*, 302–311.

Erdley, C. A., & D'Agostino, P. R. (1988). Cognitive and affective components of automatic priming effects. *Journal of Personality and Social Psychology, 54*, 741–747.

Faustman, W., & White, P. (1989). Diagnostic and psychopharmacological treatment characteristics of 536 inpatients with posttraumatic stress disorder. *The Journal of Nervous and Mental Disease, 177*, 154–159.

Fornell, C. (1992). A national customer satisfaction barometer: The Swedish experience. *Journal of Marketing, 56*, 6–21.

Frank, M. G., & Gilovich, T. (1988). The dark side of self- and social perception: Black uniforms and aggression in professional sports. *Journal of Personality and Social Psychology, 54*, 74–85.

George, J. M., Reed, T. F., Ballard, K. A., Colin, J., & Fielding, J. (1993). Contact with AIDS patients as a source of work-related distress: Effects of organizational and social support. *Academy of Management Journal, 36*, 157–171.

Gladue, B. A., & Delaney, H. J. (1990). Gender differences in perception of attractiveness of men and women in bars. *Personality and Social Psychology Bulletin, 16*, 378–391.

Goodall, J. (1986). *The chimpanzees of Gombe: Patterns of behavior*. Cambridge, MA: Belknap Press.

Goodall, J. (1990). *Through a window: My thirty years with the chimpanzees of Gombe*. Boston: Houghton Mifflin.

Haney, C., Banks, W. C., & Zimbardo, P. G. (1973). Interpersonal dynamics in a simulated prison. *International Journal of Criminology and Penology, 1*, 69–97.

Hanssel, C. E. M. (1980). *ESP and parapsychology: A critical reevaluation.* Buffalo, NY: Prometheus Books.

Harrison, L., & Gfroerer, J. (1992). The intersection of drug use and criminal behavior: Results from the national household survey on drug abuse. *Crime and Delinquency, 38*, 422–443.

Hayduk, L. A. (1983). Personal space: Where we now stand. *Psychological Bulletin, 94*, 293–335.

Heslin, R., & Boss, D. (1980). Nonverbal intimacy in airport arrival and departure. *Personality and Social Psychology Bulletin, 6*, 248–252.

Hinkle, P. E., Wiersma, W., & Jurs, S. G. (1994). *Applied statistics for the behavioral sciences* (3rd ed.). Boston: Houghton Mifflin.

Hunt, R. R., & Elliott, J. M. (1980). The role of nonsemantic information in memory: Orthographic distinctiveness effects on retention. *Journal of Experimental Psychology: General 109*, 49–74.

Isen, A. M., & Levin, P. F. (1972). Effect of feeling good on helping: Cookies and kindness. *Journal of Personality and Social Psychology, 21*, 384–388.

Kanuk, L., & Berenson, C. (1975). Mail surveys and response rates: A literature review. *Journal of Marketing Research, 12*, 440–453.

Koocher, G. P. (1977). Bathroom behavior and human dignity. *Journal of Personality and Social Psychology, 35*, 120–121.

Krippendorf, K. (1980). *Content analysis: An introduction to its methodology*. Beverly Hills, CA: Sage.

Lavrakas, P. J. (1993). *Telephone survey methods* (2nd ed.). Thousand Oaks, CA: Sage.

Lockhart, R. S., & Craik, F. I. M. (1990). Levels of processing: A retrospective commentary on the framework for memory research. *Canadian Journal of Psychology, 44*, 87–112.

Martorano, J. (1991). Case study: The use of the CEEG in treating premenstrual syndrome: An opportunity for treatment innovation. *Integrative Psychiatry, 7*, 63–64.

Mathews, K. E., Jr., & Cannon, L. K. (1975). Environmental noise level as a determinant of helping behavior. *Journal of Personality and Social Psychology, 32*, 571–577.

May, J. L., & Hamilton, P. A. (1980). Effects of musically evoked affect on women's interpersonal attraction toward and perceptual judgments of physical attractiveness in men. *Motivation and Emotion, 4*(3), 217–228.

McAninch, C. B., Austin, J. L., & Derks, P. L. (1992). Effect of caption meaning on memory for nonsense figures. *Current Psychology: Research and Reviews, 11*, 315–323.

Middlemist, R. D., Knowles, E. S., & Matter, C. F. (1976). Personal space invasions in the lavatory: Suggestive evidence for arousal. *Journal of Personality and Social Psychology, 33*, 541–546.

Middlemist, R. D., Knowles, E. S., & Matter, C. F. (1977). What to do and what to report: A reply to Koocher. *Journal of Personality and Social Psychology, 35*, 122–124.

Milgram, S. (1963). Behavioral study of obedience. *Journal of Abnormal and Social Psychology, 67*, 371–378.

Nelson, D. L., & Sutton, C. (1990). Chronic work stress and coping: A longitudinal study and suggested new directions. *Academy of Management Journal, 33*, 859–869.

Neri, D. F., Shappell, S. A., & DeJohn, C. A. (1992). Simulated sustained flight operations and performance: I. Effects of fatigue. *Military Psychology, 4*(3), 137–155.

Nolen-Hoeksema, S., & Morrow, J. (1991). A prospective study of depression and posttraumatic stress symptoms after a natural disaster: The 1989 Loma Prieta earthquake. *Journal of Personality and Social Psychology, 61*, 115–121.

Orne, M. T. (1962). On the social psychology of the psychological experiment: With particular reference to demand characteristics and their implications. *American Psychologist, 17,* 776–783.

Posavac, E. J., & Carey, R. G. (1989). *Program evaluation* (3rd ed.). Englewood Cliffs, NJ: Prentice Hall.

Robinson, J. P., Shaver, P. R., & Wrightsman, L. S. (1991). *Measures of personality and social psychological attitudes* (Vol. 1). San Diego, CA: Academic Press.

Roethlisberger, F. J., & Dickson, W. J. (1939). *Management and the worker.* Cambridge, MA: Harvard University Press.

Roper Organization. (1992). *Unusual personal experiences: An analysis of the data from three national surveys.* Las Vegas, NV: Bigelow Holding.

Rosenhan, D. L. (1973). On being sane in insane places. *Science, 179,* 250–258.

Rosenthal, R., & Rosnow, R. L. (1975). *The volunteer subject.* New York: Wiley.

Schmidt, S. R. (1985). Encoding and retrieval processes in the memory for conceptually distinctive events. *Journal of Experimental Psychology: Learning, Memory, and Cognition, 11,* 565–578.

Shaffer, D. R., Rogel, R. M., & Hendrick, C. (1975). Intervention in the library: The effect of increased responsibility on bystander willingness to prevent theft. *Journal of Personality and Social Psychology, 5,* 303–319.

Shah, I. (1970). *Tales of the Dervishes.* New York: Dutton.

Sidman, M. (1960). *Tactics of scientific research.* New York: Basic Books.

Silverman, L. H., Ross, D. L., Adler, J. M., & Lustig, D. A. (1978). Simple research paradigm for demonstrating subliminal psychodynamic activation: Effects of Oedipal stimuli on dart-throwing accuracy in college males. *Journal of Abnormal Psychology, 87,* 341–357.

Silverman, L. H., & Weinberger, J. (1985). Mommy and I are one: Implications for psychotherapy. *American Psychologist, 40,* 1296–1308.

Stagray, J. R., & Truitt, L. (1992). Monaural listening therapy for auditory disorders: Opinions and a case study. *Canadian Journal of Rehabilitation, 6,* 45–49.

Strack, F., Martin, L. L., & Stepper, S. (1988). Inhibiting and facilitating conditions of the human smile: A nonobtrusive test of the facial feedback hypothesis. *Journal of Personality and Social Psychology, 5,* 768–777.

Stroop, J. R. (1935). Studies of interference in serial verbal reactions. *Journal of Experimental Psychology, 18,* 643–662.

INDEX

Absolute value, 219
Abstract, 627–630
Addition rule, 671–672
Adjusted *k*, 513–514, 751
Alpha
  confidence intervals and size of, 381–382, 751
  for *z*-test, 346
Alternate forms, 124, 751
Alternative hypothesis (H_a)
  ANOVA and, 461
  creating, 340–342
  defined, 340
  for independent-samples *t*-test, 410
  t-test, 370, 377–378, 383
American Psychological Association (APA)
  format for research, 41. *See also* APA format
  Principles of Ethical Conduct, 98–100, 102–103
Analysis of variance (ANOVA)
  defined, 457
  experiment-wise error rate and, 460
  one-way
    between-subjects, 460–461, 469–473
    confidence interval in, 478
    describing relationship in, 478–480
    graphing results in, 478–479
    statistical notation for, 457
    steps in performing, 477
    within-subjects, 533–537, 674–678
  order of operations in, 461–462
  overview, 459–462
  power and, 480
  statistical hypotheses of, 461
  three-way, 541–545
    main effects, 542
    three-way interaction, 543–545
    two-way interactions, 542–543
  two-way
    between-subjects, 489
    assumptions of, 492
    computations, 497–507
    degrees of freedom in, 502–503
    eta squared, 516–517
    interaction effects, 495–497, 508
    logic of, 492–493
    main effects, 493–495, 507–508, 511
    mean squares, 503–504
    mixed-design, 538–541, 687–692
    overall results of, 515–516
    overview, 491–499
    statistical notation, 489
    steps in performing, 517–518
    sums of squares, 499–502
    within-subjects, 537–538, 679–685
Animal research, 95–96
  carryover effects and, 437–438
  controls with, 96
  ethics and, 102–103
Animal rights, 102
ANOVA. *See* Analysis of variance
Annual Review of Psychology, 619
APA format, 615–657
  abstract, 627–630
  Apparatus section, 632–635
  assumptions of author and reader and, 624
  common abbreviations, 638
  components of research article, 626–641
  Discussion section, 638–640
  example study, 616–617
  figures and, 636–637
  introduction, 630–631
  major sections, 623
  Materials section, 632–635
  Method section, 632
  Participants section, 632
  Procedure section, 633–635
  Reference page, 641
  research article organization, 622–626
  research literature and, 617–622
  Results section, 635–638
  rules of style, 624–626
  statistical notation. *See* Statistical notation, APA format
  tables and, 637–638
  title, 626–627
  title page, 627–628
Apparent limits, 661–662
Applied research, 13
Archival research, 112
Area under the curve
  proportion of, 152, 229
  normal curve showing, 151, 156
  standard normal curve, tables, 703–707
  total, 150
  z-scores and, 319
Association, 34
  degree of, 35
  intermediate, 258–260
  perfect, 257–258
  zero, 261
Automation
  controlling extraneous variables with, 88–89
  defined, 89
Average of the deviations, 197

Balancing participant variables, 405–407
Bar graph
  creating, 182–183
  defined, 141, 182, 751
  grouped frequency distribution, 662–663
  one-way chi square, 595–596
  relative frequency distribution, 151
  simple frequency distribution, 141–142
Barnum statements, 121, 751
Baseline design, 575–576, 751
Basic research, 13, 751
Behavior
  animal research on, 95–96
  considering context of, 55–56
  controlling, 12
  multiple baselines across, 579
  observing reliable, 85–86
  predicting, 11
  problems in inferring causes of, 69–70
  scores and, 30, 120
Beta, 359, 751
Between-subjects ANOVA
  defined, 457, 751
  one-way, assumptions of, 460–461
Between-subjects design, 403
  controlling participant variables in, 403–409
  defined, 751
  random assignment, 404–405
  within-subjects design vs., 438
Between-subjects factor, 457, 751

Bias
animal research and, 96
in field surveys, 114
multiple raters and, 111
participant variables and, 409
questionnaire title and, 125
scientific method for eliminating, 6
volunteer, 114
Biased estimators, 751
Bimodal distributions, 147–148, 166–167, 751
Binomial expansion, 672–674
Bivariate normal distribution, 384

Carryover effects
defined, 86, 751
with interviews and questionnaires, 123
nonsymmetrical, 437
with repeated measure design, 435
Case studies, 112–113, 751
Catch trials, 124–125
Causal hypothesis, 14–15, 751
Ceiling effects, 84, 91, 751
Cell
defined, 751
means, 495
Central limit theorem, 237–238, 751
Central tendency. *See also* Measure of central tendency
mean, 170–175
median, 168–170
mode, 166–168
summarizing research using, 178–184
understanding, 164–166
Chance events, 313. *See also* Probability
Changes, systematic vs. unsystematic, 59
Chi square (χ^2) procedures
critical values, 717
defined, 589, 751
one-way, 589–596
assumptions of, 591
computing chi square, 592–593
expected frequencies, 591
graphing results, 595–596
interpreting chi square, 593–594
other uses of test, 594–595
statistical hypotheses for, 590–591
two-way, 596–601
computing, 599
degrees of freedom in, 599
describing relationship in, 601
expected frequencies in, 597–599
graphing, 600
logic of, 596–597
Chi square (χ^2) tables, 717
Classification variable. *See* Qualitative variable
Class interval, 156
in grouped frequency distribution, 660, 662
Closed-ended question
defined, 117, 751
in interviews and questionnaires, 117–118
responses for, 121–123
Cluster sampling, 116, 752
Coefficient
contingency, 601
phi, 601
Coefficient of alienation, 301, 752
Coefficient of determination, 301, 752
Cohort design, 572–573, 752
Cohort effects, 572, 752
Collapsing across a variable, 406, 542–543, 680, 752
Complete counterbalancing, 531–532, 752
Complete factorial design, 490–491, 752
Complex designs
controlling participant variables in, 529–533
meta-analysis, 547–548
multivariate analysis, 547
one-way between-subjects ANOVA, 460–487
test for homogeneity of variance, 545–546
three-way ANOVA, 541–545
two-way between-subjects ANOVA, 488–527
Conceptual replication, 23, 752
Concurrent validity, 264, 752
Condition
defined, 43, 752
randomizing order of, 533
Confederates, 43, 752
Confidence interval
alpha size and, 381–382
computing, for μ, 380–381
defined, 752
for dependent samples, 445–446
for difference between two μs, 417–418
estimating population with, 379–382
in one-way ANOVA, 478
for single μ, 379
for within-subjects factor, 536–537
Confirmation, 21
Confounded comparison, 513, 752
Confounding, 81–82, 752
Confounding variables, 63–64
Consistency, 61
Construct. *See also* Hypothetical construct
component variables of, 31–32
Construct validity, 62, 640, 752
Content analysis, 118–119, 752
Content validity, 62, 640, 752
Contingency coefficient, 601, 752
Continuous scale, 137–138, 752
Control group
defined, 43, 752
nonequivalent, 565–567
two-way mixed design and, 539–540
Controlling behavior, 12
Controls
animal research and, 96
automation and, 88–89
between-subject design and, 403–409
deciding on, 68
defined, 10, 752
demand characteristics and, 92–93
descriptive studies and, 68, 109
eliminating, 35
error rate and, 460
extraneous variables and, 66–68, 88–90
field experiments and, 74
observation designs and, 110
participant variables and, 430–436
reliability and, 68
validity and, 68
Convenience sampling, 116, 752
Convergent validity, 263, 752
Correction term, 680
Correlation
multiple, 303–304
in population, 274
as relationship, 249
Correlational research, 47, 249–252
conclusions from, 250–251
correlation coefficient, 253–254
design, 752
distinguishing characteristics, 252–254
linear regression, 282–309
powerful correlational design, 272–274
reasons for using, 251–252
reliability and, 262–263
scatterplot, 252–253
two-sample experiment, 419
validity and, 263
Correlation coefficient, 253–254
computing, 264–272
defined, 752
maximizing power of, 391–392
Pearson, 265–267
point-biserial, 270–272
in research, 261–264
sampling distribution of, 385
significance tests for, 382–390
Spearman rank-order, 267–270, 710
statistical hypotheses for, 383
summary of testing, 391
with two-sample experiment, 419–420
type of relationship and, 256
zero association, 261
Counterbalancing, 86–87, 436
complete, 531–532
defined, 752
partial, 532–533
Criterion
defined, 325, 752
for z-test, 346
Criterion validity, 264, 752
Criterion variable, 285, 752

Critical value, 326–327
of chi square, 717
defined, 752–753
of *F*, 468, 711–713
of F_{max}, 716
interpolating, 669–670
of Mann-Whitney *U*, 718–721
of Spearman rank-order correlation coefficient, 710
of *t*, 708
of Wilcoxon *T*, 722–723
for *z*-test, 346
Cross-sectional design, 571–572
Cumulative frequency
defined, 153, 753
presenting in table, 153–154
Cumulative frequency distributions, 153–154
Curvilinear relationship, 255. *See also* Nonlinear relationships

D. *See* Difference score
Data
defined, 3, 753
faking, 103
ranked, nonparametric procedures for, 602–603
real, vs. ideal distributions, 148
Data collection
automation of, 88–89
critical evaluation of study and, 57–61
hypothesis testing and, 19
questionnaires for, 119
Data point
defined, 37, 753
on frequency polygon, 142
Debriefing, 100, 753
Deception, 93, 98, 753
Decision making
hypothesis testing and, 355–362
probability and, 321–323
Definitions, operational, 32–33
Degree of association, 35, 257. *See also* Strength of relationship
underestimate of, 273
Degree of consistency, 262
Degrees of freedom
defined, 206, 753
for dependent-samples *t*-test, 444
F-distribution and, 468
F-ratio and, 471–472
for one-way ANOVA, 468
for one-way chi square, 594
for Pearson *r*, 385–386
with single-sample *t*-test, 375
for *t*-distribution, 375
for two-way ANOVA, 502–503
for two-way chi square, 599
Demand characteristics, 90–95
balancing participant variables and, 407
concealing, 94–95
defined, 90, 753
general controls for, 91–92
matched-group designs and, 432
quasi-experiments and, 563
questionnaires and, 124–125
unobtrusive measures, deception and, 93–94
Dependent events, 316, 753
Dependent measure, 45, 753
Dependent samples
defined, 439, 753
Wilcoxon *T*-test for two, 605–606
Dependent-samples *t*-test, 438–447
assumptions of, 439
computing, 441–443
defined, 439, 753
effect size of, 446–447
graphing relationship from, 446
interpreting, 443–445
logic of, 439–440
power and, 447–448
statistical hypotheses for, 440–441
Dependent variable, 179, 181
between-subjects design and, 404
defined, 45–46, 753
designing, 82–87
effect size and, 446
field experiments and, 73
inferential statistics and, 338
measure of central tendency and, 179–181
measuring, 45
nonparametric procedure and, 588
qualitative, 32
quantitative, 32
Descriptive design, 46–48. *See also* Descriptive research
Descriptive hypothesis, 15, 753
Descriptive research
defined, 753
ethics and, 125–127
field surveys in, 113–114
observational studies in, 109–113
sampling techniques with, 114–117
terminology used in, 114
uses of, 109
validity and reliability issues, 68–70
Descriptive statistics
defined, 38–39, 753
frequency distributions, 139–140
measures of central tendency, 163–190
percentile, 155–156
variability measures, 191–217
z-scores, 218–246
Design, 9. *See also* Research design
baseline, 575–576
between-subjects, 403–409
choosing repeated-measures or between-subjects, 436–438
cohort, 572–573
complete factorial, 490–491
completing, for research study, 621–622
controlling participant variables with, 430–436
correlation, 47. *See also* Correlational research
cross-sections, 571–572
descriptive, 46–48
design, 753
group, 580–581
hypothetical construct, 31–32
of independent variable, 80–82
interviews and questionnaires, 117–119
issues to consider, 95
longitudinal, 570–573
matched-groups, 430–432, 529
multiple-baseline, 577–579
one-way, 457
operational definitions, 32–33
population in, 29–33
powerful, 212
pretest-posttest, 434
repeated-measures, 433–435, 529
reversal, 576
sample in, 29–30
single-subject, 573–581
time-series, 563–569
two-sample experiments and, 401–403
two-way, 489
Determinism, 7, 753
Deviation
average of, 197
around mean, 173–175
normal, 201
of score, 174
standard. *See* Standard deviation
df. *See* Degrees of freedom
Dichotomous variable, 138, 753
Differences between the means, sampling differences of, 411
Difference score (*D*), 440
Disconfirmation, 21, 753
Discrete scales, 137–138
Discriminant validity, 263
Discussion section of research article, 638–640
Distribution
bimodal, 147–148, 166–167
defined, 135, 753
frequency. *See* Frequency distribution; Simple frequency distribution
leptokurtic, 146
mesokurtic, 146
normal, 144–146, 169. *See also* Normal distribution
platykurtic, 146
probability, 315–316
real data vs. ideal, 148
rectangular, 147
sampling, of means, 236–239
skewed, 146, 148, 169, 173
tails of, 145
unimodal, 166–167
Double-barreled questions, 121, 753
Double-blind procedure, 92, 753
Duncan test, 474

Ecological validity, 65, 753
Effect size
  defined, 421, 753
  of dependent-samples *t*-test, 446–447
  eta squared and, 479
  in two-sample experiment, 421–422
Empirical probability distribution, 315, 753
Environmental variables, 56, 58, 753
Equation, linear regression, 285–291
Error. *See also* Type I error; Type II error
  margin of, 379
  prediction
    linear regression equation and, 291–298
    variance as, 209–210
  rate, experiment-wise, 460
  recall, 179
  sampling, 337
  in statistical decision making, 355–362
Error variance, 209, 292, 463, 753
Estimated population standard deviation, 205–208, 753
Estimated population variance, 205–208, 753
Estimated standard error of the mean, 371, 753–754
Estimation
  interval, 379
  point, 379
Eta (η), 479, 754
Eta squared (η^2), 479–480, 516–517
Ethics
  animal research and, 102–103
  APA Principles of Ethical Conduct, 98–100
  descriptive research and, 125–127
  of field experiments, 100–101
  participant cooperativeness and, 97
  research, 8, 96–104
  of role playing, 101–102
  scientific fraud and, 103
  of simulations, 101–102
  of unobtrusive measures, 100–101
Evaluation of a design, 57–61
Events
  dependent, 316
  independent, 316, 409
  mutually exclusive, 671
  mutually inclusive, 671
  probability and, 313, 321–323
Evidence
  empirical, 9
  flaws in, 19–21
Expected frequency, 591, 754
Expected sum of ranks, 602
Experiment
  concealing, 94–95
  defined, 42, 754
  designing powerful, 184–186
  field, 73, 94–95, 100–101
  graphing results of, 181–183
  in laboratory vs. field, 73
  single-sample, 340
  terminology used in, 46
  true vs. quasi-, 44
  two-sample, 399–454
  validity and reliability issues in, 70–75
Experimental groups, 43, 754
Experimental hypotheses, 339, 754
Experimental methods, 42–46
  dependent variable, 45–46
  independent variable, 42–44
  true vs. quasi-experiments, 44
Experimental realism, 92–93, 754
Experimenter expectancies, 91, 110, 754
Experiment-wise error rate, 754
Ex post facto research, 112, 754
External validity, 64–65, 402, 640, 754
Extraneous variable, 59–60, 402
  controlling, 66–68, 88–90
  defined, 59, 754
  strength of relationship and, 60
Extreme scores, 145

Face validity, 263, 754
Factor, 42, 457, 754. *See also* Independent variable
Factorial design
  complete, 490–491
  incomplete, 491
  planned comparisons and, 546
  simple main effects and, 546–547
Factorial symbol (!), 673
Faking data, 103
Falsifiable hypothesis, 15, 754
Fatigue effects, 435–436
F-distribution, 467–468, 754
Field experiment
  concealing and, 94–95
  defined, 73, 754
  ethics of, 100–101, 126–127
Field research, 73, 754
Field survey
  defined, 754
  flaws in, 114
  mail vs. telephone, 113–114
Figures, APA format for, 636–637
First impressions construct, 55
Fisher's protected *t*-test, 475–476, 754
Floor effects, 84, 91, 754
F-obtained (F_{obt}), 461–462, 466–468, 473–474, 504–507, 534–535
Forced-choice procedure, 45
F-ratio
  computing, 468–474
  defined, 754
  logic of, 465–467
  one-way between-subjects ANOVA and, 469–473
Fraud, scientific, 103
Frequency
  defined, 136, 754
  expected, 591
  relative, 220, 240–242
Frequency distribution
  bar graphs, 141–142
  bimodal distribution, 147–148
  cumulative, 153–154
  frequency polygons, 142–143
  graphing, 140–143
  grouped, 156–157, 660–663
  histograms, 142
  normal, 148
  real data vs. ideal distributions, 148
  rectangular distribution, 147
  relative, 148–153
  simple, 139–140. *See also* Simple frequency distribution
  skewed distributions, 146, 148
Frequency polygon, 142–143, 177, 754
Freud, Sigmund, 15
Friedman χ^2 test, 607–608, 698–700, 754
F-statistic
  ANOVA and, 461
  components of, 462–468
  critical value and, 468
  degrees of freedom and, 468
  F-distribution, 467–468
  F-ratio, 465–474
  mean square between groups, 464–465
  mean square within groups, 463
F-tables, 711–713

Gambler's fallacy, 314
Generalization, 40–41, 754
Goodness of fit test, 589–590. *See also* Chi square (χ^2) procedures, one-way
Graph, 182–183
  bar, 141–142. *See also* Bar graph
  dependent-samples *t*-test, 446
  as Figure in study, 636–637
  frequency distribution
    cumulative, 154
    grouped, 662–663
    simple, 140–143
  interaction effect in two-way ANOVA, 508
  line, 181–182
  line vs. regression, 283
  main effect in two-way ANOVA, 507–508, 511
  one-way ANOVA results, 478–479
  one-way chi square results, 595–596
  relationships, 36–38
  results of experiment, 181–183
  scatterplot, 252–253
  two-way chi square results, 600
  two-way interactions, 544
  z-distributions on, 226–227
Group designs, single-subject designs vs., 580–581
Grouped distributions, 156, 754
Grouped frequency distribution, 156–157, 660–663
  graphing, 662–663
  real vs. apparent limits and, 661–662

H_a. *See* Null hypothesis
H_0. *See* Alternative hypothesis
Habituation, 92
Hawthorne effect, 90–91
Heterogeneity of variance, 754
Heteroscedasticity, 295, 754
Histogram
 defined, 142, 754
 grouped frequency distribution, 662–663
 as relative frequency distribution, 151
Homogeneity of variance, 409, 545–546, 754
Homoscedasticity, 295, 755
Human Subjects Review Committee, 99
Hypothesis. *See also* Scientific hypotheses
 alternative, 340
 causal, 14–15
 defined, 14
 descriptive, 15
 experimental, 339
 falsifiable, 15
 null, 342–343
 parsimonious, 16
 precise, 16
 rational, 16
 scientific, 14–19
 statistical, 340
 testable, 15
 testing through research, 18–19
 two-tailed, 461
Hypothesis testing. *See also* Statistical hypothesis testing
 by discovering a relationship, 33–38
 flaws in, 21–22
 logical of statistical, 343–344
 one-tailed test, 353–355
Hypothetical construct, 31–32, 62, 755. *See also* Construct

Incomplete factorial design, 491, 755
Independent events, 316, 409, 755
Independent samples
 defined, 403, 755
 one-tailed tests on, 418
Independent-samples *t*-test, 409–418
 assumptions of, 409–410
 computing, 412–415
 formulas for, 414–415
 interpreting, 416–417
 population variance for, 412–413
 power and, 422–423
 sampling distribution for, 411–412
 standard error of the difference, 413–414
 statistical hypotheses for, 410–411
Independent variable, 42–44
 animal research and, 96
 between-subjects design and, 404
 central tendency and, 180–181
 conditions of, 43–44
 defined, 755
 designing, 80–82
 effect size and, 446
 field experiment and, 73
 power and, 422–423
 qualitative, 32
 quantitative, 32
 quasi-, 44
 true, 44
 in two-sample experiment, 401
Independent verification, 11
Individual differences, 35, 403, 755
Inferential statistics, 39–40
 defined, 40, 338
 logic of statistical hypothesis testing, 343–344
 probability, 312–335
 role in research, 337–339
 sampling error and, 337–338
 setting up procedures for, 339–344
 single-sample experiment, 340, 368–398
 statistical hypotheses, 340
 z-test, 336–367
Inflection point, 202–204, 228
Informed consent, 99–100
Instrumentation effects, 89
Interaction effect, 491
 defined, 755
 two-way ANOVA and, 495–496, 511
Interaction means, 495
 defined, 755
 table of, 514
Intermediate association, 258–260
Internal validity, 63, 402
 defined, 63, 755
 eliminating confounding and, 81
 quasi-experiment and, 559
 reporting, 640
 in true vs. quasi-experiments, 71–73
Interpolation
 on critical values, 669–670
 linear, 234, 667
 from *z*-tables, 234, 668–669
Inter-rater reliability, 111, 262, 755
Interrupted time-series design, 567–568, 755
Intersubject differences, 574
Interval estimation, 379, 755
Interval scale, 137, 755
Interval size, 156
 in grouped frequency distribution, 661
Intervening variable, 45, 755
Interviews
 administering, 125
 catch trials, 124–125
 designing, 117–119
 order effects in, 123–124
 structured, 119
 unstructured, 119
 using, 119–120
Intrasubject differences, 574
Introduction to research article, 630–631
Inverted U-shaped relationship, 255
Kruskal-Wallis *H* test, 606, 697–698
Kurtosis, 145–146

Laboratory experiments
 with animals, 102
 demand characteristics and, 91
 informed consent and, 99
 validity of, 73
Leading questions, 121, 755
Least-squares regression method, 293
Leptokurtic distribution, 146
Level, 457
Likert-type question, 45, 122, 210, 755
Limits
 real vs. apparent, 661–662
 upper real, 663
Linear interpolation, 234, 667
Linear regression, 282–309. *See also* Linear regression equation
 assumptions, 295–296
 defined, 283, 755
 line, 284
 plotting the line, 289–290
 predicting unknown scores with, 284–285
 slope, 286, 288
 standard error of the estimate, 293–295
 summary of computations, 303
 understanding, 282–285
 Y-intercept, 286–288
Linear regression equation, 285–291
 defined, 285, 755
 describing, 289
 errors in prediction and, 291–298
 predicting *Y* scores with, 290–291
Linear regression line, 284
Linear relationship, 254–255, 392, 755
Line graph, 181–182
 defined, 755
 regression graph vs., 283
Literal replication, 23, 755
Literature. *See* Research literature
Longitudinal design, 570–573, 756

Mailed survey, 113–114
Main effect
 design, 756
 graphing two-way ANOVA, 507–508, 511
 means, 493
 simple, 546–547
 of three-way ANOVA, 542
 Tukey's *HSD* for, 511–513
Manipulation
 reliable, 402
 strong, 81, 212
Manipulation check, 82
Mann-Whitney *U* test, 604, 693–694
 critical values table, 718–721
 defined, 756
Margin of error, 379, 756
Matched-groups design, 430–432, 529, 756

Materials section of research article, 632–635
Mathematical relationship, 33
extraneous variables and, 60
Mean, 170–175
cell, 495
defined, 170, 756
deviations around, 173–175
differences between the, 411
interaction, 495
main effect, 493
population, 222
regression toward, 562
sample, 170, 319–321. *See also* Sample mean
sampling distribution of, 236–239
single-sample, 369–371
standard error of, 239–240
sum of deviations around, 174
summarizing research using, 210–213
uses of, 171–173
using in research, 175–178
of z-distribution, 225
Mean difference, standard error of, 442
Mean square between groups, 464–465, 756
Mean squares
in ANOVA, 462
comparing, 465–467
defined, 756
F-ratio and, 472–473
in two-way ANOVA, 503–504
Mean square within groups, 463, 756
Measures
dependent, 45
sensitive, 83–84
unobtrusive, 93, 100–101
variability, 193–197, 756
Measure of central tendency, 164. *See also* Central tendency
Measurement, 10
valid inferences about, 62
variables, 56, 58
Measurement scales
continuous, 137–138
discrete, 138
impact of, 138–139
interval, 137
nominal, 136–137
ordinal, 137
ratio, 137
Measures of Personality and Social Psychological Attitudes, 619
Median
defined, 168, 756
uses of, 169
Mental Measurements Yearbook, The, 619
Mesokurtic distribution, 146
Meta-analysis, 547–548, 756
Method section of research article, 632
Mixed design, 687,
two-way, 539–540, 687–692
Modal score, 166
Mode, 166–168
defined, 166, 756
uses of, 167–168
Model, 17, 756
Multi-factor studies, 491
Multilevel experiments, 457–458. *See also* Analysis of variance
Multiple-baseline design, 577–579, 756
across behaviors, 579, 756
across participants, 578, 756
across situations, 579, 756
Multiple-choice questions, 117–118
Multiple correlation, 304
regression and, 303–304, 756
Multiple raters, 111, 756
Multiple regression, 304
Multiple time-series design, 569, 756
Multiple trials, 85–86, 433, 756
Multiplication rule, 671
Multivariate analysis (MANOVA), 547
Multivariate statistics, 547, 756
Murphy's Law, 75, 423
Mutually exclusive events, 671
Mutually inclusive events, 671

Naturalistic observation, 109–110, 756
Negative linear relationship, 255, 756
Negatively skewed distribution, 146, 148, 756
Nemenyi's procedure, 608, 756
Newman-Keuls test, 474
Nominal scale, 136–137, 756
Nonequivalent control group, 565–567, 756
Nonexperimental methods, 46. *See also* Descriptive design
Nonlinear relationship, 255–256, 757
Nonparametric procedures
chi square, 588–596
choosing, 603
Friedman (χ^2) test, 607–608, 698–700
Kruskal-Wallis H test, 606, 697–698
Mann-Whitney U test, 604, 693–694
parametric counterparts, 603
for ranked data, 602–608
rank sums test, 605, 695–696
reasons for using, 588–589
Wilcoxon T-test, 605–606, 696–697
Nonparametric statistics, 338, 588, 757
Nonprobability sampling, 116, 757
Nonsignificant results, 351–352, 757
Nonsymmetrical carry-over effects, 437, 757
Normal curve, 144–146
applying standard deviation to, 202–204
area under standard, 703–707
finding relative frequency using, 150–153
model, 757
showing area under the curve, 151
standard, 317–321
z-distribution and, 229–233
variations of, 145–146, 195, 203
Normal distribution, 144–146
bivariate, 384
defined, 144, 757
inflection point on, 202–204
location of median in, 169
standard deviation of, 201
Notation, statistical. *See* Statistical notation
Null hypothesis (H_0), 342–343
ANOVA and, 461
chi square and, 590–595, 597
correlation coefficient and, 383
creating, 342–343
defined, 342, 757
dependent-samples t-test and, 440–441
independent-samples t-test and, 411–412
mean square and, 466
one-tailed, 377–378
rejecting, 348
retaining, 350–351
t-distribution and, 373–374
t-test and, 370–371
two-way ANOVA and, 494
Type I errors and, 356–358
Type II errors and, 358–359, 391

Objectivity, 10, 757
Observation, 9–10
descriptive research and, 46
naturalistic, 109
participant, 110
systematic, 10
Observational research, 109–113
archival research, 112
case studies, 112–113
defined, 757
ex post facto research, 112
inter-rater reliability and, 111
multiple raters and, 111
pros and cons, 110–111
Observed frequency, 591, 594–595, 757
Observed sum of ranks, 602
Odds, 313
One-group pretest-posttest designs, 564–565
One-tailed test, 329, 339
choosing, vs. two-tailed tests, 355
for decreasing scores, 354–355
defined, 757
for increasing scores, 353–355
on independent samples, 418
of Pearson r, 387–388
with single-sample t-test, 377–378
One-way ANOVA
between-subjects
assumptions of, 460–461
computational formulas for, 469–473
within-subjects, 533–537, 674–678
One-way chi square, 589–596, 757
One-way design, 457
Open-ended question, 118–119, 757

Operational definition, 32–33, 620, 757
Order effects
  complete counterbalancing and, 531
  counterbalancing, 86–87
  defined, 757
  in interviews and questionnaires, 123–124
  with multiple trials, 434
  partial counterbalancing and, 532–533
  problem of, 86
  in repeated-measures design, 435–436, 530–531
Ordinal scales, 137
Ordinal scores. *See also* Ranked data
  bar graphs and, 662
  median and, 169–170
  range calculation and, 196

p. *See* Probability
Parameter, 164
Parametric procedures, nonparametric counterparts, 603
Parametric statistics, 338, 757
Parsimonious hypothesis, 16
Partial counterbalancing, 532–533
Participants
  changes during experiment in, 530–531
  confederates, 43
  debriefing, 100
  defined, 757
  eliminating from data, 423
  empirical evidence, 9
  ethics and cooperativeness of, 97
  habituating, 110
  informed consent of, 99–100
  instructions to, 88
  intersubject and intrasubject differences, 574
  multiple baselines across, 578
  observation of, 110
  pretest, 405–406
  protecting, 98–99
  section of research article, 632
  testing in groups, 89
  typical behavior, 120
Participant variables, 56, 58
  approach for dealing with, 408–409
  balancing, 405–407
  between-subjects design in, 403–409
  complete counterbalancing between conditions and, 531–532
  in complex designs, 529–533
  defined, 757
  designs that directly control, 430–436
  order effect in repeated-measures designs and, 530–531
  quasi-independent variables and, 560–563
  randomizing order of conditions, 533
  uncontrolled, 438
Pattern, mathematical relationship as, 33
Pavlov, Ivan, 95
Pearson correlation coefficient (*r*), 265–267, 757
  interpreting significant, 386–387
  one-tailed tests of, 387–388
  significance test for, 384
  testing, 385–386
Peer review, 103
Percentile
  defined, 155, 757
  determining score at given, 663–667
  finding for given raw score, 232
  finding raw score at given, 232–233
  grouped frequency distributions, 660–663
  using normal curve to compute, 155–156
Perfect association, 257–258
Phi (ϕ) coefficient, 601, 757
Pilot study, 89–90, 111, 123, 757
Placebo, 94, 540, 757
Planned comparisons, 546, 757
Platykurtic distribution, 146
Point-biserial correlation coefficient, 270–272
  defined, 470, 757
  significance testing of, 388–391
  two-sample experiment and, 420
Point estimation, 379, 757
Polygon
  frequency, 142–143
  grouped frequency distribution, 662–663
  relative frequency distribution, 151
Pooled variance, 412, 757
Population
  correlations in, 274
  deciding if sample represents, 321–323, 327–329
  defined, 29, 758
  estimating with confidence interval, 379–382
  hidden, 116
  identifying, 29–30
  inferring relationship in, 183
  limiting, 407–408
  of scores, 30
  z-score for score in, 222–223
Population correlation coefficient, 274
Population mean, 177–178, 222
Population standard deviation, 204–208, 222, 758
Population variance, 204–208
  defined, 204–205, 758
  for independent samples *t*-test, 412–415
Positive linear relationship, 254–255, 758
Positively skewed distribution, 146–148, 758
Post hoc comparisons, 474–477
  defined, 462, 758
  Fisher's protected *t*-test, 475–476
  Tukey's *HSD* for interaction, 513–515
  Tukey's *HSD* for main effects, 511–513
  Tukey's *HSD* multiple comparisons test, 476–477
Power
  ANOVA and, 480
  of correlation coefficient, 391–392
  defined, 758
  dependent-samples *t*-test and, 447–448
  independent-samples *t*-test and, 422–423
  of statistical test, 360–362
  of *t*-test, maximizing, 391–392
  Type II error and, 391, 447
Powerful design
  correlational research, 272–274
  defined, 185, 758
  variability and, 212
Practice effects, 86, 435, 758
Practice trials, 85, 758
Precise hypothesis, 16
Predestination, 7
Predicted *Y* score, 284
Predicting behavior, 11
Prediction, 18
  correlational design and, 251–252
  defined, 758
  hypotheses and, 33
  linear regression and, 284–285, 290–298
  research used for, 18
  sample mean for, 175–176
  variance and, 209–210
Prediction error
  linear regression equation and, 291–298
  strength of relationship and, 296–298
  variance as, 209–210
Predictive validity, 285, 758
Predictor variable, 285, 758
Pretest participants, 405–406
Pretest-posttest design, 434, 758
Probability (*p*)
  addition rule, 671–672
  computing, 315–317
  decisions based on, 321–323
  defined, 313, 758
  factors affecting, 316–317
  general formula for, 316
  logic of, 313–315
  multiplication rule, 671
  obtaining, from standard normal curve, 317–321
  of sample means, 319–321
Probability distribution
  creating, 315–316
  defined, 315, 758
  empirical, 315
  theoretical, 315–317
Probability sampling, 115, 758
Procedure section of research article, 633–635
Program evaluation, 581, 758

Proportion
  defined, 758
  finding unknown, 669
Proportion of area under the curve, 152, 229, 758
Proportion of variance accounted for, 298–303, 758. *See also* Effect size
Pseudo-explanation, 11, 630, 758
Psychological Abstracts, 618, 628, 758
Psychological attributes, z-scores defining, 235–236
Psychological Bulletin, 619
Psychological research
  applied and basic, 13
  goals of, 11–14
  role of single study in, 14
Psychology, defined, 3
Publication Manual of the American Psychological Association, 622, 758. *See also* APA format

Qualitative data, 110
Qualitative variable, 32, 84, 758
Quantitative variable, 32, 84, 758
Quasi-experiment, 44
  defined, 758
  internal validity, 71–73
  understanding, 558–560
Quasi-independent variable
  defined, 44, 758
  participant variable and, 560–563
  of passage of time, 570–573
  in quasi-experiment, 559
  time-series design and, 563–569
Questionnaires
  administering, 125
  catch trials, 124–125
  designing, 117–119
  order effects in, 123–124
  using, 119–120
Questions
  closed-ended, 117–118, 121–123
  constructing, 120
  double-barreled, 121
  leading, 121
  Likert-type, 122
  open-ended, 118
  wording, 121
Quota sampling, 116, 758

r. *See* Pearson correlation coefficient
r^2. *See* Variance, proportion accounted for
r_{pb}. *See* Point-biserial coefficient
r_s. *See* Spearman rank-order coefficient
Random assignment
  in between-subjects design, 404–405
  defined, 44, 758
  pros and cons of, 405
Randomization, 533, 758
Random sampling, 30, 115, 758
Range, 195–196
  defined, 195, 758
  restricted, 84–85, 272–274, 408
  semi-interquartile, 667
Ranked data. *See also* Ordinal scores
  nonparametric procedures for, 602–603, 693–700
Ranks, expected and observed sum of, 602
Rank sums test, 605, 695–696, 759
Raters
  defined, 111
  inter-rater reliability and, 111, 262
  multiple, 111
Rational hypothesis, 16
Ratio scale, 137, 759
Raw score, 135
  at given percentile, 232–233
  mean and, 174
  with z-distribution, 228
Reaction time, 45, 759
Reactivity, 90–91, 119
Realism, experimental, 92–93
Real limits, 661–662
  upper, 663
Recall error, 179
Rectangular distribution, 147
Reference page of research article, 641
Region of rejection, 325–327
  defined, 325, 759
  in two-tailed test, 346
Regression graph, line graph vs., 283
Regression line
  defined, 759
  with two-sample experiment, 419
Regression toward the mean, 562, 759
Regular frequency distribution, 140
Relationship
  correlation as, 249
  defined, 33, 759
  generalizing, 40–41
  graphing, 36–38
  hypothesis testing and, 33–38
  inferences about, 63–65, 183–184
  linear, 254–255
  mathematical, 60
  nonlinear, 255–256
  in one-way ANOVA, 478–480
  strength of, 35–36, 257–261
  summarizing, 179–180
  in two-sample experiment, 418–422
  types of, 254–256
Relative frequency, 220, 313
  defined, 148–149, 759
  finding, using normal curve, 150–153
  graphing, 150
  presenting in table, 149–150
  of z-score, 228
Relative frequency distributions, 148–153, 759. *See also* Bar graph; Histogram; Polygon
Relative standing, 219, 759
Reliability
  correlation research and, 262–263
  defined, 61, 759
  descriptive studies and, 68–70
  experiments and, 70–75
  inter-rater, 111, 262
  minimizing threats to, 65–68
  multiple trials for, 433
  of observed behavior, 85–86
  reporting, 640
  split-half, 262–263
  test-retest, 262
Reliability of Measures section of article, 634
Reliable manipulation, 402
Repeated-measures design, 433–436
  defined, 529
  order effects of, 530–531
Replication
  defined, 23
  Type I errors and, 357
Representative sample, 30
Research. *See also* Scientific research
  animal, 95–96, 102–103
  applied, 13
  basic, 13
  experimental methods, 42–46
  field, 73
  flow of, 40–42
  hypothesis testing through, 18
  rules for designing, 10
  unobtrusive, 126
Research article. *See also* Research literature
  components of, 626–641
  major sections of, 624
  organization of (APA format), 622–626
Research design. *See also* Design
  critical evaluation of, 57–61
  defined, 759
  example study, 55–57
  observational research, 109–113
  refining, 56–57
Researcher
  attitudes, 9
  deception by, 93–94
  observational research and, 112
  variables, 56, 58, 759
Research ethics, 8, 96–104. *See also* Ethics
Research literature. *See also* Research article
  bibliographies of, 618–619
  computerized searches for, 618
  example study, 619–622
  Psychological Abstracts, 618
  review articles, 619
  searching, 618–619
  Social Science Citation Index, 619
  testing materials references, 619
  what constitutes?, 617–618
Research study, steps in, 41
Response scale, 121, 759
Response sets
  as carryover effect, 86
  defined, 86, 759
  preventing, 124
  in repeated-measures design, 435
Restricted range, 121

Restriction of range, 84, 272–274, 759
Results section of research article, 635–638
Reversal design, 576, 759
Risks
descriptive research and, 125
field experiment and, 99–100
identifying potential, 98
informed consent and, 99–100
justifying remaining, 99
protecting participants from, 98–99
role-playing, simulations and, 101–102
r-obtained (r_{obt}), 385, 387–388
Robust procedure, 338, 759
Role playing
defined, 759
ethics of, 101–102
Rounding, 135

Sample
deciding if it represents population, 327–329
defined, 29, 758
dependent, 439
independent, 418, 403
random, 30
representative, 30
Sample mean
decisions about, 323–330
formula for, 170
probability of, 319–321
randomly selecting, 320
relative frequency of, 240–242
z-score for, 236–242
Sample standard deviation, 200–201, 759
Sample variance, 197–200
computational formula, 198–199
defined, 197, 759
Sampling
cluster, 116
convenience, 116
nonprobability, 116
probability, 115
quota, 116
random, 30, 115
snowball, 116
summary of techniques, 117
Sampling distribution, 329–330
of correlation coefficient, 385, 759
of differences between the means, 411, 759
for independent-samples *t*-test, 411–412
relative frequency of sample means and, 240–242
setting up, 324–326
for two-tailed test, 345–346
Sampling distribution of means, 236–239, 759
Sampling error
with correlation coefficients, 382–390
defined, 337, 760
Sampling techniques
nonprobability sampling, 116
probability sampling, 115
types of, 114–117
Sampling without replacement, 317, 760
Sampling with replacement, 317, 760
Scales, measurement. *See* Measurement scales
Scatterplot, 252–253
defined, 252, 760
linear relationships, 255
nonlinear relationships, 256
sampling error and, 384
strong and weak relationships, 298
with two-sample experiment, 419
Scheffe test, 474
Scholastic Aptitude Test (SAT)
correlation with grades, 285
sample mean and, 236–239, 323–329
Scientific fraud, 103
Scientific hypotheses. *See also* Hypothesis
creating, 14–15
criteria for, 15–16
sources of, 16–18
Scientific method, 2–27
assumptions of science and, 6–8
attitudes of scientists and, 8–9
criteria for scientific evidence, 9–11
defined, 6
goals of science, 12–13
hypotheses and, 14–19
introduction to, 2–5
Scientific research. *See also* Research
flaws in, 19–24
flow of, 18
Score
avoiding restrictive range of, 84
decreasing, one-tailed test for, 354–355
describing location of, 176–177
determining, at given percentile, 663–667
deviation of, 174
difference, 430, 440
extreme, 145
increasing, one-tailed test for, 353–355
individual, using *z*-distribution to describe, 227
as locations, 165
predicting, 175–176. *See also* Prediction
percentile for, 665–666
population of, 30
probability of individual, 317–318
relative location as z-score, 220–221
standard, 226
Scoring
criteria, 83
open-ended questions, 118–119
Searches. *See* Research literature, searching
Selection criteria, 405
Self-fulfilling prophecy, 91
Self-reports, 45
Semi-interquartile range, 667, 760
Sensitive measure, 83–84, 760
Serendipitous findings, 13
Sigma (Σ), 164
Significance testing
correlation coefficients, 382–390
Pearson *r*, 384
point-biserial correlation coefficient, 388–391
Spearman *r*, 388–390
Significant difference, 379
Significant results, 348–350
Simple frequency distribution
defined, 139, 760
graphing, 140–143
normal distribution, 144–146
types of, 143–148
Simple main effects, 546–547, 760
Simple random sampling, 115, 760
Simulations, ethics of, 101–102
Single-blind procedure, 92, 760
Single-sample experiment, 340
Single-sample *t*-test
calculating, 371–378
computational formulas for, 372–373
defined, 369, 760
degrees of freedom, 375
interpreting, 376–377
one-tailed hypothesis with, 377–378
sample mean and, 369–371
t-distribution, 373–375
t-tables, 375–376
Single-subject design, 573–581
argument for, 574
defined, 760
group designs vs., 580–581
logic of, 575–576
multiple-baseline designs, 577–579
other approaches, 580
pros and cons, 581
reversal design, 576
Skepticism, 8, 20
Skewed distributions, 146, 148
defined, 146, 760
location of median in, 169
measures of central tendency for, 173
Skinner, B. F., 95, 575
Slope, 286, 288, 760
Small *N* research, 392, 573, 760. *See also* Single-subject design
Snowball sampling, 116, 760
Social desirability, 91
Social Science Citation Index, 619
Sorting task, 45, 760
Spearman rank-order correlation coefficient, 267–270
critical values of, 710
defined, 267, 760
significance testing of, 388–390
Split-half reliability, 262–263, 760
Squared sum of *X*, 192, 760
Square root sign, 192

Standard deviation, 196–197, 200–204
applying to normal curve, 202–204
defined, 200, 760
interpreting, 201–202
of normal deviation, 201
of population, 204–208, 222
summarizing research using, 210–213
of *z*-distribution, 225
Standard error of the difference, 413–414, 760
Standard error of the estimate, 293–295, 760
Standard error of the mean, 239–240
defined, 239, 760
estimated, 371
Standard error of the mean difference, 442, 760
Standard normal curve
obtaining probability from, 317–321
z-distribution and, 229–233
Standard scores, 226
Statistic, defined, 164
Statistical hypotheses
for ANOVA, 461
for chi square, 590–591
for correlation coefficient, 383–384
defined, 340, 760
for dependent-samples *t*-test, 440–441
for independent-samples *t*-test, 410–411
testing, summary of, 352–353
Statistical notation
absolute value, 219
analysis of variance, 457
APA format
alpha level, 362
ANOVA results, 480–481
central tendency, 185
correlation coefficients, 274
dependent-samples *t*-test, 448
factors and interactions, 518
multifactor design, 548
multiple correlation coefficient, 304
sample standard deviation, 213
t-test results, 393
two-sample experiments, 423
z-scores, 242
chi square tests, 609
complete factorial design, 490–491
correlational analysis, 249
defined, 760–761
difference scores, 430
distributions, 135
frequency, 135
linear regression, 283
mathematical relationships, 337
parameter, 164
probability, 313
rounding, 135
Sigma (Σ), 164
squared sum of *X*, 192
square root sign, 192
Student's *t*-test, 369
subscripts, 192, 401
sum of the squared *X*s, 192
transformation, 135
two-way ANOVA, 489
Statistical procedures, role of, 38–40
Statistical tables, 703–723
critical values
of chi square, 717
of F_{max} test, 715
of Mann-Whitney *U*, 718–721
of Spearman rank-order correlation coefficient, 710
of Wilcoxon *T*, 722–723
F-tables, 711–713
Studentized range statistic values, 714–715
t-tables (critical values of *t*), 708
z-tables (area under the standard normal curve), 703–707
Statistical test, power of, 360–362
Statistics
descriptive, 38–39
inferential, 39–40. *See also* Inferential statistics
nonparametric, 338
parametric, 338
use with psychological research, 3
Stratified random sampling, 115, 761
Strength of a relationship, 257–261. *See also* Degree of association
defined, 257, 761
extraneous variables and, 60
prediction errors and, 296–298
standard deviation and, 210
in two-sample experiment, 420
variability and, 259
Strong manipulation, 81, 212, 402
Stroop interference task, 433–436
Structured interview, 119
Studentized range statistic, values of, 714–715
Student's *t*-test, 369. *See also* *t*-test
Subject history, 435
Subject maturation, 435
Subject mortality, 435
Subjects, 9. *See also* Participants
Subscripts, 192
Sum of deviations around the mean, 174
Sum of the squared *X*s, 192
Sum of squares
defined, 468, 761
in one-way ANOVA, 470–471
in two-way ANOVA, 499–502
Surveys
field, 113–114
mailed vs. telephone, 113–114
Systematic naturalistic observation, 110, 761
Systematic observations, 10
Systematic random sampling, 115, 761
Systematic variable changes, 59

Table
APA format for, 637–638
cumulative frequencies in, 153–154
grouped distribution, 157
relative frequency in, 149–150
simple frequency in, 139–140
t-distribution, 373–375
Telephone survey, 113–114
Testable hypothesis, 15
Test of independence, 596–601, 761
Test-retest reliability, 262, 761
Theoretical probability distribution, 315–317, 761
Theory, defined, 17, 761
Three-way ANOVA, 541–545
Three-way interaction, 543–545, 761
Tied rank, 269, 761
Time-series design, 563–569
defined, 564, 761
interrupted, 567–568
multiple, 569
nonequivalent control group designs, 565–564
one-group pretest-posttest designs, 564–565
Titles
of questionnaires, 125
of research articles, 626–627
t-obtained (t_{obt}), 369–385, 414–415, 447–448, 606
Total area under the curve, 150–152, 761
Transformation, 135, 761
Treatment effect, 457, 465, 474, 761
Treatment variance, 465, 761
Trial
catch, 124–125
defined, 761
multiple, 85–86, 433
practice, 85
question as, 120
True experiment
defined, 44, 761
internal validity in, 71–73
True independent variable, 44, 761
t-tables, 375–376, 708
t-test
dependent samples, 439, 761
Fisher's protected, 475–476
independent samples, 403, 409–418, 761
maximizing power of, 391–392
related-samples, 443
single-sample mean, 369–371
summary of, 382
Tukey post hoc tests
for within-subjects factor, 536–537
for multiple comparisons, 476–477, 511–515
Two-sample experiments, 399–454
defined, 401, 761
dependent-samples *t*-test, 438–447
describing relationship in, 418–422
designing, 401–403
effect size in, 421–422
independent-samples t-test, 409–418
within-subjects design, 430–438
Two-tailed hypotheses, 461

Two-tailed test
  choosing one-tailed tests vs., 355
  defined, 325, 761
  as inferential procedure, 339
  region of rejection in, 346
  sampling distribution for, 345–346
Two-way ANOVA. *See* Analysis of variance (ANOVA), two-way
Two-way between subjects design, 489, 762
Two-way chi square procedure, 596–601, 762
Two-way design, 489
Two-way mixed design, 539
Two-way interaction
  defined, 495, 762
  in three-way ANOVA, 542–543
Two-way mixed-design ANOVA, 687–692, 762
Two-way within-subjects ANOVA, 537–538, 762
Type I error, 356–358
  with analysis of variance, 460
  defined, 356, 762
  nonparametric procedures and, 588
  with *t*-distribution, 374
  post hoc tests and, 474–477
  Type II errors vs., 359–360
Type II error, 358–359
  defined, 358, 762
  post hoc tests and, 474–477
  power and, 391, 447
  Type I errors vs., 359–360
Type of relationship, 254–256

Unbiased estimators, 206, 762
Unconfounded comparison, 513, 762
Undefined terms, 121, 762
Ungrouped distribution, 156, 762
Unimodal distribution, 166–167, 762
Univariate statistics, 547, 762
Unobtrusive measure
  defined, 93, 762
  ethics of, 100–101
Unobtrusive research, ethics and, 126
Unstructured interview, 119, 762
Unsystematic changes, 59, 762
Upper real limits, 663
U-shaped relationship, 255

Validity
  concurrent, 264
  construct, 62, 640
  content, 62, 640
  convergent, 263
  correlation research and, 263
  criterion, 264
  defined, 62, 762
  descriptive studies and, 68–70
  discriminant, 263
  ecological, 65
  experiments and, 70–75
  external, 64–65, 402, 640
  face, 263
  internal, 63, 71–73, 81, 402, 640
    quasi-experiment and, 559
  in laboratory vs. field experiments, 73–74
  minimizing threats to, 65–68
Variability
  as error in predictions, 209–210
  proportion of variance accounted for, 298–303
  strength of relationship and, 259
  understanding, 193–197
Variability measures, 191–217
  population standard deviation, 204–208
  population variance, 204–208
  power of a design and, 212–213
  range, 195–196
  sample variance, 197–200
  standard deviation, 196–197, 200–204
  variance, 196–197, 209–210
Variable
  collapsing across, 406, 542–543, 680
  component, of construct, 31–32
  confounding, 63–64
  criterion, 285
  defined, 31, 762
  defining, for research study, 620–621
  dependent, 45, 82–87, 179, 181, 588
  dichotomous, 138
  environmental, 56, 58
  extraneous, 59–60, 66–68, 88–90, 402
  independent, 42–44, 80–82
  intervening, 45, 82
  measurement, 56, 58
  predictor, 285
  qualitative, 84
  quantitative, 32, 84
  quasi-independent, 559
  participant, 56, 58, 403–409. *See also* Participant variables
  researcher, 56, 58
Variance, 196–197
  analysis of. *See* Analysis of variance (ANOVA)
  defined, 197, 762
  error, 292, 463
  as error in predictions, 209–210
  homogeneity of, 409
  interpreting, 199–200
  pooled, 412
  population, 204–208. *See also* Population variance
  proportion accounted for, 298–303
  sample, 197–200
  treatment, 465
  Y scores and, 291–293
Variance between groups, 462, 762
Variance within groups, 462, 762
Verification, independent, 11
Volunteer bias, 114

Wilcoxon *T*-test, 696–697
  critical values table, 722–723
  for two dependent samples, 605–606
Within-subjects design
  between-subjects design vs., 438
  two-way, 537–538
Within-subjects factor, 457, 535–537

X axis, 36
  of bar graph, 182
  of frequency distribution, 140–143
  of line graph, 181–182
X scores, 182, 257–261. *See also* Scores
X variable, 33–34, 69–70

Y axis, 36
  of frequency distribution, 142
  of line graph, 181–182
Y-intercept, 286–289, 762
Y-scores, 182, 257–261. *See also* Scores
  predicted, 284
Y variable, 33–34, 69–70

Zero association, 261
z-distribution, 224–225
  characteristics of, 225
  comparing different distributions using, 225–227
  defined, 224, 762
  describing individual scores with, 227–236
  plotting different, on same graph, 226–227
  standard normal curve and, 229–230
z-obtained (z_{obt}), 374–352
z-score, 218–246
  computing, 221–223
  defined, 221, 763
  describing sample means with, 236–242
  finding unknown, 668–669
  interpreting with *z*-distribution, 224–225
  negative, 318
  psychological attributes and, 235–236
  raw score with known, 223
  relative frequency of, 228
  for sample mean, 240
  score's relative location as, 220–221
  understanding, 219–223
z-tables, 233–235, 703–707
  defined, 233, 763
  interpolating from, 668–669
z-test, 336–367, 345–347
  computing, 346
  defined, 336, 763
  interpreting z_{obt}, 347–352
  nonsignificant results, 351–352
  retaining H_0, 350–351
  sampling distribution for two-tailed test, 345–346
  significant results, 348–349